Parrots of the World

Parrots of the World

Joseph M. Forshaw

illustrated by
William T. Cooper

Published 1977 by T.F.H. Publications, Inc.,
P.O. Box 27, Neptune, N.J. 07753
by arrangement with Doubleday & Company, Inc.

First published 1973 by Lansdowne Press
(a division of I.P.C. Books Pty Ltd)
37 Little Bourke Street, Melbourne, 3000, Australia
© Joseph M. Forshaw 1973
Type Set by Dudley E. King Linotypers Melbourne
in 12 pt Bembo Series 270
Designed by Derrick I. Stone
ISBN 0-87666-959-3

*To our wives and families
in appreciation of their continuous support,
assistance, and encouragement*

CONTENTS

Numerals in parentheses indicate illustrations.

ABOUT THIS EDITION

The original edition of *PARROTS OF THE WORLD* was produced in 1973 in the Far East. It was a magnificent volume produced in a superb deluxe edition, with large white borders on each page, very thick binding board covers and a placement of the plates so the plates would not be facing each other. These luxuries resulted in a 1973 price of $65 per copy; a reprint of the book in the deluxe original edition might cost upwards of $100 now.

By special arrangement with the original American publishers, Doubleday & Company, Inc., T.F.H. was able to produce a lower-priced edition, printed on superb paper, with sewn binding (the same as the original edition) for permanence, and including all the color plates in the original edition except for the original cover plates; all but 27 of the plates have been reproduced at the same size as they appeared in the original edition. The location within the text of the plates has been changed in order to have the color fall on one side of the sheet, thus reducing plating and printing costs by 50% over the original edition.

One of the weaknesses of the original edition was the difficulty in locating the illustration of a particular parrot. This minor shortcoming has been corrected in this edition by (1) adding the illustration reference to each species or subspecies description and (2) by citing the page reference to the plate in both the scientific and common name indexes, contrasting it to the text page reference with the utilization of **BOLD** type numerals. *This is a completely unabridged edition of the original edition.*

FOREWORD

A few birds have always been of particular interest to mankind. Aside from the domestic assortment of the barnyard, this group is rather small—the owl, the albatross, the eagle, and as an unquestioned member of this coterie, the parrot. Though not a domestic species, the firm hold of the parrot in man's esteem derives from the tame Polly, who has been a household and sea-faring pet since ancient times. The ability of the African Grey Parrot (*Psittacus erithacus*) to mimic human speech entertained Roman nobility. Later the colourful amazons of the American tropics and the spectacular cockatoos from Australia became well known in aviary and zoo. The popularity of these 'psittacine' birds has never waned, though temporarily eclipsed a few decades ago when they were linked with a dread, if rare disease, psittacosis (derived from the Latin *Psittacus*, a parrot, hence the order Psittaciformes, and psittacine birds). But soon antibiotics made the affliction less serious; moreover, parrots were maligned—tame ducks, pigeons, in fact any birds, can carry the virus, so it is now generally termed ornithosis.

Then came the 'Budgie craze'. The Budgerigar (*Melopsittacus undulatus*), a small parakeet of the dry hinterland of Australia, differs from most others of its family in that it breeds readily in captivity. The supply soon became unlimited, the price cheap, and for a few years almost everyone, at least in the U.S.A., had one or more 'Budgies' in a cage in kitchen or dining room. This popularity fell off, perhaps unfortunately, since other species such as the Australian Cockatiel (*Nymphicus hollandicus*) were then imported in numbers, even sold in city department stores. Australia soon prohibited or regulated such traffic, but it is often a different story elsewhere. In parts of South America when the nest tree of one of the splendid macaws of that region is found, it is cut down in the hope, often vain, that the young will survive the crash. The old birds are trapped or snared, or worse yet, shot and their brilliant plumes used to make trinkets to sell in city shops. During a stay of three weeks along the upper Río Negro, in Amazonia, in 1972 I saw not a single amazon parrot; only occasionally did a pair of Blue and Yellow Macaws (*Ara ararauna*) fly over at a great height, shunning man and his nefarious ways. These large parrots, if they avoid violent death, probably live fifty years, perhaps more. This helps postpone the evil day, but only law enforcement and limitation of export to the few species that can stand the gaff will save these magnificent birds from extinction.

Like other birds, parrots differ greatly in their resilience in the face of persecution. The Carolina Parakeet (*Conuropsis carolinensis*), the only species native to the United States of America, declined rapidly to extinction. The orchards where it proved to be a pest were few and far between in those early days in Florida; the wooded swamps in which it nested vast. All to no avail, by the turn of the century it was gone. On the other hand, the Monk Parakeet (*Myiopsitta monachus*) of Argentina and neighbouring countries still flourishes even though its conspicuous stick nests—unique among parrots—are put to the torch by irate farmers. Indeed this species is now established in New York, where it seems to be spreading like wildfire.

Parrots native to islands, as with many other birds, are especially vulnerable to extinction. Several of the West Indian Islands had macaws—all became extinct shortly after the advent of Europeans. Some are known only from legends, but a few specimens of the Cuban Macaw (*Ara tricolor*) were preserved before, like the Carib Indians, it was extirpated. Now the other West Indian parrots are threatened, including the splendid Imperial Amazon (*Amazona imperialis*) of Dominica and its relatives on other isles of the Lesser Antilles.

It has been the same with other island species. The Norfolk Island Kaka (*Nestor productus*) of Norfolk Island and the Black-fronted Parakeet (*Cyanoramphus zealandicus*) from Tahiti were wiped out long ago. Whether by shooting or by the inroads of cats and other pests brought by man, the result has been the same. Now the Kakapo or Owl Parrot (*Strigops habroptilus*) of New Zealand, a truly unique creature, is tottering on the brink. At least in this case, and how seldom can it be said, we know that an enlightened government is striving to save it. But can the earlier folly of introducing polecats and other European pests into New Zealand be undone? The Kakapo, nocturnal, almost flightless, evolved over the millenia in a mammal free land—it cannot cope with new enemies.

But it is destruction of habitat that is in the long run the greatest threat to parrots as to other wildlife. In particular the short-sighted blitzing of tropical forests, with little gain and permanent loss of the thin soil—a process rampant in almost all tropical countries—makes a mockery of wise use of the land, though no parrots may remain to mock in human phrases man's stupidity.

Australia differs from the other great stronghold of Psittaciformes, South America, in that many species of its magnificent array of parrots are adapted to semi-arid country. Here too, of course, unwise land use, overstocking, or lowering of the water table by too liberal use of wells or 'bores' can destroy the trees in which they nest. But the process is a slower one, and we may hope that visitors to Australia will continue to be thrilled by flights of rose-coloured Galahs (*Eolophus roseicapillus*) or stately Red-tailed Cockatoos (*Calyptorhynchus magnificus*).

It is an interesting paradox that parrots—imitators of human speech—usually have natural calls that are piercing, almost shrieking. My companion on a visit to Mexico, the artist Don R. Eckelberry, used to shriek back at the *Aratinga* parakeets, imitating them, but in language, like their own—not fit to print! As with other birds, larger species often have lower pitched voices, and the guttural, almost raven-like croaking of the big macaws is not objectionable.

The graceful Patagonian Conure or Bank Parrot (*Cyanoliseus patagonus*) of the open, semi-arid wastes of northern Patagonia, has an almost pleasant voice. One night as we slept in a hotel in one of the small towns of the area, we woke from time to time to hear a flock of these parrots flying about and calling. Perhaps they were disturbed by an owl or other night prowler. A day or two later, driving after dark, we saw small groups of these demure brown and yellow birds roosting on telegraph wires—always within a metre of the pole where there is less movement of the wires. This parrot nests in holes in banks. Once we saw them seemingly swooping into the ground. Approaching we found a twisting little arroyo or canyon with vertical walls and no more than 13 m. in width. Somewhere, below ground level, the parrots were nesting in burrows in its walls.

A few parrots, like the one just mentioned, nest in holes in banks or cliffs, or among rocks, but most species utilize cavities in trees. These they may enlarge with their powerful beaks, but usually there is little or no attempt at nest building. The African lovebirds, so called because of the way they snuggle together on a perch, are an interesting exception. Some of them cut long shreds of thin bark or palm leaf, using the bill like a pair of scissors. These strips they tuck under the feathers of the back and carry them thus as they fly to the nest—a habit shared by no bird, other than a few parrots. Professor William Dilger of Cornell University succeeded in crossing a species having this behaviour with one that does not. The hybrids, when they were old enough to nest, were almost pathetic. They were able to cut the shreds of leaf (or in this case, brown wrapping paper) but though they attempted to tuck them under the back feathers and thus carry them to the nest-box, part of the instinctual pattern was lacking and they never succeeded. Finally, one may mention again the Monk Parakeet, which alone among parrots builds a nest in the open—a huge affair of sticks in which each of several participating pairs has its own private nesting chamber.

The distribution and evolution of parrots offers intriguing problems. Australia and tropical America are rich in species; Africa very poor and tropical Asia only somewhat less so. The northern hemisphere, to all effects and purposes, has no parrots, although as noted earlier the Carolina Parakeet formerly inhabited warmer parts of eastern United States. This does not mean that one must invoke land bridges, antarctic connections or the like to get the ancestral parrots around the world. Fossil species are known from the northern hemisphere, which had warmer climes during the ages when the group was diversifying. Even today the Kea (*Nestor notabilis*) is at home in the snows of the New Zealand Alps, while the Austral Conure (*Enicognathus ferrugineus*) reaches the raw, rain-drenched forests of Tierra del Fuego. Why parrots should be so poorly represented in Africa is problematical.

It is not surprising that parrots attracted the attention of naturalists from the earliest times. Gould's great folios did justice to the parrots of Australia and New Guinea, but he never ventured to treat the group as a whole. Audubon, with but one species to consider, produced a magnificent painting of Carolina Parakeets. But these sumptuous works are to be consulted only in major libraries. For decades, an illustrated monograph of the approximately three hundred species of parrots of the world, along the lines of modern works on such families as the pheasants, has been needed. This, Mr Forshaw has provided—first for Australia and then for the world. When he wrote to us, and later in New York told us of his plans to produce a work on the parrots of Australia fully illustrated in colour, we applauded, but with reservations. But it duly appeared, and with hand-tipped photographic plates! The American Museum's Chapman Fund had modestly aided Mr Forshaw in some of his data gathering. With this achievement behind him, he undertook the parrots of the world and was awarded a Churchill Fellowship to visit museums from Indonesia to London and New York and to seek out a few live parrots along the way. For this venture he secured the services of a talented painter of birds, Mr William T. Cooper, an artist who works more briskly than some practitioners of that calling. The result is the splendid volume before us. Joe Forshaw has the drive and ability of a Gould. He has not as yet vouchsafed to me what enterprise will next receive his attention, but one may be sure that it will be carried through with energy, enthusiasm, and elegance. I salute him!

Dean Amadon
NEW YORK
30th June, 1972

ACKNOWLEDGEMENTS

Parrots of the World was conceived by the late Dr Tom Gilliard in 1964 while the author was working in the Department of Ornithology at the American Museum of Natural History, New York, under a grant from the Chapman Memorial Fund. Since that time, while working on the project, the author has enjoyed a rewarding association with the Department and with members of the staff. It is, therefore, most gratifying that Dr Dean Amadon, Chairman of the Department, wrote the Foreword to this book.

In 1971 the author was awarded a Churchill Fellowship by the Winston Churchill Memorial Trust, Canberra, Australia, to enable him to visit various museums throughout the world to obtain data from specimens, and to carry out observations on parrots in the field in South America and on some islands in the Pacific. Much of the information in this book was gathered during the tenure of the Fellowship.

Many people are involved in one way or another in the production of a book of this kind, and we have been most fortunate to have had assistance from many sources. First and foremost, we wish to express our appreciation to the many authors whose published works form the basis for this book. In addition to these published references we have used numerous records from biologists who have supplied us personally with information about parrots occurring in their parts of the world. Their contributions are included in the text as *in litt.* or pers. comm. references. We thank the following contributors:

Salím Ali	Ornithologist resident in India.
Dean Amadon	Ornithologist from United States; familiar with South American birds in the field.
Harry Bell	Ornithologist formerly resident in Papua-New Guinea.
Robert L. Berry	Curator of Birds, Houston Zoo, Houston, United States.
Leslie Brown	Ornithologist resident in Kenya.
John Bull	Ornithologist resident in New York; has studied introduction of *Myiopsitta monachus* to that region.
Annabelle Dod	Ornithologist resident in Dominican Republic, West Indies.
Richard Donaghey	Biologist formerly resident in Papua-New Guinea.
Winston Filewood	Biologist resident in Papua-New Guinea.
Peter Fullagar	Biologist resident in Australia; has also visited New Zealand and Papua-New Guinea.
Graeme George	Biologist resident in Papua-New Guinea.
Frank Gill	Ornithologist resident in United States; has done field studies on birds of Mascarene Islands.
L. R. Guimarães	Entomologist resident in Brazil; has studied the Mallophaga from parrots.
J. R. Jackson	Ornithologist resident in New Zealand.
Cameron Kepler	Ornithologist formerly stationed on Puerto Rico; has also observed birds on other islands in the West Indies.
I. A. Earle Kirby	Government Veterinary Officer, St. Vincent, West Indies.
David Lack	British Ornithologist who has studied birds on Jamaica and other islands in the West Indies.
Eric Lindgren	Biologist resident in Papua-New Guinea.
Stephen Marchant	Ornithologist formerly resident in Ecuador, Iraq, and Nigeria.
Ken Mays	Naturalist from United States; has observed birds in the Tikal district, Guatemala.
R. Meyer de Schauensee	Ornithologist resident in United States; has observed birds in many parts of the world.
Len Robinson	Naturalist resident in Australia; has spent some time in the field in Papua-New Guinea.
Ian Rowley	Ornithologist resident in Australia; has also visited South-East Asia.
Richard Schodde	Australian ornithologist; familiar with birds of Papua-New Guinea.
Lester Short, Jr	Ornithologist from United States; familiar with South American birds in the field.
Helmut Sick	Ornithologist resident in Brazil.
Soekarja Somadikarta	Ornithologist resident in Indonesia.
Rowley Taylor	Biologist resident in New Zealand; member of Canterbury University Expedition to Antipodes Island in 1969.

Emil Urban   Ornithologist resident in Ethopia.
J. A. J. Verheijen   Ornithologist resident in Indonesia.
David Wingate   Curator Conservation Officer, Bermuda, West Indies; has studied
                             birds on other islands in the West Indies.

Searching through ornithological literature to find references dealing with parrots frequently necessitated inter-library borrowing, often with overseas institutions. These loans were arranged most efficiently by the Librarian and staff of the Divisional Library, Division of Wildlife Research, Commonwealth Scientific and Industrial Research Organization, Canberra, Australia, and to them we are extremely grateful.

We thank the following persons for assistance with translation of foreign language references: Messrs A. D'Andria, S. Marchant, and A. J. Porter, Mrs P. Ridpath and Mrs M. Marchant, and Drs M. G. Ridpath and G. F. van Tets.

Advice on nomenclatural problems was given by Dr Gene Eisenmann of the American Museum of Natural History, New York, U.S.A., and by Dr Gerlof Mees of the Rijksmuseum van Natuurlijke Historie, Leiden, The Netherlands.

The author had assistance and guidance in Guyana from Messrs Neraljan Poonai and Ram Singh, and in Brazil from Mr Bill Belton and Dr Helmut Sick. In Papua-New Guinea both of us were assisted and guided by Lt Col Harry Bell and Messrs Win Filewood, Graeme George, Tony Layton, and Roy Mackay.

Directors and staffs of the museums visited by the author gave much assistance and granted permission for types and rare or extinct specimens to be photographed. We are indebted to the directors and staffs of many museums for the loan of specimens, without which the plates could not have been painted. The museums from which specimens were borrowed are listed in the PREFACE. In addition we wish to thank the following persons for sending information about specimens in their collections: Mr John Bull and Mrs Mary LeCroy (American Museum of Natural History); Dr Frank Gill (Academy of Natural Sciencies, Philadelphia); Mr Derek Goodwin (British Museum); Mr Con Benson (Cambridge University, Museum of Zoology); Dr R. A. Paynter Jr (Museum of Comparative Zoology at Harvard); Dr Gerlof Mees (Rijksmuseum van Natuurlijke Historie, Leiden); Dr J. Steinbacher (Senckenberg Museum, Frankfurt); Dr G. Mauersberger (Zoologisches Museum, Berlin). Mrs Mary LeCroy obtained for us photographs of important specimens in the collections of the American Museum of Natural History. The illustrator acknowledges assistance and guidance given by Mr John Disney, Curator of Birds at the Australian Museum, Sydney, Australia. Some of the foreign specimens housed in Australian museums are very old and had to be thoroughly cleaned before they could be used for preparation of paintings; this cleaning was expertly carried out by Mr Kent Keith of the Division of Wildlife Research, Commonwealth Scientific and Industrial Research Organization, Canberra. Finally, we wish to thank the Chief and curatorial staff at the Division of Wildlife Research, Commonwealth Scientific and Industrial Research Organization, Canberra, for handling the administrative aspects of inter-institutional loans of specimens.

While overseas, the author visited a number of zoos to obtain from living birds the colours of soft parts. Thanks are due to Dr Norman Sholar for making possible a visit to Busch Gardens, Florida, U.S.A., and to Mr Kenton Lint, Curator of Birds at San Diego Zoological Gardens, San Diego, U.S.A., for assistance given during a visit to that zoo. Sketches were done by the illustrator from birds housed at the Taronga Park Zoological Gardens, Sydney, Australia, and we are grateful to Mr Kerry Muller, Curator of Birds, for his generous help with this work.

The illustrator is grateful to the following persons for providing plant material for backgrounds in the plates: Mr A. Clarke (Australian Paper Mills, Coffs Harbour, Australia); Mr Bill Martin (Parks and Gardens Section, Department of Interior, Canberra, Australia); Mr Graeme George (Bird of Paradise Sanctuary, Baiyer River, Papua-New Guinea); and Miss Helen Aston and Mr James Willis (National Herbarium of Victoria, Melbourne, Australia). Photographs taken by the author in the Lae Botanic Gardens, Papua-New Guinea, and the Jardim Botânico, Rio de Janeiro, Brazil, were also used.

All maps and line drawings were prepared by Mr Les Hall of the Division of Wildlife Research, Commonwealth Scientific and Industrial Research Organization, Canberra, and to him we express our gratitude for an exacting task well carried out.

The mammoth task of typing the manuscript was most capably handled by Mrs A. J. Porter to whom we are extremely grateful. Parts of the preliminary draft was typed by Mrs N. Genet. Preliminary drafts were read by Drs Salím Ali, Michael Ridpath, and Emil Urban, by Professor Lindsay Pryor, and by Mr Leslie Brown, and their valuable comments helped mould the project into its final form. Messrs B. V. Fennessy and John Calaby, and Dr Peter Fullagar of the Division of Wildlife Research, Commonwealth Scientific and Industrial Research Organization, Canberra, read the entire manuscript as it was being prepared and offered useful criticisms and comments. The author's wife, Beth, and Miss Faye Shepherd checked most of the final copy and the galley proofs.

In conclusion, we wish to pay tribute to our wives and families for the admirable manner in which they have understood, supported, and encouraged us when so much of our time and attention has been absorbed by the project.

Joseph M. Forshaw
William T. Cooper
CANBERRA,
30th June, 1972.

PREFACE

No monograph on the parrots has been published during the past century, the last authoritative book being *Die Papageien*, by Otto Finsch, which appeared in 1867–68. Since then many new species have been discovered and we have learned more about the old ones. In this book it has been my aim to bring together all published information on the parrots of the world, and to supplement this with my own field observations and the unpublished observations of other field workers. I do not suggest that the book is the last word on parrots—far from it, but I believe that it provides a comprehensive survey of our present knowledge of the parrots.

To date no attempt has been made to illustrate every species, so I am pleased that Bill Cooper has accomplished this and with such outstanding success.

For convenience I have divided the text into three sections based on the distribution of parrots. To avoid confusion with recognized faunal regions I have called these geographical units Distributions, and the three used are:

1. PACIFIC DISTRIBUTION. This Distribution has as its centre the Papuo-Australasian region, and it also includes New Zealand, islands in the Pacific, and the eastern sector of South-east Asia.

2. AFRO-ASIAN DISTRIBUTION. This Distribution comprises Africa, including nearby islands in the Indian Ocean, and Asia, as far east as Java.

3. SOUTH AMERICAN DISTRIBUTION. This Distribution includes South and Central America, the Caribbean Islands and the southern portion of North America.

Fig. 1
Geographical boundaries of the Pacific, Afro-Asian, and South American Distributions as adopted in this book.

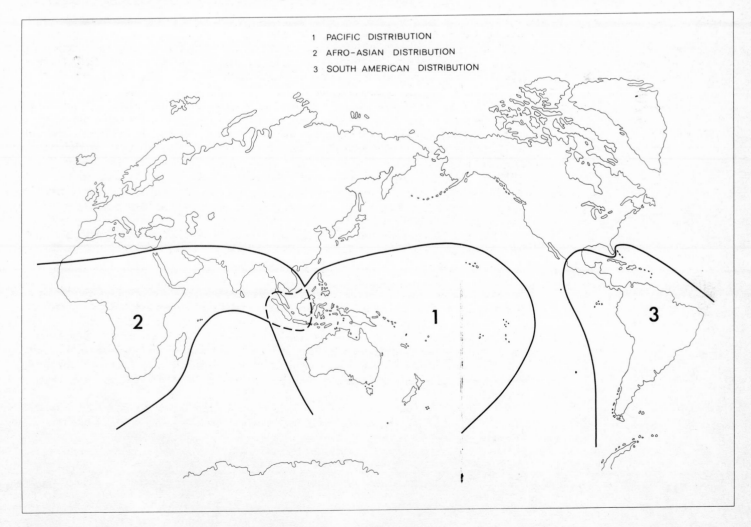

1 PACIFIC DISTRIBUTION
2 AFRO-ASIAN DISTRIBUTION
3 SOUTH AMERICAN DISTRIBUTION

These Distributions are shown in Figure 1, which also indicates that there is no precise boundary between the Pacific and Afro-Asian Distributions, but rather a zone in which are found species that could be satisfactorily placed in either Distribution. My choice of the Distribution in which these species are treated is somewhat arbitrary, but I have been guided by apparent taxonomic relationships, and this has resulted in all species except those in *Loriculus* and *Psittacula* being placed in the Pacific Distribution.

The book has been planned as a reference book and the text has been set out so that information can be found quickly. Therefore, all information pertaining to a species is given in the portion of the text covering that species, even though some habits may be very similar to those of another species. I believe that in a book of this kind it is more desirable to have repetition than to expect the reader to search back and forth trying to find the required information. The use of headings and sub-headings in the text is designed as a further aid to finding information quickly.

I decided not to include keys to identification of the parrots because I feel that in this book the detailed illustration of every species provides an adequate basis for identification. Wherever possible, diagnostic features are clearly shown in the plates. While keys are ideal for regional field guides, for large groups on a world basis they often become cumbersome and difficult to use.

PLAN OF THE TEXT

ENGLISH NAMES   The choice of English names has been a difficult problem. I have not followed any single authority, but have utilized a number of regional lists. The reason for this is that only in avicultural literature can one find English names for all species of parrots, and, in my opinion, many of these are unsuitable. My first source of names was ornithological literature from countries in which English names are used for birds, but this was only partly successful. I have adopted Australian names for Australian parrots, New Zealand names for New Zealand parrots, and, to some extent, English names used in African bird books for African parrots. The New Guinea Bird Society kindly made available a copy of the list of English names which will be adopted in that country, and with but a few exceptions I have used these. For species from parts of South-East Asia and the Pacific Islands I have had to introduce new names or adopt those used in avicultural literature.

The selection of names for South American parrots raised a particular problem. I recognized the desirability of using names proposed by Eisenmann (1955) and Meyer de Schauensee (1970), but in many cases this would have resulted in repetition of names already used for parrots from other countries; for example there would have been two Orange-fronted Parakeets, at least two Yellow-faced Parrots, two Red-capped Parrots, a Rock Parrot and a Rock Parakeet, and so on. Therefore, to overcome this problem I have adopted the collective names 'conure', 'caique' and 'amazon', which are universally used in avicultural literature; I think that these are good collective names and are just as valuable as 'macaw' for denoting New World groups.

Ducorps' Cockatoo was certainly named after Ducorps and Bonaparte's *ducrops* is probably either a *lapsus calami* or a printer's error, so I have amended it to *ducorps*.

Finally, mention must be made of the terms parrot and parakeet, and lory and lorikeet, because they often cause some confusion. There is no biological basis for distinguishing parrots from parakeets or lories from lorikeets. Generally speaking, parrots and lories are large birds with short, squarish tails, and parakeets are small birds with long, gradated tails, but in many instances these distinctions are ignored. In Australia, the terms parakeet and lory are never used. I have not been consistent with the use of these terms, being content to accept whatever is used in the various countries.

DESCRIPTION   Unless stated otherwise, the detailed description is of the nominate subspecies. I have made these descriptions from specimens. Length has been taken from a preserved specimen and is intended to be simply an indication of size, not a precise measurement. If there are no subspecies the description is followed immediately by standard taxonomic measurements from a stated number of museum specimens. These measurements are:

WING LENGTH right wing flattened against a rule.

TAIL length of tail from the base of the central feathers to the tip of the longest feather.

EXPOSED CULMEN length in a straight line from the tip of the upper mandible to the anterior edge of the cere.

TARSUS length of the tarsometatarsus *in situ*. In museum specimens it is virtually impossible to obtain accurate tarsus measurements because the legs are very shrivelled and are often permanently set in an awkward position.

The measurements are listed as a range from minimum to maximum with the average in brackets.

DISTRIBUTION   The overall range of the species is given. If there are subspecies the range is outlined only in broad, general terms, the full details being given for each subspecies. In the South American Distribution, I have used the English 'river' instead of the Spanish or Portuguese 'río' to avoid confusion with place names and names of states.

MAPS Distribution maps, based on published information, are included for all species. These maps are reproduced in tones of grey and the tones denote:

dark grey   normal range of extant species,
medium grey   range of introduced species,

light grey   former range of an extinct species or of a species extant elsewhere,
very light grey   suspected range of a species with an unknown distribution.

There is always some valid basis for criticizing distribution maps, especially when the only available data from which they can be prepared is meagre and poorly documented. Nevertheless, I believe that maps are of great value because they show clearly and at a glance the approximate range of a species.

SUBSPECIES   The distinguishing features, measurements and distribution of each subspecies are listed! All comparative phrases in the description refer back to the description of the nominate subspecies; for example, the phrase 'green of general plumage paler and more yellowish' means that the green of the general plumage in the subspecies in question is paler and more yellowish than in the nominate subspecies. The omission of any previously described subspecies means that I do not consider it to be worth retaining; this may be checked by referring to the distribution. Finally, the numbering of subspecies is not meant to suggest that they are listed in any order of importance or degree of differentiation, but is merely to show at a glance how many subspecies there are.

GENERAL NOTES   There is a regular pattern that I have followed in the opening paragraphs. Firstly, the status and habitats in the various countries are discussed. Then follows information on the general habits, and, finally, details about food, including analyses of crop and stomach contents, are given.

At this point, let me explain that I have included references in the text because the primary purpose of this book is to bring together in one volume all important published references on parrots. Furthermore, I strongly believe that the authors of the references should get credit for their observations and it would be improper of me to utilize their work in any other way. I cannot vouch for the accuracy or otherwise of the authors' published observations; that is their responsibility. I have adopted the system of author's name and the date for each reference because it incorporates the time perspective; in other words, if a reference published in 1950 is given the reader knows immediately that the observation was recorded about twenty years ago. The date is given with a reference when that reference is first mentioned within the text dealing with a species but not when the reference is used again in the text on that same species; for example, if 'Wetmore (1968)' is mentioned then each time 'Wetmore' is repeated in the text covering the same species the '(1968)' also applies, but if 'Wetmore (1957)' and 'Wetmore (1968)' are both used then each time either is repeated the date is also repeated. Full details of each reference will be found listed under author's name and date in REFERENCES CITED at the back of the book.

Sub-headings are used for paragraphs dealing with calls, nesting habits, and descriptions of eggs because these are aspects of general habits about which specific information is often required.

CALL   I am well aware of the shortcomings of describing bird calls in words or by using such terms as screech, shriek, whistle, etc., but at present there are no satisfactory alternatives. More modern methods, such as sonograms taken from recordings, are not generally understood by the average reader, and are available for very few parrots.

NESTING   I have considered eligible for inclusion in this section all facts relevant to breeding, and this includes collectors' records of gonadal enlargement in specimens. In general, very little is known about the breeding habits of most parrots, even the common species.

EGGS   I measured eggs in the Australian Museum and H. L. White Collections, but other measurements have been taken from published references. As pointed out in the INTRODUCTION the eggs of all parrots are white.

ILLUSTRATIONS

Each illustration in this book is of a particular specimen and the registration numbers for specimens are included in the captions to the plates. Preceding the number is an abbreviation denoting the museum or collection in which the specimen is housed.

AM	Australian Museum, Sydney, Australia.
AMNH	American Museum of Natural History, New York, U.S.A.
ANSP	Academy of Natural Sciences, Philadelphia, U.S.A.
BM	British Museum (Natural History), Tring, U.K.
CM	Carnegie Museum, Pittsburgh, U.S.A.
CNHM	Chicago Natural History Museum, Chicago, U.S.A.
COP	Coleccion Ornitologica Phelps, Caracas, Venezuela.
CSIRO	Division of Wildlife Research, Commonwealth Scientific and Industrial Research Organization, Canberra, Australia.
CUMZ	Cambridge University, Museum of Zoology, Cambridge, U.K.
HLW	H. L. White Collection (now held by the National Museum of Victoria), Melbourne, Australia.
JMF	Author's Collection.
LACM	Los Angeles County Museum, Los Angeles, U.S.A.
LSUMZ	Louisiana State University, Museum of Zoology, Baton Rouge, U.S.A.
MLZ	Moore Laboratory of Zoology, Occidental College, Los Angeles, U.S.A.

MM	Macleay Museum, University of Sydney, Sydney, Australia.
MP	Museu Paulista (now incorporated in the Museu de Zoologia da Universidade de São Paulo), São Paulo, Brazil.
MNHN	Museum National d'Historie Naturelle, Paris, France.
MSNG	Museo Civico di Storia Naturale, Genoa, Italy.
MZB	Museum Zoologicum Bogoriense, Bogor, Indonesia.
MZSP	Museu de Zoologia da Universidade de São Paulo, São Paulo, Brazil.
NHM	Naturhistorisches Museum, Vienna, Austria.
NHRS	Naturhistoriska Riksmuseet, Stockholm, Sweden.
NMV	National Museum of Victoria, Melbourne, Australia.
PMM	Port Moresby Museum, Port Moresby, Papua-New Guinea.
QM	Queensland Museum, Brisbane, Australia.
RMNH	Rijksmuseum van Natuurlijke Historie, Leiden, Netherlands.
USNM	United States National Museum, Washington, U.S.A.
WAM	Western Australian Museum, Perth, Australia.
YPM	Yale University, Peabody Museum, New Haven, U.S.A.
ZMB	Zoologisches Museum, Berlin, German Democratic Republic.

I would remind the reader that in the text the size of each species is denoted by the length measurement in the description.

INTRODUCTION

There are approximately eight thousand seven hundred species of birds living today, though Austin (1961) has pointed out that there is evidence to suggest that the Pleistocene bird fauna of the world may have numbered about eleven thousand five hundred species, so birds as a class possibly reached a peak some quarter to a half million years ago and have declined gradually ever since.

Bird species constitute the class Aves among vertebrates and are grouped into categories according to their similarities and differences. Thus the class Aves contains several major orders, each comprising related families, genera, and species. It is the order Psittaciformes—the parrots— that we shall be looking at in this book. Probably the most conspicuous feature making any parrot easily recognizable to even the casual observer or zoo visitor is the short, blunt, rounded bill with the curved upper mandible fitting neatly over the lower. The foot is zygodactyl, that is, two toes point forward and two are turned backwards. There are other less obvious characteristics—the head is large and broad, the neck is short, the tongue is thick and prehensile, the nostrils are set in a bare or feathered, fleshy cere at the base of the upper mandible, and there are powder downs scattered throughout the plumage.

It will be evident from even a cursory glance at the illustrations in this book that parrots come in 'all shapes and sizes'. However, despite this superficial variation they are really a very homogeneous group and, as we shall see later, this presents problems to systematists. They vary in size from the pygmy parrots of New Guinea, which are less than 9 cm. in length, to the giant macaws of South America; the Hyacinth Macaw *(Anodorhynchus hyacinthinus)*, with a total length of approximately 100 cm., is the largest of all parrots. Plumage colouration is also variable; most parrots are brilliantly coloured with green, red, and yellow predominating, but there are dull coloured species like the Vasa Parrot *(Coracopsis vasa)* from Madagascar. Tails may be long and pointed, as in the Long-tailed Parakeet *(Psittacula longicauda)* and the Princess Parrot *(Polytelis alexandrae)*; short and squarish, as in the Short-tailed Parrot *(Graydidascalus brachyurus)* and some parrotlets *(Touit* spp.), or there may be ornate feathers, as in the Papuan Lory *(Charmosyna papou)* and the racket-tailed parrots *(Prioniturus* spp.). Wings can be narrow and pointed, as in the Swift Parrot *(Lathamus discolor)* and the Cockatiel *(Nymphicus hollandicus)*, or broad and rounded as in the amazons *(Amazona* spp.). Some parrots have head crests, while others have elongated feathers on their hindnecks.

FOSSIL HISTORY

In 1861, near the Bavarian town of Pappenheim, a worker in a lithographic limestone quarry found a fossil feather on a slab and its impression on the counter slab. Later in the same year the incomplete skeleton of a feathered animal was found in the quarry. This skeleton of the oldest known bird was the first of three to be unearthed, and it provided palaeontologists with tangible evidence of the reptilian origins of birds. This bird, *Archaeopteryx lithographica*, was about the size of a crow and lived in the cycad forests of the late Jurassic period, that is, about one hundred and forty million years ago. It seems to have survived unchanged for quite some time and may have been one of the earliest of birds, judging by the number of purely reptilian features absent in all later birds. Its feathers were identical in structure to those of modern birds.

Bird bones are fragile and many are hollow, and thus easily broken and fragmented. Few land birds die where their remains can be buried in waterlaid sediments, the richest source of fossils, and it may also be assumed that many ancient birds, like those of the present, were preyed upon by carnivorous animals. Therefore, birds are poorly represented in fossil deposits and our knowledge of their evolutionary history is not as good as for reptiles and mammals. Indeed, Brodkorb has estimated that, between the time of *Archaeopteryx* and the present, up to two million species of birds probably existed, yet we have specimen evidence for the existence of less than ten thousand species, that is about half of one per cent (in Austin, 1961). However, from what we do have we are able to reconstruct sketch pictures of the early histories of most present day groups of birds.

The Eocene epoch commenced about sixty million years ago and spanned approximately twenty million years, and from this epoch onward bird fossils become increasingly plentiful. Forms closely resembling those living today had replaced the toothed birds of the Mesozoic. So many fossil birds from the early Tertiary period are assignable to living groups that most, possibly all, living orders had arisen by, or evolved during the Eocene. Of course, there were also characteristic forms which became extinct then or later (e.g. the terrestrial diatrymids).

Several authors have expressed clearly the doubts about conclusions reached by comparing fossil material with existing birds. It is widely accepted that forms related to birds living today existed as far back as the Eocene, but there have been unjustified identifications made from inadequate material. For example, Holyoak (1971b) points out that an upper mandible, fragment of skull, and two palatines of a parrot collected in Pleistocene deposits near Buenos Aires, Argentina, were assigned by Lyddekker to the genus *Conurus* (= *Aratinga*), but from the few characters it shows the specimen could represent a member of any one of fourteen living South American genera.

The earliest fossil parrot is *Archaeopsittacus verreauxi* from the upper Oligocene or lower Miocene, that is, about thirty million years ago; it was described from a tarsometatarsus found near Allier, France, but I believe that there is some doubt that the bone is from a parrot. The oldest representative of a modern genus is *Conuropsis fratercula* from the upper Miocene, that is approximately twenty million years ago; it was described from a left humerus found in Nebraska, United States of America. *Pionus ensenadensis* and *Aratinga roosevelti*, from Argentina and Ecuador respectively, date from the Pleistocene, that is, less than one million years ago, and are representatives of two widespread, living South American genera.

PARROTS AND OTHER BIRDS

Dorst (1964) says, 'Almost no other large group of birds is more sharply set apart from all others than the parrots, which form an exclusive order by themselves'. Stresemann (1927–1934) came to the conclusion that the parrots are a distinct group having no close relatives. Austin (1961) states that the parrots are a distinctive ancient group well warranting their ordinal rank. In *A Classification for the Birds of the World* (1960) Wetmore places Psittaciformes after Columbiformes (the pigeons) and before Cuculiformes (the cuckoos and touracos). Mayr and Amadon (1951) point out that the parrots are a strongly differentiated group; resemblance to Falconiformes (the hawks and eagles) is probably mere convergence and relationship to Cuculiformes must be distant. Structural similarities between the humeri of parrots and pigeons have been noted, and although this is certainly not conclusive evidence of any close affinity most authors place parrots after pigeons in their systematic lists.

I agree that there seem to be no obvious close relationships between parrots and other groups of birds, but pigeons may be nearest. While watching fruit pigeons (*Ptilinopus* spp.) feeding with fig parrots and lorikeets in large forest trees I have often noticed similarities in their actions and general behaviour. Pigeons also have fleshy ceres at the bases of their bills and the plumage patterns of some species, particularly the fruit pigeons, are like those of parrots. Of course, superficial similarities can be found in other groups of birds. For example, hawks and owls have bills somewhat resembling those of parrots. Zygodactylous feet are possessed by woodpeckers, jacamars, barbets, and toucans, all members of Piciformes; by cuckoos and touracos, both of which belong to Cuculiformes, and by the Trogoniformes, which have the inner or second instead of the outer or fourth toe turned backwards. Powder downs, which are well developed in parrots, are also present in herons—members of Ciconiformes, toucans—members of Piciformes, and in bowerbirds—members of Passeriformes.

CLASSIFICATION OF THE PARROTS

Within an order such as the Psittaciformes further categories are used by systematists to classify members of that order according to the suspected relationships and evolutionary patterns.

FAMILY (name ending in '—idae') is a grouping of similar genera; although the family is a primary category the grouping of genera within it is to a large extent subjective.

SUBFAMILY (name ending in '—inae') is a secondary category interpolated between family and genus where the genera in a family are sufficiently diverse and seem to fall into groups.

GENUS (plural genera) is a primary category representing a group of species. Mayr (1942) defines it as 'a systematic unit including one species or a group of species of presumably common phylogenetic origin, separated by a decided gap from other similar groups'. It is obligatory that every species be placed in a genus and the name of the genus (always written in italics and with a capital letter) constitutes the first word of the scientific name of a species. If there is only one species in a genus, the latter is monotypic, but if there are two or more species these are said to be congeneric and the genus polytypic.

SPECIES is the category on which present-day classification is based. It is regarded as a natural entity, whereas classification in all other categories, lower and higher, is subjective. Mayr (1940) defines species as 'groups of actually or potentially interbreeding natural populations, which are reproductively isolated from other such groups'. Amadon (1970) has rephrased the definition as follows: 'A species is a freely interbreeding population whose members do not interbreed with those of other populations'. In other words if a population of birds is breeding in a certain area in the company of another population and the members of each mate only with their own kind, then the two populations belong to separate species. For example, suppose that somewhere in Guatemala Green Conures (*Aratinga holochlora*) are commencing nesting activities, and that in the same area Orange-fronted Conures (*Aratinga canicularis*) are also breeding. The two kinds of parrots always pair within their own groups and not with members of the other group. They are separate species. However, there are obvious similarities between them so both are placed in the same genus. Species which are found breeding in the same area are said to be sympatric, while those which occur in different regions and are not found together are allopatric. As we shall see later the taxonomic treatment of allopatric populations is often subjective.

SUBSPECIES OR RACE is a category which has received much attention in recent years and its importance as an indicator of evolutionary change is now widely accepted. Mayr (1963) defines a subspecies as 'an aggregate of local populations of a species inhabiting a geographic subdivision of the range of the species and differing taxonomically from other populations of the species'.

It is a stage in the development of a species. Subspecies may be found within a continuous distribution or they may be separated by geographical or biological barriers.

(i) Subspecies occurring within a continuous distribution are illustrated by the Blue Bonnet (*Psephotus haematogaster*) from south-eastern Australia. In the southern part of its range the parrot has a yellow vent, but in the north this is red. There is no sharp geographical line of distinction but there is a narrow intermediate zone where birds have yellow vents with variable red markings.

(ii) Subspecies separated by a barrier are illustrated by the Eclectus Parrot (*Eclectus roratus*), a large parrot occurring in the Australasian area. In the southern Moluccas the female of the nominate subspecies (the first described) is red with a mauve-blue breast and collar. On Sumba, in the Lesser Sunda Islands, the female is entirely red without any mauve-blue markings. The population on Sumba Island is called an isolated subspecies, or isolate, of *Eclectus roratus* and is given a different subspecific name. The nominate subspecies then becomes *Eclectus roratus roratus* and the Sumba Island population *Eclectus roratus cornelia*.

Some doubt always exists concerning the status of isolates because one can never be certain that they would interbreed if brought together; it is a matter for taxonomic judgment. However, the prevailing practice is to emphasize affinities, and isolates are generally treated as subspecies or races of a single species. In cases where the taxonomic differences are so great as to suggest that the isolate would not interbreed with other isolates if the separating barriers were removed, the isolated populations can be treated as species within a single superspecies.

Classification is an attempt to subject living, ever-changing organisms to a static, 'pigeon-hole' type arrangement, so it is inevitable that there will be shortcomings. Differences of opinion from various taxonomists and inconsistencies in systematic lists are to be expected and should not be interpreted as evidence of failure of the system. In this book I have drawn attention to different arrangements, usually whether a certain form should be a subspecies or a species and whether a species belongs to one genus or to another. It must be remembered that although agreement on such matters is desirable it is not essential—more important is knowledge of the biological facts.

As already mentioned, Psittaciformes is a very homogeneous assemblage of forms, so differences available for separation into lower categories are minor. Systematists have always had difficulties classifying parrots and most arrangements proposed have been largely artificial, though convenient. Summing up the results from his comparative examinations of cranial osteology, Thompson (1900) remarked, 'To discover anatomical characters such as might yield or help to yield a natural classification of the Parrots has been the desire of many ornithologists, but the search has availed little'. Berlioz (1941) has expressed similar sentiments: 'Aucun caractère ostéologique no saurait être envisagé comme critère absolu pour un essai de groupement des Perroquets et la définition de leurs affinités respectives' (It has not been possible to envisage any osteological character as an absolute criterion for attempting to group the Parrots and to define their respective affinities).

Salvadori (1891) used a classification based entirely on external features, and it comprised seven families, one of which, Psittacidae, was divided into six subfamilies. Thompson followed Salvadori's classification when carrying out his osteological examinations, and although he demonstrated minor differences no major alterations were proposed. The work of these two pioneers is often criticized because emphasis was placed on what are now regarded as relatively unimportant, adaptive characters, but their classification still forms the basis for taxonomy of the Psittaciformes. Reichenow (1913) proposed a new arrangement comprising eight families and one of these, Psittacidae, was divided into three subfamilies; this was not radically different from that of Salvadori. Peters (1937) also relied strongly on Salvadori's arrangement when compiling his *Check-list*, but he used only one family separated into six subfamilies.

Verheyen (1956) analysed anatomical and ecological data, both published and original, on a number of species and proposed an arrangement comprising five families, three of which were divided into three or more subfamilies. Glenny (1957) looked at patterns in the carotid artery arrangement and recognized only one family, but this he divided into nine subfamilies. A radical arrangement was proposed by Brereton (1963) who, after considering both anatomical and ethological characters, set up two superfamilies. Inconclusive results were obtained by Gysels (1964) when he subjected extracts from eye lens and muscle to electrophoresis, but there was an indication that the one family of Peters comprised a number of separate subfamilies.

I am not a taxonomist and do not have access to large collections of specimens and anatomical material from all parts of the world so in this book there are no taxonomic discussions on the major subgroupings. I have given my opinions in a number of cases, for example, about whether *Nymphicus* is a cockatoo, and about the relationships of *Lathamus*, but these opinions are generally confined to species I know well in the field. In this book I have used an arrangement modified from that of Peters. It seems to me that *Strigops*, *Nestor*, *Micropsitta* and *Nymphicus* are genera which show differences setting them apart from related genera. There are also three major groups within the order—the lories and lorikeets, the cockatoos, and the parrots and parakeets. In other words there are two levels of distinction. To accommodate these levels nomenclaturally I have used families and subfamilies, because this is simple and makes use of widely recognized categories.

Of course, such an arrangement is largely arbitrary and probably has no worthwhile advantages over alternatives. The diagnostic characteristics for each category from family down to genus are given in the general text.

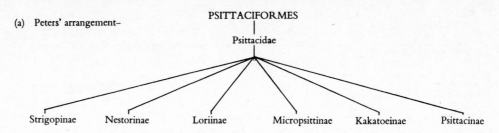

(a) Peters' arrangement–

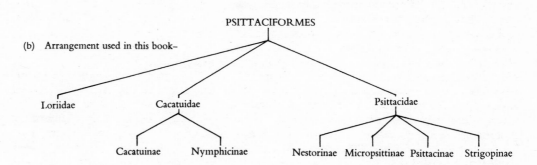

(b) Arrangement used in this book–

I shall now take a particular parrot, list the categories to which it belongs, and explain the derivation of its scientific name. The parrot is the very common Rose-ringed Parakeet from southern India and it is classified as follows:

Class: Aves
Order: Psittaciformes
Family: Psittacidae
Subfamily: Psittacinae
Genus: *Psittacula*
Species: *krameri*
Subspecies: *manillensis*

The scientific name is formed by writing the names of the last three categories followed by the name of the person who described and named it, in this case Bechstein. To signify that this parrot was placed in a different genus when originally described, the author's name is put in brackets. Therefore the scientific name of the Rose-ringed Parakeet from southern India is: *Psittacula krameri manillensis* (Bechstein).

Before ending this section on classification mention must be made of the Mallophaga, ecto-parasitic lice that live amongst the feathers of birds. The present distribution of the Mallophaga suggests that they became parasitic on the class Aves at an early stage in the evolution of that class and that they evolved with their hosts (Clay, 1964). This means that, generally speaking, the Mallophaga of related hosts are themselves related. Different species of birds do not normally come into contact with each other so there is little chance of interchange of lice populations, and this isolation has led to host restriction, so that in many cases a species of Mallophaga is found on only one host species or on a group of closely related host species. Each order of birds is parasitized by one or more mallophagan genera that are often peculiar to it, and the relationship between the species of these genera generally reflects the relationship between the hosts within the order. However, Clay points out that many factors such as discontinuous distribution of genera and species, parallel and convergent evolution, secondary infestations, and human error in interpretation of the evidence, may obscure the initial relationship between host and parasite, so that information about the occurrence of Mallophaga cannot be used as an infallible guide to relationships between the hosts.

Dr L. R. Guimarães from the Museu de Zoologia da Universidade de São Paulo has examined the Mallophaga from many species of parrots, with the notable exception of Micropsittinae. He has given me an outline of patterns of the relationships found in Ischnoceran Mallophaga, and, in my opinion, these provide a valuable guide to classification within the Psittaciformes. Mallophagan genera and their hosts are listed in Table 1, and the geographical distribution of mallophagan genera recorded from members of Psittacinae is given in Table 2.

	PARAGONIOCOTES	PSITTACONIRMUS	NEOPSITTACONIRMUS	ECHINOPHILOPTERUS	FORFICULOECUS	PSITTOECUS	THERESIELLA
LORIIDAE		●					
CACATUIDAE			●	●		●	
NESTORINAE			●	●	●		
PSITTACINAE	●		●	●			●

20

Table 2
Geographical distribution of mallophagan genera (Ischnocera) recorded from Psittacinae

	PARAGONIOCOTES	NEOPSITTACONIRMUS	ECHINOPHILOPTERUS	FORFICULOECUS	THERESIELLA
Central and South America	●				
Africa		●	●		
Madagascar		●	●		
Continental Asia		●	●		
Australian Region (including Philippines)		●	●	●	●

Parrots from the New World are parasitized only by the genus *Paragoniocotes*; it has been found on no other birds. I know of no anatomical features which suggest that Central and South American parrots are radically different from those of the Old World, but there is no doubt that they are a readily identifiable, homogeneous assemblage, which may have been isolated for a long time. The Loriidae is parasitized only by *Psittaconirmus*, and this genus has not been found on any other group of parrots. Three mallophagan genera have been recorded from Cacatuidae; *Psittoecus* has not been found on any other group of parrots, *Neopsittaconirmus* also occurs on Nestorinae and Psittacinae, and *Echinophilopterus* also on Psittacinae. Nestorinae has two genera; *Forficuloecus* also occurs on Psittacinae and *Neopsittaconirmus* also on both Psittacinae and Cacatuidae. There are five genera recorded from Psittacinae; one also occurs on Cacatuidae, another also on Nestorinae, another also on both Cacatuidae and Nestorinae, one is confined to parrots from the New World, and the newly-described *Theresiella* has been found only on *Psittacella* from New Guinea. The geographical distribution of mallophagan genera from Psittacinae is interesting; two are widespread throughout Africa, Madagascar, continental Asia and the Australasian area, two have been recorded only from the Australasian area, and one is confined entirely to Central and South America.

Summing up, we find that each of the three families Loriidae, Cacatuidae and Psittacidae has a mallophagan genus restricted to it. In the case of Loriidae there is only one genus and this has not been found on any other group of parrots. Two of the three genera found on Cacatuidae have also been recorded from Psittacidae. In Psittacidae there is a genus confined to parrots from Central and South America, another known only from *Psittacella* from New Guinea, one recorded only from Nestorinae and Psittacinae, and two that have also been found on Cacatuidae.

PHYSICAL ATTRIBUTES OF PARROTS

Some conspicuous external features of parrots have already been mentioned, but in this section these and less obvious characteristics will be described in more detail. Figures 3, 4, and 5 are an integral part of this section and are intended to replace wordy definitions and descriptions of technical terms such as nape, lower mandible, metatarsus, crop, etc. They are also designed as explanatory figures for plumage descriptions and anatomical features referred to in the main text.

PLUMAGE The plumage is the most important element in the external appearance of a bird. It plays a major role in intra-specific recognition, and parts are often specially adapted for use in display. The unit of plumage is the feather and there are about six types, of which the main two are contour feathers and down feathers. Contour feathers constitute the ordinarily visible plumage and include flight feathers, tail feathers, ear-coverts, tail-coverts and feathers on other parts of the body. Down feathers form an undercoat in most birds and are generally not visible. In parrots and some other birds there is another peculiar type of feather called a powder-down. A powder-down feather is a modified down feather which grows throughout the life of the bird, the barbs continually disintegrating into a fine powder; this powder is used by the birds for cleaning the feathers and gives the plumage a characteristic bloom.

In most birds contour feathers grow only from definite tracts of skin called pterylae, while the intervening areas, or apteria, are bare or with down but are covered by the overlapping of the contour feathers. Except in the 'ratite' birds, the penguins, and the toucans, there is a definite distribution of feather tracts and the study of the different patterns is known as pterylography or pterylosis. Pterylography is sometimes useful as a taxonomic character.

The plumage of parrots is sparse. This means that the pterylae are sparsely distributed and the apteria very prominent. Down feathers grow profusely from all parts of the skin, except on the neck where in many species the apteria are bare.

COLOUR The brilliant colours of many species of parrots demonstrate dramatically the processes of plumage colouration. In birds there are two types of colours: (i) structural colours and (ii) pigmentary colours. The structures responsible for structural colours are present in the barbs and barbules of the feathers. Dyck (1971) examined feathers from the Peach-faced Lovebird (*Agapornis roseicollis*) and came to the conclusion that in that species, and probably most other birds, blue and blue-green colours are due principally to back-scattering of light from the numerous hollow, randomly oriented keratin cylinders which make up the spongy structure of the barbs. The range of colours which may be produced by the spongy structure probably is not limited to blue and bluish-green; it is possible that other barb colours are produced by varying the dimensions of the spongy structure. He further points out that green barbs differ from blue barbs

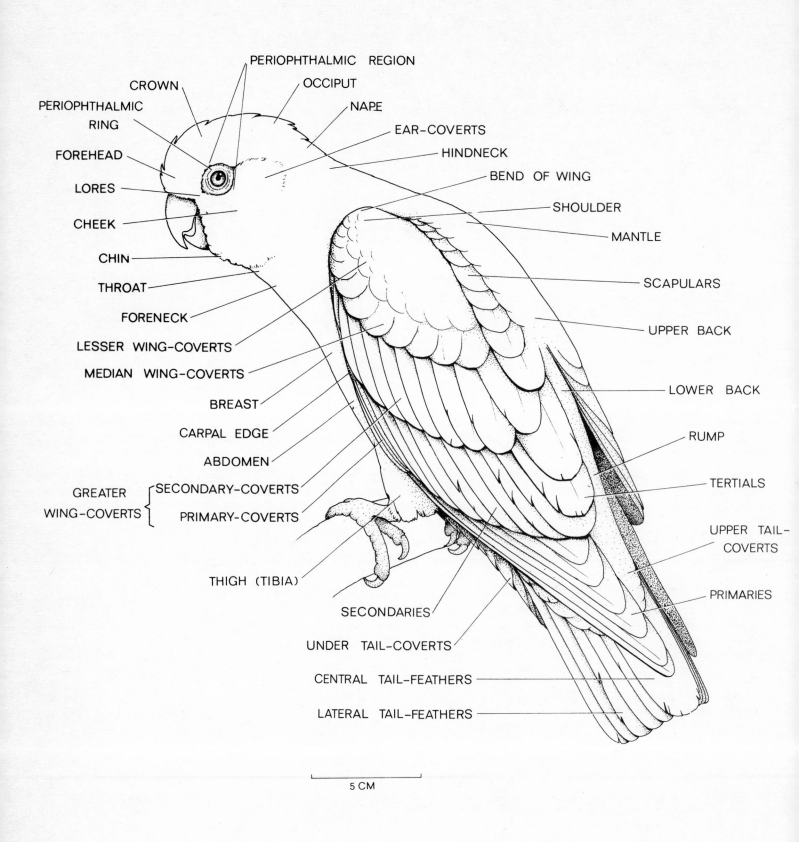

PERIOPHTHALMIC REGION

CROWN

OCCIPUT

PERIOPHTHALMIC RING

NAPE

FOREHEAD

EAR-COVERTS

LORES

HINDNECK

CHEEK

BEND OF WING

CHIN

SHOULDER

THROAT

MANTLE

FORENECK

SCAPULARS

LESSER WING-COVERTS

UPPER BACK

MEDIAN WING-COVERTS

BREAST

LOWER BACK

CARPAL EDGE

RUMP

ABDOMEN

TERTIALS

GREATER WING-COVERTS { SECONDARY-COVERTS

PRIMARY-COVERTS

UPPER TAIL-COVERTS

THIGH (TIBIA)

PRIMARIES

SECONDARIES

UNDER TAIL-COVERTS

CENTRAL TAIL-FEATHERS

LATERAL TAIL-FEATHERS

5 CM

Fig. 2a
Descriptive parts of a parrot—external features of a Galah (*Eolophus roseicapillus*).

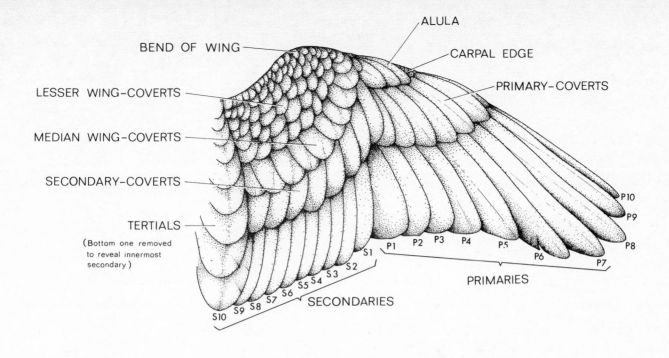

ALULA

BEND OF WING

CARPAL EDGE

LESSER WING-COVERTS

PRIMARY-COVERTS

MEDIAN WING-COVERTS

SECONDARY-COVERTS

TERTIALS

(Bottom one removed
to reveal innermost
secondary)

P10
P9
P8
P7
P6
P5
P4
P3
P2
P1
S1
S2
S3
S4
S5
S6
S7
S8
S9
S10

PRIMARIES

SECONDARIES

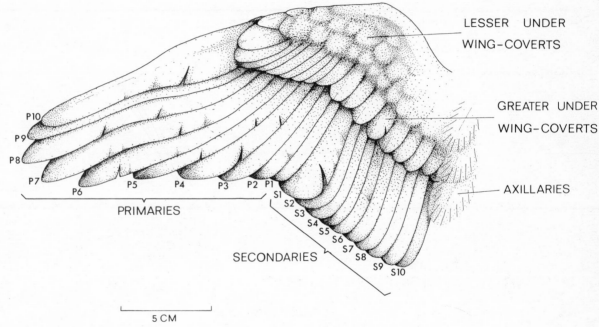

LESSER UNDER
WING-COVERTS

GREATER UNDER
WING-COVERTS

AXILLARIES

P10
P9
P8
P7
P6
P5
P4
P3
P2
P1
S1
S2
S3
S4
S5
S6
S7
S8
S9
S10

PRIMARIES

SECONDARIES

5 CM

Fig. 2b
Descriptive parts of a parrot—wing of a Galah (*Eolopus roseicapillus*). (Top) Upper side of wing. (Bottom) Under side of wing.

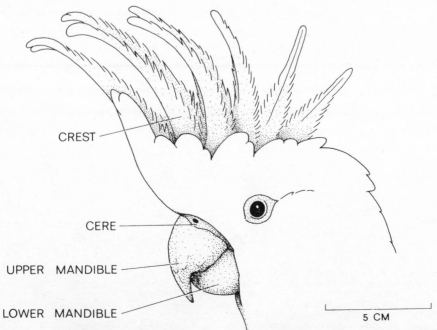

CREST

CERE

UPPER MANDIBLE

LOWER MANDIBLE

5 CM

Fig. 2c
Descriptive parts of a parrot—head of a Sulphur-crested Cockatoo (*Cacatua galerita*) showing the erectile crest.

23

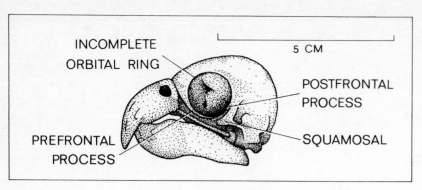

INCOMPLETE
ORBITAL RING

5 CM

POSTFRONTAL
PROCESS

PREFRONTAL
PROCESS

SQUAMOSAL

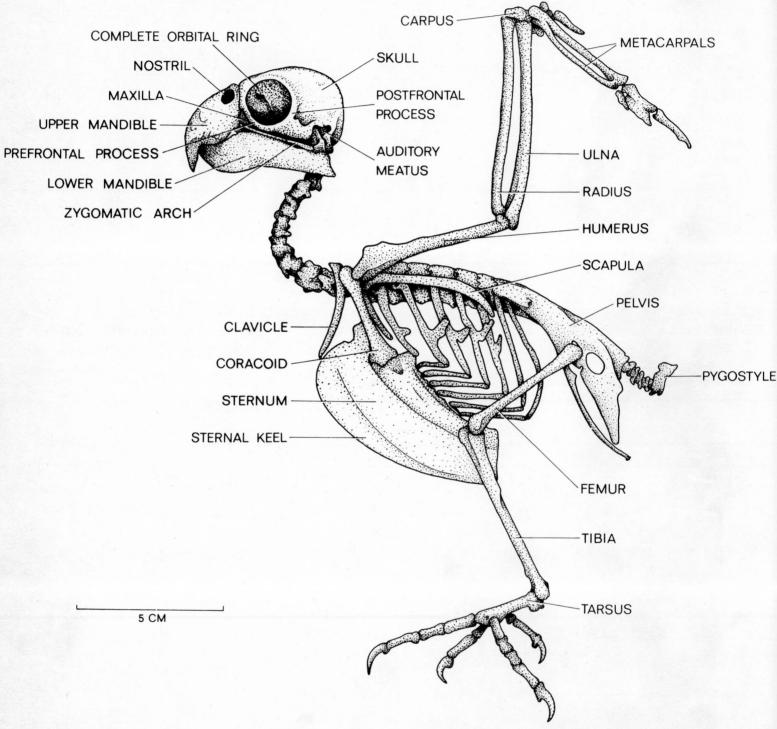

COMPLETE ORBITAL RING

NOSTRIL

MAXILLA

UPPER MANDIBLE

PREFRONTAL PROCESS

LOWER MANDIBLE

ZYGOMATIC ARCH

SKULL

POSTFRONTAL
PROCESS

AUDITORY
MEATUS

CARPUS

METACARPALS

ULNA

RADIUS

HUMERUS

SCAPULA

PELVIS

CLAVICLE

CORACOID

STERNUM

STERNAL KEEL

PYGOSTYLE

FEMUR

TIBIA

TARSUS

5 CM

Fig. 3
Descriptive parts of a parrot—skeleton of a Galah (*Eolophus roseicapillus*). Inset: Skull of an Eastern Rosella (*Platycercus eximius*) showing the incomplete orbital ring.

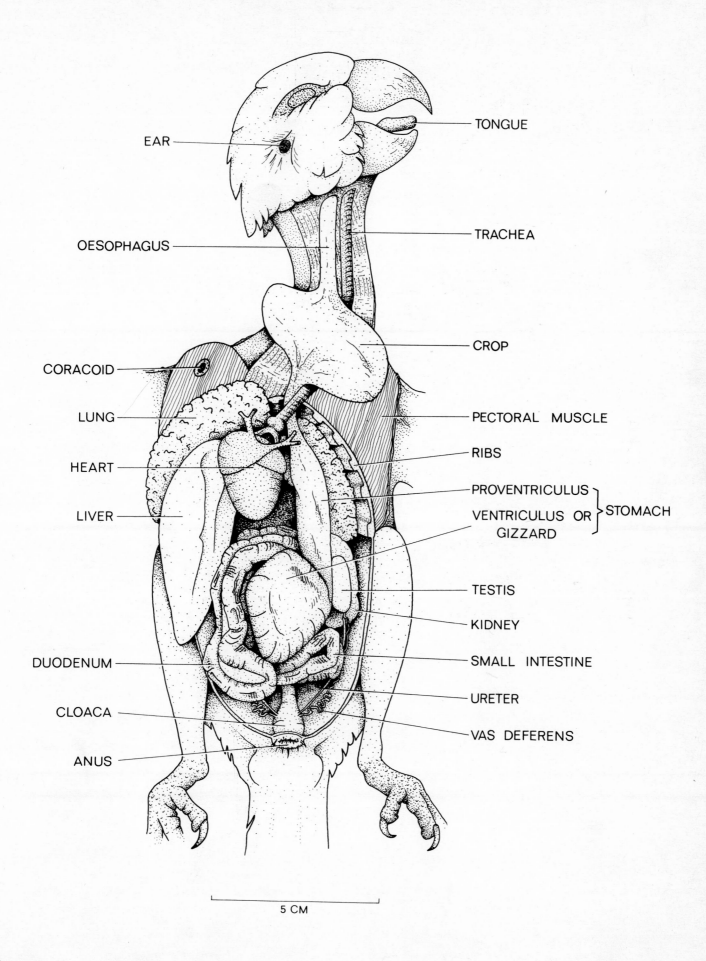

EAR

TONGUE

OESOPHAGUS

TRACHEA

CROP

CORACOID

LUNG

PECTORAL MUSCLE

HEART

RIBS

PROVENTRICULUS

LIVER

VENTRICULUS OR
GIZZARD

} STOMACH

TESTIS

KIDNEY

DUODENUM

SMALL INTESTINE

URETER

CLOACA

VAS DEFERENS

ANUS

5 CM

Fig. 4
Descriptive parts of a parrot—digestive tract and reproductive organs (male only) of a Galah (*Eolophus roseicapillus*).

in having a yellow-pigmented cortex and a denser spongy structure with wider keratin rods and correspondingly narrower air-filled channels. Vevers (1964) says that iridescent colours result from barbules being flattened for parts of their length and twisted at right angles. Pigmentary colours, as the name suggests, are due to pigments, of which the commonest is called melanin. The exact chemical composition of melanin is not known, but despite the name it is not always black and may be brown, red-brown, or even yellow. Other pigments include turacin and the carotenoids.

In parrots there are two types of pigments of unknown composition. In one type the pigment is pale yellow in visible light and fluorescent yellow-gold, sulphur-yellow, or green in ultra-violet light. Volker (1937) points out that these pigments are not present in the Loriidae or in the genus *Eclectus*, have been found in only two South American species (*Bolborhynchus lineola* and *Pionites leucogaster*), but are common in Australasian parrots and cockatoos; crest feathers of some *Cacatua* spp. are coloured by one of these pigments. The second type consists of non-fluorescent red or yellow pigments found in some parrots, including the Budgerigar (*Melopsittacus undulatus*) and the Cuban Amazon (*Amazona leucocephala*).

Many colours are due to a combination of two or more pigmentary colours or to a combination of pigmentary and structural colours. For example, purple on the head of the Plum-headed Parakeet (*Psittacula cyanocephala*) is the result of the barbules of the feathers containing red pigment and the structure of the barbs producing blue (Vevers, 1964). Dyck notes that dark green back feathers of the Peach-faced Lovebird (*Agapornis roseicollis*) reflect approximately half as much light throughout the visible spectrum as do the paler green abdominal feathers, the difference being due to variations in yellow and black pigmentation of the barbules.

BILL AND TONGUE The bill of a parrot is characteristic and comprises a down-curved upper mandible fitting neatly over a broad, up-curved lower mandible. The upper mandible is attached to the skull by a 'hinge-like' arrangement thus allowing extensive movement of both mandibles. Kinesis, that is movement of the upper mandible in relation to the skull, is present in most birds, but is especially marked in the parrots and the resulting increase in leverage enables parrots to crush the seeds and nuts that constitute the diet of so many species. There are some minor modifications in bill shape for different feeding habits, but in all species the basic structure is identical. For example, the upper mandible of the Slender-billed Corella (*Cacatua tenuirostris*) is elongated and less curved and is used to dig up roots and corms; the upper mandibles of the Slender-billed Conure (*Enicognathus leptorhynchus*) and the Red-capped Parrot (*Purpureicephalus spurius*) are also elongated and less curved and seem to be ideal for extracting certain seeds, while those species which feed extensively on pollen and nectar have narrow, protruding bills (e.g. the Loriidae, and *Loriculus* spp., *Touit* spp., and *Brotogeris* spp.).

Parrots have a thick, fleshy tongue, generally with a thick and horny epithelium towards the tip. In the Loriidae and *Lathamus discolor* it is tipped with 'brush-like' papillae used for gathering pollen (see Fig. 6).

SKULL A parrot's skull is broad and relatively large with a spacious brain cavity. Vlasblom (1953) points out that as a rule the brain is relatively small in large species and relatively large in small species. The orbits are very large and may be completely or incompletely ringed by bone. Thompson (1900) has shown which species and genera have complete or incomplete orbital rings, and his findings are included in the diagnostic features of respective genera.

DIGESTIVE TRACT The digestive tract of a bird is basically the same as that common to all vertebrates, and consists essentially of a coiled tube or gut leading from the mouth to the anus. In common with other grain-eating birds parrots have well-developed crops and gizzards, and these deserve special mention here. The crop is a thin-walled, distensible elaboration of the oesophagus, where food is stored for subsequent digestion or feeding of the young by regurgitation. The proventriculus and gizzard (ventriculus) together correspond to the stomach in mammals. The gizzard is weak and not muscular in the Loriidae, particularly in species that feed almost exclusively on pollen and nectar, but in other parrots it is highly developed with thick walls and massive muscles. Digestive juices are secreted by the glandular walls of the proventriculus.

A protein secretion similar to that originating from cells lining the crop in a pigeon and known as 'pigeon milk' has recently been described from the Budgerigar (*Melopsittacus undulatus*), though in that species it may be proventricular in origin.

NATURAL HISTORY OF PARROTS

As a rule parrots are difficult to observe in the wild state. Most are predominantly green and live in the canopy of rainforest. Often the only view one gets is a momentary glimpse when a screeching flock flashes overhead. While feeding in the treetops they can escape detection because of their protective colouration, and an observer may be unaware of their presence until they suddenly burst out from the foliage and fly off screeching loudly. Species which inhabit open country or are plentiful in the vicinity of habitation are conspicuous and there is more information on their habits. For example, we have fairly good information on the habits of such species as the Eastern Rosella (*Platycercus eximius*), the Alexandrine Parakeet (*Psittacula eupatria*), Meyer's Parrot

(*Poicephalus meyeri*) and the Monk Parakeet (*Myiopsitta monachus*), but virtually nothing is known of the habits of many forest-dwelling species like Salvadori's Fig Parrot (*Psittaculirostris salvadorii*), the Black-collared Lovebird (*Agapornis swinderniana*), the Golden-plumed Conure (*Leptosittaca branickii*) and the Spot-winged Parrotlet (*Touit stictoptera*).

In contrast to what is known about the nesting habits of most other groups of birds, information on the breeding behaviour of parrots is poor and very generalized. This is probably because nearly all species nest in hollows in trees or holes in termitaria, sites which do not facilitate observations on incubation, parental care, development of chicks, etc. Most of what is known about nesting comes from birds in captivity and there are striking individual variations in behaviour, some of which must be due to the artificial conditions.

LONGEVITY AND MORTALITY

The longevity of parrots in captivity is well known. There are records of some of the larger species living in captivity for between thirty and fifty, and even up to eighty years. I know of a Little Corella (*Cacatua sanguinea*) that was taken from a nest in central Australia in 1904 and is still living in captivity. There is very little data on the length of life in the wild state, because only in Australia have parrots been banded in any numbers. The scant information we do have from wild birds suggests that parrots are long-lived, particularly the larger species. In Table 3 I have listed longevity records obtained from banding returns submitted to the Australian Bird-Banding Scheme. The records listed refer to birds banded as adults, so these birds had already lived for an unknown number of years, and at the time of recovery they were still alive or had died from unnatural causes. In other words, the length of time between initial banding and recovery is only an unknown portion of the potential life-span of the bird.

Table 3
Longevity records from Australian banding reports

	BAND NO.	INITIAL BANDING	DATE	RECOVERY	DATE
LITTLE CORELLA (*Cacatua sanguinea*)	110–02323	Banded as adult: 34°11′ S. 142°04′ E	16th Feb., 1961	Killed by car: 34°08′ S. 142°00′ E	12th Jan., 1972
SULPHUR-CRESTED COCKATOO (*Cacatua galerita*)	120–11317	Banded as adult: 37°08′ S. 140°49′ E	19th Sept., 1960	Caught in rabbit trap: 37°14′ S. 140°44′ E	20th Sept., 1968
EASTERN ROSELLA (*Platycercus eximius*)	060–1992	Banded as adult: 30°31′ S. 151°42′ E	2nd July, 1961	Trapped and released at banding point	2nd Oct., 1970
RED-RUMPED PARROT (*Psephotus haematonotus*)	060–01609	Banded as adult: 37°08′ S. 140°49′ E	15th Sept., 1956	Trapped and released at banding point	27th June, 1964

Although there is no evidence to suggest that mortality is highest in young birds before they reach sexual maturity, I suspect that this is as true for parrots as for many other birds. Nowadays the most prevalent cause of death is probably man and his activities: parrots are shot and poisoned because of damage they do to crops, they are shot, trapped, and taken from nests for the pet trade, they are hit by cars, and they are preyed upon by feral cats and other introduced predators. I suppose that natural causes of death would include disease, predation by birds of prey, and starvation brought about by unfavourable climatic conditions such as drought.

Burnet (1939) reports that outbreaks of fatal ornithosis in wild parrots have been observed amongst Australian King Parrots (*Alisterus scapularis*) in Victoria and Eastern Rosellas (*Platycercus eximius*) in Tasmania, and in south-eastern parts of South Australia there was a highly fatal epizootic in parrots, probably Red-rumped Parrots (*Psephotus haematonotus*). In January 1939, near Adelaide, South Australia, numbers of Adelaide Rosellas (*Platycercus adelaidae*) were seen dropping dead from trees and at the time this was attributed to exceptionally hot weather and no investigations were made, but in view of the widespread epizootics of ornithosis it would seem more likely that this was another epizootic focus of the disease (Miles, 1959). During the years 1887–1888, in the Adelaide Hills, South Australia, Red-rumped Parrots (*Psephotus haematonotus*) were found to be suffering from a disease or infection which prevented feathers being renewed after moulting; naked, but otherwise healthy-looking birds were seen running about on the ground where they were easy prey to all predators (Ashby, 1907). Johnson (1967) reports that in recent years Newcastle disease has been responsible for a decline in the numbers of Slender-billed Conures (*Enicognathus leptorhynchus*) in Chile, though not on the same scale as in the case of the Chilean Pigeon (*Columba araucana*) which was almost exterminated by the virus.

It seems that even large parrots are attacked by birds of prey. I have seen a Wedge-tailed Eagle (*Aquila audax*) take a Sulphur-crested Cockatoo (*Cacatua galerita*), though at the time I suspected that the cockatoo was probably an old, weak bird. On a few occasions I have observed Peregrine Falcons (*Falco peregrinus*) take Galahs (*Eolophus roseicapillus*), and there are records of these cockatoos being killed by Little Eagles (*Hieraatus morphnoides*)

DISTRIBUTION

The three hundred and thirty-two extant species of parrots are distributed mainly in the Southern Hemisphere and are most prevalent in tropical regions. Following the extinction of the Carolina Parakeet (*Conuropsis carolinensis*), the Slaty-headed Parakeet (*Psittacula himalayana*), which inhabits the Safed Koh area in eastern Afghanistan (lat. 34°N.), is the species with the northernmost distribution. Tierra del Fuego (lat. 55°S.), inhabited by the Austral Conure (*Enicognathus ferrugineus*), is the southern limit of distribution of parrots now that the Red-fronted Parakeet (*Cyanoramphus novaezelandiae*) no longer occurs on Macquarie Island. The order is most strongly represented in Australasia and South America, though in South America there is a marked uniformity of types. There are parrots in Asia, mainly on the Indian sub-continent, and in Africa, but representation in these parts of the world is much less than might have been expected. The following list of numbers of species occurring in selected countries illustrates the pattern of distribution within the order:

Australia	52 species
New Guinea	46 ,,
Philippines	11 ,,
Central Africa	14 species
Southern Africa	10 ,,
India	10 ,,
Brazil	70 species
Colombia	49 ,,
Venezuela	48 ,,
Argentina	25 ,,
Mexico	18 ,,

Glenny (1954) considers that the present distribution of parrots, especially the concentrations in Australia and South America, is contributory evidence for the theory that Antarctica was a centre of origin of birds; movement away from Antarctica could have been by way of South America and Australia. I see no reason why the parrots could not have originated in virtually any region and ancestral forms spread to South America, Africa and Australia perhaps when those continents were much closer together and were connected by way of Antarctica, as recently as sixty-five million years ago (see Dietz and Holden, 1970).

Some parrots are widely distributed, while others have very restricted ranges. The most widely distributed species is the Rose-ringed Parakeet (*Psittacula krameri*), which occurs in Asia and northern Africa and has been introduced to parts of the Middle East and South-East Asia. Other widespread species include the Blue-headed Parrot (*Pionus menstruus*) from Central and South America and the Port Lincoln Parrot (*Barnardius zonarius*) from southern and western Australia. Most of the species with restricted ranges are confined to islands which are quite small. Antipodes Island, with a total area of approximately 38 sq. km., is inhabited by two closely related parrots, one of which, the Antipodes Green Parakeet (*Cyanoramphus unicolor*), is endemic. Another small island on which an endemic species occurs is Henderson Island, a tiny coral atoll in the Pacific Ocean that is inhabited by Stephen's Lory (*Vini stepheni*). There are species which occur in only very small areas on large land-masses, for example the Rufous-fronted Parakeet (*Bolborhynchus ferrugineifrons*) and the Tepui Parrotlet (*Nannopsittaca panychlora*), but such are not common.

HABITATS

Lowland, tropical rainforest is the habitat in which parrots are particularly plentiful, and here they may be seen climbing amongst the foliage of trees bearing flowers or fruit. In New Guinea, and in northern Australia and Guyana I have noticed that they seem to be more common along the edges of forest where it borders a watercourse or swamp, or meets a track, clearing or some similar interruption, and are not plentiful deep in the forest itself; of course, this could simply be due to the difficulty of seeing them in dense forest.

Species which inhabit open country also show a strong attachment to trees, particularly those lining watercourses, and are seldom seen far from such cover. They frequently come into botanical gardens and parklands, which are often situated well within urban boundaries. In parts of Australia Galahs (*Eolophus roseicapillus*) and Red-rumped Parrots (*Psephotus haematonotus*) are commonly seen perching on telegraph wires above city streets. In India Rose-ringed Parakeets (*Psittacula krameri*) often come down to drink from a community well in a very busy marketplace. In the Praça do República, a small park set amidst the towering buildings of central São Paulo, Brazil's largest city, I have observed small flocks of Plain Parakeets (*Brotogeris tirica*).

Generally speaking, parrots are less common at higher altitudes, and those species that do occur there are absent from or rare in neighbouring lowlands. There are some distinctive highland forms, such as the Papuan Lory (*Charmosyna papou*) and the Whiskered Lorikeet (*Oreopsittacus arfaki*) from New Guinea, Johnstone's Lorikeet (*Trichoglossus johnstoniae*) from Mindanao in the Philippines, the Derbyan Parakeet (*Psittacula derbiana*) from Tibet, the Yellow-faced Parrot (*Poicephalus flavifrons*) from Ethiopia, and the Sierra Parakeet (*Bolborhynchus aymara*) and Tepui Parrotlet (*Nannopsittaca panychlora*) from South America. Possibly the most interesting of all highland forms is the Kea (*Nestor notabilis*) from the Southern Alps of New Zealand; it is a species that has been much maligned in the literature because of its alleged sheep-killing habits. I suppose that it is somewhat incongruous to think of parrots, an essentially tropical group of birds, occurring amidst snow-covered surroundings, but the Kea even rolls about in snow and gets well covered in the process. In the Southern Alps of Australia I have often seen Gang-Gang Cockatoos (*Callocephalon fimbriatum*) wheeling about above the forest canopy while snow is falling, and Crimson Rosellas (*Platycercus elegans*) on snow-covered ground searching for exposed seed-heads.

There are a few species that occur in very specialized habitats. One of the best examples is the completely terrestrial Ground Parrot (*Pezoporus wallicus*), which is found only in coastal and contiguous mountain heathlands in southern Australia, a very restricted habitat that is rapidly disappearing. The Rock Parrot (*Neophema petrophila*) occurs along the southern seaboard of Australia and nests in crevices under overhanging slabs of rock above high-water level. There are other species which do not show such specific habitat requirements, but their habitats are dominated by a particular plant or vegetation community that seems to be indispensable to the birds, usually as a source of food or nesting sites. Examples of parrot species found in close association with particular plant species are: the Glossy Cockatoo (*Calyptorhynchus lathami*) and *Casuarina*; the Red-capped Parrot (*Purpureicephalus spurius*) and *Eucalyptus calophylla*; the Thick-billed Parrot (*Rhynchopsitta pachyrhyncha*) and *Pinus*; the Red-spectacled Amazon (*Amazona pretrei*) and *Araucaria* and the Tucuman Amazon (*A. tucumana*) and *Alnus*. Sometimes the association is obvious but the reasons obscure; for example, in the case of the Black-cheeked Lovebird (*Agapornis nigrigenis*) being confined mainly to *Colophospermum* woodland.

FEEDING

The diet of the majority of parrots comprises seeds and fruits of various kinds and these are procured in the treetops or on the ground. Lories and lorikeets are strictly arboreal and feed on pollen, nectar, and soft fruits. There are few published results from analyses of crop and stomach contents, but where this work has been done, mainly in Australia and Brazil, one interesting fact has been brought to light and that is the proportion of insect material in the contents. Insect remains have been listed in the contents from many species, even those that normally feed on grass seeds. Some of these insects could have been ingested accidentally, but I believe that parrots as a group are far more insectivorous than is generally suspected. The 'black cockatoos' from Australia (*Calyptorhynchus* spp.) feed extensively on insect larvae and for one species, the Yellow-tailed Cockatoo (*C. funereus*), these make up the staple diet.

When feeding, a parrot makes full use of both its hooked bill and zygodactylous feet. While climbing amongst the foliage of a tree in search of fruits or flowers, it often uses its bill to grasp a branch and then steps up or across from its previous position. When walking along a stout limb, it may simply press the tip of its bill firmly against the limb thus stabilising its balance and presumably allowing more rapid progress. Many species use one of their feet as a 'hand' to hold food up to the bill. Smith (1971a) has surveyed what he terms 'prehensile-footed' feeding and concludes that it is present in most, if not all, members of Loriidae, in all cockatoos except *Nymphicus*, and in the majority of the Psittacidae, exceptions in that family being mainly those species which are essentially ground-feeding birds.

Friedmann and Davis (1938) record observations on twenty captive parrots belonging to seven genera and sixteen species, the majority being neotropical. They noted for each individual the number of times it used its right or left foot to bring food to its beak. A little over 72% of the individual birds showed a tendency to use the left foot to hold food. The Orange-chinned Parakeet (*Brotogeris jugularis*), represented by three individuals, was never seen to use the right foot, while one Great-billed Parrot (*Tanygnathus megalorynchos*) used its right foot in 95% of its feedings. Of the genus *Amazona*, seven species showed a 67% use of the left foot while there was a 70.5% use of the left foot in the ten individuals involved. One Orange-winged Amazon (*Amazona amazonica*) used the left foot in 75% of its feedings. McNeil *et al.* (1971) report that of fifty-six captive Brown-throated Conures (*Aratinga pertinax*) twenty-eight consistently used the left foot to hold food and twenty-eight used the right. These birds were killed and the hindlimb segments (femur, tibiotarsus, and tarsometatarsus) were separated and measured. It was found that in the twenty-eight birds that consistently used the right foot there was a positive bilateral difference between homologue legs, the right leg being slightly longer than the left, while in the birds that used the left foot there was a less pronounced tendency for left limb segments (except the femur) to be longer.

As anyone who has watched a caged parrot shelling seeds well knows, parrots are very adept at extracting the kernel and discarding the husk. To do this the bird uses its thick tongue to steady the seed against the broad, ridged underside of its upper mandible and with the front cutting-edge of the lower mandible peels away the seed-coat.

FLIGHT

The flight of most parrots, especially the smaller ones, is swift and direct. Some have a characteristically undulating flight which is produced by each series of wingbeats being followed by a period of gliding or by a brief pause with the wings withdrawn in against the body. In the larger birds it is variable; macaws are fairly fast fliers, but the buoyant flight of 'black cockatoos' (*Probosciger* and *Calyptorhynchus*) is conspicuously slow and laboured. It is often stated that parrots are not capable of sustained flight, but I doubt that such a generalized statement can be applied. When watching evening flights of Sulphur-crested Cockatoos (*Cacatua galerita*), Eclectus Parrots (*Eclectus roratus*), and various amazons (*Amazona* spp.) returning to the roosting trees, I have been impressed by the birds' mastery of the air; they first appear as specks on the horizon and then pass high overhead giving the impression that they have come considerable distances.

Parrots found on oceanic islands sometimes fly from one island to another, but the distances usually involved are not great. The Blue-winged Parrot (*Neophema chrysostoma*) and the Swift Parrot (*Lathamus discolor*) from south-eastern Australia migrate across Bass Strait, which has an average width of approximately 200 km. and contains a number of islands, though many of these are treeless and would not provide suitable resting places for the arboreal *Lathamus*.

CALL-NOTES

The distinctly metallic call-notes of most parrots are harsh and unmelodic. Generally they are based on a simple syllable or a combination of simple syllables, and variation comes primarily from the timing of repetition. In general, the larger species have lower pitched calls. Members of the Australian platycercine genera have pleasant, whistle-like calls and one species, the Red-rumped Parrot (*Psephotus haematonotus*), often emits a prolonged trill-like whistle, almost a song.

The mimicry of captive parrots is well-known, so it is very surprising to find that there are no convincing reports of wild birds imitating other species. Nottebohm and Nottebohm (1969) sought evidence of this in Nariva Swamp, Trinidad, but found that neither the Orange-winged Amazon (*Amazona amazonica*) or the Red-bellied Macaw (*Ara manilata*), the two common species in the locality, imitated other birds. However, it was noticed that in various parts of Trinidad calls of Orange-winged Amazons varied locally, thus suggesting that individuals may have to learn the dialect of the local population.

NESTING HABITS

As stated previously, our knowledge of the nesting habits of parrots is poor and what information we do have comes largely from birds in captivity.

SEXUAL DIMORPHISM Sexual dimorphism in parrots is confined mainly to differences in plumage colouration. Females of some species in *Psittacula* have shorter central tail feathers than have the males, and in the racket-tailed Parrots (*Prioniturus* spp.) there is a slight sex difference in length of the central rackets. Sex differences in plumage colouration, including colours of soft parts, are common in parrots from Australasia and Asia, but very uncommon in African and South American species. Females of sexually dimorphic species are generally duller than males and lack some of the prominent markings, but there are two notable exceptions to this rule:
(i) the sexes of the Eclectus Parrot (*Eclectus roratus*) are so different that for nearly a century they were considered to be separate species; the male is rich green with red flanks and under wing-coverts, the female is bright red with or without blue on the underparts;
(ii) the female Rüppell's Parrot (*Poicephalus rueppellii*) is more brightly coloured than the male.

SEXUAL MATURITY The age at which parrots reach sexual maturity varies, but in general it is three or four years in the larger species and one to two years in small birds. Vane (1957) reports that a captive pair of Red-lored Amazons (*Amazona autumnalis*) started laying when they were about three years old. Licht (1968) notes that a female Festive Amazon (*Amazona festiva*), obtained as a pet when six months old, exhibited soliciting behaviour for the first time when three years old. Most *Psittacula* parrots, some rosellas (*Platycercus* spp.), and *Polytelis* species become sexually mature in their second year. Some rosellas and related groups (*Platycercus*, *Barnardius*, *Psephotus*, *Cyanoramphus*, and *Neophema* spp.), some conures (*Aratinga* and *Pyrrhura* spp.), parrotlets (*Forpus* spp.) and lovebirds (*Agapornis* spp.) will breed within the first year. There are records of Australian King Parrots (*Alisterus scapularis*) and Crimson Rosellas (*Platycercus elegans*) breeding while in immature plumage. Marshall and Serventy (1958) quote data showing that young male Budgerigars (*Melopsittacus undulatus*) may produce spermatozoa within sixty days of leaving the nest; this rapid sexual development is a physiological adaptation to an arid environment and enables very young birds to reproduce quickly when conditions are propitious.

PAIR BONDS The Kea (*Nestor notabilis*) is polygamous, but, as far as can be ascertained from observations, other species are monogamous and most mate for very long periods, perhaps for life. Pairs and family groups are readily discernible within the large flocks of gregarious parrots, such as amazons and some cockatoos. When watching flocks of Red-rumped Parrots (*Psephotus haematonotus*) resting in trees, I invariably see males sidling along branches towards their mates; individuals in each pair then chatter to each other and indulge in mutual preening. Hardy (1965) studied flocks of Orange-fronted Conures (*Aratinga canicularis*), in the wild and in captivity, and found that birds in a flock were in pairs and showed evidence of peck order; in captivity pair bonds were maintained throughout the year and were often essential to the social success and social mobility of individuals. Power (1967) reports that in captive flocks of Orange-chinned Parakeets (*Brotogeris jugularis*) there was a tendency for birds to roost and feed in pairs and this resulted in the formation of flock mates, a union that presumably would lead to the formation of breeding pairs during the breeding season; pair bonds were maintained by close and relatively continual association, and by acts of mutual preening and courtship feeding.

COURTSHIP DISPLAY Courtship displays of only a few species of parrots have been described, and most of these come from observations on captive birds. From available information I think it may be assumed that courtship displays of parrots are, as a rule, simple; even the most elaborate consist of a series of simple actions such as bowing, wing-drooping, wing-flicking, tail-wagging, foot-raising, dilation of the pupils, etc. Prominently coloured parts of the plumage of males generally feature strongly in their displays; for example, the Sulphur-crested Cockatoo (*Cacatua galerita*) and Major Mitchell's Cockatoo (*C. leadbeateri*) raise their crests, the Australian King Parrot (*Alisterus scapularis*) flicks its wings to highlight the pale green scapulars, and the Black-capped Lory (*Lorius lory*) opens its wings to expose the brilliant yellow undersides. Prior to copulation there is considerable bodily contact in the form of bill-rubbing, mutual preening, and courtship feeding. During courtship feeding the male feeds regurgitated food to the female in the same manner as the female feeds the chicks.

NEST SITES Nests are usually in hollows in trees or holes in arboreal and terrestrial termitaria, occasionally in holes in banks or in crevices among rocks. If in termitaria the tunnel and nesting chamber are excavated by the birds themselves. Natural hollows in trees or old nesting holes of other birds, such as woodpeckers and barbets, are frequently enlarged and altered to suitable dimensions, but few parrots are known to excavate fresh hollows in trees. Puget (1970) points out that in eastern Afghanistan the Slaty-headed Parakeet (*Psittacula himalayana*) nearly always nests in old nesting holes of the Scaly-bellied Woodpecker (*Picus squamatus*). There is concern for the status of the Thick-billed Parrot (*Rhynchopsitta pachyrhyncha*) from northern Mexico because of its alleged dependence on nesting holes of the very rare Imperial Woodpecker (*Campephilus imperialis*). Double-eyed Fig Parrots (*Opopsitta diophthalma*), Red-cheeked Parrots (*Geoffroyus geoffroyi*), and Red-breasted Pygmy Parrots (*Micropsitta bruijnii*) are species which do excavate fresh hollows in tree trunks, and almost certainly there are others. Crevices in walls or under the eaves of buildings are also used as nesting sites by some parrots, especially the Rose-ringed Parakeet (*Psittacula krameri*) in India. Keas (*Nestor notabilis*) and Kakapos (*Strigops habroptilus*) from New Zealand, and Patagonian Conures (*Cyanoliseus patagonus*) from southern South America dig burrows in the ground or under rocks, the Rock Parrot (*Neophema petrophila*) from Australia and the Red-fronted Conure (*Aratinga wagleri*) from South America nest in crevices in rocks, and a few Australasian species nest on the ground under or in grass tussocks. Monk Parrots (*Myiopsitta monachus*) gather twigs and dead branches to build a huge communal nest in a tree; each pair of birds has its own breeding chamber; the species is thus unique among parrots.

Most parrots do not bring lining material to the nest cavity; the eggs are simply laid on decayed wood dust or crumbled earth that accumulates on the bottom. The African lovebirds (*Agapornis* spp.) and the hanging parrots (*Loriculus* spp.) line their nests with grass, twigs, and leaves carried there by the birds in their bills or thrust among the body feathers, particularly those of the rump.

EGG-LAYING Eggs are usually laid every other day, but there is some deviation from this rule. Marchant (1960) found that in south-western Ecuador laying by the Pacific Parrotlet (*Forpus coelestis*) may have been irregular and varied from intervals of thirty-six to forty-eight hours. Lamba (1966) reports that for the Rose-ringed Parakeet (*Psittacula krameri*) intervals between eggs vary from twenty-four to forty-eight hours. I have a record of a captive Bourke's Parrot (*Neophema bourkii*) laying a clutch of four eggs with an interval of thirty-two hours between each egg. In the genus *Calyptorhynchus* there is one species that invariably lays only one egg (*C. lathami*), but the other two species sometimes lay two, the second, being laid several days after the first, generally fails to hatch, but if it does the chick is neglected and soon dies.

Clutch size varies from species to species, but is generally within the range of from two to four or five, sometimes up to eight for small species. The eggs are relatively small and are pure white.

INCUBATION AND PARENTAL CARE It is difficult to ascertain when incubation actually commences, and there is some indication that this may vary individually. As a rule it commences with or immediately after the laying of the second egg, but there are reports of captive females commencing to sit after the last egg has been laid, particularly when the clutch is larger than average. Lamba (1966) says that the female Rose-ringed Parakeet (*Psittacula krameri*) starts sitting from the very day the first egg is laid. Hardy (1963) reports that with the Orange-fronted Conure (*Aratinga canicularis*) incubation begins with the first egg. Generally the female alone incubates and while she sits is fed by the male, but there are a number of species in which males share incubation. In the Loriidae males spend considerable time in the nest with the females, but it is doubtful that they participate in incubation. Duration of incubation varies roughly in proportion to the size of the bird; for small parrots it is from seventeen to twenty-three days, but for the large macaws it can be up to five weeks.

The newly-hatched young are nidicolous and psilopaedic, that is blind and naked or with sparse dorsal down, which is white in most species. The down of *Calyptorhynchus*, *Callocephalon* and *Nymphicus* nestlings is yellow, of *Eolophus* nestlings pink, and of *Pezoporus* nestlings dark sooty grey, almost black. The eyes open seven to fourteen days after hatching. In most species the original white down is soon replaced by, or supplemented with, a dense grey down, and this gradually gives way to feathers. Newly-hatched nestlings are closely brooded and fed by the female, who in turn is fed by the male, but when they are about five to ten days old the male assists by feeding them directly.

The young birds develop slowly and remain in the nest for three to four weeks in the case of small parrots, such as *Forpus* and *Melopsittacus*, up to three or four months for the large macaws. In proportion to their size lories and lorikeets have a long nestling period. After leaving the nest young birds are fed by their parents for a brief time while learning to fend for themselves; young black cockatoos (*Calyptorhynchus* spp.) are fed by their parents for up to four months after leaving the nest. Young birds usually remain with their parents until the next breeding season thus forming the family parties often observed.

Vane (1957) records the successful rearing in captivity of a young Red-lored Amazon (*Amazona autumnalis*) by a female Grey Parrot (*Psittacus erithacus*), and all aspects of incubation and parental care were closely observed. Three eggs were placed under the brooding foster-parent and one hatched after an incubation period of twenty-five to twenty-six days. The incubating bird sat very closely and came off to feed every morning. The egg was examined the day before it hatched and definite movement was noticed inside. The next morning there was a chip in the egg and the chick could be heard squeaking inside the shell. Shortly before midday the chick emerged from the egg; it was assisted by the foster-parent who very carefully pecked the top out in a small circle, so that the chick wriggled out through a hole leaving the shell in two pieces. The foster-parent brooded the chick very closely and made no attempt to feed it, although she repeatedly cleaned it. She moved it about by lifting it bodily by the head. The first feed was given on the second day. The chick was first lifted bodily by the head, and the point of the parent's upper mandible was then gently inserted into the small opening between the chick's mandibles right at the rear. She then trickled liquid down her tongue into the opposite side of the chick's mandibles. Once the young bird commenced to take food readily the forceful procedure was abandoned and as soon as the parent clucked the chick would raise its head and would gape ready to accept food. Taking the tips of the chick's mandibles in her bill the parent applied the normal pumping action of regurgitation and one could actually watch the chick's crop fill out. At this stage feeding was carried out every two hours and the consistency of the crop milk was similar to that of ordinary milk. For much of the first two weeks the foster-parent brooded the chick continuously, but thereafter she left the nest for periods which gradually became longer as the young bird progressed. Intervals between feeds were slowly increased to three hours and when six weeks had passed the feeds were increased in frequency but decreased in bulk. During this time the consistency of the food was thickened. At about ten days after the chick had hatched its eyes commenced to open and quills began to appear. The young bird grew rapidly and at seven weeks its plumage was complete, except that the tail and flight feathers were not fully developed.

Lamba (1966) estimated that the nesting success, that is ratio of fledglings leaving the nest to number of eggs laid, for twenty-four nests of the Rose-ringed Parakeet (*Psittacula krameri*) was approximately 71.7%. Marchant (1960) studied eight nests of the Celestial Parrotlet (*Forpus coelestis*) and reported that five failed; of the three successes, two produced together seven young from twelve eggs and the third probably three from five.

JUVENILE PLUMAGE Juveniles generally resemble females or are duller than either adult sex. There are species which have a distinct juvenile plumage, for example the Crimson Rosella (*Platycercus elegans*) and some *Psittacula* species. Juveniles have shorter tails than do adults; this is especially so in the Papuan Lory (*Charmosyna papou*) and some species of *Psittacula*, adults of which have elongated central feathers, and in the racket-tailed parrots (*Prioniturus* spp.) where juveniles lack the central rackets. There is a striking difference between adults and juveniles of the Vulturine Parrot (*Gypopsitta vulturina*) from Amazonia, Brazil—in adults the bare head is sparsely covered with inconspicuous 'bristles', but in juveniles the head is well-covered with pale-green feathers.

There are general rules for differences in the colours of soft parts. Where adults have dark bills those of juveniles are usually pale, but when adults have pale bills those of juveniles are generally dark or have dark markings at the base of one or both mandibles. If the irides of adults are pale-coloured, such as orange, yellow or white, those of juveniles are generally dark.

The time taken for juveniles to attain adult plumage varies greatly from one species to another. It may be within months of leaving the nest, or it may be up to three or four years. Some species acquire adult colours rapidly with the first complete moult, while for others it is a slow, almost imperceptible process. With certain species that have a distinct juvenile plumage young males acquire the plumage of adult females and then that of adult males; for example the Red-cheeked Parrot (*Geoffroyus geoffroyi*) and the Plum-headed Parakeet (*Psittacula cyanocephala*).

MOULT

Moult is a process by which birds periodically renew their plumage or feather covering. It actually involves two separate processes; namely the loss of old feathers and the growth of new ones. Almost all birds moult at least once a year, many species twice, and a few three times. The main function of the post-nuptial moult is the renewal of worn and faded plumage so it is general and nearly always complete. The pre-nuptial moult, if present, is generally partial and intensifies secondary sexual characters by acquisition of brighter colours on certain parts of the body or by adding plumes or other adornments. In parrots pre-nuptial moult has not been found. Moult periods are closely synchronized with the reproductive cycle, so collection of specimens in moult gives some indication of the time of the year during which that species normally breeds. Keast (1968) reports that in parrots from an area in the Australian dry country the time of moult is variable, but commonly it would seem to begin in October and be largely complete by February; the species he examined normally breed in that area during the months August to December.

MOULT OF PRIMARIES In many, probably most, parrots moult of the primaries proceeds slowly; this is particularly evident in many species which occur in the equatorial belt (E. and V. Stresemann, 1966). Renewal of the entire wing is spread over several months. Old and new feathers may not be distinguishable by the degree of wear, because those renewed first could appear to be old by the time the last replacements emerge. Moult of the primaries can be terminated before the last feather has been replaced, and when the new cycle commences the residual feathers from the previous cycle also fall out. Frequently a new moult cycle may start while the previous one is still in progress. Hampe found that in *Platycercus*, *Psephotus* and *Neophema* the first complete moult commenced when the birds were seven to ten months old and renewal of the primaries took three to five months; subsequent complete moults followed each other at about yearly intervals, generally after completion of breeding (in E. and V. Stresemann, 1966).

All parrots renew primaries from the centre outwards. From the central feather, usually the sixth, it proceeds in both directions. In Loriidae and some members of Psittacinae, particularly the platycercine group, it commences with the sixth, followed by simultaneous loss of the seventh and fifth, then the eighth and fourth and so on. This regular pattern has been termed Hampe's Rule by E. and V. Stresemann and may be designated as follows:

$$\frac{7-8-9-10}{6}$$
$$5-4-3-2-1$$

In most of the Psittacinae the $5-4-3-2-1$ sequence is not followed closely, but is often modified by 'jumping' (e.g. 5 – 3 – 4 – 1 – 2); except in *Psittrichas*, *Poicephalus* and *Amazona*, the 6 – 7 – 8 – 9 – 10 sequence tends to remain constant. In Cacatuidae, Nestorinae, Micropsittinae and Strigopinae the pattern is irregular and moult may commence with a primary other than the sixth.

MOULT OF SECONDARIES Parrots have ten secondaries and the sequence of their moult in *Platycercus*, *Psephotus* and *Neophema* has been noted by Hampe (in E. and V. Stresemann, 1966). A strict descending sequence starting with s 10 and ending with s 1 was found in *Platycercus icterotis* and *P. adscitus*. However, in *Psephotus* and *Neophema* a variance was evident in the inner group (s 10 – 9 – 8)—their sequence of moult was irregular and Hampe observed the patterns 9 – 10 – 8 and 8 – 9 – 10. Renewal of secondaries started at about the same time as the dropping of the sixth primary—in other words moults of primaries and secondaries commenced at about the same time.

MOULT OF TAIL Hampe found that there was no set rule for the tail moult in the platycercine parrots that he examined (in E. and V. Stresemann, 1966). The first feather to drop out was frequently T 1 or T 6. Tail moult usually commenced after the wing moult was well advanced, but generally finished before the last primary was dropped.

MOULT OF BODY FEATHERS I know of no published information on the timing and sequence of moult of the general body feathers. My observations suggest that it commences after the first primary has been dropped and is completed before the last primary has been dropped.

PARROTS IN CAPTIVITY

The popularity of parrots as pets dates from early times. It is possible that the Rose-ringed Parakeet (*Psittacula krameri*) from northern Africa was known to the ancient Egyptians, though there appears to be no records in their writings or art. Ctesias, a Grecian slave who became court physician to Artaxerxes II in 401 B.C., gave a fairly accurate description of the Plum-headed Parakeet (*Psittacula cyanocephala*) and wrote romantically of the bird's ability to speak the language of its native India and the claim that it could be taught to speak Greek. It was probably Alexander the Great who introduced to Europe tame parrots from the Far East, and Alexandrine Parakeet, the English name for *Psittacula eupatria*, honours the warrior king. Aristotle almost certainly based his descriptions of parrots on birds brought back by the triumphant armies of his pupil, Alexander. Parrots, presumably *Psittacula* species from northern Africa and the Indian subcontinent, were well-known to the ancient Romans and talking birds were status symbols among the noble classes. The voyages of discovery to Asia and the Americas during the fifteenth and sixteenth centuries resulted in new parrot species being brought back to Europe and trading in live birds soon commenced. Nowadays the popularity of parrots is world-wide and the international trade in live birds has reached such proportions that there is urgent need for a study of its effects on wild populations.

Keeping parrots in captivity, whether it be possession of one or two household pets or the housing of many birds in elaborate breeding aviaries, is an interesting, worthwhile hobby and can give much pleasure. Probably the most satisfying reward for an aviculturist is a successful breeding in captivity. Of course, the ability of parrots to imitate speech is very well known, and owners of talking birds are invariably proud of their pets. Parrots feature prominently in the collections of most major zoos, and in various countries there are a number of excellent private collections which are open to the public.

Aviculturists have opportunities to contribute to our knowledge of parrots but, in my opinion, these opportunities are seldom utilized. Ornithologists have tended to ignore or treat with disdain information obtained from captive birds and I think that this is unfortunate. On the other hand, aviculturists have often presented incomplete or carelessly compiled data; for example take description and measurements of eggs—there are species which have been bred in captivity, sometimes on a number of occasions, but their eggs remain undescribed. As I have pointed out elsewhere, parrots are difficult to study in the wild, but many species live and breed freely in captivity so information obtained from captive birds is valuable if presented in an acceptable manner. Most of what is known about the breeding habits of parrots comes from captive birds. There are a number of avicultural journals which can be used for publication of information obtained from birds held in captivity.

There are numerous books which cover the care, management, and breeding of parrots in captivity more fully than I could possibly do here, so I shall not deal with the subject. However, I strongly believe that the management of any species in captivity should be based on the habits of that species in the wild, so for this reason I trust that information given in the text of this book will be helpful to aviculturists.

Generally speaking, parrots are easy to keep in captivity. The basic diet for most species, other than lories and lorikeets, is a seed mixture supplemented with fruit and greenfood. Proprietary foods, some containing protein additives, are now available for lories, lorikeets, and other nectar-feeding species. A few groups of parrots and some particular species, such as the *Vini* lorikeets, the Glossy Cockatoo (*Calyptorhynchus lathami*), the racket-tailed parrots (*Prioniturus* spp.), the hanging parrots (*Loriculus* spp.), the Golden-winged Parakeet (*Brotogeris chrysopterus*), and the Orange-bellied Parrot (*Neophema chrysogaster*), have proved to be somewhat unsuitable for captivity and because of the risk of high mortality trade in these species or groups is not justified. The Black-collared Lovebird (*Agapornis swinderniana*) and the pygmy parrots (*Micropsitta* spp.) have not been kept successfully despite a couple of attempts to do so, and further experiments are not warranted.

The most familiar of all parrots in captivity is without question the Budgerigar (*Melopsittacus undulatus*), a native of the interior of Australia. In 1840 John Gould returned to England with the first living Budgerigars to be seen in Europe. The lively mannerisms, bright colouring, and soft, chattering voices of these small parrots appealed to aviculturists and their popularity as cage-birds was immediate and spectacular. Demand was widespread and very high prices were paid for birds shipped from Australia. The prospect of enormous profits soon prompted continental dealers to set up breeding establishments and for a time these flourished. However, the parrots proved to be exceedingly prolific breeders in captivity and it was not long before the market was totally saturated. Interest was revived by reports that yellow and blue mutants were occasionally observed among the wild flocks, and in 1872 the first yellow mutants were received in Belgium. However, it was not until 1910 that the first pair of blue Budgerigars was seen in Europe, and this was the beginning of programmes of intense selective breeding which produced the vast range of colour variations known today. Specialist societies devoted to selective breeding were set up throughout the world, and the organization of competitive exhibitions brought about an increasing demand for pedigree birds. The Budgerigar had become a domesticated species. Exhibition Budgerigars seen on the show bench today are very different birds from those which make up the enormous flocks that wander nomadically through inland Australia.

ROLE OF AVICULTURE IN CONSERVATION
It has been claimed that the Carolina Parakeet (*Conuropsis carolinensis*) and possibly other extinct species could have been saved by breeding in captivity. This may be true, though it does presume that present-day avicultural techniques were in practice at the turn of the century. What the claim does highlight is the role of aviculture in the conservation of endangered species. I agree that breeding in captivity is important as a preservation measure for seriously endangered species, but as such it is the prerogative of government institutions and zoos, not private individuals. I support the attempts being made by the New Zealand and United States Governments to save the Kakapo (*Strigops habroptilus*) and the Puerto Rican Amazon (*Amazona vittata*) by breeding them in captivity, and suggest that similar programmes could be undertaken with other species, particularly the amazons from the Lesser Antilles. Zoos and government institutions have a public responsibility and it is possible to ensure that at all times the purpose for which the birds are held in captivity, namely preservation of the species, always remains the primary objective. On the other hand, private individuals claim that birds obtained by them are their property, a claim that is probably right and legally defensible but one that is totally alien to the objectives being pursued.

CONSERVATION
> Conservation . . . can be defined as the wise use of our natural environment; it is, in the final analysis, the highest form of national thrift—the prevention of waste and despoilment while preserving, improving and renewing the quality and usefulness of all our resources.

John F. Kennedy

MESSAGE TO CONGRESS, 1962.

'Conservation' is now a fashionable term. It figures prominently in the media and there is a growing awareness of what it means. However, we are still a long way from 'the wise use of our natural environment', and actions lag far behind words. It seems that mankind is not yet prepared to make the sacrifices that must be made if our natural resources are to be used wisely and the balance between man and his environment maintained.

Wildlife is a natural resource which has been, and still is, exploited. The number of species disappearing or becoming rare through the agency of man is steadily increasing. Parrots are not exempt from the main factors adversely affecting all wildlife throughout the world, namely loss of habitat and indiscriminate use of chemical pesticides and herbicides. In fact, they face additional pressures resulting from their alleged depredations on crops and from their popularity as pets. A number of species are seriously threatened and every effort must be made to prevent them following the Carolina Parakeet (*Conuropsis carolinensis*) along the road to extinction.

HABITAT PRESERVATION
Interference with habitat is, by far, the most important problem. Of particular concern is the widespread destruction of tropical forest, a habitat frequented by a majority of the world's parrots. First, let me mention the situation in my own country, Australia, where I am more familiar with the problem. Here, tropical rainforest occurs in only a minute fraction of the continent, but is the only habitat frequented by a number of bird species, including four parrots—Palm Cockatoo (*Probosciger aterrimus*), Double-eyed Fig Parrot (*Opopsitta diophthalma*), Red-cheeked Parrot (*Geoffroyus geoffroyi*), and Eclectus Parrot (*Eclectus roratus*). One would expect that in an advanced country like Australia such a rare and important habitat would be zealously protected, but this ideal is far removed from the actual situation for tropical rainforest has been ruthlessy destroyed and interference by pastoral and mining interests is continuing. Costin (1971) points out that in view of the paucity of uncleared rainforest in Australia, and the abundance of neglected, semi-abandoned land urgently requiring rehabilitation, it is difficult to justify further clearing and alienation of rainforest land, as is occurring in Queensland. The amount of tropical rainforest protected in national parks and reserves is negligible!

In the developing nations of South-East Asia there is intense pressure for increased food production and, of course, this is both understandable and justified. However, it would be a tragedy if in the process insufficient attention was paid to preserving viable stands of the magnificent rainforest which for centuries has been identified with that part of the world. Already in the Philippines there has been widespread clearance of forests and two distinct subspecies of the Philippine Hanging Parrot (*Loriculus philippensis*) have disappeared because of loss of habitat.

In Brazil the rapid and large-scale opening up of the Amazon Basin, the home of many species of parrots, is of great concern to biologists. The International Union for Conservation of Nature points out that this will necessarily involve major transformations of the Amazonian landscape and the consequent disappearance of wild areas (see *IUCN Bulletin*, new ser., vol. 3, no. 5, 1972). It is to be hoped that an extensive system of national parks and protected areas will be established, because on this could depend the survival of such species as the Golden Conure (*Aratinga guarouba*) and the Red-bellied Conure (*Pyrrhura rhodogaster*).

Tropical rainforest is not the only parrot habitat in danger, though it is, by far, the most important habitat for the parrots as a group. In south-eastern Brazil, *Araucaria* forest, the home of the Red-spectacled Amazon (*Amazona pretrei*), is being cleared at a rapid rate and being replaced by introduced *Eucalyptus*. In the highlands of northern Mexico there is widespread clearance of *Pinus* forest, a habitat frequented by the Thick-billed Parrot (*Rhynchopsitta pachyrhyncha*), and that parrot can no longer wander north into southern Arizona. The Ground Parrot (*Pezoporus wallicus*) is a terrestrial parrot with specialized habits and is found only in coastal heathlands of eastern and south-western Australia. As these heathlands have been greatly affected by settlement and agricultural practices the parrot has disappeared from parts of its range, and now there is emerging a new threat in the form of the mining of mineral sands and some of the remaining pockets of habitat could be irretrievably altered.

Special mention must be made of islands where the maximum limits of available habitat are finite and can in no way be extended. Birds native to small islands are particularly vulnerable to extinction. Insular forms constitute the majority of extinct parrots and many extant insular species are seriously threatened. Of special concern are the amazons occurring on islands in the West Indies. The four species confined to the Lesser Antilles are in grave danger and every effort must be made to preserve them. There are probably less than fifteen Puerto Rican Amazons (*Amazona vittata*) left in the wild and the species appears to be doomed to extinction. Kepler points out that in the case of the Puerto Rican Amazon it is important to remember that a common and wisespread insular species was brought to the verge of extinction in less than a century, due mainly to the combined effects of hunting and habitat destruction, and that a rather large forest reserve, because of its peculiar ecological characteristics, has been inadequate as a barrier against further decline of the small remnant population (*in litt.*, 1972). On the other hand, the Black Parrot (*Coracopsis nigra*), although dangerously low in numbers, appears to be surviving quite well in a forest reserve on Praslin Island, in the Seychelles.

Where the survival of a species is in the balance implementation of all possible protection measures is warranted, but it is important to bear in mind that these are more likely to be successful if they are based on knowledge of the biology of the species.

PARROTS AND AGRICULTURE

Damage to crops by parrots has been reported from many countries, but to date there has been practically no objective evaluation of the problem. I am convinced that in Australia reports of damage to crops by parrots have been exaggerated. I suspect that because the raiding of crops by parrots is so conspicuous there may be a tendency to exaggerate the problem. In other words, it may be overlooked that parrots are only one of many pests attacking crops. Often the damage done by parrots relative to that by other pests may be small and hence control of parrots would not be economically justified. However, in regions where subsistence farms come under attack from parrots the problem could take on substantial significance and crops may have to be protected.

Shooting and poisoning may produce local control of a population, but because of movement of birds into the area this effect is likely to be short-lived. Control of this type may put the whole species at risk where the entire population is already low. There is a need to consider other types of control. Encouraging results have been obtained in some parts of the world with the practice of making available in the immediate vicinity of crops favourable feeding areas and persuading the birds to utilize these by making sure that they are not disturbed whenever they do so. For example, the planting of flowering and fruit-bearing trees as windbreaks or shade trees could reduce depredations on nearby crops once the parrots became accustomed to being able to feed in these trees without being disturbed. Research into control measures is needed so that both the crops and the birds can be safeguarded.

PET TRADE

The International Union for the Conservation of Nature and the World Wildlife Fund do not oppose the use of wild animals as pets if they are adapted to domestic conditions, if their entry into the pet trade does not endanger wild populations, and if the animals pose no hazards to the importing country (see *IUCN Bulletin*, vol. 3, no. 3, 1972). I agree with this point of view. There are species of parrots which are found in reasonable abundance and are hardy and adapted to captivity—these can withstand controlled exploitation for the pet trade. However, I strongly believe that the present largely uncontrolled trade could have adverse effects on the wild populations and should not be permitted to continue. Weathersbee, writing in the *Peruvian Times*, points out that a serious drain has developed on the parrot stocks of the Amazon Basin as a result of the lifting of the ban on the importation of psittacine birds into the United States of America (see *Kingfisher*, vol. 5, no. 3, 1970). He claims that the pet trade is importing ten thousand birds annually, and this is estimated to cause the destruction of no fewer than half a million parrots in South America, because many birds perish in the time between being caught and being imported into the United States and held in quarantine. Traders systematically work the Amazon rivers, paying the Indians for birds they bring in. In many cases this has led to Indians neglecting their farming and other traditional ways of earning a living, to their own detriment when the parrot population is denuded and the traders move on. Tribal affairs have been so disrupted that some Indian chiefs are reported to have come out in opposition against the trading.

Aviculturists with a keen interest in the birds they hold in captivity can contribute to our knowledge of these species, particularly about the nesting habits. Indeed, one may make the judgement that persons holding birds in captivity have a moral obligation to learn what they can about those birds.

I acknowledge that many people like to have a pet parrot and this can give much pleasure—there are common species capable of meeting this demand. However, what cannot be allowed to continue is the present lack of control over the international pet trade. If aviculturists do not adopt a responsible attitude and denounce trade in species which are in any way endangered in the wild they must expect that legislation will be enacted to prohibit trade in such species. There is no place for 'collectors' who want a bird simply because it is rare and will go to no end of effort to obtain it.

Controls should be exercised by both the exporting and importing countries because one without the other is virtually useless. Within the exporting countries rigid protection of endangered species must be strictly enforced and controls exercised over the capture and sale of other species. Wasteful and inhumane methods of capture, such as the felling of nesting trees in the hope of securing chicks or the shooting of adults in the hope that one or two will recover from injuries, must be eliminated.

Perhaps it could be argued that the measures which I have outlined here are too idealistic and impracticable. This may be so, but I fear that unless some controls along these lines are initiated we could witness the extermination of some of the large macaws, the Golden Conure (*Aratinga guarouba*), the Golden-shouldered Parrot (*Psephotus chrysopterygius*), and amazons from the West Indies. The parrots are a resource which can be exploited but surely it is not unreasonable that limitations on the exploitation must be accepted by all concerned.

Pacific
Distribution

PACIFIC DISTRIBUTION

The Pacific Distribution as determined for this book comprises the Australasian Faunal Region and the neighbouring section of the Oriental Region. Two genera of parrots, namely *Loriculus* and *Psittacula*, although well represented in this Distribution, are treated in the Afro-Asian Distribution because, in my opinion, they are essentially Asiatic birds. On the other hand, *Psittinus* is treated here because I believe that, although it ranges up into southern Burma, its affinities are with Philippine and New Guinea genera.

Australia is the predominant land mass in the Pacific Distribution. To the north and to the east it is surrounded by many groups of islands extending through the tropics as an interrupted chain from the Malay Peninsula to Easter Island some 3,600 km. off the west coast of Chile. North of Australia there are some large islands, such as New Guinea, Celebes, Borneo and Sumatra, but to the east most islands are small. To the south-east lie New Zealand and its associated islands. Geologically, Australia has been separated from the Asiatic land mass since the early Tertiary, and perhaps since much earlier. Land connections between New Guinea and Australia existed during the early Tertiary and again at the end of the Tertiary. The past history of New Zealand is uncertain, but if land connection with the Australian continental shelf ever occurred it was probably not later than the Mesozoic (Serventy, 1964). The Polynesian archipelagos have always been isolated oceanic islands, but were possibly more extensive and more numerous during the Tertiary than at present (Mayr, 1953). Thus not only Australia itself, but the island groups surrounding it, have been cut off from the great land masses of the world, and mostly from each other, since before present day bird faunas evolved. Nevertheless, the avifaunas of Australia, New Guinea, and most of the southern Polynesian islands not only show common relationships but point to a derivation from that of Asia (Mayr, 1944). They apparently colonized originally by island-hopping across a sea barrier and have attained various levels of endemism.

Parrots are very well represented in the Pacific Distribution and show marked endemism centred on Australia, New Guinea, New Zealand and neighbouring islands. The presence of *Loriculus* and *Psittacula* is evidence of recent island-hopping colonization, while the large number of distinctive types points to earlier colonization. Lorikeets and cockatoos are restricted entirely to the Pacific Distribution, and within the Psittacidae or 'true' parrots there is a strong diversity of types (e.g. Micropsittinae in New Guinea, Nestorinae and Strigopinae in New Zealand). This diversity is in marked contrast to the uniformity found in the parrots of the Afro-Asian and South American Distributions, and has prompted some authors to refer to Australasia as 'the home of parrots'.

Within the Pacific Distribution a high degree of speciation has occurred and is occurring. One of the best examples is the Rainbow Lory (*Trichoglossus haematodus*). This polytypic species apparently originated in New Guinea and has colonized surrounding islands as well as entered Australia from southern New Guinea and possibly also from Timor (see fig. 5). Species which have followed a similar pattern include the Red-cheeked Parrot (*Geoffroyus geoffroyi*) and the Eclectus Parrot (*Eclectus roratus*). In Australia and New Guinea there are striking examples of the superspecies concept, that is, geographical replacement of one species by another closely related species (e.g. *Barnardius* and *Platycercus* in Australia, and *Chalcopsitta*, *Micropsitta*, *Psittaculirostris* and *Alisterus* in New Guinea). Serventy (1964) points out that in the Australasian Region there has been colonization by progressive invasions and I believe that certain parrots are good examples of this. An earlier colonization of Australia by *Trichoglossus* stock resulted in the development of the Scaly-breasted Lorikeet (*T. chlorolepidotus*). On Antipodes Island an early invasion of *Cyanoramphus* from New Zealand produced the endemic *C. unicolor*; then there was a subsequent invasion by the polytypic *C. novaezelandiae*.

In the adjacent table I have shown the number of species of parrots found in the major countries and the habitats in which they occur. The countries are listed as geographical, not political units (e.g. New Guinea, Moluccas, Celebes, Borneo, etc.). Extinct species are excluded, but I have included species found on offshore islands (e.g. *Tanygnathus megalorynchos* for Celebes and Philippines; *T. lucionensis* for Borneo; *Eos cyanogenia*, *E. squamata*, *Charmosyna rubrigularis* and *Tanygnathus megalorynchos* for New Guinea; *Psittacula alexandri* for Sumatra, etc.). Introduced species are also included (e.g. *Cacatua galerita*, *Platycercus elegans* and *P. eximius* for New Zealand; *Psittacula alexandri* for Borneo; *Cacatua sulphurea* and *Psittacula krameri* for Singapore, which is considered to be part of the Malay Peninsula). Oceanic islands are not listed in the table, because nearly all of those on which parrots occur are inhabited by only one species, and it is generally found in littoral habitats. Categorization of habitats is broad and arbitrary and does not take into account the actual complexities always present in the distribution of a species. Littoral habitats include rocky coastlines, coastal sand dunes, estuarine flats and swamps, coconut palms and other

Fig. 5

Possible pattern of colonisation by the Rainbow Lory (*Trichoglossus haematodus*).

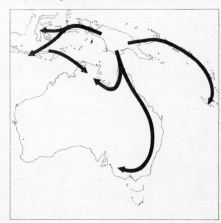

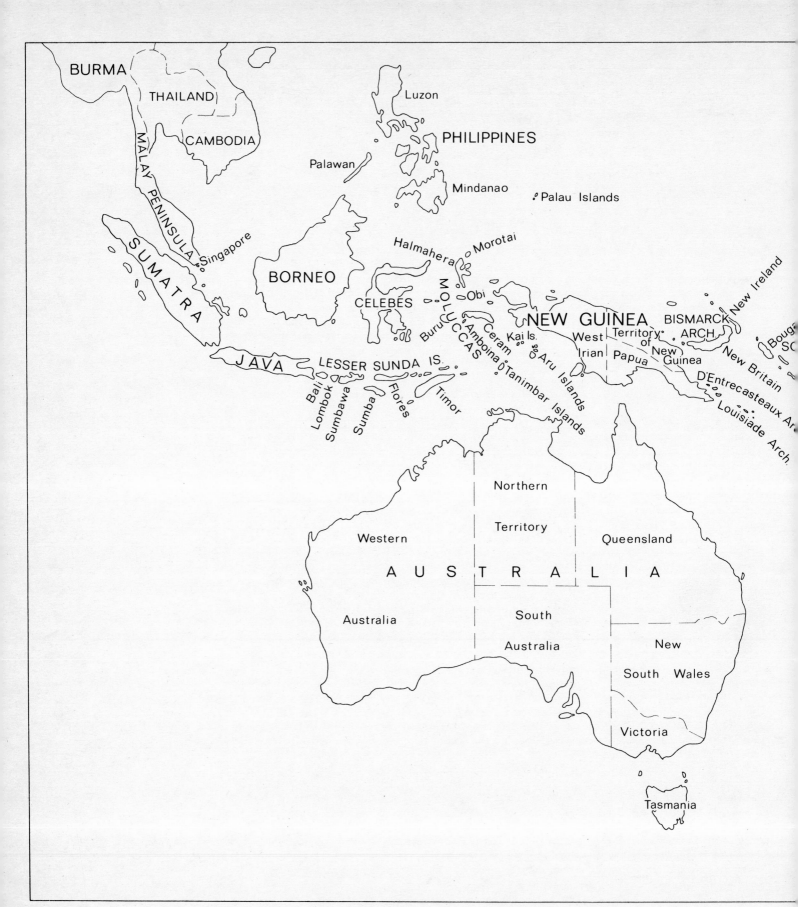

The Pacific Distribution

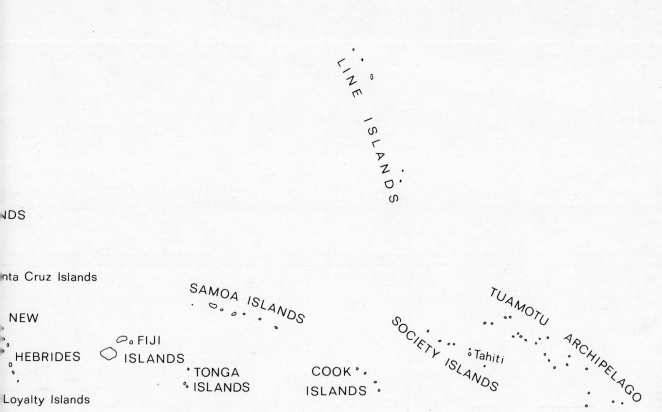

LINE ISLANDS

nta Cruz Islands

SAMOA ISLANDS

NEW

TUAMOTU ARCHIPELAGO

FIJI

SOCIETY ISLANDS

HEBRIDES

ISLANDS

Tahiti

TONGA

COOK

ISLANDS

ISLANDS

Loyalty Islands

ONIA

Henderson Is.

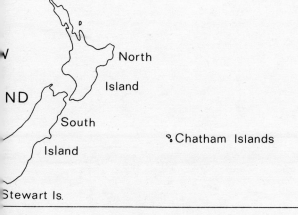

North

Island

North

ND

South

Chatham Islands

Island

Stewart Is.

trees along beaches, and mangroves. Open areas in both lowlands and highlands take in open grassland, cultivated farmland, savannah woodland, and semi-arid and arid scrublands. One aspect of distribution reflected in the figures shown in the table is the large number of species that have evolved in the vast dry interior of Australia, whereas in other countries forested areas support the majority of species.

COUNTRY	NUMBER OF SPECIES	LITTORAL HABITATS	LOWLANDS: OPEN AREAS	LOWLANDS: FORESTED AREAS	HIGHLANDS: OPEN AREAS	HIGHLANDS: FORESTED AREAS	SUBALPINE HABITATS
Australia	52	11	43	25	9	7	4
New Guinea	46	6	11	28	2	14	
Solomon Islands	11	2	6	9		5	
Fiji Islands	5	2	1	3		3	
New Caledonia	4	1	1	3		3	
New Zealand	9		2	5		6	2
Moluccas	17	6	8	12		8	
Celebes	10	2	6	4	3	3	
Borneo	5	2	3	4			
Philippines	11	1	5	6	1	4	
Malay Peninsula*	6	1	4	6	1	1	
Sumatra	4	2	4	4	1	1	
Lesser Sunda Islands	9	2	9	9		1	

Only three species, *Nestor productus*, *Cyanoramphus zealandicus* and *C. ulietanus*, have become extinct in recent time, but several others, especially *Charmosyna diadema*, *Vini peruviana*, *Psephotus pulcherrimus*, *P. chrysopterygius*, *Geopsittacus occidentalis* and *Strigops habroptilus*, are seriously endangered. Because of the high proportion of insular endemics, habitat destruction poses a most serious threat to parrots of the Pacific Distribution.

PSITTACIFORMES

Family: LORIIDAE

Parrots of the family Loriidae are known as lories and lorikeets. They have tight, glossy plumage and most are brilliantly coloured. In noisy flocks they move from one stand of flowering trees to the next. They are arboreal and rarely come near the ground. Lories feed mainly on pollen, nectar and fruits, and have anatomical modifications related to this habit. The bill is relatively elongated and narrow, and the tongue is tipped with elongated papillae forming a brush-like appendage (see fig. 6).

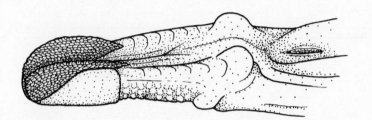 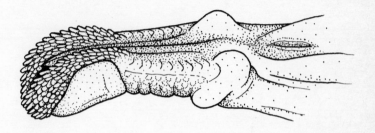

5 mm

Fig. 6
Tongue of *Trichoglossus haematodus*
(Left) 'Brush-like' papillae in the normal relaxed position. (Right) 'Brush-like' papillae erected for feeding.

Authors have nearly always referred to the brush-tipped tongue as an adaptation for extracting nectar. However, from their work with the Purple-crowned Lorikeet (*Glossopsitta porphyrocephala*) Churchill and Christensen (1970) point out that the tongue in lories is an organ for harvesting pollen and pressing it into a form suitable for swallowing, and is not primarily for gathering nectar. Nectar is collected when it flows, but it is not a substitute for pollen, which the birds continue to harvest as their source of nitrogen. At the time the birds ingest nectar they accumulate subcutaneous fat. Nectar does not reach the stomach but is held in the crop, which enlarges to accommodate it. Steinbacher (1934) notes that the ventriculus or gizzard of the Loriidae is weak and not muscular, particularly in species that feed almost exclusively on pollen and nectar, and that compound glands are arranged linearly along the walls of the proventriculus.

I am not satisfied with the usual separation of genera within the Loriidae, but a critical examination of the systematics of the family is outside the scope of this book. For the most part I have followed Peters (1937), the only major deviation being alteration to the composition of *Trichoglossus*.

Genus CHALCOPSITTA Bonaparte

Members of this genus are medium-sized parrots with rather long, rounded tails. Naked skin surrounding the base of the lower mandible is the most conspicuous external feature. There is no sexual dimorphism; immatures have pointed tips on the tail feathers.

BLACK LORY
Chalcopsitta atra (Scopoli)

Length 32 cm.
ADULTS general plumage black with a purple gloss; rump purple-blue; underside of tail feathers olive-yellow basally marked with red; bill black; iris orange-red; legs grey.
IMMATURES bare skin around eyes and base of lower mandible white instead of black; iris dark brown.

Western New Guinea and adjacent islands.

DESCRIPTION

DISTRIBUTION

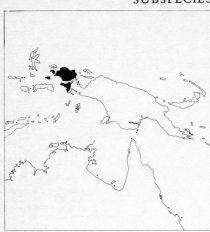

1. *C. a. atra* (Scopoli) *Illustrated on page 49.*
   13 males   wing 171–193 (185.4) mm., tail 119–151 (129.6) mm.,
            exp. cul. 20–24 (22.4) mm., tars. 22–26 (23.8) mm.
   9 females   wing 169–192 (180.0) mm., tail 114–133 (123.2) mm.,
            exp. cul. 20–24 (22.2) mm., tars. 23–25 (23.9) mm.
   Occurs in the western part of the Vogelkop, West Irian, and the nearby islands of Batanta and Salawati.

2. *C. a. bernsteini* von Rosenberg
   ADULTS reddish-purple markings on forehead and thighs, in females usually less pronounced on thighs; bluer rump.
   8 males   wing 184–203 (191.5) mm., tail 131–154 (139.9) mm.,
            exp. cul. 23–24 (23.4) mm., tars. 22–26 (24.5) mm.
   4 females   wing 182–191 (187.0) mm., tail 124–143 (134.5) mm.,
            exp. cul. 22–23 (22.5) mm., tars. 22–25 (23.3) mm.
   Confined to the island of Misool, West Irian.

3. *C. a. insignis* Oustalet *Illustrated on page 49.*
   ADULTS head streaked with greyish-blue; forehead, foreparts of cheeks, thighs and under wing-coverts red; feathers of throat and flanks margined with red; rump dull blue; under tail-coverts greyish-blue; red markings on vent and lower abdomen.
   2 males   wing 169–175 (172.0) mm., tail 130–132 (131.0) mm.,
            exp. cul. 21 (21.0) mm., tars. 23 (23.0) mm.
   1 female   wing 172 mm., tail 127 mm.,
            exp. cul. 20 mm., tars. 21 mm.
   2 unsexed   wing 176–189 (182.5) mm., tail 105–123 (114.0) mm.,
            exp. cul. 21–22 (21.5) mm., tars. 22–24 (23.0) mm.
   This subspecies is sometimes called the Rajah Lory. It is found in the eastern part of the Vogelkop, West Irian, and on adjacent Amberpon Island, and on Onin and Bomberai Peninsulas.

4. *C. a. spectabilis* van Oort
   MALE forehead, lores and upper cheeks red; head and neck black; hindneck and mantle streaked with greenish-yellow; back and wings dark greenish-brown; bend of wing violet; breast dark violet marked with red and streaked with yellow; abdomen and under tail-coverts dark green; rump bright blue; upper tail-coverts dark green; under wing-coverts red; tail olive-green above, below olive yellow basally marked with red.
   FEMALE undescribed.
   1 male **(type)** wing 176 mm., tail 109 mm.,
            exp. cul. 21 mm., tars. 22 mm.
   This race is known only from the unique type specimen, a male collected on the Mamberiok Peninsula, north-western New Guinea. Mayr (in Peters, 1937) suggests that it may be either a *C. a. insignis* x *C. s. sintillata* hybrid or an intermediate race nearer to *insignis*. I have examined the type and agree that it is intermediate between these two forms, though nearer to *insignis*, but surely its taxonomic significance cannot be assessed until further specimens are obtained.

GENERAL NOTES According to Rand and Gilliard (1967) Black Lories favour the forest edge or trees in clearings and savannah. Mayr and Meyer de Schauensee (1939c) report that on Misool specimens were collected in open grassland and the parrots seemed to prefer trees on the very edge of the forest or even the little groves of eucalypts scattered over the plain. Ripley (1964) found them in coconut palms at Arar on the west coast of the Vogelkop and in small clumps of stunted trees in an area of depauperate vegetation on the south-eastern coast of Misool.
   Rand and Gilliard say that these lories travel about in large flocks. Ripley found one such flock associating with mynahs in a flowering tree on the Warmon River, West Irian (in Mayr and Meyer de Schauensee, 1939b).

CALL A high chitter as would be expected from a much smaller bird (Ripley, 1964).

NESTING A male with enlarged gonads was collected by Ripley in December.
   Brook (1910a) gives details of a successful breeding in captivity. Two eggs were laid. Incubation commenced nearly a week after the eggs were laid and lasted about three weeks. One chick hatched and left the nest two months later. In his account of an assisted breeding in captivity Lint (1969) points out that both parents brooded and the incubation period was approximately twenty-five days.

EGGS Rounded; a single egg in the British Museum measures 31.0 × 25.7 mm. [Harrison and Holyoak, 1970].

DUYVENBODE'S LORY
Chalcopsitta duivenbodei (Dubois)

DESCRIPTION Length 31 cm.
ADULTS general plumage dark olive-brown; forehead, throat and forepart of cheeks yellow; feathers of breast margined with yellow; nape and neck streaked with dull yellow; golden yellow on bend of wing; rump violet-blue; thighs and under wing-coverts orange-yellow; yellow markings on outer tail feathers, commonly lacking in females; bill black; iris reddish; legs dark grey.
IMMATURES undescribed.

DISTRIBUTION Northern New Guinea.

SUBSPECIES

1. *C. d. duivenbodei* (Dubois)   *Illustrated on page 49.*
   9 males   wing 171–180 (176.6) mm., tail 117–138 (132.1) mm.,
               exp. cul. 21–23 (22.6) mm., tars. 22–25 (24.0) mm.
   8 females   wing 174–177 (175.3) mm., tail 123–131 (128.3) mm.,
               exp. cul. 20–23 (21.1) mm., tars. 22–24 (22.5) mm.
   Inhabits north-western New Guinea from Geelvink Bay, West Irian, east to the Aitape area, Territory of New Guinea.

2. *C. d. syringanuchalis* (Neumann)
   ADULTS head and back darker than in *duivenbodei* and often with a dark violet sheen.
   3 unsexed   wing 165–188 (177.3) mm., tail 108–123 (115.3) mm.,
               exp. cul. 21–22 (21.3) mm., tars. 20–22 (21.3) mm.
   Found in north-eastern New Guinea from the Aitape area east to Astrolabe Bay; doubtfully distinct from *duivenbodei*.

GENERAL NOTES Duyvenbode's Lory is a bird of the lowlands up to 200 m. (Rand and Gilliard, 1967). It is fairly common and pairs or small parties of up to six or eight birds are usually seen in the tops of forest trees. Nothing is known of its habits.

CALL Undescribed.

NESTING In late April Rand (1942b) saw a small group of these lories fluttering about a cavity in the trunk of a large forest tree. Two females in breeding condition were collected by him in the same month.

EGGS Undescribed.

YELLOW-STREAKED LORY
Chalcopsitta sintillata (Temminck)

DESCRIPTION Length 31 cm.
ADULTS general plumage dark green; forehead, lores, thighs, under wing-coverts and underside of tail red, less extensive on forehead in females; hindcrown, nape and ear-coverts black; head, neck and abdomen streaked with pale green, breast and mantle with bright yellow; sides of breast suffused with red; yellow band across underside of flight feathers; bill black; iris yellow to orange-red; legs dark grey.
IMMATURES less red on forehead, may be absent altogether; dusky yellow markings at base of bill; iris brown.

DISTRIBUTION Aru Islands and southern New Guinea.

SUBSPECIES

1. *C. s. sintillata* (Temminck)
   12 males   wing 160–183 (170.3) mm., tail 96–114 (106.0) mm.,
               exp. cul. 19–23 (21.0) mm., tars. 21–23 (22.1) mm.
   10 females wing 160–179 (170.4) mm., tail 97–111 (103.5) mm.,
               exp. cul. 19–22 (20.4) mm., tars. 21–24 (22.1) mm.
   Occurs in southern New Guinea from Triton Bay and the head of Geelvink Bay, West Irian, east to the lower Fly River, Papua.

2. *C. s. chloroptera* (Salvadori)   *Illustrated on page 49.*
   ADULTS narrower streaking of body feathers; under wing-coverts green or green with red markings.
   8 males   wing 168–177 (172.4) mm., tail 104–113 (108.8) mm.,
               exp. cul. 22–24 (22.4) mm., tars. 21–25 (22.4) mm.

8 females   wing 166–173 (170.0) mm., tail 102–113 (107.9) mm.,
          exp. cul. 20–23 (21.3) mm., tars. 22–23 (22.3) mm.
     Found in south-eastern New Guinea from the upper Fly River east to the Kemp Welch River.

3. *C. s. rubrifrons* G. R. Gray
    ADULTS streaking of breast wider and more orange than in *sintillata*.
    13 males   wing 176–191 (181.4) mm., tail 107–120 (113.1) mm.,
              exp. cul. 20–23 (21.8) mm., tars. 22–25 (23.1) mm.
    10 females   wing 166–186 (177.0) mm., tail 93–119 (108.2) mm.,
              exp. cul. 20–22 (21.3) mm., tars. 21–25 (23.0) mm.
      Confined to the Aru Islands.

GENERAL NOTES

The Yellow-streaked Lory is a common bird in lowland savannahs and adjacent forests (Rand and Gilliard, 1969). In the Port Moresby district it is frequently seen in rainforest and secondary growth, or in dense forests bordering streams in the savannah (Mackay, 1970). Tubb (1945) saw it in a coconut plantation at the mouth of the Kemp Welch River. It usually travels about in noisy flocks of up to thirty or more, but may also be seen singly or in pairs. According to Rand (1942a) its local abundance seems to depend on the presence of flowering trees. It has a direct, flapping flight.
     Lindgren (pers. comm., 1970) has seen these lories extracting nectar from the flowering stalks of umbrella trees (*Brassaia actinophylla*).

CALL While feeding, an occasional squeak or squeal (Mayr and Rand, 1937); in flight, a shrill screech.

NESTING A male with enlarged testes and in moult was collected in April at Baroka, south-eastern Papua (Mayr and Rand, 1937). In October, on the Lower Fly River, Rand saw two lories investigating a hollow in a dead palm stump; one bird then the other entered the cavity as if looking for a nest site, but no specimens collected were in breeding condition (in Rand, 1942a). At the Veimauri River, south-eastern Papua, a nest in a hollow in a tree about 24 m. from the ground was found in September (Mackay, 1971).

EGGS Rounded; a single egg in the British Museum measures 31.4 × 24.1 mm. [Harrison and Holyoak, 1970].

CARDINAL LORY
Chalcopsitta cardinalis (G. R. Gray)

Illustrated on page 49.

DESCRIPTION

Length 31 cm.
ADULTS general plumage red, darker and more brownish on back and wings; feathers of underparts edged with buff-yellow giving a slightly scalloped appearance; tail rusty red; bill coral with black at base of upper mandible; iris orange-red; legs dark grey.
IMMATURES paler red on back and wings; shorter, more pointed tail; bill dull orange strongly marked with black; iris dull yellow.
16 males   wing 174–186 (180.6) mm., tail 131–155 (142.0) mm.,
          exp. cul. 20–24 (21.5) mm., tars. 21–23 (21.8) mm.
10 females   wing 174–181 (176.5) mm., tail 132–145 (139.2) mm.,
          exp. cul. 20–23 (21.2) mm., tars. 20–24 (21.3) mm.

Feni, Nissan and Lavongai Islands, islands in the Tanga, Lihir, Tabor and Duke of York Groups, and the Solomon Islands (Galbraith and Galbraith, 1962).

DISTRIBUTION

GENERAL NOTES

According to Sibley (1951) the Cardinal Lory is numerous throughout the Solomon Islands. In parties of from three to ten they frequent mangroves, coastal coconut plantations and lowland forest. On Bougainville they have been collected from the canopy of tall secondary growth. Constant screeching always betrays their presence. The flight is swift and direct and Mayr (1945) says that they often fly from one island to the next.
     Sibley reports that they frequently associate with Rainbow Lories (*Trichoglossus haematodus*) to feed in fruiting forest trees or flowering coconut palms. Cain and Galbraith (1956) examined crop contents and found small berries and vegetable matter, apparently from coconut flowers.

CALL A loud, bubbling shriek like that of the Rainbow Lory (Cain and Galbraith, 1956).

NESTING In early September Cain and Galbraith observed one of a pair of lories displaying; this may have been during courtship. I know of no published information on the nesting of this common species.

EGGS Undescribed.

Genus EOS Wagler

This genus is poorly differentiated from *Chalcopsitta*; indeed *C. cardinalis* is often placed in *Eos*, presumably because of its red plumage.

There is no exposed naked skin surrounding the base of the lower mandible and the rounded tail is proportionately shorter than in *Chalcopsitta*. All species have a predominantly bright red plumage. The sexes are alike, but there is a distinctive immature plumage and young birds have pointed tips to the tail feathers.

BLACK-WINGED LORY
Eos cyanogenia Bonaparte
Illustrated on page 52.

Length 30 cm.
ADULTS general plumage bright red; bluish-purple band from eye to upper ear-coverts; black spot on flanks; upper wing-coverts, scapulars and primaries black; thighs black; central tail-feathers black, outer feathers red margined with black on outer webs; bill orange-red; iris red; legs dark grey.
IMMATURES feathers of head, neck and underparts irregularly margined with purple-black.
11 males   wing 154–169 (161.5) mm., tail 91–105 (97.8) mm.,
            exp. cul. 21–23 (21.9) mm., tars. 20–22 (20.5) mm.
9 females   wing 154–160 (157.4) mm., tail 94–101 (99.1) mm.,
            exp. cul. 20–22 (21.0) mm., tars. 20–21 (20.3) mm.

DISTRIBUTION   Islands of Biak, Numfoor, Manim and Mios Num in Geelvink Bay, West Irian.

GENERAL NOTES   The Black-winged Lory occurs on islands in Geelvink Bay, but is absent from the adjacent mainland. On Biak Ripley found that it was common only near the shore in coconut palms in and around Korrido village; he did not see it inland or in the mountains (in Mayr and Meyer de Schauensee, 1939a). The flight is swift and the parrots travel about in small flocks.

CALL A high-pitched screech (in captivity).

NESTING No published information.

EGGS Rounded; 6 eggs, 29.0 (28.7–29.6) × 23.8 (23.5–24.0) mm. [Schönwetter, 1964].

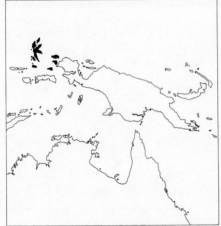

VIOLET-NECKED LORY
Eos squamata (Boddaert)

Length 27 cm.
ADULTS (plumage colouration variable); general plumage red; violet-blue collar around neck, broad and well-developed in some birds but almost entirely lacking in others; abdomen and under tail-coverts purple; scapulars dull purple tipped with black; greater wing-coverts and flight feathers margined and tipped with black; tail purple-red above, brownish-red below; bill orange-red; iris yellow to orange-red; legs grey.
IMMATURES feathers of underparts strongly margined with purple; some birds show blue on ear-coverts and crown; greenish wing-coverts; iris brown.

DISTRIBUTION   Western Papuan Islands, West Irian, and Maju Island, Weda Islands and northern Moluccas, Indonesia.

SUBSPECIES   I have followed the arrangement adopted by Mees (1965).

1. *E. s. squamata* (Boddaert)   *Illustrated on page 52.*
    8 males   wing 148–153 (150.9) mm., tail 92–105 (97.1) mm.,
                exp. cul. 18–21 (19.4) mm., tars. 19–21 (20.3) mm.
    8 females   wing 146–152 (148.9) mm., tail 91–109 (99.4) mm.,
                exp. cul. 18–20 (18.9) mm., tars. 19–21 (20.0) mm.
    Occurs on the Schildpad Islands and on Gebe, Waigeu, Batanta and Misool in the Western Papuan Islands.

2. *E. s. riciniata* (Bechstein)
    ADULTS prominent violet-grey neck collar, usually extending up to the hindcrown; some birds have violet-grey crown but red nape; red scapulars.
    11 males   wing 138–150 (143.0) mm., tail 85–101 (90.8) mm.,
                exp. cul. 17–20 (18.5) mm., tars. 17–20 (18.5) mm.

8 females   wing 133–146 (142.0) mm., tail 80–102 (92.8) mm.,
exp. cul. 17–19 (18.5) mm., tars. 17–19 (18.4) mm.
Found on Weda Islands and islands of the northern Moluccas.

3. *E. s. atrocaerulea* Jany
ADULTS similar to *riciniata* but underparts, including thighs, bluish-black; mantle black washed with blue; blue-black ear-coverts; rump darker red.
2 females   wing 143 (143.0) mm., tail 95–96 (95.5) mm.,
exp. cul. 19 (19.0) mm., tars. 18 (18.0) mm.
1 unsexed   wing 141 mm., tail 93 mm.,
exp. cul. 19 mm., tars. 19 mm.
Known only from Maju Island in the Molucca Sea, Indonesia. Mees doubts the validity of this race and suggests that it may have been based on juvenile plumage.

4. *E. s. obiensis* Rothschild
ADULTS black scapulars; variable violet-grey neck collar; some birds have violet-grey crowns and red napes.
5 males   wing 137–149 (142.6) mm., tail 89–96 (92.0) mm.,
exp. cul. 17–19 (18.0) mm., tars. 17–19 (18.2) mm.
1 female   wing 136 mm., tail 90 mm.,
exp. cul. 17 mm., tars. 18 mm.
Confined to the island of Obi in the northern Moluccas.

On Haitlal, a small island off the northern coast of Misool, Lieftinck found the Violet-necked Lory in a coconut plantation (in Mees, 1965). He also observed that each morning many birds congregated in the crowns of flowering *Erythrina* trees to feed on nectar, and in the evening shortly before sunset flocks flew back to the Misool coast, a little over 3 km. away.

CALL A shrill, discordant screech (in captivity).

NESTING No published records.

EGGS Rounded; 4 eggs, 26.8 (25.8–27.5) × 21.7 (21.5–22.0) mm. [Schönwetter, 1964].

Rajah Lory *Chalcopsitta atra insignis* 1
RMNH. Cat. 1, Reg. 1227 ad. unsexed

Black Lory *Chalcopsitta atra atra* 2
RMNH. Cat. 17, Reg. 22673 ad. ♂

Yellow-streaked Lory 3
Chalcopsitta sintillata chloroptera
CSIRO. 1638 ad. ♂

Duyvenbode's Lory 4
Chalcopsitta duivenbodei duivenbodei
AM. 035501 ad. ♂

Cardinal Lory *Chalcopsitta cardinalis* 5
CSIRO. 2975 ad. ♂

BLUE-STREAKED LORY
Eos reticulata (S. Muller)   *Illustrated on page 52.*

Length 31 cm.
ADULTS: general plumage bright red; purple-blue band from eyes across ear-coverts to mantle; mantle washed with blue-black and streaked with violet-blue; back and rump deep red variably streaked with blue; primaries, secondaries and greater wing-coverts tipped with black; tail brownish-black above, dull red below; bill coral; iris orange-red; legs grey.
IMMATURES feathers of breast variably margined with blue-black; more prominent black tips to wing-coverts; blue spots rather than streaks on mantle.
8 males   wing 168–176 (171.1) mm., tail 123–138 (129.1) mm.,
exp. cul. 19–20 (19.6) mm., tars. 21–23 (22.0) mm.
11 females   wing 156–172 (163.8) mm., tail 109–128 (118.0) mm.,
exp. cul. 18–19 (18.6) mm., tars. 20–23 (21.3) mm.

DISTRIBUTION   Tanimbar Islands, Indonesia; introduced to the Kai Islands and Damar Island, Indonesia.

GENERAL NOTES   Up to the 1920s collectors had no difficulty obtaining specimens of the Blue-streaked Lory, so presumably it was, and probably still is, quite common. There are no published details of the habits, but they are probably similar to those of the Violet-necked Lory.

CALL A shrill screech and a high-pitched whistle (in captivity).

NESTING No recorded information.

EGGS Rounded; 7 eggs, 29.1 (28.3–29.7) × 22.9 (22.3–23.6) mm. [Schönwetter, 1964].

RED AND BLUE LORY
Eos histrio (P. L. S. Müller)

DESCRIPTION   Length 31 cm.
ADULTS general plumage bright red, deeper on rump; broad purple-blue band on hindcrown; a darker blue line from eyes to mantle; mantle and back purple-blue; scapulars, flight feathers and

W. T. Cooper. 70.

thighs black; wing-coverts tipped with black; underparts red; broad blue band across breast; under tail-coverts washed with blue; tail reddish-purple above, red below; bill coral; iris red; legs grey.

IMMATURES (AMNH.616914); blue on crown, nape and below eyes; underparts red variably marked with dusky blue; thighs dull mauve-blue.

Illustrated on page 53.

Sangi, Talaud and Nenusa Islands, Indonesia.

DISTRIBUTION

1. *E. h. histrio* (P. L. S. Müller)
   - 8 males   wing 161–181 (167.8) mm., tail 111–131 (121.5) mm.,
               exp. cul. 20–22 (20.9) mm., tars. 19–23 (20.8) mm.
   - 6 females   wing 160–168 (164.0) mm., tail 108–123 (116.0) mm.,
               exp. cul. 20–23 (21.5) mm., tars. 20–23 (21.2) mm.
   - Occurs on Great Sangi and Siao Islands.

SUBSPECIES

2. *E. h. talautensis* Meyer and Wiglesworth
   ADULTS less black on wing-coverts and flight feathers.
   - 10 males   wing 160–168 (164.2) mm., tail 106–133 (119.2) mm.,
               exp. cul. 20–21 (20.4) mm., tars. 21–23 (22.1) mm.
   - 8 females   wing 161–173 (165.4) mm., tail 117–136 (125.6) mm.,
               exp. cul. 19–20 (19.6) mm., tars. 21–22 (21.5) mm.
   - Found on the Talaud Islands.

3. *E. h. challengeri* Salvadori
   .ADULTS blue band on breast less extensive and variably mingled with red; blue line from eyes does not meet blue mantle; smaller than *histrio*.
   - 2 males   wing 155–156 (155.5) mm., tail 101–107 (104.0) mm.,
               exp. cul. 19–20 (19.5) mm., tars. 19–22 (20.5) mm.
   - 1 female   wing 152 mm., tail 98 mm., exp. cul. 19 mm., tars. 23 mm.
   - Restricted to the Nenusa Islands.

Little is known of the habits of the Red and Blue Lory. When Platen visited Great Sangi Island late last century he found that it was not common and had retreated into the mountainous interior because of the spread of the coconut plantations around the coast (in Meyer and Wiglesworth, 1898). At about the same time Hickson also found that it was comparatively rare in the Sangi Islands, but very common in the Talaud Group where he saw large flocks flying from one island to the next to roost (in Meyer and Wiglesworth, 1898).

GENERAL NOTES

CALL Undescribed.

NESTING The clutch is said to be one or two eggs (in Meyer and Wiglesworth, 1898).

EGGS Undescribed.

RED LORY
Eos bornea (Linné)

Length 31 cm.
ADULTS general plumage bright red; white bases to body feathers; primaries black with a bright red speculum; secondaries tipped with black; greater wing-coverts edged with bluish-black; under tail-coverts and lower tertials blue; tail reddish-brown above, dull red below; bill dark orange; iris red; legs dark grey.
IMMATURES duller red; grey-brown bases to body feathers; lower tertials greyish, lightly marked with blue; ear-coverts sometimes lightly tinged with blue; under tail-coverts red; vent and thighs red sometimes suffused with dull blue; feathers of abdomen edged with blue; bill blackish in very young birds.

DESCRIPTION

Islands of Amboina, Saparua, Buru, Ceram, Goram, Ceramlaut and the Watubela and Kai Islands, Indonesia.

DISTRIBUTION

A revision of subspecies is outside the scope of this book so the arrangement proposed by Stresemann (1912) is followed, though I am not satisfied with it. I feel that juvenile plumage is so variable it should not be the criterion for separating subspecies. Furthermore, recognition of *bernsteini* and *rothschildi* is not practical when there are intermediate populations.

SUBSPECIES

Illustrated on page 53.

1. *E. b. bornea* (Linné)
   - 17 males   wing 160–172 (166.9) mm., tail 97–122 (112.6) mm.,
               exp. cul. 23–25 (23.6) mm., tars. 21–24 (22.3) mm.

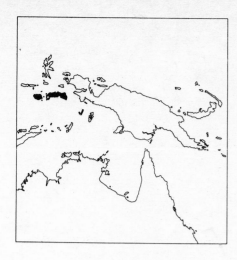

6 females   wing 159–165 (162.0) mm., tail 98–118 (109.0) mm.,
exp. cul. 22–23 (22.5) mm., tars. 22–23 (22.5) mm.
Occurs on Amboina and Saparua.

2. *E. b. cyanonothus* (Vieillot)
ADULTS   general plumage much darker.
IMMATURES   ear-coverts variably marked with blue.
11 males   wing 146–163 (154.0) mm., tail 96–112 (104.3) mm.,
exp. cul. 20–22 (20.6) mm., tars. 18–21 (19.3) mm.
13 females   wing 146–173 (154.4) mm., tail 95–109 (101.2) mm.,
exp. cul. 20–22 (20.7) mm., tars. 18–21 (19.4) mm.
Restricted to Buru.

3. *E. b. rothschildi* Stresemann
ADULTS   similar to *bornea*, but smaller.
IMMATURES   similar to *bornea*.
4 males   wing 154–160 (156.8) mm., tail 106–112 (109.5) mm.,
exp. cul. 22–23 (22.3) mm., tars. 19–21 (20.3) mm.
5 females   wing 149–153 (151.0) mm., tail 100–110 (104.2) mm.,
exp. cul. 21–23 (22.2) mm., tars. 20–21 (20.4) mm.
Found only on Ceram.

4. *E. b. bernsteini* (Rosenberg)
ADULTS   similar to *bornea*, but slightly larger.
IMMATURES   a few blue feathers above eyes; blue band from behind eye and down ear-coverts
to neck; feathers of throat narrowly margined with pale blue.
6 males   wing 158–180 (171.7) mm., tail 109–128 (123.5) mm.,
exp. cul. 21–24 (23.0) mm., tars. 21–23 (22.2) mm.
7 females   wing 165–177 (169.3) mm., tail 115–127 (118.9) mm.,
exp. cul. 22–24 (23.3) mm., tars. 22–24 (22.7) mm.
Inhabits the Kai Islands. Stresemann admits that birds from Goram, Ceramlaut and the
Watubela Islands are intermediate between this race and *rothschildi*.

GENERAL NOTES

Black-winged Lory *Eos cyanogenia*   1
RMNH. Cat. 18, Reg. 6774 ad. ♂

Blue-streaked Lory *Eos reticulata*   2
RMNH. Cat. 6 ad. ♂

Violet-necked Lory *Eos squamata riciniata*   3
AM. B2996 ad. unsexed

Stresemann (1914) reported that on Ceram the Red Lory was very common in the coastal zone
and in montane forest up to 1,250 m. Flocks of twenty or more were usually seen in flowering
trees, especially *Eugenia* sp., but at times large numbers congregated to feed. On moonlit nights
flocks often flew about screeching loudly. On Buru Toxopeus found that it was common in most
areas, particularly in mangroves, but was rare in open grassland and hilly country near the coast
(in Siebers, 1930). It visited flowering *Erythrina* trees to feed.

In the stomachs of two birds Stresemann found fragments of flowers and remains of small
insects.

CALL   A shrill, disyllabic screech (in captivity).

NESTING   In mid-December Stresemann saw several young birds taken from nests in hollows high
up in old trees.

Edworthy (1968) gives some details of a successful breeding in captivity. The clutch comprised
two eggs, but the incubation period was not determined. One young bird left the nest approximately seven weeks after hatching and the other about two weeks later. At the age of seven
months they had not acquired adult plumage, but their bills had changed to orange.

Holyoak (1970a) points out that the species *Eos goodfellowi* Ogilvie-Grant is based on juveniles
of *Eos bornea*.

EGGS   Rounded; 5 eggs 30.2 (29.8–31.2) × 24.2 (23.0–24.6) mm. [Harrison and Holyoak, 1970].

BLUE-EARED LORY
Eos semilarvata Bonaparte   *Illustrated on page 53.*

Length 24 cm.
ADULTS   general plumage bright red; white bases to body feathers; upper cheeks and ear-coverts
and band down side of neck violet-blue; abdomen and under tail-coverts blue; primaries black
with a red speculum; secondaries tipped with black; tertials black strongly suffused with blue;
tail reddish-brown above, dull red below; bill dark orange; iris orange-red; legs grey.
IMMATURES (AMNH. 616964); general plumage paler and duller red; grey-brown bases to body
feathers; pale blue restricted to ear-coverts and below eyes; scapulars brownish-grey edged with
pale blue; some feathers of abdomen margined with blue.
3 males   wing 139–145 (142.0) mm., tail 93–97 (95.0) mm.,
exp. cul. 18–19 (18.7) mm., tars. 17–19 (18.0) mm.

3 females   wing 132–138 (134.7) mm., tail 95–100 (97.7) mm.,
exp. cul. 18–19 (18.3) mm., tars. 16–17 (16.3) mm.

DISTRIBUTION   Mountains of central Ceram, Indonesia.

GENERAL NOTES   The Blue-eared Lory replaces the Red Lory in the montane forests of central Ceram above 1,500 m. (Stresemann, 1914). On the upper reaches of the Sapulewa River between Mt. Murkele and Mt. Pinaia Stresemann found it to be very common. Its habits are similar to those of the Red Lory.

CALL   A loud screech, particularly when in flight.

NESTING   No recorded information.

EGGS   Undescribed.

Genus PSEUDEOS Peters

This monotypic genus is related to *Eos*, but the tail is much shorter and there is an extensive naked area around the base of the lower mandible. The sexes are alike and immatures resemble adults, but have pointed tips to the tail feathers.

DUSKY LORY
Pseudeos fuscata (Blyth)   *Illustrated on page 56.*

Length 25 cm.
ADULTS   general plumage dusky olive-brown; crown dull yellow; feathers of hindneck and upper breast edged with dull yellow; yellow or yellow-orange band across throat, some birds have a second band across breast; abdomen and lower breast yellow or orange; thighs orange-red; under tail-coverts bluish-purple; back and rump creamy-white; under wing-coverts olive brown and dull yellow; two orange-yellow bands across undersides of flight feathers; tail dull olive-yellow marked with orange; bill dark orange; iris red; legs dark grey.
IMMATURES (CSIRO. 3855); underparts more extensively marked with yellow or orange; under tail-coverts grey black; back and rump dull yellow; bill brownish-black with yellowish base to lower mandible; iris yellowish-grey.
20 males   wing 150–168 (157.3) mm., tail 76–89 (82.0) mm.,
exp. cul. 21–23 (21.6) mm., tars. 17–21 (18.9) mm.
18 females   wing 148–166 (156.1) mm., tail 78–87 (81.9) mm.,
exp. cul. 19–23 (20.9) mm., tars. 17–21 (19.2) mm.

DISTRIBUTION   Occurs throughout New Guinea and on Salawati in the Western Papuan Islands and on Japen Island in Geelvink Bay.

GENERAL NOTES   According to Rand and Gilliard (1967) Dusky Lories inhabit both forest and open savannah, and have been recorded up to about 2,000 m. In the Port Moresby district they have been seen along the edge of rainforest on a few occasions (Mackay, 1970). Bell (pers. comm.) says that they are frequent visitors to the Lae Botanic Gardens and may breed there. When in flight or when feeding among the upper branches of flowering trees they are usually in flocks of from twenty to a hundred or more. The flight is swift and direct. While feeding they are tame and will allow a close approach. At sunset they come in to roost in a favourite tree and at dawn move out to scattered feeding areas. Hoogerwerf (1971) reports that near Manokwari on the Vogelkop, West Irian, these parrots were always seen in large parties feeding in flowering or fruiting trees, sometimes in the company of Friar Birds (*Philemon novaeguineae*) and Spangled Drongos (*Dicrurus hottentottus*).

In May 1970, near Lae, I watched flocks of these lories flying in to roost in a large tree standing in savannah adjoining secondary forest. They indulged in pre-roosting aerobatics and while some birds glided down in wide circles, others swooped down then rose high into the air again. When alighting all birds glided down into the tree. Continuous screeching accompanied these activities.

Near Lake Kutubu in Papua, Schodde and Hitchcock (1968) found these parrots feeding in a profusely flowering *Pittosporum ramiflorum*, and at Amazon Bay, south-eastern Papua, they have been observed feeding amongst coconut blossoms (Bell, 1970a). Stomach contents from birds collected at Manokwari by Hoogerwerf comprised remains of small black fruit-stones, light green pulp and fine vegetable matter, probably flower fragments.

CALL   A shrill screech, higher in pitch than the call of the Rainbow Lory.

NESTING   In the Arfak Mountains, West Irian, Bergman collected specimens with enlarged gonads during July (in Gyldenstolpe, 1955b).
There appear to be no published breeding records for this common lory.

EGGS   Rounded; 1 egg, 27.8 × 24.1 mm. [Schönwetter, 1964].

Red and Blue Lory *Eos histrio histrio*   **1**
RMNH. Cat. 5 ad. ♂

Red Lory *Eos bornea bornea*   **2**
RMNH. Cat. 25, Reg. 15120 ad. ♂

Blue-eared Lory *Eos semilarvata*   **3**
AMNH. 617003 ad. ♂

Genus TRICHOGLOSSUS Vigors and Horsefield

The lories belonging to *Trichoglossus* are small to medium-sized parrots with gradated tails comprising rather narrow, pointed feathers. There is no naked area surrounding the lower mandible. Sexual dimorphism is absent, and immatures resemble adults but have more sharply pointed tail feathers.

I have incorporated *Psitteuteles* into this genus as has been advocated by many recent authors. However, I am not convinced that *T. goldiei* belongs here and suspect that further investigations with fresh material could result in its being placed in a monotypic genus.

ORNATE LORY
Trichoglossus ornatus (Linné)

Illustrated on page 57.

Length 25 cm.
ADULTS forehead, crown and upper ear-coverts purple-blue; cheeks and lower ear-coverts bright orange-red; yellow band on side of neck behind ear-coverts; occiput red, the feathers tipped with dusky blue; throat and breast orange-red, feathers prominently margined with blue-black giving a barred appearance; abdomen and vent green variably marked with greenish-yellow; upperparts bright green; under wing-coverts yellow; tail green above, dull yellow below; bill orange-red; iris dark orange; legs greenish-grey.
IMMATURES (Meyer and Wiglesworth, 1898); occiput green lightly marked with red; narrower bluish margins to breast feathers; abdomen strongly marked with yellow; bill brownish; iris brown.
8 males   wing 127–131 (128.8) mm., tail 76–80 (78.3) mm.,
            exp. cul. 19–20 (19.4) mm., tars. 17–19 (18.3) mm.
8 females wing 125–134 (127.9) mm., tail 70–81 (75.4) mm.,
            exp. cul. 19–20 (19.6) mm., tars. 17–18 (17.5) mm.

DISTRIBUTION   Celebes and most larger offshore islands, Indonesia.

GENERAL NOTES   Heinrich says that in the Celebes the Ornate Lory is common and inhabits wooded mountain country up to about 1,000 m. (in Stresemann, 1940). It tends to avoid dense primary forest and in the flat coastal country he found it at only two localities. It is usually seen in pairs or small flocks, but in certain flowering trees very large numbers may congregate to feed. At higher altitudes it frequently associates with the Yellow and Green Lorikeet (*Trichoglossus flavoviridis*). It is tame and will allow a close approach, particularly when feeding. On Buton Island de Haan found it in teak forests and in a village near the seashore (in van Bemmel and Voous, 1951); it was locally abundant, especially along the edge of the forest bordering village gardens. The flight is swift and direct.

Food comprises pollen, nectar, fruits, blossoms and seeds. De Haan reports that on Buton it feeds on *Tectona* and *Casuarina* seeds, but I suspect that these would be supplementary to nectar and fruits.

Dusky Lory *Pseudeos fuscata*
CSIRO. 1829 ad. ♂

CALL In flight a shrill *kreet . . . kreet*; also a high-pitched *wee-oo-wee* and a variety of whistling notes (Coomans de Ruiter and Maurenbrecher, 1948).

NESTING Birds in breeding condition were collected by de Haan during September and October.
Bertagnolio (1970) gives details of a successful breeding in captivity. Two eggs were laid and both hatched after an incubation of twenty-seven days. The female sat tightly during the day and was joined by the male at night, though he probably did not participate in the incubation. The young birds left the nest eighty days after hatching.

EGGS Rounded; 3 eggs, 26.1 (23.7–27.5) × 21.7 (21.5–21.9) mm. [Harrison and Holyoak, 1970].

RAINBOW LORY
Trichoglossus haematodus (Linné)

DESCRIPTION   Length 26 cm.
ADULTS forehead, forecrown, lores and chin bluish-mauve; remainder of head brownish-black; yellowish-green nuchal collar; breast red, feathers strongly edged with blue-black giving a barred appearance; abdomen dark green; thighs and under tail-coverts greenish-yellow variably marked with dark green; upperparts green; red bases to feathers of mantle; under wing-coverts orange; broad yellow band across underside of flight feathers; tail green above, dull olive-yellow below; bill orange to dark red; iris orange-red; legs greenish-grey to dark grey.
IMMATURES duller than adults; bill brownish-black; iris brown.

DISTRIBUTION   From Bali and islands in the Flores Sea, Indonesia, east through New Guinea and adjacent islands

W. T. Cooper. 70.

W.T. Cooper. 70.

to the Solomon Islands, New Hebrides and New Caledonia and the Loyalty Islands; also in northern and eastern Australia, including Tasmania.

SUBSPECIES   I have followed the arrangement proposed by Cain (1955), but agree with Mees (1965) that *berauensis* must be synonymized with *haematodus*.

1. *T. h. haematodus* (Linné)   *Illustrated on page 60.*
   10 males   wing 135–150 (141.8) mm., tail 99–114 (108.8) mm.,
                exp. cul. 20–23 (21.4) mm., tars. 17–20 (18.8) mm.
   10 females   wing 136–146 (141.6) mm., tail 93–118 (105.2) mm.,
                exp. cul. 20–22 (21.0) mm., tars. 18–20 (19.2) mm.
   Occurs on Buru, Amboina, Ceram, Ceramlaut, the Goram, Watubela and Western Papuan Islands, islands in Geelvink Bay, except Biak, and western New Guinea along the north coast east to about Humboldt Bay and in the south to the upper Fly River; may also occur on the westernmost Kai Islands.

2. *T. h. mitchellii* G. R. Gray
   ADULTS   head dark blackish-brown with greyish-green streaking on crown and cheeks; rufous tinge on occiput; breast rich red with only slight bluish edging to the feathers in some birds; abdomen purple-black; smaller than *haematodus*.
   IMMATURES   breast paler and more orange; dark green abdomen.
   11 males   wing 129–136 (132.3) mm., tail 94–104 (98.8) mm.,
                exp. cul. 17–19 (18.1) mm., tars. 16–19 (17.3) mm.
   10 females   wing 124–133 (129.1) mm., tail 91–103 (96.4) mm.,
                exp. cul. 17–19 (17.9) mm., tars. 15–18 (16.7) mm.
   Known as Mitchell's Lorikeet, this race is found on Bali and Lombok.

3. *T. h. forsteni* Bonaparte
   ADULTS   similar to *mitchellii* but without barring on darker red breast; forehead and cheeks streaked with violet-blue; more yellowish nuchal collar; some birds have purple on hindneck below collar; abdomen purple.
   6 males   wing 132–139 (135.2) mm., tail 87–103 (97.5) mm.,
               exp. cul. 19–21 (19.8) mm., tars. 17–18 (17.5) mm.
   2 females   wing 133–139 (136.0) mm., tail 98–99 (98.5) mm.,
               exp. cul. 18–19 (18.5) mm., tars. 18 (18.0) mm.
   Forsten's Lorikeet, as this subspecies is called, occurs on Sumbawa.

4. *T. h. djampeanus* Hartert
   ADULTS   similar to *forsteni*, but head darker and more strongly streaked with violet-blue; dark purple on hindneck below collar; no trace of barring on uniformly red breast.
   8 males   wing 140–146 (142.4) mm., tail 96–112 (102.8) mm.,
               exp. cul. 18–19 (18.9) mm., tars. 17–19 (18.0) mm.
   6 females   wing 137–145 (141.7) mm., tail 101–108 (105.3) mm.,
               exp. cul. 18–19 (18.5) mm., tars. 17–19 (18.0) mm.
   Restricted to Djampea Island in the Flores Sea; doubtfully distinct from *forsteni*.

5. *T. h. stresemanni* Meise
   ADULTS   similar to *forsteni*, but breast is more orange; yellow bases to feathers of mantle; occiput tinged with green.
   3 males   wing 142–152 (148.7) mm., tail 105–124 (116.0) mm.,
               exp. cul. 20–21 (20.7) mm., tars. 19–20 (19.7) mm.
   2 females   wing 135–150 (142.5) mm., tail 93–115 (104.0) mm.,
               exp. cul. 20 (20.0) mm., tars. 18 (18.0) mm.
   Found only on Kalao tua, in the Flores Sea.

6. *T. h. fortis* Hartert
   ADULTS   forehead and cheeks streaked with violet-blue; lores, throat, line above eye, and occiput green; breast orange-yellow; abdomen dark green sometimes tinged with black; yellow under wing-coverts.
   12 males   wing 148–159 (153.3) mm., tail 111–126 (118.5) mm.,
               exp. cul. 20–22 (21.4) mm., tars. 20–21 (20.3) mm.
   9 females   wing 145–153 (148.3) mm., tail 114–124 (119.1) mm.,
               exp. cul. 20–21 (20.6) mm., tars. 19–20 (19.3) mm.
   Inhabits Sumba Island.

Ornate Lory *Trichoglossus ornatus* 1
AM. 043016 ad. ♂

Yellow and Green Lorikeet 2
Trichoglossus flavoviridis flavoviridis
RMNH. Cat. 5 ad. ♂

Johnstone's Lorikeet 3
Trichoglossus johnstoniae johnstoniae
AMNH. 618611 ad. ♂

7. *T. h. weberi* (Büttikofer)   *Illustrated on page 60.*
   ADULTS   general plumage green; breast variably marked with greenish-yellow; forehead and lores suffused with blue; smaller than *haematodus*.
   10 males   wing 125–135 (128.8) mm., tail 83–102 (94.5) mm.,
               exp. cul. 18–20 (19.3) mm., tars. 16–18 (17.1) mm.

5 females   wing 120–128 (125.0) mm., tail 84–98 (92.4) mm.,
        exp. cul. 17–19 (18.6) mm., tars. 15–18 (16.2) mm.
      Known as Weber's Lorikeet, this most distinctive subspecies is found only on Flores.

8. *T. h. capistratus* (Bechstein)
ADULTS head green; forehead, forecrown and cheeks streaked with violet-blue; breast yellow variably marked with orange; broad nuchal collar greenish-yellow; abdomen dark green; under wing-coverts yellow variably marked with orange.
9 males   wing 141–151 (146.1) mm., tail 113–119 (116.1) mm.,
        exp. cul. 19–21 (20.2) mm., tars. 17–19 (18.8) mm.
11 females wing 140–150 (144.7) mm., tail 108–119 (113.4) mm.,
        exp. cul. 18–20 (18.7) mm., tars. 17–19 (18.0) mm.
      This race is from Timor and is called Edward's Lorikeet.

9. *T. h. flavotectus* Hellmayr
ADULTS similar to *capistratus*, but breast paler yellow and seldom marked with orange; no orange on under wing-coverts.
8 males   wing 144–152 (147.9) mm., tail 107–123 (115.8) mm.,
        exp. cul. 19–20 (19.8) mm., tars. 18–19 (18.6) mm.
9 females wing 143–150 (146.7) mm., tail 103–122 (114.1) mm.,
        exp. cul. 19–20 (19.7) mm., tars. 17–19 (18.2) mm.
      Occurs on the islands of Wetar and Roma, near Timor.

10. *T. h. rosenbergii* Schlegel

Illustrated on page 60.

ADULTS similar to *haematodus*, but with a wide yellow nuchal collar bordered above by a narrow red band; head more strongly streaked with violet-blue; feathers of breast broadly edged with purple blue; abdomen purple; broad orange band on underside of flight feathers.
8 males   wing 132–150 (140.6) mm., tail 92–109 (97.5) mm.,
        exp. cul. 20–23 (22.0) mm., tars. 17–19 (18.5) mm.
3 females wing 133–144 (138.3) mm., tail 91–98 (94.3) mm.,
        exp. cul. 21–22 (21.3) mm., tars. 18–19 (18.6) mm.
      Restricted to the island of Biak in Geelvink Bay, West Irian.

11. *T. h. intermedius* Rothschild and Hartert
ADULTS similar to *haematodus*, but with less blue on the head.
10 males wing 138–154 (148.2) mm., tail 101–113 (107.3) mm.,
        exp. cul. 22–24 (23.4) mm., tars. 18–22 (20.5) mm.
9 females wing 134–144 (140.3) mm., tail 95–111 (101.0) mm.,
        exp. cul. 20–23 (21.6) mm., tars. 18–21 (19.1) mm.
      This doubtful subspecies is found in northern New Guinea from the Sepik River east to Astrolabe Bay; also on Manam Island.

12. *T. h. micropteryx* Stresemann
ADULTS general plumage paler than *haematodus*, particularly on upperparts, breast and abdomen; narrower edging to breast feathers; nuchal collar more greenish.
10 males wing 133–140 (136.6) mm., tail 94–110 (100.8) mm.,
        exp. cul. 19–22 (20.9) mm., tars. 17–19 (18.1) mm.
10 females wing 132–139 (135.0) mm., tail 85–98 (92.9) mm.,
        exp. cul. 19–22 (20.3) mm., tars. 18–20 (18.3) mm.
      Widespread in New Guinea east of the Huon Peninsula, the Wahgi Range and Hall Sound; also on Misima Island in the Louisiade Archipelago; may not be separable from *massena*.

13. *T. h. caeruleiceps* D'Albertis and Salvadori
ADULTS entire crown and sides of head pale blue; breast paler than in *micropteryx* and with narrower barring; abdomen blackish-green.
9 males   wing 134–146 (138.8) mm., tail 99–119 (108.0) mm.,
        exp. cul. 20–21 (20.2) mm., tars. 18–19 (18.6) mm.
8 females wing 133–140 (136.8) mm., tail 100–111 (105.0) mm.,
        exp. cul. 19–20 (19.3) mm., tars. 17–19 (18.0) mm.
      Found in southern New Guinea between the lower Fly River and the Princess Marianne Straits; probably not separable from *nigrogularis*.

14. *T. h. nigrogularis* G. R. Gray
ADULTS similar to *caeruleiceps*, but slightly larger; blue on head usually darker.
9 males   wing 148–161 (153.6) mm., tail 117–130 (122.8) mm.,
        exp. cul. 21–23 (21.9) mm., tars. 19–21 (22.1) mm.
8 females wing 140–155 (145.8) mm., tail 107–122 (114.9) mm.,
        exp. cul. 20–22 (21.0) mm., tars. 19–21 (19.8) mm.
      Occurs on the Aru Islands and the eastern Kai Islands.

15. *T. h. brooki* Ogilvie-Grant
ADULTS similar to *nigrogularis*, but the abdominal patch is more extensive and is black with little or no trace of green.

Red-collared Lorikeet **1**
Trichoglossus haematodus rubritorquis
CSIRO. 6375 ad. ♂

Rainbow Lory **2**
Trichoglossus haematodus haematodus
RMNH. Cat. 124 ad. ♂

Rainbow Lory **3**
Trichoglossus haematodus rosenbergii
BM. 89.1.20.134 ad. unsexed

Rainbow Lory **4**
Trichoglossus haematodus flavicans
QM. 03511 ad. unsexed

Weber's Lorikeet **5**
Trichoglossus haematodus weberi
RMNH. Cat. 3 ad. ♂

W.T. Cooper, 76.

2 males   wing 154 (154.0) mm., tail 119–124 (121.5) mm.,
          exp. cul. 22–24 (23.0) mm., tars. 18 (18.0) mm.
This subspecies is known only from the types, two cage birds said to have come from Spirit Island off the south coast of Trangan Island, Aru Islands.

16. *T. h. massena* Bonaparte
ADULTS similar to *micropteryx*, but nuchal collar less yellowish; occiput and nape strongly tinged with brown; breast paler and with narrower barring; abdomen slightly paler.
11 males   wing 138–145 (141.9) mm., tail 97–112 (105.2) mm.,
           exp. cul. 19–21 (20.4) mm., tars. 17–19 (18.5) mm.
9 females wing 131–142 (136.1) mm., tail 89–108 (99.4) mm.,
           exp. cul. 18–23 (20.1) mm., tars. 17–19 (18.0) mm.
Known as the Coconut Lory, this subspecies ranges throughout the Bismarck Archipelago and through the Solomon Islands to the New Hebrides.

17. *T. h. flavicans* Cabanis and Reichenow   *Illustrated on page 60.*
ADULTS (plumage variable); upperparts, under tail-coverts and tail vary from bronze-yellow to dull green; yellow nuchal collar; occiput reddish-brown; forehead, lores and periophthalmic region violet-blue; remainder of head black streaked with greyish-green; breast bright red with little barring.
8 males   wing 144–155 (148.9) mm., tail 110–120 (114.3) mm.,
           exp. cul. 22–24 (22.5) mm., tars. 20–21 (20.5) mm.
8 females wing 142–148 (144.5) mm., tail 97–111 (103.3) mm.,
           exp. cul. 22–23 (22.3) mm., tars. 19–21 (20.3) mm.
Occurs on New Hanover and the Admiralty Islands.

18. *T. h. nesophilus* Neumann
ADULTS similar to *flavicans* but upperparts, under tail-coverts and tail green, never varying to bronze-yellow.
7 males   wing 132–151 (141.6) mm., tail 96–114 (107.4) mm.,
           exp. cul. 19–24 (20.4) mm., tars. 18–22 (18.9) mm.
5 females wing 132–150 (140.6) mm., tail 94–116 (103.4) mm.,
           exp. cul. 18–22 (19.6) mm., tars. 17–21 (18.4) mm.
Confined to islands in the Ninigo Group, west of Manus Island.

19. *T. h. deplanchii* Verreaux and Des Murs
ADULTS differ from *massena* by having more blue on head; less brown on occiput and nape; less yellow on thighs and under tail-coverts.
8 males   wing 144–149 (145.9) mm., tail 96–113 (106.5) mm.,
           exp. cul. 19–20 (19.4) mm., tars. 17–19 (18.3) mm.
8 females wing 133–144 (138.0) mm., tail 90–111 (100.1) mm.,
           exp. cul. 18–19 (18.8) mm., tars. 17–19 (18.1) mm.
Found on New Caledonia and the Loyalty Islands.

20. *T. h. moluccanus* (Gmelin)
ADULTS head violet-blue; breast yellowish-orange with little or no barring; abdomen deep purple-blue; nuchal collar yellowish-green; under wing-coverts orange strongly washed with yellow.
10 males   wing 135–157 (150.8) mm., tail 126–142 (130.9) mm.,
           exp. cul. 17–21 (18.5) mm., tars. 15–19 (17.0) mm.
7 females wing 140–160 (146.3) mm., tail 123–133 (127.9) mm.,
           exp. cul. 18–21 (19.0) mm., tars. 15–20 (17.0) mm.
Occurs in eastern Australia from Cape York Peninsula south to Tasmania and across to Kangaroo Island and Eyre Peninsula, South Australia.

Scaly-breasted Lorikeet 1
Trichoglossus chlorolepidotus
AM. 028577 ad. ♂

Ponapé Lory *Trichoglossus rubiginosus* 2
RMNH. Cat. 5 ad. ♀

Perfect Lorikeet *Trichoglossus euteles* 3
RMNH. Cat. 20 ad. ♂

21. *T. h. rubritorquis* Vigors and Horsefield   *Illustrated on page 60.*
ADULTS throat and foreneck blackish; remainder of head violet-blue; breast paler than in *moluccanus* and without barring; abdomen greenish-black; broad orange-red nuchal collar; upper mantle dark blue variably marked with green and red.
12 males   wing 142–160 (151.1) mm., tail 127–135 (130.4) mm.,
           exp. cul. 19–22 (20.3) mm., tars. 16–19 (17.5) mm.
10 females wing 141–159 (148.4) mm., tail 129–142 (133.3) mm.,
           exp. cul. 19–21 (19.6) mm., tars. 16–19 (17.4) mm.
Known as the Red-collared Lorikeet, this race is found in northern Australia from the Kimberley division of Western Australia east to the Gulf of Carpentaria, Queensland.

GENERAL NOTES   In Australia the Rainbow Lory is primarily a lowland bird, though it is by no means uncommon in mountainous areas in north-eastern parts of the continent. It inhabits virtually all types of timbered country, and is often observed in city gardens and parklands. On offshore islands along the Queensland coast it frequents coconut palms. Throughout the north the species is abundant, and its nomadic movements are not conspicuous because there are always some birds present in most districts. However, in the south it is less common and the widespread, largely irregular movements in search of flowering trees are obvious. Sharland (1958) points out that it only rarely visits Tasmania and there are no recent records.

On Bali Rensch (1930) found the Rainbow Lory to be very common at 1,200 m. in *Erythrina* trees around Lake Bratan. He suggests that the species may have colonized Bali from nearby Lombok after the introduction of coffee brought about widespread planting of *Erythrina* as shade trees in the plantations. On Sumbawa it inhabits mainly open rainforest up to at least 1,000 m., and on Flores occurs in rainforest and *Casuarina* stands as high as 1,400 m. (Rensch, 1931). It seems to be absent from the montane forests of Lombok where there are no suitable feeding trees (Rensch, 1931). Stresemann (1914) notes that on Ceram it was common near the coast and was usually seen in flocks, but inland only ones and twos were found. On Buru Toxopeus saw large flocks in coastal coconut plantations, but did not find it in the interior or anywhere above 350 m. (in Siebers, 1930). It is very common and widespread in New Guinea, inhabiting savannah woodland, secondary forest, clearings in primary forest and trees along watercourses (Rand and Gilliard, 1967). It prefers the edges of rainforest and seems to avoid a closed canopy. It is a lowland bird, but in the Central Highlands of New Guinea I have seen it as high as 2,200 m. on the southern slopes of the Hagen Range. According to Mackay (1970) it is a very common resident in the Port Moresby district. On New Britain Gilliard found that it was common in small noisy flocks in the forest canopy below 1,000 m. (Gilliard and LeCroy, 1967a). It is very common in coastal and lowland areas throughout the Solomon Islands, though not as numerous as the Cardinal Lory (*Chalcopsitta cardinalis*), a species with which it often associates in flowering coconut palms (Mayr 1945, Sibley 1951). According to Delacour (1966) it is abundant in the forests of New Caledonia and is a frequent visitor to coffee plantations when *Erythrina* shade trees are in bloom.

Rainbow Lories are generally observed in pairs or in flocks of from a few birds to hundreds, depending on the abundance of flowering trees. They are noisy and active, continually flying about over the treetops and screeching loudly or uttering subdued chattering notes while climbing among the foliage. When feeding they are oblivious to the approach of an intruder, but at other times are rather wary. They often feed in the company of other parrots or with honeyeaters and flowerpeckers. Lavery (1970) reports that in northern Queensland, Australia, large mixed flocks of this species and the smaller Scaly-breasted Lorikeet (*Trichoglossus chlorolepidotus*) were seen feeding in ripening sorghum crops, but within the flocks the two species were mostly segregated. Flocks flying overhead respond quickly to the calls of birds feeding in trees below; they wheel about and circle once before swooping down to alight. They travel widely in search of feeding areas. Apparently they fly from New Caledonia to Lifu and Ouvea in the Loyalty Islands and MacMillan claims that on several occasions he saw flocks out at sea (in Warner, 1947).

Their diet comprises pollen, nectar, fruits, berries, seeds, leaf buds and insects and their larvae. On Guadalcanal, Solomon Islands, Donaghho (1950) found a flock of about a hundred feeding on blossoms of scarlet bottle-brush (Myrtaceae). Near Lake Kutubu, Papua, Schodde and Hitchcock (1968) found several feeding with numbers of Dusky Lories (*Pseudeos fuscata*) in a flowering *Pittosporum ramiflorum* tree. Near Port Moresby they have been seen feeding on pupae of the Poinciana Moth (*Pericyma cruegeri*) and on seeds of *Cassia* sp. and *Casuarina equisetifolia* (Bell, 1966 and 1968). In Australia they feed principally on pollen and nectar from blossoms of *Eucalyptus*, *Melaleuca* or other native trees and shrubs, particularly *Banksia*, and of some introduced trees. They are fond of cultivated fruits, especially apples and pears, and cause some damage in orchards. They also attack maize and sorghum crops to feed on the unripe 'milky' grain. Crop contents from several birds collected in South Australia consisted of nectar, fragments of flowers, flower heads from *Casuarina* sp., vegetable matter, seeds, including those of *Solanum* sp., and a small grub (Lea and Gray, 1935).

CALL In flight a sharp, rolling screech is repeated at regular intervals; while feeding a shrill chattering, and when at rest soft twittering notes are uttered.

NESTING On Ceram Stresemann was shown a nestling taken from a nest in mid-December. Verheijen (1964) records nesting on Flores during most months between February and August. A male with slightly enlarged gonads was collected on Misool by Ripley (1964) in late November, while near Tarara in southern New Guinea Rand (1942a) observed copulation in early January. In early November Sibley found an occupied nest on New Georgia in the Solomons.

In Australia the breeding season is from August to January, though in northern regions nesting has also been recorded in April and May. The nest is in a hollow limb or hole in a tree, usually at some height from the ground. The two eggs, rarely three, are laid on a bed of decayed wood dust. Although the male spends considerable time in the nesting hollow, particularly at night, it seems that he does not assist with incubation. Incubation lasts about twenty-five days and both parents feed the chicks. Young birds leave the nest approximately seven to eight weeks after hatching, but for some days return each evening to roost.

EGGS Ovate; 11 eggs, 26.9 (23.8–30.6) × 22.4 (20.6–23.9) mm. [Schönwetter 1964, Harrison and Holyoak 1970].

Purple-bellied Lory 1
Lorius hypoinochrous devittatus
AM. 022351 ad. unsexed

Black-capped Lory *Lorius lory lory* 2
RMNH. Cat. 42 ad. ♂

Black-capped Lory *Lorius lory somu* 3
CSIRO. 1365 ad. ♂

Iris Lorikeet *Trichoglossus iris iris* 1
AMNH. 345461 ad. ♂

Varied Lorikeet *Trichoglossus versicolor* 2
CSIRO. 6456 ad. ♂

Goldie's Lorikeet *Trichoglossus goldiei* 3
AMNH. 618626 ad. ♂

PONAPÉ LORY
Trichoglossus rubiginosus (Bonaparte)

Illustrated on page 61.

Illustrated on page 61.

Length 24 cm.
ADULTS general plumage deep maroon, feathers of neck and underparts edged darker giving an indistinct barred appearance; flight feathers and tail feathers olive-yellow; bill orange in male, more yellowish in female (Baker); iris yellow-orange in male, greyish-white in female (Baker); legs dark grey.
IMMATURES (Baker, 1951); similar to adults.
10 males wing 140–151 (145.5) mm., tail 91–99 (95.1) mm.,
exp. cul. 19–20 (19.6) mm., tars. 17–19 (17.9) mm.
10 females wing 136–146 (141.0) mm., tail 88–98 (93.0) mm.,
exp. cul. 16–19 (18.3) mm., tars. 17–19 (17.6) mm.

Ponapé in the Caroline Islands.

Coultas says that the Ponapé Lory is common on Ponapé and is found everywhere on the island (in Baker, 1951). It has a preference for coconut palms. It is noisy and moves about in pairs or parties of from six to eight. After sunset it emits soft crooning notes. It is inquisitive and will investigate the slightest noise, to which it responds with an excited screeching. Occasionally a lone bird may be found feeding quietly in a tree. The local name for this parrot means 'always hide out in rain' and refers to its alleged habit of sheltering from rain under a large leaf.

There are no records of feeding habits but they are probably similar to those of the Rainbow Lory.

CALL A continuous chatter when in flight (in Baker, 1951).

NESTING According to Coultas the nest is in a hollow in the top of a coconut palm or in a large forest tree and only one egg is laid. During November he collected birds with enlarged gonads.

EGGS Undescribed.

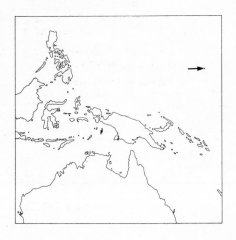

JOHNSTONE'S LORIKEET
Trichoglossus johnstoniae Hartert

Length 20 cm.
ADULTS general plumage green; forehead, upper ear-coverts and foreparts of cheeks dull rose-red; dark purple-brown band from lores to occiput; lower ear-coverts greenish-yellow; feathers of underparts yellow broadly edged with green giving a scalloped appearance; under wing-coverts and under tail-coverts yellowish-green; yellow band on underside of flight feathers; tail green above, olive-yellow below; bill orange-red; iris red; legs greenish-grey.
IMMATURES less red on upper ear-coverts; no purple-brown band across occiput; dull mauve brown marking behind eye; bare periophthalmic ring white instead of dark blue-grey; bill blackish in very young birds.

Mountains of Mindanao, Philippine Islands.

1. *T. j. johnstoniae* Hartert *Illustrated on page 57.*

Illustrated on page 57.

10 males wing 100–116 (108.8) mm., tail 65–76 (69.4) mm.,
exp. cul. 13–15 (14.1) mm., tars. 13–15 (14.1) mm.
11 females wing 99–115 (107.6) mm., tail 63–71 (67.3) mm.,
exp. cul. 12–15 (13.3) mm., tars. 13–15 (14.1) mm.
Occurs on Mt. Apo and neighbouring mountains in central and south-eastern Mindanao.

2. *T. j. pistra* Rand and Rabor.
ADULTS deeper, duller red on forehead and face; band from lores to occiput dark blue-brown; green of upperparts slightly darker; yellow of underparts slightly more vivid.
10 males wing 105–112 (108.1) mm., tail 59–70 (66.0) mm.,
exp. cul. 14–15 (14.4) mm., tars. 13–15 (14.1) mm.
7 females wing 105–111 (108.9) mm., tail 61–69 (66.6) mm.,
exp. cul. 13–15 (14.0) mm., tars. 13–15 (14.0) mm.
Known only from Mt. Malindang, western Mindanao; doubtfully distinct from *johnstoniae*.

Johnstone's Lorikeet is a bird of the montane forest. Hachisuka (1934) says that on Mt. Apo it ranges from 1,000 up to 2,500 m., while according to Rand and Rabor (1960) it occurs between 1,000 and 1,700 m. on Mt. Malindang. In his account of the discovery of the species on Mt. Apo Goodfellow (1906) reported that he found it in flocks of up to thirty or more, usually feeding in a flowering tree or shrub. He also noted that there was a daily altitudinal movement, the birds descending to lower areas each evening to roost and returning to the higher forests at sunrise. On Mt. Malindang Rabor found noisy flocks of up to fifteen in the dense forest (in Rand and Rabor, 1960).

CALL In flight a continuous *lish-lish*; feeding generally undertaken in silence (Goodfellow, 1906).

NESTING Rand and Rabor point out that collection of specimens with enlarged gonads indicates that breeding takes place between March and May.

Johnstone (1907) gives some details of a successful breeding in captivity. The nest was in a small wooden box, the bottom of which was lined with twigs and scraps of fibre taken in by the birds. Two eggs were laid and incubation lasted about three weeks. The male fed the hen and spent much time in the nest-box, but probably did not assist with incubation. The young birds left the nest approximately a month after hatching.

EGGS Rounded; 2 eggs, 22.1 (22.0–22.1) × 19.1 (19.0–19.1) mm. [Harrison and Holyoak, 1970].

Yellow-bibbed Lory *Lorius chlorocercus* **1**
RMNH. Cat. 2 ad. ♂

Purple-naped Lory *Lorius domicellus* **2**
AM. 011597 ad. unsexed

White-naped Lory *Lorius albidinuchus* **3**
AMNH. 617981 ad. ♂

YELLOW AND GREEN LORIKEET
Trichoglossus flavoviridis Wallace

Length 21 cm.
ADULTS general plumage green; forehead and crown olive-yellow; ear-coverts, cheek-patches and chin dusky green, each feather margined with yellow; nuchal collar brownish; throat, breast and upper abdomen yellow, each feather edged with dark green giving a scalloped appearance; vent and under tail-coverts yellowish-green with darker margins; under wing-coverts yellowish-green; tail green above, dull yellow below; bill orange; iris orange-yellow; legs grey.
IMMATURES (Meyer and Wiglesworth, 1898); all yellow markings more greenish; tail faintly barred with darker green near tip.

DISTRIBUTION Celebes and Sula Islands, Indonesia.

SUBSPECIES 1. *T. f. flavoviridis* Wallace *Illustrated on page 57.*
8 males   wing 111–126 (117.9) mm., tail 71–79 (74.5) mm.,
            exp. cul. 17–18 (17.4) mm., tars. 15–17 (15.6) mm.
5 females wing 112–118 (115.6) mm., tail 69–78 (71.8) mm.,
            exp. cul. 16–17 (16.4) mm., tars. 15–16 (15.8) mm.
Occurs in the Sula Islands.

2. *T. f. meyeri* Walden
ADULTS hindcrown, occiput and nape greenish-brown; feathers of breast and upper abdomen greenish-yellow margined with dark green; smaller than *flavoviridis*.
11 males   wing 98–106 (103.0) mm., tail 53–64 (57.9) mm.,
            exp. cul. 13–15 (14.2) mm., tars. 13–16 (14.0) mm.
5 females wing 96–103 (99.6) mm., tail 51–65 (57.2) mm.,
            exp. cul. 13–14 (13.8) mm., tars. 13–14 (13.4) mm.
Found in the Celebes.

GENERAL NOTES

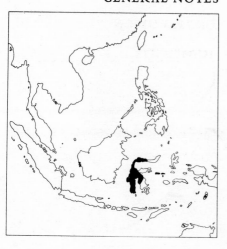

The Yellow and Green Lorikeet is probably distributed throughout the Celebes, though Stresemann (1940) pointed out that there were no records from the eastern region and I know of no subsequent reports.

According to Heinrich the Yellow and Green Lorikeet inhabits dense mountain forests between 500 and 2,000 m., being replaced in the more open areas of the lowlands by the Ornate Lory (in Stresemann, 1940). Along the edges of the forest the two species often come together to feed in flowering trees. Thinning out of the forest, rather than altitude, seems to determine the lower limits of distribution. It is shy and keeps to thick foliage where its plumage blends well with leaves and makes detection difficult. When disturbed it flies off screeching loudly.

Feeding habits are similar to those of the Ornate Lory.

CALL In flight a harsh, rasping *dra-dra-dra* repeated a few times in rapid succession then given again after a short pause (Heinrich).

NESTING Nothing is known of the breeding habits. A tame bird belonging to Platen laid an egg in November (Meyer and Wiglesworth, 1898).

EGGS Undescribed.

SCALY-BREASTED LORIKEET
Trichoglossus chlorolepidotus (Kuhl)

Illustrated on page 61.

DESCRIPTION Length 23 cm.
ADULTS general plumage green; feathers of neck, throat and breast yellow broadly margined with

W.T.Cooper. 79.

green giving a scalloped appearance; under tail-coverts, thighs and lower flanks green strongly marked with yellow; under wing-coverts and broad band across underside of flight feathers orange-red; bill coral; iris orange-yellow; legs greyish-brown.

IMMATURES similar to adults; bill dusky brown with yellow markings at base; iris pale brown.

10 males   wing 127–139 (132.4) mm., tail 92–108 (102.6) mm.,
             exp. cul. 16–17 (16.3) mm., tars. 14–16 (14.9) mm.

10 females wing 120–133 (125.2) mm., tail 94–110 (96.9) mm.,
             exp. cul. 15–17 (15.9) mm., tars. 14–16 (15.2) mm.

DISTRIBUTION   North-eastern Australia from about Cooktown, north Queensland, south to the Illawarra district of New South Wales.

GENERAL NOTES

Blue-thighed Lory *Lorius tibialis* **1**
BM. 1891.4.1.5 **type** ad. ♀

Chattering Lory *Lorius garrulus garrulus* **2**
AM. 026419 ad. ♂

Stresemann's Lory *Lorius amabilis* **3**
ZMB. 31.3582 **type** ad. ♀

The Scaly-breasted Lorikeet is mainly a lowland bird and frequents most types of country wherever there are flowering or fruiting trees and shrubs. It is common, particularly in the north-east of Australia where very large flocks may be observed.

These noisy parrots are usually seen in flocks flying high overhead or feeding among the outermost branches of a blossom-laden eucalypt. They are greedy feeders and become oblivious to the presence of an intruder as they hurriedly climb along twigs to get at flowers, often hanging upside down to reach them. Their plumage blends so well with the foliage that an observer standing under a tree and knowing almost exactly where the birds are feeding may not be able to see them. They are nomadic, the movements being governed by the flowering of trees, especially eucalypts. The flight is swift and direct.

Food consists of pollen, nectar, flowers, fruits, berries and seeds. The birds have been seen feeding among the blossoms of *Erythrina* trees, rain trees (*Pithecolobium saman*), silky oaks (*Grevillea robusta*), *Banksia serrata* and *Eucalyptus pilularis*, and on seeds of *Casuarina* and grass trees (*Xanthorrhoea*). Lavery (1970) reports large mixed flocks of this species and the Rainbow Lory (*Trichoglossus haematodus*) attacking ripening sorghum crops in north Queensland.

CALL Similar to that of the Rainbow Lory, but noticeably higher in pitch.

NESTING Breeding takes place at any time between May and February, and in the north seems to be largely dependent on rainfall. The nest is in a hollow limb or hole in a tree, generally at a considerable height. The two eggs, rarely three, are laid on a layer of decayed wood dust. Incubation last approximately twenty-five days and it seems that only the female broods. Both parents feed the young three times a day: in the morning, at midday, and again towards evening. The young leave the nest six to seven weeks after hatching.

EGGS Ovate; 3 eggs, 26.2 (25.8–26.8) × 19.5 (19.4–19.6) mm. [H. L. White Collection].

PERFECT LORIKEET

Trichoglossus euteles (Temminck)   *Illustrated on page 61.*

Length 25 cm.

ADULTS general plumage green; head olive-yellow; pale green collar around neck; breast and upper abdomen greenish-yellow; yellow band across undersides of flight feathers; under tail-coverts green tinged with yellow; tail green above, dull yellow below; bill orange-red; iris red; legs grey.

IMMATURES similar to adult but head much greener; brownish bill.

11 males   wing 126–134 (129.6) mm., tail 90–108 (100.3) mm.,
             exp. cul. 15–17 (15.8) mm., tars. 16–17 (16.5) mm.

9 females wing 123–131 (126.6) mm., tail 92–102 (98.6) mm.,
             exp. cul. 14–15 (14.7) mm., tars. 15–17 (15.6) mm.

DISTRIBUTION   Timor and the Lesser Sunda Islands from Lomblen east to Nila and Babar.

GENERAL NOTES   The Perfect Lorikeet is common, but no detailed notes on its habits have been recorded. On Timor, Stein found it up to 2,300 m. (in Mayr, 1944).

CALL A shrill screech lacking the gutteral tones so pronounced in the call of the Rainbow Lory (in captivity).

NESTING I know of no published information on nesting in the wild state. Russell (1971) reports a successful breeding in captivity. Three eggs were laid and the female brooded for about twenty-three days; the duration of the nestling period is not stated.

EGGS Oval-shaped; 2 eggs, 24.9 (24.5–25.3) × 22.8 (22.5–23.0) mm. [Harrison and Holyoak, 1970].

VARIED LORIKEET
Trichoglossus versicolor Lear

Illustrated on page 64.

Length 19 cm.
ADULTS general plumage green, more yellowish on underparts and under wing-coverts; forehead, crown and lores red, duller and less extensive in females; ear-coverts greenish-yellow; throat, cheeks and occiput dull blue streaked with yellow; upper breast dull mauve-pink streaked with yellow, duller and less pronounced in females; mantle and wing-coverts green streaked with yellow; tail green, lateral feathers margined on inner webs with yellow; naked periophthalmic ring white; bill coral; iris yellow; legs grey.
IMMATURES duller than adults with less prominent markings; red frontal band; crown green variably marked with red; bill brownish; iris brownish-grey.
10 males   wing 110–119 (115.7) mm., tail 64–72 (67.6) mm.,
            exp. cul. 12–13 (12.6) mm., tars. 14–15 (14.8) mm.
12 females   wing 108–119 (114.2) mm., tail 62–74 (66.6) mm.,
            exp. cul. 12–13 (12.5) mm., tars. 14–17 (14.8) mm.

DISTRIBUTION

Northern Australia from the Kimberley division of Western Australia to the coast of north-east Queensland.

GENERAL NOTES

Varied Lorikeets are tropical, lowland birds. They are common in most types of wooded country wherever there are flowering or fruiting trees and shrubs, but are especially attracted to paperbarks (*Melaleuca* spp.) and eucalypts lining streams or surrounding waterholes. Along the east coast of Cape York Peninsula, the north-eastern extremity of the range, they are uncommon visitors and may not arrive even though there is a wide-spread flowering of trees. Elsewhere they are nomadic, the movements being governed by the availability of blossom.

They are usually seen in family parties or small groups, but will aggregate in large flocks where trees are flowering profusely. They are not as noisy as Red-collared Lorikeets (*Trichoglossus haematodus*), a species with which they often associate, but their habits are similar. They are not timid and will generally allow a close approach. When feeding they tend to be aggressive and will drive off honeyeaters and other blossom-feeding species. The flight is swift and direct.

They have been seen feeding among the flowers of blood-woods (*Eucalyptus terminalis*), paperbarks (*Melaleuca leucodendron*), kapok trees (*Cochlospermum heteronemum*) and *Bauhinia* trees.

CALL In flight a shrill, discordant screech, similar to, but more high-pitched than that of the Red-collared Lorikeet; while feeding a sharp chattering, and when at rest soft, twittering notes.

NESTING Breeding has been recorded at all times of the year, but April to August appear to be the favoured months. The nest is in a hollow limb or hole in a tree, the bottom being lined with decayed wood dust or sometimes with *Eucalyptus* leaves. Two to four eggs are laid. Incubation lasts about twenty days and only the female broods. She sits very tightly and may wait to be lifted from the nest by hand. The young are fed by both parents and leave the nest approximately forty days after hatching.

EGGS Elliptical; 4 eggs, 24.0 (22.5–25.2) × 20.0 (19.4–20.6) mm. [H. L. White Collection].

Collared Lory *Phigys solitarius*
AM. 030548 ad. ♂

IRIS LORIKEET
Trichoglossus iris (Temminck)

DESCRIPTION

Length 20 cm.
ADULTS general plumage green, more yellowish on underparts and under wing-coverts; forehead, forecrown and behind eye orange-red; in female forecrown is green variably marked with red; reddish-violet band from eye to sides of hindneck; occiput grey-blue; ear-coverts pale bluish-green; cheek-patches green, more yellowish in female; yellow nuchal collar; feathers of breast edged with darker green giving a scalloped appearance; tail green above, dusky yellow below; bill orange; iris orange; legs bluish-grey.
IMMATURES similar to female but with less red on forecrown; bill brownish; iris brown.

DISTRIBUTION

Timor and nearby Wetar Island, Indonesia.

SUBSPECIES

Illustrated on page 64.

1. *T. i. iris* (Temminck)
    5 males   wing 112–120 (117.4) mm., tail 68–79 (73.2) mm.,
             exp. cul. 13–16 (14.8) mm., tars. 14–16 (15.1) mm.
    5 females   wing 116–120 (118.0) mm., tail 65–76 (68.6) mm.,
             exp. cul. 14–15 (14.2) mm., tars. 14–16 (15.0) mm.
    Confined to western Timor.

2. *T. i. rubripileum* (Salvadori)
ADULTS hindcrown red, sometimes slightly tinged with green; band on hindneck violet-blue; sides of head light yellowish-green.
7 males   wing 112–121 (114.9) mm., tail 66–83 (70.9) mm., exp. cul. 13–16 (14.4) mm., tars. 14–16 (15.1) mm.
4 females   wing 110–116 (113.5) mm., tail 65–71 (68.5) mm., exp. cul. 14–15 (14.5) mm., tars. 15–16 (15.2) mm.
Occurs in eastern Timor.

3. *T. i. wetterensis* (Hellmayr)
ADULTS similar to *iris*, but sides of head darker and more grass-green; larger size.
4 males   wing 124–132 (127.0) mm., tail 75–81 (79.3) mm., exp. cul. 16 (16.0) mm., tars. 16–18 (17.3) mm.
6 females   wing 121–132 (125.8) mm., tail 67–80 (74.3) mm., exp. cul. 15–17 (16.0) mm., tars. 16–18 (16.5) mm.
Restricted to Wetar Island.

GENERAL NOTES   Published information on Timor birds is scant and little is known about the Iris Lorikeet. On Timor, Stein collected specimens up to 1,500 m. (in Mayr, 1944). I suspect that its habits are similar the those of the Varied Lorikeet.

CALL   A shrill screech terminating with a pronounced downward deflection (in captivity).

NESTING   No published records.

EGGS   Undescribed.

GOLDIE'S LORIKEET
Trichoglossus goldiei Sharpe   *Illustrated on page 64.*

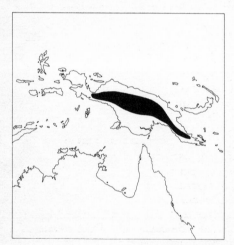

Length 19 cm.
ADULTS general plumage green, more yellowish on underparts and under wing-coverts; forehead and crown red, duller and less extensive in females; occiput blue; ear-coverts and cheeks pinkish-purple variably streaked with dark blue; neck streaked with pale green, underparts with dark green; yellow band across underside of flight feathers; tail olive-green above, yellowish-olive below; bill black; iris brown; legs greenish-brown.
IMMATURES crown green, variably marked with red.
8 males   wing 100–115 (108.4) mm., tail 70–79 (74.5) mm., exp. cul. 12–14 (13.5) mm., tars. 13–15 (13.9) mm.
8 females   wing 98–112 (104.6) mm., tail 66–83 (74.6) mm., exp. cul. 13–16 (13.5) mm., tars. 13–16 (14.3) mm.

DISTRIBUTION   Mountains of New Guinea from the Weyland Mountains near Geelvink Bay, West Irian, to south-eastern Papua.

GENERAL NOTES   According to Rand and Gilliard (1967) Goldie's Lorikeet seems to be an uncommon bird of the mid-mountain forest between 1,400 and 2,200 m. Sight records indicate that irregular movements occur to beyond both limits of this altitudinal zone. Robinson noted that in May 1970 flocks of up to sixty appeared in the Baiyer Valley at 800 m. and seemed to be attracted to a particular tree which was flowering profusely (*in litt.*, 1970). Layton (pers. comm., 1970) says that pairs and small parties are occasionally seen near sea level in the Port Moresby area, and in July 1969 a specimen was collected in the region (PMM. B653).

    Near Wapenamanda in the Western Highlands, George (pers. comm., 1970) has observed flocks of from forty to a hundred in casuarinas in open country, and at Goroka, Fullagar (pers. comm., 1970) has seen large numbers feeding in flowering eucalypts. In May 1970, on the southern slopes of the Hagen Range, also in the Western Highlands, I found pairs and small parties in disturbed *Nothofagus-Podocarpus* forest at 2,800 m. They frequented the upper storeys of trees. While light rain was falling they perched on the leafless, topmost branches and, with feathers fluffed, vigorously preened themselves. When leaving they dropped down sharply towards the ground and then levelled out in flight. The flight is swift and direct.

    Food consists of pollen, nectar, flowers, fruits and berries.

Blue-crowned Lory *Vini australis*   **1**
AM. 030590 ad. ♂

Stephen's Lory *Vini stepheni*   **2**
AMNH. 192990 ad. ♂

Kuhl's Lory *Vini kuhlii*   **3**
AM. 021742 ad. unsexed

Ultramarine Lory *Vini ultramarina*   **4**
AMNH. 195162 ad. ♂

Tahitian Lory *Vini peruviana*   **5**
AM. 035541 ad. ♀

CALL   In flight a shrill screech, much higher in pitch than that of the Rainbow Lory; while feeding a soft monosyllabic note resembling a hiss or loud whisper.

NESTING   I know of no recorded information on breeding in the wild. Plath (1951) reports that two young were successfully reared in captivity at Chicago Zoo, but the incubation and nestling periods were not determined; chicks were first noticed in early February and they left the nest in mid-March.

EGGS   Undescribed.

Genus LORIUS Vigors

The parrots belonging to this genus are medium-sized, stocky birds with short, slightly rounded tails. The bill is broader and less pointed than in other lories. Sexual dimorphism is absent, and immatures resemble adults but have pointed tips to the central tail feathers.

PURPLE-BELLIED LORY
Lorius hypoinochrous G. R. Gray

DESCRIPTION Length 26 cm.
ADULTS general plumage red, paler on breast than on upper abdomen; forehead, lores, crown and nape black with a purple-blue gloss; green wings; thighs and lower abdomen bluish-purple, lighter on thighs; some birds have dusky red bands across mantle; under wing-coverts red, outermost feathers edged with black; tail above red broadly tipped with dark blue-green, below dull olive-yellow; cere white, not grey as in *L. lory*; bill coral; iris orange-red; legs dark grey.
IMMATURES similar to adults, bill brownish.

DISTRIBUTION South-eastern New Guinea, the eastern Papuan Islands, and the Bismarck Archipelago.

SUBSPECIES 1. *L. h. hypoinochrous* G. R. Gray
8 males   wing 163–172 (167.6) mm., tail 84–92 (88.4) mm.,
        exp. cul. 23–25 (23.9) mm., tars. 21–23 (22.1) mm.
9 females   wing 164–175 (168.9) mm., tail 83–94 (88.6) mm.,
        exp. cul. 23–25 (23.9) mm., tars. 21–24 (22.2) mm.
Confined to Misima and Tagula in the Louisiade Archipelago, eastern Papuan Islands.

2. *L. h. rosselianus* Rothschild and Hartert
ADULTS similar to *hypoinochrous*, but breast is same red colour as upper abdomen.
9 males   wing 164–176 (169.8) mm., tail 87–95 (91.2) mm.,
        exp. cul. 24–26 (24.9) mm., tars. 23–24 (23.4) mm.
5 females   wing 167–175 (170.6) mm., tail 85–90 (87.8) mm.,
        exp. cul. 23–25 (23.8) mm., tars. 22–24 (23.0) mm.
Restricted to Rossel Island in the Louisiade Archipelago.

3. *L. h. devittatus* Hartert   *Illustrated on page 65.*
ADULTS similar to *hypoinochrous*, but no black margins to greater under wing-coverts.
8 males   wing 163–178 (172.0) mm., tail 82–94 (88.5) mm.,
        exp. cul. 25–27 (25.6) mm., tars. 23–25 (24.1) mm.
6 females   wing 161–173 (168.2) mm., tail 86–94 (89.7) mm.,
        exp. cul. 25–27 (25.7) mm., tars. 24–25 (24.2) mm.
Occurs in the Trobriand and Woodlark Islands, the Bismarck and D'Entrecasteaux Archipelagos, and south-eastern New Guinea west to the Angabunga River and the Huon Gulf.

GENERAL NOTES The Purple-bellied Lory is common throughout most of its range and in habits resembles the more familiar Black-capped Lory (*L. lory*). Gilliard noted that in the Whiteman Mountains on New Britain it was abundant in the upper storeys of rainforest trees (Gilliard and LeCroy, 1967a). Donaghey says that it is common on the Gazelle Peninsula, New Britain, and is generally seen in pairs flying above the forest canopy (*in litt.*, 1970). Bell (1970a) reports that at Amazon Bay on the south-eastern coast of New Guinea it was always in pairs, was very noisy, and was the most numerous of the birds visiting flowering coconut palms. On Goodenough Island he found it to be extremely abundant in secondary growth and gardens, and particularly in flowering coconut palms (Bell, 1970d). The flight is similar to that of the Black-capped Lory.

Food comprises pollen, nectar, flowers and fruits.

CALL A shrill cry that is noticeably higher in pitch and more drawn-out and mournful than that of *L. lory* (Schodde, pers. comm., 1971).

NESTING Bell has observed what may have been courtship display; one bird, perched about 1 m. away from another, was stretching its neck and bobbing its head up and down. The nesting habits are not known.

EGGS Undescribed.

Musk Lorikeet *Glossopsitta concinna* **1**
AM. 020410 ad. ♂

Purple-crowned Lorikeet **2**
Glossopsitta porphyrocephala
AM. 020417 ad. unsexed

Little Lorikeet *Glossopsitta pusilla* **3**
AM. 038634 ad. ♂

BLACK-CAPPED LORY
Lorius lory (Linné)

DESCRIPTION Length 31 cm.
ADULTS general plumage red; forehead, lores, crown and nape black with a purple gloss; dark

W.T. Cooper 71.

blue band on hindneck; mantle blue; bronze-green wings; under tail-coverts, thighs, abdomen and lower breast blue, extending up sides of breast to meet blue of mantle; under wing-coverts red; broad yellow band across underside of flight feathers; tail above red broadly tipped with blue-black, below olive-yellow; cere grey not white as in *L. hypoinochrous*; bill yellow-orange; iris yellow to orange-red; legs dark grey.

IMMATURES under wing-coverts blue, outermost feathers yellow tipped with black; bill brownish in young birds; iris brown.

New Guinea, including some of the western Papuan Islands and some islands in Geelvink Bay.

DISTRIBUTION

SUBSPECIES

1. *L. l. lory* (Linné)   *Illustrated on page 65.*
   12 males   wing 159–175 (165.9) mm., tail 92–103 (97.7) mm.,
                exp. cul. 23–27 (25.3) mm., tars. 21–26 (23.9) mm.
   11 females   wing 148–166 (157.8) mm., tail 85–98 (91.5) mm.,
                exp. cul. 22–26 (23.8) mm., tars. 22–25 (22.8) mm.
   Occurs on Waigeu, Batanta, Salawati and Misool in the western Papuan Islands, and on the Vogelkop, West Irian. I agree with Mees (1965) that *major* should be synonymized with *lory*.

2. *L. l. erythrothorax* Salvadori
   ADULTS lower breast red, blue of abdomen does not extend up sides of breast; narrower blue band on hindneck.
   25 males   wing 149–172 (163.4) mm., tail 85–98 (91.4) mm.,
                exp. cul. 23–27 (24.9) mm., tars. 22–25 (23.2) mm.
   20 females   wing 143–164 (155.2) mm., tail 84–93 (87.3) mm.,
                exp. cul. 22–26 (23.9) mm., tars. 21–23 (22.3) mm.
   Distributed from southern parts of Geelvink Bay and from the Onin Peninsula, West Irian east to south-eastern Papua and the Huon Peninsula; meets *somu* in the Fly River area (see Diamond, 1967). Because of individual variation in size and in colour of the under tail-coverts, I can see no justification for the recognition of *rubiensis*.

3. *L. l. somu* (Diamond)   *Illustrated on page 65.*
   ADULTS like *erythrothorax* but without blue on the hindneck.
   8 males   wing 149–166 (156.4) mm., tail 87–102 (93.9) mm.,
                exp. cul. 22–25 (24.0) mm., tars. 22–24 (22.6) mm.
   5 females   wing 148–152 (150.2) mm., tail 85–91 (87.2) mm.,
                exp. cul. 20–23 (22.1) mm., tars. 20–23 (21.3) mm.
   Occurs in southern New Guinea where it has been recorded from the Karimui Basin and immediately to the south, and from the mouth of the Purari River (Diamond, 1967), from the Fly River (QM. 06307), and from the Lake Kutubu area (CSIRO. 1365 and 1383).

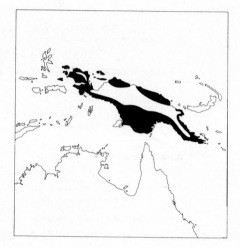

4. *L. l. salvadorii* Meyer
   ADULTS similar to *erythrothorax* but well-defined dark blue band present on hindneck; under wing-coverts dark blue; centre of abdomen and broad band across lower breast, connecting with under wing-coverts almost black.
   10 males   wing 158–170 (163.3) mm., tail 87–100 (94.5) mm.,
                exp. cul. 22–26 (24.7) mm., tars. 22–24 (23.4) mm.
   6 females   wing 157–167 (161.7) mm., tail 87–96 (92.7) mm.,
                exp. cul. 24–26 (24.7) mm., tars. 22–24 (23.1) mm.
   Found in north-eastern New Guinea from Astrolabe Bay west to the Aitape area.

5. *L. l. viridicrissalis* de Beaufort
   ADULTS like *salvadorii*, but with darker, more blackish blue on hindneck; under wing-coverts in males are mainly black with some dark blue, in females dark blue.
   8 males   wing 153–173 (161.8) mm., tail 93–102 (96.5) mm.,
                exp. cul. 24–26 (24.6) mm., tars. 21–25 (23.0) mm.
   8 females   wing 149–158 (154.8) mm., tail 82–96 (91.9) mm.,
                exp. cul. 22–25 (23.4) mm., tars. 21–24 (22.9) mm.
   Restricted to northern New Guinea between Humboldt Bay and the Mamberamo River.

6. *L. l. jobiensis* (Meyer)
   ADULTS similar to *salvadorii*, but with a rosy tinge to red breast; mantle and band across hindneck lighter blue.
   8 males   wing 165–174 (170.1) mm., tail 97–107 (102.1) mm.,
                exp. cul. 26–27 (26.5) mm., tars. 23–25 (24.0) mm.
   5 females   wing 163–174 (169.4) mm., tail 96–104 (98.6) mm.,
                exp. cul. 23–26 (24.6) mm., tars. 22–25 (23.0) mm.
   Found on Japen and Mios Num Islands in Geelvink Bay, West Irian; doubtfully distinct from *salvadorii*.

7. *L. l. cyanuchen* (S. Müller)
   ADULTS similar to *salvadorii* but without red on nape, mauve-blue of hindneck extending up to meet black of crown and occiput.

Blue-fronted Lorikeet *Charmosyna toxopei* 1
MZB. 5533 **type** ad. ♂

Red-chinned Lorikeet 2
Charmosyna rubrigularis rubrigularis
AM. 04125 ad. unsexed

Palm Lorikeet *Charmosyna palmarum* 3
AMNH. 213813 ad. ♂

Meek's Lorikeet *Charmosyna meeki* 4
CSIRO. 2907 ad. ♂

Striated Lorikeet *Charmosyna multistriata* 5
BM. 1911.12.20.623 ad. ♂

10 males   wing 164–187 (177.2) mm., tail 89–112 (105.1) mm.,
           exp. cul. 26–30 (27.8) mm., tars. 24–26 (24.7) mm.
6 females wing 161–186 (172.5) mm., tail 96–111 (102.2) mm.,
           exp. cul. 26–30 (27.8) mm., tars. 24–26 (24.7) mm.
Confined to the Island of Biak in Geelvink Bay, West Irian.

GENERAL NOTES

The Black-capped Lory frequents the upper storeys of forest trees in the lowlands and occasionally up to 1,600 m. (Rand and Gilliard, 1967). At Kutubu in the Southern Highlands district, Papua, Schodde and Hitchcock (1968) found single birds in *Pandanus* palms in swamp forest. Pairs or small parties of up to ten are usually observed flying above the treetops, but larger numbers may come together to feed in blossom-laden or fruit-bearing trees. This parrot is rather shy and seldom allows a close approach. Ripley noted that on Biak it seemed to be more solitary than on the New Guinea mainland, and single birds were seen sitting quietly in dense forest (in Mayr and Meyer de Schauensee, 1939a). In the Nomad River sub-district, Papua, Bell (1970b) noticed that there were pronounced movements at dawn and at dusk, presumably birds travelling between roosting and feeding areas.

Near Port Moresby I watched three pairs feeding in a flowering tree standing at the edge of a clearing in primary rainforest. They were paired and did not intermingle as a group. When disturbed four birds flew off, but one pair came to a tree under which we were standing and called loudly from the topmost, leafless branch. Rapid, shallow wingbeats give a characteristic fluttering appearance to the direct flight; the yellow underwings are most conspicuous in flight.

Food consists of pollen, nectar, flowers, fruits, insects and possibly seeds. Rand (1942a) says that a common food is the flower of the climbing *Freycinetia*. Stomach contents from birds collected in the Weyland Mountains comprised pollen and small insects (Rothschild, 1931).

Red-spotted Lorikeet 1
Charmosyna rubronotata rubronotata
RMNH. Cat. 3 ad. ♂

Red-flanked Lorikeet 2
Charmosyna placentis placentis
CSIRO. 3641 ad. ♂

Red-flanked Lorikeet 3
Charmosyna placentis placentis
CSIRO. 3640 ad. ♀

Red-throated Lorikeet *Charmosyna amabilis* 4
AM. A834 ad. ♂

New Caledonian Lorikeet *Charmosyna diadema* 5
MNHN. 762A **type** ad. ♀

Wilhelmina's Lorikeet *Charmosyna wilhelminae* 6
BM. 1913.3.6.81 ad. ♂

CALL A loud, ringing cry, quite unlike the screeching of the Rainbow Lory.

NESTING Males with enlarged testes have been collected in May (Rand 1942a) and in July (Gyldenstolpe 1955b, Ripley 1964). The male, when displaying, perches in a very upright position and, with wings fully spread and head turned to one side, bobs its whole body up and down (Filewood, pers. comm.). The nesting habits are not known.

Burgess (1921) gives some details of a successful breeding in captivity. Two eggs were laid but only one hatched. Incubation lasted about twenty-four days and only the female brooded, though the male roosted in the nest-box at night. The chick vacated the nest about two months after hatching.

EGGS Elliptical; one egg in the British Museum measures 27.0 × 22.0 mm. [Harrison and Holyoak, 1970].

WHITE-NAPED LORY
Lorius albidinuchus (Rothschild and Hartert)   *Illustrated on page 68.*

Length 26 cm.
ADULTS general plumage red; forehead, lores, crown and occiput black; white nuchal patch bordering black; faint yellow marking on each side of breast; green wings; under wing-coverts red; broad yellow band across underside of flight feathers; tail red broadly tipped with green; bill orange-red with dusky base to upper mandible; iris yellow to brownish-red; legs grey-black.
IMMATURES undescribed.
3 males   wing 150–152 (151.3) mm., tail 86–90 (88.3) mm.,
          exp. cul. 21–22 (21.7) mm., tars. 20–22 (21.3) mm.
6 females wing 146–162 (154.0) mm., tail 87–105 (91.7) mm.,
           exp. cul. 21–23 (21.8) mm., tars. 20–21 (20.7) mm.

DISTRIBUTION New Ireland in the Bismarck Archipelago.

GENERAL NOTES Nothing is known of the habits of the White-naped Lory. The original series was collected in the hills on the south-western coast of New Ireland.

STRESEMANN'S LORY
Lorius amabilis Stresemann
                                                        Illustrated on page 69.

DESCRIPTION Length 26 cm.
MALE undescribed.
FEMALE (ZMB. 31.3582, **type**); general plumage red, slightly darker on hindneck; green wings; under wing-coverts red; yellow band across undersides of secondaries; lower underparts and centre of abdomen dull purple-blue tinged with green, particularly on thighs; under tail-coverts

dull purple-blue marked with green and pale red; tail dark greenish-blue above, olive yellow below, and basally marked with red; bill orange; iris brownish-red (Meyer); legs yellowish-brown. IMMATURES undescribed.

1 female **(type)**   wing —, tail 90 mm.,
exp. cul. 25 mm., tars. 23 mm.

Recorded from New Britain in the Bismarck Archipelago.

Stresemann's Lory is known only from the type specimen, a female obtained by P. Otto Meyer at Nakanai, New Britain. It was almost certainly a captive bird, because the primaries have been removed, a common practice among New Guinea people to prevent flight and to obtain feathers for head adornments. I have already pointed out that the type specimen bears a striking overall similarity to *L. hypoinochrous* and interruption to a possibly simple genetic factor controlling black pigmentation could bring about all the distinguishing features (see Forshaw, 1971). I prefer to dismiss *amabilis* as a species until further specimens are obtained.

Meyer claimed that the bird inhabited primary forest at the foot of 'the volcano'.

YELLOW-BIBBED LORY

Lorius chlorocercus Gould   *Illustrated on page 68.*

Length 28 cm.

ADULTS   general plumage red; forehead, lores, crown and occiput black; bluish-black marking on each side of neck; yellow band across upper breast; violet thighs; green wings; bend of wing white variably marked with blue; under wing-coverts blue; broad rose-red band across underside of primaries; tail red broadly tipped above with green and below with dusky yellow; bill orange-red with dusky base to upper mandible; iris orange; legs dark grey.

IMMATURES   no black markings on sides of neck; little or no yellow across upper breast; thighs violet variably marked with green; bill brownish; iris brown.

15 males   wing 158–175 (165.9) mm., tail 89–100 (93.8) mm.,
exp. cul. 21–24 (22.7) mm., tars. 21–23 (22.1) mm.

10 females   wing 151–166 (159.0) mm., tail 80–94 (87.4) mm.,
exp. cul. 21–23 (21.5) mm., tars. 20–23 (21.4) mm.

DISTRIBUTION   Eastern Solomon Islands; absent from Bougainville.

GENERAL NOTES   Cain and Galbraith (1956) say that the Yellow-bibbed Lory is found in the canopy of forest and secondary growth at all altitudes. They noted that on Guadalcanal it seemed to be more plentiful in the hills than in the lowlands, and was commonest in lower mist forest. On other islands it was also seen in and around coconut plantations. It usually occurs singly, in pairs, or in parties of up to about ten, and is very active in the uppermost branches, often hanging upside-down to investigate flowers and epiphytes.

It feeds on pollen, nectar, fruits and seeds. Crop contents examined by Cain and Galbraith comprised vegetable matter with a high proportion of seeds. Caterpillars and small red seeds are given as the crop contents taken from two specimens now held in the British Museum.

CALL   A shrieking *chuik-lik* or *chu-er-wee*; also harsher, more abrupt notes (Cain and Galbraith, 1956).

NESTING   I know of no nesting records. Mayr (1931) points out that two young birds collected on Rennell Island in September are in a rather worn condition and beginning to moult their body feathers.

EGGS   Elliptical; 2 eggs, 30.0 (29.7–30.3) × 23.9 (23.9) mm. [Harrison and Holyoak, 1970].

PURPLE-NAPED LORY

Lorius domicellus (Linné)   *Illustrated on page 68.*

Length 28 cm.

ADULTS   general plumage red, darker on back; forehead, lores, crown and occiput black; variable violet or purple nuchal patch bordering black cap; variable yellow band across upper breast; thighs violet-blue; green wings; bend of wing white variably marked with blue; under wing-coverts blue; broad yellow band across underside of flight feathers; tail red broadly tipped with deep brownish-red; bill orange; iris reddish-brown to orange; legs dark grey.

IMMATURES   purple on nape deeper and more extensive; broader yellow band across breast; greater under wing-coverts margined with black; tail faintly tipped with blue; brownish bill.

10 males   wing 160–173 (165.9) mm., tail 89–105 (96.6) mm.,
exp. cul. 25–27 (26.2) mm., tars. 22–25 (23.1) mm.

3 females   wing 157–163 (160.6) mm., tail 92–97 (94.3) mm.,
exp. cul. 25–26 (25.3) mm., tars. 23–25 (23.6) mm.

Native to the Islands of Ceram and Amboina, Indonesia; introduced to Buru.

Stresemann (1914) says that on Ceram the Purple-naped Lory inhabits montane primary forest and is usually found in pairs. It is not common and is a popular pet with the local people.

In primary forest on Buru Toxopeus collected a bird with a metal ring on its left leg, obviously an escapee, and in the south-east of the island he saw another individual (in Siebers, 1931). Stresemann suggests that as Valentyn, the eighteenth-century naturalist, did not report the species from Amboina, it may have colonized that island from Ceram.

CALL Undescribed.

NESTING There appear to be no records from the wild. Spence (1955) gives details of a successful breeding in captivity. Two eggs were laid, one hatching on the twenty-fourth day, the other on the twenty-sixth. Only the female incubated. One chick was reared and it left the nest three months after hatching. At the age of about four months its bill gradually changed to orange.

EGGS Elliptical; 8 eggs, 32.0 (30.5-33.6) x 25.5 (25.0-26.6) mm. [Schönwetter, 1964].

BLUE-THIGHED LORY
Lorius tibialis Sclater   *Illustrated on page 69.*

DESCRIPTION

Length 28 cm.
MALE undescribed.
FEMALE (BM. 1891.4.1.5, **type**); general plumage red; yellow band across upper breast; green wings; bend of wing white variably marked with blue; thighs and under wing-coverts violet-blue; tail red broadly tipped with bluish-black; broad yellow band across underside of flight feathers; bill orange; iris orange (original illustration): legs pale brown.
IMMATURES undescribed.
1 female **(type)**   wing 165 mm., tail 90 mm.,
             exp. cul. 24 mm., tars. 23 mm.

Distribution unknown.

The Blue-thighed Lory is known only from the type, a female purchased as a live bird in the Calcutta market about 1867 and presented to the London Zoo. When describing the species, Sclater (1871) suggested that it may have come from the Moluccas. I have examined the type and in my opinion it is probably an aberrant specimen of *L. domicellus*.

EGGS Elliptical; 2 eggs laid in captivity in the London Zoo measure 31.3 (30.9-31.6) × 25.2 (24.5-25.8) mm. [Harrison and Holyoak, 1970].

CHATTERING LORY
Lorius garrulus (Linné)   *Illustrated on page 69.*

DESCRIPTION

Length 30 cm.
ADULTS general plumage red, darker on scapulars; thighs and wings green; bend of wing and under wing-coverts yellow; broad rose-red band across underside of primaries; tail red broadly tipped with dark green; bill orange, iris yellowish-brown to orange-red; legs dark grey.
IMMATURES similar to adults; brownish bill; iris dark brown.

DISTRIBUTION

Moluccas, Indonesia.

1. *L. g. garrulus* (Linné)
      10 males   wing 169-189 (178.5) mm., tail 99-110 (102.7) mm.,
            exp. cul. 24-27 (24.8) mm., tars. 23-25 (24.1) mm.
      4 females   wing 171-179 (175.7) mm., tail 97-108 (102.5) mm.,
            exp. cul. 24-25 (24.5) mm., tars. 22-24 (22.7) mm.
      Found on Halmahera and the Weda Islands.

2. *L. g. flavopalliatus* Salvadori
      ADULTS similar to *garrulus*, but with a well-defined yellow patch on mantle; wings brighter green.
      8 males   wing 164-180 (171.8) mm., tail 99-107 (103.5) mm.,
            exp. cul. 22-24 (23.0) mm., tars. 22-24 (22.4) mm.
      6 females   wing 164-186 (176.5) mm., tail 97-108 (101.3) mm.,
            exp. cul. 21-24 (22.7) mm., tars. 22-24 (22.8) mm.
      This race is known as the Yellow-backed Lory and occurs on Batjan and Obi.

3. *L. g. morotaianus* (van Bemmel)
      ADULTS similar to *flavopalliatus*, but yellow patch on mantle is duller and less extensive, wings darker green than in *flavopalliatus*.
      1 male **(type)**   wing 175 mm., tail 104 mm.,
            exp. cul. 24 mm., tars. 23 mm.

Known only from Morotai, but birds from nearby Raou Island probably belong to this race.

GENERAL NOTES Lendon (1946) found that the Chattering Lory was easily the most common parrot on Morotai, where it seemed to feed largely among flowering coconut palms. It was usually seen in pairs and was noticeably pugnacious when two pairs met. It was a popular pet with the local people.

CALL In flight a loud screeching, and while feeding strange gurgling notes (Lendon, 1946).

NESTING Lendon saw a pair investigating a hole in a dead tree in June, noted that a young bird had been caught in July, and observed fledged young being fed during October and November.

Collard (1965) gives details of a successful breeding in captivity. Two eggs were laid and brooded by the female, but the duration of the incubation period was not determined. Both parents fed the chicks, which left the nest seventy-six days after hatching. G. W. and G. M. Sharratt (1965) hand-reared two nestlings and reported that at four months their eyes were gradually turning lighter and their bills were almost the same as those of adults.

EGGS Elliptical; Schönwetter (1964) gives 25.8 × 21.8 mm. as the measurements of one egg.

Genus PHIGYS G. R. Gray

Amadon (1942) suggests that this monotypic genus is a specialized offshoot of *Vini*. A nuchal collar comprising elongated feathers which cover the hindneck and mantle is the most conspicuous plumage characteristic. The short tail is squarish and the central feathers are slightly shorter than the lateral ones. The body form is stockier than in *Vini*, the bill is slightly heavier, there are no shaft streaks on the crown and the cere is naked but not prominent. Sexual dimorphism is slight.

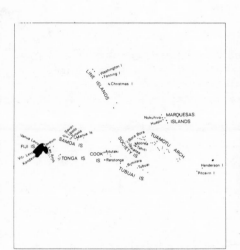

COLLARED LORY
Phigys solitarius (Suckow)   *Illustrated on page 72.*

Length 20 cm.

ADULTS forehead, lores and crown very dark purple, in females forehead is paler and more bluish and posterior of crown is washed with green; back, wings and tail green; rump yellowish-green; nuchal collar bright yellowish-green tipped with scarlet; ear-coverts, throat, breast and upper abdomen scarlet; thighs and lower abdomen purple; under wing-coverts and under tail-coverts green; bill orange; iris red; legs pink-orange.

IMMATURES feathers of breast more or less tipped with purple and with concealed yellowish-green spots; bill brownish; iris dark brown; legs pale grey.

8 males   wing 123–139 (129.4) mm., tail 62–66 (64.1) mm.,
           exp. cul. 15–17 (16.0) mm., tars. 17–19 (17.8) mm.
10 females wing 128–140 (131.2) mm., tail 61–69 (65.4) mm.,
           exp. cul. 15–17 (15.7) mm., tars. 17–18 (17.3) mm.

DISTRIBUTION Larger islands of the Fiji Group; in the Lau Archipelago it ranges south to Lakemba and Oneata.

GENERAL NOTES Mercer (1967) says that Collared Lories are common and flocks of five or eight may be seen visiting flowering trees. I have seen them feeding in flowering coconut palms lining the streets of Suva and in August 1971 saw pairs and small parties in disturbed forest adjoining wet pasture lands about 20 km. south of the city. Bahr (1912) found great numbers flitting about coconut palms on Taveuni and Oneata Islands. The flight is direct and swift with rapid, shallow wingbeats.

They feed on pollen, nectar, blossoms and soft fruits. Favourite feeding trees are coconut palms, drala (*Erythrina indica*), and African tulip, and when these are in bloom small flocks come and go constantly. When coming to feed in a coconut palm the lories alight out on the fronds and make their way down to the flowering stalks in a series of fluttering hops.

CALL In flight a shrill, disyllabic screech with the second note being more prolonged than the first; while perched a monosyllabic shriek is occasionally uttered.

NESTING Bahr obtained nestlings in December. The nest is in a hole in a tree or stump, or sometimes in a rotting coconut still attached to the tree. Two eggs are laid. Patten (1941) gives details of a successful breeding in captivity. Of the two eggs laid one hatched after about thirty days incubation. Both parents attended to the chick, but no details of the incubation are given. Almost nine weeks after hatching the young bird left the nest.

Bahr found that when the young bird was soliciting food it uttered a curious note, somewhat like the loud ticking of a clock, and agitated its whole body. He also reported that at about three months the bill and iris changed to yellow and at eight months adult plumage was acquired after a complete moult.

EGGS Broadly elliptical; a single egg in the Hamburg Museum Collection measures 25.5 × 20.0 mm. [Schönwetter, 1964].

Genus VINI Lesson

Members of this genus are small, stocky parrots with short rounded tails in which the central feathers are longer than the lateral ones. The erectile feathers of the crown are long and shaft-streaked. The bill is finer than in *Phigys* and the cere is naked but not prominent. There is no sexual dimorphism.

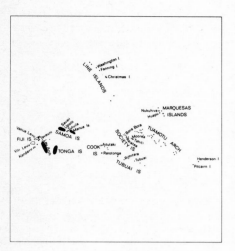

BLUE-CROWNED LORY
Vini australis (Gmelin)

Illustrated on page 73.

Length 19 cm.

ADULTS general plumage green, paler and brighter on hindneck and rump; lores, ear-coverts, throat and abdominal patch red; thighs and lower abdomen purple-blue; crown dark blue shaft-streaked with bright mauve-blue; under wing-coverts green; tail green above, greenish-yellow below; bill orange; iris yellow; legs orange.

IMMATURES shorter blue crown feathers; less red on face and throat; red abdominal patch only indicated; no purple-blue on thighs or lower abdomen; bill orange tipped with dark brown; iris brown; legs orange-brown.

8 males   wing 101–114 (107.5) mm., tail 61–69 (65.3) mm.,
            exp. cul. 11–13 (12.0) mm., tars. 14–16 (14.7) mm.

8 females wing 104–114 (109.0) mm., tail 61–69 (64.9) mm.,
            exp. cul. 11–12 (11.5) mm., tars. 14–15 (14.4) mm.

DISTRIBUTION   Samoa and Tonga Islands, several of the nearby islands in central Polynesia, and the Lau Archipelago, Fiji. Amadon (1942) points out that apparently it is absent from Tutuila Island, Samoa.

GENERAL NOTES   The Blue-crowned Lory is rare on Niue Island (Wodzicki, 1969), but according to Mayr (1945) it is abundant on Savaii, Upolu and Manua Islands in the Samoan Group. Yaldwyn (1952) says that in Samoa it is common on plantations, especially among flowering coconut palms. It associates in flocks and is said to fly from one island to another. Armstrong (1932) says that it is erratically distributed, its presence in a locality depending on the flowering of coconut palms or *Erythrina* and *Hibiscus* trees. Usually in parties of from six to a dozen or more it moves about following the blossom. In September 1953 Robert Carrick (pers. comm.) observed large numbers of these lories amongst flowering coconut palms in the Lau Archipelago. The flight is swift and direct.

CALL   A shrill whistle (Mayr).

NESTING   Little is recorded of the nesting habits. Mayr says that the nest is in a hole in a tree or in a hollow, decayed coconut still adhering to the tree.

EGGS   A single egg in the Hamburg Museum Collection measures 27.1 × 24.2 mm. [Schönwetter, 1964].

KUHL'S LORY
Vini kuhlii (Vigors)

Illustrated on page 73.

Length 19 cm.

ADULTS upperparts green, yellowish on back and rump; crown shaft-streaked with paler green; occiput dark blue shaft-streaked with mauve-blue; underparts scarlet; thighs purple; under tail-coverts greenish-yellow; under wing-coverts green; tail scarlet above, greyish below; bill orange; iris red; legs dark orange-brown.

IMMATURES underparts barred with greyish-purple; less red in tail; bill dusky brown; iris brown.

10 males   wing 120–136 (129.6) mm., tail 64–75 (69.7) mm.,
            exp. cul. 11–12 (11.3) mm., tars. 17–19 (17.8) mm.

4 females wing 124–134 (128.8) mm., tail 67–72 (69.8) mm.,
            exp. cul. 11–12 (11.3) mm., tars. 18–19 (18.3) mm.

DISTRIBUTION   Rimitara, Tubuai Islands; introduced to Washington, Fanning and Christmas Islands, Line Group.

GENERAL NOTES   When Thomas Street visited Washington Island with a United States survey expedition in 1874 he met a party of natives who had come from islands to the south to harvest coconuts. They had a number of these lories with them as pets. In this way the species was probably introduced to both Washington and Fanning Islands sometime prior to 1798. In December 1957 six lories were

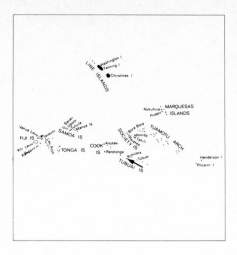

introduced to Christmas Island from Washington Island; three were still present in early 1959 (Gallagher, 1960).

There appears to be no information on Kuhl's Lory from Rimitara, but on both Washington and Fanning Islands it is quite common (Backus, 1967). It frequents coconut palms and is nearly always seen flying about singly or in pairs. Kilby (1925) found it in the company of the Kokikokiko (*Conopoderas aequinoctialis*) feeding in tahuna trees (*Tournefortia argentea*).

CALL Undescribed, but presumably similar to that of the Blue-crowned Lory.

NESTING I could not find any information on nesting in the wild state. Lee (1935) and Patten (1947) give details of breeding in captivity. No more than two eggs were laid. During incubation the male spent much time in the nest-box. Only one young bird was reared and it left the nest about seven weeks after hatching. At a little over six months the upper mandible and legs changed to orange.

EGGS Undescribed.

STEPHEN'S LORY
Vini stepheni (North)   *Illustrated on page 73.*

DESCRIPTION Length 19 cm.
ADULTS upperparts green, paler and more yellowish on rump; crown shaft-streaked with paler green; underparts scarlet; variable band of green and purple across breast; thighs and lower abdomen purple; under tail-coverts yellowish-green; under wing-coverts red and green; tail greenish-yellow; bill orange; iris yellowish; legs orange.
IMMATURES underparts green with purple and red markings on throat and abdomen; tail dark green; bill brownish; iris dark brown; legs orange-brown.
4 males   wing 126–133 (128.5) mm., tail 83–93 (87.8) mm.,
            exp. cul. 11–12 (11.5) mm., tars. 16–18 (16.8) mm.
4 females   wing 124–127 (125.8) mm., tail 85–91 (87.8) mm.,
            exp. cul. 11–12 (11.8) mm., tars. 16–18 (17.0) mm.

DISTRIBUTION Henderson Island, Pitcairn Group.

GENERAL NOTES Henderson Island is the easternmost locality for parrots within the Pacific Distribution. Stephen's Lory was discovered there in 1907, but according to Williams (1960) it is apparently not very common. Nothing is known of its habits, though presumably they are similar to those of Kuhl's Lory, a species to which it is obviously very closely allied.

CALL Undescribed.

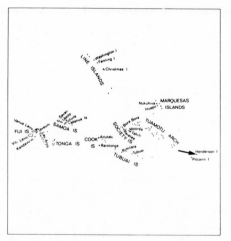

NESTING No information has been recorded. A male collected in April had enlarged gonads (AMNH. 192976). From an examination of specimens Amadon (1942) concluded that the post-juvenal moult begins on the head and the red underparts are acquired gradually.

EGGS Undescribed.

TAHITIAN LORY
Vini peruviana (P. L. S. Müller)   *Illustrated on page 73.*

DESCRIPTION Length 18 cm.
ADULTS general plumage dark mauve-blue; crown shaft-streaked with paler blue; ear-coverts, throat and upper breast white; bill orange; iris yellowish; legs orange-yellow.
IMMATURES entire underparts dark greyish-blue; greyish-white markings on chin; bill black; iris dark brown; legs dark orange-brown.
6 males   wing 108–116 (112.5) mm., tail 66–74 (68.2) mm.,
            exp. cul. 10–11 (10.5) mm., tars. 14–16 (14.8) mm.
6 females   wing 107–116 (110.8) mm., tail 65–69 (66.5) mm.,
            exp. cul. 9–11 (10.5) mm., tars. 14–15 (14.7) mm.

DISTRIBUTION Cook Islands, Society Islands and westernmost of the Tuamotu Islands.

GENERAL NOTES There is no reliable information on the present status of the Tahitian Lory, and this is largely due to the difficulty of gathering reports from so many widely scattered small islands. However, it seems to be extinct or very rare on the larger, more accessible islands and this is cause for concern. Its disappearance from Tahiti has not been documented, but about 1940 attempts were made to re-introduce it (Yealland, 1940); I do not know whether these were successful. Occasionally captive birds are seen in Tahiti and there is still some trading, but I presume that these individuals are brought from outlying islands. Amadon (1942) suggests that it may have been introduced to Aitutaki, Cook Islands, because in 1899 it was the only bird found there by Townsend and he commented that it was a common pet of the local people. Townsend found that the lory was also fairly common on Bora Bora in the Society Islands and on Rangiroa in the Tuamotu Archipelago (in Townsend and Wetmore, 1919).

On Bora Bora Wilson (1907) collected these parrots in littoral coconut palms. Their presence was indicated by the call-notes and the quick movements, but they were difficult to see amongst the foliage. There have been no recent reports from the island and in 1971 I failed to find any parrots there during three days of intensive searching. The species may be an irregular visitor to Bora Bora, though I suspect that it was a resident and has been exterminated by rats, which are so prevalent.

Tavistock (1938a and 1938b) notes that in captivity the flight was peculiarly weak and laboured, but I would be surprised if these were not swift-flying birds in the wild.

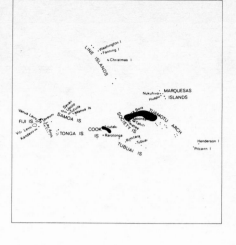

CALL A shrill chirp (Wilson) or a weak, sibilant cry (Tavistock).

NESTING The nest is in a hollow in a tree or in a rotting coconut still adhering to the tree. A normal clutch comprises two eggs. Tavistock gives details of a successful breeding in captivity. Incubation lasted a little over three weeks and both sexes brooded. It is not clear from the report whether the chick left the nest eight weeks after hatching or eight weeks from when the first egg was laid; I suspect that it was the former.

EGGS Rounded; one egg in the British Museum measures 19.4 × 17.2 mm. (Harrison and Holyoak, 1970).

ULTRAMARINE LORY
Vini ultramarina (Kuhl)

Illustrated on page 73.

Length 18 cm.

DESCRIPTION

ADULTS forehead rich blue; crown and occiput mauve-blue shaft-streaked with paler blue; upperparts dull blue, paler on rump; underparts white with dark blue markings; dark mauve-blue band across breast; thighs and under tail-coverts mauve-blue; under wing-coverts dull blue; tail pale blue tipped with white; bill dusky brown with orange at base of upper mandible; iris yellow-orange; legs orange.

IMMATURES underparts dark blue with scattered white markings on ear-coverts, breast and abdomen, and pale blue on sides of abdomen; bill black; iris dark brown; legs orange-brown.
6 males   wing 118–127 (123.3) mm., tail 71–80 (75.5) mm.,
          exp. cul. 11–12 (11.7) mm., tars. 15–16 (15.5) mm.
6 females wing 113–124 (117.2) mm., tail 70–78 (74.5) mm.,
          exp. cul. 11–12 (11.7) mm., tars. 15–17 (15.5) mm.

Nukuhiva and Huapu, Marquesas Islands.

DISTRIBUTION

Little is known of the status and habits of this beautiful parrot. Vincent (1967) mentions reports claiming that both the Ultramarine and Tahitian Lories are seriously menaced by habitat destruction, shooting and trapping. Once again Tavistock (1939) says that in captivity the flight is weak and slow.

GENERAL NOTES

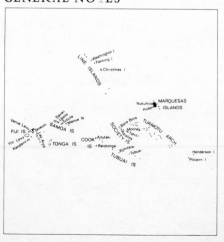

CALL A gentle, squeaky cry (Tavistock).

NESTING A male in breeding condition was collected in September (AMNH. 195162). The nest is in a hollow in a tree or in a hole in a rotting coconut still attached to the tree. Tavistock (1939) gives details of a successful breeding in captivity. The clutch comprised two eggs, but only one was laid in the nest. The incubation period was not accurately determined. Both parents incubated and cared for the chick. The young bird left the nest about eight weeks after hatching.

EGGS Rounded; 2 eggs, 22.6 (22.5–22.6) × 18.6 (18.4–18.7) mm. [Harrison and Holyoak, 1970].

Genus GLOSSOPSITTA Bonaparte

In this genus there are no shaft-streaked, erectile feathers on the crown. The small bill is fine and somewhat projecting, and the central feathers of the wedge-shaped tail are pointed. The cere is naked. Sexual dimorphism is slight in one species—*concinna*—and absent in the others.

Amadon (1942) suggested combining *Glossopsitta* with *Vini*, but I do not favour this arrangement.

MUSK LORIKEET
Glossopsitta concinna (Shaw)   *Illustrated on page 76.*

DESCRIPTION

Length 22 cm.
ADULTS general plumage bright green, lighter and more yellowish on underparts; forehead, lores and band from eyes to sides of neck red; crown and occiput blue, duller and less extensive in females; nape and mantle bronze-brown tinted with green; yellow patches on sides of breast; under wing-coverts yellowish-green; tail green with orange-red markings near bases of lateral feathers; bill black tipped with orange; iris orange; legs greenish-brown.
IMMATURES duller than adults, especially red head markings; bill blackish-brown; iris brown.
10 males   wing 126–135 (131.1) mm., tail 86–99 (89.9) mm.,
                exp. cul. 13–14 (13.9) mm., tars. 13–16 (14.9) mm.
10 females wing 121–132 (126.0) mm., tail 86–99 (92.2) mm.,
                exp. cul. 12–14 (13.0) mm., tars. 13–16 (14.8) mm.

DISTRIBUTION

Eastern and south-eastern Australia, including Tasmania and Kangaroo Island.

GENERAL NOTES

Musk Lorikeets seem to be absent from the alpine region in south-eastern Australia, but are very common elsewhere and occur at all lower altitudes. Although preferring more open habitats, such as trees bordering watercourses or surrounding farmlands, they may be found in most types of timbered country wherever there are flowering or fruit-bearing trees and shrubs. Flocks are usually seen flying high overhead or climbing amongst the branches of flowering eucalypts feeding on nectar. They are often observed in the company of other lorikeets and Swift Parrots. They are extremely noisy and, although their plumage blends with the foliage, the continuous screeching always indicates their presence. They travel about following the blossom, but the movements seem to be more predictable than those of other lorikeets.

Nectar, pollen, blossoms—particularly those of eucalypts—fruits, berries, seeds and insects and their larvae make up the diet. I have seen them feeding on the flowers of *Callistemon citrinus*, silky oak (*Grevillea robusta*) and native apple (*Angophora* sp.). Unfortunately, they sometimes become a pest in orchards and have been reported raiding maize crops to feed on unripe, 'milky' grain. Crop and stomach contents from two birds collected in South Australia comprised seeds, vegetable matter and several small caterpillars (Lea and Gray, 1935).

The direct flight is very swift and the 'whirring' of wingbeats is audible as the birds pass overhead. In flight the yellowish-green underwings distinguish this species from the other larger lorikeets and from the Swift Parrot.

CALL A shrill, metallic screech; feeding is accompanied by continuous chattering.

NESTING The breeding season lasts from August to January. The nest is in a hollow limb or hole in a tree, usually a living eucalypt near water. Both birds clean out the hollow and prepare it for laying. The two, rarely more, eggs are laid on decayed wood dust lining the bottom of the hollow. Little is known of incubation or rearing of the young.

EGGS Rounded; 4 eggs 24.6 (23.2–25.2) × 20.0 (19.4–20.6) mm. [H. L. White Coll.].

LITTLE LORIKEET
Glossopsitta pusilla (Shaw)   *Illustrated on page 76.*

Length 15 cm.
ADULTS general plumage green, lighter and more yellowish on underparts; red on forehead, lores and throat; ear-coverts shaft-streaked with pale green; nape and upper mantle bronze-brown tinted with green; under wing-coverts yellowish-green; tail green with orange-red markings near bases of lateral feathers; bill black; iris orange-yellow; legs greenish-grey.
IMMATURES facial markings duller red; bill dark olive-brown; iris brown.

10 males   wing 100–104 (101.7) mm., tail 53–65 (59.0) mm.,
                exp. cul. 10–11 (10.8) mm., tars. 12–13 (12.5) mm.

10 females wing 93–106 (99.2) mm., tail 56–65 (62.3) mm.,
   exp. cul. 10–11 (10.6) mm., tars. 12–13 (12.6) mm.

DISTRIBUTION Eastern and south-eastern Australia, including Tasmania; a doubtful record from Kangaroo Island.

GENERAL NOTES Little Lorikeets occur at all altitudes and are common in wooded country wherever there are flowering or fruit-bearing trees and shrubs. Their habits are similar to those of the Musk Lorikeet, a species with which they sometimes associate. When feeding they are remarkably tame and can be easily approached. They have been recorded feeding on the blossoms of *Melaleuca* trees and *Xanthorrhoea* spp., *Loranthus* berries and loquats (*Eriobotrya japonica* fruits). They will raid orchards but are not a serious pest.

The flight is swift and direct with rapid wingbeats. In flight the yellowish-green underwings distinguish this species from the Purple-crowned Lorikeet, the other small lorikeet in the area.

CALL A shrill, high-pitched screech, similar to but much higher than that of the Musk Lorikeet. While feeding the birds keep up a constant chatter.

NESTING Nesting usually takes place between August and January, but in the north it has been recorded as early as May. The nest is in a hollow limb or hole in a tree, generally a living eucalypt near water. Both birds clean out the hollow and prepare it for laying. The three to five eggs are laid on decayed wood dust lining the bottom of the hollow.

Lendon (1951) gives details of a successful breeding in captivity. The exact duration of incubation was unknown, but only the female brooded. She sat very tightly and was fed by the male. The two young birds left the nest about thirty days after hatching. It appeared that they were fed only by the female.

EGGS Rounded; 5 eggs, 19.5 (19.0–20.0) × 16.4 (16.0–16.7) mm. [H. L. White Coll.].

PURPLE-CROWNED LORIKEET
Glossopsitta porphyrocephala (Dietrichsen)   *Illustrated on page 76.*

DESCRIPTION Length 15 cm.
ADULTS forehead yellow-orange becoming red on lores; crown deep purple; ear-coverts pale orange washed with yellow; nape and upper mantle bronze-brown tinted with green; head and remainder of upperparts green; throat, breast and abdomen pale blue; yellow patches on sides of breast; thighs and under tail-coverts yellowish-green; under wing-coverts crimson; tail green with orange-red markings near bases of lateral feathers; bill black; iris brown; legs grey.
IMMATURES similar to adults but generally duller; in some birds purple on crown is reduced or even absent altogether.
10 males wing 100–109 (104.8) mm., tail 59–65 (62.6) mm.,
   exp. cul. 10–12 (11.3) mm., tars. 12–14 (13.1) mm.
10 females wing 98–111 (105.5) mm., tail 59–64 (61.2) mm.,
   exp. cul. 10–12 (10.9) mm., tars. 12–14 (13.4) mm.

DISTRIBUTION South-western and south-eastern Australia, excluding Tasmania.

GENERAL NOTES The Purple-crowned Lorikeet is essentially an inland species, characteristic of drier, lightly-timbered country. However, it also inhabits wooded country near the coast, particularly in areas where the inland vegetation penetrates to the seaboard. Toward the extremities of the range it is scarce, but elsewhere is quite plentiful. It is usually seen in small parties, though large flocks, sometimes comprising hundreds of birds, may congregate where there is a profuse flowering of eucalypts. Its habits are similar to those of the Musk Lorikeet and mixed flocks of the two species are often encountered. It has been reported feeding on the blossoms of various *Eucalyptus* trees, *Melaleuca* trees and boobialla (*Myoporum insulare*). It can be troublesome in orchards.

The flight is similar to, though not as swift as, that of the Little Lorikeet; the 'whirring' of the wingbeats can be heard as the birds pass overhead. In flight this species may be distinguished from the Little Lorikeet by its crimson underwings.

CALL A shrill *tsit-tsit-tsit* repeated rapidly; feeding is accompanied by a sharp chattering.

NESTING The breeding season extends from August through to December and nesting behaviour is similar to that of the Little Lorikeet. Colonial nesting has been reported, in which every available hollow in the area was being used by a breeding pair. A normal clutch comprises three or four eggs.

Johnson (1955) gives details of a successful breeding in captivity. The clutch comprised four eggs, each being laid on alternate nights. Incubation lasted seventeen days and only the female brooded; she was fed by the male and he also assisted with feeding of the chicks after they were a week old. Three chicks died in the nest, but the fourth emerged approximately eight weeks after hatching.

EGGS Rounded; 4 eggs, 20.3 (19.8–21.0) × 16.7 (16.5–16.9) mm. [H. L. White Coll.].

Genus CHARMOSYNA Wagler

Amadon (1942) treated *Charmosyna* as a subgenus in *Vini*. The two are obviously very closely allied, but I do not favour combining them until a full study is made of all genera in Loriidae.

The body form is not as stocky as in *Vini* and the tail is more gradated with narrow, pointed feathers; in one species the central tail feathers are very elongated. The bill is fine and pointed. Some species have shaft-streaked feathers on the crown, but I do not know whether these are erectile. The naked cere is prominent. Sexual dimorphism is not striking, but is present in most species and immatures generally resemble females.

PALM LORIKEET
Charmosyna palmarum (Gmelin)

Illustrated on page 77.

Length 17 cm.
MALE general plumage green, paler and more yellowish on underparts; red on chin, lores and around base of bill; mantle slightly washed with olive-brown; under wing-coverts greyish-green; no yellow band on underside of flight feathers and no red at base of tail; central tail-feathers broadly tipped with yellow, lateral tail feathers narrowly tipped with yellow; bill orange; iris yellow; legs orange-yellow.
FEMALE less red on chin and around base of bill, sometimes absent altogether; no olive-brown on mantle.
IMMATURES similar to female.
8 males: wing 91–97 (93.9) mm., tail 80–88 (82.3) mm.,
            exp. cul. 11–12 (11.4) mm., tars. 12–14 (13.4) mm.
10 females wing 88–97 (92.1) mm., tail 76–91 (81.2) mm.,
            exp. cul. 11–12 (11.3) mm., tars. 12–14 (12.5) mm.

DISTRIBUTION

The New Hebrides and the Duff, Santa Cruz and Banks Islands.

GENERAL NOTES

The Palm Lorikeet is more common in the hills than in the lowlands (Mayr, 1945). Usually in pairs or small flocks, it frequents the treetops, where it feeds on pollen, nectar, blossoms and fruits. Its small size and predominantly green colouration make it difficult to observe.

CALL A shrill, piping whistle (Mayr, 1945).

NESTING No records.

EGGS Undescribed.

RED-CHINNED LORIKEET
Charmosyna rubrigularis (Sclater)

Length 17 cm.
ADULTS general plumage green, paler and more yellowish on underparts; ear-coverts bluish-green, streaked with pale green; chin and base of lower mandible red; lores green; under wing-coverts yellowish-green; yellow band across underside of flight feathers; tail green tipped with yellow and basally marked with red, underside dusky yellow; bill orange-red; iris orange; legs yellow-orange.
IMMATURES undescribed.

DISTRIBUTION

New Britain and New Ireland in the Bismarck Archipelago, and Karkar Island off the north-eastern coast of New Guinea.

SUBSPECIES

1. *C. r. rubrigularis* (Sclater)   *Illustrated on page 77.*
    8 males   wing 92–98 (94.4) mm., tail 83–93 (88.9) mm.,
            exp. cul. 11–12 (11.8) mm., tars.11–12 (11.9) mm.
    8 females wing 86–101 (92.9) mm., tail 76–92 (84.5) mm.,
            exp. cul. 11–12 (11.8) mm., tars. 11–12 (11.6) mm.
    Occurs on New Britain and New Ireland.

2. *C. r. krakari* (Rothschild and Hartert)
    ADULTS red of chin extends down to upper throat and is bordered below by yellow.
    4 males   wing 94–100 (96.2) mm., tail 79–97 (88.0) mm.,
            exp. cul. 12–13 (12.5) mm., tars. 11–13 (11.7) mm.
    4 females wing 91–98 (94.5) mm., tail 87–95 (91.2) mm.,
            exp. cul. 12–13 (11.8) mm., tars. 11–12 (11.5) mm.
    Restricted to Karkar Island.

Gilliard and LeCroy (1967a) report that in the Whiteman Range on New Britain the Red-chinned Lorikeet is abundant in mountain forests above 500 m., being replaced in the lowlands by the Red-flanked Lorikeet (*C. placentis*). Small flocks of up to about ten frequent the upper branches of flowering trees, and are often seen in the company of honeyeaters. Food consists of pollen, nectar and probably soft fruits.

CALL Undescribed.

NESTING No records.

EGGS Undescribed.

MEEK'S LORIKEET
Charmosyna meeki (Rothschild and Hartert)   *Illustrated on page 77.*

Length 16 cm.
ADULTS general plumage green, more yellowish on underparts and under wing-coverts: crown dull greyish-blue; mantle strongly tinged with olive-brown; lower ear-coverts and sides of neck pale green streaked darker; variable yellowish-white band on underside of secondaries; tail above dark green tipped with yellow, below bright yellow; bill orange; iris yellow to orange; legs orange.
IMMATURES undescribed.
9 males   wing 77–89 (83.9) mm., tail 62–74 (67.9) mm.,
            exp. cul. 11–13 (12.1) mm., tars. 10–13 (11.4) mm.
10 females wing 74–87 (80.2) mm., tail 58–74 (63.9) mm.,
            exp. cul. 11–12 (11.4) mm., tars. 10–11 (10.9) mm.

DISTRIBUTION   Solomon Islands, where it occurs on major elevated islands.

GENERAL NOTES   Meek's Lorikeet is mainly a mountain bird (Galbraith and Galbraith, 1962). On Bougainville it has been collected in the canopy of stunted cloud forest at about 1,700 m. On Guadalcanal Cain and Galbraith (1956) found it in hill and mist forest, and saw it in the company of the Duchess Lorikeet (*C. margarethae*) in a large flowering tree on a mountain ridge; they saw small parties of three or four, but were told that large numbers may congregate to feed in a blossom-laden tree. The flight is swift and direct

It feeds on pollen, nectar and probably soft fruits. Crop contents examined by Cain and Galbraith comprised vegetable matter.

CALL Undescribed.

NESTING No records.

EGGS Undescribed.

BLUE-FRONTED LORIKEET
Charmosyna toxopei (Siebers)   *Illustrated on page 77.*

Length 16 cm.
ADULTS general plumage green, more yellowish on underparts and greater under wing-coverts; forehead green; forecrown blue, fainter and less extensive in females; chin and throat greenish-yellow; yellow band across underside of secondaries, more pronounced in females; tail green narrowly tipped with dull yellow, underside dusky yellow and basally marked with orange-red; bill orange; iris yellow-orange; legs red-orange.
IMMATURES general plumage darker and duller; chin and throat more greenish; well defined yellow band on underside of flight feathers.
2 males   wing 85–90 (87.5) mm., tail 73 (73.0) mm.,
            exp. cul. 13 (13.0) mm., tars. 11–12 (11.5) mm.
3 females wing 83–88 (85.3) mm., tail 65–77 (70.3) mm.,
            exp. cul. 12 (12.0) mm., tars. 11–12 (11.3) mm.

DISTRIBUTION   Island of Buru, Indonesia.

GENERAL NOTES   The Blue-fronted Lorikeet is known only from the original specimens collected in central Buru by Toxopeus (see Siebers, 1931). Seven birds were caught with 'bird lime' and brought in alive; they lived in captivity for about a week. The flight is direct, but not swift, and the tail is spread so that the orange-red markings on the tail-feathers are visible.

Food consists of pollen and nectar.

CALL A very shrill *ti . . . ti . . . ti . . . ti . . . ti-ti-ti* (in Siebers, 1931).

NESTING No records.

EGGS Undescribed.

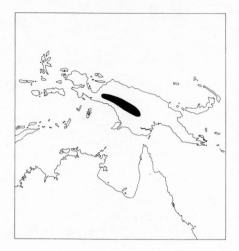

STRIATED LORIKEET
Charmosyna multistriata (Rothschild)   *Illustrated on page 77.*

Length 18 cm.
ADULTS general plumage green, more yellowish on forehead, throat and sides of head; hindcrown and nape brown, variably spotted with orange-yellow on nape; breast dark green streaked with yellowish-green; neck and lower underparts green streaked with greenish-yellow; vent red; tail above olive-green tipped with dusky yellow and basally marked with red, underside olive-yellow; upper mandible grey tipped with orange, lower orange; iris red; legs bluish-grey.
IMMATURES (Rand, 1938) head darker green; smaller orange-yellow spots on nape; duller streaks on underparts.
3 males   wing 98–102 (100.0) mm., tail 88–96 (92.3) mm.,
         exp. cul. 15–17 (16.0) mm., tars. 13–14 (13.3) mm.
3 females wing 97–102 (99.3) mm., tail 75–89 (80.0) mm.,
         exp. cul. 14–16 (15.3) mm., tars. 12–13 (12.3) mm.

DISTRIBUTION Southern slopes of the main ranges in western New Guinea between the Snow Mountains and the upper Fly River.

GENERAL NOTES The Striated Lorikeet is a rare bird known from only a few localities between 200 and 1,800 m. (Rand and Gilliard, 1967). Nothing is known of its habits.

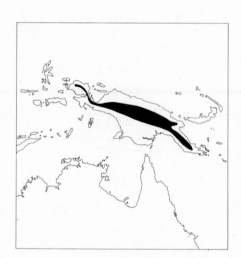

WILHELMINA'S LORIKEET
Charmosyna wilhelminae (A. B. Meyer)   *Illustrated on page 80.*

Length 13 cm.
MALE general plumage green, more yellowish on underparts; crown and nape purple-brown, nape streaked with blue; hindneck green with an olive wash in centre; lower back red; rump dark purple-blue; breast streaked with yellow; under wing-coverts red; broad red band across underside of flight feathers; tail green basally marked with red; bill orange; iris orange to red; legs grey.
FEMALE lower back green; under wing-coverts green; no red band on underside of flight feathers.
IMMATURES little or no blue streaking on crown; streaking on breast absent or only faintly indicated; males have red under wing-coverts and red band across undersides of flight feathers, but back is dull purple.
6 males   wing 67–70 (68.3) mm., tail 44–52 (47.2) mm.,
         exp. cul. 10–11 (10.2) mm., tars. 9–11 (10.0) mm.
8 females wing 65–73 (68.3) mm., tail 45–49 (47.3) mm.,
         exp. cul. 9–11 (10.3) mm., tars. 9–11 (9.9) mm.

DISTRIBUTION Highlands of New Guinea from the Arfak Mountains, West Irian, east to the Huon Peninsula and south-eastern New Guinea.

GENERAL NOTES Wilhelmina's Lorikeet is an uncommon inhabitant of mid-mountain forests between 500 and 1,800 m. (Rand and Gilliard, 1967). Mayr and Rand (1937) point out that a specimen obtained at Mafula, south-eastern New Guinea, was brought in by a native collector, who said that it was one of many feeding in a flowering tree. Its small size and predominantly green plumage would make detection difficult.

CALL Undescribed.

NESTING No records.

EGGS Rounded; 2 eggs, 16.9 (16.8–17.0) × 13.5 (13.5) mm. [Brit. Mus. Collection].

RED-SPOTTED LORIKEET
Charmosyna rubronotata (Wallace)

DESCRIPTION Length 17 cm.
MALE general plumage green, more yellowish on underparts and lower sides of neck; forehead and

forecrown red; ear-coverts purple-blue faintly streaked brighter; variable red marking on upper tail-coverts; under wing-coverts and sides of breast red; variable yellow band across underside of secondaries; tail green above, dusky yellow below, lateral feathers broadly tipped with yellow and basally marked with red; bill red; iris orange; legs red.

FEMALE forehead and forecrown green; ear-coverts green streaked with yellowish-green; under wing-coverts and sides of breast pale green.

IMMATURES undescribed.

DISTRIBUTION

Salawati and Biak Islands, and north-western New Guinea east to the Sepik River.

SUBSPECIES

1. *C. r. rubronotata* (Wallace)   *Illustrated on page 80.*
8 males   wing 80–87 (83.3) mm., tail 58–71 (65.4) mm.,
              exp. cul. 11–13 (11.9) mm., tars. 11–12 (11.1) mm.
2 females wing 82–83 (82.5) mm., tail 62–66 (64.0) mm.,
              exp. cul. 12 (12.0) mm., tars. 12 (12.0) mm.

Occurs on Salawati Island and in north-western New Guinea.

2. *C. r. kordoana* (A. B. Meyer)
    MALE red of crown paler and more extensive, ear-coverts more blue, less purple.
    FEMALE similar to *rubronotata*.
    3 males   wing 80–82 (80.7) mm., tail 65–70 (66.7) mm.,
                  exp. cul. 11–13 (12.0) mm., tars. 11–12 (11.7) mm.
    5 females wing 78–81 (79.6) mm., tail 59–69 (65.6) mm.,
                  exp. cul. 12–13 (12.2) mm., tars. 11–12 (11.2) mm.
    Restricted to Biak Island in Geelvink Bay, West Irian.

GENERAL NOTES

The Red-spotted Lorikeet is found in lowland forests up to about 850 m. (Rand and Gilliard, 1967). It feeds in the tops of flowering trees, often in the company of honeyeaters and other lorikeets. On Biak Ripley saw small, chattering flocks only among high coconut palms around a littoral village (in Mayr and Meyer de Schauensee, 1939a).

Ripley (1964) points out that in north-western New Guinea three closely related species, *C. pulchella*, *C. placentis* and *C. rubronotata*, are presumably in competition, but of these *rubronotata* seems to be far less common.

CALL Undescribed, but probably similar to that of *C. placentis*.

NESTING No records.

EGGS Undescribed.

RED-FLANKED LORIKEET
Charmosyna placentis (Temminck)

DESCRIPTION

Length 17 cm.
MALE general plumage green, more yellowish on underparts; forehead and forecrown greenish-yellow; dark blue patch on rump; lores, cheeks and upper throat dull red; ear-coverts violet blue streaked brighter; under wing-coverts, flanks and sides of breast red; yellow band across underside of flight feathers; tail above green broadly tipped with orange-yellow, below yellow, lateral feathers basally marked with red and black; bill red; iris yellow to orange; legs orange-red.
FEMALE forehead and forecrown green; red markings replaced by green; ear-coverts dull bluish-black strongly streaked with yellow.
IMMATURES like female, but males have some red on lores and greenish-yellow on forehead; iris pale yellow; legs orange-brown.

DISTRIBUTION

From the Moluccas, Kai and Aru Islands, Indonesia, through New Guinea and adjacent islands to the Bismarck Archipelago and Bougainville Island in the Solomons.

SUBSPECIES

I have followed the revision by Mees (1950)

1. *C. p. placentis* (Temminck)   *Illustrated on page 80.*
    14 males   wing 82–95 (88.3) mm., tail 60–69 (64.3) mm.,
                  exp. cul. 12–14 (12.8) mm., tars. 11–14 (12.3) mm.
    11 females wing 84–92 (88.0) mm., tail 60–71 (65.8) mm.,
                  exp. cul. 12–13 (12.5) mm., tars. 12–13 (12.4) mm.
    Occurs on Pandjang, Ceram, Amboina and Ambelau in the southern Moluccas, on the Kai and Aru Islands, and in southern New Guinea east to the Gulf District, Papua.

2. *C. p. intensior* (Kinnear)

ADULTS slightly larger than *placentis*; small patch on rump blue-violet, not blue; forehead of male slightly greener, less yellowish than in *placentis*.

13 males   wing 89–99 (93.3) mm., tail 75–85 (79.2) mm.,
 exp. cul. 12–13 (12.3) mm., tars. 12–14 (12.7) mm.
10 females wing 88–100 (92.1) mm., tail 72–83 (77.3) mm.,
 exp. cul. 11–13 (12.3) mm., tars. 11–13 (12.3) mm.

Found on North Moluccas, including Obi, and on Gebe in the Western Papuan Islands, West Irian.

3. *C. p. ornata* Mayr

ADULTS mantle slightly darker green than in *placentis*; large blue rump patch; in males red extends further down the throat.

6 males   wing 80–95 (90.3) mm., tail 67–74 (71.3) mm.,
 exp. cul. 12–14 (12.5) mm., tars. 12–14 (12.7) mm.
6 females wing 84–94 (89.3) mm., tail 66–70 (68.3) mm.,
 exp. cul. 12–13 (12.8) mm., tars. 11–13 (12.3) mm.

Occurs on Western Papuan Islands, except Gebe, and in north-western New Guinea.

4. *C. p. subplacens* (Sclater)

ADULTS no blue patch on rump.

10 males   wing 84–93 (88.7) mm., tail 56–74 (68.2) mm.,
 exp. cul. 12–13 (12.2) mm., tars. 12–14 (12.6) mm.
10 females wing 81–91 (85.3) mm., tail 56–68 (63.6) mm.,
 exp. cul. 11–13 (12.0) mm., tars. 12–14 (12.5) mm.

Inhabits eastern New Guinea east of Hall Sound in the south and the Sarmi district, West Irian, in the north.

5. *C. p. pallidior* (Rothschild and Hartert)

ADULTS similar to *subplacens*, but general plumage paler, particularly the blue ear-coverts in males.

11 males   wing 79–91 (85.6) mm., tail 67–73 (69.9) mm.,
 exp. cul. 12–13 (12.5) mm., tars. 12–13 (12.3) mm.
11 females wing 81–90 (85.4) mm., tail 63–70 (67.2) mm.,
 exp. cul. 11–13 (12.0) mm., tars. 11–12 (11.9) mm.

Found on Woodlark Island, east of New Guinea, in the Bismarck Archipelago, and on Bougainville and Fead in the Solomon Islands.

GENERAL NOTES   The Red-flanked Lorikeet is a bird of the lowland forests and savannah (Rand and Gilliard, 1967). Gilliard and LeCroy (1967a) point out that in the mountain forests of the Whiteman Range on New Britain, it is replaced by the Red-chinned Lorikeet (*C. rubrigularis*). On Bougainville it has been collected in secondary growth, especially around village gardens, and in coconut plantations. Its small size and green colouration make it inconspicuous, hence it may not be as uncommon as most reports indicate. On the label of a specimen he collected on Halmahera (MZB. 18959) de Haan has noted that the species was very common. Near Port Moresby I had a brief glimpse of a few birds as they flew into a forest tree, but once they had settled I could not find them, so well did their plumage blend with the foliage.

Mackay (1970) says that small flocks are frequently seen in the Port Moresby district. Sudbury (1969) found them in the Lae Botanic Gardens. Pairs or small parties are usually seen feeding in flowering trees or flying from one tree to the next. The flight is swift and direct.

Food comprises pollen, nectar and probably soft fruits. Stresemann (1914) noted that on Ceram flocks visited coastal districts to feed in flowering coral trees (*Erythrina indica*).

CALL In flight a shrill screech, noticeably harsher than might be expected from such a small bird; while feeding a shrill chattering.

NESTING Females in breeding condition have been collected in September and December (Rand, 1942a). On Witu Island in the Bismarck Archipelago Eichhorn found a nest containing two eggs in the growth of a 'crow's nest' fern in late July (in Hartert, 1926). In a tea-tree swamp on the middle Fly River a pair was seen excavating a tunnel, presumably for nesting, in a large arboreal termite mound (Rand, 1942a). Nothing is known of the nesting habits.

EGGS Rounded; 3 eggs, 19.0 (18.7–20.0) × 17.3 (17.0–18.0) mm. [Schönwetter, 1964].

NEW CALEDONIAN LORIKEET
Charmosyna diadema (Verreaux and Des Murs)

Length 18 cm.   *Illustrated on page 80.*
MALE undescribed.
FEMALE general plumage green, paler on forehead, lores and underparts; crown violet-blue;

cheeks and throat yellow; thighs tinged with violet-blue; green under wing-coverts; vent red; tail green above, yellow below, lateral feathers basally marked with red and black and tipped with yellow; bill orange-red; legs orange.

IMMATURES undescribed.

1 female **(type)** wing 91 mm., tail 77 mm.,
exp. cul. (damaged), tars. 16 mm.

Restricted to New Caledonia.

The New Caledonian Lorikeet is known from only two females collected before 1860; the type is now in the Paris Museum, but apparently the other specimen has been lost. Sarasin (1913) quoted reports of existence of the species in the northern forests near Oubatche.

RED-THROATED LORIKEET
Charmosyna amabilis (Ramsay)   *Illustrated on page 80.*

DESCRIPTION

Length 18 cm.

ADULTS general plumage green, paler on underparts and under wing-coverts; ear-coverts streaked with bluish-green; lores, cheeks and throat red, bordered below by a yellow band; thighs dark red; tail above green tipped with yellow, below yellowish; bill orange; iris yellow; legs orange.

IMMATURES yellow band on throat only faintly indicated; thighs dull greyish-mauve faintly tinged with red.

10 males   wing 94–100 (96.3) mm., tail 69–79 (72.8) mm.,
exp. cul. 10–11 (10.8) mm., tars. 12–13 (12.5) mm.

8 females   wing 91–96 (93.9) mm., tail 68–80 (74.0) mm.,
exp. cul. 10–11 (10.8) mm., tars. 12–13 (12.4) mm.

DISTRIBUTION

Viti Levu, Ovalau and Taveuni in the Fiji Islands.

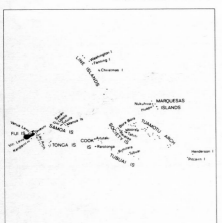

Mercer (1967) points out that the Red-throated Lorikeet is a little-known bird restricted to mountain forests. Parties of five or six are usually seen feeding in the tops of flowering trees. Blackburn (1971) points out that this parrot is a bird of the outer canopy of mountain forest and because of its small size is difficult to see; his party of observers failed to find it on Taveuni but two birds were seen in the Nausori Highlands on Viti Levu. Wood has suggested that it may be extinct on Ovalau (in Wood and Wetmore, 1926).

CALL Undescribed.

NESTING No records.

EGGS Undescribed.

DUCHESS LORIKEET
Charmosyna margarethae Tristam   *Illustrated on page 97.*

Length 20 cm.

MALE general plumage red; back, wings and under tail-coverts green; rump and upper tail-coverts olive-green; sides of rump red; hindcrown and occiput purple-black; broad yellow band across breast, continuing as narrow band on mantle; yellow of breast and mantle bordered above by a narrow purple-black line; lower breast below yellow band variably marked with dull purple; tail red tipped with yellow; bill orange; iris orange-yellow; legs orange.

FEMALE like male, but with yellow patches on sides of rump.

IMMATURES (Rothschild and Hartert, 1901) yellow band on breast and mantle ill-defined; no purple-black line above yellow band; body feathers variably edged with purple-black.

10 males   wing 106–114 (110.9) mm., tail 87–100 (93.5) mm.,
exp. cul. 14–15 (14.5) mm., tars. 14–15 (14.4) mm.

8 females   wing 98–110 (105.6) mm., tail 84–99 (88.0) mm.,
exp. cul. 13–14 (13.8) mm., tars. 13–14 (13.8) mm.

DISTRIBUTION

Solomon Islands.

GENERAL NOTES

Duchess Lorikeets are mainly mountain birds, but may also be seen in lowland forests and coastal coconut plantations (Mayr, 1945). On Bougainville they have been collected from the canopies of tall forest trees. Cain and Galbraith (1956) report that they are noisy when feeding in large groups of up to about forty. They are often seen feeding in the company of other lorikeets and honeyeaters, and are very active, often hanging upside-down to investigate blossoms. Numbers present in an area are governed by the availability of food. The flight is swift and direct.

They feed on pollen, nectar and blossoms. Crop contents examined by Cain and Galbraith comprised vegetable matter.

CALL A high-pitched, metallic *chi-chi-chi-chi* (Cain and Galbraith, 1956).

NESTING No records.

EGGS Undescribed.

FAIRY LORIKEET
Charmosyna pulchella G. R. Gray

Length 18 cm.
MALE general plumage red; back, wings and upper tail-coverts dark green; rump dull blue, sometimes marked with green; thighs and nuchal patch purple-black; yellow streaks on breast, in some birds also on lower flanks; under wing-coverts green and red; tail green at base and red and yellow towards tip, underside bright yellow; bill orange-red; iris yellow to orange; legs orange-yellow.
FEMALE like male, but with yellow patches on sides of rump.
IMMATURES thighs and nuchal patch green intermixed with black; breast variably washed with green and with little or no yellow streaking; only faint indications of grey-blue on rump; yellow band across underside of flight feathers; bill brownish; iris brown; legs brownish-grey.

DESCRIPTION

New Guinea, excluding adjacent islands.

DISTRIBUTION

1. *C. p. pulchella* G. R. Gray   *Illustrated on page 97.*
    13 males   wing 87–99 (92.5) mm., tail 79–98 (91.3) mm.,
          exp. cul. 12–13 (12.5) mm., tars. 11–14 (11.9) mm.
    8 females wing 86–92 (88.8) mm., tail 80–93 (85.9) mm.,
          exp. cul. 12–13 (12.4) mm., tars. 11–12 (11.4) mm.
    Distributed throughout most of the mountains of New Guinea from the Vogelkop, West Irian, east to the Huon Peninsula and southern Papua. I have synonymized *bella* with this subspecies.

SUBSPECIES

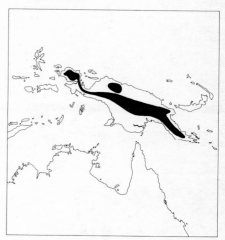

2. *C. p. rothschildi* (Hartert)
    MALE large green breast patch with yellow streaks; nuchal patch extends forward to reach posterior edge of eye; purple-black abdomen; rump green, sometimes faintly marked with grey-blue; upper tail-coverts washed with yellow.
    FEMALE broad green breast band with yellow streaks; greenish-yellow patch on side of rump.
    8 males   wing 95–99 (96.9) mm., tail 89–98 (93.5) mm.,
          exp. cul. 12–13 (12.8) mm., tars. 11–12 (11.8) mm.
    5 females wing 88–96 (93.0) mm., tail 82–92 (85.4) mm.,
          exp. cul. 12–13 (12.6) mm., tars. 11–12 (11.8) mm.
    Restricted to the Cyclops Mountains and northern slopes of mountains above the Idenburg River, West Irian.

Rand and Gilliard (1967) claim that the Fairy Lorikeet is an uncommon or locally rare resident of mid-mountain forests between 800 and 2,000 m., but Donaghey (*in litt.*) points out that the species is easily overlooked unless seen feeding in a tree and may not be rare. Near Djayapura, West Irian, it has been recorded from near sea level to 150 m. (Rand, 1942b). Pairs or small parties are generally observed, but Ripley (1964), at 100 m. at Bodim, West Irian, found large flocks feeding with other lorikeets and honeyeaters in three flowering trees. The flight is swift and direct.
    The diet consists of pollen, nectar and flowers.

GENERAL NOTES

CALL In flight a continuous repetition of high-pitched squeaks; while feeding a shrill chatter.

NESTING Males with enlarged testes and a female with a complete egg in the oviduct were collected on Mt. Misim, Territory of New Guinea, in January (in Greenway, 1935) and from this, coupled with the worn plumage of the birds, Greenway concludes that the breeding season is in late December and January followed by a post-nuptial moult in late January and February. Rand (1942b) reports that two females collected in the Snow Mountains, West Irian, in April were laying.
    Brook (1914) reports a successful breeding in captivity. Only one egg was laid, but the incubation period was not determined. The young bird vacated the nest two months after hatching.

EGGS Rounded; one egg in the British Museum measures 18.9 × 16.2 mm. [Harrison and Holyoak, 1970].

JOSEPHINE'S LORY
Charmosyna josefinae (Finsch)

DESCRIPTION   Length 24 cm.

MALE general plumage red; mantle and wings dark green; occiput and nape black, anteriorly streaked with pale lilac-blue; dusky blue patch on rump; thighs, lower flanks and lower abdomen dull black; under wing-coverts red; central tail feathers red tipped with yellow, lateral feathers red washed with green on outer webs and tipped with yellow, underside of tail yellow; bill red-orange iris yellow; legs orange.

FEMALE lower back green instead of red.

IMMATURES abdomen and nuchal patch black variably tinged with green; thighs bluish-black.

DISTRIBUTION   Mountains of western New Guinea from the Vogelkop, West Irian, east to the Sepik region.

SUBSPECIES   1. *C. j. josefinae* (Finsch)   *Illustrated on page 97.*
8 males   wing 119–125 (122.9) mm., tail 119–132 (124.5) mm.,
                exp. cul. 16–18 (17.3) mm., tars. 15–16 (15.4) mm.
8 females   wing 118–123 (120.0) mm., tail 108–129 (119.9) mm.,
                exp. cul. 16–18 (17.0) mm., tars. 15–16 (15.5) mm.
Distributed from the mountains of the Vogelkop east to the Snow Mountains.

2. *C. j. sepikiana* Neumann
MALE black of abdomen much more extensive; black nuchal patch streaked anteriorly with pale grey.
FEMALE like male, but with lower back and flanks yellow.
2 males   wing 120–123 (121.5) mm., tail 125–129 (127.0) mm.,
                exp. cul. 16 (16.0) mm., tars. 15–16 (15.5) mm.
1 female   wing 117 mm., tail 132 mm.,
                exp. cul. 16 mm., tars. 15 mm.
Confined to mountains in the Sepik region.

3. *C. j. cyclopum* Hartert
ADULTS similar to *josefinae*, but black abdominal patch and blue streaking on occiput absent or only faintly indicated.
6 males   wing 119–124 (121.5) mm., tail 94–122 (111.7) mm.,
                exp. cul. 16–18 (16.8) mm., tars. 15–17 (15.5) mm.
1 female   wing 113 mm., tail 95 mm.,
                exp. cul. 15 mm., tars. 14 mm.
Known only from the Cyclops Mountains, West Irian.

GENERAL NOTES   Josephine's Lory occurs in mountain forest between 800 and 2,000 m. (Rand and Gilliard, 1967), but has also been recorded as low as 50 m. (Rand, 1942b). In mountains above the Idenburg River, West Irian, Rand found it to be fairly common, but quiet and rather inconspicuous. In pairs or small groups it flew silently through the trees, only occasionally uttering a soft squeak, or climbed slowly among the foliage of a climbing vine feeding at the large white flowers. It could have been overlooked by a casual observer. At Sedjak, on the Vogelkop, Ripley (1964) found these lories singly and in pairs associated with Fairy Lorikeets (*C. pulchella*) in flowering trees, and noted that they could be detected by their squeaking calls.

They feed on pollen, nectar and probably soft fruits. Crops from specimens collected in the Weyland Mountains, West Irian contained pollen and flower buds (Rothschild, 1931).

CALL In flight a high-pitched, squeaking note (Rand, 1942b).

NESTING Females in breeding condition have been collected during February (Rand, 1942b). The nesting habits are not known.

EGGS Undescribed.

Fairy Lorikeet 1
Charmosyna pulchella pulchella
AMNH. 765587 ad. ♂

Duchess Lorikeet *Charmosyna margarethae* 2
AM. 030609 ad. ♂

Josephine's Lory 3
Charmosyna josefinae josefinae
RMNH. Cat. 2 ad. ♂

PAPUAN LORY
Charmosyna papou (Scopoli)

DESCRIPTION   Length (with long tail) 42 cm.

ADULTS general plumage red; mantle and wings dark green; forehead and crown red; on occiput a black patch anteriorly streaked with pale blue; nape red; narrow black line across hindneck; blue patch on rump and upper tail-coverts; yellow patches on lower flanks and sides of breast; thighs and abdominal band black; under wing-coverts red; elongated tips to primaries; tail green, tipped with yellow, underside orange-yellow; bill orange to dull scarlet; iris yellow to orange; legs orange.

IMMATURES generally duller than adults; feathers of neck and breast margined with black; abdominal patch tinged with bluish-green; blue on rump duller and less extensive; variable yellow band across underside of secondaries; tips of primaries not elongated; shorter central tail feathers; bill brownish-orange; iris pale yellow; legs brownish-orange.

DISTRIBUTION Mountains of New Guinea from the Vogelkop, West Irian to southern Papua.

SUBSPECIES

1. *C. p. papou* (Scopoli)   *Illustrated on page 100.*
   ADULTS as above, no melanistic phase.
   10 males wing 131–145 (137.8) mm., tail 200–252 (229.4) mm.,
          exp. cul. 15–17 (16.3) mm., tars. 16–18 (17.1) mm.
   8 females wing 130–139 (134.4) mm., tail 210–249 (227.6) mm.,
          exp. cul. 16–17 (16.4) mm., tars. 16–17 (16.6) mm.
   Confined to the Vogelkop, West Irian.

2. *C. p. stellae* A. B. Meyer
   MALE black patch extending from occiput to hindneck and anteriorly streaked with violet-blue; no yellow on lower flanks or sides of breast; lower flanks black; long central tail feathers yellow-orange towards tips; there is a melanistic phase in which red is replaced by black.

   FEMALE sides of rump and lower back yellow.
   10 males wing 139–151 (144.9) mm., tail 221–287 (251.1) mm.,
          exp. cul. 17–19 (17.5) mm., tars. 17–18 (17.8) mm.
   8 females wing 134–146 (139.8) mm., tail 203–267 (228.3) mm.,
          exp. cul. 16–17 (16.6) mm., tars. 17–18 (17.3) mm.
   Known as Stella's Lory, this subspecies is restricted to mountains in south-eastern New Guinea west to the Angabunga River and the Herzog Mountains.

3. *C. p. goliathina* Rothschild and Hartert   *Illustrated on page 100.*
   ADULTS similar to *stellae*, but long central tail feathers yellow towards tips; there is a melanistic phase.
   12 males wing 138–156 (147.3) mm., tail 227–301 (255.5) mm.,
          exp. cul. 17–19 (17.5) mm., tars. 17–19 (17.8) mm.
   9 females wing 135–151 (140.8) mm., tail 233–286 (267.4) mm.,
          exp. cul. 16–18 (16.7) mm., tars. 16–19 (16.7) mm.
   This race is also called Stella's Lory, and is distributed through the mountains of central New Guinea.

4. *C. p. wahnesi* Rothschild
   ADULTS like *goliathina*, but with a wide yellow band across breast; abdominal patch washed with green; there is a melanistic phase.
   3 males   wing 138–140 (138.7) mm., tail 196–235 (219.0) mm.,
          exp. cul. 17–18 (17.7) mm., tars. 16–18 (17.3) mm.
   3 females wing 120–142 (134.0) mm., tail 169–242 (210.4) mm.,
          exp. cul. 17–18 (17.3) mm., tars. 17–18 (17.3) mm.
   Restricted to mountains of the Huon Peninsula.

GENERAL NOTES The Papuan Lory inhabits montane forest between 1,500 and 3,500 m. (Rand and Gilliard 1967, Ripley 1964). Pairs or small parties are usually seen actively hopping along branches or flying through, rather than above, the trees. These birds move about in a peculiar, jerky manner, often flicking their long tail feathers. They are fairly common in most areas, though numbers may decrease or build up in accordance with the supply of food. A flash of brilliant colours and the long tail streaming behind make them conspicuous birds in flight, but when feeding among blossoms or flowering epiphytes attached to moss-covered branches they are easily overlooked. The flight is direct but not swift.

In May, 1970, on the southern slopes of the Hagen Range, in the Western Highlands, I found these lories in disturbed *Nothofagus-Podocarpus* forest at 2,800 m. They were not common and the ten to twelve birds seen were melanistic. In the company of Musschenbroek's Lorikeets (*Neopsittacus musschenbroekii*) they were feeding on fruits of a *Schefflera*, the plant depicted in the plate.

Rand (1942b) points out that on the northern slopes of the Snow Mountains, West Irian, melanistic birds predominated at mid-montane altitudes between 1,800 and 2,800 m. In mountains above the Idenburg River, West Irian, Ripley found the same correlation, but in the Bismarck and Hagen Ranges, central New Guinea, Gilliard (in Mayr and Gilliard, 1954) observed that melanistic birds were three or four times more numerous than normal ones, presumably irrespective of altitude. Skins of the species are highly treasured as head decorations by highland people and are freely traded (Donaghey, *in litt.*, 1970).

The diet consists of pollen, nectar, blossoms, fruits, berries, seeds and possibly insects and their larvae. Crop contents from a specimen collected by Dorward east of Tambul, Western Highlands, comprised remains of flowers, insects belonging to Psyllidae, Thysanoptera and Diptera, and Diptera larvae (CSIRO collection); it is probable that the insects were ingested accidentally. Crops from specimens collected in the Weyland Mountains, West Irian, contained pollen, flower

buds, and very small seeds (Rothschild, 1931), and from the Central Highlands, New Guinea, flowers and fruit pulp (Sims, 1956).

CALL In flight a soft, mellow screech, as would be expected from a much smaller bird; when hopping about in the treetops a soft *cheep . . . cheep*, and while preening or resting a prolonged, nasal *taa- - -aan*.

NESTING Females in breeding condition have been collected in October and November (Rand, 1942b). Brook (1910b) reports the successful rearing of one chick in captivity; the incubation period was about three weeks and the young bird remained in the nest for two months after hatching.

EGGS Undescribed.

Papuan Lory *Charmosyna papou papou* 1
RMNH. Cat. 3 ad. ♂

Stella's Lory *Charmosyna papou goliathina* 2
normal phase CSIRO. 1267 ad. ♂

Stella's Lory *Charmosyna papou goliathina* 3
melanistic phase CSIRO. 4639 ad. ♂

Genus OREOPSITTACUS Salvadori

This monotypic genus is unique in having fourteen tail feathers; all other parrots have twelve. The species is a small, slim parrot, with a long, strongly gradated tail and a very fine, pointed bill. Sexual dimorphism is pronounced and immatures differ from adults.

WHISKERED LORIKEET
Oreopsittacus arfaki (A. B. Meyer)

DESCRIPTION
Length 15 cm.
MALE general plumage green, more yellowish on underparts; forehead and crown red; lores and cheeks purple; double row of white streaks above purple cheeks; abdomen and lower flanks orange or red; yellow on sides of under tail-coverts; under wing-coverts and sides of breast red; yellow band across underside of secondaries; tail green tipped with rose-red, underside rose-red; bill black; iris dark brown; legs greenish-grey.
FEMALE forehead and crown green.
IMMATURES forehead red and crown green in both sexes; feathers of upper parts narrowly edged with black; less purple on cheeks and white streaks not so clearly defined; central tail feathers tipped with dull orange-yellow.

DISTRIBUTION
Mountains of New Guinea from the Vogelkop, West Irian, east to the Huon Peninsula and southern Papua.

SUBSPECIES
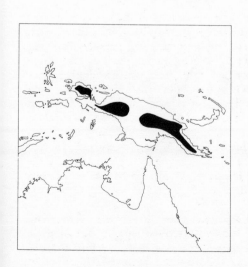

1. *O. a. arfaki* (A. B. Meyer)
   6 males   wing 72–80 (76.0) mm., tail 72–88 (77.7) mm.,
              exp. cul. 11–12 (11.2) mm., tars. 10–11 (10.8) mm.
   4 females wing 72–76 (74.0) mm., tail 74–78 (74.3) mm.,
              exp. cul. 10–11 (10.8) mm., tars. 10–11 (10.8) mm.
   Occurs only in mountains of the Vogelkop.

2. *O. a. major* Ogilvie-Grant
   ADULTS similar to *arfaki*, but larger; tail tipped with scarlet.
   11 males   wing 84–93 (88.4) mm., tail 67–86 (80.7) mm.,
              exp. cul. 12–13 (12.7) mm., tars. 11–12 (11.7) mm.
   8 females wing 79–89 (83.9) mm., tail 72–82 (78.1) mm.,
              exp. cul. 12–13 (12.4) mm., tars. 11–13 (11.8) mm.
   Confined to the Snow Mountains, West Irian.

3. *O. a. grandis* Ogilvie-Grant   *Illustrated on page 101.*
   ADULTS like *major*, but with abdomen and lower flanks green.
   14 males   wing 81–89 (85.5) mm., tail 75–89 (82.3) mm.,
              exp. cul. 11–13 (12.1) mm., tars. 11–13 (11.4) mm.
   10 females wing 81–86 (83.8) mm., tail 74–86 (81.1) mm.,
              exp. cul. 11–13 (11.9) mm., tars. 11–12 (11.5) mm.
   Distributed throughout the mountains of south-eastern New Guinea west to the Huon Peninsula and the Sepik region.

GENERAL NOTES
The Whiskered Lorikeet is a mountain bird, being common only in the mist forests between 2,000 and 3,750 m. (Rand and Gilliard, 1967). On the southern slopes of the Hagen Range, in the Western Highlands, I observed it in disturbed *Nothofagus-Podocarpus* forest at 2,800 m. It is usually seen in pairs or small flocks, often in the company of honeyeaters, flowerpeckers and other lorikeets, feeding in flowering trees. They are very active birds, continually climbing among outermost twigs and frequently reaching out or hanging upside-down to get at blossoms. They

are quiet, and while feeding will generally allow a close approach. When resting, two or more birds may huddle together. The flight is swift and direct.

Food comprises pollen, nectar, flowers, fruits and berries. George has watched these parrots feeding on *Schefflera* fruits (pers. comm., 1970).

CALL In flight a plaintive twittering, while feeding an occasional soft, squeaking note.

NESTING Females with enlarged gonads have been collected in October (Rand, 1942b). Nothing is known of the nesting habits.

Mayr and Rand (1937) quote observations on what may have been part of the mating display. One bird, apparently alone, was seen in the outermost branches of a forest tree, hopping from one branch to the next, all the while whistling to itself in a low tone and rapidly bobbing its head and body, occasionally stopping to eat a flower. A few days later a pair was seen in another tree and one was continually following the other, sometimes with wings spread to show the red markings.

EGGS Undescribed.

Musschenbroek's Lorikeet 1
Neopsittacus musschenbroekii major
CSIRO. 1040 ad. ♂

Emerald Lorikeet 2
Neopsittacus pullicauda pullicauda
CSIRO. 4580 ad. ♂

Whiskered Lorikeet *Oreopsittacus arfaki grandis* 3
CSIRO. 1195 ad. ♂

Genus NEOPSITTACUS Salvadorii

The two sibling species in this genus are small parrots with long, gradated tails. The tail feathers have rounded tips and are broader than in *Charmosyna* or *Oreopsittacus*. The bill is proportionately heavy and fairly broad. Sexual dimorphism is absent; immatures are duller than adults and have broadly pointed tips to the tail feathers.

The main external differences between the species are summarized as follows:

	N. musschenbroekii	N. pullicauda
BILL	pale yellow	orange
HEAD	prominent brown markings	little brown
TAIL	underside bright orange-yellow	underside dull olive-green
TAIL FEATHERS	tipped with yellow	not tipped with yellow
SIZE	larger of two	smaller of two

MUSSCHENBROEK'S LORIKEET
Neopsittacus musschenbroekii (Schlegel)

DESCRIPTION Length 23 cm.
ADULTS general plumage green, more yellowish on underparts; crown and nape olive-brown streaked with dull yellow; hindneck olive-brown; lores dull greenish-black; cheeks olive-brown streaked with pale green; throat, breast and centre of abdomen red; under wing-coverts and broad band across underside of flight feathers red; central tail feathers green narrowly tipped with yellow, lateral feathers green broadly tipped with yellow and basally marked with red, underside bright orange-yellow; bill pale yellow; iris red; legs grey.
IMMATURES duller than adults; head markings much less pronounced; throat and upper breast green variably washed with red; lower breast green; iris brownish-yellow to orange.

DISTRIBUTION Mountains of New Guinea from the Vogelkop, West Irian, east to southern Papua.

SUBSPECIES 1. *N. m. musschenbroekii* (Schlegel)
10 males wing 101–113 (109.0) mm., tail 80–92 (86.3) mm.,
exp. cul. 14–15 (14.8) mm., tars. 14–17 (15.5) mm.
8 females wing 106–113 (108.8) mm., tail 79–87 (84.6) mm.,
exp. cul. 14–15 (14.6) mm., tars. 14–17 (15.0) mm.
Confined to mountains of the Vogelkop.

2. *N. m. medius* (Stresemann)
ADULTS larger than *musschenbroekii*; streaking on cheeks more yellowish, less green.
11 males wing 115–125 (119.8) mm., tail 84–101(95.1) mm.,
exp. cul. 15–18 (16.7) mm., tars. 15–17 (15.4) mm.
8 females wing 112–119 (114.8) mm.. tail 90–100 (94.6) mm.,
exp. cul. 15–17 (15.9) mm., tars. 15–17 (15.8) mm.

Occurs in the Snow Mountains, West Irian; probably not separable from *major* (see Mees, 1964).

3. **N. m. major** (Neumann) *Illustrated on page 101.*

ADULTS larger than *musschenbroekii*; streaking on cheeks bright greenish-yellow; general plumage paler, particularly red of underparts which is more scarlet.

9 males   wing 111–119 (115.1) mm., tail 90–101 (96.3) mm.,
        exp. cul. 15–17 (15.9) mm., tars. 15–17 (15.3) mm.

7 females wing 110–120 (114.1) mm., tail 90–101 (94.0) mm.,
        exp. cul. 15–16 (15.3) mm.,tars. 15–17 (15.9) mm.

Distributed throughout the mountains of south-eastern New Guinea from the Sepik region and the Huon Peninsula to southern Papua.

It seems that the altitudinal ranges of this species and of the Emerald Lorikeet overlap to a much greater extent than is indicated by Rand and Gilliard (1967). Musschenbroek's Lorikeet has been collected as low as 1,450 m., or probably even 1,250 m. (Mayr and Rand, 1937), and on the southern slopes of the Hagen Range, Western Highlands, I found it at 2,800 m. It inhabits montane forests and is usually seen in pairs or small flocks, often in the company of other lorikeets. The birds seen on the Hagen Range were associating with small numbers of Papuan Lories (*Charmosyna papou*), and were feeding on *Schefflera* fruits in disturbed *Nothofagus-Podocarpus* forest. They were active in the mid and upper storeys of trees, frequently running along stout branches in a rodent-like manner. They were rather shy and when disturbed flew off screeching loudly. The flight is direct and very swift.

Food consists of pollen, nectar, blossoms, fruits, berries, seeds and possibly insects and their larvae. Crop and stomach contents from specimens collected in the Weyland Mountains, West Irian, and the Central Highlands, New Guinea, comprised fruits, berries and small hard seeds (Rothschild 1931, Sims 1956). Two seeds, very small caterpillars, and psyllid lerps were found in the crop of a bird collected near Tambul in the Western Highlands (CSIRO coll.); the insects may have been ingested accidentally.

CALL When perched, a disyllabic screech, the second note being lower in pitch than the first; in flight, a shrill, rolling screech.

NESTING A male with extremely worn plumage, but showing no signs of moult, was collected by Ripley (1964) in August and he presumed that this bird had not long completed a nesting cycle. A fledgling (AMNH. 339430) was taken near Lake Habbema, West Irian, in mid-November.

Tavistock (1950) has reported an unsuccessful nesting in captivity. Two eggs were laid, and although the male spent much time in the nest-box he probably did not assist with incubation. The incubation period was not determined and the only chick hatched died when about ten days old.

EGGS Undescribed.

EMERALD LORIKEET
Neopsittacus pullicauda Hartert

Length 18 cm.

ADULTS general plumage green, more yellowish on underparts; crown and nape lightly streaked with yellowish-green; nape slightly tinged with olive-brown; lores dull greenish-black; cheeks green streaked with greenish-yellow; throat, breast and centre of abdomen bright red; under wing-coverts and broad band across underside of flight feathers red; tail above green basally marked with red, under-side dull olive-green; bill orange; iris red; legs grey.

IMMATURES (AMNH. 339433); duller than adults, particularly on breast and abdomen where red markings are very much reduced; streaking on head not so clearly defined; brownish bill.

Mountains of New Guinea from the Snow Mountains, West Irian, and the Sepik region east to the Huon Peninsula and southern Papua; absent from the Vogelkop.

1. **N. p. pullicauda** Hartert *Illustrated on page 101.*

8 males   wing 98–108 (101.8) mm., tail 82–87 (84.8) mm.,
        exp. cul. 12–14 (13.3) mm., tars. 14–15 (14.3) mm.

8 females wing 98–104 (100.9) mm., tail 82–87 (84.3) mm.,
        exp. cul. 12–13 (12.6) mm., tars. 14–16 (14.5) mm.

Distributed through the mountains of south-eastern New Guinea west to the Sepik region.

2. **N. p. alpinus** Ogilvie-Grant

ADULTS orange-red of breast contrasting with darker red of abdomen; upperparts darker green.

8 males   wing 103–111 (105.9) mm., tail 82–93 (88.1) mm.,
        exp. cul. 12–13 (12.8) mm., tars. 14–16 (15.1) mm.

9 females wing 99–109 (104.0) mm., tail 82–94 (86.2) mm.,
        exp. cul. 12–13 (12.6) mm., tars. 14–16 (14.7) mm.

Occurs in the Snow Mountains and the ranges east to the head of the Fly River.

Palm Cockatoo
Probosciger aterrimus goliath
CSIRO. 3987 ad. ♂

3. *N. p. socialis* Mayr

ADULTS like *pullicauda*, but upperparts and sides of head darker green; less olive-brown on nape. No specimens examined.

2 males (Mauersberger, *in litt.* 1971; Paynter, *in litt.* 1971); wing 106–117 (111.5) mm., tail 86–93 (89.5) mm., exp. cul. 13–14 (13.5) mm., tars. 13 (13.0) mm.

2 females (Mauersberger, *in litt.* 1971); wing 100–104 (102.0) mm., tail 66–83 (74.5) mm., exp. cul. 13–15 (14.0) mm., tars. 13 (13.0) mm.

Known only from the Herzog Mountains and mountains on the Huon Peninsula.

GENERAL NOTES

The Emerald Lorikeet is a high mountain bird, whereas *N. musschenbroekii* is largely confined to mid-mountain forests at lower altitudes. Nevertheless, their ranges overlap considerably and both species may be found in the same area. Rand and Gilliard (1967) say that this lorikeet occurs from 2,400 m. up to 3,800 m., but Junge (1953) points out that it has been found as low as 1,750 m. and even 800 m. It is a noisy bird, commonly seen in pairs or small parties flying above the treetops or busily climbing among the foliage of flowering trees and shrubs. It is fairly tame and, while feeding, will generally allow a close approach. Numbers may build up in feeding trees, though such flocks are not cohesive units but merely aggregations of small groups. The flight is swift and direct.

The diet consists of pollen, nectar, flowers, fruits, berries and seeds.

CALL A variety of high-pitched, squeaking and twittering notes (Mayr and Rand, 1937).

NESTING A male with enlarged testes was collected during October (Rand, 1942b). Nothing is known of the nesting habits.

EGGS Undescribed.

Yellow-tailed Cockatoo 1
Calyptorhynchus funereus funereus
AM. 028666 ad. ♂

White-tailed Cockatoo 2
Calyptorhynchus funereus baudinii
CSIRO. 12232 ad. ♀

Family: CACATUIDAE

Parrots belonging to this family are called cockatoos. An erectile crest is the most obvious external feature; the bird raises it immediately after alighting and when alarmed or excited. As pointed out by Thompson (1900) there is some uniformity in the cranial osteology; all species have a complete orbit and a bridge across the temporal fossa. These birds have strong, heavy bills capable of coping with a diet of seeds, fruits and insects and their larvae. The ventriculus is thick-walled and very muscular.

Some facets of behaviour are common to all species. Cockatoos bathe by fluttering among wet foliage in the treetops or during rain showers by flying about or hanging upside-down from their perches. When cornered or aroused they emit a peculiar hissing note. Some species are strictly arboreal, but most feed either in the treetops or on the ground.

Subfamily CACATUINAE

Cockatoos in this subfamily are medium to large birds with rounded or squarish tails. The bill is strong and robust.

Red-tailed Cockatoo **1**
Calyptorhynchus magnificus magnificus
AM. 011754 ad. ♂

Red-tailed Cockatoo **2**
Calyptorhynchus magnificus magnificus
AM. 023584 ad. ♀

Genus PROBOSCIGER Kuhl

Diagnostic features of this monotypic genus are the enormous, projecting bill, the naked cheek-patches extending from the base of the lower mandible, and the bare thighs. As the mandibles do not fit together when closed the small, bi-coloured tongue is visible. The very prominent, backward-curving crest comprises narrow, elongated feathers. The cere is feathered. Sexual dimorphism is not obvious, but there is an immature plumage.

A peculiarity of the species is the ability to change the colour of the bare cheek-patches. When the cockatoo is excited or alarmed the red deepens noticeably and the bird is said to 'blush'.

PALM COCKATOO
Probosciger aterrimus (Gmelin)

Length 60 cm.

DESCRIPTION

MALE general plumage greyish-black; forehead and lores black; naked cheek-patches crimson; bare thighs bluish-grey; exposed gape red; tongue red with a black tip; bill grey-black; iris dark brown; legs, grey.
FEMALE upper mandible appreciably smaller than in the male.
IMMATURES feathers of under wing-coverts and underparts edged with pale yellow; bill tipped with white in very young birds.

DISTRIBUTION

Aru Islands, New Guinea, including some offshore islands, and Cape York Peninsula in northern Australia.

SUBSPECIES

Geographical variation is poorly documented and is in need of careful revision. I follow Mees (1957) by accepting the Aru Islands, Indonesia, as the type locality, and have already given my reason for including the Cape York Peninsula population in *aterrimus* (see Forshaw, 1969a).

1. *P. a. aterrimus* (Gmelin)
   12 males wing 318–391 (351.0) mm., tail 200–253 (237.7) mm.,
            exp. cul. 82–101 (90.0) mm., tars. 30–41 (34.5) mm.
   7 females wing 305–357 (336.7) mm., tail 205–249 (235.9) mm.,
            exp. cul. 73–91 (77.4) mm., tars. 32–38 (33.9) mm.
   Occurs on the Aru Islands, Misool in the western Papuan Islands, West Irian, southern New Guinea from about Merauke east to the Gulf of Papua, and Cape York Peninsula, northern Australia.

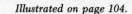

2. *P. a. goliath* (Kuhl)
ADULTS larger than *aterrimus*.
10 males wing 372–405 (384.7) mm., tail 252–276 (257.8) mm.,
exp. cul. 97–106 (101.8) mm., tars. 34–37 (35.1) mm.
8 females wing 353–373 (362.1) mm., tail 232–265 (249.4) mm.,
exp. cul. 77–85 (81.0) mm., tars. 32–35 (33.1) mm.

Found on the western Papuan Islands, except Misool, and in New Guinea from the Vogelkop, West Irian, east through central regions to south-eastern Papua; may not be separable from *aterrimus* (see Forshaw, 1969a).

3. *P. a. stenolophus* (van Oort)
ADULTS like *goliath*, but crest feathers much narrower.
12 males wing 360–406 (382.3) mm., tail 250–277 (264.5) mm.,
exp. cul. 101–118 (110.4) mm., tars. 32–40 (35.9) mm.
12 females wing 352–375 (364.5) mm., tail 247–266 (256.6) mm.,
exp. cul. 78–86 (83.0) mm., tars. 31–36 (33.8) mm.

Confined to Japen Island in Geelvink Bay, West Irian, and northern New Guinea from the Mamberamo River, West Irian, east to about Collingwood Bay in eastern Papua.

GENERAL NOTES

In New Guinea Palm Cockatoos inhabit forest and dense savannah woodland up to about 1,300 m. (Rand and Gilliard, 1967). On Cape York Peninsula their habitat is the fringe zone between dense rainforest and *Eucalyptus* woodland. Through persistent hunting they have been virtually wiped out in the vicinity of most larger towns and villages in New Guinea, but are fairly common elsewhere. Their large size, black colouration and piercing call-notes make them very conspicuous. Singly, in pairs or in small parties they are usually seen perched atop tall trees or flying above the forest canopy. On Cape York Peninsula I observed that they roosted singly in the topmost branches of tall trees, nearly always in dead or leafless uppermost branches of deciduous trees growing at the edge of rainforest. They did not stir until well after sunrise and spent some time preening before moving off. About an hour after sunrise they commenced calling to each other and soon up to six or seven would congregate in a large tree in open woodland and indulge in a variety of antics and elaborate bowing displays. I have described and figured one display which seemed to be a prominent feature of the behaviour at these congregating trees (see Forshaw, 1964). The parties left the congregating trees and fed in open woodland or along the edges of rainforest, returning to the individual roosting trees just before sunset.

I noticed that while feeding in rainforest they were confiding, but in open country were timid and seldom allowed a close approach. In the Astrolabe Bay area, northern New Guinea, Gilliard came across a lone bird as it perched quietly about 10 m. up in high rainforest, pulling with its bill at a large woody object held hand-like in the left foot; it was so engrossed in eating that when shouted at it merely turned its head briefly (Gilliard and LeCroy, 1967b).

The flight is heavy and laboured with slow, full wingbeats; the large bill is held down against the breast. On short flights the birds periodically glide on down-curved wings. When coming in to alight they glide straight into a tree and do not spiral down from above as do many other cockatoos.

These cockatoos feed on seeds, nuts, fruits, berries and leaf buds. I can find no evidence to support the claim that they extract wood-boring larvae from decaying timber. They are primarily arboreal feeders, but have been seen on the ground feeding on seeds and fallen fruits. On Cape York Peninsula they have been observed eating seeds of the kanari tree (*Canarium australasicum*) and the black bean tree (*Castanospermum australe*), and the fruits of the nonda tree (*Parinarium nonda*) and the *Pandanus* palm. Rand (1942a) reports that one bird collected in southern New Guinea had in its crop small seeds of a sedge that grew on the forest floor. Crop contents from a bird collected in the Lake Kutubu area, Papua, comprised crushed endosperm and embryos of *Terminalis* or *Myristica* or *Canarium* nuts (Schodde and Hitchcock, 1968).

CALL The normal contact call is a disyllabic whistle; the first note is mellow and deep, while the second is shrill and high-pitched, being prolonged and terminating with an abrupt, upward inflection. When alarmed a sharp, gutteral screech. Other calls are a deep, monosyllabic whistle repeated three or four times and a mournful, drawn-out, wailing cry.

NESTING On Cape York Peninsula nests containing eggs have been found as early as the first week in August and as late as the last week in January (Macgillivray, 1914). In New Guinea two females in breeding condition were collected in August (Rand, 1942a). The nest is in a hollow limb or hole in a tree, usually in the trunk of a dead tree. The bottom of the hollow is lined with a layer of splintered twigs; these are carried into the nest as long pieces and are then split and broken into short lengths. The layer may be several feet deep in some hollows but only a few inches in others. A single egg is laid on the layer. Little is known about incubation or the rearing of the chick. McLennan suspected that the young bird left the nest about sixty days after hatching (in Macgillivray, 1914).

EGGS Broadly elliptical; 3 eggs, 48.9 (44.7–54.9) × 36.5 (34.5–39.9) mm. [Aust. Mus. and H. L. White Coll.].

1 Glossy Cockatoo *Calyptorhynchus lathami*
AM. 038658 ad. ♂

2 Glossy Cockatoo *Calyptorhynchus lathami*
AM. 021224 ad. ♀

Genus CALYPTORHYNCHUS Desmarest

The 'black cockatoos' belong to this genus. They are large birds with coloured tail bands and short crests. There are no naked cheek-patches and the thighs are fully feathered. The slightly rounded tail is rather long. The cere is naked.

The bill is large and robust, but each species shows structural modifications, which are clearly adaptations related to feeding habits. *C. funereus* has a narrow, protruding bill with the tip of the upper mandible elongated and pointed, an adaptation for digging into timber to extract wood-boring insect larvae. *C. magnificus* has a broad, blunt bill, ideal for crushing seeds and hard nuts, and suitable for breaking timber rather than digging into it. *C. lathami* has a protruding, bulbous bill with an exceptionally broad lower mandible, an adaptation for tearing apart *Casuarina* cones.

1 Gang-gang Cockatoo *Callocephalon fimbriatum*
AM. 032254 ad. ♂

2 Gang-gang Cockatoo *Callocephalon fimbriatum*
AM. 09324 ad. ♀

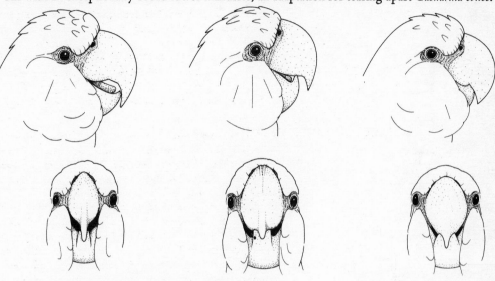

Fig. 7
Structural modifications in the bills of the species in *Calyptorhynchus*. Left: *C. funereus*. Centre: *C. magnificus*. Right: *C. lathami*.

Sexual dimorphism is slight in *funereus*, but pronounced in *magnificus* and *lathami*. Only the female incubates, but both sexes care for the young.

BLACK COCKATOO
Calyptorhynchus funereus (Shaw)

DESCRIPTION

Length 67 cm.

MALE general plumage brownish-black, duller and more brownish on underparts; feathers margined with yellow, most prominent on neck and underparts; yellow ear-coverts; central tail feathers brownish-black, lateral feathers brownish-black with a broad subterminal band of yellow variably spotted with brownish-black; naked periophthalmic ring flesh-pink; bill dark grey; iris dark brown; legs brown.

FEMALE ear-coverts brighter yellow; tail band more heavily spotted with brownish-black; naked periophthalmic ring grey; bill horn-coloured.

IMMATURES resemble female; young males have duller ear-coverts.

DISTRIBUTION

South-eastern and south-western Australia.

SUBSPECIES

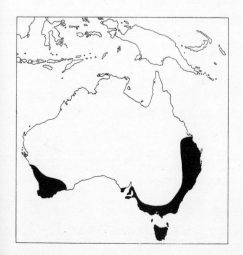

1. *C. f. funereus* (Shaw)   *Illustrated on page 105.*
   20 males   wing 359–444 (399.8) mm., tail 303–359 (346.4) mm.,
                    exp. cul. 46–73 (50.2) mm., tars. 34–38 (35.4) mm.
   20 females wing 351–457 (394.0) mm., tail 312–371 (338.6) mm.,
                    exp. cul. 45–52 (48.3) mm., tars. 32–38 (35.1) mm.
   Known as the Yellow-tailed Cockatoo, this subspecies occurs in south-eastern Australia from central Queensland through eastern New South Wales and southern Victoria to Tasmania, including larger islands in Bass Strait, and across to southern South Australia as far west as Kangaroo Island and Eyre Peninsula.

2. *C. f. baudinii* Lear   *Illustrated on page 105.*
   MALE ear-coverts and margins to body feathers dusky white; tail-band white very lightly spotted with brownish-black; legs greyish-brown.
   FEMALE ear-coverts clear white; other sex differences as in *funereus*.
   20 males   wing 352–391 (369.9) mm., tail 287–352 (330.7) mm.,
                    exp. cul. 43–57 (49.3) mm., tars. 34–37 (35.2) mm.
   20 females wing 355–386 (382.1) mm., tail 281–368 (299.8) mm.,
                    exp. cul. 42–56 (50.4) mm., tars. 35–39 (36.5) mm.
   This distinctive isolate is called the White-tailed Cockatoo. It is restricted to south-western Australia south of the Murchison River.

Black Cockatoos are noisy, conspicuous birds found in most types of timbered country at all altitudes. There is a marked difference in the habitat preferences of the two subspecies. The Yellow-tailed Cockatoo is mainly a bird of the wet coastal woodlands and mountain forests, becoming uncommon and locally distributed in drier areas. On the other hand, *baudinii* is well distributed throughout *Eucalyptus* forests, savannah woodland and dry scrublands. The species is common, particularly in south-western Australia.

Both local and seasonal movements have been recorded in eastern Australia (see Forshaw, 1969a). In the south-west movements are widespread and obvious. Davies (1966) has used sight reports to survey these movements and his results suggest that inland birds move to the south and west coasts in summer, arriving at the extreme south-west between March and May. Presumably they then return to the inner wheatbelt areas, where large numbers are recorded from April to October. Davies also notes that although there are breeding records from nearly all parts of the range of *baudinii*, results of the survey indicate that most nesting takes place in the interior away from coastal forests.

Pairs, family parties or small groups are the normal social units, but occasionally large flocks congregate to feed in *Pinus* plantations or in freshly-burnt country where they come, sometimes in association with Red-tailed Cockatoos, to extract seeds from *Banksia* cones split open by fire. The pair bond is strong and pairs or threes, comprising adults and their young, are discernible within the flock. In eastern Australia they are mainly arboreal, but in the south-east *baudinii* is frequently seen on the ground feeding on seeds. They are wary and difficult to approach; while the group is feeding one or two birds remain on the alert and at the approach of danger they screech loudly and the entire group flies off.

At dawn they leave the large roosting trees along the banks of a watercourse and after going down to drink fly off to the feeding area, where they remain all day, moving from one clump of trees to the next. During the heat of the day they shelter in the foliage of a tall tree. Toward sunset they visit a stream or waterhole to drink; a few at a time fly down from a tree, alight on the ground and then walk to the water's edge. They return to the roosting trees, but before settling down frequently indulge in excited aerobatics, flying through the treetops and wheeling about overhead.

The slow, flapping flight with full wingbeats is extremely buoyant and at times the birds seem to drift lazily along in the air. Long distance flights are at a considerable height, the cockatoos travelling far apart and calling continuously to each other. When flying from one tree to another they drop down toward the ground then glide upward before alighting. As they alight the tail is fanned and the short crest raised. When flushed these large, awkward-looking birds can twist and turn through the treetops with surprising speed. In flight the long tail is prominent.

These cockatoos feed on seeds, nuts, berries, blossoms, and insects and their larvae. They are particularly fond of seeds of *Eucalyptus*, *Acacia*, *Hakea*, *Banksia* and the introduced *Pinus* trees. In eastern Australia wood-boring larvae of cossid moths and cerambycid beetles are the staple diet of *funereus*, but in south-western Australia observations show that *baudinii* feeds mainly on seeds. In the coastal woodland of New South Wales Cooper has seen Black Cockatoos tearing apart *Banksia* inflorescences, presumably to extract nectar or to get at insects (pers. comm., 1969). In the southern highlands I have watched them digging out *Xyleutes* larvae from trunks and branches of snow gums (*Eucalyptus pauciflora*). In Western Australia they are troublesome in apple orchards, stripping developing fruit to get at the seeds, and they feed extensively on seeds of maritime pine *Pinus pinaster*), causing significant damage in plantations.

CALL In flight a prolonged, screaming *kee-ow . . . kee-ow*, a most characteristic call which cannot be mistaken for that of any other species; when alarmed a harsh screech, and while feeding a peculiar, grating note.

NESTING The courtship display of the male is simple. He raises the short crest and spreads his tail to show the tail band.

The breeding season is variable. In southern Queensland and northern New South Wales it is from March to August, but farther south it is during July to January, or even as late as February in Tasmania. In south-western Australia it is from August to November. The nest is in a spacious hollow limb or hole in a large tree, usually a eucalypt. Both birds prepare the hollow and may commence this up to six or more weeks before the first egg is laid. During the period of nest preparation courtship feeding is common. The one or two eggs are laid on a layer of decayed wood dust.

Only the female broods, but little is known of the general nesting behaviour. Incubation commences with the laying of the first egg and the second is not laid until four to seven days later. If the second egg hatches the chick is neglected and soon dies, only the first nestling being reared to maturity. The sitting female is fed three or four times a day by her mate. The incubation period has not been determined. The chick is fed by both parents early in the morning and in the late afternoon. About three months after hatching the young bird leaves the nest, but is fed by the parents for a further four months. During the second year the bill of the young male commences to darken, starting at the base of the upper mandible.

Taylor (1971) reports a successful breeding of *funereus* in captivity. Two eggs were laid, but only one hatched. The incubation period was not determined, but the young bird vacated the nest seventy-six days after hatching. Taylor also reports that the newly-hatched nestling of *funereus* is covered with yellow down whereas the down of the *baudinii* nestling is white.

Galah *Eolophus roseicapillus roseicapillus*
AM. 042503 ad. ♂

EGGS Ovate; 4 eggs, 49.9 (45.5–53.0) × 34.7 (33.4–36.1) mm. [H. L. White Coll.].

RED-TAILED COCKATOO
Calyptorhynchus magnificus (Shaw)

Length 60 cm.

MALE general plumage black, slightly washed with brown on back, nape and lower breast; central tail-feathers black, lateral feathers black with a broad subterminal band of bright red; bill dark grey; iris dark brown; legs brownish-grey.

FEMALE general plumage brownish-black, paler on underparts; numerous yellow spots on head, sides of neck, median wing-coverts and primaries; feathers of underparts margined with pale orange-yellow; tail band yellow becoming orange toward tip of tail and crossed by black bars; bill horn-coloured.

IMMATURES resemble female.

Eastern, northern and western Australia; an apparently isolated population in western Victoria and adjacent parts of south-eastern South Australia. Absent from Tasmania and Kangaroo Island.

1. *C. m. magnificus* (Shaw)   *Illustrated on page 108.*
    11 males   wing 390–449 (427.5) mm., tail 272–301 (289.5) mm.,
                exp. cul. 48–55 (50.6) mm., tars. 32–37 (35.0) mm.
    12 females wing 402–454 (422.8) mm., tail 277–321 (295.7) mm.,
                exp. cul. 47–54 (49.4) mm., tars. 33–38 (35.1) mm.
    Confined to eastern Australia from Cape York Peninsula to southern New South Wales; birds from western Victoria and south-eastern South Australia probably belong to this race.

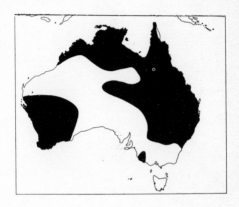

2. *C. m. macrorhynchus* Gould
    MALE similar to *magnificus* but with heavier bill.
    FEMALE tail band pale yellow with little or no orange; heavier bill.
    20 males   wing 409–451 (426.7) mm., tail 273–299 (288.4) mm.,
               exp. cul. 51–56 (53.1) mm., tars. 32–36 (34.5) mm.
    9 females wing 386–455 (410.6) mm., tail 280–311 (296.3) mm.,
               exp. cul. 48–55 (51.4) mm., tars. 33–36 (34.7) mm.
    This subspecies from northern Australia is only doubtfully distinct from *magnificus*.

3. *C. m. samueli* Mathews
    ADULTS similar to, but smaller than *magnificus*.
    10 males   wing 376–400 (390.2) mm., tail 245–270 (260.5) mm.,
               exp. cul. 45–49 (46.1) mm., tars. 33–35 (33.7) mm.
    7 females wing 374–387 (378.0) mm., tail 247–278 (257.6) mm.,
               exp. cul. 43–52 (46.7) mm., tars. 32–34 (33.3) mm.
    Found in central Australia, including south-western Queensland and far western New South Wales.

4. *C. m. naso* Gould
    ADULTS crest shorter and more rounded than in other subspecies; smaller in size than *magnificus*.
    6 males   wing 370–412 (381.3) mm., tail 239–271 (253.4) mm.,
               exp. cul. 46–53 (50.1) mm., tars. 30–33 (31.7) mm.
    6 females wing 364–402 (379.9) mm., tail 237–265 (261.1) mm.,
               exp. cul. 50–53 (51.2) mm., tars. 30–35 (32.6) mm.
    Restricted to south-western Australia. I suspect that this race is isolated from both *macrorhynchus* and *samueli*.

Northern Australia is the stronghold of the Red-tailed Cockatoo, and large flocks may be seen there in dry woodland or trees bordering watercourses. In the south, pairs, family groups or small flocks frequent *Eucalyptus* forests and savannah woodland. The species is rare in south-eastern and parts of south-western Australia, but is plentiful elsewhere. It is largely nomadic, its arrival in a particular area being unpredictable and dependent on the availability of food. In some regions it is a regular migrant.

These cockatoos are noisy and conspicuous, and their loud, raucous cries always attract attention. In heavily timbered areas they are arboreal and spend most of the day feeding among the branches of tall trees. As they split open the nuts or seed-capsules the clicking of their mandibles can be heard from some distance away. In the interior they often feed on the ground, over which they walk with an awkward, waddling gait. While feeding they are less wary than at other times, but even then seldom allow a close approach. When disturbed they fly off screeching loudly. They drink early in the morning and again toward dusk. At sundown they may be observed flying high overhead, returning from the feeding grounds to their roosting trees, generally large eucalypts on the banks of a river or creek. On moonlit nights they often fly about uttering their usual cries. The buoyant flight is similar to that of the Black Cockatoo.

They are primarily seed-eaters and there are only a few reports of them extracting larvae from branches of trees. They feed on seeds and nuts, especially those of *Eucalyptus*, *Acacia*, *Casuarina*,

Major Mitchell's Cockatoo 1
Cacatua leadbeateri leadbeateri
AM. 05566 ad. unsexed

Citron-crested Cockatoo 2
Cacatua sulphurea citrinocristata
BM. 89–1.20.20 ad. unsexed

Lesser Sulphur-crested Cockatoo 3
Cacatua sulphurea sulphurea
AMNH. 153742 ad. ♂

W. T. Cooper 70.

W.T. Cooper. 70.

Banksia, Hakea and Grevillea. In northern Australia they are said to feed extensively on *Ficus* fruits, while in the south-west they eat seeds of double-gee (*Emex australis*), a weed pest in pastoral districts. The crop contents from a specimen collected at Richmond, Queensland, comprised *Chionachne barbata* seeds, and from two collected near Wilcannia, New South Wales, seeds of storksbill (*Erodium cicutarium*).

CALL In flight a rolling, metallic *kree*, or *krurr*; when alarmed a sharp *krur-rak*. All notes are loud and harsh and can be heard from afar.

NESTING When displaying the male raises his crest and brings it forward onto the upper mandible. The cheek feathers are puffed out and brought forward to cover the bill, and the tail is spread to show the red band. Uttering a soft, growling note, he struts along the perch in front of or alongside the hen and bows toward her two or three times.

    Throughout most of the range the breeding season is from May to September. In south-eastern South Australia Attiwill (1960) recorded nesting during the months October to April, a nestling being found as late as April 24th. The nest is in a spacious hollow in a large tree, almost invariably a eucalypt standing in a forest clearing or on a river bank. A single egg is laid on a layer of decayed wood dust. Occasionally there are two eggs in the clutch, but if the second hatches the chick is neglected and soon dies.

    Incubation lasts about thirty days and only the female broods. She is fed by the male in the late afternoon and presumably in the early morning. The chick is fed by both parents twice a day. Approximately three months after hatching the young bird leaves the nest, but is fed by the parents for a further four months. Young males take four years to acquire full adult plumage (for details see Forshaw, 1969a).

EGGS Elliptical; 4 eggs, 51.1 (48.0–55.6) × 36.5 (34.6–38.2) mm. [H. L. White Coll.].

Sulphur-crested Cockatoo 1
Cacatua galerita galerita
JMF. 5 ad. ♂

Blue-eyed Cockatoo *Cacatua ophthalmica* 2
AM. A12100 ad. unsexed

GLOSSY COCKATOO
Calyptorhynchus lathami (Temminck)

Illustrated on page 109.

DESCRIPTION

Length 48 cm.
MALE head and underparts dark brown, merging into brownish-black on under tail-coverts; upperparts black, a faint brownish-green sheen on wings; central tail feathers black, lateral tail-feathers black with a broad subterminal band of bright red; bill greyish; iris dark brown; legs grey.
FEMALE tail band washed with yellow and divided by narrow black stripes; most birds have yellow feathers scattered throughout sides of head and neck.
IMMATURES similar to female, but with little or no yellow on head or neck; generally a few yellow spots on median and under wing-coverts; it is reported that some young males leave the nest with uniform red tail bands.
20 males   wing 332–370 (360.6) mm., tail 179–233 (218.5) mm.,
          exp. cul. 42–51 (46.1) mm., tars. 24–27 (25.1) mm.
20 females wing 317–360 (340.1) mm., tail 187–236 (211.4) mm.,
          exp. cul. 43–49 (45.6) mm., tars. 24–27 (25.1) mm.

DISTRIBUTION

Eastern Australia from central Queensland to eastern Victoria; an isolated, presumably relict, population on Kangaroo Island, South Australia.

GENERAL NOTES

There is a close association between Glossy Cockatoos and *Casuarina* trees, the seeds of which are their principal food, and unless on the move they are rarely found far from these trees. They inhabit dense mountain forests, temperate rainforest, coastal and dry woodland, and trees bordering water-courses. Their stronghold seems to be south-eastern Queensland and north-eastern New South Wales, where they are locally common though generally scarce. Elsewhere they are quite uncommon, but probably not as rare as is generally claimed. Throughout the coastal woodland they are more plentiful than Red-tailed Cockatoos, a species with which they are often confused.

    These cockatoos are usually seen in pairs, family parties or small groups. They rarely congregate in flocks and do not associate with other black cockatoos. The pair bond is strong and feeding groups are really loose aggregations of pairs. They are arboreal, spending most of the day feeding amongst the branches of *Casuarina* trees. Their presence is betrayed by the continual clicking of their mandibles as they tear apart cones. Underneath the trees the ground soon becomes littered with husks, twigs and leaves. While feeding they are tame and easy to approach, often allowing an observer to stand below the tree in which they are sitting. In the early morning they frequently perch on the topmost branches of tall dead trees and spend some time preening their feathers and stretching their wings.

    The flight is extremely buoyant with slow, shallow wingbeats. On long flights they fly high above the treetops. When coming to the ground to drink they glide on down-curved wings.

    They feed almost exclusively on seeds of casuarinas, particularly *Casuarina littoralis*. On Kangaroo

Island they have been seen feeding in *Casuarina stricta*. Seeds of *Eucalyptus*, *Acacia* and *Angophora* are also eaten and wood-boring insect larvae are extracted from *Casuarina* branches.

CALL A prolonged, wheezy *tarr-red . . . tarr-red*; when alarmed a series of sharp gutteral notes.

NESTING The breeding season is from March to August, eggs being most frequently found in April, May and June. The nest is in a hollow limb or hole in a tree, generally a tall dead tree standing in a forest clearing. Most nests are from 15 to 20 m. above the ground. The single egg is laid in a slight depression in a layer of decayed wood dust.

Our knowledge of the nesting behaviour is sketchy. Only the female broods and she sits very tightly. The male feeds her in the early morning and later afternoon. The incubation period has not been determined. For the first week after hatching the chick is closely brooded by the female, but thereafter is fed by both parents twice a day. They continue to feed it for some months after it has left the nest.

EGGS Ovate; a single egg in the H. L. White Collection measures 44.3 × 33.7 mm.

Genus CALLOCEPHALON Lesson

This monotypic genus is distinguished by the strange, forward-curving crest of soft, filamentary feathers. The lower mandible of the strongly curved bill is broad with a marked central indentation, almost certainly an adaptation for splitting open *Eucalyptus* seed-capsules. The tarsi are short and thick, a characteristic of an arboreal bird. The round-tipped wings are long and the squarish tail short. The cere is feathered.

Sexual dimorphism is pronounced. Both sexes incubate and care for the young.

1 Salmon-crested Cockatoo *Cacatua moluccensis*
QM. 011256 ad. ♂

2 White Cockatoo *Cacatua alba*
BM. 1901.10.5.32 ad. ♂

GANG-GANG COCKATOO
Callocephalon fimbriatum (Grant)

Illustrated on page 112.

DESCRIPTION

Length 34 cm.
MALE general plumage grey, feathers edged with pale greyish-white giving a barred appearance; head and crest orange-red; feathers of lower abdomen and under tail-coverts variably margined with orange-yellow; outer webs of wing-coverts strongly washed with dull green; primaries and tail dark grey; bill horn-coloured; iris dark brown; legs grey.
FEMALE crest and head grey; upperparts and tail barred with greyish-white; feathers of underparts broadly margined with orange and greenish-yellow.
IMMATURES resemble female, though males have the crest tipped with red and show red markings on forehead and crown; axillaries heavily barred with greyish-white; bill dark grey.
12 males   wing 241–260 (250.3) mm., tail 137–161 (149.9) mm.,
            exp. cul. 28–33 (31.2) mm., tars. 22–26 (23.3) mm.
10 females wing 249–267 (258.6) mm., tail 131–148 (137.2) mm.,
            exp. cul. 30–33 (31.2) mm.,tars. 22–25 (22.9) mm.

DISTRIBUTION

South-eastern Australia from eastern New South Wales through southern Victoria to the extreme south-east of South Australia; a rare vagrant to King Island and northern Tasmania. Introduced to Kangaroo Island, South Australia.

GENERAL NOTES

Gang-gang Cockatoos inhabit mountain forests and wooded valleys on the adjacent coastal plain. In northern and far southern New South Wales they are found in alpine woodland up to more than 2,000 m. During winter they descend to lower altitudes and move out into open forest, gardens and parklands. Their stronghold is southern New South Wales and eastern Victoria and there they are quite plentiful; elsewhere they are noticeably less numerous, becoming quite rare at the extremities of their range.

During the breeding season these cockatoos are found in pairs or family parties, but at other times they congregate in small flocks. Larger numbers often build up where there is an abundance of food; I have seen flocks of up to sixty feeding in clumps of berry-laden hawthorn bushes. They are arboreal and come to the ground only to drink or to examine fallen nuts and cones. When feeding amongst the branches of trees or shrubs they are oblivious to the approach of an intruder and can almost be touched. If disturbed they merely climb to a higher branch or fly to the next tree. For no apparent reason a feeding flock may suddenly leave a tree or bush, fly in wide circles overhead, screeching loudly all the while, then return to the same tree and continue feeding as if there had been no interruption. When rain or snow is falling they frequently fly in circles above the forest canopy, periodically swooping down through the treetops. During the hottest part of the day they either sit motionless for hours or sidle up to each other and indulge in intensive mutual preening.

The characteristic flight is heavy and laboured with slow, sweeping wingbeats. On short flights from one tree to the next the birds drop down toward the ground then rise up before alighting. At the end of long, high flights they spiral down, twisting and turning in the same way as do Galahs (*Eolophus roseicapillus*).

They feed on seeds, especially those of *Eucalyptus* and *Acacia*, berries, nuts, fruits and insects and their larvae. They are methodical feeders and will return each day to the same tree or bush until the food supply is exhausted. There is a continual noise as they crack open the seed-capsules with their strong bills and the ground underneath soon becomes littered with debris. In southern New South Wales I have seen them feeding on seeds of *Eucalyptus pauciflora*, *E. macrorrhyncha*, *E. cinerea* and *Acacia armata*. They regularly invade ornamental gardens in Canberra to attack seeds of Italian cypress (*Cupressus stricta*) and hawthorn (*Crataegus*) and *Pyracantha* berries (Forshaw, 1969b). Maddison (1910) found them eating larvae of the Emperor Gum Moth (*Artheraea eucalypti*). Crop contents from a freshly-killed bird picked up at Duntroon, Australian Capital Territory, comprised almost entirely seeds of *Crataegus monogyna* with a few seeds of a chenopod and a small caterpillar.

CALL A prolonged, rasping screech ending with an upward inflection; while feeding a soft 'growling'. The call cannot be mistaken for that of any other species.

NESTING The breeding season is from October to January. The nest is in a hole in the trunk or dead branch of a tall tree, preference being shown for a living eucalypt near water, and it is almost invariably at a great height. The birds enlarge the hollow by chewing at the sides and scraping out the chips. Two eggs are laid on a layer of chips and wood dust. Incubation lasts approximately thirty days and both sexes brood. The young leave the nest about seven weeks after hatching and are fed by the parents for a further four to six weeks. Young males acquire adult plumage over a period of three to four years (for details see Forshaw, 1969a).

EGGS Rounded-oval; 3 eggs, 35.8 (35.5–36.4) × 27.5 (26.6–28.2) mm. [H. L. White Coll.].

Goffin's Cockatoo *Cacatua goffini* **1**
RMNH. Cat. 3, Reg. 6620 ad. ♀

Little Corella *Cacatua sanguinea sanguinea* **2**
AM. 042316 ad. ♀

Long-billed Corella **3**
Cacatua tenuirostris tenuirostris
JMF. 22 ad. ♀

Genus EOLOPHUS Bonaparte

I believe that this monotypic genus is transitional between *Callocephalon* and *Cacatua*. Anatomically it closely resembles the latter, but Holyoak (1970c) has examined the cranial osteology and points out that there are structural peculiarities in the ear. Certain aspects of behaviour, particularly the flight pattern, suggest affinities with *Callocephalon*. Brereton and Immelmann (1962) note that in the method of head-scratching this bird deviates slightly from the pattern that is consistent in the Cacatuinae.

The species is a medium-sized, stocky bird with a striking pink and grey plumage. It has a short crest and a prominent naked periophthalmic ring. The cere is feathered. The round-tipped wings are long and the squarish tail short.

Sexual dimorphism is slight. Both sexes incubate and care for the young.

GALAH
Eolophus roseicapillus (Vieillot)

DESCRIPTION

Length 35 cm.
ADULTS forehead, crown and occiput white with a pink suffusion through bases of feathers; upperparts grey, very pale on rump and secondary wing-coverts; face, neck and most of underparts, including under wing-coverts, rose-pink; lower abdomen and vent pale grey; tail dark grey; naked periophthalmic ring dark greyish-red; bill horn-coloured; iris dark brown in male, pink-red in female; legs grey.
IMMATURES duller than adults; crown and breast strongly washed with grey; naked periophthalmic ring grey slightly tinted with pink; iris brown.

DISTRIBUTION

Australia generally, chiefly the interior; accidental to Tasmania.

SUBSPECIES

1. *E. r. roseicapillus* (Vieillot)
   10 males   wing 257–275 (266.9) mm., tail 135–161 (150.8) mm.,
             exp. cul. 24–30 (25.8) mm., tars. 25–27 (25.8) mm.
   10 females wing 248–282 (259.6) mm., tail 140–170 (151.2) mm.,
             exp. cul. 24–27 (25.1) mm., tars. 24–27 (25.6) mm.
   Occurs throughout eastern, central and northern Australia.

Illustrated on page 113.

2. *E. r. assimilis* (Mathews)
   ADULTS general plumage paler; crown more strongly suffused with pink; naked periophthalmic ring greyish-white.

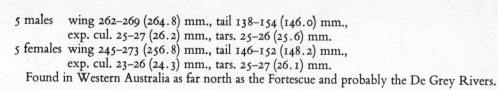

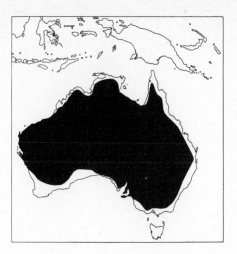

5 males   wing 262–269 (264.8) mm., tail 138–154 (146.0) mm.,
             exp. cul. 25–27 (26.2) mm., tars. 25–26 (25.6) mm.

5 females wing 245–273 (256.8) mm., tail 146–152 (148.2) mm.,
             exp. cul. 23–26 (24.3) mm., tars. 25–27 (26.1) mm.

Found in Western Australia as far north as the Fortescue and probably the De Grey Rivers.

3. E. r. kuhli (Mathews)

ADULTS similar to *assimilis*, but with grey-red periophthalmic ring.

5 males   wing 251–262 (256.6) mm., tail 125–136 (130.8) mm.,
             exp. cul. 24–25 (24.2) mm., tars. 23–25 (23.6) mm.

1 female wing 235 mm., tail 112 mm., exp. cul. 23 mm., tars. 23 mm.

Exact range is unknown, but birds from the Kimberley region, Western Australia, are probably best ascribed to this subspecies. I am provisionally accepting *kuhli* on the basis of periophthalmic ring colouration as noted on the label of one specimen from north-western Australia (AMNH. 619832). The type specimen is a very young bird and cannot be used for subspecific determination.

GENERAL NOTES

Galahs are abundant in most types of open country below 1,250 m. They are typical birds of the savannah woodlands and open grasslands of the interior, but have benefited from land-clearance and the cultivation of cereal crops and are now becoming increasingly plentiful in coastal and mountainous areas, particularly in the southern regions (for details see Forshaw, 1969a and 1969b). They are common in many urban districts, even nesting in trees in gardens and parklands. There is evidence of some local movement, the pattern and extent of which appear to be unpredictable and probably dependent on food availability and seasonal conditions.

They are usually seen in small parties or flocks, but large flocks of up to two or three hundred are common. They occasionally associate with other cockatoos and when feeding with Sulphur-crested Cockatoos (*Cacatua galerita*) respond to that bird's 'sentinel warning system', but at other times they are not shy. They spend many hours in the morning and late afternoon feeding on the ground, over which they move with a waddling gait. During the heat of the day they shelter in a tree or bush, idly stripping leaves and bark; they have been known to kill trees by removing bark from the trunks. After their evening drink they drift in small groups toward the roosting trees. At sunset they commence pre-roosting aerobatics, flying swiftly in and out through the treetops and swooping down toward the ground, screeching loudly all the while. They sometimes fly about and call at night.

The flight is moderately fast with full, rhythmic wing-beats. At the end of a long, high flight they spiral down, twisting and turning before finally darting into a tree. A flock of these cockatoos in flight is a most impressive sight as the sun highlights first the rose-pink underparts and then the soft grey of the back and wings.

Their food is seeds, grain, roots, green shoots, leaf buds and insects and their larvae. They eat sprouting shoots of wheat and attack both ripening crops and bagged grain, causing considerable damage. At Cunnamulla, Queensland, Allen (1950) investigated the feeding habits of Galahs over a period of twelve months. He found that they were feeding on seeds of grasses, mainly western button grass (*Dactyloctenium radulans*), Flinders grass (*Iseilema membranaceum*), and Mitchell grass (*Astrebla lappacea*), and each bird consumed about 15 to 20 gms. daily. Crop contents from four birds collected at Mangalore, Victoria, comprised wheat grains and seeds, including those of cape weed (*Cryptostemma calendulaceum*) and storksbill (*Erodium cicutarium*).

CALL In flight a shrill, disyllabic screech bordering on a cry; when alarmed a series of sharp shrieks. All call-notes are characteristic of the species.

NESTING The courtship display is simple and generally includes aerobatics. The male, with his crest raised and head weaving slightly from side to side, struts along a branch toward the female and utters soft, chattering notes as he approaches. The female leaves the branch and, pursued by the male, flies off, darting in and out through the trees and calling excitedly. They alight in another tree where the display is repeated and followed by mutual preening.

The breeding season varies from June to November in the north of the continent to August to January in the south. The nest is in a hollow limb or hole in a tree, generally a eucalypt growing near water. Bark is stripped from around the entrance and the bottom is lined with a layer of *Eucalyptus* leaves on which are laid two to five, normally three, eggs. Incubation lasts approximately four weeks and both parents brood. The young leave the nest five to six weeks after hatching and are fed by the parents for a further two to three weeks. Adult plumage is acquired within the first year.

EGGS Ovate; 9 eggs, 35.3 (34.5–36.2) × 26.5 (26.0–27.2) mm. [H. L. White Coll.].

Red-vented Cockatoo *Cacatua haematuropygia* 1
RMNH. Cat. 6 ad. ♀

Ducorp's Cockatoo *Cacatua ducorps* 2
CSIRO. 3230 ad. ♂

Genus CACATUA Vieillot

The so-called 'white cockatoos' belong to this genus. Their plumage is predominantly white or pale salmon-pink. They are medium to large birds with short, squarish tails and long round-tipped wings. The sexes are alike and young birds resemble adults.

There is an interesting transitional pattern in crest formation. The crests of *leadbeateri, sulphurea* and *galerita* comprise narrow, elongated, forward-curving feathers. In *ophthalmica* these feathers are broader, curve backwards, and are anteriorly bordered by elongated crown feathers; this formation is intermediate between the narrow, forward-curving and the broad, backward-curving types. The backward-curving crests of *moluccensis* and *alba* consist of very broad, elongated crown feathers. In the remaining species the formation is the same, but both the broadening and the elongation are much reduced, the least in *haematuropygia* and the most in *tenuirostris*.

MAJOR MITCHELL'S COCKATOO
Cacatua leadbeateri (Vigors)

DESCRIPTION

Length 35 cm.
ADULTS crown white suffused with salmon-pink; narrow, forward-curving crest scarlet tipped with white and with a central band of yellow, broader in females; face, neck, breast and upper abdomen salmon-pink; under wing-coverts slightly darker than breast; upperparts, tail and lower underparts white; undersides of flight and tail-feathers basally marked with deep salmon-pink; bill white; iris dark brown in males, reddish-pink in females; legs grey.
IMMATURES resemble adults; iris pale brown.

DISTRIBUTION

Interior of Australia, except the north-eastern and far south-western regions.

SUBSPECIES

1. *C. l. leadbeateri* (Vigors)   *Illustrated on page 116.*
   12 males   wing 248–280 (268.2) mm., tail 126–146 (136.6) mm.,
                  exp. cul. 29–32 (31.2) mm., tars. 24–28 (25.9) mm.
   9 females   wing 265–279 (269.9) mm., tail 129–165 (143.3) mm.,
                  exp. cul. 29–31 (30.3) mm., tars. 24–28 (24.9) mm.
   Occurs throughout the range of the species, except in mid-western Australia where it is replaced by *mollis*.

2. *C. l. mollis* (Mathews)
   ADULTS crest darker red and with little or no yellow in centre.
   2 males   wing 251–265 (258.0) mm., tail 130–135 (132.5) mm.,
                  exp. cul. 30–32 (31.0) mm., tars. 25 (25.0) mm.
   1 female   wing 265 mm., tail 137 mm.,
                  exp. cul. 30 mm., tars. 25 mm.
   Exact range undetermined; at present known only from the Carnamah district, Western Australia. I am provisionally accepting this race on the basis of darker crest colouration; the absence of yellow from the crest is occasionally seen in birds from eastern and southern Australia.

GENERAL NOTES

Major Mitchell's Cockatoo inhabits sparsely timbered grasslands, trees surrounding cereal paddocks or bordering watercourses, dry *Acacia* scrublands, and arid and semi-arid woodland, including mallee. It is generally scarce, but locally common in some districts. I believe that in the eastern States there has been a widespread decline in numbers since European settlement, due mainly to destruction of habitat. Initially, the birds may have benefited from the increase of watering places that accompanied the spread of pastoral activities, but this has probably been more than outweighed by the large-scale clearance of mallee and dry scrublands. In less arid areas these cockatoos seem to be sedentary in districts where there is permanent water. Elsewhere they are nomadic and in times of drought spectacular irruptions have been reported, presumably the result of general movements to more favourable areas. Parker (1970) points out that in southern parts of the Northern Territory, where both this species and the Little Corella (*C. sanguinea*) are common, the two show a remarkable degree of allopatry. However, it appears the where one or both species are not common the allopatry may be less pronounced; in western New South Wales I have seen mixed flocks.

These cockatoos are usually seen in pairs or small parties, sometimes in the company of Galahs (*Eolophus roseicapillus*) or Little Corellas. They rarely congregate in large flocks. Most of the day is spent on the ground or in trees and shrubs feeding on seeds. They are rather wary and will seldom allow a close approach. However, when disturbed they do not move far, generally realighting on the ground or in a tree a short distance away. They drink in the early morning and late afternoon, sometimes arriving at the waterhole before sunrise, but during very hot weather return visits may be made throughout the day. Like other cockatoos they have the habit of stripping leaves and bark from trees in which they are roosting. The flight consists of flapping wingbeats alternated with brief periods of gliding. They rarely fly high and even when travelling long distances prefer to move by a series of short flights.

Cockatiel *Nymphicus hollandicus* 1
AM. 028379 ad. ♂

Cockatiel *Nymphicus hollandicus* 2
AM. 028383 ad. ♀

They feed on seeds, nuts, fruits, berries and roots. They are particularly fond of *Callitris* and *Acacia* seeds, which they procure in the trees and on the ground underneath. In western New South Wales I have seen them feeding on seeds of paddy melons (*Cucumis myriocarpus*) and wild bitter melons (*Citrullus lanatus*) after the fruits have been split open by the summer heat. They will attack ripening wheat crops and are fond of some cultivated nuts and fruits, especially almonds.

CALL A disyllabic, quavering cry, similar to, though not as raucous as, the call of the Little Corella; when alarmed three or four harsh screeches.

NESTING When displaying the male struts along a branch towards the female. With crest raised he bobs his head up and down and swishes it from side to side in a figure-eight movement; sometimes he will lift his wings to show the richly coloured undersides. If the female becomes excited she may raise her crest and bow low towards the male.

The breeding season lasts from August to December and the nest is in a hollow limb or hole in a tree. The bottom of the hollow is lined with decayed wood dust and with strips of bark removed by the birds from around the entrance. A normal clutch comprises two to four eggs. Incubation is of approximately thirty days duration and both sexes brood, the male usually sitting during the day and the female at night. Both parents care for the young. About six to eight weeks after hatching the young birds leave the nest, but remain with the parents as a family group.

EGGS Ovate; 3 eggs, 39.1 (37.5–39.4) × 29.5 (29.0–30.0) mm. [H. L. White Coll.].

Kea *Nestor notabilis*
AM. 030418 ad. ♂

LESSER SULPHUR-CRESTED COCKATOO
Cacatua sulphurea (Gmelin)

DESCRIPTION

Length 33 cm.
ADULTS general plumage white; ear-coverts bright yellow; bases to feathers of neck and underparts yellow; undersides of flight and tail-feathers strongly suffused with yellow; narrow forward-curving crest yellow; naked periophthalmic ring creamy-white; bill grey-black; iris dark brown in males, brownish-red in females; legs dark grey.
IMMATURES similar to adults; iris pale grey.

DISTRIBUTION

Celebes and adjacent Buton Island, Sunda Islands, and islands in the Flores and Java Seas, Indonesia; probably introduced to Singapore.

SUBSPECIES

1. *C. s. sulphurea* (Gmelin)   *Illustrated on page 116.*
   10 males   wing 221–245 (231.9) mm., tail 106–115 (111.4) mm.,
              exp. cul. 38–39 (38.6) mm., tars. 22–25 (23.9) mm.
   10 females wing 217–242 (226.4) mm., tail 99–113 (107.6) mm.,
              exp. cul. 34–36 (35.1) mm., tars. 22–25 (23.7) mm.
   Confined to the Celebes and adjacent Buton Island; probably introduced to Singapore.

2. *C. s. djampeana* Hartert
   ADULTS similar to *sulphurea*, but with a smaller bill.
   6 males   wing 215–234 (225.2) mm., tail 98–112 (107.5) mm.,
              exp. cul. 33–38 (34.3) mm., tars. 22–24 (22.7) mm.
   10 females wing 211–227 (218.7) mm., tail 102–113 (107.3) mm.,
              exp. cul. 29–34 (31.3) mm., tars. 21–23 (22.0) mm.
   Occurs on the Islands of Alor, Pantar, Djampea, Kalao, Kalao tua, Madu and Kaju adi, and in the Tukangbesi Islands.

3. *C. s. abbotti* (Oberholser)
   ADULTS like *occidentalis*, but markedly larger.
   5 males   wing 263–273 (270.2) mm., tail 125–135 (129.8) mm.,
              exp. cul. 34–38 (35.4) mm., tars. 25–27 (25.8) mm.
   3 females wing 258–268 (262.0) mm., tail 130–145 (137.3) mm.,
              exp. cul. 33–35 (33.7) mm., tars. 22–26 (23.7) mm.
   Restricted to Solombo Besar Island in the Java Sea.

4. *C. s. occidentalis* Hartert
   ADULTS ear-coverts pale yellow; less yellow on bases to feathers of hindneck and underparts.
   8 males   wing 220–235 (226.5) mm., tail 103–117 (110.1) mm.,
              exp. cul. 36–38 (36.9) mm., tars. 22–25 (23.1) mm.
   7 females wing 212–228 (219.4) mm., tail 104–109 (106.4) mm.,
              exp. cul. 32–35 (34.0) mm., tars. 21–24 (22.6) mm.
   Found on Lombok, Sumbawa and Flores, and on Noesa Penida Island.

5. *C. s. parvula* (Bonaparte)
ADULTS like *occidentalis*, but with a smaller bill.
3 males   wing 227–231 (229.7) mm., tail 110–117 (112.7) mm.,
       exp. cul. 31–35 (32.7) mm., tars. 22–23 (22.7) mm.
6 females   wing 220–229 (225.2) mm., tail 110–120 (115.0) mm.,
       exp. cul. 30–32 (31.2) mm., tars. 21–24 (22.2) mm.
    Confined to Timor and neighbouring Samao Island.

6. *C. s. citrinocristata* (Fraser)   *Illustrated on page 116.*
ADULTS similar to *occidentalis*, but crest orange instead of yellow; orange ear-coverts.
8 males   wing 244–257 (251.6) mm., tail 110–130 (120.9) mm.,
       exp. cul. 35–39 (37.3) mm., tars. 24–27 (25.3) mm.
6 females   wing 231–254 (245.8) mm., tail 116–130 (122.3) mm.,
       exp. cul. 31–33 (32.0) mm., tars. 23–25 (23.7) mm.
    Occurs only on Sumba.

Illustrated on page 116.

GENERAL NOTES

Heinrich points out that the Lesser Sulphur-crested Cockatoo is very unevenly distributed in the Celebes (in Stresemann, 1941). He found that in some regions, such as the montane area between Maros and Watampone in the south and the hilly country west of the Latimodjong Mountains, it was a common bird, but in other regions was quite scarce and was absent altogether from many parts of the island. On the humid coastal plains and in the low hill-country up to about 500 m. it inhabited open woodland, cultivated fields and the edges of forest, but rarely penetrated into the interior of the forest. Around villages it was often seen in coconut palms. On Buton de Haan collected specimens in a village near the seashore and in teak forest (in van Bemmel and Voous, 1951). On Lombok, Sumbawa and Flores it is common in forests and agricultural country below 800 m., and less common up to 1,200 m. (Rensch, 1931). On Timor Stein collected specimens at 160 m. and 300 m. and on Sumba near the coast and at about 500 m. (in Mayr, 1944). In May 1969, Rowley saw small parties of cockatoos in a patch of tall rainforest in the Singapore Botanic Gardens; he believes that they were this species, not *C. galerita* (pers. comm., 1969).

These cockatoos are noisy, conspicuous birds. De Haan noted that on Buton when the forest was fresh and green their white plumage made the birds most obvious, but in the dry season when everything was pale and brown they were less striking. They are generally seen in pairs or small flocks, but larger numbers may congregate to feed. They feed mainly in the treetops, but will come to the ground. The flight is similar to that of the Sulphur-crested Cockatoo.

Food consists of seeds, nuts, berries, fruits and probably blossoms. De Haan reports that they are troublesome birds, because they destroy young fruits of *Ceiba* and *Gossampinus*, though very few are eaten, and will attack coconuts, even peeling mature nuts.

CALL A raucous screeching (Rensch, 1931), also a loud *kek-kek-kek* (Coomans de Ruiter, 1951).

NESTING Some of the specimens collected by de Haan in September and October were in breeding condition. The nest is in a hollow in a tree, and on Buton *Gossampinus* trees are favoured.

Details of breeding in captivity have been given by Allen (1924) and Kendall (1956). Up to three eggs were laid and incubation lasted about twenty-four days. Both sexes incubated, the male sitting during the day. The young birds left the nest approximately ten weeks after hatching.

EGGS Elliptical; 7 eggs, 41.2 (38.1–44.0) × 27.1 (25.7–28.4) mm. [Schönwetter, 1964].

SULPHUR-CRESTED COCKATOO
Cacatua galerita (Latham)

DESCRIPTION

Length 50 cm.
ADULTS general plumage white; ear-coverts and bases to feathers of cheeks and throat pale yellow; narrow forward-curving crest yellow; undersides of flight and tail feathers strongly washed with yellow; naked periophthalmic ring white; bill dark grey; iris dark brown in males, reddish-brown in females; legs dark grey.
IMMATURES similar to adults; very young birds have faint tinges of grey on crown, back and wings; iris brown.

DISTRIBUTION

New Guinea, including most offshore islands, Aru Islands, and northern and eastern Australia; introduced to New Zealand, the Palau Islands, and to Ceramlaut and Goramlaut, Indonesia.

SUBSPECIES

1. *C. g. galerita* (Latham)   *Illustrated on page 117.*
20 males   wing 302–391 (335.5) mm., tail 207–231 (217.2) mm.,
       exp. cul. 39–50 (44.1) mm., tars. 31–35 (32.9) mm.
20 females   wing 295–385 (337.6) mm., tail 200–236 (215.4) mm.,
       exp. cul. 34–48 (42.0) mm., tars. 30–33 (31.6) mm.
    Found in eastern and south-eastern Australia from Cape York Peninsula to King Island and

Illustrated on page 117.

Tasmania, and across to south-eastern South Australia; this is almost certainly the race introduced to New Zealand.

2. *C. g. fitzroyi* (Mathews)
ADULTS little yellow on ear-coverts and bases to feathers of cheeks and throat; naked periophthalmic ring pale plue (Lendon, 1965); blunt bill broader than in *galerita*.
10 males   wing 316–354 (332.4) mm., tail 187–234 (206.4) mm.,
           exp. cul. 38–45 (40.4) mm., tars. 31–34 (32.4) mm.
11 females wing 295–355 (328.0) mm., tail 185–221 (198.3) mm.,
           exp. cul. 36–40 (38.1) mm., tars. 31–33 (31.8) mm.
Distributed across northern Australia, including larger offshore islands, from the Fitzroy River, Western Australia, east to the Gulf of Carpentaria, where it meets *galerita*.

3. *C. g. triton* Temminck
ADULTS crest feathers broader and more rounded than in *galerita*; naked periophthalmic ring blue.
10 males   wing 261–347 (298.5) mm., tail 135–185 (154.6) mm.,
           exp. cul. 36–45 (41.9) mm., tars. 26–36 (30.6) mm.
10 females wing 272–325 (300.7) mm., tail 135–170 (154.5) mm.,
           exp. cul. 33–42 (37.4) mm., tars. 26–36 (30.2) mm.
Occurs on the western Papuan Islands, West Irian, throughout New Guinea, the islands in Geelvink Bay, the D'Entrecasteaux and Louisiade Archipelagos, and islands in the Trobriand and Woodlark Groups; introduced to Ceramlaut and Goramlaut, Indonesia, and to the Palau Islands in the Pacific.

4. *C. g. eleonora* Finsch
ADULTS similar to *triton*, but with a markedly smaller bill.
7 males   wing 267–292 (280.6) mm., tail 129–144 (136.7) mm.,
          exp. çul. 33–37 (34.1) mm., tars. 25–29 (26.4) mm.
9 females wing 261–291 (279.9) mm., tail 121–144 (132.4) mm.,
          exp. cul. 32–37 (33.6) mm., tars. 25–28 (26.3) mm.
Restricted to the Aru Islands, Indonesia. I have followed Mees (in press) in accepting this subspecies.

GENERAL NOTES   Rand and Gilliard (1967) say that in New Guinea the Sulphur-crested Cockatoo is fairly common in lowland forest and savannah country up to 1,400 m. Ripley (1964) gained the impression that in the twenty-five years since he first visited New Guinea the cockatoos had become less common and far more local possibly due in part to the strong demand for feathers, presumably for use in adornments of various kinds. I saw very few of these birds in New Guinea and was told by resident ornithologists that they are still common in remote areas, but are persistently hunted in the neighbourhood of major towns and villages. In Australia they are common inhabitants of forest, open woodland and cultivated farmlands, and are seldom found far from water. In New Zealand they are now well-established in two localities near the west coast of the North Island (Falla *et al.*, 1966), while on the Palau Islands they appear to be spreading and breeding (Ripley, 1951). The species is largely sedentary, but moves freely between offshore islands along parts of the Australian coastline, and there seems to be some altitudinal movement in the southern highlands of New South Wales.

These noisy, conspicuous birds are usually found in pairs or small family parties during the breeding season, and at other times in flocks, sometimes comprising hundreds of birds. They are wary and difficult to approach. In eastern Australia, wherever they frequent open country, the so-called 'sentinel warning system' is well-established. While the flock is feeding on the ground a few individuals remain perched atop surrounding trees. At the approach of danger these 'sentinels' rise into the air screeching loudly and the entire flock flies off. In New Guinea and northern Australia, where the cockatoos are mainly arboreal and rarely associate in large flocks, this 'warning system' has not been observed.

Each flock has its roosting site and this is rarely deserted even though long flights to and from feeding areas may become necessary. On Biak Island, behind the village of Korrido, Ripley found a roost in one or two lofty trees standing at the edge of a clearing (in Mayr and Meyer de Schauensee, 1939a). With much screeching and screaming the birds leave the roosting trees at sunrise and, after drinking at a nearby watering place, fly to the feeding grounds where they remain during the day. During the hottest part of the day they shelter in trees, idly nibbling the leaves or stripping away bark. Towards dusk they return to the roosting trees and for some time continue to jostle and squabble for perching positions; it is well after dark before the screeching gives way to occasional squawks and finally to silence.

The characteristic flight comprises a series of rapid, shallow wingbeats interspersed with gliding. When travelling to and from the roosting site they fly at a considerable height, gliding down to the trees in wide, sweeping circles.

They feed on seeds, fruits, berries, nuts, flowers, leaf buds, roots, and insects and their larvae. They are troublesome pests in cereal-growing districts, digging up newly-sown seed and raiding ripening crops; they also damage haystacks and attack bagged grain stacked in paddocks or at rail terminals awaiting transportation. On the other hand they eat the seeds of many weed pests, including Scotch thistle (*Onopordon acanthium*) and Noogoora burr (*Xanthium chinense*). Near

Adelaide, South Australia, they have been observed feeding on seeds of grass-trees (*Xanthorrhoea semiplana*) and the flowering heads of milk thistle (*Silybum marianum*). About Canberra I have frequently seen them eating hawthorn berries (*Crataegus monogyna*). Stomachs from three birds collected near Nowra, New South Wales, contained numerous seeds, including those of *Sorghum vulgare*, vegetable matter and small pieces of quartz (Cleland, 1918).

CALL A harsh, raucous screech terminating with a slight upward inflection; when alarmed a series of abrupt, gutteral screeches and while feeding an occasional sharp squawk or a shrill disyllabic whistle. I have noticed that the call of *triton* is softer than that of *galerita* and is more like an alternating cry than a screech.

NESTING The courtship display is simple and brief. The male struts along a branch towards the female. With crest raised he bobs his head up and down and swishes it from side to side in a figure-eight movement, uttering soft, chattering notes all the while. Mutual preening and touching of bills then follow.

The breeding season is somewhat variable. In southern Australia it is from August to January and in the north from May to September. In southern New Guinea a nest containing a fully fledged young bird was found in late November (Rand, 1942a), while on the northern slopes of the Snow Mountains, West Irian, a female in breeding condition was collected in February and another in March (Rand, 1942b). The nest is in a hollow limb or hole in a tree, generally high up in a tree near water. Nests have also been found in holes in cliffs and on top of a haystack. The two or three eggs are laid on decayed wood dust lining the bottom of the hollow. Incubation lasts approximately thirty days and both sexes brood. The young birds vacate the nest six to nine weeks after hatching.

EGGS Elliptical; 5 eggs, 46.5 (45.0–48.9) × 33.5 (32.0–34.4) mm. [H. L. White Coll.].

BLUE-EYED COCKATOO
Cacatua ophthalmica Sclater

Illustrated on page 117.

DESCRIPTION

Length 50 cm.
ADULTS general plumage white; backward-curving crest yellow; ear-coverts and bases to feathers of throat and cheeks suffused with yellow; undersides of flight and tail feathers washed with yellow; naked periophthalmic ring blue; bill grey-black; iris dark brown in male, reddish-brown in female; legs grey.
IMMATURES like adults.
8 males   wing 297–316 (305.8) mm., tail 163–179 (170.3) mm.,
           exp. cul. 42–45 (43.8) mm., tars. 29–32 (31.0) mm.
8 females wing 285–302 (294.0) mm., tail 149–167 (158.9) mm.,
           exp. cul. 37–45 (40.7) mm., tars. 30–33 (31.3) mm.

DISTRIBUTION

New Britain and New Ireland in the Bismarck Archipelago.

GENERAL NOTES

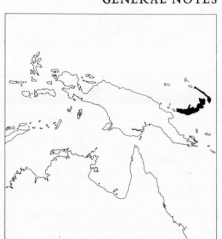

Donaghey says that the Blue-eyed Cockatoo is common in the lowland primary forests and the foothills of New Britain up to about 1,000 m. (*in litt.*, 1970). It congregates in flocks of from ten to twenty birds and is quite conspicuous, particularly towards dusk when parties fly about above the forest screeching loudly. In the Whiteman Mountains, New Britain, Gilliard found it to be abundant in tropical rainforest below 1,000 m. and becoming rare at higher altitudes (Gilliard and LeCroy, 1967a). It was usually seen in pairs flying above the forest canopy, screeching all the while. A lone bird was seen to fly down a steep mountain slope, descending nearly 300 m. before turning and twisting as though to reduce speed and disappearing into a forested canyon. The general habits are almost certainly similar to those of the Sulphur-crested Cockatoo (*C. galerita*), a species to which it is obviously very closely related. The flight consists of fluttering wingbeats interspersed with gliding.

It feeds on seeds, nuts, fruits, berries and probably insects and their larvae.

CALL A raucous, screaming note.

NESTING No details of nesting habits in the wild have been recorded.

Griffiths (1965) reports a successful breeding in captivity. Two eggs were laid, but only one hatched. The incubation period was not determined, and the chick remained in the nest for more than four months.

EGGS Elliptical; one egg measures 52.0 × 31.5 mm., and this seems abnormally large. [Schönwetter, 1964].

SALMON-CRESTED COCKATOO
Cacatua moluccensis (Gmelin)

Illustrated on page 120.

DESCRIPTION

Length 52 cm.
ADULTS general plumage pale salmon-pink; undersides of broad, backward-curving crest deep salmon-pink; undersides of flight feathers basally washed with deep salmon-pink; undersides of tail feathers basally washed with yellow-orange and deep pink; naked periophthalmic ring white tinted with blue; bill grey-black; iris dark brown; legs grey.
IMMATURES similar to adults.
10 males   wing 292–313 (303.3) mm., tail 159–182 (173.1) mm.,
            exp. cul. 42–54 (47.2) mm., tars. 33–35 (34.3) mm.
8 females wing 288–328 (301.4) mm., tail 162–189 (172.5) mm.,
            exp. cul. 44–51 (46.9) mm., tars. 33–34 (33.6) mm.

DISTRIBUTION

Ceram, Saparua and Haruku in the southern Moluccas, Indonesia; introduced to Amboina, also in the southern Moluccas.

GENERAL NOTES

The Salmon-crested Cockatoo is a popular bird in captivity, yet little has been recorded of its habits in the wild. Stresemann (1914) found that on Ceram it appeared to be common in coastal areas, but in the central mountains below 1,000 m. he encountered only small numbers. It is considered to be a pest in coconut plantations. The flight consists of a few rapid wingbeats followed by gliding and then another few wingbeats.
  Food consists of seeds, nuts, fruits, berries, and possibly insects and their larvae. The cockatoos attack young coconuts, chewing through the outer layers to get at the 'milk' and soft pulp.

CALL A loud, quavering cry (in captivity); also a shrill screech.

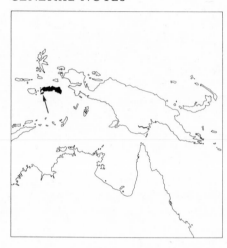

NESTING In early May Stresemann observed a pair of cockatoos in attendance at a nesting hollow about 25 m. up in the trunk of a living tree. No details of the nesting behaviour have been recorded. Lint (1951) reports that in captivity a chick hatched after an incubation of thirty days; it was removed from the nest and reared artificially. Reporting on the progress of a breeding in captivity, O'Connor (1971) states that once incubation commenced both parents were never out of the nest at the same time; the male usually, but not always, emerged at about dusk to roost in the shelter, but during the day both birds remained in the nest box at all times except when feeding.

EGGS Elliptical; 7 eggs, 50.0 (47.8–51.3) × 33.4 (32.4–34.5) mm. [Schönwetter, 1964].

WHITE COCKATOO
Cacatua alba (P. L. S. Müller)

Illustrated on page 120.

DESCRIPTION

Length 46 cm.
ADULTS general plumage white, including broad, backward-curving crest; undersides of flight feathers and tail feathers basally suffused with yellow; naked periophthalmic ring yellowish-white; bill grey-black; iris dark brown in male, reddish brown in female; legs grey.
IMMATURES like adults.
15 males   wing 272–312 (288.8) mm., tail 120–166 (148.8) mm.,
            exp. cul. 34–45 (40.8) mm., tars. 27–32 (29.5) mm.
14 females wing 252–301 (284.8) mm., tail 126–168 (146.1) mm.,
            exp. cul. 36–45 (40.9) mm., tars. 26–33 (28.8) mm.

DISTRIBUTION

Obi, Batjan, Halmahera, Ternate and Tidore in the central and northern Moluccas, Indonesia.

GENERAL NOTES

There is little recorded information on the habits of the White Cockatoo. It is said to be a fairly common bird and is generally seen in pairs or small parties flying above the treetops or sitting in the topmost branches of tall trees. Its white plumage and discordant screeching make it most conspicuous.
  The diet comprises seeds, fruits, nuts, berries and possibly insects and their larvae.

CALL A loud, raucous screech.

NESTING Guinn (1970) gives details of a successful breeding in captivity. Two eggs were laid and both hatched, but only one chick was reared. Incubation lasted about four weeks and both parents brooded. The young bird left the nest three months after hatching. Risdon (1968) also reports a successful breeding in captivity and notes that the young bird left the nest only two months after hatching. I know of no nesting records from the wild.

EGGS Elliptical; 2 eggs, 40.8 (40.5–41.0) × 30.8 (30.0–31.6) mm. [Berlin Mus. Coll.].

RED-VENTED COCKATOO
Cacatua haematuropygia (P. L. S. Müller)

Illustrated on page 124.

Length 31 cm.
ADULTS general plumage white; ear-coverts tinged with yellowish-pink; bases to feathers of crest yellow and rose-pink; undersides of flight feathers pale yellow; under tail-coverts orange-red; undersides of tail-feathers deep yellow; naked periophthalmic ring white, sometimes tinted with blue; bill greyish-white; iris dark brown in male, brownish-red in female; legs grey.
IMMATURES similar to adults; iris brown.
14 males   wing 209–231 (218.8) mm., tail 100–110 (105.1) mm.,
     exp. cul. 25–29 (27.1) mm., tars. 22–24 (23.2) mm.
15 females   wing 201–230 (210.9) mm., tail 100–110 (103.1) mm.,
     exp. cul. 23–28 (25.8) mm., tars. 22–24 (22.6) mm.

DISTRIBUTION Philippine Islands, including Palawan group in the Sulu Sea.

GENERAL NOTES The Red-vented Cockatoo is common throughout the Philippines and in the Palawan group (Delacour and Mayr, 1946). Rabor found that on Siquijor Island it frequented forest, forest edge, and secondary growth, and visited corn fields to raid ripening crops (Rand and Rabor, 1960). It is a noisy bird and is usually seen in pairs or small parties of up to about eight, but at times large numbers may congregate to feed. Potter (1953) notes that the flight is swift and direct with rapid wingbeats, though on three occasions he saw birds escape from pursuing hawks by rapid weaving and darting.

Food consists of seeds, fruits, nuts and berries. A specimen collected by Potter on Calicoan Island had its crop full of white rectangular seeds 18 mm. in length. These cockatoos attack ripening corn and may cause considerable damage to crops.

CALL A harsh, disyllabic, rasping note (in captivity).

NESTING On Masbate Island nestlings have been taken in May (in Hachisuka, 1934), while on Calicoan Island in late June Potter heard young in a nest in a hollow limb of a tree about 6 m. from the ground. No details of the nesting behaviour have been recorded.

EGGS Elliptical; one egg in the British Museum measures 37.7 × 26.7 mm. [Harrison and Holyoak, 1970].

GOFFIN'S COCKATOO
Cacatua goffini (Finsch)

Illustrated on page 121.

Length 32 cm.
ADULTS general plumage white; lores and bases to feathers of head salmon-pink; ear-coverts tinted with pale yellow; undersides of flight and tail feathers washed with yellow; naked periophthalmic ring white; bill greyish-white; iris dark brown in male, reddish-brown in female; legs grey.
IMMATURES undescribed.
7 males   wing 212–238 (221.0) mm., tail 100–114 (105.9) mm.,
     exp. cul. 29–33 (31.3) mm., tars. 23–25 (23.9) mm.
8 females   wing 210–222 (213.9) mm., tail 95–112 (100.8) mm.,
     exp. cul. 27–29 (28.3) mm., tars. 22–25 (23.0) mm.

DISTRIBUTION Tanimbar Islands, Indonesia; probably introduced to Tual in the Kai Islands, Indonesia.

GENERAL NOTES Peters (1937) and van Bemmel (1948) treat this species as a race of *C. sanguinea*. In my *Australian Parrots* I followed this arrangement, but after examining all species in *Cacatua* I have come to the conclusion that if *goffini* is considered to be conspecific with *sanguinea* then *ducorps* must also be included. Therefore, for the time being I have treated all three as specifically distinct.
Nothing has been recorded of the habits of Goffin's Cockatoo, but they are probably similar to those of the Little Corella (*C. sanguinea*).

CALL Undescribed.

NESTING No records.

EGGS Rounded; 4 eggs, 38.4 (37.6–39.6) × 28.4 (27.8–29.7) mm. [British and Berlin Mus. Colls.].

LITTLE CORELLA
Cacatua sanguinea Gould

DESCRIPTION Length 38 cm.
ADULTS general plumage white; lores and bases to feathers of crown, cheeks and throat salmon-pink; undersides of flight and tail feathers suffused with yellow; greyish-blue naked periophthalmic ring, more extensive under eye; bill white; iris dark brown; legs grey.
IMMATURES similar to adults; naked periophthalmic ring less extensive under eye.

DISTRIBUTION Northern, north-western and the interior of eastern Australia, and southern New Guinea.

SUBSPECIES 1. *C. s. sanguinea* Gould   *Illustrated on page 121.*
    11 males   wing 257–280 (267.8) mm., tail 129–160 (144.2) mm.,
              exp. cul. 29–34 (31.1) mm., tars. 28–32 (29.3) mm.
    10 females wing 254–276 (266.9) mm., tail 130–166 (149.0) mm.,
              exp. cul. 30–33 (31.3) mm., tars. 28–32 (30.1) mm.
    Distributed throughout the interior of eastern Australia, and in north-western and northern Australia, except on Cape York Peninsula and along the Gulf of Carpentaria.

    2. *C. s. normantoni* (Mathews)
    ADULTS similar to *sanguinea*, but smaller.
    6 males   wing 222–255 (240.4) mm., tail 105–120 (112.0) mm.,
              exp. cul. 28–32 (29.8) mm., tars. 23–26 (24.8) mm.
    4 females wing 239–248 (244.0) mm., tail 109–112 (110.3) mm.,
              exp. cul. 28–29 (28.8) mm., tars. 23–26 (24.8) mm.
    Occurs in southern New Guinea, and on Cape York Peninsula and around the Gulf of Carpentaria in northern Queensland.

GENERAL NOTES

In southern New Guinea Little Corellas have been recorded only in the Merauke district, West Irian, where large flocks have been seen in ricefields and along the Kumbe River (Hoogerwerf, 1964). In Australia they inhabit most types of open country, but are particularly abundant in eucalypts bordering watercourses; in the north they have been found in estuarine mangroves. They are plentiful throughout most of their range and seem to be increasing in numbers as well as extending their range southward. Like the Galah (*Eolophus roseicapillus*) they have benefited from the increase of watering places brought about by the spread of pastoral activities. They are nomadic to some extent and apart from sightings obviously related to the overall southward spread, which I have already documented (see Forshaw, 1969a), birds are occasionally seen well outside the normal range. Populations almost certainly originating from aviary escapees have become established near some major cities.

These cockatoos are noisy, conspicuous birds and are usually seen in flocks, which outside the breeding season may contain hundreds or even thousands of birds. When large flocks alight the trees acquire an immediate 'white foliage'. Their habit of invariably roosting near water was well known to early travellers, who often found waterholes by following the returning flocks at dusk. The cockatoos are astir very early and may leave the roosting trees well before sunrise. They gather at a waterhole to drink before moving out on to the open plains, where they spend most of the morning on the ground feeding on grass seeds. When a large flock is feeding on the ground all birds move along in the same direction and those at the rear are continually rising and flying up to the front. During the hottest part of the day they shelter in trees, passing the time stripping leaves and nibbling bark. They feed again in the late afternoon, and towards sunset return to the roosting trees. In flight flapping wingbeats are interspersed with brief periods of gliding.

Seeds, nuts, fruits, berries, flowers, roots and insects and their larvae make up the diet. In northern Australia the birds have been seen feeding on blossoms of *Melaleuca leucadendron*, seeds of Mitchell grass (*Astrebla lappacea*), and on roots which they dig up from around the edges of drying waterholes. In western New South Wales I have watched them eating seeds of paddy melons (*Cucumis myriocarpus*) and wild bitter melons (*Citrullus lanatus*). Along the Kumbe River, West Irian, Hoogerwerf saw them in the company of Red-winged Parrots (*Aprosmictus erythropterus*) feeding on seeding plants. Crop contents from eighteen specimens collected near Wyndham, Western Australia, comprised rice grains and seeds of ribbon grass (*Chionachne hubbardiana*), hogweed (*Boerhaavia diffusa*), barnyard millet (*Echinochloa crusgalli*) and various *Chloris* grasses (Carrick, 1956). These birds are troublesome pests in rice fields.

CALL A peculiar trisyllabic, chuckling cry; when disturbed a series of harsh shrieks.

NESTING The breeding season is variable and seems to be strongly influenced by climatic conditions. In northern Australia it commences as early as May, while in the south it is usually from August to December. However, nests have been found in most months of the year and there are reports of two or more broods being reared in favourable years. The nest is in a hollow limb or hole in a tree, generally a large eucalypt standing near water, in crevices in cliffs or occasionally in hollow, broken tops of large termites' mounds. Three or four eggs are laid on decayed wood dust lining the bottom of the hollow. Little is known of the nesting habits, but it is probable that they are similar to those of the Long-billed Corella (*C. tenuirostris*).

EGGS Ovate; 7 eggs, 38.8 (32.8–42.2) × 28.5 (25.5–31.1) mm. [H. L. White Coll.].

134

LONG-BILLED CORELLA

Cacatua tenuirostris (Kuhl)

DESCRIPTION
Length 38 cm.
ADULTS general plumage white; forehead, lores, band across throat, and bases to feathers of head, nape, mantle and upper breast bright orange-scarlet; undersides of flight and tail feathers suffused with yellow; pale greyish-blue naked periophthalmic ring, more extensive under eye; bill white; iris dark brown; legs grey.
IMMATURES like adults; shorter upper mandible.

DISTRIBUTION
South-eastern and south-western Australia.

SUBSPECIES

1. *C. t. tenuirostris* (Kuhl)   *Illustrated on page 121.*
   8 males   wing 266–284 (276.3) mm., tail 109–135 (123.5) mm.,
              exp. cul. 39–52 (44.9) mm., tars. 26–32 (27.0) mm.
   5 females wing 268–285 (276.6) mm., tail 115–122 (118.2) mm.,
              exp. cul. 40–49 (45.8) mm., tars. 27–31 (28.4) mm.
   Occurs only in south-eastern Australia from south-eastern South Australia to southern Victoria and south-western New South Wales.

2. *C. t. pastinator* (Gould)
   ADULTS no orange-scarlet band across throat; bases to feathers of nape, mantle and upper breast white; darker naked periophthalmic ring; slightly larger than *tenuirostris*.
   12 males   wing 272–337 (309.9) mm., tail 126–157 (141.5) mm.,
              exp. cul. 37–51 (46.8) mm., tars. 28–34 (31.3) mm.
   7 females wing 279–318 (303.9) mm., tail 133–180 (149.9) mm.,
              exp. cul. 38–48 (43.7) mm., tars. 31–33 (32.2) mm.
   Restricted to south-western Australia.

GENERAL NOTES
The long-billed Corella is a bird of the higher rainfall areas in southern Australia, being replaced in the drier inland and the tropical north by the closely allied Little Corella (*C. sanguinea*). In strong contrast to the latter it seems to be a declining species and is already quite rare in many districts. Initially, the decline was probably brought about by increasing aridity with the spread of drier conditions more suited to *C. sanguinea*. European settlement with its drastic land-clearance may have accelerated the decline and forced a further retreat. I have documented the decline and discussed its possible relevance to alleged hybridization between *sanguinea* and *tenuirostris* in south-western Australia (see Forshaw, 1969a). Within its restricted range local movements and fluctuations in numbers have been reported.

These cockatoos inhabit open forest, savannah woodland, grassland plains and trees bordering watercourses and surrounding pastures or cereal paddocks. They are seldom found far from water. During the breeding season they are usually seen in pairs or small groups, but at other times large flocks, sometimes comprising up to 200 or more may be encountered. They are noisy, conspicuous birds, their discordant cries generally attracting attention long before they can be seen. Very early, often well before sunrise, the birds leave the roosting trees and, after coming down to drink, move out into the neighbouring open country where they spend much of the day feeding on the ground. Their underparts become smeared with dirt and vegetable stains as they scratch about for seeds and dig up roots and bulbs. A feeding flock uses the sentinel-warning system in the same manner as does the Sulphur-crested Cockatoo (*C. galerita*), a species with which these birds sometimes associate. Towards dusk they revisit a waterhole to drink and then return to the roosting trees. They indulge in pre-roosting flights, each bird flying rapidly in and out through the trees, calling loudly. The flight consists of flapping wingbeats interspersed with short periods of gliding.

They feed on seeds, nuts, fruits, berries, roots, bulbs and probably insects and their larvae. A favourite food is corms of the introduced onion grass (*Romulea longifolia*), which the birds dig up with their elongated upper mandibles. They also dig up newly-sown grain and attack ripening maize. Carter (1912) reports that in south-western Australia they feed extensively on bulbs of a small *Drosera*.

CALL Very similar to that of the Little Corella (*C. sanguinea*).

NESTING Breeding takes place during the months August to November and the nest is in a hollow limb or hole in a tree, generally a living eucalypt standing near water. Nests are almost invariably in high, inaccessible positions. Two, rarely three, eggs are laid on decayed wood dust lining the bottom of the hollow.

Lendon has successfully bred the species in captivity (Anon., 1970). The first two eggs were laid on successive days and the third about four days later. Incubation lasted approximately twenty-four days and was shared by the parents, the male sitting during the day and the female at night.

Two chicks hatched but only one was reared and it left the nest when about seven weeks old, becoming independent some three weeks later. Both parents fed the young bird, the male assuming the major role after it had left the nest.

EGGS Ovate; 3 eggs, 33.2 (32.5–34.1) × 25.1 (24.7–25.5) mm. [H. L. White Coll.].

DUCORP'S COCKATOO
Cacatua ducorps (Bonaparte)

Illustrated on page 124.

DESCRIPTION Length 31 cm.
ADULTS general plumage white; lores white not pink as in *sanguinea*; salmon-pink bases to feathers of head and sometimes of breast, particularly noticeable on cheeks; undersides of flight and tail feathers suffused with yellow; blue naked periophthalmic ring, not extensive under eye; bill greyish-white; iris dark brown in male, reddish in female; legs grey.
IMMATURES undescribed.
8 males   wing 235–274 (253.3) mm., tail 107–121 (112.0) mm.,
            exp. cul. 29–34 (32.3) mm., tars. 24–27 (24.8) mm.
8 females wing 232–262 (241.4) mm., tail 107–117 (112.1) mm.,
            exp. cul. 27–31 (29.9) mm., tars. 24–27 (24.6) mm.

DISTRIBUTION Eastern Solomon Islands from Bougainville to Malaita; absent from the San Cristobal group.

GENERAL NOTES Ducorp's Cockatoo is a common bird, particularly in the lowlands (Mayr, 1945). Cain and Galbraith (1956) found that on Guadalcanal it occurred almost everywhere up to the lower limits of cloud forest, frequenting the forest canopy and isolated or 'second growth' trees. On Bougainville it has been collected in most lowland timbered areas, including trees in and around village gardens, and in the canopy of stunted cloud forest at about 1,700 m. It is a noisy conspicuous bird and is usually seen in pairs or small flocks flying above the treetops or perched on the topmost branches of tall trees. It is rather wary and when disturbed flies off screeching loudly. The buoyant, flapping flight consists of shallow, jerky wingbeats interspersed with gliding.

Food comprises seeds, nuts, fruits, berries, blossoms, leaf buds and insects and their larvae. Cain and Galbraith report that crop and stomach contents from birds collected on Guadalcanal comprised fruit, caterpillars and soft-bodied insects, and vegetable matter said to have been parts of a fleshy epiphyte common in the crowns of forest trees. These cockatoos raid village gardens and cause considerable damage by attacking pawpaws and digging up sweet potatoes (Mayr 1945; Cain and Galbraith 1956).

CALL A harsh *érrk-érrk . . . érrk-érrk*, often expanded into a continuous screech (Cain and Galbraith, 1956).

NESTING Nothing is known of the nesting behaviour but it is probably similar to that of the Long-billed Corella (*C. tenuirostris*).

EGGS Elliptical; 2 eggs, 37.5 (37.3–37.6) × 26.7 (25.4–27.9) mm. [Brit. Mus. Coll.].

Subfamily NYMPHICINAE

The only member of this subfamily is a medium-sized, slim bird with a long, strongly gradated tail. The wings are long and pointed and the bill is small and narrow.

Genus NYMPHICUS Wagler

The main distinguishing features of this genus are the same as for the subfamily. The fine, tapering crest is normally held erect, but can be lowered. Lendon (1951) has made the interesting observation that the pronounced sexual dimorphism is analogous to that found in *Calyptorhynchus*, especially in *C. magnificus* and *C. lathami*.

COCKATIEL
Nymphicus hollandicus (Kerr)

Illustrated on page 125.

DESCRIPTION Length 32 cm.
MALE general plumage grey, underparts paler and sometimes washed with brown; forehead, crest,

cheek-patches and throat yellow; ear-coverts orange; wing-coverts white; tail dark grey; bill dark grey; iris dark brown; legs grey.

FEMALE crown, crest and cheek-patches dull yellow tinged with grey; ear-coverts dull orange; rump, lower underparts and central tail feathers pale grey lightly marked with pale yellow; lateral tail-feathers yellow irregularly barred with dark grey.
IMMATURES similar to female.
10 males   wing 164–178 (168.7) mm., tail 157–176 (165.4) mm.,
              exp. cul. 14–15 (14.6) mm., tars. 15–17 (15.8) mm.
10 females wing 161–179 (169.1) mm., tail 155–178 (161.5) mm.,
              exp. cul. 14–15 (14.5) mm., tars. 16–17 (16.7) mm.

DESCRIPTION Australia generally, chiefly the interior; absent from Tasmania.

GENERAL NOTES

Cockatiels are found in most types of open country, particularly in the vicinity of water. They are common, especially in the north where large flocks have been reported. In northern regions they are highly nomadic, but toward the south movements become migratory. During exceptionally dry seasons movements are usually more spectacular and the birds may appear in coastal areas where they have not been recorded for many years.

In pairs or small flocks these parrots are generally seen on the ground searching for grass seeds, or flying above the scattered trees out on the open plain. They are not timid and will usually allow a close approach. If disturbed they seek refuge in a nearby tree, returning to the ground as soon as danger has passed. They have the habit of flying to large dead trees where they perch lengthways along stout limbs. While foraging on the ground, in the shade of a tree or bush, they are easily overlooked so well does their plumage blend with the ground cover. However, on the wing they are conspicuous and noisy. The flight is swift and direct, the backward-swept pointed wings being moved with deliberate, rhythmic motion; the white wing-patches are very obvious.

Food comprises seeds of grasses and herbaceous plants, grain, fruits and berries. The birds are fond of *Acacia* seeds which are procured amongst the branches or on the ground underneath. They have been seen feeding on mistletoe berries (*Loranthus* sp.), and I have seen them in mixed flocks with Red-rumped Parrots (*Psephotus haematonotus*) in stubble paddocks picking up grain. They also raid standing crops, particularly sorghum.

CALL A prolonged, warbling *queel-queel* terminating with a pronounced upward inflection.

NESTING The breeding season is variable and seems to depend largely on climatic conditions, especially rainfall. Nesting usually takes place between August and December, but may commence as early as April. The nest is in a hollow limb or hole in a tree, generally a large hollow in a eucalypt standing near water. The four to seven eggs are laid on decayed wood dust lining the bottom of the hollow. Incubation lasts twenty-one to twenty-three days and both sexes brood, the male sitting from early morning until late afternoon. They sit very tightly. Young birds leave the nest four to five weeks after hatching; males acquire the bright facial colouration of adults when about six months old, but retain the barred tail until the first complete moult.

EGGS Rounded; 6 eggs, 24.5 (23.7–25.5) × 19.0 (18.1–20.0) mm. [H. L. White Coll.].

Family PSITTACIDAE

Most parrots belong to this large, somewhat heterogeneous family. They do not have erectile crests, though in some species feathers of the crown or nape are elongated.

Subfamily NESTORINAE

There is only one genus in this subfamily. The cere is partly covered with bristle-like feathers and the tongue is tipped with a hair-like fringe. The shafts of the tail feathers are pointed and project slightly beyond the webs. The bill is longer than it is deep and on the undersides of the upper mandible there are longitudinal serrations.

Genus NESTOR

The parrots belonging to this genus are large, stocky birds with short, squarish tails. The generic characteristics are the same as for the subfamily. Sexual dimorphism is slight and young birds resemble adults.

KEA
Nestor notabilis Gould

Illustrated on page 128.

DESCRIPTION

Length 48 cm.
ADULTS general plumage olive-green, slightly paler on underparts; feathers margined with black, more pronounced on wing-coverts; crown and hindneck yellowish-green obscurely striped with black; brownish patch below eye; back and rump orange-red, feathers tipped with brownish-black; outer webs of primaries blue; under wing-coverts red-orange; orange-yellow marking on undersides of flight feathers; tail blue-green with a subterminal black band and with orange-yellow barring on inner web of each feather; bill greyish-brown (shorter and less curved in female); iris dark brown; legs dark grey.
IMMATURES crown yellowish-green; cere and eyelids yellow instead of grey; base of lower mandible orange-yellow; legs yellowish-grey.
8 males wing 315–330 (323.3) mm., tail 156–175 (164.0) mm.,
          exp. cul. 43–53 (48.8) mm., tars. 46–48 (46.6) mm.
7 females wing 302–325 (313.9) mm., tail 146–158 (152.6) mm.,
          exp. cul. 43–51 (48.0) mm., tars. 45–49 (46.7) mm.

DISTRIBUTION

Mountains of South Island of New Zealand from Fiordland north to Nelson and Marlborough Provinces.

GENERAL NOTES

Keas are mountain birds and occur from about 600 m. up to at least 2,000 m. They are fairly common inhabitants of wooded valleys and *Nothofagus* forests bordering sub-alpine scrublands. In spring and autumn they move up into sub-alpine scrub and alpine grassland to feed on seasonal fruits; they also feed out on open river flats. At Cupola Basin, Nelson Lakes National Park, Clarke (1970) found that throughout spring and summer Keas were present in the alpine scrub and grassland zones at 1,250–1,550 m., where food was most plentiful, and in autumn they were frequently seen between 1,550 and 2,000 m. eating berries and fossicking in moist ground. The movement may have been brought about by the later flowering and fruiting of plants at higher altitudes. In winter snowfalls and heavy frosts force the parrots to descend below the timberline, though some may remain in the vicinity of ski lodges. Around human habitation these parrots are extremely bold and inquisitive. They investigate all likely sources of food and have been known to cause considerable damage in huts after gaining entrance through chimneys. They feed in trees or on the ground and are frequently seen flying across mountain gorges from one feeding area to another. The flight is strong and they seem to delight in wheeling about in wide, sweeping circles, especially preceding storms when strong winds are blowing. On a fine day they enjoy rolling in snow, getting well covered in the process, and once the thaw gets under way they take to bathing in puddles. During summer months they are often active at night.

In autumn juveniles gather into wandering flocks, sometimes containing from fifty to a hundred birds; some pairs may take up territories during the following spring. Adults occupy a territory centered on the nest and nearby roost. They feed within a few kilometres of the nest, but occasionally in winter, and in summer if they fail to nest, they forage farther afield. In the early afternoon on most days throughout the year the hen will be seen sunning herself in trees close to the nest; the cock will be further away but within calling distance. A pair will join a wandering flock while it is in their territory or in a neighbouring territory, but will return to their own roost each night. Visiting birds will be tolerated within 20 m. of a nest.

Jackson (1962a) points out that Keas have a strict peck-order and are polygamous, citing an example of one dominant male being attached to at least four females. He says that there is no

surplus of males as might be expected, rather there are surplus females. But more juvenile males than females are banded so there must be a greater mortality of the former.

Leaf buds, roots, berries, fruits, seeds, blossoms, nectar and insects and their larvae make up the diet. Jackson (1960) notes that when nectar flows for a few weeks in January the parrots congregate to feed on flowering mountain flax (*Phormium colensoi*), rata (*Metrosideros* spp.), and other trees and shrubs. Then the berries ripen, one of the most important being snow totara (*Podocarpus nivalis*) which is a main food from January until it is buried in snow. At Lake Monk in Fiordland these birds have been seen eating fruits of *Coprosma ciliata* and leaves of *Senecio scorzoneroides* (Riney *et al.* 1959). Clarke found that at Cupola Basin the main food was succulent fruits of *Coprosma* spp., *Cyathodes fraseri*, *Muehlenbeckia axillaris*, *Pentachondra pumila*, *Podocarpus nivalis* and *Astelia nervosa*; successful germination of voided seeds suggested that the parrots could play a beneficial role in dispersing these soil-binding plants. Keas come to carcasses to feed on decaying flesh and to extract marrow from bones. Around settlements they scavenge in rubbish dumps.

For nearly a century landholders in the South Island high country have claimed that Keas attack and kill sheep, and in recent years this has been unduly emphasized in popular books. On the basis of this claim a bounty has been paid and in the three years 1943–1945 no less than 6,819 birds were destroyed under this scheme (Cunningham, 1948). Jackson (1962b) has examined the evidence and concludes that it is credible that Keas do attack sheep trapped in snow, sick sheep, sheep injured by falls or sheep they mistake as dead, but they are not an important predator and payment of bounties cannot be justified. The parrots are now partly protected.

CALL In flight a raucous *kee-aah*; also a variety of softer and conversational notes (Falla *et al.*, 1966).

NESTING Jackson (1963b) has found more than thirty nests and his observations provide a good overall picture of breeding activity. Nesting generally takes place during the months July to January, though eggs may be found at any time of the year except late autumn. The nest is in a crevice under rocks or among roots of a tree, or in a hollow log lying on the ground. A well-worn track leads through a narrow entrance and the wider nesting chamber is from 1 to 6 m. back. The floor of the chamber is lined with moss, lichens, leaves, twigs and chips of rotten wood, and on this layer the eggs are laid. The clutch is between two and four eggs. Incubation lasts between three and four weeks and only the female broods. While the hen is sitting and when there are chicks in the nest the male uses a stone near the entrance as a roost. The hen leaves the nest for an hour at daybreak and again at nightfall to feed and be fed by her mate. If the cock is attending to only one nesting hen he may feed her at midday also. The chicks remain in the nest for thirteen weeks. For the first month the male feeds the female and she in turn feeds the chicks, but thereafter he assists directly with feeding and takes over altogether when the young vacate the nest. Females acquire adult plumage by the end of the second year and males by the end of the third year.

Schmidt (1971) gives details of successful breedings in captivity. Clutches consisted of three eggs on one occasion and four eggs on seven. The eggs were usually laid at intervals of from three to five days, and incubation started with the laying of the third egg. Incubation periods varied from twenty to twenty-eight days, and young birds left the nest about seventy days after hatching.

EGGS Elliptical; 11 eggs, 44.8 (41.4–47.5) × 32.8 (31.0–33.5) mm. [Schönwetter, 1964].

KAKA
Nestor meridionalis (Gmelin)

Length 45 cm.

DESCRIPTION

ADULTS forehead, crown and occiput greyish-white, feathers sometimes margined with dull green; nape greyish-brown, feathers marked with olive-brown; neck and abdomen brownish-red, noticeably more crimson on hindneck where feathers are tipped with yellow and dark brown; breast olive-brown; ear-coverts orange-yellow; back and wings greenish-brown, some feathers of mantle tipped with red; rump, upper tail-coverts and under tail-coverts crimson barred with dark brown; under wing-coverts and undersides of flight feathers scarlet; tail brownish, tipped paler; bill brownish-grey (longer and more curved in male); iris dark brown; legs dark grey. IMMATURES like adults; base of lower mandible yellow.

New Zealand, including some offshore islands; formerly on Chatham Islands.

DISTRIBUTION

1. *N. m. meridionalis* (Gmelin) *Illustrated on page 145.* SUBSPECIES
   12 males   wing 265–306 (289.3) mm., tail 151–185 (164.6) mm.,
           exp. cul. 49–54 (51.7) mm., tars. 35–44 (37.7) mm.
   8 females   wing 267–304 (290.0) mm., tail 151–190 (165.4) mm.,
           exp. cul. 42–54 (48.5) mm., tars. 35–40 (37.3) mm.
   Occurs on South and Stewart Islands and on larger offshore islands.

2. *N. m. septentrionalis* Lorenz
   ADULTS generally duller and slightly smaller than *meridionalis*; back and wings darker olive-brown, feathers edged darker; breast darker brown; less crimson on hindneck; crown duller grey to greyish-white.

8 males   wing 267–272 (269.4) mm., tail 140–161 (152.1) mm.,
exp. cul. 41–50 (46.6) mm., tars. 34–36 (35.0) mm.
7 females wing 256–271 (263.0) mm., tail 146–154 (150.6) mm.,
exp. cul. 39–44 (41.3) mm., tars. 33–37 (35.1) mm.
Found on North Island and on some offshore islands.

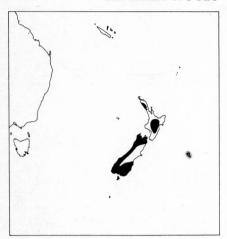

GENERAL NOTES   Kakas inhabit tracts of native forest, and due to extensive land-clearance have undoubtedly declined since European settlement. Their former presence on the Chatham Islands is known from bones found in subfossil deposits (Dawson, 1959). Although there are records of individual birds being attracted to settled districts—even to suburban gardens—by flowering and fruit-bearing trees, the species has shown little tendency to adapt to man-made habitats (Falla *et al.*, 1966), hence its protection will depend largely on forest preservation. They are fairly common birds on some offshore islands, particularly on Kapiti Island and Stewart Island, but are not plentiful elsewhere. In pairs of small parties of up to ten they are usually seen sitting in the treetops or flying above the forest canopy. They are most active in the early morning and late afternoon, and are often heard at night. They wander about and may suddenly appear in an area from which they have been absent for some time. Roberts (1953) reports that the lightkeeper on Burgess Island, in the Mokohinau Group, claimed that Kakas migrated through the island at a certain time of the year and perched near the lighthouse for only one day before moving south the following night.

During the middle of the day these parrots sit quietly in forest trees, spending the remainder of the time climbing amongst branches feeding on fruits and flowers or tearing apart rotting limbs to get at insects. They are rather quiet while feeding, but occasionally a chorus of whistling and screeching will be heard. Towards nightfall activity increases and pre-roosting flights become common. On Little Barrier Island Sibson (1947) observed that each evening parties of from eight to twelve would fly from the flat high over the ridges and sometimes out to sea and back; some birds stayed behind and called continuously from the forest. On Kapiti Island these parrots are remarkably tame and will accept food from the hands of visitors to the sanctuary.

They feed on seeds, fruits, berries, flowers, leaf buds, nectar and insects and their larvae. Fruits, such as those of miro (*Podocarpus ferrugineus*), are bitten off and held in the foot while the pulp is eaten. Tily (1951) watched one bird stripping bark from a branch in search of insects; it used its bill to force back the bark and then ran its bill up and down between the bark and limb before again seizing the bark and prising it back further.

CALL   In flight a harsh *ka-aa* and a ringing *u-wiia*; also a *chock . . . chock . . . chock* and a variety of yodelling notes (Falla *et al.*, 1966).

NESTING   The breeding season is from September through to March (Jackson, 1963a). The nest is in a large hollow limb or hole in the trunk of a tree and the entrance is frequently enlarged by the birds. A hollow may be used year after year and probably by successive pairs. Four or five eggs are laid on decayed wood dust lining the bottom of the hollow.

Jackson gives details of his observations at a nest. Four eggs were laid but only three hatched. The female brooded for about three weeks, leaving the nest each day at dawn and again at dusk to be fed by the male. The chicks left the nest nine to ten weeks after hatching.

EGGS   Elliptical; 18 eggs, 41.2 (38.3–44.5) × 31.0 (30.0–32.3) mm. [Schönwetter, 1964].

NORFOLK ISLAND KAKA
Nestor productus (Gould)

Illustrated on page 145.

Length 38 cm.
ADULTS   forehead, crown and nape brownish-grey; lores, throat and cheeks varied from yellow to orange, sometimes lightly tinged with red; upper breast varied from yellow-orange to greyish-brown; lower breast yellow or yellowish-orange; abdomen thighs and under tail-coverts dark orange or dull red marked with brownish-grey; hindneck greenish-yellow; back dark greyish-brown; wings brown, washed with dull green on coverts; rump and upper tail-coverts dark orange or dull red edged with greyish-brown; under wing-coverts dull yellow; tail brown; bill brownish-grey; iris dark brown (Gould); legs olive-brown.
IMMATURES   (Gould); like adults but breast olive-brown.
1 male: wing 259 mm., tail 130 mm.,
exp. cul. 48 mm., tars. 35 mm.
1 female   wing 261 mm., tail 128 mm.,
exp. cul. 42 mm., tars. 33 mm.
5 unsexed wing 232–259 (248.4) mm., tail 121–145 (137.6) mm.,
exp. cul. 40–49 (45.0) mm., tars. 32–38 (35.2) mm.

DISTRIBUTION   Formerly Norfolk and adjacent Phillip Island; now extinct.

GENERAL NOTES   According to Greenway (1967) the last Norfolk Island Kaka died in a cage in London sometime after 1851. It is probably that the parrots disappeared from their original haunts before this, but there are no records other than the report that they held out on Phillip Island after having been extirpated from Norfolk Island. Convicts and early settlers are said to have killed them, presumably for food.

The meagre information we have on the habits of the species comes from Gould (1865), who, during his stay in Sydney in about 1838, saw a living bird in the possession of a Major Anderson. This bird was not confined to a cage but was allowed to roam about the house; it moved along by a series of hops or leaps. Mrs Anderson told Gould that on Phillip Island the parrots were found among rocks as well as in the treetops. They were very tame and fed on the blossoms of the white-wood tree or white *Hibiscus*.

CALL Not described.

NESTING Mrs Anderson told Gould that the nest was in a hollow or hole in a tree and as many as four eggs were laid.

EGGS Undescribed.

Subfamily MICROPSITTINAE

Only the pygmy parrots belong to this subfamily. They are the smallest parrots and have structural features associated with their habit of climbing about on the faces of tree trunks. The short tail feathers have very stiff, projecting shafts similar to those found in woodpeckers (see fig. 8). The metatarsals are very long and the claws are long and curved. The bill is deeper than it is long and there is a prominent notch in the upper mandible. Steinbacher (1935) points out that both the proventriculus and ventriculus are very muscular, and underneath the base of the tongue there are extremely well-developed salivary glands.

Though common in parts of their range pygmy parrots have often been treated in the literature as if they were mythical creatures. In recent years field observers have learned much about the habits of these diminutive birds, but the aura of mystery still persists, probably because their small size makes it difficult to become familiar with them in the wild state. Of the six species five are lowland birds and seem to be largely allopatric, the sixth is a mountain bird.

Genus MICROPSITTA Lesson

The characteristics of this genus are the same for the subfamily. Sexual dimorphism is variable, though present in most species; immatures of some species have not been described.

5mm

Fig. 8
Dorsal and side view of the tail of *Micropsitta pusio* showing stiffened shafts with elongated tips.

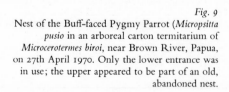

Fig. 9
Nest of the Buff-faced Pygmy Parrot (*Micropsitta pusio* in an arboreal carton termitarium of *Microcerotermes biroi*, near Brown River, Papua, on 27th April 1970. Only the lower entrance was in use; the upper appeared to be part of an old, abandoned nest.

BUFF-FACED PYGMY PARROT
Micropsitta pusio (Sclater)

DESCRIPTION Length 8.4 cm.
ADULTS general plumage green, paler and more yellowish on underparts; feathers variably edged with dusky brown; forehead and sides of head buff-brown, paler in female; in some birds there is a yellowish superciliary stripe; centre of crown and occiput deep blue, paler and less extensive in female; under tail-coverts yellow; central tail-feathers blue, lateral ones black with yellow spots near tips; bill grey; iris brown; legs greyish-pink to bluish grey.
IMMATURES crown and occiput green; buff-brown on sides of head duller and less extensive.

Bismarck Archipelago and south-eastern and northern New Guinea, including some offshore islands and some eastern Papuan Islands.

1. *M. p. pusio* (Sclater)   *Illustrated on page 149.*
    10 males   .wing 62–69 (65.3) mm., tail 24–27 (25.9) mm.,
        exp. cul. 7–8 (7.7) mm., tars. 8–10 (9.2) mm.
    10 females wing 59–65 (62.2) mm., tail 24–27 (25.9) mm.,
        exp. cul. 7–8 (7.4) mm., tars. 8–10 (8.9) mm.
    Occurs in the Bismarck Archipelago and in south-eastern New Guinea west to the Angabunga River.

2. *M. p. harterti* Mayr
    ADULTS less yellow on underparts; throat washed with blue; head markings duller than in *pusio*.
    7 males   wing 59–63 (61.1) mm., tail 25–27 (25.6) mm.,
        exp. cul. 6–8 (7.0) mm., tars. 8–9 (8.3) mm.
    2 females wing 61–63 (62.0) mm., tail 22–25 (23.5) mm.,
        exp. cul. 6–7 (6.5) mm., tars. 7–8 (7.5) mm.
    Confined to Fergusson Island in the D'Entrecasteaux Archipelago.

3. *M. p. stresemanni* Hartert
    ADULTS similar to *harterti*, but with more yellow on underparts and larger in size.
    10 males wing 62–69 (65.5) mm., tail 26–30 (27.3) mm.,
        exp. cul. 7–8 (7.4) mm., tars. 8–11 (9.1) mm.
    6 females wing 63–66 (64.8) mm., tail 23–27 (26.0) mm.,
        exp. cul. 7–8 (7.3) mm., tars. 8–9 (8.7) mm.
    Restricted to Misima and Tagula Islands in the Louisiade Archipelago.

4. *M. p. beccarii* (Salvadori)
    ADULTS general plumage darker and with less yellow on underparts; forehead and sides of head darker brown
    10 males wing 59–66 (63.1) mm., tail 24–27 (25.7) mm.,
        exp. cul. 7–8 (7.6) mm., tars. 8–9 (8.9) mm.
    8 females wing 60–64 (61.9) mm., tail 23–26 (24.6) mm.,
        exp. cul. 6–8 (7.3) mm., tars. 8–9 (8.6) mm.
    Found in northern New Guinea from west coast of Geelvink Bay, West Irian, east to the Kumusi River, and on Manam, Karkar and Rook Islands.

The Buff-faced Pygmy Parrot occurs up to about 800 m. (Mayr and Rand, 1937) but is probably quite uncommon above 400 m., the upper limit given by Rand and Gilliard (1967). It inhabits lowland forest, secondary growth, and trees around plantations or clearings. Donaghey says that it is common in forests around Port Moresby and in the foothills of the Owen Stanley Range (*in litt.* 1970). Gilliard noted that it was fairly common in lowland forests near the Whiteman Range on New Britain (in Gilliard and LeCroy, 1967a). Occasionally it is seen singly or in pairs, but generally small parties of from three to six are found in the low to mid storeys. The birds are active and noisy, moving through the branches and from tree to tree in a wave, but because of their small size they are usually heard but not seen. They are tame and will allow a close approach, particularly when feeding. The direct flight is swift and with audible wingbeats.

Near Port Moresby I watched a pair feeding in a tall tree standing in secondary growth. When first noticed they were climbing about on the face of the trunk, frequently stopping to feed on lichen. The feet were spread far apart and were at a 45° angle to the body. The projecting tail-shafts were in contact with the trunk only at their tips and there was no pressure on the tail feathers to spread them against the surface of the trunk; in other words, when feeding the parrots were using their stiffened tail feathers for support, although this was not at all obvious at first glance. While nibbling at the lichen they paused every two or three seconds to lean back from the trunk and, turning their heads right around, surveyed behind them as if aware of exposure to predators. They moved in all directions over the trunk and branches, even descending head first and upside-down on the undersides of lateral branches. Head movements were very rapid, but the birds' progress over the branches was without the jerky motions so characteristic of treecreepers, nuthatches and sittellas.

Shanahan (1969) reports that whether breeding or not these pygmy parrots roost in nests in termitaria. He found up to eight adults in a nest not being used for breeding and noticed that no nests were located in abandoned termitaria. The birds left the nests after the sun was well up and returned to roost at about 1700 hrs.; on cloudy, wet or overcast mornings they often stayed in the nest until 0800 or 0900 hrs.

There has been much discussion about the food of pygmy parrots. I have no doubt that the pair I saw near Port Moresby were feeding on lichen. It seems that this species also eats fruits, seeds and insects and their larvae. Crop and stomach contents from birds collected in south-eastern New Guinea comprised an indeterminate white, pasty mass and a few seeds (Mayr and Rand, 1937); from another taken in the Sepik district tiny black seeds and yellow fruit flesh (Gilliard and LeCroy, 1966), and from others obtained on New Britain whitish matter and black and white insect remains (Gilliard and LeCroy, 1967a).

CALL A shrill, high-pitched *tseet*, sometimes repeated two or three times in succession.

NESTING It appears that the breeding season is variable. A female with an enlarged ovary was collected in south-eastern New Guinea in May (Mayr and Rand, 1937). Near Port Moresby, in early December, Cleland found a parrot excavating a hole in a termitarium and noticed that three weeks later it was still in attendance at the hole (pers. comm. 1970). Near Lae, in late May, Bell observed a pair feeding a young bird (*in litt.* 1970). In late April, near Port Moresby, I examined a nest in an arboreal carton termitarium of *Microcerotermes biroi* about 2 m. from the ground on the trunk of a small tree in secondary growth. The termitarium extended about 1.5 m. up the trunk and in it were two entrance holes. Both entrances went in at a tangent to the face of the trunk and the one in use was some 25 cm. below and to the left of the other (see fig. 9). A parrot came to the lower hole and, although chicks could be heard calling, it did not enter to feed them.

Little is known of the nesting habits. Shanahan has taken two adults and three eggs from a nest in November and from another nest obtained two chicks.

EGGS Rounded; 11 eggs, 16.5 (15.7–17.5) × 13.7 (12.5–14.0) mm. [Schönwetter, 1964].

YELLOW-CAPPED PYGMY PARROT
Micropsitta keiensis (Salvadori)

DESCRIPTION

Length 9.5 cm.
ADULTS general plumage green, slightly paler on underparts; feathers variably margined with dusky brown; yellow crown, more dusky on forehead; face brown, gradually merging into green on lower cheeks; median wing-coverts black broadly margined with green; central tail feathers blue, lateral tail feathers black with yellow spot near tips; bill grey; iris brown; legs grey.
IMMATURES similar to female; bill yellowish with dark grey tip.

DESCRIPTION

Kai and Aru Islands, the western Papuan Islands, and western and southern New Guinea.

SUBSPECIES

1. *M. k. keiensis* (Salvadori)   *Illustrated on page 149.*
   10 males   wing 61–66 (62.6) mm., tail 25–31 (27.5) mm.,
             exp. cul. 7–8 (7.7) mm., tars. 8–9 (8.7) mm.
   6 females wing 59–62 (60.7) mm., tail 25–26 (25.7) mm.,
             exp. cul. 7–8 (7.3) mm., tars. 8–9 (8.7) mm.
   Restricted to the Kai and Aru Islands, Indonesia.

2. *M. k. viridipectus* (Rothschild)
   ADULTS general plumage darker than in *keiensis.*
   10 males   wing 57–64 (60.1) mm., tail 22–26 (24.0) mm.,
             exp. cul. 7–8 (7.1) mm., tars. 8–9 (8.6) mm.
   8 females wing 56–60 (58.1) mm., tail 21–24 (22.6) mm.,
             exp. cul. 7–8 (7.1) mm., tars. 8–9 (8.4) mm.
   Found in southern New Guinea between the Mimika and Fly Rivers; doubtfully distinct from *keiensis.*

3. *M. k. chloroxantha* Oberholser   *Illustrated on page 149.*
   MALE centre of breast and abdomen variably marked with orange-red; remainder of underparts yellowish-green.
   FEMALE entire underparts yellowish-green; crown greenish-yellow.
   9 males   wing 57–60 (58.7) mm., tail 21–25 (24.0) mm.,
             exp. cul. 7–8 (7.2) mm., tars. 8–9 (8.2) mm.
   9 females wing 56–60 (58.0) mm., tail 21–24 (22.9) mm.,
             exp. cul. 6–8 (7.0) mm., tars. 8–9 (8.1) mm.
   Occurs on the western Papuan Islands, and on the Vogelkop and Onin Peninsula, West Irian. I have examined the type of *sociabilis* and agree with Mees (in press) that that subspecies should be synonymized with *chloroxantha.*

GENERAL NOTES

The Yellow-capped Pygmy Parrot also inhabits lowland forest and geographically replaces *M. pusio.* On Misool Ripley (1964) saw small groups working their way up or around tree trunks, particularly on fig trees. Near Manokwari on the Vogelkop, West Irian, Hoogerwerf (1971) did not record these parrots often, but he points out that they are very inconspicuous and may not have been uncommon. They were usually seen in pairs in the understorey of primary forest or sometimes in light secondary growth, where they climbed on stems and branches in search of food. Their high-pitched calls attracted attention.

Also on the Vogelkop Bergman (1960) made a number of observations on these parrots. He found that a family group, comprising adults and young from previous broods, roosted in the nest in an arboreal termitarium irrespective of whether it was being used for breeding or not; in one nest he found two chicks and no less than six adults. They went to roost at about 1700 hrs. and did not emerge until approximately 0700 hrs. the following morning, when they flew straight to nearby trees and climbed on the trunks in search of food. The direct flight is swift and with audible wingbeats.

Food is probably similar to that taken by *M. pusio,* namely, lichen and fungus, seeds, fruits and insects and their larvae. Stomachs from specimens collected on Misool by Ripley contained an indeterminate white paste. Stomach and crop contents from specimens collected near Manokwari by Hoogerwerf comprised very small seeds and very fine, soft pulp, perhaps of flower fragments or small fruits.

CALL A high-pitched, squeaky *tsit* repeated at short intervals.

NESTING Ripley obtained a nestling in October and a male with enlarged gonads in November. Near Manokwari, on 24th March, Hoogerwerf found a nest containing two almost full-grown chicks in a hollow excavated in a termite nest on the stem of a small tree about 3 m. from the ground.

Bergman examined a nest in an arboreal termitarium on a bole on the trunk of a large fig tree about 4 m. from the ground. The small entrance hole was in the lower side. The nesting chamber was slightly below the centre of the termitarium, was oval in shape, and measured 20 cm. in length and 15 cm. in height. It contained no lining, but on the floor there were small pieces of white egg-shells and a few green feathers. The passage from the entrance hole to the chamber ran obliquely upwards towards the bole, on which the termitarium was fastened, then turned almost at right angles into the chamber. As well as six adults there were two nestlings in the nest; one had acquired half of its green feathers, while on the other most feathers were still in their quills, so it appeared that there was several days age difference between them or one had dominated and was receiving more food

Little is known of the nesting habits. Bergman observed that the female brooded during the day and was fed at infrequent intervals by the male. He also observed that the male seemed to do most of the feeding of young birds that had left the nest.

EGGS Undescribed.

GEELVINK PYGMY PARROT
Micropsitta geelvinkiana (Schlegel)

DESCRIPTION Length 9 cm.
MALE general plumage green, feathers of upperparts sometimes edged with dusky brown; forehead and ear-coverts brown merging into blue on neck; purple-blue crown; centre of underparts orange-yellow becoming greenish on vent; yellow under tail-coverts; median wing-coverts black broadly margined with green; central tail feathers blue, lateral ones black and green above and tipped with yellow on undersides; bill grey; iris brownish-red; legs grey.
FEMALE entire underparts greenish-yellow.
IMMATURES undescribed.

DISTRIBUTION Numfor and Biak Islands in Geelvink Bay, West Irian.

SUBSPECIES 1. *M. g. geelvinkiana* (Schlegel)   *Illustrated on page 149.*
10 males wing 56–61 (57.8) mm., tail 28–30 (28.7) mm.,
          exp. cul. 7–8 (7.8) mm., tars. 8–10 (8.7) mm.
8 females wing 54–57 (55.4) mm., tail 23–27 (24.6) mm.,
          exp. cul. 7–8 (7.3) mm., tars. 8–9 (8.4) mm.
Confined to Mumfor Island.

2. *M. g. misoriensis* (Salvadori)
MALE entire head brown with a yellow line on nape.
FEMALE no yellow on nape; feathers of crown brown edged with blue.
2 males   wing 57–58 (57.5) mm., tail 25–28 (26.5) mm.,
          exp. cul. 7–8 (7.5) mm., tars. 9 (9.0) mm.
2 females wing 54–56 (55.0) mm., tail 26–27 (26.5) mm. ,
          exp. cul. 7 (7.0) mm., tars. 8 (8.0) mm.
Found only on Biak Island.

GENERAL NOTES The Geelvink Pygmy Parrot does not occur on the New Guinea mainland, being replaced there by the closely related *M. pusio* and *M. keiensis*, and the islands to which it is restricted are seldom visited by field observers, so little is known of its habits. On Biak Ripley found it associating with flycatchers in low berry-bearing trees in primary forest (in Mayr and Meyer de Schauensee, 1939a). He also saw a couple of parties of four or five in isolated, large trees in secondary growth. They were shy and difficult to approach.

Stomach contents from a specimen collected on Numfor comprised crushed seeds (in Rothschild *et al.*, 1932). I suspect that lichen and fungus, fruits, and insects and their larvae are also eaten.

CALL In flight a rapidly repeated *tsit-tsit-tsit-tsit*; also a drawn-out *tsee . . . tsee* (in Rothschild *et al.*, 1932).

NESTING In mid-December Ripley collected a male with slightly enlarged testes. There are two nestlings collected on Numfor in mid-June (AMNH. 619111, 619112). Stein says that apparently the nest is in an arboreal termitarium (in Rothschild *et al.*, 1932).

144

W.T.Cooper, 71.

EGGS Undescribed.

MEEK'S PYGMY PARROT
Micropsitta meeki Rothschild and Hartert

Illustrated on page 149.

Length 10 cm.
ADULTS head dark grey-brown; indistinct yellow superciliary lines in most birds; underparts and neck yellow with brownish margins to feathers, especially on neck; median wing-coverts black broadly margined with green; yellow under tail-coverts; tail green above and grey and yellow below; bill horn-coloured; iris brownish-yellow; legs brown.

IMMATURES undescribed.

Admiralty, St. Matthias and Squally Islands.

1. *M. m. meeki* Rothschild and Hartert
   10 males   wing 58–65 (61.8) mm., tail 25–29 (26.9) mm.,
               exp. cul. 8–9 (8.8) mm., tars. 9–11 (9.5) mm.
   10 females wing 58–62 (59.6) mm., tail 24–30 (26.4) mm.,
               exp. cul. 7–10 (8.6) mm., tars. 9–10 (9.2) mm.
   Restricted to the Admiralty Islands.

2. *M. m. proxima* Rothschild and Hartert
   ADULTS sides of head lighter and more yellowish-grey; yellow frontal band meeting prominent yellow superciliary lines.
   8 males   wing 62–66 (64.4) mm., tail 29–31 (30.0) mm.,
              exp. cul. 8–9 (8.3) mm., tars. 9–10 (9.6) mm.
   2 females wing 61–62 (61.5) mm., tail 27–28 (27.5) mm.,
              exp. cul. 8 (8.0) mm., tars. 9–10 (9.5) mm.
   Occurs on the St. Matthias and Squally Islands.

Sibley (1951) reports that the habits of Meek's Pygmy Parrot seem to be identical with those of *M. pusio* and *M. finschii*. On Emirau Island, in the St. Matthias Group, he watched a lone bird foraging on the trunk of a smooth-barked tree. It was pecking at small warty protuberances which seemed to be a type of fungus. Stomach contents from several specimens could not be identified, but may have been this same material.

CALL A mellow, whistle-like *tseet* (Sibley, 1951).

NESTING Little is known of the nesting habits. On St. Matthias Island Eichhorn found chicks in a nest in an arboreal termitarium only 25 cm. from the ground (in Hartert, 1926a).

EGGS Undescribed.

FINSCH'S PYGMY PARROT
Micropsitta finschii (Ramsay)

Length 9.5 cm.
MALE general plumage green, paler on underparts; body feathers narrowly margined with brownish-black; blue feathers surrounding base of lower mandible; median wing-coverts black broadly margined with green; centre of abdomen orange-red; yellow under tail-coverts, longest tipped with bluish-green; central tail feathers greenish-blue with black spot near tips, lateral tail feathers black edged with green and with yellow near tips; cere pink; bill dark grey; iris orange-pink; legs grey.
FEMALE rose-pink feathers surrounding base of lower mandible; no orange-red on abdomen; cere bluish-grey.
IMMATURES (Sibley, 1951); cere grey; bill light grey with horn-coloured edges; iris reddish-brown.

Bismarck Archipelago and the Solomon Islands.

Kaka *Nestor meridionalis meridionalis* **1**
AMNH. 616676 ad. ♀

Norfolk Island Kaka *Nestor productus* **2**
NHM. 50802 ad. unsexed

1. *M. f. finschii* (Ramsay)
   Illustrated on page 148.
   10 males   wing 62–67 (64.2) mm., tail 28–34 (31.2) mm.,
               exp. cul. 7–8 (7.9) mm., tars. 9–10 (9.6) mm.
   10 females wing 61–64 (62.7) mm., tail 26–33 (29.4) mm.,
               exp. cul. 7–8 (7.8) mm., tars. 9–10 (9.6) mm.
   Occurs on Ugi, San Cristobal and Rennell in the Solomon Islands.

2. *M. f. aolae* (Ogilvie-Grant)
   ADULTS upperparts darker green than in *finschii*; blue patch on crown; males lack orange-red abdomen.
   10 males   wing 59–64 (61.6) mm., tail 27–30 (28.6) mm.,
               exp. cul. 7–8 (7.4) mm., tars. 9–10 (9.2) mm.

10 females wing 57–69 (63.9) mm., tail 24–29 (27.6) mm.,
  exp. cul. 7–8 (7.4) mm., tars. 9–10 (9.2) mm.
Confined to Guadalcanal, Malaita and the Russell Islands in the Solomon Islands.

3. *M. f. tristami.* (Rothschild and Hartert)
ADULTS like *finschii*, but males lack orange-red abdomen.
10 males wing 61–66 (63.2) mm., tail 27–29 (28.4) mm.,
  exp. cul. 8–9 (8.9) mm., tars. 9–10 (9.6) mm.
10 females wing 62–66 (63.2) mm., tail 25–29 (27.4) mm.,
  exp. cul. 8–9 (8.4) mm., tars. 9–10 (9.6) mm.
Found on Vella Lavella, Gizo, Kulambangra, New Georgia, Rubiana and Rendova in the Solomon Islands.

4. *M. f. nanina* (Tristam)   *Illustrated on page 148.*
ADULTS like *aolae*, but slightly smaller and with less blue on crown.
10 males wing 58–62 (59.8) mm., tail 24–28 (26.0) mm.,
  exp. cul. 7–8 (7.3) mm., tars. 8–10 (9.1) mm.
10 females wing 57–66 (59.8) mm., tail 23–28 (25.0) mm.,
  exp. cul. 7–8 (7.1) mm., tars. 9–10 (9.1) mm.
Occurs on Bougainville, Choiseul, Ysabel and Bugotu in the Solomon Islands.

5. *M. f. viridifrons* (Rothschild and Hartert)
ADULTS slightly larger than *aolae* and with more blue on crown; sides of head suffused with blue; some males have orange-red on abdomen, others have not.
10 males wing 58–65 (62.2) mm., tail 25–30 (28.2) mm.,
  exp. cul. 8–9 (8.2) mm., tars. 9–10 (9.3) mm.
8 females wing 59–64 (61.4) mm., tail 25–29 (26.9) mm.,
  exp. cul. 7–8 (7.9) mm., tars. 9–10 (9.3) mm.
Restricted to the Lihir Islands, and to New Hanover and New Ireland in the Bismarck Archipelago.

GENERAL NOTES

Sibley (1951) reports that on New Georgia, in the Solomon Islands, Finsch's Pygmy Parrots were common in lowland forests where they foraged in small parties of from three to six birds. Cain and Galbraith (1956) say that in the eastern Solomons they occur up to the lower limits of cloud forest, being replaced at higher altitudes by *M. bruijnii*. Bradley and Wolff (1956) point out that on Rennell Island the species seems to prefer more open patches in forest; one bird was collected and others were seen in young secondary growth covering an abandoned cultivated area. Though noisy and very active these parrots are easily overlooked because of their small size and predominantly green colouration. They are generally seen climbing about on the faces of trunks and large branches of forest trees. Their habits are similar to those of other pygmy parrots.

 Cain and Galbraith examined crop and stomach contents from birds collected in the eastern Solomons and found vegetable matter, which may have been lichen, grains of sand, and remains of insects. Stomach contents from a male collected on Rennell Island resembled crushed seeds, but may have been remnants of fungi (Bradley and Wolff, 1956).

CALL A flat, harsh *tsit* (Sibley, 1951); also a variety of squeaks, a shrill *chilp* and a soft, whispering whistle (Cain and Galbraith, 1956).

NESTING Nothing is known of the nesting habits, but the nest is probably in a termitarium. Sibley collected an immature male in late October.

EGGS Undescribed.

Finsch's Pygmy Parrot **1**
Micropsitta finschii finschii
AM. A13386 ad. ♂

Finsch's Pygmy Parrot **2**
Micropsitta finschii finschii
AM. A13387 ad. ♀

Finsch's Pygmy Parrot **3**
Micropsitta finschii nanina
CSIRO. 3026 ad. ♂

Red-breasted Pygmy Parrot **4**
Micropsitta bruijnii bruijnii
RMNH. Cat. 1 ad. ♂

Red-breasted Pygmy Parrot **5**
Micropsitta bruijnii bruijnii
AMNH. 339470 ad. ♀

RED-BREASTED PYGMY PARROT
Micropsitta bruijnii (Salvadori)

Length 9 cm.
MALE general plumage green, feathers narrowly margined with dull black; crown buff-red to brownish-orange; nape and hindneck deep blue; throat and cheeks buff-orange; dark blue line from behind eye to blue nape; sides of neck green with blue collar across lower throat; sides of breast blue; under tail-coverts and middle of abdomen and breast pale red; median wing-coverts black broadly edged with green; central tail feathers blue above, black below, lateral tail feathers black tipped with orange; cere pink; bill horn-coloured with grey towards base; iris brown; legs grey.
FEMALE crown dark blue; forehead and cheeks buff-orange; sides of breast green; middle of breast and abdomen yellowish-green; yellow under tail-coverts; cere bluish grey.
IMMATURES crown blue; forehead and lores white; cheeks and throat whitish tinged with buff; no blue on sides of breast; middle of breast and abdomen usually with some orange-red in males, entirely yellowish-green in females.

DISTRIBUTION Mountains of Buru and Ceram, New Guinea, the Bismarck Archipelago and the Solomon Islands.

SUBSPECIES

1. *M. b. bruijnii* (Salvadori)   *Illustrated on page 148.*

12 males   wing 62–70 (66.6) mm., tail 22–27 (24.8) mm.,
     exp. cul. 6–7 (6.4) mm., tars. 8–9 (8.8) mm.
9 females wing 61–66 (64.1) mm., tail 22–25 (23.7) mm.,
     exp. cul. 5–7 (6.1) mm., tars. 8–9 (8.7) mm.
   Occurs throughout the mountains of New Guinea from the Tamrau and Arfak Mountains on the Vogelkop, West Irian, east to the Owen Stanley Range in Papua.

2. *M. b. pileata* Mayr

MALE crown deeper brownish-red than in *bruijnii* and extending further down nape, thereby narrowing blue nuchal collar.
FEMALE undescribed.
3 males   wing 68–69 (68.3) mm., tail 26–27 (26.3) mm.,
     exp. cul. 6–7 (6.3) mm., tars. 8–9 (8.6) mm.
   Confined to the mountains of Buru and Ceram in the southern Moluccas, Indonesia.

3. *M. b. necopinata* Hartert

MALE crown deep brown becoming pale yellowish-brown in centre; cheeks, throat and middle of breast and abdomen reddish-orange; yellow under tail-coverts.
FEMALE similar to *bruijnii*, but crown more purplish-blue.
9 males   wing 64–70 (66.8) mm., tail 27–30 (28.1) mm.,
     exp. cul. 6–7 (6.9) mm., tars. 8–10 (9.0) mm.
2 females wing 63–64 (63.5) mm., tail 25–26 (25.5) mm.,
     exp. cul. 6–7 (6.5) mm., tars. 8–9 (8.5) mm.
   Found on New Britain and New Ireland in the Bismarck Archipelago.

4. *M. b. rosea* Mayr

MALE crown bright reddish-pink; cheeks and throat brighter and more pinkish than in *bruijnii*.
FEMALE similar to *bruijnii*
9 males   wing 65–71 (67.0) mm., tail 26–30 (27.6) mm.,
     exp. cul. 6–7 (6.7) mm., tars. 8–10 (8.9) mm.
2 females wing 59–62 (60.5) mm., tail 23–24 (23.5) mm.,
     exp. cul. 6 (6.0) mm., tars. 8–9 (8.5) mm.
   Known only from Bougainville, Guadalcanal and Kulambangra in the Solomon Islands. I have synonymized *brevis* with this race.

GENERAL NOTES

The Red-breasted Pygmy Parrot is widespread in the mountains of New Guinea between 500 and 2,300 m., but seems to be local in occurrence and abundance (Rand and Gilliard, 1967). Streseman (1914) reports that on Ceram he saw a small flock in forest at about 1,000 m. in the foothills of the central range and this was his only record. Gilliard did not see it below 780 m. on New Britain and gained the impression that it was very local and occurred in scattered, nomadic flocks (in Gilliard and LeCroy, 1967a). Its movements seem to be unpredictable, though Toxopeus was told by local villagers on Buru that it comes down from the mountain regions at the beginning of the dry season, that is, October and November (in Siebers, 1930). It inhabits cloud forest and well-timbered areas, but Sudbury (1969) found a flock of about twenty in a coffee plantation near Mt. Hagen in the central highlands of New Guinea. In the Baiyer Valley, also in the central highlands, I saw a lone male in riparian forest.

Pairs or small parties of these parrots are generally seen climbing about on sloping branches of forest trees feeding on lichen or fungus. Gilliard notes that rarely did he see them moving on purely vertical surfaces, and Robinson, who has had excellent sightings of the species in the Baiyer Valley, concurs with this observation (pers. comm. 1970). They move industriously, shuffling here and there along the tops of limbs and frequently bobbing the head over the side or around from behind the branch. Individuals in a feeding party keep close together and work over an area thoroughly before moving on. They often leap surprising distances when shifting from one branch or trunk to another. There is slight undulation in the swift flight and the wingbeats are audible from below.

As far as I know Rand (1942b) was the first to suggest that this species, and probably all pygmy parrots, feed on fungus or lichen growing on trees. He noticed that the parrots were nibbling a fungus that formed jelly-like layers on rotten wood, and stomach contents he examined resembled this fungus. Stomachs from three birds collected on New Britain contained soft vegetable matter and small black objects resembling insect remains (in Gilliard and LeCroy, 1967a).

CALL A shrill, penetrating *tsee . . . tsee* (Robinson, pers. comm. 1970).

NESTING A female in breeding condition was collected in January and two nestlings only a few days old were taken in the same month (Rand, 1942b).

Rand has described the nest in which the two nestlings were found. It was a cavity excavated by the parrots in a dead stump about 3 m. from the ground. From the entrance hole a tunnel, only 30 mm. in diameter, led inward and upward to enter, at the top and back, a chamber which was directly above the entrance. This chamber was approximately 100 mm. high and 55 mm. wide and on the floor was a layer of chips some 40 mm. deep.

Rand also saw a male excavating a similar chamber in another dead stump and suspected that this was its sleeping quarters.

EGGS Rounded; 2 eggs, 17.4 (17.3–17.5) × 14.2 (14.0–14.3) mm. [Berlin Mus. Coll.].

Buff-faced Pygmy Parrot 1
Micropsitta pusio pusio
BM. 98.12–2.177 ad. ♂

Meek's Pygmy Parrot *Micropsitta meeki* 2
RMNH. Cat. 1, Reg. 6735 ad. ♂

Yellow-capped Pygmy Parrot 3
Micropsitta keiensis keiensis
RMNH. Cat. 3, Reg. 6774 ad. ♂

Yellow-capped Pygmy Parrot 4
Micropsitta keiensis chloroxantha
AMNH. 300680 ad. ♂

Geelvink Pygmy Parrot 5
Micropsitta geelvinkiana geelvinkiana
RMNH. Cat. 2 ad. ♂

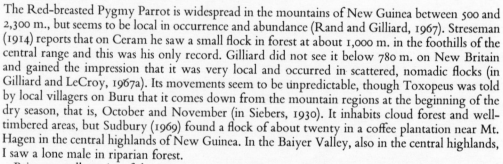

150

Subfamily PSITTACINAE

The majority of parrots belong to this diverse subfamily. In one species, *Lathamus discolor*, the tongue is tipped with poorly developed papillae, but in all others it is smooth and rounded. The shafts of the tail feathers do not project and are not stiffened. In one species, *Deroptyus accipitrinus*, elongated feathers of the nape and hindneck can be raised to form a ruff but in no species is there an erectile crest.

Genus OPOPSITTA Sclater

Holyoak (1970a) points out that *Opopsitta* and *Psittaculirostris* stand apart from other parrots in having the entoglossum deeply grooved and in having the processes of the parahyoid bone only narrowly joined and not projecting forward. He also suggests that the two genera should not be separated. I agree that the fig parrots are a readily distinguishable group, but feel that there are two component groups and these are probably best retained as separate genera.

The members of this genus are small, stocky parrots with extremely short, rounded tails. The bill is proportionately large and broad, and there is a prominent notch in the upper mandible. The cere is naked, not feathered as in *Psittaculirostris*, and there is no marked elongation of the ear-coverts. Sexual dimorphism is present in most forms and young birds resemble females.

Double-eyed Fig Parrot **1**
Opopsitta diophthalma diophthalma
RMNH. Cat. 25, Reg. 1609 ad. ♂

Double-eyed Fig Parrot **2**
Opopsitta diopthalma diophthalma
RMNH. Cat. 16 ad. ♀

Double-eyed Fig Parrot **3**
Opopsitta diophthalma virago
AMNH. 618965 ad. ♀

Double-eyed Fig Parrot **4**
Opopsitta diophthalma virago
RMNH. Cat. 1 ad. ♂

Coxen's Fig Parrot **5**
Opopsitta diophthalma coxeni
AM. A1178 ad. ♂

Red-browed Fig Parrot **6**
Opopsitta diophthalma macleayana
AM. 028423 ad. ♂

Orange-breasted Fig Parrot **7**
Opopsitta gulielmiterti gulielmiterti
RMNH. Cat. 3 ad. ♂

Orange-breasted Fig Parrot **8**
Opopsitta gulielmiterti suavissima
CSIRO. 3907 ad. ♀

Orange-breasted Fig Parrot **9**
Opopsitta gulielmiterti suavissima
CSIRO. 3887 ad. ♂

ORANGE-BREASTED FIG PARROT
Opopsitta gulielmiterti (Schlegel)

Length 13 cm.
ADULTS general plumage green, paler and more yellowish on under-wing coverts and lower underparts; forehead, crown and behind eye dark blue; lores, throat and sides of head pale yellow; variable black line on ear-coverts; breast and upper abdomen orange; concealed yellow edging on innermost wing-coverts; bill grey-black; iris dark brown; legs greenish-grey.
FEMALE cheeks yellow, bordered behind by a prominent black band and below by a greenish-blue band; orange ear-coverts; breast greenish.
IMMATURES (ANSP. 136801); similar to female, but with green breast and orange on sides of throat.

New Guinea, including Salawati in the western Papuan Islands, and the Aru Islands, Indonesia.

1. *O. g. guielmiterti* (Schlegel)   *Illustrated on page 152.*
   8 males   wing 91–97 (93.9) mm., tail 34–42 (38.3) mm.,
              exp. cul. 14–16 (14.3) mm., tars. 13–15 (14.1) mm.
   4 females wing 91–95 (93.0) mm., tail 34–40 (37.8) mm.,
              exp. cul. 14 (14.0) mm., tars. 12–14 (13.5) mm.
   Restricted to Salawati in the western Papuan Islands, and to the western part of the Vogelkc West Irian.

2. *O. g. nigrifrons* (Reichenow)
   ADULTS like *gulielmiterti*, but forehead and crown black instead of dark blue.
   No specimens examined.
   1 male   (Mauersberger, *in litt.*, 1971); wing —— (damaged), tail —— (damaged),
                   exp. cul. 15 mm., tars. 12 mm.
   1 female (**type**) (Mauersberger, *in litt.*, 1971); wing —— (damaged), tail 32 mm.,
                   exp. cul. 16 mm., tars. 12 mm.
   1 unsexed   (Mauersberger, *in litt.*, 1971); wing 91 mm., tail 37 mm.,
                   exp. cul. 16 mm., tars. 12 mm.
   Occurs in northern New Guinea between the Mamberamo and Sepik Rivers.

3. *O. g. ramuensis* Neumann
   ADULTS intermediate between *nigrifrons* and *amabilis*; similar to *amabilis*, but forehead and crown variably suffused with blue and black.
   No specimens examined.
   2 males   (Mauersberger, *in litt.*, 1971); wing 80–85 (82.5) mm., tail 31–34 (32.5) mm.,
              exp. cul. 15 (15.0) mm., tars. 11–13 (12.0) mm.
   3 females (Mauersberger, *in litt.*, 1971); wing 84–85 (84.3) mm., tail 34–35 (34.3) mm.,
              exp. cul. 15–16 (15.3) mm., tars. 10–11 (10.3) mm.
   Known only from the Ramu River district, northern New Guinea.

4. *O. g. amabilis* (Reichenow)
   MALE forehead and crown black suffused with dull, dark blue; upper abdomen, breast and sides of head pale yellow; no black markings on ear-coverts; smaller than *gulielmiterti*.

Salvadori's Fig Parrot **1**
Psittaculirostris salvadorii
MNHN. 256 ad. ♂

Salvadori's Fig Parrot **2**
Psittaculirostris salvadorii
MNHN. 254 **type** ad. ♀

Edwards' Fig Parrot **3**
Psittaculirostris edwardsii
AM. 039188 ad. ♂

Desmarest's Fig Parrot **4**
Psittaculirostris desmarestii cervicalis
AM. 030597 ad. unsexed

Desmarest's Fig Parrot **5**
Psittaculirostris desmarestii desmarestii
AM. B2989 ad. unsexed

FEMALE breast and upper abdomen orange; cheeks dusky black, extending back to ear-coverts and up to join black crown behind eye; lores and throat pale yellow, almost white.
IMMATURES like female, but breast more yellowish.
9 males   wing 80–87 (83.6) mm., tail 31–34 (32.6) mm.,
          exp. cul. 12–13 (12.8) mm., tars. 12–13 (12.1) mm.
9 females wing 79–85 (82.1) mm., tail 31–37 (33.2) mm.,
          exp. cul. 12–14 (13.0) mm., tars. 11–13 (12.2) mm.
Found in north-eastern New Guinea from the Huon Peninsula east to Milne Bay.

5. *O. g. suavissima* (Sclater)   *Illustrated on page 152.*
MALE forehead and forecrown dark blue; lores and forepart of cheeks white; remainder of cheeks black; ear-coverts pale yellow, almost white; throat, breast and upper abdomen orange; prominent yellow edging on innermost wing-coverts; yellowish-white band on underside of secondaries; smaller than *gulielmiterti*.
FEMALE hindpart of cheeks dull black tinged with blue; ear-coverts orange; throat, breast and upper abdomen dull greenish-orange.
IMMATURES similar to female.
12 males wing 74–80 (77.3) mm., tail 28–33 (30.9) mm.,
          exp. cul. 12–14 (12.3) mm., tars. 11–13 (11.7) mm.
8 females wing 73–81 (77.1) mm., tail 29–34 (31.0) mm.,
          exp. cul. 12–13 (12.3) mm., tars. 11–12 (11.8) mm.
Occurs in south-eastern New Guinea west to the Gulf of Papua.

6. *O. g. fuscifrons* (Salvadori)
ADULTS similar to *suavissima*, but forehead and forecrown brown.
17 males wing 72–88 (80.2) mm., tail 26–33 (30.4) mm.,
          exp. cul. 11–13 (11.9) mm., tars. 11–13 (11.6) mm.
9 females wing 75–84 (77.6) mm., tail 26–34 (29.6) mm.,
          exp. cul. 10–13 (11.8) mm., tars. 11–12 (11.6) mm.
Found in southern New Guinea from the Fly River, Papua, west to the Mimika River, West Irian. Along the east bank, at the mouth of the Fly River, immatures of this race show a tendency toward *suavissima*, but adults are typical *fuscifrons* (see Rand, 1938).

7. *O. g. melanogenia* (Schlegel)
ADULTS similar to *fuscifrons*, but female has a paler, more greenish breast.
7 males   wing 75–80 (77.3) mm., tail 29–32 (30.7) mm.,
          exp. cul. 11–12 (11.3) mm., tars. 11–13 (12.0) mm.
6 females wing 74–80 (76.3) mm., tail 28–32 (30.3) mm.,
          exp. cul. 11–12 (11.8) mm., tars. 11–12 (11.2) mm.
Confined to the Aru Islands, Indonesia; doubtfully distinct from *fuscifrons*.

GENERAL NOTES   Rand and Gilliard (1967) suggest that the Orange-breasted Fig Parrot is sporadically distributed throughout lowland forest and savannah, being common in some areas but seldom reported from others. This may be so, but it has been my experience that fig parrots are very easily overlooked, even in districts where they are quite abundant. Donaghey says that about Port Moresby and in the foothills of the Owen Stanley Range this species is common in primary forest up to approximately 500 m. (*in litt.*, 1970). In the Gulf District, Papua, it has been collected in *Melaleuca* swamp savannah. Near Port Moresby I saw several small parties feeding in the uppermost branches of tall forest trees.

Pairs or small groups are generally observed flying above the treetops or actively climbing amongst the foliage. When in flight they are noisy and attract attention, but while feeding are quiet and unobtrusive. The birds I saw near Port Moresby were first detected flying across a road passing through primary forest; only by closely following them and carefully watching where they alighted did I locate them in the feeding trees. The flight is swift and direct.

The feeding habits are probably very similar to those of the Double-eyed Fig Parrot. Donaghey has seen them eating fruits, probably figs, growing in clusters along the undersides of branches of forest trees.

CALL In flight a shrill, penetrating *tseet* repeated at frequent intervals. This is the only call I heard and there appeared to be no appreciable difference from the flight call of *O. diophthalma*.

NESTING Little is known of the breeding habits. In late September Donaghey observed what may have been a female inspecting a prospective nesting site. In a forest tree a male perched nearby while the female entered a hole in a bulbous growth protruding from a topmost branch. This growth appeared to be an epiphite or an abnormality in the bark. The female remained in the hollow for a few minutes then flew off with the male.

Mayr and Rand (1937) point out that young males possibly take up to three years to acquire adult plumage.

EGGS Undescribed.

DOUBLE-EYED FIG PARROT
Opopsitta diophthalma (Hombron and Jacquinot)

DESCRIPTION

Length 14 cm.

MALE general plumage green, paler and more yellowish on underparts; lores, forehead and fore-crown scarlet to deep red, bordered on hindcrown by a variable band of orange-yellow; above and in front of eye blue; scarlet to deep red cheeks, bordered below by a band of mauve-blue; flanks and sides of breast yellow; innermost wing-coverts orange-red; under wing-coverts yellowish-green; yellowish-white band on underside of secondaries; bill pale grey becoming black towards tip; iris dark brown; legs greenish-grey.

FEMALE lower cheeks buff-brown instead of red.

IMMATURES like female.

DISTRIBUTION

New Guinea, including the western Papuan Islands and some offshore islands, Aru Islands, Indonesia, and north-eastern Australia.

SUBSPECIES

I follow the arrangement proposed in my earlier revision of the subspecies (see Forshaw, 1967), but the examination of additional specimens has prompted me to synonymize *festetichi* with *coccineifrons*.

1. *O. d. diophthalma* (Hombron and Jacquinot)   *Illustrated on page 152.*
 15 males wing 81–92 (87.9) mm., tail 40–46 (42.8) mm.,
     exp. cul. 14–15 (14.6) mm., tars. 13–15 (13.6) mm.
 10 females wing 81–92 (86.2) mm., tail 34–42 (37.8) mm.,
     exp. cul. 14–15 (14.8) mm., tars. 13–14 (13.6) mm.
  Occurs in West Irian, including the western Papuan Islands, and western New Guinea east to Astrolabe Bay in the north and Etna Bay in the south.

2. *O. d. coccineifrons* (Sharpe)
 ADULTS general plumage darker than in *diophthalma*, particularly red of face and innermost wing coverts; wider and more pronounced orange-yellow band on hindcrown.
 15 males wing 83–99 (91.4) mm., tail 35–48 (43.8) mm.,
     exp. cul. 15–17 (16.2) mm., tars. 12–14 (12.8) mm.
 13 females wing 82–98 (91.4) mm., tail 34–43 (39.8) mm.,
     exp. cul. 14–17 (15.7) mm., tars. 12–14 (13.2) mm.
  Distributed throughout eastern New Guinea west to Astrolabe Bay and the Central Highlands.

3. *O. d. aruensis* (Schlegel)
 MALE blue above and in front of eye more greenish; mauve-blue bands below cheeks continue through to chin; orange-yellow band on hindcrown very much reduced or absent altogether; green of upperparts more yellowish.
 FEMALE no red markings on head, all being replaced by pale blue; no orange-yellow band on hindcrown.
 16 males wing 80–87 (85.0) mm., tail 38–44 (40.6) mm.,
     exp. cul. 14–15 (14.1) mm., tars. 12–14 (12.8) mm.
 11 females wing 80–94 (83.3) mm., tail 36–41 (38.5) mm.,
     exp. cul. 14–15 (14.2) mm., tars. 12–14 (12.8) mm.
  Occurs on the Aru Islands, Indonesia, and in southern New Guinea between the Mimika and Fly Rivers.

4. *O. d. virago* (Hartert)   *Illustrated on page 152.*
 MALE crown and cheeks paler red; no blue above and in front of eye; mauve blue bands below cheeks reduced to blue spot; green of upperparts paler than in *diophthalma*.
 FEMALE red spot on centre of forehead; remainder of forehead blue; lores and periophthalmic region green; cheeks green with variable pale blue and buff markings; no mauve-blue bands below cheeks.
 13 males wing 81–89 (85.1) mm., tail 41–48 (43.8) mm.,
     exp. cul. 13–14 (13.9) mm., tars. 12–14 (12.9) mm.
 9 females wing 82–87 (84.0) mm., tail 41–44 (42.3) mm.,
     exp. cul. 13–14 (13.8) mm., tars. 13–14 (13.7) mm.
  Restricted to Goodenough and Fergusson Islands in the D'Entrecasteaux Archipelago, Papua.

5. *O. d. inseparabilis* (Hartert)
 ADULTS similar to female *virago*, but with no blue or buff markings on cheeks.
 9 males wing 79–89 (83.8) mm., tail 37–43 (39.9) mm.,
     exp. cul. 13–14 (13.6) mm., tars. 12–14 (13.2) mm.

Blue-rumped Parrot **1**
Psittinus cyanurus cyanurus
NMV. B10520 ad. ♂

Blue-rumped Parrot **2**
Psittinus cyanurus cyanurus
NMV. B10521 ad. ♀

Blue-rumped Parrot **3**
Psittinus cyanurus abbotti
USNM. 179109 ad. ♂

Guaiabero *Bolbopsittacus lunulatus lunulatus* **4**
AMNH. 459181 ad. ♂

8 females wing 80–86 (84.6) mm., tail 37–44 (40.0) mm.,
exp. cul. 13–14 (13.5) mm., tars. 12–14 (13.3) mm.
Confined to Tagula Island in the Louisiade Archipelago, Papua.

6. *O. d. marshalli* Iredale
MALE similar to *aruensis*, but blue above and in front of eye darker and without greenish tinge.
FEMALE like *aruensis*, but forehead and forecrown deep violet-blue.
3 males   wing 84–87 (84.7) mm., tail 41–43(41.7) mm.,
exp. cul. 13–14 (13.7) mm., tars. 13–14 (13.3) mm.
3 females wing 79–86 (82.8) mm., tail 38–43 (40.7) mm.,
exp. cul. 13–14 (13.3) mm., tars. 13–14 (13.3) mm.
Occurs on Cape York Peninsula, North Queensland; exact range unknown, but probably extends from the Pascoe River and the upper reaches of the Jardine River south to the Rocky River. Commonly called Marshall's Fig Parrot.

7. *O. d. macleayana* (Ramsay)   *Illustrated on page 152.*
MALE lower cheeks and centre of forehead red; remainder of facial area blue, darker on sides of forehead, paler and more greenish around eyes.
FEMALE general plumage duller and more yellowish than in male; centre of forehead red; lower cheeks buff-brown with bluish markings.
13 males   wing 83–90 (86.7) mm., tail 34–45 (41.7) mm.,
exp. cul. 13–14 (13.3) mm., tars. 13–14 (13.6) mm.
17 females wing 79–89 (85.3) mm., tail 35–45 (42.3) mm.,
exp. cul. 13–14 (13.3) mm., tars. 13–14 (13.4) mm.
The Red-browed Fig Parrot, as this race is called, occurs in coastal areas of northern Queensland from Cooktown and the Atherton Tableland south to Cardwell, and possibly Townsville.

8. *O. d. coxeni* (Gould)   *Illustrated on page 152.*
ADULTS general plumage yellowish-green; blue marking on centre of forehead; some reddish feathers on lores and surrounding blue on forehead, less extensive in female; cheeks orange-red bordered below by a variable mauve-blue band; larger than *diophthalma*.
8 males   wing 93–100 (95.6) mm., tail 42–47 (43.8) mm.,
exp. cul. 14–16 (15.6) mm., tars. 13–16 (14.2) mm.
4 females wing 92–94 (92.8) mm., tail 42–46 (43.8) mm.,
exp. cul. 15–16 (15.5) mm., tars. 14–15 (14.8) mm.
Known as Coxen's Fig Parrot, this race is found in coastal regions of southern Queensland and northern New South Wales from Maryborough in the north to the Macleay River in the south.

GENERAL NOTES

In New Guinea the Double-eyed Fig Parrot inhabits lowland forest up to about 1,600 m. (Rand and Gilliard, 1967), and at Baiyer Valley in the Central Highlands I found it to be very common in riverine forest. I am more familiar with the species in Australia, where it is restricted to the three major tracts of tropical rainforest along the north-eastern coast. Within these three regions it is probably distributed throughout most forested areas, though Bourke and Austin (1947) found that it also frequents open woodland and partly cleared country. Near Murwillumbah, New South Wales, I have seen it in a stand of loquat trees (*Eriobotrya japonica*) in cultivated farmland. Occasionally it visits parks and gardens in Cairns and Innisfail, north Queensland. In the Claudie River district, Cape York Peninsula, I found that these fig parrots were confined mainly to rainforest; early in the morning and towards dusk birds were often seen in open woodland making their way from one patch of forest to another, but only twice were they flushed from trees in open woodland during the day, and neither of these trees was more than 10 m. from the edge of rainforest.

The general belief that this species is rare is probably due to difficulty in observing it; a small green parrot living amongst the upper branches of tall forest trees is easily overlooked. In Australia the two northern isolates, *marshalli* and *macleayana*, appear to be quite common, but the southern form, *coxeni*, has been subjected to greater loss of habitat and is now reported mainly from less accessible areas still supporting suitable forest.

Pairs or small parties are usually seen flying above the canopy or feeding amongst the branches of trees and shrubs. In flight they are noisy but while feeding seldom call, the only indications of their presence being the movement of foliage or the steady stream of discarded pieces of fruit falling to the ground. Soon after sunrise small groups leave the roosting tree and move out to the feeding areas. During bright, sunny weather they travel by means of short flights, pausing en route to preen and to stretch their wings. In overcast or wet conditions they fly straight to the feeding trees. Towards dusk they return to the roosting tree, where before nightfall many birds may congregate. At Iron Range, Cape York Peninsula, I watched more than two hundred fig parrots leave one roosting tree. The flight is swift and direct.

Fruits, particularly figs, berries, seeds, nectar, and insects and their larvae make up the diet. Bourke and Austin observed these parrots feeding on the fruits of *Ficus eugenioides* and *F. ehretii*; the parrots would bite a piece out of the fruit and gradually reduce it, discarding the unwanted portions which fell in a steady stream to the ground. At Iron Range I watched them feeding in the

Brehm's Parrot *Psittacella brehmii brehmii* **1**
RMNH. Cat. 4 ad. ♂

Brehm's Parrot *Psittacella brehmii brehmii* **2**
RMNH. Cat. 5 ad. ♀

same manner on *Ficus* and *Croton* fruits and noticed that they were eating seeds from the fruits, not the flesh. In Australia they have been observed in the company of Crimson Rosellas (*Platy-cercus elegans*) feeding on fruits of the blue fig (*Elaeocarpus grandis*) and with lorikeets extracting nectar from blossoms of silky oaks (*Grevillea robusta*). Gill (1970) reports that near Innisfail, north Queensland, a pair were seen tearing apart an old stump to feed on insect larvae. In the Baiyer Valley, New Guinea, I saw them associating with Ornate Fruit Doves (*Ptilinopus ornatus*) in a large fig tree heavily laden with fruit.

At Iron Range I watched a male feeding in a *Bletharocarya involucigera* tree growing in forest on the banks of the Claudie River. It appeared to be eating the bark or a fungal growth which may have been on the trunk. It fluttered to the upright trunk and removed some of the bark or fungus, while holding on to the face of the trunk and using its tail for support. After a few seconds it returned to a horizontal branch to crush and digest what it had taken. The entire procedure was repeated four or five times.

CALL In flight a shrill, penetrating *tseet* repeated two or three times in rapid succession; also a high-pitched, rolling screech and a sharp chattering.

NESTING The breeding season seems to be variable; in New Guinea it probably commences as early as March, but in the south not before August. One of three males collected in the Central Highlands of New Guinea between March and May had enlarged testes (Mayr and Gilliard, 1954). Nests containing eggs have been found at Maryborough, southern Queensland, in August and in the Cairns district, northern Queensland, during October. The nest is in a hollow limb or hole in a tree; the nest at Maryborough was in a rotting tree trunk lying on the ground. All reliable records indicate that the normal clutch does not exceed two eggs.

Between June and August, in the Baiyer Valley, New Guinea, Robinson carried out observations on two nests (*in litt.*, 1970). Both nests were excavated by the birds, one in a dead vertical branch and the other on the underside of an almost horizontal limb. Up to three holes were excavated, but only one was used. Males were seen feeding the brooding females, and later both parents were observed feeding the chicks. Adults always approached the nest cautiously; after alighting high up in the tree they worked their way down by short flights from one branch to the next and then, one at a time, flew straight to the nest entrance, clinging there with both feet grasping the edge of the hole. The hole was just large enough to allow the parrot to enter. While being fed the chicks kept up a constant twittering. Nothing further is known of the nesting habits.

Young males probably acquire adult plumage before the end of the first year.

EGGS Rounded; 2 eggs, 22.4 (22.1–22.7) × 19.5 (19.4–19.6) mm. [H. L. White Coll.].

Genus PSITTACULIROSTRIS Gray and Gray

This genus is very closely allied to *Opopsitta* and shows the same principal anatomical features. The members are medium-sized stocky parrots with extremely short, rounded tails. The ear-coverts are elongated, slightly in some forms of *desmarestii* but strongly in other races and in *edwardsii* and *salvadorii*. The cere is feathered. The bill is proportionately large and there is a prominent notch in the upper mandible. Sexual dimorphism is absent in *desmarestii* but present in the other two species.

As far as we know, the three species replace each other geographically and form a superspecies.

DESMAREST'S FIG PARROT
Psittaculirostris desmarestii (Desmarest)

DESCRIPTION Length 18 cm.
ADULTS general plumage green, paler and more yellowish on underparts; forehead orange-red, changing to orange-yellow on crown and nape; variable blue spot on occiput; green hindneck; cheeks green; blue spot below eye; pale blue band across breast, bordered below by an orange-brown band; blue marking on side of breast; innermost wing-coverts edged with orange; under wing-coverts bluish-green; pale yellow band across undersides of flight feathers; bill grey-black; iris dark brown; legs greyish-green.
IMMATURES crown dull yellowish.

DISTRIBUTION Western Papuan Islands, and western and southern New Guinea.

SUBSPECIES 1. *P. d. desmarestii* (Desmarest)   *Illustrated on page 153.*
  8 males   wing 108–116 (111.9) mm., tail 49–62 (54.6) mm.,
        exp. cul. 18–19 (18.6) mm., tars. 17–18 (17.8) mm.
  5 females wing 106–118 (112.0) mm., tail 49–60 (54.8) mm.,
        exp. cul. 18–20 (19.0) mm., tars. 17–18 (17.6) mm.
  Restricted to eastern regions of the Vogelkop, West Irian.

W.T. Cooper. 71.

2. **P. d. intermedia** (van Oort)

ADULTS crown and nape much more orange in colour; cheeks green with orange tips to a few feathers; ear-coverts green tipped with orange; blue absent from occiput or only slightly indicated.

6 males   wing 106–112 (109.3) mm., tail 59–62 (60.3) mm.,
        exp. cul. 18–21 (19.7) mm., tars. 16–18 (17.2) mm.
3 females wing 105–110 (108.3) mm., tail 45–59 (53.0) mm.,
        exp. cul. 18–21 (19.7) mm., tars. 17–18 (17.3) mm.

Known only from the Onin Peninsula, West Irian; doubtfully distinct from *occidentalis* (see Gyldenstolpe, 1955b).

3. **P. d. occidentalis** (Salvadori)

ADULTS cheeks, ear-coverts, and throat deep yellow instead of green; no blue on occiput; blue below eye less extensive and paler, more greenish in colour.

7 males   wing 107–114 (110.0) mm., tail 43–68 (58.1) mm.,
        exp. cul. 18–21 (19.9) mm., tars. 17–18 (17.4) mm.
1 female   wing 106 mm., tail 63 mm.,
        exp. cul. 20 mm., tars. 17 mm.
5 unsexed wing 106–111 (108.6) mm., tail 51–64 (59.2) mm.,
        exp. cul. 19–21 (20.0) mm., tars. 16–18 (17.4) mm.

Occurs in western parts of the Vogelkop, West Irian, and on Salawati and Batanta in the western Papuan Islands.

4. **P. d. blythii** (Wallace)

ADULTS like *occidentalis*, but cheeks brigher orange-yellow; no blue below eye.
IMMATURES blue subocular spot present.

2 males   wing 113–116 (114.5) mm., tail 65–66 (65.5) mm.,
        exp. cul. 20 (20.0) mm., tars. 18 (18.0) mm.
1 female   wing 118 mm., tail 63 mm.,
        exp cul. 21 mm., tars. 18 mm.
1 unsexed **(type)** wing 108 mm., tail 51 mm.,
        exp. cul. 20 mm., tars. 17 mm.

Restricted to Misool in the western Papuan Islands.

5. **P. d. godmani** (Ogilvie-Grant)

MALE no blue on occiput or below eye; crown and nape orange-red contrasting with yellow band on hindneck; cheeks and ear-coverts bright yellow, the feathers being narrow and elongated; pale blue band across breast.
FEMALE hindneck green without yellow band.
IMMATURES like female.

6 males   wing 108–119 (115.5) mm., tail 42–62 (53.3) mm.,
        exp. cul. 18–22 (19.5) mm., tars. 16–19 (17.0) mm.
5 females wing 107–115 (112.2) mm., tail 50–55 (51.8) mm.,
        exp. cul. 18–20 (19.2) mm., tars. 17–18 (17.4) mm.

Occurs in southern New Guinea from the Mimika River, West Irian, east to the Fly River, Papua, where it intergrades with *cervicalis*.

6. **P. d. cervicalis** (Salvadori and D'Albertis)   *Illustrated on page 153.*

ADULTS like *godmani*, but nape and hindneck blue; darker blue band across breast; lower breast variably tinged with orange-buff.
IMMATURES crown and nape green.

11 males   wing 105–117 (110.6) mm., tail 52–61 (56.5) mm.,
        exp. cul 19–21 (19.5) mm., tars. 16–18 (17.0) mm.
8 females wing 104–118 (111.1) mm., tail 47–58 (53.1) mm.,
        exp. cul. 19–22 (20.0) mm., tars. 16–18 (17.3) mm.

Found in south-eastern New Guinea west to the Kumusi River in the north and to the Fly and Noord Rivers in the south.

GENERAL NOTES   Rand and Gilliard (1967) point out that Desmarest's Fig Parrot seems to be an uncommon bird, or at least one which is locally distributed. Hoogerwerf (1971) claims that it is one of the commonest parrots about Manokwari on the Vogelkop, West Irian, but he does not give any details of his observations. It is primarily an inhabitant of lowland forest, where pairs or small parties frequent fruit-bearing trees, particularly fig trees. However, from the Waigani Valley, near Port Moresby, there is a record of one bird being seen in open savannah (Tubb, 1945). Around Manokwari Ripley noticed that small flocks were seen only in a certain species of *Ficus*, which had the fruit growing in clusters from the trunk (in Mayr and Meyer de Schauensee, 1939b). The flight is swift and direct.

CALL Undescribed.

NESTING Rand (1942a) reports that near the Black River, southern New Guinea, a number of these parrots were seen entering and leaving cavities in the trunk of a large, gnarled forest tree, thus suggesting the possibility of colonial nesting in such a site. This was in early July and a female collected from the tree was in breeding condition. Nothing further is known of the nesting habits.

EGGS Undescribed.

EDWARDS' FIG PARROT
Psittaculirostris edwardsii (Oustalet)

Illustrated on page 153.

Length 18 cm.

MALE general plumage green, more yellowish on sides of breast and lower underparts; forehead and crown yellowish-green; occiput olive-brown, merging into broad black band across nape to eyes; cheeks red, feathers narrow and elongated; ear-coverts yellow variably mixed and tipped with red and blue, feathers narrow and elongated; throat and breast red; blue-black band across upper breast; innermost wing-coverts edged with orange-red; under wing-coverts bluish-green; yellow band across undersides of flight feathers; bill grey-black; iris red; legs grey.

FEMALE wide band of dark blue across upper breast; remainder of breast yellow-green.

IMMATURES like female; cheeks yellow variably marked with red, feathers shorter than in adults; ear-coverts greenish-yellow, feathers narrower than in adults; iris reddish-brown.

10 males   wing 103–118 (107.7) mm., tail 50–63 (54.6) mm.,
          exp. cul. 17–20 (18.7) mm., tars. 16–18 (16.7) mm.
10 females wing 106–111 (108.8) mm., tail 47–55 (52.0) mm.,
          exp. cul. 17–20 (18.3) mm., tars. 16–17 (16.4) mm.

North-eastern New Guinea from Humboldt Bay, West Irian, east to Huon Gulf.

DISTRIBUTION

GENERAL NOTES

Edwards' Fig Parrot is an uncommon resident of lowland forest (Rand and Gilliard, 1967). In the eastern Humboldt Bay area Ripley (1964) saw a pair in the company of flocks of starlings feeding on the fruit of a very large fig tree in a village garden near the river. Rand and Gilliard report that in the foothills of the Finisterre Mountains, near Astrolabe Bay, several solitary birds were seen coming in to feed in the top of a fruit-laden tree; each bird moved quickly through the uppermost, outer branches, often hanging upside down to reach clusters of the green fruit.

CALL Undescribed.

NESTING No records. Ripley collected a juvenile in early July.

EGGS Undescribed.

SALVADORI'S FIG PARROT
Psittaculirostris salvadorii (Oustalet)

Illustrated on page 153.

Length 19 cm.

MALE general plumage green, paler and more yellowish on lower underparts; bluish-green forehead; green crown lightly streaked with blue; nape and cheeks golden yellow, feathers of cheeks narrow and elongated; blue spot behind eye; red breast; under wing-coverts pale green; innermost wing-coverts edged with orange; bill black; legs greenish-grey.

FEMALE crown green streaked with blue; hindneck yellowish-green; broad band of pale bluish-green across breast; orange-brown markings on sides of breast; yellow band on undersides of flight feathers; bluish-green under wing-coverts.

IMMATURES (MNHN. 253); duller than female; breast of male bluish marked with red.

2 males   wing 115–118 (116.5) mm., tail 58–79 (68.5) mm.,
          exp. cul. 18 mm. (damaged in one specimen), tars. 16–18 (17.0) mm.
2 females wing 109–114 (111.5) mm., tail 61–64 (62.5) mm.,
          exp. cul. 19–20 (19.5) mm., tars. 16–17 (16.5) mm.

Northern coast of West Irian from Geelvink Bay east to Humboldt Bay.

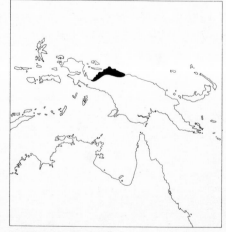

DISTRIBUTION

GENERAL NOTES

Very few specimens of the presumably rare Salvadori's Fig Parrot have been obtained. Rand (1942b) reports that a female was collected at 50 m. on the bank of the Idenburg River, West Irian. Nothing is known of its habits, but they are probably similar to those of Desmarest's Fig Parrot.

Genus BOLBOPSITTACUS Salvadori

Bolbopsittacus is a monotypic genus with superficial resemblance to *Opopsitta*. However, it seems to occupy a somewhat isolated position and the nearest relative is probably *Psittinus*. The species is a small, stocky parrot with an extremely short, rounded tail. The bill is proportionately very large and broad. The cere is naked. Sexual dimorphism is present and young birds are similar to the adult female.

GUAIABERO
Bolbopsittacus lunulatus (Scopoli)

DESCRIPTION

Length 15 cm.
MALE general plumage green, more yellowish on underparts; forehead, lores, periophthalmic region, throat and lower cheeks blue; blue collar encircles neck and meets blue cheeks; blue on bend of wing; rump and upper tail-coverts greenish-yellow; under wing-coverts yellowish-green; pale yellow band across undersides of secondaries; bill bluish-grey becoming black towards tip; iris dark brown; legs greenish-grey.
FEMALE blue only on throat and lower cheeks; yellow collar, on hindneck marked with black crescent-like bands; rump yellowish-green with black crescent-like bands.
IMMATURES like female; bill pale grey with little black towards tip.

DISTRIBUTION

Philippine Islands.

SUBSPECIES

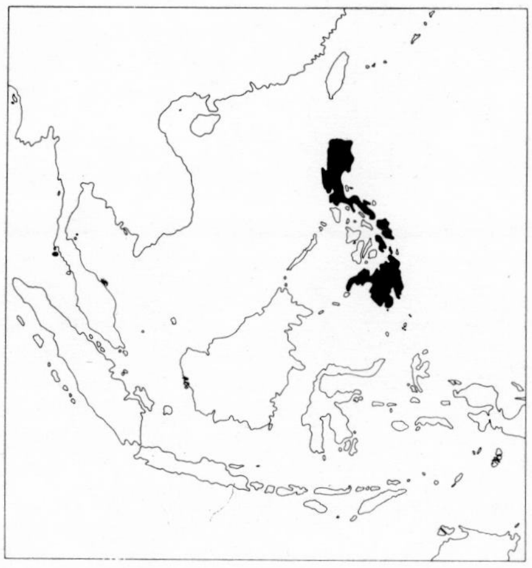

1. *B. l. lunulatus* (Scopoli)   *Illustrated on page 156.*
   10 males   wing 94–100 (97.2) mm., tail 30–35 (32.7) mm.,
               exp. cul. 16–19 (17.3) mm., tars. 14–15 (14.7) mm.
   10 females wing 94–99 (96.5) mm., tail 30–35 (32.0) mm.,
               exp. cul. 15–18 (17.0) mm., tars. 14–15 (14.6) mm.
   Confined to the Island of Luzon, Philippines.

2. *B. l. intermedius* Salvadori
   MALE underparts darker green; blue of face darker and with a purple tinge; brighter blue collar.
   FEMALE blue restricted to throat; pale green cheeks; paler green around eye; faint orange-yellow collar; green rump; thighs green instead of yellowish-green.
   10 males   wing 93–107 (101.5) mm., tail 32–35 (33.8) mm.,
               exp. cul. 17–19 (18.0) mm., tars. 14–16 (14.7) mm.
   10 females wing 95–109 (100.5) mm., tail 30–34 (32.0) mm.,
               exp. cul. 17–19 (17.8) mm., tars. 14–16 (14.7) mm.
   Occurs on Leyte in the Philippines.

3. *B. l. callainipictus* Parkes
   MALE similar to *intermedius*, but general plumage more yellowish, particularly on underparts; blue on face and nuchal collar deeper and more greenish; less blue on cheeks.
   FEMALE similar to *intermedius*, but general plumage more yellowish; brighter yellow nuchal collar and rump.
   No specimens examined.
   4 males   (Bull *in litt.*, 1971); wing 99–104 (101.8) mm., tail 46–49 (47.3) mm.,
               exp. cul. 18–21 (19.5) mm., tars. 11–14 (13.0) mm.
   4 females (Bull *in litt.*, 1971); wing 96–102 (98.0) mm., tail 40–42 (41.3) mm.,
               exp. cul. 19–21 (20.3) mm., tars. 13–15 (13.8) mm.
   Known only from Samar in the Philippines. I doubt the practical value of naming such a poorly differentiated population.

4. *B. l. mindanensis* (Steere)
   MALE green cheeks separating blue periophthalmic region from blue throat; blue collar on hindneck brighter and darker than in *lunulatus*; head has a yellowish tinge contrasting with purer green of back.
   FEMALE similar to *lunulatus*.
   7 males   wing 98–104 (101.0) mm., tail 30–35 (32.7) mm.,
               exp. cul. 18–20 (19.0) mm., tars. 14–16 (14.7) mm.
   2 females wing 95–97 (96.0) mm., tail 30–31 (30.5) mm.,
               exp. cul. 17–18 (17.5) mm., tars. 14–15 (14.5) mm.
   Known only from Mindanao and Panaon in the Philippines.

Guaiaberos are common and inhabit fairly open country, showing a marked preference for neglected clearings and low forests (Delacour and Mayr, 1946). Gilliard (1950) reports that on Bataan Peninsula, Luzon, they were common and specimens were collected from the upper branches of scattered mango trees growing on lowland pastures. Below 600 m. on Samar Island Rabor found them in fruiting trees at the edges of forests, in clearings within the forest, and in isolated fruiting trees growing in cultivated areas bordering patches of original forest or secondary growth (in Rand and Rabor, 1960).

They are usually seen in flocks and while in flight are conspicuous, but amongst the foliage of trees are difficult to detect so well does their plumage blend with the surroundings. Amadon and Jewett (1946) report that on Mt. Maquiling, near Manila, a flock of about fifty were seen swarming all over hanging vines and the lower limbs of a large jungle tree; the birds were moving quietly along the vines and limbs searching for food. The flight is swift and direct.

The birds feed primarily on berries and fruits, and are said to be particularly fond of guavas, hence the name Guaiabero. A bird collected by Amadon and Jewett had been feeding on soft, pulpy fruits, pieces of which adhered to the bill.

CALL Undescribed.

NESTING No records.

EGGS Undescribed.

Genus PSITTINUS Blyth

The species belonging to this monotypic genus is a small, stocky parrot with an extremely short, rounded tail. The bill is large and heavy and there is a notch in the upper mandible. The cere is naked. Sexual dimorphism is present and there is an immature plumage.

BLUE-RUMPED PARROT
Psittinus cyanurus (Forster)

DESCRIPTION

Length 18 cm.
MALE head greyish-blue much brighter on forehead and crown; throat and underparts pale greyish-olive; mantle and upper back blue-black faintly marked with green and grey; lower back, rump and upper tail-coverts deep blue; red on bend of wings; uppermost wing-coverts maroon-red; secondaries and greater wing-coverts dark green edged with greenish-yellow; primaries dark green; flanks and under wing-coverts red; thighs and under tail-coverts yellowish-green slightly edged with blue; tail greenish-yellow above, yellow below; upper mandible red, lower greyish-brown; iris pale yellow; legs greenish-grey.
FEMALE head brown, tinged with olive-yellow on ear-coverts; upperparts green with a small patch of blue on lower back; underparts yellowish-green with a slightly scaly appearance; entire bill greyish-brown; iris yellowish-white.
IMMATURES like female, but head green; young males usually have a tinge of blue on forehead.

DISTRIBUTION

From south-western Thailand and Tenasserim, in southern Burma, through Malaysia to Borneo and Sumatra, Indonesia.

SUBSPECIES

1. *P. c. cyanurus* (Forster)   *Illustrated on page 156.*
    12 males   wing 113–126 (119.1) mm., tail 39–45 (43.0) mm.,
            exp. cul. 19–21 (19.7) mm., tars. 13–15 (14.1) mm.
    10 females wing 111–120 (116.0) mm., tail 39–46 (42.0) mm.,
            exp. cul. 18–20 (18.9) mm., tars. 13–15 (13.8) mm.
    Ranges from south-western Thailand and Tenasserim, in southern Burma, south through the Malay Peninsula, including Singapore, to Sumatra, the Rhio Archipelago, Banka Island and Borneo.

2. *P. c. pontius* Oberholser
    ADULTS similar to *cyanurus*, but larger.
    11 males   wing 123–142 (134.4) mm., tail 45–51 (48.2) mm.,
            exp. cul. 20–23 (21.4) mm., tars. 14–17 (15.5) mm.
    8 females wing 116–136 (130.4) mm., tail 46–50 (48.8) mm.,
            exp. cul. 19–21 (20.5) mm., tars. 14–16 (15.5) mm.
    Confined to Siberut, Sipora and North and South Pagi in the Mentawai Islands, Indonesia.

3. *P. c. abbotti* Richmond

Illustrated on page 156.

MALE crown more uniformly blue; greenish feathers on forehead and around eyes; mantle and back green; rump and upper tail-coverts green; entire underparts greenish-yellow; larger size.

FEMALE entire head green; underparts greenish-yellow; larger size.

5 males   wing 140–149 (144.2) mm., tail 54–60 (57.2) mm.,
        exp. cul. 21–23 (21.8) mm., tars. 15–17 (16.0) mm.

5 females wing 134–144 (140.2) mm., tail 54–58 (56.2) mm.,
        exp. cul. 21–22 (21.2) mm., tars. 16–17 (16.4) mm.

Restricted to Simelue and Siumat Islands off the western coast of Sumatra, Indonesia.

GENERAL NOTES

Lekagul (1968) says that the Blue-rumped Parrot is common in the peninsular provinces of Thailand south of the Isthmus of Kra. According to Smythies (1953) it is only an irregular summer visitor to the extreme south of Tenasserim, southern Burma, sometimes arriving as early as late March. It is widespread, but not numerous, throughout the Malay Peninsula and on Singapore, generally in forested lowland areas (Gibson-Hill, 1949). On Borneo it is resident but rather rare in most areas (Gore, 1968; Smythies, 1968). It is a lowland bird and inhabits most types of wooded country, including orchards and plantations. Along the coast of Selangor, Malaya, large numbers have been seen in mangroves (in Robinson, 1927), while in northern Sumatra Hoogerwerf collected specimens from high trees in secondary growth surrounded by cultivated land, and from a solitary tall *Ficus* tree standing in a pasture (in Chasen and Hoogerwerf, 1941). Although sedentary in parts of its range, this species is apparently subject to some seasonal migration and considerable erratic local movements, for even in districts where it is present throughout the year marked fluctuations in numbers have been recorded (see Gibson-Hill, 1949).

Pairs or small parties are generally seen flying above the trees or feeding amongst the upper branches. Young birds are more gregarious and at the end of the breeding season large flocks visit oil-palm plantations, where they cause considerable damage (Ward and Wood, 1967). Large flocks have also been seen at other times and it has been assumed that these were migrating birds. When feeding they are fairly quiet and rely mainly on camouflage to escape detection. Their movements amongst the foliage are deliberate and rather slow, but the flight is swift and direct. They are noisy in flight and the call-notes can be heard long before the birds come into view.

Food consists of seeds, fruits and blossoms procured in the treetops. In north-eastern Sumatra they have been seen eating fruits of *Macaranga rhizinoides*, a tree of the coastal swamps (in Robinson, 1927). Crop contents from two birds collected by Hoogerwerf in northern Sumatra comprised small hard seeds. Ward and Wood report that these parrots feed on both ripe and unripe oil-palm fruits, and when present in numbers cause appreciable damage in plantations.

CALL A sharp, distinctive *chi-chi-chi* and *chew-ee* (Smythies, 1968); also a high-pitched *peep* (in captivity).

NESTING Breeding has been recorded in February and May in Perak, Malaya (in Stuart Baker, 1934), and between June and September in Borneo. The nest is in a hollow in a tree, often high up in a forest tree, and two or three eggs are laid. Stuart Baker reports that from three nests the sitting bird was taken and in each case it was the female. Nothing further is known of the nesting habits.

EGGS Rounded; 10 eggs, 24.2 (22.9–26.5) × 20.0 (17.5–21.3) mm. [Schönwetter, 1964].

Genus PSITTACELLA Schlegel

Parrots belonging to this genus are small to medium-sized, stocky birds with proportionately short, rounded tails and strongly rounded wings. The bill is robust and there is no notch in the upper mandible. The cere is naked. Sexual dimorphism is present and young birds resemble adult females.

BREHM'S PARROT
Psittacella brehmii Schlegel

Length 24 cm.

DESCRIPTION

MALE general plumage green, paler on underparts; head dark brown with slight olive tinge; yellow line on each side of neck; mantle, back and upper tail-coverts green barred with black; under tail-coverts red; blue on bend of wing; under wing-coverts green; tail green above, olive-grey below; bill bluish-grey becoming white at tip; iris red; legs grey.

FEMALE no yellow lines on sides of neck; breast yellow barred with black.

IMMATURES (Hartert, 1930); like female, but breast green narrowly barred with dull yellow.

165

Mountains of New Guinea.

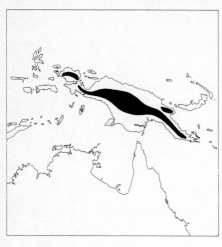

SUBSPECIES

1. *P. b. brehmii* Schlegel   *Illustrated on page 157.*
12 males   wing 118–124 (122.5) mm., tail 80–90 (85.8) mm.,
            exp. cul. 17–20 (19.5) mm., tars. 19–20 (19.3) mm.
11 females wing 119–124 (121.2) mm., tail 76–90 (81.5) mm.,
            exp. cul. 18–19 (18.5) mm., tars. 17–21 (19.2) mm.
Confined to mountains of the Vogelkop, West Irian.

2. *P. b. intermixta* Hartert
MALE like *brehmii*, but underparts more yellowish; throat and sides of head paler; mantle back and upper tail-coverts yellowish-green barred with black; slightly larger.
FEMALE abdomen more yellowish; throat and sides of head paler; mantle back and upper tail-coverts yellowish-green barred with black; slightly larger.
10 males   wing 125–138 (131.0) mm., tail 82–93 (87.6) mm.,
            exp. cul. 19–22 (20.8) mm., tars. 19–21 (20.0) mm.
10 females wing 126–134 (130.6) mm., tail 87–104 (92.4) mm.,
            exp. cul. 18–20 (19.5) mm., tars. 20–22 (20.5) mm.
Occurs in the Snow Mountains, the Weyland Mountains, and on Mt. Goliath, West Irian.

3. *P. b. harterti* Mayr
MALE like *intermixta*, but smaller and with general plumage less yellowish; head paler and more olive; bill smaller than in *pallida*.
FEMALE differences from *intermixta* and *pallida* as in male; flanks and sides of abdomen lightly barred with black and dull yellow.
2 males   wing 112–118 (115.0) mm., tail 71–78 (74.5) mm.,
           exp. cul. 18 (18.0) mm., tars. 19–20 (19.5) mm.
5 females wing 117–123 (119.6) mm., tail 70–82 (76.6) mm.,
           exp. cul. 16–17 (16.6) mm., tars. 19–20 (19.2) mm.
Restricted to the mountains of Huon Peninsula.

4. *P. b. pallida* Meyer
MALE plumage variable, but always more yellowish than in *brehmii*, particularly on underparts; some birds have blue wash on abdomen; bill narrower than in *brehmii*.
FEMALE general plumage more yellowish than in *brehmii*; flanks and sides of abdomen yellow barred with black; narrower bill.

IMMATURES (CSIRO. 2360); like female, but black barring, both above and below, narrower and duller; under tail-coverts orange-red tipped with yellowish-green; iris yellowish-brown.
16 males   wing 119–130 (123.5) mm., tail 73–90 (79.6) mm.,
            exp. cul. 18–20 (19.3) mm., tars. 18–21 (19.7) mm.
12 females wing 112–130 (120.6) mm., tail 66–88 (79.7) mm.,
            exp. cul. 17–20 (18.8) mm., tars. 18–21 (18.9) mm.
Found in mountains of eastern New Guinea west to the Sepik region; replaced by *harterti* on Huon Peninsula.

GENERAL NOTES

Brehm's Parrot is a mountain bird, and ranges from 1,700 up to 3,600 m. (Rand and Gilliard, 1967). Gyldenstolpe (1955a) reports that in the Wahgi Valley, Central Highlands, it was an uncommon inhabitant of grassland and shrub country, mostly occurring in the substage of low tree-growth. On the hillsides above the Ilaga Valley, West Irian, Ripley (1964) found it in deep *Nothofagus–Podocarpus* forest. It is usually seen singly or in pairs and is comparatively shy. When disturbed it flies a short distance to another low perch. Despite the rapid, noisy wingbeats the direct flight is not swift.

Seeds, fruits and berries make up the diet. In the Snow Mountains, West Irian, it has been seen feeding on *Podocarpus* fruits (Rand, 1942b). Stomach contents from birds collected in the Weyland Mountains, West Irian, and the Wahgi Valley, New Guinea, comprised berries and small, hard seeds (Rothschild, 1931; Sims, 1956).

CALL Undescribed.

NESTING In the Snow Mountains a male with enlarged testes was collected in January (Rand, 1942b). Two nestlings taken from a nest in the Wahgi Valley in early June showed a striking difference in development, one being well-feathered while the other had extensive patches of down (Mayr and Gilliard, 1954). Nothing further is known of the breeding habits.

EGGS Undescribed.

PAINTED PARROT
Psitacella picta Rothschild

DESCRIPTION   Length 19 cm.
MALE general plumage green, slightly paler on lower underparts; crown and occiput brownish-red; cheeks and ear-coverts greyish-brown; narrow yellow bands on sides of neck, sometimes continuing across hindneck to form a collar; chin, throat and upper breast blue; mantle and back green barred with black; rump and upper tail-coverts chestnut-red; under tail-coverts red; under wing-coverts yellowish-green; tail green above, dusky grey below; bill bluish-grey becoming white at tip; iris orange; legs dark grey.
FEMALE no yellow bands on neck; breast and sides of abdomen yellow barred with black.
IMMATURES resemble female, but head is brown with greenish edges to feathers.

DISTRIBUTION   Mountains of New Guinea east of the Snow Mountains, West Irian.

SUBSPECIES   1. *P. p. picta* Rothschild   *Illustrated on page 160.*
    11 males   wing 106–113 (108.6) mm., tail 70–73 (71.7) mm.,
                 exp. cul. 13–15 (14.2) mm., tars. 17–19 (17.9) mm.
    12 females   wing 105–114 (109.2) mm., tail 68–72 (69.3) mm.,
                 exp. cul. 12–15 (13.3) mm., tars. 17–20 (17.8) mm.
    Known from the Wharton and Owen Stanley Range in south-eastern New Guinea.

2. *P. p. excelsa* Mayr and Gilliard.
    MALE crown and occiput bright olive-brown.
    FEMALE head bright olive-brown; throat and cheeks strongly suffused with blue.
    8 males   wing 104–113 (110.1) mm., tail 65–73 (69.8) mm.,
                exp. cul. 13–15 (14.3) mm., tars. 17–20 (17.9) mm.
    4 females   wing 109–113 (110.8) mm., tail 63–75 (69.3) mm.,
                exp. cul. 12–14 (13.0) mm., tars. 18–19 (18.3) mm.
    Occurs in mountains of the Central Highlands of New Guinea.

3. *P. p. lorentzi* van Oort   *Illustrated on page 160.*
    MALE crown and occiput olive-brown; sides of head blue-green becoming darker posteriorly; throat green-blue; yellowish-green abdomen; rump and upper tail-coverts barred black and yellow.
    FEMALE differences from female *picta* same as between males.
    7 males   wing 109–120 (114.7) mm., tail 72–81 (77.3) mm.,
                exp. cul. 14–15 (14.4) mm., tars. 18–19 (18.1) mm.
    7 females   wing 109–116 (112.1) mm., tail 72–84 (76.0) mm.,
                exp. cul. 12–14 (13.6) mm., tars. 16–19 (17.7) mm.
    Found in the Snow Mountains, West Irian.

GENERAL NOTES   The Painted Parrot is a bird of the mountain forests between 2,500 and 4,000 m. (Rand and Gilliard, 1967), though Donaghey has seen it as low as 1,400 m. (*in litt.*, 1970). It is fairly common, but inconspicuous, in forested areas, particularly those adjoining open grassland. Donaghey says that it is widespread along the south-eastern divide from Mt. Albert Edward to the southern slopes of Mt. Victoria. It is usually seen singly or in pairs, but parties of up to about six have been recorded. Although showing a marked preference for low substage growth, it may be seen feeding high up in trees or may be flushed from the ground in nearby grassland. Donaghey has observed it feeding in the company of *P. madaraszi*. While feeding it is quiet, moves about slowly, and generally allows a close approach. When disturbed it flies a short distance to a low perch; in flight the red or yellow and black rump is conspicuous. The flight is direct and fairly swift.
    Food consists of seeds and berries. Rand (1942b) reports that it has been seen eating fruits of the conifer *Dacrydium*. Seeds and small, hard berries were found in the stomachs of birds collected in the Central Highlands (Sims, 1956).

CALL Undescribed.

NESTING A male with enlarged testes was collected in mid-June and another in breeding condition in August (Mayr and Rand, 1937; Rand, 1942b). Nothing is known of the nesting habits.

EGGS Undescribed.

MODEST PARROT
Psittacella modesta Schlegel

DESCRIPTION | Length 14 cm.
MALE general plumage green, more yellowish on lower underparts; forehead, lores and crown dark brown; feathers of nape and hindneck dull olive-yellow margined with brown; throat and breast pale brownish-olive; red under tail coverts; blue on bend of wing; under wing-coverts yellowish-green; tail green above, dusky grey below; bill bluish-grey becoming white at tip; iris orange; legs grey
FEMALE head brown, becoming olive on nape and hindneck; feathers of breast orange edged with dark brown; sides of abdomen barred with yellow and greenish-brown.
IMMATURES like female.

DISTRIBUTION | Mountains of western New Guinea from the Vogelkop, West Irian, east to the Central Highlands.

SUBSPECIES | 1. *P. m. modesta* Schlegel   *Illustrated on page 177.*
7 males   wing 91–97 (93.3) mm., tail 48–59 (54.9) mm.,
            exp. cul. 13–14 (13.4) mm., tars. 15–17 (15.6) mm.
7 females wing 91–95 (92.4) mm., tail 47–58 (50.7) mm.,
            exp. cul. 13–14 (13.3) mm., tars. 15–16 (15.6) mm.
Confined to mountains of the Vogelkop, West Irian.

2. *P. m. collaris* Ogilvie-Grant
MALE like *modesta*, but with an irregular yellowish collar below brown on hindneck; more rufous tinge on throat and sides of head.
FEMALE like *modesta*, but with indistinct yellow markings on hindneck.
4 males   wing 92–101 (96.0) mm., tail 53–56 (54.8) mm.,
            exp. cul. 13–14 (13.3) mm., tars. 16–17 (16.5) mm.
5 females wing 90–101 (93.6) mm., tail 54–58 (56.0) mm.,
            exp. cul. 12–13 (12.4) mm., tars. 16–17 (16.6) mm.
Occurs on the southern slopes of the Snow Mountains, West Irian.

3. *P. m. subcollaris* Rand   *Illustrated on page 177.*
MALE similar to *collaris*, but yellow collar is narrower and brighter; head darker brown and upperparts slightly darker green.
FEMALE similar to *modesta*, but head is darker brown; some birds have an indistinct yellow collar on hindneck.
5 males   wing 93–102 (96.2) mm., tail 55–64 (59.4) mm.,
            exp. cul. 13–14 (13.4) mm., tars. 15–17 (15.8) mm.
7 females wing 92–104 (96.7) mm., tail 53–68 (59.9) mm.,
            exp. cul. 12–14 (13.0) mm., tars. 16–18 (16.7) mm.
Distributed from the northern slopes of the Snow Mountains, West Irian, east to the Hindenburg Range in western New Guinea; birds from further east, that is, Central Highlands, may be *subcollaris* or an undescribed race (see Rand and Gilliard, 1967).

GENERAL NOTES | The Modest Parrot inhabits montane forests between 1,700 and 2,800 m. (Rand and Gilliard, 1967). Rand (1942b) reports that on the northern slopes of the Snow Mountains, West Irian, it was uncommon, being found singly or in pairs in the lower part of forest trees where it fed on seeds and small fruits. Nothing further is known of its habits, though they are probably similar to those of *P. madaraszi*.

CALL Undescribed.

NESTING No records.

EGGS Undescribed.

MADARASZ'S PARROT
Psittacella madaraszi Meyer

Length 14 cm.
MALE very much like *P. modesta*, but always without yellow collar on hindneck; head paler, more olive-brown and more strongly marked with yellow; lower back and rump generally more strongly barred with black; stouter bill; bill blue-grey becoming white at tip; iris brownish-red; legs bluish-grey.

FEMALE general plumage green, paler and more yellowish on underparts; forehead strongly suffused with blue; occiput, nape and hindneck barred with orange and black; rump and lower back barred with black and yellowish-green; red under tail-coverts; blue on bend of wing; tail green above, dusky grey below; iris scarlet.
IMMATURES similar to female.

DISTRIBUTION   Mountains of New Guinea, east of the Weyland Mountains, West Irian.

SUBSPECIES   1. *P. m. madaraszi* Meyer   *Illustrated on page 177.*
   17 males   wing 83–95 (89.9) mm., tail 47–55 (50.5) mm.,
                   exp. cul. 13–15 (14.1) mm., tars. 14–17 (15.5) mm.
   14 females wing 86–94 (88.9) mm., tail 47–54 (50.3) mm.,
                   exp. cul. 12–15 (13.9) mm., tars. 14–18 (15.5) mm.
       Occurs in the mountains of south-eastern New Guinea west in the south to the Angabunga River and in the north to Mt. Misim.

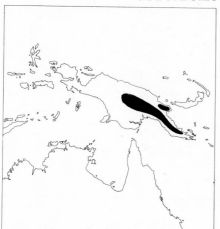

   2. *P. m. huonensis* Mayr and Rand
      MALE brown of crown more yellowish than in *madaraszi*.
      FEMALE no orange on occiput, nape and hindneck; less black barring on upperparts.
   1 male   wing 94 mm., tail 48 mm.,
                      exp. cul. 14 mm., tars. 15 mm.
   1 female **(type)** wing 91 mm., tail 53 mm.,
                      exp. cul. 14 mm., tars. 18 mm.
       Confined to mountains of the Huon Peninsula.

   3. *P. m. hallstromi* Mayr and Gilliard
      MALE general plumage darker than in *madaraszi*; head darker brown with narrower yellow markings.
      FEMALE barring on nape and hindneck brighter with wider black bands and darker, more reddish-orange margins.
      IMMATURES (CSIRO. 2255); like female, but with paler and less extensive barring on nape and hindneck; faint indications of yellow and brownish barring on breast; barring on rump and upper tail-coverts less pronounced; iris brownish-yellow.
   10 males   wing 83–103 (92.9) mm., tail 50–59 (54.9) mm.,
                   exp. cul. 14–16 (14.6) mm., tars. 15–16 (15.4) mm.
   7 females wing 86–96 (91.0) mm., tail 49–59 (53.0) mm.,
                   exp. cul. 13–14 (13.6) mm., tars. 15–16 (15.4) mm.
       Occurs in the Central Highlands and on the Hindenburg Range.

   4. *P. m. major* Rothschild
      ADULTS similar to *madaraszi*, but slightly larger.
   2 males   wing 95–97 (96.0) mm., tail 52–54 (53.0) mm.,
                   exp. cul. 13–15 (14.0) mm., tars. 16 (16.0) mm.
   4 females wing 90–102 (94.8) mm., tail 53–56 (55.3) mm.,
                   exp. cul. 14–15 (14.3) mm., tars. 15–17 (16.3) mm.
       Found in the Weyland Mountains and on the northern slopes of the Snow Mountains, West Irian.

GENERAL NOTES   Madarasz's Parrot inhabits montane forests from 1,250 up to 2,500 m. though Rand and Gilliard (1967) suggest that it may be more prevalent at slightly lower altitudes than is *P. modesta*. In July 1969 a specimen was collected in lowland rainforests near Port Moresby (NGM. B664). Hitchcock (pers. comm., 1969) found it in primary *Nothofagus* forest at about 2,500 m. in the Kubor Range, Central Highlands, while in the Morobe district, Papua, it has been collected along the margins of primary forest at about 2,000 m. It is a quiet, unobtrusive bird, and is generally seen singly or in pairs in the lower branches of forest trees. Gyldenstolpe (1955a) observed a solitary male in the upper half of a huge tree growing in a patch of heavy forest near a creek. At about 1,400 m. in the Owen Stanley Range Donaghey saw two birds in the company of a pair of Painted Parrots feeding amongst the topmost branches of a small, slender tree (*in litt.*, 1970).
   It feeds on fruits, berries, seeds and vegetable matter. There was fruit and leaf pulp in the stomach of the bird collected near Port Moresby, and Sims (1956) reports that crop contents from birds collected in the Central Highlands comprised seeds and pieces of hard berries.

CALL Undescribed.

NESTING A female taken in south-eastern New Guinea in mid September was laying, and a male with enlarged testes was collected in the Central Highlands in June (Mayr and Rand, 1937; Sims, 1956). Nothing further is known of the breeding habits.

EGGS Undescribed.

Genus GEOFFROYUS Bonaparte

The parrots in this genus are medium-sized, stocky birds with short, squarish tails and pointed wings. The robust bill is projecting and there is no distinct notch in the upper mandible. The cere is naked. Thompson (1900) points out that the skull is very similar to that of *Eclectus*, both having a prefrontal which reaches, but does not join, the squamosal, and a deeply and narrowly notched auditory meatus. Sexual dimorphism is pronounced and there is a juvenile plumage.

RED-CHEEKED PARROT
Geoffroyus geoffroyi (Bechstein)

DESCRIPTION

Length 21 cm.
MALE general plumage green, more yellowish on underparts and upper tail-coverts; forehead, throat and sides of head rose-red; crown and occiput mauve-blue; variable reddish-brown marking on median wing-coverts; blue under wing-coverts; tail yellowish-green above, more yellowish below; upper mandible coral, lower brownish-grey; iris pale yellow; legs greenish-grey.
FEMALE throat and lower cheeks olive-brown; remainder of head rich brown; entire bill brownish-grey
IMMATURES head green; throat and cheeks tinged with brown; bill brownish-grey.

DISTRIBUTION

Widely distributed from the Moluccas and Lesser Sunda Islands, Indonesia, to New Guinea and Cape York Peninsula, Australia.

SUBSPECIES

1. G. g. geoffroyi (Bechstein)   *Illustrated on page 180.*
   10 males   wing 138–154 (147.7) mm., tail 68–75 (72.8) mm.,
             exp. cul. 18–19 (18.4) mm., tars. 16–17 (16.6) mm.
   11 females wing 136–150 (142.5) mm., tail 71–75 (72.6) mm.,
             exp. cul. 17–19 (18.2) mm., tars. 16–18 (16.7) mm.
   Confined to Timor, Samao and Wetar in the Lesser Sunda Islands, Indonesia.

2. G. g. floresianus Salvadori
   MALE general plumage darker than in *geoffroyi*; darker brown patch on wing-coverts; violet-blue of crown darker and extending down to nape; under wing-coverts darker blue; larger with a larger bill.
   FEMALE brown of crown darker and extending down to nape; remaining differences as in male.
   11 males   wing 158–178 (165.3) mm., tail 73–90 (80.2) mm.,
             exp. cul. 20–22 (21.2) mm., tars. 17–19 (18.1) mm.
   10 females wing 159–176 (167.2) mm., tail 72–87 (78.6) mm.,
             exp. cul. 19–23 (21.0) mm., tars. 18–20 (18.7) mm.
   Occurs on Lombok, Sumbawa, Flores and Sumba in the Lesser Sunda Islands, Indonesia.

3. G. g. cyanicollis (S. Müller)   *Illustrated on page 180.*
   MALE general plumage darker than in *geoffroyi*; violet-blue of crown extending down to hind-neck where it meets a prominent blue collar; mantle and back variably tinged with bronze-brown, in some birds very pronouned on back; upper breast and lower abdomen bluish-green; no brown marking on wing-coverts; darker blue under wing-coverts; larger size.
   FEMALE head darker brown, less chestnut than in *geoffroyi*; blue nape; violet wash on crown; remaining differences as in male.
   10 males   wing 174–184 (178.8) mm., tail 80–101 (91.1) mm.,
             exp. cul. 22–24 (22.9) mm., tars. 18–20 (19.2) mm.
   9 females wing 171–180 (175.9) mm., tail 90–101 (94.8) mm.,
             exp. cul. 22–24 (22.9) mm., tars. 19–21 (19.8) mm.
   Occurs on Morotai, Halmahera and Batjan in the northern Moluccas, Indonesia.

4. G. g. obiensis (Finsch)
   ADULTS like *cyanicollis*, but with wider blue collar across hindneck and nape and extending up almost to the eye; violet-blue or brown of crown does not extend below occiput; lower back and rump reddish-brown.
   5 males   wing 175–183 (179.4) mm., tail 89–97 (94.2) mm.,
             exp. cul. 21–23 (22.2) mm., tars. 18–20 (19.0) mm.
   6 females wing 164–185 (176.7) mm., tail 91–98 (94.7) mm.,
             exp. cul. 21–23 (21.7) mm., tars. 18–20 (19.3) mm.
   Found on the Obi Group in the central Moluccas, Indonesia.

5. *G. g. rhodops* (Schlegel)
MALE like *floresianus*, but much larger; general plumage darker; dark brownish-red patch on wing-coverts; red of face sharply set apart from blue crown; darker blue under wing-coverts. FEMALE crown very dark chestnut-brown; other differences as in male.

22 males   wing 175–195 (184.8) mm., tail 80–96 (89.2) mm.,
exp. cul. 22–26 (24.2) mm., tars. 19–22 (20.3) mm.
22 females wing 169–192 (179.9) mm., tail 75–101 (85.6) mm.,
exp. cul. 20–27 (23.1) mm., tars. 19–22 (20.4) mm.

Occurs on Buru, Ceram, Amboina, Saparua, Haruku and Ceramlaut in the southern Moluccas, Indonesia.

6. *G. g. explorator* Hartert
ADULTS like *rhodops*, but female has paler brown forecrown.

4 males   wing 170–172 (171.3) mm., tail 76–82 (78.0) mm.,
exp. cul. 22–25(23.8) mm., tars. 18–19 (18.3) mm.
3 females wing 171–174 (172.7) mm., tail 76–81 (78.7) mm.,
exp. cul. 22–23 (22.7) mm., tars. 19–20 (19.7) mm.

Found on the Goram Islands, between Ceram and the Kai Islands, Indonesia; doubtfully distinct from *rhodops*.

7. *G. g. keyensis* Finsch
MALE like *floresianus*, but larger; general plumage more yellowish, especially the tail; ear-coverts rose-red washed with mauve-blue; red bases to blue feathers of crown; under wing-coverts pale blue; central tail-feathers greenish-yellow edged with pale green. FEMALE head paler chestnut-brown; other differences as in male.

10 males   wing 182–201 (190.9) mm., tail 86–99 (92.7) mm.,
exp. cul. 22–25 (24.1) mm., tars. 19–22 (20.6) mm.
11 females wing 184–195 (188.6) mm., tail 89–100 (94.1) mm.,
exp. cul. 21–25 (23.1) mm., tars. 18–21 (19.8) mm.

Known only from the Kai Islands, Indonesia.

8. *G. g. timorlaoensis* A. B. Meyer
ADULTS smaller than *keyensis*, but otherwise similar.

7 males   wing 172–181 (174.7) mm., tail 81–90 (86.1) mm.,
exp. cul. 21–23 (21.9) mm., tars. 18–20 (19.1) mm.
4 females wing 169–177 (173.3) mm., tail 84–87 (85.5) mm.,
exp. cul. 21–23 (21.8) mm., tars. 18–20 (18.8) mm.

Confined to the Tanimbar Islands, Indonesia.

9. *G. g. aruensis* (G. R. Gray)
ADULTS like *floresianus*, but general plumage paler, especially on underparts which are more yellowish; under wing-coverts variable, but generally darker than in *floresianus*.

11 males   wing 143–165 (154.5) mm., tail 65–71 (68.7) mm.,
exp. cul. 19–21 (20.2) mm., tars. 18–20 (18.9) mm.
10 females wing 148–160 (153.7) mm., tail 62–72 (66.9) mm.,
exp. cul. 19–22 (19.9) mm., tars. 18–20 (18.7) mm.

Occurs on the Aru Islands, Indonesia, in southern New Guinea east of the Mimika River in the south and the Kumusi River in the north, on Fergusson and Goodenough Islands in the eastern Papuan Islands, and north of the Rocky River on the eastern side of Cape York Peninsula, Queensland.

10. *G. g. orientalis* A. B. Meyer
ADULTS very similar to *aruensis*, but blue of under wing-coverts paler; paler blue crown in male.

3 males   wing 163–170 (166.0) mm., tail 70–73 (71.0) mm.,
exp. cul. 20–24 (21.7) mm., tars. 17–18 (17.7) mm.
1 female wing 154 mm., tail 66 mm.,
exp. cul. 20 mm., tars. 18 mm.

Restricted to the Huon Peninsula, north-eastern New Guinea; doubtfully distinct from *aruensis*.

11. *G. g. sudestiensis* De Vis
ADULTS like *aruensis*, but general plumage is slightly more yellowish; no reddish-brown marking on wing-coverts; crown and nape of female are dark green.

8 males   wing 161–168 (165.4) mm., tail 79–85 (81.8) mm.,
exp. cul. 20–21 (20.3) mm., tars. 16–19 (18.1) mm.
6 females wing 165–170 (167.7) mm., tail 82–85 (83.2) mm.,
exp. cul. 20–22 (20.7) mm., tars. 17–19 (18.2) mm.

Known only from Misima and Tagula Islands in the Louisiade Archipelago, Papua.

12. *G. g. cyanicarpus* Hartert

MALE similar to *sudestiensis*, but general plumage darker green; cheeks and ear-coverts strongly washed with mauve-blue; blue edge to wing from bend to outermost primary.

FEMALE similar to *sudestiensis*, but general plumage darker green; crown and nape brown slightly tinged with green; blue edge to wing from bend to outermost primary.

7 males   wing 170–182 (177.1) mm., tail 83–91 (86.3) mm.,
       exp. cul. 21–22 (21.3) mm., tars. 18–20 (19.1) mm.

4 females wing 172–177 (174.0) mm., tail 84–88 (85.8) mm.,
       exp. cul. 19–21 (20.0) mm., tars. 19–20 (19.5) mm.

Restricted to Rossel Island in the Louisiade Archipelago, Papua.

13. *G. g. minor* Neumann

MALE like *aruensis*, but lower back and rump brownish-red; red of face darker and less rose; mantle lightly washed with bronze-brown.

FEMALE head slightly darker brown; other differences as in male.

9 males   wing 156–167 (161.3) mm., tail 68–77 (72.2) mm.,
       exp. cul. 20–22 (21.0) mm., tars. 18–21 (19.3) mm.

8 females wing 151–161 (155.6) mm., tail 62–71 (67.8) mm.,
       exp. cul. 19–21 (20.4) mm., tars. 18–20 (18.8) mm.

Occurs in northern New Guinea from the Mamberamo River, West Irian, east to Astrolabe Bay.

14. *G. g. jobiensis* (A. B. Meyer)

ADULTS like *minor* but with paler blue under wing-coverts and much reduced reddish-brown marking on wing-coverts; back brighter red, less brownish than in *minor*; males have red of forehead extending back to forecrown.

8 males   wing 162–178 (169.9) mm., tail 69–79 (74.1) mm.,
       exp. cul. 21–23 (22.3) mm., tars. 18–19 (18.8) mm.

7 females wing 157–177 (165.4) mm., tail 66–78 (72.4) mm.,
       exp. cul. 19–22 (21.0) mm., tars. 17–20 (18.7) mm.

Confined to Japen and Meos Num Islands in Geelvink Bay, West Irian.

15. *G. g. mysoriensis* (A. B. Meyer)   *Illustrated on page 180.*

MALE like *minor*, but with violet-blue of crown extending down over hindneck and red of face down to throat; no bronze-brown tinge on mantle; more extensive reddish-brown marking on wing-coverts; dark blue under wing-coverts; rump and lower back darker red and less brownish.

FEMALE brown of crown extends down over hindneck; other differences as in male.

10 males   wing 159–175 (167.4) mm., tail 70–80 (76.8) mm.,
       exp. cul. 20–22 (20.9) mm., tars. 17–19 (18.5) mm.

10 females wing 158–172 (166.2) mm., tail 71–80 (75.5) mm.,
       exp. cul. 19–22 (20.9) mm., tars. 17–19 (18.3) mm.

Known only from Biak and Numfoor Islands in Geelvink Bay, West Irian.

16. *G. g. pucherani* Souancé

ADULTS like *minor*, but reddish-brown marking on wing-coverts absent or only slightly indicated; less bronze-brown suffusion on mantle; rump and lower back very dark brownish-red; dark blue under wing-coverts.

10 males wing 156–167 (161.5) mm., tail 65–77 (71.4) mm.,
       exp. cul. 21–23 (21.9) mm., tars. 17–19 (17.8) mm.

9 females wing 152–165 (159.0) mm., tail 68–76 (71.6) mm.,
       exp. cul. 20–22 (20.8) mm., tars. 18–20 (18.6) mm.

Found on the western Papuan Islands and in north-western New Guinea east to Etna Bay, West Irian.

GENERAL NOTES   Red-cheeked Parrots are widespread common inhabitants of lowland forests and savannah woodland. Bell (1970c) says that in New Guinea they occur in lowland tropical rainforest and the lower oak forests of the foothills up to 800 m., and although plentiful in both primary and man-induced savannah, their presence there seems to depend on the presence of scattered small patches of forest or vine-scrub. Bell also points out that on Goodenough Island they are very common even in mangroves, a habitat apparently not frequented on the mainland of New Guinea. On Flores, Lombok and Sumbawa they occur up to 500 m., mainly in rainforest and drier monsoon forest, but are also seen in cultivated farmlands (Rensch, 1931). On Timor Stein collected specimens as high as 720 m. and on Sumba up to about 500 m. (in Mayr, 1944). Stresemann (1914) reports that they were common in open country throughout coastal regions of Ceram but were rare in the interior. On Buru Toxopeus found them to be very widely distributed along the coast and in the adjacent hills but the Buru Racket-tailed Parrot (*Prioniturus mada*) seemed to take over their habitat at higher elevations (in Siebers, 1930). Lendon (1946) recalls that on Morotai, northern Moluccas, these parrots were very common, being exceeded in numbers only by the extremely abundant Chattering Lory (*Lorius garrulus*). Most reports claim that they are common birds in

New Guinea; I found them to be plentiful in the vicinity of both Port Moresby and Lae. Mackay (1970) says that around Port Moresby they are most common in rainforest and secondary growth, but are frequently seen in savannah where nesting has also been recorded. Hoogerwerf (1971) reports that they are very common in the Manokwari district on the Vogelkop, West Irian, and heavy forests are their favourite haunts. Although their range on Cape York Peninsula is very restricted, they are common in suitable forested areas (Thomson, 1935; Forshaw, 1966).

Red-cheeked Parrots are noisy conspicuous birds when in flight and their strident call-notes attract attention. Family parties are generally seen dashing about above the forest canopy, but flocks will congregate in a heavily-laden fruiting tree or at some other concentrated source of food. They are strictly arboreal and spend much of the day feeding amongst the uppermost branches of tall trees where their predominantly green plumage blends so well with the foliage. In contrast to their behaviour when on the move they are silent while feeding, but an observer standing near the tree will see them fluttering from one branch to another or hanging upside-down to get at fruits. Another indication of their presence is the discarded pieces of fruit falling to the ground.

I noticed that at Iron Range, Cape York Peninsula, Red-cheeked Parrots showed a regular pattern in their daily movements. In the early morning they left the roosting positions in tall trees by the river and flew out to feeding areas. En route many birds alighted on the very tops of leafless uppermost branches of tall deciduous trees and called loudly for two or three minutes. When calling they adopted an upright stance with the bill lifted slightly skyward; the wings were raised, but not spread, and were vibrated in accompaniment to the call (for illustration see Forshaw, 1969a). Only twice did I see two or more birds calling from the same tree, but up to ten were seen calling from neighbouring trees. As far as I could determine the parrots did not use regular calling perches, though from New Guinea Bell reports the consistent use of a calling perch by what may have been the same bird. The passage to the feeding trees was over by about 1000 hrs., and only scattered feeding parties were seen during the remainder of the day. The return flight near dusk was brief and direct, and the birds did not pause en route to call. It is noteworthy that the calling behaviour is common in New Guinea (Bell, 1970c), but the only indication of regular daily movements is the comment by Schodde and Hitchcock (1968) that in the Lake Kutubu area, Papua, calling was particularly clamorous between 0800 and 1000 hrs. each morning.

Pre-roosting aerobatics are commonly performed and during the day groups of birds may also be seen fluttering up and down above the forest canopy. Shallow rapid wingbeats are characteristic of the swift direct flight.

The birds feed on seeds, nuts, fruits, berries, flower buds, blossoms and probably insects and their larvae. Bell reports that most of his observations are of birds eating small fruits, but on one occasion he watched a parrot taking seeds from what appeared to be ripe fruits of *Eucalyptus papuana* and on another occasion a party of eleven birds were seen tearing apart unripened fruits of *Casuarina papuana* to get at the partly-formed seeds. At Iron Range I watched a pair eating fruits of scaly ash (*Ganophyllum falcatum*). They hopped from one branch to another and edged out towards the extremities to get at the fruit. They stretched out, bit off either the entire fruit or pieces of it and then withdrew back to the normal sitting position to crush and eat it; at no time were the feet used to hold fruit. Crop contents from specimens collected near Manokwari by Hoogerwerf comprised purple fruit pulp, remnants of fruit stones and remains of crushed seeds.

CALL In flight or when perched atop a tall tree a shrieking, metallic *aank . . . aank . . . aank . . . aank* repeated rapidly; also a disyllabic variation *aank-aank . . . aank-aank . . . aank-aank* terminating with an upward inflection, a repetitive *kik-kik-kik-kik*, and a variety of gutteral, chattering notes and shrill screeches. The parrots respond readily to imitations of their calls.

NESTING Breeding has been recorded in the Lesser Sunda Islands between April and August (Rensch, 1931; Verheijen, 1964), in north-western New Guinea in February (Mayr and Meyer de Schauensee, 1939b), in southern New Guinea in April and from October to December (Rand, 1942a; Bell, 1970c), and on Cape York Peninsula during August to December (see Forshaw, 1969a). The nest is in a hollow limb or hole in a tree, often in a hole excavated by the birds in a decaying trunk of a dead tree. Rand describes a nest found in southern New Guinea. It was in an excavation made by the birds in a large dead trunk standing in riverine forest and was approximately 10 m. from the ground. On a layer of fresh wood chips there were three eggs.

Little is known of the nesting behaviour. Bell examined two nestlings taken from a nest in advanced second-growth oak forest and found that there was a marked disparity in size; the larger was well-feathered, but the other was only little more than half the size and had a bare breast and the head covered with pin-feathers. Rensch points out that young birds remain with their parents in family groups for quite some time, perhaps even into the second year, and my observations on Cape York Peninsula support this.

Young males acquire the brownish head of the female before attaining the red and blue colouration, probably in the second year. Maclennan saw a male with plumage similar to that of the female feeding a young bird which apparently had recently left the nest, so it seems that males are capable of breeding before acquiring adult plumage, or the young of the previous year assist at the nest (see Macgillivray, 1918).

EGGS Rounded; average measurements of 3 eggs were 29.0 × 25.0 mm. (Rand, 1942a).

BLUE-COLLARED PARROT
Geoffroyus simplex (A. B. Meyer)

DESCRIPTION Length 22 cm.
MALE general plumage green, paler and more yellowish on underparts; forehead and throat yellowish-green; greyish-blue collar encircling neck; bronze-brown marking on median wing-coverts; inner edges of flight feathers narrowly margined with pale yellow, particularly prominent on secondaries; greater wing-coverts margined with yellowish-green; dark blue under wing-coverts; tail green above, dusky yellow below; bill grey-black; iris creamy-white; legs olive-grey.
FEMALE no blue collar encircling neck; crown and occiput tinged with blue.
IMMATURES like female, but without blue tinge on crown and occiput; bill brownish-grey; iris greyish-white.

DISTRIBUTION Mountains of New Guinea.

SUBSPECIES 1. *G. s. simplex* (A. B. Meyer)　　　　　　　　　*Illustrated on page 181.*
2 males　wing 148–157 (152.5) mm., tail 68–75 (71.5) mm.,
　　　　　exp. cul. 20 (20.0) mm., tars. 18 (18.0) mm.
2 females wing 152 (152.0) mm., tail 67–71 (69.0) mm.,
　　　　　exp. cul. 20–21 (20.5) mm., tars. 17 (17.0) mm.
Known only from the Arfak and Tamrau Mountains on the Vogelkop, West Irian.

2. *G. s. buergersi* Neumann
MALE collar less bright and more lilac-coloured than in *simplex*, and more extensive on hindneck; under wing-coverts more violet-blue.
FEMALE like *simplex*, but under wing-coverts more violet-blue.
10 males　wing 158–171 (162.9) mm., tail 68–77 (73.1) mm.,
　　　　　exp. cul. 21–23 (21.4) mm.,tars. 16–19 (17.6) mm.
6 females wing 151–161 (155.8) mm., tail 68–73 (71.2) mm.,
　　　　　exp. cul. 19–21 (20.2) mm., tars. 16–19 (17.7) mm.
Also called the Lilac-collared Parrot, this race occurs in the mountains of New Guinea from the Snow Mountains, West Irian, east to the Owen Stanley Range in south-eastern Papua.

GENERAL NOTES The Blue-collared Parrot is found in montane forests between 600 and 1,800 m., though there are also occasional records from near sea level. In the Owen Stanley Range, north of Amazon Bay in south-eastern Papua, Hitchcock collected specimens at about 600 m. in secondary forest on Nowata Plateau and at about 1,000 m. in primary ridge forest on Mt. Moiba (pers. comm., 1970). The species may be locally common, but is generally scarce. Rand (1942a) reports that above the Idenburg River on the northern slopes of the Snow Mountains it was fairly common and, singly or in pairs, frequented the tops of forest trees. Grant remarks that in the mountains above the Iwaka River, West Irian, flocks of up to twenty were seen flying back and forth above the forest canopy (in Ogilvie-Grant, 1915). It is noisy when in flight but is silent while feeding and could then be easily overlooked because of its predominantly green plumage. It is shy and when disturbed darts about above the trees, calling loudly, before settling once again. The flight is swift and direct.
　　Food consists of seeds, fruits and berries procured in the treetops. One of the specimens collected by Hitchcock had its crop full of seeds.

CALL A sharp, abrupt cry repeated often (Rand); also a variety of whistling notes (Grant).

NESTING In early January a nest containing three chicks was found at 1,800 m. on the northern slopes of the Snow Mountains (Rand, 1942b). It was in a hole, apparently excavated by the birds, some 10 m. up near the top of a large rotten stump standing in the forest. The entrance was about 80 mm. in diameter and a short tunnel only 70 mm. long led to a nest chamber measuring 200 mm. in width by 400 mm. in height. The young birds were of different sizes and were covered with short, grey down through which some feathers were just appearing. Nothing further is known of the nesting habits.

EGGS Undescribed.

SINGING PARROT
Geoffroyus heteroclitus (Hombron and Jacquinot)

DESCRIPTION Length 25 cm.
MALE general plumage green, paler and more yellowish on underparts; head yellow bordered

below by a greyish-mauve collar encircling neck; reddish-brown marking on median wing-coverts; pale yellow margins on inner edges of flight feathers, particularly prominent on innermost secondaries; violet-blue under wing-coverts; tail green above, dusky yellow below; upper mandible pale yellow, lower dark grey; iris pale yellow; legs greyish-green.

FEMALE crown and occiput grey variably tinged with blue; cheeks olive-grey becoming dull yellowish-green on throat; nape and collar around hindneck green, darker than mantle; upper mandible dark grey.

IMMATURES similar to female, but crown and occiput pale bluish-grey tinged with green.

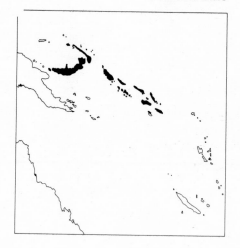

DISTRIBUTION   Bismarck Archipelago and the Solomon Islands.

SUBSPECIES   1. *G. h. heteroclitus* (Hombron and Jacquinot)   *Illustrated on page 181.*
   18 males   wing 150–170 (161.2) mm., tail 73–86 (84.4) mm.,
         exp. cul. 19–22 (20.2) mm., tars. 18–20 (18.8) mm.
   10 females wing 149–167 (157.0) mm., tail 75–83 (79.1) mm.,
         exp. cul. 19–21 (20.0) mm., tars. 18–19 (18.7) mm.
      Occurs on Lavongai Island, the Lihir Group, New Ireland and New Britain in the Bismarck Archipelago, and throughout the Solomon Islands except Rennell Island.

2. *G. h. hyacinthinus* Mayr
   MALE greyish-mauve of collar extends down to mantle and lower breast, sometimes even to flanks and abdomen; bend of wing bluish; pronounced bluish margins to primary-coverts.
   FEMALE bluish-grey of head deeper in colour and extending to neck and cheeks; pronounced bluish margins to primary-coverts.
   4 males   wing 173–176 (174.5) mm., tail 85–101 (93.8) mm.,
         exp. cul. 21–22 (21.8) mm., tars. 18–19 (18.8) mm.
   4 females wing 171–176 (174.8) mm., tail 93–103 (97.3) mm.,
         exp. cul. 21 (21.0) mm., tars. 20–21 (20.5) mm.
      Confined to Rennell Island in the Solomons.

GENERAL NOTES   The Singing Parrot is a bird of lowland forests and secondary growth, though on Bougainville it has also been collected in village gardens up to 500 m. Gilliard and LeCroy (1967a) point out that it appeared to be very uncommon in the Whiteman Mountains on New Britain. Cain and Galbraith (1956) report that in the eastern Solomons it is found in the lowlands and higher valleys, and pairs are generally seen in the topmost branches of tall trees, either isolated or in the forest. The predominantly green plumage makes this parrot most inconspicuous amongst the foliage and this, coupled with its secretive behaviour when entering or leaving trees, makes it easy to overlook. However, the shrill call-notes are distinctive and always betray its presence. Donaghho (1950) reports that small flocks were seen on Tulagi Island and in riverine forest on Guadalcanal; birds perched on the topmost branches of tall trees to call and did so for long periods, usually on bright sunny days, although one bird was seen calling when the weather was overcast. The flight is swift and direct.

The diet comprises seeds, fruits, blossoms and flower buds procured in the treetops. The Singing Parrot is said to be fond of bananas and will raid village gardens to feed on ripening fruits. Crop contents from two specimens collected by Cain and Galbraith consisted of small, seedy fruit.

CALL In flight a harsh *ee-ah . . . ee-ah . . . ee-ah* (Bradley and Wolff, 1956); also a shrill *chee* and a series of disyllabic whistling notes repeated rapidly on an ascending scale (Cain and Galbraith, 1956). The variety of call-notes given by this parrot is responsible for its vernacular name.

NESTING I know of no published records, but the breeding habits are probably similar to those of *G. geoffroyi.*

EGGS Undescribed.

Genus PRIONITURUS Wagler

Racket-tailed parrots belonging to *Prioniturus* are distinguished, as their name implies, by an elongation of the central tail feathers in the form of bare shafts terminating in spatules (see fig. 10). During the second or third moult these feathers commence to grow and frequently appear before the old ones have been lost. From an examination of specimens it appears that in adult birds feathers have bare shafts and spatulated tips from the time of emergence. The parrots are medium-sized, stocky birds bearing a resemblance to *Geoffroyus* spp., to which they are probably closely allied. Apart from the elongated rackets, the tail is decidedly squarish. The bill is robust and proportionately large with a distinct, but not pronounced, notch in the upper mandible. The cere is closely bordered by feathers, only the nares being naked. Sexual dimorphism is pronounced in some species, but slight in others; young birds resemble or are duller than females and lack the racket-tails.

20 mm

Fig. 10
Dorsal view of the tail of *Prioniturus flavicans* showing elongated rackets.

GREEN RACKET-TAILED PARROT
Prioniturus luconensis Steere

Illustrated on page 184.

Length 29 cm.
MALE general plumage yellowish-green, paler on head and mantle; under wing-coverts yellowish-green; undersides of flight feathers greenish-blue; white margins to inner edges of secondaries; central tail-feathers above green with spatules black variably tinged with blue, lateral tail feathers above dark blue tipped with black, entire underside of tail greenish-blue; bill pale bluish-grey becoming horn-coloured towards tip; iris dark brown; legs bluish-grey.
FEMALE generally darker and less yellowish; bare shafts of central tail feathers shorter.
IMMATURES like adults but central tail feathers tipped with blue and having pointed tips but without rackets.
8 males   wing 143–150 (147.0) mm., tail 125–155 (142.5) mm.,
          exp. cul. 16–19 (17.3) mm., tars. 16–18 (16.8) mm.
8 females wing 148–158 (151.9) mm., tail 114–134 (125.6) mm.,
          exp. cul. 16–19 (17.3) mm., tars. 16–18 (16.9) mm.

Confined to Luzon and Marinduque in the Philippine Islands.

The Green Racket-tailed Parrot is common in northern and central Luzon (Delacour and Mayr, 1946) but surprisingly little has been recorded about its habits. Gilliard (1950) reports that on Bataan Peninsula, Luzon, it was fairly common in the canopy of primary tropical forest. Hachisuka (1934) says that in northern Luzon it also frequents cornfields, where it feeds on both flowers and grain.

CALL Undescribed.

NESTING Young have been obtained in May (Whitehead, 1899). The nest is in a hollow limb or hole in a tree. No further details of the nesting habits have been published.

EGGS Undescribed.

BLUE-CROWNED RACKET-TAILED PARROT
Prioniturus discurus (Vieillot)

Length 27 cm.
MALE general plumage green, paler and more yellowish on underparts; crown, occiput and nape blue; wings slightly darker green than back; under wing-coverts green; undersides of flight feathers greenish-blue; pale yellow margins to inner edges of secondaries; central tail feathers above green with spatules black tinged with blue, lateral tail feathers above blue edged on outer webs with green and tipped with black, entire underside of tail greenish-blue; bill pale bluish-grey becoming white towards tip; iris greyish-brown; legs bluish-grey.
FEMALE similar to male but with shorter tail rackets.
IMMATURES blue on crown and nape absent or only slightly indicated; central tail-feathers with pointed tips but without rackets.

Philippine Islands, including Jolo Island in the Sulu Archipelago.

1. *P. d. discurus* (Vieillot)   *Illustrated on page 185.*
   11 males   wing 151–166 (156.4) mm., tail 103–137 (120.6) mm.,
              exp. cul. 20–21 (20.7) mm., tars. 15–18 (16.9) mm.
   9 females wing 148–159 (152.8) mm., tail 102–113 (106.9) mm.,
              exp. cul. 20–21 (20.2) mm., tars. 17–19 (17.6) mm.
   Found on Mindanao, Olutanga, Basilan, Guimaras, Luzon, and Jolo Island in the Sulu Archipelago, Philippines.

2. *P. d. whiteheadi* Salomonsen
   ADULTS blue on crown less extensive and not sharply defined, gradually merges into green of head.
   14 males   wing 153–170 (162.2) mm., tail 118–155 (142.1) mm.,
              exp. cul. 19–22 (20.3) mm., tars. 15–20 (18.2) mm.
   12 females wing 157–175 (167.3) mm., tail 100–143 (127.2) mm.,
              exp. cul. 20–22 (20.6) mm., tars. 18–20 (18.8) mm.
   Occurs on Negros, Bohol, Samar, Leyte, Masbate and Cebu in the Philippines.

3. *P. d. nesophilus* Salomonsen
ADULTS like *whiteheadi*, but with even less blue on crown, usually only a blue wash on centre of crown; darker green underparts.
1 male (**type**): wing 150 mm., tail 124 mm.,
exp. cul. 19 mm., tars. 18 mm.
Found on Catanduanes, Sibuyan and Tablas in the Philippines.

4. *P. d. mindorensis* Steere
ADULTS forecrown green without any blue; hindcrown and nape deep bluish-mauve; lores and cheeks more yellowish-green.
11 males   wing 161–174 (167.7) mm., tail 124–144 (131.8) mm.,
exp. cul. 19–22 (21.1) mm., tars. 16–20 (18.2) mm.
10 females 151–171 (161.0) mm., tail 109–133 (121.3) mm.,
exp. cul. 20–23 (21.2) mm., tars. 18–20 (18.8) mm.
Confined to Mindoro in the Philippines.

5. *P. d. platenae* Blasius   *Illustrated on page 184.*
MALE entire head and most of underparts blue, a little duller on underparts where feathers have yellow bases; under tail-coverts greenish-yellow tipped with green; tail spatules black tinged with green.
FEMALE blue restricted to crown and sides of head; underparts pale green with traces of blue.
17 males   wing 152–164 (158.4) mm., tail 105–156 (131.4) mm.,
exp. cul. 17–20 (19.1) mm., tars. 16–19 (17.5) mm.
10 females wing 154–164 (157.3) mm., tail 115–128 (121.3) mm.,
exp. cul. 18–21 (19.2) mm., tars. 17–19 (18.0) mm.
Occurs on Busuanga, Palawan, Dumaran and Balabac in the Philippines.

GENERAL NOTES

The Blue-crowned Racket-tailed Parrot is common and widely distributed in the Philippines (Delacour and Mayr, 1946). Small flocks are often seen flying high above the forest canopy. They are noisy, especially when in flight. Ripley and Rabor (1958) report that on Mindoro small groups of from five or six up to a dozen were commonly encountered in primary forest below about 1,750 m., and less frequently in cleared areas or cultivated fields where there were small remnants of forest trees in fruit or a banana grove in full fruit. An entire group often alighted in a particular fruiting tree to feed. Their constant screeching could be heard from afar. Potter (1953) gives some evidence of movements, for on Calicoan, off the southern tip of Samar, the species was not seen until mid-summer, but from then through to October it was increasingly common. Throughout September and early October the parrots could be seen at any time in forested areas. They were very noisy, screeching while in flight and when feeding in the treetops, often in the company of cockatoos, pigeons and coletos. The flight seems laboured, but is fast with rapid wingbeats.

They feed on fruits, berries, nuts and seeds. Ripley and Rabor report that these birds are very fond of bananas, and in newly-cleared land adjacent to forest are destructive to the green maturing fruit.

CALL A shrill screeching while in flight and less frequently when feeding.

NESTING Females with enlarged gonads have been collected in April (Ripley and Rabor, 1958). Goodfellow took three eggs from a hollow in early April (Ogilvie-Grant, 1906). It has been reported that this species nests in colonies in tall, dead trees, (Hachisuka, 1934; Delacour and Mayr, 1946). Nothing is known of the breeding behaviour.

EGGS Rounded, without gloss; 3 eggs, 31.3 (30.2–31.9); × 25.9 (25.4–26.6) mm. [Harrison and Holyoak, 1970].

Modest Parrot *Psittacella modesta modesta* 1
RMNH. Cat. 4 ad. ♀

Modest Parrot *Psittacella modesta modesta* 2
RMNH. Cat. 5 ad. ♂

Modest Parrot *Psittacella modesta subcollaris* 3
AMNH. 339620 ad. ♂

Madarasz's Parrot *Psittacella madaraszi madaraszi* 4
CSIRO. 4488 ad. ♀

Madarasz's Parrot *Psittacella madaraszi madaraszi* 5
QM. MAC6747 ad. ♂

MOUNTAIN RACKET-TAILED PARROT
Prioniturus montanus Ogilvie-Grant

DESCRIPTION

Length 30 cm.
MALE general plumage green, noticeably duller and darker on upperparts; in some birds feathers of rump very lightly edged with olive-brown; forehead, forecrown, lores and foreparts of cheeks blue, bases of feathers being green; large red spot on crown; green under wing-coverts; undersides of flight feathers greenish-blue; tail green above, greenish-blue below with spatules black tinged with blue; bill pale bluish-grey becoming white towards tip; iris dark brown; legs bluish-grey.
FEMALE entire head green with tinge of blue on forehead and around eyes; shorter tail rackets.
IMMATURES similar to female, but central tail feathers have pointed tips and no rackets.

Philippine Islands, including islands in the Sulu Archipelago.

SUBSPECIES

1. *P. m. montanus* Ogilvie-Grant   *Illustrated on page 188.*
   13 males   wing 161–171 (164.8) mm., tail 121–147 (135.6) mm.,
              exp. cul. 18–21 (19.8) mm., tars. 16–19 (17.6) mm.
   12 females   wing 152–172 (160.8) mm., tail 98–132 (117.8) mm.,
              exp. cul. 18–20 (19.1) mm., tars. 16–19 (17.8) mm.
   Known only from the mountains of Luzon, Philippines.

2. *P. m. verticalis* Sharpe
   MALE forehead, sides of head and nape green; entire crown blue with a central patch of scarlet; underparts greenish-yellow, more yellow on breast.
   FEMALE similar to *montanus*, but without any blue on head.
   7 males   wing 163–185 (174.6) mm., tail 125–146 (136.0) mm.,
              exp. cul. 21–22 (21.6) mm., tars. 18–20 (18.9) mm.
   4 females   wing 171–176 (174.0) mm., tail 119–127 (122.0) mm.,
              exp. cul. 21–24 (22.3) mm., tars. 18–21 (19.5) mm.
   Found on Jolo, Bongao, Tawi Tawi and Sibutu in the Sulu Archipelago, Philippines.

3. *P. m. waterstradti* Rothschild   *Illustrated on page 188.*
   ADULTS forehead to eyes pale blue, bases to feathers green; lores and cheeks greenish-blue; hindcrown and nape green; mantle and back green with a slight brownish tinge; lower back pale greenish-brown; tinge of blue on bend of wing; dull black spatules.
   11 males   wing 152–160 (155.7) mm., tail 114–147 (131.1) mm.,
              exp. cul. 18–20 (19.0) mm., tars. 16–18 (16.8) mm.
   11 females   wing 151–164 (155.5) mm., tail 98–147 (122.1) mm.,
              exp. cul. 17–19 (18.0) mm., tars. 15–18 (16.9) mm.
   Known only from Mounts Apo, Katanglad and McKinley on Mindanao in the Philippines.

4. *P. m. malindangensis* Mearns
   ADULTS like *waterstradti*, but with paler blue on forehead and forecrown; occiput and nape brighter green; brighter, paler blue on cheeks; less brownish tinge on mantle.
   6 males   wing 153–161 (158.2) mm., tail 136–140 (138.0) mm.,
              exp. cul. 18–19 (18.5) mm., tars. 15–18 (16.5) mm.
   7 females   wing 149–158 (153.7) mm., tail 107–147 (118.3) mm.,
              exp. cul. 17–19 (18.0) mm., tars. 14–18 (16.0) mm.
   Known only from the Mt. Malindang district on Mindanao in the Philippines; may not be distinct from *waterstradti* (see Ripley and Rabor, 1961).

GENERAL NOTES

The Mountain Racket-tailed Parrot seems to favour higher altitudes but is by no means confined to them. Hachisuka (1934) says that on Mt. Apo it is found in primary forest above about 2,000 m., but Rand and Rabor (1960) report that on Mt. Malindang specimens were collected between 850 and 1,700 m., and Meyer de Schauensee and Du Pont (1962) record a specimen from Anakan at 470 m. It is common and is usually seen in small flocks flying above the forest screeching all the while. It feeds in fruiting trees, sometimes in association with pigeons and other parrots. Soon after sunrise these parrots seem to delight in dashing through the trees and wheeling about high overhead to the accompaniment of continuous screeching. They occasionally fly about on moonlit nights. The flight is swift and direct with deliberate wingbeats.

Fruits, seeds, berries and nuts make up the diet. Sometimes, in the company of the Green Racket-tailed Parrot (*P. luconensis*), the birds raid cornfields to feed on ripening grain.

CALL A shrill, screeching note.

NESTING No published records.

EGGS Undescribed.

Red-cheeked Parrot *Geoffroyus geoffroyi cyanicollis*   **1**
         AM. B1998 ad. ♂

Red-cheeked Parrot *Geoffroyus geoffroyi cyanicollis*   **2**
         RMNH. Cat. 27, Reg. 2479 ad. ♀

Red-cheeked Parrot   **3**
Geoffroyus geoffroyi mysoriensis
         AMNH. 620826 ad. ♂

Red-cheeked Parrot *Geoffroyus geoffroyi geoffroyi*   **4**
         RMNH. Cat. 8 ad. ♀

Red-cheeked Parrot *Geoffroyus geoffroyi geoffroyi*   **5**
         RMNH. Cat. 5 ad. ♂

RED-SPOTTED RACKET-TAILED PARROT
Prioniturus flavicans Cassin   *Illustrated on page 188.*

Length 37 cm.

MALE general plumage green, paler and more yellowish on lower underparts and sides of head; neck olive-yellow extending down to breast and mantle; crown and occiput blue with a central patch of red; green under wing-coverts; undersides of flight feathers greenish-blue; central tail-feathers above green with black spatules, lateral tail feathers above green tipped with black, entire underside of tail greenish-blue; bill pale bluish-grey becoming white towards tip; iris dark brown; legs bluish-grey.

FEMALE no red on crown and blue less extensive.

IMMATURES like female, but blue on crown represented by blue edging to only a few feathers; central tail-feathers with pointed tips but no rackets.

11 males wing 176–194 (184.4) mm., tail 150–181 (164.7) mm.,
           exp. cul. 22–25 (23.4) mm., tars. 19–21 (19.9) mm.
5 females wing 179–191 (186.2) mm., tail 132–160 (142.4) mm.,
           exp. cul. 22–25 (23.2) mm., tars. 18–20 (19.4) mm.

DISTRIBUTION Northern regions of the Celebes, and on Peleng and the Togian Islands, Indonesia; said also to occur on Great Sangir Island, Indonesia, but this needs confirmation.

GENERAL NOTES Stresemann (1940) points out that the Red-spotted Racket-tailed Parrot has been recorded only from the northern peninsula of the Celebes, but it may occur on the eastern peninsula because specimens have been collected on nearby Peleng Island. Heinrich reports that in northern Celebes it inhabits primary montane forest below about 1,000 m., but is occasionally seen in clumps of trees in cultivated land (in Stresemann, 1940). It appears to be less common than the Golden-mantled Racket-tailed Parrot (*P. platurus*) but the habits of the two species are similar.

CALL A drawn-out screech with an alternating pitch, similar to the call of *P. platurus* but not as harsh (Heinrich, in Streseman, 1940).

NESTING No records.

EGGS Undescribed.

GOLDEN-MANTLED RACKET-TAILED PARROT
Prioniturus platurus (Vieillot)

DESCRIPTION Length 28 cm.

MALE general plumage green, paler and more yellowish on lower underparts; long under tail-coverts yellowish-green bordered with yellow; dull pink-red marking on hindcrown bordered behind by a dull grey-blue patch extending down to nape; variable orange-yellow band across upper mantle; lower mantle bluish-grey, sometimes tinged with green; wing-coverts dull grey; pale yellow margins to inner webs of secondaries; green under wing-coverts; undersides of flight feathers greenish-blue; central tail feathers above green with spatules black tinged with green, lateral tail feathers above green tipped with black and blue, entire underside of tail greenish-blue; bill pale bluish-grey becoming dark grey towards tip; iris dark brown; legs greenish-grey.

FEMALE entire upperparts green; shorter tail rackets.

IMMATURES like female; central tail-feathers with pointed tips but no rackets.

DISTRIBUTION Celebes and nearby islands, Indonesia.

SUBSPECIES 1. *P. p. platurus* (Vieillot)   *Illustrated on page 185.*
24 males   wing 170–187 (179.8) mm., tail 121–183 (152.4) mm.,
            exp. cul. 22–26 (23.4) mm., tars. 17–21 (19.0) mm.
12 females wing 166–184 (173.5) mm., tail 111–144 (125.5) mm.,
            exp. cul. 21–24 (22.3) mm., tars. 17–20 (18.8) mm.
Occurs on the Celebes, the Togian and Lembeh Islands, Siao Island, Peleng Island, Banggai Island, and Muna and Buton Islands, Indonesia.

2. *P. p. talautensis* Hartert
MALE generally darker than *platurus*, particularly on mantle and wing-coverts which are more greenish; head darker green; underparts less yellowish.
FEMALE like *platurus*.
12 males   wing 177–191 (180.8) mm., tail 101–152 (132.4) mm.,
           exp. cul. 22–25 (23.5) mm., tars. 18–21 (19.1) mm.
6 females wing 169–186 (175.7) mm., tail 101–129 (117.7) mm.,
           exp. cul. 22–24 (23.0) mm., tars. 18–21 (19.7) mm.
Confined to the Talaud Islands, Indonesia.

3. *P. p. sinerubris* Forshaw
MALE (MZB. 21881, **type**); no pink marking on hindcrown; mantle and wing-coverts green lightly tinged with grey; bend of wing and lesser wing-coverts washed with violet; smaller size.

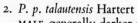

Singing Parrot *Geoffroyus heteroclitus heteroclitus* 1
CSIRO. 3218 ad. ♂

Singing Parrot *Geoffroyus heteroclitus heteroclitus* 2
CSIRO. 2939 ad. ♀

Blue-collared Parrot *Geoffroyus simplex simplex* 3
RMNH. Cat. 1, Reg. 22692 ad. ♂

FEMALE undescribed.
2 males wing 158–159 (158.5) mm., tail 126–132 (129.0) mm.,
exp. cul. 21 (21.0) mm., tars. 17–18 (17.5) mm.
This distinct subspecies is at present known only from Taliabu in the Sula Islands, Indonesia.

Heinrich says that the Golden-mantled Racket-tailed Parrot is found throughout the Celebes, but is most common in mountainous regions between 1,800 and 2,000 m. (in Stresemann, 1940). He reports that on clear days birds have been seen flying up to 100 m. above the highest peak of Mt. Latimojong. On Muna Island de Haan collected a specimen at the edge of forest and reported that the species occurred mostly in flocks of about ten, but was more often heard than seen (in van Bemmel and Voous, 1951). Van Bemmel and Voous suggest that on Muna and Buton numbers may have declined because of trapping for the local cage-bird trade. On the labels of the specimens he collected on Taliabu, de Haan has noted that the parrots were common.

These parrots are strong fliers and small parties of from five to ten are often seen in flight, even during the night. They move about widely in search of fruit-bearing trees. While feeding in the treetops they are difficult to observe, so well does their predominantly green plumage blend with the foliage. If disturbed they become silent and sit still amongst the leaves or behind a stout limb; if the disturbance persists they will suddenly dart out from the tree screeching loudly.

They feed on fruits, seeds and probably blossoms. Heinrich notes that they are very fond of mangoes and come down from the mountains to lowland villages to feed on these fruits. There are also reports that at night they attack ripening corn crops.

CALL A harsh screech with an alternating pitch (Heinrich); also a *kak ... kak* (in Seth-Smith, 1903).

NESTING In October a female in breeding condition was collected on Muna Island by de Haan. The nest is in a hollow limb or hole in a tree, but little is known of the breeding behaviour. Males probably take up to two years to acquire adult plumage and the tail rackets develop before the wing-coverts are grey or other adult plumage is attained (see Seth-Smith, 1903).

EGGS Undescribed.

Green Racket-tailed Parrot *Prioniturus luconensis* 1
AMNH. 620928 ad. ♂

Blue-crowned Racket-tailed Parrot 2
Prioniturus discurus platenae
AMNH. 620973 ad. ♂

Buru Racket-tailed Parrot *Prioniturus mada* 3
AMNH. 621031 ad. ♂

BURU RACKET-TAILED PARROT

Prioniturus mada Hartert
Illustrated on page 184.

DESCRIPTION

Length 32 cm.
MALE general plumage green, paler and more yellowish on underparts; yellow under tail-coverts; nape, hindneck, mantle and lower back bluish-purple, duller on mantle; bluish-green on throat; lesser wing-coverts bluish-purple; blue on edge of forewing; pale yellow margins to inner webs of secondaries; green under wing-coverts; undersides of flight feathers greenish-blue; central tail feathers above green with spatules dark blue tinged with green, lateral tail feathers above green tipped with dark blue, entire underside of tail greenish-blue; bill bluish-grey becoming darker towards tip; iris brown; legs grey.
FEMALE no bluish-purple on hindneck, mantle and back, slightly indicated on nape; shorter tail rackets.
IMMATURES (MZB. 13580); no bluish-purple markings, except slight tinge on nape in males; blue on bend of wing; central tail feathers with pointed tips but no rackets.
11 males wing 169–186 (178.3) mm., tail 121–151 (130.0) mm.,
exp. cul. 20–23 (20.8) mm., tars. 18–20 (18.9) mm.
4 females wing 169–182 (173.5) mm., tail 112–119 (115.8) mm.,
exp. cul. 20–21 (20.8) mm., tars. 19–20 (19.5) mm.

DISTRIBUTION

Confined to Island of Buru, Indonesia.

GENERAL NOTES

Stresemann (1913) reports that the Buru Racket-tailed Parrot was common in the mountains of Buru above 1,000 m., and was seen flying about in flocks. Almost all we know of the habits of this species has been reported by Toxopeus, who saw it frequently in the mountains and to a lesser extent in the lowlands (in Siebers, 1930). At Wai Eken, about 300 m., a group of adults and immatures was seen feeding in a fruiting tree and on the following day birds were seen near Mefa, almost on the coast. As a rule the species replaces the Red-cheeked Parrot (*Geoffroyus geoffroyi*) at higher elevations.

Food consists of seeds and fruits. The birds are said to be particularly fond of a particular fruit, which abounds throughout the mountains and is known locally as 'ka'keha'.

CALL A repetition of pleasant, whistling notes; nestlings give a soft *tee-wee ... tee-wee* and a harsh *kai-kai-kai-kai* (Toxopeus, in Siebers, 1930).

NESTING The breeding season is from December to February and the nest is in a hollow limb or

hole in a tree. Little is known of the breeding habits. Toxopeus found that there was remarkable variation in the development of chicks from the same nest; one nest contained five young birds, the smallest of which was covered with down, three others had down adhering to their emerging feathers, and the fifth was well-feathered without any traces of down. It seems that young birds acquire adult plumage before they are two years old, but within a few months of leaving the nest males show bluish-purple on occiput and nape.

EGGS Undescribed.

Genus TANYGNATHUS Wagler

Thompson (1900) points out that although the cranial osteology of *Tanygnathus* is broadly similar to that of *Geoffroyus* and *Eclectus* there are numerous distinguishing features, principally in the orbital and auditory regions. The parrots belonging to this genus are medium to large birds with very large, heavy bills and proportionately short slightly rounded tails giving them a 'top-heavy' appearance. There is no prominent notch in the upper mandible and the cere is naked. Sexual dimorphism is slight or absent, and young birds are duller than adults.

Blue-crowned Racket-tailed Parrot **1**
Prioniturus discurus discurus
USNM. 161123 ad. ♀

Golden-mantled Racket-tailed Parrot **2**
Prioniturus platurus platurus
AMNH. 298714 ad. ♂

Golden-mantled Racket-tailed Parrot **3**
Prioniturus platurus platurus
RMNH. Cat. 43, Reg. 12464 ad. ♀

GREAT-BILLED PARROT
Tanygnathus megalorynchos (Boddaert)

DESCRIPTION

Length 41 cm.
ADULTS head, upper mantle and upper tail-coverts bright green; feathers of lower mantle dull green tipped with pale blue; back and rump bright pale blue; underparts greenish-yellow, becoming green on thighs; under wing-coverts and sides of breast yellow; yellow across under-sides of flight feathers; scapulars and lesser wing-coverts black; median wing-coverts black broadly margined with deep yellow; greater wing-coverts green edged with greenish-yellow; primaries and secondaries blue narrowly margined on outer webs with green; tail above green tipped with greenish-yellow, below dusky yellow; bill red, paler towards tip; iris yellowish-white; legs greenish-grey.
IMMATURES like adults, but scapulars and lesser wing-coverts green with little or no black; narrow, paler yellow margins to median wing-coverts.

DISTRIBUTION

The western Papuan, Tanimbar and Lesser Sunda Islands, the Moluccas, and islands to the north and south of the Celebes, Indonesia; also on Balut Island in the Philippines where possibly introduced (see Hachisuka, 1934).

SUBSPECIES

1. *T. m. megalorynchos* (Boddaert)   *Illustrated on page 189.*
   13 males wing 233–251 (243.8) mm., tail 140–158 (150.0) mm.,
         exp. cul. 42–52 (48.2) mm., tars. 25–27 (26.2) mm.
   9 females wing 232–248 (238.4) mm., tail 131–150 (141.8) mm.,
         exp. cul. 41–48 (44.3) mm., tars. 23–26 (25.1) mm.
   Occurs on the Talaud and Sangir Islands and surrounding small islands north of the Celebes, and throughout the northern and central Moluccas, including Majau Island in the Molucca Sea, the western Papuan Islands, and small islands off the western coast of the Vogelkop, West Irian; possibly introduced to Balut Island off the southern coast of Mindanao in the Philippines.

2. *T. m. affinis* Wallace
   ADULTS head with a bluish tinge and contrasting with green of hindneck; entire underparts green with little yellowish suffusion; under wing-coverts and sides of breast more greenish than in *megalorynchos*; green scapulars; bend of wing blue; greenish-blue lesser wing-coverts.
   10 males   wing 235–250 (241.9) mm., tail 136–149 (141.1) mm.,
         exp. cul. 44–48 (45.9) mm., tars. 24–27 (25.5) mm.
   10 females wing 225–239 (232.7) mm., tail 130–140 (134.5) mm.,
         exp. cul. 40–47 (42.8) mm., tars. 23–26 (24.4) mm.
   Found on Buru, Ceram, Amboina and Haruku in the southern Moluccas.

3. *T. m. subaffinis* Sclater
   ADULTS similar to *affinis*, but with little or no blue on tips of feathers of mantle; rump tinged with very pale blue; median wing-coverts not so bright or blackish and with paler yellow margins.

10 males wing 234–249 (239.9) mm., tail 136–147 (141.6) mm.,
            exp. cul. 44–47 (45.8) mm., tars. 25–28 (26.3) mm.
5 females wing 234–242 (236.4) mm., tail 132–148 (140.2) mm.,
            exp. cul. 44–47 (45.6) mm., tars. 22–27 (25.4) mm.
    Known only from the Tanimbar Islands.

4. *T. m. hellmayri* Mayr
MALE like *affinis*, but without blue margins to feathers of mantle; bend of wing green not blue; margins to median wing-coverts narrower and pale greenish-yellow instead of deep yellow; head more yellowish, without a pronounced bluish tinge and not contrasting with hindneck.
FEMALE similar to *affinis*, but with less black on lesser wing-coverts; bend of wing and greater wing-coverts more greenish.
1 male **(type)** wing 236 mm., tail 147 mm.,
            exp. cul. 43 mm., tars. 26 mm.
1 female   wing 229 mm., tail 131 mm.,
            exp. cul. 42 mm., tars. 25 mm.
    Confined to westernmost Timor and nearby Semao Island.

5. *T. m. viridipennis* Hartert
ADULTS like *megalorynchos*, but primaries and secondaries green instead of blue.
5 males   wing 239–254 (244.4) mm., tail 140–154 (144.8) mm.,
            exp. cul. 43–48 (45.0) mm., tars. 25–28 (26.2) mm.
7 females wing 232–240 (237.1) mm., tail 133–148 (142.6) mm.,
            exp. cul. 40–44 (42.4) mm., tars. 25–27 (25.7) mm.
    Restricted to Kalao tua and Madu Islands, south of the Celebes.

6. *T. m. djampeae* Hartert
ADULTS similar to *floris*, but with paler blue rump; primaries more greenish.
2 males   wing 239–245 (242.0) mm., tail 152–156 (154.0) mm.,
            exp. cul. 47–49 (48.0) mm., tars. 26 (26.0) mm.
3 females wing 231–256 (241.0) mm., tail 137–156 (147.7) mm.,
            exp. cul. 41–49 (44.3) mm., tars. 26 (26.0) mm.
    Found on the Islands of Djampea and Kalao, south of the Celebes.

7. *T. m. floris* Hartert
ADULTS like *sumbensis*, but crown and occiput lighter green; less blue on back and wings, but rump is deep blue as in *sumbensis*; underparts slightly more yellowish.
No males examined.
8 females wing 222–245 (233.3) mm., tail 132–150 (142.1) mm.,
            exp. cul. 42–48 (43.9) mm., tars. 24–26 (25.1) mm.
    Restricted to Flores in the Lesser Sunda Islands.

8. *T. m. sumbensis* A. B. Meyer
ADULTS similar to *megalorynchos*, but underparts less yellow and more greenish, especially on breast; under wing-coverts more greenish; more prominent blue tips to feathers of mantle; darker blue rump.
6 males   wing 245–261 (252.3) mm., tail 132–160 (154.7) mm.,
            exp. cul. 49–52 (50.3) mm., tars. 25–28 (26.2) mm.
3 females wing 246–256 (251.0) mm., tail 158–172 (162.7) mm.,
            exp. cul. 45–51 (47.3) mm., tars. 26 (26.0) mm.
    Confined to Sumba in the Lesser Sunda Islands.

Mountain Racket-tailed Parrot 1
Prioniturus montanus montanus
AMNH. 620982 ad. ♂

Mountain Racket-tailed Parrot 2
Prioniturus montanus waterstradti
USNM. 192135 ad. ♂

Red-spotted Racket-tailed Parrot 3
Prioniturus flavicans
NMV. 10076 ad. ♂

GENERAL NOTES   The Great-billed Parrot favours small islands and coastal areas on larger islands. Stresemann (1914) reports that on Ceram it appeared to be totally absent from some districts and extremely numerous in others, particularly along the coast wherever *Sonneratia alba* grew as a beach tree; apparently the large green fruits were a favourite food. Rensch (1931) notes that the species is well-known to local people on the south coast of Flores, but he did not see it in the mountains. On Timor Stein collected specimens at 160 and 300 m. (in Mayr, 1944). Toxopeus records that on Buru this parrot was usually seen either singly or in small parties. However, each evening hundreds of birds, in parties of twenty or more, could be seen flying in an easterly direction along the northern shores of Lake Rana towards the mountains, presumably to roost because next morning they would return before the early mists had dissipated (in Siebers, 1930). In the Schildpad Islands, off the western coast of the Vogelkop, Ripley found these parrots wandering from island to island in search of the fruit of a certain large glossy-leaved tree growing only along the shore (in Mayr and Meyer de Schauensee, 1939c). Rapid wingbeats are a noticeable feature of the flight (Lendon, 1946).

These parrots feed primarily on fruits and nuts. The fruits being eaten on the Schildpad Islands were about the size of a lemon, the skin being green and the flesh like that of an olive; the yellow stony seeds, about 25 mm. long, were discarded by the parrots and littered the ground under the trees. Toxopeus says that they also attack corn crops.

CALL In flight a shrill cry (Lendon, 1946).

NESTING Toxopeus estimated that on Buru breeding occurred about December. Nests were in hollows high up in tall trees. Nothing is known of the nesting habits.

EGGS Broadly elliptical; a single egg in the British Museum measures 38.8 × 28.4 mm. [Harrison and Holyoak, 1970].

BLUE-NAPED PARROT
Tanygnathus lucionensis (Linné)

DESCRIPTION Length 31 cm.
ADULTS general plumage green, noticeably more brilliant on head and rump; hindcrown and occiput blue; bend of wing and lesser wing-coverts black, latter narrowly margined with blue; median wing-coverts black broadly margined with dull orange-yellow; scapulars, tertials and secondary-coverts blue edged with yellowish-green; back variably suffused with blue; under wing-coverts green; tail green above, dusky yellow below; bill red, paler towards tip; iris pale yellow; legs greenish-grey.
IMMATURES general plumage darker, duller green; little or no blue on crown and occiput; wing-coverts green margined with greenish-yellow; lower back tinged with blue.

DISTRIBUTION Philippine Islands, islands off northern and eastern Borneo, and islands north of the Celebes, Indonesia.

SUBSPECIES Rand and Rabor (1960) point out that the considerable geographical variation in this species presents a difficult nomenclatural problem. Insular populations similar to each other are separated by islands on which occur different populations. To overcome this Rand and Rabor have grouped all green-backed forms under *T. l. talautensis* Meyer and Wiglesworth, the oldest name, and I follow this arrangement.

1. *T. l. lucionensis* (Linné)
    10 males   wing 179–202 (188.4) mm., tail 107–131 (117.4) mm.,
                exp. cul. 27–33 (30.8) mm., tars. 18–21 (19.3) mm.
    10 females wing 186–198 (191.1) mm., tail 106–119 (114.1) mm.,
                exp. cul. 29–33 (30.5) mm., tars. 20–25 (21.0) mm.
    Confined to Luzon and Mindoro in the Philippines.

2. *T. l. hybridus* Salomonsen
    ADULTS similar to *lucionensis*, but blue on head much paler and reduced to occiput; feathers of back and rump green broadly tipped with pale blue; mantle green without any blue; wing-coverts green margined with yellowish-green, broadest on median and lesser coverts, and more brownish on lesser coverts.
    2 males   wing 194–195 (194.5) mm., tail 124–132 (128.0) mm.,
               exp. cul. 33–34 (33.5) mm., tars. 21–22 (21.5) mm.
    1 female   wing 195 mm., tail 116 mm.,
               exp. cul. 30 mm., tars. 22 mm.
    Known only from Polillo in the Philippines.

3. *T. l. talautensis* Meyer and Wiglesworth   *Illustrated on page 189.*
    ADULTS back green without traces of blue; blue on crown and occiput variable.
    IMMATURES like *lucionensis*, and blue is often present on back.
    10 males   wing 171–200 (183.8) mm., tail 100–126 (110.1) mm.,
                exp. cul. 30–38 (32.6) mm., tars. 20–23 (21.0) mm.
    10 females wing 170–202 (186.1) mm., tail 100–123 (110.9) mm.,
                exp. cul. 29–36 (31.4) mm., tars. 19–22 (21.0) mm.
    Occurs throughout central and southern Philippines, including Palawan and the Sulu Archipelago, on Mantanani and Siamil Islands and the Maratua Islands, off north-eastern Borneo, and on Siau and Great Sangir Islands and the Talaud Islands, north of the Celebes, Indonesia.

Great-billed Parrot 1
Tanygnathus megalorynchos megalorynchos
RMNH. Cat. 61, Reg. 2479 ad. unsexed

Blue-naped Parrot 2
Tanygnathus lucionensis talautensis
USNM. 201826 ad. ♂

GENERAL NOTES The Blue-naped Parrot is very common in the Philippines, where it frequents forests but often comes out into open country (Delacour and Mayr, 1946). Rand and Rabor (1960) report that on Siquijor, in the Philippines, it was found in forest and secondary growth but also came out into cultivated fields to feed on grain. It is a popular cage-bird and Kloss (1930) suggests that it may have been introduced to islands off the Borneo coast by sailing craft from the Sulu Archipelago. However, after discovering the species on Siamil Island, Thompson (1966) came to the conclusion that it was probably a naturally-established resident on these islands. He estimated that there were from thirty to one hundred birds on Siamil Island, and noted that flocks of from ten to twenty were seen in the remnant of forest on the north side, but birds were rarely observed in the coconut groves that covered most of the island. There is a specimen from the Lawas River in north-eastern Borneo but this was almost certainly a captive bird (see Hachisuka, 1934).

Little has been recorded about the bird's habits, though they are probably similar to those of Müller's Parrot. Fruits, seeds, berries and nuts make up the diet. Grain is also eaten and the birds can be troublesome in corn-growing areas.

CALL A harsh drawn-out metallic note (in captivity); very different from the call of *T. sumatranus*.

NESTING On Samar, in the Philippines, nesting in holes in trunks of old trees was observed in June (Whitehead, 1899). There are no other published details of the breeding habits.

EGGS Broadly elliptical; 7 eggs, 38.7 (36.0–40.9 × 27.0 (25.0–28.4) mm. [Harrison and Holyoak, 1970].

MÜLLER'S PARROT
Tanygnathus sumatranus (Raffles)

Length 32 cm.
MALE general plumage green, brighter on head and upper tail-coverts, more yellowish on mantle and underparts; rump and lower back blue; lesser and primary wing-coverts green margined with blue; median and secondary wing-coverts green margined with yellowish-green; under wing-coverts yellowish-green; tail above green tipped with greenish-yellow; below dusky yellow; bill red, paler towards tip; iris pale yellow; legs greenish-brown.
FEMALE mantle darker green, less yellowish; little blue on margins of lesser wing-coverts; white bill.
IMMATURES similar to female.

Philippine Islands, including the Sulu Archipelago, the Talaud and Sangir Islands and the Celebes and nearby islands, Indonesia.

1. *T. s. sumatranus* (Raffles). *Illustrated on page 192.*
   10 males   wing 201–221 (208.4) mm., tail 116–128 (121.9) mm.,
               exp. cul. 32–35 (32.9) mm., tars. 22–23 (22.5) mm.
   10 females wing 201–211 (206.5) mm., tail 114–125 (119.2) mm.,
               exp. cul. 29–32 (29.6) mm., tars. 21–23 (22.2) mm.
   Occurs in the Celebes, including small islands off the northern peninsula, on the Togian and Sula Islands, the Banggai Archipelago, and on Muna and Buton Islands.

2. *T. s. sangirensis* Meyer and Wiglesworth.
   ADULTS like *sumatranus*, but generally more blue on bend of wing and lesser wing-coverts.
   6 males   wing 210–226 (215.3) mm., tail 127–143 (134.2) mm.,
              exp. cul. 29–33 (31.8) mm., tars. 22–23 (22.8) mm.
   5 females wing 210–222 (215.8) mm., tail 116–138 (131.0) mm.,
              exp. cul. 30–32 (30.8) mm., tars. 23–26 (23.8) mm.
   Found on the Sangir and Talaud Islands; doubtfully distinct from *sumatranus*.

3. *T. s. burbidgii* Sharpe.
   ADULTS general plumage darker green, slightly yellowish on underparts; head and neck yellowish-green, contrasting with darker green mantle; back and rump deep blue; all upper wing coverts green very narrowly margined with yellowish-green; tail above dark green.
   7 males   wing 212–229 (219.4) mm., tail 145–156 (148.7) mm.,
              exp. cul. 33–37 (35.3) mm., tars. 22–25 (23.4) mm.
   3 females wing 210–217 (214.0) mm., tail 138–146 (142.3) mm.,
              exp. cul. 31–37 (34.0) mm., tars. 22–25 (23.7) mm.
   Restricted to the Sulu Archipelago in the Philippines.

4. *T. s. everetti* Tweeddale.
   ADULTS like *burbidgii*, but head darker green and underparts more yellowish; neck yellowish-green forming a collar; feathers of mantle green margined with dark blue; back and rump slightly darker blue; tail above green tipped with greenish-yellow.
   14 males   wing 187–208 (201.6) mm., tail 112–135 (127.4) mm.,
              exp. cul. 30–35 (32.9) mm., tars. 19–24 (21.3) mm.
   10 females wing 182–206 (199.8) mm., tail 110–138 (125.8) mm.,
              exp. cul. 29–33 (31.6) mm., tars. 19–23 (21.4) mm.
   Found on Panay, Leyte, Samar, Negros and Mindanao in the Philippines.

5. *T. s. duponti* Parkes.
   ADULTS similar to *everetti*, but with blue of lower back and blue margins to feathers of mantle paler; under wing-coverts decidedly yellowish.

DESCRIPTION

DISTRIBUTION

SUBSPECIES

Müller's Parrot **1**
Tanygnathus sumatranus sumatranus
NMV. 18931 ad. ♂

Black-lored Parrot *Tanygnathus gramineus* **2**
MSNG. 25584 ad. ♀

Rufous-tailed Parrot *Tanygnathus heterurus* **3**
MSNG. 19034 **type** unsexed

W.T. Cooper. 71.

No specimens examined.

2 males (Bull, *in litt.* 1971); wing 201–204 (202.5) mm., tail 142–149 (145.5) mm.,
       exp. cul. 37–39 (38.0) mm., tars. 21–23 (22.0) mm.

1 female (Bull, *in litt.* 1971); wing 199 mm., tail 144 mm.,
       exp. cul. 37 mm., tars. 25 mm.

1 unsexed (Bull, *in litt.* 1971); wing 202 mm., tail 153 mm.,
       exp. cul. 33 mm., tars 23 mm.

Restricted to Luzon in the Philippines. I doubt the practical value of naming such poorly differentiated populations.

6. *T. s. freeri* McGregor.

ADULTS similar to *everetti*, but larger and with longer tail; general plumage more yellowish, particularly on neck; paler blue margins to feathers of mantle; crown lighter green.
No specimens examined.

Confined to Polillo in the Philippines.

Red-sided Eclectus Parrot **1**
Eclectus roratus polychloros
CSIRO. 1421 ad. ♀

Red-sided Eclectus Parrot **2**
Eclectus roratus polychloros
CSIRO. 1434 ad. ♂

GENERAL NOTES

Heinrich says that Müller's Parrot appears to be distributed throughout the Celebes, but is far more prevalent in the humid lowlands up to about 500 m. (in Stresemann, 1940). It favours the edges of forest and clumps of trees in cultivated land, and is rarely seen in the interior of the forest. It is active at night and is frequently heard screeching as it flies overhead. Ripening corn is a favourite food and Heinrich reports that on the Minahassa large flocks caused considerable damage in corn crops in newly-cleared land adjoining forest. Coomans de Ruiter (1951) noted that in the Bodjo River region, southern Celebes, the arrival of these parrots about the middle of November coincided with the ripening of corn in the numerous village gardens. They caused much damage in the gardens, but were difficult to control because they came at night. On Muna Island de Haan collected a specimen at the edge of a forest and noted that birds were often seen in *Leptospermum* and fruit-bearing *Ficus* trees (in van Bemmel and Voous, 1951). During the hottest part of the afternoon they rested amongst the foliage of *Bauhinia* trees, which were scattered throughout the savannah. Even on dark moonless nights they could be heard screeching loudly as they flew high overhead. According to Delacour and Mayr (1946) this species appears to be less common than the Blue-naped Parrot in the Philippines, and is a more timid inhabitant of dense forest. Van Bemmel and Voous suggest that on Muna and Buton numbers may have declined because of large-scale trapping, but elsewhere it seems to be a fairly common bird.

It feeds on fruits, seeds, nuts and berries procured in the treetops, and attacks ripening corn.

CALL In flight a harsh *ki–ek . . . ki–ek . . . ki–ek* (Coomans de Ruiter, 1951); very different from the call of *T. lucionensis*.

NESTING Heinrich gives some details of a nest from which he took two chicks in early November. The nest was in a hollow in a tree about 30 m. from the ground. The two young birds were still naked, but differed markedly in size. Nothing further has been recorded of the breeding habits.

EGGS Broadly elliptical; one egg in the British Museum measures 41.9 × 29.7 mm. [Harrison and Holyoak, 1970].

RUFOUS-TAILED PARROT

Tanygnathus heterurus Salvadori

Illustrated on page 192.

Length 30 cm.

TYPE SPECIMEN (unsexed): general plumage green, paler on head; olive-brown suffusion on throat, neck and upper mantle; feathers of lower mantle strongly tipped with blue; lower back blue; bend of wing dull blue; greater and median wing-coverts green edged with greenish-yellow; primaries blue broadly margined with green; feathers of under wing-coverts green edged with olive-yellow; tail green above, olive-red below; white bill; greenish-grey legs.

1 unsexed **(type)** wing 211 mm., tail 123 mm.,
     exp. cul. 35 mm., tars. 23 mm.

DISTRIBUTION

Unknown, thought to be the Celebes or nearby islands, Indonesia.

GENERAL NOTES

The Rufous-tailed Parrot is known only from the type specimen, which was in a collection from the Celebes and New Guinea sent to the Genoa Museum by Bruijn. There was no information accompanying the specimen. I have examined the type and in my opinion it is probably an aberrant specimen of *T. sumatranus*.

194

BLACK-LORED PARROT
Tanygnathus gramineus (Gmelin)

Illustrated on page 192.

DESCRIPTION   Length 40 cm.

ADULTS general plumage green, slightly more yellowish on underparts and lower cheeks; nape and hindneck brighter green than back; upper cheeks greyish-green; crown bluish-grey, bases of feathers dull green; black line from forehead to eyes; primaries and primary-coverts blue broadly edged with green; secondaries, secondary-coverts and median-coverts green narrowly edged with brighter green; tail above green tipped with greenish-yellow, underside dusky yellow; bill red in male, greyish-white in female; iris yellow; legs dark grey.

IMMATURES undescribed.

1 male   wing 255 mm., tail — (damaged),
               exp. cul. 34 mm., tars. 26 mm.

2 females   wing 259–263 (261.0) mm., tail 149–161 (155.0) mm.,
               exp. cul. 33–35 (34.0) mm., tars. 25 (25.0) mm.

DISTRIBUTION   Restricted to the Island of Buru, Indonesia.

GENERAL NOTES   Very little is known about the Black-lored Parrot and it seems that there are only three specimens in existence. Toxopeus met with it only in mountains above 700 m., and noted that it was largely, if not exclusively, nocturnal in habits (in Siebers, 1930). It was more frequently heard than seen, but on a moonlit night he did get a good view of one bird as it flew past. The only specimen obtained was a badly injured male which fell from a tree, supposedly after a fight with another bird, and was brought in by natives; this incident occurred in the early afternoon.

     The only information about feeding is the statement made to Toxopeus by a native chief that he had caught these parrots with nooses when fruits on certain trees were ripening.

CALL Higher in pitch and more drawn-out than that of the Great-billed Parrot (Toxopeus in Siebers, 1930).

NESTING No records.

EGGS Undescribed.

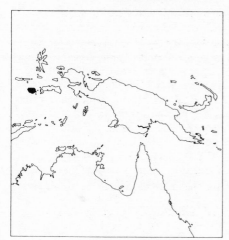

Genus ECLECTUS Wagler

A relationship between this monotypic genus and *Geoffroyus* is indicated by similarities in cranial osteology; both have a pre-frontal which reaches, but does not join, the squamosal, and both have a deeply and narrowly notched auditory meatus (Thompson, 1900). The species is a large stocky parrot with a short square tail and long round-tipped wings. A tight interlocking of the hair-like feathers produces a sleek, glossy plumage. The bill is large and projecting, and there is a notch in the upper mandible.

     The extreme sexual dimorphism in colour is such that for many years the male and female were regarded as separate species. Young birds resemble the adults.

Grand Eclectus Parrot *Eclectus roratus roratus*   1
RMNH. Cat. 48, Reg. 15139 ad. ♀

Eclectus Parrot *Eclectus roratus riedeli*   2
AMNH. 620326 ad. ♀

ECLECTUS PARROT
Eclectus roratus (P. L. S. Müller)

Length 35 cm.

MALE general plumage green, slightly tinged with yellow on head; bend of wing blue; outer webs of primaries mauve-blue; under wing-coverts and sides of body red; under tail-coverts yellowish-green; central tail feathers green narrowly tipped with yellowish-white, lateral tail feathers green suffused with blue towards tips and tipped with yellowish-white, outermost tail feathers more strongly suffused with blue on outer webs, underside of tail grey-black tipped with yellowish-white; upper mandible coral with yellowish tip, lower mandible black; iris orange; legs grey.

FEMALE general plumage red, darker and more brownish on back and wings; lower breast, abdomen and band across upper mantle dull purple; bend of wing mauve-blue; outer webs of primaries dull mauve; under wing-coverts dull purple; under tail-coverts red with yellowish tips to longer feathers; tail above red tipped with orange-yellow, below dusky orange tipped with orange-yellow; bill black; iris yellowish-white.

IMMATURES resemble adults; upper mandible dark brownish-grey becoming dull yellow towards tip; iris brown.

DISTRIBUTION   Moluccas and Lesser Sunda, Tanimbar, Aru and Kai Islands, Indonesia, New Guinea, including offshore islands, Cape York Peninsula, Australia, Admiralty Islands and from Bismarck Archipelago east through the Solomon Islands; introduced to Goram Islands, Indonesia, and Palau Archipelago in the Pacific.

W.T. Cooper 71.

1. *E. r. roratus* (P. L. S. Müller)   *Illustrated on page 196.*

    8 males   wing 237–247 (241.6) mm., tail 115–133 (122.1) mm.,
              exp. cul. 37–40 (38.0) mm., tars. 22–24 (23.3) mm.
    8 females wing 228–234 (230.8) mm., tail 105–119 (111.1) mm.,
              exp. cul. 34–37 (36.3) mm., tars. 22–24 (23.1) mm.

    Known as the Grand Eclectus Parrot, this race occurs on Buru, Ceram, Amboina, Saparua and Haruku in the southern Moluccas; birds from Ceram show a tendency towards *vosmaeri*.

2. *E. r. vosmaeri* (Rothschild)

    MALE similar to *roratus*, but more pronounced yellowish tinge on head and neck; under tail-coverts noticeably yellowish; tail strongly suffused with blue and tipped with bright yellow; larger size.
    FEMALE like *roratus*, but back and wings slightly brighter red; under tail-coverts yellow; tail red broadly tipped with yellow; larger size.
    8 males   wing 265–282 (272.6) mm., tail 125–138 (130.8) mm.,
              exp. cul. 38–42 (39.5) mm., tars. 24–27 (24.6) mm.
    8 females wing 255–272 (260.4) mm., tail 127–139 (131.6) mm.,
              exp. cul. 36–37 (36.3) mm., tars. 24–27 (25.4) mm.

    Found on the larger islands in northern and central Moluccas.

3. *E. r. westermani* (Bonaparte)

    MALE like *roratus*, but smaller; general plumage duller and more bluish; less red on sides of body.
    FEMALE like *roratus*, but smaller.
    8 males   wing 210–231 (219.4) mm., tail 100–115 (104.8) mm.,
              exp. cul. 35–42 (37.6) mm., tars. 22–27 (24.0) mm.
    3 females wing 212–222 (216.7) mm., tail 92–103 (97.0) mm.,
              exp. cul. 33–35 (34.0) mm., tars. 22–23 (22.7) mm.

    This subspecies is known only from aviary specimens; if it is an aberrant form due to captivity, and I doubt this, then it must be of *roratus*, not *riedeli* as claimed by Meyer (in Salvadori, 1891).

4. *E. r. cornelia* Bonaparte

    MALE similar to *roratus*, but larger; most feathers of upperparts bordered with lighter green; head and neck paler green; tail more strongly suffused with blue.
    FEMALE entirely red, paler on head and darker, more brownish on back and wings; tail narrowly tipped with yellow; larger than *roratus*.
    4 males   wing 262–272 (266.8) mm., tail 146–155 (149.3) mm.,
              exp. cul. 38–42 (39.3) mm., tars. 23–25 (24.3) mm.
    11 females wing 248–264 (253.8) mm., tail 120–150 (134.1) mm.,
              exp. cul. 35–39 (36.0) mm., tars. 23–26 (24.4) mm.

    Confined to Sumba in the Lesser Sunda Islands.

5. *E. r. riedeli* A. B. Meyer   *Illustrated on page 196.*

    MALE like *roratus*, but decidedly smaller; neck and lower cheeks more bluish-green; broad yellow tip to tail.
    FEMALE entirely red, darker and more brownish on back and wings; under tail-coverts yellow; tail broadly tipped with yellow; smaller than *roratus*.
    9 males   wing 209–224 (216.9) mm., tail 105–113 (108.6) mm.,
              exp. cul. 34–37 (35.1) mm., tars. 22–24 (23.2) mm.
    3 females wing 209–218 (214.0) mm., tail 104–118 (109.0) mm.,
              exp. cul. 34–36 (34.7) mm., tars. 21–25 (23.7) mm.

    Restricted to Tanimbar Islands.

Pesquet's Parrot *Psittrichas fulgidus*
CSIRO. 4106 ad. ♂

6. *E. r. polychloros* (Scopoli)   *Illustrated on page 193.*

    MALE like *roratus*, but larger; little yellow tinge to green plumage; central tail feathers green tipped with pale yellow, lateral ones blue tipped with pale yellow and suffused on outer webs with green, little green on outermost tail feathers.
    FEMALE general plumage red, brighter on head and upper breast, duller and more brownish on back and wings; narrow blue ring around eyes; abdomen, lower breast and band across upper mantle blue, more purple on breast in some birds; under tail-coverts entirely red; tail red tipped with orange.
    30 males   wing 240–279 (256.2) mm., tail 103–137 (121.1) mm.,
              exp. cul. 38–46 (41.6) mm., tars. 22–26 (24.1) mm.
    30 females wing 225–258 (245.8) mm., tail 98–123 (114.4) mm.,
              exp. cul. 34–43 (40.2) mm., tars. 22–26 (24.4) mm.

    Often called the Red-sided Eclectus Parrot, this subspecies is distributed throughout the Kai and western Papuan Islands, New Guinea and offshore islands, Trobriand Islands, and

D'Entrecasteaux and Louisiade Archipelagos; introduced to Goram Islands, Indonesia, and Palau Islands in the Pacific.

7. *E. r. biaki* (Hartert)
ADULTS like *polychloros*, but smaller; in females hindneck and underparts generally brighter red.
7 males   wing 229–242 (237.3) mm., tail 104–120 (114.0) mm.,
        exp. cul. 36–38 (37.4) mm., tars. 22–24 (23.0) mm.
2 females wing 215–216 (215.5) mm., tail 103–104 (103.5) mm.,
        exp. cul. 35 (35.0) mm., tars. 21–22 (21.5) mm.
Confined to Biak Island in Geelvink Bay, West Irian; doubtfully distinct from *polychloros*.

8. *E. r. aruensis* G. R. Gray
ADULTS like *polychloros*, but tail of male more broadly tipped with yellow and tail of female brighter red and less blackish towards base.
19 males wing 256–283 (267.3) mm., tail 121–140 (131.1) mm.,
        exp. cul. 41–46 (42.9) mm., tars. 25–30 (26.9) mm.
8 females wing 247–265 (259.4) mm., tail 113–135 (124.3) mm.,
        exp. cul. 39–43 (40.3) mm., tars. 25–27 (25.8) mm.
Restricted to the Aru Islands; doubtfully distinct from *polychloros*.

9. *E. r. macgillivrayi* Mathews
ADULTS like *polychloros*, but larger.
10 males wing 276–296 (284.6) mm., tail 146–162 (154.1) mm.,
        exp. cul. 40–46 (43.4) mm., tars. 28–30 (29.4) mm.
10 females wing 267–288 (276.6) mm., tail 140–160 (147.0) mm.,
        exp. cul. 39–43 (41.2) mm., tars. 27–30 (28.6) mm.
Confined to the coastal area of eastern Cape York Peninsula, Australia, from the Pascoe River south to the Rocky River and its tributaries.

10. *E. r. solomonensis* Rothschild and Hartert
ADULTS like *polychloros*, but smaller in size and with smaller bills, green of males generally more yellowish.
30 males wing 215–255 (253.6) mm., tail 93–115 (102.6) mm.,
        exp. cul. 34–46 (38.9) mm., tars. 22–25 (23.7) mm.
30 females wing 210–246 (227.2) mm., tail 89–108 (96.3) mm.,
        exp. cul. 35–41 (37.9) mm., tars. 21–25 (23.0) mm.
Distributed throughout the Admiralty Islands, the Bismarck Archipelago and the Solomon Islands; there is a west to east cline of decreasing size.

GENERAL NOTES

Eclectus Parrots are birds of lowland forests and, to a lesser extent, clumps of tall trees in savannah. Stresemann (1914) reports that on Ceram they were seen in pairs in primary forest below 625 m., but were not very common. Toxopeus found that they were common on Buru and apparently were distributed from the coast up to high mountain districts, though his remarks about birds being present in montane areas seem vague (in Siebers, 1930). Lendon (1946) recalls that on Morotai, northern Moluccas, they were fairly common and were most often seen singly flying high above coconut plantations. On Sumba Stein collected specimens on the coast and at about 500 m. (in Mayr, 1944). Gilliard found that they were fairly common in the lowlands of New Britain (in Gilliard and LeCroy, 1967a). Mayr (1945) says that throughout the Solomon Islands they are common in primary forest and secondary growth. Ripley (1951) reports that a male was collected on Aulupsechel Island, in the Palau Archipelago, and a flock of ten was seen on another island, so the species is probably established as a breeding resident.

According to Rand and Gilliard (1967) Eclectus Parrots are fairly common, conspicuous birds in the rainforests of New Guinea up to about 1,000 m. Mackay (1970) says that in the Port Moresby district they are very common in rainforests, being frequently seen and heard flying overhead. Schodde and Hitchcock (1968) report that they were common birds in the Lake Kutubu area, Papua, being seen singly or in small parties of from four to six in the canopy of tall secondary and primary forest. Hoogerwerf (1971) says that in the Manokwari district on the Vogelkop, West Irian, they were amongst the most common parrots and were found in almost any locality where there were tall trees. Ripley (1964) reports that they were common in the lowlands of Misool and Waigeu, western Papuan Islands, and around Djyapura, West Irian. I saw very few of these parrots in New Guinea and got the impression that they were not plentiful in the immediate vicinity of large centres of population, possibly because of hunting.

I became familiar with Eclectus Parrots in the wild on Cape York Peninsula, where they are particularly abundant in the Iron Range district. Within walking distance of my camp there were three roosting sites and one was occupied by more than eighty birds. They were noisy, conspicuous parrots, their loud, raucous cries being a familiar sound in the rainforest. Single birds or pairs were occasionally seen resting in tall eucalypts in open country, but they were probably moving from one patch of rainforest to another. In the early morning pairs and small parties left the roosting tree and moved out into the surrounding forest to feed. Larger flocks sometimes congregated to feed in fruit-laden trees. They were wary and when disturbed flew out from the opposite side of the tree, but before flying off frequently circled back high overhead, screeching loudly. Return flights to the roosting tree commenced towards dusk and the parrots travelled in threes or fours,

1 Red Shining Parrot
Prosopeia tabuensis atrogularis
AM. 027892 ad. ♀

2 Red Shining Parrot
Prosopeia tabuensis splendens
AM. 030546 ad. ♀

3 Masked Shining Parrot *Prosopeia personata*
MM. B1792 ad. ♂

males generally flying in front of females. As each group came into the tree it joined in the screeching and squawking, which continued until after nightfall.

The birds are strong fliers and on long flights, such as to and from roosting trees, they fly high above the forest canopy. The flight is rather slow with full deliberate wingbeats interspersed with brief periods of gliding. In flight the wings are not raised above body level and the resulting pattern of wing movement is a good field characteristic.

Observers have frequently remarked on the preponderance of males, and it has been my experience that away from roosting sites females are seen in far fewer numbers than are males. It would be interesting to know whether females are more timid because of their showy red plumage.

Eclectus Parrots feed on fruits, nuts, seeds, berries, leaf buds, blossoms and nectar procured in the treetops. On Buru Toxopeus saw them in casuarinas eating new leaf shoots. Gut contents from specimens collected in the eastern Solomons comprised soft, mainly fig-like, fruit (Cain and Galbraith, 1956), and from birds collected near Manokwari, West Irian, by Hoogerwerf, fruit pulp and many small fruit stones.

CALL In flight a harsh, screeching *krraach-krraak* repeated three or four times; while feeding a disyllabic, wailing cry or a mellow, flute-like *chu-wee . . . chu-wee*, the latter also being given sometimes in flight. I have heard females uttering the strange, bell-like *chee-ong . . . chee-ong*, but Cain and Galbraith state that it is given by paired birds.

NESTING In southern New Guinea nests have been found in August and late November (Bell 1970b; Rand 1942a), and in the Solomon Islands in June and in early April and early August (Cain and Galbraith 1956; Donaghho 1950). In the Solomon Islands copulation has been observed during late October (Cain and Galbraith, 1956). In November I flushed a female from a nesting hollow in a tree beside the Claudie River, Cape York Peninsula, and in January noticed birds in attendance at what I was told were regular nesting trees, though, judging from the large numbers using roosting trees, breeding must have been almost finished by then; two recently-fledged birds were collected from one roosting tree. From all parts of the range there are reports that nests are attended by groups of up to seven or eight birds of both sexes. There were four males and two females present at the nest I found at Iron Range in November.

The nest is in a hole in the trunk of a tall tree standing near the edge of the forest or in a clearing in the forest. It is invariably in a high inaccessible position. Rand says that a nest found in southern New Guinea was in a natural cavity in a tea-tree about 20 m. from the ground. Macgillivray (1918) looked at a number of nests on Cape York Peninsula and estimated that the lowest was about 14 m. from the ground, the highest approximately 22 m. The entrance is usually about 25 to 30 cm. in diameter and the depth varies from 30 cm. to more than 600 cm. The two eggs are laid on wood chips lining the bottom of the hollow. Cain and Galbraith report that at the nest which they had under observation the sitting female was fed at frequent intervals by the male; he would alight on a branch near the nest and call, whereupon the female would emerge and go to his perch to be fed, returning to the hollow immediately or sometimes, after being preened by the male.

Indge (1953) gives details of a successful breeding in captivity. Two eggs were laid, both hatched but one chick soon disappeared. Only the female brooded and she sat very tightly for twenty-six days. She left the nest about twice a day to be fed by the male. The young bird, a male, left the nest a little over twelve weeks after hatching.

EGGS Broadly ovate, slightly glossy; 10 eggs, 40.2 (38.3–43.4) × 31.0 (30.3–31.7) mm. [Schönwetter, 1964].

Genus PSITTRICHAS Lesson

Thompson (1900) claims that the cranial osteology of this monotypic genus indicates that it is an isolated form. The orbit is incomplete and both the prefrontal and postfrontal processes are small. The squamosal is extremely stout and broad, there are diagnostic structural characteristics in the auditory meatus, and there is no interorbital vacuity. I believe that, despite these differences and its peculiar external appearance, this parrot is related to *Eclectus*. The species is a large parrot with a relatively short, squarish tail and long, rounded wings. The most striking external feature is the absence of feathers from the forepart of the head. The bill is narrow and very projecting, and there is no notch in the upper mandible. Sexual dimorphism is very slight and young birds resemble adults.

PESQUET'S PARROT
Psittrichas fulgidus (Lesson)

Illustrated on page 197.

Length 46 cm.
ADULTS general plumage black; naked throat and forepart of head grey-black with some scattered bristle-like feathers; lanceolate feathers on hindcrown, nape and neck; red spot behind eye, absent

Australian King Parrot 1
Alisterus scapularis scapularis
AM. 05316 ad. ♂

Australian King Parrot 2
Alisterus scapularis scapularis
AM. 03387 ad. ♀

DESCRIPTION

in females; feathers of breast and abdomen brownish-black broadly tipped with pale grey; under wing-coverts and lower underparts red; median and greater wing-coverts scarlet; bill black; iris dark reddish-brown; legs grey.

IMMATURES like adults, but red of plumage generally duller.

15 males   wing 285–318 (304.5) mm., tail 154–184 (171.7) mm.,
           exp. cul. 38–44 (40.9) mm., tars. 29–34 (31.3) mm.

10 females wing 285–315 (299.7) mm., tail 160–198 (169.3) mm.,
           exp. cul. 36–39 (37.7) mm., tars. 28–33 (30.6) mm.

DISTRIBUTION   Mountains of New Guinea, excluding offshore islands.

SUBSPECIES   Mayr (1937) points out that there is much altitudinal variation in size, but no subspecies are recognizable.

GENERAL NOTES   Pesquet's Parrot inhabits montane forest between 800 and 2,000 m., but is occasionally found in the foothills and nearby lowlands down to sea level (Rand and Gilliard, 1967). It seems to be irregularly distributed, being quite plentiful in some districts but uncommon and local in others. Rand (1942a and b) reports that it was fairly common on the upper Fly River, in southern Papua, and on the northern slopes of the Snow Mountains, in West Irian. It was conspicuous, and was seen singly, in pairs and in small parties flying above the forest or sitting in the topmost branches of tall trees. Schodde and Hitchcock (1968) report that at Lake Kutubu in the Southern Highlands, Papua, it was frequently seen singly or in small groups of up to twenty birds in tall secondary forest about the margins of the lake, and when disturbed usually flew through the forest trees rather than above their canopy. Bell (1969) found pairs and small parties in oak forest at Derongo in the Western Highlands, Papua, and noted that a tall solitary tree close to the Ok Menga River was used regularly as a roosting site.

Goodfellow says that, when not feeding, these parrots rest in the tallest trees, preferring dead ones which tower above the surrounding forest canopy, and here they perch for hours in rain or sunshine (in Ogilvie-Grant, 1915). They do not climb from one branch to another but jump with a jerky motion and a rapid flicking of the wings. In flight they are very noisy and their calls can be heard from afar. Their flight comprises rapid, shallow wingbeats interspersed with gliding, and this—coupled with the flight silhouette of short tail, broad wings and slender outstretched neck— is a very distinctive characteristic of the species.

The birds feed on soft fruits, particularly figs, blossoms, and probably nectar. Rand records that on the northern slopes of the Snow Mountains two birds were seen eating the flowers of a *Freycinetia*, and there were figs in the stomachs of two birds collected in the upper Fly River area. Specimens collected usually have fruit pulp caked around the base of the bill, and it has been suggested that, since there are fewer feathers on the head the plumage is prevented from becoming matted with food.

CALL A harsh, screeching *aa-ar . . . aa-ar . . . aa-ar*, somewhat similar to that of the Sulphur-crested Cockatoo (*Cacatua galerita*) but more high-pitched and not as raucous (Schodde and Hitchcock, 1968).

NESTING Nothing is known of the nesting habits. A male with enlarged testes was collected in the upper Fly River area in May (Rand, 1942a); on the northern slopes of the Snow Mountains a female collected in February was laying and another taken in April had an enlarged ovary (Rand, 1942b).

EGGS Undescribed.

Amboina King Parrot **1**
Alisterus amboinensis amboinensis
RMNH. Cat. 9, Reg. 15148 ad. ♂

Green-winged King Parrot **2**
Alisterus chloropterus chloropterus
CSIRO. 8411 ad. ♀

Green-winged King Parrot **3**
Alisterus chloropterus chloropterus
CSIRO. 7828 ad. ♂

Genus PROSOPEIA Bonaparte

This genus introduces an assemblage of broadtailed parrots usually referred to as the platycercine parrots after *Platycercus*, one of the component genera. The assemblage is centred in Australia, where recent diversification is apparent. There are two principal groups in the assemblage and within each the genera are obviously closely related. The groups are rather more loosely allied to each other and there are some specialized genera, such as *Lathamus* and *Pezoporus*, which I believe to be offshoots from the *Platycercus-Neophema* group.

Prosopeia, Alisterus, Aprosmictus and *Polytelis* make up what is called the 'king parrot group'. Thompson (1900) points out that there are similarities in the cranial osteology of these genera, particularly in the postorbital and squamosal processes, and that the group is related to *Platycercus* and its near allies. The parrots belonging to *Prosopeia* are rather large, slim birds with long, rounded tails and short, rounded wings. The bill is massive and there is a notch in the upper mandible. The cere is naked. The sexes are alike in plumage colouration, but females are smaller than males and have smaller bills; young birds resemble the adults. They are called shining parrots because of an obvious sheen on the back and wings.

RED SHINING PARROT
Prosopeia tabuensis (Gmelin)

DESCRIPTION Length 45 cm.

ADULTS forehead, lores and foreparts of cheeks reddish-black; feathers surrounding base of lower mandible faintly tipped with blue; remainder of head brownish-red, darker on cheeks; underparts deep maroon; collar of dark blue across upper mantle; wings, back and rump bright green; outer webs of primaries mauve-blue; tail above green suffused with blue, below grey-black; bill grey-black; iris yellow; legs dark grey.

IMMATURES like adults; bill paler with horn-coloured markings; iris brown.

DISTRIBUTION Fiji Islands; introduced to Tongatabu and Eua, Tonga Islands, but apparently no longer present on Tongatabu.

SUBSPECIES Amadon (1942) shows quite clearly why it is necessary to restrict the name *tabuensis* to the introduced, variable populations on Eua, Tonga Islands, and Ngau, Fiji Islands. This means that the name *atrogularis* must be revived for the birds from Vanua Levu and Kio, Fiji Islands.

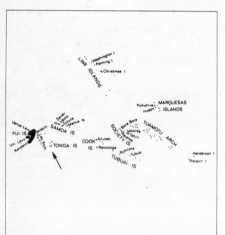

1. *P. t. atrogularis* (Peale)   *Illustrated on page 200.*
   8 males   wing 237–258 (244.0) mm., tail 191–226 (212.0) mm.,
             exp. cul. 29–33 (30.8) mm., tars. 26–28 (27.0) mm.
   9 females wing 219–225 (222.0) mm., tail 187–208 (198.8) mm.,
             exp. cul. 26–28 (26.8) mm., tars. 26–27 (26.2) mm.
   This subspecies, as described above, occurs on Vanua Levu and the adjacent small island of Kio, Fiji Islands.

2. *P. t. koroensis* (Layard)
   ADULTS blue band across upper mantle absent or very narrow and interrupted; rump feathers extensively tipped with maroon.
   10 males wing 220–242 (232.5) mm., tail 192–218 (204.8) mm.,
             exp. cul. 31–34 (32.3) mm., tars. 26–28 (27.3) mm.
   9 females wing 216–228 (222.1) mm., tail 190–204 (197.8) mm.,
             exp. cul. 27–32 (28.1) mm., tars. 24–28 (25.9) mm.
   Confined to Koro, Fiji Islands.

3. *P. t. taviunensis* (Layard)
   ADULTS no blue band across upper mantle; little or no maroon tips to feathers of rump; forehead and lores less blackish; smaller size.
   9 males   wing 211–227 (217.9) mm., tail 180–195 (186.0) mm.,
             exp. cul. 30–33 (31.3) mm., tars. 26–28 (27.1) mm.
   8 females wing 196–208 (201.5) mm., tail 161–182 (172.1) mm.,
             exp. cul. 24–26 (25.6) mm., tars. 22–27 (24.5) mm.
   Occurs on Taveuni and Ngamea, Fiji Islands.

4. *P. t. tabuensis* (Gmelin)
   ADULTS plumage colouration variable but basically intermediate between *atrogularis* and *koroensis*.
   8 males   wing 230–258 (241.9) mm., tail 212–236 (224.3) mm.,
             exp. cul. 29–35 (33.0) mm., tars. 25–27 (26.4) mm.
   7 females wing 230–241 (234.4) mm., tail 204–230 (220.1) mm.,
             exp. cul. 26–30 (27.9) mm., tars. 25–27 (25.9) mm.
   Found on Ngau, Fiji Islands, and on Eua and formerly on Tongatabu, Tonga Islands; presumed to be a mixture resulting from the introduction of two or more races by man.

5. *P. t. splendens* (Peale)   *Illustrated on page 200.*
   ADULTS head and underparts crimson; broad blue collar across upper mantle; forehead, lores and feathers around base of lower mandible red.
   10 males wing 221–245 (228.3) mm., tail 193–223 (204.0) mm.,
             exp. cul. 28–32 (29.9) mm., tars. 25–27 (26.2) mm.
   10 females wing 213–224 (219.6) mm., tail 194–228 (202.6) mm.,
             exp. cul. 24–30 (26.2) mm., tars. 25–27 (25.8) mm.
   Restricted to Kandavu, Fiji Islands; introduced to Viti Levu, Fiji Islands, but seems to be very scarce there.

GENERAL NOTES Mercer (1967) says that Red Shining Parrots associate in small parties and feed on fruits and berries. Porter (1935) reports that on Kandavu the parrots were quite plentiful, even around villages, and were not timid. Blackburn (1971) reports that on Taveuni they are numerous throughout the rainforest and are usually seen singly or in pairs. He also reports that on Kandavu they are abundant in the Gasele forest, and in the Vunisea district they were seen from the mangroves up to the high hills; a number frequented the village itself and one periodically visited the local store for its ration of biscuit. They are noisy birds, and when perched below the forest canopy they are remarkably conspicuous. Recent sightings from the highlands of Viti Levu are also recorded by Blackburn. According to Porter the undulatory flight comprises flapping wingbeats interspersed with brief periods of gliding.

The diet of these birds consists of fruits, berries and seeds procured in the treetops. Near Talaulia, on Kandavu, Porter saw them in mango trees feeding on ripe fruit. It is said that they are also fond of pawpaws and bananas. Early observers have spoken of large flocks doing considerable damage to maize and other crops (see Bahr, 1912).

CALL A raucous screech given once or repeated twice in rapid succession; also a shrill cry (in captivity). Blackburn says that the calls of *splendens* are more high-pitched than those of the other subspecies.

NESTING On Kandavu, in August, Wood found a nest containing eggs (in Wood and Wetmore, 1926). It was in a stump about 140 cm. high and 35 cm. in diameter. The decayed centre was hollow to a depth of approximately 130 cm. and at the bottom, on a layer of chips and rotten wood, were three eggs. Collins (1944) records a successful breeding in captivity and notes that the incubation period was about three weeks. Bahr says that when young birds are approximately six months old their irides change from brown to yellow.

EGGS Rounded; 5 eggs, 38.4 (36.1–41.0) × 30.1 (28.9–32.0) mm. [Schönwetter, 1964].

Superb Parrot *Polytelis swainsonii* **1**
AM. 033442 ad. ♀

Superb Parrot *Polytelis swainsonii* **2**
AM. 033443 ad. ♂

Regent Parrot *Polytelis anthopeplus* **3**
AM. 033596 ad. ♂

Princess Parrot *Polytelis alexandrae* **4**
AM. 037491 ad. ♂

MASKED SHINING PARROT
Prosopeia personata (G. R. Gray)

Illustrated on page 200.

DESCRIPTION

Length 47 cm.
ADULTS general plumage bright green, slightly paler on underparts and under wing-coverts; forehead, lores and facial area black; centre of breast yellow, becoming orange on centre of abdomen; outer webs of primaries deep blue; tail above green suffused with blue, below grey-black; bill grey-black; iris orange; legs dark grey.
IMMATURES resemble adults; bill paler with horn-coloured markings; iris brown.
10 males   wing 236–250 (243.7) mm., tail 203–259 (224.8) mm.,
            exp. cul. 30–34 (31.8) mm., tars. 26–28 (27.3) mm.
10 females wing 225–238 (228.8) mm., tail 200–245 (215.0) mm.,
            exp. cul. 25–28 (26.8) mm., tars. 25–29 (26.8) mm.

DISTRIBUTION

Known only from Viti Levu, Fiji Islands, though there are early published reports from nearby islands of Ovalau and Mbau.

GENERAL NOTES

There is confusion in the literature concerning the status of the Masked Shining Parrot. Probably basing his assessment on early published reports, Vincent (1966) says that the species must be nearing extinction. These early reports claimed that depredations by the introduced mongoose and shooting by fruit-growers to protect their crops would soon bring about the extinction of the species. On the other hand, B. and J. Morgan (1965) state that the Masked Shining Parrot is the common large parrot on Viti Levu and is usually seen in dense forest. B. Morgan says that land clearance would certainly affect the parrots but he saw them in forest country and did not get the impression that they were rare (pers. comm., 1970). Blackburn (1971) reports that in the Nausori Highlands birds were seen and heard very frequently, and in the vicinity of Nausori Village they were common in the forest and in adjoining gardens where they fed on banana flowers. Mercer (1967) points out that the species is considered a pest in some fruit-growing areas but gives no information about its present status. In 1971, I observed these parrots in disturbed forest adjoining wet pasture lands about 20 km. south of Suva, and they were fairly common there. I suspect that the species is locally common but generally scarce, and in my opinion its survival depends on preservation of tracts of virgin forest.

In pairs or small parties these parrots may be seen in forest country and timber bordering watercourses. They are noisy and their raucous cries can be heard from afar. They keep mainly to the uppermost branches of tall trees but will come down to feed on cultivated fruits and ripening grain. They are timid and I found them difficult to observe; the call-notes indicated where a parrot was sitting but at my approach it generally flew out from the opposite side of the tree and soon disappeared in the forest. The undulating flight consists of flapping wingbeats alternating with gliding.

The parrots feed on seeds, fruits and berries procured in the treetops. I watched one bird eating small newly-formed guavas from a tree standing in a pasture about 100 m. from the edge of the forest. They are fond of cultivated fruits, particularly bananas, and can cause damage to crops. Stomach contents from an unspecified number of birds comprised broken seeds and comminuted wild figs (Wood and Wetmore, 1926).

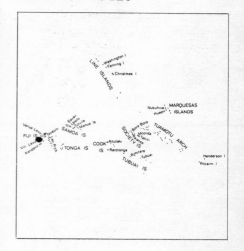

CALL In flight a harsh screech; also a series of peculiar, cackling notes and a variety of strident shrieks, the latter like some of the call-notes of *Eclectus*.

NESTING There appear to be no published records, but nests are said to be in hollow limbs or holes high up in tall forest trees.

EGGS Rounded or broadly elliptical; 10 eggs, 37.9 (33.1–39.7) × 30.1 (27.9–30.8) mm. [Schönwetter, 1964].

Genus ALISTERUS Mathews

The parrots in this genus are similar to those in *Prosopeia*, but have much smaller bills and proportionately longer, less rounded wings. Sexual dimorphism is slight in one species, *amboinensis*, but pronounced in *chloropterus* and *scapularis*; in the sexually dimorphic species young birds are similar to adult females, but in *amboinensis* there is an immature plumage.

AUSTRALIAN KING PARROT
Alisterus scapularis (Lichtenstein)

DESCRIPTION

Length 43 cm.
MALE head and underparts scarlet; under tail-coverts greenish-black broadly margined with scarlet; mantle, upper back and wings dark green; scapulars bright pale green; narrow blue band across upper mantle; upper tail-coverts, rump and lower back deep blue; under wing-coverts dark green tinged with blue; central tail feathers above black slightly tinged with green, lateral tail feathers above greenish-black tinged with blue, underside of tail grey-black; bill black with orange-red at base of upper mandible; iris yellow; legs grey.
FEMALE head green; throat and breast dull greyish-green with reddish tinge on throat, abdomen and lower breast scarlet; under tail-coverts green broadly margined with scarlet; scapulars dark green, occasionally tinged with pale green; rump and lower back blue tinged with green; upper tail-coverts green; central tail feathers above dark green, lateral tail feathers above bluish-green; undersides grey-black narrowly tipped with rose-red; bill entirely brownish-black; iris pale yellow.
IMMATURES like adult female; bill pale brown; iris brown.

Coastal and contiguous mountain regions of eastern Australia from northern Queensland to southern Victoria.

DISTRIBUTION

1. *A. s. scapularis* (Lichtenstein)   *Illustrated on page 201.*   SUBSPECIES
   8 males   wing 210–233 (216.9) mm., tail 176–218 (205.1) mm.,
          exp. cul. 22–23 (22.6) mm., tars. 24–26 (24.9) mm.
   8 females wing 206–219 (213.5) mm., tail 193–223 (206.3) mm.,
          exp. cul. 19–22 (20.8) mm., tars. 24–26 (25.1) mm.
   Found in eastern Australia from the Otway Ranges, southern Victoria, north to about Cardwell, northern Queensland.

2. *A. s. minor* Mathews
   ADULTS similar to *scapularis*, but smaller.
   14 males wing 185–202 (193.9) mm., tail 165–195 (184.7) mm.,
          exp. cul. 19–23 (21.6) mm., tars. 20–23 (21.4) mm.
   5 females wing 183–203 (194.0) mm., tail 165–191 (179.6) mm.,
          exp. cul. 20–22 (20.8) mm., tars. 20–22 (21.0) mm.
   Confined to north-eastern Queensland from Cooktown and the Atherton Tableland south to Cardwell, where it merges with *scapularis*.

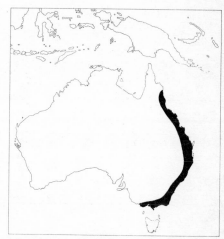

Australian King Parrots inhabit tropical rainforest, *Eucalyptus* woodland and dense scrublands bordering watercourses from sea level up to about 1,600 m. Occasionally they are found in savannah woodland where it adjoins riparian forest, and outside the breeding season they frequently come to feed in parks and gardens, orchards, and cultivated farmlands: Although they are common they seem to have disappeared from some districts because of land-clearance and afforestation programmes, the latter often resulting in eucalypts being replaced by *Pinus radiata* or other exotic species. In some areas, particularly in the south, flocks descend from the mountain forests in late autumn and remain in the valleys and coastal lowlands until September. In the lowlands the species seems to be sedentary, though banding recoveries suggest that there are some movements (see

GENERAL NOTES

Forshaw, 1969a). Observations show that it is mainly birds in immature plumage that move about; fully-coloured males are seldom seen in wandering flocks.

These parrots are usually observed in pairs or small parties, but in autumn immatures tend to band together in flocks of up to twenty or thirty birds. At other times many may congregate to take advantage of a concentrated source of food, such as a heavily-laden fruit tree or a ripening maize crop. They are occasionally seen around barns and stockyards feeding on spilled grain. In the morning and late afternoon they feed amongst the outer branches of trees or shrubs, and during the heat of the day they sit quietly amongst the foliage. On the ground they walk with an awkward, waddling gait. They are rather wary and noticeably more difficult to approach than are the rosellas. When disturbed they fly off through the forest and rarely alight until well out of sight. Occasionally they associate with Crimson Rosellas (*Platycercus elegans*) and Gang-Gang Cockatoos (*Callocephalon fimbriatum*) to feed. They are not as noisy or active as most parrots, their movements being somewhat slow and deliberate. The direct flight is heavy with sweeping deliberate wingbeats, and when flying through the trees the birds frequently make sharp turns by tilting the entire body. They are strong fliers and move through even the densest forest or scrub with surprising ease and swiftness. The tail is fanned slightly when alighting.

Food consists of fruits, berries, nuts, seeds, particularly those of eucalypts and acacias, nectar, blossoms and leaf buds. I have seen these parrots feeding on fruits of *Solanum nigrum* and the introduced *Phytolacca octandra*, and in the company of Brown Pigeons (*Macropygia phasianella*) eating berries of wild tobacco (*Solanum auriculatum*). Cooper (pers. comm., 1970) has often seen them feeding on seeds of sunshine wattle (*Acacia botrycephala*), while Chisholm (1934) reports that in the Comboyne district, New South Wales, they are especially fond of the seeds of blackwood wattle (*Acacia melanoxylon*). Unfortunately, they also raid orchards and maize crops, often causing damage, and have been reported attacking potatoes left out in paddocks to dry.

CALL In flight a shrill *crassak . . . crassak*; when alarmed a harsh, metallic screech. Feeding is usually undertaken in silence with only the occasional utterance of gutteral, cackling notes. While perched, males often give a series of soft, though penetrating, high-pitched whistling notes.

NESTING The courtship display is quite elaborate. The male puffs the feathers on his head, draws tight the remainder of his body plumage and displays the pale green scapulars by rapidly flicking his wings. With dilated eyes he perches before the female and gives the normal contact call. The hen puffs her head feathers, draws tight the remainder of her body plumage, contracts the pupils of her eyes, calls intermittently and solicits courtship feeding by continually bobbing her head. Courtship feeding generally follows.

The breeding season is from September to January. The nest is in a hollow limb or hole in a tree, usually in the trunk of a tall tree standing in dense forest. Most nesting hollows are very deep, the eggs being laid near ground level. Favaloro (1931) examined a nest in which young had been reared the previous year. The entrance was about 10 m. from the ground, and he was told that when the tree was struck with a stick the female could be heard inside as she scrambled up to the entrance; apparently the eggs were only about 60 cm. above ground level. The three to six, usually five, eggs are laid on decayed wood dust lining the bottom of the hollow.

Incubation lasts about twenty days and only the female broods. The male is always in close proximity to the nest and roosts in an adjacent tree. He feeds the hen at regular intervals throughout the day. The young leave the nest approximately five weeks after hatching, but remain with their parents to form family parties. Males acquire adult plumage through a slow moult beginning when they are a little over sixteen months old and continuing for a further fourteen or sixteen months. However, males are capable of breeding while in immature plumage.

EGGS Rounded; 6 eggs, 32.8 (32.0–33.7) × 26.8 (24.7–27.7) mm. [H. L. White Coll.].

GREEN-WINGED KING PARROT
Alisterus chloropterus (Ramsay)

DESCRIPTION Length 36 cm.

MALE head and underparts scarlet; variable mauve-blue band across upper mantle and extending up on to hindneck and nape; mantle, scapulars and tertials greenish-black; lesser and median wing-coverts pale yellowish-green forming a band across wing; remainder of wing dark green; back, rump and upper tail-coverts mauve-blue; under tail-coverts scarlet with dark blue bases; under wing-coverts mauve-blue; tail above black strongly tinged with blue, below grey-black; bill grey-black with orange at base of upper mandible; iris orange; legs dark grey.

FEMALE head, back and wings dull green; feathers of throat and breast dull olive-green edged with brownish-red; under wing-coverts dull green; tail above green becoming black towards tip and suffused with blue, below grey-black; base of upper mandible duller and more brownish.

IMMATURES like female, but no brownish-red edges to feathers of throat and breast, bill brownish-black tipped paler; iris brown.

DISTRIBUTION New Guinea east of the Weyland Mountains, West Irian.

1. *A. c. chloropterus* (Ramsay)   *Illustrated on page 204.*
   8 males   wing 187–194 (190.8) mm., tail 200–218 (209.6) mm.,
            exp. cul. 20–23 (21.1) mm., tars. 20–21 (20.4) mm.
   8 females wing 183–193 (188.5) mm., tail 202–229 (214.4) mm.,
            exp. cul. 20–22 (21.0) mm., tars. 20–22 (20.5) mm.
   Occurs in eastern New Guinea west in the north to the Huon Peninsula and in the south to Hall Sound, Papua.

2. *A. c. callopterus* (D'Albertis and Salvadori)
   MALE like *chloropterus*, but with narrow blue band across upper mantle not extending up on to hindneck and nape.
   FEMALE similar to *chloropterus*.
   6 males   wing 191–202 (193.5) mm., tail 193–200 (197.3) mm.,
            exp. cul. 21–23 (21.8) mm., tars. 21–23 (21.5) mm.
   2 females wing 182–185 (183.5) mm., tail 192–207 (199.5) mm.,
            exp. cul. 19–21 (20.0) mm., tars. 19–21 (20.0) mm.
   Found in central New Guinea from the upper Fly River, the Central Highlands and the Sepik River area west to the Weyland Mountains, West Irian.

3. *A. c. moszkowskii* (Reichenow)
   MALE similar to *callopterus*.
   FEMALE like male and very different from female *chloropterus*; blue band across upper mantle absent or only slightly indicated; mantle and back dull green; green on sides of breast.
   IMMATURES similar to female, but yellowish-green wing band narrower and duller; breast strongly marked with green.
   10 males   wing 185–194 (189.4) mm., tail 174–200 (187.3) mm.,
            exp. cul. 22–23 (22.3) mm., tars. 19–21 (20.2) mm.
   10 females wing 185–196 (190.7) mm., tail 184–212 (195.5) mm.,
            exp. cul. 19–22 (20.7) mm., tars. 19–21 (20.1) mm.
   Restricted to northern New Guinea from Geelvink Bay, West Irian, east to the Aitape district.

GENERAL NOTES   The Green-winged King Parrot inhabits lowland and mid-mountain forest. Rand (1942b) gives records up to 1,400 m. on the northern slopes of the Snow Mountains, West Irian, while at Aiyura in the Central Highlands, New Guinea, Donaghey (*in litt.*, 1970) observed a lone male at 1,700 m. Rand and Gilliard (1967) claim that it is rather uncommon, but it is not a conspicuous bird and I suspect that it could be more numerous than is indicated by observations. Mackay (1970) notes that it is reasonably common in the rainforests of the Port Moresby district. Donaghey says that at Brown River, near Port Moresby, it is seemingly uncommon, but is probably often overlooked (*in litt.*, 1970).

At Brown River and at Sogeri, also near Port Moresby, I saw single birds in dense forest, and found that unless seen in flight across tracks or clearings they were most inconspicuous. They showed a marked preference for small trees and the lower branches of taller trees, and were not seen high up in the canopy. They were quiet and allowed a close approach, but were seldom detected until they took flight and then they soon disappeared through the trees. The flight is direct, and with deliberate, rhythmic wingbeats.

The parrots feed on seeds, berries, nuts, fruits, buds, blossoms and possibly insects and their larvae. Stomach contents from birds collected in the Weyland Mountains consisted of berries and small seeds (Rothschild, 1931).

CALL   In flight and when alarmed a series of shrill, metallic shrieks; while perched or feeding an occasional mellow, flute-like note. All calls are similar to those of the Australian King Parrot, but are noticeably higher in pitch.

NESTING   Ripley (1964) reports that a male showing slight gonadal enlargement was collected at Bodim, West Irian, in late July. I know of no published nesting records.

EGGS   Undescribed.

AMBOINA KING PARROT
Alisterus amboinensis (Linné)

DESCRIPTION   Length 35 cm.
ADULTS head and underparts red; bend of wing, lesser wing-coverts and mantle through to upper tail-coverts deep purple-blue; wings dull green; under tail-coverts black broadly edged with red;

under wing-coverts purple-blue; tail above black strongly suffused with purple-blue, below grey-black with broad edging of dull pink on inner webs of three outermost feathers; bill grey-black with orange at base of upper mandible; iris orange; legs dark grey.

IMMATURES like adults, but mantle green; lateral tail feathers tipped with dull rose-red; bill brownish-black, paler at tip; iris brown.

DISTRIBUTION

SUBSPECIES

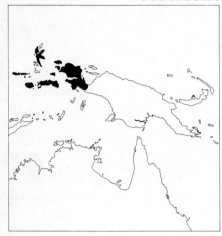

Peleng Island and the Sula Islands, Indonesia, east through the Moluccas to the western Papuan Islands and western New Guinea.

1. *A. a. amboinensis* (Linné)   *Illustrated on page 204.*
    9 males   wing 200–214 (206.1) mm., tail 208–232 (222.6) mm.,
             exp. cul. 21–24 (22.7) mm., tars. 21–25 (22.4) mm.
    5 females wing 202–210 (205.8) mm., tail 215–235 (224.8) mm.,
             exp. cul. 23–24 (23.6) mm., tars. 22–23 (22.6) mm.
    Confined to Amboina and Ceram in the southern Moluccas, Indonesia.

2. *A. a. sulaensis* (Reichenow)
    ADULTS like *amboinensis*, but with variable green band across blue mantle; no pink edging to inner webs of lateral tail feathers.
    2 males   wing 187–195 (191.0) mm., tail 194–200 (197.0) mm.,
             exp. cul. 20–21 (20.5) mm., tars. 20–22 (21.0) mm.
    2 females wing 195–197 (196.0) mm., tail 196–201 (198.5) mm.,
             exp. cul. 21–22 (21.5) mm., tars. 21 (21.0) mm.
    Confined to the Sula Islands, Indonesia.

3. *A. a. versicolor* Neumann
    ADULTS differ from *sulaensis* by having mantle blue without any green markings; smaller than *amboinensis*.
    2 males   wing 175–183 (179.0) mm., tail 170–178 (174.0) mm.,
             exp. cul. 21–23 (22.0) mm., tars. 21 (21.0) mm.
    1 female wing 177 mm., tail 184 mm.,
             exp. cul. 21 mm., tars. 23 mm.
    2 unsexed wing 195–205 (200.0) mm., tail 177–179 (178.0) mm.,
             exp. cul. 20 (20.0) mm., tars. 19–20 (19.5) mm.
    Restricted to Peleng Island, Indonesia.

4. *A. a. buruensis* (Salvadori)
    ADULTS similar to *sulaensis*, but outermost tail feathers broadly margined with pink on undersides of inner webs, next two pairs narrowly margined; bill grey-black in both sexes.
    10 males wing 206–228 (213.1) mm., tail 215–240 (228.9) mm.,
             exp. cul. 21–24 (22.0) mm., tars. 22–23 (22.4) mm.
    10 females wing 203–211 (207.9) mm., tail 209–245 (225.4) mm.,
             exp. cul. 21–23 (22.2) mm., tars. 21–23 (22.0) mm.
    Confined to Buru in the southern Moluccas, Indonesia.

5. *A. a. hypophonius* (S. Müller)
    ADULTS like *amboinensis*, but wings deep blue instead of green; lesser wing-coverts brighter blue than remainder of wing; no pink on undersides of lateral tail feathers.
    9 males   wing 186–201 (193.7) mm., tail 182–196 (188.8) mm.,
             exp. cul. 21–24 (23.0) mm., tars. 20–23 (21.2) mm.
    4 females wing 195–201 (198.3) mm., tail 177–206 (190.5) mm.,
             exp. cul. 22–23 (22.7) mm., tars. 21–23 (22.3) mm.
    Restricted to Halmahera in the northern Moluccas, Indonesia.

6. *A. a. dorsalis* (Quoy and Gaimard)
    ADULTS similar to *amboinensis*, but without pink on undersides of lateral tail feathers; red of head and underparts slightly darker.
    IMMATURES undersides of tail-feathers narrowly tipped with pink.
    10 males wing 175–193 (182.8) mm., tail 168–197 (178.2) mm.,
             exp. cul. 20–23 (21.6) mm., tars. 19–21 (20.1) mm.
    10 females wing 176–186 (180.0) mm., tail 177–191 (183.3) mm.,
             exp. cul. 19–24 (21.1) mm., tars. 19–21 (20.4) mm.
    Occurs on the western Papuan Islands and in north-western New Guinea east to Etna Bay and the Weyland Mountains, West Irian.

GENERAL NOTES   The Amboina King Parrot is a bird of lowland and mid-mountain forests. Stresemann (1914) says that on Ceram it was common inland from Wahai and seemed to be also common in the mountains of central and western Ceram; specimens were collected up to 1,400 m. On Buru Toxopeus found it to be fairly common on the eastern coast and inland in the Rana district; the highest record was a sighting south of Fakal at 1,450 m. (in Siebers, 1930). Gyldenstolpe (1955b) remarks that, judging by the number of specimens collected by Bergman in lowland and montane forests of the Arfak Mountains, the species must be quite common throughout the Vogelkop, West Irian. Hoogerwerf (1971) says that along Geelvink Bay, West Irian, it is probably more common than it seems on account of its quiet and rather silent behaviour. Stein found that it was scarce in the Weyland Mountains, West Irian (in Rand and Gilliard, 1967).

These parrots are usually seen singly or in pairs quietly feeding amongst dense foliage on lower branches of forest trees. They are seldom noticed until they fly off screeching loudly. The flight is direct, and with deliberate, rhythmic wingbeats.

Seeds, fruits, berries and buds make up the diet. Stresemann reports that in the montane forests of Ceram the parrots seemed to feed almost exclusively on acorns from a very common *Quercus* tree; crops and stomachs from two specimens collected on Mt. Sofia were filled with partly-digested acorns. Stomach contents from four birds collected near Geelvink Bay, West Irian, comprised crushed hard seeds, crushed fruit-stones, some with pulp attached, and millet-like grains (Hoogerwerf, 1971).

CALL A high-pitched, sharp *kree . . . kree* (Toxopeus in Siebers, 1930).

NESTING Males with enlarged testes were collected in the Arfak Mountains during late February (Gyldenstolpe, 1955b). Rand and Gilliard report that in the Weyland Mountains Stein observed a pair investigating a stump in the forest as though in search of a nest site. Nothing further is known of the breeding behaviour.

EGGS Broadly elliptical; 9 eggs, 33.4 (31.5–37.2) × 26.1 (24.1–28.1) mm. [Harrison and Holyoak, 1970].

Genus APROSMICTUS Gould

Aprosmictus resembles *Alisterus*, but the tail is squarish and proportionately shorter. The two species are medium-sized parrots with predominantly green plumage colouration. Sexual dimorphism is pronounced and young birds are similar to adult females.

RED-WINGED PARROT
Aprosmictus erythropterus (Gmelin)

Length 32 cm.
MALE head bright pale green, slightly tinged with blue on hindcrown and occiput; upper tail-coverts and entire underparts bright yellowish-green; scapulars, mantle and upper back black, becoming dark green on tertials; lower back blue, becoming paler on rump; lesser, median and secondary wing-coverts red; remainder of wing green; bend of wing and under wing-coverts pale green; tail above green tipped with yellow, below dark grey tipped with yellowish-white; bill coral; iris orange-red; legs grey.
FEMALE general plumage dull green, yellowish on underparts and upper tail-coverts; red markings restricted to outermost wing-coverts; rump and lower back paler blue; underside of tail paler grey tipped with yellowish-white and lateral feathers margined with very pale rose-pink on inner webs; iris pale brown.
IMMATURES similar to adult female; bill yellowish in very young birds.

Northern and north-eastern Australia and southern New Guinea.

1. *A. e. erythropterus* (Gmelin)
   Illustrated on page 205.

   8 males   wing 183–208 (200.1) mm., tail 139–152 (145.8) mm.,
       exp. cul. 18–20 (18.7) mm., tars. 21–23 (21.9) mm.
   6 females   wing 190–204 (197.5) mm., tail 143–150 (147.0) mm.,
       exp. cul. 16–18 (16.8) mm., tars. 22–23 (22.5) mm.
   Occurs in eastern Australia from about Cooktown, northern Queensland, south to north-eastern South Australia and the interior of northern New South Wales.

2. *A. e. coccineopterus* (Gould)
   MALE hindcrown and occiput strongly washed with blue; general plumage slightly paler than in *erythropterus*; slightly smaller size.
   FEMALE general plumage, particularly dull green of upper back, slightly paler than in *erythropterus*; slightly smaller size.

10 males   wing 175–198 (185.9) mm., tail 124–132 (127.6) mm.,
          exp. cul. 17–20 (18.3) mm., tars. 19–22 (20.7) mm.
8 females   wing 176–199 (184.6) mm., tail 122–135 (128.5) mm.,
          exp. cul. 17–18 (17.5) mm., tars. 20–22 (21.1) mm.

  This poorly-differentiated subspecies is found in northern Australia, including some offshore islands, from the Kimberley division of Western Australia east to Cape York Peninsula and the interior of northern Queensland, where it merges with *erythropterus*.

3. *A. e. papua* Mayr and Rand
 MALE similar to *coccineopterus*, but mantle and scapulars tinged with green.
 FEMALE not distinguishable from *coccineopterus*.
6 males   wing 185–194 (189.0) mm., tail 123–131 (126.7) mm.,
          exp. cul. 18–19 (18.7) mm., tars. 19–20 (19.7) mm.
6 females wing 181–191 (187.2) mm., tail 127–138 (131.5) mm.,
          exp. cul. 18–19 (18.7) mm., tars. 19–21 (20.3) mm.

  Confined to coastal southern New Guinea from Princess Marianne Straits, West Irian, east to the Oriomo River, Papua; probably not distinct from *coccineopterus*.

GENERAL NOTES

In Australia Red-winged Parrots are common inhabitants of open *Eucalyptus* forest, timber bordering water-courses, *Melaleuca* woodland, arid *Acacia* scrublands and groves of *Casuarina* or *Callitris* trees along rocky ridges or dispersed throughout open sandy country. Along the northern coastline they also occur in mangroves. Though they avoid dense forest, there are occasional records of birds being seen in extensive clearings surrounded by primary rainforest. In southern New Guinea these parrots are fairly common in wooded savannah within about 50 km. of the seaboard, but not farther inland (Rand and Gilliard, 1967). Throughout most of their range in Australia they are sedentary, but along the fringes of distribution there are irregular movements and fluctuations in numbers. Irregular movements may also take place in southern New Guinea, judging from the report quoted by Rand (1942a) that flocks of up to several hundred were seen at Mabadauan in April.

  These parrots are generally seen in pairs or family parties, although flocks of from fifteen to twenty may be noted during the non-breeding season. On rare occasions flocks may build up to contain sixty or more individuals, but this is usually brought about by seasonal movements or by a concentrated food supply, such as a heavy flowering of eucalypts in a small area. I know of no reports from Australia of very large flocks like those recorded in southern New Guinea. The parrots are wary and difficult to approach. When disturbed they rise into the air and, calling loudly, fly to the next grove of trees. They are sometimes seen in the company of other parrots, especially the Pale-headed Rosella (*Platycercus adscitus*) and the Mallee Ringneck Parrot (*Barnardius barnardi*). They are arboreal, spending most of the day feeding or resting in the outermost branches of trees and shrubs, and coming to the ground only to drink or occasionally to feed on fallen seeds and fruits. The characteristic, flapping flight is buoyant and slightly erratic with full, deliberate wing-beats. A parrot descending suddenly from a height comes down by a series of plunging drops with a momentary pause between each.

  Food consists of fruits, berries, seeds, nuts, blossoms, nectar, and insects and their larvae. They are particularly fond of seeds of eucalypts and acacias, berries of mistletoe (*Loranthus* spp.), and seeds of hopbush (*Dodonaea* spp.). Near Mitchell, Queensland, I have seen a party of fifteen feeding on seeds of *Acacia salicina*; some birds were clambering amongst the outer branches extracting seeds from the pods, often hanging upside down while doing so; others were on the ground underneath the bush picking up fallen seeds. In the same district Fullagar (pers. comm., 1968) found them eating galls from the leaves of rosewood (*Heterodendron oleaefolium*). Crop contents from a specimen collected by Thomson (1935) on the Coleman River, Cape York Peninsula, comprised seeds of a *Grevillea*, and from specimens collected by Cleland (1919) in the Pilliga scrub, northern New South Wales, comprised manna lerps (*Spondyliaspis eucalypti*) and their scales.

CALL In flight a sharp, metallic *crillik-crillik* repeated three or four times; when alarmed a series of harsh screeches. Feeding is occasionally accompanied by a soft, mellow chattering.

NESTING When courting, the male, chattering softly, undertakes short flights around the female. He alights on the same branch or on an adjacent one and droops his wings, thus exposing the blue rump and lower back. He draws tight his body plumage and, with contracted pupils, takes two or three slow, deliberate steps towards the female. Courtship feeding occurs at infrequent intervals.

  The breeding season is variable. Nesting usually takes place between August and February, but in the north may commence as early as May. Thomson claims that on Cape York Peninsula this species breeds in the dry season, generally from April to July. The nest is in a hollow limb or hole in a tree, usually in a eucalypt standing near water. Most nesting hollows are very deep, the eggs being near ground level. On Cape York Peninsula a young bird was taken from a hollow in a tree by cutting into the trunk about 90 cm. from the ground, yet the entrance was at a height of more than 10 m. (in White, 1922). Three to five, occasionally up to six, eggs are laid on decayed wood dust lining the bottom of the hollow.

  Incubation lasts about three weeks and only the female broods. Early in the morning and again towards late afternoon she leaves the nest to feed with, and be fed by, the male. The young leave the nest approximately five weeks after hatching, but remain with the parents to form the family parties usually observed. Males do not acquire adult plumage until they are more than two years old. I know of no published breeding records involving males in immature plumage, but it is probable that this does occur.

EGGS Rounded; 7 eggs, 31.2 (30.3–32.0) × 25.9 (25.2–26.4) mm. [H. L. White Coll.].

TIMOR RED-WINGED PARROT
Aprosmictus jonquillaceus (Vieillot)

DESCRIPTION
Length 35 cm.
MALE head, underparts and upper tail-coverts bright yellowish-green; mantle and upper back dark green with pronounced blue margins to feathers; rump and lower back blue; bend of wing blue; inner median and lesser wing-coverts yellow slightly tinged with green; outer median and greater wing-coverts red; remainder of wing green, darker on primaries; under wing-coverts yellowish-green; tail green above and grey-black below, all feathers tipped with greenish-yellow and lateral feathers edged with same colour on inner webs; bill coral with yellowish tip; iris orange; legs dark grey.
FEMALE like male, but no blue margins to feathers of mantle and upper back; bend of wing green; iris brownish-orange.
IMMATURES like female, but inner median and lesser wing-coverts green with little or no traces of yellow; iris pale brown.

DISTRIBUTION
Timor and Wetar Island in the Lesser Sundas, Indonesia.

SUBSPECIES
1. *A. j. jonquillaceus* (Vieillot)   *Illustrated on page 205.*
   7 males   wing 183–191 (186.1) mm., tail 145–169 (161.4) mm.,
           exp. cul. 19–21 (20.0) mm., tars. 20–21 (20.4) mm.
   5 females wing 173–189 (182.2) mm., tail 161–175 (168.0) mm.,
           exp. cul. 17–20 (18.6) mm., tars. 19–21 (20.0) mm.
   Confined to Timor.

2. *A. j. wetterensis* (Salvadori)
MALE like *jonquillaceus*, but inner median and lesser wing-coverts green with a little suffusion of yellow; less extensive red markings on greater wing-coverts; slightly smaller.
FEMALE similar to *jonquillaceus*, but upper wing-coverts darker green; slightly smaller.
   5 males   wing 172–180 (177.2) mm., tail 149–158 (154.0) mm.,
           exp. cul. 19–21 (19.8) mm., tars. 19–20 (19.6) mm.
   6 females wing 172–181 (176.2) mm., tail 152–166 (157.8) mm.,
           exp. cul. 18–20 (18.8) mm., tars. 19–21 (19.8) mm.
   Known only from Wetar Island.

GENERAL NOTES
Little is recorded about the Timor Red-winged Parrot, but its habits are probably similar to those of *A. erythropterus*. On Timor Stein collected specimens from the coast up to about 2,600 m. on Mt. Ramelan (in Mayr, 1944).

CALL Similar to that of *A. erythropterus*, but not as raucous (in captivity).

NESTING No records.

EGGS Undescribed.

Genus POLYTELIS Wagler

This genus is transitional between the *Prosopeia-Alisterus-Aprosmictus* group and the *Platycercus* group, although general external appearances are markedly different from either. Despite superficial similarities to *Psittacula* I do not think that it is closely allied to that Afro-Asian genus. Cain (1955) points out that in wing structure it shows affinities to *Alisterus* and *Aprosmictus* as well as to *Neophema*. Thompson (1900) says that the cranial osteology is similar to that of *Prosopeia*, *Alisterus* and *Aprosmictus*, the last two being considered as one genus.

   The parrots belonging to *Polytelis* are medium-sized birds with extremely long, strongly gradated tails. All tail-feathers are narrow and have finely tapered tips; the central pair are much longer than the adjacent pair. The wings are long and pointed, the three outermost primaries being narrow and of these the inner two are scalloped; the adult male Princess Parrot has the third primary of each wing terminating in an elongated spatule. The bill is small and slender. Sexual dimorphism is pronounced in two species—*swainsonii* and *anthopeplus*—but less conspicuous in *alexandrae*; young birds are similar to adult females.

SUPERB PARROT
Polytelis swainsonii (Desmarest)

Illustrated on page 208.

Illustrated on page 208.

DESCRIPTION

Length 40 cm.

MALE general plumage green, more yellowish on underparts; hindcrown washed with blue; forehead, throat and cheeks yellow; a wide scarlet band across foreneck; under wing-coverts green; outer webs of primaries dull blue; tail green above, glossy black below; bill coral; iris yellow-orange; legs grey.

FEMALE head green; facial area pale bluish-green; chin and throat greyish-green; thighs orange-yellow; margins and undersides of lateral tail-feathers rose-pink; iris yellow.

IMMATURES similar to female; iris pale brown.

11 males   wing 174–192 (183.1) mm., tail 209–261 (236.3) mm.,
        exp. cul. 14–17 (15.6) mm., tars. 19–21 (19.7) mm.

7 females wing 173–189 (178.1) mm., tail 196–219 (209.6) mm.,
        exp. cul. 15–16 (15.8) mm., tars. 19–22 (20.1) mm.

DISTRIBUTION

Interior of New South Wales and northern Victoria; largely a riparian species closely associated with the Murrumbidgee River and Castlereagh River systems.

GENERAL NOTES

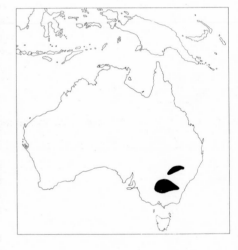

Superb Parrots frequent riverine eucalypts, especially where they form woodlands on flood plains radiating out from the watercourses. Toward the eastern extremity of their range the parrots are less dependent on the rivers and may be seen in open forest and trees surrounding pastures. They are fairly common and as the region has been an agricultural stronghold for a long time there should be little further alteration to the habitat (Frith and Calaby, 1953). Despite the restricted range these birds seem to be partly nomadic, their arrival in some areas coinciding with the flowering of eucalypts.

Small flocks are generally encountered and there is little apparent separation into pairs even during the breeding season. The parrots are most active early in the morning and towards late afternoon, when they are usually seen on the ground searching for seeds or in the treetops feeding on blossoms. While feeding they will allow a close approach, but are rather timid if disturbed when away from suitable cover.

They feed on seeds, fruits, nuts, berries, nectar and blossoms. Recorded food items include seeds of barley grass (*Hordeum murinum*), burr medic (*Medicago denticulata*), spiky wattle (*Acacia armata*), flowering heads of milk thistle (*Sonchus oleraceus*) and *Eucalyptus* blossoms. Sometimes in the company of Cockatiels (*Nymphicus hollandicus*) they visit stubble paddocks to pick up fallen wheat.

The swift, direct flight seems effortless, the backward-swept wings being moved with deliberate precision. On long flights the birds travel at a considerable height and the narrow, pointed wings and very long, gradated tail give a characteristic, streamlined flight silhouette.

CALL A prolonged warbling note terminating abruptly is given at frequent intervals during flight. It resembles the call of the Cockatiel but is deeper and has no upward inflection. A series of soft twittering notes is occasionally given while the bird is feeding or sitting in the treetops.

NESTING When courting the male may make brief flights around the hen, bowing as he alights. He fluffs out his head feathers, draws tight the remainder of his body plumage, partly spreads his wings and, with contracting pupils, races to and fro uttering a series of chattering notes. The female crouches low on her perch, fluffs out her head feathers, partly spreads her wings and emits soft, begging calls. Courtship feeding follows.

The breeding season is from September to December. The nest is in a hollow limb or hole in a tree, generally in a riverine eucalypt at a considerable height. On a layer of decayed wood dust four to six eggs are laid. Incubation lasts approximately twenty-two days and only the female broods. She is fed by the male two or three times a day. The young vacate the nest about thirty days after hatching and remain with their parents. Young males attain adult plumage with a slow moult, which normally begins when they are between six and nine months old and is completed when they are a little over twelve months old.

EGGS Rounded; 5 eggs, 28.7 (28.0–30.0) × 23.3 (23.0–23.7) mm. [H. L. White Coll.].

REGENT PARROT

Polytelis anthopeplus (Lear)

Illustrated on page 208.

DESCRIPTION

Length 40 cm.

MALE general plumage yellow, more olive on crown and hindneck; back dark olive-green; a broad red band across inner wing-coverts; outer wing-coverts bluish-black; dark blue on outer webs of primaries; under wing-coverts yellow; tail blue-black; bill coral; iris orange-brown; legs grey.

FEMALE head and breast dull olive-yellow; median wing-coverts yellow; under tail-coverts dull olive-green; tail dark bluish-green, lateral tail feathers margined and tipped on undersides with rose pink.

IMMATURES similar to female.

8 males   wing 193–200 (197.8) mm., tail 213–226 (220.4) mm.,
exp. cul. 18–19 (18.4) mm., tars. 20–23 (21.4) mm.

8 females wing 184–198 (188.7) mm., tail 200–214 (206.8) mm.,
exp. cul. 17–19 (18.5) mm., tars. 20–23 (21.8) mm.

DISTRIBUTION

South-western Australia and interior of south-eastern Australia from far south-western New South Wales and north-western Victoria to eastern South Australia.

SUBSPECIES

Birds from south-western Australia tend to be duller and more greenish, but, in my opinion, are not subspecifically distinct because the differences are not constant within the population. Near Kojonup, Western Australia, I have observed brightly-coloured, yellow birds.

GENERAL NOTES

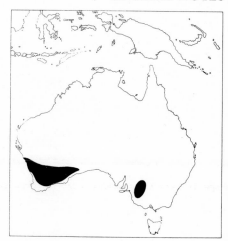

In south-eastern Australia the Regent Parrot replaces the Superb Parrot geographically. It is a bird of the flooded-zone *Eucalyptus* woodland and neighbouring arid scrublands. In south-western Australia its habitat preferences are far less specialized and it occurs in most types of timbered country; it has even penetrated the forested south-western corner by colonizing scattered cleared areas. In the eastern States it is uncommon, having retreated away from increasing land-clearance and settlement. In south-western Australia the reverse has happened; it is very abundant and has extended its range since settlement of the wheat-belt.

Pairs or small parties are generally seen, but in south-western Australia flocks of up to one hundred have been reported. At night the parrots roost in tall trees growing along a river bank, beside a stream, or around a stock-watering place. Early in the morning they often spend some time in the topmost branches preening themselves or quietly chattering. After drinking they fly off to feed. They may travel considerable distances to the feeding grounds. Most of the day is spent on the ground searching for grass seeds or feeding amongst the foliage of eucalypts and acacias. During the middle of the day they shelter in a tree or bush; while sheltering from the heat they are reluctant to fly and will allow a close approach, but at other times they are rather wary. Towards dusk they return to the roosting area, where they gather at the water's edge to drink before settling down for the night. In the breeding season males band together in small parties.

Seeds, nuts, fruits, berries, leaf buds, nectar and blossoms make up the diet. The birds are particularly fond of seeds of *Eucalyptus* and *Acacia*, but also eat wheat and cultivated fruits and in Western Australia are often troublesome to farmers. They have been seen feeding on seeds of *Acacia acuminata*. Near Balranald, New South Wales, I watched a small party in the company of Yellow Rosellas (*Platycercus flaveolus*) feeding on seeds of *Eucalyptus camaldulensis*.

The flight is similar to that of the Superb Parrot.

CALL Similar to, but noticeably harsher than, the call of the Superb Parrot; for a couple of minutes after alighting a soft twittering is emitted.

NESTING The courtship display is not as elaborate as that of the Superb Parrot, but the general nesting behaviour is similar. The breeding season is from August to January. Most nests are in large hollows down the main trunks of trees and the eggs may be up to 5 m. from the entrance. A normal clutch is four to six, usually four, eggs. On leaving the nest young males usually have a slightly more yellow tinge on the head. They begin a slow moult at the age of six months, full adult plumage being acquired when they are about fourteen or fifteen months old.

EGGS Rounded; 4 eggs, 31.0 (30.1–32.0) × 24.4 (22.8–25.1) mm. [H. L. White Coll.].

PRINCESS PARROT

Polytelis alexandrae Gould

Illustrated on page 208.

Length 45 cm.

MALE crown and nape light blue; forehead and sides of head pale bluish-grey; chin, throat and foreneck rose-pink; breast and abdomen bluish-grey tinged with green and yellow; thighs and lower flanks rose-pink, remainder of flanks washed with blue; under tail-coverts olive-yellow; back pale olive-green; wing-coverts bright yellow-greenish; secondaries and primary-coverts dull pale blue; primaries bluish-green narrowly edged with yellow; under wing-coverts green; rump violet-blue; central tail feathers olive-green washed with blue toward tips, lateral feathers blue-grey margined with rose-pink; bill coral; iris orange; legs dark grey.

FEMALE crown greyish-mauve; rump greyish-blue; wing-coverts duller and more greenish; shorter central tail feathers.

IMMATURES resemble female.

8 males   wing 167–198 (185.3) mm., tail 260–292 (276.4) mm.,
           exp. cul. 14–17 (15.6) mm., tars. 20–23 (20.8) mm.

8 females wing 163–180 (173.0) mm., tail 203–214 (208.7) mm.,
           exp. cul. 14–16 (15.0) mm., tars. 19–22 (20.4) mm.

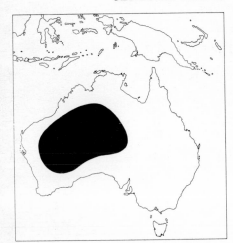

DISTRIBUTION   Interior of central and western Australia.

GENERAL NOTES   Princess Parrots are rare, little-known inhabitants of the arid interior. They frequent *Casuarina* trees scattered throughout open sandy country, dry *Acacia* scrublands and eucalypts bordering watercourses. They are highly nomadic. At irregular intervals, perhaps more than twenty years apart, they appear on a tree-lined watercourse, remain to breed, and then disappear as abruptly as they arrived. Storr (1967) says that in the Northern Territory their movements seem to be governed by the occurrence of ephemeral waters and the flowering of acacias.

Pairs or small groups of up to fifteen or twenty are usually seen, but larger flocks have been reported. They spend most of the day on the ground picking up grass seeds. Observers who have watched these parrots say that they are tame and will allow a close approach. When disturbed they fly to a nearby tree, where they will often perch lengthwise along a stout limb, presumably to escape detection.

All reports indicate that they feed on seeds, procured on or near the ground but fruits, berries and blossoms are probably also taken. Seeds of spinifex (*Triodia* spp.) are an important food item. Crops from birds collected in the Northern Territory contained seeds of *Triodia mitchelli*, mulga grass (*Danthonia bipartita*), *Portulaca oleracea*, *Calandrinia* sp., and fine grit (North 1896; Forshaw 1969a).

The flight is not as swift as that of the Superb Parrot and there is slight undulation. Before alighting the birds seem to pause momentarily in mid-air and then drop to the ground with a fluttering of wings. When travelling long distances they fly high, but short flights are close to the ground.

CALL A loud, unmelodic rolling note and peculiar cackling notes; a soft twittering when flushed into trees or bushes. These parrots are quiet and seldom call.

NESTING The courtship display is similar to that of the Superb Parrot, though males erect a few frontal feathers like a tiny crest.

The breeding season is from September to January and during this time several pairs may congregate to form a small colony. The nest is in a hollow limb or hole in a tree, generally in a large hollow in a riverine eucalypt, but nests have been found in *Casuarina* trees away from water. As many as ten nests have been found in one tree. A normal clutch comprises four to six eggs. Incubation lasts approximately twenty-three days and only the female broods. The young leave the nest some five weeks after hatching and accompany their parents when they depart almost immediately from the breeding area. Adult plumage is acquired by males slowly and imperceptibly early in the second year.

EGGS Rounded, highly glossy; 3 eggs, 27.4 (26.0–28.2) × 22.2 (21.3–23.1) mm. [Aust. Mus. Coll.].

Genus PURPUREICEPHALUS Bonaparte

A narrowing of the anterior of the cranium, a long, projecting bill, and a distinctive plumage pattern are the conspicuous characteristics of this monotypic genus. In common with other genera in the *Platycercus* group adult females and immatures show a 'wing-stripe' formed by a series of white spots on the underside of the flight feathers.

I have summarized the various theories put forward to explain the development of *Purpureicephalus* (see Forshaw, 1969a). Most authors agree that it is a relict form, which was once more widely distributed. However, I cannot accept the suggestion that overspecialization of the bill was solely responsible for the disappearance of any eastern representative.

RED-CAPPED PARROT
Purpureicephalus spurius (Kuhl)

Illustrated on page 225.

DESCRIPTION

Length 36 cm.
MALE forehead, crown and occiput deep crimson; rich green upperparts; cheek-patches, rump and upper tail-coverts bright yellow-green; breast and abdomen blue-violet; flanks and under tail-coverts red variably intermixed with green; under wing-coverts and outer webs of primaries blue; central tail feathers green marked with blue, lateral feathers pale blue tipped with white; wing-stripe absent; bill greyish; iris dark brown; legs brown.
FEMALE duller than male; more green on flanks and under tail-coverts; wing-stripe present.
IMMATURES crown dark green; rust-coloured frontal band; breast and abdomen dull cinnabar-brown; flanks and under tail-coverts heavily marked with green; wing-stripe present.
9 males   wing 152–166 (161.5) mm., tail 187–217 (194.3) mm.,
           exp. cul. 21–25 (22.5) mm., tars. 20–23 (21.8) mm.
5 females wing 152–163 (155.2) mm., tail 192–213 (197.6) mm.,
           exp. cul. 21–23 (21.8) mm., tars. 21–24 (22.6) mm.

DISTRIBUTION

South-western Australia south of the Moore River near Perth.

GENERAL NOTES

The Red-capped Parrot is a bird of the marri (*Eucalyptus calophylla*) forests and trees surrounding cultivated farmlands or bordering roads and watercourses; it also visits parklands and orchards. It is quite common and is sometimes seen in the suburbs of Perth. It is sedentary but in a particular area numbers may fluctuate with the availability of food, thus denoting local movement. Early in the morning and towards evening pairs or small parties may be seen on the ground searching for seeds or feeding amongst the outer branches of a eucalypt. During the day they sit quietly in the forest trees, where, despite their brilliant plumage, they are difficult to observe. They are most reluctant to leave the trees; normally they fly from one tree to another just ahead of the intruder. The slightly undulating, swift flight comprises rapid wing-beats interspersed with gliding, thus producing a somewhat buoyant or fluttering effect. There is no overall curve towards the ground terminating in an upward glide. Before landing the tail is only slightly fanned.

I have described in detail how the projecting bill is used to extract seeds from the fruits of marri, the most important food (Forshaw, 1969a). It is also used to remove seeds from the fruits of jarrah (*Eucalyptus marginata*), *Grevillea*, *Hakea*, *Casuarina* and the woody pear (*Xylomelum sp.*). Seeds of grasses, blossoms and leaf buds, and insects and their larvae, particularly psyllid lerps, are also eaten. The parrots may attack apples, pears and citrus fruits.

CALL A grating, disyllabic *crrr-uk* repeated several times is given regularly during flight; when alarmed a series of sharp shrieks. Feeding is usually done in silence.

NESTING The mating display lacks the tail-wagging and 'squaring' of the shoulders so typical of *Platycercus* spp. The male erects the red crown feathers and droops his wings thus exposing the bright yellow-green rump, the feathers of which are fluffed. He then slowly raises the fanned tail towards the back.

Nesting usually commences in August and continues through to early December. The nest is in a hollow limb or hole in a tree, generally a marri, at a considerable height. Four to seven, usually five, eggs are laid on a layer of decayed wood dust. Incubation lasts about twenty days and only the female broods. The young leave the nest approximately five weeks after hatching and remain with their parents for some months. Acquisition of adult plumage is slow, commencing at the age of five months and continuing over the next nine months.

EGGS Rounded; 5 eggs, 26.3 (25.8–27.0) × 22.6 (22.3–23.0) mm. [Aust. Mus. Coll.].

219

Genus BARNARDIUS Bonaparte

Barnardius is a genus based primarily on colour-pattern. Peters (1937) dismissed it altogether and incorporated all forms as a single species in *Platycercus*. However, Condon (1941) points out that there are structural differences in the auditory region of the crania of the two genera. I favour the retention of *Barnardius* as a distinct genus.

There are two species. They are medium-sized birds with long, gradated tails. There is no 'mottled' pattern on the back and the blue cheek-patches are ill-defined. The most conspicuous plumage characteristic is a narrow yellow collar encircling the hindneck. The white wing-stripe is present in most, though not all, immatures, and is variable in adults. The upper mandible is notched and is heavier than in *Platycercus*. The difference in the width of the mandible between the sexes is less marked than in *Platycercus*.

The flight pattern, general habits and nesting behaviour of these parrots are similar to those of the *Platycercus* species. There is, however, one notable difference; *Barnardius* parrots rarely congregate in flocks and are generally seen in pairs or family parties.

MALLEE RINGNECK PARROT
Barnardius barnardi (Vigors and Horsfield)

DESCRIPTION

Length 33 cm.
MALE crown and nape bright green; red frontal band; bluish cheek-patches; brownish band across occiput; narrow yellow collar encircling hindneck; underparts turquoise-green; irregular orange-yellow band across abdomen; back and mantle deep blackish-blue; median wing-coverts yellow; rump green; wings green with blue on outer webs of primaries; central tail-feathers green marked with blue, lateral feathers pale blue tipped with white; wing-stripe absent; bill greyish-white; iris dark brown; legs grey.
FEMALE duller than male; back and mantle dark greyish-green; wing-stripe generally present.
IMMATURES crown and nape brownish; back and mantle greyish-green; wing-stripe generally present.

DISTRIBUTION

Interior of eastern Australia east of 138°E.

SUBSPECIES

1. *B. b. barnardi* (Vigors and Horsfield)   *Illustrated on page 228.*
   11 males   wing 153–170 (163.4) mm., tail 169–186 (177.3) mm.,
            exp. cul. 18–19 (18.4) mm., tars. 20–22 (20.8) mm.
   11 females wing 153–163 (157.6) mm., tail 171–180 (173.3) mm.,
            exp. cul. 17–18 (17.6) mm., tars. 20–21 (20.3) mm.
   Occurs in the interior of south-eastern Australia except in the range of *whitei*.

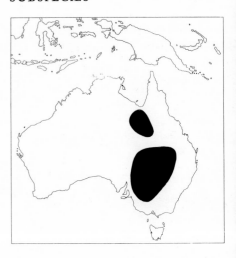

2. *B. b. whitei* (Mathews)
   ADULTS back and mantle dark greyish-green; crown and occiput brownish.
   4 males   wing 160–177 (170.3) mm., tail 179–194 (185.7) mm.,
            exp. cul. 18–20 (19.0) mm., tars. 20–23 (21.5) mm.
   4 females wing 155–181 (168.0) mm., tail 170–189 (179.0) mm.,
            exp. cul. 17–18 (17.5) mm., tars. 21–22 (21.5) mm.
   Confined to the Flinders Ranges, South Australia; towards the east it merges with *barnardi*. In the Flinders Range this race meets and, to some extent, probably hybridizes with *B. zonarius*, but, as with some *Platycercus* spp. also involved in hybridization, I prefer to retain specific status for each taxon.

3. *B. b. macgillivrayi* (North)   *Illustrated on page 228.*
   ADULTS general plumage pale green; no red frontal band; lower ear-coverts bright pale blue; very wide uniform abdominal band of pale yellow.
   5 males   wing 154–160 (157.6) mm., tail 169–187 (175.6) mm.,
            exp. cul. 17–18 (17.6) mm., tars. 20–22 (20.6) mm.
   5 females wing 157–165 (160.8) mm., tail 164–188 (173.8) mm.,
            exp. cul. 17–18 (17.2) mm., tars. 20–22 (20.8) mm.
   This distinctive isolate is known as the Cloncurry Parrot. It is found in north-western Queensland and the adjacent eastern area of the Northern Territory.

GENERAL NOTES

Mallee Ringneck Parrots frequent low *Eucalyptus* scrubland (mallee), open woodland and trees bordering water-courses. *B. b. macgillivrayi* appears to differ somewhat from the other subspecies by showing a marked preference for large eucalypts growing along the banks of rivers and creeks. Unlike *B. zonarius* this species does not seem to be able to withstand encroaching settlement. As the mallee and open woodland are cleared for grazing or cultivation the parrots gradually retreat. They are still considered to be common but in some areas numbers do appear to be declining.

Because of the isolated habitat there is little published information about *macgillivrayi* but observers have told me that it is plentiful along the upper tributaries of the Diamantina River. In pairs or small family parties the parrots are usually seen feeding on the ground or amongst the outer branches of a tree. They are not shy birds and when disturbed usually fly to a nearby tree. The flight is undulating with an overall drop towards the ground and a glide upwards before alighting; the tail is fanned when landing.

Seeds, fruits, berries, blossoms, leaf buds, and insects and their larvae make up the diet. They seem to be particularly fond of the seeds of paddy melons (*Cucumis myriocarpus*), wild bitter melons (*Citrullus lanatus*) and fruits of the introduced tobacco tree (*Nicotiana glauca*). Grit, sand and small pieces of charcoal are also eaten, presumably as an aid to digestion.

CALL A shrill *kwink* repeated many times in rapid succession; when alarmed a harsh, metallic note. Feeding in the branches of trees is often accompanied by a subdued chattering but when on the ground the parrots are silent.

NESTING When displaying, the male crouches before the female and 'squares' his shoulders, vibrating them slightly; the tail is spread and moved quickly from side to side and this action is accompanied by an almost continuous chattering. The commencement of the breeding season is marked by squabbling and fighting amongst males.

Nesting begins about August but may be delayed, or even prevented altogether, by adverse climatic conditions, particularly drought. The nest is in a hollow limb or hole in a tree, the bottom of the cavity being lined with decayed wood dust. A normal clutch comprises four to six, usually five, eggs. Incubation lasts approximately twenty days and only the female broods. She leaves the nest early in the morning and again towards dusk. The cock sits in a nearby tree and warns of any approaching danger. About five weeks after hatching the young leave the nest but remain with their parents to form the family parties usually observed. Adult plumage is attained when twelve to fifteen months old.

EGGS Rounded; 4 eggs, 29.2 (27.1–30.7) × 22.8 (22.2–23.5) mm. [Aust. Mus. Coll.].

PORT LINCOLN PARROT
Barnardius zonarius (Shaw)

DESCRIPTION   Length 38 cm.
MALE head dull black; red frontal band in some birds; lower ear-coverts violet-blue; narrow yellow collar encircling hindneck; back, wings and rump brilliant green; under wing-coverts blue; throat and breast bluish-green; abdomen yellow; vent and under tail-coverts yellowish-green; central tail feathers dark green marked with blue, lateral feathers pale blue tipped with white; wing-stripe absent; bill greyish-horn; iris brown; legs grey.
FEMALE similar to male; head generally more brownish; wing-stripe usually absent.
IMMATURES duller than adults; pronounced brownish tint on head; wing-stripe present in females but absent in most males.

DISTRIBUTION   Central and western Australia.

SUBSPECIES   1. *B. z. zonarius* (Shaw)   *Illustrated on page 228.*
12 males   wing 168–185 (176.8) mm., tail 165–218 (193.2) mm.,
                exp. cul. 18–22 (20.1) mm., tars. 21–24 (22.1) mm.
8 females   wing 164–178 (168.7) mm., tail 157–199 (173.7) mm.,
                exp. cul. 17–21 (19.1) mm., tars. 20–23 (21.2) mm.
Ranges throughout central and southern Australia west from Eyre Peninsula, South Australia, and Tennant Creek, Northern Territory, to the central regions of Western Australia where it meets *semitorquatus* and *occidentalis*.

2. *B. z. semitorquatus* (Quoy and Gaimard)
MALE abdomen green instead of yellow; prominent crimson frontal band; larger size.
FEMALE duller than male, frontal band smaller and paler, sometimes absent altogether.
10 males   wing 185–202 (192.0) mm., tail 197–226 (218.4) mm.,
                exp. cul. 21–24 (22.3) mm., tars. 23–26 (24.4) mm.
5 females   wing 181–190 (184.3) mm., tail 199–210 (205.2) mm.,
                exp. cul. 20–24 (21.9) mm., tars. 23–26 (23.8) mm.
This subspecies is known as the Twenty-eight Parrot. It is restricted to south-western Australia south of Perth and east to Albany.

3. *B. z. occidentalis* (North)

ADULTS head pale greyish-black; lower ear-coverts pale blue; abdomen and vent lemon-yellow; smaller than *semitorquatus*.

4 males   wing 161–166 (163.5) mm., tail 174–192 (185.6) mm.,
      exp. cul. 19–21 (20.3) mm., tars. 21–24 (22.0) mm.
6 females wing 159–170 (165.2) mm., tail 177–195 (192.6) mm.,
      exp. cul. 18–20 (18.7) mm., tars. 20–22 (21.0) mm.

This distinct pallid race occurs in Western Australia from the Pilbara region in the north to the Murchison River in the south.

GENERAL NOTES

The Port Lincoln Parrot is a most successful species, being quite common throughout more than one third of the Australian continent. It occurs in a wide variety of habitats including the dense coastal forests of the south-west, the semi-arid *Eucalyptus*-dominant wheatbelt and the arid scrublands and sparsely-vegetated plains of the interior. It has retreated from the more settled parts of Eyre Peninsula but seems to have increased in the wheatbelt of Western Australia, where it is now extremely abundant. Generally seen in pairs or small groups, these parrots are most striking birds when observed in the field. The black head bordered by a vivid yellow collar stands out strongly against the natural surroundings. Unlike *B. barnardi* they are noisy and this further aids detection. They spend much of the day feeding on the ground or amongst the branches of trees and shrubs. When disturbed they call excitedly and investigate the danger before flying away. Flight is similar to that of *B. barnardi*.

Normally a sedentary species the Port Lincoln Parrot sometimes moves in inland areas, depending on the availability of water; in prolonged dry periods the birds from the desert and sandhill country move into the large rock-holes which hold permanent water. The provision of stock-watering dams in pastoral country has benefited the birds.

There is some variation in feeding habits. The birds from the drier inland areas feed on seeds of grasses and herbaceous plants, while those in the south-western forests show a marked preference for fruits of *Eucalyptus* and other trees. I have seen *semitorquatus* feeding on the berries of white cedar trees (*Melia azederach*) planted as ornamental borders along streets and driveways. Robinson (1960) gives a detailed account of feeding on the fruit of the marri (*Eucalyptus calophylla*); the parrots tear the fruit apart when it is half ripe or remove the outer covering just prior to ripening—unlike the Red-capped Parrot (*Purpureicephalus spurius*) they are not interested in the hardened, ripe nuts. Jenkins (1969) observed them eating corms of onion grass (*Romulea longifolia*), leaves of capeweed (*Cryptostemma calendula*) and grub larvae of the sawfly (*Perga* sp.). They are very fond of cultivated fruits and grain and can be a pest in farmlands. They also eat nectar; Nicholls (1905) collected a specimen from a flock feeding on the blossoms of a karri (*Eucalyptus diversicolor*) and when it was held up by the feet nectar flowed from the bill.

CALL Similar to, but slightly higher in pitch than the calls of *B. barnardi*. In addition *semitorquatus* gives a trisyllabic call ending with an upward inflection; this is said to resemble the words 'twenty-eight'.

NESTING The courtship display and nesting behaviour resemble those of *B. barnardi*. The normal breeding season for the central and southern populations extends from August to February and if conditions are favourable two broods may be reared. Birds in the northern parts of the range generally commence breeding as early as June or July. A clutch comprises four to seven, usually four, eggs.

EGGS Rounded; 4 eggs, 29.4 (29.3–30.0) × 24.1 (24.0–24.2) mm. [Aust. Mus. Coll.].

Genus PLATYCERCUS Vigors

Parrots belonging to this genus are collectively known as rosellas and all show two plumage characteristics: well-defined cheek-patches and a pronounced 'mottling' on the back. They are medium-sized birds with long, gradated tails. There is a notch in the upper mandible; males have a noticeably wider, heavier upper mandible than do females. In all but one species—*icterotis*—the sexes are alike in plumage. The white underwing-stripe is present but is variable according to the species.

The rosellas are an interesting assemblage of closely related parrots. There are two species groups differentiated by immature plumage patterns. The *caledonicus-elegans-adelaidae-flaveolus* group, in which immatures are predominantly dull green, is confined to eastern Australia including Tasmania. In the more widespread *eximius-adscitus-venustus-icterotis* group immatures resemble both or one of the adults. Species from within a group replace each other geographically and may hybridize at the borders of their ranges. However, every species from the *caledonicus* group is sympatric with a species from the *eximius* group and hybridization rarely occurs.

The swift, undulating flight is interspersed with brief periods of gliding, during which the wings may be either extended or withdrawn in to the body. In flight the birds drop down towards the ground then glide upwards before alighting; the tail is spread when landing. These parrots are primarily seed-eaters and spend much of the day on the ground searching for food.

GREEN ROSELLA
Platycercus caledonicus (Gmelin)

Illustrated on page 229.

DESCRIPTION Length 36 cm.

MALE red frontal band; head and underparts rich yellow, the latter sometimes washed with orange-red; cheek-patches deep blue; feathers of nape, back and wings black margined with dark green; rump olive-green; median wing-coverts greenish-black; under wing-coverts and outer webs of flight feathers blue; central tail feathers green marked with blue, lateral feathers pale blue tipped with white; wing-stripe absent; bill horn-coloured; iris brown; legs grey.

FEMALE smaller size with smaller bill; throat generally washed with orange-red; wing-stripe usually absent.

IMMATURES head and underparts dull greenish-yellow; blue cheek-patches; back and wings dull green; wing-stripe present.

10 males wing 180–193 (183.7) mm., tail 186–199 (192.1) mm.,
      exp. cul. 17–19 (18.3) mm., tars. 24–26 (24.8) mm.
7 females wing 165–176 (169.9) mm., tail 170–189 (178.1) mm.,
      exp. cul. 15–19 (16.7) mm., tars. 21–23 (21.9) mm.

DISTRIBUTION Tasmania and the larger islands in Bass Strait.

GENERAL NOTES

According to Ridpath and Moreau (1966) Green Rosellas occur in all habitats in Tasmania except heathlands and cleared croplands devoid of tracts of timber. They are common and during the non-breeding season flocks are a familiar sight even within urban limits. Green (1969) says that they are widely distributed on Flinders Island and are plentiful in most habitat types. Because of the sombre colouration of their upperparts they are inconspicuous when on the ground seeking seeds or when in the tall eucalypts feeding on blossoms. Only in flight is the rich yellow of the underparts fully displayed. They are noisy birds and this draws attention to their presence. Immatures tend to band together in groups of up to twenty, while adults associate in smaller parties of four or five. These parrots are not shy and will usually allow a close approach. They are sedentary. The flight is strong with less undulation than that of the other rosellas. Rapid wing-beats are interspersed with only brief periods of gliding; when alighting the tail is fanned.

The diet comprises seeds, blossoms, berries, nuts, fruits, and insects and their larvae. During winter months flocks congregate on hawthorn hedges to feed on the berries. They also feed extensively on the berries of *Coprosma* and *Cyathodes* shrubs. I have seen them eating leaf buds of the introduced basket willows (*Salix viminalis*). On the north coast of Tasmania Green and Swift (1965) observed a small mixed flock of Green and Eastern Rosellas feeding on psyllids of the genus *Schedotrioza*. Small seeds, vegetable matter, minute scraps of charcoal, sand and insect larvae have been found in crop contents (Lea and Gray, 1935).

CALL A disyllabic *cussik-cussik* given regularly in flight; also a variety of flute-like whistles. When alarmed the bird emits a rapid succession of shrill piping notes.

NESTING When displaying the male droops his wings, 'squares' his shoulders, fluffs up his breast and upper tail-coverts and moves his fanned tail from side to side; he either holds his head high and tilts it back or he bows slightly. The display is accompanied by a constant chattering.

Breeding lasts from September through to January or February. The nest is in a hollow limb or hole in a tree, usually a eucalypt. Sharland (1956) found nests in crevices in ruins of convict buildings. Up to six, usually four or five eggs are laid on decayed wood dust lining the bottom of the hollow. Incubation is of three weeks duration and only the female broods. She leaves the nest for a brief period each morning to feed with her mate and to be fed by him. About five weeks after hatching the young leave the nest, remain with their parents for another four or five weeks then band together with other immatures. At about fourteen months adult plumage is acquired after the first complete moult, but birds in their first year are capable of breeding.

EGGS Rounded; 6 eggs, 30.5 (29.7–31.8) × 24.4 (24.0–24.6) mm. [R. H. Green Coll.].

CRIMSON ROSELLA
Platycercus elegans (Gmelin)

DESCRIPTION Length 36 cm.

ADULTS general plumage rich crimson; cheek-patches violet-blue; feathers of nape, back and wings black broadly margined with crimson; median wing-coverts black; under wing-coverts, bend of wing and outer webs of flight feathers blue; central tail feathers blue slightly washed with green, lateral feathers pale blue tipped with white; wing-stripe absent; bill greyish-white; iris dark brown; legs grey.

IMMATURES crown, throat, upper breast, thighs and under tail-coverts red; remainder of under-parts dull greyish-green; cheek-patches violet blue; upperparts bright olive-green; wing-stripe present.

DISTRIBUTION

Eastern and south-eastern Australia; introduced to Norfolk Island and New Zealand.

SUBSPECIES

1. *P. e. elegans* (Gmelin)　　　　　　　　　　　　　　*Illustrated on page 232.*
   14 males　wing 169–188 (181.7) mm., tail 176–199 (190.7) mm.,
   　　　　　exp. cul. 18–20 (18.6) mm., tars. 21–24 (22.1) mm.
   12 females　wing 164–176 (170.7) mm., tail 170–201 (184.1) mm.,
   　　　　　exp. cul. 16–17 (16.8) mm., tars. 21–24 (22.3) mm.
   Occurs in south-eastern Australia from south-eastern Queensland to south-eastern South Australia. This is almost certainly the race introduced to Norfolk Island and New Zealand.

2. *P. e. nigrescens* Ramsay
   ADULTS general plumage colouration darker; narrower margins to feathers give back and wings black appearance; smaller size.
   IMMATURES similar to adults, not predominantly green as in other subspecies.
   11 males　wing 154–168 (160.3) mm., tail 141–178 (158.4) mm.,
   　　　　　exp. cul. 16–19 (17.7) mm., tars. 19–22 (20.2) mm.
   7 females　wing 147–160 (154.1) mm., tail 154–171 (161.5) mm.,
   　　　　　exp. cul. 15–17 (16.3) mm., tars. 19–21 (19.7) mm.
   Confined to north-eastern Queensland. This subspecies is almost certainly an isolate, the known southern limit of its range being some 640 km. north of the northernmost records for *elegans*.

3. *P. e. melanoptera* North
   ADULTS back more heavily marked with black.
   10 males　wing 175–182 (177.7) mm., tail 175–211 (186.7) mm.,
   　　　　　exp. cul. 17–19 (18.1) mm., tars. 21–24 (22.8) mm.
   6 females　wing 168–178 (172.4) mm., tail 172–187 (177.5) mm.,
   　　　　　exp. cul. 16–17 (16.5) mm., tars. 21–24 (21.8) mm.
   Found only on Kangaroo Island, South Australia; doubtfully distinct from *elegans*.

GENERAL NOTES

Turner *et al.* (1968) report that the Crimson Rosella is now well established and very common on Norfolk Island. Hamel (1970) says that in New Zealand it has been recorded from the Dunedin district in the South Island and from about Wellington in the North Island, but it has never been common. In eastern Australia it is a bird of the coastal and adjacent mountainous forests from sea level to the alpine woodlands above 1,900 m. It is plentiful, even occurring in numbers in the outer suburbs of large towns and cities. In some areas along the fringes of its range nomadic movements during the winter months have been reported but elsewhere the species is sedentary. It is forced to retreat by extensive land-clearance and is replaced by the Eastern Rosella. Immatures tend to congregate in small flocks while adults remain in pairs or groups of up to five birds. These parrots are not shy and will usually allow a close approach. Most of the day is spent feeding in the treetops or on the ground. The flight is more undulating and noticeably slower than that of the Green Rosella. The parrots normally fly close to the ground and glide upward into a tree; when alighting the tail is fanned.

They eat seeds, fruits, blossoms, and insects and their larvae. I have frequently seen them feeding on the seeds of native pines (*Callitris endlicheri*), the introduced sweetbriar (*Rosa rubiginosa*) and sorrel (*Rumex* sp.). Crop contents from two birds comprised seeds of *Rumex acetosella*, *Helichrysum scorpioides*, *Danthonia* spp., *Stellaria media* and *Trifolium dubium*, and some *Hemiptera* insects (Forshaw, 1969a). Some damage is done to orchards in the apple and pear-growing districts of southern New South Wales (Forshaw, 1969b).

CALL A low-pitched *kweek . . . kweek . . . kweek*, the middle note on a lower scale; when alarmed a series of shrill, metallic screeches. A soft chattering generally accompanies feeding.

NESTING The courtship display and general nesting behaviour closely resemble those of the Green Rosella. Breeding commences in late August or early September and continues through until January or February. The normal clutch comprises five to eight, usually five, eggs. Adult plumage is acquired over a period of some sixteen months; there are reports of young birds leaving the nest with an almost completely red plumage.

EGGS Rounded; 6 eggs, 29.4 (28.5–30.0) × 24.2 (24.0–24.5) mm. [Aust. Mus. Coll.].

YELLOW ROSELLA
Platycercus flaveolus Gould

Illustrated on page 229.

Length 33 cm.
MALE head and entire underparts pale yellow; throat and upper breast often lightly marked with red; orange-red frontal band; cheek-patches violet-blue; feathers of nape, back and wings black broadly margined with pale yellow; rump and upper tail-coverts dull yellow; median wing-coverts black; under wing-coverts and outer webs of flight feathers blue; central tail feathers blue strongly washed with green, lateral feathers pale blue tipped with white; wing-stripe absent; bill greyish-white; iris dark brown; legs grey.
FEMALE similar to male; wing-stripe generally present.
IMMATURES back and wings dull olive-green with little or no black on feathers; underparts pale yellow-green; rump olive-green; wing-stripe present.
13 males   wing 160–178 (168.7) mm., tail 167–199 (184.0) mm.,
                exp. cul. 15–19 (16.3) mm., tars. 20–25 (22.2) mm.
10 females wing 152–172 (162.9) mm., tail 162–189 (174.0) mm.,
                exp. cul. 15–17 (16.1) mm., tars. 20–23 (21.7) mm.

Interior of south-eastern Australia; a riparian species closely associated with the Murray-Murrumbidgee-Lachlan Rivers system in southern New South Wales, northern Victoria and eastern South Australia.

GENERAL NOTES

The Yellow Rosella frequents riverine eucalypts, especially where they form savannah woodland on flood plains extending some distance from the watercourses. Throughout the restricted range it is quite common, but early reports suggest that prior to the development of large-scale irrigation along the rivers it was more widespread and numerous. These reports also indicate that there were nomadic movements into fringe areas from which the species has now disappeared. Pairs or small parties are generally observed feeding amongst the outer branches of tall eucalypts or on the ground searching for seeds. They seem to be more arboreal than other rosellas. In the treetops their plumage blends extremely well with the foliage and, despite the chattering call-notes, an observer usually has difficulty locating them. They are less confiding than other rosellas and generally move well ahead of an intruder. The flight is swifter and less undulating than that of the Crimson Rosella; the flight path is direct and lacks the inverted arc.

The diet comprises seeds, fruits, berries, blossoms, nectar, nuts, and insects and their larvae. I have seen these parrots feeding on seeds of paddy melons (*Cucumis myriocarpus*); other records include the seeds of the water pepper (*Polygonum hydropiper*), the introduced Scotch thistle (*Onopordon scanthium*), and the larvae of the cup moth (*Limacodes longerans*).

CALL Similar to, but of a slightly higher pitch than the calls of the Crimson Rosella.

NESTING The breeding season extends from late August to December or early January. General nesting behaviour, including courtship display, is very similar to that of the Green Rosella. The nesting hollow is generally high up in a very large eucalypt and four or five eggs are laid. Adult plumage is acquired over about fourteen months, but many young birds leave the nest as duller versions of the adults.

EGGS Rounded; 5 eggs, 27.3 (27.0–27.8) × 22.9 (22.5–23.2) mm. [Aust. Mus. Coll.].

ADELAIDE ROSELLA
Platycercus adelaidae Gould (hybrid population)

Illustrated on page 233.

DESCRIPTION

Red-capped Parrot *Purpureicephalus spurius*
AM. 020360 ad. ♂

Length 36 cm.
ADULTS (much variation in plumage); forehead and crown red; nape and sides of head dull orange-yellow; cheek-patches violet blue; feathers of mantle, back and wings black broadly margined with olive-yellow and red; rump olive-yellow with variable red markings; median wing-coverts black; underparts orange-yellow variably marked with red; under wing-coverts and outer webs of flight feathers blue; central tail feathers blue strongly washed with green, lateral feathers pale blue tipped with white; wing-stripe absent; bill greyish-white; iris dark brown; legs grey.
IMMATURES crown, throat, upper breast, thighs and under tail-coverts dull red; violet-blue cheek-patches; breast and abdomen dull greyish-green; upperparts olive-green; wing-stripe present.
10 males   wing 156–190 (173.0) mm., tail 181–196 (187.5) mm.,
                exp. cul. 16–18 (17.3) mm., tars. 21–24 (22.2) mm.
10 females wing 163–172 (167.6) mm., tail 173–184 (180.5) mm.,
                exp. cul. 16–17 (16.4) mm., tars. 20–24 (21.5) mm.

DISTRIBUTION	Southern South Australia from the southern Flinders Ranges to the Fleurieu Peninsula south of Adelaide. Condon (1968) points out that there is a break of some 70 km. separating the northern and southern populations.

SUBSPECIES

Two taxonomic arrangements have been proposed for the Adelaide Rosella. Both make it an intermediate form between *P. elegans* and *P. flaveolus*, but differ in the nomenclature. Some authors treat all three forms as subspecies of *P. elegans*, while others regard them as distinct species. In my opinion the Adelaide Rosella is a hybrid population so I use the name *P. adelaidae* merely for convenience not as an indication of specific status.

GENERAL NOTES

Within their very restricted range Adelaide Rosellas are abundant. They inhabit tall types of timbered country and are often seen in suburban gardens and parklands in Adelaide. They are sedentary. Flocks of immatures and pairs or small parties of adults are generally found in the treetops or clambering over shrubs and bushes feeding on seeds and berries, or on the ground searching for grass seeds. They regularly visit farm-houses and haystacks to pick up spilled grain. Boehm (1959) reports that they are fond of the seeds of the slender thistle (*Carduus tenuiflorus*). Crop and stomach contents from about forty birds comprised seeds—including those of *Solanum nigrum*, *Xanthorrhoea spatha*, clover (*Trifolium glomeratum*), and *Acacia* sp.—grains of wheat, vegetable matter, fine grit and pieces of charcoal, remains of small caterpillars, and insects (Lea and Gray, 1935).

The flight is similar to that of the Crimson Rosella.

CALL All call-notes are similar to those of the Crimson Rosella.

NESTING The breeding season extends from September through to December. Nesting behaviour, including courtship display, closely resembles that of the Green Rosella. The nesting hollow is in a living or dead eucalypt and four or five, rarely up to seven, eggs are laid. Adult plumage is acquired at about sixteen months, but over the next few years the colours become richer and red margins appear on some of the back feathers.

EGGS Rounded; 7 eggs, 29.2 (29.0–30.3) × 24.1 (24.0–24.4) mm. [Aust. Mus. Coll.].

EASTERN ROSELLA
Platycercus eximius (Shaw)

Length 30 cm.
MALE head and breast red; white cheek-patches; lower breast yellow merging into pale green on abdomen; vent and under tail-coverts red; feathers of back and wings black margined with greenish-yellow; median wing-coverts black; rump pale green; under wing-coverts and outer webs of flight feathers blue; central tail feathers green washed with blue, lateral feathers pale blue tipped with white; wing-stripe absent; bill greyish-white; iris dark brown; legs grey.
FEMALE red on head and breast duller and less extensive; wing-stripe present.
IMMATURES similar to female; nape and hindcrown green; wing-stripe present.

South-eastern Australia including Tasmania; introduced to New Zealand.

1. *P. e. eximius* (Shaw) *Illustrated on page 232.*
 10 males   wing 152–161 (156.1) mm., tail 147–178 (162.6) mm.,
              exp. cul. 15–17 (16.0) mm., tars. 19–21 (20.2) mm.
 10 females wing 138–156 (147.6) mm., tail 146–170 (159.1) mm.,
              exp. cul. 14–16 (14.8) mm., tars. 19–22 (20.6) mm.
 Occurs in south-eastern New South Wales, throughout Victoria and in south-eastern South Australia. This is probably the race introduced to New Zealand where it is now strongly established in the vicinity of Auckland; there is also a small population near Dunedin in the South Island (Falla *et al.*, 1966).

2. *P. e. cecilae* (Mathews)
 ADULTS head and breast darker red; feathers of back and wings margined with rich golden yellow; rump bluish-green.
 6 males   wing 152–167 (161.0) mm., tail 160–177 (166.8) mm.,
            exp. cul. 16–17 (16.3) mm., tars. 21–23 (22.1) mm.
 6 females wing 145–160 (151.7) mm., tail 145–170 (156.0) mm.,
             exp. cul. 15–16 (15.3) mm., tars. 19–21 (19.7) mm.
 Found in south-eastern Queensland and north-eastern New South Wales south to the Hunter River region where it meets *eximius*.

3. *P. e. diemenensis* North
 ADULTS larger white cheek-patches; red on head and breast darker and more extensive.

Cloncurry Parrot **1**
Barnardius barnardi macgillivrayi
AM. 033698 ad. ♂

Mallee Ringneck Parrot **2**
Barnardius barnardi barnardi
CSIRO. 10044 ad. ♂

Port Lincoln Parrot **3**
Barnardius zonarius zonarius
CSIRO. 10323 ad. ♂

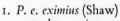

5 males   wing 147–162 (153.3) mm., tail 164–182 (172.2) mm.,
           exp. cul. 17–18 (17.8) mm., tars. 22–23 (22.8) mm.
3 females wing 147–156 (152.7) mm., tail 148–158 (152.3) mm.,
           exp. cul. 15–16 (15.7) mm., tars. 21–22 (21.3) mm.
   Confined to Tasmania.

GENERAL NOTES

Hamel (1970) reports that in New Zealand the Eastern Rosella has become established mainly in the north of the North Island and around the Dunedin district of Otago in the South Island; it has occasionally increased to pest proportions. According to Rostron (1969) it is slowly building up in numbers and is spreading into new areas in New Zealand. In Tasmania it is not numerous (Green, 1959) but elsewhere in south-eastern Australia it is extremely abundant. It inhabits lightly timbered country up to about 1,250 m. and is a familiar bird in gardens and parklands on the outskirts of towns and cities. It has benefited greatly from the establishment of pasture lands and the cultivation of cereal crops. Pairs or small groups are often seen feeding on spilled grain around haystacks, storage sheds or in fowl pens. Despite their showy plumage they are not conspicuous on the ground and may not be noticed until they rise up in front of the observer. They are often flushed from the roadside and are frequently killed by moving vehicles. During winter they congregate in flocks of eight to twenty birds, occasionally up to one hundred, but in early spring pairs leave to set up breeding territories. Except for the middle of the day, when they shelter from the heat amongst the outermost branches of a eucalypt, they spend most of their time in the treetops feeding on seeds and blossoms or on the ground seeking grass seeds. The undulating flight is comparatively swift. The inverted arc path is usually followed, but on a long flight, particularly over open grassland, the birds fly at a considerable height and do not drop towards the ground.

They are troublesome in orchards and Rostron points out that in New Zealand they are already causing damage to citrus crops. Often in the company of Red-rumped Parrots they visit stubble paddocks after harvesting to pick up fallen grain. Other notable food items include the berries of hawthorn and *Pyracantha* bushes, seeds of clover and Scotch thistle (*Onopordon scanthium*)—the latter a serious weed pest—and psyllids. Crop contents from six birds comprised wheat grains, seeds of *Cerastium vulgatum*, *Oxalis* sp. and *Melilotus alba*, some fine charcoal and a *Paropsis* beetle (Lea and Gray 1935, Forshaw 1969a).

CALL A loud *kwink . . . kwink . . . kwink* on an ascending scale or a metallic piping note repeated twice; when alarmed a shrill screech. Feeding is usually accompanied by a subdued chattering. All call-notes are noticeably higher in pitch than those of the Crimson Rosella.

NESTING The courtship display and general nesting behaviour are similar to those of the Green Rosella. The breeding season lasts from September to January but nests have also been found in April and May. The nest is in a hollow in a living or dead tree, or in a fence post, stump or log lying on the ground; nests have even been found in rabbit burrows. A clutch of four to nine, usually five, eggs are laid. Unless a second nesting is imminent the young birds remain with their parents for many months after leaving the nest. Adult plumage is acquired within the first year.

EGGS Rounded; 7 eggs, 26.9 (25.7–28.1) × 21.7 (21.3–22.1) mm. [Aust. Mus. Coll.].

Green Rosella *Platycercus caledonicus* **1**
AM. 028301 ad. ♂

Yellow Rosella *Platycercus flaveolus* **2**
AM. 028293 ad. ♂

Northern Rosella *Platycercus venustus* **3**
AM. 037525 ad. ♂

PALE-HEADED ROSELLA
Platycercus adscitus (Latham)

DESCRIPTION

Length 30 cm.
MALE head white with tinges of yellow; cheek-patches violet-blue below, white above; feathers of back and wings black margined with dusky yellow; rump dusky yellow; upper breast yellow tinged with blue, lower breast and abdomen blue; vent and under tail-coverts red; median wing-coverts black; under wing-coverts and outer webs of flight feathers blue; central tail feathers green strongly washed with blue, lateral feathers pale blue tipped with white; wing-stripe absent, bill horn-coloured; iris dark brown; legs grey.
FEMALE similar to male; wing-stripe present.
IMMATURES duller than female; usually some red or grey markings on head; wing-stripe present.

North-eastern Australia; introduced to Hawaii in 1877 but not recorded since 1928 (Munro, 1960).

DISTRIBUTION

1. *P. a. adscitus* (Latham)   *Illustrated on page 233.*   SUBSPECIES
   6 males   wing 140–160 (146.5) mm., tail 143–164 (154.7) mm.,
              exp. cul. 16–18 (17.1) mm., tars. 19–21 (19.5) mm.
   4 females wing 142–154 (147.3) mm., tail 142–154 (148.5) mm.,
              exp. cul. 15–16 (15.4) mm., tars. 19–21 (19.7) mm.
      Restricted to the northern extremity of the range from Cape York Peninsula south to the Mitchell River and Cairns, where it intergrades with *palliceps*.

230

2. *P. a. palliceps* Lear

ADULTS white cheek-patches; feathers of back and wings margined with rich golden yellow; rump greenish-blue.

11 males   wing 148–169 (160.4) mm., tail 161–175 (167.8) mm.,
            exp. cul. 15–18 (17.1) mm., tars. 20–23 (21.1) mm.
5 females wing 148–156 (152.2) mm., tail 162–187 (168.9) mm.,
            exp. cul. 16–18 (16.8) mm., tars. 20–22 (21.3) mm.

Widely distributed from northern Queensland, south of Cairns and the Mitchell River, to northern New South Wales.

GENERAL NOTES

The Pale-headed Rosella is a lowland bird inhabiting most types of timbered country including clearings in heavy forest or the forest itself where it adjoins open grassland. It is abundant throughout most of its range and, like the Eastern Rosella, has benefited from the clearing of farmlands and the cultivation of cereal crops. In drier western regions the provision of stock-watering facilities has ameliorated the habitat. If present in numbers the species may become a pest in orchards or amongst maize crops. It is sedentary. The general habits are similar to those of the Eastern Rosella. While these parrots are feeding on the ground their 'mottled' backs blend extremely well with the grass coverage and an observer may be unaware of their presence until they fly up in front of him. The flight resembles that of the Eastern Rosella.

In southern Queensland I have seen these birds associated with Mallee Ringneck and Red-winged Parrots feeding on *Callitris* and *Acacia* seeds. They have also been recorded eating *Melaleuca* blossoms and the seeds of *Eucalyptus camaldulensis*, *Casuarina cunninghamiana*, *Melaleuca linariifolia* and *Xanthium chinense*, the last being a weed pest.

CALL   All call-notes are similar to those of the Eastern Rosella.

NESTING   In the south the breeding season lasts from September to December, while in the north it is from February through to June, that is, after the wet season, but if good rains fall at other times some birds will breed. The nest is in a deep hollow in a living or dead tree, preferably one standing near a river or stream. A clutch of three to five eggs is laid. The nesting behaviour resembles that of the Green Rosella. After leaving the nest young birds remain with their parents to form family parties. Adult plumage is acquired gradually and is not complete until the first full moult at the age of sixteen months.

EGGS   Rounded; 5 eggs, 26.2 (25.5–27.2) × 21.4 (21.0–21.6) mm. [Aust. Mus. Coll.].

Crimson Rosella *Platycercus elegans elegans*   1
CSIRO. 84 Imm. ♂

Crimson Rosella *Platycercus elegans elegans*   2
AM. 028319 ad. ♂

Eastern Rosella *Platycercus eximius eximius*   3
CSIRO. 12672 ad. ♂

NORTHERN ROSELLA
Platycercus venustus (Kuhl)

Illustrated on page 229.

Length 28 cm.

ADULTS forehead, crown and nape black, sometimes with red markings; cheek-patches white above, violet-blue below; feathers of back and wings black broadly margined with pale yellow; median wing-coverts black; rump and underparts pale yellow, the feathers narrowly edged with black; under tail-coverts scarlet; under wing-coverts and outer webs of flight feathers blue; central tail feathers blue washed with green, lateral feathers pale blue tipped with white; wing-stripe absent; bill greyish-white; iris dark brown; legs grey.

IMMATURES duller than adults; red markings often on head or breast; central tail feathers bronze green; wing-stripe generally present.

6 males   wing 143–152 (148.5) mm., tail 141–163 (153.0) mm.,
           exp. cul. 15–17 (16.2) mm., tars. 18–19 (18.7) mm.
8 females wing 138–154 (143.2) mm., tail 142–165 (151.0) mm.,
           exp. cul. 14–17 (15.4) mm., tars. 18–20 (18.8) mm.

DISTRIBUTION

North-western and northern Australia from the Kimberleys, Western Australia, east to the Northern Territory—Queensland border; occurs on Bathurst, Melville and Milingimbi Islands.

GENERAL NOTES

Northern Rosellas inhabit savannah woodland, timber bordering watercourses, littoral forests and occasionally coastal mangroves. They are locally common but generally scarce (Storr, 1967) and are rarely encountered in any numbers. Pairs or small parties of up to six or eight birds are usually seen in the treetops or on the ground searching for seeds. They are more difficult to approach than are most of the other rosellas and when flushed from the ground fly to the topmost branch of a nearby tree where they wait until the danger has passed before returning to feed. During the heat of the day they sit quietly amongst the uppermost branches of a tree, their plumage blending well with the foliage. They are sedentary. The undulating flight is surprisingly swift and somewhat erratic; they normally fly close to the ground, gliding up into a tree and then fanning their tails before alighting.

Seeds of grasses, shrubs and trees, principally eucalypts, melaleucas and acacias and fruits, berries,

W. T. Cooper. '70.

and blossoms constitute the diet. I am not aware of any report of this species eating insects and their larvae, but it probably does so.

CALL A disyllabic, high-pitched note repeated three or four times. When feeding in the treetops a soft chattering is emitted.

NESTING Nesting has been recorded during June, July and August. The courtship display and general nesting behaviour are similar to those of the other rosellas. The nesting hollow is generally in a tree standing near water. Only two to four eggs are laid. After leaving the nest young birds remain with their parents to form family parties. Acquisition of adult plumage is a slow and inconspicuous process lasting about twelve months.

EGGS Rounded; 2 eggs, 25.4 (25.0–25.7) × 20.6 (20.1–21.1) mm. [H. L. White Coll.].

WESTERN ROSELLA
Platycercus icterotis (Kuhl)

DESCRIPTION Length 25 cm.
MALE head and entire underparts red; yellow cheek-patches; feathers of back and wings black broadly margined with dark green, in some birds scattered red margins; rump green, occasionally marked with red; median wing-coverts black; under wing-coverts and outer webs of flight feathers blue; central tail feathers green tinged with blue, lateral feathers pale blue tipped with white; wing-stripe generally absent; bill grey; iris dark brown; legs brownish-grey.
FEMALE head and upper breast green with faint yellow and red markings; red frontal band; lower underparts dull red strongly suffused with green; duller cheek-patches; wing-stripe present.
IMMATURES resemble female, but lack the yellow cheek-patches and most of the red from the underparts; wing-stripe present.

DISTRIBUTION South-western Australia.

SUBSPECIES 1. *P. i. icterotis* (Kuhl)   *Illustrated on page 233.*
    10 males wing 133–150 (139.5) mm., tail 142–149 (145.6) mm.,
          exp. cul. 13–15 (13.8) mm., tars. 18–20 (19.2) mm.
    6 females wing 130–143 (135.7) mm., tail 121–146 (135.5) mm.,
          exp. cul. 12–14 (13.0) mm., tars. 17–18 (17.7) mm.
    Restricted to coastal areas.

2. *P. i. xanthogenys* Salvadori
ADULTS very pale yellow cheek-patches; feathers of back and wings margined with red and greyish-buff in male and with buff in female; rump greyish-olive; central tail-feathers blue with no noticeable tints of green.
    5 males wing 137–168 (144.8) mm., tail 141–156 (147.0) mm.,
          exp. cul. 13–15 (14.0) mm., tars. 17–19 (18.2) mm.
    3 females wing 132–136 (133.7) mm., tail 146–157 (150.3) mm.,
          exp. cul. 12–13 (12.7) mm., tars. 18–19 (18.3) mm.
    This race inhabits the drier interior of south-western Australia; there is a zone of intergradation with *icterotis*.

Open forest, trees surrounding croplands or lining roadways, timber bordering watercourses, grasslands and cultivated farmlands are inhabited by the Western Rosella; in heavy forest it is not a common bird, being largely restricted to clearings and roadside areas. It is common, though not plentiful, and seems to be benefiting from increased cultivation of cereal crops. Unlike other rosellas it is a quiet and unobtrusive bird, often remaining unnoticed as it shelters from the heat of the day in a tree or moves over the ground searching for grass seeds. Pairs or small family parties are generally seen, but sometimes there is an aggregation at a concentrated food supply such as a stubble paddock after harvesting. They are confiding birds and become very tame around farm buildings where they come to feed on spilled grain. In some areas local movements have been reported, but the species is largely sedentary. The buoyant, fluttering flight differs markedly from the heavy flight of other rosellas; between wingbeats there are only very brief periods of gliding. Flights are usually over short distances, the parrots preferring to move from one tree to another rather than fly above an expanse of open land.

The diet comprises seeds of grasses and herbaceous plants, fruits, berries and insects and their larvae.

CALL The call is soft and melodious, comprising a series of whistle-like notes repeated rapidly; it lacks the harsh, metallic tones common to the calls of other rosellas.

Western Rosella *Platycercus icterotis icterotis* 1
AM. 028318 ad. ♂

Western Rosella *Platycercus icterotis icterotis* 2
WAM. A2521 ad. ♀

Pale-headed Rosella *Platycercus adscitus adscitus* 3
QM. 04026 ad. ♂

Adelaide Rosella *Platycercus adelaidae* 4
CSIRO. 10252 ad. ♂

NESTING The breeding season extends from August through to December, September being the main month for egg-laying. In a hollow limb or hole in a *Eucalyptus* tree three to seven, usually five eggs are laid. Only the female broods and while she is sitting the male remains in the immediate vicinity of the nest. Incubation lasts about twenty-five days and the young leave the nest after a further thirty days. During the first autumn and winter young birds commence to show a little red on the head and breast and yellow on the cheeks, but the full adult plumage is not attained until they undergo a rapid, complete moult when about fourteen months old.

EGGS Rounded; 17 eggs, 25.9 (24.6–27.7) × 21.6 (20.3–22.5) mm. [Serventy and Whittell, 1967].

Genus PSEPHOTUS Gould

Members of this genus are small to medium-sized, slim parrots with uniformly coloured backs and long, strongly gradated tails. There are no well-marked cheek-patches and the bills are smaller and less robust than those of the rosellas. Except for one rather aberrant species—*haematogaster*—sexual dimorphism is pronounced. The white wing-stripe is present, though variable in extent according to the species.

Some authors place *P. haematogaster* in a monotypic genus, *Northiella*, because of its different wing formula.

Red-rumped Parrot **1**
Psephotus haematonotus haematonotus
AM. 028408 ad. ♂

Red-rumped Parrot **2**
Psephotus haematonotus haematonotus
AM. 033153 ad. ♀

Mulga Parrot *Psephotus varius* **3**
AM. 026232 ad. ♂

Mulga Parrot *Psephotus varius* **4**
AM. A18502 ad. ♀

RED-RUMPED PARROT
Psephotus haematonotus (Gould)

DESCRIPTION

Length 27 cm.
MALE general plumage green, duller and more bluish on back and wings; yellow abdomen; vent and under tail-coverts white; red-rump; median wing-coverts yellow; under wing-coverts and outer webs of primaries blue; central tail feathers green tinged with blue, lateral feathers blue tipped with white; wing-stripe absent; bill black; iris dark brown; legs grey.
FEMALE head and upperparts olive-green; neck and breast dull yellowish-olive; abdomen, vent and under tail-coverts white; median wing-coverts pale blue; green rump; wing-stripe present; bill grey.
IMMATURES similar to, but duller than adults; in males nape and back are dull green without bluish tinge; females have yellowish bills, males dull grey; wing-stripe present.

Interior of south-eastern Australia.

DISTRIBUTION

SUBSPECIES

1. *P. h. haematonotus* (Gould)   *Illustrated on page 236.*
   12 males   wing 126–141 (131.4) mm., tail 138–158 (148.2) mm.,
          exp. cul. 12–13 (12.2) mm., tars. 15–18 (16.4) mm.
   12 females   wing 120–131 (124.3) mm., tail 129–155 (142.0) mm.,
          exp. cul. 11–13 (11.8) mm., tars. 14–18 (15.8) mm.
      Occurs in the interior of south-eastern Australia; probably meets *caeruleus* north of the Flinders Range, South Australia.

2. *P. h. caeruleus* Condon
   MALE general plumage paler and more bluish; rump pale red; central tail feathers strongly washed with pale blue.
   FEMALE decidedly paler than *haematonotus*; nape and upper mantle greyish instead of olive-green.
   3 males   wing 120–124 (122.3) mm., tail 152–158 (154.2) mm.,
          exp. cul. 12–13 (12.7) mm., tars. 15–17 (16.3) mm.
   3 females   wing 120–123 (121.3) mm., tail 140–153 (145.7) mm.,
          exp. cul. 12–13 (12.7) mm., tars. 15–17 (16.0) mm.
      Known only from about Innamincka, South Australia, the type locality.

GENERAL NOTES

The Red-rumped Parrot frequents lightly-timbered grasslands, open plains and cultivated farmlands below 1,250 m. It is seldom seen far from permanent water and in drier areas is replaced by the Mulga Parrot and Blue-Bonnet. It benefits from the clearing of forests and the establishment of cereal crops and is now extending its range. There is some indication of irregular movements at higher altitudes, but elsewhere the species seems to be sedentary. A common bird, it is often seen around farm buildings and in parklands within city limits. Pairs or small parties are usually encountered, but in western parts of the range large flocks are not uncommon. They spend most of the time on the ground searching for seeds. The flock moves over the ground like sandpipers on a tidal flat, the birds scurrying here and there to pick up seeds and fluttering from the shade of one

tree to that of another. When resting amongst the green foliage of a tree or when feeding on the ground they are inconspicuous because the colours of their upperparts blend so well with the surroundings. While feeding they are unwary and simply run ahead of the intruder. During the breeding season males band together in groups until the young hatch and then they assist at the nest. They usually fly high. The flight is strong and rather swift with some undulation; when alighting the tail is slightly fanned.

These parrots feed on the seeds of grasses and herbaceous plants and green vegetable matter, particularly the leaves of various thistles. Crop contents from birds collected in south-eastern South Australia and near Canberra comprised vegetable matter, scraps of charcoal, fine grit, wheat, and seeds of a saltbush (*Chenopodiaceae*), chickweed (*Stellaria media*), *Echinochloa crusgalli* and *Linum* sp. (Lea and Gray 1935, Forshaw 1969a).

CALL A disyllabic, shrill whistle with an upward inflection repeated three or four times. When perched in the treetops they emit a pleasant, trill-like whistle, almost a song. When squabbling or defending a nesting hollow they give a grating chatter.

NESTING The mating display differs only slightly from that of the rosellas. Nesting takes place between August and December, but following good rains in northern and western districts eggs have been found as early as May. The nest is in a hollow limb or hole in a tree, preferably a eucalypt standing near water. Nests have also been found in fence posts and under the eaves of farm buildings. When a tree contains only one nest that tree is defended, but when there are two or more nests only the limb containing the hollow is defended. The four to seven, usually five, eggs are laid on a layer of decayed wood dust. Only the female broods and incubation lasts about three weeks. She is fed by the male at almost hourly intervals. The young leave the nest approximately thirty days after hatching. Adult plumage is acquired with a complete moult when the birds are about three months old, but young males retain the wing-stripes for a further twelve months.

Blue-Bonnet **1**
Psephotus haematogaster haematogaster
AM. 028392 ad. ♂

Naretha Blue-Bonnet **2**
Psephotus haematogaster narethae
CSIRO. 5693 ad. ♂

EGGS Rounded; 6 eggs, 23.5 (22.8–24.0) × 19.2 (18.5–20.0) mm. [H. L. White Coll.].

MULGA PARROT
Psephotus varius Clark   *Illustrated on page 236.*

DESCRIPTION Length 27 cm.
MALE general plumage green, paler on lower breast; forehead yellow; red patch on crown; abdomen and thighs yellow variably marked with orange-red; red patch on upper tail-coverts with a yellowish-green band and a bluish line above; median wing-coverts yellow; under wing-coverts and outer webs of primaries blue; central tail feathers dark blue washed with green, lateral feathers blue tipped with white; wing-stripe absent; bill dark grey; iris brown; legs brownish-grey.
FEMALE forehead dull orange-yellow; dull red patch on crown; head and breast brownish-green; underparts pale green; median wing-coverts dull red; wing-stripe present; bill brownish-grey.
IMMATURES duller than adults; males have a little red on abdomen; wing-stripe present.
8 males   wing 126–145 (135.4) mm., tail 163–174 (166.8) mm.,
             exp. cul. 12–14 (12.8) mm., tars. 15–17 (15.7) mm.
8 females wing 125–132 (129.4) mm., tail 155–168 (162.4) mm.,
             exp. cul. 12–13 (12.1) mm., tars. 16–17 (16.4) mm.

DISTRIBUTION Interior of southern Australia.

GENERAL NOTES

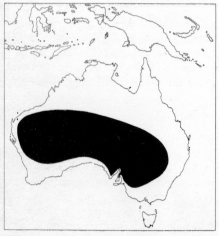

Throughout their extensive range Mulga Parrots are generally common, but locally may be rather scarce. Unlike Red-rumped Parrots they do not associate in flocks, but pairs or family parties may come together to feed at a concentrated supply of food such as spilled grain at a railway siding. They inhabit sparsely-timbered grasslands, arid scrublands and groves of mulga, myall or stunted eucalypts. Pairs or small family parties are generally observed on the ground feeding in the shade of trees. They are confiding and if disturbed merely fly to a nearby tree. They are unobtrusive birds lacking the bustling activities so characteristic of *P. haematonotus*. During the hottest part of the day they sit quietly amongst the branches of a tree, their plumage blending with the foliage. In arid central regions the occurrence of these parrots is unpredictable and I believe that this is because they prefer to remain within travelling distance of a reliable water supply, many of such watering places being only seasonal. The buoyant, fluttering flight is surprisingly swift; the birds usually fly close to the ground and when alighting spread their tails.

Their food comprises seeds of grasses and herbaceous plants, fruits, berries and green vegetable matter. They have been observed feeding on the seeds of mulga (*Acacia aneura*), while near Leonora, Western Australia, Sedgwick (1952) found them eating the seeds of *Loranthus murrayi* and the developed, but unripe, pods of *Acacia tetragonophylla*. Crops from birds collected in South Australia contained scraps of charcoal, fine grit, vegetable matter and numerous seeds including those of ruby saltbush (*Enchylaena tomentosa*) and mouse-ear chickweed (*Cerastium glomeratum*) and a plant of the family Caryophyllaceae (Lea and Gray, 1935).

CALL A soft whistle repeated three or four times in quick succession.

NESTING The nesting behaviour is similar to that of the Red-rumped Parrot. The breeding season lasts from July to December, but nesting may take place at almost any time of the year following good rains. Most trees are small and stunted and this means that nesting hollows are often ill-formed apertures close to the ground. A normal clutch comprises four to six, usually five, eggs.

EGGS Rounded; 5 eggs, 24.2 (24.0–24.5) × 18.8 (18.4–19.2) mm. [H. L. White Coll.].

BLUE-BONNET
Psephotus haematogaster (Gould)

DESCRIPTION Length 28 cm.
ADULTS forehead, lores and forepart of crown mauve-blue; paler blue cheek-patches; upperparts olive-brown; breast pale olive-brown marked with buff-yellow; abdomen yellow with central patch of red; vent and under tail-coverts yellow; wing-coverts bright olive; under wing-coverts and outer webs of flight feathers blue; central tail-feathers bronze-green washed with blue, lateral feathers blue tipped with white; wing-stripe absent in male, present in female; bill greyish-horn; iris grey-brown; legs grey.
IMMATURES duller than adults; smaller red abdominal patch; wing stripe present.

DISTRIBUTION Interior of south-eastern and southern Australia.

SUBSPECIES

Paradise Parrot *Psephotus pulcherrimus* **1**
AM. 017835 ad. ♂

Paradise Parrot *Psephotus pulcherrimus* **2**
AM. 021244 ad. ♀

Golden-shouldered Parrot **3**
Psephotus chrysopterygius chrysopterygius
AM. 027895 ad. ♂

Golden-shouldered Parrot **4**
Psephotus chrysopterygius chrysopterygius
HLW. 528 ad. ♀

Hooded Parrot **5**
Psephotus chrysopterygius dissimilis
AM. 032988 ad. ♂

1. *P. h. haematogaster* (Gould)   *Illustrated on page 237.*
   8 males   wing 122–140 (129.2) mm., tail 163–187 (172.2) mm.,
              exp. cul. 16–18 (16.4) mm., tars. 20–21 (20.8) mm.
   12 females wing 118–133 (125.1) mm., tail 147–182 (165.0) mm.,
              exp. cul. 14–17 (14.9) mm., tars. 19–21 (19.8) mm.
   Occurs in western and southern New South Wales, north-western Victoria and south-eastern South Australia; meets *haematorrhous* in the north and *pallescens* in the west.

2. *P. h. haematorrhous* Gould
   ADULTS median and greater wing-coverts reddish-chestnut; pale green on bend of wing; red extends from abdomen through to thighs, vent and under tail-coverts.
   8 males   wing 125–145 (135.4) mm., tail 172–181 (176.9) mm.,
              exp. cul. 16–17 (16.2) mm., tars. 20–22 (21.3) mm.
   10 females wing 119–133 (126.2) mm., tail 170–179 (174.4) mm.,
              exp. cul. 14–17 (15.8) mm., tars. 19–22 (20.8) mm.
   Found in southern Queensland and northern New South Wales.

3. *P. h. pallescens* Salvadori
   ADULTS upperparts and breast very pale; median wing-coverts olive-yellow.
   6 males   wing 126–138 (131.8) mm., tail 157–168 (163.0) mm.,
              exp. cul. 15–16 (15.7) mm., tars. 19–21 (20.2) mm.
   4 females wing 125–129 (126.8) mm., tail 149–165 (156.5) mm.,
              exp. cul. 15–16 (15.3) mm., tars. 18–20 (19.0) mm.
   This pale desert race from the Lake Eyre Basin, South Australia, is the counterpart of *Psephotus haematonotus caeruleus* from the same area.

4. *P. h. narethae* H. L. White   *Illustrated on page 237.*
   MALE forehead, lores and upper cheek-patches greenish-blue; lower cheek-patches mauve-blue; head and breast pale brown 'mottled' with pale buff; upperparts greyish-olive; rump olive-yellow; abdomen yellow; under tail-coverts red; lesser wing-coverts greenish-blue; median wing-coverts scarlet; central tail-feathers dull olive-green washed with blue.
   FEMALE much duller than male; colours on cheek-patches, wing-coverts and abdomen paler and less extensive.
   8 males   wing 117–126 (122.8) mm., tail 147–155 (150.9) mm.,
              exp. cul. 13–15 (13.8) mm., tars. 18–20 (19.1) mm.
   5 females wing 105–120 (112.8) mm., tail 141–152 (145.4) mm.,
              exp. cul. 12–14 (13.2) mm., tars. 18–20 (19.4) mm.
   The exact range of this distinct subspecies from southern Australia has not been determined; records are from near Ceduna, South Australia, to east of Kalgoorlie, Western Australia, and north 140 km. from Rawlinna, Western Australia. Further investigations into the Ceduna population are required because there are unconfirmed reports that birds illegally trapped in Western Australia were released near Ceduna. If *narethae* is found to be naturally sympatric

W.T. Cooper. '71.

with *pallescens* in the Ceduna district, then the two forms will have to be treated as separate species.

GENERAL NOTES   Blue-Bonnets are found in lightly-timbered grasslands, open plains, arid scrublands, and trees bordering watercourses or surrounding cereal paddocks. They are fairly common and are often seen around farm buildings and stock-watering troughs. Pairs or small parties are usually seen on the ground feeding in the shade of trees. I have often flushed them from the roadside. They also visit railway sidings to feed on spilled wheat. When moving over the ground they run quickly and adopt a curious upright stance, appearing to stretch themselves to their maximum height. They are rather wary. While roosting during the hottest part of the day they are extremely quiet, but if disturbed call excitedly, raise the frontal feathers on their heads and lift their folded wings. The erratic flight is undulating and like that of the rosellas. The birds generally fly close to the ground.

Seeds of grasses and herbaceous plants, fruits, berries, blossoms and nectar constitute the diet. Fine grit and pieces of charcoal are also eaten, presumably as an aid to digestion. In western New South Wales I have seen Blue-Bonnets feeding on the seeds of saltbush (*Atriplex vesicarum*) and bluebush (*Kochia sedifolia*). Crop contents from birds collected in northern New South Wales comprised pieces of charcoal, flower stamens and seeds of *Amaranthus* and *Atriplex* spp. (Cleland, 1918).

CALL   A harsh abrupt *cluck-cluck* repeated at regular intervals. When alarmed the birds give the same call with a more rapid repetition. While perched they occasionally give a high-pitched, piping whistle. *P. h. narethae* has a soft, flute-like note resembling *cloote-cloote*, as well as a loud *ack-ack-ack*.

Antipodes Green Parakeet
Cyanoramphus unicolor
AM. 037314 ad. ♂

NESTING   The mating display resembles that of the rosellas but the general stance is very upright and the frontal feathers are raised in the form of a small crest. The breeding season is from July to December, but this species is to some extent an opportunist breeder and may nest at other times of the year following good rains. The nest is in a hollow in a tree, often only a small hole in a stunted tree. The four to seven, usually five, eggs are laid on decayed wood dust. Incubation lasts twenty-two days and only the female broods; she sits very tightly. About thirty days after hatching the young leave the nest, but remain with the parent to form the family parties usually observed. Adult plumage is attained through a complete moult when the birds are about three or four months old.

EGGS   Rounded; 5 eggs, 23.4 (22.5–24.1) × 19.4 (19.1–19.8) mm. [Aust. Mus. Coll.].

GOLDEN-SHOULDERED PARROT
Psephotus chrysopterygius Gould

DESCRIPTION   Length 26 cm.
MALE forehead and lores pale yellow; crown and nape black; underparts turquoise blue; lower abdomen, thighs and under tail-coverts scarlet tipped with white; upperparts brown; rump turquoise blue; median wing-coverts golden-yellow; under wing-coverts and outer webs of flight feathers blue; tail greenish-blue; lateral feathers tipped with white; wing-stripe absent; bill greyish; iris dark brown; legs greyish-brown.
FEMALE crown and nape pale bronze-brown; upperparts and breast dull yellowish-green; lower underparts pale blue with some red and white markings towards vent; wing-stripe present.
IMMATURES resemble female; males are brighter on sides of head and under tail-coverts; wing-stripe present.

DISTRIBUTION   Southern Cape York Peninsula, Queensland, and north-eastern region of Northern Territory.

SUBSPECIES   1. *P. c. chrysopterygius* Gould   *Illustrated on page 240.*
    3 males   wing 112–113 (112.3) mm., tail 150–157 (152.7) mm.,
        exp. cul. 11–13 (11.8) mm., tars. 14–15 (14.6) mm.
    3 females wing 106–110 (108.3) mm., tail 133–151 (144.0) mm.,
        exp. cul. 12–13 (12.6) mm., tars. 14–15 (14.6) mm.
    Confined to southern parts of Cape York Peninsula, chiefly the interior.

    2. *P. c. dissimilis* Collett   *Illustrated on page 240.*
    MALE forehead, lores, crown and nape black; upperparts darker brown; yellow on wing-coverts brighter and more extensive; no red markings on lower underparts; under tail-coverts salmon-pink with faint white markings.
    FEMALE forehead, crown and sides of face pale greyish-green; vent and under tail-coverts salmon-pink.
    3 males   wing 120–122 (120.4) mm., tail 153–162 (158.0) mm.,

exp. cul. 12–13 (12.6) mm., tars. 14–15 (14.6) mm.
5 females wing 115–127 (119.6) mm., tail 148–153 (150.8) mm.,
exp. cul. 12–14 (13.1) mm., tars. 16–18 (16.6) mm.
Known as the Hooded Parrot, this distinctive isolate occurs in north-eastern regions of the Northern Territory from the Arnhem Land Plateau east to the Macarthur River.

GENERAL NOTES Golden-shouldered Parrots are found in semi-arid savannah woodland and open forest. In 1917 *chrysopterygius* was collected in mangroves along the banks of the Watson River. About Borroloola *dissimilis* has been observed in eucalypts growing along rocky ridges bordering watercourses. This species seems to have disappeared from parts of its range and is now quite rare. On Cape York Peninsula illegal trapping of adults and removal of young birds from nests have endangered *chrysopterygius*, and rigid enforcement of protection laws is urgently needed to save it from extinction. Within their restricted ranges the parrots are somewhat nomadic; observers have told me that on Cape York Peninsula the movements of *chrysopterygius* seem to have a predictable pattern, with most birds travelling to western parts of the Cape after completion of breeding.

Pairs or small parties are generally seen feeding on the ground. They are not shy and when disturbed merely fly to the nearby trees to await the passing of danger and then return to the ground. During the hottest part of the day they rest quietly in the treetops. When sitting in trees their plumage blends well with the foliage, especially with the greyish-green foliage of melaleucas.

They feed on seeds of grasses and herbaceous plants and on blossoms and leaf buds. Robinson has seen them extracting nectar from blossoms of *Grevillea pteridifolia* and biting off the stamens, presumably to take pollen; he also observed birds removing bark or some growth on the bark of *Eucalyptus* trees (*in litt.*, 1971). The crop from a bird collected near Port Stewart contained numerous small grass seeds (Thomson, 1935).

Orange-fronted Parakeet **1**
Cyanoramphus malherbi
AM. 030426 ad. ♂

Red-fronted Parakeet **2**
Cyanoramphus novaezelandiae novaezelandiae
AM. 030422 ad. ♂

Yellow-fronted Parakeet **3**
Cyanoramphus auriceps auriceps
AM. 030427 ad. ♂

CALL The call of *chrysopterygius* in flight is a whistle-like *fweep-fweep* repeated two or more times in succession and sometimes drawn-out to a *few-weep . . . few-weep*; while perched a repetition of an abrupt *weet* is given and also a disyllabic *fee-oo* may be emitted (Robinson, *in litt.*, 1971). The distress call of *chrysopterygius* is a disyllabic *cluk-cluk* (in captivity). The calls of *dissimilis* are a harsh *chissik-chissik* and a soft flute-like whistle (in captivity).

NESTING When courting the male makes short flights around the female, and then with breast feathers puffed out and the frontal feathers raised in a small crest he struts along the perch towards her. The breeding season is from May to January. The nest is in a hole excavated by the birds in a terrestrial termites' mound. No nesting material is used, the four to six eggs being laid on crumbled earth. Incubation lasts about twenty-three days and only the female broods. At intervals during the day the male comes to the nest and calls to the brooding female; she emerges and flies off with the male, presumably to be fed by him. Both parents feed the chicks. Young birds leave the nest some five weeks after hatching and remain with their parents to form the family parties usually seen. Young birds undergo a moult of body feathers when about four months old, but males do not begin to attain adult plumage for some time thereafter, the transition being completed when they are almost sixteen months. Robinson has seen a breeding pair at the nest and the male was still in immature plumage (*in litt.*, 1971).

EGGS Rounded; 6 eggs, 21.3 (20.5–22.2) × 18.4 (18.2–18.7) mm. [H. L. White Coll.].

PARADISE PARROT
Psephotus pulcherrimus (Gould)

Illustrated on page 240.

DESCRIPTION Length 27 cm.
MALE forehead red; crown and nape brownish-black; upperparts brown; underparts turquoise blue, often suffused with green on breast; lower abdomen, thighs and under tail-coverts scarlet; rump turquoise-blue; median wing-coverts red; under wing-coverts and outer webs of flight feathers blue; tail bronze-green tinged with blue, lateral feathers tipped with white; wing-stripe absent; bill greyish; iris brown; legs greyish-brown.
FEMALE crown and nape dark brown; forehead yellowish-white faintly tipped with red; face and breast buff-yellow with brownish-orange markings; lower underparts palest blue with some red markings; little red on wing-coverts; wing-stripe present.
IMMATURES similar to female; males show some blue or green on face and breast and have darker crown and wing-coverts; wing-stripe present.
21 males wing 121–135 (127.9) mm., tail 143–182 (158.5) mm.,
exp. cul. 12–14 (12.8) mm., tars. 16–19 (16.7) mm.
6 females wing 122–126 (124.7) mm., tail 144–168 (161.5) mm.,
exp. cul. 12–14 (12.6) mm., tars. 16–18 (16.6) mm.

DISTRIBUTION Central and southern Queensland and northern New South Wales; possibly northern Queensland.

GENERAL NOTES There is only unsubstantiated evidence suggesting that the Paradise Parrot still exists. Probably it

was never very common and as a species was declining prior to the advent of European settlement. At the turn of the century it was locally common, though generally scarce. Then came a steady decline in numbers, and in 1915 searches were carried out in its old haunts without success. Disappearance of the birds was attributed to the loss of seeding grasses brought about by two years without a wet season followed immediately by a severe drought in 1902, and by widespread heavy stocking. The last authenticated sighting was in November 1927, though other possible observations have been reported since. Small populations probably survive in some remote areas, but until there is some tangible proof of this the species must be regarded as being extremely rare, if not already extinct.

Paradise Parrots frequented open savannah woodland and scrubby grasslands where termites' mounds were prevalent; river valleys were their stronghold. Pairs or small parties spent most of the day on the ground feeding. They were rather tame and would allow a close approach before flying to a nearby tree. The flight was rather swift with slight undulation.

They fed on seeds of grasses and herbaceous plants. The method of feeding was to seize a blade of grass near the base and run the bill over the stem thus removing the seeds. If the stem was thick the parrot would climb on and bend it down with its weight.

CALL A series of soft, whistle-like notes repeated three or four times; when alarmed a sharp, metallic note was given once or twice.

NESTING Nesting was recorded in September, December and March. The nest was in a hollow excavated in a terrestrial termites' mound, or occasionally in a hole in a creek bank or in a hollow in a tree. In the mound or creek bank a large nesting chamber was hollowed out at the end of a tunnel. No nesting material was used, the four or five eggs being laid on a mat of crumbled earth. Incubation lasted approximately three weeks and only the female brooded. At intervals during the day the male would alight at the tunnel entrance and call softly. The female would emerge and the pair would fly off together, presumably to feed. Nothing further is known of the nesting habits.

EGGS Rounded; 5 eggs, 21.2 (20.3–21.8) × 17.6 (17.3–18.0) mm. [H. L. White Coll.].

Genus CYANORAMPHUS Bonaparte

This genus also lacks both the mottled back and the well-defined cheek-patches. The species are small to medium-sized, stocky parrots with long, gradated tails. The tarsi are rather long and there is no notch in the upper mandible. Males are larger than females, but there are no plumage differences. The white wing-stripe is prominent in immatures and adult females, but slight or absent altogether in adult males.

Black-fronted Parakeet 1
Cyanoramphus zealandicus
MNHN. 136 ad. unsexed

Society Parakeet *Cyanoramphus ulietanus* 2
BM. 21.R.28.1.84 ad. unsexed

ANTIPODES GREEN PARAKEET
Cyanoramphus unicolor (Lear)

Illustrated on page 241.

Illustrated on page 241.

Length 30 cm.
ADULTS general plumage green, noticeably lighter and more yellowish on underparts; crown and facial area brilliant emerald green; outer webs of flight feathers violet-blue; tail margined with yellow; bill pale bluish-grey becoming dark grey towards tip; iris orange; legs greyish-brown.
IMMATURES undescribed.
11 males   wing 144–157 (150.1) mm., tail 116–147 (135.3) mm.,
            exp. cul. 19–24 (22.0) mm., tars. 25–28 (26.1) mm.
12 females wing 141–153 (146.8) mm., tail 125–150 (137.1) mm.,
            exp. cul. 19–23 (19.9) mm., tars. 25–28 (26.1) mm.

DESCRIPTION

Antipodes Island.

DISTRIBUTION

GENERAL NOTES

It is interesting that two closely related parrots should be found on Antipodes Island, which has an area of only 38 sq. km. The Antipodes Green Parakeet is endemic to the island, whereas the other species, *C. novaezelandiae*, is widely distributed throughout New Zealand and on islands north to New Caledonia. Taylor visited Antipodes Island in 1969 with the Canterbury University Expedition and observed both species; he has made comparative notes on their habits (*in litt.*, 1971). He says that both are common and occur on all parts of the island, though relative densities differ according to habitat. *C. unicolor* was found to be more common in areas of tall dense *Poa litorosa* tussock, especially on the coastal slopes, whereas *C. novaezelandiae* predominated on open parts of the central elevated plateau and along the south coast. He also points out that, at least during the breeding season, a wide ecological separation exists between the two species and no instances of direct inter-specific competition were seen. No flocking behaviour was observed in either species, the parrots being encountered singly, in pairs, or in small groups of up to five. They were fearless of man and, if approached quietly, would remain feeding less than 2 m. from an observer. *C. unicolor* occasionally gave the impression of being inquisitive and attracted by human activity. When disturbed it gave a very brief call or remained silent and disappeared into the nearest thick vegetation; this furtive behaviour was particularly characteristic of males. On the other hand when *C. novaezelandiae* was disturbed it usually called in alarm and then took flight, continuing to call as it flew. When feeding intently both species moved by climbing over, under and among the vegetation. Red-fronted Parakeets tended to fossick much more, mixing seeds with flowers and other items, while *C. unicolor* was often watched for long periods feeding solely on *Poa* leaves.

Both species are capable of strong flight and on calm days could be seen swooping about the slopes and flying at heights of more than 30 m. above the central plateau. However, they flew much less during wet or windy weather.

Taylor notes that distribution of the two species on the island was correlated with the availability of the different foods being eaten at the time of his visit. Feeding observations from all parts of the island showed that 65% of the diet of *C. unicolor* was leaves of *Poa* tussock and sedges, with other important foods being seeds (12%), berries (9%), and fragments from corpses of penguins and other birds (7%). By comparison, 60% of the food of *C. novaezelandiae* was seeds, mainly those of *Carex appressa*, and the remainder comprised flowers (14%), berries (10%), and invertebrates (10%).

CALL Oliver (1955) reports that this parrot makes a low chattering sound as it walks about. According to Turbott all calls are similar to those of *C. novaezelandiae*, though some notes seem softer and deeper (in Falla *et al.*, 1966).

NESTING Taylor states that by February *C. unicolor* had finished nesting and all chicks seen were flying and partly feeding themselves. However, *C. novaezelandiae* was still feeding young in the nest and some chicks were still in down. Thus it appears that *C. unicolor* breeds earlier than *C. novaezelandiae* and the difference in timing could be associated with the availability of preferred foods. The two species used different nesting sites: *C. novaezelandiae* in tunnels in the crowns of tall tussocks or clumps of ferns and *C. unicolor* in burrows in the fibrous peat beneath the vegetation.

EGGS Nearly spherical; 2 eggs, 26.2 (25.4–27.0) × 23.0 (23.0) mm. [Oliver, 1955].

Horned Parakeet *Eunymphicus cornutus cornutus* **1**
AMNH. 337745 ad. ♂

Horned Parakeet *Eunymphicus cornutus uvaeensis* **2**
AM. 027722 ad. ♂

RED-FRONTED PARAKEET
Cyanoramphus novaezelandiae (Sparrman)

Length 27 cm.
ADULTS general plumage green, lighter and more yellowish on underparts; forehead, crown, band behind eyes and patch on each side of rump crimson-red; outer webs of flight feathers violet-blue; bill pale bluish-grey becoming dark grey towards tip; iris red; legs greyish-brown.
IMMATURES red markings on head less extensive; shorter tail; iris pale brown.

DESCRIPTION

New Zealand and outlying islands, Norfolk Island, and New Caledonia; formerly on Macquarie and Lord Howe Islands.

DISTRIBUTION

1. *C. n. novaezelandiae* (Sparrman)   *Illustrated on page 244.*
   8 males   wing 129–139 (134.9) mm., tail 122–158 (137.5) mm.,
              exp. cul. 14–17 (15.9) mm., tars. 20–22 (21.5) mm.
   8 females wing 125–133 (128.6) mm., tail 115–130 (123.0) mm.,
              exp. cul. 14–17 (14.8) mm., tars. 19–21 (19.9) mm.
   Distributed throughout New Zealand on North, South and Stewart Islands, on most offshore islands, and on Auckland Islands.

SUBSPECIES

2. *C. n. cyanurus* Salvadori
   ADULTS more blue on flight feathers; green of general plumage less yellowish, particularly on underparts; bluish-green tail.
   9 males   wing 132–147 (139.3) mm., tail 118–154 (132.8) mm.,
              exp. cul. 17–19 (18.2) mm., tars. 21–23 (21.9) mm.
   8 females wing 133–145 (136.6) mm., tail 120–162 (132.9) mm.,
              exp. cul. 14–18 (15.8) mm., tars. 21–22 (21.8) mm.
   Occurs on Kermadec Islands.

3. *C. n. chathamensis* Oliver
   ADULTS similar to *novaezelandiae*, but with bright emerald green facial area.
   1 male   wing 140 mm., tail 144 mm.,
              exp. cul. 17 mm., tars. 22 mm.
   10 unsexed wing 126–141 (132.9) mm., tail 124–140 (132.7) mm.,
              exp. cul. 14–18 (15.8) mm., tars. 21–23 (22.0) mm.
   Found on Chatham Islands.

W. T. Cooper. 7.

4. *C. n. hochstetteri* (Reischek)
ADULTS plumage distinctly more yellowish; orange-red markings on head and each side of rump; faint blue on flight feathers; larger size.
11 males wing 135–150 (143.4) mm., tail 116–131 (126.3) mm.,
exp. cul. 18–19 (18.7) mm., tars. 23–26 (24.6) mm.
1 female wing 129 mm., tail 117 mm.,
exp. cul. 15 mm., tars. 22 mm.
Restricted to Antipodes Island.

5. *C. n. erythrotis* (Wagler)
ADULTS plumage paler and more yellowish; blue on flight feathers paler and washed with green; doubtfully distinct from *hochstetteri*.
2 unsexed wing 142–145 (143.5) mm., tail 128–158 (143.0) mm.,
exp. cul. 15–20 (17.5) mm., tars. 21–24 (22.5) mm.
Formerly found on Macquarie Island, now extinct.

6. *C. n. cookii* (G. R. Gray)
ADULTS larger than *novaezelandiae*, but otherwise similar.
18 males wing 138–150 (145.5) mm., tail 138–183 (154.5) mm.,
exp. cul. 20–23 (21.3) mm., tars. 21–25 (23.4) mm.
15 females wing 128–137 (134.1) mm., tail 136–169 (145.1) mm.,
exp. cul. 17–19 (17.4) mm., tars. 21–23 (22.2) mm.
Confined to Norfolk Island.

7. *C. n. subflavescens* Salvadori
ADULTS plumage more yellowish than *cookii*, especially on cheeks and underparts; less extensive red markings on head.
1 male wing 147 mm., tail 145 mm.,
exp. cul. 19 mm., tars. 21 mm.
1 female wing 149 mm., tail 162 mm.,
exp. cul. 22 mm., tars. 22 mm.
Formerly found on Lord Howe Island, now extinct.

8. *C. n. saissetti* Verreaux and Des Murs
ADULTS face and underparts more yellowish than in *novaezelandiae*; paler, brighter red on crown.
15 males wing 114–135 (127.8) mm., tail 133–170 (156.5) mm.,
exp. cul. 15–18 (16.2) mm., tars. 19–21 (19.9) mm.
13 females wing 114–126 (121.6) mm., tail 130–160 (142.8) mm.,
exp. cul. 13–18 (14.5) mm., tars. 17–21 (19.1) mm.
Occurs on New Caledonia.

GENERAL NOTES At the time of European settlement in New Zealand Red-fronted Parakeets inhabited mainland forests at all altitudes. In the 1880s they were reported in great numbers and irruptions took place in Marlborough, over the Canterbury Plains and in several other localities. Then there was a spectacular decline and now they are rare on the mainland, being found only in the larger tracts of forest. However, on most of the outlying islands they are still common and seem to be doing quite well. Turbott (1961) says that they are common birds on Little Barrier Island, while according to Oliver (1955) they are fairly numerous in the Auckland Islands. Taylor says that they are common on Antipodes Island (*in litt.*, 1971); his observations on their habits are given in the text covering the Antipodes Green Parakeet because they are an integral part of a comparative study on the two species. On Norfolk Island these parrots are now very scarce and are restricted to two small remnants of virgin rainforest, though they have been seen in adjoining *Eucalyptus* plantations and they visit gardens to feed on ripening fruit, especially peaches (Turner *et al.*, 1968; Smithers and Disney, 1969). They disappeared from Lord Howe Island about 1870 and from Macquarie Island about 1890; I have previously outlined the recorded history of their extermination from these islands (see Forshaw, 1969a). Delacour (1966) reports that they are rare on New Caledonia.

These parrots show a remarkable adaptation to habitat. In New Zealand and on the larger islands they frequent forests, where most of the day is spent feeding in the treetops or amongst the outer branches of shrubs. They often come to the ground to feed on seeds. On smaller islands they inhabit low, stunted scrub, while on treeless Macquarie Island they were completely terrestrial, living and breeding amongst tussocks along the seaboard. They are tame and will allow a close approach. Indeed, it has been reported that on some islands they may be caught by hand. The flight is swift and very slightly undulating.

On the labels of specimens he collected in New Caledonia Macmillan has noted his field observations (AMNH Collection). He says that the parrots inhabit mountain forests in the north-western region, but they are not common. They seem to be rather silent birds so they may be more plentiful than is thought, but they are seldom seen even by local people. They are not timid and fly fairly swiftly. They generally feed in the middle and lower storeys of the forest, but often perch or rest high up in the canopy. In 1964 I made a brief search in an area in New Caledonia where a pair of parrots had been seen a few days earlier, but was not successful.

Seeds, fruits, berries, nuts, blossoms, leaves and grass shoots are the staple diet. On Hen Island

1 Bourke's Parrot *Neophema bourkii*
AM. 033570 ad. ♂

2 Elegant Parrot *Neophema elegans*
AM. 028414 ad. ♂

3 Blue-winged Parrot *Neophema chrysostoma*
AM. 017853 ad. ♂

flocks have been seen feeding on the seeds of flax (*Phormium tenax*). From one of the Poor Knights Islands comes an interesting report of many parrots congregating to feed on seeds of toetoe (*Cortaderia toetoe*) which had grown profusely after fire; parrots were even attracted from a neighbouring island. Seeds of *Mariscus ustulatus, Uncinia uncinata* and other sedges, fruits of *Acaena* and *Mesembryanthemum*, and blossoms of *Olearia* and *Senecio huntii* have been recorded as food. Taylor says that on Antipodes Island an important food is the seeds of *Carex appressa*. Crop contents from specimens collected on New Caledonia by Macmillan comprised yellow-fruit-pulp, fragments of seeds, and small white melon-like seeds.

CALL A rapidly repeated *ki-ki-ki-ki* is given in flight; while perched a trisyllabic, shrill note or a soft *tu-tu-tu-tu*. A subdued chattering may accompany feeding.

NESTING The breeding season seems to be affected by climatic conditions. Nests may be found at anytime between October and April, but eggs are usually laid during October, November and December. The nest is in a hollow limb or hole in a tree, in a hole in a cliff, in a crevice between rocks, in a burrow in the ground or in a hole in the matted base of a tussock. A normal clutch comprises five to nine eggs. Incubation commences with the laying of the second egg and lasts about twenty days; only the female sits. Both parents attend to the chicks, though the male prefers to transfer food to the female. The young leave the nest five to six weeks after hatching.

Orange-bellied Parrot *Neophema chrysogaster* **1**
AM. 035544 ad. ♂

Rock Parrot *Neophema petrophila* **2**
JMF. 17 ad. ♂

EGGS Broadly elliptical: 12 eggs, 25.8 (23.4–28.2) × 21.3 (19.2–23.7) mm. [Schönwetter, 1964].

YELLOW-FRONTED PARAKEET
Cyanoramphus auriceps (Kuhl)

DESCRIPTION Length 23 cm.
ADULTS general plumage green, more yellowish on underparts; crimson frontal band extending to eyes; crown golden yellow; crimson patch on each side of rump; outer webs of flight feathers violet-blue; bill pale bluish-grey becoming dark grey at tip; iris orange-red; legs greyish-brown.
IMMATURES shorter tail; iris pale brown.

DISTRIBUTION New Zealand and outlying islands.

SUBSPECIES 1. *C. a. auriceps* (Kuhl)   *Illustrated on page 244.*
  10 males wing 108–112 (109.9) mm., tail 114–120 (116.6) mm.,
      exp. cul. 13–15 (14.4) mm., tars. 19–22 (20.5) mm.
  8 females wing 106–112 (109.0) mm., tail 107–113 (110.5) mm.,
      exp. cul. 11–14 (12.8) mm., tars. 17–20 (18.6) mm.
  North, South and Stewart Islands, some offshore islands, and the Auckland Islands.

2. *C. a. forbesi* Rothschild
ADULTS larger size; brighter plumage with more yellowish underparts; sides of face emerald green; frontal band does not reach eyes; outer webs of flight feathers greenish-blue.
  6 males wing 121–131 (128.2) mm., tail 115–152 (130.5) mm.,
      exp. cul. 13–15 (14.4) mm., tars. 19–22 (20.5) mm.
  4 females wing 121–126 (122.5) mm., tail 108–135 (123.3) mm.,
      exp. cul. 13–14 (13.3) mm., tars. 20–21 (20.5) mm.
  3 unsexed wing 122–129 (126.0) mm., tail 128–158 (139.7) mm.,
      exp. cul. 15–16 (15.7) mm., tars. 21–24 (22.7) mm.
  Occurs on Chatham Islands; formerly on three islands in the group, but now reduced to a small population on Little Mangere Island.

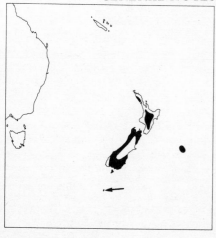

GENERAL NOTES Yellow-fronted and Red-fronted Parakeets are easily confused in the field. Mixed parties have been reported, though it seems that where both occur one or the other is conspicuously more numerous. This species may be distinguished by the absence of red from behind the eye, by the yellow crown and by its smaller size.

These parakeets were also plentiful and widely distributed in New Zealand at the time of European settlement. After a period of marked decline they now appear to be expanding their range and according to Falla *et al.* (1966) recent reports suggest that they are fairly common in larger tracts of mountain forest. However on Little Mangere Island *forbesi* is represented by a population of only about one hundred birds frequenting scrub and low forest near the summit of the main elevated peak.

Pairs or small parties are usually seen feeding in the treetops or amongst the outer branches of shrubs. Observers have remarked that the parrots are often found accompanying flocks of whiteheads (*Mohoua albicilla*). Their habits are similar to those of Red-fronted Parakeets, though they seem to be more arboreal and less dependent on ground plants for food.

They eat seeds, fruits, berries and vegetable matter. Crop contents of a bird collected in the East Coast district, New Zealand, comprised fragments of *Coprosma* berries and seeds of tawari (*Ixerbia brexioides*)

CALLS All calls are similar to, though weaker and more high-pitched than, those of the Red-fronted Parakeet; this is particularly noticeable with the *ki-ki-ki-ki* given in flight (Falla *et al.*, 1966).

NESTING Once again there is a prolonged breeding season and nests may be found at anytime between July and April, though October, November and December are the important months. The nesting behaviour is similar to that of the Red-fronted Parakeet. The male comes to the nest, escorts the sitting female away to feed her and then brings her back to the hollow, which is invariably in a tree or decaying stump.

EGGS Broadly elliptical; 7 eggs, 22.9 (21.6–24.2) × 18.9 (17.8–20.0) mm. [Schönwetter, 1964].

Turquoise Parrot *Neophema pulchella* 1
AM. 033530 ad. ♂

Turquoise Parrot *Neophema pulchella* 2
AM. 033450 ad. ♀

Scarlet-chested Parrot *Neophema splendida* 3
AM. 035545 ad. ♂

ORANGE-FRONTED PARAKEET
Cyanoramphus malherbi Souancé

Illustrated on page 244.

Length 20 cm.
ADULTS general plumage green, only slightly paler on underparts; orange frontal band, becoming paler towards eyes; crown pale yellow; orange patch on each side of rump; outer webs of primaries violet-blue; bill pale bluish-grey becoming dark grey towards tip; iris orange-red; legs brown.
IMMATURES (Souancé); similar to adults, but frontal band barely distinguishable.
7 males   wing 95–114 (105.7) mm., tail 101–119 (111.1) mm.,
           exp. cul. 11–15 (13.3) mm., tars. 18–19 (18.4) mm.
9 females wing 97–110 (102.4) mm., tail 107–119 (111.0) mm.,
           exp. cul. 11–13 (11.7) mm., tars. 17–20 (18.3) mm.

DISTRIBUTION   South Island, New Zealand; may have occurred on North, Stewart and Auckland Islands, but records are doubtful (see Harrison, 1970).

GENERAL NOTES

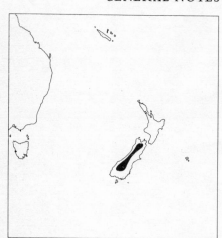

The little-known Orange-fronted Parakeet is a rare bird confined to forests and subalpine scrub of the South Island from Nelson to Fiordland. Harrison points out that it is not restricted to subalpine areas, having been recorded at about 600 m. and in the Canterbury district. Although records show that since European settlement this species has never been as common as the other two New Zealand parakeets, it was much more widespread in the 1880s. It was present in the large mixed flocks of parakeets that invaded the Canterbury district in the summer of 1884–85 and was said to be common in the forests about Nelson (Buller, 1888). Along with the other two species it declined drastically in the 1890s and has since been sighted very infrequently. After a lapse of thirty years it was rediscovered in 1965 in the Nelson Lakes National Park by wildlife officers.

Virtually nothing is known of its habits. Records of food include seeds, berries, and insects and their larvae.

CALL Apparently closely resembling that of the Red-fronted Parakeet (Falla *et al.*, 1966).

NESTING The only information on nesting habits is from breeding in captivity and suggests that the behaviour is similar to that of the Red-fronted Parakeet (see Harrison, 1970).

EGGS Broadly elliptical; 2 eggs, 21.5 (21.2–21.8) × 18.0 (18.0) mm. [Oliver, 1955].

BLACK-FRONTED PARAKEET
Cyanoramphus zealandicus (Latham)

Illustrated on page 245.

Length 25 cm.
ADULTS general plumage green, paler and somewhat bluish on underparts and tail; black forehead; lores and stripe behind eye scarlet; red rump; outer webs of flight feathers violet-blue; bill pale bluish-grey becoming black towards tip; legs greyish-brown.
IMMATURES (Rothschild, 1907); forehead dull bluish-black; head brownish; greyish-green underparts; brown markings on back; eye-stripe and rump markings chestnut-red.
2 unsexed wing 136–145 (140.5) mm., tail 135–144 (139.5) mm.,
          exp. cul. 15–19 (17.0) mm., tars. 25 (25.0) mm.

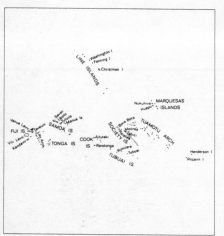

DISTRIBUTION   Formerly Tahiti, Society Islands; now extinct.

GENERAL NOTES   Lieutenant de Marolles collected the last specimen of the Black-fronted Parakeet in 1844 and this is now in the Paris Museum. It is probable that the species became extinct about this time and there is no longer any tradition among the local people about its existence. Indeed, there is reason to believe that it was rare as early as 1773 when, during Captain Cook's second voyage, the first two specimens were obtained.

I do not know the basis for Rothschild's description of immatures so cannot vouch for its authenticity.

SOCIETY PARAKEET
Cyanoramphus ulietanus (Gmelin)

Illustrated on page 245.

Length 25 cm.
ADULTS head blackish-brown, paler towards neck; back and wings brown; rump and upper tail-coverts brownish-red; underparts olive-yellow; under wing-coverts and outer webs of flight feathers mauve-grey; central tail feathers brownish-olive, lateral ones mauve-grey; bill grey; legs grey-brown.
IMMATURES undescribed.
2 unsexed wing 130–145 (137.5) mm., tail 132–133 (132.5) mm.,
    exp. cul. 19 (19.0) mm., tars. 22–25 (23.5) mm.

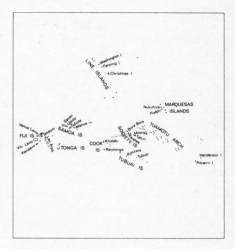

DISTRIBUTION

Formerly Raiatea, Society Islands; now extinct.

SUBSPECIES

The naturalists in Captain Cook's party discovered the Society Parakeet in 1773. They collected two specimens, the only ones known, and presumably the species became extinct soon after.

Genus EUNYMPHICUS Peters

A peculiar, coronal crest is diagnostic of this monotypic genus. Not a true, moveable crest as found in the cockatoos, it is simply an elongation of a few crown feathers.

The species is a medium-sized parrot, similar in general appearance to *Cyanoramphus*. There is a notch in the upper mandible and the loreal region is less densely feathered. There is no sexual dimorphism. I have no information on the wing-stripe.

HORNED PARAKEET
Eunymphicus cornutus (Gmelin)

Length 32 cm.
ADULTS general plumage green, more yellowish on underparts; rump greenish-yellow; ear-coverts and hindneck yellowish; forehead and forepart of crown red; face black; crest of two feathers black tipped with red; outer webs of primaries violet-blue; bill pale bluish-grey becoming black towards tip; iris orange-red; legs dark grey.
IMMATURES (AMNH. 337749); facial markings greyish and less extensive; feathers of forehead and forecrown black tipped with red; ear-coverts pale green; hindneck olive-green; bill horn-coloured; iris brownish.

New Caledonia and Ouvea, Loyalty Islands.

DISTRIBUTION

SUBSPECIES

1. *E. c. cornutus* (Gmelin)
    10 males wing 154–171 (162.2) mm., tail 139–175 (163.8) mm.,
        exp. cul. 19–21 (20.4) mm., tars. 19–22 (21.2) mm.
    6 females wing 151–161 (156.7) mm., tail 150–166 (156.2) mm.,
        exp. cul. 17–21 (18.7) mm., tars. 20–22 (20.5) mm.
    Occurs on New Caledonia.

Illustrated on page 248.

2. *E. c. uvaeensis* (Layard and Layard)

Illustrated on page 248.

    ADULTS ear-coverts and hindneck green; red on centre of forehead only; face blackish-green; crest of six green feathers.
    8 males   wing 151–169 (161.3) mm., tail 136–158 (151.0) mm.,
        exp. cul. 19–22 (20.9) mm., tars. 19–22 (20.5) mm.
    13 females wing 149–167 (155.0) mm., tail 127–155 (146.8) mm.,
        exp. cul. 18–22 (19.3) mm., tars. 18–21 (19.5) mm.
    Confined to Ouvea, Loyalty Islands.

Swift Parrot *Lathamus discolor* AM. 028243 ad. ♂

Vincent (1967) claims that populations of the Horned Parakeet are low enough to cause concern. Delacour (1966) says that it is fairly well distributed in the humid forests of New Caledonia, particularly in the Blue River region. It is shy and difficult to observe, but is not infrequently heard and pairs or family groups may be seen flying above the treetops. During 1944 and 1945 Warner (1947) found it to be fairly common in more inaccessible areas above 470 m., but he remarked that numbers must have declined drastically since 1882 when the Layards reported it from all forested areas. For a long time the people of Ouvea have taken chicks of *uvaeensis* from nests to sell as cage birds. This race is also seriously threatened by increasing destruction of the forest habitat. Delacour reports that protective measures have recently been taken and a number of parrots have been transferred to the neighbouring island of Lifou. According to Macmillan this had also been done about 1925 but was not successful; the birds flew back to Ouvea (in Delacour, 1966).

Warner found pairs and groups of four or more in the *Agathis-Araucaria* forests; once he saw a flock of ten feeding on the fruits of a small tree about 3 m. high. They were always shy and difficult to approach. When disturbed they would fly a hundred yards or so and alight in the tops of tall trees where they perched quietly. If pursued they would fly off silently, flocks dispersing in pairs. They roosted in the treetops or in hollows and were astir about an hour before dawn. When a group moved off to feed one bird usually took the lead.

The flight is swift and slightly undulating.

They feed on fruits and seeds. Macmillan spent a couple of hours watching a pair feed on the berries of vines and the seeds of various trees and shrubs, especially seeds of the 'penubre tree'. While feeding they occasionally displayed to each other, bowing several times, ruffling up their feathers and calling intermittently (in Warner, 1947). These parrots are fond of ripe pawpaw (*Carica papaya*) and a method used to catch them is to place a noose around a hole pecked in the fruit so that when the bird returns to feed it will be snared by the neck. Crop and stomach contents from four birds collected by Macmillan comprised remains of flowers, large milky seed kernels, and yellow fruit-pulp with melon-like seeds.

CALL A raucous *ko-kot . . . ko-kot*; while perching or feeding a peculiar chuckling is given and when alarmed a series of sharp shrieks.

NESTING In courtship the birds bow before each other as described above. When the head is dropped the crest feathers shake and fall forward.

Every nest found by Macmillan was in a hollow limb or hole in a living 'teak' tree (*Metrosideros demonstrans*). Most breeding takes place in November or December, but eggs have been found in October. The clutch is from two to four eggs, but usually only two chicks are reared (in Warner, 1947). Nothing further is known of the nesting behaviour.

EGGS Rounded; 5 eggs, 26.4 (25.4–28.0) × 21.7 (20.3–23.6) mm. [Schönwetter, 1964].

Genus NEOPHEMA Salvadori

Because of their semi-terrestrial habits the parrots belonging to this genus are often called 'grass-parrots'. They are small birds with gradated tails; the central tail feathers and the next pair are of equal length. The upper mandible is not distinctly notched and the white wing-stripe is variable in extent according to the species. Sexual dimorphism is pronounced in *pulchella* and *splendida*, but slight in other species.

All species are strong fliers, the flight being swift and somewhat erratic. Immelmann (1968) points out that the zig-zag pattern with occasional sharp changes of direction is like the flight of sandpipers.

BOURKE'S PARROT
Neophema bourkii (Gould)

Illustrated on page 249.

DESCRIPTION Length 19 cm.

ADULTS forehead blue in males, in females white sometimes tinged with blue; upperparts earth-brown; lores and periophthalmic region dusky white; throat and breast brownish margined with pink, narrower margins in female; abdomen rose-pink; thighs, under tail-coverts, flanks and sides of rump pale blue; wing-coverts brown edged with yellowish-white; under wing-coverts pale blue; outer webs of primaries violet-blue; tail brown washed with blue, lateral feathers tipped with white; wing-stripe absent in males, present in females; bill greyish-horn; iris brown; legs greyish-brown.

IMMATURES similar to female, but with less pink on abdomen; wing-stripe absent or slight in males, pronounced in females

7 males   wing 106–120 (114.0) mm., tail 98–110 (105.2) mm.,
          exp. cul. 9–12 (10.7) mm., tars. 14–15 (14.8) mm.

7 females wing 108–119 (112.4) mm., tail 88–102 (96.2) mm.,
exp. cul. 10–12 (10.3) mm., tars. 13–14 (13.6) mm.

DISTRIBUTION Interior of southern and central Australia.

GENERAL NOTES Bourke's Parrot is an inhabitant of the dry *Acacia* scrubland. It is fairly common and in some inland pastoral districts seems to be increasing, probably because of the stock-watering facilities. It is usually seen in pairs or small parties, though in times of drought flocks of up to a hundred may congregate around water. They are quiet and very tame, merely fluttering off to a nearby tree when disturbed. Most of the day is spent either feeding on the ground or sitting in low bushes, their plumage blending remarkably well with the surroundings. They have the strange habit of coming in to drink before dawn and well after sunset, sometimes as late as 2100 hrs. These parrots are nomadic; they often remain in one locality for many years then move away.

They feed on seeds of grasses and herbaceous plants, procured on the ground or in bushes. They have also been seen eating emerging grass shoots brought on by rains after a long dry spell.

CALL A mellow *chu-wee* is given in flight. While perched they occasionally give a soft, rolling whistle; the alarm call is a shrill, metallic note.

NESTING When courting the male bows slightly before the female, then immediately stretches up to his full height, raising his wings slightly to show the blue flanks. The breeding season is largely governed by rainfall, but nesting generally occurs between August and December. The nest is in a hollow in a tree from 1 to 3 m. above the ground. The three to six eggs are laid on a lining of decayed wood dust. Only the female broods and she sits very tightly. Incubation lasts about eighteen days and the young leave the nest approximately four weeks after hatching. They acquire adult plumage with the first complete moult when about four or five months old.

EGGS Rounded; 4 eggs, 20.3 (20.0–20.7) × 16.6 (16.5–16.8) mm. [H. L. White Coll.].

BLUE-WINGED PARROT
Neophema chrysostoma (Kuhl)

Illustrated on page 249.

DESCRIPTION Length 20 cm.

MALE crown dull golden-yellow; frontal band, not extending to eyes, ultramarine blue edged above with pale greenish-blue; upperparts dull olive-green; throat and breast pale green, remainder of underparts yellow; wing-coverts deep blue, paler on innermost secondaries; under wing-coverts blue; tail bluish-grey, lateral feathers tipped with yellow; wing-stripe absent; bill bluish-grey; iris brown; legs brownish-grey.

FEMALE crown dull olive-green; smaller frontal band; blue on wings duller and slightly suffused with green; underparts tinged with dull green; wing-stripe absent or slight.

IMMATURES duller than female; no frontal band; dull slaty-blue wings; wing-stripe may be absent in some males, but is pronounced in all females.

8 males   wing 105–115 (110.1) mm., tail 104–117 (110.8) mm.,
        exp. cul. 9–12 (10.4) mm., tars. 14–16 (15.3) mm.
7 females wing 105–113 (107.6) mm., tail 100–124 (111.6) mm.,
        exp. cul. 9–11 (9.9) mm., tars. 14–16 (14.9) mm.

DISTRIBUTION South-eastern Australia, including Tasmania and islands in Bass Strait but not Kangaroo Island.

GENERAL NOTES The Blue-winged Parrot is distinguished from the Elegant Parrot by the extensive blue wing markings, by the almost uniformly dark frontal band which does not extend above the eyes, and by the pale green upper breast. I have always found that in the field it appears to be noticeably duller with less yellow on the underparts.

These parrots are the least specialized of the Neophemas and may be found in a variety of habitats, including forested valleys, sparsely-timbered grasslands, coastal sand-dunes, *Acacia* scrublands, and arid saltbush (*Atriplex*) plains. They are common, especially in Tasmania. Breeding has not been recorded from New South Wales or south-western Queensland, the parrots being migratory visitors during autumn and winter. They move back and forth across Bass Strait, though it appears that in recent years more birds have remained in Tasmania throughout the winter.

Depending on the season and the locality, Blue-winged Parrots are generally seen in pairs or small flocks. They are very social and even during the breeding season groups of up to twenty may be observed; within the flocks there is a marked absence of quarrelling. Sometimes they associate with Elegant or Orange-bellied Parrots. In the morning and toward late afternoon they spend most of the time on the ground feeding on grass seeds. While foraging amongst the grass they are difficult to see, so well does their plumage blend with the surroundings. They are tame and will allow a close approach. When disturbed all birds in the flock rise simultaneously and fly to nearby trees to await the passing of danger before returning to the ground in twos and threes. During the middle of the day they sit quietly in a tree, often on the leafless uppermost branches of a tall eucalypt, their heads all turned to face into the prevailing wind; they also commonly perch on fences and telegraph wires.

They feed on seeds, blossoms, berries, fruits, green vegetable matter and insects and their larvae. In Tasmania they are said to be particularly fond of the seeds of wallaby grasses (*Danthonia*), silver grass (*Aira caryophyllea*), and hairy sundew (*Drosera peltata*). In Victoria they have been seen with the introduced goldfinch (*Carduelis carduelis*) feeding on the flowers and seeds of cape weed (*Cryptostemma calendulaceum*). I have seen a flock feeding on seeds of *Poacaespitosa*. Lea and Gray (1935) examined crop contents from two birds collected in South Australia and found a few seeds, soft vegetable matter, fragments of spiders, fine grit and sand.

CALL A soft, melodic tinkling is usually given in flight; the alarm call is a sharp, high-pitched disyllabic note. Feeding is sometimes accompanied by a soft twittering.

NESTING During courtship feeding the male stretches up to his full height, droops his wings to show the blue markings and regurgitates food with a bobbing of the head, at the same time uttering a soft twittering. The breeding season is from October to January. The nest is in a hollow limb or hole in a tree, or in a hole in a stump, fence post, or log lying on the ground. Several nests may be in one tree. On a layer of decayed wood dust lining the hollow four to six eggs are laid. Incubation is of approximately eighteen days duration and only the female broods; she sits very tightly. The young leave the nest about four weeks after hatching, but remain with their parents for some time. They acquire adult plumage when eight or nine months old.

EGGS Rounded; 6 eggs, 23.6 (22.9–24.7) × 19.1 (18.7–19.6) mm. [R. H. Green Coll.].

ELEGANT PARROT
Neophema elegans (Gould)

Illustrated on page 249.

Length 23 cm.

DESCRIPTION

ADULTS crown and upperparts rich golden-olive, dull olive in females; frontal band deep blue, bordered above by a pale blue line extending over and beyond the eyes; underparts yellow, greenish on breast; median wing-coverts pale greenish-blue, other wing-coverts blue; under wing-coverts dark blue; tail blue washed with olive, lateral feathers tipped with yellow; wing-stripe absent, sometimes slight in females; bill greyish-black; iris brown; legs greyish-brown. IMMATURES similar to female; frontal band absent or only slight; wing-stripe absent or slight, may be pronounced in some females.

10 males   wing 105–115 (110.6) mm., tail 110–119 (115.4) mm.,
            exp. cul. 9–11 (10.3) mm., tars. 14–16 (14.5) mm.
7 females wing 104–114 (108.7) mm., tail 106–120 (114.8) mm.,
            exp. cul. 10–11 (10.4) mm., tars. 14–16 (14.7) mm.

South-western and south-eastern Australia, excluding Tasmania but including Kangaroo Island.

DISTRIBUTION

The differences between this species and *N. chrysostoma* are listed under the Blue-winged Parrot.

GENERAL NOTES

Elegant Parrots inhabit open country, including coastal sand-dunes, lightly-timbered grasslands and cultivated paddocks, dry scrublands, and saltbush (*Atriplex*) plains. They are common, particularly in south-western Australia where they are both increasing in numbers and expanding their range, reputedly because of land-clearance and the widespread use of subterranean clover (*Trifolium subterraneum*) in pastures. During the breeding season they are usually found in pairs or small parties, but at other times they congregate in flocks of from twenty to a hundred, sometimes in the company of Blue-winged Parrots. While on the ground searching for seeds their plumage blends extremely well with the grass coverage. When alarmed they often sit motionless and fly off only at the last moment. They fly to a nearby tree or alight again on the ground behind a bush or tussock, but if followed persistently or if disturbed away from shelter they rise high into the air and soon disappear from sight. They are partly nomadic, particularly along the fringes of the range.

Seeds, vegetable matter, berries and fruits make up the diet. They are very fond of seeds of clover and *Paspalum* grasses and have been seen feeding on seeds and fruits of several kinds of twinleaf (*Zygophyllum*). Crop contents from eighteen birds collected in South Australia comprised numerous seeds, vegetable matter and fine grit (Lea and Gray, 1935).

CALL A sharp *tsit* is emitted in flight; while feeding they are usually quiet, but may utter a plaintive twittering.

NESTING The courtship display and nesting behaviour resemble those of the Blue-winged Parrot. The breeding season is from August to November and the nest is in a hollow in a tree, usually at some height from the ground. A normal clutch comprises four or five eggs. Young birds acquire adult plumage when only three or four months old.

EGGS Rounded; 5 eggs, 20.7 (20.4–21.2) × 17.6 (16.7–18.1) mm. [Serventy and Whittell, 1967].

ROCK PARROT
Neophema petrophila (Gould)

Illustrated on page 252.

Length 22 cm.

ADULTS crown and upperparts dull brownish-olive; frontal band dark blue with pale blue outer edges; lores, periophthalmic region and foreparts of cheeks pale blue, less extensive in female; breast dull greyish-olive, very dull in female; abdomen and vent yellow; under wing-coverts and outer webs of flight feathers blue; tail dull blue washed with olive, lateral feathers tipped with yellow; wing-stripe slight; bill greyish; iris dark brown; legs greyish.

IMMATURES duller than adults; no frontal band; foreparts of cheeks greyish-olive; wing-stripe present.

15 males   wing 104–114 (110.1) mm., tail 102–117 (109.2) mm.,
        exp. cul. 10–12 (10.7) mm., tars. 14–17 (15.5) mm.
10 females wing 104–115 (110.2) mm., tail 105–113 (108.8) mm.,
        exp. cul. 10–12 (10.8) mm., tars. 15–18 (16.7) mm.

DESCRIPTION

Coastline and offshore islands of southern Australia east to Robe, South Australia.

DISTRIBUTION

The Rock Parrot is the dullest member of the genus and may be identified by the blue on the lores and foreparts of the cheeks. In habitat preference it is the most specialized species, frequenting coastal sand-dunes and bleak, rocky islets up to 20 km. offshore; it has been seen as far as 10 km. inland but such records are uncommon. It is plentiful in most areas.

GENERAL NOTES

Pairs or small parties are generally encountered, but sometimes flocks of up to a hundred congregate on an islet to feed or nest. They are inconspicuous as they forage for seeds amongst low bushes or tall grass and their presence is easily overlooked until they rise into the air. When feeding they are tame and will allow a close approach. While a blustery wind is blowing they are reluctant to leave the shelter of rocks or low shrubs and when disturbed merely fly low over the ground for a short distance. However, on a still day they circle high overhead, calling intermittently, then alight on a rock or shrub and pause briefly before dropping to the ground. They feed early in the morning and toward late afternoon, passing the remainder of the day sitting on a crag or in a bush growing near the seashore. When perched they adopt a rather upright stance and if restless bob their heads slightly.

They feed on seeds and fruits of grasses, shrubs, and halophytic plants growing amongst the rocks, on tidal flats, or near brackish watercourses. They are particularly fond of seeds of the pigfaces, *Carpobrotus aequilaterus* and *C. crystallinum*. Near Adelaide, South Australia, I have seen them feeding on seeds of a halophytic samphire, *Arthrocnemum arbuscula*. In 1959 Storr found these parrots very plentiful near Jurien Bay, Western Australia, where they were feeding largely on seeds of the introduced strand daisy (*Arctotheca nivea*). At Albany and Esperance, Western Australia, they sometimes come into railway yards to pick up spilled wheat.

CALL A plaintiff, though penetrating, *tsit-tseet* repeated frequently; while feeding an occasional subdued *titter-titter*.

NESTING Courtship feeding has been described by Warham (1955). The male bobs his head jerkily while the female keeps up her *tsit-tsit* begging cries. Their bills are interlocked for the transfer of food and up to eight feeds may occur in succession, each one lasting about two seconds.

The breeding season is from August to October and in favourable years two broods are sometimes reared. The four or five eggs are laid in a crevice under an overhanging slab of rock above high-water level. Incubation lasts about eighteen days and only the female sits. Partly-feathered nestlings often scramble out of the crevice or hole to meet the parent coming in to feed them. The young leave the nest about thirty days after hatching and maintain a loose association with their parents within the flock. Adult plumage is attained rapidly with a moult which the birds undergo when three or four months old.

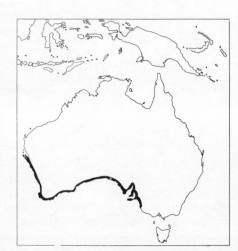

EGGS Elliptical: 5 eggs, 24.1 (23.8–24.6) × 19.6 (19.0–20.2) mm. [H. L. White Coll.].

ORANGE-BELLIED PARROT
Neophema chrysogaster (Latham)

Illustrated on page 252.

Length 20 cm.

MALE crown and upperparts bright grass-green; frontal band blue, bordered above by a faint blue line; underparts yellow with a bright orange patch on lower abdomen; under wing-coverts and

DESCRIPTION

outer webs of flight feathers blue; median wing-coverts paler blue; tail green washed with blue, lateral feathers tipped with yellow; wing-stripe absent; bill greyish-brown; iris brown; legs greyish.

FEMALE dull green feathers scattered throughout back; paler frontal band without upper border; wing-stripe variable.

IMMATURES duller than female; well-marked but smaller abdominal patch; wing-stripe present.

4 males   wing 106–111 (108.2) mm., tail 100–110 (104.7) mm.,
      exp. cul. 10–11 (10.5) mm., tars. 15–17 (15.9) mm.

3 females wing 107–110 (108.3) mm., tail 97–104 (100.7) mm.,
      exp. cul. 10–11 (10.7) mm., tars. 15–16 (15.7) mm.

DISTRIBUTION Tasmania, mainly in western regions, some islands in Bass Strait, and coastal areas of south-eastern South Australia and western Victoria east to Port Phillip Bay; formerly near Sydney, New South Wales.

GENERAL NOTES Because other species of *Neophema* occasionally show orange abdominal markings they are easily mistaken for Orange-bellied Parrots. The most reliable field character of *chrysogaster* is the bright grass-green upperparts; the unique alarm call is also a valuable aid to identification.

This species is also a coastal bird, but has a wider habitat tolerance than has the Rock Parrot. It frequents open grassland and light scrub, sand-dunes, tidal flats, cultivated paddocks and swamp-lands; it has been found up to 60 km. inland. It is very rare, but early accounts of abundance and more widespread distribution may have been due to abnormal numbers following extremely favourable breeding conditions (see Forshaw, 1969a).

Orange-bellied Parrots may breed in south-eastern South Australia, though the evidence is not conclusive. They are absent from Victoria between November and March, and it seems that they migrate to Tasmania to breed. Recent observations have indicated that birds from both Victoria and Tasmania probably breed in south-western Tasmania, not on islands in Bass Strait as I have previously suggested (Forshaw, 1969a).

They are generally seen singly, in pairs or in small flocks. They spend most of the day on the ground either searching for seeds or quietly sitting under a tussock or small bush, their plumage blending extremely well with the surroundings. They may commence feeding before sunrise and in the evening continue until after dusk. They are rather wary and difficult to approach. If disturbed they rise high into the air, calling loudly, then drop again and move away just above ground or water level, soon disappearing from sight. They have been seen in the company of Elegant and Blue-winged Parrots, sometimes perching on fence posts or telegraph wires.

They feed on seeds, fruits and berries. Hinsby (1947) reports that they eat decaying kelp and are particularly fond of *Coprosma* berries and seeds of *Poa billardieri*. I have seen them feeding on seeds of sea heath (*Frankenia pauciflora*). The crop contents of a specimen from Victoria comprised seeds, including those of *Suaeda maritima* and *Atriplex cinerea* (Jarman, 1965).

CALL A series of soft tinkling notes not unlike the call of *N. chrysostoma*; when alarmed a *chitter-chitter* repeated so rapidly it becomes almost a 'buzzing' sound.

NESTING The few nesting records we have are for November and December. All nests found have been in hollows in trees, but Gould suspected that on offshore islands nests would be on the ground under rocks or tussocks. Clutches of four and six eggs have been found. Little is known of the nesting behaviour. Lendon (1951) believes that young birds do not attain adult plumage until late spring, probably eight or nine months after they leave the nest.

EGGS Rounded; 4 eggs, 21.2 (20.3–22.5) × 17.4 (17.1–17.9) mm. [Tas. Mus. Coll.].

TURQUOISE PARROT
Neophema pulchella (Shaw)

Illustrated on page 253.

DESCRIPTION Length 20 cm.

MALE crown and upperparts bright green; face blue, paler on cheeks; underparts yellow; chestnut-red band across inner wing-coverts; lesser and median wing-coverts turquoise blue; under wing-coverts and outer webs of flight feathers dark blue; tail green, lateral feathers tipped with yellow; wing-stripe absent; bill greyish-black; iris brown; legs grey.

FEMALE face pale blue; lores yellowish-white; foreneck and breast green; no reddish band on wing-coverts; wing-stripe present.

IMMATURES duller than adults; males have faint chestnut marking on wing-coverts; wing-stripe present.

10 males wing 100–113 (109.6) mm., tail 93–110 (101.4) mm.,
      exp. cul. 10–11 (10.7) mm., tars. 14–16 (14.5) mm.

7 females wing 102–112 (108.0) mm., tail 97–106 (100.2) mm.,
exp. cul. 10–12 (10.7) mm., tars. 14–16 (14.6) mm.

DISTRIBUTION   South-eastern Australia from south-eastern Queensland to northern Victoria; no longer has a continuous distribution, occurring only in scattered areas.

GENERAL NOTES   Turquoise Parrots are found in open forest and timbered grasslands on mountain slopes, ridges or along water-courses. They are rare, but not endangered unless interference with habitat increases drastically. There is evidence of some local movement but they are largely sedentary. They are generally seen singly, in pairs, or in small parties, but occasionally flocks of up to thirty have been reported. Between noon and mid-afternoon they sit quietly in trees or shrubs, the rest of the day being spent on the ground searching for seeds. They come to drink only once a day and approach the waterhole cautiously. When feeding they are very tame, being content to walk away from the intruder, feeding as they go. Amidst green herbage they are inconspicuous, but toward late summer, when the grass dries off, their green upperparts become obvious.

Food comprises seeds and vegetable matter procured on or near the ground. They have been seen feeding on seeds of bearded heath (*Leucopogon microphyllus*), chickweed (*Stellaria media*), barley grass (*Hordeum murinum*), wallaby grass (*Danthonia semiannularis*), and *Paspalum* grass. Small parties have been found along the roadside feeding on sorghum spilled from trucks.

CALL   A soft, though penetrating, disyllabic whistle; while feeding a weak, high-pitched twittering.

NESTING   The breeding season is from August to December. The nest is in a hollow in a tree, stump, fence post, or log lying on the ground. The four or five eggs are laid on a lining of decayed wood dust. Incubation lasts approximately twenty days and only the female broods; she sits very tightly. The young vacate the nest some four weeks after hatching. Adult plumage is acquired when they are about four months old.

Chaffer and Miller (1946) observed a female stripping the aromatic leaves from a *Leptospermum* and placing them beneath her feathers. It is probable that this species, as well as *N. splendida*, carries leaves to the nest under the rump feathers.

EGGS   Broadly elliptical; 17 eggs, 20.5 (19.6–21.8) × 16.7 (16.4–17.2) mm. [laid in captivity].

SCARLET-CHESTED PARROT
Neophema splendida (Gould)   *Illustrated on page 253.*

Length 19 cm.
MALE upperparts bright green; head blue, deeper on throat and cheeks; sides of neck and breast green; foreneck and middle of breast scarlet; lower underparts yellow; wing-coverts pale blue; under wing-coverts and outer webs of flight feathers dark blue; tail green; lateral feathers blue tipped with yellow; wing-stripe absent; bill greyish-black; iris brown; legs brownish-grey.
FEMALE paler blue on forehead and face; lores blue (not white as in *pulchella*); breast green; wing stripe variable, may be absent.
IMMATURES similar to female; males have darker blue on face; wing-stripe variable.
8 males   wing 109–123 (113.1) mm., tail 92–102 (96.8) mm.,
exp. cul. 9–10 (9.9) mm., tars. 14–16 (14.6) mm.
5 females wing 108–113 (110.0) mm., tail 88–102 (96.6) mm.,
exp. cul. 9–10 (9.6) mm., tars. 14–16 (14.7) mm.

DISTRIBUTION   Interior of southern Australia.

GENERAL NOTES   Scarlet-chested Parrots inhabit dry *Eucalyptus* or *Acacia* scrublands, clumps of trees and shrubs growing along stony ridges, and open saltbush (*Atriplex*) or spinifex (*Triodia*) plains. They are rare, but periodically large numbers have been reported from scattered localities. I believe that they are nomadic and this could account for the paucity of records. They are usually seen in isolated pairs or small parties rarely exceeding ten birds, but in 1939 and 1966, when irruptions occurred in distant parts of South Australia, flocks of more than a hundred were recorded. They are unobtrusive birds, spending most of the time on the ground or in low bushes searching for seeds. Most observers have pointed out that they are extremely quiet and unless flushed may be easily overlooked. They are said to be tame, though the only time that I have seen the species was a sighting of three birds and they were timid, probably because of the absence of suitable cover. They are often found far from water and it has been claimed that they get moisture by drinking dew or chewing water-bearing plants such as *Calandrinia*. They feed on seeds procured on or near the ground; whilst taking seeds from standing grass they hold the stalk down by placing one foot on it.

CALL   A feeble, twittering note lacking the penetration so marked in calls of other Neophemas.

NESTING The breeding season is somewhat variable, depending on climatic conditions and the availability of food, but is generally from August to December or January. The nesting behaviour is similar to that of the Turquoise Parrot and there are three to five, rarely six, eggs in a normal clutch. About two or three months after leaving the nest males show a few red feathers on the breast and three months later they resemble the adults. However, the blue on the face and crown and scarlet on the breast do not develop fully until well into the second year.

In captivity female Scarlet-chested Parrots will place green leaves under the rump feathers and carry them into the nesting hollow. Preference is shown for aromatic leaves. Only a few leaves are taken so presumably they are not for nest-building as is the case with *Agapornis* and *Loriculus* parrots.

EGGS Rounded; 2 eggs, 23.0 (23.0) × 18.9 (18.7–19.2) mm. [H. L. White Coll.].

Genus LATHAMUS Lesson

A relationship between this monotypic genus and the platycercine genera is indicated by certain anatomical features, including osteology of the skull, pelvis and legs, the same rounded cere, the presence of a superficial left carotid, and pterylosis (feather distribution). The crude brush tongue and the sharply-pointed wings, characteristics so well marked in lorikeets, are probably due to convergence. Furthermore, the variable wing-stripe and the red under tail-coverts suggest that it is either an aberrant member of the platycercine group or a remnant of the stock from which the group has developed. All of these points have been discussed fully by Forbes (1879).

The species is a medium-sized parrot with a strongly-gradated tail comprising narrow, pointed feathers. The bill is fine and there is a notch in the upper mandible. Sexual dimorphism is slight; the wing-stripe is present in immatures but variable in adults.

SWIFT PARROT
Láthamus discolor (White)

Illustrated on page 256.

DESCRIPTION
Length 25 cm.
ADULTS general plumage green, more yellowish on underparts; face red, duller and less extensive in females; crown blue; lores yellow; under tail-coverts red; under and lesser wing-coverts dark red; outer webs of flight feathers blue; tail dull brownish-red; wing-stripe variable; bill horn-coloured; iris yellow; legs brownish.
IMMATURES duller than adults; less red on throat and under tail-coverts; wing-stripe present; iris brownish.
8 males   wing 116–124 (120.0) mm., tail 110–125 (119.1) mm.,
           exp. cul. 12–14 (12.9) mm., tars. 15–17 (15.9) mm.
4 females wing 118–123 (120.2) mm., tail 105–120 (113.8) mm.,
           exp. cul. 12 (12.0) mm., tars. 14–16 (15.0) mm.

DISTRIBUTION
South-eastern Australia, including Tasmania and some islands in Bass Strait.

GENERAL NOTES
Swift Parrots are migratory. They breed only in Tasmania and on some islands in Bass Strait, arriving in August and September then returning to the mainland between January and May. Thomas (1970) reports that some birds remain in Tasmania during the winter months, but I know of no summer records from the mainland. Their habits closely resemble those of lorikeets and mixed flocks are commonly found feeding in the same tree. They may be distinguished by their call-notes which differ strongly from the screeching of lorikeets. In flight the red under wing-coverts together with the narrow, pointed tail are diagnostic. Furthermore, no Australian lorikeet has red under tail-coverts.

These parrots inhabit most types of timbered country wherever there are flowering trees. They are common visitors to gardens and parklands and have often been seen in trees lining the streets of towns and cities. They are scarce at the highest altitudes but plentiful elsewhere. In small parties, or occasionally large flocks, they are generally seen feeding amongst the topmost branches of flowering trees or flying high overhead. They are noisy and seem to be always on the move, clambering about amongst the foliage, hanging upside down to get at blossoms, and darting from one tree to the next. While feeding they are oblivious to intruders. They are arboreal, coming to ground only to drink or examine seeds and fallen blossoms. After feeding they often rest on the topmost leafless branches of tall trees. As the name implies their direct flight is extremely swift. An audible 'whirring' is made by the wingbeats and the flocks move in the air with remarkable precision.

Although pollen and nectar are staple foods, the birds also feed extensively on insects and their larvae and on fruits, berries, seeds and vegetable matter. They are voracious feeders and their plumage may become completely matted with nectar. The major source of pollen and nectar is *Eucalyptus* blossoms and the parrots follow the flowering of these trees. They have also been seen

feeding on *Banksia* and *Xanthorrhoea* flowers, and on berries of the introduced red cedar (*Juniperus virginiana*). They are particularly fond of psyllid lerps (small insects which attack *Eucalyptus* leaves) and in many areas arrival of the parrots coincides with infestations. Crop and stomach contents from one bird collected in Tasmania and three collected in South Australia comprised small caterpillars, lerps and lerp-scales, seeds and some vegetable matter.

CALL A mellow *clink-clink-clink* repeated rapidly; while feeding a subdued chattering.

NESTING While breeding Swift Parrots remain gregarious and more than one nest may be found in a tree. The breeding season is from late September to January. The nest is in a hollow limb or hole in a eucalypt. In Launceston City Park I was shown a nest in a crevice in a concrete wall. The three to five eggs are laid on a layer of decayed wood dust. Incubation lasts approximately twenty days and it seems that although males may spend time in the nest only the female broods. Little is known of the rearing of the young, but the nestling period is said to be longer than that of the rosellas.

Tavistock (1936) gives some details of a successful breeding in captivity. Three eggs were laid but only two young birds were reared. The incubation period was not determined. The young birds left the nest approximately ten weeks after the first egg was laid. Tavistock claims that young birds undergo a partial moult with assumption of brighter plumage when a few months old, full adult plumage being attained in the following autumn (in Lendon, 1951).

EGGS Somewhat spherical; 35 eggs, 24. 6(23.0–26.5) × 20.2 (19.0–22.0) mm. [R. H. Green Coll.].

Genus MELOPSITTACUS Gould

I believe that this monotypic genus is transitional between *Neophema* and *Pezoporus*. The predominantly green plumage with black and yellow barring on the upperparts suggests affinities with the latter, while the general appearance and habits in the field are not unlike those of the Neophemas.

The species, so well-known as a cage bird, is a small parrot with a strongly-gradated tail. Blue is found on some feathers of the cheeks, but there are no well-defined cheek-patches. The sexes are alike. Adults and immatures of both sexes have a white wing-stripe.

BUDGERIGAR
Melopsittacus undulatus (Shaw)   *Illustrated on page 265.*

DESCRIPTION Length 18 cm.
ADULTS upperparts barred with black and yellow; rump and underparts green; forehead and face yellow; feathers of cheeks tipped with violet-blue; a series of black spots across throat; under wing-coverts green; tail greenish-blue, lateral feathers centrally banded with yellow; bill olive-grey; cere blue, brownish in breeding female; iris white; legs greyish-blue.
IMMATURES duller than adult; black spots on throat ill-defined or absent; barring on forehead; iris greyish.
8 males   wing 93–100 (95.4) mm., tail 91–103 (95.8) mm.,
                exp. cul. 9–10 (9.8) mm., tars. 13–15 (13.7) mm.
9 females wing 93–104 (97.0) mm., tail 88–99 (93.4) mm.,
                exp. cul. 9–11 (9.9) mm., tars. 14–15 (14.2) mm.

DISTRIBUTION Australia generally, chiefly the interior; absent from Tasmania. Introduced to Florida, United States of America.

GENERAL NOTES Because of their world-wide popularity as cage birds Budgerigars are undoubtedly the best known of all parrots. They have found their way to virtually every country and are eagerly sought by persons wanting household pets or by fanciers interested in the many colour varieties now available. In the section dealing with parrots in captivity I have given more detailed information about domesticated Budgerigars. These parrots must have escaped from captivity many times and in many different countries, but it seems that only in central Florida, United States of America, have they become established.

Budgerigars inhabit timber bordering watercourses, sparsely timbered grasslands, dry scrublands, and open plains. Although numbers fluctuate enormously in accordance with the prevailing conditions, Immelmann (1968) believes that they are the most abundant of Australian parrots and, indeed, one of the most abundant of all birds on the continent. The sizes of flocks encountered in the interior during favourable years have become legendary and observers have seen the sky darkened by myriads of these small parrots. Elsewhere they generally congregate in small parties. They are extremely nomadic, the movements and fluctuations in numbers being governed by the availability of water and seeding grasses.

Normally these parrots are not shy and will allow a close approach. During early morning and late afternoon they are most active, visiting waterholes to drink, scurrying through the grass searching for seeds, or flying from one tree to the next. They spend the remainder of the day sitting in trees or tall bushes and may be easily overlooked, but flocks on the move are conspicuous because of their noise; they are generally heard before being seen. The swift, erratic flight of flocks is characterized by remarkable precision, the entire flock twisting and turning as one. The flight of small groups is slower with even turns.

They feed on seeds procured on or near the ground. Important food items are seeds of spinifex (*Triodia*) and Mitchell grass (*Astrebla*). Lea and Gray (1935) examined crop contents from three birds collected in south-eastern Australia and found seeds—mainly grass seeds and a few seeds of *Portulaca oleracea*—and fine grit.

CALL A pleasant warble generally given in flight, also a subdued, disyllabic screech; feeding often accompanied by a subdued chattering.

NESTING Nesting generally takes place between August and January in the south and from June to September in the north, but the parrots are opportunist breeders and will nest at any time following good rains. The nest is in a hollow in a tree, stump, fence post, or log lying on the ground. The four to six, occasionally up to eight, eggs are laid on decayed wood dust. The female broods for about eighteen days and the young leave the nest some thirty days after hatching. Adult plumage is acquired when three or four months old.

EGGS Rounded; 6 eggs, 18.6 (18.3–19.8) × 14.2 (13.7–14.7) mm. [H. L. White Coll.].

Genus PEZOPORUS Illiger

In my opinion this monotypic genus is a member of a relict group that also includes *Geopsittacus* and probably *Strigops*. On the other hand it is also related to *Melopsittacus* and through it to other platycercine genera.

The species is a medium-sized, slim parrot with a long, strongly gradated tail comprising narrow, pointed feathers. The wings are short and rounded. There is a narrowing of the anterior of the cranium. The tarsi are long and the claws extremely long and only slightly curved. There is no notch in the upper mandible.

Sexual dimorphism is absent; all birds show a pale yellow wing-stripe.

Budgerigar *Melopsittacus undulatus*
AM. 042268 ad. ♂

GROUND PARROT
Pezoporus wallicus (Kerr)

DESCRIPTION
Length 30 cm.
ADULTS general plumage green, strongly 'mottled' with black and yellow; lower underparts greenish-yellow transversely barred with black; narrow orange-red frontal band; tail green and yellow barred with brownish-black; wing-stripe present; bill brownish; iris dull yellow; legs brown.
IMMATURES no red frontal band; wing-stripe present.

DISTRIBUTION
Coastal regions of south-western and south-eastern Australia, including Tasmania.

SUBSPECIES
1. *P. w. wallicus* (Kerr)
13 males wing 118–139 (128.6) mm., tail 161–195 (177.6) mm., *Illustrated on page 268.*
exp. cul. 12–15 (13.7) mm., tars. 25–27 (25.9) mm.
12 females wing 120–138 (128.9) mm., tail 158–200 (177.4) mm.,
exp. cul. 13–15 (13.6) mm., tars. 24–27 (25.9) mm.
Occurs in south-eastern Australia including Tasmania and possibly some islands in Bass Strait; distribution no longer continuous, but made up of isolated pockets of suitable habitat.

2. *P. w. flaviventris* North
ADULTS abdomen bright yellow with indistinct, interrupted black barring.
2 males wing 135–138 (136.5) mm., tail 164–176 (170.0) mm.,
exp. cul. 14–15 (14.5) mm., tars. 26–30 (28.0) mm.
3 females wing 118–133 (127.0) mm., tail 145–176 (165.3) mm.,
exp. cul. 13–15 (14.3) mm., tars. 26–28 (27.3) mm.
A doubtfully distinct isolate confined to southern coastline of south-western Australia; formerly it ranged farther north.

GENERAL NOTES
Ground Parrots are terrestrial and largely nocturnal. Their plumage colouration and pattern blend remarkably well with the ground cover making them most difficult to observe. Little is

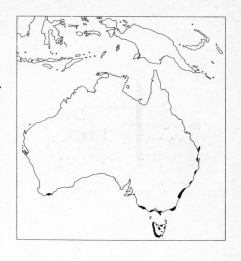

known of their habits. They frequent heathlands, estuarine flats, swamps and, in some localities, grasslands and pastures. Loss of habitat is the main reason the species is rare and unless suitable areas are set aside and managed it could disappear from much of its already reduced range.

These parrots are shy, elusive birds and to see them it is necessary to methodically tramp through vegetation in the hope of flushing one or two. With an audible flutter they rise up about 5 m. away and fly 30 m. or more before dropping back into cover. They run quickly and, because of their long legs, they lack the waddling gait so characteristic of most parrots. When disturbed they crouch low and run through vegetation, frequently pausing and stretching into a fully upright stance to check on the danger. I have never seen them perch, though it is claimed that they can stand on a stout branch or log. Toward nightfall they become active and commence calling. While calling they may be seen fluttering above the vegetation. They call again at sunrise, but during the day are silent even when flushed. Because of their supposedly weak flight it is widely believed that these parrots are sedentary. In fact, they are strong fliers and probably move about to some extent. The swift, erratic flight comprises rapid wingbeats alternated by periods of gliding when the bird tilts its body.

They feed on seeds and green shoots. They are particularly fond of seeds of button-grass (*Gymnoschoenus sphaerocephalus*) and I have seen them eating seeds of slender twine-rush (*Leptocarpus tenax*).

CALL A thin, high-pitched *tee . . . tee . . . stit* or *tee . . . tee . . . tee . . . stit* followed occasionally by a number of sharper notes on an ascending scale terminating with a prolonged note (*tee . . . tee . . . tee . . . tee———ee*).

NESTING The breeding season lasts from September to December. The nest is a shallow excavation in the soil lined with chewed stalks or leaves. Nests are generally situated near the base of a tussock or small bush and are always well-hidden by surrounding vegetation. The normal clutch comprises three or four eggs. Little is known of the nesting behaviour. Young birds leave the nest a little over three weeks after hatching and shelter in nearby vegetation until they can fly.

EGGS Slightly spherical; 8 eggs, 27.9 (27.0–28.4) × 22.0 (21.4–22.6) mm. [R. H. Green Coll.].

Genus GEOPSITTACUS Gould

When describing this monotypic genus Gould remarked how much it reminded him of a diminutive *Strigops*. I believe that, despite marked osteological differences, the New Zealand genus is related to both *Geopsittacus* and *Pezoporus*, more closely to this genus than to *Pezoporus*.

The species is a medium-sized bird with a short, slightly gradated tail comprising narrow, pointed feathers. The head is broad and there is no narrowing of the anterior of the cranium. The bill is flat and compressed, somewhat similar to that of *Strigops*, and there is no notch in the upper mandible. The naked cere is large and fleshy. In front of and below the cere there are a number of short, hair-like feathers. The wings are long and pointed. The tarsi are long, but the claws are curved and very short.

Sexual dimorphism is absent. Both sexes show a yellowish-white wing-stripe.

1 Ground Parrot
Pezoporus wallicus wallicus
AM. 028466 ad. ♂

2 Night Parrot *Geopsittacus occidentalis*
AM. 017832 ad. ♀

NIGHT PARROT

Geopsittacus occidentalis Gould

Illustrated on page 268.

DESCRIPTION

Length 23 cm.
ADULTS general plumage yellowish-green 'mottled' with dark brown, black and yellow; lower underparts rich yellow; under wing-coverts pale green; tail dark brown marked with yellow and green; yellowish-white wing-stripe present; bill horn-coloured; iris black (Gould); legs brown.
IMMATURES (Bourgoin, in Wilson 1937); said to be dull and very plain with some yellow on throat and neck.

4 males	wing 142–150 (147.0) mm., tail 92–113 (103.0) mm.,	
	exp. cul. 13–14 (13.3) mm., tars. 20–23 (21.8) mm.	
3 females	wing 136–145 (137.3) mm., tail 95–106 (98.6) mm.,	
	exp. cul. 12–13 (12.3) mm., tars. 22–23 (22.3) mm.	
11 unsexed	wing 132–153 (143.5) mm., tail 88–115 (99.6) mm.,	
	exp. cul. 10–14 (12.5) mm., tars. 20–24 (22.2) mm.	

DISTRIBUTION

Interior of Australia.

GENERAL NOTES

The Night Parrot remains one of Australia's most mysterious birds. The only specimen collected this century was taken in September, 1912 at Nichol Spring, Western Australia, but it deteriorated and has since been lost (see Wilson, 1937). Recent probable sightings from localities as far apart as

W.T. Cooper. 71.

Partacoona, South Australia (Powell, 1970) and the Pilbara Region in Western Australia (Ives, 1971) are, in my opinion, good evidence that the species still exists, even though there have been no authentic records for more than fifty years. Unlike the Paradise Parrot, Australia's other 'missing' parrot, this species is an inconspicuous bird with extremely secretive habits. Furthermore, it is nocturnal and occurs in virtually uninhabited country. I believe that, although numbers have almost certainly declined because of loss of habitat, it will eventually be found.

Most observers have pointed out the close association between this species and spinifex grass (*Triodia*); Bourgoin found it amongst thick spinifex on limestone hills. It has also been seen and collected amongst samphire bushes on salt lakes.

Night Parrots are nocturnal. During the day they are supposed to shelter in a tunnel in the base of a spinifex tussock. It is said that they bite off stems to form the tunnel and then pull the strips in to conceal the entrance. They may also shelter in hollow logs and rocky caves or burrow into sandy soil. They have been observed singly or in pairs, but occasionally small groups of up to eight were seen coming to water well after nightfall (Andrews, 1883). Whitlock (1924) was told that the parrots were poor fliers in daylight and could be run down and caught once driven into the open. However, at night they are apparently strong fliers because Andrews claimed that they would fly up to four or five miles to water. The flight is erratic, but without undulation, and the birds rarely rise more than a few metres above the vegetation. They are probably nomadic; Andrews claimed that numbers fluctuated in accordance with the seasons.

A Night Parrot caught in the Gawler Ranges, South Australia, in 1867 lived for some months in the London Zoo. It moved along in a series of jumps, but at times ran about with considerable agility.

They feed on seeds, particularly those of spinifex. The crop of a specimen collected by Bourgoin in Western Australia was filled with seeds of spinifex and limestone herbage. The captive bird at London Zoo showed a marked preference for greenfood.

CALL A low, disyllabic whistle, sometimes prolonged into a mournful note; when alarmed a peculiar croaking note like the loud croak of a frog.

NESTING Little is known of the breeding behaviour. The nest is a small platform of sticks placed on or near the ground in the centre of a tussock. It is in an enlarged cavity at the end of a tunnel similar to that used for shelter. McDonald took four nestlings from one nest and said that he had seen others containing four white eggs (in McGilp, 1931).

EGGS Undescribed.

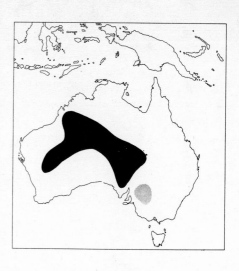

Kakapo *Strigops habroptilus* AM. 030428 ad. ♂

Subfamily STRIGOPINAE

I have retained this monotypic subfamily, though I have doubts about the value of doing so. As already pointed out I believe that the species is probably related to *Geopsittacus* and *Pezoporus*.

The presence of only a rudimentary keel to the sternum is the most distinctive characteristic. The lower mandible of the stout, blunt bill is strongly ridged. There is a markedly swollen cere and the feathers at the base of the bill have the shafts prolonged into hairs.

Genus STRIGOPS G. R. Gray

The distinguishing features are the same as for the subfamily. The species is a large, heavy parrot with a rather long, rounded tail. There is no sexual dimorphism in plumage, but females average smaller than males and have smaller, slighter bills.

KAKAPO
Strigops habroptilus G. R. Gray

Illustrated on page 269.

DESCRIPTION

Length 64 cm.

ADULTS upperparts bright green irregularly barred and streaked with brown and yellow; underparts greenish-yellow similarly marked; wings and tail green with brown and yellow barring; irregular yellow stripe from lores to above the eye; forehead and prominent facial disc yellowish-brown, faintly streaked paler; bill yellowish-white, marked with brown at base of upper mandible; iris dark brown; legs brownish-grey.
IMMATURES said to be much duller.

10 males   wing 265–284 (272.6) mm., tail 203–250 (222.6) mm.,
        exp. cul. 34–43 (38.0) mm., tars. 45–57 (51.8) mm.
10 females wing 252–285 (269.1) mm., tail 205–238 (220.3) mm.,
        exp. cul. 35–37 (36.4) mm., tars. 46–56 (49.6) mm.

DISTRIBUTION   New Zealand; formerly the mountain ranges of North, South and Stewart Islands. Subfossil remains from Chatham Island. Now greatly reduced, the only known population being confined to the Cleddau watershed in Fiordland, South Island.

GENERAL NOTES   The Kakapo is now extremely rare and most of the information we have on its habits and life history comes from the writings of early naturalists. The last bird held in captivity by the New Zealand Wildlife Service died in February 1968 and there have been no further sightings in the field. Williams (1963) points out that subfossil remains show that the range had shrunk considerably prior to European settlement and perhaps even before Polynesian colonization. Settlement and the land-clearance that goes with it almost certainly accelerated the decline, and the introduction of stoats, weasels and deer may have also contributed to it. The parrots were still widespread and locally common along the west coast of South Island during the latter half of the last century (Reid, 1970). The last record from North Island seems to be the sighting of a single bird in the Huiara Range in 1927. In 1949 a Wildlife Service field officer caught a Kakapo on Stewart Island; feathers were found near the same spot two years later, but there have been no further records. Apparently the species disappeared from Chatham Island well over 150 years ago.

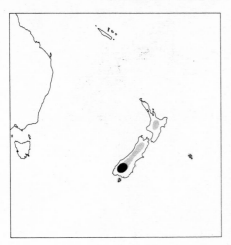

Kakapos have been found at all altitudes below 1,250 m. Williams says that they are primarily birds of the mossy beech (*Nothofagus*) forests, particularly those adjoining open ground along river flats, or the subalpine scrub belt bordering the snow tussock (*Danthonia*) meadows above the tree line. During the day they shelter amongst the foliage of low trees, in crevices in rocks, under shrubs, or in burrows under the roots of trees. They become active at dusk. There are some records of feeding during the day, but these parrots are almost totally nocturnal in habits. They cannot fly, but do flap their wings when jumping from trees down to the ground. They are agile climbers, using feet and bill and balancing with their wings. When travelling downhill they can move with surprising speed by alternately running with their awkward, clumsy gait and gliding short distances. When moving up to the subalpine areas to feed they walk along well-defined tracks traversing the tops of spurs, sometimes in single file one behind the other. These tracks were conspicuous landmarks in areas where the parrots were locally common. Accounts in the early literature give the impression that Kakapos were largely solitary birds, but Lyall (1852) says that according to the Maoris they congregated together in large numbers in caves during winter.

Food comprises fruits, berries, nuts, seeds, green shoots, leaf buds, fern roots, moss, some fungi, and probably insects and their larvae. They are said to be particularly fond of the fruits of kotukutuku (*Fuchsia excorticata*). The method of feeding on leaves and stems is peculiar and produces characteristic signs of the birds' presence in an area. They chew the leaves or stems, extracting the juices, and then leave behind hanging on the plant tight balls of macerated, fibrous material which are subsequently bleached white by the sun. Crops examined by von Haast were filled with moss (in Stivens, 1964).

CALL Lyall describes the call as a hoarse croak, varied occasionally by a discordant shriek; Stivens claims that they are noisy feeders, croaking and muttering all the time. However, the call commonly referred to is a very loud, ventriloquial 'booming' which commences quietly as a few short grunts but rapidly builds up in volume. Williams points out that although no birds have ever been seen 'booming', that they do so is established beyond doubt by observations on a captive bird in 1904; this bird called only at night or when in its shelter.

NESTING There is no evidence supporting the claim made by Henry (1903) that Kakapos breed only every two years and in any locality the season is synchronized. From early accounts it appears that eggs are usually laid in January and February with the odd nest being found as early as December or as late as mid-May, the latter possibly a re-nesting. The nest is in a burrow in a large crevice between rocks or tree roots. A chamber 30 cm. or so high and up to 60 cm. in diameter is excavated and lined with decayed wood chips or a few feathers. The normal clutch is one or two, rarely three, eggs. Lyall found chicks in nests during the latter half of February and the first half of March; there was generally only one, never more than two, but in one nest there were two chicks and an addled egg. The chicks in a nest were of different ages, some being nearly fully fledged while others were covered only with white down and Lyall concluded that there was a long interval between laying of the first and second eggs. It is said that only the female incubates and cares for the young.

EGGS Ovoid, more pointed at one end; 13 eggs, 50.5 (48.2–54.5) × 36.3 (35.0–37.8) mm. [Schönwetter, 1964].

Mascarene Parrot *Mascarinus mascarinus*
MNHN. 211 **type** ad. unsexed

W.T. Cooper. 72.

Vasa Parrot *Coracopsis vasa drouhardi* 1
AM. 015875 ad. unsexed

Black Parrot *Coracopsis nigra nigra* 2
AM. B2525 ad. ♂

Afro-Asian
Distribution

Cape Parrot *Poicephalus robustus robustus* 1
USNM. 159514 ad. ♂
Cape Parrot *Poicephalus robustus suahelicus* 2
NHM. 6784 ad. ♂

Grey Parrot *Psittacus erithacus erithacus*
AM. 023415 ad. unsexed

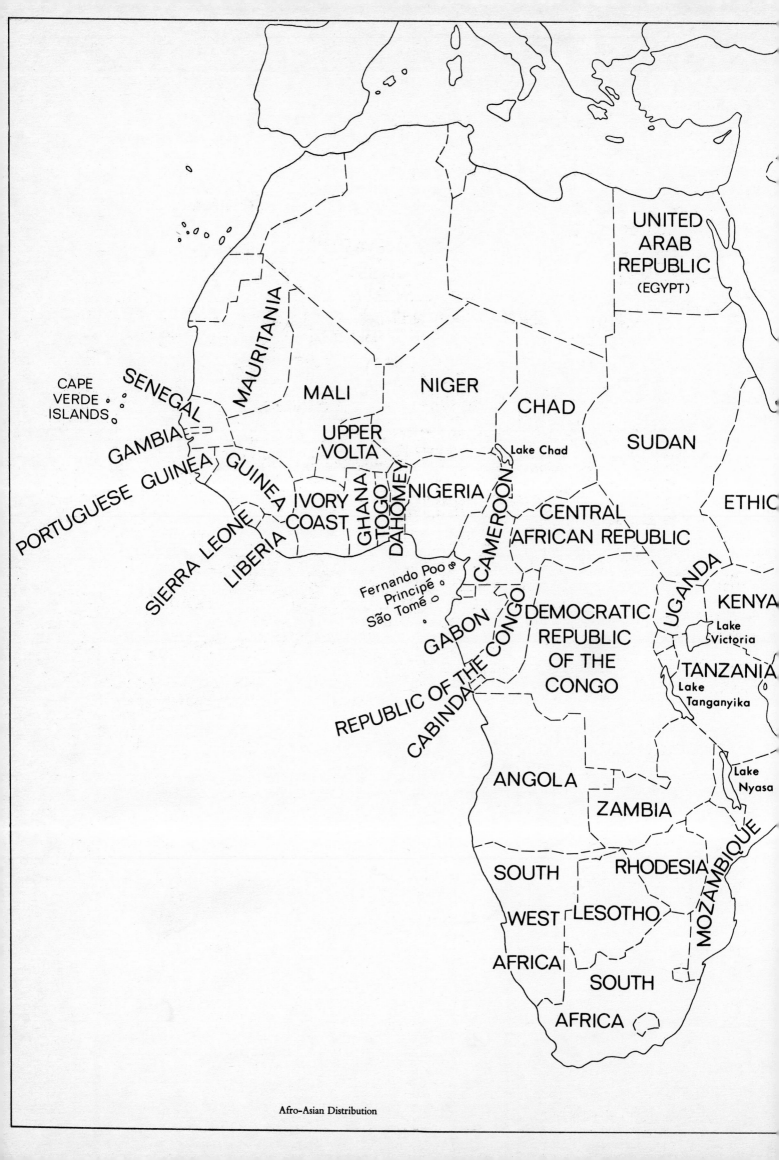

Afro-Asian Distribution

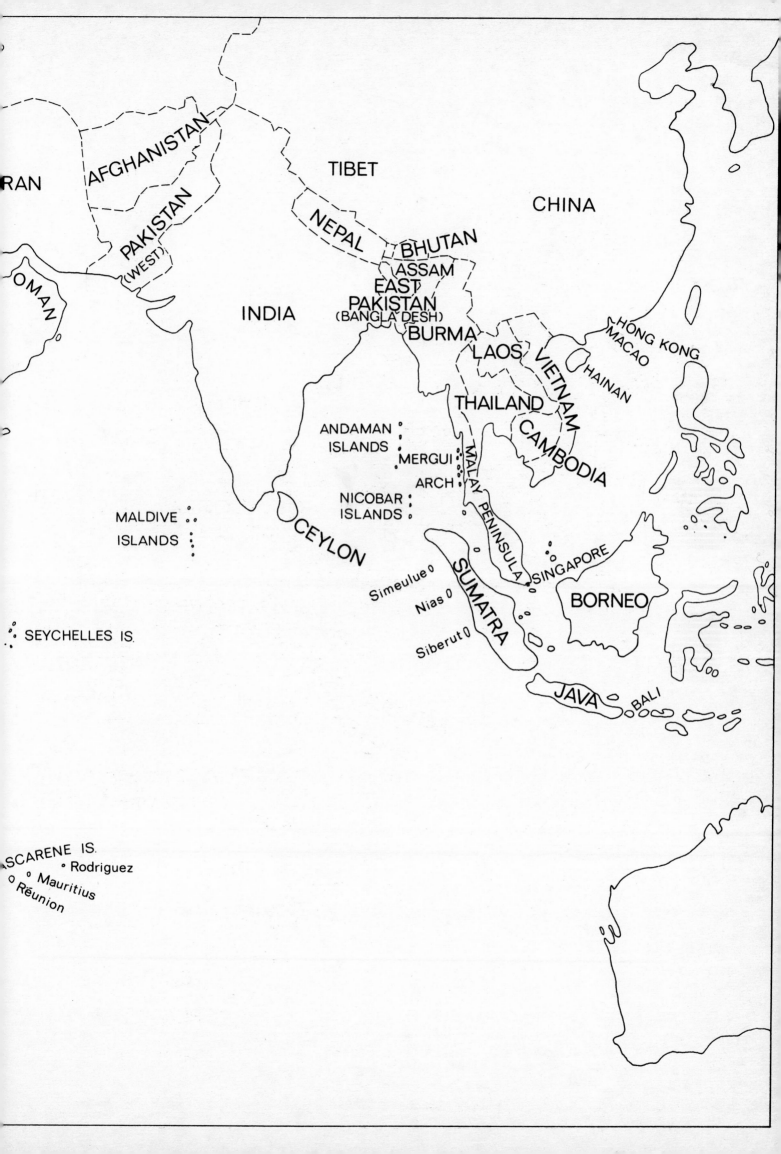

W.T. Cooper. 71.

AFRO-ASIAN DISTRIBUTION

The Afro-Asian Distribution includes the Malagasy and Ethiopian Faunal Regions, most of the Oriental Region and some southernmost parts of the Palearctic Region. It extends from Africa east to Indochina and the Malay Peninsula. Two genera of parrots, *Psittacula* and *Loriculus*, range into the Pacific Distribution, particularly *Loriculus* which occurs in New Guinea, but they are essentially Asiatic birds so all species are treated here. *Psittinus* comes north into southern Burma, but is treated in the Pacific Distribution because I believe that its affinities are with Philippine and New Guinea genera. Within this Distribution the major land masses are Africa and the Indian sub-continent, and it is on these that most parrots occur.

Moreau (1964) says that it seems certain that through most of avian history the continent of Africa has maintained its present outline, though the climatic belts have changed their locations somewhat, thus influencing the present distribution of birds. Therefore, the continent must have been a principal scene of continuous evolution of both forest and non-forest species (e.g., all but two of the eighteen species of parrots belong to only two genera, *Poicephalus* and *Agapornis*). There is recent geological evidence that great ecological disruption, no doubt with corresponding influences on extinction and on the later stages of evolution, has taken place during the latter half of the Pleistocene, presumably by no means for the first time. In Africa there are few endemic bird groups above generic level, and although some groups are extremely well represented others, including the parrots, are represented by fewer species than might have been expected.

To the east of southern Africa lies the important large island of Madagascar and farther east in the Indian Ocean are the Mascarene Islands, a group of small oceanic islands. The Comoro Islands are also small oceanic islands and are situated at the northern end of the Mozambique Channel between Madagascar and the African mainland. To the north-east of Madagascar are the Seychelles Islands, which on geological grounds are probably a continental relict but from the ornithological point of view are oceanic. Moreau points out that it is often claimed that Madagascar has been isolated since the Miocene, but it seems that there is no evidence for any land connection later than the Secondary. The majority of Madagascar avifaunal stock probably came from Africa, and some of the existing birds indicate that immigrant stock has continued to establish itself at long intervals. *Coracopsis* is a parrot genus without obvious affinities to any extant African genera, and contains two sibling species; *Agapornis cana*, the third species found on the island, is a 'primitive' representative of an African genus. Benson (1960) says that the avifauna of the Comoro Islands is transitional between Madagascar and Africa; both species of *Coracopsis* occur there and are subspecifically distinct from the populations on Madagascar.

The Mascarene Islands have become famous as the former home of the Dodo (*Raphus cucullatus*) and other unique extinct birds, some of them parrots. The origins of these parrots are most obscure, but they could have been Asiatic rather than African. It is interesting to note that the predominantly Asiatic genus *Psittacula* is represented in the Mascarenes by an endemic species on Mauritius and another formerly occurred on Rodriguez.

The two parrots recorded from the Seychelles Islands indicate that colonization came from Asia and from the Comoro Islands: the extinct *Psittacula wardi* was very closely allied to *P. eupatria* from India, and the extant small population of *Coracopsis nigra* is only doubtfully distinct from birds on the Comoro Islands.

The Oriental Region, of which the important component is the Indian Peninsula, lies largely within the tropics and its avifauna is of mainly Ethiopian and Palearctic origins. There are only two genera of parrots: *Loriculus*, a genus related to *Agapornis* from Africa, and *Psittacula*, of which *P. krameri*, the most widely distributed of all parrots, occurs in both India and Africa. The Region is dominated by the Himalayas, its northern boundary. The southern aspect of the main chain with its associated hills and subsidiary ranges extends from Afghanistan east through northern India, Nepal and Bhutan to south-eastern Tibet and south-western China. Here are found typically highland parrots such as *Psittacula derbiana*, *P. himalayana* and *P. alexandri*. The Peninsula itself stretches southward from the Himalayan foothills and includes the Island of Ceylon. In the south-west there is a tropical, humid zone where are found some endemic forms including the parrot *Psittacula columboides*. Ali (1964) points out that Ceylon was alternately joined to and separated from peninsular India during various geological epochs, and under periods of prolonged isolation many endemic forms have developed. The parrots provide a good example of the results of this: *Loriculus beryllinus* and *Psittacula calthorpae* are endemic to the island, but *Psittacula eupatria*, *P. krameri* and *P. cyanocephala* are racially identical with populations from the southern sector of the Peninsula.

Special mention must be made of the Andaman and Nicobar Islands, which form the eastern boundary to the Bay of Bengal. The Andaman Islands have avifaunal affinities with both nearby

Jardine's Parrot *Poicephalus gulielmi guli* .. 1
MNHN. CG1947,524 ad. ♂

Yellow-faced Parrot 2
Poicephalus flavifrons flavifrons
USNM. 210664 ad. ♂

Burma and the Malaysian area; *Loriculus vernalis, Psittacula eupatria, P. alexandri* and *P. longicauda* occur there. The Nicobar Islands lie off the western tip of Sumatra and the avifauna is more allied to that of the Malaysian area; all three species of parrots, including the endemic *Psittacula caniceps*, are from Malaysian stock.

The birds of Burma and Indochina are of mainly Indian origin and there is a Palearctic influence, chiefly through the migrants; *Loriculus vernalis* occurs throughout and there are two or more *Psittacula* species in most areas. In the Malaysian area there is a blending of Indian and Australasian forms: *Loriculus* reaches its peak of development in this eastern sector of the Distribution.

Parrots are poorly represented in the Afro-Asian Distribution and divergence above specific level is slight. In the table below I have listed the number of parrots found in the major countries and the habitats in which they occur. The countries are given as geographical, not political, units (e.g., India includes Pakistan, Nepal and Bhutan; Indochina includes Cambodia, Laos and Vietnam). For convenience Africa is divided arbitrarily into three sectors and these are as follows:

(i) Southern Africa occupies the area below a line drawn across the northern borders of Mozambique, Malawi, Zambia and Angola.

(ii) Central Africa extends up to a line drawn across the northern borders of Kenya, Uganda, Democratic Republic of Congo, Central African Republic, Cameroon, Nigeria, Dahomey, Upper Volta, Ivory Coast, Guinea and Senegal; included are the offshore islands of Zanzibar, Pemba, the Mafia Islands and islands in the Gulf of Guinea.

(iii) Northern Africa extends up to the Red and Mediterranean Seas; the important country for parrots is Ethiopia.

Extinct species are excluded but introduced species are included (e.g. *Agapornis cana* for the Mascarene, Comoro and Seychelles Islands; *Psittacula krameri* for the Mascarene Islands, Iraq and Iran; *P. alexandri* for Borneo). Categorization of habitats is broad and arbitrary and does not take into account the actual complexities always present in the distribution of a species. Littoral habitats include estuarine flats and swamps, coconut palms and other trees along beaches, and mangroves. Open areas in both lowlands and highlands take in open grassland, cultivated farmland, savannah woodland and semi-arid and arid scrublands. Subalpine habitat refers to the coniferous-oak forests high up on the slopes of the Himalayas, where *Psittacula derbiana* is a summer visitor.

COUNTRY	NUMBER OF SPECIES	LITTORAL HABITATS	LOWLANDS: OPEN AREAS	LOWLANDS: FORESTED AREAS	HIGHLANDS: OPEN AREAS	HIGHLANDS: FORESTED AREAS	SUBALPINE HABITATS
Northern Africa	8		5	2		2	
Central Africa	14	3	7	8	2	2	
Southern Africa	10	1	8	7		1	
Madagascar	3	1	2	2			
Comoro Islands	3		2	2			
Mascarene Islands	3		2	1		1	
Seychelles Islands	2		1	1			
Iraq	1		1				
Iran	1		1				
Afghanistan	3		1	1		1	
India	10		4	5		5	
Ceylon	5	1	4	4		1	
Tibet	1					1	1
China	3			1		3	1
Burma	7	1	4	6		2	
Indochina	5	1	3	4		1	
Andaman Islands	4	2	2	4		2	
Nicobar Islands	3	1	3	3		3	
Thailand	6		3	5	2	2	
Malay Peninsula	6	1	4	6	1	1	
Borneo	5	2	3	4			
Sumatra	4	2	4	4	1		1

Since the arrival of European man in the Seychelles and Mascarene Islands some endemic forms have been exterminated, particularly in the Mascarenes. Another species, *Psittacula echo* from Mauritius, is seriously endangered. In Africa some lovebirds (*Agapornis* spp.) have very restricted ranges so need protection, but here and in India most species are common and widely distributed.

Subfamily PSITTACINAE

Genus LOPHOPSITTACUS Newton

This extinct monotypic genus is known only from subfossil bones and a detailed sketch in the original manuscript kept by Wolphart Harmanzoon during a voyage to Mauritius in 1601–1602. Of the skeletal material, the most striking bones are the very large lower mandibles, and it is from these that the species derives its vernacular name (see fig 12). From the size of the limb bones and sternum it is apparent that the parrot was a very large bird with an enormous bill. The sketch shows that the tail was moderately long and rounded, and the frontal feathers immediately behind the bill were elongated and stiffened to form a crest. Holyoak (1971a) points out that the reduced keel on the sternum, the very short wings and the size of the bird, indicate that it was incapable of strong flight and was probably totally flightless. He also claims that size differences in fully ossified bones suggest that there may have been a remarkable sexual dimorphism in size.

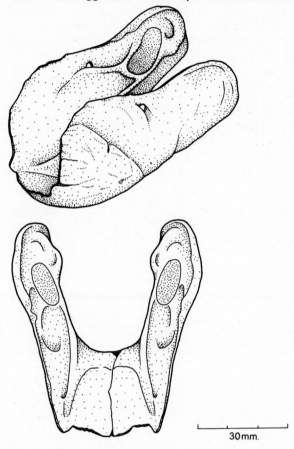

30mm.

Fig. 11
Lower mandible of the Broad-billed Parrot (*Lophopsittacus mauritianus*): (upper), lateral view; (lower), dorsal view.

BROAD-BILLED PARROT
Lophopsittacus mauritianus (Owen)

Length probably more than 70 cm.
ADULTS general plumage colouration was either grey or blue. We have not illustrated this parrot because there are no specimens; for an illustration based on Harmanzoon's sketch see plate 7 in *Extinct Birds*, by Lord Rothschild, 1907.

Formerly Mauritius, Mascarene Islands; now extinct.

Holyoak claims that the Broad-billed Parrot was last seen alive about 1638. There is no reference to it in journals of explorers who visited the island during the second and third decades of the eighteenth century.

Hachisuka (1953) says that there are reasons for believing that this parrot was nocturnal, but he does not give them and I know of no supporting evidence.

Holyoak says that examination by X-rays of the lower mandibles discloses a loose and open arrangement of the tissue. This, together with the strikingly wide bill and narrow palatines shows that the bill of *Lophopsittacus* was weakly constructed, despite its large size, suggesting that the bird ate fruit or some other soft food.

DISTRIBUTION

GENERAL NOTES

283

Genus NECROPSITTACUS Milne-Edwards

This extinct genus has also been described from subfossil skeletal material. Distinguishing features were a singularly depressed cranium and structural modifications in the occipital region. The species was a large parrot with a massive bill.

RODRIGUEZ PARROT
Necropsittacus rodericanus (Milne-Edwards)

Length probably about 50 cm.
ADULTS external appearance not known, though Hachisuka (1953) suggests that it was uniformly green.

DISTRIBUTION   Formerly Rodriguez, Mascarene Islands; now extinct.

GENERAL NOTES   It is not known when the Rodriguez Parrot became extinct, but it was reported by the anonymous writer of a manuscript dated 1731. He wrote 'The perroquets are of three kinds and in quantity. The largest are larger than a pigeon and have a very long tail, the head large as is the bill. Most of them live on islets that lie to the southward of the island, where they eat a little black seed, which produces a small tree, the leaves of which have an odour of lemon, and come to the large island to drink water. The others stay on the large island where they are found in small trees.' The largest species mentioned in this text is thought to be *N. rodericanus*.

   N. borbonicus from Réunion and *N. francicus* from Mauritius are hypothetical species named by Rothschild (1907) from vague descriptions in early writings. If they did exist there is no proof that they differed from *N. rodericanus*.

Genus MASCARINUS Lesson

The systematic position of this extinct, monotypic genus is uncertain, though affinities with *Eclectus* and *Tanygnathus* have been advocated by some authors, seemingly because of the massive red bill. I believe that it was probably related to the other extinct Mascarene genera and possibly to *Coracopsis*.

   The cranium was depressed and protruded anteriorly. The species was a medium sized parrot with a fairly long, rounded tail. The cere was feathered and there was a patch of thick, velvety feathers around the base of the bill.

MASCARENE PARROT
Mascarinus mascarinus (Linné)

Illustrated on page 272.

Length 35 cm.
ADULTS general plumage brown, paler and more yellowish on underparts; face black; head greyish-lilac; tail brown with white at base of lateral feathers; bill red; legs brownish.
IMMATURES undescribed.
1 unsexed **(type)** wing 211 mm., tail 152 mm.,
            exp. cul. 32 mm., tars. 24 mm.
1 unsexed   wing—(damaged), tail 144 mm.,
            exp. cul. 36 mm., tars. 22 mm.

DISTRIBUTION   Formerly Réunion and possibly Mauritius, Mascarene Islands; now extinct.

GENERAL NOTES   The Mascarene Parrot became extinct sometime after 1834 when the last known living bird died in the garden of the King of Bavaria (Greenway, 1967).

   The two specimens are in a poor state of preservation and plumage colours have faded; the greyish-lilac on the head is not clearly discernible. The illustration in Rothschild's *Extinct Birds* (1907) has been used as an added source of information in the preparation of the painting in this book.

284

Genus CORACOPSIS Wagler

Because of their strange, sombre plumage colouration the two species belonging to this genus are most distinctive. Other external features are a heavy, broad bill and a long, slightly rounded tail. The naked cere and periophthalmic ring are very prominent. An osteological characteristic is the almost complete orbital ring formed by the prefrontal reaching to, but not joining the squamosal; Thompson (1900) points out that the postfrontal process is almost obsolete. Sexual dimorphism is absent.

VASA PARROT
Coracopsis vasa (Shaw)

DESCRIPTION

Length 50 cm.
ADULTS general plumage brownish-black, somewhat greyish on upperparts; under tail-coverts grey variably shaft-streaked with black; faint darker band across centre of tail; bill pale horn-coloured, may be greyish after moult; iris brown; legs flesh-brown.
IMMATURES general plumage more brownish; feathers of underparts edged with chestnut; grey bill.

DISTRIBUTION

Madagascar and Comoro Islands; introduced to Réunion, Mascarene Islands, but there are no reports of its continued presence there so the introduction was probably unsuccessful.

SUBSPECIES

1. *C. v. vasa* (Shaw)
   10 males wing 300–322 (311.0) mm., tail 190–209 (196.7) mm.,
             exp. cul. 35–40 (37.3) mm., tars. 31–34 (31.8) mm.
   8 females wing 299–316 (306.1) mm., tail 185–202 (194.1) mm.,
             exp. cul. 34–38 (35.8) mm., tars. 31–33 (32.0) mm.
   Confined to eastern Madagascar.

2. *C. v. drouhardi* Lavauden   *Illustrated on page 273.*
   ADULTS slightly smaller; paler colouration, particularly on underparts which are grey; under tail-coverts whitish.
   10 males wing 276–299 (287.1) mm., tail 168–200 (181.5) mm.,
             exp. cul. 33–35 (33.6) mm., tars. 29–31 (29.6) mm.
   8 females wing 277–303 (288.4) mm., tail 160–200 (178.9) mm.,
             exp. cul. 30–34 (31.5) mm., tars. 28–31 (29.8) mm.
   Occurs in western Madagascar.

3. *C. v. comorensis* (Peters)
   ADULTS plumage colouration paler; brown under tail-coverts.
   4 males   wing 256–295 (281.3) mm., tail 185–193 (191.0) mm.,
             exp. cul. 29–31 (30.3) mm., tars. 27–28 (27.5) mm.
   4 females wing 272–294 (281.8) mm., tail 177–200 (187.3) mm.,
             exp. cul. 28–29 (28.8) mm., tars. 26–29 (27.5) mm.
   Found on Grand Comoro, Moheli and Anjouan in the Comoro Islands.

GENERAL NOTES

On Madagascar Vasa Parrots are noisy, conspicuous birds found in forests and savannah below 1,000 m., being more abundant at the lower altitudes (Rand, 1936). On the Comoro Islands Benson (1960) found that they are largely dependent on evergreen forest above 300 m., frequently visiting open country to feed but probably not remaining there permanently. They are usually seen in small parties, though large numbers may congregate to feed or roost. Rand found between one and two hundred roosting in tall trees around a lake; as the parrots came and departed they flew high above the plateau, their wings reflecting the rays of the setting or rising sun.

They may be heard calling or seen flying about on moonlit nights. During the day they feed in the treetops and groups of up to ten or fifteen may be seen resting high up in a solitary dead tree. They are tame and approachable. Forbes-Watson (1969) reports that on Grant Comoro he stood watching a pair eating fruit in a tree about 3 m. from him. When coming to and going from the roosting trees they fly high above the forest canopy. Rand also saw them flying about high over open ground. The heavy flight with slow, flapping wingbeats is characteristic. Forbes-Watson points out that in flight the bird looks quite unlike any African parrot, and reminded him of an elongated ragged crow with a truncated head.

They feed on fruits, nuts, berries and seeds. Rand found small numbers in the company of bulbuls and starlings feeding in fruit-bearing trees and saw flocks feeding on the ground in open savannah. He reported that they were pests in cornfields, attacking the standing crops. They also fed on a millet-like grain grown by the local people; the entire seed-head was bitten off and carried in the bill to a nearby perch where it was held in the foot and the seeds eaten. On Anjouan

Island, Benson watched one parrot feeding on the fruits of a *Cussonia* tree. Stomach contents from birds collected by Benson in the Comoro Islands comprised small seeds.

CALL A low, prolonged *pee-aw* or *fee-eu* on a descending scale; also a harsh squawk and a raucous *kraaar . . . kraaar* (Benson, 1960). Benson also heard a *cho-cho-chi-chi-chi* .song-call which may have been confined to the breeding season.

NESTING Little is known of the breeding habits. A female which appeared to have laid recently (MNHN. CG 1959, 404) was collected on Anjouan, Comoro Islands, by Benson in late October. Rand reports that on Madagascar the breeding season probably includes at least the months of October to December. In early December he found a nest containing three young birds. The nest was in a hollow limb of a tree, the chamber being down in the trunk. The three chicks had many pin-feathers showing but not a trace of down. Rand also noticed that females in breeding condition had lost most of their crown feathers.

EGGS Slightly elliptical; 6 eggs, 46.2 (44.5–48.0) × 34.2 (32.8–36.5) mm. [Schönwetter, 1964].

BLACK PARROT
Coracopsis nigra (Linné)

DESCRIPTION

Length 35 cm.
ADULTS general plumage blackish-brown; inconspicuous greyish markings on under tail-coverts; outer webs of primaries grey; bill pale horn-coloured, may be greyish after moult; iris dark brown; legs grey.
IMMATURES undescribed.

DISTRIBUTION

Madagascar, Comoro Islands, and Praslin Island in the Seychelles.

SUBSPECIES

1. *C. n. nigra* (Linné)   *Illustrated on page 273.*
   10 males wing 230–252 (242.6) mm., tail 146–164 (158.0) mm.,
           exp. cul. 23–24 (23.7) mm., tars. 24–26 (24.6) mm.
   8 females wing 216–239 (226.5) mm., tail 135–157 (150.1) mm.,
           exp. cul. 21–23 (22.4) mm., tars. 22–25 (23.1) mm.
   Occurs in eastern Madagascar, intergrading with *libs* in the north-west and south-west.

2. *C. n. libs* Bangs
   ADULTS entire plumage paler; underparts browner; greyish back.
   10 males wing 227–260 (243.8) mm., tail 143–170 (157.0) mm.,
           exp. cul. 21–24 (22.5) mm., tars. 24–26 (24.5) mm.
   8 females wing 221–254 (237.3) mm., tail 149–174 (159.6) mm.,
           exp. cul. 21–23 (22.4) mm., tars. 23–25 (23.8) mm.
   Inhabits the drier western region of Madagascar.

3. *C. n. sibilans* Milne-Edwards and Oustalet
   ADULTS smaller size; general plumage pale brown; no grey on outer webs of primaries; bill brownish-grey.
   4 males   wing 188–193 (190.5) mm., tail 137–142 (139.3) mm.,
           exp. cul. 19–20 (19.3) mm., tars. 19–23 (20.3) mm.
   2 females wing 188–189 (188.5) mm., tail 126–145 (135.5) mm.,
           exp. cul. 18–20 (19.0) mm., tars. 19–20 (19.5) mm.
   Found on Grand Comoro and Anjouan in the Comoro Islands; may not be distinct from *barklyi* (see Gaymer *et al.*, 1969).

4. *C. n. barklyi* E. Newton
   ADULTS similar to *sibilans*; greyish-blue reflections on outer webs of primaries; inconspicuous pale brown spots on crown.
   10 males wing 177–203 (191.9) mm., tail 122–138 (132.4) mm.,
           exp. cul. 19–21 (20.0) mm., tars. 21–22 (21.5) mm.
   9 females wing 181–202 (190.4) mm., tail 125–139 (130.3) mm.,
           exp. cul. 18–20 (19.1) mm., tars. 19–21 (20.4) mm.

   Restricted to Praslin Island in the Seychelles.

GENERAL NOTES

Rand (1936) and Benson (1960) report that Black Parrots are woodland birds, favouring denser forest and brush than does *C. vasa*. Forbes-Watson (1969) points out that they are more inclined to feed in the mid-stratum than are Vasa Parrots. In north-western Madagascar they have been seen in mangrove swamps. They are not as common as Vasa Parrots.
    On Praslin Island, Seychelles, *C. n. barklyi* is very rare and is virtually confined to the Vallée de

Mai Reserve, a reserve set aside primarily for the unique Coco de Mer Palms (*Laodicea maldivicum*). There does not seem to be any close association between the parrots and these trees, though they do nest in decayed trunks; rigid protection enforced in the reserve is probably responsible for the parrots' presence there. Past records from Praslin and Marianne Islands (the latter rather doubtful) show that the birds were more widespread. Habitat destruction through land clearance or, as suggested by Honegger (1966), by forest fires, almost certainly brought about the decline. Actual numbers are difficult to ascertain but Penny (1968) claims that there may be only thirty to fifty parrots on the island. They are strictly protected and positive conservation measures being taken include the provision of artificial nesting logs and planting of fruit trees for food.

In small parties Black Parrots are generally seen feeding in the treetops or flying about above the forest canopy. They are noisy birds, frequently being heard before they are seen. They are active on moonlit nights. They are not timid, but when disturbed quietly climb to a position more sheltered among the foliage. The flight is graceful, comprising long glides alternating with strong, rhythmic wingbeats.

The feed on seeds, fruits, berries and blossoms. On Praslin Island they are very fond of the introduced guavas (*Psidium cattleanum*) and eat flowers and fruits of *Ficus*, *Neowormia*, *Northea*, *Eugenia* and *Deckenia* (Gaymer et al., 1969). They are said to raid ripening mangoes along the coast. On Madagascar, Rand saw one bird eating a mango that was hanging on the tree. Benson was told that on Grand Comoro Island the birds are pests in cacao plantations, attacking young pods in which the seeds have not formed. Stomach contents from birds collected by Benson on the Comoro Islands consisted solely of small seeds.

CALL A high-pitched, whistling *dir-tee-jo* or *dir-tee* . . . *dir-tee* . . . *dir-tee-jo- - - -o*, also a *cark* . . . *caark*, softer and not as harsh as that of *C. vasa* (Rand, 1936). Benson noted a supposed breeding song-call, *kwa*, repeated up to six times followed by a shrill *kwü* also repeated up to six times.

NESTING Little is known of the breeding biology. On Praslin Island, Gaymer et al. observed courtship in February: one bird approached another and with outstretched neck and fanned tail gave a stiff, formal bow, tucking in the chin at the last moment; the recovery movement was faster and some contact of bills was observed. Rand collected specimens in breeding condition in early January and Benson collected a male with enlarged testes on 1st October. Legrand (1964) describes two nests found on Praslin Island. One was in a hollow in the trunk of a dead *Albizzia* tree and the other in a dead *Pandanus* palm. The first contained two eggs on a layer of decayed wood dust at the bottom of a vertical hollow. The second contained three chicks.

EGGS A single egg in the Senckenberg Museum Collection measures 38.6 × 30.5 mm. [Schönwetter, 1964].

Genus PSITTACUS Linné

The most conspicuous external feature of this monotypic genus is the bare facial area with very short, hair-like bristles. Osteologically, the orbital ring is incomplete due to poor development of the prefrontal process (Thompson, 1900).

The species, so widely known throughout the world as a cage bird, is a rather large, stocky parrot with a very short, square tail. The cere is naked. There is no sexual dimorphism.

GREY PARROT
Psittacus erithacus Linné

DESCRIPTION
Length 33 cm.
ADULTS general plumage pale grey; feathers of head and neck margined with greyish-white, those of abdomen with dark grey; rump very pale grey; primaries very dark grey, almost black; facial area whitish; tail and adjacent tail-coverts red; bill black; iris pale yellow; legs dark grey.
IMMATURES tail dark red towards tip; under tail-coverts tinged with grey; iris grey.

DISTRIBUTION
Central Africa from Gulf of Guinea Islands and the west coast east to western Kenya and northwestern Tanzania; possibly on Mt. Kilimanjaro, Tanzania.

SUBSPECIES
1. *P. e. erithacus* Linné   *Illustrated on page 276.*
     10 males   wing 234–252 (242.5) mm., tail 80–95 (86.8) mm.,
                 exp. cul. 32–39 (35.7) mm., tars. 25–28 (27.4) mm.
     8 females   wing 232–259 (241.6) mm., tail 79–95 (85.6) mm.,
                 exp. cul. 32–37 (34.5) mm., tars. 26–28 (26.8) mm.

Widespread in equatorial Africa from south-eastern Ivory Coast east to western Kenya and south to northern Angola, southern regions of the Congo and to north-western Tanzania.

There is a sight record from Mt. Kilimanjaro, Tanzania (in Bangs and Loveridge, 1933) but no specimens have been collected. Mackworth-Praed and Grant (1952) point out that this locality is so isolated the birds may belong to a different subspecies.

2. *P. e. princeps* Boyd Alexander
ADULTS similar to *erithacus*, but general plumage darker.
10 males   wing 230–250 (241.9) mm., tail 88–100 (94.3) mm.,
                exp. cul. 34–40 (37.3) mm., tars. 26–28 (26.7) mm.
10 females wing 225–251 (234.2) mm., tail 85–100 (91.6) mm.,
                exp. cul. 32–42 (35.3) mm., tars. 25–27 (26.1) mm.
Restricted to the Islands of Principé and Fernando Poo in the Gulf of Guinea; this subspecies is probably not distinct from *erithacus* (see Amadon, 1953).

3. *P. e. timneh* Fraser
ADULTS general plumage dark grey, lighter on rump and abdomen; under tail-coverts dark grey tinged with red; tail dark maroon edged with brownish; upper mandible reddish tipped with black, lower mandible black; smaller size.
4 males   wing 206–225 (216.5) mm., tail 74–84 (80.3) mm.,
                exp. cul. 30–33 (31.3) mm., tars. 22–23 (22.8) mm.
3 females wing 203–212 (208.3) mm., tail 80–81 (80.7) mm.,
                exp. cul. 29–31 (29.7) mm., tars. 23–26 (24.3) mm.
This very distinct subspecies is confined to southern Guinea, Sierra Leone, Liberia and westernmost parts of Ivory Coast.

GENERAL NOTES   Though Grey Parrots visit savannah woodland and open country to feed, they are primarily birds of the lowland forests. In Nigeria and Cameroon they also inhabit coastal mangroves (Maclaren, 1952; Serle, 1965). They are generally common but may be locally scarce, especially around towns and villages. In southern Nigeria Marchant (1942) found them to be rather uncommon and attributed this to exploitation and destruction of the forest. They appear to be extending their range in eastern Africa (Mackworth-Praed and Grant, 1952).

Large flocks congregate at roosting sites, generally very tall trees on the edge of the forest, in a clearing in the forest, or on a small island in a river or lake, the last being a particularly favoured locality. Chapin (1939) describes a roost in a forest clearing, where up to two hundred parrots perched on a few palm trees, their weight having permanently bent the fronds. At Lake Tumba, Congo, Curry-Lindahl (1960) saw great flocks congregating at dusk to roost in the inundated forest, and at Barombi Lake, Cameroon, Serle (1965) found a roost of several hundred in a silk-cotton tree. At sunrise, even before the early morning mists have lifted, pairs and small groups leave the roosting trees for their feeding grounds. They fly high above the treetops calling loudly. Towards dusk the return journeys commence and may continue until well after nightfall. They follow regular routes. The flight is swift and direct with rapid, shallow wingbeats. These parrots are shy birds, and rarely allow a close approach.

The diet comprises seeds, nuts, fruits, and berries, mostly procured in the treetops. When feeding the parrots prefer to climb from one branch to another rather than fly. They are particularly fond of fruits of the oil palm (*Elaeis guinensis*). From west Africa come reports of them raiding maize crops, often causing considerable damage. Chapin noted that bits of quartz are occasionally found in the stomach contents and to get these the parrots must come to the ground.

CALL A medley of high-pitched screams and prolonged whistling notes; when alarmed a harsh screech.

NESTING The breeding season seems to be variable. In Uganda it is from July to September (Mackworth-Praed and Grant, 1952). In the Congo Chapin found eggs in early August. Serle (1957) says that in eastern Nigeria it is in the dry season; he obtained eggs in early January. In Liberia young birds have been seen in April (Rand, 1951). A nest described by Serle was about 30 m. from the ground in a knot hole in a huge *Terminalia* tree; three well-incubated eggs lay on a bed of decayed wood dust about 60 cm. from the entrance.

Langberg (1958) and Lister (1962) give details of successful breedings in captivity. Four and three eggs were laid and only the female brooded. In the first report the incubation period is given as thirty days while in the other it is said to have been only twenty-one days, a surprising difference. Newly-hatched chicks were closely brooded by the female, all being fed by the male. Thereafter, both parents attended to the nestlings. The young birds left the nest nearly ten weeks after hatching.

EGGS Rounded ovate, somewhat glossy; 3 eggs, 39.4 (38.7–39.7) × 31.0 (30.7–31.5) mm. [Serle, 1957].

Genus POICEPHALUS Swainson

Parrots belonging to this genus are small to medium-sized, stocky birds with short, squarish tails and proportionately robust bills. There is no bare patch on the face. The naked cere is prominent. Notable osteological features of the skull are a small post-orbital process and a straight, rather short squamosal (Thompson, 1900). Sexual dimorphism is present in some species but absent in most.

A good aid to field identification of *Poicephalus* parrots is the flight pattern; all wing movement seems to be below the body level.

CAPE PARROT
Poicephalus robustus (Gmelin)

DESCRIPTION

Length 33 cm.
ADULTS (plumage variable); head and neck greenish to yellowish-brown flecked with darker brown and dull green; lores, chin and lower cheeks blackish-brown sometimes with variable dull pink markings; reddish frontal band sometimes present in males, generally well-defined in females; feathers of back and wing-coverts black broadly margined with dark green; rump and underparts green variably suffused with dull blue and dusky grey; thighs and outer edge of wing orange-red; under wing-coverts blackish and green; tail blackish-brown; bill horn-coloured; iris brown; legs bluish-grey.
IMMATURES (Lang, 1969); no orange-red on thighs or wings; head and neck brownish-olive; sometimes marked with pink; tail dark green.

DISTRIBUTION

Southern and central Africa.

SUBSPECIES

1. *P. r. robustus* (Gmelin)   *Illustrated on page 277.*
   11 males wing 204–223 (213.1) mm., tail 81–97 (89.3) mm.,
         exp. cul. 31–37 (34.1) mm., tars. 21–25 (22.0) mm.
   6 females wing 201–218 (208.5) mm., tail 83–93 (88.3) mm.,
         exp. cul. 32–35 (33.5) mm., tars. 21–23 (22.3) mm.
   Restricted to extreme south-eastern Africa from Knysna and eastern Cape Province to Natal, western Zululand, western Swaziland and eastern Transvaal.

2. *P. r. suahelicus* Reichenow   *Illustrated on page 277.*
   MALE head and neck silvery-grey; reddish frontal band rarely present.
   FEMALE forehead and forepart of crown pinkish-red with a slight silvery wash.
   9 males wing 211–235 (221.6) mm., tail 88–96 (92.8) mm.,
         exp. cul. 40–46 (43.1) mm., tars. 22–24 (23.0) mm.
   9 females wing 210–229 (218.3) mm., tail 84–95 (89.2) mm.,
         exp. cul. 37–43 (40.3) mm., tars. 22–24 (22.6) mm.
   Distributed from Mozambique, Rhodesia, northern Lesotho (Bechuanaland) and northern regions of South-West Africa to Angola, southern Congo and central Tanzania.

3. *P. r. fuscicollis* (Kuhl)
   ADULTS similar to *suahelicus*, but green of body plumage more bluish, particularly on rump and lower back.
   3 males wing 203–213 (207.0) mm., tail 84–88 (86.3) mm.,
         exp. cul. 43–44 (43.3) mm., tars. 22–25 (23.3) mm.
   4 females wing 200–222 (207.5) mm., tail 78–88 (84.5) mm.,
         exp. cul. 39–41 (40.0) mm., tars. 22–23 (22.5) mm.
   Occurs in western Africa from Gambia and southern Senegal to northern Ghana and Togo.

GENERAL NOTES

The Cape Parrot may be locally common but is generally scarce. Skead (1964) claims that it must be an extremely rare vagrant in the Knysna forests and probably was never a permanent resident; Clancey (1965) suggests that it may be extinct in that locality. In some parts of the Transkei region, eastern South Africa, there is widespread removal of young birds from nests and trapping of adults for sale as pets, and it has been suggested that this could be contributing to the noticeable decline in numbers (in Skead, 1971). Cawkell and Moreau (1963) suspect that its numbers have declined in Gambia where it had previously been reported to be more numerous than anywhere else. Traylor (1963) reports that in Angola it is locally distributed below 1,250 m. in southern Huila, north to Quilengues and along the escarpment to Quindumbo, Benguela, and also in northern Bié, along the upper Cuango River, and in Cuanza Norte.

It is a forest bird. In eastern Cape Province, South Africa, it roosts and breeds in mountain *Podocarpus* forests above 1,000 m., wandering into coastal forests and wooded valleys to feed (Skead, 1964). When these are long-distance movements the parrots may remain in the lowland areas for days or weeks before returning to the higher altitudes. In Malawi, Benson (1940) found it in well-wooded country between 600 and 1,200 m. Presumably referring to a much earlier report from Hopkinson, Bannerman (1953) says that in Gambia it does not wander far from the river or its tributaries and keeps to the mangroves. Harvey and Harrison (1970) state that it is apparently a rare parrot in the north of Ghana, but at the Mole Game Reserve in the south they recorded it on nineteen occasions flying above riverine forest, apparently during daily feeding movements.

Skead (1964 and 1971) has given a detailed account of the habits of this species in eastern Cape Province and Natal, South Africa. It occupies regular roosting sites, invariably tall forest trees on a mountain ridge. Early in the morning, before the mists have lifted, pairs or threes and fours fly off to feeding grounds, which may be nearby at the foot of the mountain or distant remnant patches of forest in open scrubland. Some birds usually remain near the roosting trees. They fly high and call almost continuously. They lose height in a steady, descending glide or in a rapid, downward spiral. The day is spent feeding in the treetops and resting on the uppermost branches of tall, dead trees. They are extremely wary and difficult to approach. They climb among the foliage with slow, deliberate movements, using their bills to hook branches onto which they are about to step. When feeding they are silent, but there is an audible clicking from their mandibles and a steady patter of discarded fruit and husks falling to the ground. The return flights to the roosting trees commence towards dusk and may continue until after nightfall. Pairs and groups will often fly back together as loose flocks.

In Gambia, Hopkinson (1910) encountered a party of Cape Parrots in mangroves. At sunrise they commenced screeching in the treetops and then darted down to drink and bathe in a shallow part of the creek.

The flight is swift and direct with rapid, regular wing-beats. A group on the wing will make minor swerves to the right and then back to the left and so on. In flight the large bill gives the bird a top-heavy appearance.

These parrots feed on seeds, nuts, berries, fruits and nectar. Skead (1964) points out that seed-kernels are eaten, the skin and flesh being discarded. In South Africa the main food is seeds of yellow-woods (*Podocarpus falcatus* and *P. latifolius*), kaffir plum (*Harpephyllum caffrum*), wild olive (*Olea capensis*) and *Commiphora caryaofolia*; *Podocarpus* is particularly important and has a great influence on movements (Skead, 1964). Skead (1971) also notes that a favourite seasonal food is seeds of the introduced black wattle (*Acacia mollissima*), which is widespread throughout eastern Cape Province and in some districts is grown commercially. North of King William's Town, eastern Cape Province, he has seen a flock of parrots feeding on nectar from kaffirboom (*Erythrina caffra*). Hopkinson reports that in Gambia they raid harvested peanuts left in heaps to dry.

CALL A high-pitched *zzkeek* or a disyllabic *zzk-eek*; also a variety of combined notes such as *zwree-ank* or *zwree-enk* (Skead, 1964).

NESTING Dean (1971) lists two September breeding records from Natal and Zululand; one nest contained a clutch of two eggs, the other a clutch of four. Benson and Stuart Irwin (1967) list records from Zambia and Rhodesia indicating egg-laying from late March to July. Breeding has been recorded from January possibly to April or May in Malawi, in October, November and May in Rhodesia, and in December in eastern Cape Province, South Africa (Mackworth-Praed and Grant, 1962). According to Bannerman the breeding season in Gambia is March and April. In Rhodesia Vincent (1946) found a nest in May; it was about 6 m. from the ground in a hole in the trunk of a *Brachystegia* tree and about 30 cm. from the entrance three eggs were lying on bare wood in a cavity approximately 18 cm. across.

Lang (1969) gives some details of a successful breeding in captivity. The incubation period was about twenty-six days and the young birds left the nest nine to eleven weeks after hatching.

EGGS Rounded, glossy surface; 9 eggs, 35.1 (32.8–39.2) × 28.8 (26.6–30.2) mm. [McLachlan and Liversidge, 1970].

JARDINE'S PARROT
Poicephalus gulielmi (Jardine)

DESCRIPTION   Length 28 cm.
ADULTS general plumage green; forehead, crown, thighs and outer edges of wings orange-red; lores black; feathers of back and wings brownish-black broadly margined with green; rump yellowish-green; under wing-coverts blackish broadly margined with green; tail brownish-black; upper mandible horn-coloured becoming blackish towards tip, lower blackish; iris reddish-orange; legs greyish-brown.
IMMATURES (Friedmann, 1930); forehead dusky brown; crown buff-brown, the feathers narrowly tipped with greenish; narrower margins to feathers of mantle and wings; no orange-red on thighs, wings or head; underparts more bluish.

DISTRIBUTION   Central Africa.

1. *P. g. gulielmi* (Jardine)
    6 males   wing 197–214 (203.3) mm., tail 72–84 (78.0) mm.,
                 exp. cul. 34–35 (34.3) mm., tars. 21–23 (22.0) mm.
    6 females wing 194–208 (200.0) mm., tail 82–85 (83.5) mm.,
                 exp. cul. 33–35 (34.0) mm., tars. 21–23 (22.3) mm.
    Distributed from southern Cameroon and Central African Republic to northern Angola.

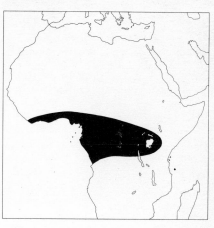

2. *P. g. fantiensis* Neumann
    ADULTS forehead and crown orange instead of orange-red; thighs and edges of wings some-times, but not always, orange; broader green margins to feathers of back and wings; smaller size.
    2 males   wing 189–191 (190.0) mm., tail 75–83 (79.0) mm.,
                 exp. cul. 31 (31.0) mm., tars. 21 (21.0) mm.
    No females examined.
    Ranges from Cameroon west to Liberia (see Hald-Mortensen, 1971).

3. *P. g. massaicus* (Fischer and Reichenow)
    ADULTS like *gulielmi*, but general plumage paler; less orange-red on forehead and crown.
    9 males   wing 201–213 (207.8) mm., tail 85–92 (88.0) mm.,
                 exp. cul. 26–31 (29.3) mm., tars. 19–22 (20.6) mm.
    10 females wing 197–207 (202.3) mm., tail 77–91 (85.1) mm.,
                 exp. cul. 26–29 (27.5) mm., tars. 19–22 (20.5) mm.
    Inhabits the highlands of southern Kenya and northern Tanzania.

4. *P. g. permistus* Neumann
    ADULTS intermediate between *gulielmi* and *massaicus*; green margins to feathers of back and wings broader than in *gulielmi*; orange-red frontal patch smaller than in *gulielmi* but larger than in *massaicus*.
    No specimens examined.
    This doubtful race is confined to the highlands of Kenya, except in the south.

Illustrated on page 280.

GENERAL NOTES

Jardine's Parrot is a forest bird and has been recorded up to about 3,500 m. It is common in eastern Africa but appears to be scarce in the west. In the Congo, Chapin (1939) found that it was not as plentiful or as conspicuous as the Grey Parrot. Brunel and Thiollay (1969) point out that it is rare in the Ivory Coast. In northern Angola it frequents only tropical forest and the tall shade trees in coffee plantations (Heinrich, 1958; Traylor, 1963), while in Kenya and Tanzania it inhabits mountain *Podocarpus* forests (Pitman, 1928).

Pairs or small parties of up to ten are usually encountered, but large flocks may build up where there is an abundance of food. Brown says that when flying to and from the feeding grounds or while feeding in treetops they are at times noisy and conspicuous (*in litt.*, 1967). However, he finds them shy and difficult to observe for any length of time; no matter how cautiously you approach the tree in which they are feeding some see you and become silent and alarmed, soon leaving and taking the others with them. The flight is fast and direct.

Meinertzhagen (1937) says that on Mt. Kenya they roosted at about 2,500 m., descending to 2,200 m. each day to feed. Pitman gives details of daily movements in the Cherangani Hills, Kenya. Just after sunrise the parrots left the forests of the hills and flew some 50 to 60 km. across *Acacia* plains to feed in forests on Mt. Elgon, returning each evening to roost. When traversing the plains they normally followed tree-lined rivers and streams.

Seeds, nuts, fruits and berries make up the diet. In eastern Africa these parrots feed mainly on wild olives and fruits of *Podocarpus* and *Cedrus*. Bates (1930) has observed them extracting seeds from *Spathodea* pods and says that they constantly revisit certain trees to feed. When feeding on wild olives they are often in the company of Rameron Pigeons (*Columba arquatrix*) and Sharpe's Starlings (*Pholia sharpii*). Cunningham-van Someren (1969) reports that in Kenya they feed on flowers and probably also on seeds of the introduced silky oak (*Grevillea robusta*). In Cameroon they are fond of oil palm nuts and soft fruits (Serle, 1954). In one stomach Chapin found pieces of a few insects.

CALL A conversational, screeching chatter in flight and while feeding; when alarmed a high-pitched screech (Brown, *in litt.*, 1967).

NESTING Little is known of the nesting habits. According to Mackworth-Praed and Grant (1952) breeding in Kenya appears to be at higher elevations, about 2,500 m., and has been recorded in June and probably also September to November. A specimen collected by Chapin in the Congo in October showed some enlargement of the gonads, and during the same month in the following year he was given a brood of four nestlings taken from a hollow in a tree. These were covered with greyish-white down and the green plumage was commencing to appear. Bowen (1932) suspects that young of the previous year remain with the parents until the following breeding season.

EGGS Undescribed.

BROWN-HEADED PARROT
Poicephalus cryptoxanthus (Peters)

DESCRIPTION

Length 22 cm.

ADULTS general plumage green, paler on underparts and lower back; paler green margins to feathers of underparts, more pronounced towards thighs and vent; rump bright yellowish-green; head and neck dusky brown becoming greenish on mantle; under wing-coverts yellow; blue on outer webs of primaries; tail olive-brown edged and tipped with green; upper mandible bluish-grey becoming darker towards tip, lower almost white; iris yellow; legs greyish-black.

IMMATURES duller; neck and upper breast suffused with yellowish-olive.

DISTRIBUTION

South-eastern Africa.

SUBSPECIES

1. *P. c. cryptoxanthus* (Peters)   *Illustrated on page 297.*
   8 males   wing 147–164 (154.6) mm., tail 60–68 (63.3) mm.,
              exp. cul. 20–22 (20.8) mm., tars. 16–18 (17.0) mm.
   8 females wing 145–152 (148.5) mm., tail 58–66 (61.9) mm.,
              exp. cul. 19–22 (19.6) mm., tars. 15–18 (16.6) mm.
   Ranges from Zululand, eastern Swaziland, eastern Transvaal, southern Mozambique and south-eastern Rhodesia north to Malawi, coastal Tanzania and coastal Kenya.

2. *P. c. tanganyikae* Bowen
   ADULTS general plumage paler; head more olive-brown; rump and underparts brighter and more yellowish.
   5 males   wing 147–152 (150.4) mm., tail 59–63 (61.0) mm.,
              exp. cul. 21–22 (21.6) mm., tars. 16–18 (17.2) mm.
   5 females wing 145–159 (149.6) mm., tail 58–65 (61.0) mm.,
              exp. cul. 20–22 (20.8) mm., tars. 15–17 (16.2) mm.
   This subspecies is restricted to the interior of Tanzania. It has been rejected by some authors, but Clancey (1964) says that it seems perfectly valid on the basis of a series from the Kilosa region, the type locality.

3. *P. c. zanzibaricus* Bowen
   ADULTS darker brown head; rump and underparts bluish-green.
   3 males   wing 152–173 (159.3) mm., tail 60–70 (64.0) mm.,
              exp. cul. 20–24 (21.3) mm., tars. 18–19 (18.3) mm.
   2 females wing 146–166 (156.0) mm., tail 64–73 (68.5) mm.,
              exp. cul. 20–23 (21.5) mm., tars. 16–19 (17.5) mm.
   Occurs on Zanzibar and Pemba Islands; doubtfully distinct from *cryptoxanthus*.

GENERAL NOTES

The Brown-headed Parrot replaces Meyer's Parrot in the south-east of Africa. It is locally common in lowlands, particularly near the coast. Vaughan (1930) reports that on Zanzibar it was far less common than on nearby Pemba Island. Clancey says that in Zululand and Mozambique it inhabits dry woodland and *Acacia* scrub, and is common in cashew nut plantations and the edges of primitive cultivation. In Malawi it is common in *Acacia* woodland below 1,000 m. (Williams, 1963). Along the coast it also frequents coconut plantations.

When in flight it is a noisy, conspicuous bird, but while feeding in the treetops is difficult to see because the green plumage blends with the foliage; even in a dead tree it sits concealed behind another branch. Pairs or small parties of up to ten are generally observed. It is rather wary and keeps to the mid and upper storeys of trees. It has been observed coming to drink about noon. The flight is very fast and direct.

These parrots feed on seeds, fruits, nuts, berries and nectar. While camping by a river in Mozambique Porter (1927) saw large numbers feeding on nectar from the huge red flowers of the 'German sausage' tree. Vaughan reports that on Zanzibar and Pemba they often feed on coconut inflorescences. In eastern Tanzania they are very fond of mkwata fruits (*Ficus*) and will attack ripening maize crops (Fuggles-Couchman, 1939). In Mozambique, Vincent (1934) found a small party persistently attacking some millet fields.

CALL In flight a harsh, sharp screech; feeding is accompanied by conversational chattering (Mackworth-Praed and Grant, 1952).

NESTING Little is known of the nesting habits. Breeding has been recorded between May and July and in September and October (Mackworth-Praed and Grant, 1952). In Malawi, at about 600 m., Benson (1942) found a nest in early June; it was in a hole in a baobab tree about 10 m. from the ground and the cheeping of young birds could be heard. In Tanzania Loveridge (1922) found three eggs in an old woodpecker's nesting hollow in a tree in late June. In early June Paget-Wilkes took two newly-hatched nestlings from a hole in a horizontal branch of a dead tree (in Prestwich, 1955); they uttered a continuous rasping alarm-note.

EGGS Slightly elliptical, glossy: a single egg in the British Museum Collection measures 27.2 × 22.9 [Schönwetter, 1964].

NIAM-NIAM PARROT

Poicephalus crassus (Sharpe)

Illustrated on page 297.

DESCRIPTION Length 25 cm.

ADULTS general plumage green, darker on back and wings; head and neck brown tinged with olive-yellow; silver-grey ear-coverts; throat and breast olive-brown; feathers of mantle brownish broadly margined with dark green; under wing-coverts green; outer webs of flight feathers bluish-green; tail olive-brown margined and tipped with green; upper mandible greyish-brown becoming black towards tip, lower yellowish-horn; iris red; legs greyish-black.

IMMATURES (BM. 1936.9.17.1); crown and nape greyish-brown strongly marked with olive-yellow; underparts paler and more yellowish than in adult; innermost secondaries edged with yellow; upper mandible yellowish tipped with dark grey, lower yellowish.

3 males   wing 164–168 (166.7) mm., tail 64–73 (68.0) mm.,
                   exp. cul. 24–25 (24.7) mm., tars. 19–20 (19.3) mm.

1 unsexed (type); wing 168 mm., tail 75 mm.,
                  exp. cul. 24 mm., tars. 18 mm.

DISTRIBUTION Central-western Africa between 4°N. and 7°N. from eastern Cameroon to Bahr el Ghazal and Equatoria Provinces, south-western Sudan.

GENERAL NOTES

The Niam-Niam Parrot is a little known bird of the forests and savannah woodlands. According to Blancou (1939) it is not rare in the upper Ouham River area, Central African Republic, near the Cameroon border. Cave and Macdonald (1955) say that it is rare in south-western Sudan, being recorded only a few times from about Yambio. There are very few reports from other parts of the range.

Near Bozoum, Central African Republic, Blancou found a number of these parrots in trees around a waterhole and in patches of forest scattered throughout the region. He concluded that they frequented mountain forests or were attracted to the mountains, where they fed and roosted in the tall trees. Elsewhere there were probably local movements. He found them in pairs or small groups. They were wary and difficult to approach. If disturbed they usually flew off calling loudly, but sometimes remained still and silent, relying on the foliage for cover. At Guedoko, about 42 km. from Bozoum, there were regular daily movements.

They feed on seeds. Stomach contents from specimens collected near Bozoum by Blancou comprised partly digested millet and pale yellow seeds.

CALL A continuous very sharp, cheeping cry, the tone of which changes when the bird is alarmed (Blancou, 1939).

NESTING Nothing is known of the breeding habits, but Blancou suspected that nesting took place during the August-September rains.

EGGS Undescribed.

SENEGAL PARROT

Poicephalus senegalus (Linné)

Illustrated on page 297.

DESCRIPTION Length 23 cm.

ADULTS general plumage green, paler and more yellowish on rump; lores, crown and nape dark grey; remainder of head paler grey, more silvery on ear-coverts; lower breast and abdomen yellow, more or less tinged with orange; under wing-coverts and under tail-coverts bright yellow; tail brownish-green; bill grey; iris yellow; legs brownish.

IMMATURES duller than adults; brownish head with dull grey ear-coverts; iris dark brown.

DISTRIBUTION Central-western Africa.

SUBSPECIES 1. *P. s. senegalus* (Linné)

      8 males   wing 151–160 (155.6) mm., tail 64–70 (66.9) mm.,
                   exp. cul. 20–26 (23.3) mm., tars. 17–21 (18.8) mm.
      6 females   wing 151–157 (154.5) mm., tail 65–70 (67.2) mm.,
                   exp. cul. 21–24 (22.5) mm., tars. 18–19 (18.3) mm.

     Distributed from Senegal and Gambia to Guinea, including the Los Islands, and southern Mali.

     2. *P. s. versteri* Finsch

      ADULTS upperparts darker green; red abdomen.

      11 males   wing 146–160 (154.9) mm., tail 54–70 (64.0) mm.,
                   exp. cul. 22–26 (23.8) mm., tars. 16–19 (17.9) mm.

3 females wing 151–155 (153.7) mm., tail 64–67 (65.0) mm.,
exp. cul. 20–23 (21.7) mm., tars. 17–18 (17.7) mm.
Ranges from Ivory Coast and Ghana east to western Nigeria.

3. *P. s. mesotypus* Reichenow
ADULTS green of upperparts and breast paler and extending further down toward abdomen;
orange abdomen.
7 males wing 148–161 (155.6) mm., tail 63–71 (66.4) mm.,
exp. cul. 24–28 (25.1) mm., tars. 17–20 (18.3) mm.
5 females wing 144–159 (149.8) mm., tail 60–69 (64.9) mm.,
exp. cul. 21–22 (21.8) mm., tars. 17–19 (17.8) mm.
Confined to eastern and north-eastern Nigeria, northern Cameroon and south-western
Chad.

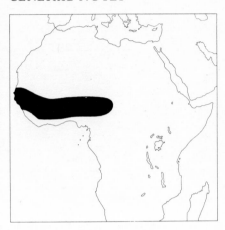

Senegal Parrots inhabit savannah woodland and open forest. In northern Nigeria they are found almost anywhere where there are tall trees, but prefer forest in which baobab (*Adansonia digitata*) or locust-bean trees (*Parkia filicoidea*) are numerous (Hutson and Bannerman, 1931). Brown says that they are frequent rather than common in most of the Nigerian savannahs; only two or three pairs are seen in a day's walking (*in litt.*, 1967). They must be very rare in south-western Chad because Salvan (1968) has never recorded them and considers a report from the Chari River to be quite extraordinary. Harvey and Harrison (1970) report that at the Mole Game Reserve, in southern Ghana, these were the most common parrots, and were observed almost every day flying over the motel during what appeared to be daily feeding movements. Descarpentries and Villiers (1969) state that in the central Ferlo region of Senegal they were very common everywhere. According to Bates (1934) there is a seasonal movement in southern Mali, the birds going south during the driest part of the year. Elsewhere, fluctuations in numbers seem to depend on food availability; in some areas flocks arrive when crops are ripening and are most conspicuous as they travel from one farm to the next searching for grain.

They are generally seen singly, in pairs or in small parties of ten to twenty. Brown says that they are shy and difficult to approach; all one generally sees is a parrot flying away screeching loudly. They are noisy, but among the branches their plumage blends well with the foliage. The direct flight with full, deliberate wingbeats is not as swift as that of other *Poicephalus* species.

These parrots feed on seeds, grain, fruits and leaf buds. They are particularly fond of figs and seeds of locust bean trees, mahogany (*Kaya senegalensis*), madobia (*Pterocarpus erinaceus*), dinya (*Vitex cienkowskii*), and shea butter trees (*Butyrospermum parkii*), and the shrub *Sclerocarya birroea* (Hutson and Bannerman 1931; Bouet 1961). In Ivory Coast they have been seen eating young buds of the *Kassia* tree (Traylor and Parelius, 1967). Near Mopti, Mali, where *Acacia albida* is a rather large tree, Bates found these parrots feeding so extensively on the green seeds that the ground underneath was littered with debris. They also raid ripening millet and maize crops and attack harvested peanuts set out to dry.

CALL A series of short screeches and rather high-pitched whistles; when alarmed these notes become harsh and raucous.

NESTING Breeding takes place towards the end of the rains, that is, from September to November. The nest is in a hollow in a tree, often a baobab, at a considerable height from the ground. A nest containing two chicks was found in November (Hutson and Bannerman, 1931); one nestling was double the size of the other and had acquired pin feathers on the head, breast and wings, the other chick was covered with grey down.

Petersen (1957) gives details of a successful breeding in captivity. The clutch comprised three eggs, each being laid at two-day intervals, but only two hatched. Incubation lasted about twenty-five days. Both parents stayed in the nest, only one at a time coming out to feed. One chick died; the other left the nest nine weeks after hatching.

EGGS A single egg in the British Museum measures 29.4 × 26.4 mm. [Harrison and Holyoak, 1970].

RED-BELLIED PARROT
Poicephalus rufiventris (Rüppell)

Length 22 cm.
MALE head, upperparts and upper breast greyish-brown, variably tinted with orange on cheeks and breast; rump yellowish-green washed with blue; lower breast, abdomen and under wing-coverts orange; thighs and vent pale green, variably tinted with yellow and orange; bill greyish-black; iris orange-red; legs grey.
FEMALE throat and under wing-coverts greyish; breast and abdomen green.
IMMATURES resemble female but males have orange under wing-coverts and orange markings on abdomen.

North-eastern Africa.

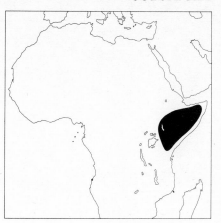

1. *P. r. rufiventris* (Rüppell)   *Illustrated on page 300.*
   11 males wing 149–156 (152.7) mm., tail 69–76 (71.6) mm.,
             exp. cul. 21–26 (24.5) mm., tars. 18–20 (18.6) mm.
   9 females wing 148–158 (152.0) mm., tail 69–76 (73.4) mm.,
             exp. cul. 22–23 (22.4) mm., tars. 17–19 (18.0) mm.
   Ranges from central Ethiopia south to the Pangani district in north-eastern Tanzania.

2. *P. r. pallidus* van Someren
   ADULTS head and upper breast paler than in *rufiventris*.
   5 males   wing 145–154 (150.6) mm., tail 68–78 (71.0) mm.,
             exp. cul. 22–24 (23.0) mm., tars. 18–19 (18.4) mm.
   5 females wing 144–153 (148.6) mm., tail 69–73 (71.6) mm.,
             exp. cul. 21–22 (21.6) mm., tars. 17–19 (18.0) mm.
   Confined to Somalia and eastern Ethiopia; probably not separable from *rufiventris* (see Berlioz and Roche, 1963).

GENERAL NOTES

The Red-bellied Parrot is a bird of the lowlands, where it frequents dry thornbush and *Acacia* scrublands, particularly those in which baobab trees are present. Brown found that in the Embu district, Kenya, it largely avoids open *Combretum* savannah and keeps to *Commiphora* thornbush country, while in Nyanza Province, also in Kenya, it is replaced by Meyer's Parrot as the common inhabitant of savannahs (*in litt.*, 1967). Thesiger and Meynell (1935) report that about Afdam and along the Mullu River in northern Ethiopia it is numerous in large flat-topped *Acacia* trees, while around Yavello in the south Benson (1945) found it to be fairly common on the arid plains up to 1,400 m. Archer and Godman (1961) claim that in Somalia it occurs at 1,000 to 1,300 m., but during the months July to September when the *Ficus* fruits are ripe it ascends to 2,000 m.

Its habits are very similar to those of the Senegal Parrot. It is observed in pairs or small groups, seldom in large flocks. It is not a conspicuous bird and is shy and difficult to approach. Archer and Godman note that it seems to be always on the move, flashing by just below tree-top level. They also report that it prefers to perch on the branch of a dead tree. The very swift flight is direct and with rapid wingbeats.

Recorded food includes seeds, fruits and maize. In Somalia it feeds on *Ficus* fruits and *Acacia* seeds (Archer and Godman, 1961).

CALL In flight a shrill screech (Mackworth-Praed and Grant, 1952).

NESTING Breeding has been recorded in October, January, March and May to July. The nest is in a hole in a tree, often at some height in a baobab, or in an arboreal or terrestrial termites' mound not more than 2 to 3 m. from the ground. Near Armaleh, Somalia, two nests were found in late January; one contained two advanced chicks and the other a fresh egg. Nothing further is known of the nesting behaviour.

EGGS Rounded; 2 eggs, 26.8 (26.6–27.0) × 23.1 (22.7–23.4) mm. [Harrison and Holyoak, 1970].

MEYER'S PARROT
Poicephalus meyeri (Cretzschmar)

DESCRIPTION Length 21 cm.
ADULTS head, upperparts and upper breast ash-brown; a variable yellow band across crown; rump and underparts bluish-green, sometimes more bluish than green; bend of wing, thighs and under wing-coverts yellow; tail brown; bill dark grey; iris orange-red; legs greyish-black.
IMMATURES general plumage greenish-brown; no yellow on crown or thighs; less yellow on bend of wing; under wing-coverts brown and green with little or no yellow; rump brighter blue; underparts green with no bluish tinge; iris dark brown.

DISTRIBUTION Central and eastern Africa.

SUBSPECIES
1. *P. m. meyeri* (Cretzschmar)   *Illustrated on page 297.*
   10 males wing 141–149 (144.5) mm., tail 56–67 (63.2) mm.,
             exp. cul. 21–25 (23.3) mm., tars. 16–19 (17.2) mm.
   8 females wing 141–149 (145.1) mm., tail 55–68 (62.5) mm.,
             exp. cul. 20–24 (21.9) mm., tars. 16–17 (16.5) mm.
   Distributed from southern Chad and north-eastern Cameroon through northern parts of Central African Republic to central and southern Sudan and western Ethiopia.

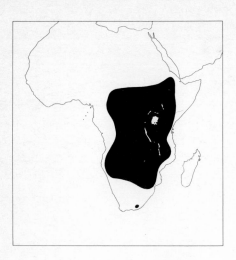

Niam-Niam Parrot *Poicephalus crassus* **1**
MNHN. CG1935,670 ad. ♂

Meyer's Parrot *Poicephalus meyeri meyeri* **2**
MNHN. CG1936,1090 ad. ♂

Brown-headed Parrot **3**
Poicephalus cryptoxanthus cryptoxanthus
AMNH. 620205 ad. ♂

Senegal Parrot *Poicephalus senegalus senegalus* **4**
RMNH. Cat. 4, Reg. 5739 ad. ♂

2. *P. m. saturatus* (Sharpe)
ADULTS darker upperparts; rump green washed with pale blue.
10 males   wing 144–158 (149.4) mm., tail 63–73 (68.6) mm.,
           exp. cul. 19–22 (20.8) mm., tars. 16–17 (16.6) mm.
10 females wing 144–156 (149.2) mm., tail 65–71 (68.1) mm.,
           exp. cul. 17–20 (18.7) mm., tars. 16–18 (16.8) mm.
Occurs in Uganda, Rwanda, Burundi, western Tanzania and the interior of Kenya. Intergrades with *matschiei* in Tanzania.

3. *P. m. matschiei* Neumann
ADULTS darker upperparts; rump bright blue; underparts suffused with blue.
10 males   wing 142–160 (152.4) mm., tail 60–71 (67.7) mm.,
           exp. cul. 20–22 (20.7) mm., tars. 16–18 (17.0) mm.
6 females wing 140–160 (150.5) mm., tail 60–71 (65.3) mm.,
           exp. cul. 18–19 (18.7) mm., tars. 16–18 (16.8) mm.
Ranges from south-eastern Kenya to northern Malawi, Zambia and south-eastern regions of the Congo.

4. *P. m. transvaalensis* Neumann
ADULTS paler brown upperparts.
10 males   wing 144–157 (151.5) mm., tail 60–75 (67.7) mm.,
           exp. cul. 19–21 (20.4) mm., tars. 17–18 (17.3) mm.
10 females wing 141–160 (151.7) mm., tail 61–73 (66.9) mm.,
           exp. cul. 18–21 (19.4) mm., tars. 16–19 (17.0) mm.
Distributed from northern Mozambique through Rhodesia and eastern Lesotho to Transvaal. An isolated population in eastern Cape Province, South Africa, probably originated from escapees (Clancey, 1965).

5. *P. m. reichenowi* Neumann
ADULTS upperparts dark brown; no yellow on crown.
8 males   wing 154–174 (160.9) mm., tail 70–75 (72.6) mm.,
           exp. cul. 20–21 (20.6) mm., tars. 16–18 (17.1) mm.
10 females wing 148–165 (154.5) mm., tail 63–76 (69.5) mm.,
           exp. cul. 17–20 (18.7) mm., tars. 16–19 (17.3) mm.
Restricted to northern and central Angola and adjacent parts of the Congo.

6. *P. m. damarensis* Neumann
ADULTS paler brown upperparts; no yellow on crown.
11 males   wing 149–160 (155.8) mm., tail 67–74 (69.6) mm.,
           exp. cul. 18–23 (20.5) mm., tars. 17–19 (17.8) mm.
8 females wing 154–158 (156.0) mm., tail 65–70 (67.5) mm.,
           exp. cul. 17–22 (18.9) mm., tars. 16–19 (17.5) mm.
Occurs in southern Angola (Da Rosa Pinto, 1968), northern and central South West Africa, and north-western Lesotho. Birds from the Okavango region, Lesotho, are intermediate between this race and *transvaalensis* (Traylor, 1965).

GENERAL NOTES   Meyer's Parrot is widely distributed and inhabits most types of timbered country, including savannah woodland, tall trees along watercourses, secondary growth about cultivation, and dry *Acacia* scrubland. In dry scrubland it shows a preference for the scattered taller trees, particularly baobabs. In Eritrea it is a riparian species closely associated with *Tamarindus* and *Adansonia* (baobab) along river valleys below 1,250 m. (Smith, 1957). It is locally common, but is often absent from apparently suitable localities (Williams, 1963). Cave and Macdonald (1955) point out that in Sudan it is more common in the south than in the north. It is quite common in southern Chad (Salvan, 1968). In south-central Transvaal it is regularly recorded at only a few localities and is sporadic elsewhere (Tarboton, 1968). Traylor (1963) reports that it is common in the woodlands of northern Angola, but does not reach the coastal plain. Williams says that it is a local resident and partial migrant; according to Jackson (1938) there are local movements in Kenya and Uganda, but Salvan says that the species is very sedentary in southern Chad, and Ruwet (1964) reports that it is common throughout the year on the Lufira plains, Congo.

Pairs or small flocks are generally seen, but large numbers may congregate where food is plentiful. In Zambia, White (1945) reported large flocks raiding maize crops in December and January; each evening the return flight was along a regular route across the bottom of his garden. They roost in holes in trees (Prozesky, 1970). They are seldom found far from water. They are shy and when disturbed in a tree dive steeply out of it on the opposite side before flying off. The flight is swift and direct, and the birds usually travel low near the ground.

Seeds, nuts, berries and fruits make up the diet. Grain crops are sometimes attacked.

CALL   A high-pitched *chee-chee-chee*; also a disyllabic clinking call, one note higher than the other (McLachlan and Liversidge, 1970).

NESTING   Breeding has been recorded in all months between June and December, but it is generally earlier in the south than in the north. Traylor (1963) reports that a young bird about to leave the

nest was taken at Chitau, Angola, in late August. The nest is in a hole in a tree, often in an old nesting hole of a wood-pecker or barbet. Two to four eggs are laid on a layer of decayed wood dust.

Greenway (1967) gives some details of a successful breeding in captivity. Three eggs were laid and two hatched after approximately thirty days incubation. Only one chick was reared and it left the nest eight weeks after hatching.

A hand-reared nestling, acquired when it was about ten days old, flew free, but returned each evening to roost in a house. It was accompanied by a wild bird, presumably of the opposite sex, which did not enter the house. When the tame bird was fifteen months old it had only a few yellow feathers on the crown (Brown, *in litt.*, 1967).

EGGS Glossy, slightly ovate; 12 eggs, 25.4 (24.7–27.8) × 20.0 (19.3–21.0) mm. [McLachlan and Liversidge, 1970].

RÜPPELL'S PARROT
Poicephalus rueppellii (G. R. Gray)   *Illustrated on page 300.*

Illustrated on page 300.

DESCRIPTION

Length 22 cm.
MALE general plumage dusky earth-brown; silver-grey ear-coverts; rump and under tail-coverts slightly washed with blue; under wing-coverts and edges of wings yellow; thighs yellow, variably tinged with orange; bill greyish-black; iris orange-red; legs brownish-grey.
FEMALE lower back, rump and upper tail-coverts bright blue; vent and lower abdomen dull blue.
IMMATURES similar to female but brighter blue on rump and paler on lower abdomen; edges of wings yellow-brown; wing-coverts edged with yellowish-white; duller under wing-coverts.
10 males   wing 146–157 (147.8) mm., tail 71–77 (73.3) mm.,
        exp. cul. 21–25 (22.6) mm., tars. 17–19 (18.0) mm.
10 females wing 138–156 (145.3) mm., tail 62–75 (69.5) mm.,
        exp. cul. 20–22 (21.1) mm., tars. 17–19 (17.7) mm.

DISTRIBUTION

South-western Africa from southern Angola south to about Otjimbingwe, South West Africa.

GENERAL NOTES

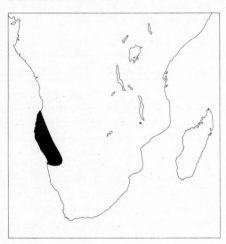

Along the upper reaches of the Huab River, South West Africa, Macdonald (1957) found Rüppell's Parrot in tall trees bordering the dry river bed. In Angola it is found below 1,250 m. in dry woodland, most commonly along streams, and ranges north to southern and western Huila and up the coastal plain to Luanda (Traylor, 1963). In southern Angola, Heinrich (1958) also recorded it in dry forest where *Euphorbia* was prevalent. Meyer de Schauensee (1933) remarks that in Damaraland it was plentiful wherever there were large trees.

It is a local and inconspicuous bird, usually found in small flocks in the tops of tall trees. It is shy and difficult to observe, generally being detected by the call. When disturbed it immediately adopts an upright stance and calls loudly before flying off. The flight is swift and direct.

Food comprises insect larvae, berries, young shoots and seeds, including those of melons. McLachlan and Liversidge (1970) state that buds and pods of acacias are also eaten.

CALL A sharp *quaw*; when alarmed a continuous, shrill screech increasing in pitch and volume (Mackworth-Praed and Grant, 1962).

NESTING Breeding has been recorded in February. Of the very few nests found most have been in old woodpeckers' holes in acacias about 5 m. from the ground. According to Mackworth-Praed and Grant three eggs are laid.

Woolridge (1969) gives some information on the breeding of a *P. meyeri* × *P. rueppellii* hybrid in captivity. Three eggs were laid and only the hen Rüppell's Parrot incubated. The incubation period was not determined, but the one chick hatched was fed by both parents and left the nest about four months after the first egg was laid.

EGGS Rounded; average measurements of three eggs have been recorded as 27.3 × 24.0 mm. [see Schönwetter, 1964].

YELLOW-FACED PARROT
Poicephalus flavifrons (Rüppell)

DESCRIPTION

Length 28 cm.
ADULTS general plumage green, paler and brighter on rump, back and lower underparts; forehead, crown and upper cheeks yellow; thighs and edges of wings sometimes marked with yellow;

upper mandible brownish-grey, lower almost white; iris orange-red; legs dark brownish-grey. IMMATURES (Friedmann, 1930); crown and upper cheeks dull yellowish olive-green.

Ethiopia.

1. *P. f. flavifrons* (Rüppell)   *Illustrated on page 280.*
    10 males   wing 166–180 (173.3) mm., tail 71–92 (75.2) mm.,
                  exp. cul. 24–27 (25.4) mm., tars. 18–20 (18.9) mm.
    8 females wing 161–173 (167.9) mm., tail 72–82 (76.5) mm.,
                  exp. cul. 22–25 (23.5) mm., tars. 18–20 (18.9) mm.
    Occurs in northern and central Ethiopia as far west as the Gurafarda Mountains.

2. *P. f. aurantiiceps* Neumann
    ADULTS forehead, crown and upper cheeks orange.
    4 males   wing 163–175 (169.5) mm., tail 74–82 (78.5) mm.,
                  exp. cul. 25–26 (25.5) mm., tars. 18–20 (18.8) mm.
    2 females wing 160–170 (165.0) mm., tail 78–84 (81.0) mm.,
                  exp. cul. 22–24 (23.0) mm., tars. 19–20 (19.5) mm.
    Known only from the Masango area and the Gila River, south-western Ethiopia; doubtfully distinct from *flavifrons*.

According to Urban (1966) the Yellow-faced Parrot is a bird of the highland *Hagenia* forests. Brown says that it occurs quite commonly in the cedar-podocarp forests of Bale and Arussi Provinces (*in litt.*, 1967). Neumann gives its altitudinal range as from 1,000 to 3,000 m. (in Friedmann, 1930).

These parrots are usually seen in small flocks of from fifteen to twenty, often in the company of Black-winged Lovebirds (*Agapornis taranta*). They spend much of the time noisily feeding in the treetops. If approached too closely they suddenly become very quiet and then fly off screeching loudly. Each night they return to the same roosting trees. They have a fast, rushing flight. Their food comprises seeds, grain and fruits.

CALL A shrill, unmusical whistle (Mackworth-Praed and Grant, 1952).

NESTING Nothing is known of the breeding behaviour, but Brown suspects that the nest is in a hole in a tree and the breeding range is up to 3,000 m. (*in litt.*, 1967).

EGGS Undescribed.

Genus AGAPORNIS Selby

Because of their conspicuous indulgence in mutual preening the parrots in this genus are known as lovebirds. Being extremely popular as cage birds they are now familiar throughout the world. They are small, stocky parrots with very short, rounded tails. Most species have proportionately large bills. The most notable osteological features of the cranium are the very narrow auditory meatus and the extremely small post-frontal process (Thompson, 1900).

The lovebirds are an interesting assemblage of closely related and almost totally allopatric forms, which hybridize readily in captivity. There are two well-differentiated groups, one intermediate species—*roseicollis*—and one little known, aberrant species—*swinderniana*. The *cana-pullaria-taranta* group is regarded by Moreau (1948) and Dilger (1960) as the more 'primitive' group. In this group there are no naked, periophthalmic rings (though in *pullaria* and *taranta* there are feathered rings) and sexual dimorphism is present. Females in this group carry very small pieces of nesting material, many at a time, thrust amidst the feathers of the entire body. In the *fischeri-personata-lilianae-nigrigenis* group there are prominent naked periophthalmic rings and no sexual dimorphism. Females in this group carry large pieces of nesting material in their bills. In *roseicollis* there is no periophthalmic ring, sexual dimorphism is absent, and females carry variably-sized pieces of nesting material tucked under the feathers of the rump and lower back. In *swinderniana* there is an inconspicuous feathered periophthalmic ring and sexual dimorphism is absent; nothing is known of the nesting habits.

1 Red-bellied Parrot
   Poicephalus rufiventris rufiventris
   USNM. 243695 ad. ♂

2 Red-bellied Parrot
   Poicephalus rufiventris rufiventris
   USNM. 243680 ad. ♀

3 Ruppell's Parrot *Poicephalus rueppellii*
   ANSP. 93502 ad. ♀

4 Ruppell's Parrot *Poicephalus rueppellii*
   ANSP. 93505 ad. ♂

GREY-HEADED LOVEBIRD
Agapornis cana (Gmelin)

Length 14 cm.
MALE general plumage green, brighter on rump and more yellowish on underparts; head, neck and breast light grey; under wing-coverts black; tail green, lateral feathers marked with yellow and subterminally barred with black; bill pale grey; iris dark brown; legs grey.

FEMALE head, neck and breast green; green under wing-coverts.

IMMATURES (Düger, 1960); resemble adults, but males have greenish wash on nape (some males said to have green heads and breasts): bill yellowish marked with black on base of upper mandible.

DISTRIBUTION Madagascar; introduced to Rodriguez, Mauritius, Comoro Islands, Seychelles, Zanzibar and Mafia Islands, and possibly to Natal.

SUBSPECIES 1. *A. c. cana* (Gmelin) *Illustrated on page 301.*

10 males   wing 91–101 (95.6) mm., tail 41–50 (46.9) mm.,
        exp. cul. 11–12 (11.6) mm., tars. 13–14 (13.3) mm.
10 females wing 88–95 (91.8) mm., tail 41–48 (45.1) mm.,
        exp. cul. 11–12 (11.3) mm., tars. 12–14 (13.2) mm.

Occurs in Madagascar, except the central plateau and the south-western arid zone; introduced to Mascarene Islands, Comoro Islands, Mahé in the Seychelles, and Zanzibar and Mafia Islands. According to Clancey (1964) there was possibly an unsuccessful attempt to introduce this subspecies to Natal in the late 1890s.

2. *A. c. ablectanea* Bangs.

ADULTS general plumage darker bluish-green with noticeably less yellow; head and breast of male purer grey with a violet tinge.

7 males   wing 93–101 (96.3) mm., tail 44–51 (46.9) mm.,
        exp. cul. 11–12 (11.6) mm., tars. 13–14 (13.6) mm.
6 females wing 90–95 (93.2) mm., tail 43–54 (47.5) mm.,
        exp. cul. 11–12 (11.3) mm., tars. 13–14 (13.3) mm.

Confined to the south-western arid zone of Madagascar, intergrading with *cana* about Bekopata and Ankavandra (Moreau, 1948).

GENERAL NOTES In Madagascar, Rand (1936) found Grey-headed Lovebirds on the coastal plain and inland mountain slopes below 1,000 m. They were common and frequented brush and open ground on the edge of the forest, following clearings into the forest on the mountain slopes. In the arid south-west they were locally distributed in open desert brush, being more common about grassy areas in the vicinity of trees. Benson (1960) reports that on the Comoro Islands they were fairly common in open country, particularly around cultivation, but were never seen in or near evergreen forest. Elsewhere introductions of the species have not been successful; it has apparently disappeared altogether from Mauritius, Zanzibar and Mafia, and is present in only small numbers on Rodriguez and Réunion (Gill, 1967). Gaymer et al., (1969) point out that it was introduced to Mahé, in the Seychelles, in 1906 and was once common there, but the initial success was not maintained and it is now found in small numbers only near the south-western coast of the island.

These lovebirds are generally seen in small groups of from five to twenty, but large flocks of fifty and eighty have been reported. Sometimes in the company of *Foudia* and *Lonchura* finches, they spend much of the time on the ground feeding on grass seeds. They are rather shy and when disturbed fly some distance away. They have a swift, twisting flight. Rand noticed that they often perched on the tops of trees along the edge of the forest as well as in bushes and on telegraph wires.

They feed mainly on grass seeds procured on the ground. Along the trails they pick up spilled grain and around villages raid rice spread out to dry (Rand, 1936).

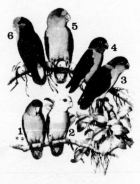

Grey-headed Lovebird *Agapornis cana cana* **1**
AM. A4270 ad. ♀

Grey-headed Lovebird *Agapornis cana cana* **2**
AM. 030557 ad. ♂

Black-collared Lovebird **3**
Agapornis swinderniana swinderniana
RMNH. Cat. 8, Reg. 9701 ad. ♂

Black-collared Lovebird **4**
Agapornis swinderniana zenkeri
AMNH. 468738 ad. ♂

Black-winged Lovebird *Agapornis taranta* **5**
RMNH. Cat. 5, Reg. 5747 ad. ♂

Red-faced Lovebird *Agapornis pullaria pullaria* **6**
AM. 034074 ad. ♂

CALL A sharp, metallic note; when alarmed a series of high-pitched notes.

NESTING Little is known of nesting in the wild state. Benson suspects that on the Comoro Islands the lovebirds breed during the rains, that is between November and April. In north-eastern Madagascar, Rand watched courtship feeding involving four males and a female sitting at the entrance to a large hollow in a tree.

Dilger (1960) gives details of nesting in captivity. The bottom of the nest-box is lined with small pieces of bark, grass, leaves, or seed husks carried by the female tucked amidst her body feathers. In a slight depression in this lining three to six, usually three or four, eggs are laid. The eggs are laid every other day and incubation, which lasts twenty-three days, commences with the laying of either the first or second egg. Only the female broods, though the male may sit in the nest with her. Both parents feed the chicks. The young leave the nest forty-three days after hatching. Young males acquire full adult plumage with completion of the post-juvenal moult, that is at about four months.

EGGS Rounded; 10 eggs, 19.2 (18.0–21.2) × 16.0 (14.1–16.5) mm. [Schönwetter, 1964].

RED-FACED LOVEBIRD
Agapornis pullaria (Linné)

DESCRIPTION Length 15 cm.

MALE general plumage green, more yellowish on underparts; forehead and facial area orange-red;

rump bright blue; under wing-coverts black; tail green, lateral feathers marked with red and yellow and subterminally barred with black; bill coral-red; iris dark brown; legs grey.
FEMALE forehead and facial area more orange than red; green under wing-coverts.
IMMATURES forehead and facial area yellow; under wing-coverts black in males, green in females; bill reddish-brown lightly marked with black near base of upper mandible.

Illustrated on page 301.

DISTRIBUTION

Central and central-western Africa; extinct on Principé and Fernando Poo Islands in the Gulf of Guinea (Amadon, 1953; Amadon and Basilio, 1957).

SUBSPECIES

1. *A. p. pullaria* (Linné)
   8 males   wing 84–92 (88.4) mm., tail 36–41 (37.9) mm.,
              exp. cul. 13–14 (13.9) mm., tars. 12–14 (12.9) mm.
   8 females wing 86–98 (89.0) mm., tail 35–39 (36.0) mm.,
              exp. cul. 13–14 (13.1) mm., tars. 12–14 (12.8) mm.
   Occurs in western Africa from northern Angola north to Guinea, and central Africa east to South-western Sudan and Lake Albert on the Congo-Uganda border; also on Sao Tomé and formerly Principé and Fernando Poo, Gulf of Guinea.

2. *A. p. ugandae* Neumann
   ADULTS rump paler blue than in *pullaria*.
   11 males   wing 87–95 (91.1) mm., tail 34–41 (37.6) mm.,
              exp. cul. 13–14 (13.8) mm., tars. 12–13 (12.6) mm.
   8 females wing 88–92 (90.5) mm., tail 37–40 (38.3) mm.,
              exp. cul. 13–14 (13.3) mm., tars. 12–13 (12.4) mm.
   Distributed from south-western Ethiopia and south-eastern Sudan south to the Kigoma region, Tanzania.

GENERAL NOTES

Red-faced Lovebirds are lowland birds probably restricted to below 1,400 m. (Moreau, 1948). They frequent secondary forest, savannah woodland and lightly timbered grasslands, particularly in the vicinity of cultivation; they penetrate primary forest only where there are accessible grass-covered clearings. In Cabinda and northern Angola they are rare and inhabit open grasslands near gallery forest (Traylor, 1963). Irving Gass (1954) points out that they still occur in coastal Ghana, though his records indicate that they are not common about Accra. They are very scarce around Lagos, Nigeria (Sander, 1956). Brown found them to be uncommon in the savannahs of Ilorin and Kabba districts, Nigeria, but plentiful on the Niger flood plain in the Benin district, where savannah and forest are mixed (*in litt.*, 1967). According to Cave and Macdonald (1955) they are common in the south-western Sudan. In Uganda they are resident, but there are local movements governed by food supply (Jackson, 1938).

Although large flocks may congregate to raid ripening crops, pairs or small groups of from fifteen to twenty are the normal social units. During the day they wander far and wide searching for food and toward evening return to their favourite roosting trees. Dilger (1960) points out that in captivity this species typically sleeps hanging upside down as do the hanging parrots (*Loriculus*). Much of the time is spent on or near the ground feeding on grass seeds. They are often seen clinging to the seeding heads of grasses or cereal plants, frequently hanging upside down to get at the seeds. They are shy and difficult to approach (Marchant, 1942). The direct flight is very swift.

These parrots feed on seeds, fruits, berries and leaf buds. They are troublesome in crop-growing districts, attacking both green and ripening grain. Chapin (1939) reported that they sometimes attack guavas. Figs are also eaten.

CALL In flight or when perched a twittering *si-si-si-si* (Mackworth-Praed and Grant, 1952).

NESTING In Uganda and Tanzania breeding has been recorded during May to July (Mackworth-Praed and Grant, 1952), and at Mugera, Uganda, a male with slightly enlarged testes was collected in February (Friedmann and Williams, 1969). In Nigeria Serle (1957) found a nest containing four well-fledged young in early October. In the Congo Chapin was given a brood of five taken from a nest in October. The nest is in a hole excavated in an arboreal, or rarely a terrestrial, termitarium. Serle describes a nest; it was in a spherical chamber at the end of a tunnel leading from a rounded entrance hole.

Dilger summarizes published details of breeding in captivity. It seems that only the female excavates the nesting chamber; the male is often eager to assist but inefficiency renders his efforts useless. The bottom of the chamber is generally lined with seed husks or small pieces of bark, grass, or leaves carried by the female amidst her body feathers. The general nesting behaviour is similar to that of the Grey-headed Lovebird. Incubation lasts twenty-two days and the young leave the nest about forty-two days after hatching (Nielsen, 1964). Adult plumage is acquired on completion of the post-juvenal moult, that is at about four months.

Fischer's Lovebird *Agapornis fischeri* 1·
RMNH. Cat. 9, Reg. 6488 ad. ♂

Nyasa Lovebird *Agapornis lilianae* 2
RMNH. Cat. 1, Reg. 6130 ad. ♂

Peach-faced Lovebird 3
Agapornis roseicollis roseicollis
JMF. 12 ad. ♂

Black-cheeked Lovebird *Agapornis nigrigenis* 4
AM. 032845 ad. ♂

Masked Lovebird *Agapornis personata* 5
AM. 034877 ad. ♀

EGGS Rounded; 15 eggs, 21.4 (20.0–22.4) × 16.8 (16.0–18.0) mm. [Schönwetter, 1964].

303

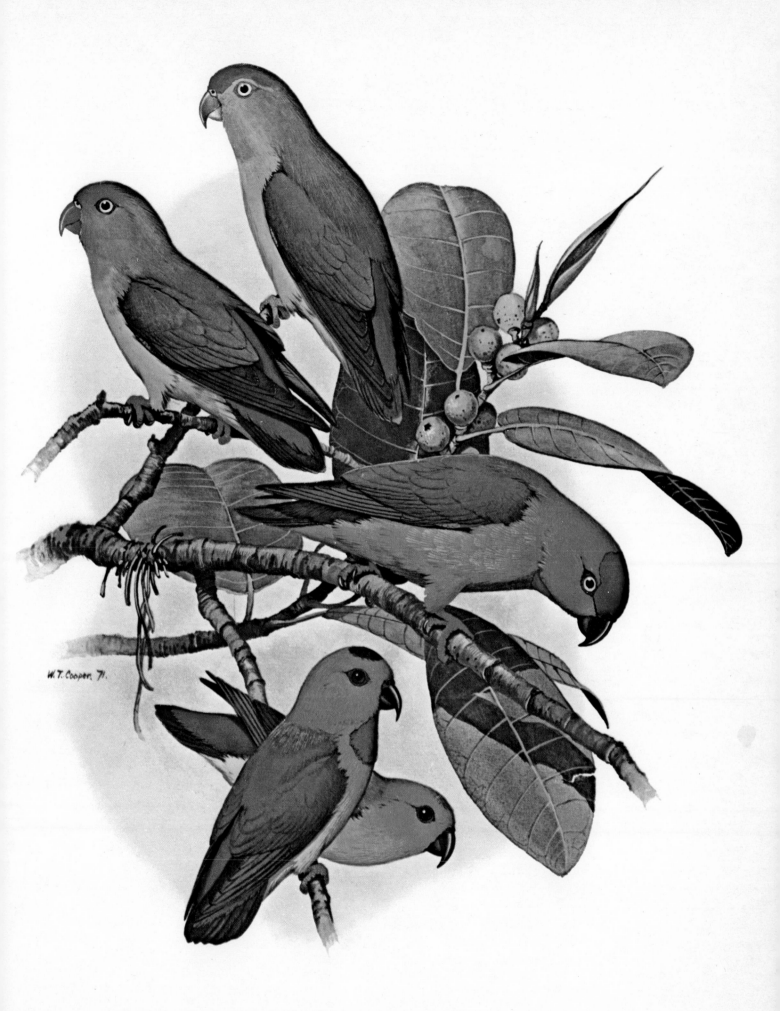

BLACK-WINGED LOVEBIRD
Agapornis taranta (Stanley)

Illustrated on page 301.

Length 16.5 cm.

MALE general plumage green, slightly more yellowish on underparts; forehead, lores and periophthalmic ring red; black flight feathers; under wing-coverts black; tail green, lateral feathers marked with yellow and subterminally barred with black; bill coral-red; iris dark brown; legs grey.

FEMALE forehead, lores and periophthalmic ring green; under wing-coverts green, sometimes with black markings.

IMMATURES resemble female, but males have black under wing-coverts; bill dusky yellow basally marked with black.

10 males   wing 97–106 (101.5) mm., tail 41–53 (46.6) mm.,
        exp. cul. 17–18 (17.8) mm., tars. 14–15 (14.7) mm.
10 females wing 95–105 (101.5) mm., tail 43–48 (45.5) mm.,
        exp. cul. 16–18 (17.1) mm., tars. 14–15 (14.2) mm.

DISTRIBUTION   Highlands of Ethiopia.

GENERAL NOTES   Like the Yellow-faced Parrot (*Poicephalus flavifrons*) the Black-winged Lovebird is essentially a bird of the highland forests of the Ethiopian Plateau between 1,300 and 3,200 m. However, it does descend to lower altitudes to feed on figs (Urban, 1966). It inhabits juniper, podocarp, *Hagenia* and *Hypericum* forests, but may also be seen in acacias and euphorbias (Urban, *in litt.*, 1967). Benson (1945) noted that it was found associated with the edge of evergreen forest. In Eritrea, Smith (1957) recorded it in junipers on the plateau and in *Combretum* and *Euphorbia* woodlands on the central mountains and escarpments up to 1,600 m. It is common wherever suitable habitat exists.

Brown says that he has always found these lovebirds in small flocks of less than twenty, often less than ten, but several flocks may aggregate to feed in one tree, for example a fruit-laden fig tree (*in litt.*, 1967). They appear to roost in hollows (possibly old nesting holes of woodpeckers or barbets) in dead limbs. The holes are used for roosting throughout the year and are occupied by small groups perennially. The birds leave their roosting holes soon after dawn and fly to feeding grounds. About an hour before dark they return to roost.

They feed on seeds, berries and fruits. A favourite food is fruits of the sycamore fig (*Ficus sycamorus*). Smith reports that they also eat juniper berries.

Ceylon Hanging Parrot *Loriculus beryllinus* 1
AMNH. 622366 ad. ♂

Vernal Hanging Parrot *Loriculus vernalis* 2
USNM. 449954 ad. ♂

Celebes Hanging Parrot 3
Loriculus stigmatus stigmatus
RMNH. Cat. 39 ad. ♂

Blue-crowned Hanging Parrot 4
Loriculus galgulus galgulus
AM. 030553 ad. ♂

Blue-crowned Hanging Parrot 5
Loriculus galgulus galgulus
RMNH. Cat. 34 ad. ♀

CALL In flight a high-pitched *kseek* (Brown, *in litt.*, 1967); also a shrill twittering call (Mackworth-Praed and Grant, 1952).

NESTING In early October Benson collected a female almost ready to lay. At Dangila a nest containing young was found in late October (Cheesman and Sclater, 1935). Brown has seen a pair inspecting a hollow limb in November, and in March has watched a pair feeding a young bird. These observations suggest that the species has a protracted breeding season, and this is confirmed by Stresemann and Stresemann (1966) who examined a series of twelve specimens from Maracò district and found that commencement of wing moult was present in birds collected as early as mid-January and as late as July. The nest is in a hollow limb or hole in a tree, the bottom of which is lined with small pieces of twigs, grass or leaves carried by the female amidst her body feathers. The general nesting behaviour is similar to that of the Grey-headed Lovebird.

In captivity incubation lasts twenty-five days and the young leave the nest about fifty days after hatching (Dilger, 1960). Males acquire adult plumage with the first complete moult when about four months old.

EGGS Rounded; 6 eggs, 24.3 (23.7–25.0) × 18.9 (18.6–19.0) mm. [Schönwetter, 1964].

BLACK-COLLARED LOVEBIRD
Agapornis swinderniana (Kuhl)

DESCRIPTION   Length 13 cm.

ADULTS general plumage green, slightly duller and paler on head and underparts; narrow black collar around nape; below collar the entire neck is yellow, sometimes with an olive tinge; rump and lower back deep mauve-blue; outer webs of flight feathers black; green under wing-coverts; tail green, lateral feathers strongly marked with orange and subterminally barred with black; bill greyish-black; iris yellow; legs dusky greenish-yellow.

IMMATURES black nuchal collar absent or represented by a few black feathers on each side of neck; bill pale grey basally marked with black; iris brown.

DISTRIBUTION   West and central Africa.

SUBSPECIES   1. *A. s. swinderniana* (Kuhl)   *Illustrated on page 301.*
    6 males wing 90–94 (91.7) mm., tail 32–36 (34.3) mm.,
        exp. cul. 13–14 (13.3) mm., tars. 11–13 (12.0) mm.
    1 female wing 88 mm., tail 33 mm.,
        exp. cul. 13 mm., tars. 11 mm.
    Known only from the forests of Liberia.

    2. *A. s. zenkeri* Reichenow.   *Illustrated on page 301.*
    ADULTS below black nuchal collar the entire neck is reddish-brown extending as a suffusion on to the breast.
    7 males wing 92–97 (94.7) mm., tail 31–35 (33.3) mm.,
        exp. cul. 14 (14.0) mm., tars. 12–14 (12.6) mm.
    1 female wing 89 mm., tail 32 mm.,
        exp. cul. 12 mm., tars. 12 mm.
    Distributed from Cameroon and Gabon east to western regions of the Central African Republic and the Congo.

    3. *A. s. emini* Neumann.
    ADULTS less extensive reddish-brown markings on neck and breast; bill more strongly curved; there may be a difference in the primary/secondary length ratio (see Parkes, 1960).
    11 males wing 92–100 (95.0) mm., tail 30–36 (32.2) mm.,
        exp. cul. 13–15 (13.8) mm., tars. 12–13 (12.5) mm.
    10 females wing 90–98 (93.5) mm., tail 30–35 (32.6) mm.,
        exp. cul. 13–15 (13.3) mm., tars. 12–13 (12.3) mm.
    Occurs in central Congo east to far western Uganda; may be isolated from *zenkeri* as there are no records from the Mayombe or Kasai districts (see Chapin, 1939).

Black-collared Lovebirds are little-known inhabitants of lowland evergreen forests. In far western Uganda they regularly ascend the mountains to about 1,800 m. to feed (Cunningham-van Someren, 1948). Parkes notes that they have probably not been collected in Liberia for more than fifty years, and there seems to be only one record from Gabon, two birds having been collected near Lastoursville in April 1958 (Berlioz, 1959). In the east these lovebirds may not be as rare as is generally claimed; in the Ituri forest near the Congo-Uganda border Curry-Lindahl (1960) found that they were fairly common, but, because of their arboreal habits, would have been overlooked were it not for the call-notes.

Small flocks of from fifteen to twenty may be seen flying above the forest canopy. They feed in the treetops, rarely coming near the ground, and their plumage blends extremely well with the foliage. Sometimes they visit fig trees near villages or in secondary forest, but generally they feed in the strangling figs growing upon large trees, often at the edges of clearings (Chapin, 1939). The flight is swift and direct.

They feed almost exclusively on figs. Williams (1963) says that they also visit farmlands to feed on grain, especially millet. In the Congo, Father Hutsebout was able to keep them alive in captivity only if wild figs were provided; they would not accept substitute foods and if deprived of figs would die within three or four days (in Bouet, 1961). Crop and stomach contents examined by Chapin comprised *Ficus* seeds, pieces of insects, a caterpillar and some white insect larvae. In far western Uganda, Cunningham-van Someren observed many birds feeding on *Ficus* fruits, but crops from two specimens contained also green 'milky' maize.

CALL   Relatively subdued twittering notes; shriller calls in flight (Williams, 1967).

NESTING   Chapin suspected that in the vicinity of Medje, Congo, the breeding season was about July. Males coming into breeding condition were collected in western Uganda in July by Cunningham-van Someren. Bouet suggests that the nest is in an arboreal termitarium. Nothing further is known of the nesting habits.

EGGS   Undescribed.

Philippine Hanging Parrot 1
Loriculus philippensis chrysonotus
USNM. 314910 ad. ♂

Philippine Hanging Parrot 2
Loriculus philippensis philippensis
USNM. 201837 ad.♂

Philippine Hanging Parrot 3
Loriculus philippensis philippensis
AMNH. 459206 ad. ♀

Philippine Hanging Parrot 4
Loriculus philippensis bonapartei
RMNH. Cat. 1 ad. ♂

Philippine Hanging Parrot 5
Loriculus philippensis siquijorensis
USNM. 210956 ad. ♂

PEACH-FACED LOVEBIRD
Agapornis roseicollis (Vieillot)

DESCRIPTION   Length 15 cm.
ADULTS general plumage green, decidedly more yellowish on underparts; forehead and behind eyes red; lores, cheeks, throat and upper breast rose-pink; rump bright blue; under wing-coverts green tinged with blue; tail green above, bluish below, lateral feathers marked with orange and basally and subterminally barred with black; bill horn-coloured tinged with green, especially along cutting edges and on lower mandible; iris dark brown; legs grey.
IMMATURES forehead tawny-green tinged with rose-pink; frontal area very pale rose-pink suffused with greyish-blue; bill strongly marked with black on base of upper mandible.

DISTRIBUTION   South-western Africa.

W.T. Cooper, '71.

1. *A. r. roseicollis* (Vieillot)   Illustrated on page 304.

   8 males   wing 102–108 (105.1) mm., tail 44–50 (46.8) mm.,
       exp. cul. 17–18 (17.5) mm., tars. 15–17 (16.0) mm.
   8 females wing 98–110 (103.5) mm., tail 44–48 (46.3) mm.,
       exp. cul. 17–19 (17.6) mm., tars. 14–16 (15.1) mm.

     Occurs in South-West Africa south to the Orange River and in northern Cape Province, and inland to Lake Ngami, Lesotho.

2. *A. r. catumbella* Hall

   ADULTS general plumage brighter; slightly deeper red on forehead; pink of cheeks and throat more heavily suffused with red.
   4 males   wing 99–105 (102.0) mm., tail 46–47 (46.7) mm.,
       exp. cul. 17–18 (17.5) mm., tars. 15 (15.0) mm.
   4 females wing 99–102 (100.3) mm., tail 43–46 (44.8) mm.,
       exp. cul. 17–18 (17.5) mm., tars. 14–16 (15.0) mm.

     Known with certainty only from the type locality, Benguella district in southern Angola, but birds from elsewhere in southern Angola probably belong to this race.

According to Moreau (1948) Peach-faced Lovebirds are found in dry country from sea level up to more than 1,600 m. Traylor (1963) says that in Angola they range throughout southern and western Huila north to Sá de Bandeira, and up the arid coastal plain north to Novo Redondo; they are found in open country, but never far from water. Bowen (1932) found them in a palm grove a few miles north of Lobite, southern Angola. Along the Guab River, South-West Africa, Macdonald (1957) found them to be fairly common; small flocks were frequently seen going to and from an open water storage tank at the side of the dry river bed.

   These parrots are noisy, gregarious birds and are plentiful in most parts of their range. They prefer dry, mountainous or open country, but are very dependent on water, which may be located by watching evening flights of the birds to their drinking pools.

   In flight they twist in and out through the trees with remarkable speed and dexterity; one catches glimpses of their reddish foreparts as they approach and their blue rumps as they fly away. They are usually seen in small flocks, but at certain times of the year, when maize is ripening or there is an abundance of favoured seeds, flocks of many hundreds may be seen.

   They feed on seeds and berries. Mackworth-Praed and Grant (1962) claim that they are pests in some grain-growing areas.

CALL A shrill, metallic *shreek* repeated several times in quick succession; when alarmed the repetition becomes more rapid (McLachlan and Liversidge, 1970).

NESTING Breeding has been recorded in February and March, and the birds nest colonially. Nests are in crevices in cliffs or buildings, or more commonly in communal nests of weavers. Each of these communal nests contains many breeding chambers, some of which are taken over by the parrots, the remainder being used by the weavers. At Sindi, South-West Africa, in early December Niven observed parrots taking possession of nest-chambers and denying entrance to the rightful owners (in Winterbottom, 1969). In most areas nests of the Social Weaver (*Philetairus socius*) are used, but where this species does not occur nests of the Stripe-breasted Sparrow-weaver (*Plocepasser mahali*) are used. Hoesch (1940) points out that there are structural similarities in the nests of these two species. The parrots do not add new nesting material to these nests, but in crevices in cliffs do construct rather elaborate cup-shaped nests.

   Dilger (1960) gives details of breeding in captivity. In the nest-box a cup-shaped nest is built from long strips of bark, leaves, or grass carried by the female tucked under her rump feathers. The general nesting behaviour resembles that of the Grey-headed Lovebird. Incubation lasts twenty-three days and the young leave the nest forty-three days after hatching. Adult plumage is acquired at about four months of age.

EGGS Rounded; 25 eggs, 23.8 (21.0–26.3) × 17.6 (16.8–19.0) mm. [Schönwetter, 1964].

Moluccan Hanging Parrot **1**
Loriculus amabilis amabilis
AMNH. 303098 ad. ♂

Moluccan Hanging Parrot **2**
Loriculus amabilis sclateri
AMNH. 622465 ad. ♂

Orange-fronted Hanging Parrot **3**
Loriculus aurantiifrons meeki
CSIRO. 8599 ad. ♂

Orange-fronted Hanging Parrot **4**
Loriculus aurantiifrons tener
AMNH. 622552 ad. ♂

Green Hanging Parrot *Loriculus exilis* **5**
NHM. 50247 ad. ♂

Wallace's Hanging Parrot *Loriculus flosculus* **6**
BM. 1873.5.12.1555 **type** ad. unsexed

Yellow-throated Hanging Parrot *Loriculus pusillus* **7**
RMNH. Cat. 61, Reg. 45251 ad. ♂

FISCHER'S LOVEBIRD

Agapornis fischeri Reichenow

Illustrated on page 304.

Length 15 cm.

ADULTS general plumage green, more yellowish on underparts; forehead, cheeks and throat orange-red; remainder of head dull olive-green, tinged with reddish on occiput; upper breast and collar around neck yellow; upper tail-coverts washed with pale blue; under wing-coverts blue and green; tail green, lateral feathers marked with yellow and basally and subterminally barred with black; naked periophthalmic ring white; bill red; iris brown; legs pale grey.

IMMATURES duller than adults, particularly on the head; small blackish markings on base of upper mandible.

   8 males   wing 88–98 (93.8) mm., tail 38–44 (40.9) mm.,
       exp. cul. 16–17 (16.6) mm., tars. 14–15 (14.6) mm.

8 females wing 90–95 (92.9) mm., tail 40–42 (40.5) mm.,
exp. cul. 16–18 (17.0) mm., tars. 14–16 (15.1) mm.

DISTRIBUTION Northern Tanzania from Kome and Ukerewe Islands, Lake Victoria, and southern shores of the Lake to Nzega, about 200 km. to the south, and Singida, 500 km. to the south-east; possibly occurs naturally in southern Kenya, though most reports indicate that it originated from aviary escapees (see Zimmerman, 1967; Cunningham-van Someren, 1969). Introduced to the Tanga area on the coast some time prior to 1928 (Mackworth-Praed and Grant, 1952).

GENERAL NOTES Fischer's Lovebird inhabits the inland plateau between 1,100 and 1,700 m. (Moreau, 1948). In the east it frequents grassland with scattered *Acacia*, *Commiphora* and *Balanites* trees, and toward the west heavily cultivated country dotted with baobabs (*Adansonia*). It is a common resident generally seen in small flocks, but in crop-growing areas large flocks of more than a hundred may congregate to feed on grain. They are noisy birds, their call-notes often being heard before the birds are sighted. The direct flight is very swift.

They feed on seeds procured on or near the ground and will attack ripening crops, particularly millet and maize.

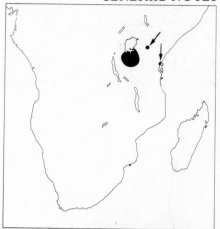

CALL A shrill whistle and a high-pitched twittering.

NESTING Breeding is colonial and has been recorded during May to July, possibly earlier. The nest is in a hole in a tree, in a cavity in a building, or among the bases of palm fronds. Turner and Pitman (1965) found these lovebirds roosting in communal nests of the Rufous-tailed Weaver (*Histurgops ruficauda*), but did not find any eggs or chicks; it is probable that the parrots do breed in these nests. Inside the cavity or among the fronds a bulky dome-shaped nest with an entrance at the side is constructed from long twigs and strips of bark carried by the female in her bill.

In captivity the general nesting behaviour is similar to that of the Grey-headed Lovebird; incubation is of twenty-three days duration and the young leave the nest thirty-eight days after hatching (Dilger, 1960).

EGGS Rounded; 10 eggs, 23.3 (20.2–24.5) × 17.0 (16.5–18.0) mm. [Schönwetter, 1964].

Seychelles Parakeet *Psittacula wardi* **1**
UMZC. 18/Psi/67/g/3 **syntype** ad. ♂

Alexandrine Parakeet **2**
Psittacula eupatria nipalensis
AMNH. 176731 ad. ♂

Black- Newton's Parakeet *Psittacula exsul* **3**
UMZC. 18/Psi/67/h/2 ad. ♂

MASKED LOVEBIRD

Agapornis personata Reichenow *Illustrated on page 304.*

Length 14.5 cm.
ADULTS general plumage green; forehead, lores, crown and anterior of cheeks brownish-black; remainder of head dusky olive; throat reddish-orange; upper breast and collar around neck yellow; upper tail-coverts pale blue; under wing-coverts greyish-blue and green; tail green, lateral feathers marked with orange-yellow and basally and subterminally barred with black; naked periophthalmic ring white; bill red; iris dark brown; legs grey.
IMMATURES duller than adults, particularly on head; small blackish markings on base of upper mandible.
8 males wing 94–98 (96.3) mm., tail 39–45 (42.0) mm.,
exp. cul. 16–19 (17.1) mm., tars. 14–15 (14.8) mm.
8 females wing 90–97 (93.5) mm., tail 39–45 (41.1) mm.,
exp. cul. 16–18 (17.4) mm., tars. 12–16 (14.5) mm.

DISTRIBUTION North-eastern Tanzania from Lake Manyara south to the Iringa Highlands; introduced to Dar es Salaam about 1928 (Mackworth-Praed and Grant, 1952) and recently to Nairobi, Kenya (Cunningham-van Someren, 1969).

GENERAL NOTES Moreau (1948) points out that the range of the Masked Lovebird is an inland plateau varying between 1,100 and 1,700 m., and bordered in the east by the Pangani Valley and in the south by forested mountains. Its habitat is wooded grasslands dominated by acacias. This species occurs to within 65 km. of the range of Fischer's Lovebird, but apparently the two do not meet. Moreau suggests that the barrier may be *Brachystegia-Isoberlinia* woodland, which is largely devoid of seeding grasses and shrubs—the food of these parrots.

The habits and ecology are similar to those of Fischer's Lovebird.

CALL A high-pitched twittering.

NESTING Breeding is colonial and has been recorded between March and August. The nest is in a hole in a tree, especially a baobab, or in crevices in buildings or even in an old swift's nest. A bulky, dome-shaped nest is constructed from long twigs and strips of bark carried by the female in her bill.

The general nesting behaviour resembles that of the Grey-headed Lovebird; incubation lasts twenty-three days and the young leave the nest about forty-four days after hatching (Dilger, 1960).

EGGS Rounded; 4 eggs, 23.3 (22.4–24.0) × 17.0 (16.7–17.2) mm. [Schönwetter, 1964].

NYASA LOVEBIRD

Agapornis lilianae Shelley

Illustrated on page 304.

DESCRIPTION
Length 13.5 cm.

ADULTS general plumage green, more yellowish on underparts and rump; forehead and throat orange-red merging into salmon-pink on crown, lores, cheeks and upper breast; tail green, lateral feathers marked with yellowish-orange and basally and subterminally barred with black; naked periophthalmic ring white; bill coral-red; iris dark reddish-brown; legs greyish-brown.

IMMATURES blackish suffusion on cheeks; small black markings on base of upper mandible.

8 males wing 90–95 (92.8) mm., tail 36–41 (38.4) mm.,
 exp. cul. 14–15 (14.5) mm., tars. 13–15 (14.1) mm.
8 females wing 89–94 (91.9) mm., tail 35–38 (36.8) mm.,
 exp. cul. 14–16 (14.8) mm., tars. 13–15 (13.9) mm.

DISTRIBUTION
Southernmost parts of Tanzania and north-western Mozambique south through Malawi and eastern Zambia to northernmost Rhodesia along the Zambesi River Valley; introduced to Lundazi, Zambia (Benson and White, 1957). Records from southern South West Africa are of aviary escapees (Clancey, 1965).

GENERAL NOTES

The Nyasa Lovebird is a low-altitude bird confined to river valleys between 600 and 1,000 m. (Moreau, 1948), occasionally wandering up to the higher plateau when not breeding (White, 1942). It is closely associated with mopane (*Colophospermum mopane*) woodland, though Smithers *et al.* (1957) claim that on the flood plain of the Zambesi Valley it also inhabits open *Acacia* woodland where there are large trees. Benson and Stuart Irwin (1967) point out that this species is isolated from *nigrigenis* by a 160 km. wide strip of *Brachystegia* woodland between Kanchindu and Livingstone. There is considerable local movement and at times the lovebirds are common in cultivated farmlands (Winterbottom, 1949).

These parrots are gregarious, noisy birds, usually seen in flocks of from twenty to a hundred or more. They spend much of the time on the ground searching for grass seeds or in the treetops feeding on seeds and buds. During the day they make frequent visits to water. The flight is swift and direct.

They feed on seeds, grain, berries, fruits and leaf buds. They are sometimes troublesome in crop-growing areas, being particularly fond of ripening grain, especially millet. They have also been seen feeding on blossoms of *Acacia albida* (Benson pers. comm., 1971).

CALL When perched or in flight a shrill chatter, reminiscent of the rattling of a metal chain, though more high-pitched (Benson and Benson, 1948).

NESTING Breeding in the wild state is very poorly documented. Birds introduced to the Lundazi area nest under the eaves of houses and lay during January and February (Benson and White, 1957). It has been claimed that in the Luangwa Valley, Zambia, these lovebirds breed in nests of the Buffalo Weaver (*Bubalornis albirostris*).

In captivity a bulky, dome-shaped nest is built from long stalks and strips of bark carried into the nest-box by the female in her bill. The general nesting behaviour is similar to that of the other lovebirds; incubation lasts twenty-two days and the young leave the nest about forty-four days after hatching (Dilger, 1960).

EGGS Slightly elliptical; 8 eggs, 20.6 (19.7–22.0) × 16.6 (16.0–17.0) mm. [Schönwetter, 1964].

BLACK-CHEEKED LOVEBIRD

Agapornis nigrigenis Sclater

Illustrated on page 304.

DESCRIPTION
Length 13.5 cm.

ADULTS general plumage green, more yellowish on rump and underparts; forehead and forecrown reddish-brown; hindcrown and nape dark yellowish-green; lores, throat and cheeks brownish-black; upper breast pale orange-red; tail green, lateral feathers marked with orange-yellow and basally and subterminally barred with black; naked periophthalmic ring white; bill coral-red; iris brown; legs grey-brown.

IMMATURES similar to adults; small blackish markings at base of upper mandible; iris pale brown.

8 males wing 91–97 (94.6) mm., tail 40–45 (42.3) mm.,
 exp. cul. 14–15 (14.6) mm., tars. 13–14 (13.5) mm.
8 females wing 90–98 (94.5) mm., tail 40–45 (42.8) mm.,
 exp. cul. 14–16 (14.9) mm., tars. 13–14 (13.8) mm.

DISTRIBUTION
Confined to south-western Zambia along the Zambesi River Valley east to about Livingstone and north to Senanga and the Kafue National Park (Benson and Stuart Irwin, 1967); possibly also in far north-western Rhodesia about Victoria Falls.

The Black-cheeked Lovebird has the most restricted range of the Agapornids. Moreau (1948) says that it is a lowland bird inhabiting river valleys between 600 and 1,000 m. Like the Nyasa Lovebird it is closely associated with mopane (*Colophospermum mopane*) woodland, the vegetation type typical of the flat alluvial soils of the river valleys. It is subject to local movements, some of which appear to be seasonal; it is said to be an annual visitor to Senanga (see Winterbottom, 1942).

Mackworth-Praed and Grant (1962) claim that these lovebirds have been heavily reduced in numbers by trapping for the live bird trade, surely a threat to any species with such a restricted range. The habits and general ecology are similar to those of the Nyasa Lovebird.

They feed on seeds, fruits, berries and leaf buds. In Kafue National Park they have been seen feeding on seeds of *Rhus quartiniana* and *Syzygium guineense* and on seeds of *Hyparrhenia* grass (in Benson and Stuart Irwin, 1967).

CALL A shrill, high-pitched note, said to be like that of the Peach-faced Lovebird (Mackworth-Praed and Grant, 1962).

NESTING Nothing is known of breeding in the wild state. In captivity a bulky, dome-shaped nest is built from long stalks and strips of bark carried into the nest-box by the female in her bill. The general nesting behaviour is similar to that of the other lovebirds; incubation lasts twenty-four days and the young leave the nest about forty days after hatching (Dilger, 1960).

EGGS Slightly elliptical; 20 eggs, 21.4 (20.0–23.6) × 16.8 (15.7–17.7) mm. [Schönwetter, 1964].

Genus LORICULUS Blyth

The members of *Loriculus*, a genus closely related to *Agapornis* (Dilger, 1960), are small parrots with very short, rounded tails and extremely fine, pointed bills. The tail is so short that it is sometimes hidden by the tail-coverts. The cere is naked.

The popular nome hanging parrot refers to the birds' strange roosting habit of hanging upside down. Females carry nesting material amidst their rump feathers, a habit shared by the lovebirds.

Except in the Celebes, where there are two species, all forms replace each other geographically.

VERNAL HANGING PARROT
Loriculus vernalis (Sparrman)

Illustrated on page 305.

Length 13 cm.

MALE general plumage green, noticeably paler on underparts and brighter on head; blue patch on throat; rump and upper tail-coverts red; undersides of flight feathers greenish-blue; tail green above, bluish below; bill dull coral with yellowish tip; iris pale yellowish-white; legs pale orange.
FEMALE slightly duller; little or no blue on throat.
IMMATURES forehead and cheeks dull greyish-green; green feathers on rump; bill pale orange; iris brown; legs pale brownish.

10 males   wing 87–94 (91.0) mm., tail 35–38 (36.5) mm.,
           exp. cul. 11–13 (11.8) mm., tars. 11–12 (11.5) mm.
10 females wing 86–92 (89.6) mm., tail 33.37 (35.4) mm.,
           exp. cul. 10–12 (10.9) mm., tars. 11–13 (11.6) mm.

South-western India, south of Bombay, and up the eastern coast to Bengal and the eastern Himalayas from eastern Nepal to Assam, then east through Burma and Thailand, north of lat. 10°N. on the Malay Peninsula, to Cambodia, southern Laos and southern Vietnam; also on the Andaman Islands and islands in the Mergui Archipelago.

In India the Vernal Hanging Parrot inhabits well-wooded country and cultivated plantations below 2,000 m. (Ali 1946, Ripley 1961); it is common but, because of its small size and predominantly green colouration, may be easily overlooked. It is uncommon in Nepal (Fleming and Traylor, 1968) and is sparingly distributed in Burma (Smythies, 1953), but seems to be plentiful elsewhere. Deignan (1945) says that in northern Thailand it may be found in open evergreen woodland, dry deciduous jungle and bamboo thickets, both on the plains and in the hills up to at least 1,400 m. In southern Vietnam it occurs mainly in secondary forest near cultivated areas, especially where there are flowering trees (Wildash, 1968). Ali and Ripley (1969) point out that in India there are local migrations, which are apparently not altogether connected with food supply; some districts are visited during the wet season, others during the winter.

Pairs, family parties or small flocks are usually seen, but large numbers may congregate where trees are in heavy blossom. At such times the trees may be literally swarming with these small parrots; they present a scene of intense activity as they climb about among the foliage, often

hanging upside down to get at flowers. They are very agile when clambering about in the treetops, and have a curious way of ascending a branch in a spiral course around it. The entire flock may suddenly leave the tree, wheel about overhead calling loudly, and then dart back into the tree to continue feeding. While feeding they are quite tame and take no notice of people or traffic passing underneath. Their diminutive size and predominantly green colouration make them difficult to observe in the canopies of tall trees, so they are generally seen when dashing from one tree to another. The swift, undulating flight comprises rapid wingbeats periodically interrupted by short pauses with the wings closed against the body.

Food consists of soft fruits and berries, chiefly wild figs (*Ficus*), supplemented by nectar and seeds. Ali and Ripley state that in India favourite sources of nectar are blossoms of silk-cotton trees (*Salmalia malabarica*), coral trees (*Erythrina* spp.), the many introduced eucalypts, and of the parasitic Loranthaceae. They also eat seeds of casuarinas, bamboo, and teak (*Tectona grandis*) in forests and plantations, and attack guavas (*Psidium* sp.) and loquats (*Eriobotrya japonica*) in orchards, often causing damage. They are fond of coconut palm toddy which they take from the collecting pots, sometimes in such quantity that they become stupefied.

CALL In flight a sharp *chee-chee-chee* repeated every few seconds or a shrill *tsit-tsit*; when feeding an occasional soft twittering (Smythies, 1953).

NESTING The breeding season is from January to April. The nest is in a hollow in a tree or an old rotten stump, often low down near ground level. On the Andaman Islands, Abdulali (1964) found a nest containing two newly-hatched chicks; the bottom of the hollow was about 60 cm. from the entrance and was lined with green leaves. Leaves and strips of bark used as nest-lining are carried by females tucked under their rump feathers. A normal clutch comprises two to four eggs. Little is known about the nesting behaviour. Ali and Ripley state that apparently both sexes incubate, but I suspect that although the male may enter the nest he probably does little, if any, brooding. The female sits very tightly, often allowing herself to be lifted from the nest. Both parents feed the nestlings (Ali and Ripley, 1969).

Buckley (1968) reports that five birds in immature plumage received into captivity in November had developed bright orange bills and incomplete, light blue throat patches by the following March.

EGGS Broadly ovate; 30 eggs, 19.1 (17.5–21.0) × 15.8 (15.1–17.0) mm. [Stuart Baker, 1927].

CEYLON HANGING PARROT
Loriculus beryllinus (J. R. Forster)

Illustrated on page 305.

Length 13 cm.
ADULTS general plumage green, paler on underparts; forehead, crown, rump and upper tail-coverts scarlet; nape and mantle tinged with golden-orange; lores and cheeks slightly suffused with pale blue; pale blue patch on chin and throat, less prominent in females; undersides of wings and tail greenish-blue; bill dark orange, paler at tip; iris pale yellowish-white; legs orange-yellow.
IMMATURES forehead greenish-grey; crown green slightly tinged with orange; mantle green; only a faint bluish tinge on throat; bill pale orange; iris brown.
10 males   wing 92–95 (93.7) mm., tail 38–42 (39.8) mm.,
                exp. cul. 12–13 (12.3) mm., tars. 11–12 (11.4) mm.
8 females   wing 87–94 (91.1) mm., tail 38–42 (40.4) mm.,
                exp. cul. 12–13 (12.3) mm., tars. 11–12 (11.3) mm.

DISTRIBUTION Ceylon.

GENERAL NOTES

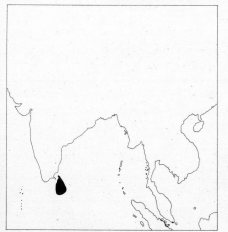

The Ceylon Hanging Parrot is widespread in the lowlands and hills up to 1,250 m., ascending up to about 1,600 m. during the north-east monsoons (Henry, 1971). It is most plentiful in the south-west of the Island, is almost absent from the arid northern regions and is locally distributed in the northern forest tract (Wait, 1925). It frequents gardens, plantations, and wooded country, wherever there are flowering or fruit-bearing trees.

Usually seen singly, in pairs or in small groups, it spends most of the day feeding in the treetops, where its green colouration blends very well with the foliage. Its habits are similar to those of the Vernal Hanging Parrot. The swift, undulating flight comprises rapid wingbeats interrupted by brief pauses with the wings closed against the body.

Food consists of fruits, berries, nectar and seeds. When the intoxicating coconut palm toddy is being collected in pots the parrots consume such quantities that they become temporarily stupefied and are easily caught. A favourite food is nectar from flowers of *Erythrina* and *Salmalia* trees. Salim Ali says that they also feed on nectar from blossoms of introduced eucalypts (*in litt.*, 1967). Henry has observed them extracting seeds from *Casuarina* cones.

CALL In flight a sharp *twit-twit-twit* ... *twit-twit-twit*; while feeding a series of squeaky, warbling notes (Henry, 1971).

NESTING According to Henry this species breeds in the first half of the year and sometimes again in July to September. When courting the male struts along a perch in front of the female. The bill is held high in the air, the blue throat feathers are puffed out, the tail is spread, and the red rump feathers are raised and spread. These actions are accompanied by a warbling note.

The nest is in a hollow in a tree, preferably a long, narrow cavity with a small entrance hole. The bottom of the hollow is lined with strips of green leaves carried by the female amidst her rump feathers. On this layer two or three eggs are laid. Only the female incubates and she sits very tightly.

Bloom (1960) gives details of the breeding in captivity of hybrids from a female Ceylon Hanging Parrot and a male Blue-crowned Hanging Parrot. A clutch of four eggs was laid and incubated by the female for nineteen days. During this time she was fed at the nest-box by the male. The two chicks reared left the nest five weeks after hatching.

EGGS Ovate; 3 eggs, 18.7 (18.4–18.9) × 14.9 (14.8–15.0) mm. [Stuart Baker, 1927].

PHILIPPINE HANGING PARROT
Loriculus philippensis (P. L. S. Müller)

DESCRIPTION   Length 14 cm.
MALE general plumage green, paler and more yellowish on underparts; forehead and forepart of crown bright red bordered behind by a narrow yellow line and on the occiput by a dusky yellow patch; golden-orange band on nape; red patch on throat and centre of upper breast; rump and upper tail-coverts bright red; pale blue marking on each side of rump; greater under wing-coverts blue; undersides of wings and tail greenish-blue; bill orange-red; iris brown; legs orange.
FEMALE no red patch on throat and breast; anterior of cheeks and around base of bill tinged with blue.
IMMATURES similar to female but little or no red on forehead.

DISTRIBUTION   Philippine Islands, including the Sulu Archipelago.

SUBSPECIES   1. *L. p. philippensis* (P. L. S. Müller)   *Illustrated on page 308.*
  10 males wing 91–96 (93.6) mm., tail 40–44 (42.0) mm.,
     exp. cul. 13–14 (13.8) mm., tars. 11–12 (11.8) mm.
  10 females wing 89–100 (93.0) mm., tail 40–44 (42.7) mm.,
     exp. cul. 13–14 (13.2) mm., tars. 11–13 (11.7) mm.
  Inhabits the Islands of Luzon, Polillo, Marinduque, Catanduanes and Banton.

2. *L. p. mindorensis* Steere
MALE no yellow on crown; very faint orange band on nape.
FEMALE breast light yellow.
  11 males wing 93–101 (96.2) mm., tail 39–44 (41.6) mm.,
     exp. cul. 14–15 (14.9) mm., tars. 12–13 (12.5) mm.
  10 females wing 94–100 (96.6) mm., tail 40–47 (43.3) mm.,
     exp. cul. 13–15 (14.2) mm., tars. 12–14 (13.1) mm.
  Confined to Mindoro Island.

3. *L. p. bournsi* McGregor
MALE small yellow patch behind scarlet forecrown.
FEMALE very little blue suffusion on face.
  6 males wing 90–99 (93.8) mm., tail 40–45 (42.7) mm.,
     exp. cul. 12–15 (13.3) mm., tars. 12–13 (12.3) mm.
  6 females wing 88–96 (91.5) mm., tail 42–47 (44.8) mm.,
     exp. cul. 13–14 (13.3) mm., tars. 12–13 (12.2) mm.
  Occurs on Tablas, Romblon and Sibuyan Islands.

4. *L. p. panayensis* Tweeddale
MALE similar to male *bournsi*, but has more yellow on crown.
FEMALE similar to female *bournsi*.
  9 males wing 89–95 (92.2) mm., tail 39–44 (42.0) mm.,
     exp. cul. 13–14 (13.6) mm., tars. 11–13 (11.8) mm.
  9 females wing 89–97 (92.9) mm., tail 38–45 (42.2) mm.,
     exp. cul. 12–13 (12.8) mm., tars. 11–13 (11.7) mm.
  Found on Islands of Ticao, Masbate and Panay.

5. *L. p. regulus* Souancé
   MALE entire hindcrown golden-yellow.
   FEMALE hindcrown green tinged with yellow.
   11 males   wing 90–100 (95.7) mm., tail 41–45 (43.1) mm.,
         exp. cul. 13–15 (13.7) mm., tars. 11–13 (12.0) mm.
   9 females wing 92–102 (98.2) mm., tail 42–47 (44.0) mm.,
         exp. cul. 12–14 (13.0) mm., tars. 11–12 (11.8) mm.
      Occurs on Guimaras and Negros Islands.

6. *L. p. chrysonotus* Sclater   *Illustrated on page 308.*
   MALE entire hindcrown, nape and upper back rich golden yellow.
   FEMALE mantle and upper back green slightly washed with golden orange.
   7 males   wing 96–104 (100.0) mm., tail 44–51 (47.0) mm.,
         exp. cul. 14–15 (14.4) mm., tars. 11–14 (13.0) mm.
   8 females wing 95–104 (99.8) mm., tail 45–56 (49.6) mm.,
         exp. cul. 12–15 (13.4) mm., tars. 12–14 (13.4) mm.
      Formerly occurred on Cebu Island; probably extinct.

7. *L. p. worcesteri* Steere
   MALE mantle slightly tinged with orange; entire crown scarlet, becoming orange on nape.
   FEMALE entire crown scarlet; cheeks and upper throat pale blue.
   10 males wing 90–100 (94.1) mm., tail 38–47 (42.8) mm.,
         exp. cul. 13–15 (14.2) mm., tars. 11–12 (11.8) mm.
   7 females wing 89–99 (94.6) mm., tail 41–47 (44.3) mm.,
         exp. cul. 13–15 (13.7) mm., tars. 11–13 (12.6) mm.
      Inhabits Islands of Samar, Leyte and Bohol.

8. *L. p. siquijorensis* Steere.   *Illustrated on page 308.*
   MALE hindcrown and nape green; smaller red throat patch.
   FEMALE sides of forehead, lores, cheeks, chin and upper throat pale blue.
   5 males   wing 97–100 (98.6) mm., tail 41–50 (45.8) mm.,
         exp. cul. 14–15 (14.8) mm., tars. 13–14 (13.2) mm.
   6 females wing 98–104 (101.3) mm., tail 45–51 (48.2) mm.,
         exp. cul. 13–15 (13.3) mm., tars. 13–15 (14.0) mm.
      Formerly found on Siquijor Island; probably extinct.

9. *L. p. apicalis* Souancé
   MALE entire crown scarlet, becoming orange on nape; mantle washed with golden yellow;
   rump bright scarlet.
   FEMALE lores, cheeks, chin and upper throat pale blue, crown and nape as in male; mantle
   faintly tinged with golden yellow.
   10 males   wing 86–99 (94.8) mm., tail 38–43 (40.2) mm.,
         exp. cul. 13–15 (13.7) mm., tars. 10–12 (11.1) mm.
   11 females wing 85–100 (94.8) mm., tail 40–48 (43.4) mm.,
         exp. cul. 12–14 (13.3) mm., tars. 11–13 (11.7) mm.
      Found on the Islands of Mindanao, Dinagat and Bazol. I have examined the female of
   L. salvadorii Hachisuka in the British Museum and another similar specimen in the Academy
   of Natural Sciences, Philadelphia, and must agree with the suggestion made by Peters (1937)
   that they are aberrant specimens of *L. p. apicalis*.

10. *L. p. dohertyi* Hartert
    ADULTS similar to *apicalis*, but mantle strongly washed with orange.
    7 males   wing 90–100 (96.0) mm., tail 39–50 (43.0) mm.,
          exp. cul. 13–14 (13.9) mm., tars. 12 (12.0) mm.
    5 females wing 89–97 (93.6) mm., tail 41–46 (43.2) mm.,
          exp. cul. 12–13 (12.6) mm., tars. 12–13 (12.4) mm.
       Confined to Basilan Island.

11. *L. p. bonapartei* Souancé   *Illustrated on page 308.*
    MALE hindcrown and nape strongly washed with orange; bill black; legs dusky grey.
    FEMALE crown and nape as in male; lores and cheeks pale blue; bill black; legs dusky grey.
    10 males   wing 91–97 (94.7) mm., tail 43–48 (45.6) mm.,
          exp. cul. 13–14 (13.7) mm., tars. 12–14 (12.6) mm.
    10 females wing 91–99 (95.0) mm., tail 42–51 (46.8) mm.,
          exp. cul. 12–14 (12.8) mm., tars. 12–14 (12.7) mm.
       This distinctive subspecies is found on the Islands of Jolo, Bongao and Tawitawi in the Sulu
    Archipelago.

GENERAL NOTES   According to Rand and Rabor (1960) the Philippine Hanging Parrot is primarily a forest bird, wandering out into secondary growth and coconut plantations to feed. On Bataan Peninsula, Luzon, Gilliard (1950) found it to be abundant in high bushes, vines, bamboo clumps and fruit trees throughout the lowland farmlands, and also along the edges of secondary forest near villages. It is more common at lower altitudes, becoming scarce above 1,250 m., but on Mt. Apo, Mindanao, Goodfellow collected it at 2,500 m. (in Hachisuka, 1934).

Throughout most of the Islands the species is common. Amadon and Jewett (1946) noted that on Luzon it was the most common parrot. However, two subspecies are very rare or may be already extinct. Rand and Rabor suspect that *siquijorensis* from Siquijor Island may be extinct, pointing out that a specimen collected in late 1954 proved to be *regulus* from Guimaras and Negros Islands, almost certainly introduced as a cage bird. After McGregor collected *chrysonotus* on Cebu in 1906 nothing was heard of it until 1929 when some live birds became available in Britain and the United States; evidently the subspecies existed in some numbers on Cebu until at least 1929, and in captivity at the London Zoo until 1943 (Rand, 1959). It seems that clearing of primary forest was probably responsible for the decline of these two forms. These parrots are very popular as cage birds and are freely traded between the islands.

Philippine Hanging Parrots are usually seen singly, in pairs, or infrequently in small parties. They are arboreal, spending most of the day feeding in the middle and top storeys of trees. Gilliard reports that they may be also found near the ground in shaded bushes growing on steep banks. They are sometimes observed feeding in the company of greybirds, coletos and glossy starlings. In the forests they are rather shy, but when feeding in coconut groves are exceedingly bold. The flight is said to be peculiarly undulating (Hachisuka, 1934; Delacour and Mayr, 1946), but Potter (1953) claims that, although laboured, it is swift and direct without undulation.

Food comprises nectar, seeds, blossoms and soft fruits. The birds visit coconut palms to feed on nectar when it is being harvested from the flowering stalks by fitting joints of bamboo over the cut ends. Ripley and Rabor (1958) observed them feeding on *Ficus* fruits.

CALL   A high-pitched, rapid whistle.

NESTING   Little is known of the breeding habits. On Bohol specimens with enlarged gonads were collected in April and May and three nestlings were taken from a hole 12 m. above the ground in a dead tree standing at the edge of a small clearing in primary forest (Rand and Rabor, 1960).

EGGS   Rounded; 3 eggs, 18.7 (18.4–19.0) × 16.4 (16.2–16.7) mm. [Harrison and Holyoak, 1970].

BLUE-CROWNED HANGING PARROT
Loriculus galgulus (Linné)

Illustrated on page 305.

DESCRIPTION   Length 12 cm.
MALE general plumage green, slightly paler on underparts; crown deep blue; triangular patch of golden yellow on mantle; yellow band across lower back; throat, rump and upper tail-coverts scarlet; under wing-coverts and undersides of wings and tail greenish-blue; bill black; iris dark brown; legs buff-brown.
FEMALE duller with more yellowish underparts; lacks red throat and yellow band across lower back; blue on crown and yellow on mantle only slightly indicated.
IMMATURES general plumage dull green, feathers with narrow dusky margins; forehead grey tinged with blue; blue crown and yellow mantle absent; rump green margined with dull red; throat green; bill pale horn-coloured; legs pale flesh-brown.
10 males   wing 80–88 (84.0) mm., tail 30–34 (32.4) mm.,
               exp. cul. 11–12 (11.3) mm., tars. 10–12 (10.9) mm.
10 females wing 79–89 (83.6) mm., tail 29–36 (32.6) mm.,
               exp. cul. 10–11 (10.5) mm., tars. 10–11 (10.8) mm.

DISTRIBUTION   The Malay Peninsula south of lat. 10°N., and on Singapore, Anamba Islands, Borneo and some offshore islands, the Riau Archipelago, Bangka and Belitung Islands, and on Sumatra and the outlying Islands of Nias, Siberut, Sipora and Enggano.

GENERAL NOTES   The Blue-crowned Hanging Parrot is widespread and locally common in lightly wooded areas of the lowlands of the Malay Peninsula south of Wellesley Province (Gibson-Hill, 1949). In the southernmost provinces of Thailand it is common in evergreen forests (Lekagul, 1968). According to Smythies (1968) it is the only species of parrot that is common throughout the lowlands of Borneo. It is primarily a bird of the lower altitudes and as a rule is not found in heavy jungle, but there are records from as high as 1,250 m. and Robinson (1927) gives a sighting from the summit of Gunong Tahan, the highest mountain on the Peninsula. In May, 1969, at Ulu Gombak, on the Malay Peninsula, a banding party, of which a colleague was a member, netted the species in forest with bamboo regrowth (Rowley, pers. comm., 1969). At Poelou Moenteh, North Sumatra, specimens were collected in primary hill forest (Chasen and Hoogerwerf, 1941). It has also been

seen in coconut plantations, orchards and gardens. I have no information on its present status on Singapore; Gibson-Hill (1950) claims that it is a resident, very small numbers inhabiting lightly wooded areas, but Ward (1968) does not include it in his list.

Throughout Malaysia these little parrots are very popular as cage-birds and numbers are often caught with 'bird-lime'. Singly, in pairs, or infrequently in small flocks, they are generally seen flying above the treetops or feeding in flowering trees and bushes. When climbing they take extraordinarily long strides, the whole body being turned as each leg is stretched forward; the bill is used to grasp a twig and the tail may be depressed against a branch for support in much the same way as with woodpeckers. When hanging upside-down the feet are together, the tail depressed against a branch, and the body arched far back so that the head may be behind the feet. The flight is direct with fast-whirring wingbeats.

The diet consists of nectar, fruits, seeds, blossoms and possibly small insects. While feeding the birds constantly brush their bills on twigs or leaves.

CALL A sharp, penetrating note sometimes uttered in flight; also a sharp, high screech (Smythies, 1968).

NESTING Breeding has been recorded between January and July. The nest is in a hollow in a living or dead tree. Edgar describes a nest found in a hollow in a living tree about 12 m. from the ground (in Chasen, 1939): the entrance hole was nearly 8 cm. in diameter, but the cavity was about 45 cm. deep and 30 cm. wide; it was lined with a very thick layer of pieces of leaves and bracken fronds and on this were three eggs.

Norgaard-Olesen (1968) gives some details of a successful breeding in captivity. The incubation period was not determined, but the one chick reared left the nest approximately five weeks after hatching.

EGGS Rounded-oval; 10 eggs, 18.0 (16.4–19.9) × 15.5 (13.8–16.1) mm. [Schönwetter, 1964].

CELEBES HANGING PARROT
Loriculus stigmatus (S. Müller)

DESCRIPTION
Length 15 cm.
MALE general plumage green, paler and more yellowish on underparts; forehead and crown red; nape and mantle tinged with orange-yellow; green occiput; red patch on chin and throat; red marking on edge of forewing; dark red rump and upper tail-coverts, latter not extending to tip of tail; undersides of flight feathers greenish-blue; tail above green tipped paler, below greenish-blue; bill black; iris pale yellow; legs orange.
FEMALE forehead and crown green, sometimes with red bases to feathers; iris brown.
IMMATURES forehead and crown green; throat patch yellow suffused with red; edge of forewing greenish-yellow; bill horn-coloured; legs yellowish-brown.

DISTRIBUTION
Celebes, Togian Islands and islands of Butung and Muna, Indonesia.

SUBSPECIES
1. *L. s. stigmatus* (S. Müller)   *Illustrated on page 305.*
   11 males   wing 91–97 (95.0) mm., tail 35–41 (38.0) mm.,
               exp. cul. 11–12 (11.7) mm., tars. 12–13 (12.2) mm.
   11 females wing 91–99 (95.0) mm., tail 37–43 (40.2) mm.,
               exp. cul. 10–11 (10.7) mm., tars. 11–13 (11.8) mm.
   Confined to the Celebes.

2. *L. s. quadricolor* Walden
   ADULTS only mantle tinged with orange-yellow; underparts more yellowish.
   2 males   wing 94–95 (94.5) mm., tail 38–39 (38.5) mm.,
              exp. cul. 11 (11.0) mm., tars. 12 (12.0) mm.
   3 females wing 91–92 (91.7) mm., tail 37–42 (39.3) mm.,
              exp. cul. 11 (11.0) mm., tars. 11–13 (12.0) mm.
   1 unsexed wing 95 mm., tail 38 mm.,
              exp. cul. 11 mm., tars. 12 mm.
   Occurs on the Togian Islands.

3. *L. s. croconotus* Jany
   ADULTS similar to *quadricolor*, but wings and tail brighter green.
   5 males   wing 89–95 (92.6) mm., tail 39–43 (41.0) mm.,
              exp. cul. 11–12 (11.2) mm., tars. 11–12 (11.8) mm.
   2 females wing 90–96 (93.0) mm., tail 38–44 (41.0) mm.,
              exp. cul. 10 (10.0) mm., tars. 13 (13.0) mm.
   This doubtful subspecies is found on the Islands of Butung and Muna.

The Celebes Hanging Parrot is widely distributed in the Celebes, where it frequents open country on the coastal plain and the hill country up to 800 m. (in Stresemann, 1940). Singly, in pairs, or in small flocks, it is generally seen in flowering trees about villages or in coconut plantations. It seems to be nomadic, or may be even migratory; Coomans de Ruiter and Maurenbrecher (1948) note that near Makassar it was most numerous between October and December, that is, the end of the dry season and beginning of the rains. It is a common bird, but is inconspicuous because of its small size, predominantly green colouration and soft call-notes.

It feeds on nectar and soft fruits. Coomans de Ruiter (1951) reports that it is fond of nectar from blossoms of djuwet (*Eugenia* sp.) and djambu (*E. malaccensis*) and he often saw parrots in these trees. On Muna and Butung it feeds extensively on flowers of *Ceiba pentandra* and on fruits of *Ficus religiosa* and *Tamarindus indica* (in van Bemmel and Voous, 1951); stomachs of specimens collected always contained a sticky fluid, and sometimes this flowed from bills of the birds.

CALL In flight a high-pitched *siet-siet*; also a very high *siet-suu* (Coomans de Ruiter, 1951).

NESTING According to Platen this species breeds twice a year—in February and August (in Meyer and Wiglesworth, 1898). In south-eastern Celebes a nest was found in early February; it contained two newly-hatched chicks and was about 4 m. from the ground in a broken tree trunk standing in a clearing.

EGGS Almost spherical; 4 eggs, 19.4 (18.7–21.1) × 16.2 (14.1–17.0) mm. [Schönwetter, 1964].

MOLUCCAN HANGING PARROT
Loriculus amabilis Wallace

DESCRIPTION

Length 11 cm.
MALE general plumage green, paler and more yellowish on underparts; forehead, crown and occiput crimson-red; back and lower mantle tinged with golden-orange; edge of forewing dark red; crimson-red patch on chin and throat; dark red rump and upper tail-coverts, latter extending to tip of tail; tail green above, greenish-blue below, feathers tipped with greenish-yellow; bill black; iris pale-yellowish-white; legs orange.
FEMALE crown green; reddish spots on forehead; two or three irregular red spots on throat; iris brown.
IMMATURES throat patch and edge of forewing yellowish; iris pale brown.

Moluccas, Great Sangi Island, Sula Islands, and Islands of Peling and Banggai, Indonesia.

DISTRIBUTION

SUBSPECIES

1. *L. a. amabilis* Wallace
   9 males   wing 74–84 (77.2) mm., tail 30–33 (31.3) mm.,
        exp. cul. 9–10 (9.2) mm., tars. 9–11 (10.2) mm.
   3 females wing 71–80 (75.7) mm., tail 31–33 (32.0) mm.,
        exp. cul. 9 (9.0) mm., tars. 10–11 (10.3) mm.
   Found on Halmahera and Batjan in the northern Moluccas.

Illustrated on page 309.

2. *L. a. catamene* Schlegel
   ADULTS edge of forewing yellowish-green; under tail-coverts orange-red narrowly margined with green; tail-feathers tipped with red; slightly larger size.
   2 males   wing 82 (82.0) mm., tail 36–38 (37.0) mm.,
        exp. cul. 10 (10.0) mm., tars. 10 (10.0) mm.
   1 female wing 82 mm., tail 34 mm.,
        exp. cul. 10 mm., tars. 11 mm.
   This distinct subspecies is confined to Great Sangi Island.

3. *L. a. sclateri* Wallace
   ADULTS in both sexes forehead green with reddish-brown bases to feathers; crown green; a triangular orange patch on back; larger size.
   11 males   wing 89–102 (93.9) mm., tail 35–41 (37.4) mm.,
        exp. cul. 11–13 (12.1) mm., tars. 11–13 (12.1) mm.
   5 females   wing 88–106 (93.6) mm., tail 36–40 (38.0) mm.,
        exp. cul. 11–13 (12.0) mm., tars. 12–13 (12.4) mm.
   1 unsexed **(type)** wing 91 mm., tail 41 mm.,
        exp. cul. 12 mm., tars. 12 mm.
   Occurs on the Sula Islands.

Illustrated on page 309.

4. *L. a. ruber* Meyer and Wiglesworth
   ADULTS similar to *sclateri*, but with scarlet on mantle.
   2 males   wing 86–88 (87.0) mm., tail 34–38 (36.0) mm.,
        exp. cul. 12 (12.0) mm., tars. 12–13 (12.5) mm.

2 females   wing 89–91 (90.0) mm., tail 38–39 (38.5) mm.,
exp. cul. 11 (11.0) mm., tars. 13 (13.0) mm.
5 unsexed   wing 88–99 (93.4) mm., tail 33–39 (36.2) mm.,
exp. cul. 11–12 (11.2) mm., tars. 11–13 (12.0) mm.
Inhabits islands of Peling and Banggai in the Celebes group.

GENERAL NOTES   The habits and general ecology of the Moluccan Hanging Parrot are similar to those of the Philippine Hanging Parrot. In pairs or small parties it is generally seen in flowering or fruit-bearing trees in secondary forest, along the edge of primary forest, or in village gardens. Platen noted that on Great Sangi Island it was not particularly plentiful (in Meyer and Wiglesworth, 1898).

CALL   A weak, sibilant cry (Tavistock, 1931a).

NESTING   I know of no published information on nesting habits, but presumably they resemble those of the other species.
   Tavistock gives details of an unsuccessful breeding attempt in captivity. The female carried nesting material tucked among the feathers of her rump and flanks; three eggs were laid but all were infertile.

EGGS   Rounded; 2 eggs, 17.1 (16.9–17.3) × 14.6 (14.5–14.8) mm. [Berlin Mus. Coll.].

GREEN HANGING PARROT
Loriculus exilis Schlegel

Illustrated on page 309.

Length 10.5 cm.
ADULTS   general plumage green, yellowish on underparts and darker on wings; an elongated spot of red on throat, reduced or even absent in females; greenish-blue surrounding red spot on throat; rump and upper tail-coverts red, basally suffused with yellow; undersides of wings greenish-blue; tail green above, greenish-blue below, lateral feathers tipped with greenish-yellow; bill coral-red; iris yellow in male, brown in female; legs orange.
IMMATURES   no red on throat; bill yellowish-brown; iris pale brown; legs yellowish.
5 males   wing 64–69 (67.4) mm., tail 24–32 (27.8) mm.,
exp. cul. 7–8 (7.4) mm., tars. 8–9 (8.8) mm.
4 females   wing 64–68 (66.0) mm., tail 25–28 (26.8) mm.,
exp. cul. 7–8 (7.5) mm., tars. 9–10 (9.3) mm.

DISTRIBUTION   Restricted to northern and south-eastern parts of Celebes, Indonesia.

GENERAL NOTES   The Green Hanging Parrot is a little-known bird. It is probably not rare, but its very small size and green colouration would make it difficult to observe among the foliage (in Stresemann, 1940). Furthermore, it is probably nomadic and follows the flowering of trees. In March 1871, Meyer saw only one pair near Manado, but in May large flocks suddenly appeared and frequented mangrove bushes along the seaboard (in Meyer and Wiglesworth, 1898). It has been recorded up to and beyond 800 m.
   Meyer found nectar in stomachs from specimens collected near Manado.

CALL   Similar to, but more high-pitched than that of the Celebes Hanging Parrot (in Stresemann, 1940).

NESTING   According to Platen breeding takes place twice a year, in February and August, and the nest is in a hole in a dead palm tree (in Meyer and Wiglesworth, 1898).

EGGS   Rounded; 3 eggs, 19.3 (18.9–19.6) × 15.0 (14.3–15.7) mm. [Harrison and Holyoak, 1970].

WALLACE'S HANGING PARROT
Loriculus flosculus Wallace

Illustrated on page 309.

DESCRIPTION   Length 12 cm.
ADULTS   general plumage green, noticeably lighter on underparts; nape tinged with orange; rump and upper tail-coverts crimson; elongated red spot on throat, reduced or even absent in females; undersides of wings greenish-blue; tail above green tipped with pale green slightly stained with red, below greenish-blue; bill red; iris orange in males, brown in females (Wallace); legs orange.
IMMATURES   undescribed.

1 unsexed **(type)** wing 79 mm., tail 33 mm.,
exp. cul. 11 mm., tars. 12 mm.

DISTRIBUTION   Confined to Flores in the Lesser Sunda Islands, Indonesia.

GENERAL NOTES   Wallace's Hanging Parrot is a mysterious bird, about which almost nothing seems to be known. The type is the only specimen that I could locate. Fr. Verheijen says that neither he nor his two co-missionaries on Flores have seen the bird or been able to get any information about it from local people (*in litt.*, 1972). Their observations were carried out mainly in the western part of the island, but even if the species is confined to eastern Flores it would be surprising if people in the west had no knowledge whatever of it.

CALL Undescribed.

NESTING I know of no published information on nesting habits.

EGGS Rounded; 3 eggs, 19.7 (19.5–20.0) × 16.0 (15.5–16.3) mm., [Schönwetter, 1964].

YELLOW-THROATED HANGING PARROT
Loriculus pusillus G. R. Gray

Illustrated on page 309.

DESCRIPTION   Length 12 cm.
ADULTS general plumage bright green, paler and more yellowish on underparts; mantle slightly tinged with yellow; rump and upper tail-coverts red; orange-yellow patch on throat, markedly reduced in female; undersides of wings greenish-blue; tail green above, greenish-blue below; bill orange; iris yellowish-white; legs dusky yellow.
IMMATURES undescribed.
9 males   wing 82–89 (85.0) mm., tail 31–37 (33.7) mm.,
exp. cul. 9–10 (9.8) mm., tars. 10–11 (10.8) mm.
8 females wing 82–90 (85.6) mm., tail 32–36 (34.3) mm.,
exp. cul. 9–10 (9.5) mm., tars. 10–11 (10.8) mm.

DISTRIBUTION   Islands of Java and Bali, Indonesia.

GENERAL NOTES   Hoogerwerf (1947) points out that on Java Yellow-throated Hanging Parrots have been recorded up to at least 1,850 m. He says that they are probably not rare, but are easily overlooked because they keep to the treetops in forested areas. In the Tjibodas area he once saw them flying above garden trees and also found a large flock feeding in a *Ficus* tree near the river (Hoogerwerf, 1949). On Bali these parrots have been seen feeding in flowering *Erythrina* trees at 1,200 m. (Rensch, 1930). The flight is very swift and the 'whirring' of wingbeats can be heard as the birds pass overhead.

The parrots feed on nectar, blossoms, leaf buds, and possibly seeds. On the Udjung Kulon Reserve, Java, Hoogerwerf (1970) has seen small groups of these parrots feeding on the flowers of *Cassia siamea*.

CALL A shrill *sree-ee* (Hoogerwerf, 1949).

NESTING Breeding has been recorded in April and May. The nest is in a hollow in a tree, often in the trunk of a palm tree, or in an old nesting hole of a barbet. Hoogerwerf (1949) found a nest in a hollow in the top of a tree fern standing on the edge of primary forest. The hollow is lined with leaf fragments, presumably carried by the female amidst her body feathers. A normal clutch comprises two eggs. The female sits very tightly and may be lifted from the nest.

EGGS Broad-oval, without gloss; 5 eggs, 19.3 (18.3–20.7) × 15.2 (15.0–15.6) mm. [Hellebrekers and Hoogerwerf, 1967].

ORANGE-FRONTED HANGING PARROT
Loriculus aurantiifrons Schlegel

DESCRIPTION   Length 10 cm.
MALE general plumage green, paler and more yellowish on underparts; forehead and forecrown rich golden-yellow; a bright red patch on throat; rump and upper tail-coverts red; yellow markings on sides of rump; undersides of wings greenish-blue; tail above green tipped with greenish-yellow, below greenish-blue; bill black; iris pale yellowish-white; legs brownish.

322

FEMALE forehead and forecrown bluish-green, bases of feathers reddish; cheeks strongly tinged with blue; smaller red patch on throat; iris brown.
IMMATURES like female but lacking red throat patch; bill pale brown.

Misool Island, New Guinea, including some offshore islands, and Bismarck Archipelago.

DISTRIBUTION

SUBSPECIES

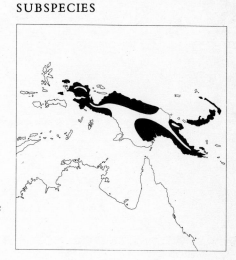

1. *L. a. aurantiifrons* Schlegel
    2 males wing 65–69 (67.0) mm., tail 26–27 (26.5) mm.,
        exp. cul. 7 (7.0) mm., tars. 9–11 (10.0) mm.
    No females examined.
    Confined to Misool in the western Papuan Islands.

2. *L. a. batavorum* Stresemann
    MALE less yellow on forehead and forecrown.
    FEMALE similar to *aurantiifrons*.
    8 males   wing 64–72 (67.3) mm., tail 24–31 (28.0) mm.,
        exp. cul. 6–8 (6.9) mm., tars. 8–10 (9.0) mm.
    7 females wing 65–69 (67.6) mm., tail 26–29 (27.9) mm.,
        exp. cul. 6–8 (7.1) mm., tars. 8–9 (8.7) mm.
    Found on Waigeu, western Papuan Islands, and in north-western New Guinea east on the north coast to the Sepik region and on the south to the Setekwa River.

3. *L. a. meeki* Hartert   *Illustrated on page 309.*
    MALE similar to *batavorum* but larger.
    FEMALE bases of feathers of forehead and forecrown yellowish-brown; larger than *batavorum*.
    9 males   wing 69–76 (72.7) mm., tail 28–31 (29.2) mm.,
        exp. cul. 6–7 (6.7) mm., tars. 9–10 (9.2) mm.
    10 females wing 69–75 (72.4) mm., tail 27–30 (28.5) mm.,
        exp. cul. 6–7 (6.4) mm., tars. 9–10 (9.2) mm.
    Occurs on Fergusson and Goodenough Islands and in south-eastern New Guinea east of Huon Peninsula in the north and Lake Kutubu in the south.

4. *L. a. tener* Sclater   *Illustrated on page 309.*
    MALE forehead and forecrown green; orange-red patch on throat; rump and upper tail-coverts yellowish-green.
    FEMALE similar to male, but forehead, forecrown and cheeks tinged with greenish-blue.
    10 males   wing 64–67 (65.1) mm., tail 25–30 (27.7) mm.,
        exp. cul. 6–7 (6.8) mm., tars. 8–10 (9.0) mm.
    4 females wing 64–70 (66.3) mm., tail 25–29 (27.0) mm.,
        exp. cul. 6–7 (6.5) mm., tars. 9–10 (9.3) mm.
    This distinct race is sometimes listed as a separate species; it is found on New Hanover, New Ireland, Duke of York Islands, and New Britain in the Bismarck Archipelago.

The Orange-fronted Hanging Parrot seems to be a rather rare bird and little is known of its habits. It frequents lowland forest up to about 800 m., though Shaw Mayer collected one specimen at 1,600 m. in the Weyland Mountains (see Rothschild, 1931). Gilliard and LeCroy (1967) report that on Mt. Uali, New Britain, one of these parrots flew into a mist net set up on a sharp ridge between two steep valleys; it was probably travelling from the lowlands on one side of the ridge to those on the other. It is generally seen singly or in pairs. Bell (1970d) reports that on Goodenough Island two to four birds were observed coming to a littoral *Casuarina* tree early each morning; they ran their bills along the 'needles' as if feeding, possibly on lerps.
    Stomach contents from the specimen collected by Shaw Mayer comprised remains of flower buds.

GENERAL NOTES

CALL Undescribed.

NESTING In September, 1948, at Fakal, Misool, a male was seen entering a hole in a huge term-itarium attached to a tree trunk about 2 m. from the ground; it may have been breeding or simply retiring for the night (in Mees, 1965). At Moro, near Lake Kutubu, in October, 1961, a female was taken from its nest in a small hollow about 12 m. from the ground in a slender tree standing in primary forest; it was said to be incubating a clutch of four eggs (Schodde and Hitchcock, 1968). Near Djayapura, West Irian, two fledglings were brought in by natives in July (Rand, 1942b). Nothing further is known of the nesting habits.

EGGS Undescribed.

Genus **PSITTACULA** Cuvier

A strongly gradated tail, in which the feathers, particularly the long central pair, are narrow, is the most conspicuous external characteristic of this genus. The bill is heavy and robust with a distinct notch in the upper mandible. Thompson (1900) points out that in the skull there is a wide interruption to the orbital ring and a rather large postfrontal process arching downward.

I believe that this genus is related to *Tanygnathus*, *Eclectus* and *Psittrichas*, but do not agree with Immelmann (1968) who includes *Polytelis* and *Alisterus* in the group. In my opinion those two Papuo-Australian genera are allied to the platycercine group, similarities between *Polytelis* and *Psittacula* being only superficial.

Psittacula is a widely distributed genus and includes one species, *P. krameri*, which is the most widely distributed of all parrots.

ALEXANDRINE PARAKEET
Psittacula eupatria (Linné)

DESCRIPTION
Length 58 cm.
MALE general plumage green; occiput and cheeks suffused with greyish-blue; faint blackish stripe from cere to eyes; broad black stripe across lower cheek-patches; wide rose-pink collar encircling hindneck; dark purple-red patch on secondary coverts; tail green tipped with yellow, underside yellowish; bill red, tipped paler; iris pale yellow; legs greenish-grey.
FEMALE duller than male; no black stripe across cheek-patches; no rose-pink collar; shorter central tail feathers.
IMMATURES resemble female, but males usually larger; short central tail feathers.

DISTRIBUTION
Ceylon, eastern Afghanistan and western Pakistan through India to Indochina; also in the Andaman Islands.

SUBSPECIES

1. *P. e. eupatria* (Linné)   *Illustrated on page 312.*
   8 males   wing 198–215 (204.3) mm., tail 218–355 (289.1) mm.,
             exp. cul. 32–36 (34.3) mm., tars. 20–22 (20.6) mm.
   8 females wing 189–200 (194.9) mm., tail 215–258 (240.4) mm.,
             exp. cul. 29–32 (30.1) mm., tars. 19–22 (20.3) mm.
   Found in Ceylon and southern India north to about Hyderabad, Andhra Pradesh.

2. *P. e. nipalensis* (Hodgson)
   ADULTS occiput and cheeks tinged with blue; larger than *eupatria*.
   8 males   wing 214–238 (227.1) mm., tail 298–328 (314.6) mm.,
             exp. cul. 35–39 (36.1) mm., tars. 21–24 (22.1) mm.
   8 females wing 200–228 (219.8) mm., tail 286–376 (317.4) mm.,
             exp. cul. 31–37 (33.5) mm., tars. 20–22 (21.4) mm.
   Distributed from eastern Afghanistan and southern and eastern regions of West Pakistan east through northern and central India, Nepal, Bhutan and East Pakistan to Assam.

3. *P. e. magnirostris* (Ball)
   MALE narrow blue band on hind-neck above rose-pink collar; brighter patch on wing-coverts; larger, heavier bill.
   FEMALE similar to *eupatria*, but with larger, heavier bill.
   7 males   wing 216–225 (220.0) mm., tail 266–347 (318.1) mm.,
             exp. cul. 38–42 (39.7) mm., tars. 21–23 (21.7) mm.
   5 females wing 200–213 (204.6) mm., tail 250–328 (286.6) mm.,
             exp. cul. 32–37 (35.0) mm., tars. 20–23 (21.8) mm.
   Confined to the Andaman Islands.

4. *P. e. avensis* (Kloss)
   ADULTS reduced blue band on hindneck; neck yellowish; smaller bill.
   5 males   wing 199–221 (208.2) mm., tail 320–336 (325.6) mm.,
             exp. cul. 34–38 (36.2) mm., tars. 18–22 (20.2) mm.
   5 females wing 194–204 (199.8) mm., tail 281–313 (301.2) mm.,
             exp. cul. 30–33 (31.8) mm., tars. 19–20 (19.8) mm.
   Occurs in the Cachar district of Assam and throughout Burma south to about Amherst.

5. *P. e. siamensis* (Kloss)
   MALE occiput and nape washed with blue; paler, more reddish wing-patches; face and neck bright yellowish; slightly smaller than *avensis*.

Seychelles Parakeet *Psittacula wardi*   **1**
UMZC. 18/Psi/67/g/3 **syntype** ad. ♂

Alexandrine Parakeet   **2**
Psittacula eupatria nipalensis
AMNH. 176731 ad. ♂

Newton's Parakeet *Psittacula exsul*   **3**
UMZC. 18/Psi/67/h/2 ad. ♂

FEMALE face and neck yellowish; slightly smaller than *avensis*.

10 males   wing 187–204 (198.6) mm., tail 256–298 (280.1) mm.,
              exp. cul. 33–36 (34.1) mm., tars. 19–20 (19.5) mm.
9 females   wing 179–190 (185.8) mm., tail 200–254 (224.4) mm.,
              exp. cul. 30–34 (32.7) mm., tars. 19–21 (19.9) mm.
Found in western and northern Thailand, and in Laos, Cambodia and Vietnam.

GENERAL NOTES   In northern India the Alexandrine Parakeet is common and widely distributed up to about 800 m., though along the Himalayan foothills it has been recorded up to about 1,600 m. (Ali and Ripley, 1969). It is only sporadically distributed throughout peninsular India south of 18°N. latitude, and Ali (1969) points out that its occurrence in Kerala requires confirmation. Populations around such major cities as Karachi, Bombay and Calcutta may have originated from escapees, though Eates (1937) suggests that wandering parties could occasionally reach Karachi. Puget (1970) observed three birds in an orange orchard on the outskirts of Jalalabad, in eastern Afghanistan, but claims that it is unlikely that these had escaped from captivity. In Ceylon it is locally, though widely, distributed throughout the lowlands, particularly in the north, but is occasionally found above 300 m. (Wait, 1925). Henry (1971) claims that its range in Ceylon has declined in recent years, possibly due to the spread of cultivation and the collection of nestlings for the pet trade, but the parrots are still numerous in jungle districts, especially to the east and south of the mountains. According to Abdulali (1964) the species is quite common in the Andaman Islands, where large flocks have been seen roosting in coastal mangroves. Ripley (1950) says that in Nepal it seems to be local, being confined to fairly heavy forest or in proximity to heavy forest. It is sparingly distributed throughout the lowlands of Burma (Smythies, 1953), seems to be irregularly distributed in northern Thailand (Deignan, 1945), and is not very common in southern Vietnam (Wildash, 1968). In the Sukkur district, West Pakistan, Eates noted a regular north to south movement commencing with the onset of cold weather in November, while according to Frome (1947) it is chiefly a spring visitor to Delhi, being common between March and May; elsewhere the species is sedentary, though there are some nomadic movements and fluctuations in numbers governed chiefly by the food supply.

During the day these rather wary parrots are usually seen in parties or small flocks. They inhabit moist and dry deciduous forest, well-wooded country, cultivated farmlands, parks and gardens, coconut plantations, and trees around towns and villages. Ali and Ripley point out that they are also present in older canal-irrigated desert settlements with established trees and forest plantations, such as those in the Punjab. They are common in some urban areas. Toward dusk flocks come together and hundreds, sometimes thousands, go to roost in a grove of trees or section of forest. Throughout the non-breeding season these roosting sites are used continuously by the entire population in an area. At dawn, amidst an almost incessant chorus of screeching, flocks leave the roosting trees and move off to feed. Feeding grounds may be some miles away and, when travelling these distances, the parrots band together in close formation and fly at a considerable height. Sleek bodies and long, tapering tails give them a streamlined appearance in the air. Deliberate, rhythmic wingbeats are a characteristic feature of the swift, direct, flight.

Food comprises seeds, nuts, fruits, berries, blossoms, leaf buds and nectar. Ali and Ripley state that the parrots feed avidly on nectar from *Salmalia*, *Butea* and *Erythrina* flowers, and another favourite food is the fleshy petals of mhowa blossoms (*Bassia latifolia*). Eates says that in Karachi they feed extensively on *Casuarina* seeds. They raid ripening crops, especially maize, wheat and rice, and cause considerable damage in orchards where their wasteful feeding habits result in the destruction of much more fruit than is actually eaten.

CALL   A loud, screaming *kee-ak* or a screeching *kee-arr*, which are deeper and more sonorous than the call-notes of *P. krameri* (Ali and Ripley, 1969).

NESTING   The male, when courting, perches beside the female and continually turns his head from side to side, occasionally 'flicking' his wings, all to the accompaniment of a soft chattering.

The breeding season is from November to April and the nest is in a hole in a tree or rarely in a crevice in a chimney or wall, or under the roof of a building. The hollows are often excavated by the birds themselves in the trunk of a palm or large softwood tree such as *Salmalia malabarica*. Sometimes several holes in the trunk of one tree will be occupied by breeding pairs. Old nesting holes of barbets and woodpeckers are also used, although the parrots frequently enlarge these hollows.

Two to four eggs are laid on a layer of decayed wood dust. Ali (1946) says that incubation lasts about twenty-one days, but Heydon (1929) found that in captivity it commenced with the laying of the first egg and continued for twenty-eight days after the laying of the last egg; both sexes brooded. Young birds leave the nest approximately six weeks after hatching; they soon acquire the long central tail-feathers, but males do not attain adult plumage until the second year.

EGGS   Broad-oval, slightly glossy; 12 eggs, 34.0 (30.5–35.9) × 26.9 (24.1–28.0) mm. [Schönwetter, 1964].

SEYCHELLES PARAKEET
Psittacula wardi (Newton)

Illustrated on page 312.

Illustrated on page 312.

Length 41 cm.

ADULTS general plumage green, more yellowish on underparts; occiput and nape tinged with blue; obscure black line from cere to eyes; in male broad black stripes across lower cheeks, absent in female; dull red patch on secondary wing-coverts; central tail feathers light blue tipped with yellowish-green, lateral feathers green; bill red; iris yellow; legs dusky grey.

IMMATURES resemble female, but with shorter central tail feathers.

1 male **(syntype)** wing 204 mm., tail 187 mm.,
exp. cul. 33 mm., tars. —.
1 male wing 208 mm., tail 184 mm.,
exp. cul. 34 mm., tars. 22 mm.
6 females wing 182–204 (194.5) mm., tail 200–261 (228.0)mm.,
exp. cul. 29–34 (31.7) mm., tars. 20–22 (21.0) mm.
2 unsexed wing 188–200 (194.0) mm., tail 136–194 (165.0) mm.,
exp. cul. 32 (32.0) mm., tars. 19–22 (20.5) mm.

DESCRIPTION

Formerly the Islands of Mahé and Silhouette, Seychelles; now extinct.

DISTRIBUTION

The Seychelles Parakeet disappeared sometime prior to 1906, the year in which Nicoll could find no trace of it (Greenway, 1967). In 1870 a few skins were sent to Cambridge University, and the latest authentic record seems to be the two specimens collected by H. M. Warry in June 1881 (one is in the Liverpool Museum and the other is in the American Museum of Natural History). In 1866 Newton was told that it had been nearly exterminated through ruthless shooting because of the damage it did to maize crops (Newton, 1867). He failed to find it on Mahé, but on Silhouette saw it at 200 m. along the edge of forest adjoining a maize field; it was a wary bird and could not be approached. He mentions hearsay reports that the species occurred on Praslin Island, but if so it probably disappeared at an earlier date. A. and E. Newton (1876) claim that the clearing of forest to make way for coconut plantations, as well as indiscriminate shooting and trapping, brought about the extermination of these parrots.

GENERAL NOTES

CALL Undescribed.

NESTING No details have been recorded.

EGGS Undescribed.

ROSE-RINGED PARAKEET
Psittacula krameri (Scopoli)

Length 40 cm.

MALE general plumage green, more yellowish on under wing-coverts and lower underparts; narrow black line from cere to eyes; black chin and broad black stripes across lower cheeks; rose-pink collar encircling hindneck; nape variably suffused with blue; central tail-feathers bluish tipped with yellowish-green, lateral feathers green; upper mandible dark red becoming black towards tip, lower mandible black with dark red markings near base; iris pale yellow; legs greenish-grey.

FEMALE no black markings on chin or cheeks; no rose-pink collar; black line from cere to eye much less prominent; nape not suffused with blue; shorter central tail-feathers.

IMMATURES similar to female; short central tail-feathers; bill coral pink with pale tip; iris greyish-white; legs grey.

DESCRIPTION

Central and north-eastern Africa, Afghanistan, West Pakistan through India and Nepal to central Burma, and Ceylon; introduced to Mauritius, Zanzibar, Egypt, Aden and Oman, Kuwait, Iraq, Iran, Hong Kong and Macao, and Singapore. There is an early record from the Cape Verde Islands and unconfirmed reports from south-eastern China, Indochina and Lebanon.

DISTRIBUTION

1. *P. k. krameri* (Scopoli) *Illustrated on page 329.*
12 males wing 144–157 (150.3) mm., tail 194–278 (231.4) mm.,
exp. cul. 18–21 (19.6) mm., tars. 15–17 (15.8) mm.
10 females wing 143–152 (147.6) mm., tail 177–240 (198.2) mm.,
exp. cul. 18–21 (19.8) mm., tars. 15–17 (16.2) mm.
Distributed in western Africa from Guinea, Senegal and southernmost regions of Mauritania east to western Uganda and the White Nile in southern Sudan. There is a specimen (BM. 1910.5.6.156) collected on São Tiago, Cape Verde Islands, in 1909, but no mention is made of the species by D. and W. Bannerman (1968) in their treatment of the birds from those

SUBSPECIES

Illustrated on page 329.

islands. Parrots seen in the Nairobi National Park, Kenya, may represent an eastern extension of range by this race, but are more likely to have originated from aviary escapees (see Cunningham-van Someren, 1969).

2. *P. k. parvirostris* (Souancé)

ADULTS head and cheeks greener, less yellow, than in *krameri*; smaller bill with predominantly red upper mandible.

10 males   wing 146–160 (153.0) mm., tail 215–246 (233.7) mm.,
         exp. cul. 19–21 (19.6) mm., tars. 16–17 (16.6) mm.
8 females   wing 148–160 (153.4) mm., tail 184–218 (196.4) mm.,
         exp. cul. 19–21 (19.6) mm., tars. 14–17 (15.6) mm.

Ranges from the Sennar district, Sudan, east through northern Ethiopia to north-western Somalia.

3. *P. k. borealis* (Neumann)

ADULTS sides of head behind ear-coverts lightly suffused with blue; underparts greyish-green; bill entirely coral red, lower mandible often marked with black; larger than *krameri* and with a larger bill.

9 males   wing 170–177 (173.9) mm., tail 226–253 (239.2) mm.,
         exp. cul. 22–25 (23.2) mm., tars. 17–18 (17.7) mm.
8 females   wing 170–175 (172.4) mm., tail 211–230 (220.0) mm.,
         exp. cul. 21–24 (23.0) mm., tars. 18–19 (18.3) mm.

Occurs in north-western West Pakistan, along the Himalayan foothills, throughout northern India north of lat. 20°N., and from Nepal through to central Burma. The populations of this subspecies in Hong Kong and Macao are of uncertain origin; La Touche (1931) suggests that they may have reached there from neighbouring south-eastern China, but I tend to agree with the claim made by Herklots (1940) that they were introduced sometime between 1903 and 1913. This parrot has also been introduced to Mauritius.

Vaurie (1965) claims that *borealis* has been introduced to Oman, Iraq, Egypt and Zanzibar. Guichard and Goodwin (1952) point out that a female collected at Khaburah, Oman, is inseparable from *borealis*, but Meyer de Schauensee and Ripley (1953) ascribe Oman birds to *manillensis* because of their large size. Etchecopar (1969) summarised his sight records from the Middle East and suggested that the species may be a naturally-occurring resident of at least some areas, but subsequently he altered this view and claimed that the species was certainly introduced to Afghanistan, Iran, Iraq and Kuwait (in Hüe and Etchecopar, 1970). Further investigations into this confusing problem are required.

4. *P. k. manillensis* (Bechstein)

ADULTS larger than *krameri*; in males facial markings and rose collar are more prominent; larger bill; lower mandible black.

8 males   wing 162–180 (170.0) mm., tail 203–235 (219.0) mm.,
         exp. cul. 22–25 (23.3) mm., tars. 18–19 (18.3) mm.
8 females   wing 153–167 (162.6) mm., tail 174–210 (193.3) mm.,
         exp. cul. 21–24 (22.6) mm., tars. 17–18 (17.8) mm.

Inhabits Ceylon, Rameswaram Island, and the Indian Peninsula south of lat. 20°N. Introduced to Singapore some time prior to 1951 (see Gibson-Hill, 1952).

GENERAL NOTES   In India and Africa Rose-ringed Parakeets are common inhabitants of lightly timbered areas, cultivated farmlands and the vicinity of habitation. They are common residents of woodland in western and southern Sudan (Cave and Macdonald, 1955). Brown says that he has a few records of these parrots in savannah regions of Nigeria, but they are rare in the areas that he knows (*in litt.*, 1967). Etchecopar and Hüe (1967) point out that the parrots were introduced in the Giza district of Lower Egypt, but may no longer survive there. Near Khaburah, Oman, Guichard and Goodwin found them feeding on seeds of *Acacia arabica*, and were told that, to the south near Suwaik they were common and fed extensively on dates. About Batah, Oman, Meyer de Schauensee and Ripley observed that these parakeets were very common in the tops of palm trees. In late 1959, Marchant (1961) saw three birds at Karradah Sharqiyah, Iraq, and comments that the species was fairly often recorded in the Baghdad area between 1938 and 1952, but the paucity of recent records suggests the decline of a local colony probably originating from escapees. Marchant says that the birds he saw were in market gardens with scattered trees (pers. comm., 1966). Etchecopar observed these parrots in city gardens in Teheran, Iran, in *Acacia* scrubland several kilometres from Bandar Abbas on the Persian Gulf, in man-made gardens near Ahmadi, Kuwait, and at Kut, Iraq. Niet-hammer and Niethammer (1967) saw two birds at Jalalabad, Afghanistan, in May 1965, and point out that the species could occur naturally in the area. Puget (1970) has seen several flocks of from twelve to fifteen birds in gardens at Kabul and several parties in and around Jalalabad; he believes that the species breeds at both localities. In India they are abundant in deciduous woodland, light secondary jungle, semi-desert scrubland, and in gardens, orchards and cultivated farmlands in the neighbourhood of human habitation (Ali and Ripley, 1969); they are extraordinarily plentiful in and around some of the larger northern cities like Lahore, New Delhi and Kanpur. According to Henry (1971) these parrots are common throughout the lowland dry zone of Ceylon, especially near the coast, but they avoid the hills and are scarce in wet areas. In Burma they are fairly common on the plains and uplands of the dry zone (Smythies, 1953).

Rose-ringed Parakeets are usually seen in small flocks, but at a concentrated source of food or in roosting trees hundreds, or even thousands, may congregate. They are sedentary, though in intensely cultivated regions there are local movements governed by the ripening of crops. They are noisy, fearless birds, always attracting attention by their continuous screeching and squabbling. The flight is swift and direct with rapid wingbeats.

They feed on seeds, berries, fruits, blossoms, and nectar, and are serious pests in orchards, coffee plantations, and croplands. Ali and Abdulali (1938) note that about Bombay they were invariably present in flowering *Erythrina* and *Salmalia* trees, biting off the petals and eating the nectar. Dilger (1954) reports that in India large flocks comprising thousands of birds assemble after the breeding season and descend upon standing fruit and grain, causing tremendous damage. They also attack grain stored at railway sidings, tearing open the bags and causing severe losses through spillage. Wilson (1949) reports that in Sudan damage to crops is not widespread, being confined mainly to areas where croplands adjoin patches of forest inhabited by the birds. Crop contents from specimens collected near Fika, Nigeria, comprised *Ficus* fruits, seeds, millet grains and fragments of flowers (Bannerman, 1951).

CALL A loud, screeching *kee-ak . . . kee-ak . . . kee-ak* is given while at rest and in flight (Ali, 1946).

NESTING The breeding season is variable. In Africa it is from August to November (Mackworth-Praed and Grant, 1952; Cunningham-van Someren, 1969), in India from December to May (Lamba, 1966), and in Ceylon from November to June or even later (Henry, 1971). In India the commencement of the breeding season sees a marked reduction in the numbers of birds at the roosting trees as pairs leave to seek nesting sites.

The courtship display is elaborate. Uttering a low, twittering note, the female spreads her wings slightly, rolls her eyes, moves her head from side to side in semicircles, and rubs bills with the male. The male struts toward her, feeds her by regurgitation, draws himself up to full height and repeatedly raises one foot. This display continues for some minutes and is often followed by copulation.

In Africa the nest is always high up in a hollow limb or hole in a tree. In India it may also be in a cavity under the roof of a house or in a hole in a wall even within a congested market place (Ali, *in litt.*, 1967). Old nesting hollows of barbets and woodpeckers are sometimes enlarged, or the parrots may excavate a hollow in a soft-wooded tree. Two to six, usually three or four, eggs are laid on a layer of debris or decayed wood dust. Incubation commences with the laying of the first egg and lasts twenty-two to twenty-four days (Lamba, 1966). Both sexes brood, but the female sits more closely than the male. Young birds leave the nest six to seven weeks after hatching; the long central tail-feathers are acquired soon after leaving the nest but males do not attain adult plumage until the second complete moult when about three years old (Tavistock, 1954). There are nesting records involving males in sub-adult plumage.

EGGS Broad-oval, without gloss; 39 eggs, 30.7 (29.0–33.0) × 23.8 (23.0–25.0) mm. [Lamba, 1966].

MAURITIUS PARAKEET
Psittacula echo (Newton and Newton)

Illustrated on page 329.

DESCRIPTION Length 42 cm.
MALE general plumage bright green, slightly more yellowish on underparts and under wing-coverts; narrow black line from cere to eyes; broad black stripes across lower cheek-patches and on to sides of neck; broad rose-pink collar encircling nape and hindneck; occiput strongly tinged with blue; tail green above, dusky yellow below; upper mandible dark red, lower black; iris pale yellow, legs grey.
FEMALE no blue on occiput; rose-pink replaced by a yellowish-green collar on hindneck; dark green stripes across lower cheek-patches; central tail feathers washed with blue; bill entirely black.
IMMATURES (USNM.487076); similar to female.
8 males wing 177–190 (184.3) mm., tail 164–200 (185.9) mm.,
exp. cul. 22–24 (23.5) mm., tars. 19–22 (20.1) mm.
5 females wing 175–182 (180.0) mm., tail 162–186 (170.2) mm.,
exp. cul. 21–23 (22.4) mm., tars. 20–22 (20.8) mm.

DISTRIBUTION Confined to Mauritius in the Mascarene Islands; may have formerly occurred on Réunion Island.

SUBSPECIES Peters (1937) and most recent authors treat this form as a subspecies of *P. krameri*, but Gill (pers. comm., 1971) says that its behaviour is distinct enough to warrant its being considered a separate species. In my opinion this separation is supported by morphological features; *echo* is a larger, heavier bird, and its distinctly shorter, broader tail and sexual dimorphism in bill colouration are features also present in *exsul*, the other Mascarene species.

GENERAL NOTES The Mauritius Parakeet is rare and is confined to remote scrublands and forests of the island's

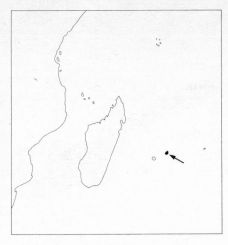

south-western plateau (Rountree *et al.*, 1952). Introduction of *P. krameri*, which has multiplied rapidly and is now locally common in the south and the east, could prove to be a further threat.

Gill reports that it is a quiet, unobtrusive bird, spending much of the day sitting quietly in the treetops, and this is in marked contrast to the noisy behaviour of *P. krameri* (pers. comm., 1971). Pairs are usually seen flying above the forest canopy or across forested gorges, and this is the only time that the call is given. Nothing further is known of its habits.

CALL In flight a disyllabic *aak-aak*, which is very different from the call of *P. krameri* (Gill, pers. comm., 1971).

NESTING Newton and Newton (1876) report that two eggs and the sitting female were taken from a nest in a hole in a tree. There appears to be no further information on nesting habits.

EGGS According to Hartlaub eggs measure 30.0–31.5 × 26.0–26.5 mm. [in Schönwetter, 1964].

NEWTON'S PARAKEET
Psittacula exsul (A. Newton)   *Illustrated on page 312.*

Length 40 cm.
MALE general plumage pale greenish-blue with a greyish cast, paler and brighter on underparts; head noticeably darker and without greyish suffusion; fine black line from cere to eyes; chin black; broad black stripes across lower cheeks to sides of neck then becoming narrow and continuing up to nape; primaries deep greenish-blue; tail bluish-green above, greyish below; upper mandible red, lower black; iris yellow (Vandorous); legs grey.
FEMALE very faint black line on forehead; black stripes not extending beyond sides of neck; crown suffused with grey; upper mandible black.
IMMATURES undescribed.

1 male   wing 199 mm., tail 207 mm. (abraded),
                   exp. cul. 25 mm., tars. 22 mm.
1 female **(type)** wing 192 mm., tail 212 mm.,
                   exp. cul. 24 mm., tars. 23 mm.

DISTRIBUTION Formerly the Island of Rodriguez; now extinct.

GENERAL NOTES Only two specimens of Newton's Parakeet were collected, the last being shot by a Mr Vandorous on 14th August 1875 and given to a Mr Caldwell who forwarded it to Mr E. Newton (A. and E. Newton, 1876). Caldwell (1876) remarked that he himself had seen several birds but could not get near one. Writing to Professor A. Newton, a Mr Slater said that on 30th September, 1874 he saw a single bird in forest towards the south-western end of the island (in Newton, 1875). Gill (1967) says that the species is almost certainly extinct and presumably has been for most of this century.

CALL Undescribed.

NESTING No records.

EGGS Undescribed.

Malabar Parakeet *Psittacula columboides* **1**
AM. 030563 ad. ♂

Rose-ringed Parakeet *Psittacula krameri krameri* **2**
MNHN. CG1962,3563 ad. ♂

Mauritius Parakeet *Psittacula echo* **3**
AMNH. 621312 ad. ♂

Emerald-collared Parakeet *Psittacula calthorpae* **4**
AMNH. 621601 ad. ♂

SLATY-HEADED PARAKEET
Psittacula himalayana (Lesson)

Length 40 cm.
ADULTS general plumage green with a bluish tinge, particularly on breast and upperparts; head dark grey with a bluish tinge; chin, stripes across lower cheeks, and narrow line on side of neck black; hindneck tinged with bluish-green; deep maroon patch on wing-coverts, almost always absent in females; under wing-coverts bluish-green; tail feathers green and blue tipped with yellow; upper mandible red with yellowish tip, lower yellowish; iris white; legs pale greenish-grey.
IMMATURES cheeks brownish-green, remainder of head green; faint band of pale green on hindneck; bill horn-coloured with brownish marking near base of lower mandible.

DISTRIBUTION Eastern Afghanistan through northern India and Nepal to Burma, Thailand, Indochina and south-western China.

SUBSPECIES

1. *P. h. himalayana* (Lesson)   *Illustrated on page 332.*

9 males   wing 162–177 (169.4) mm., tail 211–243 (228.6) mm.,
exp. cul. 21–23 (22.1) mm., tars. 15–17 (16.3) mm.
8 females wing 158–170 (163.3) mm., tail 192–224 (208.5) mm.,
exp. cul. 20–22 (20.9) mm., tars. 15–17 (16.0) mm.

Distributed from eastern Afghanistan to northern India, Nepal and Assam north of the Brahmaputra River (Vaurie, 1965).

2. *P. h. finschii* (Hume)   *Illustrated on page 332.*

ADULTS head purer grey with less blue; general plumage more yellowish than in *himalayana*, particularly on upperparts; under wing-coverts darker bluish-green; central tail-feathers violet-blue tipped with dull yellowish-white; smaller size with narrower, proportionately longer central tail-feathers.

10 males   wing 144–152 (146.7) mm., tail 198–276 (216.4) mm.,
exp. cul. 20–22 (20.8) mm., tars. 15–16 (15.4) mm.
7 females wing 141–145 (143.3) mm., tail 187–203 (197.1) mm.,
exp. cul. 20–21 (20.3) mm., tars. 15–16 (15.6) mm.

Ranges from Assam south of the Brahmaputra River east to Burma, northern Thailand, Laos, Vietnam and northern Yunnan in south-western China (Vaurie, 1965).

Husain (1959a) suggests that *himalayana* and *finschii* are sympatric in the Himalayan foothills between Bhutan and northern Bengal, so should be treated as distinct species. However, he does admit that study of further specimens from the area is necessary. Pending clarification of this problem and proof that the two forms nest in the same area I prefer to follow Ripley (1961) and Vaurie (1965) and treat the two forms as subspecies.

GENERAL NOTES

The Slaty-headed Parakeet is a highland bird, though in central Nepal it has been found as low as 240 m. (see Biswas, 1960); in the Likiang Range, Yunnan, it ascends to at least 3,800 m. (Vaurie, 1965). Vielliard (1969) reports that in eastern Afghanistan it seems to be fairly nomadic and around Kunar appears to favour cultivated areas where there are large trees. Puget (1970) reports that in eastern Afghanistan he saw large numbers in oak and cedar groves. About Mussoorie, in the Himalayan foothills of northern India, Fleming (1967) recorded it in subtropical, coniferous, and oak forests. Ali and Ripley (1969) point out that in northern India it occurs chiefly between about 600 m. and 2,500 m., occasionally descending down to 250 m., and inhabits well wooded slopes and valleys, particularly deodar forest and the vicinity of terraced cultivation or hillside orchards. Smythies (1953) says that in Burma it is more a bird of the forest than are other parakeets, and though scarce in the north becomes common farther south. In northern Thailand it is common in the more open mixed deciduous forests, cleared areas and along the wider trails between 600 m. and 1,200 m. (Deignan, 1945). In Vietnam it occurs in forests on the western slopes of the central mountain chain and is seldom seen near cultivation (Wildash, 1968). Throughout the Himalayan Region there is a marked altitudinal movement, the birds descending to lower areas in winter (Hudson, 1930; Wright, 1957; Puget, 1970), but elsewhere the species is resident though often irregularly distributed and subject to local nomadic movements governed by food supply.

These noisy parakeets generally move about in family parties or small flocks. Fleming notes that in the Mussoorie district flocks of up to fifty gather towards the end of the monsoon season to feed on *Viburnum* berries. They have been recorded in mixed groups with Rose-ringed, Plum-headed and Blossom-headed Parakeets. The flight is swift and direct. A flock in flight is an attractive sight; the birds twist and turn through the trees in unison and with remarkable agility, and then suddenly swing upwards to alight in the uppermost branches of a tall tree.

Their food comprises seeds, nuts, fruits, berries, blossoms and leaf buds. Wright reports that in the Dehra Dun area, northern India, they are attracted to berries on the *Duranta* hedges, and to camphor berries, seeds of *Terminalia myriocarpa*, *Bauhinia purpurea* flowers, and in February to the dry pods on shisham trees (*Dalbergia* sp.). Fleming reports that in the Mussoorie district the main food items are acorns, and *Cornus* and *Viburnum* berries. Ali and Ripley claim that the parrots are a pest in maize fields of the upland valleys, and are destructive to walnuts, apples, and pears in the hillside orchards. Near Henzada, Burma, Stanford (1935) watched them feeding on seeds of *Dendrocalamus longispathus*. Smythies quotes a report of numbers of parakeets having been seen eating grit from a dry creek bed in the Mandalay district.

CALL A high-pitched *scree-scree* and a long, drawn-out *wee . . . eenee* (Wright, 1957); also a variety of softer and more musical, chattering notes. All call-notes are harsher than those of *P. cyanocephala*.

Slaty-headed Parakeet 1
Psittacula himalayana finschii
MNHN. CG1924,819 ad. ♂

Slaty-headed Parakeet 2
Psittacula himalayana himalayana
AMNH. 778629 ad. ♂

Intermediate Parakeet *Psittacula intermedia* 3
AMNH. 621540 ad. ♂

NESTING Surprisingly little is known about the nesting of this common species. In central and southern Burma the breeding season is from January to March (Smythies, 1953) and in India between March and May (Ali and Ripley, 1969). Puget says that in eastern Afghanistan breeding takes place during spring, that is, from March to May, and nests are nearly always in old nesting holes of the Scaly-bellied Woodpecker (*Picus squamatus*). Nests are in hollow limbs or holes in trees and two or more may be found in one tree. A normal clutch comprises four or five eggs. Apparently young birds acquire the slaty head after the first winter (Smythies, 1953; Ali and Ripley, 1969).

EGGS Rounded; 43 eggs, 28.3 (27.2–30.5) × 22.2 (21.2–25.0) mm. [Schönwetter, 1964].

PLUM-HEADED PARAKEET

Psittacula cyanocephala (Linné)

Illustrated on page 333.

DESCRIPTION

Length 33 cm.

MALE plumage predominantly green, brighter and more yellowish on mantle and underparts; head deep red, strongly tinged with bluish-purple on hindcrown, nape and lower cheeks; chin, broad stripes across lower cheeks, and narrow nuchal collar black; wide bluish-green band on neck; rump bluish-green; under wing-coverts greenish-blue; dark red patch on wing-coverts; long central tail feathers blue broadly tipped with white, lateral feathers yellow-green tipped with yellow; upper mandible orange-yellow, lower brownish-black; iris yellowish-white; legs greenish-grey.

FEMALE head dull bluish-grey, more greyish on forehead and cheeks; black markings replaced by a variable yellow collar; no red wing-patch; upper mandible pale yellow, lower greyish.

IMMATURES green head, sometimes tinged with grey near chin; bill pale yellow.

10 males   wing 134–146 (140.0) mm., tail 174–225 (202.5) mm.,
       exp. cul. 17–19 (17.7) mm., tars. 13–15 (14.4) mm.

10 females   wing 126–138 (134.1) mm., tail 152–194 (165.1) mm.,
       exp. cul. 16–18 (17.1) mm., tars. 14–15 (14.3) mm.

DISTRIBUTION

Ceylon, Rameswaram Island, and most of India, east of about Rawalpindi in West Pakistan, and Nepal east to Bhutan and West Bengal.

SUBSPECIES

Biswas (1951) has listed three subspecies, but from the measurements given I must agree·with Rand and Fleming (1957) that *rosa* is a synonym of *bengalensis*, which in turn seems inseparable from *cyanocephala* though there is an obvious south-north clinal increase in size.

GENERAL NOTES

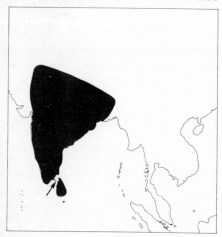

In Ceylon the Plum-headed Parakeet is the common parakeet of the lower hill zone up to about 1,000 m., or somewhat higher on the eastern side of the mountain massif (Henry, 1971); it may also occur in isolated wooded hills in the dry zone, but Henry believes that its range has decreased since the turn of the century. In India it is found in wooded plains and foothills up to about 1,300 m., or even 1,500 m. in certain areas (Ali and Ripley, 1969); it is particularly common in forests surrounding cultivation. In far western Nepal, Fleming and Traylor (1968) found large groups in tall trees in the more open areas above cultivated fields. Whistler claims that it is a generally distributed and fairly common species, being resident in some parts of its range but only a seasonal visitor in other areas (in Ali, 1934). Ali and Ripley point out that the marked local movements are governed mainly by food supply.

Family parties or small groups are usually seen, though in forested areas near cultivation very large flocks of several hundred may collect to feed on ripening grain. These parrots have the habit of alighting on the topmost branches of trees and when perched adopt a very upright stance. At dusk groups come into a large communal roosting site, such as a bamboo clump or a patch of forest, and there is continual screeching and chattering until after nightfall. The flight is swift and flocks twist and turn through the forest with astonishing ease.

These parrots feed on seeds, fruits, nuts, blossoms, especially those of *Salmalia*, *Butea* and *Bassia*, and leaf buds. Whistler notes that, besides grain, favourite food items are figs, the small black drupes of *Zizyphus oenoplia*, and *Butea* flowers; one specimen collected by the Hyderabad survey party had pollen adhering to its throat feathers. They can be serious pests in orchards and rice fields.

CALL In flight a shrill *too-i . . . too-i* (Ali, 1946); also a variety of melodic notes while perched.

NESTING According to Ali and Ripley the breeding season in India is from December to April. Henry says that in Ceylon it is from February to May, and often again in August-September. The nest is in a hollow limb or hole in a tree. Lowther (1940) claims that almost invariably the birds excavate the hollow, often in large 'knots' so characteristic of *Bassia* trees, but there are records of nests in old woodpeckers' and barbets' holes and in crevices in walls of buildings. Several pairs may nest in the same tree or in closely adjoining trees; colonial nesting has been reported. A normal clutch is from four to six eggs. Lowther says that both sexes incubate and care for the young, but according to Betts (1951) the male does not assist. An account of breeding in captivity gives the impression that only the female brooded, though this is not clearly stated (Eaves, 1945).

Further information from breeding in captivity includes a description of the courtship display and duration of the nestling period. The display by the male consisted of a series of neat bows, followed by a jerking of the tail and running up and down the perches. Only one chick was reared and it left the nest seven weeks after hatching. According to Tavistock (1954) young birds attain a plumage similar to that of the female with their first moult and males come into full colour with the second complete moult when in their third year.

Plum-headed Parakeet *Psittacula cyanocephala*   **1**
AMNH. 621483 ad. ♂

Plum-headed Parakeet *Psittacula cyanocephala*   **2**
CNHM. 229440 ad. ♀

Blossom-headed Parakeet   **3**
Psittacula roseata roseata
AMNH. 621502 ad. ♂

EGGS Spherical, without gloss: 60 eggs, 25.0 (22.2–27.2) × 20.4 (19.1–22.0) mm. [Schönwetter, 1964].

BLOSSOM-HEADED PARAKEET
Psittacula roseata Biswas

Length 30 cm.
MALE similar to *P. cyanocephala*; general plumage green, yellowish on underparts; forecrown, cheeks and ear-coverts rose-pink; crown and nape pale bluish-lilac; chin, broad stripes across lower cheeks, and narrow nuchal collar black; green rump; brownish-red patch on wing-coverts; under wing-coverts green; long central tail feathers blue tipped with pale yellow, lateral feathers yellow-green tipped with pale yellow; upper mandible orange-yellow, lower grey; iris palest yellow; legs greenish-grey.
FEMALE head dull bluish-grey; black markings replaced by a variable yellow collar; small red wing-patch; upper mandible yellow, lower greyish-white.
IMMATURES head green, occasionally tinged with grey near chin; no red wing-patch; bill pale yellow.

From lower Himalayas in West Bengal and Assam east to Indochina.

Illustrated on page 333.

1. *P. r. roseata* Biswas
   10 males wing 137–148 (143.2) mm., tail 151–179 (168.2) mm.,
       exp. cul. 18–20 (18.9) mm., tars. 14–16 (14.9) mm.
   8 females wing 128–143 (137.9) mm., tail 141–157 (148.1) mm.,
       exp. cul. 17–19 (17.8) mm., tars. 14–15 (14.5) mm.
   Ranges from the Lower Himalayas in West Bengal and Assam south and east to East Pakistan and northern Burma; intergrades with *juneae* in the Tripura area, southern Assam.

2. *P. r. juneae* Biswas
   ADULTS general plumage more yellowish than in *roseata*; central tail-feathers less bluish, lateral feathers more yellowish; red wing-patch larger.
   8 males wing 133–142 (137.4) mm., tail 145–170 (157.4) mm.,
       exp. cul. 17–18 (17.3) mm., tars. 13–15 (14.1) mm.
   8 females wing 126–141 (133.6) mm., tail 129–158 (145.1) mm.,
       exp. cul. 16–17 (16.8) mm., tars. 13–15 (14.0) mm.
   Distributed from southernmost Assam and south Burma east through Thailand, north of Prachuap, to Laos, Cambodia and Vietnam.

The habits and general behaviour of the Blossom-headed Parakeet are similar to those of the very closely allied Plum-headed Parakeet. It is usually seen in family groups or small flocks, sometimes in the company of Moustached Parakeets (*P. alexandri*). Smythies (1953) says that the species is sparingly distributed through most of Burma, frequenting cultivation and the outskirts of forests. Christison *et al.* (1946) report that in coastal Arakan and the Yomas foothills, south-western Burma, it was generally scarce and locally migratory, being very common at Ruywa in March and April. It is a common forest bird in Thailand (Lekagul, 1968), but in southern Vietnam is uncommon and inhabits mainly open timbered regions at the edge of cultivation (Wildash, 1968).

CALL Similar to that of the Plum-headed Parakeet.

NESTING In Burma nesting has been recorded during March and April (Smythies, 1953). McClure (1968) points out that during March, April and May nestlings and juvenile birds are offered for sale in the Bangkok market. Presumably, the nesting behaviour is similar to that of the Plum-headed Parakeet.
   Hargreaves (1960) gives some details of a successful nesting in captivity. The incubation period was not determined, but the two young reared left the nest about six weeks after hatching. About two months after leaving the nest they went through a body moult and acquired silvery-grey heads.

EGGS Almost spherical; 8 eggs, 25.1 (24.2–26.7) × 21.0 (20.0–21.6) mm. [Harrison and Holyoak, 1970].

INTERMEDIATE PARAKEET
Psittacula intermedia (Rothschild)

Illustrated on page 332.

Length 36 cm.
MALE general plumage green, brighter on rump and more yellowish on underparts; forehead and periophthalmic region rufous pink; remainder of head slaty-purple; chin, broad stripes across lower cheeks, and narrow collar around nape black; ill-defined bluish-green band on neck; maroon patch on wing-coverts; under wing-coverts bluish-green; tail feathers bluish-green tipped with yellow.

DESCRIPTION

DISTRIBUTION

SUBSPECIES

GENERAL NOTES

Derbyan Parakeet *Psittacula derbiana* **1**
MNHN. CG1897,99 ad. ♂

Blyth's Parakeet *Psittacula caniceps* **2**
USNM. 178500 ad. ♂

DESCRIPTION

FEMALE undescribed.

IMMATURES undescribed.

1 male wing 155 mm., tail 206 mm.,
 exp. cul. 20 mm., tars. —.

1 male wing 155 mm., tail —,
 exp. cul. 19 mm., tars. —.

3 males wing 151–160 (156.0) mm., tail 167–195 (180.7) mm.,
 exp. cul. 18–21 (19.7) mm., tars. 14–16 (15.0) mm.

DISTRIBUTION   Unknown; thought to be the Himalayan region, northern India.

GENERAL NOTES   The Intermediate Parakeet was described by Rothschild in 1895 from a single skin sent to him from Bombay, and he thought that it probably came from the Western Provinces. He remarked that it was intermediate between *P. himalayana* and *P. cyanocephala*. Hartert (1924) examined six skins (all males) sent to him by a London skin dealer and fully agreed with Rothschild's remark about the intermediate appearance. No further specimens have been obtained.

Biswas (1959b) believes that *intermedia* is a distinct species that has escaped the notice of ornithologists because of its probable localized distribution. On the other hand, Husain (1959) suggests that it is a hybrid between the Slaty-headed and Plum-headed Parakeets. I have examined six specimens in the Rothschild Collection at the American Museum of Natural History; in my opinion, one is almost certainly an immature specimen of *P. himalayana* and the other five, all adult males, are hybrids as suggested by Husain.

MALABAR PARAKEET
Psittacula columboides (Vigors)

Illustrated on page 329.

DESCRIPTION   Length 38 cm.

MALE head, neck, breast and back grey with a variable rose tint; lores and periophthalmic region green, tinged with blue on forecrown; chin, stripes across lower cheeks, and narrow nuchal collar black; bluish-green band on neck; bluish-green rump; wing-coverts dark green with pale margins; flight feathers blue; lower abdomen and vent yellowish-green washed with blue; under wing-coverts green; central tail feathers blue tipped with yellow, lateral feathers green tipped with yellow; upper mandible red tipped with yellow, lower brownish; iris yellow; legs pale grey.

FEMALE no bluish-green band on neck; lacks green forehead; mantle, breast and abdomen pale green, sometimes washed with grey; bill dusky black.

IMMATURES grey replaced by green; no bluish-green neck band; black markings faintly indicated; pale orange-red bill in very young birds.

10 males wing 144–160 (150.2) mm., tail 212–266 (237.4) mm.,
 exp. cul. 22–25 (23.2) mm., tars. 15–17 (16.0) mm.

10 females wing 135–143 (141.1) mm., tail 171–201 (188.9) mm.,
 exp. cul. 22–23 (22.3) mm., tars. 15–17 (16.1) mm.

DISTRIBUTION   The Western Ghats strip in south-western India from about 19°N. lat., north of Bombay, south to Kerala.

GENERAL NOTES   Malabar Parakeets inhabit tropical evergreen and moist deciduous forest (Ripley, 1961). They are most abundant in the hills between 450 and 1,000 m., but are occasionally seen in the lowlands and also as high as 1,600 m., where they completely replace Plum-headed Parakeets (Ali, 1969). They are birds of the wetter areas, but in mixed forests do associate with *P. cyanocephala*, their counterpart in the drier zone.

These noisy parrots are usually seen in family parties of four or five, or in small flocks. They are particularly common in secondary jungle on old forest clearings or abandoned coffee and rubber plantations. They are largely arboreal, spending most of the day feeding in the treetops. Where cultivation adjoins hillside forest they will come to the ground to attack ripening crops.

Food comprises seeds, nuts, fruits, berries, nectar and leaf buds; figs are an important food item. They frequently visit flowering *Erythrina* and *Grevillea* trees—so widely cultivated as shade trees in tea and coffee plantations—to extract pollen and nectar. They also raid vetches (*Dolichos*) and other crops cultivated in forest clearings, and are destructive in orchards (Ali and Ripley, 1969).

In flight a harsh, disyllabic cry, which is easily distinguished from the call of *P. cyanocephala* (Ali and Ripley, 1969).

Moustached Parakeet **1**
Psittacula alexandri alexandri
ANSP. 57059 ad. ♂

Long-tailed Parakeet **2**
Psittacula longicauda longicauda
AM. 030565 ad. ♂

NESTING The breeding season is from January to March and the nest is in a hollow limb or hole high up in a tall tree. A marked preference is shown for lofty ironwood trees (*Mesua ferrea*). Old nesting hollows of woodpeckers and barbets are sometimes enlarged and used. Three or four eggs are laid on a layer of decayed wood dust lining the bottom of the hollow.

Jaywardene (1963) gives some details of a successful breeding in captivity. The incubation period was not determined, but only the female brooded. The male did not assist with feeding of the chicks until a few days before they left the nest, six weeks after they hatched. Further information from another breeding in captivity is given by Curr (1971); the incubation period was about twenty-seven days and the young birds left the nest approximately eight weeks after hatching.

Tavistock (1929b) has described plumage changes in young birds. They attain full adult plumage with the first complete moult, not with the second as in most other members of the genus. On leaving the nest they have orange-red bills, but these soon become black, and in males change back to red within the first year.

EGGS Spherical, slightly glossy; 30 eggs, 28.3 (27.0–30.3) × 24.5 (22.3–25.1) mm. [Schönwetter, 1964].

Hyacinth Macaw *Anodorhynchus hyacinthinus*
AM. 043712 ad. unsexed

EMERALD-COLLARED PARAKEET
Psittacula calthorpae (Blyth)

Illustrated on page 329.

Length 29 cm.
ADULTS head dark bluish-grey; forehead, lores and periophthalmic region suffused with green, duller in female; chin and stripes across lower cheeks black; narrow nuchal collar blue; underparts and broad band on neck rich green, latter tinged with blue; mantle, back and rump bluish-grey, strongly washed with violet-blue on rump; lesser wing-coverts grey; wings green, yellowish on median coverts; under wing-coverts green; tail rich blue tipped with yellow; in males upper mandible coral red tipped with yellow, in females entirely greyish-black, lower brownish in both sexes; iris yellowish-white; legs greenish-grey.
IMMATURES grey replaced by green; ill-defined band of brighter green on neck; rump greyish-blue; bill orange-red.
10 males   wing 135–145 (140.2) mm., tail 125–135 (129.3) mm.,
            exp. cul. 21–23 (21.8) mm., tars. 16–17 (16.3) mm.
10 females wing 135–140 (137.4) mm., tail 117–123 (119.9) mm.,
            exp. cul. 20–21 (20.5) mm.; tars. 16–17 (16.5) mm.

DISTRIBUTION Ceylon; there is an unconfirmed sight record from the Maldive Islands (see Ali and Ripley, 1969).

GENERAL NOTES Henry (1971) points out that although Emerald-Collared Parakeets occur near sea level in parts of the wet zone of Ceylon, they are primarily birds of the hills up to about 1,600 m.; at times they ascend to 2,000 m., but probably do not breed at this altitude. In pairs or small flocks they frequent most types of well-wooded country, particularly the forest edge surrounding clearings. They are common but locally distributed, and numbers in an area may fluctuate with the availability of food.

These parrots are arboreal in habits. During the morning, while feeding in the treetops, they are tame and easy to approach. They have been seen in the company of Brahminy Mynahs (*Sturnus pagodarum*) feeding on the fruits of the kanda tree (*Macaranga tomentosa*). After feeding they become restless and noisy. Small parties congregate in shady trees and emit an almost continuous chatter. Towards evening they feed again. Before going to roost they wander about, calling loudly, and frequently pause momentarily on the topmost branches of tall, conspicuous trees. The flight is swift and direct, and the birds are very adept at weaving in and out through the forest.

They feed on seeds, fruits, berries, nectar, blossoms and leaf buds, generally procured in the treetops.

CALL While in flight a harsh, chattering *ak-ak-ak-ak-ak* (Henry, 1971).

NESTING According to Henry the breeding season is from January to May, and often again between July and September. The nest is in a hollow limb or hole in a tree, usually at a considerable height. Three or four eggs are laid on a layer of decayed wood dust at the bottom of the cavity.

Jindasa (1961) gives some details of a successful breeding in captivity. The incubation period was about three weeks and the young left the nest seven weeks after hatching.

EGGS Rounded; 9 eggs, 24.7 (23.0–26.0) × 19.3 (19.0–19.7) mm. [Stuart Baker, 1927].

DERBYAN PARAKEET
Psittacula derbiana (Fraser)

Illustrated on page 336.

DESCRIPTION Length 50 cm.
MALE forehead, lores and lower cheeks black; forecrown suffused with bright blue; periophthalmic region tinged with bluish-green; remainder of head blue-violet; upperparts green, paler on nape and median wing-coverts; throat, underparts and under wing-coverts lavender-purple; thighs and vent green variably margined with blue; central tail feathers blue tinged with green near base, lateral feathers green narrowly edged with blue; upper mandible red with a yellowish tip, lower black; iris yellowish-white; legs greenish-grey.

FEMALE no blue on forecrown; brownish-pink band behind ear-coverts; upper mandible black.
IMMATURES head green instead of blue; general plumage much duller; very young birds have
orange-red bills.

13 males   wing 208–228 (220.3) mm., tail 225–266 (250.1) mm.,
         exp. cul. 30–35 (32.8) mm., tars. 19–22 (20.9) mm.
10 females   wing 211–221 (215.6) mm., tail 207–245 (227.0) mm.,
         exp. cul. 29–34 (30.9) mm., tars. 19–23 (20.6) mm.

North-eastern Assam near the Tibet border (Stoner, 1952), south-eastern Tibet west to about
93°E. long. in the Tsangpo Valley, and western China in the mountains of western Szechwan and
north-western Yunnan.

DISTRIBUTION

GENERAL NOTES

The Derbyan Parakeet inhabits a region seldom visited by ornithologists so little is known of its
habits. It is a mountain bird, frequenting coniferous forests, mixed pine and oak forests and
rhododendron alpine forests up to 4,000 m. (Ripley 1961, Vaurie 1965). In the Mishmi Hills, north-
eastern Assam, Stoner found it as low as 1,250 m. Ludlow (1951) notes that in south-eastern Tibet
it is resident, being present as high as 3,300 m. in mid-winter. Vaurie says that there is slight
altitudinal movement, and I suspect that this would be prevalent at the highest elevations.

In the Tsangpo Valley, south-eastern Tibet, Kinnear found flocks of up to fifty birds in cultivated
areas in the main valley and in coniferous forests high up the side valleys; he reported that they
were noisy birds and strong fliers (in Ludlow, 1944). In the Mishmi Hills, Stoner saw several flocks
in pine forest near a small village.

Food consists of seeds, fruits, berries and leaf buds. Kinnear noticed that early in the year the
parakeets were feeding in poplar trees (*Populus ciliata*), and in autumn they raided the barley fields
and peach groves. Food items listed by Ali and Ripley (1969) include seeds of *Pinus tabulaeformis*
and cultivated fruits. Stoner was told by local villagers that in late summer the parrots descended
on their maize crops.

CALL A prolonged, raucous, metallic cry (in captivity).

NESTING Kinnear says that these parrots breed in mid-June and the nest is in a hole in a tree,
especially a poplar.

Tavistock (1929a) observed the courtship display of captive birds. The male, after walking toward
the female with his bill rubbing against the perch, stands erect before her and then, while vibrating
the lower mandible, bows several times. He then lifts each foot in much the same way as does the
Rose-ringed Parakeet (*P. krameri*), and then, with lateral tail-feathers fanned and pupils contracted,
bows slowly and gracefully towards the hen.

Ezra (1933) gives some details of a successful breeding in captivity. One chick hatched thirty-one
days after the first of two eggs was laid, and remained in the nest for about fifty days. Payne (1956)
also bred the species in captivity and believes that the incubation period may have been only
eighteen to twenty days. The bills of very young birds are red, but soon change to blackish and
later change back to red in males, the cycle being completed in fifteen to eighteen months (Norris,
1954).

EGGS A single egg in the Hamburg Museum measures 36.1 × 27.7 mm. [Schönwetter, 1964].

MOUSTACHED PARAKEET
Psittacula alexandri (Linné)

Lear's Macaw *Anodorhynchus leari*   1
AMNH. 474100 ad. ♂

Glaucous Macaw *Anodorhynchus glaucus*   2
USNM. 256884 ad. unsexed

Length 33 cm.
ADULTS upperparts green; median wing-coverts greenish-yellow; hindneck emerald green; head
grey with a variable bluish tinge; periophthalmic region washed with green; chin, lower cheeks,
and line from forehead to eyes black; throat, breast, and upper abdomen bright salmon pink,
duller in females; lower abdomen and vent green washed with blue; under wing-coverts pale
green; central tail feathers blue tipped with yellowish-green, lateral feathers bluish-green; bill
coral red; iris pale yellow; legs greenish-grey.
IMMATURES crown and entire underparts green; lower cheeks dark brown; sides of head washed
with brownish-grey; median wing-coverts green margined with yellowish-green; shorter tail;
bill pale red in very young birds.

From the lower Himalayas in northern India and Nepal, through Assam, Burma, the Andaman
Islands, southern China, Hainan Island, and Indochina to Java, Bali and islands off western Sumatra;
probably introduced to southern Borneo (Symthies, 1968), and there is a sight record from Hong
Kong (Dove and Goodhart, 1955).

DISTRIBUTION

1. *P. a. alexandri* (Linné)
   12 males   wing 149–155 (152.3) mm., tail 139–191 (160.8) mm.,
         exp. cul. 24–25 (24.7) mm., tars. 15–17 (16.3) mm.

Illustrated on page 337.

SUBSPECIES

10 females wing 145–166 (152.8) mm., tail 129–153 (138.2) mm.,
exp. cul. 23–25 (24.0) mm., tars. 15–17 (15.9) mm.

Restricted to Java and Bali, Indonesia; also occurs in southern Borneo where it was probably introduced from Java.

2. *P. a. kangeanensis* Hoogerwerf
ADULTS similar to *alexandri*, but with less blue in grey of head; bill slightly heavier than in *dammermani*; males have brighter and more extensive yellowish wing-patch than *alexandri* or *dammermani*; bill colouration as in *alexandri*.
2 males wing 159–161 (160.0) mm., tail 179–180 (179.5) mm.,
exp. cul. 26–27 (26.5) mm., tars. 18–19 (18.5) mm.
2 females wing 158–159 (158.5) mm., tail 153–168 (160.5) mm.,
exp. cul. 25 (25.0) mm., tars. 17 (17.0) mm.

Confined to the Kangean Islands, Indonesia.

3. *P. a. dammermani* Chasen and Kloss
ADULTS like *alexandri*, but larger and with a more robust bill; tend to be more bluish on crown; bill colouration as in *alexandri*.
1 male wing 179 mm., tail 218 mm.,
exp. cul. 26 mm., tars. 17 mm.
1 female wing 172 mm., tail 161 mm.,
exp. cul. 23 mm., tars. 18 mm.

Found on the Karimundjawa Islands, Indonesia.

4. *P. a. perionca* (Oberholser)
ADULTS similar to *major*, but slightly smaller in size; lower abdomen and vent of males brighter than in *major*; bill colouration as in *fasciata*.
5 males wing 183–194 (189.0) mm., tail 169–227 (194.2) mm.,
exp. cul. 28–30 (29.0) mm., tars. 18–20 (19.2) mm.
5 females wing 171–185 (179.6) mm., tail 159–170 (164.6) mm.,
exp. cul. 27–29 (27.8) mm., tars. 19 (19.0) mm.

Confined to Nias Island, Indonesia.

5. *P. a. major* (Richmond)
ADULTS similar in colouration to *cala*, but larger in size; also larger than *perionca*; less bluish suffusion on lower abdomen and vent of males than in *cala*; bill colouration as in *fasciata*.
5 males wing 189–203 (196.0) mm., tail 178–227 (208.0) mm.,
exp. cul. 29–31 (29.4) mm., tars. 19–21 (20.2) mm.
2 females wing 187–188 (187.5) mm., tail 199–200 (199.5) mm.,
exp. cul. 27–28 (27.5) mm., tars. 18 (18.0) mm.

Found on Lasia and Babi Islands, Indonesia.

6. *P. a. cala* (Oberholser)
ADULTS smaller than both *major* and *perionca*; resemble *abbotti* but the pink of the breast, particularly in females, is less suffused with lilac; differs from *fasciata* in its larger size, absence of green from the forecrown, and paler green of the back; bill colouration as in *fasciata*.
7 males wing 173–185 (177.6) mm., tail 162–197 (182.0) mm.,
exp. cul. 25–27 (25.7) mm., tars. 17–19 (18.1) mm.
7 females wing 168–179 (173.3) mm., tail 159–185 (171.9) mm.,
exp. cul. 23–27 (24.9) mm., tars. 17–19 (18.0) mm.

Occurs only on Simeulue Island, Indonesia.

7. *P. a. abbotti* (Oberholser)
ADULTS differ from *fasciata* by an overall paler colouration and a larger size; bill colouration as in *fasciata*.
9 males wing 173–181 (176.9) mm., tail 161–206 (179.6) mm.,
exp. cul. 24–27 (25.8) mm., tars. 17–18 (17.6) mm.
7 females wing 163–178 (170.9) mm., tail 160–185 (171.6) mm.,
exp. cul. 23–26 (24.7) mm., tars. 16–19 (17.4) mm.

Found on the Andaman Islands.

8. *P. a. fasciata* (P. L. S. Müller)
MALE like *alexandri*, but head grey strongly tinged with blue; breast and abdomen darker pink washed with lilac-blue; upper mandible red, lower blackish.
FEMALE deep pink of breast less suffused with lilac and continuing up side of neck in front of emerald green hindneck; head less tinged with blue; bill black.
12 males wing 153–171 (160.2) mm., tail 157–194 (176.3) mm.,
exp. cul. 23–26 (24.3) mm., tars. 17–19 (17.3) mm.
10 females wing 153–161 (156.8) mm., tail 140–170 (151.2) mm.,
exp. cul. 22–25 (23.2) mm., tars. 16–17 (16.7) mm.

Spix's Macaw *Cyanopsitta spixii*
ANSP. 100760 ad. unsexed

Distributed from the Dehra Dun area, northern India, east through Nepal and the lower Himalayas to Assam, East Pakistan, Burma, as far south as Tenasserim and the Mergui Archipelago, and to Thailand, Indochina, Hainan Island, and southernmost China in the provinces of Yunnan and Kwangsi.

GENERAL NOTES The Moustached Parakeet is a bird of the foothills and lowland plains, rarely ascending above 2,000 m. In the Himalayan region it avoids dense evergreen forest in favour of moist deciduous forest, light secondary jungle, and woodland in the neighbourhood of cultivation (Ali and Ripley, 1969). Smythies (1953) says that it is common throughout the forests of Burma and is one of the two parrots characteristic of teak forests, the other being the Slaty-headed Parakeet. It is common in the Andaman Islands where it is often seen in Port Blair and in fields and open country (Abdulali, 1964). According to Lekagul (1968) it is a common forest bird in every part of Thailand; in the northern provinces, Deignan (1945) found that it was the commonest parrot, occurring irregularly in every town and village and in any type of vegetation. It is by far the most common parrot in southern Vietnam and is often found close to habitation (Wildash, 1968). In southern China it frequents evergreen broad-leaved forests in the foothills (Cheng, 1963). Meyer de Schauensee and Ripley (1940) report that on Nias Island it was common in groves of coconut palms. Somadikarta says that on Java it is found mainly in mountain forests and has become scarce around cities and major towns (pers. comm., 1971); in 1971 during a visit of three days to the Bogor Botanic Gardens I saw only one immature bird, and there are reports that the species was a common resident there (see Hoogerwerf and Siccama, 1938).

Throughout most areas these parrots are sedentary, but there are local irregular movements, often coinciding with the ripening of crops, and numbers may fluctuate greatly. To the south of Muang Fang, northern Thailand, Deignan saw a flock of more than ten thousand on a small rice plain and remarked that such congregations must cause serious damage. Cheng reports that in southern China large flocks move out into the fields during the autumn harvest. An indication of regular movements comes from Stevens (1925) who reports that the species was only seen in the Rungbong Valley, Sikkim, during 'the cold weather'.

Flocks of from ten to fifty of these very noisy parrots are generally seen flying low over the open fields then rising up above taller vegetation. They alight with outspread tails and much fluttering of the wings. They call just as loudly and just as frequently while perched as when in flight. However, while feeding in the treetops they are usually quiet and their presence is indicated only by falling husks and the occasional fluttering of wings as a bird moves from one branch to another. They roost communally and outside the breeding season very large numbers may congregate in a tree, a clump of trees, or a bamboo thicket. The flight is slower than that of other *Psittacula* parrots and the rounded wings are noticeable.

The birds feed on seeds, nuts, fruits, berries, nectar, blossoms and leaf buds, and, as mentioned, are serious pests in rice fields. On Java they feed extensively on nectar and flowers of peteh (*Parkia speciosa*) and coral (*Erythrina variegata*) trees and on *Albizzia* seeds (Kuroda, 1936; Hoogerwerf and Siccama, 1938). Seeds, fruits and nuts, principally chestnuts (*Castanea* sp.), were found in the stomachs of seventeen birds collected in southern Yunnan during winter (Cheng, 1963).

CALL A raucous, trumpet-like scream that can be heard from a great distance (Smythies, 1953); also a shrill *ek-ek* and a variety of shrieks and whistles (Hoogerwerf and Siccama, 1938). On the Andaman Islands, Abdulali (1964) noted a plaintive, but distinctive *kewn*, and heard a female utter a nasal *kaink*.

NESTING In India, Burma, the Andaman Islands, and probably most of Indochina, the breeding season is from December to April, varying locally with altitude and other conditions. On Java nesting has been recorded in all months except April (Hoogerwerf, 1949). The nest is in a hollow limb or hole in a tree and several pairs may nest in the same or in adjacent trees. Old nesting holes of woodpeckers and barbets are frequently enlarged and used. Three or four eggs are laid on a layer of wood dust at the bottom of the hollow.

Vane (1953) gives details of a successful breeding in captivity. The incubation period was approximately twenty-eight days and only the female brooded. Only one chick hatched and it left the nest fifty-one days later. On leaving the nest its bill was pale red, but changed to black within a month. Hoogerwerf and Siccama point out that four months after leaving the nest young birds have acquired most of the adult plumage colouration, though they are much duller and after a further two months the central tail-feathers are fully developed.

EGGS Broad-oval, slightly glossy; 24 eggs, 29.5 (28.4–31.4) × 24.2 (23.6–24.8) mm. [Hoogerwerf, 1949].

BLYTH'S PARAKEET
Psittacula caniceps (Blyth)   *Illustrated on page 336.*

DESCRIPTION Length 56 cm.
ADULTS general plumage green, brighter on rump; crown and nape grey, slightly tinged with blue

in males, strongly tinged with blue in females; chin, lower cheeks, forehead and lores black; upper cheeks and ear-coverts yellowish-grey becoming dull mauve-grey towards hindneck; tail green, central tail-feathers strongly tinged with grey and tipped with yellow; upper mandible red in males, black in females, lower black in both sexes; iris orange-red; legs greenish-grey.
IMMATURES undescribed, but probably similar to female.
10 males   wing 209–222 (215.3) mm., tail 316–378 (341.9) mm.,
            exp. cul. 29–32 (29.8) mm., tars. 21–23 (21.6) mm.
10 females wing 202–219 (211.4) mm., tail 241–357 (286.4) mm.,
            exp. cul. 28–33 (29.6) mm., tars. 21–23 (21.8) mm.

Islands of Great Nicobar, Little Nicobar, Montschall and Kondul in the Nicobar Islands.

Little is known of the habits of Blyth's Parakeet. Abdulali (1967) found it to be common at Campbell Bay, Great Nicobar Island, but had difficulty collecting specimens because of its preference for perching in leafy trees rather than on bare branches. It is arboreal and generally keeps to the topmost branches of the tallest trees. Pairs or small parties are usually seen, and they are very noisy. They are popular as pets and many are caught for sale. The flight is swift and direct.
    Abdulali (1964) says that these parrots feed extensively on ripe fruits of *Pandanus*, which is abundant on the inhabited islands.

CALL A harsh, raucous *kraan . . . kraan*, somewhat like the call of a crow and very different from the screeching calls of *P. longicauda* (Abdulali, 1967).

NESTING I know of no published records.

EGGS Rounded; one egg in the British Museum measures 38.2 × 25.6 [Harrison and Holyoak, 1970].

LONG-TAILED PARAKEET
Psittacula longicauda (Boddaert)

Length 42 cm.
MALE general plumage green, darker on crown and paler, more yellowish on underparts; lores and line through eye bluish-black; sides of head and wide nuchal band rose-red; chin and lower cheeks black; mantle and upper back dull yellow washed with bluish-grey; rump and lower back pale blue; under wing-coverts yellowish; central tail feathers blue tipped with yellow, lateral feathers green; upper mandible red, lower brownish; iris yellowish-white; legs greenish-grey.
FEMALE crown darker green, posterior of ear-coverts washed with blue; upper cheeks dull orange-red; lower cheeks dark green; shorter central tail feathers; entire bill brownish.
IMMATURES predominantly green, darker on crown and lower cheeks; sides of head variably tinged with orange-red; rump slightly washed with blue in males; short central tail feathers; brownish bill.

Malay Peninsula, Borneo, Sumatra and adjacent islands, and the Andaman and Nicobar Islands.

1. *P. l. longicauda* (Boddaert)   *Illustrated on page 337.*
    10 males   wing 147–155 (150.7) mm., tail 215–270 (240.7) mm.,
                exp. cul. 21–24 (22.0) mm., tars. 15–17 (16.2) mm.
    8 females   wing 143–148 (145.4) mm., tail 154–201 (173.1) mm.,
                exp. cul. 20–22 (21.1) mm., tars. 16–17 (16.4) mm.
    Found on the Malay Peninsula south of Kedah, and on Singapore, Borneo, Sumatra, Nias Island, Bangka Islands and the Anambas Islands.

2. *P. l. defontainei* Chasen
    ADULTS like *longicauda*, but crown more yellowish; upper cheeks deeper in colour in both sexes.
    9 males   wing 148–164 (159.3) mm., tail 149–251 (220.3) mm.,
               exp. cul. 21–25 (22.9) mm., tars. 16–18 (17.1) mm.
    4 females wing 148–155 (150.8) mm., tail 196–211 (205.8) mm.,
               exp. cul. 21–22 (21.8) mm., tars. 15–18 (16.5) mm.
    Occurs on the Natuna Islands, the Riau Archipelago, and Bintan, Karimata and Belitung Islands, Indonesia.

3. *P. l. modesta* (Fraser)
    MALE larger than *longicauda*; crown dull red with a greenish tinge; nape distinctly paler than ear-coverts.

FEMALE larger than *longicauda*; crown greenish-brown; bluish band bordering reddish ear-coverts.

10 males   wing 192–208 (202.8) mm., tail 180–231 (209.5) mm.,
           exp. cul. 27–30 (28.4) mm., tars. 20–22 (21.1) mm.
7 females   wing 192–206 (199.9) mm., tail — (damaged),
           exp. cul. 27–29 (27.9) mm., tars. 19–21 (20.1) mm.
1 female   wing 190 mm., tail 208 mm.,
           exp. cul. 28 mm., tars. 19 mm.
    Restricted to Enggano Island, Indonesia.

4. *P. l. tytleri* (Hume)
MALE nape, mantle and upper back yellowish-green strongly suffused with greyish-mauve; breast slightly tinged with same colour; rump and lower back green; larger than *longicauda*.
FEMALE no greyish-mauve on nape, back or breast; larger than *longicauda*.
8 males   wing 172–182 (176.5) mm., tail 206–249 (223.0) mm.,
           exp. cul. 22–24 (23.4) mm., tars. 18–19 (18.3) mm.
7 females   wing 166–180 (173.7) mm., tail 160–193 (175.0) mm.,
           exp. cul. 21–24 (22.9) mm., tars. 17–19 (18.1) mm.
    Occurs on the Andaman Islands.

5. *P. l. nicobarica* (Gould)
ADULTS crown bright green; nape yellowish-green, tinged with lilac in males; ear-coverts and upper cheeks bright red; entire upperparts green, in males there is a slight bluish suffusion on mantle; much larger than *longicauda*.
9 males   wing 190–200 (194.9) mm., tail 250–275 (259.2) mm.,
           exp. cul. 24–28 (25.6) mm., tars. 19–21 (19.9) mm.
8 females   wing 190–206 (194.6) mm., tail 197–250 (221.3) mm.,
           exp. cul. 24–25 (24.3) mm., tars. 18–20 (19.3) mm.
    Found on the Nicobar Islands.

GENERAL NOTES

Glenister (1951) says that Long-tailed Parakeets are common in suitable localities on the Malay Peninsula. They seem to prefer the edge of high jungle, dead trees standing in swampy areas, and other types of open country. They are probably passage migrants on Singapore and are seen mostly between May and July, when they are fairly common in tall trees in suburban gardens (Ward, 1968). On Borneo they are resident but local, chiefly near the coast where they frequent clearings and mangrove forests (Gore, 1968; Smythies, 1968). Abdulali (1964 and 1967) reports that they are common in the South and Middle Andamans, and were frequently noted at all camps in the Nicobar Islands. In all regions they can be unpredictable in their movements; large flocks may build up in an area or suddenly arrive from elsewhere, and then leave and be absent for years.

They are restless birds and seem to be always on the move, dashing from one tree to another and clambering through the foliage. They are noisy and their raucous screeching attracts attention as they speed through the air, swerving gracefully to avoid branches. Outside the breeding season they roost communally; towards late afternoon parties converge on an assembly point from which, accompanied by continuous screeching, they indulge in aerobatics before leaving as one large flock to settle in a favoured clump of trees or bamboo. From observations of flocks visiting oil-palm plantations in Johore, Malaysia, Ward and Wood (1967) found that the parrots fed for an hour or two after dawn and again in the late afternoon, and probably spent the remainder of the day roosting in rainforest trees. The flight is swift and direct.

Seeds, fruits, nuts, berries, nectar, blossoms and leaf buds make up the diet. In the Nicobar Islands they have been seen feeding on the outer covering of betel nuts (*Areca catechu*), papaya (*Carica papaya*), and ripe *Pandanus* fruit (Ali and Ripley, 1969). Smythies reports that in Borneo they have been observed eating fruits of kapor trees (*Dryobalanops* sp.) and *Dillenia speciosa*. Robinson (1927) remarks that around Kuala Lumpur, Malaysia, they are particularly fond of the flowers of an *Acacia* originally planted as shade trees in coffee plantations. Ward and Wood point out that these parrots can be serious pests in oil-palm plantations; they pluck ripe fruits from the bunch and carry them out along the leaf rachids or to an adjacent palm where they remove and eat the soft mesocarp while holding the fruits in one of their feet.

CALL A shrill screech repeated rapidly.

NESTING On the Andaman and Nicobar Islands eggs and nestlings have been taken during February and March (in Stuart Baker, 1927), while on the Malay Peninsula eggs have been found in February and chicks in July (in Chasen, 1939). The nest is in a hollow limb or hole in a tree, often in a tall, dead tree. The two or three eggs are laid on a mat of strips of bark or decayed wood dust. Presumably, nesting behaviour does not differ greatly from that of other species in the genus. According to Tavistock (1931b) young birds acquire a plumage similar to that of the adult female with the first moult and retain it for about one year.

EGGS Rounded, highly glossy; 30 eggs, 30.6 (28.4–34.2) × 24.7 (23.0–26.1) mm. [Stuart Baker, 1927].

South American Distribution

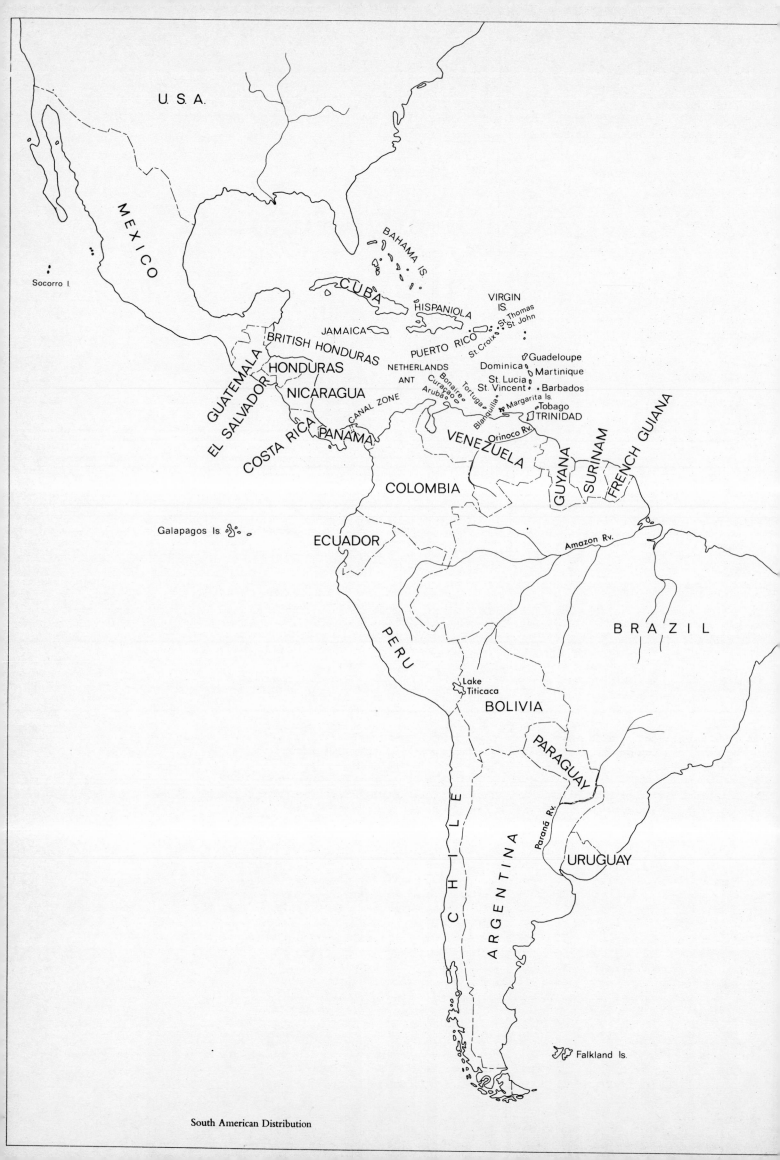

South American Distribution

SOUTH AMERICAN DISTRIBUTION

The South American Distribution includes the Neotropical Faunal Region and the southern sector of the Nearctic Region, though for practical purposes the latter may be omitted because its only parrot species, the Carolina Parakeet (*Conuropsis carolinensis*), is now extinct. Parrots are very well represented in this Distribution and include some of the most familiar groups such as macaws (*Ara* spp.) and amazons (*Amazona* spp.). The dominant geographical feature is the South American continent and it is there that the majority of parrots occur. The other geographical components, namely Central America and the Caribbean Islands, are, from the avifaunal point of view, merely subsidiary outliers.

Topographical features of the South American continent are on a grand scale. They include the greatest mountain range in the world—the Andes, the largest river—the Amazon, and vast tropical forests. Also on a grand scale is the avifauna, which is the richest in the world, particularly in tropical elements. Mayr (1964) points out that the avifauna is not only extremely rich and varied, but its distribution is remarkably uniform throughout the continent; there are no latitudinal barriers anywhere east of the Andes, and the Andes themselves have served as a distributional pathway, permitting the colonization of the lower latitudes by temperate elements. Altitude plays an important role in bird distribution on the continent and a number of altitudinal zones are generally recognized. Meyer de Schauensee (1970) lists these zones as follows:

tropical zone   = sea level to 1,400–1,550 m.
subtropical zone   = 1,400–1,550 to 2,350–2,670 m.
temperate zone   = 2,350–2,670 to 2,970–3,600 m.
páramo or puna zone = 2,970–3,600 m. to snow line.

Parrots are found in all of these zones, though their presence in the páramo zone is confined to the lower limits and is largely seasonal (e.g. *Bolborhynchus aymara* in Bolivia, *B. aurifrons* in northern Chile, and *B. orbygnesius* in central Peru). They are most numerous in forests of the tropical zone, especially in the vast rainforests that cover so much of the Amazon Basin. As pointed out by Mayr, the continent is dominated by tropics and subtropics, the southern sector being so narrow that it leaves little space for a temperate element fauna.

Parrots are a conspicuous component of the avifauna of the Amazonian rainforests; some species which occur there have a much wider distribution (e.g. *Ara ararauna*, *Ara macao*, *Pionus menstruus*, and *Amazona ochrocephala*), whereas other species are restricted to the region (e.g. *Aratinga guarouba*, *Pyrrhura perlata*, *Gypopsitta vulturina*, *Amazona festiva*, and *Deroptyus accipitrinus*). Highland avifauna, in which parrots are well represented, is for the most part confined to the Andes and subsidiary ranges, especially in the north. Some typical mountain parrots are *Leptosittaca branickii*, *Ognorhynchus icterotis*, *Pyrrhura calliptera*, *Hapalopsittaca melanotis* and *H. amazonina*, *Pionus tumultuosus* and *P. seniloides*, *Amazona mercenaria*, and all species in *Bolborhynchus*. East of the Andes there are two major mountainous regions; the isolated Venezuela-Guyana highlands and the eastern Brazilian mountains. The mountainous region of southern Venezuela, the adjacent border of Brazil, and Guyana comprises isolated tabletop mountains and has been designated as Pantepui by Mayr and Phelps (1967). Among the highland endemics of Pantepui are two parrots, *Pyrrhura egregia* and *Nannopsittaca panychlora*. The importance of the eastern Brazilian mountains in bird distribution is largely artificial; eastern Brazil has been subjected to widespread deforestation and it is mainly in the mountains that remnants of forest are serving as refuges for woodland birds, including parrots such as *Pyrrhura cruentata*, *Touit melanonota*, *Amazona dufresniana*, and *Triclaria malachitacea*. There are extensive savannahs north of the Amazon River, particularly in the upper Orinoco Basin of Venezuela and north-eastern Colombia, and more extensive ones in the south from Mato Grosso, Brazil, down into Patagonia. Some parrots typical of these savannah regions are *Ara auricollis*, *Aratinga acuticaudata*, *Aratinga pertinax*, *Aratinga aurea*, *Nandayus nenday*, *Forpus xanthopterygius*, and *Amazona xanthops*. In the south the savannahs tend to become less wooded and two parrots confined to southern latitudes, *Cyanoliseus patagonus* and *Myiopsitta monachus*, have curious nesting habits, presumably developed to overcome the shortage of trees. Also at southern latitudes, near the coasts, are found *Araucaria* and *Nothofagus* forests and there is in each of these specialized woodland types an endemic parrot; *Amazona pretrei* is largely restricted to *Araucaria* forest and *Enicognathus ferrugineus* inhabits *Nothofagus* forest.

Mayr cites parrots and trogons as examples of pantropical groups in which adaptive radiation has taken place since they immigrated into South America. Conditions favouring radiation must have been prevalent on the continent because we find that in many groups, including parrots, speciation has been rampant. Haffer (1970) suggests that alternating humid and dry climatic periods of the Pleistocene and post-Pleistocene probably caused the repeated shrinkage and later expansion of the Amazonian forest. During arid phases forest birds were restricted to a number of isolated humid refuges where the forests survived, and in these many new species and subspecies probably developed. The latest differentiation of the Amazonian bird fauna at the genus and species level is, geologically speaking, very recent and occurred rather rapidly.

Central America contains a strongly mixed fauna made up of an old indigenous element and numerous post-Pliocene invaders from South America (Mayr, 1964). The parrots are clearly of South American origin and endemism is mainly at the subspecific and specific level. *Rhynchopsitta*, the only endemic genus, is, in my opinion, closely allied to *Ara*.

Bond (1963) claims that the avifauna of the Caribbean Islands is derived for the most part from Central America. The South American element is comparatively recent and has entered the Caribbean Antilles mainly via Jamaica and Grenada. Three genera of Psittacidae have reached the Islands. These are *Ara* (now extinct), *Aratinga*, and *Amazona*, all of which probably originated in South America and subsequently invaded Central America as far north as northern Mexico. They represent for the most part a comparatively old South American element on the Antilles. *Amazona leucocephala*, *A. ventralis*, and *A. collaria* comprise a superspecies related to *A. albifrons* and *A. xantholora* from Central America, and, together with *A. vittata* of Puerto Rico and *A. agilis* of Jamaica, were doubtless derived from Central America. On the other hand, the ancestors of the four *Amazona* species found in the Lesser Antilles probably came from South America. The indigenous Caribbean parrots of the genus *Aratinga* are closely allied to Central American species; *A. chloroptera* and *A. euops* are related to the continental *A. finschi*, while *A. nana* of Jamaica is, I believe, conspecific with *A. astec* of Central America.

As I have pointed out in the Introduction there is a uniformity of types in parrots of the South American Distribution and this is in marked contrast to the diversity present in parrots of the Pacific Distribution. The uniformity is well illustrated by the fact that of the one hundred and thirty-eight extant species in the South American Distribution no less than ninety-two belong to only six genera, of which two (*Ara* and *Aratinga*) are closely related. I agree with the oft quoted claim that some genera, particularly monotypic ones, are poorly differentiated and probably not worth retaining, but I am cautious about changing species to subspecies because so little is known about the distribution and habits of the birds. Furthermore, speciation has been pronounced in other major South American groups.

In the table below I have listed the number of parrots found in the main countries and the habitats in which they occur. Introduced species are included (e.g. *Myiopsitta monachus*, *Brotogeris versicolorus* and *Amazona ventralis* for Puerto Rico, and *Forpus passerinus* for Jamaica), but extinct species are excluded. Categorisation of habitats is broad and arbitrary and does not take into account the actual complexities always present in the distribution of a species. Littoral habitats include estuarine flats and swamps, coconut palms and other trees along beaches, and mangroves. Open areas in both lowlands and highlands comprise open grassland, cultivated farmland, savannah woodland, and semi-arid and arid scrublands. Subalpine habitat refers to the lower limits of the páramo zone in the Andes, where *Bolborhynchus* spp. are summer visitors.

COUNTRY	NUMBER OF SPECIES	LITTORAL HABITATS	LOWLANDS: OPEN AREAS	LOWLANDS: FORESTED AREAS	HIGHLANDS: OPEN AREAS	HIGHLANDS: FORESTED AREAS	SUBALPINE HABITATS
Cuba	2			2		2	
Jamaica	4		2	2		3	
Hispaniola	2		2	2	1	2	
Puerto Rico	4		2	2		1	
Trinidad	8		1	7			
Mexico	18	2	9	4	1	4	
Guatemala	12		7	7	1	1	
Honduras (excluding British Honduras)	13	2	6	7		1	
Costa Rica	16	1	10	9		3	
Panama	20	2	9	15		3	
Colombia	49		13	29	2	13	
Venezuela	48	1	12	29		12	
Guianas (Guyana, Surinam, and French Guiana)	29	2	9	23		2	
Brazil	70	3	27	54		1	
Ecuador	38		8	20	1	11	
Peru	41		11	22	4	9	1
Bolivia	38		15	21	5	8	1
Paraguay	17		12	11			
Uruguay	6		4	3			
Argentina	25		13	15	4	2	
Chile	4		3	2	2	1	1

Extinction of parrot species has not been prevalent in the South American Distribution, but there could be an increase in the near future. Since the arrival of European man, *Conuropsis carolinensis* from the United States of America and *Ara tricolor* from Cuba have become extinct. Other species may have occurred formerly in the Caribbean Islands, but no specimens have been preserved. Several extant species are seriously endangered, especially in the Caribbean Islands and in eastern Brazil. During the past four decades there has been a dramatic increase in man-made changes to the natural face of the South American continent. Land-clearance has even penetrated the vast Amazonian rainforests, so long considered to be one of the last major undeveloped regions on earth.

Subfamily PSITTACINAE

There are no anatomical characters to separate New World parrots from Psittacinae, but they are a very homogeneous group easily distinguishable from Old World species. In the Introduction I have pointed out that there are features which suggest that they have been isolated for a long time.

Genus ANODORHYNCHUS Spix

Parrots belonging to this genus are very large birds with long, gradated tails. Their plumage is predominantly blue. There is a prominent naked periophthalmic ring and a variable naked area at the base of the lower mandible, but the lores and facial area are feathered. Thompson (1900) points out that the orbital ring is incomplete and there are other notable osteological features in the skull, chiefly in the auditory region. The sexes are alike and young birds probably resemble the adults.

Anodorhynchus purpurascens Rothschild is based entirely on the description of a macaw in the writings of an early traveller to Guadeloupe, in the Lesser Antilles. Although there is no reason to doubt the description it is not supported by specimens, and there is no proof that the now extinct species belonged to this genus.

HYACINTH MACAW
Anodorhynchus hyacinthinus (Latham)

Illustrated on page 340.

Length 100 cm.
ADULTS general plumage rich cobalt-blue, slightly darker on wings; underside of tail dark grey; naked periophthalmic ring and naked area surrounding base of lower mandible yellow; bill grey-black; iris dark brown; legs dark grey.
IMMATURES like adults, but with shorter tail.
10 males wing 388–426 (407.5) mm., tail 461–562 (509.4) mm.,
        exp. cul. 87–94 (90.4) mm., tars. 38–46 (43.3) mm.
8 females wing 392–411 (400.0) mm., tail 433–530 (492.4) mm.,
        exp. cul. 83–93 (87.8) mm., tars. 38–44 (41.9) mm.

DISTRIBUTION Interior of southern Brazil from the Tapajós River east to Maranhão and south through western Bahia and Goiás to Minas Gerais and Mato Grosso.

GENERAL NOTES The majestic Hyacinth Macaw is the largest of all parrots. It is a common bird in captivity, yet little is known of its habits in the wild state. Meyer de Schauensee (1970) lists its habitats as swamps, forests, and palm groves. Sick (1965) says that it is a bird typical of stands of palms, from which it regularly travels to the surrounding hills and secondary forest where it nests. Cherrie notes that in many parts of Mato Grosso visited by the Roosevelt-Rondon Expedition in 1916 the species was abundant, and was invariably seen in pairs (in Naumburg, 1930). On the flood plain or pantanal in the Descalvados district, Mato Grosso, Rehn found that it was fairly common and was always in pairs; several groups seen contained from one to eight pairs (in Stone and Roberts, 1935). When disturbed they would circle overhead screeching loudly, and at the passing of danger would settle on the topmost branches of tall trees. Stager (1961) reports that in central Goiás, between Peixe and the Serra Dourada, small flocks of from three to six individuals were seen. In this area there are stands of heavy cerrado, which is a specialized vegetation community dominated by low, semi-deciduous trees, and these are intersected by watercourses bordered with gallery forest or stands of the large burity palm (*Mauritia vinifera*). It was in close proximity to these watercourses that all macaws were seen. The flight is direct with shallow wingbeats, and is, for such a large bird, quite swift. In flight these birds, with their long tails streaming behind, make a most impressive sight.

Food consists of seeds, nuts and fruits. Crop and stomach contents from a specimen collected at Miranda Estate, Mato Grosso, comprised crushed palm nuts, and from another specimen taken at the same locality, three fruits, possibly *Ficus* sp. (Schubart *et al.*, 1965).

CALL A harsh, discordant screech (in captivity).

NESTING I know of no published records, but the nest is probably in a hollow in the trunk of a palm tree.

EGGS Undescribed.

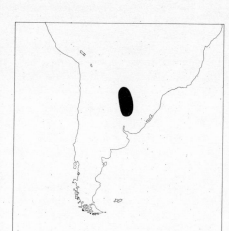

GLAUCOUS MACAW
Anodorhynchus glaucus (Vieillot)

Illustrated on page 341.

Length 72 cm.

ADULTS general plumage greenish-blue, more greenish on underparts; head and neck with a pronounced greyish-green tinge; throat dark greyish-brown becoming a suffusion on cheeks and upper breast; tail above greenish-blue, below dark grey; naked periophthalmic ring yellow and naked area at base of lower mandible paler yellow; bill grey-black; iris dark brown; legs dark grey.
IMMATURES undescribed.

5 males   wing 360–373 (365.0) mm., tail 361–375 (370.6) mm.,
            exp. cul. 64–68 (66.8) mm., tars. 34–40 (36.6) mm.
1 female   wing 353 mm., tail 352 mm.,
            exp. cul. 66 mm., tars. 36 mm.
3 unsexed   wing 352–364 (360.0) mm., tail 340–381 (354.3) mm.,
            exp. cul. 63–68 (65.3) mm., tars. 35 (35.0) mm.

DISTRIBUTION   Paraguay, north-eastern Argentina in the provinces of Misiones and Corrientes, and north-western Uruguay in the province of Artigas; formerly in extreme south-eastern Brazil.

GENERAL NOTES   The Glaucous Macaw is an extremely rare, little-known bird. Sick (1969) says that it is already extinct in south-eastern Brazil, and points out that there have been no recent reports from other parts of its range (pers. comm., 1971). Cuello and Gerzenstein (1962) quote early records from Artigas in north-western Uruguay, and state that, although the species probably occurs there, they know of no specimens taken in the country. According to Olrog (1959) it is very rare in north-eastern Argentina, where it frequents subtropical forest. Meyer de Schauensee (1970) lists forests and palm groves as its habitats.

CALL   Undescribed.

NESTING   Orifila (1936) quotes a report given by Azara in 1805 stating that nesting occurs in hollows in trees or holes in cliffs, and two eggs are laid. Nothing further is known of the nesting habits.

EGGS   Undescribed.

LEAR'S MACAW
Anodorhynchus leari Bonaparte

Illustrated on page 341.

Length 75 cm.

ADULTS head, neck and underparts greenish-blue, feathers of underparts with obscure paler tips; back, wings and upper side of tail rich cobalt-blue; underside of tail dark grey; bare periophthalmic ring yellow and bare area at base of lower mandible paler yellow; bill grey-black; iris dark brown; legs dark grey.
IMMATURES undescribed.

4 males   wing 374–391 (384.8) mm., tail 354–371 (362.0) mm.,
            exp. cul. (abnormal growth) 66–73 (68.5) mm., tars. 34–36 (35.0) mm.
1 female   wing 389 mm., tail 343 mm.,
            exp. cul. (abnormal growth) 65 mm., tars. 40 mm.
2 unsexed   wing 396–406 (401.0) mm., tail 376–481 (428.5) mm.,
            exp. cul. (abnormal growth) 67–71 (69.0) mm., tars. 38–41 (39.5) mm.

DISTRIBUTION   Exact range unknown, but probably north-eastern Brazil in the states of Pernambuco and Bahia.

GENERAL NOTES   Lear's Macaw is a mysterious bird known only from specimens held in captivity. Voous (1965) suggests that it could be a hybrid between *Anodorhynchus hyacinthinus* and *A. glaucus*, but this I cannot accept. In my opinion *leari* is closely related to *glaucus*, and indeed they may be isolates of the one species, but both are clearly distinct from *hyacinthinus*. *A. hyacinthinus* is a larger bird with a unique pattern of bare skin around the base of the lower mandible.

For more than a century European and American zoos have occasionally received specimens of Lear's Macaw in consignments of Hyacinth Macaws. Most shipments originated from Pará, probably from the port of Belém, but the locality from which the rare smaller macaws came could not be established. About 1950 Pinto visited the Santo Antão Municipality in Pernambuco and was shown a captive Lear's Macaw that had come from Joazeiro, a town on the left bank of the São Francisco River which separates Pernambuco and Bahia (Pinto, 1950); it is probable that the species occurs in this region. Sick (1969) points out that the species must be regarded as rare, though there is the possibility that further populations may be discovered.

CALL A strong, guttural screech similar to, but not as raucous as the call of *A. hyacinthinus* (in captivity).

NESTING No records.

EGGS An egg laid by a bird at the London Zoo is now in the British Museum Collection and measures 57.0 × 38.4 mm. [Harrison and Holyoak, 1970].

Genus CYANOPSITTA Bonaparte

In this monotypic genus the lores and periophthalmic ring are bare, but the remainder of the face is feathered. The species is a medium sized parrot with a long, gradated tail. The plumage is predominantly blue. There is no sexual dimorphism and young birds resemble adults.

SPIX'S MACAW
Cyanopsitta spixii (Wagler)

Illustrated on page 344.

Length 56 cm.
ADULTS general plumage blue, darker on back, wings and upper side of tail; forehead and ear-coverts grey tinged with blue; remainder of head and neck greyish-blue; slight greenish tinge on breast and abdomen; underside of tail dark grey; naked lores and periophthalmic ring black; bill grey-black; iris yellow; legs dark grey.
IMMATURES (MZSP. 43.409); general plumage darker blue, particularly on upperparts; shorter tail; bill grey-black with horn-coloured marking along culmen.
3 males   wing 261–299 (274.7) mm., tail 313–355 (335.0) mm.,
             exp. cul. 31–33 (32.3) mm., tars. 23–26 (24.3) mm.
6 females wing 247–286 (273.0) mm., tail 265–378 (322.8) mm.,
             exp. cul. 31–35 (32.7) mm., tars. 22–27 (24.3) mm.

GENERAL NOTES Spix's Macaw is a very rare bird, about which little is known (Sick, 1969). Meyer de Schauensee (1970) says that it inhabits palm groves. Hellmayr (1929) reports that a few individuals were observed by Reiser in June 1903 in the vicinity of Parnaguá, Piauí, but no further details are given. Sick notes that live birds offered for sale had formerly been taken from the nest, but now they are generally aviary bred.

CALL A sharp, rolling *kraa*———*ark* terminating with an upward inflection (in captivity).

NESTING No records.

EGGS A single egg in the British Museum Collection measures 34.9 × 28.7 mm. [Harrison and Holyoak, 1970].

Genus ARA Lacépède

The most conspicuous external feature of parrots belonging to this genus is the bare facial area. In most species it is totally devoid of feathers, but in some it is traversed by widely spaced rows of short feathers. The species are small to very large birds with long gradated tails. The orbital ring is complete, except perhaps in *A. ararauna*, and its posterior portion is somewhat broad and flattened (Thompson, 1900). The sexes are alike and young birds resemble adults.

It is clear from the writings of early travellers that macaws, in addition to *Ara tricolor*, formerly occurred in the West Indies, but there is supporting evidence only from the Virgin Islands. Other species have been named, but it cannot be established with certainty that any were members of this genus or were, in fact, different from extant species found in Central and South America.

ST. CROIX MACAW
Ara autocthones Wetmore

External appearance not known.

DISTRIBUTION Formerly St. Croix in the Virgin Islands; now extinct.

GENERAL NOTES The St. Croix Macaw is known only from a sub-fossil left tibiotarsus found in kitchen middens at Concordia near Southwest Cape, St. Croix Island.

BLUE AND YELLOW MACAW
Ara ararauna (Linné)

Illustrated on page 361.

DESCRIPTION

Length 86 cm.

ADULTS forehead and forecrown green; remainder of upperparts and upper side of tail rich blue; bare lores and cheeks creamy-white, latter traversed by lines of greenish-black feathers; throat black with greenish tinge towards breast; ear-coverts, sides of neck, underparts, and under wing-coverts yellow-orange; underside of tail olive-yellow; bill grey-black; iris yellow; legs dark grey.

IMMATURES (Risdon 1965; F. and P. Brooks 1970); like adults; iris brown.

10 males   wing 366–392 (384.8) mm., tail 490–519 (500.8) mm.,
               exp. cul. 61–69 (65.6) mm., tars. 35–39 (36.6) mm.

10 females wing 360–386 (371.7) mm., tail 451–524 (496.2) mm.,
               exp. cul. 63–66 (64.4) mm., tars. 33–38 (35.9) mm.

DISTRIBUTION

From eastern Panama south through Colombia, except the Cauca Valley and western Nariño, to eastern and western Ecuador and possibly northern Peru, east through Venezuela, mainly south of the Orinoco River, to the Guianas and Trinidad, and south through Brazil to the states of São Paulo and Rio de Janeiro, and to Bolivia, Paraguay and possibly northern Argentina (see comments under *Ara caninde*).

SUBSPECIES

Ara caninde from Paraguay and northern Argentina could be a subspecies of *A. ararauna*.

GENERAL NOTES

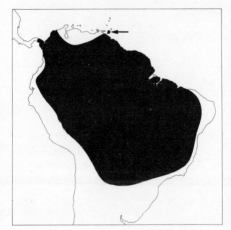

Blue and Yellow Macaws are still common in forests in more remote parts of their range, but have declined in numbers or disappeared altogether from accessible regions. Wetmore (1968) says that in eastern Panama they are locally distributed and are present in small numbers in the less settled areas from the upper Bayano River to eastern Darién; in 1959 he found them to be fairly common in the Tuira Valley and along the Chucunaque River near the mouth of the Tuquesa. On Trinidad they are apparently confined to Nariva Swamp on the eastern part of the island and they keep to the more inaccessible sectors; as early as forty years ago they were rare (Belcher and Smooker, 1936), but F. and M. Nottebohm (1969) point out that at present only about fifteen birds survive in the swamp, and the species may soon disappear from the island. Snyder (1966) says that in Guyana they are widespread in savannahs and forests along some coastal rivers and in the interior; I failed to see them in the vicinity of Georgetown or in the Mabaruma district in the interior, and was told by local people that they are not plentiful in these areas. According to Haverschmidt (1954 and 1968) they are still the most numerous of the large macaws in coastal Surinam, though the clearance of forest has brought about their disappearance from the neighbourhood of Paramaribo. They are very locally distributed in Venezuela, and north of the Orinoco River have been recorded only in the state of Monagas (Phelps and Phelps, 1958). Todd and Carriker (1922) note that they were common in the lowland forest region of tropical Colombia between the Sierra Nevada on one side and the Cienaga Grande and Magdalena River on the other. Haffer (1959) reports that in the vicinity of the Golfo de Urabá, extreme north-western Colombia, between June and August 1958, Blue and Yellow Macaws were frequently seen in open country to the north-west of Montería, and here they appeared to be more plentiful than the Scarlet Macaw (*Ara macao*) which is the common large macaw of the region. Stager (1961) found that in the Chapada dos Veadeiros and Serra Dourada areas in central Goiás, Brazil, they were very abundant in tall palms lining watercourses. Pinto and Camargo (1948) point out that in Mato Grosso, Brazil, they are generally very common along those rivers that flow towards Uruguay and those that flow towards Paraguay, and in many localities are the only macaws to be found.

These splendid parrots inhabit forests and tall palms growing in swamps or along watercourses. Dugand (1947) reports that in Atlántico, Colombia, they generally do not leave the dense forest, particularly in the dry months, but during the rainy season they move about over considerable distances. Young (1929) recalls that on the western side of the Abary River, Guyana, the macaws frequented a large swamp covered with palms and from here they often travelled some 25 km. to feed in secondary forest, particularly when jabillo trees (*Hura crepitans*) were bearing fruit.

Blue and Yellow Macaws associate in pairs, and even when large flocks are observed paired birds are readily discernible as they fly close together, their wings almost touching. They are generally seen flying above the forest canopy or feeding amongst the branches of tall trees. At the approach of danger they rise into the air screeching loudly. Young reports that when they were feeding in sand-box trees near Blairmont, Guyana, it was possible to approach them if care was exercised and he was able to stand under the tree in which they were feeding. They have regular roosting sites and in the early morning the flocks leave to fly to the feeding grounds, which may be some distance away; return flights commence just before sunset. These flights to and from the roosting trees are quite spectacular and have been described by many writers. Haverschmidt (1954) recalls that while travelling down the Coppename River, Surinam, late one day in August he witnessed a return flight to roosting trees and counted several hundreds of these birds crossing the river. Young describes a similar spectacle when birds flew across open savannah on their way to a stand of jabillo trees. Wetmore describes a memorable sighting during an early morning journey in a small plane, when between El Real and La Palma, Panama, they passed above a pair of these birds in flight with the blue of their backs and wings showing clearly in the rays of the rising sun, against a background of green forest. The characteristic flight silhouette is largely due to the long tail streaming behind. The flight is direct with slow, shallow wingbeats and is quite fast for such a large bird.

Their diet consists of seeds, fruits, nuts and probably vegetable matter. In the Coronie district, Surinam, Haverschmidt (1954) has seen them feeding in jabillo trees and a specimen collected had its stomach full of seeds from this tree. A specimen collected at Caicara, north-eastern Venezuela, also had *Hura crepitans* seeds in its stomach (Friedmann and Smith, 1950). Brabourne (1914) reports that about 65 km. north of Villarrica, Paraguay, numbers of these macaws congregated to feed on the yellow fruits of a low palm that was widespread on grassy clearings in the forest. Schubart *et al.* (1965) point out that published feeding records show that Blue and Yellow Macaws prefer fruits of burity palms (*Mauritia vinifera*) and other palms such as *Astrocaryum*, *Bactris* and *Maximilianea*.

CALL A loud, screeching *rraa* ——— *aa.*

NESTING According to Herklots (1961) breeding takes place in Trinidad during April and May and nests are in holes in dead ité (*Mauritia*) and cabbage (*Oreodoxa*) palms. Wetmore does not give the time of breeding in Panama, but states that pairs were occasionally seen at hollows near the tops of tall dead trees. In Guyana the breeding season is rather variable, though most nesting takes place during the months February to May or June and the nest is in the trunk of a large dead palm, the entrance probably being through the decayed top of the trunk (McLoughlin, 1970). Haverschmidt (1968) reports that in Surinam breeding has been recorded in February and nests are in hollows in dead moriché palms (*Mauritia flexuosa*).

Risdon (1965) gives details of a successful breeding in captivity. Two eggs were laid with an interval of two days between each. The hen covered the first egg most of the time, but commenced sitting closely with the laying of the second egg. The male was never found incubating, though he often joined the female in the nest-box when someone approached. One egg hatched after an incubation period of from twenty-four to twenty-six days. The young bird left the nest thirteen weeks after hatching. At the age of six months it could be distinguished from the adults only by its dark eyes.

EGGS Elliptical; 17 eggs, 46.4 (40.6–50.7) × 35.9 (33.0–37.7) mm. [Schönwetter, 1964].

CANINDE MACAW
Ara caninde (Wagler)

Illustrated on page 361.

Length 85 cm.
ADULTS entire upperparts, including forehead and forecrown, blue, paler and more greenish than in *A. ararauna*; bare facial area smaller than in *ararauna* and bordered on throat by a broad bluish band which extends up to the ear-coverts; feathered lines across lores and cheeks broader than in *ararauna* and dark green instead of black; underparts and under wing-coverts orange-yellow; tail blue above, olive-yellow below; bill grey-black; legs dark grey.
2 unsexed (BM); wing 362–363 (362.5) mm., tail 453–454 (453.5) mm.,
        exp. cul. 53–56 (54.5) mm., tars. 31–32 (31.5) mm.
1 unsexed (CM); wing 350 mm., tail 480 mm.,
        exp. cul. 50 mm., tars. 31 mm.
1 male (CM);   wing 330 mm., tail 422 mm.,
        exp. cul. 47 mm., tars. 31 mm.

DISTRIBUTION Bolivia (known from the Buenavista district), Paraguay, and northern Argentina in the province of Chaco.

SUBSPECIES The Caninde Macaw is a mysterious bird and its status remains unresolved. In my opinion there are three possibilities to be considered:
    (i) it is a valid species sympatric with *A. ararauna* in Bolivia and Paraguay;
    (ii) it is the juvenile of *A. ararauna*;
    (iii) it is a subspecies of *A. ararauna* distinguished by its strikingly different juvenile plumage.
I have included the two Carnegie Museum specimens from Buenavista, Bolivia, though they do not agree entirely with the British Museum specimens from Paraguay; their throats are darker. One of the Bolivian specimens is labelled as a juvenile male, the other is not sexed. According to Orfila (1936) there is a fifth specimen in the Museo Argentino de Ciencias Naturales.

GENERAL NOTES I am not familiar with either *ararauna* or *caninde* so cannot make any judgement on the status of the latter. However, I am inclined to treat it as a subspecies of *ararauna*, the diagnostic character being a distinct juvenile plumage. In other words all five specimens are juveniles. There is in the Carnegie Museum a typical *ararauna* from the same locality as the two specimens of *caninde*. Risdon (1965) and F. and P. Brooks (1970) have bred *ararauna* in captivity and point out that juveniles differ from adults only by their eye colour. It is likely that captive birds would come from northern Brazil, so if *caninde* is the juvenile of *ararauna* the distinction is present only in the southern population.

MILITARY MACAW
Ara militaris (Linné)

Length 70 cm.
ADULTS general plumage green with a slight olive tinge on back and wings; head slightly paler green than body; inconspicuous bluish tinge on hindneck; forehead and feathered lines on bare lores red; bare facial area white tinged with flesh-pink and traversed by lines of small greenish-black feathers; throat olive-brown; lower back, rump and upper tail-coverts blue; green under wing-coverts; outer edges of primaries blue; upper side of tail brownish-red broadly tipped with blue; undersides of tail and flight feathers olive-yellow; bill grey-black; iris yellow; legs dark grey.
IMMATURES undescribed, but probably similar to adults.

Mexico, except the forested south-east, western Colombia, north-western Venezuela, Ecuador, northern Peru and Bolivia to north-western Argentina.

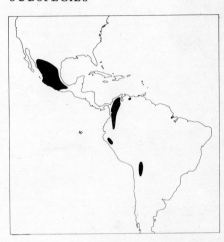

1. *A. m. militaris* (Linné)
    10 males wing 345–374 (360.1) mm., tail 375–419 (387.9) mm.,
           exp. cul. 53–59 (56.9) mm., tars. 32–33 (32.6) mm.
    7 females wing 346–369 (356.7) mm., tail 330–387 (357.4) mm.,
           exp. cul. 50–57 (54.3) mm., tars. 30–34 (32.3) mm.
    Occurs in the tropical zone of Colombia from the Dagua Valley east across the northern part of the country to the middle Magdalena and the Santa Marta regions and to north-western Venezuela, and south to eastern Ecuador and Lambayeque and Cajamarca provinces in northern Peru; Colombian records from east of the Andes are from the Sierra Macarena and Putumayo.

2. *A. m. mexicana* Ridgway.   *Illustrated on page 364.*
    ADULTS similar to *militaris*, but larger.
    14 males   wing 350–392 (375.8) mm., tail 352–426 (388.1) mm.,
           exp. cul. 55–67 (60.4) mm., tars. 34–37 (34.5) mm.
    11 females wing 352–385 (369.0) mm., tail 327–392 (374.2) mm.,
           exp. cul. 55–61 (58.2) mm., tars. 32–35 (33.9) mm.
    Found in Mexico north to south-eastern Sonora, north-eastern Sinaloa and south-western Chihuahua, but absent from the humid forests of the Caribbean lowlands, Chiapas and Oaxaca south of the Isthmus of Tehuantepec; doubtfully distinct from *militaris* (see Todd and Carriker 1922; Bond and Meyer de Schauensee 1943).

3. *A. m. boliviana* Reichenow.
    ADULTS like *militaris*, but throat reddish-brown; feathers of ear-coverts with reddish bases; darker blue on outer webs of primaries and tip of tail.
    4 males   wing 366–375 (369.5) mm., tail 326–380 (364.3) mm.,
           exp. cul. 55–63 (61.5) mm., tars. 33–36 (33.8) mm.
    6 females wing 350–367 (358.5) mm., tail 351–390 (374.7) mm.,
           exp. cul. 53–56 (54.5) mm., tars. 30–35 (32.0) mm.
    3 unsexed wing 345–371 (358.7) mm., tail 343–345 (344.3) mm.,
           exp. cul. 50–57 (54.0) mm., tars. 34–36 (34.7) mm.
    Restricted to tropical parts of Bolivia and extreme north-western Argentina in the provinces of Jujuy and Salta; doubtfully distinct from *militaris* (see Zimmer 1930; Bond and Meyer de Schauensee 1943).

According to Blake (1953) the Military Macaw is widely distributed in arid and semi-arid regions of Mexico, and occurs both in the coastal slopes and up to 2,500 m. in pine and oak forests; in the lowland humid forests of the south and along the Caribbean coast it is replaced by the Scarlet Macaw (*Ara macao*). It frequents forests of the tropical zone in Colombia and north-western Venezuela (Phelps and Phelps 1958; Meyer de Schauensee 1964).
    These macaws inhabit dry forest, open woodland and trees bordering watercourses in semi-arid and arid areas. They generally avoid tropical rainforest. They are locally common, particularly in more remote districts, but in common with the other large macaws have suffered from shooting and collecting of nestlings so are now rare in the vicinities of larger centres of habitation. Schaldach (1963) says that they are not common in Colima, Mexico, but during the dry season, that is November to June, small flocks of up to about ten birds are occasionally seen in dense thorn forest. Sutton and Burleigh (1940b) report that near Tamazunchale in San Luis Potosí, Mexico, scattered pairs were seen in wooded ravines leading off from the Moctezuma River. Stager (1954) notes that in south-western Chihuahua, Mexico, they were present between 900 and 1,350 m., that is the arid tropical zone, in the Barranca de Cobre, one of the major canyons of the Sierra Madre Occidental. Fleming and Baker (1963) point out that the macaws are characteristic of the barranca country and pairs or small groups of up to twenty may be seen flying high above the canyons, their raucous cries echoing down to the floor below. Todd and Carriker (1922) claim that these are the most common macaws in the vicinity of Santa Marta, Colombia, where they range from sea level up to at least 1,600 m., the lower limit of the subtropical zone. Near Rio Frio, also in the Santa Marta district, Darlington (1931) recorded three species of macaws, but noticed that only *Ara militaris* ranged into the foothills where on one occasion he saw thirty-five scattered about the sky and feeding in trees on wooded ridges.

Blue and Yellow Macaw *Ara ararauna* **1**
AMNH. 474188 ad. ♂

Caninde Macaw *Ara caninde* **2**
BM. 25.P.7.1.84 unsexed

In the early morning the parrots can be seen flying high overhead on their way from roosting sites to the feeding ground. The return flights commence towards dusk. Fleming and Baker could not determine whether birds travelled from the barranca country of Durango, Mexico, west to the Pacific lowlands of Sinaloa and Nayarit to feed during the day, but this seemed to be the practice of birds seen near San Blas, Nayarit. Soon after sunrise one morning in January 1965, near San Blas, I observed a pair of Military Macaws flying high overhead in a westerly direction. As well as these conspicuous daily flights to and from feeding grounds, seasonal movements governed by food supply have been recorded. M. Koepcke (1961) reports that in northern Peru these parrots are found mainly on the eastern side of the Andes, especially in the Marañón region where they ascend to considerable heights, but at a certain time of the year, normally during September and October, they visit the mountain forests of Taulis on the Pacific slope to feed on special fruits; the isolated position of this tract of forest means that the macaws must fly across great stretches of puna grasslands (H. W. Koepcke, 1963).

These macaws remain paired within the flocks and this is readily discernible to the observer. When resting they often perch atop conspicuous tall trees, such as dead pines on the side of a canyon. If approached they screech loudly and then rise into the air, their yellow underwings flashing conspicuously. The direct flight is quite swift for such large birds and is characterized by slow, shallow wingbeats.

They feed on seeds, nuts, berries, fruits and probably vegetable matter procured in the treetops. McLellan (1925) reports hearing flocks in roadside forest near Tepic, Mexico, where they were attracted by fruit-bearing palms and *Ficus* trees.

CALL A raucous, drawn-out *kraa——— aak*.

NESTING Fleming and Baker were told by residents at Rancho Las Margaritas, Durango, that nesting commenced in March. Near Vicente Guerrero, also in Durango, a nest in a dead pine tree was located in early July. The tree was felled by woodcutters who wanted young birds to sell as pets, but the hollow contained two freshly-incubated eggs which were crushed when the tree came down. The hollow was approximately 20 m. from the ground and had been originally excavated by an Imperial Woodpecker (*Campephilus imperialis*). It had a maximum inner diameter of 33 cm. and the bottom was lined with coarse wood dust. Nothing further is known of the nesting habits.

EGGS Elliptical; 2 eggs, 46.4 (45.8–46.6) × 32.8 (29.7–35.8) mm. [Brit. Mus. Coll.].

BUFFON'S MACAW
Ara ambigua (Bechstein)

DESCRIPTION   Length 85 cm.
ADULTS similar to *A. militaris*, but green of general plumage paler and more yellowish; forehead and feathered lines on lores scarlet; lower back, rump, and upper tail-coverts pale blue, decidedly paler than in *militaris*; tail above pale brownish-red broadly tipped with very pale blue; undersides of tail and flight feathers olive-yellow; bare facial area white suffused with flesh-pink and traversed with lines of black feathers; bill grey becoming paler towards tip; iris dull yellow; legs grey.
IMMATURES duller than adults, particularly on underparts; indistinct yellowish margins on scapulars and inner secondaries; central tail feathers tipped with dull yellow; brown iris.

DISTRIBUTION   Central America from Nicaragua to western Colombia and western Ecuador.

SUBSPECIES   1. *A. a. ambigua* (Bechstein)   *Illustrated on page 364.*
12 males   wing 356–422 (391.6) mm., tail 330–468 (399.1) mm.,
          exp. cul. 65–81 (71.6) mm., tars. 34–41 (37.3) mm.
12 females wing 372–407 (392.2) mm., tail 385–459 (426.2) mm.,
          exp. cul. 64–74 (68.5) mm., tars. 34–39 (36.2) mm.
Distributed from Nicaragua through Costa Rica and Panama to western Colombia as far south as the Baudó Mountains.

2. *A. a. guayaquilensis* Chapman.
ADULTS similar to *ambigua*, but with a smaller, narrower bill; undersides of tail and flight feathers more greenish.
No males examined.
2 females wing 355–393 (374.0) mm., tail 396–414 (405.0) mm.,
          exp. cul. 64–68 (66.0) mm., tars. 38–40 (39.0) mm.
Restricted to western Ecuador and possibly south-western Colombia; seems to be isolated from *ambigua* (see Meyer de Schauensee, 1949).

GENERAL NOTES   Wetmore (1968) says that Buffon's Macaw is locally distributed in forests of the tropical and subtropical zones of Panama; it has disappeared from areas in the vicinity of human habitation

spread in Honduras, occurring in the arid lowlands of the Pacific slope, in the interior below 1,100 m., and in the Caribbean lowland rainforest; it is uncommon in most parts of the country, particularly on the Caribbean slope, but is fairly common locally in portions of the arid Pacific lowlands. In Honduras it is found not only in the vicinity of forests but also in the scrubby growth along the Pacific coast, and it frequently forages in open, often cultivated country. Huber (1933) reports that in the vicinity of Eden, north-eastern Nicaragua, it was rather common and could be seen every day. It is primarily an inhabitant of the Pacific slope of Costa Rica though it does cross low sections of the continental divide to the Caribbean side, where it is now far less common than formerly (Slud, 1964). It does not penetrate far into the forest, but frequents forest borders, patches of woodland, and open or semi-open country with scattered stands of tall trees. Wetmore (1968) points out that the species was formerly present on the Caribbean slope of the Canal Zone in Panama and on the Pacific side in western Chirquí, but is now restricted to Isla Coiba and the lower Azuero Peninsula in south-western Los Santos; there are recent records from Isla Ranchería and Isla Canal de Afuera. Birds may fly from Isla Ranchería to the mainland (see Wetmore, 1968). It has been, and presumably still is, common on Isla Coiba.

Meyer de Schauensee (1964) says that in Colombia it inhabits open woodland and savannah of the tropical zone in north-eastern regions, the lower Magdalena Valley and east of the Andes south to Amazonas. Haffer (1959) reports that it is the common large macaw of the Golfo de Urabá region, extreme north-western Colombia. In Atlántico, north-western Colombia, Dugand (1947) has found that it wanders about and is often observed in semi-arid forest during summer. It occurs in open woodland and savannah in the tropical zone of Venezuela (Phelps and Phelps, 1958). The species must be extremely rare in Trinidad because Herklots (1961) lists only two records; a pair seen at Nariva Swamp in 1934 and a party of five at Waller Field in 1943. Snyder (1966) claims that it is distributed in both forest and savannah throughout Guyana, but McLoughlin (1970) says that it rarely visits the coast. In Guyana, I gained the impression from what local residents told me that the Scarlet Macaw is now uncommon in the vicinity of settlements. Haverschmidt (1968) points out that in Surinam it is more a bird of the hilly forests of the interior than is the Blue and Yellow Macaw (*A. ararauna*), though there is some overlapping and both species can be found in the same habitat.

These spectacular macaws are generally seen in pairs, family parties, or small flocks of up to about thirty, and many writers have described their vivid impressions of observing them in the wild state. Huber says that without doubt they are the most striking of tropical birds and seeing them fly overhead was always a memorable event of the day. In certain lights against the deep green foliage of the forest they appeared dark and inconspicuous as they flew across the valley, but in other lights their brilliant colours stood out in all their glory. Slud remarks that when feeding in the treetops they adorn the foliage like gigantic, gaudy flowers. Wetmore (1944) recalls that while doing field work at the Hacienda Santa María, north-western Costa Rica, one of the delights experienced was the sight each day of Scarlet Macaws flying past, fairly glowing with colour in the morning sun. They came daily to feed in wild fruit trees in a little coffee plantation behind the house, and if something startled them forty or fifty would fly around the house screeching loudly.

As with the other large macaws there is a strong pair bond and this is most evident as flocks pass overhead—paired birds fly close together, their wings almost touching. They undertake conspicuous daily flights from their roosting sites to scattered feeding grounds. Wetmore (1957) reports that on Isla Coiba, each morning soon after sunrise, groups came flying over the forest and pasturelands from their roosts somewhere in the south, and each evening as sunset was near they returned. At Laguna Ocotal, Chiapas, Mexico, Paynter (1957) noted small flocks flying over quite regularly in the morning and evening, but they did not seem to feed in the vicinity of the lake so rarely alighted. During the day they feed or rest in the topmost branches of tall trees. In districts where they are not molested they may be tame, but as a rule they are extremely wary and at the slightest sign of danger rise into the air screeching loudly. The flight is direct and with steady, shallow wingbeats.

They feed on seeds, fruits, nuts, berries and probably vegetable matter procured in the treetops. Dickey and van Rossen note that in El Salvador during August and September the macaws feed extensively on fruits of the jocote tree (*Spondias mombin*). At El Paraiso, Colombia, Dugand has seen them feeding on fruits of the jabillo tree (*Hura crepitans*). Schubart *et al.* (1965) point out that published feeding records show that Scarlet Macaws favour *Lecythis* fruits and fruits of juvia or Pará chestnut (*Bertholletia excelsa*) and of licuri palms (*Syagrus coronata*). McLoughlin says that in Guyana they may be seen in the company of Blue and Yellow Macaws feeding in the same tree.

CALL A loud, harsh *rraa* ——— *aar* (Haverschmidt, 1968); feeding is done in silence.

NESTING In early April, near Eden, north-eastern Nicaragua, a pair was found nesting in a hollow in a large tree (Huber, 1933). The hollow was about 16 m. from the ground and went straight down the trunk: when the female entered she disappeared completely, even her long tail being hidden from view. In mid-March another nest was found in deep jungle south of the Coatzacoalcos River, Veracruz, Mexico (Lowery and Dalquest, 1951). It was in a hollow in the trunk of a dead tree about 10 m. from the ground; as seen from below the entrance to the hollow was approximately 60 cm. in diameter. Wetmore (1957) reports that on Isla Coiba young birds accompanying their parents on daily flights were first noticed at the beginning of February. Nothing further is known of the nesting habits.

EGGS Elliptical; 13 eggs, 47.0 (43.7–52.3) × 33.9 (32.6–36.0) mm. [Schönwetter, 1964].

Military Macaw *Ara militaris mexicana* 1
NMV. R1143 ad. unsexed

Buffon's Macaw *Ara ambigua ambigua* 2
USNM. 209785 ad. ♂

A.F. Poder 72

Herklots notes that in the Nariva Swamp on Trinidad they rest during the day and become active about 1600 hrs. when pairs and small flocks fly about before finally alighting to feed in palm trees. They generally keep to themselves, though at times flocks may associate with flocks of Orange-winged Amazons (*Amazona amazonica*). Along the Orinoco River in north-eastern Venezuela Smith has seen flocks of over a hundred of these macaws feeding in palms and notes that, despite their size, they are difficult to see amidst the foliage (in Friedmann and Smith, 1955). Haverschmidt says that in Surinam noisy flocks are often seen flying above the savannahs to settle in palms to feed. The flight is direct with rapid, rhythmic wingbeats. The long, pointed tail and slightly backward curved wings give these birds a streamlined appearance in the air.

They feed extensively on the fruits of *Mauritia* palms.

CALL In flight a shrill screech or a loud *wrr —— rake . . . wrr —— rake*; also a variety of squawks and while feeding a 'purring' sound (Snyder, 1966).

NESTING In Guyana breeding usually takes place between February and May or June and the nest is in a hollow in a dead palm (McLoughlin, 1970). The base of the palm is generally under water for part of the year and this may give some protection against predators. Herklots says that in Trinidad nests are in old woodpeckers' holes in trunks and two eggs are laid.

EGGS Undescribed.

Blue-crowned Conure **1**
Aratinga acuticaudata acuticaudata
MNHN. CG1960, 253 ad. ♀

Golden Conure *Aratinga guarouba* **2**
AM. 044049 ad. unsexed

ILLIGER'S MACAW
Ara maracana (Vieillot)

Illustrated on page 369.

DESCRIPTION Length 43 cm.
ADULTS general plumage green, tinged with olive on rump and upper tail-coverts; forehead rose-red; head, nape, and lower cheeks greenish-blue, darker on crown; a red patch on the lower back and another on the middle of the abdomen; primaries and primary-coverts blue; secondaries and outermost upper wing-coverts blue edged with green; carpal edge bluish-green; under wing-coverts olive-green; tail above blue, becoming reddish-brown towards base; undersides of flight and tail feathers olive-yellow; naked facial area very pale yellow; bill black; iris orange; legs yellow.
IMMATURES red on forehead paler and less extensive; red on abdomen and lower back more yellowish; green of upperparts duller and more greyish.
10 males wing 204–227 (216.8) mm., tail 181–217 (200.1) mm.,
     exp. cul. 31–37 (34.6) mm., tars. 20–24 (21.6) mm.
7 females wing 208–219 (213.6) mm., tail 189–206 (198.0) mm.,
     exp. cul. 33–36 (34.0) mm., tars. 20–22 (21.0) mm.

DISTRIBUTION Eastern Brazil from Pará and Maranhão south to Mato Grosso and Rio Grande do Sul, and through Paraguay to Misiones in north-eastern Argentina.

GENERAL NOTES Illiger's Macaw is a bird of the forests, particularly in close proximity to watercourses, and is fairly common throughout much of its range, particularly in the north. I did not see it in Rio Grande do Sul and was told by local observers that it is not common in the state. Mitchell (1957) suggests that since the turn of the century this species may have been forced to retreat inland because of the destruction of coastal forests. It is usually seen in pairs or small parties, and its habits are similar to those of the other small macaws. However, according to Eckelberry (1965) its distinctive flight is not direct like that of other macaws; the bird pitches up in flight, not in an undulatory manner but in a peculiarly jerky, rearing motion.

CALL A guttural screech similar to, but deeper than, the call of *Ara auricollis* (in captivity).

NESTING I know of no published record of breeding in the wild state. The species is commonly kept in captivity and has probably bred on a number of occasions, yet the only published information that I can find is the statement attributed to Russ and quoted by Butler (1905) that the incubation period is of twenty-four days duration.

EGGS Rounded; Nehrkorn gives the measurements of three eggs as 37.1 (36.5–38.0) × 29.9 (29.6–30.0) mm. [Schönwetter, 1964].

BLUE-HEADED MACAW
Ara couloni Sclater

Illustrated on page 369.

DESCRIPTION Length 41 cm.
ADULTS general plumage green, slightly more yellowish on underparts; entire head, except bare

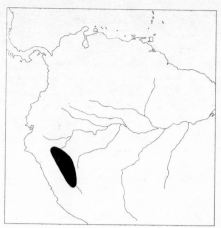

facial area, blue; primaries and primary-coverts blue; secondaries and outermost upper wing-coverts blue edged with green; upper side of tail blue; undersides of flight and tail feathers dusky yellow; naked facial area grey; bill grey-black becoming horn-coloured on culmen and at tip of upper mandible; iris yellow; legs flesh-pink.
IMMATURES undescribed.
5 males   wing 224–233 (226.2) mm., tail 203–243 (223.2) mm.,
      exp. cul. 37–42 (38.6) mm., tars. 21–25 (22.2) mm.
5 females wing 218–225 (220.4) mm., tail 188–223 (204.2) mm.,
      exp. cul. 37–39 (37.6) mm., tars. 22–23 (22.4) mm.

Eastern Peru, where recorded in the Huallaga Valley from Loreto to Huánuco and in the Ucayali, Apurímac, and Purús river drainages; almost certainly occurs in adjacent western Brazil (O'Neill, 1969).

GENERAL NOTES

Traylor (1958) points out that the Blue-headed Macaw is apparently a representative of *Ara maracana*, but the differences are so striking that the two should be treated as separate species.

There is virtually no recorded information on the habits of this macaw. O'Neill says that at Balta, on the Curanja River at about 300 m., it was seen in pairs or groups of three and did not associate with the more common Chestnut-fronted Macaw (*A. severa*).

RED-SHOULDERED MACAW
Ara nobilis (Linné)

DESCRIPTION

Length 30 cm.
ADULTS general plumage green, more yellowish on lower underparts; forehead and forecrown blue; carpal edge, bend of wing, and greater under wing-coverts red; remainder of under wing-coverts green; outer web of outermost primary tinged with dull blue; remaining wing feathers entirely green; undersides of tail and flight feathers dull olive-yellow; naked facial area white; bill dark grey; iris dark orange; legs dark grey.
IMMATURES no blue on forehead and forecrown; red absent from bend of wing and carpal edge, but present on under wing-coverts; iris brown.

DISTRIBUTION

From the Guianas and eastern Venezuela south to southern Brazil.

SUBSPECIES

Green Conure *Aratinga holochlora holochlora* **1**
MLZ. 40221 ad. ♂

Green Conure *Aratinga holochlora rubritorquis* **2**
AMNH. 326000 ad. ♂

Finsch's Conure *Aratinga finschi* **3**
AMNH. 389263 ad. ♂

1. *A. n. nobilis* (Linné)   *Illustrated on page 372.*
8 males   wing 164–177 (169.4) mm., tail 127–148 (139.4) mm.,
      exp. cul. 26–27 (26.8) mm., tars. 17–18 (17.3) mm.
8 females wing 163–177 (169.6) mm., tail 122–152 (141.0) mm.,
      exp. cul. 25–27 (26.0) mm., tars. 16–18 (17.1) mm.
Occurs in the Guianas, eastern Venezuela, and in Brazil north of the Amazon in the states of Roraima and Pará.

2. *A. n. cumanensis* (Lichtenstein)
ADULTS larger than *nobilis*; upper mandible horn-coloured, lower mandible grey.
8 males   wing 174–190 (182.3) mm., tail 140–173 (159.8) mm.,
      exp. cul. 29–31 (29.9) mm., tars. 18–19 (18.5) mm.
8 females wing 173–189 (181.3) mm., tail 143–170 (155.8) mm.,
      exp. cul. 27–32 (29.4) mm., tars. 17–21 (18.4) mm.
Found in Brazil south of the Amazon in the states of Pará, Maranhão, Piauí, and Bahia; intergrades into *longipennis* in central Goiás (Stager, 1961).

3. *A. n. longipennis* (Neumann)
ADULTS similar to *cumanensis*, but larger.
9 males   wing 181–200 (191.9) mm., tail 155–182 (165.1) mm.,
      exp. cul. 30–33 (30.9) mm., tars. 18–19 (18.6) mm.
8 females wing 182–196 (189.8) mm., tail 153–173 (165.5) mm.,
      exp. cul. 30–33 (31.1) mm., tars. 19–20 (19.3) mm.
Occurs in Brazil in the states of Mato Grosso, Goiás, Minas Gerais, São Paulo and Espírito Santo; doubtfully distinct from *cumanensis*. Stager points out that south of the Amazon there is a north-south cline of increasing size and this, coupled with the minor differences in measurements, suggests to me that *longipennis* should be synonymized with *cumanensis*.

GENERAL NOTES

The Red-shouldered Macaw is the smallest of all macaws. According to Snyder (1966) it is widespread in the sand-belt forests of Guyana; in the coastlands it also inhabits forest-fringed savannahs and plantations. I found it to be quite abundant in a variety of wooded habitats in coastal Guyana. Haverschmidt (1968) says that in Surinam it is common and fairly large, noisy flocks frequent scattered bushes and palm groves on the sandy savannahs, occasionally visiting the coastal region during September and October. In Venezuela it is very locally distributed in palm groves in the tropical zone in the extreme east of Monagas and south of the Orinoco River in

W.T.Cooper 72.

Bolívar (Phelps and Phelps, 1958). Stager reports that in the Serra Dourada region, Goiás, visited by the Machris Expedition in 1956, it was very common and showed a marked preference for cultivated clearings at the edge of primary forest, and for cerrado, which is a specialized vegetation community dominated by low, semi-deciduous trees.

Flocks of these macaws are generally seen weaving their way through the trees or dashing across open country to disappear into adjoining woodland. Young (1929) says that when feeding they are tame and can be approached, but they are so silent and so well does their plumage blend with the foliage that an intruder may not be aware of their presence until they dart out from a tree to the accompaniment of much screeching. In May 1971, I observed many small parties of up to ten in trees along the banks of the Mahaicony River in coastal Guyana. On an uppermost branch of one tree there was a group of six huddled close together and engrossed in mutual preening. In the air they are extremely noisy and the screeching call-notes always attract attention. The flight is swift and direct with rapid, jerky wingbeats. In flight the blue forehead and white, naked face are conspicuous.

They feed on seeds, berries, fruits, nuts and blossoms, procured in the treetops. Young says that favourite foods are berries of the black-sage bush (*Cordia aubletis*) and the paste trees (*Cordia* spp.), and flowers of the sandkoker tree (*Erythrina glauca*), all of which abound in secondary growth, the first two in particular being a feature of abandoned canefields. McLoughlin (1970) reports that birds he observed feeding on some green berries were eating only the very small kernels and rejecting the rest, and when captive birds were given 'native guavas' they picked out the small hard seeds and ate little, if any, of the flesh. Crop and stomach contents from a specimen collected on the São Francisco River, Minas Gerais, comprised 1.2 gms. of seeds, and from another collected on the Haúna River, Espírito Santo, remains of seeds (Schubart *et al.*, 1965).

CALL A shrill *kreek-kreek* repeated intermittently and a harsh *ark-ark-ark-ark*.

NESTING In Guyana nesting presumably takes place during the normal breeding season for most birds, that is between February and May or June (McLoughlin, 1970). A favourite nest site is a hole in the trunk of a living palm at the base of one of the fronds, and two nests have been found in one palm tree. Nests have also been found in a hollow near the top of a dead palm and in an arboreal termitarium.

Vane (1950) gives details of a successful breeding in captivity. Four eggs were laid over a period of eight days and incubation lasted twenty-four days. The sexes were identical so observations on nesting behaviour were difficult, but it did appear that only the female incubated, though the male joined her in the nest-box at night. The young birds left the nest sixty days after hatching.

EGGS Rounded; 2 eggs, 32.8 (32.3–33.2) × 26.9 (26.7–27.1) mm. [Harrison and Holyoak, 1970].

Genus ARATINGA Spix

The name Conure, which is applied to many long-tailed parrots from the New World, is derived from *Conurus*, an invalid name formerly given to this genus. Members of this genus are small to medium-sized parrots with long, gradated tails and proportionately broad, heavy bills. They have prominent naked or partly-feathered periophthalmic rings, but the lores and upper cheeks are fully feathered. The cere is naked in some species, but in others it is largely hidden by feathers and only the nostrils are exposed. According to Thompson (1900) the orbital ring is incomplete, though the imperfection is slight and the prefrontal process extends back almost to meet the postfrontal. The sexes are alike and immatures generally resemble adults.

Aratinga labati, a form presumed to have formerly inhabited Guadeloupe, is known from the writings of Père Labat, who described and figured it in 1724. It was a green parrot with a few red feathers on the head. Marien and Koopman (1955) suggest that it was a locally differentiated form, but Bond (1956) points out that Labat's description could have been of a captive specimen of *A. euops*.

BLUE-CROWNED CONURE
Aratinga acuticaudata (Vieillot)

DESCRIPTION Length 37 cm.

ADULTS general plumage green, more yellowish on underparts; forehead, crown, lores, cheeks, and ear-coverts dull blue; breast sometimes tinged with blue; outer webs of flight feathers bluish-brown becoming chestnut on the coverts; under wing-coverts dusky olive; undersides of flight feathers olive-bronze; long central tail feathers green above, lateral feathers brownish-red tipped with golden-olive; underside of tail brownish-red; creamy-white periophthalmic ring; upper mandible horn-coloured becoming grey towards tip, lower mandible grey-black; iris yellow; legs pink-brown.

IMMATURES blue restricted to forehead and crown; tinge of blue never present on breast.

From eastern Colombia and northern Venezuela south to Paraguay, Uruguay, and northern Argentina; also on Margarita Island, Venezuela.

I have followed the arrangement advocated by Blake and Traylor (1947), but draw attention to the claim made by Phelps and Phelps (1958) that *neoxena* (Cory) is not synonymous with *haemorrhous* Spix.

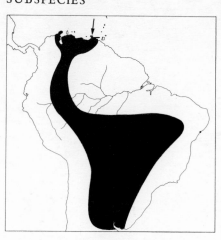

1. *A. a. acuticaudata* (Vieillot)   *Illustrated on page 373.*

   10 males   wing 185–200 (193.1) mm., tail 170–189 (180.9) mm.,
                exp. cul. 26–29 (27.2) mm., tars. 18–21 (19.6) mm.
   10 females wing 181–197 (189.3) mm., tail 165–185 (175.0) mm.,
                exp. cul. 25–29 (27.4) mm., tars. 18–20 (18.9) mm.

    Ranges from extreme south-western Mato Grosso, Brazil, and the lowlands of eastern Bolivia south to Uruguay and the provinces of Buenos Aires and La Pampa in Argentina.

2. *A. a. haemorrhous* Spix.

ADULTS blue of head paler and restricted to forehead and forecrown; no bluish wash on breast; lower mandible horn-coloured like the upper.

IMMATURES blue on forehead only, or replaced by a rufous-brown tinge.

   10 males   wing 180–197 (186.1) mm., tail 160–175 (164.2) mm.,
                exp. cul. 28–31 (28.7) mm., tars. 19–20 (19.7) mm.
   10 females wing 179–193 (180.5) mm., tail 147–171 (157.6) mm.,
                exp. cul. 25–29 (27.3) mm., tars. 19–20 (19.3) mm.

    Distributed from northern Venezuela, including Margarita Island, and adjacent eastern Colombia south to south-western Mato Grosso, Brazil, and east to Piauí and northern Bahia, Brazil. Steinbacher (1962) points out that birds from some parts of Mato Grosso and neighbouring areas in Bolivia are intermediate between *haemorrhous* and *acuticaudata*.

3. *A. a. neumanni* Blake and Traylor.

ADULTS like *haemorrhous*, but darker, less golden-green above and below; darker blue on crown and extending back to nape; larger than *haemorrhous*.

IMMATURES probably similar to adults.

   9 males   wing 193–207 (197.8) mm., tail 175–188 (180.8) mm.,
              exp. cul. 27–29 (28.1) mm., tars. 18–20 (18.9) mm.
   9 females wing 195–206 (198.7) mm., tail 177–188 (182.8) mm.,
              exp. cul. 27–30 (28.1) mm., tars. 18–20 (19.1) mm.

    Known only from intermediate altitudes (1,500–2,650 m.) in the provinces of Cochabamba, Santa Cruz, and probably Chuquisaca and Tarija, Bolivia.

Todd and Carriker (1922) point out that the Blue-crowned Conure is a bird of the arid tropical zone in Venezuela with western limits in the Guajira region, Colombia. Phelps and Phelps (1958) state that in Venezuela it is locally distributed in scattered thickets in the tropical zone north of the Orinoco River, and south of the Orinoco has been recorded only in northern Bolívar. Haffer (1967a) says that it does not occur beyond the arid Guajira Peninsula in northern Colombia, but has a wider ecological range east of the Andes, where it extends south into the grassland savannahs of the Orinoco and Meta plains. Friedmann and Smith (1950) report that in north-eastern Venezuela it was present throughout the year in savannah and along the edges of forest, but there was considerable seasonal variation in numbers, particularly at Cantaura, Anzoátegui. It was quite rare between March and July, but in late August flocks of up to a hundred were present and remained until January, when peak flocks of over two hundred were recorded. In February numbers decreased rapidly and by March the species was rare again. In south-eastern Bolivia, Eisentraut (1935) met with it at the end of the dry season, but never regularly at any one locality; at the beginning of October he flushed a flock of several hundred from near a lagoon. Unger says that when sorghum is being harvested in western Paraguay this species moves about in large flocks and consequently is conspicuous; during the breeding season it is seldom seen, presumably because nesting pairs are more secretive (in Steinbacher, 1962). Seasonal movements have been reported by Hoy (1968) who says that at the beginning of October large numbers of parrots, including this species, migrate into the Lerma Valley, north-western Argentina, to feed on ripening berries. According to Barattini (1945) it is a rare bird in Uruguay, and his specimens seem to be the only ones obtained in the country (in Cuello and Gerzenstein, 1962). Wetmore (1926) found it to be quite common in open forest at Tapia, Tucumán, and near Victoria, La Pampa, two localities in northern Argentina. Pereyra (1937) says that there has been a decline in numbers in the Pampeanos Mountains, northern Argentina.

    These parrots associate in flocks and are generally seen flying overhead or feeding in trees and bushes. They are not shy and generally will allow a close approach. Wetmore reports that near Tapia, each morning and evening, flocks were seen flying down to the river to drink; they often flew at a considerable height and as they passed overhead their long tails and pale bills and feet were conspicuous.

    Food consists of seeds, fruits, berries and nuts procured in bushes or in trees. Cherrie (1916) notes that at Ciudad Bolívar, Venezuela, flocks were seen feeding in mango trees bearing ripe fruit. In northern Argentina Wetmore found them feeding on piquillín berries (*Condalia lineata*), fruits of large tree cacti, and various seeds and berries. Wetmore also notes that in most specimens collected the distal end of the bill was considerably worn, thus indicating that it is used extensively for cutting. Unger reports that in Paraguay the species causes widespread damage to ripening sorghum crops though this is counter-balanced to some extent by its consumption of seeds of noxious weeds.

CALL A loud *cheeah-cheeah* repeated rapidly (Friedmann and Smith, 1950).

NESTING The nest is in a hollow in a tree. In Chaco, northern Argentina, Venturi found a nest containing two fresh eggs in late December (in Hartert and Venturi, 1909). A nest found at Orán, north-western Argentina, by Hoy on 15th December was in a hollow in a tree about 7 m. from the ground and contained two fresh eggs. No further details of nesting habits have been recorded.

EGGS Rounded; 2 eggs, 32.9 (32.5–33.2) × 24.0 (23.6–24.3) mm. [Hoy, 1968].

GOLDEN CONURE
Aratinga guarouba (Gmelin)

Illustrated on page 373.

Length 34 cm.
ADULTS general plumage rich yellow; primaries, secondaries and outer wing-coverts dark green; under-sides of flight feathers dusky yellow; bill horn-coloured; iris brown; legs flesh-pink.
IMMATURES (BM. 1950.25.1); cheeks and ear-coverts dark green; crown, nape, and upperparts strongly marked with dull green; breast lightly marked with dull green; upper side of tail feathers dark green margined on inner webs with yellow.
10 males   wing 200–218 (208.8) mm., tail 141–165 (153.2) mm.,
           exp. cul. 35–37 (36.2) mm., tars. 19–23 (21.2) mm.
10 females wing 202–218 (211.8) mm., tail 146–162 (154.0) mm.,
           exp. cul. 35–37 (35.9) mm., tars. 20–23 (21.1) mm.

DISTRIBUTION   Restricted to north-eastern Brazil from the Xingú River, Pará, east to north-western Maranhão.

GENERAL NOTES

The Golden Conure is well-known, though uncommon, in captivity, but little is known of its habits in the wild state. It frequents tropical rainforest, where pairs and small groups may be seen feeding in the treetops. Pinto (1946) says that it is becoming increasingly rare. The plumage of wild birds becomes stained and matted with fruit juices, particularly on the underparts.
    It feeds on fruits, berries, seeds, and nuts, procured in the treetops. On the label attached to a specimen (10.273) in the Museu Paráense Emilio Goeldi, Belém, Brazil, the stomach contents are given as having been 'cultivated berries'. One crushed seed was found in the stomach of a specimen collected on the Gurupi River, Pará (Schubart *et al.*, 1965).

CALL A shrill, metallic *keek-keek-keek* repeated rapidly many times; while feeding an occasional *keek* is uttered (in captivity).

NESTING Snethlage (1935) reports that a completely formed egg was found in the oviduct of a specimen collected on the Tocatins River, Pará, on 13th October 1912.
    Turner (1940) gives details of a successful breeding in captivity. Two eggs were laid, but one chick died soon after hatching. The length of the incubation period was not precisely determined, but was about one month. Only the female brooded, though the male roosted with her in the nest-box at night. The young bird vacated the nest three months after hatching. Hill (1939) also reports a successful breeding in captivity and records a nestling period of only six to eight weeks, which seems more like what should be expected.

EGGS Snethlage says that the egg removed from the oviduct of a specimen was almost round, but gives no measurements.

GREEN CONURE
Aratinga holochlora (Sclater)

DESCRIPTION   Length 32 cm.
ADULTS general plumage green, paler and more yellowish on underparts; in some birds there are a few red feathers on the head; under wing-coverts dull yellowish-green; undersides of tail and flight feathers olive-yellow; naked periophthalmic ring pale beige; bill horn-coloured; iris orange-red; legs brownish.
IMMATURES similar to adults, but iris brown.

DISTRIBUTION   Socorro Island, off the west coast of Mexico, and Central America from north-western Mexico south to northern Nicaragua.

SUBSPECIES

1. A. h. holochlora (Sclater)   *Illustrated on page 376.*
14 males   wing 163–175 (167.5) mm., tail 122–135 (127.9) mm.,
    exp. cul. 24–26 (24.9) mm., tars. 17–18 (17.4) mm.
12 females wing 160–175 (167.4) mm., tail 107–141 (121.1) mm.,
    exp. cul. 23–25 (24.3) mm., tars. 15–19 (17.0) mm.
Occurs in the foothills and mountains of eastern and southern Mexico from Neuvo León south to Veracruz, Oaxaca, and Chiapas.

2. A. h. brevipes (Lawrence)
ADULTS similar to *holochlora*, but underparts darker green without yellowish tinge; tenth primary shorter than the seventh instead of vice versa in *holochlora* and other subspecies.
8 males   wing 165–173 (167.9) mm., tail 142–155 (149.0) mm.,
    exp. cul. 27–29 (27.9) mm., tars. 17–19 (18.0) mm.
4 females wing 162–174 (165.3) mm., tail 136–148 (141.8) mm.,
    exp. cul. 26–28 (27.0) mm., tars. 17–18 (17.5) mm.
Confined to Socorro Island in the Revilla Gigedo Group, off the west coast of Mexico.

3. A. h. brewsteri Nelson.
ADULTS like *holochlora*, but general plumage darker green with less yellowish tinge; bluish suffusion on crown.
5 males   wing 168–173 (170.8) mm., tail 115–135 (125.2) mm.,
    exp. cul. 24–25 (24.4) mm., tars. 17–19 (17.8) mm.
3 females wing 164–170 (166.7) mm., tail 112–122 (117.0) mm.,
    exp. cul. 23–24 (23.7) mm., tars. 17–18 (17.3) mm.
Occurs in the mountains, chiefly between 1,250 and 2,000 m. in Sonora, Sinaloa and Chihuahua, north-western Mexico.

4. A. h. strenua (Ridgway)
ADULTS similar to *holochlora*, but larger and with heavier bill and stouter legs.
7 males   wing 174–184 (179.4) mm., tail 123–150 (138.9) mm.,
    exp. cul. 26–29 (27.3) mm., tars. 18–20 (18.9) mm.
13 females wing 173–185 (178.8) mm., tail 127–149 (141.2) mm.,
    exp. cul. 26–30 (27.5) mm., tars. 18–20 (19.1) mm.
Ranges along the Pacific slopes of Central America from Oaxaca, Mexico, south to northern Nicaragua.

Bangs and Peters (1928) claim that both *strenua* and *holochlora* were collected at the same locality in Oaxaca, so the former should be regarded as specifically distinct. Griscom (1932) supported this and pointed out that bill width measurements are diagnostic. I have found intergradation between *holochlora* and *strenua* in all measurements, including bill width, so in my opinion *strenua* is nothing more than a poorly-differentiated race. If, as has been predicted, *strenua* and *rubritorquis* are found to be sympatric in Guatemala then it is *rubritorquis* that should be considered a separate species.

5. A. h. rubritorquis (Sclater)   *Illustrated on page 376.*
ADULTS smaller than *holochlora*; throat and foreneck red; variable red markings on lower cheeks and sides of neck.
8 males   wing 157–162 (159.0) mm., tail 116–126 (121.3) mm.,
    exp. cul. 23–26 (24.0) mm., tars. 16–18 (17.3) mm.
8 females wing 152–163 (155.9) mm., tail 111–124 (115.6) mm.,
    exp. cul. 22–24 (23.4) mm., tars. 15–17 (16.1) mm.
Found in the highlands of eastern Guatemala, El Salvador, and northern Nicaragua.

GENERAL NOTES

Griscom (1950) says that in Mexico the Green Conure is characteristic of the arid tropics of the Pacific lowlands, but is also widespread in montane pine forests. Blake (1953) says that, although it ascends up to 2,200 m. in Mexico, it is most abundant in the lowlands and at medium altitudes. On Socorro Island, Brattstrom and Howell (1956) found that it was common in all forested areas, that is in the higher parts of the island and in the forested canyons that extend down to the sea on the north side. In Guatemala it is fairly common from near sea level up to 2,600 m. in drier parts of the Pacific subtropical zone and lowlands, the arid interior, and the highlands, and inhabits moist woodland, scrubby open woodland, farmlands, and plantations (Land, 1970). Dickey and van Rossem (1938) claim that it is a common resident throughout the arid lower tropical zone of El Salvador and ascends locally to 1,400 m. Monroe (1968) reports that in Honduras it is fairly common to common in the interior highlands above 900 m., occasionally descending to 300 m. in the nonbreeding season, and although it seems to prefer pine forests it can be found in any woodland habitat, even in cloud forest.

These parrots travel about in noisy flocks, the sizes of which seem to vary in accordance with the availability of food. Edwards and Lea (1955) report that on the Monserrate Plateau, Chiapas, Mexico, the flocks became larger and more noisy in early April when they moved into *Mimosa* trees to feed on the developing seeds. Sutton and Pettingill (1942) report that in the Gomez Farias region of south-western Tamaulipas, Mexico, the parrots were seen every day, but numbers fluctuated with the food supply. They are usually seen flying back and forth above the treetops, or coming from their roosting trees in the early morning and returning in the evening. They generally fly high and the shrieking call-notes always attract attention. The flight is direct and very swift.

They feed on seeds, fruits, nuts, berries and probably vegetable matter, procured in the treetops or amongst the outer branches of bushes. They also raid corn crops. On Volcán de San Miguel, El Salvador, Dickey and van Rossem found them feeding extensively on ripening fruits of the waxberry (*Myrica mexicana*). Wetmore (1941) notes that above Tecpam, Guatemala, flocks came in to feed in corn fields and two specimens collected had their crops filled with corn.

CALL In flight a shrill, metallic screech repeated rapidly.

NESTING A male collected at Usumatlán, Guatemala, at the beginning of August had enlarged testes, and another taken in mid-December was moulting in the primaries (Land, 1962b). In south-western Tamaulipas, Mexico, at the end of April, Sutton watched a single bird fly silently to a large hollow in a cypress, climb along the edge using both bill and feet, and disappear inside (in Sutton and Pettingill, 1942). Dickey and van Rossem suggest that in El Salvador breeding probably takes place in February and March, because in late January they observed pairs at work excavating holes in termites' mounds. Birds were also seen entering and leaving old woodpeckers' holes and roosting in crevices in the walls of a partly-built church, though no nesting was recorded at the second site. The post-juvenal moult was almost complete in a specimen collected in mid-August. Nothing further is known of the nesting habits.

EGGS Rounded; a single egg in the British Museum Collection measures 29.9 × 24.7 mm. [Harrison and Holyoak, 1970].

FINSCH'S CONURE
Aratinga finschi (Salvin)

Illustrated on page 376.

DESCRIPTION

Length 28 cm.
ADULTS general plumage green, paler and more yellowish on underparts; forehead and anterior of lores red (red does not extend back to eyes); edge of wing, carpal edge and outermost under wing-coverts red, often with an orange tinge; greater under wing-coverts yellow; innermost under wing-coverts green; thighs marked with red; undersides of tail and flight feathers olive-yellow; naked periophthalmic ring creamy-white; bill horn-coloured; iris orange; legs greyish-brown.
IMMATURES red of forehead much reduced or absent altogether; less red on under wing-coverts; greater under wing-coverts dusky olive; edge of wing and carpal edge green; no red on thighs.
8 males   wing 162–176 (168.5) mm., tail 132–136 (133.6) mm.,
                exp. cul. 25–27 (25.8) mm., tars. 17–20 (18.5) mm.
8 females wing 162–171 (166.0) mm., tail 132–139 (134.9) mm.,
                exp. cul. 25–26 (25.6) mm., tars. 18–20 (18.4) mm.

DISTRIBUTION

Tropical Central America from southern Nicaragua south to western Panama; absent from most of western Costa Rica.

GENERAL NOTES

Finsch's Conure occurs primarily on the Caribbean side of Costa Rica, and its centre of distribution seems to follow the foothills and lower slopes in the upper tropical and lower subtropical belts the full length of the country (Slud, 1964). On the western or Pacific side it is resident only in the lowlands on the peninsular coast of the Golfo Dulce in the far south-west. During the dry season it appears in good numbers, perhaps only seasonally, on the Pacific side of the Guanacaste Cordillera and on the Pacific side of the central plateau as far as San José and the neighbouring slopes up to more than 1,400 m. In western Panama it is distributed locally in the tropical and subtropical zones up to at least 1,600 m. (Wetmore, 1968).

Slud says that these parrots prefer semi-open agricultural or pasture lands in which woodland alternates with clearings; they do not enter the forest except on the peripheral canopy. In heavily forested sectors of the Caribbean lowlands of Costa Rica they seem to occur irregularly or seasonally, even in suitable secondary growth habitats. They are generally observed in flocks of from six or ten up to a hundred or more and these seem to wander widely during much of the year. Within the flocks paired birds are readily discernible by their frequent indulgence in mutual preening and by their flying close together.

In Panama Wetmore has observed evening and morning flights to and from regular roosting sites. From mid-January to early March, 1958, at Almirante, numbers came each evening to roost in palms in the residential area. Pairs and small groups commenced to arrive at sunset and started a shrill chattering which built up steadily as more birds arrived. There was intense activity until dark, with some birds climbing about and others swinging upside-down from the extremities of the fronds. Squabbling over roosting positions was also common. As darkness fell the noise subsided and, except for an occasional squawk, all remained quiet until dawn when the exodus got under way. When heavy rain fell just prior to sunrise the parrots were far quieter than usual, and if the morning was overcast and continued to be so they remained in the palms for an hour or more after the normal time of departure. Although more than five hundred birds were roosting in the palms at night it was difficult to find feeding groups during the day, thus suggesting that they dispersed over a wide area. Local residents told Wetmore that the parrots first appeared in the roosts in 1944 and had increased greatly in numbers since 1950.

Birds in a flock fly in unison, twisting and turning almost as one individual. The flight comprises shallow rapid wingbeats and the path is erratic with frequent changes in direction. The birds come to a fluttering halt on the crowns of trees and sink from sight in the foliage.

They feed on seeds, fruits, nuts, berries and probably vegetable matter, generally procured in trees and bushes. Near Puerto Armuelles, Panama, in February and March 1966, Wetmore found them occasionally feeding in fields where corn had been harvested.

CALL A raucous *kaa-kaa-kaa* (Slud, 1964). On first arriving at the roosting tree birds give a loud, harsh, guttural note with a mellow undertone, *keerr-keerr*, sometimes more elaborately *kew-kee-kee-kee-kee . . . kew-keerr* (Eisenmann, 1957).

NESTING Wetmore was told that in the Almirante district, Panama, nesting took place in July and this coincided with a reduction in the number of birds at the roosting site. Blake (1958) reports that birds with slightly enlarged gonads were collected in extreme western Panama in late November. No details of the nesting behaviour have been recorded.

EGGS Undescribed.

RED-FRONTED CONURE
Aratinga wagleri (G. R. Gray)

Length 36 cm.

ADULTS general plumage green, paler and more yellowish on underparts; forehead, crown, and anterior of lores red (red not extending to eyes); sometimes a red band or some red feathers across the throat; bend of wing and carpal edge green; greater under wing-coverts olive-yellow, remaining under wing-coverts green; undersides of flight and tail feathers olive-yellow; naked periophthalmic ring buff-white; bill horn-coloured; iris yellow; legs brownish.
IMMATURES red on head and throat reduced or even absent altogether.

DISTRIBUTION From northern Venezuela through Colombia to western Ecuador and southern Peru.

SUBSPECIES

1. *A. w. wagleri* (G. R. Gray)   *Illustrated on page 393.*
   8 males wing 172–191 (180.9) mm., tail 134–158 (146.0) mm.,
         exp. cul. 26–29 (27.6) mm., tars. 17–20 (18.1) mm.
   6 females wing 171–185 (177.8) mm., tail 134–150 (139.8) mm.,
         exp. cul. 26–28 (26.8) mm., tars. 18–19 (18.5) mm.
   Occurs in north-western Venezuela and in Colombia west of the Eastern Andes and south to northern Nariño (see Lehmann, 1960).

2. *A. w. transilis* Peters.
   ADULTS similar to *wagleri*, but general plumage, including red on head, darker; red on head more restricted posteriorly.
   6 males wing 168–178 (172.5) mm., tail 129–146 (135.2) mm.,
         exp. cul. 24–26 (25.2) mm., tars. 17–20 (18.3) mm.
   3 females wing 170–171 (170.3) mm., tail 131–142 (135.0) mm.,
         exp. cul. 23–25 (24.3) mm., tars. 18–19 (18.3) mm.
   Found in northern Venezuela east to Sucre, and in eastern Colombia where it has been recorded from Belén, Caquetá (see Meyer de Schauensee, 1944).

3. *A. w. frontata* (Cabanis)
   ADULTS red of forehead and crown extending to lores and eyes; thighs, bend of wing, edge of forewing, and carpal edge red; larger size.
   8 males wing 216–235 (224.8) mm., tail 175–205 (195.1) mm.,
         exp. cul. 29–33 (30.4) mm., tars. 19–23 (21.4) mm.
   4 females wing 218–224 (221.3) mm., tail 182–200 (189.8) mm.,
         exp. cul. 29–31 (30.0) mm., tars. 18–21 (19.5) mm.
   Occurs in western Ecuador and western Peru south to about Chuquibamba, Arequipa.

4. *A. w. minor* Carriker.
   ADULTS like *frontata*, but smaller; general plumage, both above and below, darker green without the bronze-yellow shade so conspicuous in *frontata*; red on thighs paler, but more extensive; notch on upper mandible more rounded, less angular.
   2 males wing 203–204 (203.5) mm., tail 174–183 (178.5) mm.,
         exp. cul. 29–30 (29.5) mm., tars. 19–20 (19.5) mm.
   4 females wing 188–199 (194.5) mm., tail 167–171 (169.3) mm.,
         exp. cul. 25–28 (26.8) mm., tars. 18–20 (18.8) mm.
   Replaces *frontata* in central and southern Peru from the Marañón Valley south to about Ayacucho.

The Red-fronted Conure is very locally distributed in forests in the subtropical zone of north-western Venezuela, but becomes more generally distributed towards the east (Phelps and Phelps, 1958). Schafer and Phelps (1954) report that in north-central Venezuela it ranges up into the highest belts of the sub-temperate zone at 2,000 m. and occurs in almost all humid, timbered habitats, but prefers virgin forest. It is the most abundant parrot in subtropical cloud forests in the vicinity of the Rancho Grande Reserve, Aragua, north-central Venezuela, and between January and July from five hundred to fifteen hundred may be seen each day flying back and forth through Portachuelo Pass; during September to December it is almost entirely absent from the region. Lehmann (1960) says that the species is widely distributed in Colombia and frequents the tropical and subtropical zones, ascending almost to the temperate zone in some areas; he has recorded nesting at 2,500 m. According to M. Koepcke (1970) it is not common in the Department of Lima, Peru, and occurs between 1,000 and 3,000 m. where it inhabits the Andean slopes, from which it moves out into patches of woodland and cacti in cultivated fields and orchards. Carriker (1933) reports that it was abundant at Chagual, 1,400 m. on the floor of the upper Marañón Valley, and was seen as high as 2,800 m. above Soquián. Morrison (1948) found it to be very common about Ayacucho, southern Peru, where it greatly outnumbered the Mitred Conure (*Aratinga mitrata*).

These noisy parrots undertake regular daily flights between their roosting sites and feeding grounds, and these movements are very obvious. Todd and Carriker (1922) report that in the vicinity of Las Vegas, northern Colombia, the parrots roosted on the mountainside and came down into the valley below to feed. Miller (1947) notes that at Villavieja, central-western Colombia, flocks of up to seventy birds passed overhead every day, but only once were they seen at close quarters when a group of four alighted in a small tree at the edge of woodland after flying across arid open country. Lehmann says that on the Valle del Cauca plateau, south-western Colombia, large flocks of up to three hundred birds are seen, particularly in the evening as they fly to their roosts. Sometimes these roosts are on the mountain slopes, but generally they are on rocks in the foothills of the Cordillera Occidental. Irregular local movements during the day are reported by Beebe who noticed that at Rancho Grande, north-central Venezuela, flocks of various sizes were continually flying back and forth through the Portachuelo Pass in the coastal range, irrespective of weather conditions. The flight is swift and direct with rapid, shallow wingbeats.

Food consists of seeds, fruits, berries and nuts, generally procured in the treetops.

CALL Loud and strident cries are given (M. Koepcke, 1970). Morrison points out that the call-notes are much more high-pitched than those of the Mitred Conure (*A. mitrata*).

NESTING Schafer and Phelps report that in north-central Venezuela breeding takes place between April and June. In western Colombia these parrots nest in holes in rocks (Lehmann, 1960). Along the Vinagre River at Puracé, Cauca, there is a nesting colony which Lehmann has been watching for more than twenty-five years; the nests are in rocks but are inaccessible because the rock face is from 150 to 250 m. high. Near Pereira, Caldas, Melton has found six to eight occupied nesting holes in a rock about 15 to 20 m. in height and situated above a road (in Lehmann, 1960). Nothing further is known of the breeding habits.

EGGS Undescribed.

MITRED CONURE
Aratinga mitrata (Tschudi)

DESCRIPTION Length 38 cm.
ADULTS general plumage green, paler and more yellowish on underparts; forehead brownish-red merging into paler and brighter red on forecrown, lores, cheeks and sides of neck; sometimes part of ear-coverts also red; scattered red feathers often present on hindneck, mantle, throat, thighs, and bend of wing; under wing-coverts olive-green; undersides of tail and flight feathers olive-yellow; naked periophthalmic ring creamy-white; bill horn-coloured; iris orange-yellow with an inner grey ring (Orfila, 1936); legs brownish.
IMMATURES little or no red on cheeks or sides of neck; brown iris.

DISTRIBUTION From central and southern Peru south through eastern Bolivia to La Rioja and western Cordoba in north-western Argentina.

SUBSPECIES 1. *A. m. mitrata* (Tschudi)   *Illustrated on page 393.*
    10 males   wing 198–207 (203.3) mm., tail 160–182 (168.7) mm.,
             exp. cul. 31–32 (31.5) mm., tars. 19–21 (20.3) mm.
    10 females wing 192–206 (200.2) mm., tail 156–170 (161.8) mm.,
             exp. cul. 29–31 (30.0) mm., tars. 19–21 (20.1) mm.
    Distributed from the subtropical zone of central Peru, east of the Andes, south through eastern Bolivia to north-western Argentina.

2. *A. m. alticola* Chapman.   *Illustrated on page 393.*
    ADULTS like *mitrata*, but general plumage darker green, particularly on upperparts which are

glaucous; red restricted to a narrow frontal band and a few feathers on lores and sides of head; no red on thighs.

1 male (**type**); wing 196 mm., tail 153 mm.,
exp. cul. 28 mm., tars. 19 mm.

No females examined.

Known only from the temperate zone in the Cuzco region, central Peru; treated as a separate species by Olrog (1968).

GENERAL NOTES   There is little published information on the habits of the Mitred Conure, but they are probably similar to those of *Aratinga wagleri*. At Ninabamba and Ahuayro, southern Peru, Morrison (1948) recorded both species, and although *mitrata* was common it was seen in twos and threes and was greatly outnumbered by the flocks of *wagleri*. Chapman (1921) notes that this species has been collected between 1,000 and 2,600 m. in Bolivia, while in the Cuzco region, central Peru, *alticola* was collected at 3,400 m. He mentions the claim that in central Peru these parrots visit the temperate zone at certain seasons to raid grain crops, but points out that birds in the temperate zone are clearly separable as *alticola*. In south-eastern Bolivia, Eisentraut (1935) observed it only once, when, in the middle of January, what appeared to be a wandering, post-breeding flock alighted in a food tree. Orfila (1936) says that the species is abundant in the province of Tucumán, north-western Argentina. Hoy (1968) reports that at the beginning of October large numbers of parrots, including this species, migrate into the Lerma Valley, north-western Argentina, to feed on ripening berries.

CALL   Similar to, but very much deeper and harsher than that of *A. wagleri* (Morrison, 1948).

NESTING   At Orán, north-western Argentina, Hoy found a nest containing two well-incubated eggs on 20th December. It was in a hollow in a tree about 10 m. from the ground. The hollow was fairly open, though not visible from below, and was lined with pieces of decayed wood. Nothing further is known of the nesting habits.

EGGS   Broad-oval; a single egg, taken from the nest described above, measures 33.2 × 26.5 mm. [Hoy, 1968].

RED-MASKED CONURE
Aratinga erythrogenys (Lesson)   *Illustrated on page 393.*

DESCRIPTION   Length 33 cm.
ADULTS general plumage green, paler and more yellowish on underparts; forehead, crown, lores, and foreparts of cheeks red (red completely encircles eye); bend of wing, carpal edge, outermost under wing-coverts, and thighs red; remaining under wing-coverts olive-yellow; undersides of flight and tail feathers dusky-yellow; naked periophthalmic ring creamy-white; bill horn-coloured; iris yellow; legs grey.
IMMATURES (ANSP. 118069); head entirely green without any red markings; thighs green; carpal edge greenish-yellow with a few red feathers; bend of wing and outermost under wing-coverts red, but not as extensive as in adults.

10 males   wing 171–186 (178.7) mm., tail 138–150 (142.5) mm.,
exp. cul. 26–29 (27.7) mm., tars. 18–20 (18.7) mm.
8 females   wing 173–180 (176.9) mm., tail 138–146 (141.9) mm.,
exp. cul. 26–28 (27.0) mm., tars. 18–19 (18.3) mm.

DISTRIBUTION   Restricted to the arid zone of western Ecuador and north-western Peru south to Lambayeque.

GENERAL NOTES   Within its restricted range the Red-masked Conure seems to be quite common and to some extent nomadic. Little has been recorded of its general habits, but they are probably similar to those of the closely-related *Aratinga wagleri*. Marchant (1958) reports that on the Santa Elena Peninsula, south-western Ecuador, it was a scarce to numerous non-breeding visitor, numbers varying from year to year. For instance, in 1955 no birds were seen, though there were hearsay reports of small flocks, but in 1956 the first arrivals were noted in late May and large parties were present until August, chiefly in the valleys. In 1957 some birds were seen in early February, then none till late April and thereafter it was common in large flocks at least till August and was much more widespread than in previous years. It certainly did not breed in the area, but visited it presumably after breeding elsewhere.

CALL   A disyllabic, rasping call, the second note being more drawn-out (in captivity).

NESTING   I know of no published records of nesting in the wild. Shore-Baily (1925) gives some details of a breeding in captivity. Four eggs were laid and two hatched after an incubation of approximately a month's duration. The young birds left the nest about six weeks after hatching.

EGGS   Rounded; 2 eggs, 31.1 (31.0–31.1) × 25.6 (25.6–25.7) mm. [Schönwetter, 1964].

WHITE-EYED CONURE
Aratinga leucophthalmus (P. L. S. Müller)

Length 32 cm.

ADULTS general plumage green, slightly paler on underparts; variable scattering of red feathers on head and neck; red on carpal edge and on edge of forewing; outermost lesser under wing-coverts red, innermost green; outermost greater under wing-coverts yellow, innermost olive; undersides of tail and wing feathers olive; naked periophthalmic ring greyish-white; bill horn-coloured; iris orange; legs brownish-grey.

IMMATURES like adults but carpal edge and edge of forewing yellowish-green; outermost lesser under wing-coverts green washed with red; outermost greater under wing-coverts olive-green.

From the Guianas, Venezuela, and eastern Colombia south to northern Argentina and northern Uruguay.

Separation of the subspecies of *A. leucophthalmus* and establishing their respective distributions is very difficult. Authors have generally oversimplified subspecific differences and not taken into consideration the pronounced overlapping and intergradations between populations. Variation in size, even from the same locality is striking and this undermines the value of size differences as a racial character. I tend to agree with the arrangements proposed by Gyldenstolpe (1951), but am not convinced that the diagnostic characters are as clear as is indicated by him. For instance, I accept *callogenys* because of its heavier, more robust bill and its slightly darker plumage, not because of its alleged larger size and the more constant presence of red feathers on the head. The acceptance of *propinquus* is provisional and depends on the acquisition of further specimens, but I expect that it will eventually prove to be invalid. Finally, *nicefori* is of little consequence until further specimens are obtained; it could prove to be an aberrant specimen of *callogenys*.

1. *A. l. leucophthalmus* (P. L. S. Müller)　　*Illustrated on page 396.*
　　10 males　wing 166–178 (172.5) mm., tail 134–157 (145.0) mm.,
　　　　exp. cul. 24–28 (26.0) mm., tars. 18–20 (18.6) mm.
　　10 females wing 166–188 (173.7) mm., tail 135–162 (147.6) mm.,
　　　　exp. cul. 24–28 (25.2) mm., tars. 17–20 (18.3) mm.
　　Distributed from the Guianas, eastern Venezuela, and eastern Colombia, south of Meta, south through Brazil, except the upper Amazon region and the extreme south-east, to Bolivia, Paraguay, and northern Argentina, as far south as Catamarca and northern Santa Fe and Entre Ríos, and into northern Uruguay.

2. *A. l. callogenys* (Salvadori)
　ADULTS like *leucophthalmus*, but general plumage slightly darker; heavier, more robust bill.
　　12 males　wing 171–186 (182.2) mm., tail 143–160 (153.2) mm.,
　　　　exp. cul. 28–32 (30.0) mm., tars. 19–22 (20.3) mm.
　　11 females wing 170–184 (176.6) mm., tail 144–160 (151.9) mm.,
　　　　exp. cul. 26–31 (28.6) mm., tars. 19–21 (20.0) mm.
　　Occurs in the tropical zone of eastern Ecuador, north-eastern Peru, and the upper Amazon region in north-western Brazil; there is considerable intergradation with *leucophthalmus*.

3. *A. l. propinquus* (Sclater)
　ADULTS like *leucophthalmus*, but larger.
　　3 males　wing 182–188 (185.7) mm., tail 160–164 (162.3) mm.,
　　　　exp. cul. 27–28 (27.3) mm., tars. 20 (20.0) mm.
　　2 females wing 178–195 (186.5) mm., tail 154–171 (162.5) mm.,
　　　　exp. cul. 26 (26.0) mm., tars. 19–20 (19.5) mm.
　　1 unsexed wing 192 mm., tail 180 mm.,
　　　　exp. cul. 29 mm., tars. 19 mm.
　　At present known only from extreme south-eastern Brazil in the states of Santa Catarina and Rio Grande do Sul and north-eastern Argentina in Misiones and Corrientes; doubtfully distinct from *leucophthalmus*.

4. *A. l. nicefori* Meyer de Schauensee.
　ADULTS similar to *callogenys*, but general plumage paler and more yellowish; red band across forehead.
　No specimens examined.
　　1 unsexed (**type**) (Meyer de Schauensee, 1946); wing 190 mm., tail 159 mm.,
　　　　exp. cul. 29 mm., tars. —.
　　Known only from the unique type collected at Guaicaramo on the Guavio River, about 100 km. north-east of Villavicencio, Meta, Colombia.
　　Meyer de Schauensee (1946) claims that *nicefori* is intermediate between *A. l. callogenys* and *A. finschi*, so the latter should be treated as a subspecies of *leucophthalmus*. In my opinion the collection of a unique specimen does not justify this arrangement.

Haverschmidt (1968) says that in Surinam the White-eyed Conure is locally distributed, and he has recorded it as fairly common only from the coastal region in the Nickerie district where flocks live in mangroves. There is a small group that roosts in palms along the Nickerie River and specimens have been collected on the Surinam River, so the species probably wanders about to some extent. Its status in Guyana is not known, but Snyder (1966) lists only the specimen collected by Schomburgk in about 1837 and I know of no recent records. In Venezuela it is very locally distributed in open forests and palm groves in the tropical zone in the extreme east of the country, where it has been recorded north of the Orinoco River in only Anzoátegui and Monagas and south of the Orinoco in Delta Amacuro and Bolívar (Phelps and Phelps, 1958). Friedmann and Smith (1950) report that between January and June flocks of from ten to twenty birds were seen regularly near stands of moriché palms (*Mauritia flexuosa*) on the savannah near Cantaura, Anzoátegui, but apparently the species is rare in that district because local residents were not familiar with it. Meyer de Schauensee (1964) says that in the tropical zone of south-eastern Colombia it inhabits open forests and palm groves. Pinto (1946) reports that it is one of the most common parrots in central Brazil. It was abundant in the region about Descalvados, Mato Grosso, Brazil, visited by the Roosevelt-Cherrie Expedition in 1916 and at that time, during November and December, it was associating in large flocks (Naumburg, 1930); indeed it was one of the most widely distributed and abundant birds observed during the course of the expedition. According to Orfila (1936) it is common in northern Argentina. In Uruguay it occurs in mountains in the north of the country (Cuello and Gerzenstein, 1962).

These parrots are generally seen in pairs, family parties, or flocks of from ten to thirty individuals. Friedmann (1927) reports that at San Joaquin, northern Argentina, he observed two birds in a low tree; they flew down to the ground as if to feed but quickly returned to the tree as he approached. In north-eastern Venezuela Smith found them associating with Blue-crowned Conures (*Aratinga acuticaudata*), but when mixed flocks flew overhead he was able to differentiate between the two species by their call-notes (in Friedmann and Smith, 1950).

They feed on seeds, nuts, fruits, berries, blossoms, vegetable matter and insects and their larvae, procured both on the ground and in the treetops. Venturi says that in the Ocampo district, Santa Fe, Argentina, they fed extensively on flowers of ceibo trees (*Erythrina* sp.) and on fruits of cacti (in Hartert and Venturi, 1909). At Caicara, Monagas, Venezuela, Smith found a flock feeding on the flowers of *Erythrina glauca* (in Friedmann and Smith, 1955). Crop and stomach contents from a specimen collected on the upper São Francisco River, Minas Gerais, Brazil, comprised one hundred and eighty grass seeds weighing 2.8 gms., from another taken at the same locality six hundred grass seeds with a total weight of 5.3 gms., and from a specimen collected at Salobra, Mato Grosso, fifty seeds, fruit remnants, and remains of insects (Schubart *et al.*, 1965):

CALL In flight a sharp, metallic *che–chek* and a shrill screech similar to, but more high-pitched than that of *A. acuticaudata* (Friedmann and Smith 1950 and 1955).

NESTING Venturi says that in the Ocampo district, northern Argentina, these parrots retreated into the forests at the beginning of November to breed and returned with their young at the end of December (in Hartert and Venturi, 1909). A male with slightly enlarged testes was collected at the end of January at San Joaquin, also in northern Argentina (Friedmann, 1927). Penard and Penard (1908) claim that in the Guianas nesting takes place in February, and three or·four eggs are laid in a hollow in a palm tree. Nothing further is known of the breeding habits.

EGGS According to Penard and Penard the eggs average 31.0 × 25.0 mm.

HISPANIOLAN CONURE
Aratinga chloroptera (Souancé)

DESCRIPTION
Length 32 cm.
ADULTS general plumage green, slightly paler and more yellowish on underparts; outermost under wing-coverts red; greater under wing-coverts green variably marked with red, remaining under wing-coverts green; red on bend of wing and edge of forewing; some birds show a few red feathers on head; undersides of tail and flight feathers dull olive-yellow; naked periophthalmic ring creamy-white; bill horn-coloured; iris yellow; legs brownish.
IMMATURES like adults, but no red on bend of wing or edge of forewing; less red on greater under wing-coverts.

DISTRIBUTION
The Island of Hispaniola in the West Indies; formerly on Mona Island and possibly Puerto Rico, but now extinct.

SUBSPECIES
1. *A. c. chloroptera* (Souancé)   *Illustrated on page 396.*
    10 males   wing 167–185 (175.7) mm., tail 132–147 (139.3) mm.,
           exp. cul. 26–27 (26.4) mm., tars. 16–18 (17.2) mm.
    10 females wing 170–182 (173.7) mm., tail 120–151 (143.3) mm.,
           exp. cul. 26–27 (26.3) mm., tars. 17–20 (18.0) mm.
    Occurs on Haiti and the Dominican Republic which together make up the Island of Hispaniola in the West Indies.

2. *A. c. maugei* (Souancé)

ADULTS like *chloroptera*, but green of underparts faintly duller; greater under wing-coverts more extensively marked with red.

1 female wing 163 mm., tail 153 mm.,
    exp. cul. 27 mm., tars. 18 mm.
2 unsexed wing 174 (174.0) mm., tail 152–166 (159.0) mm.,
    exp. cul. 28–29 (28.5) mm., tars. 19–21 (20.0) mm.

Formerly found on Mona Island, midway between Hispaniola and Puerto Rico, and possibly on Puerto Rico, but now extinct; doubtfully distinct from *chloroptera*.

GENERAL NOTES

The last known specimen of the Hispaniolan Conure from Mona Island was collected by W. W. Brown in 1892 and is now in the Field Museum of Natural History, Chicago. Its former occurrence on Puerto Rico is based on hearsay evidence and, if it did occur there, it must have disappeared prior to 1883 (see Greenway, 1967). Bond (1946) suggests that it may have been extirpated by pigeon hunters, who visited the island in the last century.

Dod reports that on Hispaniola this species occurs in all habitats, including the arid lowlands, but is most numerous in the mountains (*in litt.*, 1972). Wetmore and Swales (1931) state that it is common in the high mountains of the interior, but is locally distributed elsewhere and has been recorded less frequently in Haiti than in the Dominican Republic. Danforth (1929) reports that between San Juan, Dominican Republic, and Mirebalais, Haiti, it was most abundant and thousands were seen every day, mostly in flocks of from ten to a hundred or more. Bond (1929a) found it to be abundant in the pine belt in northern Haiti. Kepler says that in the Dominican Republic he observed it in small groups of from four to eight individuals, always in close proximity to mountain forest (*in litt.*, 1971).

These noisy parrots are generally seen flying overhead, when their screeching call-notes attract attention. While feeding in the treetops they are far less conspicuous, because their green plumage blends well with the foliage. They undertake regular flights to and from roosting sites. At San Juan, Dominican Republic, Danforth noticed that every morning many large flocks flew over the town to the east and at evening returned to the west. Within the flocks paired birds are readily discernible because they fly close together. While feeding they are tame and somewhat oblivious to the approach of an intruder, but at other times are wary and difficult to approach. The flight is swift and direct.

They feed on seeds, fruits, nuts, berries, and probably blossoms and leaf buds. Danforth observed them feeding on *Ficus* fruits. It has been reported that they raid ripening maize crops (see Wetmore and Swales, 1931).

CALL In flight a shrill screech is given almost continuously (Danforth, 1929).

NESTING Wetmore and Swales quote early reports which claimed that nests are in old woodpeckers' holes or other hollows in trees and three to five, rarely seven, eggs are laid. Bond (1929a) describes a nest found on Morne Salnave, northern Haiti, but gives no date; it was in a hole in a dead pine tree at least 25 m. from the ground. No further details of the nesting habits have been recorded.

EGGS Undescribed.

CUBAN CONURE
Aratinga euops (Wagler)

Illustrated on page 396.

Length 26 cm.

ADULTS general plumage green, paler and more yellowish on underparts; scattered red feathers on head and underparts; occasional red feather on bend of wing and on thighs; lesser under wing-coverts and edge of forewing red; greater under wing-coverts olive-yellow; undersides of tail and flight feathers olive-yellow; naked periophthalmic ring white; bill horn-coloured; iris yellow; legs brownish.

IMMATURES like adults but with less red on under wing-coverts; edge of forewing yellowish-green; brown iris.

10 males wing 132–147 (137.4) mm., tail 120–131 (127.1) mm.,
    exp. cul. 18–19 (18.7) mm., tars. 13–16 (15.1) mm.
8 females wing 132–140 (136.4) mm., tail 119–132 (125.0) mm.,
    exp. cul. 18–19 (18.8) mm., tars. 13–16 (15.0) mm.

DISTRIBUTION

Cuba and formerly the Isle of Pines, West Indies.

GENERAL NOTES

The Cuban Conure disappeared from the Isle of Pines soon after the beginning of this century. At the turn of the century Gundlach stated that it was formerly very abundant on the island, but at the rate it was being taken for the cage-bird trade it would be only a few years before it was exterminated (in Todd, 1916). Apparently the prediction was fulfilled soon after (Bangs and Zappey, 1905).

On Cuba the species is common in the wilder, heavily forested regions, and is occasionally seen in open country well away from the normal habitat (Bond, 1956). Ripley and Watson (1956) give a record of a flock of twenty-five being found associated with a flock of Cuban Amazons (*Amazona leucocephala*) at Santa Tomás in the Zapata Swamp. Barbour (1943) says that it was formerly more widespread and plentiful, but has disappeared from, or declined in numbers in, many districts, largely because of the destruction of forests. It seems to wander about and to some extent these movements may be seasonal. Davis (1941) notes that in the region around Cienfuegos flocks occasionally come down from the Trinidad Mountains in September and October, and Barbour says that birds from these mountains also occasionally visit the Soledad Botanic Gardens, especially when fruit of the jobo (*Spondias luteus*) is ripe.

Family parties or small flocks of these parrots are generally seen flying overhead or feeding in the treetops. When sitting quietly in a tree they are very difficult to see, so well does their plumage blend with the foliage, but normally their presence is betrayed by intermittent chattering and by the movement of leaves as they clamber about amongst the branches. They are fairly tame and will usually allow a close approach. The flight is swift and direct.

They feed on fruits, seeds, berries, nuts and probably blossoms and leaf buds, generally procured in the treetops.

CALL In flight a shrill screeching is given almost continuously; while feeding or at rest a sharp chattering is emitted.

NESTING Barbour says that nests are in hollows in trees, especially in palms, or in old wood-peckers' holes. Holes excavated in arboreal termitaria by Cuban Green Woodpeckers (*Xiphidiopicus percussus*) are often used.

Near Guasimal in southern Las Villas province, Bauzá has found many nests in deserted wood-peckers' holes or in natural hollows in palms (in Bond, 1958). Eggs were collected in late June, mid July, and in early and late August, but as there were many young birds present on these dates it would appear that eggs are generally laid during May. Nests contained from two to five eggs or young birds.

EGGS Rounded; 3 eggs, 27.3 (26.4–27.9) × 22.1 (21.6–22.6) mm. [Bond, 1958].

GOLDEN-CAPPED CONURE
Aratinga auricapilla (Kuhl)

DESCRIPTION

Length 30 cm.
ADULTS general plumage dark green, paler and more yellowish on cheeks, ear-coverts, throat, and upper breast; forehead, lores, and periophthalmic region orange-red; forecrown golden-yellow; in some birds cheeks washed with yellow; abdomen and lower breast red with green bases to feathers generally showing through; feathers of rump and lower back variably edged with red; outer webs of primaries, primary-coverts and secondaries blue; under wing-coverts orange-red; upper side of tail olive-green tipped with blue; undersides of tail and flight feathers grey; bill grey-black; iris brown; legs grey.
IMMATURES head markings less pronounced, particularly yellow on forecrown; cheeks deeper green; little or no red edgings to feathers of rump and lower back; red on underparts confined to flanks and centre of abdomen.

Eastern Brazil from Bahia south to Rio Grande do Sul.

DISTRIBUTION

SUBSPECIES

1. *A. a. auricapilla* (Kuhl)
    4 males   wing 160–169 (165.0) mm., tail 132–152 (142.0) mm.,
              exp. cul. 22–25 (23.5) mm., tars. 16–18 (17.0) mm.
    4 females wing 161–169 (165.0) mm., tail 128–145 (138.5) mm.,
              exp. cul. 22–25 (23.5) mm., tars. 16–18 (17.3) mm.
    Confined to northern and central parts of Bahia, north-eastern Brazil; birds from southern Bahia tend to be intermediate between this race and *aurifrons* (see Pinto, 1935).

2. *A. a. aurifrons* Spix.   *Illustrated on page 397.*
    ADULTS like *auricapilla*, but sides of head, throat and upper breast deeper green without any yellowish tinge; no red margins to feathers of rump and lower back.
    10 males wing 163–172 (167.0) mm., tail 131–146 (139.6) mm.,
              exp. cul. 23–25 (24.5) mm., tars. 16–19 (17.4) mm.
    8 females wing 160–167 (165.3) mm., tail 120–142 (137.1) mm.,
              exp. cul. 22–25 (23.5) mm., tars. 16–18 (17.0) mm.
    Occurs in south-eastern Brazil from Minas Gerais and southern Goiás, south to northern Rio Grande do Sul.

Virtually nothing has been recorded about the Golden-capped Conure, but its habits are probably similar to those of the very closely-related *Aratinga jandaya*. It inhabits forest, open woodland and

GENERAL NOTES

savannah. I suspect that the species is now rare south of Rio de Janeiro because of the extensive land-clearance that has taken place in that region.

CALL Undescribed.

NESTING No records.

EGGS Broadly elliptical; 3 eggs, 30.4 (30.0–30.7) × 23.5 (21.4–24.5) mm. [Harrison and Holyoak, 1970].

JANDAYA CONURE
Aratinga jandaya (Gmelin)

Illustrated on page 397.

Length 30 cm.
ADULTS head and neck yellow, tinged with orange on forehead, ocular region, cheeks, and throat; back, wings and upper tail-coverts green; feathers of rump and lower back green variably edged with red; breast and abdomen orange-red; under tail-coverts green; outer webs of primaries, primary-coverts, and secondaries blue; under wing-coverts orange-red; upper side of tail olive tipped with blue; undersides of tail and flight feathers grey; bill grey-black; iris grey-brown; legs grey.
IMMATURES head and neck pale yellow variably marked with green; paler orange-red on breast and abdomen.
10 males   wing 153–165 (159.7) mm., tail 129–146 (136.2) mm.,
            exp. cul. 23–25 (23.8) mm., tars. 15–18 (16.6) mm.
8 females wing 153–162 (157.3) mm., tail 130–146 (137.5) mm.,
            exp. cul. 22–23 (22.4) mm., tars. 16–18 (17.0) mm.

DISTRIBUTION   North-eastern Brazil from Alagoas, Pernambuco, Ceará and Maranhão south through Piauí to northern Goiás.

GENERAL NOTES   Stager (1961) points out that the Jandaya Conure seems to be sporadically distributed in Goiás and has been missed by most workers in the area. In central Goiás he found it only in the Serra Dourada and it was not common. It was seen singly, in pairs, or in small flocks of ten to fifteen birds, always in primary forest at the margins of clearings. Lamm (1948) reports that it is fairly common in coastal coconut palms near Recife, Pernambuco, and is usually seen in small flocks of up to a dozen birds; it does not occur in the arid scrublands of the interior of the state. The flight of this parrot is swift and direct.

It feeds on seeds, fruits, berries and probably vegetable matter. The stomach from a specimen collected on the Mearim River, Maranhão, contained seven small fruits and a small quantity of crushed seeds (Schubart *et al.*, 1965).

CALL A screeching *kink-kink-kank*, the last note being of a higher pitch (in captivity).

NESTING I know of no records from the wild state. Jones (1955) gives details of a successful breeding in captivity. Three eggs were laid, but the hen did not commence sitting until two or three days after the last egg had been laid. She alone incubated and sat very tightly. The cock entered the nest-box frequently and generally slept in it at night. The incubation period was not determined precisely, but was about twenty-six days. Both parents fed the chicks. The young birds left the nest approximately eight weeks after hatching, and some five weeks later were still occasionally fed by both parents.

EGGS Rounded; 2 eggs, 28.4 (26.9–29.8) × 22.6 (21.1–24.0) mm. [Harrison and Holyoak, 1970].

SUN CONURE
Aratinga solstitialis (Linné)

Illustrated on page 397.

Length 30 cm.
ADULTS general plumage yellow, variably tinged with orange on forehead, sides of head, lower abdomen, rump and lower back; under tail-coverts green tinged with yellow; mantle, lesser and median upper wing-coverts and under wing-coverts yellow variably marked with green; secondary coverts green; outer webs of primary coverts blue; primaries and secondaries green, former becoming blue towards tips; upper side of tail olive tipped with blue; undersides of tail and flight feathers olive-grey; bill grey; iris dark brown; legs grey.
IMMATURES crown marked with green; upper back and scapulars green slightly edged with yellow; rump and lower back tinged with red; upper tail-coverts green with a yellow tinge; greenish throat; breast and abdomen orange; under tail-coverts green margined with paler green; lesser and median upper wing-coverts green edged with yellow; paler bill.

14 males   wing 146–160 (153.1) mm., tail 131–146 (137.6) mm.,
exp. cul. 21–25 (22.8) mm., tars. 16–18 (16.9) mm.
8 females wing 150–162 (156.4) mm., tail 121–146 (133.1) mm.,
exp. cul. 19–24 (21.5) mm., tars. 16–18 (16.8) mm.

DISTRIBUTION The Guianas, extreme south-eastern Venezuela, and north-eastern Brazil in Roraima, northern Amazonas and Pará, and probably in north-western Amapá. Not recorded south of the Amazon River; Pinto (1966) points out that the specimen reputedly collected by Garbe at Santarem came from the Monte Alegre district on the northern bank.

SUBSPECIES *Aratinga solstitialis*, *A. jandaya*, and *A. auricapilla* are probably conspecific. However, I am not familiar with the birds and it is apparent from the literature that the distribution of each form has not been precisely determined, so for the present I prefer to treat each as a separate species.

GENERAL NOTES Haverschmidt (1968) says that the Sun Conure occurs in flocks on the savannahs of southern Surinam, but has not been recorded in the north of the country. I did not see it in Guyana and was told that it is locally distributed and not very common in the country. Its occurrence in south-eastern Venezuela is based solely on Schomburgk's record from Cerro Roraima in 1848 (Phelps and Phelps, 1958).

This brilliantly coloured parrot frequents open forests, savannahs, and palm groves, and is generally seen in flocks. Sometimes quite large flocks congregate to feed in trees bearing ripening fruits. It is a noisy bird and the screeching call-notes always betray its presence. The flight is swift and direct.

Seeds, fruits, nuts, berries and probably blossoms make up the diet.

CALL A shrill, disyllabic screech repeated a number of times in rapid succession (in captivity).

NESTING Haverschmidt reports that at Sipalwini, Surinam, a nest containing young birds was found in a hole in a moriché palm (*Mauritia flexuosa*) in February. Nothing further is known of the nesting habits.

Nieremberg (1972) gives details of a successful breeding in captivity. Four eggs were laid at two day intervals. The hen incubated day and night, leaving only for brief periods of feeding. Three eggs hatched, the first four weeks after it was laid. Both parents fed the chicks. The young birds vacated the nest approximately eight weeks after hatching.

EGGS Rounded; 3 eggs, 29.5 (28.4–31.4) × 23.5 (22.8–24.0) mm. [Schönwetter, 1964].

DUSKY-HEADED CONURE
Aratinga weddellii (Deville)

Illustrated on page 400.

Length 28 cm.
ADULTS general plumage green, paler and more yellowish on underparts; head brownish-grey, the feathers tipped with dull greyish-blue; outer webs of primaries and secondaries blue; tail above green broadly tipped with blue, below grey; naked periophthalmic ring creamy-white; bill black; iris yellowish-white; legs grey.
IMMATURES undescribed, but probably similar to adults.
10 males   wing 139–152 (145.0) mm., tail 100–119 (109.9) mm.,
exp. cul. 21–22 (21.7) mm., tars. 16–18 (16.7) mm.
11 females wing 136–148 (142.4) mm., tail 97–112 (104.7) mm.,
exp. cul. 20–22 (20.7) mm., tars. 15–18 (16.5) mm.

DISTRIBUTION From south-eastern Colombia south through eastern Ecuador to eastern Peru and north-eastern Bolivia in Beni and Cochabamba; also in western Mato Grosso, Brazil, and in Amazonian Brazil in southern Amazonas from the Juruá River east to the Maderia River.

GENERAL NOTES Olrog (1968) says that the Dusky-headed Conure frequents patches of forest in savannah. There is a specimen collected in forest at 750 m. in the province of Sara, Bolivia (AMNH. 474301). In Colombia it occurs in forest in the tropical zone east of the Andes (Meyer de Schauensee, 1964). Terborgh and Weske (1969) report that in the Apurímac Valley, central Peru, it was found in primary forest, in a coffee plantation adjacent to forest, and in matorral, which is a riparian woodland of varied composition. Virtually nothing has been recorded on the habits of this seemingly common parrot.

CALL Undescribed.

NESTING Bond and Meyer de Schauensee (1943) report that a male collected at Todos Santos, Bolivia, in early August was in breeding condition. I know of no published nesting records.

EGGS Undescribed.

OLIVE-THROATED CONURE
Aratinga nana (Vigors)

DESCRIPTION

Length 26 cm.
ADULTS general plumage green, brighter on rump, cheeks and ear-coverts; orange-yellow feathers surrounding nostrils; throat and breast olive-brown, becoming more olive on lower breast and abdomen; under tail-coverts green; outer webs of primaries and secondaries blue; under wing-coverts pale green; undersides of flight feathers grey; underside of tail olive-yellow; naked periophthalmic ring white; bill horn-coloured; iris orange; legs grey.
IMMATURES similar to adults; brown iris.

DISTRIBUTION

Jamaica and the Caribbean slope of tropical Central America from Tamaulipas, Mexico, south to extreme western Panama.

SUBSPECIES

1. *A. n. nana* (Vigors)   *Illustrated on page 400.*
    7 males   wing 137–145 (141.9) mm., tail 128–132 (130.3) mm.,
            exp. cul. 21–22 (21.6) mm., tars. 16–17 (16.6) mm.
    7 females wing 139–144 (142.0) mm., tail 123–128 (125.7) mm.,
            exp. cul. 21–22 (21.7) mm., tars. 14–17 (15.4) mm.
    Confined to Jamaica in the West Indies.

2. *A. n. astec* (Souancé)   *Illustrated on page 400.*
    ADULTS smaller than *nana*, but with proportionately longer wings; green of general plumage paler, more yellowish, particularly on lower underparts; paler brown on throat, breast and abdomen; smaller bill.
    10 males   wing 132–147 (139.1) mm., tail 92–113 (105.9) mm.,
            exp. cul. 17–19 (18.3) mm., tars. 13–15 (14.1) mm.
    8 females wing 133–142 (136.9) mm., tail 102–118 (107.9) mm.,
            exp. cul. 17–19 (18.0) mm., tars. 14–15 (14.4) mm.
    This race is known as the Aztec Conure and is often treated as a separate species. It is distributed along the tropical zone of the Caribbean slope from Veracruz, Mexico, south to the Almirante Bay region in extreme western Panama; replaced by the doubtfully distinct *melloni* in Honduras.

3. *A. n. vicinalis* (Bangs and Penard)
    ADULTS like *astec*, but general plumage brighter green; throat, breast, and abdomen much greener and less brownish.
    8 males   wing 137–148 (143.0) mm., tail 107–119 (112.6) mm.,
            exp. cul. 18–19 (18.4) mm., tars. 14–15 (14.8) mm.
    8 females wing 132–143 (137.3) mm., tail 109–115 (112.4) mm.,
            exp. cul. 18–19 (18.3) mm., tars. 14–15 (14.9) mm.
    Restricted to north-eastern Mexico from central Tamaulipas south to north-eastern Veracruz.

4. *A. n. melloni* Twomey.
    ADULTS similar to *astec*, but paler on breast, abdomen, and flanks; duller olive cast to throat and breast; green of flanks paler and slightly tinged with grey; olivaceous cast on crown; paler green back.
    5 males   wing 134–142 (137.6) mm., tail 102–114 (107.2) mm.,
            exp. cul. 17–18 (17.6) mm., tars. 13–15 (14.2) mm.
    4 females wing 133–141 (137.5) mm., tail 103–125 (113.5) mm.,
            exp. cul. 17–18 (17.5) mm., tars. 13–15 (14.3) mm.
    Confined to Honduras; probably not separable from *astec* (see Monroe, 1968).

GENERAL NOTES

Bond (1956) says that the Olive-throated Conure is common in many parts of Jamaica, occurring chiefly in the lowlands, in wooded hills, and on lower mountain slopes; it is rare in, or absent from, the higher mountains. Lack has recently completed an extensive field study on the birds of the island and he reports that this species is most abundant in the mid-level wet limestone forests, except the very wet forests of the John Crow Mountains (*in. litt.*, 1971). It is also common in wooded cultivation and less arid secondary forest in the lowlands, but is absent from both forest and cultivation in the Blue Mountains and the John Crow Mountains.

Loetscher (1941) says that it is a common to abundant resident of the tropical zone of Veracruz, Mexico, both in humid and semi-arid districts up to about 780 m. Paynter (1955) reports that it is by far the most common parrot on the Yucatán Peninsula, Mexico, where its principal habitat is deciduous forest and scrub, though it also occurs in clearings in rainforest. In British Honduras it is widely distributed in all wooded habitats and in semi-open country, but is least common in the heart of rainforest (Russell, 1964). Monroe says that in Honduras it is a fairly common to common inhabitant of the Caribbean lowlands below 1,100 m., occurring primarily in and around areas of rainforest, though during the day flocks may disperse widely throughout adjacent open or cultivated country, both humid and arid. It is a common resident in the Caribbean lowlands of Guatemala and is fairly common in the Petén up to 750 m. (Land, 1970); it inhabits forest edges and scrublands in humid areas and ranges out into plantations and cultivated farmlands. Smithe

(1966) points out that it is uncommon at Tikal, Guatemala, although flocks of from four to twelve are occasionally seen and heard flying across the airstrip and into the bordering forest. At Eden, north-eastern Nicaragua, Huber (1933) found it to be very common in flocks of from ten to thirty birds. It is largely restricted to the humid tropical lowlands and foothills along the Caribbean slope of Costa Rica and is locally distributed in both partially deforested and heavily forested areas (Slud, 1964); it does not enter the forest but keeps mainly to the forest edge and to neighbouring clearings and plantations with trees of various sizes. Only four specimens have been collected in western Panama, all in 1927, and Wetmore (1968) points out that these may have been wanderers from farther north.

These parrots are generally seen in pairs or flocks of from five to thirty individuals, but larger numbers will congregate when certain fruits are ripening. Lowery and Dalquest (1951) report that in Veracruz great flocks of both this species and the Green Conure (*Aratinga holochlora*) gather when the 'nanchi' fruit is ripe, but *A. nana* is by far the more numerous. Lack notes that they visit the arid forests of the southern lowlands of Jamaica when certain fruits are available, but at other times are absent. At Lumsden, western Jamaica, Danforth (1928) found large flocks being attracted to fruit-bearing guava trees. They tend to keep to the middle and lower storeys of trees and do not fly about above the canopies. Flocks comprise paired birds, which are nearly always discernible when at rest by their intensive mutual preening. The flight is swift and an observer frequently gets little more than a glimpse as the birds flash past and continue on, twisting and turning through the forest.

They feed on seeds, fruits, berries, blossoms and probably vegetable matter, generally procured in trees and bushes. They often cause considerable damage to corn crops. Stomachs from two specimens collected at Lumsden, western Jamaica, were filled mainly with pulp and seeds of guava fruits (Danforth, 1928).

CALL In flight a high-pitched screech; also a sustained, harsh twittering terminating with an upward inflection (Slud, 1964).

NESTING Russell points out that in British Honduras breeding in April and May is indicated by the enlarged gonads of specimens collected in these months. A female in breeding condition was collected at Tikal, Guatemala, in mid-May (Smithe and Paynter, 1963). The nest is in a hole excavated by the birds in an arboreal termitarium.

EGGS Rounded; one egg in the Nehrkorn Collection measures 25.3 × 20.5 mm. (Schönwetter, 1964).

Red-masked Conure *Aratinga erythrogenys* 1
AMNH. 175100 ad. ♂

Red-fronted Conure *Aratinga wagleri wagleri* 2
ANSP. 145091 ad. ♂

Mitred Conure *Aratinga mitrata mitrata* 3
ANSP. 143652 ad. ♂

Mitred Conure *Aratinga mitrata alticola* 4
AMNH. 129136 **type** ad. ♂

ORANGE-FRONTED CONURE
Aratinga canicularis (Linné)

DESCRIPTION

Length 24 cm.
ADULTS general plumage green, broad orange frontal band extending down to lores; forecrown dull blue; throat and breast pale olive; abdomen, under tail-coverts and under wing-coverts greenish-yellow; outer webs of primaries green, becoming blue towards tips; outer webs of secondaries blue; tail above green, below dusky olive-yellow; naked periophthalmic ring dull orange-yellow; bill horn-coloured; iris pale yellow; legs greyish-brown.
IMMATURES like adults, but with narrower orange frontal band; brown iris.

DISTRIBUTION

Western Central America from Sinaloa, Mexico, south to western Costa Rica.

SUBSPECIES

1. *A. c. canicularis* (Linné)   *Illustrated on page 404.*
11 males   wing 130–142 (136.5) mm., tail 95–112 (102.4) mm.,
            exp. cul. 17–19 (18.4) mm., tars. 13–15 (14.0) mm.
10 females wing 129–139 (135.1) mm., tail 97–103 (100.1) mm.,
            exp. cul. 17–19 (17.7) mm., tars. 13–15 (14.1) mm.
   Distributed along the Pacific slope of Central America from Chiapas, south-western Mexico, south to western Costa Rica.

2. *A. c. eburnirostrum* (Lesson)
ADULTS like *canicularis*, but with narrower orange frontal band; underparts more green, less yellowish; brownish spot on each side of base of lower mandible.
10 males   wing 130–140 (134.2) mm., tail 95–106 (100.3) mm.,
            exp. cul. 18–20 (19.0) mm., tars. 14–15 (14.4) mm.
10 females wing 126–139 (133.2) mm., tail 95–112 (102.9) mm.,
            exp. cul. 17–19 (17.9) mm., tars. 13–15 (14.1) mm.
   Restricted to south-western Mexico from extreme eastern Michoacán south through Guerrero to Oaxaca.

3. *A. c. clarae* Moore.
ADULTS similar to *eburnirostrum*, but orange frontal band greatly restricted, so that blue of

392

W.T.Cooper 72.

crown continues anteriorly in front of eye and down to lores; lower throat and breast greener, less yellowish-olive; darker more blackish spot on each side of base of lower mandible.

10 males   wing 130–141 (136.7) mm., tail 102–114 (108.4) mm.,
             exp. cul. 18–20 (18.5) mm., tars. 13–15 (14.5) mm.
12 females wing 130–142 (134.3) mm., tail 100–118 (109.6) mm.,
             exp. cul. 17–19 (18.4) mm., tars. 13–16 (14.2) mm.

Confined to western Mexico from Sinaloa south to Colima and inland to western Durango and central Michoacán.

GENERAL NOTES   Hardy (1963) points out that the distribution of the Orange-fronted Conure closely approximates the northern part of the range of the colonial termite *Nasutitermes nigriceps*. The parrots nest in holes excavated in termitaria. Although it is reported that natural hollows and old woodpeckers' holes in trees may be used if termitaria are not available (Dickey and van Rossem, 1938), the general rule seems to be that the parrots are totally dependent upon the termitaria for nesting sites. It appears that *Aratinga canicularis* does not occur as a breeding resident outside the geographic range of the termite.

Orange-fronted Conures are common throughout most of their range in Mexico. McLellan (1927) reports that they were quite abundant at Labrados, Sinaloa, large flocks being attracted to a fruit-bearing *Ficus* tree, while around San Blas, Nayarit, they were seen in swamps and in the hilly district east of the town. In 1964 I found them to be fairly common, though irregularly distributed, in Nayarit and southern Sinaloa, mainly in deciduous forest and trees lining watercourses. South of Mazatlán, Sinaloa, I observed two birds in arid scrubland, but they could have been on their way to a small patch of forest bordering a stream about 3 km. away. In the vicinity of San Blas, Nayarit, I found small flocks along the edges of forest beside the road. Zimmerman and Harry (1951) report that they were abundant in tropical deciduous forest south of Autlán, Jalisco, and flocks of up to eighty birds were seen repeatedly. Paynter (1956) says that in the Jorullo region, Michoacán, they were seen frequently, particularly in trees standing within fields. Schaldach (1963) notes that they are among the most abundant of resident birds in the tropical areas of Colima, occurring from the coastal plain at least as high as the oak woodland on the upper slopes of La Medialuna in the centre of the state. In Oaxaca they are very common, permanent residents from sea level up to 1,360 m. in tropical semi-deciduous and deciduous forests, humid gallery forest, and arid tropical scrub along the Pacific coast and inland through the Tehuantepec River basin (Binford, 1968). Edwards and Lea (1955) report that on the Monserrate plateau, Chiapas, these parrots were common during July and August, but were never as numerous as *Aratinga holochlora*.

They are common residents in the Pacific lowlands and arid interior of Guatemala from sea level up to 1,050 m., and occur on the edges of woodland and out into neighbouring scrubby open areas (Land, 1970). According to Monroe (1968) they are the most common parrots in the arid lowlands of the Pacific slope of Honduras; they also occur in the arid interior highlands up to 1,500 m. and in the Comayagua Valley on the Caribbean drainage, but are most common below 600 m. They are common residents throughout the arid lower tropical zone of El Salvador, wandering after the breeding season to much higher elevations, such as 1,400 m. on Volcán de San Salvador (Dickey and van Rossem, 1938); the centre of abundance is on the coastal plain, but the birds are very numerous almost anywhere in the arid lower tropical zone. Slud (1964) says that in Costa Rica their presence is indicative of tropical dry forest, and they are distributed throughout the northern half of the Pacific slope from the lowlands to lower subtropical elevations on the Guanacaste Cordillera and across the central plateau to San José; they are most abundant in Guanacaste and on the Nicoya Peninsula, becoming increasingly less common away from these centres of distribution.

These noisy, conspicuous parrots congregate in flocks during the non-breeding season and at that time seem to be somewhat nomadic, the numbers present in an area being governed by the availability of food. Pairs remain apart while engaged in nesting activities, but will often associate with other pairs to form small groups of from four to eight birds to feed at frequent intervals during the day. In districts where the species is common some very large flocks have been recorded during the non-breeding season. Wetmore (1944) reports that near Liberia, Guanacaste, Costa Rica, he saw a flock of two hundred birds, and an even larger flock was seen by his assistant. Slud notes that in Costa Rica flocks of from several individuals to several score are generally seen. On the central plateau an observer meets wandering groups, some apparently being seasonal residents in the plazas of towns, whereas in the north-west large concentrations are encountered. At Finca El Cacahuito, south-eastern Guatemala, Tashian (1953) found these parrots in large mixed flocks of frugivorous birds feeding in wild fig trees in a coffee plantation. It is in the late evening and early morning, when screeching flocks pass overhead on their way to and from the roosting sites, that the presence of this species in an area is most evident. The swift, direct flight comprises rapid wingbeats interspersed with very brief periods of gliding.

Near Tuxtla Gutierrez, Chiapas, Mexico, and at Tehuantepec, Oaxaca, Mexico, Hardy (1965) carried out observations on the daily activities of these parrots. Near Tuxtla Gutierrez flocks were present on the mountain slopes in tropical deciduous forest which was disturbed considerably by agriculture. Here they were attracted to feed on the fruits of two common trees—a small, scrubby myrrh (*Bursera* sp.) bearing large numbers of small, fleshy, pod-like fruits, and scattered large fig trees (*Ficus* sp.), from 7 to 16 m. in height, and bearing small, fleshy, round fruits ranging from unripe to ripe. On the flat, coastal plain at Tehuantepec they frequented scrubland, but spent most of the day in mango and coconut plantations adjacent to the town, their roosting places being trees and tree cacti on low hillsides about 2 km. away. Although the feeding area appeared suitable for roosting, it was always deserted about an hour before dusk when the birds flew directly to the roosting sites. Soon after sunrise activity commenced with the birds flying from the roosting trees and milling about noisily before moving off to the feeding area. They became quiet once feeding had commenced and could be detected only by careful investigation of trees at close range. Small groups sat mainly in the tops of trees, feeding and calling in soft, conversational notes. When an intruder or predator was discovered the group became quiet and ceased feeding. This pause in activity sometimes spread to other groups in the tree. If the intruder or predator approached further the birds would screech loudly and fly off. Feeding was interrupted at approximately half-hourly intervals by breaks when the birds rested, preened each other, or simply flew about. As the day progressed the rate of feeding diminished while resting and mutual preening became dominant. From about 1100 hrs. until mid-afternoon some birds continued feeding and some rested in the food trees, but many retired to the thickest groves of trees away from the feeding areas to rest quietly for more than an hour at a time. The feeding rate increased in the late afternoon, but never reached the intensity of morning activity.

They feed on fruits, particularly wild figs (*Ficus* sp.), seeds, nuts, berries, blossoms and possibly insects and their larvae. In Sinaloa, Mexico, Hardy (1963) found them feeding on the fleshy blossoms of *Combretum farinosum* and suspected that these were an important component of the regurgitated food being fed to nestlings.

CALL Normally a raucous *can-can-can* repeated frequently (Slud, 1964); also a shrill screeching, and while feeding a subdued chatter.

NESTING Schaldach says that in Colima, Mexico, the flocks begin to break up about the middle of April when the birds commence nesting activities. In the Sierra Madre del Sur, Oaxaca, Mexico, a nest containing two young, nearly ready to leave, was found on 15th May (Rowley, 1966). Hardy (1963) points out that at northern latitudes the breeding season probably commences in February; two specimens collected by Lamb in mid-March 1934, near San Ignacio, Sinaloa, were in breeding condition, one having contained an egg in the oviduct. Specimens with enlarged gonads were collected in south-eastern Guatemala by Tashian during December. Dickey and van Rossem report that at Rio San Miguel, El Salvador, parrots were seen digging out nesting hollows during February, but the collection of recently-fledged young on 18th March showed that in some cases laying must take place about the middle of January.

The nest is in a hole excavated by the birds in an arboreal carton termitarium of *Nasutitermes nigriceps*. Only an occupied termitarium will be used and rarely is it utilized by more than one pair. Dickey and van Rossem claim that in the absence of suitable termitaria natural hollows and old woodpeckers' holes in trees may be used. The entrance hole is about 7 cm. in diameter and is situated near the bottom of the termitarium. A tunnel goes straight up through the hard outer shell for about 30 cm. before making a sharp turn inward and downward into the softer core where it leads to a chamber some 15 to 20 cm. in diameter. Both sexes participate in excavation, though the male performs most of the work until the entrance tunnel has been completed and digging of the nesting chamber commences. The parrots dig only with their bills and the task requires about one week. For a period of approximately a week after completion of excavation the birds do not visit the nest, possibly to allow the termites to seal off the nesting area.

Von Hagen (1938) reports that over half of the carton termitaria he examined had the centres hollowed out by parrots. Although not all of these would disintegrate, the greater proportion would lose most of their durability due to destruction of the humid or heat-generating part. Furthermore, after the birds have left a termitarium ants invariably take up occupation and eventually overrun it.

Three to five eggs make up the normal clutch, but clutches of from one to three eggs have been recorded. Eggs are laid every other day and incubation commences with the laying of the first egg. Incubation lasts approximately thirty days and only the female broods (Hardy, 1963). The male enters the nest only to roost and accompanies the female when she leaves the nest to feed. Newly-hatched nestlings are fed only by the female, but as they progress the male takes over part of the feeding duties. Young birds leave the nest about six weeks after hatching.

EGGS Rounded; one egg taken from a nest at Rio San Miguel, El Salvador, measured 22.7 × 19.6 mm. [Dickey and van Rossem, 1938].

Cuban Conure *Aratinga euops* 1
AMNH. 399400 ad. ♂

Hispaniolan Conure 2
Aratingua chloroptera chloroptera
ANSP. 22349 ad. ♂

White-eyed Conure 3
Aratinga leucophthalmus leucophthalmus
AM. 043401 ad. ♂

BROWN-THROATED CONURE
Aratinga pertinax (Linné)

Length 25 cm.
ADULTS general plumage green, paler and more yellowish on underparts; forehead, lores and sides of head orange-yellow; forecrown dull greenish-blue; throat and breast pale olive-brown; variable orange marking across centre of abdomen; under wing-coverts yellowish-green; outer webs of primaries green, becoming dull blue towards tips; outer webs of secondaries dull blue; tail above green narrowly tipped with greenish-blue, below dusky olive-yellow; naked periophthalmic ring buff-white; bill brownish; iris yellow; legs grey.

IMMATURES (Hartert, 1893); cheeks brownish, sometimes with a few orange-yellow feathers; forehead tinged with green and brownish; throat and upper breast tinged greenish; upper mandible pale horn-coloured.

DISTRIBUTION Panama, northern South America, and islands off the northern coast of Venezuela; introduced to St. Thomas in the Virgin Islands, West Indies.

SUBSPECIES A thorough revision of the races of this species is most desirable. It seems to me that in some cases diagnostic differences are minor and may be clinal.

1. *A. p. pertinax* (Linné) *Illustrated on page 401.*
   8 males   wing 137–145 (140.5) mm., tail 115–124 (119.0) mm.,
       exp. cul. 19–20 (19.8) mm., 14–17 (15.1) mm.
   9 females wing 134–143 (138.1) mm., tail 111–123 (116.7) mm.,
       exp. cul. 18–19 (18.8) mm., tars. 14–15 (14.3) mm.
   Occurs on the Island of Curaçao in the Netherlands Antilles, off the northern coast of Venezuela; introduced to St. Thomas in the Virgin Islands, West Indies.

2. *A. p. xanthogenia* (Bonaparte)
   ADULTS like *pertinax*, but orange-yellow of forehead continuing back on to crown and replacing dull-greenish-blue.
   IMMATURES crown green, sometimes with a few orange-yellow feathers; trace of orange-yellow on forehead; cheeks tinged with brown.
   4 males   wing 142–147 (143.8) mm., tail 111–122 (117.0) mm.,
       exp. cul. 21–22 (21.8) mm., tars. 15–16 (15.8) mm.
   6 females wing 135–142 (138.2) mm., tail 103–125 (113.0) mm.,
       exp. cul. 20–21 (20.3) mm., tars. 15–16 (15.2) mm.
   Confined to the Island of Bonaire in the Netherlands Antilles, off the northern coast of Venezuela.

3. *A. p. arubensis* (Hartert)
   ADULTS orange-yellow restricted to periophthalmic region, more extensive below eye; forehead pale yellow; crown dull greenish-blue, extending almost to occiput; lores, cheeks, and sides of head mixed light brown and very pale orange-yellow; feathers of ear-coverts yellow edged with brown; throat and upper breast yellowish-brown.
   4 males   wing 136–147 (139.5) mm., tail 112–118 (114.8) mm.,
       exp. cul. 17–19 (18.3) mm., tars. 15–17 (15.8) mm.
   4 females wing 131–141 (134.3) mm., tail 107–116 (111.5) mm.,
       exp. cul. 18–19 (18.5) mm., tars. 14–16 (15.0) mm.
   Restricted to the Island of Aruba in the Netherlands Antilles, off the northern coast of Venezuela.

4. *A. p. aeruginosa* (Linné)
   ADULTS like *arubensis*, but with very little pale yellowish-buff on forehead; orange-yellow restricted to a narrow line encircling eye; throat, breast and sides of head slightly darker and more brownish; greenish-blue of crown extending back to nape.
   8 males   wing 133–139 (135.8) mm., tail 98–104 (100.1) mm.,
       exp. cul. 18–20 (19.0) mm., tars. 14–15 (14.3) mm.
   8 females wing 127–141 (134.5) mm., tail 98–108 (102.6) mm.,
       exp. cul. 18–19 (18.5) mm., tars. 14–15 (14.3) mm.
   Found in northern Colombia from the Caribbean coast east through Magdalena and the Guajira Peninsula to Zulia, north-western Venezuela.

5. *A. p. griseipecta* Meyer de Schauensee.
   ADULTS like *aeruginosa*, but cheeks, throat and upper breast olive-grey, merging into green of lower breast; no yellow shaft-streaks on feathers of ear-coverts; very little blue on green crown.
   1 male (**type**); wing 132 mm., tail 103 mm.,
       exp. cul. 19 mm., tars. 14 mm.
   1 unsexed   wing 135 mm., tail 106 mm.,
       exp. cul. 20 mm., tars. 15 mm.
   Known only from the Sinú River valley in north-eastern Colombia.

Sun Conure *Aratinga solstitialis* 1
QM. 011485 ad. unsexed

Jandaya Conure *Aratinga jandaya* 2
MNHN. CG1958,666 ad. ♂

Golden-capped Conure 3
Aratinga auricapilla aurifrons
MNHN. CG1968,440 ad. ♂

6. *A. p. lehmanni* Dugand.
   ADULTS similar to *aeruginosa*, but with much broader orange-yellow area around eye; greenish-blue restricted to forecrown and not extending to nape; only very faint tints of blue along central portions of tips of central tail feathers; throat slightly darker than in *chrysophrys* and outer webs of flight feathers more green, less bluish.
   7 males   wing 135–140 (137.7) mm., tail 88–110 (104.4) mm.,
       exp. cul. 17–19 (18.1) mm., tars. 13–16 (14.9) mm.
   5 females wing 134–139 (136.2) mm., tail 91–106 (99.2) mm.,
       exp. cul. 17–19 (18.2) mm., tars. 14–16 (14.6) mm.

Occurs in eastern Colombia from Sierra Macarena and the plains of Meta east to the Orinoco River.

7. *A. p. tortugensis* (Cory)
ADULTS like *aeruginosa* but with more orange-yellow on sides of head; throat and sides of head below orange-yellow are paler; under wing-coverts more yellowish-green; larger size.
8 males   wing 141–148 (145.4) mm., tail 119–130 (123.3) mm.,
       exp. cul. 19–21 (19.9) mm., tars. 14–15 (14.6) mm.
8 females wing 140–146 (143.1) mm., tail 109–127 (117.8) mm.,
       exp. cul. 18–20 (19.1) mm., tars. 14–16 (14.6) mm.
Confined to Tortuga Island, off the northern coast of Venezuela.

8. *A. p. margaritensis* (Cory)
ADULTS forehead whitish; forecrown dull greenish-blue; lores, cheeks, and ear-coverts olive-brown; periophthalmic region orange-yellow, more extensive under eye; throat and upper breast pale olive.
10 males   wing 133–145 (140.8) mm., tail 116–130 (122.5) mm.,
       exp. cul. 19–21 (19.6) mm., tars. 14–18 (15.6) mm.
10 females wing 137–143 (140.7) mm., tail 103–121 (114.2) mm.,
       exp. cul. 18–20 (19.2) mm., tars. 14–16 (15.2) mm.
Restricted to Margarita and Los Frailes Islands, off the northern coast of Venezuela.

9. *A. p. venezuelae* Zimmer and Phelps.
ADULTS like *margaritensis*, but upperparts paler, more yellowish; inner webs of tail feathers basally edged with yellow; less orange on abdomen than in *chrysophrys*.
10 males   wing 131–140 (135.8) mm., tail 92–127 (105.1) mm.,
       exp. cul. 17–21 (18.8) mm., tars. 13–16 (14.8) mm.
10 females wing 128–139 (134.9) mm., tail 95–113 (105.3) mm.,
       exp. cul. 16–19 (18.1) mm., tars. 14–16 (14.7) mm.
Generally distributed throughout Venezuela except the extreme north-west which is inhabited by *aeruginosa*, Delta Amacuro in which *surinama* occurs, and the Cerro Roraima area occupied by *chrysophrys*.

10. *A. p. chrysophrys* (Swainson)   *Illustrated on page 401.*
ADULTS similar to *margaritensis*, but throat and cheeks darker, brighter brown; forehead pale brownish-yellow.
12 males   wing 135–150 (141.3) mm., tail 92–111 (103.1) mm.,
       exp. cul. 18–20 (19.0) mm., tars. 14–16 (15.1) mm.
13 females wing 129–142 (137.8) mm., tail 91–125 (107.3) mm.,
       exp. cul. 18–20 (18.6) mm., tars. 14–16 (14.9) mm.
Occurs in the interior of Guyana, the Cerro Roraima district, south-eastern Venezuela, and extreme northern Roraima, Brazil.

11. *A. p. surinama* Zimmer and Phelps.
ADULTS like *chrysophrys*, but orange-yellow extending from below eyes down on to cheeks and forward to base of bill; narrow orange-yellow frontal band; throat and breast pale yellowish-green instead of brownish.
6 males   wing 126–140 (134.8) mm., tail 99–112 (105.5) mm.,
       exp. cul. 18–20 (19.2) mm., tars. 14–16 (15.0) mm.
6 females wing 130–137 (133.0) mm., tail 92–112 (100.2) mm.,
       exp. cul. 18–19 (18.8) mm., tars. 14–15 (14.3) mm.
Distributed from French Guiana and Surinam along the coast of Guyana to Delta Amacuro, north-eastern Venezuela.

12. *A. p. chrysogenys* (Massena and Souancé)
ADULTS general plumage darker than in other races; no pale frontal band; crown dark greenish-blue; outer webs of flight feathers extensively marked with dark blue; throat, breast and sides of head dark brown; centre of abdomen extensively tinged with dark orange.
9 males   wing 126–142 (136.0) mm., tail 92–110 (99.0) mm.,
       exp. cul. 18–20 (18.9) mm., tars. 13–16 (14.9) mm.
5 females wing 132–139 (135.0) mm., tail 85–98 (91.8) mm.,
       exp. cul. 17–19 (18.0) mm., tars. 14–16 (14.4) mm.
Exact range undetermined; at present known only from the Negro River region, north-western Brazil.

13. *A. p. paraensis* Sick.
ADULTS forehead and crown bluish-green; hindneck dark green, feathers slightly edged with brownish-yellow; upperparts dark green; outer webs of primaries and secondaries dark blue; throat, breast and sides of head brown, dark on ear-coverts and above eye; periophthalmic region orange-yellow; lower underparts dark orange-yellow with brown and green markings on upper abdomen; flanks, thighs and under tail-coverts green; underside of tail dull greenish-yellow; iris red.

Dusky-headed Conure *Aratinga weddellii* 1
AMNH. 474301 ad. ♂

Olive-throated Conure *Aratinga nana nana* 2
AMNH. 474525 ad. ♂

Aztec Conure *Aratinga nana astec* 3
AMNH. 389268 ad. ♂

9 males   wing 133–145 (139.7) mm., tail 87–102 (97.0) mm.,
         exp. cul. 19–20 (19.6) mm., tars. 13–15 (13.9) mm.
4 females wing 132–140 (136.3) mm., tail 85–103 (92.5) mm.,
         exp. cul. 18–20 (19.0) mm., tars. 13–14 (13.5) mm.

    Known only from the Tapajós River and its tributary, the Cururu, in the Amazon Basin, northern Brazil.

14. *A. p. ocularis* (Sclater and Salvin)   *Illustrated on page 401.*

    ADULTS entire crown and forehead green, lightly tinged with dull blue in some specimens; orange-yellow in front of and below eye, more extensive below; lores and sides of head buff-brown; throat and upper breast brownish, paler than sides of head; underparts yellowish-green, becoming more yellow on abdomen.

    IMMATURES no orange-yellow in front of and below eye; throat and foreneck more greenish, less brown.

7 males   wing 129–135 (131.6) mm., tail 98–109 (102.1) mm.,
         exp. cul. 18–20 (18.7) mm., tars. 14–15 (14.3) mm.
10 females wing 130–139 (133.9) mm., tail 99–111 (103.9) mm.,
         exp. cul. 18–20 (18.8) mm., tars. 14–17 (14.9) mm.

    Confined to the Pacific lowlands of Panama from western Chiriquí east to the western sector of the province of Panama and formerly to the Canal Zone and Panama City.

There appears to be no knowledge of how and when the Brown-throated Conure was introduced to St. Thomas in the Virgin Islands, West Indies, but it must have been well over a century ago. The oldest specimen I could locate was collected in 1860 (NHRS. 13936) but there are probably others that pre-date this. Nichols (1943) says that it was once common on the island, but was almost wiped out by the hurricanes of 1926 and 1928. It subsequently increased, but remained largely confined to the eastern half of the island where it inhabited high scrub, descending at certain times to feed on seasonally-ripening fruits. According to Leopold (1963) the species has now extended its range to most parts of St. Thomas, and the population is estimated to be about four hundred birds. On Curacao, Bonaire, and Aruba, Netherlands Antilles, it is an abundant, well-known bird found in virtually all types of habitats, particularly semi-deserts with cacti and acacias, fruit plantations, manchineel (*Hippomane mancinella*) thickets, and mangroves (Voous, 1955). Flocks of more than one hundred birds may be observed in fruit plantations and in farmlands, where they raid ripening millet crops. On Margarita Island, Lowe·(1907b) found that it was common on the coastal lowlands as well as in the inland hills, and large flocks were seen regularly in the evening as they flew overhead on their way from tall mangroves, lining a lagoon at the western end of the island, to the foothills, where apparently they roosted.

    The species is locally common in the savannahs of western Panama and is generally encountered in pairs or small flocks (Wetmore, 1968). Eisenmann and Loftin (1968) point out that there are no recent records from the Canal Zone. In Colombia it inhabits open woodland, dry scrubland, and cultivated farmlands in the tropical zone, and is generally common. Todd and Carriker (1922) state that it is a common resident of the littoral tropical zone from Dibulla, north-eastern Colombia, east into the Guajira Peninsula and local variations in abundance indicate that it prefers the more arid areas. Haffer (1961) notes that it is rather common on the arid plains of the Guajira Peninsula and groups of four to eight were frequently encountered in stands of cacti. Dugand (1947) says that it is abundant throughout Atlántico, northern Colombia, in both forested and arid areas. Darlington (1931) reports that it is common in the semi-arid region and in dry pastures about Rio Frio, Magdalena, northern Colombia, but there seems to be a partial seasonal movement into more humid areas during the dry season, that is from December to May. In Venezuela it is generally distributed in open forest, scrubland, and savannah in the tropical zone, though in the Mount Roraima area in the extreme south-east it is occasionally recorded in the subtropical zone (Phelps and Phelps, 1958). Smith found that in Monagas and Anzoátegui, north-eastern Venezuela, it was the commonest parrot, and, though present throughout the year in all types of habitat, it was most numerous at the edges of dry woodland where flocks of from ten to twenty or more birds were encountered (in Friedmann and Smith, 1950). Schafer and Phelps (1954) state that at Rancho Grande, a large nature reserve in northern Venezuela, it is common on both sides of the cordilleras, up to 500 m. on the northern slope and up to 700 m. on the southern side, and is found in almost all dry habitats, including dry woodland. Haverschmidt (1968) points out that in Surinam it is very common in mangroves, cultivated areas on the coastal belt wherever there are scattered trees, and in the savannah region adjoining the coastal belt. Snyder (1966) claims that it is probably the commonest parrot in Guyana, particularly on the coast where it is widespread and abundant. My observations in Guyana support this claim, because I found it virtually everywhere in open country, especially in farmlands along coastal rivers. Near Mabaruma, north-western Guyana, I saw a pair in a patch of secondary growth surrounded by primary forest and this was my only record of the species occurring in close proximity to rainforest.

    These parrots are generally observed in pairs or small parties, but large flocks may congregate at a concentrated food supply. Dugand reports that serious damage is done to maize crops in Atlántico, northern Colombia, when flocks are present. They are tame, being frequently found in and around towns and villages. They are very noisy, particularly while in the air, and have the habit of perching on the topmost leafless branch of a dead or deciduous tree to call. In the late evening they fly about, screeching almost incessantly, before moving off to their roosting place. The flight is swift and erratic with unpredictable sharp changes of direction.

GENERAL NOTES

Brown-throated Conure   **1**
Aratinga pertinax pertinax
CNHM. 38019 ad. ♂

Brown-throated Conure   **2**
Aratinga pertinax ocularis
USNM. 188411 ad. ♂

Brown-throated Conure   **3**
Aratinga pertinax chrysophrys
AM. 043411 ad. ♂

The diet is made up of seeds, fruits, nuts, blossoms, and possibly insects and their larvae. Voous (1957) reports that crop and stomach contents from specimens collected in the Netherlands Antilles comprised fruits and seeds, among which those of *Caesalpinia*, *Acacia*, *Prosopis*, and organpipe cacti (*Cereus repandus*) were most numerous; birds were also observed eating the fruits of *Malpighia* and flowers of *Gliricidia sepium*, the latter well-known as a rich source of nectar. In north-eastern Venezuela, Smith saw the birds feeding on the fruits of mapurite (*Fagara caribaea*) and chaparro (*Curatella americana*). In May 1971, at Mabaruma, north-western Guyana, I watched a pair feeding alongside five Yellow-crowned Amazons (*Amazona ochrocephala*) in a kanakudiballi tree (*Cochlospermum orinocense*); the amazons were biting off the entire fruit, holding it in one foot, and scooping out the seeds with the lower mandible, but the conures simply perched beside fruits and picked out seeds with their bills.

CALL In flight a shrill *crik-crik . . . crak-crak* repeated rapidly a number of times; when perched a disyllabic *cherr-cheedit*, the second note being sustained and then terminated abruptly.

NESTING On St. Thomas, Virgin Islands, Nichols found a nest containing eggs in late March. Voous (1957) points out that there seems to be no definite breeding season in the Netherlands Antilles, and nesting apparently commences whenever conditions are favourable. Females with swollen oviducts and developing eggs in the ovary were collected at various dates between mid-November and early April, and many nests containing eggs or young were found between mid-December and late January. On the other hand Rutten recorded full breeding activity in May and Koelers found one nest with eggs and another with chicks in mid-August (in Voous, 1957). At Rancho Grande, northern Venezuela, nesting takes place between February and April (Schafer and Phelps, 1954). Haverschmidt notes that in Surinam nests have been found in all months except February, May, October and December; a nest with eggs was found in late July and another with three almost fully feathered nestlings in early March. Haverschmidt suspects that at times two females may lay in the same nest, because nine eggs were found in one nest; in my opinion there could be another explanation, probably a female took over a deserted nest in which eggs had already been laid. The nest is in a hole excavated by the birds in an arboreal termitarium, or occasionally in holes in trees, in natural crevices and holes in limestone rocks, or in holes excavated in earthen banks. On Curaçao and Aruba, Netherlands Antilles, Voous (1957) found birds nesting in small colonies—four or five nesting holes had been excavated in the decayed trunk of a date palm and a number of nests were found in holes dug out in a steep, sandy wall bordering a road. Nests in termitaria had more or less rounded entrance holes of from 7 to 10 cm. in diameter, and one that was opened for examination comprised a tunnel, nearly 50 cm. in length, terminating in a chamber with a diameter of approximately 25 cm. A clutch consists of four to seven eggs.

Shore-Baily (1915) gives details of a successful breeding in captivity. Five eggs were laid and three hatched. The first chick hatched twenty-three days after the laying of the first egg. Only the female incubated during the day; she was joined by the male at night, but it was not ascertained whether he assisted with incubation. The young birds left the nest approximately six weeks after hatching.

EGGS Rounded; without gloss and of a rough and chalky texture; 11 eggs, 26.4 (25.0–28.1) × 21.7 (21.0–22.3) mm. [Nichols, 1943; Voous, 1957].

Peach-fronted Conure *Aratinga aurea aurea* 1
NMV. 23518 ad. unsexed

Orange-fronted Conure 2
Aratinga canicularis canicularis
MLZ. 4841 ad. ♂

Cactus Conure *Aratinga cactorum cactorum* 3
AMNH. 474497 ad. ♂

CACTUS CONURE
Aratinga cactorum (Kuhl)

DESCRIPTION

Length 25 cm.
ADULTS upperparts green; crown pale brown, the feathers with paler edges; green ear-coverts; lores, cheeks, throat, sides of neck and upper breast brown; yellow line below eye; lower breast and abdomen dull orange-yellow; flanks, thighs, and under tail-coverts yellowish-green; outer webs of flight feathers bluish green, more bluish on secondaries; under wing-coverts yellow-green; tail above green narrowly tipped with blue, below dusky olive-yellow; naked periophthalmic ring white; bill horn-coloured, iris orange, legs greyish-brown.
IMMATURES crown green with little or no brown tinge; throat and upper breast olive; lower breast and abdomen olive with orange tips to many feathers.

DISTRIBUTION

North-eastern Brazil.

SUBSPECIES

1. *A. c. cactorum* (Kuhl)   *Illustrated on page 404.*
   6 males   wing 136–140 (138.3) mm., tail 114–125 (117.8) mm.,
           exp. cul. 18–20 (18.8) mm., tars. 13–15 (14.0) mm.
   6 females wing 136–140 (138.2) mm., tail 94–114 (104.7) mm.,
           exp. cul. 18–19 (18.5) mm., tars. 14–15 (14.3) mm.
   Restricted to the state of Bahia, south of the São Francisco River, and adjacent parts of Minas Gerais, north-eastern Brazil.

W. T. Cooper. 72

2. *A. c. caixana* Spix.

ADULTS general plumage, both above and below, paler; throat and breast buff-brown; centre of abdomen less orange, more yellow.

8 males wing 135–143 (139.3) mm., tail 106–124 (113.8) mm.,
     exp. cul. 18–19 (18.4) mm., tars. 14–16 (14.5) mm.
8 females wing 134–141 (137.8) mm., tail 105–118 (111.1) mm.,
     exp. cul. 17–19 (18.1) mm., tars. 14–16 (15.1) mm.

Occurs in north-eastern Brazil from north-western Bahia, north of the São Francisco River, and western Pernambuco through Ceará, Piauí, and Maranhão to the Belém region in eastern Pará.

GENERAL NOTES

Sick (1965) points out that the Cactus Conure is a typical bird of the inland caatinga, a specialized arid vegetation community characterized by deciduous, thorny scrub with many cacti and other succulents. It also frequents open forest and savannah. Lamm (1948) reports that it is found only in the interior of Pernambuco, where it is very common. It is generally seen in pairs or in small parties of up to eight individuals.

Food consists of seeds, berries, fruits, nuts and probably flowers, procured both in bushes and on the ground.

CALL Undescribed.

NESTING I know of no records from the wild state. Lovell-Keays (1914a) gives some details of a successful breeding in captivity. Four eggs were laid and were incubated only by the female, who in turn was fed by the male. The incubation period was not determined, but the young birds left the nest approximately six weeks after hatching.

EGGS Broadly elliptical; 2 eggs, 25.4 (25.2–25.5) × 19.6 (19.5–19.7) mm. [Vienna Mus. Coll.].

PEACH-FRONTED CONURE
Aratinga aurea (Gmelin)

DESCRIPTION

Length 26 cm.
ADULTS general plumage green; forehead and forecrown yellow-orange; hindcrown and occiput dull blue; throat and cheeks pale olive, sometimes with a slight bluish tint; breast pale olive; abdomen, under tail-coverts and under wing-coverts greenish-yellow; outer webs of primaries and primary-coverts green, becoming blue towards tips; outer webs of secondaries blue; upper side of tail green, slightly tipped with blue; undersides of flight and tail feathers olive-yellow; feathered periophthalmic ring orange; bill grey-black; iris yellowish-orange; legs grey.
IMMATURES similar to adults, but with narrower orange frontal band and less blue on crown; paler bill; greyish iris.

DISTRIBUTION

Brazil, mainly south of the Amazon River, south to eastern Bolivia, northern Paraguay and extreme north-western Argentina.

SUBSPECIES

1. *A. a. aurea* (Gmelin)   *Illustrated on page 404.*
 12 males wing 137–151 (146.1) mm., tail 110–130 (120.5) mm.,
      exp. cul. 17–19 (18.3) mm., tars. 14–16 (15.1) mm.
 12 females wing 133–146 (142.7) mm., tail 109–119 (115.4) mm.,
      exp. cul. 16–18 (17.1) mm., tars. 14–16 (14.8) mm.

Occurs throughout most of Brazil south of the Amazon River and north of it along the Jamundá River (see Pinto, 1947), and in the provinces of Beni, Sara and Santa Cruz, eastern Bolivia, and in Salta, extreme north-western Argentina; recorded from Caviana Island at the mouth of the Amazon River (Brodkorb, 1937).

2. *A. a. major* (Cherrie and Reichenberger)
 ADULTS similar to *aurea*, but larger.
 1 male (**type**); wing 164 mm., tail 139 mm.,
        exp. cul. 18 mm., tars. 18 mm.
 1 female wing 160 mm., tail 140 mm.,
        exp. cul. 17 mm., tars. 14 mm.

Exact range undetermined, but recorded from northern Paraguay; possibly extends into neighbouring southern Bolivia, south-western Mato Grosso, and north-western Argentina. Further specimens are needed to establish the validity of this race because, as pointed out by Pinto (1947), there seems to be a north-south cline of increasing size.

Nanday Conure *Nandayus nenday*
AM. 043423 ad. ♀

The Peach-fronted Conure is common in open country throughout most of Brazil south of the Amazon River, but is absent from the south-east. Pinto suggests that it will become more widespread in the Amazon Basin as land-clearance increases. Lamm (1948) says that in Pernambuco and Paraiba, north-eastern Brazil, it is common in semi-open country where there are sufficient trees to provide cover, and it is occasionally seen in large flocks. In the Chapada dos Veadeiros and the Serra Dourada, central Goiás, Brazil, Stager (1961) found that it was common in cerrado, a vegetation community dominated by stunted deciduous trees, and flocks of thirty to fifty birds were encountered every day. According to Olrog (1959) it is rare in northern Argentina.

These parrots are generally seen in pairs or in flocks of from ten to thirty or more. They spend much of the day in trees and bushes or on the ground searching for seeds and fruits, and the plumage of their underparts often becomes soiled and abraded from contact with the ground. They are fairly tame and will normally allow a close approach. The flight is swift and buoyant.

They feed on seeds, fruits, berries, nuts, and insects and their larvae. Crop and stomach contents from a specimen collected at Cachimbo, Pará, and another collected on the Paraná River, Mato Grosso, comprised seeds and fruit remains, from a specimen collected on the Maranhão River, Goiás, a small quantity of seeds of two species, and from a specimen collected on the upper São Francisco River, Minas Gerais, six crushed seeds, one Geometridae larva, one Coleoptera pupa, and 1,030 Diptera larvae, th ˙ last possibly due to ingestion of infested fruit (Schubart et al., 1965).

CALL A shrill screech is given in flight.

NESTING There is very little recorded information on the nesting habits of this common species. The nest is in a hollow limb or hole in a tree and two or three eggs make up the normal clutch (Orfila, 1936).

EGGS Rounded; 6 eggs, 27.4 (26.2–29.0) × 22.0 (21.2–23.0) mm. [Schönwetter, 1964].

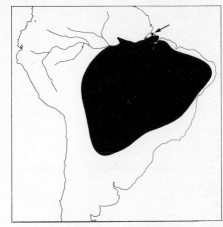

Genus NANDAYUS Bonaparte

The species belonging to this monotypic genus is a medium-sized parrot with a long, strongly-gradated tail. The projecting bill is longer than it is deep, and there is a notch in the upper mandible. The cere is only partly feathered, the nares being exposed. There is no sexual dimorphism and young birds resemble adults.

NANDAY CONURE
Nandayus nenday (Vieillot)

Illustrated on page 405.

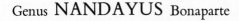

1 Golden-plumed Conure *Leptopsittaca branickii*
   ANSP. 92799 ad. ♀

2 Yellow-eared Conure *Ognorhynchus icterotis* .
   YPM. 24004 ad. ♂

DESCRIPTION

Length 30 cm.
ADULTS general plumage green, paler and more yellowish on underparts; head black; throat and upper breast washed with blue; thighs red; rump, lower back, and under wing-coverts yellowish-green; outer webs of flight feathers blue; upper side of tail olive-green tipped with blue; undersides of flight and tail feathers grey; bill black; iris dark brown; legs brownish-pink.
IMMATURES similar to adults, but generally with less blue on throat and upper breast; shorter tail.
10 males   wing 170–190 (178.9) mm., tail 139–172 (152.6) mm.,
            exp. cul. 23–26 (24.3) mm., tars. 17–20 (18.3) mm.
10 females wing 172–188 (179.0) mm., tail 148–178 (163.9) mm.,
            exp. cul. 22–24 (23.0) mm., tars. 18–19 (18.6) mm.

DISTRIBUTION

Occurs in south-eastern Bolivia, southern Mato Grosso, Brazil, Paraguay, and northern Argentina in the provinces of Formosa, Chaco, and occasionally Santa Fe.

GENERAL NOTES

Olrog (1968) says that the Nanday Conure frequents savannahs and palm groves, and sometimes appears in very large flocks. Cherrie observed it at many localities in Mato Grosso, and to the east of Descalvados it was nesting and very common during the last half of November (in Naumburg, 1930). Unger claims that it has benefited from land settlement and crop-growing in Paraguay and is now abundant, particularly in the south where it causes damage to sunflower and maize crops (in Steinbacher, 1962).

In western Paraguay, Wetmore (1926) found the species to be fairly common, especially in open palm forests where there was a plentiful supply of food in the form of palm nuts. It was seen in flocks of from ten to twelve or more and their approach was always heralded by the screeching call-notes. Occasionally the flocks fed on the ground under palm trees that had dropped their seeds, and they were regularly seen going to waterholes to drink; when coming to drink the birds would alight in bushes standing in pools and then sidle down the branches until they could reach the water. Wetmore also saw a few birds in central Formosa, Argentina, but here they were very wary. The strong, direct flight is fairly swift and comprises rapid wingbeats.

Food consists of seeds, fruits, nuts, berries, and probably vegetable matter.

CALL A raucous, screeching *kree-ah . . . kree-ah* is given in flight; while perched the birds often emit a shrill chatter.

NESTING Cherrie recorded nesting during late November at Fedegoso, east of Descalvados, Mato Grosso. Small parties of from four to a dozen birds were often observed searching for nesting sites, a favourite place being hollows in the tops of fence posts in cattle yards. Four or five of the party would perch on the top of a post and closely inspect the hollow centre; one bird sometimes scrambled tail first down into the hollow. After much chattering the party would fly off, only to return later to continue examining prospective sites. A nest containing four fresh eggs was found in a hollow in the top of a fence post. Nesting material was not taken into the hollow, the eggs being laid on pieces of rotten wood. No further details of nesting habits have been recorded.

EGGS Ovate; 3 eggs, 29.0 (28.5–29.5) × 23.2 (23.0–23.5) mm. [Naumburg, 1930].

Genus LEPTOSITTACA Berlepsch and Stolzmann

The most conspicuous external feature of this monotypic genus is a tuft of elongated feathers extending beyond the ear-coverts. The species is a medium-sized parrot with a long, strongly-gradated tail. The cere is partly feathered. There is no sexual dimorphism.

GOLDEN-PLUMED CONURE
Leptosittaca branickii Berlepsch and Stolzmann   *Illustrated on page 408.*

DISTRIBUTION

Length 35 cm.
ADULTS general plumage green, paler and more yellowish on underparts; orange frontal band; lores, line below eye, and elongated feathers above ear-coverts yellow; abdomen variably suffused with orange; undersides of flight feathers dull yellow; tail feathers above green with dull red on inner webs, below dull red; bill horn-coloured; iris orange; legs dark grey.
IMMATURES undescribed.
10 males   wing 178–194 (189.1) mm., tail 175–201 (187.4) mm.,
          exp. cul. 25–27 (26.0) mm., tars. 18–20 (19.5) mm.
7 females wing 181–187 (184.1) mm., tail 165–190 (180.1) mm.,
          exp. cul. 23–26 (24.3) mm., tars. 19–21 (19.3) mm.

Recorded from the central Andes of Colombia, and the Andes in the provinces of El Oro and Loja, south-western Ecuador, and the province of Junín, central Peru.

GENERAL NOTES

Virtually nothing is known of the habits of the Golden-plumed Conure. Meyer de Schauensee (1970) says that it is an inhabitant of forests in the temperate zone. Most specimens have been collected at altitudes around 3,200 m. Lehmann (1957) notes that he has seen the species on several occasions and mentions the sighting of a small flock at 3,200 m. near Páramo de Puracé, southern Colombia.

Genus OGNORHYNCHUS Bonaparte

The species in this monotypic genus is a medium-sized parrot with a long, strongly-gradated tail. The proportionately large, heavy bill is much deeper than it is long, and there is a notch in the upper mandible. The feathers of the ear-coverts are elongated. Sexual dimorphism is absent.

YELLOW-EARED CONURE
Ognorhynchus icterotis (Massena and Souancé)   *Illustrated on page 408.*

Length 42 cm.
ADULTS upperparts, sides of neck, and lower cheeks dark green; forehead, lores, upper cheeks, and ear-coverts yellow; underparts yellowish-green, becoming darker green on thighs and under tail-coverts; under wing-coverts greenish-yellow; undersides of flight feathers dull yellow; tail above green, below dusky orange-red; bill dark grey; iris orange; legs grey.
IMMATURES undescribed.
7 males   wing 218–233 (225.1) mm., tail 162–220 (192.3) mm.,
          exp. cul. 33–37 (35.0) mm., tars. 20–22 (21.1) mm.
10 females wing 216–231 (225.0) mm., tail 161–207 (186.2) mm.,
          exp. cul. 33–37 (35.0) mm., tars. 20–23 (21.2) mm.

Known only from the Andes of Colombia and the Andes in the provinces of Imbabura and Pichincha, northern Ecuador.

DISTRIBUTION

The Yellow-eared Conure is a little-known bird. Meyer de Schauensee (1964) says that in Colombia it is locally distributed in the subtropical and temperate zones wherever there are wax palms (*Ceroxylon andicolum*). Most specimens have been collected between 2,500 and 3,200 m. Chapman (1917) found it to be common in Colombia, and in some areas it was quite abundant. Lehmann (1957) reports that he has obtained several specimens, mainly in the Moscopán region, Cauca, Colombia, where the species has been relatively common. However, in that region it seems to have declined in numbers, and during a ten day visit in July 1956 only one bird was seen flying high overhead early one morning. The apparent decline could have been due to seasonal movements because earlier visits had been made between December and April, but local residents claimed that even during these months fewer birds were being seen.

CALL Undescribed.

NESTING A male with enlarged testes and a female that was laying were collected at Moscopán, Cauca, Colombia, in early March (YPM Collection). In May, along the Quindío Trail above the Tochecito and Toché Rivers, Colombia, Chapman found the species nesting in colonies in holes more than 25 m. up in wax palms.

EGGS Undescribed.

Genus RHYNCHOPSITTA Bonaparte

I believe that this monotypic genus is closely related to *Ara*. The skull resembles that of *Ara*, the orbital ring being complete (see Olsen, 1967). The species is a large parrot with a short, slightly-gradated tail and a large, greatly-compressed bill. The cere is feathered. There is no sexual dimorphism and young birds resemble adults.

THICK-BILLED PARROT
Rhynchopsitta pachyrhyncha (Swainson)

Length 38 cm.
ADULTS general plumage bright green, lighter and more yellowish on cheeks and ear-coverts; forehead, forecrown and broad superciliary stripe red; brownish marking in front of eye; bend of wing, carpal edge, and thighs red; greater under wing-coverts yellow; undersides of flight and tail feathers greyish; bill black; iris orange-yellow; legs grey.
IMMATURES no red superciliary stripe; bend of wing and carpal edge green; less red on thighs; bill horn-coloured with dark grey at base of upper mandible.

Highlands of northern and central Mexico; formerly a non-breeding visitor to the mountains of southern Arizona and south-western New Mexico, United States of America.

1. *R. p. pachyrhyncha* (Swainson)   *Illustrated on page 425.*
   10 males   wing 254–276 (267.1) mm., tail 162–177 (170.4) mm.,
                exp. cul. 36–41 (38.7) mm., tars. 21–24 (22.6) mm.
   10 females wing 254–265 (259.0) mm., tail 160–178 (169.4) mm.,
                exp. cul. 37–39 (38.1) mm., tars. 22–24 (22.7) mm.
   Occurs in the highlands of north-western and central Mexico from the Sierra Madre Occidental in Chihuahua and eastern Sonora south over the central plateau to Michoacán; formerly ranged south-east into Veracruz, Mexico, and north-west into southern Arizona and south-western New Mexico, United States, but there have been no recent records from either of these extralimital regions (see Loetscher, 1941; and Phillips *et al.*, 1964).

2. *R. p. terrisi* Moore   *Illustrated on page 425.*
   ADULTS general plumage darker green; forehead, forecrown, superciliary line, and marking in front of eye maroon-brown; bend of wing, carpal edge, and thighs brownish-red; greater under wing-coverts grey with slight olive tint; larger size.
   4 males   wing 287–290 (287.8) mm., tail 185–204 (193.8) mm.,
                exp. cul. 40–42 (41.3) mm., tars. 23–24 (23.8) mm.
   1 female   wing 283 mm., tail 188 mm.,
                exp. cul. 40 mm., tars. 24 mm.
   This very distinct race is called the Maroon-fronted Parrot and is often treated as a separate species (see Hardy, 1967). It is known from two localities in the Sierra Madre Oriental in central-west Neuvo León, Mexico, namely the Sierra Potosí at about 2,340 m. and an area at 1,875 m. approximately 10 km. south-east of Galeana, and from the Mesa de las Tablas and at about 3,100 m. near San Antonia de las Alazanas, both in south-eastern Coahuila, Mexico.
   Hardy and Dickerman (1955) suspected that the Coahuilan specimens were intermediate between *terrisi* and *pachyrhyncha*. I have examined the type series of *terrisi* from Nuevo León

and one of the Coahuilan specimens (LSUMZ. 31532), and in the latter could not detect any obvious tendency towards *pachyrhyncha*.

GENERAL NOTES That Thick-billed Parrots formerly occurred as far north as northern Arizona is indicated by references to 'parrots' in an account of the Espejo expedition of 1582–1583 (see Wetmore, 1931) and, to a lesser extent, by archaeological material dating back to 1250 and recovered from Indian sites (see Hargrave, 1939). In late historic times they have been known as irregular visitors, mainly during winter, to the mountains of south-eastern Arizona and south-western New Mexico. A large flock, estimated to contain between seven hundred and one thousand birds, was observed by miners at Bonita Park in the Chiricahua Mountains, south-eastern Arizona, in August 1904; the birds were extremely tame during their stay of four days and were seen feeding on *Pinus* seeds, both in the trees and on the ground below (Smith, 1907). There was a large-scale invasion during 1917–1918 and the last reliable reports were in 1922 and 1935, though rumours persisted up until 1945. Phillips *et al.* (1964) point out that rapid clearance of pine forests in Sonora and Chihuahua will almost certainly prevent these parrots from ever again being seen in the United States.

The large-scale invasion during 1917–1918 gave the best information on the habits of these parrots. The information came from reports made by local observers and has been summarized by Wetmore (1935). Thick-billed Parrots were first observed in Pinery Canyon, Chiricahua Mountains, on 20th August 1917, a party of six or eight being found feeding in a pine tree. Numbers increased steadily until by 1st September about three hundred were present. Some of the birds disappeared during autumn as cold weather came on, but others remained throughout the entire winter, although at one time snow covered the ground for more than two weeks and the parrots were forced to seek food on the ground wherever the snow had been partly blown away. The last record from Pinery Canyon was on 26th or 27th March 1918, when a flock of ten or twelve was seen. To the south, in Rucker Canyon, the parrots were more abundant. Here they were first recorded during the first week of July 1917, when a flock of fifty or sixty was seen, and numbers increased steadily until by early autumn there were one thousand or possibly fifteen hundred birds present. By November numbers had decreased but a few remained throughout the winter until March 1918, though they wandered much and occasionally were not observed for a week at a time. During the same period, that is July 1917 to March 1918, parrots were observed in neighbouring mountain ranges, including Animas Peak in south-western New Mexico. In the Dragoon Mountains a considerable flock arrived in Cochise Stronghold Canyon at the end of July and stayed for about six weeks. These birds were seen to fly directly out across the flats to the east each morning and return at night, so it is possible that they may have crossed each day to the Chiricahua Mountains to feed. During late autumn and winter, in the Chiricahua Mountains, they came down into the foothills between 1,550 and 1,700 m., having been confined to the higher basins during earlier months.

On arrival in the Chiricahua Mountains the parrots began to attack the cones of Chihuahua pine (*Pinus chihuahuana*) and continued to eat the seeds until the entire crop had been consumed. Wetmore found evidence that there had been some feeding on seeds of yellow pine (*Pinus brachyptera*), but this must have been rare. When the supply of pine seeds was exhausted the parrots ate acorns (*Quercus* spp.) and these were the staple food during autumn and winter. At first they fed in the trees, and then later descended to the ground to pick up fallen nuts. Apparently there was no damage to crops or fruit even though parrots were frequently seen feeding in oak trees bordering maize fields and surrounding apple orchards. At night they gathered in flocks to roost and then dispersed in small parties to feed during the day. In Pinery Canyon they roosted somewhere on the upper mountain slopes during summer and autumn, but as colder weather came on the roosting place was changed to one at a lower altitude. In the morning and at evening two large flocks were always seen. In Rucker Canyon, where there were more than one thousand birds present, the morning and evening flights were most spectacular. In winter small feeding parties sometimes came down to sit on sandstone ledges where they clambered about or basked in the sun. In Rucker Canyon, toward evening, flocks were often seen flying down to the river to drink before going to roost. They were noisy and the raucous calls could be heard from afar. When a bird of prey appeared entire flocks would rise into the air and fly about in circles, screeching loudly all the while.

Thick-billed Parrots are characteristic of the highland pine forests of Mexico, though they also occur locally in the foothills (Blake, 1953). Vincent (1967) claims that they are decreasing, mainly because of widespread clearance of the Sierra Madre forests, and both subspecies are said to be rare and endangered, particularly *terrisi* which is thought to be nearing extinction. This is a fairly generalized statement, but it does demonstrate the urgent need for a comprehensive survey to ascertain the present status of these fine birds as a forerunner to the implementation of conservation measures. Most records are from localities between 1,560 and 3,400 m., but the parrots have been found also in lowlands where there are extensive *Pinus* stands. Marshall (1957) reports that in the 1950s, during visits of a few weeks duration to the Sierra Madre Occidental in north-western Chihuahua, he saw pairs, small parties, and a couple of flocks of up to fifty or sixty. It was obvious that there were local movements and fluctuations in numbers. Several days could pass without any birds being seen. Only twice were they seen in the Sierra Madre in 1955, though flocks had been present a few years earlier, and in 1954 they were numerous in the Sierra Huachinera, where none had been seen the previous year. Stager (1954) encountered a flock of about twenty-five at Cumbre on the Barranca de Cobre in the Sierra Madre Occidental, Chihuahua, and of the several specimens collected males outnumbered females by two to one; the flock remained feeding in the area during the entire eight days Stager was there. Burleigh saw small flocks on the summit of

Diamante Pass, southern Coahuila, but although noisy and conspicuous they were wary and could not be observed at close quarters (in Burleigh and Lowery, 1942). Near San Antonio de las Alazanas, Coahuila, Dickerman found a large flock of about three hundred in conifer-aspen woodland (in Urban, 1959). Fleming and Baker (1963) mention possible seasonal movements in Durango; they did not see parrots during their summer field trips to the Sierra Madre Occidental, but were told by local residents that the birds occurred at certain localities during winter. Blake and Hanson (1942) report that they were locally distributed in the Cerro de Tancítaro area, Michoacán, from the lowlands to the highest reaches of the mountain and were moderately common in tropical deciduous forest.

Daily flights to and from roosting sites were observed by Hoogstraal in the Cerro de Tancítaro area, Michoacán, where the birds roosted in tropical deciduous forest and each morning and evening flew to the pine forests of the higher slopes to feed (in Blake and Hanson, 1942). Marshall says that not only do the parrots fly rapidly with their shallow wingbeats, but they also glide for long distances. When two pairs fly in company the individuals in each pair fly close together, one slightly ahead of the other, but between the pairs a distance of two or three metres is maintained. In the Sierra Madre, Chihuahua, one small flock seen was in a compact 'V' formation and a flock of sixty was in several 'V' subdivisions but proceeding as one overall unit. In the Sierra Huachinera, Chihuahua, the birds spent much time in pines along the summits and groups generally flew along or parallel to the ridges. One flock was seen to rise with much screeching from the bottom of a deep canyon and spiralled slowly upward, the birds gaining altitude each time they soared into the breeze until finally they were high enough to clear the ridge in level flight.

These parrots feed primarily on *Pinus* seeds and their plumage often becomes matted with resin. They also eat acorns (*Quercus* spp.), other seeds, fruits, and vegetable matter. The birds observed by Stager in Chihuahua were eating terminal buds of *Pinus chihuahuana* and *P. lumholtzii*. Blake and Hanson report that in the Cerro de Tancítaro area, Michoacán, the fruit of a local cherry tree (*Prunus capuli*) was eaten, and the crop and stomach from one bird contained seeds of an unidentified leguminous plant.

CALL A harsh, raucous *kurr-rak . . . kurr-rak* and a loud *kuk-kuk-kuk-kuk-kuk* (in captivity).

NESTING Nesting has been recorded as high as 3,125 m. on Mount Mohinora, south-western Chihuahua, Mexico (in Friedmann *et al.*, 1950). There are no records from the United States. Bent (1940) says that eggs have been found between early May and late August. Thayer (1906) describes ten nests found in Chihuahua between 11th and 28th August 1905. The nests were in holes high up in tall pines, one being in a live tree that had been struck by lightning, the others in dead trees. It has been presumed that all of these nests were in old nesting holes of Imperial Woodpeckers (*Campephilus imperialis*), but in the field notes quoted by Thayer such is claimed for only one nest; I see no reason why these parrots could not enlarge old nesting hollows of smaller woodpeckers. The entrances to the hollows were usually circular and 15 to 18 cm. in diameter. The depth varied from 45 to 60 cm. and the diameter of the nesting chambers from 20 to 25 cm. Eggs were laid on a layer of decayed wood dust lining the bottom of each hollow. One nest, found on 20th August, contained two large nestlings and one 'fresh' egg, another, found on 28th August, contained two chicks, and in each of the remaining nests, found between 11th and 25th August, there were one or two eggs.

Lint (1966) gives details of a successful breeding in captivity. One egg was laid and hatched after an incubation lasting twenty-eight days. Only the female brooded, and while sitting she was fed regurgitated food by the male. The young bird was removed from the nest and reared by hand.

Another successful breeding in captivity is reported by Dyson (1969). For the first eleven days after hatching the chick was closely brooded by the female, but from that date onward both parents visited the nest-box to feed the young bird. It left the nest prematurely thirty-eight days after hatching, so was returned by the keeper and subsequently vacated the nest fifty-nine days after hatching.

EGGS Ovate to rounded-ovate, glossy; 20 eggs, 39.5 (37.6–42.0) × 30.6 (29.0–32.0) mm. [Bent, 1940].

Genus CONUROPSIS Salvadori

The extinct, monotypic genus *Conuropsis* was probably closely related to *Aratinga*. The species was a medium-sized parrot with a long, gradated tail and long, pointed wings. The cere was completely feathered. The bill was proportionately large and broad with a prominent notch in the upper mandible. Sexual dimorphism was not present and young birds were duller than adults.

CAROLINA PARAKEET
Conuropsis carolinensis (Linné)

DESCRIPTION   Length 30 cm.

ADULTS general plumage green, paler on underparts; forehead, lores, periophthalmic region and upper cheeks orange; remainder of head and upper part of neck yellow; scapulars, greater wing-coverts and tertials tinged with olive and margined with greenish-yellow; primary-coverts deep green edged with yellowish-green; outer webs of primaries basally marked with yellow; bend of wing, carpal edge, and thighs yellow; undersides of flight and tail feathers greyish; bill horn-coloured; iris brown; legs flesh-brown.

IMMATURES forehead, lores, and periophthalmic region tawny-orange; remainder of head and neck green; bend of wing and carpal edge yellowish-green; no yellow on thighs.

DISTRIBUTION   Formerly eastern United States of America; now extinct.

SUBSPECIES   1. *C. c. carolinensis* (Linné)   *Illustrated on page 428.*
   21 males   wing 177–201 (187.0) mm., tail 131–158 (147.6) mm.,
         exp. cul. 22–24 (23.5) mm., tars. 16–20 (17.8) mm.,
   13 females   wing 178–194 (185.5) mm., tail 125–157 (142.7) mm.,
         exp. cul. 22–24 (23.3) mm., tars. 16–19 (17.9) mm.
      Formerly confined to south-eastern United States from Florida north to southern Virginia and occasionally as a visitor to Pennsylvania and possibly New York.

2. *C. c. ludovicianus* (Gmelin)
   ADULTS like *carolinensis*, but green of rump, lower hindneck, and sometimes the wing-coverts decidedly more bluish; green of underparts less yellowish; greater wing-coverts, inner secondaries, and basal sections of outer webs of primaries more extensively marked with brighter yellow.
   6 males   wing 185–196 (190.2) mm., tail 121–163 (146.7) mm.,
         exp. cul. 24–26 (24.7) mm., tars. 17–20 (18.0) mm.
   5 females   wing 180–196 (187.6) mm., tail 124–157 (143.6) mm.,
         exp. cul. 22–24 (23.2) mm., tars. 17–19 (18.0) mm.
   1 unsexed wing 190 mm., tail 145 mm.,
         exp. cul. 24 mm., tars. 19 mm.

      Formerly distributed throughout the Mississippi-Missouri drainage in the eastern interior of the United States from the Gulf of Mexico between eastern Texas and Mississippi, or possibly western Alabama, north to the southern shores of the Great Lakes from western New York to southern Wisconsin and to eastern Colorado, southern Nebraska, and possibly to South and North Dakota; now extinct.

GENERAL NOTES   The extinction of the Carolina Parakeet, the only parrot native to the United States, was a tragedy. The last known specimen died at the Cincinnati Zoo on 21st February 1918 (Laycock, 1969), but the species may have survived a few years longer in the wild. Greenway (1967) says that the last specimen collected in the wild was taken at Padget Creek in Brevard County on the east coast of Florida on 18th April 1901, but there is a report of a parakeet being taken opposite Platte County, at Potter, Atchison County, Kansas, in August 1904 (see McKinley, 1960). There is an unquestion-able sight record from April 1904, when Frank Chapman saw two flocks and a total of thirteen birds at Taylor's Creek on the north-eastern side of Lake Okeechobee, Florida. Further sightings were recorded as late as 1920, when a flock of about twenty was reported from near Fort Drum Creek, Florida, by a local resident. In the spring of 1926 Charles Doe, then curator of birds at the University of Florida, located three pairs of parrots in Okeechobee County, Florida, and identified them as Carolina Parakeets. No birds were collected, but he did find and take five eggs which are now in the university museum. Nicholson (1948) points out that the eggs could be those of a Mexican species, a number of which were reported to have escaped from captivity in Miami, and as no birds were collected the authenticity of the record cannot be established. Reported sightings during 1934–1935 in wild swamp country along the Santee River, South Carolina, prompted two eminent ornithologists, Alexander Sprunt and Robert Porter Allen, to visit the area in late 1936 and attempt to find the birds. Details of their sightings of parrots, as given in Allen's report for the National Audubon Society, did not convince other ornithologists, notably Ludlow Griscom who dismissed the records. Allen later changed his mind and rejected the records, saying that birds observed flying overhead at dusk were probably Mourning Doves (*Zenaidura macroura*). On the other hand, Sprunt maintained that they were Carolina Parakeets. The habitat in this area was eventually destroyed by a power project.

   The complete story behind the disappearance of these parrots will never be known because documentation of their decline was sketchy. There seems little doubt that man and his effects on the environment were responsible, but the factors directly involved remain something of a mystery. Greenway points out that during a period of about ninety years the range of *Conuropsis* gradually contracted from east to west, toward the Mississippi River, and the dates of final records from the various regions coincide well with the spread of settlement and the destruction of forests. Persistent persecution and destruction of habitat are widely accepted as having been the direct causes of the extirpation of the parrots. However, McKinley (1966) says that it is almost too easy to say that they were such pests of fruit and grain crops that they were relentlessly exterminated. I agree that there were probably more subtle primary causes involved, and the species may have been a naturally declining one, but the importance of persecution as a secondary pressure on the species should not be under-rated. The decline of these birds was quite perceptible, for as early as 1831 Audubon wrote:

> Our Parakeets are very rapidly diminishing in number; and in some districts, where twenty-five years ago they were plentiful, scarcely any are now to be seen . . . . I should think that along the Mississippi there is not now half the number that existed fifteen years ago.

When their extreme rarity became evident and Florida was proving to be the last stronghold, collectors and trappers eagerly sought out the remaining flocks—as is so often the case when something becomes rare the demand increases dramatically and the final sprint to extinction is accelerated!

How important was persecution as a cause of extinction? Was it so intense and widespread that the death rate for the species exceeded the birth rate over the entire range? These questions can never be answered from the recorded evidence we have, but what is obvious is that parrots were shot and because of their gregarious habits it was possible to destroy large numbers with little effort. An account by Audubon is probably somewhat overdramatic, but it does give us a picture of what was happening; in 1831 he wrote:

> The Parrot does not satisfy himself with Cockle-burs, but eats or destroys almost every kind of fruit indiscriminately, and on this account is always an unwelcome visitor to the planter, the farmer or the gardener. The stacks of grain put up in the field are resorted to by flocks of these birds, which frequently cover them so entirely, that they present to the eye the same effect as if a brilliantly coloured carpet had been thrown over them. They cling around the whole stack, pull out the straws, and destroy twice as much of the grain as would suffice to satisfy their hunger. They assail the Pear and Apple-trees, when the fruit is yet very small and far from being ripe, and this merely for the sake of the seeds. As on the stalks of Corn, they alight on the Apple-trees of our orchards, or the Pear-trees in the gardens, in great numbers; and, as if through mere mischief, pluck off the fruits, open them up to the core, and, disappointed at the sight of the seeds, which are yet soft and of a milky consistence, drop the apple or pear, and pluck another, passing from branch to branch, until the trees which were before so promising, are left completely stripped, like the ship water-logged and abandoned by its crew, floating on the yet agitated waves, after the tempest has ceased. They visit the Mulberries, Pecan-nuts, Grapes, and even the seeds of the Dog-wood, before they are ripe, and on all commit similar depredations. The Maize alone never attracts their notice.
>
> Do not imagine, reader, that all these outrages are borne without severe retaliation on the part of the planters. So far from this, the Parakeets are destroyed in great numbers, for whilst busily engaged in plucking off the fruits or tearing the grain from the stacks, the husbandman approaches them with perfect ease, and commits great slaughter among them. All the survivors rise, shriek, fly round about for a few minutes, and again alight on the very place of most imminent danger. The gun is kept at work; eight or ten, or even twenty, are killed at every discharge. The living birds, as if conscious of the death of their companions, sweep over their bodies, screaming as loud as ever, but still return to the stack to be shot at, until so few remain alive, that the farmer does not consider it worth his while to spend more of his ammunition. I have seen several hundreds destroyed in this manner in the course of a few hours, and have procured a basketful of these birds at a few shots, in order to make choice of good specimens for drawing the figures by which this species is represented in the plate now under your consideration.

When common the parrots were seen in large flocks, sometimes containing two or three hundred birds, but as they became rare the sizes of the flocks diminished and eventually only small parties, pairs, and occasionally single birds were sighted. Their favourite habitats were heavily forested river valleys, trees bordering streams, and extensive cypress swamps, but they ranged far and wide in search of food. McIlhenny claimed that they arrived in southern Louisiana in late April when the black mulberries were ripening (in Bendire, 1895). They were most active in the early morning and late afternoon, the remainder of the day being spent resting amongst the foliage of large shady trees. In the early morning, just before sunrise, they would assemble in the roosting trees and, to the accompaniment of much chattering, climb to the topmost branches. As soon as the sun rose small flocks flew off in all directions to the feeding areas. After feeding for two or three hours they often went to a nearby stream to drink and bathe, and then retreated to a grove of trees where they sheltered during the hotter part of the day. In the late afternoon they returned to the feeding areas, remained until dusk, and then made their way back to the roosting site, once again to the accompaniment of much screeching. A favourite roosting place was inside a large hollow stump or branch of a tree where each bird hung attached to the wall by its bill and feet. They also roosted in large cypress trees growing in swamps. The flight was swift and direct, the flocks darting in and out through the trees with remarkable precision. When coming to feeding trees the birds would spiral down from above until they almost reached the ground and then rise up to alight on the branches.

Their food consisted of seeds, fruits, nuts, blossoms, and probably leaf buds. They ate sand and gravel, presumably as an aid to digestion, and were said to be fond of saline earth. A favourite food was seeds of the cocklebur (*Xanthium strumarium*) which still grows abundantly in marginal and waste lands. Audubon gave a description of a parrot feeding on these seeds:

> It alights upon it, plucks the bur from the stem with its bill, takes it from the latter with one foot, in which it turns it over until the joint is properly placed to meet the attacks of the bill, when it bursts it open, takes out the fruit, and allows the shell to drop. In this manner, a flock of these birds, having discovered a field ever so well filled with these plants, will eat or pluck off all their seeds, returning to the place day after day until hardly any are left.

They also ate seeds of burgrass (*Cenchrus tribuloides*), a very serious weed pest, seeds of a thistle (*Cirsium lecontei*), blossoms from maple trees (*Acer rubrum*), *Asimina* fruit, mulberries, wild grapes, and berries of various kinds, and nuts from sycamore (*Platanus*), cypress (*Taxodium*), pecan (*Carya*), and beech (*Fagus*) trees (in Bendire, 1895). They attacked cultivated fruits and grain. In the vicinity of Fort Smith, Arkansas, during the autumn and winter of 1860–1861, Bendire frequently saw flocks in large osage orange trees (*Maclura pomifera*) biting off the fruit and feeding on the tender buds. Cottam and Knappen (1939) report that stomach contents from one bird comprised 'two rabbit hairs, two bits of the bird's own feathers' (both surely ingested accidentally), two fragments of an ant and the remains of seeds of loblolly pine (*Pinus taeda*).

CALL In flight a loud, screeching *qui . . . qui . . . qui . . . qui . . . qui ——— ii*, each note terminating with an upward inflection and the last being drawn-out (in Bendire, 1895); while feeding the birds kept up a constant chatter and when resting subdued, twittering notes were sometimes uttered.

NESTING Very little is known of the nesting habits. In the United States National Museum, Washington, there are two eggs taken in St. Mary's Parish, Louisiana, in March 1878, and in the American Museum of Natural History, New York, there are two eggs collected on 26th April 1855 at an unnamed locality in Georgia (in Bendire, 1895). The eggs from Georgia were found on a layer of a few chips at the bottom of a hollow in a tree. Most of the other eggs in collections were laid in captivity. There are also reports that the parrots built nests of twigs in the forks of trees, but these claims have generally been discounted.

Carolina Parakeets bred in captivity, but few details are recorded. They had the reputation of being inattentive parents and the nesting failure rate was very high. Nowotny (1898) reported that eggs laid in captivity hatched after an incubation of nineteen or twenty days, but the chicks eventually died because of parental neglect. Bent (1940) points out that birds in immature plumage were collected between early October and early April, indicating that this plumage was maintained all through the first winter. Specimens taken in February show yellow feathers appearing on the head, and it seems that progressive changes toward maturity continued all through the spring months until, by summer, the yellow head was acquired.

EGGS Ovate, slightly glossy; 24 eggs, 34.2 (32.1–37.0) × 27.8 (25.8–30.2) mm. [Bent, 1940].

Genus CYANOLISEUS Bonaparte

The species belonging to this monotypic genus is a large parrot with a long, gradated tail and a proportionately small bill, which is often partly concealed by the cheek feathers. The cere is feathered. There is no sexual dimorphism and young birds resemble adults.

I have examined the type of *Cyanoliseus whitleyi* (Kinnear) [BM. 1937.6.13.3] and agree entirely with the suggestion made by Delacour (in Peters, 1937) that it is a hybrid. It was an aviary bird and appears to have been a hybrid between *C. patagonus* and one of the large, predominantly green conures, probably *Aratinga wagleri*.

PATAGONIAN CONURE
Cyanoliseus patagonus (Vieillot)

DESCRIPTION Length 45 cm.
ADULTS head, neck, back and scapulars olive-brown with a variable tinge of green, particularly on scapulars; lower back, rump, upper tail-coverts, and lower underparts yellow with slight olive tinge; thighs and centre of abdomen orange-red; under tail-coverts olive-yellow; throat and breast greyish-brown; whitish marking on each side of upper breast, rarely extending as a band across upper breast; upper and under wing-coverts olive; outer webs of primaries and primary-coverts blue; outer webs of secondaries bluish-green; tail above olive-green tinged with blue, below brown; bill grey; iris yellowish-white; legs flesh-pink.
IMMATURES like adults, but with horn-coloured upper mandible; iris pale grey.

DISTRIBUTION Central Chile, northern and central Argentina, and possibly Uruguay.

SUBSPECIES 1. *C. p. patagonus* (Vieillot)
Illustrated on page 429.
  8 males   wing 239–252 (245.5) mm., tail 226–263 (239.6) mm.,
         exp. cul. 28–31 (29.5) mm., tars. 23–25 (24.0) mm.,
  7 females wing 232–248 (239.1) mm., tail 215–245 (230.9) mm.,
         exp. cul. 27–29 (28.1) mm., tars. 23–24 (23.6) mm.
   Occurs as a breeding resident in Córdoba, central Argentina, and in southern Argentina from Chubut north to southern Neuquén and southern Buenos Aires; in winter southern birds migrate north to Mendoza, Entre Ríos and possibly Uruguay.

2. *C. p. andinus* Dabbene and Lillo.
  ADULTS general plumage duller than in *patagonus*; little or no yellow on lower underparts;

centre of abdomen washed with dull orange-red; very faint whitish marking on side of upper breast.

1 male   wing 240 mm., tail 222 mm.,
           exp. cul. 30 mm., tars. 25 mm.
3 females   wing 238–243 (240.0) mm., tail 190–231 (214.3) mm.,
           exp. cul. 27–28 (27.7) mm., tars. 23–25 (24.0) mm.

Confined to north-western Argentina from Salta south to San Luis. Bó (1965) points out that birds from San Luis show a tendency toward *patagonus*.

3. *C. p. byroni* (J. E. Gray)

ADULTS yellow on lower underparts more extensive and brighter than in *patagonus*; thighs and centre of abdomen brighter red; prominent whitish band across upper breast; larger size.

6 males   wing 249–270 (260.5) mm., tail 199–260 (232.3) mm.,
           exp. cul. 33–35 (34.2) mm., tars. 27–29 (27.5) mm.
5 females   wing 255–266 (261.4) mm., tail 253–262 (257.4) mm.,
           exp. cul. 31–33 (32.2) mm., tars. 26–29 (27.6) mm.

Formerly occurred in central Chile from Atacama south to Valdiva, but now restricted to a few localities in the central provinces.

GENERAL NOTES

Johnson (1967) says that the Patagonian Conure was once widespread and quite abundant in central Chile, but because of persecution is now rare and reduced to a few isolated breeding colonies in the foothills of the Andes and in the coastal ranges between Atacama and Colchagua. Housse (1949) claims that adults are shot and young birds are taken from the nest because they are considered to be a delicacy. At the end of November mountain hunters, equipped with ladders, ropes, and long hooks, raid the nests to obtain nearly-fledged young for a feast traditionally held in honour of Saint Andrew. Any chicks too small for eating are reared as pets. Housse further remarks that the effects of this persistent persecution are well demonstrated in the Riviére-Claire Valley, Colchagua, where many deserted nesting burrows can be seen along the cliff faces. Barros (1934) reported that in February 1933 a population of approximately three hundred birds was found in the Cordilleras del Estero Peuco, central Chile, and this was regarded as an important discovery of a 'healthy colony' of such a rare species. Johnson describes how well the parrots respond to protection: in 1940 a nesting colony reduced to only six breeding pairs was given protection by the landholder on whose property it was situated, and in 1952 a flock of at least five hundred parrots was seen on this same property. The species has now been granted legal protection in Chile (Johnson, 1967) so it is to be hoped that the decline in numbers can be halted.

In Argentina these parrots are locally common, but generally much less abundant than in the past (Conway, 1965). Rarely are wintering birds seen north of Bahía Blanca, southernmost Buenos Aires, whereas at the turn of the century they ranged north to the Paraná River (Hudson, 1920). Pereyra (1938) says that they were formerly very common in ravines along the Atlantic coast of the province of Buenos Aires, but are now scarce. It is doubtful whether there are any valid recent records from Uruguay (see Cuello and Gerzenstein, 1962). The parrots inhabit most types of open country, especially in the vicinity of streams and rivers. In Río Negro, southern Argentina, Wetmore (1926) found them out on the flood plain of the river and among nearby gravel hills. As well as the seasonal migration in eastern Argentina, movements governed by seasonal availability of food have been reported in north-western Argentina and in Chile there are altitudinal movements. Hoy (1968) reports that in the Lerma Valley, north-western Argentina, flocks of parrots, including this species, appear at the beginning of October to feed on certain ripening berries. In the Cordilleras del Estero Peuca, central Chile, Barros found that these parrots ascended up to 1,900 m. during summer, the last birds leaving the valleys during February, and returned to the lowlands in May or June, after the first major snowfalls of the winter.

Very large flocks of these gregarious parrots were once recorded in most parts of their range, but now observers generally report only small parties. Zapata (1969) notes that along San Jorge Gulf in southern Chubut, Argentina, groups of from eleven to thirteen birds were seen during December 1964. They are usually seen feeding on the ground or in trees and bushes, or they may be flushed from beside small watercourses. Most of the day is spent foraging for seeds and fruits, or resting quietly in trees where their plumage blends well with the foliage. At sunset small flocks come in from all directions to a central roosting place, sometimes a grove of trees but more often their burrows in sandstone cliff faces. In southern Argentina Amadon has seen them roosting on telegraph wires in towns (pers. comm., 1964). At the roosting place the scene is one of intense activity with the birds jostling for perching positions; it is well after dark before all is quiet. They have been seen flying about at night and Conway reports hearing screeching flocks flying overhead at 0300 hrs., well before dawn. At sunrise there is an outbreak of screeching and chattering as birds emerge from burrows or flutter from branch to branch. They rise into the air, go to a watercourse to drink, and then disperse in small groups to feed. Housse says that when travelling to and from roosting sites the parrots generally fly high in long, drawn-out, irregular formations, and their continuous screeching can be heard from afar. During the day, while moving about locally, they usually fly low, close to the ground. The direct fairly swift flight comprises rhythmic, shallow wingbeats. When flushed from the ground, these birds present an impressive sight as their sleek streamlined appearance is enhanced by the flashes of blue from the wings shown when they rise up into a tree and then spread their tails just before alighting.

They feed on seeds, berries, fruits, and probably vegetable matter. Hudson says that they are fond of the berries of *Empetrum rubrum* and the seeds of the giant thistle (*Carduus mariana*). Wetmore reports that in Río Negro, southern Argentina, they were seen feeding on the ripe berries of *Lycium salsum* and *Discaria* sp. They can be pests in crop-growing districts; in Río Negro and Neuquén, southern Argentina, flocks congregate during autumn to raid ripening maize crops (Sick, 1968).

CALL A shrill, rollicking screech is given in flight; while perched a guttural cry is occasionally uttered.

NESTING Housse says that in Chile nesting commences in September; nests with eggs have been found in October and November. Peters (1923) claims that birds he saw in Río Negro, Argentina, in late December and late January were nesting at the time. The nests are in burrows excavated by the birds in sandstone or limestone cliff faces, sometimes at a great height from the ground and overlooking the sea or a river. The burrows have entrances ranging from 8 to 18 cm. in diameter, and they penetrate up to 3 m. into the sandstone before terminating in a nesting chamber, which is usually about 40 cm. long and 15 cm. high. The birds nest in colonies and their burrows follow zig-zag paths, frequently meeting each other to form an inter-connecting labyrinth. Two, rarely three, eggs make up the normal clutch.

Johnson describes the return of the parrots to the burrows. In groups of up to a dozen the parrots approach the cliff face and increase the rate of their wingbeats to gain speed. They wheel about in close formation and then glide straight in toward the burrow entrances. Just as they reach the cliff face the wings are closed and each bird enters its burrow on the run.

Partridge (1964) gives details of a successful breeding in captivity. Three eggs were laid. The incubation period was not determined precisely, but was estimated to have been approximately twenty-four or twenty-five days. Only the female incubated and the male was not seen to enter the nest-box until after the chicks had hatched; from this time onward he was regularly observed entering the nest, presumably to feed the hen, and later the chicks as well. The young birds left the nest eight weeks after hatching, but were fed by the parents for a further several weeks.

EGGS Almost spherical, slightly glossy; 3 eggs, 36.4 (35.0–37.4) × 29.4 (27.0–30.8) mm. [Schönwetter, 1964].

Genus PYRRHURA Bonaparte

Parrots belonging to *Pyrrhura* are small to medium-sized birds with long, gradated tails. The bill is rather broad and there is a notch in the upper mandible. The naked cere is very prominent. In the skull there is a complete orbital ring (Thompson, 1900). Sexual dimorphism is absent and young birds resemble adults.

BLUE-THROATED CONURE
Pyrrhura cruentata (Wied)   *Illustrated on page 432.*

Length 30 cm.
ADULTS general plumage green; feathers of crown and nape dark brown narrowly edged with buff-yellow, edging becoming more prominent on nape; frontal band, lores, periophthalmic region, and ear-coverts brownish-red; yellowish-orange marking on each side of neck; cheeks green; throat, upper breast, and collar around hindneck blue; broad dark red patch on rump and lower back; red on centre of abdomen; bend of wing bright red; outer webs of primaries blue; undersides of flight feathers grey with olive on inner webs; tail above olive, below brownish-red; bill greyish-brown; iris yellow-orange; legs grey.
IMMATURES duller than adults; less red on bend of wing.
8 males   wing 145–152 (148.6) mm., tail 127–136 (132.3) mm.,
      exp. cul. 19–21 (19.6) mm., tars. 15–17 (15.8) mm.
8 females wing 144–152 (148.9) mm., tail 124–134 (128.8) mm.,
      exp. cul. 18–20 (19.1) mm., tars. 15–17 (16.0) mm.

DISTRIBUTION Occurs in eastern Brazil from southern Bahia and Minas Gerais south to north-eastern São Paulo.

GENERAL NOTES There is very little recorded information on the habits of the Blue-throated Conure. Pinto (1935) says that it is a forest bird and is locally common, though the range is quite restricted. Sick (1969) lists it as an endangered species, but gives no further details. I suspect that the decline has been brought about by the extensive land-clearance that has taken place in the region.

CALL Undescribed.

NESTING No records.

EGGS Rounded; 2 eggs, 27.7 (27.5–27.8) × 19.9 (19.4–20.3) mm. [Harrison and Holyoak, 1970].

BLAZE-WINGED CONURE
Pyrrhura devillei (Massena and Souancé)

Illustrated on page 436.

Length 26 cm.

ADULTS general plumage green, paler and more yellowish on rump and upper tail-coverts; narrow brownish-black frontal band; crown ash-brown, continuing to nape where variably marked with green; cheeks green; ear-coverts greyish-brown; breast and sides of neck olive-brown, each feather edged with a whitish band then a dusky brown one giving a barred appearance; abdomen variably marked with red; brownish-red markings on lower back; bend of wing, carpal edge, and lesser under wing-coverts scarlet; greater under wing-coverts olive-yellow; primary-coverts bluish-green; outer webs of primaries deep blue; tail above olive, below brownish-red; bill grey; iris brown; legs grey.

IMMATURES undescribed.

3 males   wing 123–127 (125.7) mm., tail 116–132 (123.7) mm.,
       exp. cul. 15–17 (16.3) mm., tars. 14 (14.0) mm.
4 females wing 122–130 (125.8) mm., tail 117–128 (122.5) mm.,
       exp. cul. 15–17 (16.0) mm., tars. 13–15 (14.0) mm.

DISTRIBUTION   Restricted to eastern Bolivia, northern Paraguay, and south-western Mato Grosso, Brazil.

SUBSPECIES   Short claims that *P. devillei* hybridizes with *P. frontalis* in northern Paraguay, so the two are probably conspecific (pers. comm., 1971).

GENERAL NOTES   There is virtually no recorded information on the habits of the Blaze-winged Conure, but they are probably similar to those of the Maroon-bellied Conure. Crop and stomach contents from two specimens collected at Salobra, Mato Grosso, Brazil, comprised crushed seeds and the remains of fruits (Schubart *et al.*, 1965).

MAROON-BELLIED CONURE
Pyrrhura frontalis (Vieillot)

Length 26 cm.

ADULTS general plumage green, paler and more yellowish on lower underparts; few red feathers behind cere; narrow rufous frontal band; lores black; greyish-brown ear-coverts; sides of neck, throat and breast olive, feathers margined with dull yellow then tipped with olive-brown giving a barred appearance; centre of abdomen brownish-red; variable brownish-red markings on lower back; bend of wing and under wing-coverts green; primary-coverts bluish-green; outer webs of primaries blue, becoming greenish towards tips; tail above olive broadly tipped with brownish-red, below dull brownish-red; bill greyish-brown; iris dark brown; legs grey.

IMMATURES similar to adults, but general plumage duller; shorter tail.

DISTRIBUTION   South-eastern Brazil, Uruguay, Paraguay, and northern Argentina.

SUBSPECIES   I have followed the arrangement proposed by Laubmann (1932).

Illustrated on page 436.

1. *P. f. frontalis* (Vieillot)
   6 males   wing 127–141 (134.2) mm., tail 120–131 (126.3) mm.,
       exp. cul. 16–18 (17.2) mm., tars. 14–16 (14.8) mm.
   8 females wing 127–140 (132.8) mm., tail 122–127 (125.5) mm.,
       exp. cul. 16–17 (16.4) mm., tars. 14–15 (14.5) mm.
   Confined to south-eastern Brazil from south-eastern Bahia through eastern Minas Gerais to Espírito Santo and Rio de Janeiro.

2. *P. f. kriegi* Laubmann
   ADULTS similar to *frontalis*, but tail very narrowly tipped with brownish-red; bend of wing green, in some birds faintly tinged with orange-red.
   8 males   wing 128–140 (133.4) mm., tail 116–127 (121.3) mm.,
       exp. cul. 16–18 (16.8) mm., tars. 14–15 (14.4) mm.
   8 females wing 129–145 (136.1) mm., tail 110–126 (117.3) mm.,
       exp. cul. 15–17 (16.3) mm., tars. 14–15 (14.4) mm.
   Occurs in south-eastern Brazil from western Minas Gerais through São Paulo and Paraná to Rio Grande do Sul.

3. *P. f. chiripepe* (Vieillot)
   ADULTS like *frontalis*, but upper side of tail entirely olive, without brownish-red tip; in most birds bend of wing variably marked with orange-red.
   6 males   wing 129–137 (134.3) mm., tail 122–131 (126.2) mm.,
       exp. cul. 16–17 (16.3) mm., tars. 14–16 (15.0) mm.
   3 females wing 131–135 (133.0) mm., tail 126–129 (127.7) mm.,
       exp. cul. 16–17 (16.3) mm., tars. 14–15 (14.7) mm.

Found in Paraguay, Uruguay, and northern Argentina in the provinces of Salta, Chaco, Formosa, Corrientes, and Misiones.

Olrog (1968) says that Maroon-bellied Conures inhabit forests, and large flocks may be seen in the treetops. They are common throughout most of their range. Wetmore (1926) found them to be common at Las Palmas, Chaco, northern Argentina, and on a low wooded hill near Puerto Pinasco, Paraguay. Eckelberry (1965) notes that they seem to be the most common of the parrots found in Misiones, northern Argentina. In northern regions of Rio Grande do Sul, south-eastern Brazil, between 800 and 1,300 m., I found them to be the most common and widely distributed of parrots. They occurred in all types of woodland, except *Eucalyptus* plantations, but seemed to be particularly common in *Araucaria* forest in valleys penetrating open, undulating grassland. Pairs were occasionally seen, but generally they were in flocks of from ten to about forty birds. In May 1971, near Gramado, Rio Grande do Sul, I saw a small flock feeding during the late afternoon in a large *Araucaria* tree standing in disturbed woodland; it was the only large *Araucaria* tree in the immediate vicinity and the birds were reluctant to leave it, persistently returning each time they were flushed. Near Bom Jesus, Rio Grande do Sul, I found a party quietly resting during the middle of the day; in pairs, and threes and fours they were sitting huddled close together on thick, main branches near the trunk of the tree, and were preening each other. At sunrise the next morning I observed post-roosting aerobatics; screeching flocks were flying up and down a forested valley.

These parrots are very noisy when in flight, but are silent while feeding in the treetops. Their plumage blends extremely well with the foliage and quite often I became aware of their presence in a tree only after they had darted out from the other side, shrieking in alarm as they went. At times it was difficult to locate them in the forest canopy even though I had seen them alight. The flight is swift and somewhat erratic. When coming to alight they glide past the tree then swoop back and down into it.

They feed on seeds, fruits, nuts, berries, blossoms and possibly insects and their larvae. Mitchell (1957) has seen them eating palm nuts of various kinds, the black berries of a cypress-like evergreen, and the fruits of the jaboticaba (*Myrciara* sp.); she also observed them in the Rio de Janeiro Botanic Gardens where they were in the company of Plain Parakeets (*Brotogeris tirica*) in flowering trees, biting off the blossoms and letting them fall to the ground, but it was not ascertained whether any part of the flower was being eaten. They can cause considerable damage in orange orchards (Wetmore, 1926), and will attack 'milky' maize (Sick, 1968).

CALL In flight a shrill screech, much louder than would be expected from a small bird; when alarmed a sharp, staccato *aack-aack-aack-aack*.

NESTING Early reports from Argentina claim that the nest is in a hollow in a tree and up to five eggs are laid (see Orfila, 1937).

Dalborg-Johansen (1954) reports a successful breeding in captivity. The incubation period was not determined precisely, but was estimated to have been approximately thirty days. Only the female incubated, but the chicks were fed by both parents. The young birds left the nest forty-five days after hatching and were fed for a further fortnight by the parents, especially the male.

EGGS Rounded; 3 eggs, 25.8 (24.9–26.5) × 21.0 (20.6–21.3) mm. [Schönwetter, 1964].

PEARLY CONURE
Pyrrhura perlata (Spix)

DESCRIPTION   Length 24 cm.
ADULTS general plumage green; crown and occiput brown; darker brown frontal band; feathers of nape brown margined with buff; variable blue collar on hindneck, reduced to a few feathers in some birds; cheeks dull blue, slightly tinged with green towards lores; buff ear-coverts; feathers of sides of neck, throat and upper breast brown broadly margined with buff then tipped with dark brown giving a barred appearance, on upper breast also suffused with blue; flanks and thighs suffused with blue; under tail-coverts greenish-blue; faint red markings on abdomen; bend of wing and lesser under wing-coverts red; primary-coverts and outer webs of primaries deep blue; outer webs of secondaries bluish-green; tail brownish-red basally marked with olive on upper side; bill grey; iris reddish-brown; legs dark grey.
IMMATURES like adults, but pale margins to feathers of nape less pronounced; bill and legs paler grey.

DISTRIBUTION   North-eastern Brazil.

SUBSPECIES   1. *P. p. lepida* (Wagler)   *Illustrated on page 433.*
    5 males   wing 126–131 (127.8) mm., tail 106–111 (109.2) mm.,
               exp. cul. 16 (16.0) mm., tars. 13–16 (14.4) mm.
    5 females wing 118–124 (120.2) mm., tail 104–116 (109.4) mm.,
               exp. cul. 15–16 (15.2) mm., tars. 13–14 (13.6) mm.

I unsexed wing 125 mm., tail 111 mm.,
    exp. cul. 15 mm., tars. 14 mm.
    This race, as described above, is distributed from Belém and the Capim River, Pará, east to Cumã Bay, Maranhão.

2. *P. p. coerulescens* Neumann
ADULTS like *lepida*, but crown and nape paler brown; upper cheeks green merging into blue on lower cheeks; upper breast more strongly tinged with blue and extending up to throat; lower underparts green, slightly tinged with blue on under tail-coverts.
3 males   wing 122–130 (127.3) mm., tail 108–124 (115.7) mm.,
    exp. cul. 16–17 (16.3) mm., tars. 13–15 (14.0) mm.
3 females wing 125–133 (128.3) mm., tail 111–119 (114.0) mm.,
    exp. cul. 15–16 (15.3) mm., tars. 13–15 (14.0) mm.
Known only from the type locality, Miritiba, near the coast of northern Maranhão.

3. *P. p. anerythra* Neumann
ADULTS like *lepida*, but crown paler brown; lores and upper cheeks green, merging into blue on lower cheeks; no blue tinge on upper breast; abdomen and lower breast tinged with red; under wing-coverts and bend of wing green; in some birds there are red markings on carpal edge, but in most this is entirely green.
5 males   wing 126–138 (133.6) mm., tail 101–121 (115.0) mm.,
    exp. cul. 16–18 (16.8) mm., tars. 14–15 (14.4) mm.
2 females wing 125–135 (130.0) mm., tail 113–116 (114.5) mm.,
    exp. cul. 16 (16.0) mm., tars. 14–15 (14.5) mm.
2 unsexed wing 120–127 (123.5) mm., tail 113–116 (114.5) mm.,
    exp. cul. 16 (16.0) mm., tars. 13 (13.0) mm.
Recorded from the Fresco River, a tributary of the Xingú, the Pracupi River in the vicinity of Portel, and from Arumattra on the left bank of the Tocatins River, all in Pará.

4. *P. p. perlata* (Spix)
ADULTS like *lepida*, but cheeks greenish-yellow; olive-brown frontal band; sides of neck, throat, and upper breast pale buff, the feathers narrowly margined with brown.
No specimens examined.
    Range unknown. This race is known from only two specimens, which, as their wings are clipped, probably came from captivity.

GENERAL NOTES   The Pearly Conure inhabits humid forests, but there is virtually no recorded information on its habits. Three seeds were found in the stomach from a specimen collected on the Gurupi River, Pará (Schubart *et al.*, 1965).

CALL Undescribed.

NESTING I know of no records from the wild state. Low (1967 and 1968) gives details of successful breeding in captivity. In the first year there were four eggs in the clutch, and in the next year three; three chicks hatched on both occasions. Incubation lasted twenty-three days and it seems that only the female incubated; the male entered the nest-box at night to roost. The young birds left the nest approximately seven weeks after hatching.

EGGS Undescribed.

CRIMSON-BELLIED CONURE
Illustrated on page 432.
Pyrrhura rhodogaster (Sclater)

Length 24 cm.
ADULTS forehead brown variably tinged with blue; crown, nape, sides of neck, throat, and upper breast brown, each feather with a paler tip thus giving a barred appearance; upper cheeks yellowish-green, becoming blue on lower cheeks; variable blue collar encircling hindneck; mantle, median and lesser wing-coverts, lower back, middle of rump, and central upper tail-coverts green; scapulars and secondary-coverts greenish-blue; bend of wing, lesser under wing-coverts, lower breast, and abdomen crimson; thighs, flanks, under tail-coverts, and lateral upper tail-coverts blue; primary-coverts and outer webs of primaries deep blue; outer webs of secondaries greenish-blue; tail above brownish-red basally marked with green and tipped with blue, below greyish; bill brownish-grey; iris dark brown; legs grey.
IMMATURES undescribed.
8 males   wing 127–140 (136.1) mm., tail 96–109 (102.3) mm.,
    exp. cul. 17–18 (17.4) mm., tars. 15–16 (15.4) mm.
5 females wing 125–138 (132.8) mm., tail 100–106 (102.6) mm.,
    exp. cul. 16–18 (16.6) mm., tars. 15–17 (15.6) mm.

Confined to northern Brazil, south of the Amazon River, between the Madeira and Tapajós Rivers, east along the Jamauchim River, and south to northern Mato Grosso.

While in northern Mato Grosso with the Roosevelt-Rondon Expedition in 1916 Cherrie found large flocks of Crimson-bellied Conures along the Roosevelt River (in Naumburg, 1930). If undisturbed they kept up a constant chatter while fluttering about in the treetops, but at the same time they were very watchful and wary. When approached the birds would suddenly become silent and sit motionless amidst the foliage where, despite their bright plumage, it was difficult to detect them. Nothing further is known of their habits.

GREEN-CHEEKED CONURE
Pyrrhura molinae (Massena and Souancé)

Length 26 cm.

ADULTS general plumage green; reddish-brown forehead; crown and nape brown tinged with green; cheeks green; ear-coverts greyish-brown; sides of neck, throat, and upper breast pale brown sometimes tinged with dull green, each feather broadly margined with pale greyish-buff or dull yellow and tipped with dark brown thus giving a barred appearance; some blue feathers on hindneck, rarely forming an indistinct collar; brownish-red patch on centre of abdomen; under tail-coverts green lightly washed with blue; primary-coverts and outer webs of primaries blue; outer webs of secondaries greenish-blue; tail above brownish-red tipped with blue and slightly marked with green at base, below dull brownish-red; bill grey; iris brown; legs dark grey.
IMMATURES undescribed.

West-central and southern Mato Grosso, Brazil, northern and eastern Bolivia from La Paz to Tarija, and north-western Argentina.

A critical revision of the subspecies is required. It seems extraordinary that a species with a fairly restricted distribution should show such geographical variation. Furthermore, some of the diagnostic features are not convincing.

1. *P. m. molinae* (Massena and Souancé)   *Illustrated on page 436.*
    11 males   wing 130–139 (134.9) mm., tail 119–142 (129.3) mm.,
               exp. cul. 17–19 (18.0) mm., tars. 14–17 (15.4) mm.
    10 females   wing 129–140 (135.4) mm., tail 121–142 (134.8) mm.,
               exp. cul. 16–18 (17.7) mm., tars. 14–17 (15.5) mm.
    According to Todd (1947) this race is restricted to the highlands of eastern Bolivia.

2. *P. m. phoenicura* (Schlegel)
    ADULTS like *molinae*, but upper side of tail broadly marked with green.
    1 male   wing 126 mm., tail 122 mm.,
             exp. cul. 16 mm., tars. 15 mm.
    1 female wing 128 mm., tail 129 mm.,
             exp. cul. 17 mm., tars. 16 mm.
    Confined to west-central Mato Grosso, Brazil, and neighbouring north-eastern Bolivia.

3. *P. m. sordida* Todd.
    ADULTS similar to *molinae*, but general plumage duller; crown paler brown; green of cheeks paler and less extensive; barring on breast indistinct because of paler centres to feathers; brownish-red abdominal patch paler and less prominent; outer webs of primaries paler blue; under tail-coverts suffused with blue.
    7 males   wing 126–136 (131.9) mm., tail 123–143 (135.9) mm.,
             exp. cul. 16–18 (17.1) mm., tars. 13–15 (14.4) mm.
    4 females   wing 123–135 (128.5) mm., tail 117–145 (129.8) mm.,
             exp. cul. 15–18 (16.3) mm., tars. 14–15 (14.5) mm.
    Occurs in southern Mato Grosso, Brazil, and in neighbouring easternmost Bolivia.

4. *P. m. restricta* Todd.
    ADULTS like *molinae*, but green of cheeks tinged with blue; blue collar on hindneck always prominent; feathers of sides of neck, throat, and upper breast very broadly margined with greyish-white instead of greyish-buff; brownish-red abdominal patch duller in colour and less extensive; flanks and under tail-coverts strongly tinged with blue.
    2 males   wing 135–137 (136.0) mm., tail 132–136 (134.0) mm.,
             exp. cul. 16–17 (16.5) mm., tars. 16 (16.0) mm.
    2 females wing 142–143 (142.5) mm., tail 138–144 (141.0) mm.,
             exp. cul. 16–18 (17.0) mm., tars. 15–17 (16.0) mm.
    Known only from Palmarito, Chiquitos, Bolivia, the type locality.

5. *P. m. australis* Todd.
    ADULTS similar to *molinae*, but with more pronounced brownish-red abdominal patch; underparts duller green and under tail-coverts green with little blue.

7 males   wing 128–134 (131.7) mm., tail 122–131 (127.0) mm.,
           exp. cul. 16–17 (16.3) mm., tars. 14–15 (14.4) mm.
6 females wing 126–133 (129.5) mm., tail 108–137 (123.7) mm.,
           exp. cul. 16–17 (16.3) mm., tars. 13–14 (13.8) mm.
           Occurs in Tarija, southern Bolivia, and in the provinces of Salta, Jujuy, and occasionally Tucumán, north-western Argentina.

GENERAL NOTES   The Green-cheeked Conure is a forest bird and is generally seen in large flocks in the tops of trees (Olrog, 1968). Orfila (1937) says that it is not uncommon to find flocks of twenty or more in the forests of north-western Argentina. Neithammer (1953) reports that at 2,000 m. in the 'yungas', or forested valleys, around Pojo and Irupana, Bolivia, this species and the Red-billed Parrot (*Pionus sordidus*) are the dominant parrots.

   It feeds on seeds, fruits, nuts, berries and probably vegetable matter.

CALL   Undescribed.

NESTING   Near Orán, Salta, north-western Argentina, a nest containing three freshly-laid eggs was found at the beginning of February (Hoy, 1968). It was in a hollow in a tree at about 5 m. from the ground. The entrance to the hollow was a fairly large opening and at the bottom of the cavity there were a few straws and pieces of moss, presumably left by some other bird that had previously nested there. Nothing further is known of the nesting habits.

EGGS   Rounded; 3 eggs, 24.2 (23.5–24.8) × 19.6 (19.2–20.0) mm. [Hoy, 1968].

YELLOW-SIDED CONURE
Pyrrhura hypoxantha Salvadori

Illustrated on page 436.

Length 25 cm.
MALE undescribed.
FEMALE (AMNH. 474758, **type**); crown brown, darker on forehead; feathers of nape brown edged with buff; indistinct blue collar across hindneck; greyish-brown ear-coverts; cheeks green, becoming yellowish posteriorly; feathers of sides of neck, throat, and upper breast yellowish-white narrowly tipped with pale brown thus giving a barred appearance; feathers of lower breast yellow narrowly tipped with pale brown; orange-red patch on centre of abdomen; flanks and thighs yellow, each feather faintly margined with green; under tail-coverts yellow, longest feathers washed with blue; under wing-coverts yellow; mantle, upper back, and wings green; lower back, rump, and upper tail-coverts green marked with yellow; primary-coverts and outer webs of primaries blue; outer webs of secondaries bluish-green; tail brownish-red tipped with bluish-green; bill brownish; legs grey.
IMMATURES undescribed.
1 female (**type**); wing 134 mm., tail 136 mm.,
           exp. cul. 17 mm., tars. 14 mm.
2 unsexed   wing 131–136 (133.5) mm., tail 123–146 (134.5) mm.,
           exp. cul. 16–17 (16.5) mm., tars. 14–15 (14.5) mm.

DISTRIBUTION   Recorded from Urucúm and Corumbá, localities about 18 km. apart, south-western Mato Grosso, Brazil.

GENERAL NOTES   The Yellow-sided Conure is known only from three specimens. I agree with the suggestion made by a number of authors that these specimens are merely aberrant examples of *P. molinae*. The two original specimens were collected from a flock of *P. molinae* and there was another seen but not taken (Salvadori, 1900).

WHITE-EARED CONURE
Pyrrhura leucotis (Kuhl)

DESCRIPTION   Length 23 cm.
ADULTS general plumage green; crown and nape brown, suffused with blue on forecrown; narrow frontal band, lores, periophthalmic region, and upper cheeks maroon; lower cheeks dull blue; ear-coverts brownish-white; throat dull bluish; feathers of sides of neck and upper breast green broadly margined with buff and narrowly tipped with brown giving a barred appearance; brownish-red patch on centre of abdomen; bend of wing red; under wing-coverts green; brownish-red patch extending from lower back to upper tail-coverts; primary-coverts greenish-blue; outer webs of primaries blue; tail above brownish-red marked with green, below dull brownish-red; bill greyish-brown; iris brown; legs grey.
IMMATURES like adults.

Northern Venezuela and eastern Brazil; introduced to the Rio de Janeiro Botanic Gardens.

SUBSPECIES

1. *P. l. leucotis* (Kuhl) *Illustrated on page 437.*
   8 males   wing 118–125 (120.9) mm., tail 106–115 (110.0) mm.,
         exp. cul. 14–15 (14.6) mm., tars. 13–14 (13.4) mm.
   8 females wing 115–123 (118.8) mm., tail 97–111 (104.9) mm.,
         exp. cul. 13–15 (14.1) mm., tars. 13–14 (13.3) mm.
      Occurs in coastal regions of eastern Brazil from southern Bahia to São Paulo; not previously recorded from Guanabara, but now well-established in and around the Rio de Janeiro Botanic Gardens where confiscated birds were released by fauna authorities (Sick pers. comm., 1971).

2. *P. l. griseipectus* Salvadori
   ADULTS like *leucotis*, but ear-coverts more purely white with little brownish edging; feathers of sides of neck and upper breast dusky grey broadly margined with buff and tipped with brown; no blue suffusion on forecrown.
   4 males   wing 116–122 (119.3) mm., tail 106–110 (108.3) mm.,
         exp. cul. 15–17 (15.5) mm., tars. 14–15 (14.3) mm.
   4 females wing 116–127 (120.3) mm., tail 107–125 (113.0) mm.,
         exp. cul. 15–17 (15.5) mm., tars. 14–15 (14.3) mm.
      Confined to north-eastern Brazil in the state of Ceará.

3. *P. l. pfrimeri* Ribeiro.
   ADULTS similar to *griseipectus*, but forehead and sides of head, including ear-coverts, chestnut-red; crown and nape dull blue; feathers of throat dull greenish-blue margined with white.
   3 males   wing 121–125 (123.3) mm., tail 105–115 (110.3) mm.,
         exp. cul. 14–16 (15.0) mm., tars. 12–14 (13.0) mm.
   3 females wing 115–118 (117.0) mm., tail 107–119 (112.3) mm.,
         exp. cul. 13–15 (14.0) mm., tars. 13–14 (13.3) mm.
      Known only from Santa Maria de Taguatinga, Goiás, north-eastern Brazil, the type locality.

4. *P. l. emma* Salvadori
   ADULTS similar to *leucotis*, but blue collar of hindneck extending up on to nape; lower cheeks and throat more bluish; broader buff margins to feathers of sides of neck and upper breast.
   10 males   wing 114–122 (117.7) mm., tail 90–116 (109.2) mm.,
         exp. cul. 14–16 (15.3) mm., tars. 13–15 (14.0) mm.
   10 females wing 112–120 (115.6) mm., tail 105–115 (109.4) mm.,
         exp. cul. 14–15 (14.6) mm., tars. 13–14 (13.4) mm.
      Distributed along the coastal range of northern Venezuela from Yaracuy east through the Federal District to Miranda.

5. *P. l. auricularis* Zimmer and Phelps.
   ADULTS like *emma*, but with larger and clearer white ear-coverts; green of back and flanks slightly deeper, less yellowish.
   10 males   wing 112–119 (115.8) mm., tail 100–121 (110.9) mm.,
         exp. cul. 14–17 (15.3) mm., tars. 13–15 (13.8) mm.
   7 females wing 113–120 (117.0) mm., tail 107–120 (112.9) mm.,
         exp. cul. 14–16 (14.7) mm., tars. 13–15 (14.3) mm.
      Occurs in the coastal range of north-eastern Venezuela in Sucre, Anzoátegui, and Monagas.

GENERAL NOTES   In northern Venezuela White-eared Conures inhabit forests in the tropical zone and in the lower belt of the sub-tropical zone (Phelps and Phelps, 1958). Pinto (1935) says that in eastern Brazil they are forest birds, but gives no further details of their habits. Schafer and Phelps (1954) report that in the Rancho Grande Reserve, northern Venezuela, these parrots are irregular vagrants in moist forests of the subtropical zone. Sightings are recorded only from the cloud forests around Portachuelo during July and August, the time of the year when Red-eared Conures (*P. hoematotis*) are also most plentiful. They travel about in flocks of from fifteen to twenty and favour the forest canopy.

In May 1971, I found them to be quite common in the Rio de Janeiro Botanic Gardens, where pairs and small parties were seen flying from tree to tree. A group of five, comprising a pair and three birds, was observed sitting in the topmost leafless branches of a small deciduous tree. These birds were spasmodically engaged in self and mutual preening. One was fed in turn by birds sitting on either side but then the bird on the left moved away and sat alone on a lower branch, thus leaving two pairs. While the parrots are perching, the red abdomen and white ear-coverts contrasted against the dark head are most conspicuous. The flight is swift and direct.

They feed on seeds, fruits, nuts, berries, and possibly insects and their larvae. Some ants were found in the stomach of a specimen collected at Linhares, Espírito Santo, Brazil, but these must have been ingested accidentally (Schubart *et al.*, 1965).

CALL   The contact call is not as loud as that of related species and is a sharp *teer-teer* repeated rapidly three or four times; while perched an occasional *teet* is uttered.

NESTING   I know of no published breeding records from the wild. Restall (1970) quotes information obtained from three successful breedings in captivity. The clutch comprised five to nine eggs, and these were normally laid on alternate days. The incubation period was approximately twenty-seven days and only the female brooded; she remained in the nest throughout the entire nesting period, that is from the commencement of laying until all young birds had left the nest. The young remained in the nest for an undetermined period, and after leaving were fed by the parents for a further two weeks. Brook (1907) also successfully bred this species in captivity and noted that the young birds left the nest about five weeks after hatching.

EGGS Broadly elliptical; 3 eggs, 26.3 (25.9–26.9) × 20.5 (20.0–20.9) mm. [Harrison and Holyoak, 1970].

PAINTED CONURE
Pyrrhura picta (P. L. S. Müller)

DESCRIPTION

Length 22 cm.
ADULTS general plumage green; crown and nape dark brown, strongly suffused with blue on forecrown; forehead, lower cheeks, and indistinct collar on hindneck blue; lores and upper cheeks reddish-brown; ear-coverts buff-white; feathers of sides of neck, throat, and upper breast dusky brown broadly edged with greyish-buff thus giving a scalloped appearance; brownish-red patch on centre of abdomen; bend of wing red; green under wing-coverts; brownish-red patch extending from lower back to upper tail-coverts; primary-coverts and outer webs of primaries blue; tail above brownish-red becoming green towards base, below dull brownish-red; bill brownish-grey; iris brown; legs grey.
IMMATURES like adults, but bend of wing green with only a few red feathers scattered here and there.

DISTRIBUTION

Distributed from the Guianas to Venezuela, south of the Orinoco River, and south through the Amazon Basin, northern Brazil, to south-eastern Peru and northern Bolivia; also in northern Colombia.

SUBSPECIES

A critical revision of the subspecies is needed. I agree with Phelps and Phelps (1958) that *orino-censis* and *cuchivera* are synonymous with *picta*, and have followed Gyldenstolpe (1945) in recognizing *roseifrons* as distinct from *lucianii*, though this is rejected by Pinto (1947).

1. *P. p. picta* (P. L. S. Müller)   *Illustrated on page 437.*
   25 males   wing 116–130 (122.4) mm., tail 95–115 (106.3) mm.,
               exp. cul. 14–17 (15.2) mm., tars. 13–16 (14.0) mm.
   10 females wing 115–125 (120.0) mm., tail 90–108 (100.7) mm.,
               exp. cul. 14–16 (14.3) mm., tars. 13–14 (13.8) mm.
   Distributed from Amapá, northern Brazil, through the Guianas to Venezuela, south of the Orinoco River in Delta Amacuro, Bolívar, and in eastern Amazonas in the mountains of Yaví and Parú.

2. *P. p. amazonum* Hellmayr.
   ADULTS blue suffusion on forecrown extending back only to anterior edge of eye; ear-coverts bright brownish-buff; feathers of breast dull green, not dusky brown, more broadly edged with greyish-buff or rufous-buff; bend of wing green, sometimes a few feathers tipped with red; less green towards bases of tail-feathers.
   15 males   wing 116–128 (121.3) mm., tail 90–112 (99.8) mm.,
               exp. cul. 14–15 (14.7) mm., tars. 12–15 (13.5) mm.
   11 females wing 120–125 (122.6) mm., tail 96–111 (102.7) mm.,
               exp. cul. 14–15 (14.4) mm., tars. 13–15 (13.5) mm.
   Known only from the northern banks of the Amazon River between Obidos and Monte Alegre, Pará, northern Brazil.

3. *P. p. microtera* Todd
   ADULTS similar to *amazonum*, but with less blue on forehead and forecrown; feathers of throat and breast dusky, rather than green, broadly edged with greyish-buff; smaller size.
   .15 males   wing 104–117 (110.8) mm., tail 81–102 (90.9) mm.,
               exp. cul. 13–15 (13.9) mm., tars. 12–15 (13.1) mm.
   10 females wing 105–113 (109.9) mm., tail 83–97 (89.8) mm.,
               exp. cul. 13–15 (13.9) mm., tars. 12–14 (12.9) mm.
   Occurs south of the Amazon River from the Tapajós River east to the Tocatins River, Pará, and south to northernmost Goiás, northern Brazil.

4. *P. p. lucianii* (Deville)
   ADULTS (plumage variable); like *picta*, but with little or no blue on forehead and forecrown; some birds show red on forehead, lores, and as a superciliary stripe; blue collar on hindneck restricted to faint bluish wash; little or no red on bend of wing; feathers of lower breast strongly centred with green.

13 males wing 113–130 (121.3) mm., tail 93–107 (99.9) mm.,
exp. cul. 14–16 (14.6) mm., tars. 13–14 (13.5) mm.
14 females wing 118–128 (122.3) mm., tail 89–106 (99.6) mm.,
exp. cul. 14–15 (14.6) mm., tars. 13–15 (13.6) mm.

Distributed along the upper Amazon River in Amazonas, north-western Brazil, and neighbouring north-eastern Peru, and along the Purús and Madeira Rivers and their tributaries, Amazonas, Brazil, south to La Paz, Bolivia, and to south-eastern Peru.

5. *P. p. roseifrons* (G. R. Gray)   *Illustrated on page 437.*

ADULTS like *lucianii*, but forehead, lores, forecrown and sometimes upper cheeks red, extending on to crown and nape in old birds; upperparts paler green; flanks and under tail-coverts more olive; brownish-red patches on abdomen and rump more red, less brownish.
IMMATURES less red on head, but generally more extensive than in adults of *lucianii*.
13 males wing 120–129 (124.7) mm., tail 98–110 (102.4) mm.,
exp. cul. 14–16 (15.0) mm., tars. 13–15 (13.8) mm.
11 females wing 119–127 (122.1) mm., tail 95–103 (99.5) mm.,
exp. cul. 14–16 (14.8) mm., tars. 13–16 (14.0) mm.

Known only from the upper Juruá River, Amazonas, north-western Brazil.

6. *P. p. subandina* Todd

ADULTS frontal band and lores reddish-brown; cheeks bluish-green; ear-coverts yellowish-brown; feathers of sides of neck, throat, and upper breast dusky broadly edged with greyish-buff; iris yellowish-brown.
9 males wing 111–117 (115.1) mm., tail 93–111 (104.1) mm.,
exp. cul. 14–16 (14.9) mm., tars. 12–14 (13.3) mm.
12 females wing 112–124 (116.3) mm., tail 95–108 (103.2) mm.,
exp. cul. 14–16 (15.0) mm., tars. 12–14 (12.8) mm.

Known only from the lower Sinú valley, north-western Colombia.

7. *P. p. caeruleiceps* Todd   *Illustrated on page 437.*

ADULTS similar to *subandina*, but crown blue; ear-coverts greyish-white; lores and frontal band red, becoming more brownish on upper cheeks and periophthalmic region; feathers of sides of neck, throat, and upper breast more broadly edged with greyish-buff.
3 males wing 119–126 (123.0) mm., tail 102–120 (112.7) mm.,
exp. cul. 14–16 (15.0) mm., tars. 12–13 (12.7) mm.
3 females wing 120–123 (121.0) mm., tail 113–116 (114.3) mm.,
exp. cul. 13–15 (14.3) mm., tars. 13–14 (13.3) mm.

Known only from the western slopes of the eastern Andes in Magdalena and Norte de Santander, northern Colombia.

Thick-billed Parrot 1
Rhynchopsitta pachyrhyncha pachyrhyncha
AMNH. 703756 ad. ♂

Maroon-fronted Parrot 2
Rhynchopsitta pachyrhyncha terrisi
MLZ. 42496 ad. ♂

The Painted Conure is common in most parts of its range, the apparent notable exception being northern Colombia, yet there is little recorded information on its habits. According to Haverschmidt (1968) it is not uncommon in Surinam, where it occurs in flocks in the forests of the sand ridges in the coastal region and in the interior. In Guyana it frequents coastal rivers and forests in the interior, being recorded as common at Nappi in the south-east (Snyder, 1966). In Venezuela and northern Colombia it inhabits forests in the tropical zone (Phelps and Phelps, 1958; Meyer de Schauensee, 1964).

Food consists of seeds, fruits, nuts, berries, and possibly insects and their larvae. The stomach from a specimen collected at Cachimbo, Pará, Brazil, contained crushed seeds, and from another specimen collected on the Xingú River, also in Pará, thirteen Diptera larvae which were probably ingested in infested fruit (Schubart *et al.*, 1965).

CALL A monosyllabic *eek*; also flocking screams *ee-ee-m* on a descending scale (Snyder, 1966).

NESTING Bond and Meyer de Schauensee (1943) report that a female collected at Teoponte, La Paz, Bolivia, in mid-August was in breeding condition. A male with enlarged testes (USNM. 372611) was collected in mid-June near El Carmen, Norte de Santander, northern Colombia. In Surinam, eggs have been found in February (Hellebrekers, 1941). Penard and Penard (1908) claim that the normal clutch comprises three or four eggs.

EGGS Elliptical; 26.5 × 19.1 mm. are the average measurements of two eggs in the Leiden Museum Collection [Hellebrekers, 1941].

SANTA MARTA CONURE
Pyrrhura viridicata Todd   *Illustrated on page 433.*

DESCRIPTION Length 25 cm.
ADULTS general plumage green; narrow red frontal band; purplish-brown ear-coverts; feathers of

hindneck conspicuously tipped with purplish-brown; feathers of sides of neck, throat, and breast very faintly tipped with purplish-brown; abdomen variably and irregularly marked with orange-red; bend of wing and under wing-coverts yellow variably marked with orange-red; primary-coverts greenish-blue; outer webs of primaries blue; tail above green, below dusky reddish-brown; bill horn-coloured; iris brown; legs grey.
IMMATURES undescribed.

 10 males wing 140–146 (142.1) mm., tail 108–123 (114.2) mm.,
    exp. cul. 16–17 (16.5) mm., tars. 14–16 (14.6) mm.
 8 females wing 137–143 (139.4) mm., tail 104–118 (113.0) mm.,
    exp. cul. 15–17 (16.0) mm., tars. 14–16 (15.0) mm.

DISTRIBUTION Known only from the Santa Marta Mountains, northern Colombia.

GENERAL NOTES Very little is known of the habits of the Santa Marta Conure. Meyer de Schauensee (1970) says that it inhabits forests and grassy mountain scrub in the subtropical zone. Most, if not all, specimens, have been collected between 2,100 and 2,400 m. In November 1920, on the summit of San Lorenzo, Carriker collected a female from a flock of about sixteen and found that all birds were very timid (in Todd and Carriker, 1922).

CALL Undescribed.

NESTING A male with enlarged testes (USNM.386844) was collected in mid-September. Nothing is known of the nesting habits.

EGGS Undescribed.

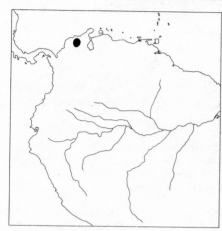

FIERY-SHOULDERED CONURE
Pyrrhura egregia (Sclater)

DESCRIPTION Length 25 cm.
ADULTS general plumage green; narrow brown frontal band; feathers of crown, nape and lores brown edged with green; reddish-brown ear-coverts; feathers of sides of neck, throat and upper breast green edged with yellowish-white and tipped with dusky brown, thus giving a barred appearance; centre of abdomen variably suffused with brownish-red, well-defined in some birds and almost absent in others; bend of wing, carpal edge, and under wing-coverts yellow extensively marked with orange; primary-coverts, and outer webs of primaries and secondaries blue; tail above dark reddish-brown basally marked with green, below greyish; bill horn-coloured; iris hazel; legs grey.
IMMATURES yellow and orange-red on bend of wing much reduced; carpal edge and lesser under wing-coverts green; crown and nape uniformly green; less pronounced barring on throat and breast.

DISTRIBUTION South-eastern Venezuela and adjoining regions of western Guyana and extreme north-eastern Roraima, Brazil.

SUBSPECIES 1. *P. e. egregia* (Sclater)   *Illustrated on page 433.*
 10 males wing 129–139 (133.9) mm., tail 108–116 (112.7) mm.,
    exp. cul. 15–17 (16.3) mm., tars. 13–14 (13.7) mm.
 10 females wing 125–133 (128.5) mm., tail 99–117 (108.2) mm.,
    exp. cul. 15–17 (16.2) mm., tars. 13–14 (13.5) mm.
 Occurs in western Guyana and neighbouring south-eastern Venezuela in the vicinity of Mount Roraima, Bolívar.

 2. *P. e. obscura* Zimmer and Phelps
 ADULTS like *egregia*, but upperparts darker green and lower parts slightly darker green.
 8 males wing 122–130 (126.9) mm., tail 105–117 (112.8) mm.,
    exp. cul. 15–17 (16.3) mm., tars. 14–15 (14.3) mm.
 8 females wing 127–131 (128.5) mm., tail 95–113 (106.9) mm.,
    exp. cul. 16–17 (16.4) mm., tars. 14–15 (14.1) mm.
 Confined to extreme north-eastern Roraima, Brazil (see Pinto, 1966), and adjacent extreme south-eastern Venezuela in the Gran Sabana, Bolívar, except in the vicinity of Mount Roraima where *egregia* occurs.

Mayr and Phelps (1967) point out that the Fiery-shouldered Conure is a characteristic bird of the Pantepui area, that is the isolated tabletop mountains in southern Venezuela, though in neighbouring western Guyana it does occur at tropical altitudes. Snyder (1966) says that it inhabits forested areas of western Guyana. Nothing is known of its habits.

Carolina Parakeet
Conuropsis carolinensis carolinensis
USNM. 132094 ad. ♂

MAROON-TAILED CONURE
Pyrrhura melanura (Spix)

Length 24 cm.

ADULTS general plumage green; reddish-brown forehead; feathers of crown brown edged with green; ear-coverts and cheeks green; feathers of sides of neck, throat, and upper breast green narrowly edged with greyish-buff and tipped with dusky brown, thus giving a barred appearance; under wing-coverts green; outermost primaries blue narrowly margined on outer webs with green; primary-coverts red tipped with yellow, the yellow increasing on innermost coverts; tail above brownish-red narrowly marked with green towards base, below greyish; prominent naked periophthalmic ring white; bill grey; iris dark brown, legs grey.
IMMATURES like adults.

From Colombia, except the Santa Marta region, and southern Venezuela south to the Negro River, Amazonas, north-western Brazil, and through Ecuador to north-eastern Peru.

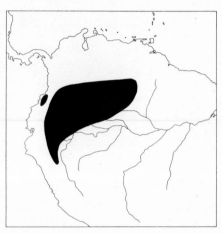

1. *P. m. melanura* (Spix)
   6 males   wing 128–133 (130.8) mm., tail 106–111 (108.5) mm.,
              exp. cul. 15–16 (15.3) mm., tars. 14–15 (14.3) mm.
   6 females wing 125–134 (128.8) mm., tail 98–110 (108.5) mm.,
              exp. cul. 15–16 (15.2) mm., tars. 13–15 (13.7) mm.

   Confined to north-eastern Peru, extreme eastern and southern Columbia, north-western Amazonas, Brazil, and southernmost Venezuela in southern Amazonas and central Bolívar.

2. *P. m. souancei* (Verreaux)   *Illustrated on page 457.*
   ADULTS like *melanura*, but breast feathers broadly margined with greyish-white; no yellow tips to red primary-coverts; carpal edge orange-red; abdomen tinged with brownish-red, forming an indistinct patch in some birds; upper side of tail more broadly marked with green towards base.
   7 males   wing 130–136 (133.0) mm., tail 98–117 (108.4) mm.,
              exp. cul. 15–16 (15.6) mm., tars. 14–15 (14.3) mm.
   6 females wing 128–137 (132.3) mm., tail 102–115 (108.3) mm.,
              exp. cul. 15–16 (15.3) mm., tars. 13–14 (13.8) mm.

   Occurs east of the Andes in Meta and Caquetá, Colombia, in eastern Ecuador, and in northern Peru. Bond (1955) points out that intergradation with *melanura* is to be expected in northern Peru.

3. *P. m. berlepschi* Salvadori   *Illustrated on page 457.*
   ADULTS similar to *souancei*, but feathers of sides of neck, throat, and breast more broadly margined with buff-white and tipped with dusky brown; cheeks brighter green with an olive tinge; abdomen more consistently tinged with brownish-red.
   No males examined.
   1 female (**type**); wing 135 mm., tail 105 mm.,
                        exp. cul. 16 mm., tars. 14 mm.

   Known only from the Huallaga River valley, eastern Peru. The status of this form is uncertain; it is generally regarded as a distinct species, but I suspect that specimens may be merely aberrant examples of *souancei*.

4. *P. m. pacifica* Chapman
   ADULTS like *melanura*, but forehead and forecrown green; no yellow tips to primary-coverts; feathers of breast very narrowly margined with buff-white; no reddish-brown on abdomen; upper side of tail more red, less brownish; shorter tail; no prominent naked periophthalmic ring.
   5 males   wing 125–136 (129.2) mm., tail 90–100 (95.2) mm.,
              exp. cul. 16–17 (16.4) mm., tars. 14–15 (14.6) mm.
   1 female   wing 124 mm., tail 92 mm.,
              exp. cul. 16 mm., tars. 15 mm.

   Known only from the Pacific slopes of the Andes in Nariño, south-western Colombia. This is the only form of *Pyrrhura* found west of the Andes.

Patagonian Conure
Cyanoliseus patagonus patagonus
AM. 08885 ad. unsexed

5. *P. m. chapmani* Bond and Meyer de Schauensee
   ADULTS like *souancei*, but feathers of throat, breast, and entire neck, including hindneck, brown margined with greyish-white; upper mantle with bluish tinge; forehead and forecrown brown; reddish-brown bases to ear-coverts showing through; more pronounced reddish-brown marking on abdomen; upper side of tail narrowly marked with green towards base.
   12 males   wing 137–145 (140.3) mm., tail 111–128 (121.8) mm.,
              exp. cul. 17–18 (17.2) mm., tars. 14–16 (14.4) mm.
   14 females wing 132–147 (139.0) mm., tail 110–132 (120.1) mm.,
              exp. cul. 16–18 (17.2) mm., tars. 13–16 (14.1) mm.

   Confined to the subtropical zone between 1,600 and 2,800 m. on the eastern slope of the Central Andes in southern Colombia from Belén, Caquetá, north to Gaitania, Tolima.

In southern Venezuela the Maroon-tailed Conure is locally distributed in forests of the tropical zone (Phelps and Phelps, 1958). In Colombia it is generally distributed in forests of the tropical zone, except in the south on the eastern slopes of the Central Andes where *chapmani* is confined to forests in the subtropical zone. Lehmann (1957) points out that in the Moscopán region, Cauca, he has not found *chapmani* below 1,950 m. According to Chapman (1926) it occurs in the subtropical zone of eastern Ecuador. It is common throughout most of its range. Dugand and Borrero (1948) report that in the vicinity of Tres Esquinas, Caquetá, southern Colombia, it and the Cobalt-winged Parakeet (*Brotogeris cyanoptera*) are the most common parrots.

Lehmann says that these parrots fly about in groups of from six to twelve individuals, at times in large flocks. They often pause to rest in trees for a few minutes before continuing their journey. They frequent tall and medium-sized forest trees, but will come into low ones to feed. They are restless and loquacious but at the approach of danger will freeze and suddenly become silent. When passing over cleared land they occasionally fly close to the ground and Lehmann remarks that at times they have almost brushed against him.

They feed on seeds, fruits, nuts, berries and probably blossoms.

Blue-throated Conure *Pyrrhura cruentata* 1
NMV. 23519 ad. ♂

Crimson-bellied Conure *Pyrrhura rhodogaster* 2
NHM. 40872 ad. ♂

CALL In flight a shrieking note is given at regular intervals.

NESTING At the headwaters of the Napo River, eastern Ecuador, nesting has been recorded in April, May, and June (Goodfellow, 1900).

Rhodes (1970) gives details of a successful breeding in captivity. Four eggs were laid, but only two hatched. The incubation period was not determined precisely, but was estimated to have been approximately twenty-five days. The first young bird to leave the nest did so seven weeks after hatching, and the second left a week later.

EGGS Undescribed.

BLACK-CAPPED CONURE
Pyrrhura rupicola (Tschudi)

DESCRIPTION

Length 25 cm.
ADULTS general plumage green; forehead, crown, and occiput brownish-black; sides of head, including superciliary line, green; feathers of hindneck brownish-black narrowly edged with buff-white; feathers of sides of neck, throat, and upper breast dark brown edged with buff-white or with dull yellow on lower breast, thus giving a scalloped appearance; bend of wing green; carpal edge and primary-coverts red; under wing-coverts green; outer webs of primaries green slightly tinged with blue; tail green above, greyish below; bill grey; iris brown; legs dark grey.
IMMATURES similar to adults, but carpal edge green with a few red feathers.

DISTRIBUTION

Central and south-eastern Peru, northern Bolivia, and extreme north-western Brazil.

SUBSPECIES

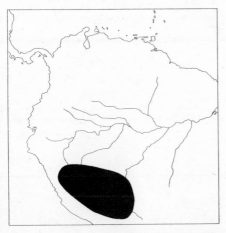

1. *P. r. rupicola* (Tschudi)
   4 males   wing 129–133 (131.0) mm., tail 110–120 (116.5) mm.,
             exp. cul. 16–17 (16.3) mm., tars. 13–16 (14.5) mm.
   3 females wing 124–135 (128.7) mm., tail 105–119 (110.7) mm.,
             exp. cul. 16–17 (16.4) mm., tars. 14–15 (14.4) mm.
   Confined to central Peru.

2. *P. r. sandiae* Bond and Meyer de Schauensee   *Illustrated on page 440.*
   ADULTS like *rupicola*, but with narrower buff-white edges to feathers of neck and breast, particularly on hindneck where almost absent.
   5 males   wing 123–126 (125.2) mm., tail 96–109 (102.8) mm.,
             exp. cul. 15–16 (15.8) mm., tars. 13–14 (13.8) mm.
   5 females wing 119–135 (126.4) mm., tail 96–123 (108.0) mm.,
             exp. cul. 14–17 (15.6) mm., tars. 13–16 (15.0) mm.
   Distributed from Junín and southern Loreto, south-eastern Peru, to Acre, extreme north-western Brazil, and Beni, northern Bolivia; probably not distinct from *rupicola* (Bond, 1955; Meyer de Schauensee pers. comm., 1971).

GENERAL NOTES

Very little is known of the habits of the Black-capped Conure. In southern Loreto, south-eastern Peru, it has been collected at about 300 m. (LSUMZ Collection), and in northern Bolivia at about 170 m. (NHRS Collection).

WHITE-NECKED CONURE

Pyrrhura albipectus Chapman

Illustrated on page 440.

Length 24 cm.

ADULTS general plumage green; very narrow reddish-brown frontal band; crown and nape greyish-brown, feathers finely tipped with buff-white; ear-coverts orange-yellow; cheeks green, feathers tipped with pale yellow; white collar encircling neck, on foreneck merging into yellow of breast; abdomen tinged with reddish-brown; bend of wing green with a few scattered red feathers; carpal edge and primary-coverts red; under wing-coverts green; outer webs of primaries deep blue; outer webs of secondaries bluish-green; bill greyish-brown; iris brown; legs dark grey.

IMMATURES undescribed.

1 male	wing 141 mm., tail 100 mm., exp. cul. 17 mm., tars. 16 mm.
1 female (**type**);	wing 135 mm., tail 107 mm., exp. cul. 17 mm., tars. 15 mm.

DISTRIBUTION   Known only from south-eastern Ecuador.

GENERAL NOTES   The White-necked Conure is an inhabitant of the subtropical forests (Meyer de Schauensee, 1970), but virtually nothing is known of its habits.

BROWN-BREASTED CONURE

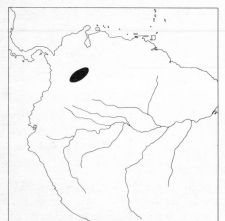

Pyrrhura calliptera (Massena and Souancé)

Illustrated on page 440.

Length 22 cm.

ADULTS general plumage green; crown and nape dusky brown tinged with dull blue and green, particularly on crown; ear-coverts reddish-brown; cheeks green, dusky bases to feathers showing through; feathers of sides of neck, throat, and upper breast rufous edged with pale brown and tipped with dusky black, thus giving an indistinct barring; abdomen tinged with reddish-brown; bend of wing green; carpal edge and primary-coverts yellow; outer webs of primaries greenish-blue; under wing-coverts green with some yellow feathers; tail brownish-red more dusky below; bill horn-coloured; iris yellowish-brown; legs brownish.

IMMATURES like adults, but primary-coverts green.

7 males	wing 134–156 (142.1) mm., tail 96–113 (103.3) mm., exp. cul. 16–18 (16.7) mm., tars. 14–16 (15.1) mm.
1 female	wing 141 mm., tail 113 mm., exp. cul. 18 mm., tars. 15 mm.

Has been recorded from Boyacá and Cundinamarca, central Colombia.

The Brown-breasted Conure is a forest bird and occurs in the subtropical and lower temperate zones along the eastern Andes (Meyer de Schauensee, 1964). Chapman (1917) remarks that it was common in the subtropical zone of the Eastern Andes. Olivares (1969) says that in Cundinamarca it inhabits cold, montane moorlands; at Páramo de Guasca he collected a female that was with four other birds in stubble. Little is known of its habits, though presumably they are similar to those of other species in the genus.

Santa Marta Conure *Pyrrhura viridicata*   **1**
USNM. 386837 ad. ♀

Fiery-shouldered Conure   **2**
Pyrrhura egregia egregia
COP. 4087 ad. ♂

Pearly Conure *Pyrrhura perlata lepida*   **3**
ANSP. 22391 ad. unsexed

RED-EARED CONURE

Pyrrhura hoematotis Souancé

Length 25 cm.

ADULTS general plumage green; forehead and forecrown brown, feathers variably edged with dull blue; occiput and nape olive-green variably tinged or marked with dull brownish-yellow; cheeks green; ear-coverts brownish-red; feathers of sides of neck margined with brownish-grey; throat and upper breast green tinged with olive, feathers faintly tipped with dusky grey; centre of abdomen variably suffused with brownish-red; under tail-coverts bluish-green; under wing-coverts green; carpal edge greenish-blue; primary-coverts and outer webs of primaries blue; tail brownish-red tipped with olive-green; bill brownish-grey; iris brown; legs grey.

IMMATURES undescribed.

DISTRIBUTION   Northern Venezuela.

GENERAL NOTES   1. *P. h. hoematotis* Souancé   *Illustrated on page 457.*

10 males	wing 121–132 (128.4) mm., tail 98–121 (112.3) mm., exp. cul. 16–18 (16.6) mm., tars. 13–15 (14.0) mm.
10 females	wing 125–133 (129.3) mm., tail 109–119 (114.2) mm., exp. cul. 15–17 (16.1) mm., tars. 13–15 13.8) mm.

Generally distributed along the coastal range of north-central Venezuela from Aragua through the Federal district to Miranda.

2. *P. h. immarginata* Zimmer and Phelps
ADULTS like *hoematotis*, but without brownish-grey margins to feathers of sides of neck; no brownish-yellow tinge or markings on occiput and nape; feathers of breast with light subterminal bands but not dusky grey margins.
1 male   wing 137 mm., tail 103 mm.,
         exp. cul. 17 mm., tars. 16 mm.
2 females   wing 135–138 (136.5) mm., tail 103–110 (106.5) mm.,
         exp. cul. 17 (17.0) mm., tars. 15 (15.0) mm.
Known only from Cubiro, Lara, northern Venezuela, the type locality.

The Red-eared Conure inhabits forests in the subtropical zone (Phelps and Phelps, 1958). Schafer and Phelps (1954) point out that it is characteristic of mountain forests, and occurs mainly on the southern slopes from 1,600 m. up to the highest peaks. It frequents both the montane forests and the high subtemperate savannah woodland, and occasionally even subtropical cloud forest where it is replaced by the Red-fronted Conure (*Aratinga wagleri*). At Rancho Grande Reserve it is quite common, particularly between December and March and in July, and flocks of from ten to one hundred may be seen in the forest canopy. Its brownish-red tail is conspicuous in flight.

Food comprises seeds, fruits, nuts, and berries. The stomach from a specimen collected at Rancho Grande was filled with reddish fruit (Beebe, 1947).

CALL Undescribed.

NESTING Schafer and Phelps state that at Rancho Grande nesting takes place in August, but no details are given.

EGGS Rounded; 4 eggs, 24.1 (24.0–24.5) × 21.3 (21.0–22.0) mm. [Schönwetter, 1964].

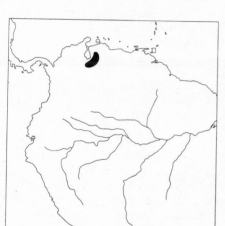

Green-cheeked Conure   1
Pyrrhura molinae molinae
ANSP. 143670 ad. ♂
Maroon-bellied Conure   2
Pyrrhura frontalis frontalis
USNM. 350843 ad. ♀
Blaze-winged Conure *Pyrrhura devillei*   3
MP. 18290 ad. ♀
Yellow-sided Conure *Pyrrhura hypoxantha*   4
AMNH. 474758 **type** ad. ♀

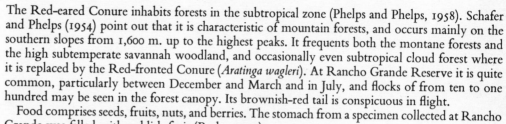

ROSE-CROWNED CONURE
Pyrrhura rhodocephala (Sclater and Salvin)   *Illustrated on page 440.*

Length 24 cm.
ADULTS general plumage green; forehead, crown, and occiput rose-red; ear-coverts maroon; reddish tinge on chin; cheeks green; feathers of sides of neck, throat, and breast green with dusky bases and faintly tipped with brown, thus giving a slight barring; centre of abdomen tinged with brownish-red; bend of wing green, sometimes with a few scattered orange feathers; carpal edge orange tinged with white; primary-coverts white; under wing-coverts green; outer webs of flight feathers violet-blue; tail brownish-red, dusky below; bill horn-coloured; iris brown; legs dark grey.
IMMATURES crown green tinged with dull blue and with scattered rose-red feathers; primary-coverts blue; upper side of tail basally tinged with green.
9 males   wing 130–142 (137.0) mm., tail 97–115 (107.9) mm.,
       exp. cul. 16–18 (16.6) mm., tars. 14–15 (14.6) mm.
7 females   wing 130–137 (134.0) mm., tail 100–110 (105.3) mm.,
       exp. cul. 16–17 (16.4) mm., tars. 14–16 (14.6) mm.

DISTRIBUTION   Known only from the Cordillera de Mérida in Táchira, Mérida, and Trujillo, western Venezuela.

GENERAL NOTES   The Rose-crowned Conure inhabits forests in the subtropical zone (Phelps and Phelps, 1958), but very little is known of its habits.

HOFFMAN'S CONURE
Pyrrhura hoffmanni (Cabanis)

DESCRIPTION   Length 24 cm.
ADULTS (plumage variable); general plumage green; feathers of head and throat variably shaft-streaked and tipped with yellow; ear-coverts dark red; reddish spot on chin; feathers of throat and breast with faint dusky or dull orange-yellow tips; outer webs of outermost primaries blue, becoming green towards tips; primary-coverts, inner primaries, and outer secondaries yellow becoming green towards tips; under wing-coverts green; undersides of flight feathers dull olive-yellow; tail above reddish-olive margined with green, below dull brownish-red tipped with olive; bill horn-coloured; iris brown to pale greyish-white; legs grey.
IMMATURES similar to adults.

DISTRIBUTION   Southern Costa Rica and western Panama.

W.T.Cooper. 72.

1. *P. h. hoffmanni* (Cabanis)
   10 males   wing 132–140 (134.4) mm., tail 105–111 (107.6) mm.,
        exp. cul. 16–18 (16.9) mm., tars. 13–15 (14.4) mm.
   8 females   wing 126–133 (130.4) mm., tail 102–106 (105.0) mm.,
        exp. cul. 16–17 (16.5) mm., tars. 14–15 (14.5) mm.

Illustrated on page 457.

   Occurs in the highlands of southern Costa Rica north to the hilly Caribbean approaches to the central plateau, but apparently does not quite reach the Cordillera Central.

2. *P. h. gaudens* Bangs
   ADULTS like *hoffmanni*, but feathers of crown and occiput shaft-streaked with greenish-yellow and orange red, and faintly tipped with dull red; underparts slightly darker green, less yellowish.
   IMMATURES like *hoffmanni* as there are no orange-red or dull red markings on crown and occiput.
   10 males   wing 133–148 (137.6) mm., tail 106–114 (108.8) mm.,
        exp. cul. 15–18 (16.5) mm., tars. 14–15 (14.7) mm.
   10 females   wing 130–140 (136.0) mm., tail 104–111 (108.2) mm.,
        exp. cul. 15–18 (16.2) mm., tars. 14–15 (14.7) mm.

   Confined to the mountains of western Panama in western Chiriquí and on the Caribbean slope in Bocas del Toro.

In Costa Rica Hoffmann's Conure is found from the middle of the subtropical belt well into the lower montane belt, though at times it occurs a little lower to about 1,000 m. (Slud, 1964). It normally frequents forested ridges and hillsides in partly wooded country. In montane oak forest at La Chonta, 2,380 m. on the Cordillera de Talamanca, Orians (1969) found that it frequented closed forest and secondary growth, where it fed in the canopies of tall forest trees and the smaller understorey trees. According to Wetmore (1968) its range in Panama is along the middle elevations of the great Chiriquí volcano, including Cerro Pando and the westward spurs to the Quebrada Santa Clara; he points out that it has been recorded from above Boquete, at about 500 m., up to 3,000 m., though its normal limit seems to be about 2,430 m. A specimen collected near Cricamola in February 1928 is the only lowland record.

These parrots are generally seen in pairs or small flocks and are most conspicuous when flying through open tree growth. In dense forest they are difficult to locate and an observer gets little more than a fleeting glimpse as they disappear through the trees. At times they can be seen flying low across semi-open country. As they fly past the red of their ear-coverts is often visible or their wings flash yellow in the sunlight. They are normally wary and difficult to approach, but sometimes feeding birds will remain seemingly oblivious to an observer standing within a few metres of the branches in which they are sitting. The flight is swift and direct.

They feed on seeds, fruits, nuts, berries, and blossoms, procured in trees and shrubs. Near Cerro Punta, Chiriquí, western Panama, Leck and Hilty (1968) observed them in the company of many other fruit-eating birds feeding on the fruits of the shrub *Leandra subseriata*.

CALL Slud says that these parrots chatter without screaming, and the unparrot-like cries of a flock can sound like a whirring or bring to mind a noisy group of songbirds; at times they emit a harsh continuous *ack-ack-ack-ack*, which is similar to the call of the Orange-chinned Parakeet (*Brotogeris jugularis*).

NESTING Blake (1958) reports that a male collected in the Chiriquí volcano area in mid-May had enlarged testes, although it was still in immature plumage. Nothing further is known of the nesting habits.

EGGS Undescribed.

Genus ENICOGNATHUS G. R. Gray

I have followed Peters and Blake (1948) by incorporating *Microsittace* Bonaparte in this genus.

The two species in *Enicognathus* are medium-sized parrots with long, gradated tails. The bill is proportionately small, and in one species the upper mandible is less curved and elongated. The cere is completely feathered. The plumage colouration is remarkably similar in the two species, and is characterized by dark edging to the feathers, thus giving a barred appearance. Sexual dimorphism is absent and young birds resemble adults.

AUSTRAL CONURE
Enicognathus ferrugineus (P. L. S. Müller)

Length 33 cm.

Painted Conure *Pyrrhura picta roseifrons*   1
NHRS. 552779 ad. ♂

Painted Conure *Pyrrhura picta picta*   2
QM. 012122 ad. ♂

Painted Conure *Pyrrhura picta caeruleiceps*   3
USNM. 372611 ad. ♂

White-eared Conure *Pyrrhura leucotis leucotis*   4
USNM. 368164 ad. ♂

ADULTS general plumage dull green, all feathers with dusky tips thus giving a barred appearance; crown slightly tinged with blue and feathers broadly tipped with greyish-black; forehead and lores dull reddish-brown; brownish-red patch in centre of abdomen; primaries and primary-coverts green tinged with blue; tail brownish-red faintly tipped with green; bill grey; iris reddish-brown; legs grey.

IMMATURES similar to adults, but reddish markings on forehead and abdomen duller and less extensive.

DISTRIBUTION

SUBSPECIES

GENERAL NOTES

Brown-breasted Conure *Pyrrhura calliptera* **1**
CM. 21986 ad. ♂

Black-capped Conure *Pyrrhura rupicola sandiae* **2**
LSUMZ. 63929 ad. ♂

Rose-crowned Conure *Pyrrhura rhodocephala* **3**
CM. 28871 ad. ♂

White-necked Conure *Pyrrhura albipectus* **4**
ANSP. 167552 ad. ♂

From Colchagua, Chile, and Neuquén, Argentina, south to Tierra del Fuego; the most southerly distributed of all parrots.

1. *E. f. ferrugineus* (P. L. S. Müller)
   10 males wing 187–203 (195.6) mm., tail 153–177 (169.1) mm., exp. cul. 19–21 (19.9) mm., tars. 17–19 (17.8) mm.
   10 females wing 190–204 (197.8) mm., tail 148–178 (167.1) mm., exp. cul. 19–21 (20.0) mm., tars. 17–19 (18.2) mm.
   Confined to southernmost Chile in the province of Magallanes and to the eastern slopes of the Andes in southern Argentina from south-western Chubut south to Tierra del Fuego.

2. *E. f. minor* (Chapman)   *Illustrated on page 460.*
   ADULTS general plumage darker green, less yellowish; brownish-red abdominal patch darker and less extensive; slightly smaller size.
   8 males wing 176–190 (181.3) mm., tail 151–169 (160.9) mm., exp. cul. 18–21 (19.4) mm., tars. 17–19 (17.5) mm.
   8 females wing 177–193 (183.5) mm., tail 148–170 (159.0) mm., exp. cul. 18–21 (19.5) mm., tars. 17–19 (17.6) mm.
   Occurs in southern Chile from Colchagua south to Aysén and the eastern slopes of the Andes in south-western Argentina from Neuquén south to western Chubut.

Austral Conures are common inhabitants of the *Nothofagus* forests of southern Chile and Argentina. They also frequent other wooded areas and semi-open country. Housse (1949) claims that they are more numerous in continental Chile, where conditions are more favourable than in Tierra del Fuego and islands in the Straits of Magellan. Johnson (1967) quotes a report claiming that in recent years they have greatly increased in numbers in forests of oak and canelo (*Drimys winteri*) in the Cordillera de Lontué, southern Chile. Olrog (1948) reports that they were abundant in the southern forests of Tierra del Fuego and in every forested locality in Valdivia province, southern Chile, visited by the Swedish Museum Expedition during 1939–1941. Bernath (1965) records sightings of numerous flocks at several localities along the Straits of Magellan and north to Lake Balmaceda, Magallanes, southernmost Chile. Johansen (1966) says that the parrots are very common in all forests and in parklands on the 'estancias' or ranches throughout Tierra del Fuego; he found them to be most abundant during January 1964 in tall beech (*Nothofagus pumilio*) forests near Lapataia on the Beagle Channel and at Viamonte, both localities on Isla Grande in Argentinian territory. Humphrey *et al.* (1970) point out that on Isla Grande they are most common in southern forested districts along the Beagle Channel and there are relatively few records from northern parts of the island. In southernmost parts of their range these parrots are resident throughout the year, despite the very severe winter, but in the north there are irregular seasonal movements. Referring to *minor*, the northern subspecies, Housse says that the parrots are found up to about 1,200 m. in the Andes during September to March, and then large flocks come down to the foothills and disperse across the coastal valley. In July and August they move farther westward eventually reaching the wooded hills close to the Pacific coast. These movements are irregular with respect to time of the year, distances travelled, and numbers of birds involved; the severity of winter conditions in the mountains seems to be the major influencing factor, though availability of food in the lowlands almost certainly has an important bearing on local distribution. In the coastal valley, where they can cause considerable damage to crops, their distribution is sporadic and unpredictable; they may be absent altogether from some areas for up to three or five years.

These parrots associate in flocks of from ten to a hundred or more. They are largely arboreal and spend much of the day in trees and shrubs searching for food. While feeding in the treetops they scramble about with their bodies low, close to the branches, and this, coupled with their predominantly green plumage, makes them quite inconspicuous. They usually alight on the topmost branches of a tree and make their way down into the canopy to feed. When not feeding a flock will often perch on the uppermost branches of a dead tree, each bird facing into the wind. Housse claims that they roost hanging upside down from a thin branch, but I know of no other reference to such an unusual habit. They are tame and will normally allow a close approach, especially while feeding. They are noisy when in flight and their screeching call-notes attract attention as flocks fly past. The flight is swift and direct; sometimes they will fly only 2 or 3 m. above the ground, rising over or detouring around low bushes and then continuing on their straight path.

Food consists of seeds, fruits, berries, leaf buds, and bulbous roots. They are fond of grass seeds, acorns, and the leaf buds of *Nothofagus* and colihués (*Chusquea quila*). A favourite food is the seeds of *Araucaria araucana* and swarms of parrots come into the *Araucaria* forests when these seeds are ripe. In farmlands considerable damage can be done when these parrots raid ripening crops to feed on grain.

439

CALL In flight or when disturbed in the treetops the parrots give a raucous, metallic, interrupted screech, somewhat like the call of the Monk Parakeet (*Myiopsitta monachus*).

NESTING Johnson reports that nesting takes place in December. The nest is in a hollow or hole in a tree, favourite sites being natural hollows or deserted woodpeckers' holes in large, old oak trees that have been killed by forest fires. If the hollow is deep the birds will almost fill it with broken twigs and then add a few dry leaves and some feathers. Undisturbed nesting hollows are used for several years. Housse says that if hollows in trees are not available the parrots will build a nest of twigs or even grass stems amongst the dense foliage of the bamboo-like *Chusquea*. Four to seven, occasionally eight, eggs are laid, but nothing further is known of the breeding behaviour.

EGGS Rounded, slightly glossy; 7 eggs, 30.8 (30.0–32.0) × 24.9 (24.5–25.3) mm. [Johnson, 1967].

SLENDER-BILLED CONURE
Enicognathus leptorhynchus (King)

Illustrated on page 460.

DESCRIPTION

Length 40 cm.
ADULTS general plumage dull green, a little brighter on head, all feathers tipped with dusky brown; feathers of crown broadly edged with greyish-black; forehead, lores, and periophthalmic region dull crimson-red; brownish-red tinge on abdomen; primary-coverts bluish-green; outer webs of primaries green tinged with blue towards tips; tail brownish-red faintly tipped with green; bill brownish-grey; iris red; legs brownish.
IMMATURES like adults, but general plumage darker green, less yellowish; shorter upper mandible, and bill tipped horn-coloured; skin surrounding eye whitish instead of grey.
10 males wing 212–226 (218.9) mm., tail 160–197 (179.3) mm.,
      exp. cul. 32–37 (33.9) mm., tars. 21–23 (22.1) mm.
10 females wing 206–219 (212.9) mm., tail 150–185 (170.9) mm.,
      exp. cul. 27–34 (30.7) mm., tars. 21–25 (22.4) mm.

DISTRIBUTION

Confined to central Chile from Aconcagua south to Chiloé Island and occasionally to northern Aysén.

GENERAL NOTES

Slender-billed Conures are essentially forest birds, though they may be also found in semi-open country and farmlands, especially during winter when they are more prevalent in the lowlands. Johnson (1967) points out that their centre of distribution lies between Cautín and Chiloé Island, that is from latitudes 38° to 43° South. Away from this region they become less common and more sporadically distributed, being confined mainly to forested mountain ranges and adjacent valleys. Although still fairly common, there has been a marked decline in numbers, partly as a result of loss of habitat through clearing of forests, partly on account of excessive hunting, and in recent years also due to Newcastle disease, though not on the same scale as in the case of the Chilean Pigeon (*Columba araucana*) which was almost exterminated by the virus (Johnson, 1967). Housse (1949) points out that there are seasonal altitudinal movements; in May the parrots leave the hills and mountains to spend winter in the coastal lowlands, returning to the mountains in September.

These noisy parrots are very gregarious, remaining in flocks even while breeding. They are generally seen in the treetops or on the ground searching for seeds and berries, or flying overhead, and their continuous screeching attracts attention. Housse says that when coming down from the mountains they fly high in flocks of from fifty to three hundred. Each flock adopts a haphazard formation of three or four loosely-arranged lines, one behind the other. At times one or two birds will suddenly deviate to the right or left and confusion follows; those birds nearest the turn quickly follow and regroup, but those on the opposite end of the flock formation are left behind and take some time to wheel about and eventually catch up. In the lowlands their local distribution is centred on the roosting sites, which are patches of forest or dense stands of trees, including groves of introduced eucalypts. Housse describes one such roosting place found several kilometres from Los Angelès, Bio-Bio, in 1933. It was being used by about two thousand parrots, and at evening the noise was deafening as screeching flocks came in from all directions to join the large numbers of birds already there. It was dark before the noise died down. If a hawk appeared above the roost all parrots would rise into the air, screeching loudly, and circle overhead several times before gradually spiralling back down into the treetops. Birds have also been found roosting in the Santiago Botanic Gardens.

Early in the morning the parrots leave the roosting place, once again with continuous screeching, and disperse in all directions to their feeding areas. Here they spend the day feeding and periodically resting in trees. They are wary, and while the flock is feeding sentinels perch high up in neighbouring trees to warn of approaching danger. The flight is swift and direct with rapid wingbeats.

They feed on seeds, fruits, berries, nuts, leaf buds, and roots of various kinds. A favourite food is the nuts of *Araucaria araucana* and during March and April, when these are ripe, swarms of parrots come into the *Araucaria* forests; with their elongated bills they easily extract nuts from the cones. Sick (1968) says that at other times they feed extensively on seeds of *Nothofagus*, one of the dominant trees in the region; in early April, at Valdivia, he saw them eating acorns. They come to the ground to forage for seeds of grasses and thistles and to dig up bulbous roots. They attack ripening crops, often causing considerable damage, and will tear apart unripe apples to get at the pips.

CALL In flight or when disturbed these parrots keep up an almost incessant screeching; feeding is accompanied by a shrill chattering. All call-notes are raucous and can be heard from afar.

NESTING Johnson says that breeding occurs during November or December. The nest is in a hollow limb or hole in a tree and several occupied hollows may be found in one tree. Undisturbed hollows will be used for several years. Johnson says that nesting material is not used, but Housse reports that deep vertical hollows will be filled to within 20 cm. of the entrance with dry twigs which the birds bite off into small lengths and then drop inside.

Housse also claims that crevices in rocky cliff faces are sometimes used as nesting sites, and if no hollows are available the parrots will build a nest from dry twigs amongst the dense foliage of a tree or *Chusquea* clump. He describes a nest constructed by a female that lived at semi-liberty in a garden in Santiago. On branches of a box tree this parrot placed a number of twigs in a roughly criss-crossed pattern. Each day it added more twigs so that at the end of a week there was a roughly cylindrical structure about 50 cm. high and 20 cm. wide. Approximately 35 cm. up from the base an opening was made and this led to a platform which was lined with blades of grass and feathers.

Two to five, rarely six, eggs make up the clutch. According to Housse the female does most of the incubating, but for several hours during the day the male takes over while she goes to feed. Little is known of incubation or care of the young, but throughout the nesting period one parent always remains in close proximity to the nest.

EGGS Broadly ovate, glossy; 4 eggs, 31.4 (29.0–34.0) × 25.2 (23.2–26.5) mm. [Schönwetter, 1964].

Genus MYIOPSITTA Bonaparte

The species in this monotypic genus is a medium-sized parrot with a long, gradated tail. The heavy, robust bill is very broad with a somewhat rounded tip to the upper mandible, and there is a distinct notch in the upper mandible. The cere is completely feathered. Thompson (1900) points out that the orbital ring is incomplete and the auditory meatus narrow. There is no sexual dimorphism and young birds resemble adults.

MONK PARAKEET
Myiopsitta monachus (Boddaert)

Length 29 cm.

ADULTS forehead bluish-grey becoming brownish on crown and occiput; lores, cheeks, and throat pale grey; breast feathers brownish-grey tipped with greyish-white, thus giving a distinct barred appearance; olive-yellow band across upper abdomen; lower abdomen, flanks, thighs, and under tail-coverts bright yellowish-green; nape and hindneck bright green, contrasting with brownish-green of mantle; wings dull green; lower back, rump, and upper tail-coverts yellowish-green; lesser under wing-coverts green; greater under wing-coverts and inner webs of undersides of flight feathers pale blue; primary-coverts violet-blue; outer webs of primaries and secondaries deep blue narrowly margined with green; tail above green with blue down centre of each feather, below pale green with dull greyish-blue at base of each feather; bill brownish; iris dark brown; legs grey.
IMMATURES like adults, but grey forehead tinged with green.

From central Bolivia and southern Brazil south to central Argentina; recently introduced to, and apparently now established in, Puerto Rico and north-eastern United States.

1. *M. m. monachus* (Boddaert)
   10 males   wing 151–161 (156.7) mm., tail 126–144 (135.7) mm.,
         exp. cul. 19–21 (19.7) mm., tars. 18–21 (19.3) mm.
   8 females   wing 146–155 (149.8) mm., tail 122–145 (136.8) mm.,
         exp. cul. 18–20 (19.3) mm., tars. 17–19 (18.0) mm.

   Illustrated on page 461.

   Distributed from southern Rio Grande do Sul, extreme south-eastern Brazil, through Uruguay to north-eastern Argentina in the provinces of Entre Ríos, Santa Fe, Córdoba, and Buenos Aires.

2. *M. m. calita* (Jardine and Selby)
   ADULTS similar to *monachus*, but smaller in size and with smaller bill; head darker grey, without bluish tinge on forehead and forecrown; feathers of lower abdomen with marginal bluish tint; wing-coverts tinged with grey.
   3 males   wing 136–139 (137.7) mm., tail 119–131 (126.0) mm.,
         exp. cul. 17–18 (17.3) mm., tars. 15–16 (15.3) mm.
   2 females   wing 136–144 (140.0) mm., tail 129–130 (129.5) mm.,
         exp. cul. 17 (17.0) mm., tars. 17 (17.0) mm.

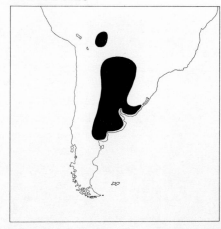

442

Occurs in western Argentina from Salta, Santiago del Estero and western Córdoba south to Mendoza and La Pampa; birds from Río Negro probably belong to this race.

3. **M. m. cotorra** (Vieillot)

ADULTS like *calita*, but upperparts distinctly brighter green; abdomen less yellowish.

10 males wing 133–147 (138.3) mm., tail 123–130 (126.8) mm.,
  exp. cul. 15–18 (16.8) mm., tars. 15–18 (16.2) mm.
10 females wing 131–140 (135.9) mm., tail 114–129 (120.7) mm.,
  exp. cul. 15–17 (16.4) mm., tars. 15–17 (16.4) mm.

Ranges from Tarija, south-eastern Bolivia, Paraguay, and southern Mato Grosso, Brazil, south to northern Argentina in Formosa and Chaco.

4. **M. m. luchsi** (Finsch)   *Illustrated on page 461.*

ADULTS forehead and forecrown uniformly pale grey, almost white; breast uniformly pale grey without barring; band across upper abdomen purer yellow, less olive; outer webs of primaries pale blue without green margins; tail above dark green with dark blue down centre of each feather, below greyish-blue; small size; narrower, more pointed bill.

10 males wing 150–163 (154.6) mm., tail 132–151 (142.1) mm.,
  exp. cul. 17–19 (18.5) mm., tars. 15–18 (16.6) mm.
8 females wing 146–151 (148.6) mm., tail 129–145 (138.1) mm.,
  exp. cul. 17–19 (17.8) mm., tars. 15–17 (15.9) mm.

This distinct subspecies is known only from Cochabamba province, central Bolivia.

GENERAL NOTES The Monk Parakeet is a familiar, abundant bird throughout most of its range and is common in captivity in many countries of the world. It is primarily a lowland bird, rarely occurring above 1,000 m., and is found in low rainfall areas in open forest, trees along watercourses, savannah woodland, dry *Acacia* scrubland, palm groves, farmlands, and orchards. It is particularly common in the vicinity of human habitation. The race *luchsi* from central Bolivia is an exception to these generalizations, being little-known and seldom recorded; at approximately 1,560 m., at Ele-Ele, Cochabamba, Carriker observed several flocks, always in heavy vegetation along the river in what was otherwise an arid region (in Bond and Meyer de Schauensee, 1943). The species is very common throughout the Chaco region of western Paraguay, south-eastern Bolivia, and north-western Argentina but towards the west becomes rare in the foothills of the Andes (see Eisentraut, 1935; Laubmann, 1930). Unger says that in western Paraguay it is common and has increased greatly with the spread of settlement (in Steinbacher, 1962). In south-western Mato Grosso, Brazil, Cherrie found it to be abundant at many points along the Paraguay River, particularly north of the mouth of the São Lourenco River (in Naumburg, 1930). It is common and widespread in Argentina, especially in the north where very large numbers are often encountered. Cuello and Gerzenstein (1962) point out that it is very abundant and generally distributed throughout Uruguay.

In many areas, the extensive planting of introduced trees, mainly *Eucalyptus*, has undoubtedly benefited these parrots by changing treeless plains into suitable habitat (see Gibson, 1919). In southern Uruguay and north-eastern Argentina Wetmore (1926) found Monk Parakeets in open country wherever trees offered shelter, especially in eucalypts around 'estancias' or ranches, in lowland palm groves, in open pastures studded with trees, and in dense forest bordering the Cebollati River; at Lavalle, Buenos Aires, north-eastern Argentina, a small colony was found inhabiting a clump of eucalypts in town. At the Río de Gastone, Tucumán, north-western Argentina, Friedmann (1927) found them in fairly open *Acacia*-dotted plains east of the river. Cherrie found that along the Paraguay River in south-western Mato Grosso, Brazil, the parrots frequented the narrow forested strip of high land separating the main river channel from vast marshlands extending out for many kilometres on either side (in Naumburg, 1930); however, Stone and Roberts (1935) report that in this region birds are found in isolated trees in the drier areas just as frequently as in the fringe of riverine forest. In late May 1971, near Camaquã, southern Rio Grande do Sul, Brazil, I saw them in fields of rice stubble throughout which were scattered groves of introduced *Eucalyptus* trees.

Kepler reports that about fourteen birds have been seen near San Juan, Puerto Rico, and the species is apparently established as a resident (in Bond, 1971b). There is now a resident population in south-eastern New York and the neighbouring regions of New Jersey and Connecticut, north-eastern United States (Bull pers. comm., 1972). Nests have been recorded from these areas and from Massachusetts, Virginia, and Florida, but to date actual breeding successes are known only from the New York metropolitan area. Bump (1971) points out that there are no records of attempts having been made to acclimatize the species in the United States and it is probable that the birds were turned loose, escaped from their owners, or were inadvertently liberated through handling mishaps at airports. Survival during winter is almost certainly assisted by the availability of food at numerous suburban bird-feeding stations. Summing up the present situation, Bull concludes that the species appears to be fairly well established in parts of north-eastern United States, but is only very locally distributed.

Movements have been reported from along the fringes of its range, but elsewhere the species seems to be sedentary. Eisentraut notes that in the vicinity of Villa Montes and the nearby foothills, Tarija, south-eastern Bolivia, it is present only during the dry season when isolated small flocks can be observed. Commenting on his observations of it at the Río de Gastone, Tucumán, north-western Argentina, Friedmann noted that no nests were found and the birds seemed to be wandering about aimlessly as he never saw them twice in the same place on successive days. In the Camaquã district, Rio Grande do Sul, southern Brazil, local residents told us that the parrots are absent during winter, thus indicating that a north to south movement takes place at a time when climatic conditions would be expected to produce the reverse. Furthermore, I gained the impression that the species may not breed in southern Rio Grande do Sul; occupants of a farm-house alongside a *Eucalyptus* tree in which there were three nests told us that they had looked for young birds in these nests, but none had been reared there during the past two years. I examined a fourth nest that had fallen from the tree during the previous night and found it to be quite loosely constructed, thus suggesting that it may have been used only for roosting.

Monk Parakeets are highly gregarious and associate in flocks of from ten to a hundred or more. Their presence in an area is known with certainty because of the enormous nests constructed from twigs and placed in the topmost branches of trees; these structures are unmistakable and cannot be overlooked. The nests are the foci of the birds' daily activities; some individuals are always in attendance and there is a scene of constant confusion as parrots continuously come and go, jostle and squabble with each other, and enter or emerge from entrance tunnels, all to the accompaniment of an incessant chattering. Small groups go out from the nesting trees and band together in large flocks to feed in open grassland or cultivated fields. While feeding away from shelter they are wary and difficult to approach; sentinels are usually perched atop nearby trees and at the appearance of danger they screech loudly causing the entire flock to fly off. Around the nesting trees they show alarm at being disturbed, but rarely move away altogether; at the approach of an intruder they abruptly cease chattering to watch intently for some time before rising into the air and circling overhead, screeching loudly all the while. The appearance of hawks in the sky above produces the same noisy reaction. They fly swiftly with rather rapid wingbeats and seldom rise more than 10 m. above the ground.

They feed on seeds, fruits, berries, nuts, leaf buds, blossoms, and insects and their larvae. Favourite foods include seeds of thistles, grasses, and various trees, especially tala (*Celtis tala*), and palm nuts. Friedmann reports that stomach contents from birds collected in Santa Fe, north-eastern Argentina, comprised soft green leguminous seeds. At Riacho Pilaga, north-western Argentina, Wetmore found these parrots feeding in a large field where recent ploughing had brought to the surface discarded sweet potatoes left from the previous years harvest. In La Pampa, central Argentina, Pereyra (1938) has seen them eating meat left hanging from trees to dry. However, it is their depredations on crops that have brought these parrots into conflict with man. Flocks descend on ripening cereal crops, particularly maize and sorghum, frequently causing widespread damage; they also raid citrus orchards. Present control measures, which include shooting and destruction of nests by setting them alight with petrol-soaked rags attached to long poles, are unsuccessful, largely because they are not based on a sound knowledge of the biology of the species.

CALL In flight or when active about the nest the parrots emit almost continuously a loud, staccato shrieking; feeding is accompanied by a high-pitched chattering.

NESTING Breeding commences in October. Eisentraut reports that in south-eastern Bolivia recently-hatched nestlings were present at the beginning of December, and in mid-December a nest was found to contain young of different ages, some being almost ready to leave. A female collected at the end of December had a strongly developed ovary, thus indicating that some birds may rear two broods in a season. At Fedegoso, south-western Mato Grosso, Brazil, a clutch of five eggs was taken from a nest at the end of November; one was just at the point of hatching, one was fresh, and the remaining three were in various stages of incubation (in Naumburg, 1930). Friedmann reports that birds in breeding condition were collected in Santa Fe, north-eastern Argentina, in mid-January. Pereyra says that in Buenos Aires province, north-eastern Argentina, incubation of eggs commences in mid-November.

The nest of this species is unique among parrots. It is a large, bulky structure built from dry twigs and placed in the topmost branches of a tree. Preference is shown for thorny twigs, presumably because they bind together better and provide extra protection against predators. Nests with a single chamber and occupied by only one pair are not uncommon, but it is the enormous communal nests occupied by many pairs that are so conspicuous. These are probably formed over a number of years as pairs build their nests alongside or on top of existing nests. Each pair has its own chamber or compartment with an entrance tunnel, and there are no connections between compartments. Nests containing up to twenty compartments have been recorded, and Hudson (1920) says that some nests could weigh as much as 200 kg.

Conway (1965) describes a nest found on the ground underneath a *Eucalyptus* tree near Castelli, Buenos Aires, north-eastern Argentina. Although broken it still measured more than 2m. from top to bottom and had four, possibly five compartments. The entrance to each compartment was on the lower side or underneath the nest and pointed obliquely downward, thus hindering access by predators. From the entrance a short tunnel led to a slightly wider 'porch' which in turn opened out into the brood chamber.

Birds use the nests throughout the year as roosting quarters, but with the approach of the breeding season they begin to add to them and to repair sections damaged by wind or rain. Despite its overall untidy, loose appearance the nest is strongly constructed from tightly inter-woven twigs. This strength is well demonstrated by the fact that a number of species of large birds, including Jabirus (*Jabiru mycteria*), Chimango Caracaras (*Milvago chimango*), and tree-ducks (*Dendrocygna* spp.), often nest on top of larger nests of Monk Parakeets.

444

Five to eight eggs are laid on a bed of twigs. It is very difficult, even in captivity, to observe what takes place in the brood chamber so little is known of incubation and care of the young. Such (1964) reports a successful breeding in captivity. Five eggs were laid and all hatched, but the incubation period was not determined. The young birds left the nest approximately six weeks after hatching.

EGGS Ovate; 37 eggs, 28.1 (26.0–31.0) × 21.5 (19.0–22.9) mm. [Schönwetter, 1964].

Genus BOLBORHYNCHUS Bonaparte

I have followed Meyer de Schauensee (1966) by incorporating *Amoropsittaca* and *Psilopsiagon* in this genus.

The five species belonging to *Bolborhynchus* are small parrots with broad, blunt bills. The cere is naked. There is a transitional pattern in tail structure—in *aymara* and *aurifrons* the tail is long and strongly gradated, in *lineola* it is short and slightly gradated, and in *orbygnesius* and *ferrugineifrons* it is short and rounded. Sexual dimorphism is present in *aurifrons* and to a slight degree in *lineola*, but is absent in the remaining species.

SIERRA PARAKEET
Bolborhynchus aymara (d'Orbigny)

Illustrated on page 464.

Illustrated on page 464.

DESCRIPTION

Length 20 cm.
ADULTS forehead, lores, periophthalmic region, ear-coverts, crown, and nape brownish-grey; remainder of upperparts green, darker on wings and tail; cheeks, throat, and breast pale grey, increasingly tinged with pale blue towards lower breast; upper abdomen pale bluish-grey intermixed with yellowish-green; lower abdomen and under tail-coverts bluish-green; flanks and under wing-coverts yellowish-green; underside of tail dusky green; bill flesh-pink; iris brown; legs brownish.
IMMATURES like adults, but with shorter tail.
11 males wing 93–101 (97.0) mm., tail 80–106 (97.0) mm.,
          exp. cul. 10–12 (10.8) mm., tars. 12–14 (12.6) mm.
10 females wing 92–99 (96.1) mm., tail 89–104 (97.7) mm.,
          exp. cul. 10–12 (10.3) mm., tars. 12–14 (12.9) mm.

DISTRIBUTION

Distributed along the eastern slopes of the Andes from La Paz and Cochabamba, central Bolivia, south to Mendoza and western Córdoba, north-western Argentina.

GENERAL NOTES

Sierra Parakeets are mountain birds, and are characteristic of dry, shrubby hillsides and sparsely vegetated valleys. Orfila (1938) says that they reach altitudes of more than 4,000 m., and in Tucumán, north-western Argentina, they descend to 1,200 m. during winter. In Bolivia specimens have been collected between 1,700 and 3,600 m. [ANSP and NHRS Collections]. Wetmore (1926) reports that in March 1921 these parakeets were observed on the slopes above the city of Mendoza, north-western Argentina, and by following back along the line of flight of a small flock a waterhole was located in what was an otherwise wholly arid tract of country. Above Potrerillos, Mendoza, north-western Argentina, at nearly 2,000 m., Wetmore found that they were common and small parties ranged over the hills feeding in berry-bearing bushes or foraging for fallen seeds in the grass below. They are highly gregarious, being usually seen in parties and sometimes in large flocks (Wetmore, 1926; Olrog, 1968). Their flight is swift and direct.

They feed on seeds, berries, fruits, and probably vegetable matter.

CALL Wetmore reports that their twittering call-notes are high-pitched, and at times resemble those of agitated Barn Swallows (*Hirundo rustica*).

NESTING Little is known of the breeding habits in the wild. Olrog says that the nest is in a hole excavated in an earthen bank and four to six eggs are laid.

Beckett (1964) gives details of a successful breeding in captivity. Seven eggs were laid and were incubated by the hen for twenty-eight days, sitting apparently commencing with the laying of the first egg. Four eggs hatched and the chicks left the nest six weeks after hatching.

EGGS Undescribed.

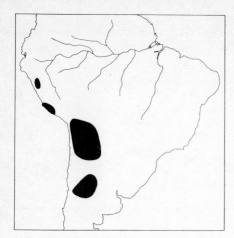

MOUNTAIN PARAKEET
Bolborhynchus aurifrons (Lesson)

Length 18 cm.

MALE general plumage green, paler and more yellowish on underparts; forehead, lores, foreparts of cheeks, and throat bright yellow; cheek-patches emerald green; sides of breast yellow; lower breast and upper abdomen strongly tinged with yellow; under wing-coverts bluish-green; primary-coverts and outer webs of secondaries bluish-green; outer webs of primaries violet-blue; tail green above, bluish-grey below; bill horn-coloured; iris brown; legs brownish.

FEMALE no yellow on forehead and lores; foreparts of cheeks, throat, and sides of breast tinged with yellow, but not as prominent as in male; green of underparts darker, less yellowish than in male.

IMMATURES similar to female.

DISTRIBUTION Central and southern Peru, central-western Bolivia, and northernmost Chile south to north-western Argentina thence west to central Chile.

SUBSPECIES 1. *B. a. aurifrons* (Lesson)   *Illustrated on page 464.*
    10 males wing 89–99 (93.3) mm., tail 75–90 (82.5) mm.,
           exp. cul. 11–12 (11.7) mm., tars. 13–14 (13.4) mm.
    7 females wing 91–95 (93.0) mm., tail 75–84 (79.1) mm.,
           exp. cul. 11–12 (11.3) mm., tars. 13–14 (13.3) mm.
    Confined to coastal regions and adjacent western slopes of the Andes in central Peru.

2. *B. a. robertsi* (Carriker)
MALE like *aurifrons*, but underparts, except chin and throat, darker green without the strong yellow wash; chin and throat bright yellow, contrasting strongly with green of remainder of underparts.
FEMALE like *aurifrons*, but underparts darker green.
    2 males   wing 93–94 (93.5) mm., tail 91–94 (92.5) mm.,
           exp. cul. 11 (11.0) mm., tars. 13 (13.0) mm.
    1 female wing 91 mm., tail 82 mm.,
           exp. cul. 11 mm., tars. 13 mm.
    Known only from Soquián in the Marañón Valley, Libertad, north-western Peru, the type locality.

3. *B. a. margaritae* Berlioz and Dorst
ADULTS both sexes similar to female *aurifrons*; larger size, but with shorter tail.
    10 males wing 100–109 (105.0) mm., tail 66–78 (72.3) mm.,
           exp. cul. 11–13 (11.9) mm., tars. 14–15 (14.3) mm.
    8 females wing 101–108 (104.4) mm., tail 68–80 (71.8) mm.,
           exp. cul. 11–12 (11.8) mm., tars. 13–15 (13.9) mm.
    Distributed from southern Peru and Cochabamba and Oruro, central-western Bolivia, south through Tarapacá and Antofagasta, northern Chile, to extreme north-western Argentina in the provinces of Jujuy, Salta, and Tucumán.

4. *B. a. rubrirostris* (Burmeister).
ADULTS like *margaritae*, but head and underparts darker, not yellowish, green and tinged with blue; bill flesh-pink.
    8 males   wing 102–108 (104.4) mm., tail 73–76 (74.8) mm.,
           exp. cul. 12–13 (12.4) mm., tars. 13–15 (14.4) mm.
    8 females wing 102–108 (105.1) mm., tail 73–82 (77.4) mm.,
           exp. cul. 12–13 (12.3) mm., tars. 13–15 (13.9) mm.
    Occurs on the eastern slopes of the Andes in north-western Argentina from Catamarca south to Mendoza and western Córdoba, and across on the western slopes only in Santiago province, central Chile.

GENERAL NOTES Mountain Parakeets are common, conspicuous birds in parts of their range, yet surprisingly little is known of their habits. Koepcke (1970) says that in Lima province, central Peru, they are common on the steppes and in open shrubby country on the coastal plain and Andean slopes, even appearing in flocks in cultivated fields, tree plantations, gardens, and in the city parks of Lima. Dorst (1956) reports that they are locally abundant in the high plateaux of southern Peru. In the Maritime Range, a coastal range in Arequipa province, southern Peru, Hughes (1970) found them to be locally common at high altitudes wherever native bushes and small trees were prevalent. Johnson (1967) claims that they are rare in northern Chile, being found only in the mountains above 3,000 m. He encountered small parties of fifteen to twenty birds in the Lake Huasco and Collacagua regions of Tarapacá in January and at Putre, Arica, in November. However, Peña (1961) says that they are rather common breeding residents in the Antofagasta Ranges, northern Chile; he observed flocks at three localities between 3,030 and 4,100 m.

In winter these parrots descend to lower altitudes (Olrog, 1968). Koepcke reports that during winter in Lima province, central Peru, they are abundant on coastal hills and in wooded and shrubby places with fog vegetation. Hughes indicates that there may be seasonal fluctuations in numbers in the Maritime Range, southern Peru; he observed parrots at all seasons, although most frequently between June and November. Housse (1949) claims that they migrate into the mountains of central Chile along 33° South lat. between September and December, remain to breed, and then depart in March. Johnson quotes a report stating that the parrots arrive regularly in the mountains of Santiago province, central Chile, during September and may be seen there throughout the summer.

Food comprises seeds, fruits, berries, and probably vegetable matter. It has been reported that in the Moreno district, Jujuy, north-western Argentina, buds and seeds from tola bushes (*Leptophyllum* sp.) are a favourite food (Lönnberg, 1903).

CALL Undescribed, though Lönnberg refers to large flocks 'which fly about screaming loudly'.

NESTING In the mountains of Santiago province, central Chile, Johnson has observed birds going in and out of nesting burrows in December. Lönnberg describes two nests, presumably found in Jujuy, north-western Argentina; each was in a burrow excavated in an earth bank and comprised an upward sloping tunnel about 2 m. in length and leading to two chambers, the first contained the eggs and was 20 to 30 cm. in front of the second. Nothing further is known of the nesting habits.

EGGS Broadly elliptical; 4 eggs, 28.4 (27.3–29.4) × 20.1 (19.8–20.5) mm. [Schönwetter, 1964].

BARRED PARAKEET
Bolborhynchus lineola (Cassin)

DESCRIPTION

Length 16 cm.
MALE general plumage green, noticeably bluish on forecrown and olive on upperparts; all feathers of upperparts, except crown, margined with black, thus giving a barred appearance; flanks and sides of breast olive-green barred with greenish-black; throat, centre of breast, and abdomen yellowish-green; under tail-coverts yellowish-green with dark green spot at tip of each feather; bend of wing black; lesser and median wing-coverts broadly margined with black; outer webs of flight feathers bright green; under wing-coverts and undersides of flight feathers bluish-green; tail above dark green broadly tipped with black, below dusky green; bill pale horn-coloured with a pink tinge; iris dark brown; legs pink.
FEMALE like male, but with narrower black margins to feathers of upperparts, particularly on rump and lesser wing-coverts; tail above dark green very narrowly tipped with black.
IMMATURES similar to adults, but general plumage paler green and black barring less distinct; more extensive bluish tinge on head.

DISTRIBUTION

Central America from southern Mexico south to western Panama, and north-western South America from westernmost Venezuela south to central Peru.

SUBSPECIES

1. *B. l. lineola* (Cassin)   *Illustrated on page 464.*
    5 males   wing 104–107 (105.2) mm., tail 53–58 (55.6) mm.,
                exp. cul. 12–13 (12.4) mm., tars. 13–14 (13.2) mm.
    5 females wing 102–107 (104.0) mm., tail 55–57 (55.4) mm.,
                exp. cul. 11–12 (11.8) mm., tars. 12–13 (12.8) mm.
    Ranges from southern Mexico south to Chiriquí region, western Panama.

2. *B. l. tigrinus* (Souancé)
    ADULTS similar to *lineola*, but general plumage darker and more strongly barred with black.
    6 males   wing 101–113 (107.5) mm., tail 50–62 (57.5) mm.,
                exp. cul. 12 (12.0) mm., tars. 12–14 (12.5) mm.
    10 females wing 100–111 (104.9) mm., tail 52–60 (56.2) mm.,
                exp. cul. 11–12 (11.8) mm., tars. 12–14 (12.7) mm.
    Exact range not determined but to date recorded from the mountains of Táchira and Mérida, north-western Venezuela, the Andes of Colombia from Norte de Santander south to Cauca, and the Andes of central Peru in Cuzco and Ayacucho.

GENERAL NOTES

Barred Parakeets are considered to be uncommon or rare in most parts of their range, but I suspect that this may be due to their small size and protective colouration making them so difficult to detect in mountain forest. Blake (1953) says that they are rare in southern Mexico, occurring only in dense forests at high altitudes. Davis (1945) found that they were moderately common at 1,400 m. in forested areas along the Banderillo River, Veracruz, southern Mexico, and flocks were seen in the taller trees eating what appeared to be berries. At about 1,660 m. near Pueblo Nuevo, Chiapas, southern Mexico, Amadon and Eckelberry (1955) often saw small groups of up to ten flying high above the mountain forest. Monroe (1968) says that in Honduras these parrots breed mostly above 1,500 m., descending as low as 600 m. in the non-breeding season, and, although locally distributed, they are very common where they do occur, flocks of more than one hundred being frequently observed. They prefer cloud forest or montane rainforest, but in winter often inhabit lowland rainforest. From 17th February to 4th March 1963 large flocks appeared in the rainforest of Finca Fé, western Honduras, at an elevation of 610 m., a locality from which the species was totally absent during the preceding six months and the following two months. Land (1970) points out that there are only two records of the species from Guatemala, one from 1,850 m. in the highlands and the other from 400 m. in the arid interior. In Costa Rica these parrots are known mainly from the central highlands, though they are also present in unknown numbers along the Cordillera de Talamanca (Slud, 1964); there are no records from either the Cordillera de Guanacaste or the Cordillera de Tilaran, both in the north-west of the country. They normally range from the mountaintops down to the lower subtropical belt, where they are local, but Slud has found them several times in January at upper tropical-belt elevations near Buenos Aires, south-western Costa Rica. They favour well-wooded, partly-cleared areas, including the park-like pastures with tall trees on the larger volcanoes. Wetmore (1968) says that in western Panama they are forest birds, local in occurrence, and to date recorded only in small numbers from the sub-tropical zone on both the Pacific and Caribbean slopes of the Volcán de Chiriquí. In early February 1960, at 1,500 m. on the Silla de Cerro Pando, Chiriquí, western Panama, he found a small group feeding quietly in a tree crown in the forest.

According to Phelps and Phelps (1958) they are locally distributed in open areas in the sub-tropical zone of north-western Venezuela. Meyer de Schauensee (1964) says that in Colombia they inhabit open forest and savannah in the subtropical zone. In February 1941, Niceforo (1945) saw a flock of fifteen near Cucuta, Norte de Santander, and was told by local residents that the parrots frequently visited the district just prior to the time of the maize harvest. Lehmann (1957) reports that in June and July at Paso de Las Cruces, above San Antonio, Cali, at 2,000 m., he saw small flocks flying through the mist which frequently covers that area; he has not recorded them there during other months of the year despite repeated searches.

These small parrots are generally observed in pairs or small flocks of less than twenty, though at times large flocks of a hundred or more have been reported. It is only while flying above the treetops, their twittering call-notes attracting attention, that they are conspicuous, because when at rest or while feeding among the topmost branches of trees their mottled plumage blends remarkably well with the foliage. While feeding they are tame and will allow a close approach; Davis reports that when specimens were collected from a feeding flock the remaining birds merely circled overhead two or three times and then returned to the same tree to continue feeding. Their flight is direct and very swift.

They feed on seeds, fruits, berries, nuts, and probably leaf buds and blossoms, procured in the treetops.

CALL In flight or while feeding they emit a high-pitched twittering, similar to notes normally given by songbirds.

NESTING Nothing is known of nesting in the wild. Blake (1958) reports that a male and a female with slightly enlarged gonads were collected during December at Lerida, Chiriquí, western Panama.

Prestwich (1954) describes what may have been a courtship display by captive birds. The pair would stand facing each other, stretch vertically to the fullest possible extent, and with bills interlocked remain in this position for a few moments. This pair subsequently nested, laying four eggs and hatching one chick which was successfully reared, but no details are given.

EGGS Schönwetter (1964) gives 19.5 × 19.2 mm. as the measurements of an egg in the Nehrkorn Collection, but Wetmore points out that these are almost certainly incorrect because the length seems to be too small for a bird of this size.

ANDEAN PARAKEET
Bolborhynchus orbygnesius (Souancé)

Illustrated on page 464.

Illustrated on page 464.

Length 17 cm.
ADULTS general plumage green, duller and slightly yellowish on underparts; forehead and lores tinged with yellow, absent or less pronounced in females; outer webs of primaries bluish-green; lesser under wing-coverts green; greater under wing-coverts and undersides of flight feathers bluish-green; tail green; bill pale greenish-yellow with grey at base; iris dark brown; legs pale brown.
IMMATURES undescribed, but probably similar to adults.
13 males   wing 101–115 (108.8) mm., tail 56–68 (63.8) mm.,
      exp. cul. 12–13 (12.4) mm., tars. 14–16 (14.8) mm.
8 females   wing 105–112 (108.9) mm., tail 58–65 (63.1) mm.,
      exp. cul. 11–13 (12.1) mm., tars. 14–16 (14.8) mm.

DESCRIPTION

Highlands of Peru and northern Bolivia from Cajamarca south to Cochabamba.

DISTRIBUTION

GENERAL NOTES　Meyer de Schauensee (1970) says that the Andean Parakeet frequents bushy mountain slopes in the subtropical and temperate zones. Koepcke (1970) notes that it is a species characteristic of the Peruvian Andes, and in Lima province, central Peru, it occurs only above 1,500 m. Griswold reports that in June, when the weather became noticeably warmer and the rains eased, this species arrived at Maraynioc in a valley ranging from 5,000 to 6,250 m., to the north-east of Tarma, Junín province, central Peru (in Peters and Griswold, 1943). In the Pampas River Valley, Ayacucho, southern Peru, Morrison (1948) found it to be common and large flocks were seen in temperate woodland. Dorst (1961) reports that in the Sandia Valley, Puno, southernmost Peru, the species is very common and occurs in numerous flocks which show a marked preference for low shrubs.

These small parrots are generally encountered in flocks of from five to fifty. They spend much of the day in shrubs or on the ground foraging for seeds, fruits, and berries. At Maraynioc, central Peru, Griswold saw them feeding on wild raspberries. When disturbed they usually fly a short distance and alight on the tops of bushes. The flight is swift and direct.

CALL　Undescribed.

NESTING　Olrog (1968) claims that the nest is in a burrow excavated in an earth bank. I know of no published nesting records.

EGGS　Undescribed.

RUFOUS-FRONTED PARAKEET
Bolborhynchus ferrugineifrons (Lawrence)　　　　*Illustrated on page 464.*

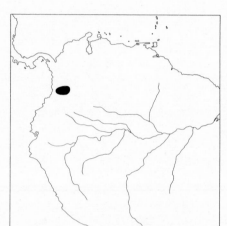

Length 18 cm.
ADULTS general plumage green, paler on underparts and slightly tinged with olive-yellow on upper breast; narrow frontal band, lores, and surrounding base of lower mandible rufous; outer webs of primaries bluish-green; lesser under wing-coverts green; greater under wing-coverts and undersides of flight feathers bluish-green; tail green above, bluish-green below; bill grey with yellowish-horn tip; iris dark brown; legs yellowish-grey.
IMMATURES undescribed.

5 males	wing 121–125 (122.6) mm., tail 57–71 (65.4) mm., exp. cul. 13–15 (14.0) mm., tars. 15–17 (15.6) mm.
1 female	wing 124 mm., tail 68 mm., exp. cul. 13 mm., tars. 16 mm.
1 unsexed (**type**);	121 mm., tail 75 mm., exp. cul. 14 mm., tars. 16 mm.

DISTRIBUTION　Known only from the Central Andes in Tolima and Cauca, Colombia.

GENERAL NOTES　Nothing is known of the habits of the Rufous-fronted Parakeet. Meyer de Schauensee (1970) says that it inhabits scrubby mountain slopes in the temperate zone. It has been recorded as high as 3,750 m. (ANSP. 154716).

A male with enlarged testes (CNHM. 249549) was collected in mid-January.

Genus FORPUS Boie

The species in this genus are small, stocky parrots with very short, wedge-shaped tails. The bill is large and there is a distinct notch in the upper mandible. Sexual dimorphism is present and young birds resemble adults.

Brereton (1963) postulates that the *Forpus-Bolborhynchus* group may be allied to the platycercine group from Australia, but I find such a theory difficult to accept and doubt its validity as an argument for a faunal connection between Australasia and South America. The behaviour of these South American species in the wild is in no way similar to that of platycercine parrots.

MEXICAN PARROTLET
Forpus cyanopygius (Souancé)

DESCRIPTION　Length 13 cm.
MALE general plumage green, paler and more yellowish on forehead, sides of head, and underparts; underparts also with slight bluish tinge in some birds; lower back, rump, under wing-coverts, and axillaries turquoise-blue; primary-coverts, secondaries, and bases of shorter primaries blue; undersides of tail and flight feathers bluish-green; bill pale horn-coloured; iris brown; legs greyish.

449

FEMALE all blue marking replaced by yellowish-green; underparts without bluish tinge and more yellowish than in male.

IMMATURES like adults; male has blue of rump, under wing-coverts, and axillaries mixed with green, and has primary-coverts green with blue along median line.

North-western Mexico, including the Tres Marías Islands.

Illustrated on page 465.

1. *F. c. cyanopygius* (Souancé)
   8 males   wing 88–91 (89.5) mm., tail 38–42 (40.8) mm.,
        exp. cul. 12–13 (12.8) mm., tars. 11–13 (12.3) mm.
   8 females wing 88–90 (88.9) mm., tail 38–42 (40.4) mm.,
        exp. cul. 12–13 (12.8) mm., tars. 11–13 (12.3) mm.
   Occurs in north-western Mexico from Sinaloa and western Durango south to Colima.

2. *F. c. pallidus* (Brewster)
   ADULTS general plumage paler than in *cyanopygius*; upperparts with ash-grey tinge, underparts paler and more yellowish.
   6 males   wing 88–93 (90.0) mm., tail 38–41 (39.7) mm.,
        exp. cul. 12–14 (13.3) mm., tars. 11–13 (12.0) mm.
   4 females wing 86–88 (87.0) mm., tail 38–41 (39.5) mm.,
        exp. cul. 12–14 (13.0) mm., tars. 11–14 (12.8) mm.
   Known only from south-eastern Sonora and northernmost Sinaloa, north-western Mexico; probably not distinct from *cyanopygius*.

3. *F. c. insularis* (Ridgway)
   MALE similar to *cyanopygius*, but upperparts darker green; underparts glaucous green contrasting with yellowish-green of sides of head; blue of rump and lower back darker.

   FEMALE like *cyanopygius*, but with darker green upperparts.
   6 males   wing 87–91 (89.2) mm., tail 41–43 (42.0) mm.,
        exp. cul. 13–14 (13.7) mm., tars. 12–13 (12.7) mm.
   5 females wing 87–92 (89.2) mm., tail 41–43 (42.0) mm.,
        exp. cul. 13–14 (13.6) mm., tars. 12–13 (12.4) mm.
   Confined to the Tres Marías Islands, off the coast of Nayarit, western Mexico.

Mexican Parrotlets are common in the arid tropical zone of western Mexico from sea level up to approximately 1,320 m. (Friedmann *et al.*, 1950); birds with enlarged gonads have been collected at elevations up to 1,000 m. They inhabit tropical deciduous woodland and most types of open country. Van Rossem (1945) says that in the tropical zone foothills of south-eastern Sonora they are resident and rather common, particularly in the vicinity of Alamos, and most records are from the narrow altitudinal range of 375 to 470 m.; sight records from a locality at 100 m. in the lowlands were probably of seasonal vagrants. In January 1965, on the outskirts of Alamos, I found them frequenting trees lining a dry seasonal watercourse (see Forshaw, 1965). To the north of San Blas, Nayarit, McLellan (1927) found large flocks, which apparently frequented tall trees bordering open country, but they were not conspicuous birds in the area. Schaldach (1963) reports that they are not abundant in Colima, even in the dry season; they probably indulge in a good deal of local wandering throughout the region, in search of various ripening fruits and seeds, and this would account for the apparent scarcity of these birds at times.

The endemic subspecies on the Tres Marías Islands seems to have declined since the turn of the century and is now quite scarce. Reports of sightings ceased in about 1930, and in 1955 Stager (1957) failed to find it despite a thorough search on all four islands. However, Grant and Cowan (1964) report that it was found on Maria Magdalena in each year from 1960 to 1963, and on Maria Cleofas in 1963, but no more than ten birds were seen on any one day; a marked contrast to the flocks of fifty or more frequently reported at the turn of the century.

These parrots are generally seen in flocks of from ten to fifty, though pairs and single birds are occasionally recorded. They are not conspicuous, being easily overlooked unless the observer is familiar with their call-notes. They are active in the early morning and late afternoon, and are most likely to be encountered at these times as they fly to and from feeding areas or watering places. They sometimes associate with other species; Zimmerman and Harry (1951) report that south of Autlán, Jalisco, in late June and early July, flocks of from ten to twenty were usually seen in the early morning with flocks of Orange-fronted Conures (*Aratinga canicularis*) that came to feed in large *Ficus* trees. While on the ground or in the treetops searching for fruits, berries, and grass seeds, they are fairly tame and will allow a close approach, but at other times they are rather wary. The very swift, direct flight is undertaken with rapid wingbeats and there is no noticeable gliding.

In the Alamos district I observed flocks generally containing about forty birds. They gave fine displays of precision flying when on the wing, each flock twisting and turning in almost perfect unison. Flying at only two or three metres above the ground they showed flashes of bright green while darting through the trees and over lower shrubs. On leaving the uppermost branches of a tree the flock would dive down toward the ground, then continue to fly at the characteristically low level, and finally rise suddenly to alight once again in the upper branches of another tree. I watched two flocks fly into a large *Ficus* tree and I immediately took up a position underneath that tree to observe feeding behaviour. However, it was virtually impossible to locate individual birds, so well did their plumage blend with the foliage. When I struck the trunk of the tree with a piece of wood all birds took fright and flew to a neighbouring tree and adopted a very upright stance so that males showed very clearly their blue rumps. After some five or ten minutes when they returned in twos and threes to continue feeding, I watched a group of three males move into the feeding tree and observed their feeding behaviour. Before settling down to feed there was much calling and fluttering. Feeding was very methodical and the parrots worked their way through the outermost branches examining, or even tasting, all the fruits and eating those that had reached a satisfactory stage of development. Judging by pieces falling to the ground there was a preference for fruits which, although still green, were beginning to ripen. A continual shower of falling pieces of fruit and the occasional emission of the high-pitched call were the only obvious indications of feeding.

CALL When perched in a tree or flying overhead the parrots give their contact call, a high-pitched, rolling screech that is surprisingly penetrative and can be heard from a considerable distance; while feeding they emit an occasional shrill, monosyllabic squeak.

NESTING Breeding has been recorded during June and July (Grant, 1966), but little is known of the nesting habits. A young male just assuming its first winter plumage was collected near San Blas, Nayarit, by McLellan in mid-October.
   Goddard (1927) gives details of a successful breeding in captivity. In the nest-box a nest was made from dry grass and old seed-heads of millet with a lining of feathers which the female may have plucked from her breast. Three eggs were laid and subsequently hatched, but the incubation period was not determined. The young birds left the nest approximately five weeks after hatching.

EGGS Undescribed.

GREEN-RUMPED PARROTLET
Forpus passerinus (Linné)

DESCRIPTION

Length 12 cm.
MALE general plumage yellowish-green, decidedly paler and brighter on forehead, cheeks, underparts, lower back, and rump; greyish tinge on nape and hindneck; in some birds rump and lower back washed with pale blue; primary-coverts, bases of shorter primaries, and under wing-coverts violet-blue; secondaries pale blue; undersides of flight feathers bluish-green; tail green, paler below; bill horn-coloured; iris dark brown; legs brownish.
FEMALE like male but blue markings replaced by green; forehead more yellowish than in males.
IMMATURES similar to adults.

DISTRIBUTION

Trinidad and the Guianas west through northern and central Venezuela to northern Colombia; northern Brazil along the upper Branco River and along the Amazon River from the lower Madeira River, eastern Amazonas, east to the Anapú River, Pará, and to Macapá, Amapá. Introduced to Curaçao in the Netherlands Antilles, and to Jamaica, Barbados, and possibly Martinique in the West Indies; it has not survived on Martinique.

SUBSPECIES

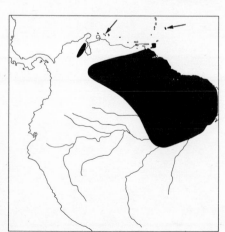

1. *F. p. passerinus* (Linné)   *Illustrated on page 465.*
   9 males   wing 79–86 (82.4) mm., tail 31–39 (35.6) mm.,
                exp. cul. 11–13 (11.7) mm., tars. 11–12 (11.4) mm.
   10 females wing 77–84 (80.2) mm., tail 31–41 (35.9) mm.,
                exp. cul. 11–12 (11.6) mm., tars. 11–12 (11.2) mm.
   Confined to Guyana, Surinam, and French Guiana. A specimen captured on Martinique, West Indies, is referred to this race by Bond (1952), who suggests that birds were probably brought to the island from French Guiana but were subsequently extirpated.

2. *F. p. viridissimus* (Lafresnaye)
   MALE similar to *passerinus*, but green of general plumage darker throughout; upper sides of wings darker and more strongly tinged with bluish; under wing-coverts and axillaries bluish-green with patch of violet blue on lesser under wing-coverts.
   FEMALE similar to *passerinus*.
   10 males   wing 79–84 (82.3) mm., tail 35–42 (38.2) mm.,
                exp. cul. 11–13 (12.0) mm., tars. 11–12 (11.5) mm.
   10 females wing 75–83 (79.3) mm., tail 36–41 (38.4) mm.,
                exp. cul. 11–12 (11.6) mm., tars. 10–12 (11.4) mm.
   Occurs on Trinidad and is distributed across northern Venezuela from Delta Amacuro and northern Bolívar, south of the Orinoco River, east to the Zulia River valley in Norte de Santander, northern Colombia; introduced to Curaçao, Netherlands Antilles. This is probably the subspecies introduced to Jamaica and Barbados in the West Indies.

3. *F. p. cyanophanes* (Todd)

MALE like *viridissimus*, but with more extensive violet-blue on primary and secondary coverts thus forming a conspicuous patch on the closed wing; more extensive violet-blue marking on under wing-coverts.

FEMALE like *passerinus*.

3 males   wing 81–84 (82.0) mm., tail 38–40 (39.0) mm.,
             exp. cul. 12–13 (12.3) mm., tars. 11–12 (11.7) mm.

1 female   wing 80 mm., tail 43 mm.,
             exp. cul. 11 mm., tars. 11 mm.

Found in the arid tropical zone of northern Colombia east of the Santa Marta Mountains extending southward between this range and the Sierra de Perijá into the Césare River valley as far as Camperucho.

4. *F. p. cyanochlorus* (Schlegel)

ADULTS similar to *passerinus*, except that in female the green of general plumage is more yellowish particularly on underparts, rump and lower back.

2 males   wing 80–81 (80.5) mm., tail 40–41 (40.5) mm.,
             exp. cul. 11 (11.0) mm., tars. 11–12 (11.5) mm.

1 female   wing 78 mm., tail 39 mm.,
             exp. cul. 11 mm., tars. 12 mm.

Restricted to northernmost Brazil, where known only from the upper Branco River, Roraima.

5. *F. p. deliciosus* (Ridgway)

MALE similar to *passerinus*, but rump and lower back emerald green tinged with pale blue; upper tail-coverts greenish-yellow; secondaries violet-blue narrowly edged with pale green; greater upper wing-coverts pale blue becoming violet-blue along shafts.

FEMALE like *passerinus*, but with conspicuous yellow tinge on forehead.

10 males   wing 79–84 (81.6) mm., tail 36–43 (38.0) mm.,
             exp. cul. 11–13 (11.7) mm., tars. 12–14 (12.6) mm.

8 females wing 78–82 (79.5) mm., tail 36–39 (37.5) mm.,
             exp. cul. 11–12 (11.1) mm., tars. 12–13 (12.4) mm.

Occurs in northern Brazil along both banks of the Amazon River from the lower Madeira River, eastern Amazonas, east to the Anapú River, Pará, and farther east along the north bank to the vicinity of Macapá, Amapá.

GENERAL NOTES

Since its introduction to Jamaica in about 1918 the Green-rumped Parrotlet has steadily increased its range and is now widespread in lowland open country on the southern side of the island (Bond, 1971a). To the south-west of Kingston, Oelke (1968) observed that it regularly visits semi-arid coastal *Acacia*-cactus scrubland to feed. Bond (1971a) reports that it is rare and evidently decreasing on Barbados, and the introduction to Martinique has apparently been unsuccessful. It was first recorded on Trinidad in 1916 and is now widespread and common, particularly in mangrove swamps, palm groves in savannah woodland, and clearings in lowland forests, but it seems to be absent from the wet, high forests of the Northern Range (Herklots, 1961). Ffrench and Ffrench (1966) point out that a pair of birds found breeding on Tobago were undoubtedly introduced from Trinidad as cage birds. It seems to be quite scarce on Curaçao; Voous (1957) observed only one pair on the island despite a thorough search, but he quotes a report stating that in the spring of 1954 small parties of up to six individuals suddenly appeared on Curacao where they were observed in various localities between 27th February and 20th March after which time they disappeared just as suddenly and were not sighted again until 11th September 1955. Snyder (1966) says that it is widely distributed in both coastal and inland regions of Guyana, and may be found in the vicinities of centres of population. During a stay of ten days in Guyana in early May 1971 I recorded the species only once; a party of seven birds was seen in low bushes near the Timehri Airport, 40 km. from Georgetown. According to Haverschmidt (1968) it is quite common in Surinam, being found in open country wherever there are scattered trees. In northern Venezuela it is generally distributed in savannah, farmlands, and semi-arid scrublands in the tropical zone, and occasionally up to 1,800 m. in the subtropical zone (Phelps and Phelps, 1958). In Monagas and Anzoátegui, north-eastern Venezuela, Smith found it to be fairly common in all habitats except open savannah, and noted that it showed a preference for the edges of both wet and dry forest (in Friedmann and Smith, 1950). Near Maracay, Aragua, north-western Venezuela, Wetmore (1939) recorded several flocks in pastures dotted with trees and shrubs. Shafer and Phelps (1954) report that in the Rancho Grande district, Aragua, north-western Venezuela, it occurs on both sides of the range in almost all wooded biotopes from the coast up to the dry deciduous woodlands at 500 m. on the southern slopes, but it does show a marked preference for man-made habitats such as gardens, parklands, cultivated fields, and tree-lined avenues in the proximity of settlement. There appear to be seasonal movements in this region for Schafer and Phelps point out that the species is a rare visitor to the Rancho Grande Reserve in May and it rarely crosses the Portachuelo Pass, though when this does take place it is invariably between late February and June. In northern Colombia it inhabits dry and semi-arid areas in the tropical zone (Meyer de Schauensee, 1964). Todd and Carriker (1922) report that it was very common around Río Hacha in the Santa Marta region, and inhabited both open woodland and dry scrubland in which thornbush and cacti predominated. Niceforo (1945) recalls that he found it in many localities along the Cucuta to Puerto Santander railway line and in both the Cucuta valley and near the Zulia River.

These parrots associate in flocks of from five to thirty, or occasionally up to fifty, but because of their small size and predominantly green plumage colouration they are not conspicuous and may be overlooked unless the observer is familiar with their call-notes. Haverschmidt reports that in Surinam they roost in low fully-leaved trees and frequently move out into open grassland to feed; to get at the seed-heads they settle on long grass stems which often bend under their weight. The birds seen by me near Timehri Airport, Guyana, were in a group sheltering in a dense bush during a heavy rainstorm and were it not for their constant twittering I would have failed to notice them. While feeding in berry-laden shrubs or amongst the branches of trees they are fairly tame and will generally allow a close approach. The flight is swift and the parrots fly in close formation, twisting and turning considerably.

Food comprises seeds, berries, fruits, leaf buds, and probably blossoms. Haverschmidt reports that in Surinam the parrots feed on grass seeds, the berries of Loranthaceae in trees, and the seeds of *Lagerstroemia indica*. Stomach contents from a bird collected on Trinidad comprised seeds and vegetable matter (Williams, 1922), and the crops of two birds taken on Curaçao contained grass seeds only (Voous, 1957).

CALL A shrill *chee . . . chee . . . chee*, similar to the call-notes of small passerine birds (Friedmann and Smith, 1950); also a penetrating disyllabic *tsup-tsup* accented on the second note (Snyder, 1966). When feeding or resting in a tree or shrub the birds keep up a constant twittering.

NESTING Herklots says that on Trinidad breeding takes place during April and other months, but gives no further information about the other months. In Surinam nesting has been recorded in February, June, and August (Haverschmidt, 1968), while in Venezuela it occurs between May and August (Friedmann and Smith, 1950 and 1955; Schafer and Phelps, 1954). In the Cucuta valley and near the Zulia River, northern Colombia, Niceforo found nests in May and June. The nest is in a hollow limb or hole in a tree, or in a hole excavated in an arboreal termitarium. Two unusual nest sites have been recorded; one was in a hole excavated in the thick base of a palm frond (Belcher and Smooker, 1936) and the other was in the hollow end of a piece of 75 mm. wide pipe used as the cross-arm of a clothesline support, 2 m. above the ground (Friedmann and Smith, 1955). Two to seven eggs make up the normal clutch.

Cherrie (1916) describes a nest found at Quiribana de Caicara, Venezuela, in late April. It was in a hollow in an old stump, about 4 m. from the ground. The nesting chamber was approximately 60 cm. down from the entrance. There was no nest lining, and the five eggs and two newly-hatched chicks rested on pieces of decayed wood.

Smith observed the behaviour of the birds at the nest in the clothesline support. This nest was composed of twigs, but these could have been rearranged by the parrots from a previous nest of the Saffron Finch (*Sicalis flaveola*). The pair had a well-established morning ritual. Consistently at 0630 hrs., never deviating from this time by more than two or three minutes, the incubating bird would leave the nest and, accompanied by its mate, circle the area at top speed, twittering all the while. One bird then entered the nest hole immediately, while the other remained beside the entrance for a short period before also entering to spend five to ten minutes inside and then departing.

Enehjelm (1951) gives details of a successful breeding in captivity. Seven eggs were laid and all subsequently hatched. From the dates listed it seems that the incubation period was approximately eighteen days and the young birds left the nest about five weeks after hatching. Wildeboer (1926) also bred this species in captivity and reports that the female incubated during the day and was joined by the male at night, but I suspect that he merely roosted in the nest-box and did not participate in incubation.

EGGS Spherical to elliptical, without gloss; 9 eggs, 17.5 (17.2–18.3) × 14.3 (13.3–14.9) mm. [Hellebrekers, 1941].

BLUE-WINGED PARROTLET
Forpus xanthopterygius (Spix)

DESCRIPTION Length 12 cm.
MALE general plumage green, paler and more yellowish on underparts; generally a few violet-blue feathers on bend of wing; primary and secondary-coverts violet-blue; outer webs of secondaries green becoming violet-blue towards bases; under wing-coverts deep violet-blue; bright emerald green feathers surrounding eye; lower back and rump violet-blue; tail bright green above, dusky green below; bill horn-coloured with grey at base of upper mandible; iris dark brown; legs grey.
FEMALE no blue markings, all being replaced by green; forehead and facial area greenish-yellow; similar to female *passerinus*, but more yellowish on underparts, particularly on flanks.
IMMATURES like adults, but males have less extensive blue markings on wings, and the under wing-coverts and rump are green variably intermixed with violet-blue.

DISTRIBUTION North-western Colombia; from central and north-eastern Peru east along both sides of the Amazon River to eastern Amazonas, northern Brazil; eastern Brazil from Maranhão and Ceará south to Rio Grande do Sul and north-eastern Argentina in Misiones and Corrientes, thence north through Paraguay to eastern Bolivia and central-eastern Peru.

SUBSPECIES

1. *F. x. xanthopterygius* (Spix)   *Illustrated on page 465.*
10 males   wing 81–88 (84.3) mm., tail 34–42 (38.4) mm.,
exp. cul. 11–13 (11.7) mm., tars. 11–13 (11.4) mm.
12 females   wing 80–89 (85.3) mm., tail 36–44 (41.8) mm.,
exp. cul. 11–13 (11.4) mm., tars. 11–12 (11.4) mm.
Ranges from Paraguay and north-eastern Argentina in Misiones and Corrientes north through central and mid-eastern Brazil to northern Bahia where it intergrades into *flavissimus*.

2. *F. x. flavissimus* (Hellmayr)
MALE like *xanthopterygius*, but general plumage paler, more yellowish-green; forehead, cheeks, and throat bright lemon yellow; violet-blue on wings, lower back, and rump slightly paler.
FEMALE similar to *xanthopterygius*, but general plumage paler and more yellowish-green, particularly on forehead, facial area, and lower underparts.
9 males   wing 80–85 (82.7) mm., tail 33–40 (36.1) mm.,
exp. cul. 11–12 (11.8) mm., tars. 10–12 (11.0) mm.
8 females   wing 78–85 (80.8) mm., tail 35–41 (37.9) mm.,
exp. cul. 11–12 (11.6) mm., tars. 10–12 (11.0) mm.
Occurs in north-eastern Brazil from Maranhão, Ceará, and Paraiba south to northern Bahia.

3. *F. x. olallae* Gyldenstolpe
MALE similar to *crassirostris*, but violet-blue of wings, rump, and lower back darker, while that of under wing-coverts is paler; green of upperparts averages slightly darker.
FEMALE similar to *crassirostris*.
7 males   wing 73–78 (76.6) mm., tail 31–33 (31.4) mm.,
exp. cul. 11–12 (11.9) mm., tars. 11 (11.0) mm.
2 females   wing 76–79 (77.5) mm., tail 30–35 (32.5) mm.,
exp. cul. 11–12 (11.5) mm., tars. 11 (11.0) mm.
Confined to north-western Brazil, where at present known from only two localities, Codajas and near Itacoatiara, both on the north bank of the Amazon River in eastern Amazonas; doubtfully distinct from *crassirostris* (see Pinto, 1945).

4. *F. x. crassirostris* (Taczanowski)
MALE like *xanthopterygius*, but all blue markings paler; primary-coverts pale greyish violet-blue contrasting with darker violet-blue secondary-coverts; upper mandible compressed laterally at the centre; smaller size.
FEMALE like *xanthopterygius*, but green of general plumage less yellowish; smaller size.
11 males   wing 75–80 (77.1) mm., tail 31–40 (33.6) mm.,
exp. cul. 11–12 (11.8) mm., tars. 10–12 (11.2) mm.
6 females   wing 72–80 (75.5) mm., tail 32–34 (33.0) mm.,
exp. cul. 11–12 (11.5) mm., tars. 11–12 (11.7) mm.
Distributed from north-eastern Peru and extreme south-eastern Colombia east along both banks of the Amazon River and its tributaries to central Amazonas, north-western Brazil.

5. *F. x. spengeli* (Hartlaub)
MALE similar to *xanthopterygius*, but lower back and rump pale turquoise blue; innermost primary-coverts violet-blue; secondary-coverts and bases of secondaries turquoise blue; under wing-coverts and axillaries turquoise blue intermixed with violet-blue.
FEMALE like *xanthopterygius*, but with yellowish forehead more conspicuous.
No specimens examined.
6 males   (Gill *in litt.*, 1972; LeCroy *in litt.*, 1972); wing 79–86 (82.5) mm., tail 36–42 (38.0) mm., exp. cul. 12–13 (12.5) mm., tars. 10–11 (10.8) mm.
5 females   (Gill *in litt.*, 1972; LeCroy *in litt.*, 1972); wing 74–84 (79.0) mm., tail 35–44 (39.0) mm. exp. cul. 11–12 (11.8) mm., tars. 10–11 (10.8) mm.
Confined to northern Colombia where it is distributed from the Caribbean coastal region west and south-west of the Santa Marta Mountains at Atlántico thence south along the lower Magdalena River to northern Bolívar.

6. *F. x. flavescens* (Salvadori)
MALE like *xanthopterygius*, but green of general plumage paler and more yellowish; forehead, cheeks, and underparts distinctly greenish-yellow; lower back and rump much paler blue.
FEMALE similar to *xanthopterygius*, but general plumage paler and more yellowish, particularly on forehead and facial area.
5 males   wing 81–86 (83.6) mm., tail 36–38 (37.2) mm.,
exp. cul. 11–12 (11.2) mm., tars. 12–14 (12.6) mm.
4 females   wing 81–86 (82.8) mm., tail 36–40 (37.8) mm.,
exp. cul. 11 (11.0) mm., tars. 12 (12.0) mm.
Occurs in the provinces of Santa Cruz and Beni, eastern Bolivia, and in south-eastern and central-eastern Peru.

The Blue-winged Parrotlet is sporadically distributed in most types of open country throughout its wide range, being common in some districts but quite scarce in others. Furthermore, it seems to wander about locally. Meyer de Schauensee (1964) says that in Colombia it is found in dry and semi-arid regions in the tropical zone. Dugand (1947) reports that in Atlántico, northern Colombia, it is common, except in extremely arid districts, and is particularly abundant on the tree-covered plains along the Magdalena River and the southern lakes. At El Paraiso, Atlántico, he recorded it almost daily in orchards and very frequently in trees in gardens. In the vicinity of Río Frio, Magdalena, northern Colombia, Darlington (1931) found that it occurred rather sparingly in forest and semi-open country and in the shade trees of the town, but in open forest at Aracataca and in cactus thickets at Servillano it was more numerous. Lamm (1948) reports that in Pernambuco and Paraiba, north-eastern Brazil, the species is fairly common in semi-open country and somewhat less so in the fringe of coconut palms along the coast; it was also seen a number of times in the dry interior. It is very common in Bahia, though there are local fluctuations in numbers and seasonal movements, the latter presumably correlated with food supply (Pinto, 1935). Sick and Pabst (1968) state that it often visits Guanabara, eastern Brazil, sometimes appearing in Santa Teresa and other suburbs near the centre of Rio de Janeiro. Mitchell (1957) reports that while she was living in the São Paulo suburb of Brooklyn during September and October 1954, it was a common bird in the neighbourhood, flocks being recorded daily flying up and down a shallow valley overlooked by the house. In May 1971, I observed two pairs in parkland near the Museu Ipiranga, São Paulo, and heard others in neighbouring trees. Olrog (1959) says that in north-eastern Argentina it frequents subtropical scrublands. Chubb (1910) recorded it as a common resident in Paraguay and claimed that it favours clumps of low bushes in open country. Terborgh and Weske (1969) report that in the Apurímac River valley, central-eastern Peru, the species inhabits matorral, an extremely patchy and varied riparian vegetation community dominated by scattered trees and dense thickets. In Santa Cruz, Bolivia, it has been collected at 400 m. (Bond and Meyer de Schauensee, 1943).

These parrots are generally seen in small parties of from five to twenty, but occasionally flocks of up to fifty or more are encountered, particularly at a concentrated source of food such as a grove of fruit-laden trees. They are active birds and spend much of the day on the ground foraging for grass seeds or in trees and bushes feeding on berries, always to the accompaniment of a constant twittering and it is this that attracts attention. At Lajes, in the state of Rio de Janeiro, Brazil, Mitchell came across a number of birds resting silently in a tree, the individuals preening themselves and each other, but as she approached they burst from the tree and, shrieking continuously, flew off across the hilly countryside, wheeling and twisting in the air like a flock of finches. The flight is swift and erratic.

They feed on seeds of grasses and herbaceous plants, berries, fruits, leaf buds and probably blossoms.

CALL A plaintive, though penetrating *tseet . . . tseet . . . tseet*; while feeding the birds keep up a constant twittering.

NESTING Surprisingly little has been recorded about the nesting habits of this widespread and common species. I suspect that in the north breeding takes place at about the middle of the year, while in the south it probably commences much later. The nest is in a hollow limb or hole in a tree, or in a deserted nest of the Rufous Hornero or Ovenbird (*Furnarius rufus*). These large, dome-shaped mud nests are used extensively by the parrots; they cover the floor of the nesting chamber with grass stems and on this lay three to seven eggs.

Watson (1905) gives details of a successful breeding in captivity. Eight eggs were laid. The incubation period was not determined precisely, but was estimated to have been approximately eighteen days. Only the female brooded, and she alone fed the chicks. The young birds vacated the nest about four weeks after hatching.

EGGS Spherical to elliptical; 20 eggs, 18.9 (17.0–21.5) × 15.2 (14.0–16.0) mm. [Schonwetter, 1964].

SPECTACLED PARROTLET
Forpus conspicillatus (Lafresnaye)

Length 12 cm.
MALE upperparts dull green; forehead, cheeks, and throat bright yellowish-green; underparts dull yellowish-green with slight greyish tinge on breast; periophthalmic region cobalt-blue; lower back, rump, carpal edge, primary and secondary-coverts, secondaries, under wing-coverts, and axillaries violet-blue, darker on rump; primaries green with violet-blue on bases of innermost feathers; upper tail-coverts green; undersides of flight feathers bluish-green; tail green above, dusky green below; bill horn-coloured tinged with brown; iris dark greyish-brown; legs brownish.
FEMALE all blue markings replaced by green; upperparts brighter green than in male; lower back, rump, and periophthalmic region emerald-green; underparts yellowish-green, duller on under wing-coverts.

IMMATURES males have emerald-green periophthalmic region and yellowish-green under wing-coverts; green intermixed with blue on rump, lower back, and wing-coverts; females resemble adult female.

DISTRIBUTION
Eastern Panama, Colombia, except the south-east, and along the Meta River in western Venezuela.

SUBSPECIES

1. *F. c. conspicillatus* (Lafresnaye)   *Illustrated on page 465.*
   8 males   wing 75–83 (79.3) mm., tail 36–41 (38.1) mm.,
           exp. cul. 11–12 (11.6) mm., tars. 9–11 (10.4) mm.
   5 females wing 78–84 (80.2) mm., tail 36–38 (36.6) mm.,
           exp. cul. 11–12 (11.4) mm., tars. 10–11 (10.8) mm.
   Locally distributed in Darién, eastern Panama, and ranges from northern Colombia, at about 10° North lat., south to Huila and western slopes of the Eastern Andes in Boyacá and Cundinamarca, central Colombia.

2. *F. c. metae* Borrero and Camacho
   MALE similar to *conspicillatus*, but underparts brighter and more yellowish-green; head brighter green, particularly on throat and cheeks which are more yellowish; bend of wing more yellowish; blue periophthalmic ring much reduced, being restricted mainly to a partial superciliary line.
   FEMALE very similar to *conspicillatus*, but general plumage slightly more yellowish.
   11 males wing 74–80 (75.9) mm., tail 31–36 (34.3) mm.,
           exp. cul. 11–12 (11.2) mm., tars. 10–12 (10.9) mm.
   5 females wing 72–82 (75.0) mm., tail 33–39 (36.0) mm.,
           exp. cul. 11–12 (11.6) mm., tars. 10–12 (10.8) mm.
   Ranges from the eastern slopes of the Eastern Andes in Boyacá, Cundinamarca, and Meta, central Colombia, east to western Venezuela along the Meta River.

3. *F. c. caucae* (Chapman)
   MALE like *conspicillatus*, but blue of lower back, rump, and upper and under wing-coverts paler, less violet; heavier, more robust bill.
   FEMALE like *conspicillatus*, but with heavier, more robust bill.
   5 males   wing 81–85 (83.0) mm., tail 38–41 (39.6) mm.,
           exp. cul. 12–13 (12.2) mm., tars. 11–12 (11.6) mm.
   4 females wing 78–83 (79.8) mm., tail 37–40 (38.8) mm.,
           exp. cul. 12–13 (12.5) mm., tars. 11–12 (11.8) mm.
   Occurs west of the Andes in Cauca and Nariño, south-western Colombia. Birds from the upper Patía valley, Nariño, have been separated as *F. c. pallescens* Lehmann and Haffer, but I have not seen a published description or examined specimens (see Haffer, 1967a).

GENERAL NOTES
Wetmore (1968) points out that the Spectacled Parrotlet is a locally-distributed resident of the lower Tuira River valley, Darién, eastern Panama, where it has been recorded to date only from El Real, at the former village site of Tapalisa on the lower Pucro River, and near Pucro. At Pucro he collected a pair in low trees bordering an old ricefield, and near El Real secured another pair at the border of a field near the Pirre River. Meyer de Schauensee (1964) says that in Colombia it is found in open forest in the tropical zone, though it has been recorded up to 1,600 m. Olivares (1969) reports that there are occasional records from the savannah around Bogotá, but in the tropical and subtropical zones the species is abundant. Miller (1947) reports that in the upper Magdalena River valley, central-western Colombia, it was abundant in open forest and in thorn bushes even where these were widely spaced in barren country.

During the non-breeding season flocks of these parrots are generally seen in trees and bushes feeding on berries or on the ground searching for grass seeds. Pairs are often encountered during the breeding season, though at this time flocks are also common. Miller notes that flocks feeding in trees suggested North American crossbills in their deliberate movements and in their rapid departure by dropping steeply in their take-off. The flight is swift and erratic.

Food consists of seeds of grasses and herbaceous plants, berries, fruits, leaf buds, and probably blossoms. Wetmore reports that the two birds collected near El Real, eastern Panama, had their crops filled with soft grass seeds.

CALL Miller points out that the twittering of flocks somewhat resembles that of the common North American Tree Swallow (*Iridoprocne bicolor*).

NESTING A female that was laying was collected by Wetmore on 8th February at Pucro, eastern Panama. On 26th January, in the upper Magdalena River valley, central-western Colombia, Miller found a nest in a hole in a stump, about 2 m. from the ground. This hole had not been excavated by the birds, but had rotted out naturally; it was approximately 50 cm. deep and at the bottom on large rough chips of wood and a few feathers there were four eggs. Another bird was flushed from a nesting hole in the top of a fence post. Olivares reports that at Fusagasuga, Cundinamarca, central Colombia, two chicks were found in a hole in a fence post, but no date is given; while this nest was being examined both parents showed obvious concern and perched only a few metres from the post. Nothing further is known of the nesting behaviour.

EGGS Spherical to elliptical; 4 eggs, 18.1 (17.6–18.5) × 16.0 (15.4–16.4) mm. [Schönwetter, 1964].

SCLATER'S PARROTLET
Forpus sclateri (G. R. Gray)

Length 12.5 cm.

MALE general plumage dark green, distinctly darker than in any other species; forehead and cheeks emerald green; underparts glaucous green, slightly tinged with olive on breast and with yellow on under tail-coverts; lower back and rump blue-violet, much darker than in any other species; upper tail-coverts dark green; primary and secondary-coverts, secondaries, and under wing-coverts blue-violet; outer webs of innermost primaries blue-violet towards bases; undersides of flight feathers bluish-green; tail dark green above, bluish-green below; upper mandible grey, lower horn-coloured; iris brown; legs greyish-brown.

FEMALE all blue markings replaced by green; general plumage paler than in male, particularly underparts which are yellowish-green; forehead, forecrown, and cheeks greenish-yellow.

IMMATURES undescribed, but probably similar to adults.

French Guiana, western Guyana, Venezuela in Carabobo, Bolívar, and southernmost Amazonas, and from about Belém, Pará, northern Brazil, west through the Amazon Basin to south-eastern Colombia, north-eastern Ecuador, eastern Peru, and northernmost Bolivia.

1. *F. s. sclateri* (G. R. Gray)   *Illustrated on page 465.*
   18 males   wing 78–86 (81.3) mm., tail 32–39 (35.5) mm.,
           exp. cul. 10–12 (11.1) mm., tars. 10–12 (11.0) mm.
   8 females wing 79–81 (80.1) mm., tail 33–40 (36.6) mm.,
           exp. cul. 11–12 (11.1) mm., tars. 10–12 (11.0) mm.

   Distributed from about Belém, Pará, northern Brazil, west through the Amazon Basin to Amazonas and Caquetá, south-eastern Colombia, thence south through the Napo River region, north-eastern Ecuador, and eastern Peru to extreme southern Acre, western Brazil, and northernmost Bolivia.

2. *F. s. eidos* Peters.
   MALE like *sclateri*, but green of general plumage lighter and more yellowish, particularly on underparts; paler blue-violet on rump and lower back.
   FEMALE similar to *sclateri*, but green of general plumage lighter and more yellowish, especially on breast.
   3 males   wing 80–88 (84.0) mm., tail 36–42 (39.7) mm.,
           exp. cul. 11 (11.0) mm., tars. 11–12 (11.7) mm.
   3 females wing 79–80 (79.7) mm., tail 34–40 (36.0) mm.,
           exp. cul. 10–11 (10.7) mm., tars. 11–12 (11.3) mm.

   Occurs in French Guiana, western Guyana, Venezuela in Bolívar and Carabobo, and in the upper Negro River region of Amazonas, Brazil, Guainía, extreme eastern Colombia, and southernmost Amazonas, Venezuela.

There appear to be no recent records of Sclater's Parrotlet from French Guiana, and there are only two specimens from Guyana, the first described by Schomburgk in 1848 and the second collected in the North-West District in 1949. In Venezuela and Colombia the species inhabits forests in the tropical zone (Phelps and Phelps, 1958; Meyer de Schauensee, 1964). In the vicinity of Belém, Pará, northern Brazil, Bond found it to be common (in Stone, 1929).

These parrots are widely distributed and, judging by the number of specimens in collections, must be quite common in the Amazon Basin, yet virtually nothing has been recorded about their habits. I suspect that being forest birds they are more arboreal than other species in the genus.

CALL Undescribed.
NESTING No published records.

EGGS Spherical to elliptical; 4 eggs, 18.2 (17.5–18.7) × 14.8 (14.4–15.2) mm. [Schönwetter, 1964].

Maroon-tailed Conure   **1**
Pyrrhura melanura souancei
AMNH. 230878 ad. ♂

Maroon-tailed Conure   **2**
Pyrrhura melanura berlepschi
BM. 69.6.25.106 **type** ad. ♀

Hoffman's Conure *Pyrrhua hoffmanni hoffmanni*   **3**
CM. 29230 ad. ♂

Red-eared Conure   **4**
Pyrrhura hoematotis hoematotis
CM. 104385 ad. ♂

PACIFIC PARROTLET
Forpus coelestis (Lesson)   *Illustrated on page 465.*

Length 12.5 cm.

MALE general plumage dull green, much brighter and more yellowish on forehead, crown, cheeks, and throat; blue line behind eye; occiput and nape bluish-grey; upper back, scapulars, innermost wing-coverts, and innermost secondaries greenish-grey; lower back, rump, under wing-coverts, and axillaries deep cobalt-blue, darker on rump; upper tail-coverts greenish-blue; primary and secondary-coverts, outer secondaries, and bases of inner primaries deep cobalt-blue; underparts green, tinged with grey on flanks and sides of breast; undersides of flight feathers bluish-green; tail dull green above, dusky green below; bill horn-coloured; iris brown; legs brownish.

FEMALE all blue markings replaced by emerald green, though some birds show blue tinge behind eye and have rump washed with turquoise-blue; upperparts less greyish and brighter green than in male; forehead, crown, cheeks, and throat less yellowish.

IMMATURES similar to adults, though male has paler, more restricted blue line behind eye, less blue on wings, and blue of rump and lower back intermixed with bluish-green.

10 males   wing 79–88 (83.6) mm., tail 38–42 (39.4) mm.,
            exp. cul. 12–13 (12.6) mm., tars. 11–13 (12.1) mm.
10 females wing 80–85 (81.6) mm., tail 37–44 (40.2) mm.,
            exp. cul. 12–13 (12.8) mm., tars. 11–13 (11.8) mm.

DISTRIBUTION

Along the Pacific side of the Andes from the Chone River region, western Ecuador, south to about Trujillo, Libertad, north-western Peru.

GENERAL NOTES

The Pacific Parrotlet is an abundant inhabitant of dry scrublands and secondary growth in the tropical zone (Chapman, 1926). Marchant (1958) lists it as a common resident of the Santa Elena Peninsula, south-western Ecuador.

Toward the end of the breeding season these parrots are generally seen in family parties of from five to ten birds frequenting low bushes and scattered trees in dry country. The parties persist throughout the dry season and sometimes amalgamate to form quite large flocks. They are noisy birds and their chattering attracts attention. When not on the ground searching for grass seeds or in trees feeding on berries, they sit quietly amongst the foliage of a tree or bush preening themselves and each other. Their general habits are similar to those of the other species.

CALL The call usually heard from flocks is a high-pitched chattering.

NESTING Marchant (1960) reports that in south-western Ecuador the breeding season commences in late January, after the rains, and continues through until late May. Two broods are sometimes reared and the second nesting may start only seven or eight days after successful fledging from the first. Nest sites are many and extremely varied and include hollow branches and holes in trees, and holes in fence posts, in telephone poles, in electricity installations on oilfields, hollow ends to pipes and bamboo rafters of houses, in deserted woodpeckers' holes, in old mud nests of the Pale-legged Hornero (*Furnarius leucopus*), and in the large stick nests of the Necklaced Spinetail (*Synallaxis stictothorax*) and the Fasciated Wren (*Campylorhynchus fasciatus*). In the nests examined Marchant found no lining, the eggs being laid on the bare floor of the hole.

Marchant points out that the normal clutch appears to be four to six eggs. These are laid at two-day intervals, though this can vary between 36 and 48 hours. Incubation commences early, perhaps usually with the laying of the second egg, and only the female sits during the day. Incubation lasts seventeen days and the young hatch over a period of at least three days. The chicks hatch naked, quills begin to show after about ten days and green feathers at about twenty days. Approximately thirty days after hatching the young leave the nest. Boorer (1964) bred the species in captivity and noted that during incubation, and for the first three weeks or so after hatching, the hen left the nest-box only once each day, usually at about noon; the male spent much time in the nest-box, but could always be seen sitting just inside the entrance hole so it is certain that he did not participate in incubation.

EGGS Ovate, smooth and without gloss; 13 eggs, 19.4 (17.6–21.0) × 16.0 (15.2–17.3) mm. [Schönwetter, 1964].

Austral Conure *Enicognathus ferrugineus minor* 1
MNHN. CG1964,829 ad. ♂

Slender-billed Conure 2
Enicognathus leptorhynchus
MNHN. CG1953,223 ad. ♂

YELLOW-FACED PARROTLET

Forpus xanthops (Salvin)   *Illustrated on page 465.*

Length 14.5 cm.

MALE crown, cheeks, and throat yellow; occiput and nape violet-grey, extending as a stripe to eye; upper back and wings greenish-grey; lower back, rump, and upper tail-coverts cobalt-blue; primary and secondary coverts and inner secondaries violet-blue, paler on secondary-coverts; inner primaries washed with blue on bases; underparts greenish-yellow; under wing-coverts deep blue; undersides of flight feathers bluish-green; tail green above, dusky green below; bill horn-coloured with grey at base of upper mandible; iris brown; legs brown.

FEMALE like male, but lower back and rump pale blue; primary and secondary-coverts, secondaries, and bases to primaries green tinged with blue.

IMMATURES undescribed, but probably similar to adults.

10 males   wing 89–94 (91.1) mm., tail 43–48 (45.3) mm.,
            exp. cul. 14–15 (14.6) mm., tars. 12–15 (13.8) mm.
10 females wing 89–93 (90.9) mm., tail 40–48 (45.3) mm.,
            exp. cul. 14–15 (14.6) mm., tars. 12–15 (13.5) mm.

DISTRIBUTION

Known only from the Marañón Valley in Libertad, north-western Peru.

W.T. Cooper. 72.

The Yellow-faced Parrotlet has a very restricted known range, and virtually nothing is known of its habits, though I believe that they would not differ greatly from those of other species in the genus. Meyer de Schauensee (1971) says that it inhabits dry, open scrub in the subtropical and upper tropical zones. It has been collected at 1,720 m.

Genus BROTOGERIS Vigors

A narrow, protruding bill is the most conspicuous external feature of this genus; there is a wide, rounded notch in the upper mandible, and the lower mandible is strongly curved. The species are small parrots with short, gradated tails, though in two species—*tirica* and *versicolorus*—the central feathers are elongated. Thompson (1900) points out that the characteristic features of the skull are the incomplete orbital ring with a very small postfrontal process and large squamosal, and the presence of a large mandibular foramen. There is no sexual dimorphism and young birds resemble adults.

PLAIN PARAKEET
Brotogeris tirica (Gmelin)   *Illustrated on page 468.*

Length 23 cm.
ADULTS general plumage green, brighter and more yellowish on crown, cheeks, and underparts; bluish tinge on hindneck and mantle; upper back slightly tinged with bronze-olive; bend of wing and upper wing-coverts olive-brown; primary-coverts, primaries, and outer secondaries dull violet-blue edged with green; flanks, axillaries, and under wing-coverts greenish-yellow; undersides of flight feathers bluish-green; tail dark green above, dusky bluish-green below; bill brownish becoming pale horn-coloured towards base; iris dark brown; legs pink.
IMMATURES like adults, but with only tinges of blue on predominantly green primary-coverts, primaries, and outer secondaries; shorter tail; bill darker brown.
10 males   wing 116–128 (122,2) mm., tail 106–122 (114.9) mm.,
             exp. cul. 16–18 (17.0) mm., tars. 13–15 (13.7) mm.
8 females   wing 120–123 (121.8) mm., tail 107–131 (115.4) mm.,
             exp. cul. 16–18 (16.5) mm., tars. 13–15 (13.9) mm.

Eastern Brazil from eastern Bahia and southern Goiás to Rio Grande do Sul.

The Plain Parakeet has not been recorded from western and extreme northern Bahia, but is common throughout the remainder of the state (Pinto, 1935). Sick and Pabst (1968) point out that it is always present in the Rio de Janeiro Botanic Gardens, and is sometimes seen in parks elsewhere in the city; it has been recorded in the Quinta da Bôa Vista in September. Mitchell (1957) says that it is a widely distributed species in eastern Brazil, and inhabits more open country than does the Maroon-bellied Conure (*Pyrrhura frontalis*), another common species in the region; she recorded it in greater numbers in park lands, and saw it less often in such localities as the wooded slopes of Mt. Itatiaia, Rio de Janeiro. Mitchell also recorded it in flocks in the Rio de Janeiro Botanic Gardens throughout the year; in late May 1971 I made a number of visits to these Gardens but saw the species only once—two birds were flushed from a tall tree and they flew off towards Corcovado. I found it to be common in and around São Paulo. It was often seen in palm trees lining the entrance driveway to the Museu Ipiranga, and it was always present in the Praça da República.

The Praça da República is a park taking up a square block in the centre of the business sector of the city of São Paulo. It is completely surrounded by towering commercial buildings, and is a very busy place. Office workers use it for relaxation during lunch hour, and there is a never-ending stream of pedestrian traffic. On Sundays art exhibitions and musical recitals are staged there. Finally, there are the countless numbers of cars, buses, and trucks that roar past on all sides day and night. This park was the last place I expected to find parrots, yet small flocks of Plain Parakeets could always been seen there. They were usually seen flying from one tree to the next or climbing among the branches, but on one occasion I watched a flock leave the park and fly between multi-storey office buildings before returning to trees on the opposite side.

These parakeets are extremely difficult to locate when they are sitting or feeding in the treetops, so well does their plumage blend with the foliage. I often had trouble finding them even though I had seen them fly into the tree. Mitchell noticed that when feeding they seemed to be less active than Maroon-bellied Conures, and they moved about slowly among the branches, climbing rather than fluttering from one to the other. I saw them singly, in pairs, and in small parties. They are very noisy, particularly when in flight. The flight is swift and direct.

They feed on seeds, fruits, berries, blossoms, nectar, and possibly insects and their larvae.

CALL In flight a shrill, rolling screech; while feeding or resting in the treetops a harsh, disyllabic, rasping note is given.

Monk Parakeet *Myiopsitta monachus monachus* **1**
AMNH. 321560 ad. ♂

Monk Parakeet *Myiopsitta monachus luchsi* **2**
ANSP. 143696 ad. ♀

DESCRIPTION

DISTRIBUTION

GENERAL NOTES

NESTING Little is known of the nesting habits of this common species. Near Juiz de Fora, southern Minas Gerais, in early September, Mitchell found a pair nesting in a hollow in a tree, and during late January, in a park in São Paulo, she saw young birds being fed by adults.

Lovell-Keays (1914b) gives details of a successful breeding in captivity. Four eggs were laid and all hatched. It was estimated that incubation lasted about twenty-six days and only the female brooded; she was fed by the male. The young birds left the nest seven weeks after hatching.

EGGS Rounded; 7 eggs, 25.3 (22.3–26.9) × 21.4 (19.2–22.7) mm. [Schönwetter, 1964].

CANARY-WINGED PARAKEET
Brotogeris versicolorus (P. L. S. Müller)

DESCRIPTION Length 22 cm.

ADULTS general plumage dull green, darker on back and scapulars; forehead, periophthalmic region, and foreparts of cheeks tinged with bluish-grey; lores bare with scattered bluish-grey feathers; primary-coverts dark blue; outer webs of first four primaries green washed with blue towards bases, remaining primaries white; secondaries white tinged with yellow; secondary-coverts yellow; under wing-coverts dull green; undersides of flight feathers bluish-green; tail green above, dusky greenish-blue below; bill horn-coloured with pronounced yellow tinge; iris dark brown; legs greyish-pink.

IMMATURES fewer primaries are white and these have green tips; secondary-coverts yellow edged with green.

DISTRIBUTION From French Guiana, the Amazon Basin in northern Brazil, south-eastern Colombia, and eastern Ecuador south to northern Argentina, Paraguay, and south-eastern Brazil; introduced to the Lima area, central Peru, and to Puerto Rico, West Indies.

SUBSPECIES 1. *B. v. versicolorus* (P. L. S. Müller)   *Illustrated on page 472.*

11 males   wing 117–125 (122.2) mm., tail 80–94 (87.1) mm.,
           exp. cul. 14–17 (15.3) mm., tars. 14–15 (14.5) mm.
10 females   wing 116–124 (120.3) mm., tail 81–94 (86.8) mm.,
           exp. cul. 14–16 (15.0) mm., tars. 13–15 (14.1) mm.

Distributed from eastern Ecuador, north-eastern Peru, and south-eastern Colombia east through the Amazon Basin to the Belém area, Pará, and Mexiana Island at the mouth of the Amazon River, northern Brazil, and to French Guiana. According to Koepcke (1970) it is this race that has been introduced to the Lima area, central Peru. Kepler does not identify the subspecies seen in Puerto Rico (in Bond, 1971b), but I suspect that it was probably *versicolorus*.

2. *B. v. chiriri* (Vieillot)   *Illustrated on page 472.*

ADULTS general plumage green, paler and more yellowish on underparts; no bluish-grey tinge on forehead, periophthalmic region, or foreparts of cheeks; lores fully feathered; primaries green tinged with blue towards bases; secondaries green; secondary-coverts yellow; tail bright green above, yellowish-green below.

IMMATURES like adults.

10 males   wing 116–128 (122.0) mm., tail 87–106 (94.2) mm.,
           exp. cul. 15–17 (16.2) mm., tars. 13–15 (14.2) mm.
10 females   wing 115–125 (118.3) mm., tail 85–100 (91.8) mm.,
           exp. cul. 14–16 (14.9) mm., tars. 12–14 (13.3) mm.

Occurs in the interior of eastern and southern Brazil from Ceará, Maranhão, and southern Pará south to Rio de Janeiro, western São Paulo and Mato Grosso, and in northern and eastern Bolivia, Paraguay, and northern Argentina in Chaco, Formosa and Misiones.

Pinto and Camargo (1957) point out that three specimens from Cachimbo on the east bank of the Tapajós River in southern Pará, northern Brazil, show no tendency toward *versicolorus*, although the locality is almost within the range of the nominate race. This suggests that *chiriri* may be specifically distinct from *versicolorus*.

3. *B. v. behni* Neumann

ADULTS similar to *chiriri*, but larger; green of general plumage lacks yellowish tinge; underside of tail bluish-green.

9 males   wing 127–138 (131.3) mm., tail 98–112 (104.3) mm.,
           exp. cul. 15–17 (15.9) mm., tars. 14–15 (14.4) mm.
8 females   wing 123–133 (129.3) mm., tail 98–117 (102.8) mm.,
           exp. cul. 14–15 (14.9) mm., tars. 13–14 (13.8) mm.

Known only from central and southern Bolivia, though birds from Salta, north-western Argentina probably belong to this race. If *chiriri* is treated as a distinct species this race will belong to it.

The Canary-winged Parakeet is a common inhabitant of most types of wooded country in the

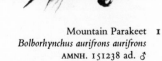

Mountain Parakeet   1
Bolborhynchus aurifrons aurifrons
AMNH. 151238 ad. ♂

Sierra Parakeet *Bolborhynchus aymara*   2
ANSP. 143990 ad. ♂

Barred Parakeet *Bolborhynchus lineola lineola*   3
AMNH. 326014 ad. ♂

Rufous-fronted Parakeet   4
Bolborhynchus ferrugineifrons
ANSP. 154716 ad. ♂

Andean Parakeet *Bolborhynchus orbygnesius*   5
LSUMZ. 37268 ad. ♂

W.T.Cooper. 72.

Mexican Parrotlet **1**
Forpus cyanopygius cyanopygius
AMNH. 474911 ad. ♂

Blue-winged Parrotlet **2**
Forpus xanthopterygius xanthopterygius
NHRS. 552780 ad. ♂

Sclater's Parrotlet *Forpus sclateri sclateri* **3**
NHRS. 552781 ad. ♂

Sclater's Parrotlet *Forpus sclateri sclateri* **4**
NHRS. 552782 ad. ♀

Pacific Parrotlet *Forpus coelestis* **5**
AMNH. 185566 ad. ♂

Pacific Parrotlet *Forpus coelestis* **6**
AMNH. 185568 ad. ♀

Yellow-faced Parrotlet *Forpus xanthops* **7**
AMNH. 474976 ad. ♂

Green-rumped Parrotlet **8**
Forpus passerinus passerinus
RMNH. Cat. 54, Reg. 28045 ad. ♂

Spectacled Parrotlet **9**
Forpus conspicillatus conspicillatus
AMNH. 71554 ♂

tropical zone. In Cochabamba, central Bolivia, it has been collected at 1,560 m., the upper limit of the tropical zone (in Bond and Meyer de Schauensee, 1943). Dugand and Borrero (1946) report that it is perhaps the most common parrot in the vicinity of Leticia, extreme south-eastern Amazonas, Colombia; they saw large flocks in all places visited. I know of no recent reports from eastern Ecuador, but at the turn of the century Goodfellow (1900) reported seeing many thousands roosting in trees along the banks of the lower Napo River. Koepcke says that it is very common in the Peruvian lowlands, east of the Andes. Meyer de Schauensee found it to be common in the Belém district, Pará, northern Brazil, and on one occasion in mid-May he encountered a flock of approximately one thousand birds (in Stone, 1929). Stager (1961) says that in central Goiás, northern Brazil, it is abundant in gallery forest association on the Chapada dos Veadeiros and in patches of primary forest along the Serra Dourada. Pabst and Sick (1968) report that it sometimes visits Guanabara, eastern Brazil, and it has been observed in parklands on the outskirts of Rio de Janeiro. Mitchell (1957) points out that this species was probably common in the state of Rio de Janeiro in the 1850s, but appears to have subsequently retreated inland; she saw a single bird in the Rio de Janeiro Botanic Gardens. Cherrie noted that it was common at almost every locality in Mato Grosso, western Brazil, visited by the Roosevelt-Rondon Expedition in 1916 (in Naumburg, 1930). In the Descalvados district, Mato Grosso, Rehn found that it was numerous, mainly in small groups and usually in dry scrub (in Stone and Roberts, 1935). Olrog (1959) says that in northern Argentina it frequents subtropical forests.

A small population originating from escaped cage birds is now established in the Lima district, central Peru, and birds are regularly offered for sale in the Lima markets (Koepcke, 1970). Kepler reports the sighting of hundreds of these parrots on Puerto Rico, so the species is apparently established as a resident (in Bond, 1971b).

Canary-winged Parakeets are generally seen in flocks of from eight or ten up to fifty, though occasionally very large flocks containing hundreds of birds are encountered. In Mato Grosso, western Brazil, Cherrie found that during November large flocks were seen, but by January these had broken up into pairs which were investigating prospective nesting sites They are very noisy birds and their presence in an area cannot be overlooked, though while resting or feeding in the treetops they are difficult to detect because their plumage blends extremely well with the foliage. When in the air birds belonging to the nominate race are easily identified from below by the translucent white flight feathers. The flight is swift and direct.

These parrots feed on seeds, fruits, berries, blossoms, and vegetable matter. Dugand and Borrero report that in the Leticia district, south-eastern Colombia, numbers of birds gathered daily in gardens and patios to feed on ripe *Inga* fruits. Stomach contents from two birds collected at Cachimbo, Pará, northern Brazil, comprised seeds and fruits; from another taken on the upper São Francisco River, Minas Gerais, central Brazil, 3.3 gms. of seeds, of which about twenty-five were whole, and from two specimens collected at Salobra, Mato Grosso, western Brazil, tiny seeds, vegetable matter and fragments of rotten wood (Schubart *et al.*, 1965).

CALL In flight or when perched a rapid repetition of a shrill, metallic note; when feeding a high-pitched chattering is given.

NESTING Goodfellow concluded that along the lower Marañón River, north-eastern Peru, nesting must have taken place during July because at about that time local people had numbers of young birds. In Mato Grosso, western Brazil, Cherrie saw pairs seeking nest sites in January. The nest is in a hollow limb or hole in a tree or in a hole excavated in an arboreal termites' mound.

Vane (1954) gives details of a successful breeding in captivity. Five eggs were laid and all hatched. Incubation commenced with the laying of the second egg and lasted approximately twenty-six days. Only the female brooded; the male joined her in the nest-box at night, but probably did not assist with incubation. The young birds left the nest eight weeks after hatching.

EGGS Rounded; 9 eggs, 22.8 (21.0–23.1) × 18.8 (17.5–19.6) mm. [Schönwetter, 1964].

GREY-CHEEKED PARAKEET
Brotogeris pyrrhopterus (Latham)

Illustrated on page 469.

Length 20 cm.
ADULTS general plumage green, paler and more yellowish on underparts; forehead greyish; crown bluish-green; sides of head and chin pale grey; slight brownish tinge on lesser and median wing-coverts; primary-coverts dark blue; primaries green slightly tinged with blue; under wing-coverts and axillaries orange; undersides of flight feathers bluish-green; tail green, feathers narrowly edged with yellow on inner webs; bill horn-coloured slightly tinged with orange; iris dark brown; legs pale pink.
IMMATURES like adults, but crown green without bluish suffusion.
10 males wing 112–125 (117.8) mm., tail 65–75 (69.5) mm.,
    exp. cul. 16–18 (17.2) mm., tars. 13–15 (13.9) mm.
8 females wing 115–120 (117.3) mm., tail 63–70 (67.1) mm.,
    exp. cul. 16–17 (16.3) mm., tars. 13–15 (13.8) mm.

West of the Andes from the Chone River district, western Ecuador, south to Piura, extreme DISTRIBUTION north-western Peru.

GENERAL NOTES

Meyer de Schauensee (1970) says that the Grey-cheeked Parakeet inhabits arid scrublands in the tropical zone. Apparently it is quite common within its restricted range, yet little has been recorded about its habits. Brosset (1964) reports that it is very common in western Ecuador and can be seen in large flocks, particularly in the vicinity of banana plantations. Stomach contents from a specimen collected by Brosset in western Ecuador comprised seeds and fruits.

CALL A shrill, metallic note repeated rapidly (in captivity).

NESTING Hampe (1939) quotes details given by Hood of a successful breeding in captivity. Five eggs were laid over a period of eight days, and four chicks hatched. Incubation lasted approximately four weeks, and the young birds left the nest about five weeks after hatching.

EGGS Rounded; 6 eggs, 22.8 (21.4–25.5) × 17.9 (16.7–18.6) mm. [Schönwetter, 1964].

ORANGE-CHINNED PARAKEET
Brotogeris jugularis (P. L. S. Müller)

Length 18 cm.

ADULTS general plumage green, paler and yellowish on throat, breast, and abdomen; crown and occiput tinged with blue; orange chin; mantle washed with olive; lower back and rump tinged with blue; lesser and median wing-coverts olive-brown; primary-coverts violet-blue; primaries bluish-green; thighs and under tail-coverts bluish-green; carpal edge and under wing-coverts greenish-yellow; undersides of flight feathers bluish-green; tail above green tinged with blue, below dusky bluish-green; bill horn-coloured; iris dark brown; legs pale yellowish-brown. IMMATURES similar to adults.

Plain Parakeet *Brotogeris tirica* **1**
NMV. B10907 ad. unsexed

Cobalt-winged Parakeet **2**
Brotogeris cyanoptera gustavi
ANSP. 118071 ad. ♂

Cobalt-winged Parakeet **3**
Brotogeris cyanoptera cyanoptera
NMV. 24826 ad. unsexed

South-western Mexico south to northern Colombia and northern Venezuela.

DISTRIBUTION

SUBSPECIES

1. *B. j. jugularis* (P. L. S. Müller)
   10 males   wing 105–112 (108.6) mm., tail 55–67 (61.1) mm.,
             exp. cul. 15–17 (16.0) mm., tars. 13–14 (13.2) mm.
   10 females wing 105–111 (108.3) mm., tail 55–68 (61.0) mm.,
             exp. cul. 15–17 (15.5) mm., tars. 13–14 (13.3) mm.

   Illustrated on page 469.

   Distributed from south-western Mexico south through Central America, mainly on the Pacific side, to northern Colombia, as far south as Chocó, Tolima, and Santander, and to north-western Venezuela east to the Cordillera de Mérida; absent from British Honduras.

2. *B. j. exsul* Todd
   ADULTS similar to *jugularis*, but thighs and under tail-coverts bright green without blue tinge; orange marking on chin paler and less extensive; more pronounced olive suffusion on mantle; lesser and median wing-coverts darker olive-brown.
   5 males   wing 110–113 (111.4) mm., tail 59–65 (61.0) mm.,
            exp. cul. 15–17 (15.8) mm., tars. 13–14 (13.2) mm.
   5 females wing 110–113 (111.2) mm., tail 59–63 (60.6) mm.,
            exp. cul. 15–16 (15.4) mm., tars. 12–14 (13.0) mm.

   Occurs in north-western Venezuela, between the Orinoco River in Guárico and Apure and the Cordillera de Mérida, and in Arauca, north-eastern Colombia.

GENERAL NOTES

According to Blake (1953) the Orange-chinned Parakeet is a very abundant and conspicuous inhabitant of the arid Pacific lowlands in Guerrero, Oaxaca, and Chiapas, south-western Mexico. Binford (1968) reports that in Oaxaca it is an uncommon permanent resident in humid gallery forest, and perhaps other habitats, of the Pacific lowlands and adjoining foothills up to 250 m. Monroe (1968) says that it occurs in the arid Pacific lowlands and arid interior of Honduras up to 900 m. elevation; it is found in the same situations as the Orange-fronted Conure (*Aratinga canicularis*), but is less common than that species and does not associate with it in mixed flocks. It has been recorded from Isla Tigre in the Golfo de Fonseca, Honduras (see Stone, 1933). In Guatemala it is a fairly common resident of the Pacific lowlands up to 500 m., and is found in scrublands, secondary growth, and open woodland (Land, 1970). Dickey and van Rossem (1938) state that in El Salvador it is a common resident of wooded areas in the arid tropical zone, the centre of abundance being the coastal plain; it wanders locally, and after the breeding season may ascend up to 1,400 m. Howell (1957) reports that at El Recreo, on the humid Caribbean slope of southern Nicaragua, this species was commonly seen in large trees left standing in fields and at the edges of clearings. Slud (1964) points out that in Costa Rica it is nearly confined to the Pacific slope along the length of the country and has two centres of distribution, one in the dry-forested north-west, the other in the Térraba-Golfo Dulce region of the far south-west; the species is abundant in semi-open and partly deforested areas in the tropical zone, though along the Guanacaste Cordillera,

W.T.Cooper '76.

and perhaps also the Cordillera de Tilarán, it is resident in the lower subtropical zone. It reaches the northern and north-western Caribbean lowlands of Costa Rica by way of the southern shores of Lake Nicaragua. At three localities in the Pacific lowlands Orians (1969) recorded it in secondary growth and closed forest. In Panama it is a common resident of the tropical zone on both the Pacific and Caribbean slopes, though not recorded to date from Bocas del Toro or northern Veraguas (Wetmore, 1968); it occurs on Isla Coiba, Isla Cébaco, and Isla Taboga, though on the last it may have been introduced from the mainland. It is found in lowlands wherever there are trees, and, although more common in open country, it does frequent heavy forest, where it is not easily detected in the treetops. On Isla Coiba it is fairly common, though not nearly so abundant as in many mainland localities (Wetmore, 1957). At Paracoté, on the Azuero Peninsula, Panama, Aldrich and Bole (1937) found that it was common in and around a coconut plantation and was often seen feeding in the tops of tall trees at the edge of the forest. Eisenmann (1952) says that it is common on Barro Colorado Island, Panama Canal Zone, and outside the breeding season, which extends from January to May, large flocks frequently gather, particularly in the afternoon, in the clearing surrounding the laboratory buildings. Meyer de Schauensee (1964) reports that in Colombia it inhabits open woods in the tropical zone. Dugand (1947) points out that in Atlántico, northern Colombia, it was seen only in western forested regions, including the shores of Lake Tocahagua, the wooded plains of Puerto Giraldo along the Magdalena River, and forests bordering the southern lakes; it seems to avoid semi-arid districts. Darlington (1931) says that in the Santa Marta region, northern Colombia, this parrot is one of the first of local birds to be seen by casual visitors because it is abundant in the shade and fruit trees of the various towns as well as being common throughout semi-open country. In the upper Magdalena Valley, central Colombia, Miller (1947) found it in woodlands along watercourses. In north-western Venezuela it is generally distributed in the vicinity of Lake Maracaibo and is locally distributed elsewhere; it inhabits wooded clearings and farmlands in the tropical zone (Phelps and Phelps, 1958).

During the breeding season these parakeets are generally observed in pairs or family parties, but at other times flocks of from ten to thirty are usually encountered. Flocks often come together where there is an abundance of food in a confined area or at a roosting site and hundreds of birds may be present. Screeching flocks circling above the treetops or flying swiftly across semi-arid scrublands are a conspicuous component of the local avifauna. Van Tyne (1950) observed these parrots on Barro Colorado Island, Panama Canal Zone, and noticed that each flock was an aggregation of many pairs, a fact that became obvious when the flock alighted and birds perched close to each other in twos and somewhat apart from others. Slud reports that they often sit on high bare branches of tall trees in clearings. When they are perching, especially if they have just alighted or are about to take flight again, they are usually silent, but on the wing they keep up a constant chatter. Wetmore (1968) remarks that when they alight they seem to disappear as they crouch motionless amid the green leaves that match their plumage. While feeding in trees or shrubs they present a scene of intense activity as they flutter from one branch to another and clamber about amongst the foliage, often hanging upside-down to get at fruits or flowers. They fly very rapidly with many twists and changes of direction; often they alternate series of wingbeats with brief periods of gliding. Wetmore (1968) reports measuring their flight speed by speedometer at 72 km. per hour when they were flying alongside his car on a highway in Panama.

They feed on fruits, nectar, blossoms, seeds, and vegetable matter, procured in trees and shrubs. Aldrich and Bole report that at Paracoté, on the Azuero Peninsula, Panama, the birds were seen feeding in the tops of tall trees bearing small red fruits which were obviously much to their liking. Eisenmann (1961) notes that on Barro Colorado Island, Panama Canal Zone, they have been seen eating the tips of catkins of guarumo trees (*Cecropia mexicana*). Wetmore (1957) reports that on Isla Coiba, Panama, there were guayabo trees scattered through the pastures and when these came into blossom the parrots visited them regularly to feed on nectar; three specimens collected had their throats completely filled with nectar. In Panama they have also been observed eating fleshy parts of balsa flowers, and tearing apart pods of barrigón (*Bombax* sp.) to get at the small seeds (Wetmore, 1968). Darlington reports that in the Santa Marta region, northern Colombia, they are partial to *Cecropia* catkins, and they cause much damage to cultivated fruits. Stomachs from two specimens collected in the Panama Canal Zone contained fruit fragments and vegetable matter, and from another taken in the same region about twenty soft white seeds with an average diameter of 6.4 mm. (Hallinan, 1924). Olson and Blum (1968) report finding seeds of *Muntingia calabura* in the crop of a parrot collected on Barro Colorado Island, Panama Canal Zone.

CALL These parrots give a variety of shrill screeches, squawks, and chattering notes; the normal call given in flight is a harsh, rasping continuous chatter of quick notes on the same level and sounding like *ack-ack-ack-ack* (Slud, 1964). Antiphonal singing or antiphonal dueting, that is vocalizing by two individuals such that distinct or similar phrases or syllables are uttered alternately, has been recorded in captive birds (Power, 1966).

NESTING On Barro Colorado Island, Panama Canal Zone, Van Tyne noticed that in late winter the flocks broke up into rather widely scattered breeding pairs and then reassembled in late spring after nesting had finished; thus, in February 1926 there were but three pairs in the laboratory clearing instead of the usual large flock, and the first small post-breeding flock did not appear until mid-May. Dickey and van Rossem (1938) report that a female collected in El Salvador in late January was laying, and in the same month at Puerto del Triunfo, also in El Salvador, pairs were seen widening and digging out natural cavities such as knot-holes and shallow cracks in dead trees; at one stump, completely rotted out in the centre and with one side open, about a

Golden-winged Parakeet 1
Brotogeris chrysopterus chrysopterus
RMNH. Cat. 20, Reg. 35363 ad. ♂

Orange-chinned Parakeet 2
Brotogeris jugularis jugularis
AM. A13424 ad. unsexed

Grey-cheeked Parakeet *Brotogeris pyrrhopterus* 3
BM. 1940.12.5.1050 ad. ♀

Tui Parakeet *Brotogeris sanctithomae takatsukasae* 4
ANSP. 91091 ad. unsexed

Tui Parakeet *Brotogeris sanctithomae sanctithomae* 5
AMNH. 791775 ad. ♂

dozen pairs were found working at nesting sites on the inside of the shell. The birds also nest in old woodpeckers' holes and in holes excavated in arboreal termites' mounds. Wetmore (1968) has seen as many as eight fledglings taken from one nest.

Power (1967) describes how captive parrots excavated nesting cavities in artificial cork termitaria. Male and female shared equally in the excavation of the nest, digging alternately at the outset and simultaneously when the cavity was large enough to accommodate both birds. A nest consisted of a short tunnel, which began on the lower half of the outside of the termitarium and inclined upwardly to open near the top of a spherical or ellipsoidal chamber in the heart of the termitarium. Much of the daily resting and all nocturnal roosting by pairs were inside the nesting cavities as soon as each was large enough to accommodate both birds.

Hood (1961) gives details of a successful breeding in captivity. Four eggs were laid and all hatched. Incubation lasted approximately three weeks and for most of that time the male sat beside the female in the nest-box, though at times he stood guard at the entrance. The nestling period is not given.

EGGS Rounded; 2 eggs, 23.7 (23.3–24.1) × 19.6 (18.8–20.3) mm. [Harrison and Holyoak, 1970].

Canary-winged Parakeet **1**
Brotogeris versicolorus versicolorus
NMV. 24817 ad. ♂

Canary-winged Parakeet **2**
Brotogeris versicolorus chiriri
AMNH. 475078 ad. ♂

Tepui Parrotlet *Nannopsittaca panychlora* **3**
BM. 1922.3.5.1307 ad. unsexed

COBALT-WINGED PARAKEET
Brotogeris cyanoptera (Pelzeln)

Length 18 cm.
ADULTS general plumage green, darker on back and wings; forehead and lores yellow, duller and less extensive in female; crown and nape tinged with blue; orange chin; primary-coverts and secondaries violet-blue; outermost primaries violet-blue edged with green, remaining primaries violet-blue; carpal edge and under wing-coverts green; undersides of flight feathers bluish-green; central tail-feathers dark blue margined with green, next pair green edged with blue, remaining tail-feathers green; underside of tail yellowish-green; bill pale horn-coloured; iris dark brown; legs pale flesh-brown.
IMMATURES undescribed, but probably similar to adults.

DISTRIBUTION Western Amazon Basin from southern Venezuela, south-eastern Colombia, north-eastern Peru, and eastern Ecuador south to north-western Bolivia.

SUBSPECIES

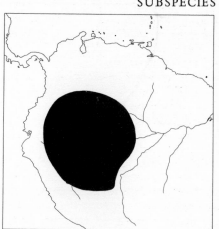

1. *B. c. cyanoptera* (Pelzeln)   *Illustrated on page 468.*
   10 males   wing 114–120 (116.4) mm., tail 50–64 (56.6) mm.,
           exp. cul. 15–18 (16.5) mm., tars. 13–15 (14.2) mm.
   10 females wing 113–123 (117.3) mm., tail 49–63 (56.1) mm.,
           exp. cul. 15–18 (16.5) mm., tars. 13–15 (13.9) mm.
   Distributed from the Negro and Purús Rivers, Amazonas, Brazil, west to the upper Orinoco Valley, southern Venezuela, south-eastern Colombia north to Meta and Cundinamarca, eastern Ecuador, and eastern Peru; intergrades with *gustavi* in the lower Huallaga River valley, north-eastern Peru, and with *beniensis* in northern Bolivia.

2. *B. c. gustavi* Berlepsch   *Illustrated on page 468.*
   ADULTS greenish-yellow tinge on forehead; very little blue suffusion on crown and nape; bend of wing and carpal edge yellow; outermost primary-coverts green, inner primary-coverts violet-blue.

   1 male   wing 119 mm., tail 58 mm.,
               exp. cul. 18 mm., tars. 15 mm.
   1 female   wing 121 mm., tail 58 mm.,
               exp. cul. 16 mm., tars. 14 mm.

   1 unsexed (**type**); wing 111 mm., tail 61 mm.,
               exp. cul. 16 mm., tars. 14 mm.
   Restricted to the upper Huallaga River valley in northern Peru; Traylor (1958) points out that birds from the lower Huallaga River valley are intermediate between this race and *cyanoptera*.

3. *B. c. beniensis* Gyldenstolpe
   ADULTS like *gustavi*, but general plumage paler, more yellowish-green; forehead and lores distinctly tinged with yellow; strong bluish tinge on crown and nape; bend of wing, carpal edge, and primary-coverts yellow.
   5 males   wing 116–121 (119.2) mm., tail 54–60 (57.2) mm.,
           exp. cul. 16–18 (17.6) mm., tars. 14–16 (14.4) mm.
   4 females wing 113–119 (116.5) mm., tail 53–62 (57.0) mm.,
           exp. cul. 16–18 (16.8) mm., tars. 14–15 (14.3) mm.
   Known only from Beni province, northern Bolivia; Bond and Meyer de Schauensee (1943) report that in the vicinity of Rurrenabaque, Beni, this race intergrades with *cyanoptera*.

The Cobalt-winged Parakeet is widely distributed and seems to be quite common throughout much of its range, yet there is very little recorded information on its habits. I suspect that its habits are very similar to those of the closely-allied *B. jugularis*. In Venezuela it occurs in open country in the tropical zone (Phelps and Phelps, 1958). Meyer de Schauensee (1964) says that in Colombia it inhabits savannah in the tropical zone. Dugand and Borrero (1948) report that in the vicinity of Tres Esquinas, Caquetá, south-eastern Colombia, this species and the Maroon-tailed Conure (*Pyrrhura melanura*) were the most common parrots, and flocks of the former were seen every day. In northern Bolivia specimens have been collected in the lowlands up to about 300 m. (Bond and Meyer de Schauensee, 1943).

CALL Undescribed.

NESTING No published records.

EGGS Rounded; 6 eggs, 23.1 (22.1–23.9) × 18.5 17.0–19.8) mm. [Schönwetter, 1964].

GOLDEN-WINGED PARAKEET
Brotogeris chrysopterus (Linné)

Length 16 cm.
ADULTS general plumage green, slightly darker on back and wings; blackish-brown frontal band; crown tinged with blue; cheeks dark bluish-green; orange-brown chin spot; primary-coverts orange; primaries violet-blue broadly margined and tipped with green; under wing-coverts green; undersides of flight feathers bluish-green; tail above green tinged with blue, below dusky green; bill pale horn-coloured; iris dark brown; legs pale yellowish-brown.
IMMATURES like adults, but primary-coverts green.

Amazonian Brazil, eastern Venezuela, and the Guianas.

1. *B. c. chrysopterus* (Linné)
    8 males   wing 107–111 (109.1) mm., tail 50–63 (56.6) mm.,
           exp. cul. 17–18 (17.4) mm., tars. 13–14 (13.4) mm.
    8 females wing 103–110 (106.8) mm., tail 53–66 (58.1) mm.,
           exp. cul. 15–17 (16.5) mm., tars. 13–14 (13.5) mm.

Illustrated on page 469.

    Occurs in the Guianas, eastern Venezuela from Sucre and Monagas south to Bolívar and north of the Amazon River in northernmost Brazil from Roraima to Amapá.

2. *B. c. tuipara* (Gmelin)
    ADULTS like *chrysopterus*, but narrow frontal band and chin spot orange; lateral tail-feathers narrowly edged with yellow.
    8 males   wing 112–123 (117.3) mm., tail 56–67 (62.0) mm.,
           exp. cul. 17–19 (17.6) mm., tars. 14–15 (14.1) mm.
    8 females wing 111–120 (115.3) mm., tail 52–64 (58.5) mm.,
           exp. cul. 17–18 (17.3) mm., tars. 13–15 (14.0) mm.

    Distributed along the southern side of the Amazon River, northern Brazil, from the lower Tapajós River, Pará, east to Isla de Marajó and the Belém district, and along the coastal forest belt to north-eastern Maranhão.

3. *B. c. chrysosema* Sclater
    ADULTS forehead and lores yellowish-orange; orange chin spot; primary-coverts yellow; larger size.
    5 males   wing 118–124 (121.0) mm., tail 55–66 (62.4) mm.,
           exp. cul. 17–18 (17.6) mm., tars. 13–15 (14.2) mm.
    4 females wing 118–120 (119.3) mm., tail 56–60 (58.0) mm.,
           exp. cul. 17–18 (17.5) mm., tars. 14–15 (14.3) mm.

    Restricted to the Madeira River and its tributaries in Amazonas and northern Mato Grosso, Brazil.

4. *B. c. solimoensis* Gyldenstolpe
    ADULTS like *chrysopterus*, but frontal band paler, more reddish-brown; paler, yellowish-brown chin spot.
    8 males   wing 111–118 (113.5) mm., tail 57–65 (58.9) mm.,
           exp. cul. 16–18 (16.8) mm., tars. 12–14 (13.0) mm.
    6 females wing 109–114 (111.7) mm., tail 56–63 (57.8) mm.,
           exp. cul. 16–18 (17.0) mm., tars. 12–14 (13.0) mm.

    Known only from the upper Amazon River in the Codajas and Manaus districts, Amazonas, northern Brazil.

5. *B. c. tenuifrons* Friedmann
    ADULTS similar to *tuipara*, but has practically no frontal band and what little there is, is brownish, almost as in *chrysopterus*.

          2 males   wing 109–111 (110.0) mm., tail 53–60 (56.5) mm.,
                        exp. cul. 16–17 (16.5) mm., tars. 13–14 (13.5) mm.
          1 female   wing 109 mm., tail 55 mm.,
                        exp. cul. 16 mm., tars. 13 mm.
          Known only from the upper Negro River at Santa Isabel and the mouth of the Cauaburi
River, Amazonas, north-western Brazil.

GENERAL NOTES   Haverschmidt (1968) says that in Surinam the Golden-winged Parakeet is quite common in forests
on the coastal sand ridges, in the adjoining savannah region, and in the interior. Apparently it
wanders to some extent because in the last ten days of July 1964 flocks appeared in trees on the
outskirts of Paramaribo, and small numbers were observed in trees in the centre of town. In
Guyana it is generally seen in the forest canopy or flying above the treetops (Snyder, 1966).
Phelps and Phelps (1958) point out that it is locally distributed in eastern and southern regions of
Venezuela. Smith reports that he collected a specimen in heavy lowland forest at Quiriquire,
Monagas, north-eastern Venezuela, and this was the only place at which the species was
encountered (in Friedmann and Smith, 1955). Beebe (1916) found it to be quite common in forest
on the outskirts of Belém, Pará, northern Brazil, and his notes give a good account of its general
habits.

Beebe observed that these noisy parakeets were restless forest birds shifting from one feeding
place to another, always gorging themselves and tearing off bunches of berries but wasting much
more than they ate. They were quite common, and half an hour would seldom pass without a
pair or small flock dashing past high overhead, screeching loudly. While feeding they showed
little fear and could be easily approached. In the evening they collected in flocks of thirty or forty
and circled about high in the air before flying off in a south-westerly direction toward some
distant roost.

Food consists of fruits, berries, seeds, blossoms, nectar, and probably vegetable matter procured
in the treetops. Beebe collected a specimen near Belém and found twenty-three berries in its crop.

CALL   A high-pitched *chil . . . chil . . . chil* or *chit-chit* (Snyder, 1966).

NESTING   In Surinam, Haverschmidt has recorded nesting in November, February, and April.
The nest is in a hollow limb or hole in a tree or in a hole excavated in an arboreal termites' mound.
The normal clutch comprises three or four eggs (Penard and Penard, 1908). Nothing further is
known of the nesting habits.

EGGS   Penard and Penard claim that the eggs are rounded and average 23 × 18 mm.

TUI PARAKEET
Brotogeris sanctithomae (P. L. S. Müller)

DESCRIPTION   Length 17 cm.
ADULTS general plumage green, paler and more yellowish on underparts, under wing-coverts,
lower back, rump and upper tail-coverts; slight bluish cast on cheeks and nape; forehead, lores,
and forecrown yellow; primaries dark green; undersides of flight feathers bluish-green; tail green
above, yellowish-green below; bill brownish; iris grey; legs pale greyish-brown.
IMMATURES like adults.

DISTRIBUTION   Amazon Basin from Amapá, northernmost Brazil, west to eastern Ecuador and northern Bolivia.

SUBSPECIES   1. *B. s. sanctithomae* (P. L. S. Müller)   *Illustrated on page 469.*
          10 males   wing 106–114 (109.6) mm., tail 52–61 (57.3) mm.,
                        exp. cul. 13–15 (14.4) mm., tars. 13–14 (13.6) mm.
          10 females wing 101–115 (107.6) mm., tail 52–62 (57.1) mm.,
                        exp. cul. 12–14 (13.6) mm., tars. 12–14 (13.1) mm.
          Distributed from the upper Amazon River at the mouth of the Madeira River, eastern
Amazonas, Brazil, west through south-eastern Colombia and north-eastern Peru to easternmost Ecuador, and along the Madeira River and its tributaries to northernmost Bolivia.

2. *B. s. takatsukasae* Neumann   *Illustrated on page 469.*
          ADULTS like *sanctithomae*, but with yellow streak behind eye; generally, though not always,
more extensive yellow marking on forehead and forecrown.
          10 males   wing 98–110 (104.3) mm., tail 46–60 (52.7) mm.,
                        exp. cul. 13–15 (13.7) mm., tars. 12–14 (13.0) mm.
          10 females wing 99–106 (102.4) mm., tail 43–59 (50.4) mm.,
                        exp. cul. 13–14 (13.4) mm., tars. 12–13 (12.7) mm.
          Restricted to the Amazon region of northern Brazil from about the mouth of the Madeira
River, eastern Amazonas, east along the north bank to Amapá and along the south bank to the
mouth of the Curuá River or possibly to the Belém district, Pará (see Pinto, 1947).

Tui Parakeets are common in captivity and appear to be quite abundant in the wild state, but there is little recorded information on their habits. Meyer de Schauensee (1970) says that they inhabit forest in the tropical zone. Novaes (1957) reports that in Acre, north-western Brazil, they are common in open country and flocks of from eight to ten birds were seen in manoic and sugarcane plantations. During the breeding season pairs or family parties are usually seen, while throughout the remainder of the year they associate in flocks. They are very noisy and spend much of the day in the treetops feeding on fruits, berries, nectar, blossoms, and seeds.

CALL A series of shrill, screaming notes and a rapid repetition of high-pitched shrieks (in captivity).

NESTING In July, Goodfellow (1900) recorded nesting along the lower Marañón River in north-eastern Peru. Six young birds were taken from a hollow in the bend of a branch of a tree about 6 m. from the ground; there was marked variation in the development of these nestlings, some being almost fully feathered while others were about half the size and with very few feathers showing.

EGGS According to Neunzig the eggs average 23 × 17 mm. [in Schönwetter, 1964].

Genus NANNOPSITTACA Ridgway

Mayr and Phelps (1967) claim that *Nannopsittaca* is allied to *Forpus*, *Touit*, and *Brotogeris*, and there are no obvious peculiarities to justify its separation as a monotypic genus; however, they do not synonymize it with any of the related genera and recent authors have continued to accept it. The species is a small parrot with a short squarish tail; the tail feathers are broad and have pointed tips. The protruding bill is slender and the upper mandible noticeably less downcurved than in related genera. The cere is naked. There is no sexual dimorphism.

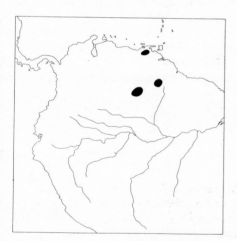

TEPUI PARROTLET
Nannopsittaca panychlora (Salvin and Godman)   *Illustrated on page 472.*

Length 14 cm.
ADULTS general plumage green, paler on underparts; periophthalmic region yellow, more extensive under eye; forehead, lores, chin, and under tail-coverts tinged with yellow, generally less pronounced in female; carpal edge pale yellow; undersides of flight feathers bluish-green; tail green above, bluish-green below; bill dusky; iris dark brown; legs pale brown.
IMMATURES undescribed, but probably similar to adults.
11 males   wing 89–98 (94.4) mm., tail 37–43 (41.0) mm.,
            exp. cul. 12–13 (12.1) mm., tars. 12–14 (12.4) mm.
10 females wing 88–98 (93.1) mm., tail 37–43 (39.7) mm.,
            exp. cul. 11–13 (11.9) mm., tars. 12–13 (12.2) mm.

DISTRIBUTION   The higher mountain peaks in eastern Venezuela, south of the Orinoco River in Amazonas and Bolívar and north of it only on Cerro Papelón in Sucre, and in the Mount Roraima district of extreme eastern Venezuela and westernmost Guyana.

GENERAL NOTES   The Tepui Parrotlet is an old element of the avifauna of the Pantepui area; that is, the isolated tabletop mountains in southern Venezuela, even though it also occurs in Sucre in north-eastern Venezuela so is not strictly an endemic (Mayr and Phelps, 1967). It is entirely restricted to cool, humid subtropical forests on the summits and slopes of the isolated mountains and does not enter the intervening tropical lowlands. Nothing is known of its habits.

Genus TOUIT G. R. Gray

Parrots belonging to *Touit* are small, stocky birds with short, square tails. The tail feathers are broad and have slightly pointed tips. The bill is proportionately large, though rather narrow, and there is no distinct notch in the upper mandible. The naked cere is quite prominent. Sexual dimorphism is present in most species.
    Touit is a poorly-known genus and most species are considered to be rare, mainly because few specimens have been collected. However, I believe that, as with *Opopsitta diophthalma* in Australia, the small number of specimens collected and the paucity of sight records may not be true indicators of the status of the birds but merely of the difficulty in detecting them in the forest canopy.

SEVEN-COLOURED PARROTLET
Touit batavica (Boddaert)

Illustrated on page 489.

Length 14 cm.
ADULTS forehead, lores, and foreparts of cheeks yellow; remainder of head and neck greenish-yellow, feathers of nape and sides of neck edged with black thus producing a scalloped appearance; back, rump, scapulars, and lesser and median wing-coverts black; upper tail-coverts black becoming yellowish-green towards tail and flanks; greater wing-coverts greenish-yellow becoming green and then blue towards outer and inner feathers; outer webs of tertials greenish-yellow; primary-coverts black; primaries and secondaries green; carpal edge rose-red; foreneck pale blue tinged with green; breast pale bluish-green merging into yellowish-green of abdomen, thighs, and under tail-coverts; under wing-coverts blue marked with yellow and red towards carpal edge, and bordered with black along leading edge; undersides of flight feathers bluish-green; central tail-feathers violet, lateral tail-feathers mauve-violet subterminally barred with black; bill yellowish with grey towards base; iris yellow; legs yellowish-brown.
IMMATURES undescribed, but presumably similar to adults.

8 males   wing 101–119 (111.9) mm., tail 43–47 (44.5) mm.,
            exp. cul. 15–16 (15.5) mm., tars. 12–14 (12.6) mm.
5 females   wing 108–112 (110.0) mm., tail 43–48 (45.4) mm.,
            exp. cul. 15–16 (15.2) mm., tars. 12–13 (12.4) mm.

Surinam, Guyana, and Venezuela, north of the Orinoco River from Sucre west to Mérida and south of the Orinoco River in eastern Bolívar; also on Trinidad and Tobago.

DISTRIBUTION

GENERAL NOTES

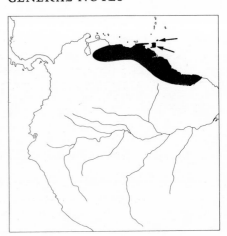

Herklots (1961) says that on Trinidad Seven-coloured Parrotlets are relatively abundant in lowland forests and in valleys of the Northern Range up to about 625 m. Nesting has been recorded at approximately 560 m., on Spring Hill Estate, Trinidad (Belcher and Smooker, 1936). Haverschmidt (1968) reports that they are irregular wanderers in the coastal region of Surinam; between the end of March and mid-April 1962, a flock frequented and roosted in a fruit-bearing tree at Slootwijk and several specimens were collected, all being in non-breeding condition and with very worn plumage. They are forest birds in Guyana (Snyder, 1966). In May 1971, at Marabuma, north-western Guyana, I found them in secondary forest and disturbed primary forest; a flock of about fifteen birds flew diagonally across the road and alighted in the canopy of a tall tree towering above surrounding trees in a small patch of forest on a hill. They are locally distributed in forests of the tropical and subtropical zones along the ridges of northern Venezuela from Sucre west to Mérida and south of the Orinoco River in Bolívar (Phelps and Phelps, 1958). Schafer and Phelps (1954) report that in the vicinity of the Rancho Grande Reserve, northern Venezuela, these parrotlets occur on both sides of the cordillera from the dry deciduous forests at 400 m. up to the subtemperate mountain forests at 1,700 m.; they are most common in humid tropical forests at 400 m. and during the rainy season in higher mountain forests at 800 m. They prefer dense forest and as a rule avoid open fields or plantations. They wander about locally and at the Rancho Grande Reserve birds can be seen moving through Portachuelo Pass almost every day, except between February and May when presumably they are nesting. Beebe (1947) recalls seeing a party of four birds flying through the Pass and pausing en route in a *Cecropia* tree.

These small parrots are gregarious and outside the breeding season associate in flocks of from ten to thirty, though much larger flocks have occasionally been recorded. They are strictly arboreal and keep to the canopies of tall forest trees. They are difficult to detect while feeding amongst the foliage so are generally observed flying overhead, often very high above the treetops. They are noisy when on the wing, but usually feed in silence. While feeding they may hang upside-down to get at blossoms or fruits. Herklots notes that they feed mainly in the early morning. Rapid, shallow wingbeats are a feature of the swift, direct flight.

Food consists of flowers, nectar, buds, fruits, berries, and seeds.

CALL When in flight flocks give a continuous plaintive, though penetrating, squeaking call resembling *ee—e th . . . ᵓe—th*; a series of soft chattering notes may also be uttered (Snyder, 1966). Belcher and Smooker report that on Trinidad breeding takes place during February and March, and the nest is in a hole excavated in an arboreal termites' mound or in a hollow limb or hole in a tree. On 13th March 1924, at Spring Hill Estate, Trinidad, five half-fledged young were found in a hole in a tree, and, on 8th March 1928, a set of six slightly-incubated eggs was taken from a hole, probably made by a woodpecker, in a tree at approximately 4 m. from the ground. Belcher was shown a hole in a termitarium from which young birds had been taken, and he watched a pair of parrots investigating another active termitarium. Nothing further is known of the nesting habits.

EGGS Almost spherical, slightly glossy; 6 eggs, 22.0 (21.5–22.8) × 19.3 (18.9–19.8) mm. [Belcher and Smooker, 1936].

SCARLET-SHOULDERED PARROTLET

Touit huetii (Temminck)

Illustrated on page 492.

DESCRIPTION

Length 15.5 cm.

MALE general plumage green, paler and more yellowish on underparts; forehead and lores bluish-black; anterior of cheeks violet-blue; ear-coverts and crown pale olive-brown; nape and hindneck green tinged with olive-brown; mantle and sides of neck dark green; thighs dull blue; under tail-coverts yellow; bend of wing, under wing-coverts and axillaries scarlet; lesser, median, and outer secondary-coverts violet-blue; primary-coverts black; primaries and outer secondaries black edged on outer webs with green; central tail-feathers green broadly tipped with black, lateral tail-feathers crimson tipped with black; bill yellowish with grey towards base; iris dark brown; legs greenish-grey.

FEMALE like male, but lateral tail-feathers greenish-yellow tipped with black.

IMMATURES similar to adult female, but without bluish-black on forehead and lores.

11 males wing 108–125 (113.7) mm., tail 40–45 (42.3) mm.,
     exp. cul. 13–15 (14.3) mm., tars. 12–13 (12.4) mm.
4 females wing 107–112 (109.8) mm., tail 40–43 (41.0) mm.,
     exp. cul. 13–14 (13.5) mm., tars. 11–12 (11.8) mm.

DISTRIBUTION

Occurs in northern Guyana, north-eastern and southern Venezuela in Monagas, western Bolívar, and Amazonas, the Guapaya River area, Meta, south-eastern Colombia, eastern Ecuador, eastern Peru in Loreto and Huánuco, and north-eastern Brazil south of the Amazon River between the lower Tocatins River and Belém, Pará, south to Araguatins, northernmost Goiás, and the Serra do Cachimbo, southern Pará; its presence in French Guiana and on Trinidad requires confirmation.

GENERAL NOTES

The Scarlet-shouldered Parrotlet is a little-known bird that has been recorded from scattered localities over a wide range, though it probably occurs in at least some, if not all, intervening areas. Snyder (1966) says that in Guyana it inhabits tropical forest, and large flocks have been recorded recently at Mabaruma and Wineperu, two localities in the northern sector. In Venezuela it frequents forests in the tropical zone and is only known from one locality in Monagas, two in western Bolívar, and one in western Amazonas (Phelps and Phelps, 1958). It seems that in Colombia the species is only known from a few specimens, all collected in the Guapaya River area at the foot of the Sierra Macarena in Meta (see Blake, 1962; Niceforo and Olivares, 1966), but almost certainly it also occurs in the extreme east adjoining the Venezuela border at San Fernando de Atabapo. At the turn of the century Goodfellow (1900) met with it below Baeza in eastern Ecuador, but I know of no recent records from that country.

O'Neill (1969) reports that at Santa Elena, Huánuco, eastern Peru, a flock of about fifty of these parrotlets frequented large fruiting trees and roosted in the thickest portion of the crown of a somewhat smaller tree across a narrow valley from the house in which he was staying. While in a tree the birds were never heard to utter a sound, and were almost undetectable because they moved about by climbing. When in flight the flock was always tightly compact and the birds called softly, the disyllabic notes resembling pronounciation of the generic name. Near Pucallpa, Loreto, eastern Peru, Maria Koepcke found a pair silently climbing among branches in the understorey of the forest (in O'Neill, 1969).

CALL In flight a high-pitched *witch-witch* (Snyder, 1966).

NESTING No records. A male with enlarged testes (COP.21455) was collected in early April at San Fernando de Atabapo, western Amazonas, Venezuela.

EGGS Undescribed.

RED-WINGED PARROTLET

Touit dilectissima (Sclater and Salvin)

Length 17 cm.

MALE general plumage green, paler and more yellowish on underparts; narrow frontal band, lores, and streak below eye red; forecrown and band from lores across upper cheeks to ear-coverts dull blue; hindcrown and nape bronze-green; bend of wing, lesser wing-coverts, outer median and inner primary-coverts, and forewing scarlet; outer primary-coverts black; primaries black, edged on outer webs with green; secondaries black; under wing-coverts yellow; undersides of flight feathers dull bluish-green; central tail-feathers black with green towards bases, lateral tail-feathers greenish-yellow tipped with black; bill yellowish with grey towards base; iris brown; legs grey.

FEMALE like male, but with little or no red on lesser wing-coverts and outer median wing-coverts; inner primary-coverts black.

IMMATURES similar to adult female, but forecrown green with scattered blue feathers; red frontal band and lores only slightly indicated; no red or blue below eye; iris grey.

DISTRIBUTION

DISTRIBUTION   Southern Costa Rica and neighbouring western Panama, and eastern Panama to north-western Venezuela and south to western Ecuador.

SUBSPECIES   1. *T. d. dilectissima* (Sclater and Salvin)   *Illustrated on page 492.*
    10 males   wing 111–120 (114.8) mm., tail 41–49 (44.6) mm.,
         exp. cul. 15–18 (15.9) mm., tars. 12–14 (12.7) mm.
    7 females   wing 110–116 (113.4) mm., tail 42–48 (44.0) mm.,
         exp. cul. 15–17 (14.3) mm., tars. 12–13 (12.6) mm.
    Distributed from Darién, eastern Panama, east through northern Colombia to north-western Venezuela, as far east as Trujillo, and south through western Colombia, inland to the western slopes of the eastern Andes, to north-western Ecuador, where recorded from El Barro, Quevedo.

    2. *T. d. costaricensis* (Cory)   *Illustrated on page 492.*
    ADULTS like *dilectissima*, but forecrown red; paler blue on cheeks; throat distinctly greenish-yellow; darker red on wings.
    IMMATURES similar to adults, but red of forecrown mixed with green.
    2 males   wing 119–121 (120.0) mm., tail 42–45 (43.5) mm.,
         exp. cul. 16–17 (16.5) mm., tars. 13 (13.0) mm.
    3 females   wing 111–118 (114.7) mm., tail 37–42 (39.3) mm.,
         exp. cul. 15–16 (15.3) mm., tars. 12–13 (12.7) mm.
    Known only from near Puerto Limón and the Turrialba Volcano region, south-eastern Costa Rica, and from Cocoplum, Bocas del Toro, and Boquete, Chiriquí, in western Panama.

GENERAL NOTES   Slud (1964) points out that the Red-winged Parrotlet is undoubtedly rare in south-eastern Costa Rica, and is probably a bird of the cool and wet lower middle altitudes; the four specimens from Puerto Limón could have been collected from a wandering group in the foothills. He met with it twice in October 1953, at Matrículas de Pavones situated on a 900 m. high forested ridge over-looking the Reventazón River valley and within sight of Turrialba Volcano. The few birds observed at this locality were in medium-sized trees at the forest border and were with Red-headed Barbets (*Eubucco bourcierii*) and Blue and Gold Tanagers (*Buthraupis aracei*), both indicative of cool, very wet portions of the hilly subtropical belt. Slud suggests that although the species has not been recorded between the Puerto Limón-Turrialba Volcano region and western Panama it probably occurs along the Caribbean slopes of the Talamanca Cordillera in southern Costa Rica. Its status in Panama is unknown, but very few specimens have been collected (Wetmore, 1968); in western Panama *costaricensis* has been recorded only twice, one specimen having been collected at 1,250 m. in Chiriquí, and in eastern Panama *dilectissima* is known only from the subtropical and upper tropical zones on Cerro Pirre, Darién. Wetmore says that in Darién a pair has been collected at 1,600 m. elevation along the headwaters of the Limón River, and on 6th February 1961, he saw several birds at about 600 m. elevation along the Seteganti River. In Venezuela the species occurs in forests in the subtropical zone and is locally distributed along ridges in the Sierra de Perijá, north-western Zulia, and along the Cordillera de Mérida in Táchira, Mérida, and Trujillo (Phelps and Phelps, 1958). Meyer de Schauensee (1964) says that in Colombia it frequents forest in the tropical zone; it has been collected at Pueblo Nuevo, above Ocaña, Norte de Santander, northern Colombia at 1,720 m. (Dugand, 1948), and in the south-west in coastal forests bordering Nariño (Olivares, 1957). Carriker (1959) reports that on 12th August 1959, to the east of La Guayacana, Nariño, at an elevation of 225 m. a male was collected from a small flock found feeding in trees in old, more or less open secondary growth; the species was not recorded in the area again during his stay of two months.

    Olivares reports that Red-winged Parrotlets seen in coastal forests bordering Nariño, south-western Colombia, were in flocks and were very wary; stomach contents from the specimen collected comprised small fruits. Wetmore recalls that at the Seteganti River, Darién, eastern Panama, three birds flew past in close formation, swung swiftly around him several times, and then disappeared; two eventually alighted in the top of a red-flowered tree but were hidden among the green leaves and could not be located. In flight the black wing markings were prominent, and when a bird passed nearby the red around its eyes could be seen.

CALL   Slud notes that the only sound heard from these parrotlets was a chatter.

NESTING   No records.

EGGS   Undescribed.

SAPPHIRE-RUMPED PARROTLET
Touit purpurata (Gmelin)

DESCRIPTION   Length 17 cm.
    MALE general plumage green, paler and more yellowish on underparts; crown and occiput olive-brown merging into green on nape; brownish tinge on ear-coverts; scapulars and tertials

dark brown; lower back and rump blue; upper tail-coverts, sides of rump, and flanks bright green; sides of body greenish-yellow; flight feathers green; carpal edge violet-blue; under wing-coverts green; undersides of flight feathers dull bluish-green; central tail-feathers green tipped with black, lateral tail-feathers violet-red tipped and margined on outer webs with black; bill yellowish with grey towards base; iris grey; legs greenish-grey.

FEMALE like male, but with paler brown scapulars and tertials; lateral tail-feathers subterminally banded with green and tipped with black; no black margins to outer webs of lateral tail-feathers. IMMATURES (Penard and Penard, 1908); like adult female, but generally duller in colour; rump olive-brown with little or no blue.

DISTRIBUTION Guianas and northernmost Brazil west to south-eastern Colombia and eastern Ecuador.

SUBSPECIES

1. *T. p. purpurata* (Gmelin)
   13 males   wing 115–123 (119.1) mm., tail 43–50 (46.1) mm.,   *Illustrated on page 489.*
              exp. cul. 14–16 (15.1) mm., tars. 12–15 (13.4) mm.
   12 females wing 110–120 (114.7) mm., tail 42–49 (44.8) mm.,
              exp. cul. 13–15 (14.3) mm., tars. 12–14 (12.6) mm.

   Distributed from the Guianas and northern Brazil between Amapá and the Capim River region, eastern Pará, west to the lower Negro River, north-eastern Amazonas, Brazil, and southern Venezuela in south-eastern Bolívar and eastern Amazonas. Chapman (1929) points out that there is a marked tendency towards *viridiceps* in a specimen from the Merumé Mountains, western Guyana.

2. *T. p. viridiceps* Chapman
   ADULTS like *purpurata*, but crown, occiput and nape green; deeper greenish-yellow on sides of body.
   9 males   wing 115–126 (120.9) mm., tail 47–50 (48.7) mm.,
              exp. cul. 14–16 (14.6) mm., tars. 12–14 (12.7) mm.
   2 females wing 112–121 (116.5) mm., tail 46–51 (48.5) mm.,
              exp. cul. 14 (14.0) mm., tars. 13 (13.0) mm.

   Restricted to the upper Negro River and its tributaries, north-western Amazonas, Brazil, the upper Orinoco River and its tributaries, west of Cerro Duida, Amazonas, southern Venezuela, and south-eastern Colombia in Guainía, Vaupés, Caquetá, and probably Putumayo; probably, the race occurring in eastern Ecuador, but this has not been confirmed.

   Sassi (1947) claims that specimens in the Natterer Collection, now in the Naturhistorisches Museum, Vienna, show that *viridiceps* is not separable from *purpurata*. In March 1971, I examined these same specimens and came to the opposite conclusion. Of the five specimens with adequate locality data only one is from the upper Negro River region, and it is clearly referable to *viridiceps*.

GENERAL NOTES In Surinam the Sapphire-rumped Parrotlet is an uncommon bird of the savannah forests and forests on the coastal sand ridges (Haverschmidt, 1968). Snyder (1966) says that in Guyana it has been recorded mainly from forested areas in northern and western districts. In southern Venezuela it is locally distributed in forests of the tropical zone, occasionally up to the lower subtropical zone (Phelps and Phelps, 1958). Meyer de Schauensee (1964) says that in south-eastern Colombia it inhabits forest in the tropical zone. Dugand and Borrero (1948) report that very few birds were seen in the vicinity of Tres Esquinas, Caquetá, south-eastern Colombia.

Very little is known of the habits of this species. Dugand and Borrero state that in the Tres Esquinas area, south-eastern Colombia, it was a rather silent bird and spent much of the time in the leafy canopies of *Ficus* trees feeding on figs. In the savannah forests of Surinam Haverschmidt has found small groups feeding on the fruits of *Clusia grandiflora*.

CALL Penard and Penard claim that the call resembles *keree-ke-ke*.

NESTING A male with enlarged testes (COP.21459) was collected in southern Venezuela in March. Haverschmidt reports that on 11th April 1962, in forest on a sand ridge in the Commewijne district, Surinam, a parrot was observed entering a hole in an arboreal termitarium; it was collected and proved to be a male in breeding condition. Penard and Penard state that nests are in holes excavated in arboreal termites' mounds or in old woodpeckers' holes in trees, and three to five eggs make up the normal clutch.

EGGS Undescribed.

BROWN-BACKED PARROTLET
Touit melanonota (Wied)   *Illustrated on page 489.*

Length 15 cm.
ADULTS general plumage green, paler and brighter on forehead, lores, cheeks and underparts; obscure brown marking on ear-coverts; mantle and tertials dark brown; scapulars and back brownish-black; upper tail-coverts and rump green; flanks and sides of lower breast pale bluish-grey, generally duller and less pronounced in females; primary-coverts brown tinged with green;

obscure dull reddish marking on carpal edge; under wing-coverts green; undersides of flight feathers dull bluish-green; central tail-feathers green, lateral tail-feathers red tipped with black; bill yellowish with grey towards base; iris greyish; legs brownish-grey.
IMMATURES undescribed.
6 males wing 107–116 (111.7) mm., tail 41–46 (43.0) mm.,
     exp. cul. 14–15 (14.2) mm., tars. 11–13 (11.7) mm.
1 female wing 111 mm., tail 43 mm.,
     exp. cul. 14 mm., tars. 12 mm.

DISTRIBUTION
Confined to south-eastern Brazil from southern Bahia south to southern São Paulo.

GENERAL NOTES
Pinto (1946) says that the Brown-backed Parrotlet was formerly common at times in the coastal forests of São Paulo, but it is now one of the rarest species within the whole littoral belt of south-eastern Brazil. However, Sick (1969) points out that it is resident in Guanabara, and may be more common than is generally believed; he gives a sight record from the Floresta da Tijuca, a reserve on the outskirts of Rio de Janeiro, dating from October 1966, and mentions other observations from the Serra do Mar in the state of Rio de Janeiro.

Virtually nothing is recorded about the habits of this species. It is said to associate in small flocks and keep to the canopies of forest trees.

GOLDEN-TAILED PARROTLET
Touit surda (Kuhl)

Illustrated on page 492.

DESCRIPTION
Length 16 cm.
MALE general plumage green, paler and more yellowish on underparts; narrow frontal band, lores, chin, anterior portion of cheeks and line below eye golden yellow; slight olive tinge on hindneck; scapulars and upper tertials olive-brown; rump pale bluish-green; primary-coverts dark brown; primaries and secondaries brown margined on outer webs with green; obscure dull bluish marking on carpal edge; flanks and sides of lower breast greenish-yellow; under wing-coverts green; undersides of flight feathers dull green; central tail feathers green faintly tipped with black, lateral tail feathers greenish-yellow tipped with black; bill yellowish with grey towards base; iris grey; legs greenish-grey.
FEMALE like male, but lateral tail feathers greenish-yellow margined and tipped with dull green.
IMMATURES undescribed.

DISTRIBUTION
Eastern Brazil from Pernambuco to São Paulo.

SUBSPECIES

1. *T. s. surda* (Kuhl)
   10 males wing 115–130 (119.7) mm., tail 46–53 (48.8) mm.,
       exp. cul. 14–16 (15.0) mm., tars. 12–13 (12.8) mm.
   6 females wing 115–123 (118.3) mm., tail 46–50 (48.2) mm.,
       exp. cul. 14–16 (15.2) mm., tars. 12–14 (13.2) mm.
   Occurs in south-eastern Brazil from southern Bahia, and possibly southern Goiás, south to Rio de Janeiro and possibly São Paulo. Pinto (1935) points out that its occurrence in São Paulo and southern Goiás needs confirmation.

2. *T. s. ruficauda* Berla
   ADULTS similar to *surda*, but lateral tail feathers brownish-yellow instead of greenish-yellow.
   2 males wing 110–113 (111.5) mm., tail 48–50 (49.5) mm.,
       exp. cul. 15 (15.0) mm., tars. 12–13 (12.5) mm.
   1 female wing 112 mm., tail 49 mm.,
       exp. cul. 15 mm., tars. 13 mm.
   Known only from the vicinity of Recife, Pernambuco, eastern Brazil. I believe that further specimens must be obtained before the validity of this race, and especially its alleged smaller size, can be established.

GENERAL NOTES
The Golden-tailed Parrotlet is a little-known inhabitant of coastal and adjacent mountain forests. I suspect that it has decreased in recent years because of the extensive land-clearance that has taken place along the eastern coast of Brazil. It associates in family groups or small flocks, and keeps to the upper branches of forest trees where its predominantly green plumage blends well with the foliage. Nothing further is known of its habits.

SPOT-WINGED PARROTLET
Touit stictoptera (Sclater)

Illustrated on page 492.

DESCRIPTION
Length 17 cm.
MALE general plumage green, slightly paler and more yellowish on underparts; lores and periophthalmic region greenish-yellow; bend of wing blackish-brown; scapulars, lesser wing-coverts,

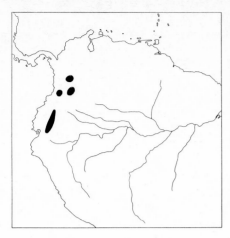

and median wing-coverts, except outer two, brown tipped with buff-white thus giving a spotted appearance; outer two median wing-coverts dull orange; secondaries and secondary-coverts dark brown; primary-coverts blackish-brown, outer webs of inner feathers narrowly edged with green; primaries blackish-brown edged on outer webs with green; under wing-coverts green; undersides of flight feathers bluish-green; tail above green with reddish-brown on inner webs of lateral feathers, below olive-yellow; bill grey becoming yellowish towards tip; iris yellowish-brown; legs bluish-grey.

FEMALE all wing-coverts green with exposed black bases to feathers; lores and foreparts of cheeks brighter yellow; primary-coverts brown broadly edged with green; primaries and secondaries green.

IMMATURES similar to adult female.

3 males   wing 131–134 (133.0) mm., tail 52–54 (53.0) mm.,
          exp. cul. 16 (16.0) mm., tars. 13–14 (13.3) mm.
3 females wing 123–130 (127.0) mm., tail 50–56 (52.7) mm.,
          exp. cul. 16 (16.0) mm., tars. 14–15 (14.3) mm.

DISTRIBUTION   Known only from Colombia on the western slopes of the Central Andes in Cauca, the western slopes of the Eastern Andes in Cundinamarca, and the Macarena Mountains in Meta, and from the eastern slopes of the Andes in Ecuador.

GENERAL NOTES   Meyer de Schauensee (1970) says that the Spot-winged Parrotlet occurs in forest in the subtropical and upper tropical zones. Dugand (1945) records the collection of specimens in mid-November 1944, below Fusagasugá, Cundinamarca, central-western Colombia, at about 1,600 m. He also mentions the claim by people in the district that this species is found occasionally feeding in *Ficus* and *Clusia* trees in the mountains above Fusagasugá, close to 2,200 or 2,300 m., and frequently it raids maize crops when the grain is ripening. The stomach of one of the specimens collected contained numerous small fruits of a Loranthaceae. Dugand suggests that it may be only a seasonal visitor to the Fusagasugá district because a thorough search by one of his assistants in April 1945 failed to locate it, and the American Museum of Natural History Expedition did not record it there during late March and early April 1913. At the turn of the century Goodfellow (1902) met with it in forest below Baeza, eastern Ecuador, but I know of no recent records from that country. Nothing further is known of its habits or life history.

Genus PIONITES Heine

It has been pointed out that there are some similarities in the behaviour of the parrots belonging to this genus and the conures now placed in *Aratinga* and *Pyrrhura* (Tavistock, 1954; Smith, 1971b). When examining the skulls, Thompson (1900) noticed similarities in the quadrate bones, but he did not suggest that these were indicative of a relationship between *Pionites*, then known as *Caica*, and the old genus *Conurus*, now separated into *Aratinga* and *Pyrrhura*. Members of this genus are called Caiques, and are medium-sized parrots with short, square tails. The bill is relatively narrow with a strongly ridged upper mandible and there is a notch in the upper mandible. The cere is naked. Notable features of the skull are the incomplete orbital ring with an extremely reduced postfrontal process and a well developed squamosal, and the narrow auditory meatus (Thompson, 1900). There is no sexual dimorphism.

BLACK-HEADED CAIQUE
Pionites melanocephala (Linné)

DESCRIPTION   Length 23 cm.
ADULTS forehead, crown, and nape black; lores and streak under eye green; cheeks and throat orange-yellow; broad rufous-orange band across hindneck, bordered above and below by a few bluish feathers; back, wings, rump, and upper tail-coverts green; breast and centre of abdomen creamy-white suffused with buff; thighs, sides of abdomen, and flanks orange; under wing-coverts green; axillaries reddish-orange; under tail-coverts yellowish-orange; primary-coverts and primaries violet-blue narrowly edged with green; carpal edge greenish-yellow; tail above green tipped with yellow, below dull olive-yellow; bill grey-black; iris orange; legs grey.
IMMATURES breast and centre of abdomen pale yellow; thighs more yellowish and streaked with green; all orange and yellow parts of plumage noticeably paler than in adults; bill horn-coloured with black markings at base of upper mandible; iris dark brown.

DISTRIBUTION   From the Guianas and northern Pará, Brazil, west to southern Colombia, eastern Ecuador and north-eastern Peru.

SUBSPECIES   1. *P. m. melanocephala* (Linné)
10 males   wing 137–147 (142.5) mm., tail 66–75 (68.9) mm.,
           exp. cul. 22–28 (24.7) mm., tars. 17–19 (18.1) mm.

Illustrated on page 493.

7 females wing 133–142 (137.9) mm., tail 66–72 (68.4) mm.,
exp. cul. 21–25 (23.3) mm., tars. 18–19 (18.4) mm.

Ranges from the Guianas and north of the Amazon River in northern Pará, Brazil, west through north-eastern and southern Venezuela and Roraima and northernmost Amazonas, Brazil, to Meta, south-eastern Colombia, where it intergrades with *pallida* (see Dugand and Borrero, 1948).

2. *P. m. pallida* (Berlepsch)
ADULTS like *melanocephala*, but throat, flanks, and thighs clear yellow; breast and centre of abdomen white with little or no creamy-buff suffusion; paler orange-yellow band across hind-neck.

4 males   wing 130–143 (137.0) mm., tail 61–68 (65.0) mm.,
exp. cul. 23–24 (23.5) mm., tars. 17–18 (17.8) mm.
4 females wing 135–140 (137.5) mm., tail 63–66 (64.3) mm.,
exp. cul. 22–23 (22.8) mm., tars. 17–18 (17.8) mm.

Distributed from southern Colombia, east of the Andes in Meta and west of the Andes in Nariño (Niceforo and Olivares, 1966), south to north-eastern Peru and eastern Ecuador. Traylor (1958) points out that two specimens from Sarayacu, eastern Ecuador, are intermediate between this race and *melanocephala*.

GENERAL NOTES

The Black-headed Caique inhabits forest and savannah in the tropical zone (Meyer de Schauensee, 1970). Haverschmidt (1968) says that in Surinam it is quite common in forests on the coastal sand ridges, in savannah forests, and in the extensive forests of the interior. In Guyana it is widespread and fairly common in high forest and along the edges of forest (Snyder, 1966). Phelps and Phelps (1958) state that in Venezuela it frequents open forest in the tropical zone and is generally distributed south of the Orinoco River, but north of this river it is known only from southern Sucre. Meyer de Schauensee (1964) says that in south-eastern Colombia it is found in forests in the tropical zone, and Dugand (1948) reports that it is abundant in the flat savannah woodlands of Meta.

These noisy parrots associate in family parties or flocks of up to thirty, and keep to the upper branches of trees where they spend much of the day feeding on fruits, berries, and seeds. They are rather wary and when disturbed fly off through the forest, screeching loudly.

CALL Smith (1971b) describes what he terms 'crowing' and suggests that it is a contact call. This is performed by birds while perching. The wings are raised and held momentarily above the head, thus displaying the bright reddish-orange axillaries. While the wings are held in the highest position the bird gives a piping *toot*, which is often repeated rapidly to form a disyllabic note.

Other calls emitted include a screaming *heeyah . . . heeyah* and *wheech-wheech-wheech* (Snyder, 1966), as well as a variety of shrieks and squawks. The alarm note is a shrill *wey-ak*.

NESTING Little is known of nesting in the wild. A male with active, enlarged testes was collected in April at Cerro Yapacana on the upper Orinoco River, Amazonas, Venezuela (Friedmann, 1948). One of seven specimens collected in coastal Surinam during February, March, and April had in its oviduct one fully developed, hard-shelled egg and four others in various stages of development (Bangs and Penard, 1918). Haverschmidt (1972) reports that on 9th October and 13th November 1969 he observed two different pairs nesting in holes in very big and tall trees at the edge of the forest at Phedra, Surinam. Penard and Penard (1908) claim that the normal clutch comprises two to four eggs.

Smith gives details of a successful breeding in captivity. The nest-box was lined with chips of wood removed from the inside walls by the male. Three eggs were laid, but only one hatched. The male sat beside the brooding female at times during the day, but did not cover the eggs, and at night he roosted with her in the nest-box. Incubation lasted approximately twenty-seven days and the young bird left the nest seventy-three days after hatching.

EGGS A fully developed, hard-shelled egg removed from the oviduct of a specimen collected in Surinam was ovate and measured 31.5 × 22.5 mm. (Bangs and Penard, 1918). Smith gives 29.5 × 23.5 mm. as the average measurements of a clutch of three eggs.

WHITE-BELLIED CAIQUE
Pionites leucogaster (Kuhl)

DESCRIPTION

Length 23 cm.
ADULTS crown, nape, hindneck, and upper ear-coverts orange; lores, throat, and sides of head yellow; back, wings, rump, and upper tail-coverts green; breast and abdomen creamy-white; flanks and thighs green; under tail-coverts yellow; axillaries reddish-orange; under wing-coverts green; primary-coverts and primaries violet-blue narrowly edged with green; bill pale horn-coloured; iris red; legs pink.
IMMATURES crown and nape brownish with scattered black feathers; bill horn-coloured with grey markings towards base; iris brown; legs grey.

Northern Brazil between the Amazon River and northern Mato Grosso west to northern Bolivia, eastern Peru, and eastern Ecuador.

1. *P. l. leucogaster* (Kuhl)   *Illustrated on page 493.*
   8 males   wing 137–140 (138.8) mm., tail 63–70 (67.3) mm.,
           exp. cul. 24–25 (24.3) mm., tars. 18–19 (18.3) mm.
   7 females   wing 133–142 (137.9) mm., tail 61–74 (67.9) mm.,
           exp. cul. 22–25 (23.7) mm., tars. 17–19 (18.1) mm.
   Occurs in northern Brazil between the Amazon River in the Belém district, Pará, and north-eastern Mato Grosso west to about the Madeira River region in eastern Amazonas; specimens from the Serra do Cachimbo and upper Xingú River in southern Pará and from the upper Xingú River in northern Mato Grosso show a marked tendency towards *xanthurus*.

2. *P. l. xanthurus* Todd
   ADULTS general plumage paler, particularly on crown and nape; thighs, flanks, under tail-coverts and entire tail yellow; rump and upper tail-coverts yellow variably marked with green.
   4 males   wing 140–147 (144.0) mm., tail 65–70 (67.8) mm.,
           exp. cul. 24–25 (24.3) mm., tars. 19–20 (19.3) mm.
   3 females   wing 135–142 (139.0) mm., tail 65–77 (69.0) mm.,
           exp. cul. 22–23 (22.7) mm., tars. 18–19 (18.7) mm.
   Occurs in north-western Brazil where known only from the Machados River on the Rondônia-Amazonas border, Hyutanahán and Nova Olinda on the Purús River, Amazonas, and the Juruá River, Amazonas; a specimen from the Manaus region, eastern Amazonas, is intermediate between this race and *xanthomeria*.

3. *P. l. xanthomeria* (Sclater)
   ADULTS like *leucogaster*, but with thighs and flanks yellow instead of green; tail green as in *leucogaster*.
   6 males   wing 137–144 (140.5) mm., tail 65–72 (67.7) mm.,
           exp. cul. 23–24 (23.7) mm., tars. 18–19 (18.3) mm.
   4 females   wing 138–142 (140.0) mm., tail 67–70 (68.0) mm.,
           exp. cul. 22–24 (23.0) mm., tars. 17–19 (18.0) mm.
   Distributed along the southern bank of the upper Amazon River in Amazonas, Brazil, west to eastern Ecuador thence south-east to northernmost Bolivia in Beni province; birds from the upper Juruá River in south-western Amazonas, Brazil, show a tendency towards *xanthurus*.

White-bellied Caiques inhabit forest in the tropical zone (Meyer de Schauensee, 1970). They show a preference for trees bordering watercourses. Fry (1970) reports that in the Serra do Roncader, north-eastern Mato Grosso, they were found only in dry forest and four was the maximum number of birds seen in any one day. They are generally seen in pairs, family parties, or small flocks, and are very noisy, their screeching call-notes attracting attention as they fly from one patch of forest to another. They keep to the forest canopy, where much of the day is spent feeding on fruits, berries and seeds. When disturbed they fly off through the forest, screeching loudly.

CALL A variety of squawks, flute-like whistles, and screaming notes, all essentially similar to those given by *P. melanocephala*.

NESTING At Murutucu, Pará, Brazil, a nest containing two eggs was found on 1st January 1924 (Pinto, 1954). It was in a hollow in a tree, about 30 m. from the ground, and the female was incubating.
   Poltimore (1936) gives details of the successful rearing in captivity of a *P. melanocephala* × *P. leucogaster* hybrid. Four eggs were laid and all subsequently hatched, but only one chick was reared. Incubation lasted approximately four weeks and only the female brooded. The young bird left the nest about ten weeks after hatching; it resembled the male *P. melanocephala* but the thighs were green as in the female *P. leucogaster*.

EGGS Pinto notes that the two eggs taken from the nest at Murutucu measured 31 × 25 mm. and 30 × 25 mm.

Genus PIONOPSITTA Bonaparte

Members of this genus are medium-sized, stocky parrots with short, slightly rounded tails and broad, pointed wings. The tail-feathers are broad with almost pointed tips. The bill has a bulbous base, and there is a notch in the upper mandible. The naked cere is quite prominent, and the lores are only partly feathered. Sexual dimorphism is present in *pileata*, a rather aberrant species, but is absent in other species; young birds differ from adults. As well as being sexually dimorphic, *pileata* has a number of distinct features; its bill is less projecting and is not laterally compressed towards the tip, its tail is proportionately longer and the tail-feathers narrower, and its wings are narrower and more pointed.

Haffer (1970) points out that, with the exception of *pileata*, all species probably originated from a common ancestor and evolved in isolation in forest refuges during the alternating humid and dry climatic periods of the Pleistocene and post-Pleistocene. He claims that they now belong to the *Pionopsitta caica* superspecies or species group; *Gypopsitta* is also included in this group. The component species replace each other geographically and hybridization has not been recorded. Two species, *haematotis* and *pyrilia*, may be locally sympatric in north-western Colombia, but this requires confirmation (see Meyer de Schauensee, 1950).

PILEATED PARROT
Pionopsitta pileata (Scopoli)

Illustrated on page 496.

Length 22 cm.
MALE general plumage green, slightly tinged with blue on chin and throat: forehead, lores, crown, and periophthalmic region red; nape tinged with olive; ear-coverts brownish-purple; bend of wing, carpal edge, primary-coverts, and outer lesser under wing-coverts violet-blue; primaries dark blue edged with green; under wing-coverts bluish-green; undersides of flight feathers greenish-blue; thighs and under tail-coverts yellowish-green; central tail feathers above green tipped with blue, lateral tail feathers above violet-blue edged with green, underside of tail feathers dull bluish-green; bill greyish-green becoming horn-coloured towards tip; iris dark brown; legs grey.
FEMALE like male, but lores, crown, and periophthalmic region green; forehead green tinged with blue; more pronounced bluish suffusion on throat.
IMMATURES similar to adult female, but without blue suffusion on forehead; ear-coverts green.
10 males   wing 141–152 (147.0) mm., tail 67–76 (71.0) mm.,
           exp. cul. 17–19 (17.7) mm., tars. 14–16 (15.1) mm.
10 females wing 141–148 (144.6) mm., tail 64–76 (71.0) mm.,
           exp. cul. 17–18 (17.3) mm., tars. 15–16 (15.4) mm.

DISTRIBUTION   South-eastern Brazil from southern Bahia south to Rio Grande do Sul, eastern Paraguay, and north-eastern Argentina in Misiones and Corrientes.

GENERAL NOTES

The Pileated Parrot is a forest bird, and Sick (1969) points out that, like so many of the forest birds from the littoral belt of south-eastern Brazil, it has suffered greatly from loss of habitat through widespread land-clearing and increasing urbanization; he lists it as one of Brazil's threatened species. I did not see it in Rio Grande do Sul, but was told by local people that at times it is fairly common in the vicinity of Bom Jesus, particularly in orchards when fruit is ripening. Olrog (1959) says that in north-eastern Argentina it frequents subtropical forest, and Eckelberry (1965) reports that it was seen regularly near Tobunas, Misiones.

These parrots are generally found in pairs or small flocks. They keep to the treetops where they are inconspicuous as they silently climb about among the branches, feeding on fruits, berries, and seeds. They are rather tame and will usually allow a close approach. If disturbed they remain motionless for a moment before flying off, screeching as they go. The flight is swift and direct with rapid wingbeats.

CALL In flight the parrots give a staccato repetition of a relatively subdued, metallic note; while feeding or at rest they occasionally emit a soft chirruping call.

NESTING Von Ihering (1902) records the receipt of two eggs taken from a hole in the trunk of a tree; the entrance to the hollow was at the top of the tree.

EGGS Rounded, glossy; 2 eggs, 26.0 (26.0) × 22.3 (22.0–22.5) mm. [Von Ihering, 1902].

BROWN-HOODED PARROT
Pionopsitta haematotis (Sclater and Salvin)

DESCRIPTION   Length 21 cm.
ADULTS general plumage green; crown and nape dark greyish-brown, each feather broadly tipped with olive; ear-coverts dark brownish-red; sides of neck, cheeks, and throat grey, becoming almost black towards sides of neck and paler on cheeks; hindneck dull olive-yellow, continuing round on to breast where it becomes more greenish; lesser wing-coverts, carpal edge, and outermost secondary-coverts violet-blue; primary-coverts black, lightly tinged on outer webs with violet-blue; primaries dull black narrowly edged on outer webs with pale buff; under wing-coverts greenish-blue; undersides of flight feathers dull bluish-green; axillaries and sides of body red; under tail-coverts yellowish-green; central tail feathers green tipped with dark blue, lateral tail feathers green broadly tipped with dark blue and marked with dull red on inner webs; bill horn-coloured tinged with pale brownish-yellow; iris yellow; legs yellowish-brown.

484

IMMATURES like adults, but head colouration much paler; olive-yellow of hindneck much reduced; breast more greenish; no brownish-red on ear-coverts; iris brown.

DISTRIBUTION Central America, mainly on the Caribbean side, from southernmost Mexico south to north-western Colombia.

SUBSPECIES

1. *P. h. haematotis* (Sclater and Salvin)   *Illustrated on page 496.*
    10 males   wing 145–153 (148.3) mm., tail 58–65 (62.0) mm.,
                exp. cul. 19–20 (19.4) mm., tars. 17–18 (17.2) mm.
    8 females   wing 145–151 (147.5) mm., tail 57–62 (59.8) mm.,
                exp. cul. 17–20 (18.5) mm., tars. 16–18 (17.3) mm.
    Ranges from Veracruz and Oaxaca, southern Mexico, south to western Panama in northern Coclé and western Colón, where apparently it intergrades with *coccinicollaris* (see Wetmore, 1968).

2. *P. h. coccinicollaris* (Lawrence)
    ADULTS lower foreneck and extreme upper breast variably marked with red, often forming a prominent band in males but generally less developed in females.
    7 males   wing 144–155 (148.1) mm., tail 61–70 (64.9) mm.,
               exp. cul. 18–20 (19.3) mm., tars. 17–18 (17.7) mm.
    7 females wing 145–155 (149.7) mm., tail 62–70 (66.3) mm.,
               exp. cul. 18–19 (18.1) mm., tars. 17–18 (17.7) mm.
    Restricted to eastern Panama, east of the Canal Zone, and north-western Colombia, east to Bolívar.

GENERAL NOTES Observers consistently point out that Brown-hooded Parrots are easily overlooked and consequently their status may be under-estimated. Blake (1953) says that in southern Mexico they are abundant locally, but often remain undetected as they feed quietly in the tops of large forest trees. According to Loetscher (1941) they are uncommon residents of forests in the tropical zone of southern Veracruz, Mexico, and range from near sea level up to an elevation of approximately 800 m.; though fairly widespread over the southern half of the state, they are among the least common of local parrots and in 1939 he found them only at the edge of a patch of forest between Jesús Carranza and Ubero. Andrle (1967) notes that they seem to be rare on the Sierra de Tuxtla in southern Veracruz. In Oaxaca, southern Mexico, they are fairly common residents of cloud forest and dense tropical evergreen forest in northern regions, and have been recorded up to 1,675 m. (Binford, 1968). Thompson (1962) suggests that their presence on the higher slopes of Oaxaca may be the result of post-breeding movements. Paynter (1955) reports that they are fairly common in heavy rainforest at the base of Yucatán Peninsula, Mexico, but their detection is almost always a matter of chance. In Guatemala they are fairly common in humid forest and along the edges of forest in the Caribbean lowlands and in the Petén, ranging up to about 1,000 m. in the foothills (Land, 1970). Smithe (1966) reports that they are common residents of the forest canopy at Tikal, northern Guatemala. They are inconspicuous, but common residents of the tall forests of British Honduras (Russell, 1964). Monroe (1968) points out that they are uncommon to fairly common in Honduras and are resident in lowland rainforest, occurring up to 1,200 m. in low montane rainforest; he has observed small flocks in low montane rainforest between 900 and 1,200 m. elevation, and in dense rainforest near sea level. Huber (1933) reports that in the Eden district, north-eastern Nicaragua, at about 530 m. elevation, a single specimen was collected in dense forest high up on a hillside. Slud (1964) notes that these parrots are widely, though unevenly distributed in humid to very wet forests and along the edges of forest on both the Caribbean and Pacific slopes of Costa Rica up to approximately 3,100 m.; they are locally uncommon in some areas, abundant in others, but in general are more numerous in the tropical zone on the Caribbean side than on the Pacific side. On the southern slopes of the Volcán Rincón de la Vieja in Guanacaste province, northern Costa Rica, Wetmore (1944) found birds in a shade tree in a coffee plantation. In Panama they are residents of forests in the tropical and subtropical zones, and have been recorded up to about 1,900 m. (Wetmore, 1968). Meyer de Schauensee (1964) says that in north-western Colombia they are found in forest in the tropical zone.

These parrots are generally found in pairs or small groups of from about five to fifteen or twenty. They are most frequently observed flying above the forest canopy or over open country on their way from one patch of forest to another. Their secretive habits are well emphasized by Russell when he says that small flocks may feed unnoticed high in the treetops until their presence is made known by an occasional warbling call or by falling pieces of fruit. At times they rest quietly among the foliage, occasionally giving forth a soft warble. Commenting on the bird he collected at Eden, north-eastern Nicaragua, Huber describes how it was first seen flying from one tree to another, but after alighting it remained perfectly motionless and could not be located; it remained concealed for at least ten minutes before moving. Wetmore (1968) reports that a female collected at El Uracillo, western Panama, was in company with a female Blue-headed Parrot (*Pionus menstruus*); the two were preening each other, and apparently had been using the same hollow in a tree. At times Brown-hooded Parrots feed in company with other parrots, particularly amazons, and with toucans. While feeding they are tame, and do not readily take alarm. If disturbed they remain quiet and still, taking flight only when the threat is persistent or prolonged. The flight is swift and direct; in flight the birds display their red axillaries.

They feed on fruits, berries, and seeds, usually procured in the treetops, though, as noted by Slud, birds will occasionally descend to the understorey in heavy forest. Wetmore (1968) reports that near Puerto Armuelles, Chiriquí, western Panama, they were seen feeding on figs in high forest. Land says that they will attack corn crops. The stomach of a specimen collected in the Panama Canal Zone contained fruit seeds (Hallinan, 1924).

CALL They utter *pileek-pileek* notes alternating with rough *zapp-zapp* calls when in flight; also a variety of gurgling and squeaky notes and a call transcribed as *kree—ee . . . tee . . . yer* (Slud, 1964; Smithe, 1966).

NESTING Little is known of the nesting habits. Males with enlarged testes have been collected in Campeche, Mexico, in mid-February (Paynter, 1955), at Tikal, northern Guatemala, during May and July (Smithe and Paynter, 1963), and in Chiriquí, western Panama, in mid-August (Blake, 1958). Smithe says that the nest is in a hole in a tree.

EGGS Undescribed.

ROSE-FACED PARROT
Pionopsitta pulchra Berlepsch

Illustrated on page 496.

Illustrated on page 496.

DESCRIPTION

Length 23 cm.

ADULTS general plumage green; crown and nape dark greyish-brown, each feather lightly margined with olive; lores, superciliary line, ear-coverts, and posterior of cheeks rose-pink; anterior of cheeks and chin pale rose; hindneck dull olive-yellow, continuing round on to breast and there becoming more greenish; bend of wing and lesser wing-coverts mixed orange and yellow; median wing-coverts blue; carpal edge and outermost secondary-coverts violet-blue; primary-coverts black, lightly tinged on outer webs with violet-blue; primaries dull black narrowly edged on outer webs with pale buff; under wing-coverts greenish-blue; undersides of flight feathers dull bluish-green; axillaries and sides of body green; under tail-coverts yellowish-green; central tail feathers green tipped with dark blue, lateral tail feathers red on inner webs and with broad blue tips; bill horn-coloured; iris yellow; legs pale yellowish-brown.

IMMATURES rose-pink restricted to superciliary line and ear-coverts; cheeks and chin greenish-brown; crown and nape more greenish; breast green tinged with olive-yellow; olive-yellow on hindneck much reduced; iris brown.

11 males wing 151–173 (160.2) mm., tail 55–67 (62.5) mm.,
   exp. cul. 19–22 (20.4) mm., tars. 17–20 (18.3) mm.
8 females wing 151–164 (157.5) mm., tail 57–66 (62.3) mm.,
   exp. cul. 18–22 (19.5) mm., tars. 18–19 (18.8) mm.

DISTRIBUTION

Occurs west of the Andes from the upper Atrato River in Chocó, western Colombia, south to western Ecuador. Haffer (1967b) points out that this species and the very closely related *P. haematotis* are separated by a narrow gap, approximately 100 km. wide, and specimens from the northern extremity of its range, that is Mutatá, on the eastern side of the Atrato Valley in the Baudo mountains, show no approach toward *haematotis coccinicollaris*.

GENERAL NOTES

There is little recorded information on the habits of the Rose-faced Parrot, but I suspect that they are very similar to the habits of *P. haematotis*. Meyer de Schauensee (1964) says that it occurs in forest in the tropical zone, and occasionally in the subtropical zone; it has been recorded up to 2,100 m. Olivares (1957) reports seeing many flocks in the vicinity of Guapí, south-western Cauca, Colombia, and says that there the species is often found around banana plantations where it causes some damage.

In the Gaupí district a female was collected on 26th November, a pair on 30th December, and in all three the gonads were well-developed. Stomach contents from two of these specimens comprised small fruits and pieces of green banana.

BARRABAND'S PARROT
Pionopsitta barrabandi (Kuhl)

DESCRIPTION

Length 25 cm.

ADULTS general plumage green, slightly tinged with blue on abdomen; head black, except orange-yellow cheeks; throat and breast olive; thighs yellow; bend of wing and lesser wing-coverts orange-yellow, bases to feathers red; primaries and primary-coverts black, tinged with dark blue on outer webs; secondaries and outer secondary-coverts blue edged with green; carpal edge and under wing-coverts orange-red; undersides of flight feathers dull bluish-green; tail green tipped with blue, inner webs of lateral tail feathers yellow; bill grey-black; iris brown; legs pale grey.

IMMATURES crown brown; feathers of forehead, nape, cheeks and chin olive margined with brown; bend of wing and lesser wing-coverts green with a few yellow feathers; some green feathers along carpal edge and in under wing-coverts; primaries edged with yellow towards tips of outer webs.

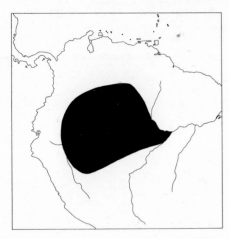

DISTRIBUTION   Upper Amazon Basin from southern Venezuela south to north-western Mato Grosso, Brazil, and west to eastern Ecuador.

SUBSPECIES   1. *P. b. barrabandi* (Kuhl)
    8 males   wing 157–171 (161.4) mm., tail 63–71 (67.6) mm.,
              exp. cul. 19–21 (20.0) mm., tars. 17–19 (17.5) mm.
    8 females wing 147–171 (158.1) mm., tail 62–71 (66.0) mm.,
              exp. cul. 18–20 (18.5) mm., tars. 17–19 (17.8) mm.
      Distributed north of the upper Amazon River from the Negro River region, eastern Amazonas, Brazil, and southern Venezuela, in Amazonas and southern Bolívar, west to south-eastern Colombia as far north as Caquetá; probably intergrades with *aurantiigena* in northern-most Peru and in north-eastern Ecuador.

2. *P. b. aurantiigena* Gyldenstolpe   *Illustrated on page 497.*
    ADULTS like *barrabandi*, but cheeks, bend of wing and lesser wing-coverts, and thighs deep orange instead of yellowish.
    11 males wing 158–170 (163.5) mm., tail 56–72 (65.6) mm.,
              exp. cul. 20–22 (20.5) mm., tars. 17–20 (18.1) mm.
    8 females wing 159–165 (162.4) mm., tail 61–71 (67.6) mm.,
              exp. cul. 19–21 (20.0) mm., tars. 18–19 (18.3) mm.
      Distributed south of the upper Amazon River from north-western Mato Grosso and the Madeira River region, Amazonas, Brazil, west to eastern Ecuador and north-eastern Peru as far south as the Curanja River in southern Loreto.

GENERAL NOTES   Barraband's Parrot inhabits forest in the tropical zone (Meyer de Schauensee, 1970). Gyldenstolpe (1951) points out that it has a rather extensive range, but wherever found it appears to be rare and locally distributed. Phelps and Phelps (1958) state that it is very locally distributed in tropical forest in southern Venezuela. It has been collected on very few occasions in south-eastern Colombia (Dugand and Borrero, 1948). O'Neill found it to be an uncommon inhabitant of hilly country, at about 300 m. elevation, in the vicinity of Balta, on the Curanja River, Loreto, eastern Peru (in Haffer, 1970).

    It is a bird of the forest canopy, where it feeds on fruits, berries, and seeds. No further information on its habits has been recorded.

CALL Undescribed.

NESTING No records. A male with slightly enlarged testes (COP.29204) was collected in southern Venezuela during April.

EGGS Undescribed.

SAFFRON-HEADED PARROT
Pionopsitta pyrilia (Bonaparte)   *Illustrated on page 497.*

DESCRIPTION   Length 24 cm.
ADULTS general plumage green, paler and more yellowish on underparts; entire head and throat deep yellow; ear-coverts washed with orange; neck and upper breast olive; some yellow and red feathers on thighs; lesser wing-coverts yellow, bases to the feathers red; median wing-coverts strongly washed with blue; secondary-coverts blue edged with green; primary-coverts black; primaries black tinged with blue and narrowly edged with bluish-green; secondaries black tinged with blue and broadly edged with green on outer webs; bend of wing, carpal edge, under wing-coverts, axillaries, and sides of body scarlet; undersides of flight feathers dull bluish-green; tail green tipped with blue, inner webs of lateral tail feathers yellow; bill horn-coloured; iris dark brown; legs grey.
IMMATURES head green, cheeks and ear-coverts strongly tinged with olive; throat olive, like upper breast; lesser wing-coverts green; carpal edge green with a few red feathers; lesser under wing-coverts red but greater under wing-coverts green; primaries have narrow yellow edges towards tips.
    8 males   wing 140–151 (146.6) mm., tail 61–70 (67.0) mm.,
              exp. cul. 16–18 (17.6) mm., tars. 16–18 (16.8) mm.
    8 females wing 135–148 (142.9) mm., tail 60–74 (68.0) mm.,
              exp. cul. 16–19 (17.5) mm., tars. 15–18 (16.6) mm.

DISTRIBUTION   From Darién, eastern Panama, through northern Colombia, south to about 5°N. lat., to the east slopes of the Eastern Andes in Santander, thence to north-western Venezuela in the provinces of Zulia, Táchira, Mérida, and Lara.

Wetmore (1968) points out that in Panama the Saffron-headed Parrot is known from only two specimens collected in the lower Tuira area, Darién, in 1915. In north-western Venezuela it is locally distributed in forests in the tropical and lower subtropical zones (Phelps and Phelps, 1958). Meyer de Schauensee (1964) says that in northern Colombia it is found in forests from the tropical up to the upper subtropical zone. Olivares (1969) reports that he has frequently seen the species in the Magdalena River valley in Caldas, northern Colombia, so almost certainly it is also common on the opposite side of the river in Cundinamarca.

Virtually nothing has been recorded about the habits of this parrot. It keeps to the forest canopy where it feeds on fruits, berries and seeds.

CAICA PARROT
Pionopsitta caica (Latham)

Illustrated on page 497.

Length 23 cm.
ADULTS general plumage green, paler on underparts; head brownish-black; collar around hind-neck rusty olive-yellow, each feather edged with brown thus producing a scalloped appearance; throat and upper breast dull olive-brown; under tail-coverts yellowish-green; primary-coverts deep blue edged with green on outer webs; primaries black broadly edged with green on outer webs; under wing-coverts green; undersides of flight feathers dull bluish-green; tail green tipped with blue, inner webs of lateral tail feathers yellow; bill horn-coloured; iris orange; legs greenish-grey.
IMMATURES crown and occiput green; cheeks olive-green; dull yellowish collar around hindneck, but feathers not edged with brown; throat and upper breast green suffused with olive-yellow.
8 males   wing 148–158 (153.0) mm., tail 63–67 (65.8) mm.,
            exp. cul. 19–20 (19.5) mm., tars. 17–20 (17.9) mm.
8 females wing 146–161 (149.6) mm., tail 60–68 (65.1) mm.,
            exp. cul. 18–19 (18.6) mm., tars. 16–19 (17.1) mm.

DISTRIBUTION   From Bolívar, eastern Venezuela, and the Guianas south to the Amazon River between Roraima and Amapá, north-eastern Brazil.

GENERAL NOTES   The Caica Parrot occurs in forests in the tropical zone (Meyer de Schauensee, 1970). Haverschmidt (1968) says that in Surinam it inhabits the forests of the interior. According to Snyder (1966) it is not common in Guyana, but is widespread from the coastal rivers inland to localities which lie roughly along the foothills of the western mountain ranges. In eastern Venezuela it is very locally distributed in tropical forests in the Gran Sabana and neighbouring areas in south-eastern Bolívar (Phelps and Phelps, 1958).

These parrots are usually observed in pairs or small flocks. They are birds of the treetops, where they feed on fruits, berries, and seeds. Nothing further is known of their habits.

CALL A medium to low-pitched, nasal *wee-uck* and *wo-cha* (Snyder, 1966).

NESTING No records.

EGGS Undescribed.

Genus GYPOPSITTA Bonaparte

The bare head in adults is the most conspicuous external feature of this monotypic genus. Undoubtedly, this is a unique characteristic, but its validity as the diagnostic feature of a genus is doubtful because in immatures only the lores and periophthalmic region are naked. Griscom and Greenway (1941) point out that plumage colouration of the species so closely resembles that of *Pionopsitta barrabandi* as to suggest that the two are representative forms with complementary ranges. Haffer (1970) incorporates *Gypopsitta* into *Pionopsitta* and claims that *G. vulturina* is merely a member of the *P. caica* superspecies.

The species is a medium-sized, stocky parrot with a short, squarish tail. The bill is broad at the base and laterally compressed along the culmen; there is no distinct notch in the upper mandible. The naked cere is prominent in both adults and immatures. Sexes are alike, but there is a different immature plumage.

Seven-coloured Parrotlet *Touit batavica* 1
AMNH. 475361 ad. ♂

Brown-backed Parrotlet *Touit melanonota* 2
ANSP. 22602 ad. ♂

Sapphire-rumped Parrotlet 3
Touit purpurata purpurata
AMNH. 475373 ad. ♂

VULTURINE PARROT
Gypopsitta vulturina (Kuhl)

Illustrated on page 500.

DESCRIPTION   Length 23 cm.
ADULTS general plumage green, noticeably tinged with blue on abdomen and lower breast; bare forehead brownish-yellow, covered with pale hair-like bristles; remainder of bare head black,

W.T. Cooper. 72.

covered with black hair-like bristles; bright yellow collar encircling neck; hindneck and sides of neck, below yellow collar, black; upper breast dull olive-yellow, each feather lightly tipped with black thus giving an indistinct scalloped effect; thighs green variably marked with orange-yellow; under tail-coverts yellowish-green; bend of wing and lesser wing-coverts reddish-orange; outermost median wing-coverts dark blue; primary-coverts black with narrow edging of violet-blue on outer webs; primaries black tinged with violet-blue and narrowly margined with green; carpal edge, under wing-coverts, and axillaries red; undersides of flight feathers dull green; tail green tipped with dark blue; inner webs of lateral tail feathers yellow; bill greenish-grey with yellowish marking at base of upper mandible; iris orange; legs greenish-grey.

IMMATURES naked lores and periophthalmic region brownish-yellow; remainder of head covered with dull green feathers, the yellow bases of which show through; no yellow collar encircling neck; upper breast dull yellowish-green; underparts paler green with less blue suffusion; thighs green; bend of wing and lesser wing-coverts orange-yellow; bill yellowish in very young birds.

11 males   wing 151–165 (157.1) mm., tail 60–73 (66.9) mm.,
       exp. cul. 18–20 (19.0) mm., tars. 16–18 (17.4) mm.
6 females   wing 150–156 (152.7) mm., tail 64–71 (67.0) mm.,
       exp. cul. 18–20 (18.5) mm., tars. 17–18 (17.2) mm.

DISTRIBUTION   North-eastern Brazil, south of the Amazon River, from the east bank of the lower Madeira River, eastern Amazonas, east to the Gurupi River, which forms the Pará-Maranhão border, and south to the Serra do Cachimbo in southern Pará; erroneously recorded from Guyana and Venezuela.

GENERAL NOTES   The Vulturine Parrot inhabits forests in the tropical zone, but little is known of its habits. Bond and Meyer de Schauensee found it to be quite common in the vicinity of Belém and along the Gurupi River (in Stone, 1929); they noticed that it moved about in groups of six or eight and was very quiet while feeding.

Food consists of fruits, berries and seeds, procured in the treetops. It has been suggested that absence of feathers from the head prevents the plumage becoming matted with fruit pulp.

CALL   Bond and Meyer de Schauensee report that this species gives a curious, rather liquid cry of two notes, which is easily distinguishable from the call of any other parrot (in Stone, 1929).

NESTING   No records.

From an examination of specimens in the Museu Emilio Goeldi Paráense, Belém, it is apparent that acquisition of adult plumage is gradual. Feathers are lost from the head and the exposed skin is almost uniformly buff-brown; the hair-like bristles are pale on the forehead and lores, those areas which remain pale in the adult, but are black elsewhere. The yellow collar, the olive-yellow upper breast, and the strong blue suffusion on the underparts are then acquired. Finally, the bare head gradually takes on the black and yellowish pattern of the adult.

EGGS   Undescribed.

Genus HAPALOPSITTACA Ridgway

This genus is obviously closely allied to *Pionopsitta*, and the two species resemble the species in that genus. They are medium-sized, stocky parrots with short, slightly rounded tails. The bill is proportionately smaller and narrower than in *Pionopsitta*, and there is no notch in the upper mandible. The naked cere is prominent, but the lores are fully feathered. There is no sexual dimorphism.

BLACK-WINGED PARROT
Hapalopsittaca melanotis (Lafresnaye)

DESCRIPTION   Length 24 cm.
ADULTS general plumage green, paler and more yellowish on underparts; lores and narrow frontal band blue; crown and entire neck strongly suffused with blue, latter forming a distinct collar; ear-coverts black; periophthalmic region emerald green; all upper wing-coverts and outermost secondaries black; inner secondaries black edged with green on outer webs; primary-coverts dark violet-blue tipped with black; primaries dark blue narrowly edged with dull green; carpal edge bluish-green tinged with black; under wing-coverts bluish-green; undersides of flight feathers greenish-blue; tail above green tipped with violet-blue, below dusky bluish-green; bill bluish-grey; iris brown; legs pale bluish-grey.
IMMATURES undescribed, but probably similar to adults.

DISTRIBUTION   Central Peru and central-western Bolivia.

1. *H. m. melanotis* (Lafresnaye)   *Illustrated on page 501.*
    11 males   wing 156–162 (159.5) mm., tail 80–92 (84.2) mm.,
            exp. cul. 17–19 (18.4) mm., tars. 17–19 (17.5) mm.
    4 females   wing 148–156 (152.5) mm., tail 79–84 (81.0) mm.,
            exp. cul. 17–18 (17.5) mm., tars. 17–19 (18.0) mm.
    Restricted to La Paz and Cochabamba provinces, central-western Bolivia.

2. *H. m. peruviana* (Carriker)
    ADULTS like *melanotis*, but ear-coverts brownish-yellow; blue suffusion on foreneck restricted to a narrow band across lower throat.
    1 male (**type**); wing 162 mm., tail 90 mm.,
            exp. cul. 17 mm., tars. 17 mm.
    1 female   wing 161 mm., tail 88 mm.,
            exp. cul. 17 mm., tars. 17 mm.
    Known only from two localities in Junín province, central Peru; Auquimarca on the Paucartambo River (the type locality), and Chilpes, about 60 km. farther south.

GENERAL NOTES

The Black-winged Parrot is a little-known inhabitant of forests in the temperate zone. Bond and Meyer de Schauensee (1943) report that at an elevation of 2,500 m. in Cochabamba, Bolivia, specimens were collected at Incachaca in wet forest interspersed with boggy meadows. In Junín, central Peru, specimens have been collected at 2,800 and 3,100 m. (Peters and Griswold, 1943).

RUSTY-FACED PARROT
Hapalopsittaca amazonina (Des Murs)

DESCRIPTION

Length 23 cm.
ADULTS general plumage green, paler and more yellowish on lower underparts; forehead dull orange-red, becoming rufous on forecrown; lores pale yellow; chin and anterior of cheeks dull orange-red; hindcrown olive slightly tinged with rufous red; slightly elongated feathers of ear-coverts and posterior of cheeks olive with yellowish shaft-streaks; throat and breast olive, becoming more yellowish towards abdomen; bend of wing and lesser wing-coverts red; outer median and secondary wing-coverts dark blue; primary-coverts violet-blue tinged with black; primaries brownish-black with bases of outer webs violet-blue; secondaries blue broadly edged with green on outer webs; carpal edge and lesser under wing-coverts pale red; greater under wing-coverts and undersides of flight feathers greenish-blue; tail brownish-red tipped with violet-blue; bill horn-coloured with bluish-grey marking at base of upper mandible; iris greenish-yellow; legs dark grey.
IMMATURES yellowish streaks on ear-coverts and posterior of cheeks scarcely visible; face duller red; secondaries green.

Western Venezuela, central Colombia, and western Ecuador.

1. *H. a. amazonina* (Des Murs)   *Illustrated on page 501.*
    9 males   wing 149–157 (151.4) mm., tail 71–83 (76.2) mm.,
            exp. cul. 17–18 (17.2) mm., tars. 15–18 (16.9) mm.
    5 females   wing 144–154 (148.4) mm., tail 75–82 (78.0) mm.,
            exp. cul. 16–17 (16.6) mm., tars. 15–17 (16.0) mm.
    Restricted to the western slopes of the Eastern Andes in central Colombia from Cundinamarca north to Norte de Santander and neighbouring extreme south-western Táchira in north-western Venezuela.

2. *H. a. theresae* (Hellmayr)
    ADULTS like *amazonina*, but forehead, chin and anterior of cheeks much darker brownish-red; ear-coverts and posterior of cheeks darker olive; throat and breast rusty olive-brown; upperparts darker green.
    8 males   wing 147–155 (150.5) mm., tail 68–83 (78.3) mm.,
            exp. cul. 15–18 (16.8) mm., tars. 15–17 (16.4) mm.
    5 females   wing 145–153 (149.8) mm., tail 66–81 (76.6) mm.,
            exp. cul. 16–17 (16.2) mm., tars. 16–18 (16.6) mm.
    Confined to the Cordillera de los Andes in Táchira and Mérida, north-western Venezuela.

3. *H. a. fuertesi* Chapman.   *Illustrated on page 501.*
    ADULTS like *amazonina*, but forehead and anterior of cheeks greenish-yellow; crown blue; chin green; red marking on abdomen; bend of wing and lesser wing-coverts crimson, darker and more maroon in female; outer median coverts violet-blue broadly edged with pink.
    4 males   wing 151–157 (153.5) mm., tail 77–94 (83.3) mm.,
            exp. cul. 15–17 (15.8) mm., tars. 16–18 (17.3) mm.
    1 female   wing 150 mm., tail 86 mm.,
            exp. cul. 17 mm., tars. 17 mm.
    Known only from the Central Andes in Caldas, Colombia.

Scarlet-shouldered Parrotlet *Touit huetii*   1
COP. 21455 ad. ♂

Golden-tailed Parrotlet *Touit surda*   2
NMV. B10519 ad. ♂

Red-winged Parrotlet   3
Touit dilectissima costaricensis
CNHM. 44476 ad. ♂

Red-winged Parrotlet   4
Touit dilectissima dilectissima
COP. 54477 ad. ♂

Spot-winged Parrotlet *Touit stictoptera*   5
ANSP. 159823 ad. ♂

Spot-winged Parrotlet *Touit stictoptera*   6
ANSP. 159822 ad. ♀

W.T.Cooper. 72.

4. *H. a. pyrrhops* (Salvin)

Illustrated on page 501.

ADULTS forehead, forecrown, anterior of cheeks, and chin darker red; crown and nape green tinged with blue, turning into yellowish towards forecrown; yellowish shaft-streaks on ear-coverts; throat and breast more greenish and not so strongly set apart from lower underparts; some feathers of middle of abdomen sometimes tipped with red; bend of wing, lesser wing-coverts, outer median coverts, and under wing-coverts rose-red; undersides of flight feathers blue; tail above violet-blue with green towards base, below dusky blue.

1 unsexed   wing 142 mm., tail 93 mm.,
          exp. cul. 16 mm., tars. 17 mm.
1 unsexed (LeCroy *in litt.*, 1972); wing 143 mm., tail 76 mm. (abraded),
          exp. cul. 17 mm., tars. 16 mm.
Restricted to the Andes in western Ecuador.

Phelps and Phelps (1958) state that in the mountains of north-western Venezuela the Rusty-faced Parrot is very locally distributed in forests in the subtropical and temperate zones. In Colombia it inhabits forests in the upper subtropical and temperate zones (Meyer de Schauensee, 1964). Chapman (1917) reports that it was a common bird at El Roble in the subtropical zone above Fusugasugá, Cundinamarca. There is no recorded information on its habits.

Black-headed Caique   **1**
Pionites melanocephala melanocephala
AM. A13428 ad. unsexed

White-bellied Caique   **2**
Pionites leucogaster leucogaster
ANSP. 22618 ad. unsexed

Genus GRAYDIDASCALUS Bonaparte

The species in this monotypic genus is a medium-sized, stocky parrot with an extremely short, squarish tail. The proportionately large bill is swollen laterally and there is no distinct notch in the upper mandible. The naked cere is prominent. Thompson (1900) points out that the orbital ring is incomplete with the postfrontal process being extremely reduced; the well-developed squamosal is long and straight and nearly meets the prefrontal process. Sexual dimorphism is absent and young birds resemble adults.

SHORT-TAILED PARROT
Graydidascalus brachyurus (Kuhl)

Illustrated on page 504.

Length 24 cm.
ADULTS general plumage green, paler on underparts and upper tail-coverts; primaries and primary-coverts darker green; secondaries, greater wing-coverts, and tertials edged with yellowish-green; dark red marking on carpal edge; under wing-coverts green edged with yellowish-green; undersides of flight feathers bluish-green; central tail feathers green, lateral tail feathers yellowish-green basally banded with red; bill greenish-grey; iris red; legs grey.
IMMATURES (Wagler); like adults but without red on bases of lateral tail-feathers.
10 males   wing 145–160 (151.9) mm., tail 49–55 (51.4) mm.,
     exp. cul. 23–26 (24.9) mm., tars. 17–19 (18.4) mm.
10 females wing 144–151 (148.1) mm., tail 45–53 (50.5) mm.,
     exp. cul. 23–26 (24.8) mm., tars. 17–20 (18.5) mm.

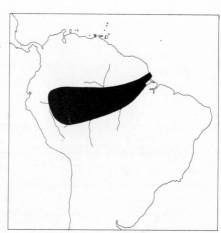

From Caquetá and Amazonas, south-eastern Colombia, south through eastern Ecuador to eastern Peru, and east through the Amazon Basin to the mouth of the Amazon River and the coast of Amapá, northernmost Brazil.

DISTRIBUTION

The Short-tailed Parrot inhabits forests in the tropical zone (Meyer de Schauensee, 1970). It seems to be quite common, at least in certain areas, yet few details of its habits have been recorded. Gyldenstolpe (1951) reports that at Itaboca, Amazonas, Brazil, the species was apparently abundant, but it was not obtained by his collectors at any other locality in the Purús River region. Goodfellow (1902) met with it at the Coca River in Napo, north-eastern Ecuador, where large flocks were congregating at dusk to roost in tall trees along the river banks.

  Masticated tubers were found in the stomach of a specimen collected on the Autaz Mirim River, Amazonas, Brazil (Schubart *et al.*, 1965).

GENERAL NOTES

Genus PIONUS Wagler

The parrots belonging to this genus are medium-sized birds with short, squarish tails. There is a distinct notch in the upper mandible of the stout bill, and the naked cere is prominent. A notable osteological feature of the skull is the complete orbital ring, and the bar formed by the fusion of the prefrontal and postfrontal processes is strong and broad with an abrupt angular lower border (Thompson, 1900). There is no sexual dimorphism, but young birds differ from adults.

  The wingbeat pattern is an excellent aid to field identification of *Pionus* parrots. The wingbeats are deep, but all movement is below the body level and at the end of each stroke the flight feathers are pointing almost straight down.

BLUE-HEADED PARROT
Pionus menstruus (Linné)

Length 28 cm.

ADULTS general plumage green; head and neck blue; feathers of throat with pink-red bases, usually showing through to produce an indistinct band; ear-coverts dull black; upper breast green tinged with olive-brown and feathers edged with blue giving an overall blue appearance; under tail-coverts red tipped with bluish-green; lesser wing-coverts olive-brown; median wing-coverts green broadly edged with olive-brown; outermost primaries margined on outer webs with greenish-blue; under wing-coverts and undersides of flight feathers dull green; tail green, lateral feathers tipped and margined with blue and basally barred with red; bill dark grey with red markings at base of both mandibles; iris dark brown; legs pale greenish-grey.

IMMATURES (COP.48681); head, throat and breast pale green; crown feathers narrowly edged with blue; bases to feathers of throat dull pink; under tail-coverts yellowish-green variably marked with rose-red.

Southern Costa Rica south to northern Bolivia and central Brazil; also on Trinidad.

1. *P. m. menstruus* (Linné)   *Illustrated on page 505.*

 12 males wing 175–194 (184.7) mm., tail 67–78 (74.6) mm.,
     exp. cul. 23–27 (25.3) mm., tars. 18–22 (19.8) mm.
 12 females wing 171–190 (179.4) mm., tail 65–76 (71.5) mm.,
     exp. cul. 22–25 (23.9) mm., tars. 18–21 (19.8) mm.

 Ranges from the Guianas west to the Eastern Andes in Colombia, thence south through eastern Ecuador, eastern Peru, and northern Brazil, to northern Bolivia, and central Brazil in Mato Grosso and Goiás; also on Trinidad.

2. *P. m. reichenowi* (Heine)

ADULTS like *menstruus*, but head, neck, and throat darker blue; no pink-red bases to feathers of throat; feathers of back and rump darker green edged with blue, especially on rump; feathers of breast and abdomen olive broadly tipped with blue; flanks, thighs, and sides of breast green suffused with pale blue; under tail-coverts red tipped with blue instead of green; under wing-coverts edged with blue.

 5 males wing 174–180 (176.6) mm., tail 67–75 (71.2) mm.,
     exp. cul. 24–26 (25.4) mm., tars. 18–21 (19.2) mm.
 3 females wing 169–182 (174.7) mm., tail 65–76 (71.3) mm.,
     exp. cul. 23–24 (23.3) mm., tars. 18–20 (19.0) mm.

 Known only from coastal north-eastern Brazil from Alagoas south to Espírito Santo and possibly Rio de Janeiro.

3. *P. m. rubrigularis* Cabanis

ADULTS similar to *menstruus*, but blue of head and neck duller; red bases to feathers of throat more extensive and quite conspicuous; upperparts darker green.

 10 males wing 173–186 (180.2) mm., tail 63–77 (72.3) mm.,
     exp. cul. 24–26 (24.7) mm., tars. 18–21 (19.6) mm.
 10 females wing 171–180 (175.8) mm., tail 66–74 (69.9) mm.,
     exp. cul. 22–25 (23.5) mm., tars. 18–20 (18.9) mm.

 Distributed from southern Costa Rica through Panama to western Colombia, west of the Eastern Andes, and western Ecuador.

Slud (1964) reports that in southern Costa Rica the Blue-headed Parrot is primarily a Caribbean species and is uncommon to fairly common in lightly timbered country in the tropical belt north to about the Pacurare River; on the Pacific side it has been recorded only from the Coto River in the wet-forested Golfo Dulce region near the Panama border. In Panama it is a widespread, fairly common resident of the tropical zone on both the Caribbean and Pacific slopes, and has been recorded up to about 575 m. in the foothills of Cerro Pirre, Darién (Wetmore, 1968). Eisenmann and Loftin (1968) report that it is present in the Panama Canal Zone, where, according to Eisenmann (1952), it is common in forests on Barro Colorado Island. It is common on Isla Coiba and visits islands in the Archipiélago de las Perlas, Panama (Wetmore, 1957 and 1968). Meyer de Schauensee (1964) says that in Colombia it inhabits forest in the tropical zone. Dugand (1947) reports that in Atlántico, north-western Colombia, the species was seen only in forested areas in the west where it was abundant, particularly along the banks of the Tocahagua River. Todd and Carriker (1922) state that it was found to be fairly common in lowlands all around the Sierra Nevada in Magdalena, north-western Colombia, and Darlington (1931) lists it as an abundant, forest-dwelling species in the vicinity of Rio Frio, also in Magdalena. In the Guapí district, Cauca, south-western Colombia, Olivares (1957) found it to be the most common parrot, and although a resident of dense forest it came out into open farmlands to feed. It occurs throughout most of Venezuela and is generally distributed in forests of the tropical zone, though also accidental to the subtropical zone (Phelps and Phelps, 1958); to date it has not been recorded from Delta Amacuro or from southern Amazonas. Friedmann and Smith (1955) report that around Caicara, Monagas, north-eastern Venezuela, it was usually seen in the heaviest forest and, like the Blue and Yellow

Brown-hooded Parrot **1**
Pionopsitta haematotis haematotis
LSUMZ. 27413 ad. ♂

Pileated Parrot *Pionopsitta pileata* **2**
LACM. 66551 ad. ♂

Pileated Parrot *Pionopsitta pileata* **3**
LACM. 46937 ad. ♀

Rose-faced Parrot *Pionopsitta pulchra* **4**
BM. 1901.10.14.2 ad. ♂

Macaw (*Ara ararauna*), seemed to be at the extreme edge of its preferred habitat, namely the dense lowland forest of Quiriquire and Caripito. In Guyana it is widespread and moderately common in forested areas (Snyder, 1966). Haverschmidt (1968) says that it is common in the forests of Surinam. At the turn of the century Goodfellow (1902) recorded it as being common along the Napo River in eastern Ecuador and north-eastern Peru, and I presume that it is still plentiful in this fairly remote region. Terborgh and Weske (1969) report that at a locality on the Apurímac River, central Peru, the species was observed only in a tract of primary forest and in an adjoining coffee plantation. Pinto (1954) points out that there appear to be no records of *P. menstruus* from the Belém district, Pará, northern Brazil, but it seems to be a common bird farther west on the lower Tocatins River. Herklots (1961) notes that it has been recorded from several localities on Trinidad and claims that it is now definitely increasing on the island, due largely to its fondness for seeds of teak trees (*Tectona grandis*), plantations of which are being established in southern and central regions.

Outside the breeding season Blue-headed Parrots band together in flocks and move about in search of food. In some regions the movements follow regular patterns and the birds are present only as non-breeding visitors. Wetmore (1968) notes that on Isla San José and Isla Pedro González in the Archipielago de las Perlas, Panama, the parrots were absent between February and April, the nesting period, but at the beginning of May a few pairs appeared, and by June they were present in noisy flocks and were attracted especially by the ripening fruits of membrillo trees. Haverschmidt says that between June and August, but mostly in July, flocks arrive in the coastal region of Surinam where they feed extensively on seeds of jabillo trees (*Hura crepitans*).

During the nesting season these parrots are generally seen singly or in pairs and are silent and wary, but at other times noisy flocks are normally encountered. They occupy regular roosting sites, and each morning fly out to widely scattered feeding areas; these daily flights are at times very spectacular. Bangs and Barbour (1922) describe flights which took place at nightfall and about dawn every day on the lower Jesusito River, Darién, Panama; flock after flock whirred past overhead until the entire forest resounded with their screams, but the birds seldom paused to rest where they could be observed. Wherever there is an abundance of food the parrots tend to remain quietly throughout the day, periodically feeding and resting in the treetops. In districts where they are persistently persecuted they are timid and will seldom allow a close approach, but in other districts they will often rely on plumage colouration for concealment and if disturbed will sit motionless among the foliage. Although essentially birds of the forest canopy, they commonly visit open country, particularly cornfields where they cause considerable damage to ripening crops. They are strong fliers and on long-distance flights, such as to and from roosting places, they fly high above the treetops with characteristic rhythmic wingbeats.

Food consists of fruits, berries, seeds, and blossoms, generally procured among the higher branches of trees. Corn has become an important part of the birds' diet and they also attack bananas. Crop contents from a specimen collected at Caicara, Monagas, north-eastern Venezuela, comprised corn (Friedmann and Smith, 1955), and stomachs from two specimens collected at Cachimbo, Pará, Brazil, and three collected at Salobra, Mato Grosso, Brazil, contained seeds, crushed seeds, and fruit remains (Schubart *et al.*, 1965).

CALL The parrots give a variety of high-pitched screeches and harsh screaming notes. Eisenmann (1952) records a harsh, high-pitched *kee—weenk . . . kee—weenk . . . kee—weenk*; calls reported by Snyder are a rather high-pitched *krit-krit* or *chitty-wit-wit* and a more liquid *chil-chil*.

NESTING Wetmore (1968) reports that in Panama the breeding season is from February to April; a female collected at Almirante on 6th February was laying, young were seen in the possession of Chocó women on 29th March, and all through the first half of April pairs were active about their nesting holes. On Barro Colorado Island, Panama Canal Zone, Gilliard found young in a nest on 12th April (in Eisenmann, 1952). In the Guapí district, Cauca, south-western Colombia, Olivares found that some specimens had enlarged gonads, whereas other collected on the same day or within two or three days had small gonads; a female taken on 6th December was in breeding condition, and a male with enlarged testes was collected on 15th December. Young birds were taken from a nest at Cachaví, north-western Ecuador, on 26th December (Hartert, 1898). Along the upper Orinoco River in Venezuela Cherrie (1916) found a nest containing three chicks on 13th March, but he gives no definite locality. Haverschmidt records a nest with small nestlings in Surinam during October.

Nests are in hollow limbs or holes in trees. The nest described by Cherrie was in a natural hollow in a tree about 6 m. from the ground. The hole was approximately 60 cm. deep and no nesting material had been taken in by the birds. The oldest of the three young birds was nearly as large in body size as the adults but was naked, and judging from size differences there must have been at least four or five days between the hatching of the oldest and of the youngest.

EGGS Pointed oval, slightly glossy; 4 eggs, 31.5 (30.5–32.0) × 25.1 (25.0–25.1) mm. [Belcher and Smooker, 1936].

Saffron-headed Parrot *Pionopsitta pyrilia* 1
MM. B1825 ad. ♀

Caica Parrot *Pionopsitta caica* 2
AM. B5774 ad. unsexed

Barraband's Parrot 3
Pionopsitta barrabandi aurantiigena
AM. A13426 ad. unsexed

RED-BILLED PARROT
Pionus sordidus (Linné)

DESCRIPTION Length 28 cm.

ADULTS head olive-green, feathers of crown and occiput broadly edged with dark blue; cheeks olive, feathers tipped with blue; chin and band across throat blue; breast buff-olive, each feather subterminally tinged with dull mauve-pink; abdomen buff-olive slightly suffused with dull pink; under tail-coverts red; upperparts dull olive-green, each feather margined with paler olive-brown; primary-coverts and flight feathers green, outermost primary edged with blue on outer web; under wing-coverts and undersides of flight feathers green; central tail feathers green, lateral tail feathers blue basally barred with red; bill red; iris yellow; legs dark grey.

IMMATURES head, throat and breast pale green; feathers of crown narrowly edged with blue; under tail-coverts yellowish-green variably marked with red.

DISTRIBUTION From northern Venezuela and western Colombia south through Ecuador and eastern Peru to northern Bolivia.

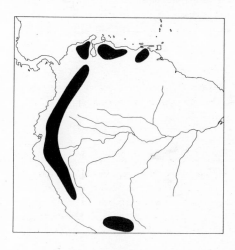

SUBSPECIES

1. *P. s. sordidus* (Linné)
    6 males   wing 175–184 (178.3) mm., tail 75–81 (77.8) mm.,
                exp. cul. 24–26 (24.8) mm., tars. 18–20 (18.7) mm.
    6 females wing 174–179 (176.0) mm., tail 76–81 (77.8) mm.,
                exp. cul. 24–26 (24.8) mm., tars. 19–20 (19.3) mm.
    Confined to the mountains of north-western Venezuela from Lara and Falcón east to the Caracas district.

2. *P. s. antelius* Todd.
    ADULTS like *sordidus*, but general colouration paler and more yellowish-green; throat green with little or no blue band; no mauve-pink tinge on breast; abdomen olive-yellow with paler yellow edges to feathers; smaller size.
    6 males   wing 160–167 (163.5) mm., tail 70–77 (73.0) mm.,
                exp. cul. 22–26 (24.7) mm., tars. 18–20 (19.0) mm.
    5 females wing 156–166 (161.8) mm., tail 70–74 (71.2) mm.,
                exp. cul. 23–24 (23.4) mm., tars. 18–20 (18.8) mm.
    Restricted to the mountains of north-eastern Venezuela in Anzoátegui, Sucre, and Monagas.

3. *P. s. ponsi* Aveledo and Ginés.
    ADULTS similar to *saturatus*, but lesser wing-coverts and upper tail-coverts darker, less.yellowish-green; abdomen and flanks darker olive-green.
    3 males   wing 182–187 (184.7) mm., tail 81–85 (82.3) mm.,
                exp. cul. 25–26 (25.7) mm., tars. 20–22 (20.7) mm.
    1 female   wing 182 mm., tail 82 mm.,
                exp. cul. 26 mm., tars. 20 mm.
    Known only from the Sierra de Perijá, Zulia, extreme north-western Venezuela, and in neighbouring Magdalena, northern Colombia, west to the Sierra Nevada foothills.

4. *P. s. saturatus* Todd.
    ADULTS general plumage, both above and below, much darker green than in *sordidus*; feathers of upperparts without paler olive-brown margins; underparts darker, more uniform green with little or no mauve-pink tinge.
    4 males   wing 182–193 (189.3) mm., tail 77–86 (82.5) mm.,
                exp. cul. 23–27 (24.8) mm., tars. 19–20 (19.8) mm.
    1 female   wing 181 mm., tail 82 mm.,
                exp. cul. 24 mm., tars. 20 mm.
    Confined to the Sierra Nevada de Santa Marta in Magdalena, northern Colombia.

5. *P. s. corallinus* Bonaparte.   *Illustrated on page 505.*
    ADULTS general plumage, both above and below, dull green without paler edges to feathers; feathers of head edged with blue; feathers of mantle and upper back tinged with grey and tipped with dusky blue; chin and band across throat purple-blue; darker margins to upper wing-coverts; larger than *sordidus*.
    8 males   wing 187–206 (196.9) mm., tail 64–85 (78.9) mm.,
                exp. cul. 22–25 (23.5) mm., tars. 19–21 (19.6) mm.
    6 females wing 195–201 (197.7) mm., tail 79–85 (81.5) mm.,
                exp. cul. 22–25 (23.3) mm., tars. 18–21 (19.3) mm.
    Distributed from the Eastern Andes in Colombia south through eastern Ecuador and Peru to northern Bolivia; absent from the lowlands of Loreto, north-eastern Peru and to date not recorded from southern Peru.

6. *P. s. mindoensis* Chapman.
    ADULTS similar to *corallinus*, but general colouration paler, more yellowish-green; narrower blue margins to feathers of head; no greyish-blue tinge to feathers of mantle and upper back; no darker margins to upper wing-coverts.
    1 male   wing 197 mm., tail 84 mm.,
                  exp. cul. 25 mm., tars. 21 mm.
    1 female (**type**); wing 196 mm., tail 77 mm.,
                  exp. cul. 26 mm., tars. 20 mm.

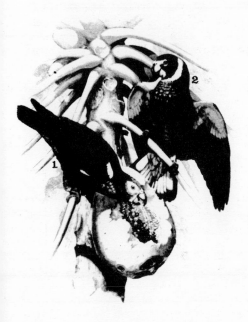

Vulturine Parrot *Gypopsitta vulturina* **1**
AMNH. 288262 imm. ♂

Vulturine Parrot *Gypopsitta vulturina* **2**
AMNH. 429164 ad. ♂

W.T.Cooper. '72.

Known only from the mountains of western Ecuador; probably not distinct from *corallinus* (see Bond and Meyer de Schauensee, 1943).

The Red-billed Parrot is a bird of the mountain forests. It is not well-known, and judging from published records is local in occurrence. In Columbia it inhabits forests in the subtropical zone of the Eastern Andes and the Santa Marta mountains, and in the upper tropical zone in the Santa Marta foothills (Meyer de Schauensee, 1964). Todd and Carriker (1922) give 1,875 m. as the upper limit of its distribution in the Santa Marta mountains. Phelps and Phelps state that in Venezuela it is found in forests in the tropical and subtropical zones. Phelps and Schafer (1954) report that in the Rancho Grande region, north-central Venezuela, it is resident in humid forests on both sides of the main range, and has been recorded down to 306 m. on the southern slope. Niethammer (1953) reports that in the eastern foothills of the Andes in northern Bolivia this species is one of the most common parrots in forests, but it is easily overlooked; at approximately 2,000 m. in the vicinity of Irupana, La Paz, and Pojo, Cochabamba, he found it and the Green-cheeked Conure (*Pyrrhura molinae*) to be the dominant species.

This species is usually encountered in pairs or flocks of up to forty, but local movements involving larger flocks have been recorded. Phelps and Schafer point out that at Rancho Grande, north-central Venezuela, during the dry season, especially from November to February, flocks of thirty to fifty come up from the valley forests each day as soon as the evening mists commence to fall. Beebe (1947) describes a spectacular flight observed in the same area in early March; a compact flock of more than ninety birds was seen flying low, silhouetted against the forest, and headed straight up the valley toward Portachuelo Pass.

Beebe reports that at the Rancho Grande Reserve these parrots seemed to be common residents of the subropical zone and occasionally pairs or small flocks were seen feeding in the forest canopy. However, more frequently they were seen going through Portachuelo Pass; several flocks would appear from the south and fly directly through and on into the north valley, and then at about noon these or others would return, or they might come into view, wheel around and return in the direction from which they had come. Their call-notes always attracted attention and could be heard before the birds were sighted.

They feed on fruits, berries, and seeds, procured in the treetops.

CALL Beebe describes the flight call as *pee-unt*.

NESTING Phelps and Schafer state that at Rancho Grande, north-central Venezuela, nesting takes place at the end of the dry season, which I presume would be about April. Near San Juan Mayu, La Paz, Bolivia, Niethammer found an occupied nest in late October; it was in a hole in the trunk of an old tree, approximately 6 m. from the ground.

EGGS Rounded; a single egg in the British Museum Collection measures 33.0 × 22.7 mm. [Harrison and Holyoak, 1970].

Black-winged Parrot **1**
Hapalopsittaca melanotis melanotis
NHRS. 552783 ad. ♂

Rusty-faced Parrot **2**
Hapalopsittaca amazonina amazonina
USNM. 392023 ad. ♂

Rusty-faced Parrot **3**
Hapalopsittaca amazonina fuertesi
AMNH. 111476 ad. ♀

Rusty-faced Parrot **4**
Hapalopsittaca amazonina pyrrhops
BM. 90.6.1.241 ad. unsexed

SCALY-HEADED PARROT
Pionus maximiliani (Kuhl)

Length 29 cm.
ADULTS general plumage dull green, paler and more bronze-brown on underparts; forehead and lores nearly black; cheeks green, each feather edged with bluish-grey; feathers of head margined with dark grey giving a scaly appearance; chin and band across lower throat dull blue; feathers of back, wings, rump, breast, and abdomen edged with dusky olive-brown; under tail-coverts red, longest narrowly edged with yellowish-green; outermost primary margined with greenish-blue on outer web; under wing-coverts and undersides of flight feathers dull green; central tail feathers green, lateral tail feathers predominantly blue and basally barred with red; bill yellowish-horn with dark grey at base of upper mandible; iris dark brown; legs grey.
IMMATURES head paler green with less pronounced dark edging to feathers; reddish forehead; blue band on throat poorly developed.

From northern Argentina north to Ceará, Piauí and Goiás, Brazil.

I have followed the arrangement proposed by Smith (1960).

1. *P. m. maximiliani* (Kuhl). *Illustrated on page 509.*
   13 males   wing 170–180 (175.2) mm., tail 72–83 (78.2) mm.,
           exp. cul. 23–27 (25.2) mm., tars. 18–21 (19.5) mm.
   8 females   wing 168–175 (171.1) mm., tail 69–85 (76.4) mm.,
           exp cul. 23–25 (24.0) mm., tars. 18–20 (18.9) mm.
   Restricted to north-eastern Brazil from Ceará and Piauí south to Espírito Santo, central Minas Gerais and southern Goiás.

2. *P. m. melanoblepharus* Ribeiro.
   ADULTS like *maximiliani*, but chin and throat band much darker blue; back and underparts darker green; larger size.

502

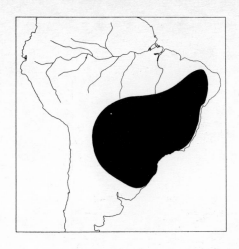

10 males   wing 185–198 (191.1) mm., tail 76–90 (85.8) mm.,
          exp. cul. 24–28 (26.1) mm., tars. 19–21 (19.9) mm.
10 females wing 182–203 (189.3) mm., tail 77–99 (87.0) mm.,
          exp. cul. 24–27 (25.1) mm., tars. 19–21 (20.0) mm.

Ranges from southernmost Goiás and southern Minas Gerais, central Brazil, south to eastern Paraguay and to Misiones and Corrientes in north-eastern Argentina; intergrades with *siy* in eastern Mato Grosso, Brazil.

3. *P. m. siy* Souancé.

ADULTS similar to *melanoblepharus*, but chin and throat band reddish-purple with blue tips to some feathers; green of back and underparts paler and bronze in colour.

20 males   wing 176–199 (190.5) mm., tail 77–96 (86.9) mm.,
          exp. cul. 23–28 (25.2) mm., tars. 18–21 (20.5) mm.
20 females wing 170–196 (182.6) mm., tail 77–95 (86.2) mm.,
          exp. cul. 23–27 (24.6) mm., tars. 19–21 (19.9) mm.

Occurs in Mato Grosso, Brazil, central and eastern Bolivia, Paraguay, except the eastern sector, and northern Argentina in Formosa and Chaco where it intergrades with *lacerus*.

4. *P. m. lacerus* (Heine).

ADULTS like *siy*, but throat band more extensive and bluer in colour; slightly larger size.

8 males   wing 194–209 (199.4) mm., tail 85–96 (91.1) mm.,
          exp. cul. 22–26 (24.9) mm., tars. 19–22 (20.4) mm.
2 females wing 193–200 (196.5) mm., tail 87–90 (88.5) mm.,
          exp. cul. 22–24 (23.0) mm., tars. 19–20 (19.5) mm.

Confined to north-western Argentina in Salta and Tucumán, and probably extending into Santiago de Estero and Catamarca.

GENERAL NOTES   The Scaly-headed Parrot is a widespread and fairly common inhabitant of lowland forest and open woodland. Stager (1961) reports that in central Goiás, Brazil, it occurred commonly in the Serra Dourada and was found to be fairly plentiful in gallery forest areas of the Chapada dos Veadeiros. Pinto (1935) says that it was one of the commonest parrots in the forests of southern Bahia, Brazil, that he visited. Sick and Pabst (1968) point out that it still occurs in the forests of Guanabara, Brazil, though in reduced numbers, and occasionally groups of four to six are seen flying over the outer suburbs of Rio de Janeiro that are near forests. In early June 1971, I saw two pairs flying over suburbs bordering the Floresta da Tijuca. Mitchell (1957) notes that at Lajes, in the state of Rio de Janeiro, Brazil, this species was heard frequently, and quite large flocks of up to fifty often passed overhead, morning and evening, as though coming from or going to a roost. Stone and Roberts (1935) report that in Mato Grosso, Brazil, small flocks were seen frequently, and usually they were feeding in trees. Near Villa Montes, southernmost Bolivia, Eisentraut (1935) found pairs and small groups in forest, but in general the species was not recorded very often and was not seen at all in forested areas farther down the Pilcomayo River. Olrog (1959) says that in northern Argentina it frequents subtropical forests and the characteristic woodlands of the Chaco. Wetmore (1926) recorded it as being common in forest in the vicinity of Puerto Pinasco, Paraguay, and in late July 1920 saw it near Las Palmas, Chaco, northern Argentina.

In May 1971, I observed these parrots between 800 and 1,300 m. in north-eastern Rio Grande do Sul, southern Brazil, and they seemed to be quite common in the region. Near Gramado, I saw them in disturbed woodland on a ridge behind the edge of forest which came up from the surrounding valleys. Singly, in pairs, and in small groups of up to eight they flew back and forth across the road en route to and from a patch of forest on a nearby hillside. They were rather timid and when approaching them I had to use the trunks of trees for cover. A party of six birds was observed at very close quarters; they were in the uppermost branches of a small tree at the edge of the forest, well below the top of the ridge, and all were preening themselves in a very thorough manner. Another two were sitting on a dead limb of a neighbouring tree and seemed to be basking in the late afternoon sun. In the same area two were flushed, together with a flock of Maroon-bellied Conures (*Pyrrhura frontalis*), from an *Araucaria* tree in which they may have been feeding. Near Bom Jesus, also in Rio Grande do Sul, I found them in *Araucaria* forest; one bird was seen calling from the topmost branch of a towering dead tree, and a group of about ten were observed clambering about in the crown of a large *Araucaria* tree. I noticed that in the field their pale-tipped bills and red under tail-coverts were easily discernible and proved to be excellent aids to identification.

Scaly-headed Parrots are generally seen in pairs or small flocks as they fly across open country on their way from one patch of forest to another. When in the crowns of forest trees they are easily overlooked because their plumage blends so well with the foliage. In flight they are noisy and often will be heard before being sighted, but while feeding or resting they only occasionally give a soft chatter.

Food consists of fruits, berries, seeds, and probably blossoms, procured in the treetops. Stone and Roberts report that in Mato Grosso, Brazil, the parrots appeared to be fond of wild figs, *Figueira* fruits, and the purple berries of another tree. In south-eastern Brazil they feed extensively on *Araucaria* nuts.

CALL   In flight a resonant *choik-choik* . . . *choik-choik* . . . *choik-choik*, which can be heard from afar; when the birds are alarmed these notes are repeated very rapidly.

Short-tailed Parrot *Graydidascalus brachyurus*
AMNH. 284873 ad. ♂

503

W.T.Cooper 72.

Blue-headed Parrot *Pionus menstruus menstruus* 1
NMV. 22472 ad. ♂

Red-billed Parrot *Pionus sordidus corallinus* 2
ANSP. 79072 ad. ♂

NESTING Naumburg (1930) reports that at Fort Wheeler, Paraguay, a female with a fully formed egg in the oviduct was collected on 4th October. The nest from which this bird flew was a natural hollow in the trunk of a large tree, about 10 m. from the ground.

EGGS Broadly elliptical to short ovate; 3 eggs, 32.2 (31.4–32.9) × 24.4 (24.1–25.0) mm. [Schönwetter, 1964].

PLUM-CROWNED PARROT
Pionus tumultuosus (Tschudi)

Illustrated on page 508.

Length 29 cm.
ADULTS general plumage green, paler on underparts; feathers of sides of head red with white bases showing through, particularly on lores and below eyes, and tipped with purple; crown and nape dark red; hindneck, sides of neck, and breast reddish-purple, becoming less reddish on breast; under tail-coverts red tinged with purple and edged with yellowish-green; under wing-coverts and undersides of flight feathers dull green; central tail feathers green, lateral tail feathers green tipped with violet-blue and basally barred with red; bill olive-yellow; iris brown; legs greenish-grey.
IMMATURES nape and hindcrown dark green like back; throat rose-red as in adult, but cheeks and breast green; under tail-coverts yellowish-green basally marked with pink.
10 males   wing 178–190 (182.9) mm., tail 76–85 (79.7) mm.,
exp. cul. 23–24 (23.3) mm., tars. 19–22 (20.6) mm.
10 females   wing 175–181 (178.4) mm., tail 75–86 (79.1) mm.,
exp. cul. 21–23 (22.4) mm., tars. 19–21 (19.9) mm.

DISTRIBUTION   Mountains of eastern Peru, west of the Andes at Taulis, Cajamarca, and Bolivia in La Paz and Cochabamba.

GENERAL NOTES   Little is known of the habits of the Plum-crowned Parrot. According to Meyer de Schauensee (1970) it inhabits forest in the upper tropical and subtropical zones. Griswold recorded it as being common at about 2,000 m., in the vicinity of Chilpes, Junín, central Peru, and observed that it was fairly tame when feeding in large groups (in Peters and Griswold, 1943). Carriker collected specimens at elevations between 2,500 and 2,800 m. in La Paz and Cochabamba, Bolivia (in Bond and Meyer de Schauensee, 1943).

WHITE-HEADED PARROT
Pionus seniloides (Massena and Souancé)

Illustrated on page 508.

DESCRIPTION   Length 30 cm.
ADULTS general plumage green, slightly paler on lower underparts; feathers of forehead and crown white becoming greyish towards orange-red tips; feathers of occiput, nape, and sides of neck white at base, then greyish-blue and margined with violet-black; ear-coverts dark grey with pink centres; feathers of hindneck pinkish-white; feathers of lores and cheeks white edged with grey, the edgings becoming darker and more pronounced towards posterior of cheeks; feathers of anterior of cheeks sometimes edged with orange-red; pink band on throat merging into reddish-mauve on breast, which in turn blends into brown of abdomen; under tail-coverts red; under wing-coverts and undersides of flight feathers dull green; central tail feathers green, lateral tail feathers green tipped with dull purple and basally marked with red; bill pale olive-yellow; iris brown, legs greenish-grey.
IMMATURES feathers of head green with white bases, those of crown also narrowly edged with dull red; feathers of sides of head white margined with green; throat and breast green, feathers with dull reddish-mauve centres.
10 males   wing 182–199 (190.0) mm., tail 71–83 (76.7) mm.,
exp. cul. 23–26 (24.9) mm., tars. 18–21 (19.9) mm.
8 females   wing 179–200 (189.1) mm., tail 72–80 (76.8) mm.,
exp. cul. 23–26 (24.3) mm., tars. 20–21 (20.5) mm.

DISTRIBUTION   From mountains of north-western Venezuela, in Táchira and Mérida, west to the Central Andes of Colombia then south through western Ecuador almost to the border of Peru.

GENERAL NOTES   In north-western Venezuela the White-headed Parrot is locally distributed in forests of the subtropical and temperate zones along the Cordillera de los Andes (Phelps and Phelps, 1958). Meyer de Schauensee (1964) says that in Colombia it inhabits forest in the subtropical and temperate zones.
At the turn of the century Goodfellow (1902) met with this species between 1,250 and 1,560 m. in the mountains of Ecuador. At San Nicolas, on the western slopes of the Andes, it was seen in

flocks in the early morning among maize fields on the hillsides, and it probably caused considerable damage to crops. The flocks sheltered in surrounding forests during the day. At Baeza, on the eastern slopes of the Andes in northern Ecuador, local people claimed that the parrots arrived there in large numbers about October. There is very little published information about its habits, but they are probably similar to those of other members of the genus.

WHITE-CAPPED PARROT
Pionus senilis (Spix)

Illustrated on page 508.

Illustrated on page 508.

Length 24 cm.

DESCRIPTION

ADULTS general plumage green, paler and more yellowish on lower underparts; forehead and forecrown white; white patch on chin and middle of throat; ear-coverts dark blue; feathers of remainder of head green broadly edged with blue; feathers of breast olive-brown edged with purple-blue, gradually becoming green towards abdomen; under tail-coverts red edged with yellowish-green and tinged with blue towards tips; primary-coverts and primaries violet-blue, latter becoming green towards tips; secondaries blue edged with green on outer webs; lesser and median wing-coverts golden-brown centred with dull green; under wing-coverts bluish-green; undersides of flight feathers dull green; central tail feathers green tipped with blue, lateral tail feathers blue basally marked with red; bill greenish-yellow with grey at base; iris dark brown to orange-brown; legs pink.

IMMATURES feathers of forehead and forecrown green edged with buff-white; feathers of remainder of head green with little or no blue margins; no white patch on chin and middle of throat; little or no purple-blue margins to feathers of breast; lesser and median wing-coverts green slightly margined with olive-brown; under tail-coverts yellowish-green.

15 males   wing 171–192 (178.7) mm., tail 68–78 (70.8) mm.,
        exp. cul. 23–27 (25.1) mm., tars. 19–21 (19.4) mm.
12 females wing 166–177 (170.8) mm., tail 61–75 (69.0) mm.,
        exp. cul. 23–26 (24.0) mm., tars. 18–20 (18.9) mm.

From San Luis Potosí and southern Tamaulipas, south-eastern Mexico, south to western Panama; occurs mainly on the Caribbean slopes.

DISTRIBUTION

Loetscher (1941) claims that the White-capped Parrot is a fairly common resident of rainforests in the humid tropical zone of southern Veracruz, south-eastern Mexico, and sometimes it wanders up to as high as 1,250 m. Dalquest found it to be rather uncommon in Veracruz (in Lowery and Dalquest, 1951); in the southern sector of the state a few pairs were noted in low trees along the banks of the Coatzacoalcos River, and one flock of about ten birds was seen, but in the north it was more common and flocks of from six to ten were often observed. Binford (1968) says that in Oaxaca, southern Mexico, it is fairly common in tropical evergreen forest in the Atlantic region from 100 up to 600 m., and probably higher. Tashian (1952) found it to be common in the Palenque district, north-eastern Chiapas, extreme southern Mexico, while Edwards and Lea (1955) report that at El Fénix, also in Chiapas, flocks of from ten to twenty birds were seen occasionally in pine-oak woodlands and cloud forest. Paynter (1955) reports that it is relatively common in heavier rainforest at the base of Yucatán Peninsula, south-eastern Mexico, but has not been reliably recorded from the state of Yucatán, towards the tip of the Peninsula. In nearly every part of British Honduras the species is a noisy and conspicuous resident of forests, especially near their borders, semi-open country, and savannah woodland in which *Pinus caribaea* predominates (Russell, 1964). Monroe (1968) says that in Honduras it is a fairly common resident of lowland rainforest, primarily below 1,100 m. on the Caribbean slope, though there are records from the interior of the country up to 1,600 m. thus suggesting that the species may follow riverine forests to this elevation. In northern Guatemala, including the Eastern Highlands, it is a fairly common resident of humid forest, edges of woodland, and open woodland from sea level up to 2,300 m. (Land, 1970). Smithe and Paynter (1963) state that it is probably the most common parrot in the vicinity of Tikal, in the Petén, northern Guatemala. Howell (1964) points out that in Nicaragua it is now found only on the Caribbean slope, and two specimens collected in 1943 at El Carmen, on the Pacific slope, may have been escapees from captivity or could be proof that the species did occur in gallery forest on the western side before the region was so extensively altered by agricultural practices. Huber (1933) found it to be very common about Eden, north-eastern Nicaragua, and saw it in isolated trees in clearings as well as in dense forest. Slud (1964) reports that it is abundant in the humid lowlands and subtropical areas along both the Caribbean and Pacific slopes in Costa Rica, though it decreases rapidly above the subtropical belt and reaches its upper limit at approximately the transition to the lower montane belt; it is typically an inhabitant of semi-open areas with remnant stands of trees, such as have been partly cleared for plantations and crops. Occasionally it is found well inside forest, in the crowns of tall trees and flying over the canopy. Wetmore (1968) says that in western Panama it is a rare resident of the tropical and lower subtropical zones in western Chiriquí and the tropical zone in Bocas del Toro; he has recorded it between 1,100 and 1,800 m. on the southern side of Cerro Pando near the Costa Rican border.

Local movements, which may have been seasonal, have been recorded in Mexico. Davis (1952) reports that at Xilitla, San Luis Potosí, all parrots seen in the winter of 1950 were between 1,250

GENERAL NOTES

White-capped Parrot *Pionus senilis* **1**
LSUMZ. 10960 ad. ♂

Plum-crowned Parrot *Pionus tumultuosus* **2**
ANSP. 143767 ad. ♂

Bronze-winged Parrot **3**
Pionus chalcopterus chalcopterus
ANSP. 157617 ad. ♀

White-headed Parrot *Pionus seniloides* **4**
ANSP. 118064 ad. ♂

507

and 1,560 m., while in the winter of 1951 most were seen between 160 and 300 m. Binford points out that local migration in Oaxaca is indicated by records from a point at 100 m. elevation, 2 km. south-west of Valle Nacional, where the species was not recorded from 14th February through to 25th March 1961, but was fairly common thereafter.

White-capped Parrots generally associate in small flocks of from a few birds up to about fifteen, though at times large flocks of a hundred or more may be seen, especially where there is an abundance of food. Slud notes that during the breeding season lone birds may be observed within close proximity of the nesting tree. The parrots are arboreal and spend most of their time in the treetops where they move about deliberately and climb from one branch to another in what appears to be a most purposeful manner. While in the treetops they are normally silent and this, together with their predominantly green plumage, makes detection difficult. However, in flight they are noisy and conspicuous, and it is while flying above the forest canopy or across open country from one stand of trees to another that they are generally seen. They are rather wary and when disturbed fly off, screeching loudly. They fly rapidly and turn in unison when making frequent alterations to the line of flight. When birds pass by fairly close their white caps and throats are clearly discernible.

They feed on fruits, seeds, berries, nuts, and probably blossoms. They are also fond of corn and can cause considerable damage to ripening crops.

CALL In flight these parrots keep up an almost incessant shrill screeching. The begging call of recently-fledged birds is a continuous wailing note.

NESTING Russell reports that a male with enlarged testes was collected in May at Augustine, British Honduras, occupied nesting hollows were found in the colony in late February and March, and another nest containing three eggs was found in mid-April; the hollows were from 5 to 8 m. above the ground. Smithe and Paynter recall that near Tikal, Guatemala, birds were seen going into a hole in a dead tree during the last week of March, and it appeared that a nest was being prepared; two males collected at the same season three years earlier had slightly enlarged testes.

Yealland (1935) describes the hand-rearing of a young bird hatched in captivity. He gives little information about the nesting habits, but does indicate that only the female incubated.

EGGS Broadly elliptical; 4 eggs, 34.9 (33.8–35.6) × 25.4 (23.8–26.2) mm. [Harrison and Holyoak, 1970].

Scaly-headed Parrot 1
Pionus maximiliani maximiliani
CNHM. 103953 ad. ♂

Dusky Parrot *Pionus fuscus* 2
NMV. 3233 ad. unsexed

BRONZE-WINGED PARROT
Pionus chalcopterus (Fraser)

Length 29 cm.

ADULTS general appearance dark violet-blue; feathers of head and neck bronze-brown broadly tipped with dark violet-blue and with white bases, latter sometimes showing through on crown and nape; chin white; feathers of throat edged with dull pink, producing a narrow band; feathers of back, mantle, and scapulars dark bronze-green indistinctly edged with blue; lower back and rump deep blue; upper tail-coverts brownish-green edged with blue; feathers of underparts dark green broadly edged with dark violet-blue; under tail-coverts red, more or less blue along shafts; upper wing-coverts and tertials bronze-brown; primary-coverts, primaries, and outer secondaries purple-blue; inner secondaries purple-blue edged with brown; under wing-coverts blue; undersides of flight feathers bluish-green; tail dark blue with red on bases of lateral tail feathers; bill yellowish; iris brown; legs brownish.

IMMATURES head and upperparts greenish; feathers of underparts brown edged with dark green and tinged with blue; upper wing-coverts brown with paler tips and edged with green.

DISTRIBUTION Mountains of north-western Venezuela, western Colombia, Ecuador, and north-western Peru.

SUBSPECIES 1. *P. c. chalcopterus* (Fraser) *Illustrated on page 508.*
    10 males wing 193–204 (198.9) mm., tail 77–86 (81.8) mm.,
        exp. cul. 25–26 (25.3) mm., tars. 19–21 (19.9) mm.
    8 females wing 190–200 (194.8) mm., tail 74–81 (77.9) mm.,
        exp. cul. 24–27 (25.4) mm., tars. 19–22 (20.0) mm.
    Occurs in the mountains of extreme north-western Venezuela and in the Andes of Colombia, except in Nariño.

2. *P. c. cyanescens* Meyer de Schauensee
    ADULTS like *chalcopterus*, but underparts purer blue, less bronze-green in tone; slightly smaller size.
    10 males wing 182–192 (187.0) mm., tail 65–81 (74.3) mm.,
        exp. cul. 24–27 (25.4) mm., tars. 18–21 (19.3) mm.
    2 females wing 181–183 (182.0) mm., tail 75–76 (75.5) mm.,
        exp. cul. 24–26 (25.0) mm., tars. 19–20 (19.5) mm.
    Ranges from north-western Peru north through western Ecuador to Nariño, south-western Colombia; doubtfully distinct from *chalcopterus*.

In Venezuela the Bronze-winged Parrot is restricted to the Sierra de Perijá, along the border with Colombia, and is generally distributed in forests in the tropical and lower sub-tropical zones (Phelps and Phelps, 1958). Meyer de Schauensee (1964) says that in Colombia it inhabits forests in the upper tropical and subtropical zones.

Judging from published reports and the number of specimens in collections this species must be quite common, yet there is little recorded information on its habits. Yepez (1953) says that in the Sierra de Perijá, north-western Venezuela, it is generally found in pairs or small flocks. It flies rapidly and for long distances, constantly emitting its shrill screech. At the turn of the century, Goodfellow (1900) met with it in the vicinity of Santo Domingo, western Ecuador; he usually saw only one or two pairs together and never encountered it in any numbers. Small seeds were found in the crop of a specimen collected at Pallatanga, western Ecuador (Sclater, 1860).

NESTING Yepez reports that in the Sierra de Perijá, north-western Venezuela, breeding takes place about March, and the nest is in a hollow in a dead tree.

EGGS A single egg in the British Museum Collection measures 29.3 × 23.7 mm. [Harrison and Holyoak, 1970].

DUSKY PARROT
Pionus fuscus (P. L. S. Müller)

Illustrated on page 509.

DESCRIPTION Length 26 cm.

ADULTS head dull slaty-blue; red spot on either side of forehead; ear-coverts black; feathers of throat and sides of neck tipped with dusky white thus producing an indistinct collar; feathers of chin edged with dull pink; upperparts dark brown with paler edges to feathers; underparts brown, feathers variably edged with purple-red or reddish-blue; under tail-coverts dull red; primary-coverts and flight feathers purple-blue; under wing-coverts and undersides of flight feathers deep violet-blue; tail dark blue with red at bases of lateral tail feathers; bill dark grey with yellow towards base of upper mandible; iris brown; legs grey.

IMMATURES like adults, but some upper wing-coverts edged with green; greenish tinge on secondaries.

11 males   wing 160–178 (168.8) mm., tail 63–75 (67.7) mm.,
          exp. cul. 22–25 (23.9) mm., tars. 18–21 (19.6) mm.
14 females wing 161–180 (165.9) mm., tail 65–73 (68.5) mm.,
          exp. cul. 22–26 (24.1) mm., tars. 18–21 (19.4) mm.

DISTRIBUTION Occurs in the Guianas, in southern Venezuela north to the Orinoco River, in the Sierra de Perijá, extreme north-eastern Colombia, and in northern Brazil, north of the Amazon River from Amapá inland to the Negro River, and south of the Amazon River from Maranhão west to the Madeira River.

GENERAL NOTES Haverschmidt (1968) says that in Surinam the Dusky Parrot is common in forests on sand ridges near the coast, in adjoining savannah forests, and in the forests of the interior, though overall it is less numerous than the Blue-headed Parrot (*Pionus menstruus*). He further reports that each year noisy flocks come to the coastal belt especially in July and August, and in late June 1963, when the species was numerous on the coast, a lone parrot alighted on a fishing trawler well out to sea (Haverschmidt, 1963). Snyder (1966) says that it is widespread and moderately common in dense forest throughout Guyana. In May 1971, near Mabaruma, north-western Guyana, I observed a pair of these parrots in disturbed primary forest surrounding small cornfields. Phelps and Phelps (1958) state that in Venezuela it is locally distributed in forests in the tropical zone in eastern and north-western Bolívar. In extreme north-eastern Colombia it is known only from forests in the upper tropical zone of the Sierra de Perijá (Meyer de Schauensee, 1964). Pinto (1954) points out that early in the century Lorentz Müller found it to be extremely abundant along the Acará River, Pará, northern Brazil. I did not see it in the vicinity of Belém, Pará, in May 1971, but was told that in certain parts of the district it is quite common.

Published information on the habits of these parrots is very scant indeed. The pair that I observed in north-western Guyana were quiet, unobtrusive birds, even in flight, and this confirms the comments made by Beebe and Beebe (1910) about behaviour at a nesting tree; they watched the tree, morning and afternoon for several days, often for an hour at a time, but neither saw nor heard anything of the birds.

Yellow-billed Amazon *Amazona collaria* **1**
AMNH. 475361 ad. ♀

Puerto Rican Amazon *Amazona vittata vittata* **2**
USNM. 232250 ad. ♂

Black-billed Amazon *Amazona agilis* **3**
USNM. 236743 ad. ♀

CALL Undescribed.

NESTING Beebe and Beebe describe a nest found at Aremu, Guyana, at the beginning of April. It was in a hole about 12.5 m. up in a tall dead tree. It contained four young birds, each at a different stage of development. The youngest was covered only in pin-feathers, the second had feathers appearing on the scapulars, crown, breast, and tail, the third was well-feathered, except for the face, throat, underwings, and flanks, and the oldest was fully-feathered, but had a very short tail.

W.T. Cooper '76

EGGS Pinto draws attention to a difference in size and shape between eggs in a clutch of three, now in the Carlos Estevão Collection; the longest measures 35.0 × 27.0 mm., and the most spherical 34.0 × 27.5 mm. A single egg in the British Museum Collection measures 36.2 × 28.9 mm. [Harrison and Holyoak, 1970].

Genus AMAZONA Lesson

Species in this genus are called amazons, and are probably the best-known of all New World parrots. They are medium-sized to large, stocky birds with strong, heavy bills and short, slightly rounded tails. The naked cere is prominent and there is a distinct notch in the upper mandible. The wings are broad and rounded; in some species the flight feathers barely extend beyond the tertials when the wing is folded. Thompson (1900) points out that the complete orbital ring and associated osteological features of the skull are similar to the arrangement present in *Pionus*. Sexual dimorphism is absent or slight, and although there is an immature plumage in most species the differences are not striking.

Two species, probably belonging to *Amazona*, are supposed to have occurred formerly in the Lesser Antilles, but no specimens have been preserved. *Amazona violacea* (Gmelin) from Guadeloupe is based on the writings of Du Tertre, Labat, and Brisson, while *A. martinica* Clark from Martinique is based chiefly on the account of Labat.

The characteristic flight silhouette of *Amazona* parrots reminds me of the flight of ducks, and is a good aid to field identification. The wingbeats are shallow, and all movement of the wings is below body level.

YELLOW-BILLED AMAZON
Amazona collaria (Linné)   *Illustrated on page 512.*

Illustrated on page 512.

DESCRIPTION

Length 28 cm.
ADULTS general plumage green, paler and more yellowish on underparts; feathers of head, except forehead, distinctly edged with black; forehead and line around eye dull white, forecrown dull blue, each feather edged with black; feathers of lores and upper cheeks pale blue with buff bases showing through; ear-coverts dull greyish-blue tinged with green; throat, anterior of cheeks, and sides of neck rose-red, most feathers lightly edged with green or dull blue; lower back and rump pale green merging into bright yellowish-green on upper tail-coverts; primaries and primary-coverts blue; outer webs of secondaries dull blue margined with green; under wing-coverts green; undersides of flight feathers bluish-green; tail green tipped with greenish-yellow, lateral feathers basally marked with red and outermost feathers narrowly edged with blue; bill yellowish-horn; iris dark hazel; legs pale pink.
IMMATURES similar to adults.
8 males   wing 180–193 (187.3) mm., tail 92–101 (97.5) mm.,
           exp. cul. 24–30 (26.1) mm., tars. 20–22 (20.9) mm.
8 females wing 173–186 (180.1) mm., tail 88–102 (94.0) mm.,
           exp. cul. 24–27 (25.6) mm., tars. 18–22 (20.5) mm.

Jamaica, West Indies.

DISTRIBUTION

GENERAL NOTES

Lack says that the Yellow-billed Amazon is typically a bird of the mid-level wet, limestone forests, being common in the John Crow Mountains, on Mount Diablo, and in the 'Cockpit Country' (*in litt.*, 1971); it is absent from the montane forests of the Blue Mountains, except on the eastern side where it appears to be a daily visitor from the neighbouring John Crow Mountains. Lack also reports that it is an occasional visitor, but probably does not breed, in wooded cultivation in the higher parts of the southern lowland hills. Although essentially a forest bird, it frequently comes out into cultivated areas to feed. Bond (1971a) points out that it is more widespread than the Black-billed Amazon (*Amazona agilis*).

These parrots are generally found in flocks of from five or six up to thirty or more. They sometimes associate in mixed flocks with Black-billed Amazons. While feeding in the treetops they are easily overlooked because their predominantly green plumage blends so well with the foliage, but when flying above the forest canopy they are conspicuous and their screeching call-notes always attract attention. They are rather wary and will seldom allow a close approach.

Food comprises fruits, berries, and seeds, procured in the treetops. The parrots sometimes raid orchards and gardens, causing considerable damage to ripening fruit.

CALL A guttural, rolling screech repeated at irregular intervals; while feeding or preening a soft, guttural call is emitted (in captivity).

NESTING Little is known of the nesting habits. Danforth (1928) says that during June and July young birds are taken from nests for sale as cage birds. The nest is in a hollow limb or hole in a tree, usually at a considerable height, and two or three, sometimes four, eggs are laid (Gosse, 1847; Porter, 1936).

EGGS Rounded; 4 eggs, 36.0 (35.6–36.2) × 29.2 (28.1–30.1) mm. [Schönwetter, 1964].

Cuban Amazon *Amazona leucocephala palmarum* **1**
YPM. 58046 ad. ♂

Hispaniolan Amazon *Amazona ventralis* **2**
YPM. 58267 ad. ♂

CUBAN AMAZON
Amazona leucocephala (Linné)

DESCRIPTION

Length 32 cm.

ADULTS general plumage green, the feathers edged with black; forehead, forecrown, and around eyes white; lores, cheeks, and throat rose-red; rose-red feathers sometimes present on breast; ear-coverts dull black; abdomen dull red, feathers edged with greenish-black; upper and under tail-coverts yellowish-green, former faintly edged with black; primary-coverts, primaries, and carpal edge blue; secondaries dull blue, narrowly edged on outer webs with green; under wing-coverts green; undersides of flight feathers bluish-green; tail green tipped with greenish-yellow, lateral feathers basally marked with red and outermost feathers edged with blue; bill horn-coloured; iris pale olive-green; legs pink.

IMMATURES like adults, but with less pronounced black edging to body feathers; little dull red on abdomen.

DISTRIBUTION

Bahamas, Cuba, and nearby islands, West Indies.

SUBSPECIES

1. *A. l. leucocephala* (Linné)
   8 males   wing 183–204 (193.6) mm., tail 102–111 (107.6) mm.,
             exp. cul. 23–27 (24.6) mm., tars. 21–23 (21.9) mm.
   8 females wing 186–197 (191.0) mm., tail 100–110 (105.4) mm.,
             exp. cul. 23–26 (24.6) mm., tars. 21–23 (21.9) mm.
   Confined to eastern and central Cuba.

2. *A. l. palmarum* Todd   *Illustrated on page 513.*
   ADULTS like *leucocephala*, but general plumage averaging darker green; red abdominal patch darker, more purplish, and more extensive; throat deeper red.
   10 males   wing 189–202 (195.7) mm., tail 106–113 (109.9) mm.,
              exp. cul. 25–27 (26.2) mm., tars. 21–24 (22.6) mm.
   10 females wing 187–199 (191.5) mm., tail 100–113 (106.3) mm.,
              exp. cul. 25–27 (25.7) mm., tars. 22–24 (22.8) mm.
   Restricted to western Cuba and nearby Isle of Pines; doubtfully distinct from *leucocephala* (see Peters, 1928; Parkes, 1963).

3. *A. l. caymanensis* (Cory)
   ADULTS similar to *leucocephala*, but general plumage more yellowish-green; less pronounced black edging to feathers; white of forehead less extensive posteriorly; green on sides of neck extended so as to separate rose-red of throat from that of cheeks; red abdominal patch much reduced; slightly larger size.
   8 males   wing 199–207 (203.6) mm., tail 110–120 (114.1) mm.,
             exp. cul. 25–27 (25.8) mm., tars. 21–24 (22.8) mm.
   8 females wing 192–204 (197.6) mm., tail 102–115 (107.6) mm.,
             exp. cul. 24–26 (24.6) mm., tars. 21–24 (22.9) mm.
   Confined to Grand Cayman Island; doubtfully distinct from *leucocephala* (see Fisher and Wetmore, 1931).

4. *A. l. hesterna* Bangs
   ADULTS like *leucocephala*, but general plumage more yellowish-green; abdominal patch more extensive and more purplish-red; cheeks and throat deeper red; smaller size.
   2 males   wing 171–178 (174.5) mm., tail 98–99 (98.5) mm.,
             exp. cul. 23–27 (25.0) mm., tars. 21–22 (21.5) mm.
   1 female wing 185 mm., tail 104 mm.,
             exp. cul. 26 mm., tars. 20 mm.
   Occurs on Little Cayman and Cayman Brac Islands.

5. *A. l. bahamensis* (Bryant)
   ADULTS like *leucocephala*, but red abdominal patch more restricted or entirely absent; white of crown more extensive posteriorly and below eyes to lores and upper cheeks; less red on bases of lateral tail-feathers; slightly larger.
   2 males   wing 205–211 (208.0) mm., tail 120–124 (122.0) mm.,
             exp. cul. 29–30 (29.5) mm., tars. 23 (23.0) mm.
   6 females wing 201–217 (208.2) mm., tail 110–123 (116.0) mm.,
             exp. cul. 26–30 (28.5) mm., tars. 21–24 (23.0) mm.
   Occurs on Great Inagua, Abaco, and possibly Acklin Islands, in the Bahamas; formerly present on Long, Crooked, and Fortune Islands, also in the Bahamas.

White-fronted Amazon **1**
Amazona albifrons albifrons
MNHN. CG1936,1553 ad. ♂

Yellow-lored Amazon *Amazona xantholora* **2**
MNHN. CG1953,481 ad. ♂

GENERAL NOTES

Bond (1956) says that the Cuban Amazon is common in the more remote woodlands of Cuba, both in mountains and in the lowlands, and in the southern sector of the Isle of Pines. Garrido and Schwartz (1968) report that it is abundant on Guanahacabibes Peninsula, westernmost Cuba, and noisy flocks are very conspicuous. Walkinshaw and Baker (1946) found it to be fairly common on the Isle of Pines. Reports on the status of the species on the Cayman Islands are somewhat conflicting. According to Bond (1956) it is common on Grand Cayman, particularly in the north,

Red-spectacled Amazon *Amazona pretrei* **1**
AMNH. 321809 ad. ♂

Tucuman Amazon *Amazona tucumana* **2**
ANSP. 143752 ad. ♂

and in western Cayman Brac, but on Little Cayman it is very rare. On the other hand, Johnston *et al.* (1971) report that it is a resident of the wilder parts of Grand Cayman, and is not uncommon in central regions of both Cayman Brac and Little Cayman. Lack has seen it on Grand Cayman, and says that it is common in the arid lowland forest (*in litt.*, 1971). The species is now locally distributed on only one island in the Bahamas, namely Great Inagua, and its status is causing concern; there have been no recent records from Acklin Island and only a single sighting on Abaco Island, so the population on Great Inagua, presently estimated to be less than one thousand birds, could be the last remnant of *bahamensis* (Fisher *et al.*, 1969).

Outside the breeding season these parrots travel about in pairs or flocks of from five or six up to thirty or more. While nesting is taking place flocks are noticeably smaller and single birds are frequently encountered. In proximity to habitation they are timid, presumably because of persistent persecution, but in remote areas they will often allow a close approach, especially while feeding. They are generally very noisy, particularly when in flight, but at times they may feed or rest silently in the treetops, and an observer might be unaware of their presence until they fly off, screeching loudly. Fisher and Wetmore (1931) report that quite a number of parrots were seen on Grand Cayman Island and they were rather silent, except when individuals of a flock became separated from one another.

Fruits, berries, seeds, nuts, leaf buds, and blossoms make up the diet. On Cuba and the Isle of Pines the parrots feed extensively on seeds of palms and on seeds and tender shoots of pines. They occasionally visit orchards and gardens to feed on cultivated fruit. Walkinshaw and Baker report that on the Isle of Pines flocks were observed in grapefruit orchards, where they often sat twisting the stems of the unripe grapefruit until the fruit dropped to the ground. Fisher and Wetmore note that on Grand Cayman Island the birds appeared to be eating the internal soft parts of flowers.

CALL A variety of harsh screeches and shrill, metallic shrieks (in captivity).

NESTING Barbour (1943) says that on Cuba nesting commences in late March and extends well into summer. Todd (1916) reports that on the Isle of Pines a nest was found in early April, another containing three eggs in mid-April, and one containing young as late as 27th June. On Grand Cayman Island four eggs were taken from a nest on 12th May (Bangs, 1916). The nest is in a hollow limb or hole in a tree, generally about 6 m. from the ground in an old woodpeckers' nesting hole in the trunk of a palm. Three or four eggs constitute the normal clutch.

Boosey (1957) reports a successful breeding in captivity, but gives only meagre details. The female commenced to sit about the middle of May and the two young birds left the nest at the end of August.

EGGS Rounded; 7 eggs, 35.0 (33.4–36.9) × 28.2 (27.0–28.9) mm. [Schönwetter, 1964].

HISPANIOLAN AMAZON
Amazona ventralis (P. L. S. Müller)   *Illustrated on page 513.*

DESCRIPTION
Length 28 cm.
ADULTS general plumage green, feathers of head, breast, and upperparts distinctly edged with black; forehead and lores white; crown and upper cheeks dull blue, feathers edged with black; ear-coverts and superciliary line black; rose-red spot on chin; variable maroon patch on lower abdomen; upper and under tail-coverts yellowish-green; primaries and primary-coverts blue becoming darker towards tips; secondaries and secondary-coverts blue narrowly edged on outer webs with green; under wing-coverts green; undersides of flight feathers bluish-green; tail green tipped with yellow, lateral feathers basally marked with red and outermost feathers margined with blue; bill horn-coloured; iris dark brown; legs pale pink.
IMMATURES similar to adults, but with little or no blue on crown; abdominal patch paler red.
12 males   wing 183–202 (189.4) mm., tail 92–105 (101.6) mm.,
            exp. cul. 24–29 (26.8) mm., tars. 19–24 (21.3) mm.
10 females wing 171–191 (183.4) mm., tail 91–100 (97.3) mm.,
            exp. cul. 25–27 (25.7) mm., tars. 19–23 (21.1) mm.

DISTRIBUTION
Hispaniola and some offshore islands, West Indies; introduced to Puerto Rico.

GENERAL NOTES
Dod points out that at present the Hispaniolan Amazon is locally abundant on Hispaniola, but there is an increasing threat to its status from land-clearance and the spread of settlement (*in litt.*, 1972). It occurs in virtually all wooded habitats and the only limiting factor appears to be the availability of food; it is present in both the arid lowlands and the high montane forests, though more common in the latter where settlement is sparse. Bond (1956) reports that on Gonâve Island, Haiti, it is found only at higher elevations. Schwartz (1970) records the species for the first time from Saona Island, off south-eastern Dominican Republic, and suggests that the lack of previous reports may mean that the island has been colonized recently from the adjacent mainland; it appears to be quite a common bird on the island. It is commonly hunted for food, is often shot because of damage done to crops, and is popular as a cage bird, many nestlings being taken for sale in markets.

The species is now well-established on Puerto Rico and two nests have been seen at San Germán (in Bond, 1971b). Dod reports that the introduction was unintentional. Several hundred young parrots were captured in the Dominican Republic and taken by boat to Puerto Rico for sale. However, Puerto Rican authorities would not allow importation because there was no health clearance. Return of the birds to the Dominican Republic could have resulted in legal action being taken against the persons responsible for their capture, so all were released outside the port of Mayaguez and many reached land.

There are conspicuous local movements which seem to be governed by food supply. In some areas arrival of the parrots coincides with the ripening of certain fruits. However, on the Samaná Peninsula, north-eastern Dominican Republic, they are present throughout the year, both at sea level and in the high mountains, so presumably there is a continuous source of food (Dod *in litt.*, 1972).

Hispaniolan Amazons are generally seen in pairs, family groups, or flocks and are conspicuous as they fly low above the forest canopy, screeching loudly all the while. The call-notes carry well and usually are heard before the birds are sighted. At times the parrots are cautious and will not allow a close approach, while at other times they are almost absurdly tame. Dod gives an excellent first-hand description of their daily activities. When the first rays of early morning light fall on the roosting trees the parrots wake, begin to climb about among the topmost branches, and commence to chatter, the chorus gradually building up to almost deafening levels if large numbers of birds are present. Soon after sunrise the majority leave as one main group, and then the remainder follow behind as stragglers in twos and threes. While on Hispaniola, Kepler observed these parrots flying from the Dominican Republic across into Haiti, presumably to feed in the fields (*in litt.*, 1971); in about an hour approximately two hundred passed by, travelling mostly in pairs or trios rather than in big groups, and the pairs were generally many metres apart. The birds spend most of the day feeding or quietly resting in the treetops, where they are well-camouflaged amongst the foliage. Wetmore and Swales (1931) remark that when the parrots fly into the branches of even a fairly open deciduous tree they seem to disappear entirely, so well does the green of their plumage blend with the leaf colour. Sometimes they alight in dead trees where they clamber about and squabble in the usual parrot manner. Dod says that in the late afternoon the flocks return to their roosting trees, and it is a most impressive sight to see the large branches of the big trees bend over with the weight of the birds. In April, at the commencement of the breeding season, the flocks break up and pairs, or sometimes groups of three, are encountered, the trio presumably resulting from an unattached individual associating with a pair. The pairs select a tree and during the day regularly visit it to rest or sit in the sun, often spending up to half an hour or more preening their feathers or idly chattering. The flight is not fast and comprises characteristic shallow wingbeats; when flying low over trees the parrots frequently glide for short distances on motionless, down-curved wings.

They feed on fruits and seeds, particularly those of palms, berries, nuts, and probably blossoms. Dod says that in the arid lowlands fruits from various cacti and guayacan trees (*Caesalpinia* sp.) make up a large part of their diet, while in humid areas and in the mountains they eat guavas (*Psidium* spp.), bananas, and plantains, and will attack some cultivated crops such as maize and pigeon peas or guandules.

CALL In flight a loud screeching is emitted almost continuously; while feeding or resting the parrots frequently chatter or 'growl' softly. Dod reports that at the onset of breeding males can be heard repeating a regular, somewhat melodic, chattering.

NESTING Records in the literature indicate that the breeding season is somewhat variable, though nesting usually commences in late april. According to local lore young birds leave the nest on Ascension Day, so prior to this date there is widespread searching for nestlings to sell as pets (Dod *in litt.*, 1972). The nest is in a hole in a tree, generally in an old woodpeckers' hole in the trunk of a palm at moderate heights from the ground. Two or three, rarely four, eggs make up the normal clutch.

On 5th March, a nest containing two chicks was found by Abbott at Laguna on the Samaná Peninsula, north-eastern Dominican Republic (in Wetmore and Swales, 1931). It was in a hollow about 23 cm. in diameter in a partly dead tree standing in a clearing approximately 100 m. from the edge of woodland. The entrance hole was about 9 m. from the ground and the trunk of the tree was hollow for most of its length, the lower part being filled with wet debris.

Gates (1971) gives details of a successful breeding in captivity. Three eggs were laid, but only one hatched. Only the female brooded, the male feeding her at regular intervals throughout the day. The incubation period was not determined precisely, but was estimated to have been approximately twenty-five days. The chick was first heard in the nest on 15th May and it emerged from the nest-box on 15th July.

EGGS An addled egg with one end damaged was taken from a hollow in a palm tree on the Samaná Peninsula, Dominican Republic, and it measured 35.7 × 27.6 mm. [Wetmore and Swales, 1931].

Lilac-crowned Amazon *Amazona finschi woodi* **1**
ANSP. 129258 ad. ♂

Green-cheeked Amazon *Amazona viridigenalis* **2**
ANSP. 77272 ad. ♂

WHITE-FRONTED AMAZON
Amazona albifrons (Sparrman)

Length 26 cm.

DESCRIPTION

MALE general plumage green, feathers of head, neck, breast, and upperparts narrowly edged with dusky black; lores and periophthalmic region red; forehead and forecrown white, sometimes tinged with yellow; crown and occiput dull blue, feathers edged with dusky black; upper and under tail-coverts yellowish-green; alula and primary-coverts red; outer webs of primaries green towards bases and becoming blue at tips; outer webs of secondaries blue; under wing-coverts green; undersides of flight feathers bluish-green; tail green tipped with yellowish-green, lateral feathers with red towards bases; bill yellowish; iris pale yellow; legs light grey.

FEMALE like male, but alula and primary-coverts green.

IMMATURES similar to adults, but in males the alula is green; in both sexes red of the face is restricted to loral region and white of forehead and forecrown is tinged with yellow.

DISTRIBUTION   Mexico to western Costa Rica.

SUBSPECIES

1. *A. a. albifrons* (Sparrman).   *Illustrated on page 516.*
    10 males wing 178–190 (183.6) mm., tail 82–101 (92.6) mm.,
            exp. cul. 25–28 (26.4) mm., tars. 19–22 (20.5) mm.
    8 females wing 170–178 (173.4) mm., tail 81–95 (87.5) mm.,
            exp. cul 23–25 (24.1) mm., tars. 18–21 (20.0) mm.
        Ranges from Nayarit, central-western Mexico, south along the Pacific side to southern Chiapas and south-western Guatemala.

2. *A. a. saltuensis* Nelson.
    ADULTS like *albifrons*, but green of general plumage, particularly on back and sides of neck, strongly suffused with blue; blue of crown and occiput extending down to nape.
    11 males wing 175–190 (184.3) mm., tail 81–96 (89.8) mm.,
            exp. cul. 24–27 (25.6) mm., tars. 19–22 (20.3) mm.
    5 females wing 176–185 (180.2) mm., tail 87–95 (92.0) mm.,
            exp. cul. 23–25 (24.0) mm., tars. 20–21 (20.2) mm.
        Confined to Sinaloa, western Durango, and southern Sonora, north-western Mexico.

3. *A. a. nana* W. de W. Miller.
    ADULTS similar to *albifrons*, but smaller.
    8 males   wing 164–172 (167.3) mm., tail 73–86 (79.3) mm.,
            exp. cul. 25–27 (26.0) mm., tars. 19–21 (20.1) mm.
    10 females wing 155–175 (163.0) mm., tail 73–91 (81.7) mm.,
            exp. cul. 23–25 (24.3) mm., tars. 18–21 (19.6) mm.
        This poorly-differentiated subspecies is distributed from extreme south-eastern Veracruz and north-eastern Chiapas, southern Mexico, south to north-western Costa Rica.

GENERAL NOTES   The White-fronted Amazon is very common in dry parts of both coastal slopes of Mexico (Blake, 1953). Van Rossem (1945) says that in southern Sonora it is a common breeding resident of the lowlands, foothills, and lower mountains south of about 28° North lat., and it is found in a wide variety of habitats ranging from stands of giant cacti in the north to woodlands in the south; Van Rossem has observed it in pines at 1,560 m., near Rancho Santa Barbara. In January 1965, near Alamos, Sonora, I saw a party of five birds in trees bordering a seasonal watercourse. Lewis (1971) found it to be common in parts of Nayarit, namely the dry country near Rosa Morada, the thorn brush around Navarrete, and the dense palm-*Ficus* forest along the coast. In the vicinity of the Aguacatillo River, Guerrero, Davis (1944) found it to be abundant at about 300 m. in upland thickets, especially near cornfields. Binford (1968) says that along the entire Pacific slope of Oaxaca and north to Matías Romero in the Atlantic region the species is a common permanent resident in tropical deciduous forest and arid tropical scrub from sea level up to 1,000 m. Paynter (1955) reports that on Yucatán Peninsula it occurs most commonly in rainforest of moderate height, less commonly in deciduous forest, and rarely in tall rainforest; it seems to be less common than its sibling species the Yellow-lored Amazon (*A. xantholora*), but this may be merely because it is often found in habitats where detection is not easy.

    In Guatemala this species inhabits dry woodland and secondary growth up to 1,850 m., and is a fairly common resident in the Pacific lowlands and subtropics, the arid interior, and the northern Petén, but apparently is absent from the humid Caribbean lowlands (Land, 1970). Smithe (1966) says that it is uncommon around Tikal, in the Petén, and although it may be more plentiful than is indicated by sight records it certainly has been difficult to find. Russell (1964) points out that in British Honduras it is uncommon and inhabits high secondary growth, the edges of rainforest, pinelands, and open country with scattered tall trees; it is possible that this species and the very similar *Amazona xantholora* have often been confused in the field. Monroe (1968) says that in Honduras it is found in the arid Pacific lowlands, the arid interior below 1,800 m., and arid and sometimes more humid open areas of the interior valleys and Caribbean lowlands, even occasionally entering more open sections of rainforest, and wherever it occurs it is usually the most frequently observed small parrot. Dickey and van Rossem (1938) found it to be generally common and locally abundant in El Salvador. Slud reports that it is confined to the Pacific north-west of Costa Rica where it is one of the common indicators of dry-forested regions of Guanacaste province, being found in open and semi-open country with scattered trees and upward into the subtropical belt on the deforested slopes of Guanacaste Cordillera; its distribution in Costa Rica appears to be controlled by climate rather than by the presence or absence of competing species. Wetmore

(1944) found it to be common around Liberia, Guanacaste, and daily flights to and from the roosting sites were conspicuous. Orians (1969) notes that to the south of Cañas, Guanacaste, the species was found in open savannah, secondary growth, and closed forest.

Seasonal movements have been reported from some regions. Land (1962a) notes that during July and August flocks of up to twenty parrots were seen daily in the foothills of the Sierra de las Minas, eastern Guatemala, but they were not seen during the dry winter months. Dickey and van Rossem point out that these parrots are spring and summer visitors to the arid lower tropical zone in extreme western El Salvador.

During the day pairs or small groups of White-fronted Amazons are generally found feeding or resting in the treetops. The birds I saw near Alamos, Sonora, Mexico, were quiet and unobtrusive, and this is in agreement with comments made by other observers. They were tame and did not fly off when I stood under the tree in which they were sitting. However, like most parrots, they are noisy in flight, especially when travelling to and from roosting sites. It is on these daily flights that the birds are most conspicuous because the small parties then come together to form flocks, sometimes containing hundreds of birds, and their passage overhead cannot be overlooked. Wetmore reports that at sunset one evening in mid-November a flock of two hundred flew in scattered formation over the town of Liberia, Guanacaste, north-western Costa Rica. At Champotón, Campeche, Mexico, Klaas (1968) found them with Yellow-lored Amazons (*A. xantholora*) in large mixed flocks. Dickey and van Rossem found a roost in tall trees on a mangrove island in the main lagoon at Barra de Santiago, El Salvador. This roost was being used by several thousand parrots. Each evening at about sundown the first flocks began to arrive and by dusk the sky was filled with screeching lines and groups, the uproar from which could be heard from a long distance away. Stragglers were still coming in well after dark and with the arrival of each new group there was a fresh outbreak of squabbling and jostling for perching positions, all to the accompaniment of much noise. At first light they left the roosting trees and, in flocks of about ten up to fifty or more, headed straight inland, to be seen no more until near the end of the day. Slud points out that in flight the shallow wingbeats, not rising above body level, are typical of the genus, but the continually veering flight path is not and is more like that of an *Aratinga* conure.

They feed on fruits, nuts, seeds, berries, blossoms and probably leaf buds, procured in the treetops. In Nayarit, Mexico, Lewis observed large numbers of parrots congregating in *Ficus* trees to feed on figs. They can be troublesome in crop-growing districts; Davis reports that along the Aguacatillo River, in Guerrero, Mexico, the parrots commonly congregated around cornfields in the early morning and again in the evening to feed on ripening grain.

CALL A raucous, sometimes shrill *ca-ca-ca-ca*, and a barking *yack-yack . . . yack-yack* (Slud, 1964; Smithe, 1966).

NESTING Paynter notes that several of the specimens collected in Campeche, southern Mexico, in early February were just beginning to show gonadal activity. A female with a slightly enlarged ovary was collected in November at Hill Bank, British Honduras (Russell, 1964). Van Tyne (1935) reports that a breeding pair was collected on 3rd April at Uaxactun, northern Petén, Guatemala. Nothing further is known of the nesting habits.
EGGS Rounded; 2 eggs in the British Museum Collection measure 30.3 (30.0–30.5) × 22.7 (22.4–22.9) mm. [Schönwetter, 1964].

YELLOW-LORED AMAZON
Amazona xantholora (G. R. Gray)

Illustrated on page 516.

DESCRIPTION Length 26 cm.
ADULTS general plumage green, feathers distinctly edged with dusky black; forehead and forecrown white; hindcrown dull blue, feathers edged with black; lores yellow; periophthalmic region and upper cheeks red; ear-coverts black; upper and under tail-coverts yellowish-green; primary-coverts red; primaries green becoming violet-blue towards tips; secondaries violet-blue; under wing-coverts and undersides of flight feathers bluish-green; tail green tipped with yellowish-green, lateral feathers basally marked with red; bill yellowish-horn; iris yellowish-brown; legs pale grey.
IMMATURES forehead and forecrown dull blue, not white; lores yellow with scattered green feathers; periophthalmic region and upper cheeks green with scattered red feathers; primary-coverts green or green intermixed with red.
7 males   wing 164–177 (172.0) mm., tail 73–85 (79.0) mm.,
            exp. cul. 25–26 (25.7) mm., tars. 19–20 (19.7) mm.
5 females wing 165–172 (169.4) mm., tail 76–82 (79.0) mm.,
            exp. cul. 24–25 (24.4) mm., tars. 19–20 (19.6) mm.

DISTRIBUTION Confined to Yucatán Peninsula, especially the eastern and central sectors, and offshore Cozumel Island in extreme south-eastern Mexico, British Honduras, and on Roatán in the Bay Islands, Honduras.

The restricted range of the Yellow-lored Amazon is almost encircled by that of the more widely distributed sibling species *Amazona albifrons*. Where the two are sympatric *A. xantholora* seems to be more common and there are apparent differences in habitat prefererence, though these are minor and there is considerable overlap. The two species are so alike in general appearance that they are easily confused in the field.

Paynter (1955) points out that on Yucatán Peninsula this species is a bird of deciduous forest, occurring less frequently in light rainforest, the preferred habitat of *A. albifrons*, and apparently absent from heavy rainforest. It seems to be more common that *A. albifrons*, but this could be due to its being found in a habitat where detection is not difficult. The two species may occur in the same general area, but seldom do they come together in mixed flocks. Paynter never found them associated in a single flock, and always one species was more abundant than the other, depending on the nature of the habitat. On the other hand, Klaas (1968), reports that in the vicinity of Champotón, Campeche, the Yellow-lored Amazon was plentiful, and to the south of the village it occurred in large flocks with *A. albifrons*. Griscom (1926) found that this parrot was not a permanent resident of Cozumel Island, but a daily visitor from the adjacent shore of Yucatán Peninsula, approximately 15 km. away; soon after sunrise every morning flocks of various sizes came streaming in across the sea, scattered over the island, and then returned to the mainland just before sunset. Early this century Peck found the species in considerable numbers in pine ridges near the Sibun River and Manatee Lagoon, British Honduras (in Russell, 1964). Monroe (1968) points out that in Honduras it is known from only one specimen collected in 1947 on Roatán, in the Bay Islands, where it is apparently confined to the pine ridges, and is probably rare.

Large flocks of these parrots assemble each night at regular roosting places, from which they disperse every day into surrounding woodland, where, in small groups, they feed and rest in the treetops. Paynter reports that at Champotón, Campeche, Mexico, a minimum of fifteen hundred birds roosted nightly in a small area of secondary growth, and in the late afternoon they could be approached quite closely.

They feed on fruits, berries, nuts, seeds, blossoms, and probably leaf buds, procured in the treetops.

CALL Said to resemble the call of *Amazona albifrons* (Griscom, 1926)

NESTING Paynter reports that a male taken on Yucatán Peninsula in mid-March was in breeding condition. Young birds were present in each of four nests found by Peck during April and May in British Honduras (in Russell, 1964).

EGGS Undescribed.

BLACK-BILLED AMAZON
Amazona agilis (Linné)   *Illustrated on page 512.*

Length 25 cm.
ADULTS general plumage green, paler and more yellowish on underparts; feathers of neck lightly edged with dusky black; generally a few red feathers on forehead; under tail-coverts yellowish-green; primary-coverts red, in females some coverts green; primaries violet-blue; secondaries dark blue becoming green towards bases; under wing-coverts and undersides of flight feathers bluish-green; tail green, lateral feathers basally marked with red on inner webs, outermost feathers margined with blue; bill grey becoming paler towards base; iris dark brown; legs greenish-grey.
IMMATURES like adults, but primary-coverts green.
5 males   wing 170–176 (172.6) mm., tail 80–89 (85.4) mm.,
           exp. cul. 23–25 (24.4) mm., tars. 20–21 (20.2) mm.
4 females wing 159–166 (161.0) mm., tail 75–80 (77.0) mm.,
           exp. cul. 23–24 (23.8) mm., tars. 20–21 (20.3) mm.

Jamaica, West Indies.

It is remarkable that there should be two *Amazona* species occurring together on Jamaica, when the two neighbouring large islands, Cuba and Hispaniola, are each inhabited by only one species. Lack (*in litt.*, 1971) reports that the Black-billed Amazon is common in the mid-level wet limestone forests of Mount Diablo and the 'Cockpit Country', where counts showed it to be just as plentiful as the Yellow-billed Amazon (*Amazona collaria*). However, he did not see it anywhere else, either in wooded cultivation or in the John Crow Mountains, so it is much more restricted in range than is *A. collaria*. Towards the end of last century it was reported as being common in the John Crow Mountains, which is still the least disturbed area on Jamaica, but no ornithologist seems to have observed the species there recently.

Flocks of from five or six up to thirty or more of these parrots are generally seen flying back and forth above the forest canopy, their screeching call-notes attracting attention. When feeding or resting in the treetops they are extremely difficult to locate, so well does their plumage blend with the foliage, and an observer may be unaware of their presence until they suddenly burst from a tree, screeching loudly in alarm. Lack often saw these parrots in mixed flocks with Yellow-billed

Amazons, but rarely observed them feeding so could not determine whether the two species took the same or different foods.

Food consists of fruits, berries, seeds, nuts, blossoms and probably leaf buds, normally procured by the birds high up in forest trees. Gosse (1847) has pointed out that these parrots will come low down to feed on ripe plantain fruits (*Musa* spp.) and to extract seeds from the aromatic berries on pimento trees (*Pimenta officinalis*).

CALL A sharp, rolling screech, similar to, but more high-pitched than the call of *Amazona collaria* (in captivity); when feeding or preening the birds often give a soft 'growl'.

NESTING Little is known of the breeding habits. The nest is in a hollow in a tree, often in an old woodpeckers' hole high up in the trunk, and two to four eggs are laid (Gosse, 1847).

EGGS Undescribed.

PUERTO RICAN AMAZON
Amazona vittata (Boddaert)

Length 29 cm.
ADULTS general plumage green, paler and more yellowish on underparts; feathers edged with dusky black, particularly on head and neck; lores and frontal band red; under tail-coverts yellowish-green; feathers of abdomen sometimes slightly tinged with dull red; primary-coverts and primaries dark blue; outer webs of outermost secondaries blue narrowly edged with dull green; under wing-coverts green; undersides of flight feathers bluish-green; tail green narrowly tipped with yellowish-green, lateral feathers basally marked with red on inner webs and outermost feathers edged with blue; bill yellowish-horn; iris brown; legs yellowish-brown.
IMMATURES similar to adults.

DISTRIBUTION Puerto Rico, and formerly nearby Culebra Island, West Indies.

SUBSPECIES

1. *A. v. vittata* (Boddaert).   *Illustrated on page 512.*
8 males   wing 182–193 (188.5) mm., tail 90–103 (96.9) mm.,
           exp. cul. 27–30 (28.5) mm., tars. 21–24 (22.1) mm.
5 females wing 178–196 (185.6) mm., tail 93–104 (98.2) mm.,
           exp. cul. 27–28 (27.2) mm., tars. 22–24 (23.0) mm.
1 unsexed wing 203 mm., tail 105 mm.
           exp. cul. 32 mm., tars. 24 mm.
Occurs on Puerto Rico; may have occurred formerly on offshore Vieques Island.

2. *A. v. gracilipes* Ridgway.
ADULTS similar to *vittata*, but smaller and with relatively smaller, more slender feet.
2 males   wing 169–173 (171.0) mm., tail 93–95 (94.0) mm.,
           exp. cul. 26 (26.0) mm., tars. 20–21 (20.5) mm.
1 female   wing 175 mm., tail 100 mm.,
           exp. cul. 23 mm., tars. 20 mm.
1 unsexed wing 173 mm., tail 90 mm.,
           exp. cul. 27 mm., tars. 22 mm.
This poorly-differentiated subspecies formerly inhabited Culebra Island, to the east of Puerto Rico; now extinct.

GENERAL NOTES Puerto Rican Amazons were last recorded on Culebra Island in 1899 when A. B. Baker collected three specimens, all of which are now in the United States National Museum, Washington; I do not know the origin of the specimen in the Naturhistorisches Museum, Vienna. Wetmore (1927) reports that on Vieques Island, in 1912, he was told that parrots were seen formerly in heavy forests on the southern part of the island and it was thought that they came from Puerto Rico; no specimens are known from Vieques Island and if the species did occur there it has almost certainly been extinct since the turn of the century.

It seems that *Amazona vittata* is doomed to extinction because the decline in numbers is continuing and the few surviving birds may not constitute a viable population. Wetmore points out that Moritz, in 1836, reported great flocks of parrots on Puerto Rico, and, in 1864, Taylor found them to be common. It seems that until the turn of the century they were plentiful, particularly in the interior, but, in February 1912, Wetmore could find only small populations in the mountains of western Puerto Rico, in lowland areas near the mouth of the Mameyes River, and in the Luquillo forests. From August 1953 until March 1956, a census was carried out in the Luquillo National Forest Reserve, eastern Puerto Rico, which by then was the last stronghold of the species. In the course of the census no larger flock than two hundred parrots was ever seen and this same flock occurred at the same place at almost the same date in two consecutive years, so it seems likely that it contained most, if not all, of the parrots that occurred in the forest (Rodriguez-Vidal, 1959). Recher and Recher (1966) mention a further drastic decline in numbers, pointing out that the largest flock seen personally or reported to them was a group of thirteen observed during December 1965; they estimated that the population in existence at that time probably did not exceed fifty individuals, and the species was on the verge of extinction. To determine the present status, distribution, and ecology of *Amazona vittata*, and to develop a management plan to perpetuate the species have been the objectives of a project carried out during 1968–1970 by Dr Cameron Kepler, and most of what we know about the present status and habits of the parrots comes from his findings. The project was commenced anew in 1972 by Dr Noel Snyder.

The parrots are virtually confined to the Luquillo National Forest, which comprises 11,200 hectares (28,000 acres) of tropical forest that is also set aside as a bird refuge. Kepler found that the decline in numbers recorded historically, and documented by comparisons between the 1953–1956 census and present-day studies, is clearly continuing and each year fewer parrots are seen. There may be less than fifteen parrots remaining in the wild state in Puerto Rico and if the decline continues at the present rate they will certainly become extinct. Kepler concludes that if his population estimates reflect absolute numbers, and this is a distinct possibility, the wild population cannot be expected to survive more than five years. The original deline was almost certainly brought about by deforestation and widespread hunting, but factors now affecting the population are more subtle. When a population declines to such small numbers all adverse pressures acting upon it are potentially catastrophic. Kepler points out that nesting may have been more successful in 1970 than in the previous year, but overall numbers continued to fall, suggesting that some factor is resulting in appreciable mortality among adult birds. Interactions between parrots and hawks, namely Red-tailed Hawks (*Buteo jamaicensis*), Broad-winged Hawks (*B. platypterus*), and Sharp-shinned Hawks (*Accipiter striatus*), have been seen and any successful attack would have a major impact on the present small population. Predation on eggs and nestlings has been recorded. Rodriguez-Vidal says that the black rat (*Rattus rattus*) is the worst predator and in 1956 four out of six nests were destroyed by these rodents. Another threat is the Pearly-eyed Thrasher (*Margarops fuscata*), an aggressive bird which competes with the parrots for nesting sites and food, and which may also prey upon eggs and chicks. The thrashers have become much more abundant and widespread in recent years, thus aggravating the threat to the parrots. Rodriguez-Vidal reports that, on 30th March 1955, a parrot's nest containing two eggs was found, and on 22nd April a parrot was incubating these eggs. However, on 25th April the parrots were observed well away from the nesting tree and a pair of thrashers was seen going in and out of the hollow; broken parrot eggs were later found on the ground near the tree and the thrashers subsequently nested in the hollow. Kepler found that thrashers readily used artificial nest-boxes, so these were provided, but the end result was an increase in the thrasher population and likewise an increase in competition for natural hollows; the nest-boxes had to be removed. In 1956, a feral cat destroyed one nest by eating not only the eggs, but the brooding parrot as well. Three birds are now held in captivity at the Patuxent Research Centre, Maryland, U.S.A., where attempts will be made to establish a breeding stock. It is also planned to establish another captive population at the Luquillo Forest Reserve.

A flock of no more than fifteen Puerto Rican Amazons, possibly the last survivors, resides in the La Mina area in the centre of the Luquillo Forest, and from this location birds regularly move into the drainages of nearby rivers. They are frequently sighted in El Verde, especially between September and December when tabonuco (*Dacryodes excelsa*) is in fruit. Kepler (1970) reports that the parrots are highly regular in their daily activities. Throughout most of the year they call loudly for one or two hours at dawn and then disperse to feeding sites. If food is available locally, they fly to this food source day after day, generally at the same time, and return to their roosting places over the same route. Such a feeding area may be regularly visited over a period of weeks, despite the presence of fruiting trees of the same species at a closer location. When the birds shift to a new site the same procedures are followed. They use regular flight paths when travelling from one valley to another. Kepler noticed that one such path skirted the higher ridges extending up to El Yunque Peak, the parrots obviously preferring to fly around, rather than over, these ridges, possibly because of the cloud cover that often envelops the higher sections. They regularly fly distances of 1 km. from roosting to feeding places, and they commonly fly 4 to 5 km. when moving down the Espiritu Santo River valley.

Rodriguez-Vidal lists more than fifty species of fruiting plants, the fruits of which are used as food by the parrots. The most common food plant noted by him was the sierra palm (*Euterpe globosa*), reflecting perhaps its long fruiting period (November to June), its abundance in the La Mina area, and the relative ease with which parrots can be seen in the rather open palm stands. Other important food plants were the bejuco de rana vine (*Marcgravia sintenisii*), and camasey de paloma (*Miconia sintenisii*), tabonuco (*Dacryodes excelsa*), cafeillo (*Casearia guianensis*), guara (*Cupania triquetra*), and hueso blanco (*Mayepea domingensis*) trees. Kepler (1970) has seen parrots extracting nectar from fleshy bracts below the flower clusters on *Marcgravia* vines, and found that in the La Mina area they fed in *Clusia krugiana* trees more than in any other tree. On 2nd July 1969, he watched one parrot eat eighteen marble-sized *Clusia* fruits in less than three minutes. Kepler also points out that it is possible that some food essential to the parrots is not found within the Forest Reserve and this could account for the reported flights from the forest during summer months.

CALL In flight a rapid, strident *kar . . . kar*, that can be heard up to 2 km. away, and when feeding the parrots frequently utter low chuckling notes (Wetmore, 1927). Kepler says that there are distinct take-off calls, flight calls, and a series of contact calls, including duetting between pair members (*in litt.*, 1971).

NESTING Kepler (1970) says that the breeding seasons extends from February to June, that is during the annual dry season and when the palms are fruiting. The nest is in a hollow in a tree, and in the Luquillo Forest Reserve all nests found have been in Colorado trees (*Cyrilla racemiflora*). The upper branches of these large trees are susceptible to rotting, and they fall in rain or wind, leaving behind holes extending into the trunk; here the parrots nest, choosing sites more than 6 m. from the ground. Holes facing south are preferred because there is more protection from wind and rain. The parrots prepare the nest by cleaning out the interior, but they do not add lining material. In six nests, found during 1955, the entrance hole ranged from 10 to 23 cm. in diameter, the depth of the cavity from 43 to 64 cm., and the height of the nest above ground from 7 to 15 m.; the locality was about 650 m. above sea level. A normal clutch generally comprises three eggs, though nests are occasionally found with two eggs or even with only one egg.

Kepler found one nest in 1970. It contained two eggs on 15th March and three on 23rd March. One chick had hatched by 5th April. When checked again on 5th May there were three young and all had fledged by 27th May. On 29th May, a group of five birds, comprising a pair followed by a line of three, was seen about 3 km. from this nest site, and was almost certainly the nesting pair with their young.

Twenty nests were reported between 1953 and 1969. In nineteen nests for which the fate of eggs or chicks is known, forty eggs produced eighteen fledged young; that is, a breeding success of forty-five per cent and is equivalent to about one young per pair per year. Fifteen of the eggs were either destroyed or infertile. Of the twenty-five eggs that hatched, seven young were lost to predation or died when the tree fell or the nesting cavity filled with rainwater. Predation thus accounted for thirteen of the twenty-two nest losses, or in other words fifty-nine per cent. In the three breeding seasons, 1969 to 1971, four of five known nests were unsuccessful—two of these nests were found in 1971, and both were destroyed by predators (Kepler *in litt.*, 1972).

EGGS A single egg in the Nehrkorn Collection measures 35.7 × 28.7 mm. [Schönwetter, 1964].

TUCUMAN AMAZON
Amazona tucumana (Cabanis)

Illustrated on page 517.

Length 31 cm.

DESCRIPTION

ADULTS general plumage green, feathers strongly edged with black; forehead and forecrown red; upper and under tail-coverts yellowish-green; thighs orange; primary-coverts red; primaries green becoming blue towards tips; outermost secondaries blue on outer webs, inner secondaries more greenish towards base; under wing-coverts green; undersides of flight feathers olive-green; tail green tipped with yellowish-green; bill horn-coloured; iris orange-yellow; legs pale greyish-pink.

IMMATURES like adults, but thighs green.

11 males wing 202–223 (211.5) mm., tail 90–112 (102.5) mm.,
      exp. cul. 20–23 (21.3) mm., tars. 20–22 (21.0) mm.
8 females wing 198–215 (206.5) mm., tail 98–106 (103.1) mm.,
      exp. cul. 20–22 (20.8) mm., tars. 20–23 (21.2) mm.

Occurs in Chuquisaca and Tarija, south-eastern Bolivia, and in northern Argentina from Jujuy east to Misiones.

DISTRIBUTION

Tucuman Amazons are typically birds of the alder (*Alnus jorullensis*) forests along the eastern slopes and foothills of the Andes, and probably occur in north-eastern Argentina only as non-breeding visitors. Hoy (1968) reports that in the vicinity of Orán, Salta, north-western Argentina, flocks come down from the mountains into lower valleys at the commencement of October. Orfila (1938) says that they are very common, and flocks are generally seen flying above the forest canopy or feeding in the treetops. Between 1,800 and 2,000 m. elevation on the Sierra de San Xavier, above Tafi Viejo, Tucumán, Wetmore (1926) found them to be common in flocks that passed screeching over the forested slopes or worked about in dense forest growth, well hidden by heavy limbs and thick foliage; the flocks were wild and seldom allowed a close approach.

GENERAL NOTES

Food consists of fruits, seeds, nuts, berries, and probably blossoms and leaf buds, procured in the treetops.

CALL In flight a shrill screeching note.

NESTING Bond and Meyer de Schauensee (1943) report that a female taken at Padilla, Chuquisaca, Bolivia, on 12th January, was incubating a clutch of four eggs.

EGGS Rounded; 4 eggs, 34.5 (33.6–36.2) × 26.7 (25.3–27.5) mm. [Bond and Meyer de Schauensee, 1943].

RED-SPECTACLED AMAZON
Amazona pretrei (Temminck)

Illustrated on page 517.

DESCRIPTION   Length 32 cm.
ADULTS general plumage green, paler and brighter on head, neck and underparts; feathers distinctly edged with black; forehead, lores, crown, and periophthalmic region red; upper and under tail-coverts yellowish-green; thighs red; bend of wing, carpal edge, alula, and primary-coverts red; primaries and secondaries green becoming blue towards tips; under wing-coverts and undersides of flight feathers green; tail green broadly tipped with yellowish-green, small red spots on bases of inner webs of three outermost feathers; bill horn-coloured; iris orange-yellow; legs pale yellowish-brown.
IMMATURES like adults, but red restricted to forehead, forecrown and lores; periophthalmic region green with scattered red feathers; carpal edge green.
5 males   wing 210–220 (215.4) mm., tail 100–120 (110.2) mm.,
            exp. cul. 22–25 (23.8) mm., tars. 20–21 (20.6) mm.
2 females   wing 204–206 (205.0) mm., tail 107–108 (107.5) mm.,
            exp. cul 23 (23.0) mm., tars 20–22 (21.5) mm.

DISTRIBUTION   Occurs in south-eastern Brazil, from southern São Paulo to Rio Grande do Sul, and in Misiones, north-eastern Argentina; possibly found also in northern Uruguay and extreme south-eastern Paraguay.

GENERAL NOTES   The Red-spectacled Amazon inhabits *Araucaria* forests, and is considered by most authorities to be very uncommon throughout its restricted range. Widespread clearance of the forests is responsible for the apparent general decline in numbers and the disappearance of the species from some of its former haunts. Pinto (1946) doubts that it is still found in the state of São Paulo. Sick (1969) lists it as a threatened species and remarks that it was formerly common in the *Araucaria* forests of Rio Grande do Sul; he (1968) says that it was extremely nomadic, wandering through the once extensive forests in search of ripening seeds, but now it appears to be scarce in Brazil. It has been recorded from nothern Uruguay, but this needs confirmation (see Cuello and Gerzenstein, 1962).

In May 1971, I observed these parrots near Vacaria, Rio Grande do Sul, and am able to report that they are in no immediate danger of extinction provided there is adequate preservation of *Araucaria* forest. The area was undulating open grassland intersected by valleys which almost invariably supported dense stands of *Araucaria* forest; the birds inhabited these forested valleys. Many thousands of parrots were observed congregating in a stand of trees surrounding a marsh prior to going to roost in an adjacent patch of forest. It is impossible to say how many were present; estimates by members of our party ranged from ten thousand to thirty thousand, but I am sure that the lower figure is conservative. The farmer, on whose property the congregating site was situated, said that some parrots were resident there throughout the year, but the vast majority arrived in April and departed in July. They came to feed on ripe *Araucaria* seeds.

From late afternoon until well after sunset small groups flew in over open grassland toward the congregating site, sometimes pausing en route in forested valleys. We were standing on a hill overlooking the congregating site and incoming parrots passed low overhead, enabling us to differentiate clearly adult birds and those in immature plumage; it seemed that many of the groups were family parties. The parrots were restless in the congregating trees and were difficult to approach. At times thousands would rise into the air and circle above the treetops, to the accompaniment of an incredible volume of screeching; this was a most memorable sight. It was after nightfall when they began to move across to the roosting trees and the transfer was still in progress when we reluctantly departed. The strong, buoyant flight is characterized by shallow, rapid wing-beats, and at times birds tumbled and swerved erratically in the air.

The most important food is *Araucaria* seeds, but I presume that when these are not available other seeds, as well as fruits, berries, and probably blossoms, are eaten.

CALL   The call given in flight is a disyllabic metallic note, the second being lower in pitch than the first, and this is repeated twice in rapid succession.

NESTING Sick (1969) says that nesting was recorded near Erechim, Rio Grande do Sul, in 1960/61. A male with slightly enlarged testes (AMNH 321809) was collected west of São Lourenço, Rio Grande do Sul, in mid-October. Nothing further is known of the nesting habits.

EGGS Undescribed.

GREEN-CHEEKED AMAZON
Amazon viridigenalis (Cassin)

Illustrated on page 520.

DESCRIPTION   Length 33 cm.
ADULTS general plumage green, paler and more yellowish on underparts; feathers edged with dusky black, particularly on neck; forehead, crown and lores crimson, bases of feathers yellow;

violet-blue band from above eyes down sides of neck; cheeks and ear-coverts bright green, no black egding to feathers; primary-coverts green; outer webs of primaries violet-blue becoming green towards bases; red marking at base of outer webs of first five secondaries; secondaries green becoming blue towards tips; carpal edge green; under wing-coverts and undersides of flight feathers green; tail green broadly tipped with yellowish-green; bill yellowish-horn; iris yellow; legs pale greenish-grey.

IMMATURES like adults, but with only forehead and lores crimson.

8 males   wing 200–213 (207.5) mm., tail 103–116 (108.6) mm.,
     exp. cul. 27–31 (28.9) mm., tars. 22–25 (23.8) mm.
8 females wing 194–205 (200.4) mm., tail 97–109 (102.4) mm.,
     exp. cul. 27–29 (27.6) mm., tars. 22–24 (22.9) mm.

DISTRIBUTION
North-eastern Mexico from Nuevo León and Tamaulipas through San Luis Potosí to northern Veracruz.

GENERAL NOTES

Blake (1953) says that the Green-cheeked Amazon is rather common in north-eastern Mexico, and being a noisy, conspicuous bird it is not likely to be overlooked by even a casual observer. Sutton and Pettingill (1942) report that it was seen daily throughout the Gomez Farias region in south-western Tamaulipas. Martin et al. (1954) point out that in the Sierra de Tamaulipas, southern Tamaulipas, this species is not confined to the arid tropical lowlands, but ranges over the dry open pine-oak ridges where are found many typically temperate birds; it is common on these pine-oak ridges as well as in the tropical deciduous forest of the canyons. In San Luis Potosí, Sutton and Burleigh (1940a and 1940b) found it to be uncommon in the vicinity of Valles, and infrequently noted it in heavier woodlands along the Axtla River and about 10 km. upstream from Tamazunchale along the Moctezuma. Loetscher (1941) says that in northern Veracruz it is a rather common resident of wooded parts of the tropical zone. In Veracruz, Dalquest found it to be less abundant than either Amazona autumnalis or A. ochrocephala, and saw it most often in the northern sector where the jungle is low and dense; it was not recorded from the slopes of the Mexican Plateau, and was seen only a few times on the coastal plain of central Veracruz (in Lowery and Dalquest, 1951).

Dalquest reports that these parrots gather in large flocks of from twenty to one hundred individuals and pairs are not always discernible. The flocks are active throughout the day, usually resting or feeding in the tops of adjoining trees, for varying lengths of time, and then taking flight and wheeling about in compact formation before alighting in other trees, screeching all the while. They are noisy in the morning, while feeding, and in the evening just before going to roost. Sutton and Pettingill mention that they disturbed roosting flocks at night, but on one occasion a screeching flock that had not been disturbed flew past in the moonlight. Sutton and Pettingill also report seeing Ornate Eagle-Hawks (Spizaetus ornatus) swooping down upon screaming flocks of these parrots, and parrot feathers were found under trees used regularly by the raptors.

They feed on fruits, seeds, nuts, berries, buds and flowers, and are very wasteful, often biting only a small piece from a fruit and letting the remainder fall to the ground. They can be troublesome pests in cornfields. Pine seeds were in the crop and stomach of a specimen collected in the Sierra de Tamaulipas, southern Tamaulipas (Martin et al., 1954).

CALL Usual cry is a harsh kee-craw . . . craw . . . craw (Sutton and Pettingill, 1942).

NESTING Sutton and Pettingill report that in mid-March courtship was going on in the Gomez Farias region, south-western Tamaulipas. Many birds were paired, while others were squabbling and chasing each other. Birds sometimes came to grips in mid-air, fluttering upward as if climbing an invisible wire. Males were seen to walk the entire length of a branch in presenting some tidbit to their mates. In late March there was considerable bickering over nesting sites. On 31st March, Sutton watched one pair finally defeat other contenders and occupy an old woodpeckers' hole in a big cypress, about 20 m. from the ground. A pair and their nest were discovered near Tamazunchale, San Luis Potosí, on 20th April, and two days later, in the same state, a breeding female was collected along the Axtla River (Sutton and Burleigh, 1940b).

EGGS Rounded; 2 eggs, 35.7 (35.0–36.4) × 27.5 (27.1–27.9) mm. [Schönwetter, 1964].

LILAC-CROWNED AMAZON
Amazona finschi (Sclater)

DESCRIPTION
Length 33 cm.

ADULTS general plumage green, paler and more yellowish on underparts; feathers edged with dusky black; forehead, forecrown, and lores deep maroon; hindcrown, sides of nape, and hindneck bluish-mauve, feathers edged with dusky black; cheeks and ear-coverts yellowish-green without dusky black edges to feathers; primaries violet-blue becoming green towards bases; red speculum at bases of inner webs of first five secondaries; secondaries green becoming blue towards tips; under wing-coverts and undersides of flight feathers green; tail green tipped with yellowish-green, outermost feathers edged with blue on outer webs towards bases; bill horn-coloured; iris orange; legs greenish-grey.

IMMATURES similar to adults, but iris dark brown.

1. *A. f. finschi* (Sclater).
   10 males wing 191–208 (197.9) mm., tail 100–120 (112.3) mm.,
        exp. cul. 29–30 (29.5) mm., tars. 21–23 (22.5) mm.
   10 females wing 185–202 (195.4) mm., tail 108–124 (113.8) mm.,
        exp. cul. 27–30 (28.9) mm., tars. 21–23 (22.2) mm.
   Occurs in central-western and south-western Mexico from southern Sinaloa and Durango
   south to Oaxaca.

2. *A. f. woodi* Moore.   **Illustrated on page 520.**
   ADULTS like *finschi*, but green of general plumage less yellowish; maroon on forecrown and
   forehead narrower, more restricted, and somewhat duller.
   10 males wing 198–215 (206.6) mm., tail 109–124 (116.8) mm.,
        exp. cul. 29–32 (30.3) mm., tars. 21–24 (22.3) mm.
   9 females wing 193–208 (200.8) mm., tail 104–124 (114.6) mm.,
        exp. cul. 27–31 (29.2) mm., tars. 22–23 (22.4) mm.
   This poorly differentiated race is confined to north-western Mexico from extreme south-
   eastern Sonora and south-western Chihuahua south to central-eastern Sinaloa and Durango.

DISTRIBUTION

SUBSPECIES

GENERAL NOTES

Although sometimes found at sea level, the Lilac-crowned Amazon is more abundant in wooded foothills and mountains, ascending locally to an altitude of about 2,200 m. (Blake, 1953). Van Rossem (1945) says that it is a fairly common, but rather local, resident of foothills and mountains above 375 m. in the extreme south-eastern corner of Sonora; at Rancho Santo Bárbara it was observed in pine and pine-oak associations up to 1,720 m. Stager (1954) found it to be fairly plentiful in the Barranca de Cobre region, south-western Chihuahua, and noted that it was common even in the arid tropical growth at the bottom of the Barranca at 900 m. elevation. In January 1965, I recorded the species inland from San Blas, Nayarit, but it was not common; one or two small flocks passed overhead soon after sunrise on most mornings, and once a party of seven alighted in a nearby tree thus enabling me to make positive identification. It is an abundant resident of Colima, and occurs from sea level up to the montane oak woodlands (Schaldach, 1963). Hoogstraal found it in large flocks in deciduous forest near Apatzingan, Michoacán, but did not record it elsewhere in that state (in Blake and Hanson, 1942). Binford (1968) says that in Oaxaca it is a very uncommon resident of humid and semi-arid pine-oak forests in the Pacific region, west of the Isthmus of Tehuantepec, wandering into the lowlands, including the Isthmus, during autumn; it has been recorded from sea level up to 1,530 m.

Outside the breeding season these parrots are generally seen in flocks, particularly at roosting places. Schaldach reports that in Colima during the dry season, namely November to June, flocks containing as many as two to three hundred birds are sometimes encountered. Stager recalls making camp in a stand of oaks at the 1,470 m. level in the Barranca de Cobre, south-western Chihuahua, and then finding that this particular grove of oaks must have been a parrot roost of long standing because just before dark several hundred Lilac-crowned Amazons came streaming in from their feeding grounds and began settling into the trees for the night.

They feed on fruits, especially wild figs, seeds, nuts, berries, buds, and blossoms, procured in the treetops. Schaldach says that in parts of Colima the parrots are greatly detested because of the damage they do at times to corn crops and to ripening bananas.

CALL In flight a harsh, rolling screech.

NESTING At El Muerto, south-western Chihuahua, on 9th May, Stager collected a male in pre-breeding condition. Near La Mesita, Chihuahua, on 28th May, a brooding female and her two newly-hatched chicks were taken from a nest (MLZ Collection). In Colima, Schaldach noted breeding activity as early as February; a pair was seen investigating an old woodpeckers' hole in a hollow, dead *Ficus* tree standing in tall tropical deciduous forest.

Lint (1952) records a successful hatching in captivity. The incubation period was twenty-eight days, and the one chick hatched was taken from the nest when five days old and reared by hand.

EGGS Rounded; 4 eggs, 37.0 (36.4–38.1) × 29.2 (27.9–30.2) mm. [Schönwetter, 1964].

RED-LORED AMAZON
Amazona autumnalis (Linné)

Length 34 cm.
ADULTS general plumage green; forehead and lores red; feathers of crown, occiput and nape green with lilac-blue towards tips and edged with dusky black; upper cheeks and ear-coverts yellow, concealed bases of feathers red; carpal edge yellowish-green; primaries green becoming dark blue towards tips; red speculum at bases of first five secondaries; secondaries green becoming blue

DESCRIPTION

towards tips; under wing-coverts and undersides of flight feathers green; tail green, lateral feathers broadly tipped with yellowish-green and outermost feathers edged with blue on outer webs; bill grey with yellowish-horn on upper mandible; iris orange; legs greenish-grey.

IMMATURES like adults, but with less red on forehead and lores; upper cheeks and ear-coverts sometimes marked with green; iris dark brown.

DISTRIBUTION   Central America from eastern Mexico south to the Amazon Basin and western Ecuador.

SUBSPECIES   1. *A. a. autumnalis* (Linné).   *Illustrated on page 537.*

    8 males   wing 200–211 (206.1) mm., tail 103–120 (111.6) mm.,
            exp. cul. 27–32 (30.0) mm., tars. 23–25 (24.5) mm.
    8 females wing 195–215 (202.0) mm., tail 96–119 (110.4) mm.,
            exp. cul. 28–31 (29.4) mm., tars. 23–26 (24.4) mm.
    Distributed along eastern or Caribbean slope from Tamaulipas, Mexico, south to northern Nicaragua where it intergrades with *salvini*; present on the Bay Islands, Honduras.

2. *A. a. salvini* (Salvadori).
ADULTS similar to *autumnalis*, but without yellow on upper cheeks and ear-coverts, these being green; bases of lateral tail feathers red on inner webs.
    8 males   wing 199–230 (215.9) mm., tail 107–126 (116.6) mm.,
            exp. cul. 28–35 (31.6) mm., tars. 23–27 (25.3) mm.
    8 females wing 200–217 (210.3) mm., tail 111–122 (117.8) mm.,
            exp. cul. 29–34 (31.3) mm., tars. 24–27 (25.1) mm.
    Ranges from south-eastern Nicaragua and eastern and south-western Costa Rica south to western Colombia and extreme north-western Venezuela; intergrades with *autumnalis* in north-eastern Nicaragua (see Howell, 1957) and with *lilacina* in extreme south-western Colombia (see Olivares, 1957).

3. *A. a. lilacina* Lesson.
ADULTS like *salvini*, but red of forehead and lores extends over eyes forming superciliary lines; feathers of crown green with lilac tips and edged with reddish-violet; cheeks yellowish-green.
No specimens examined.
    1 male (Bull *in litt.*, 1972);   wing 201 mm., tail 133 mm.,
                         exp. cul. 22 mm., tars. ——.
    1 unsexed (Bull *in litt.*, 1972);   wing 197 mm., tail 121 mm.,
                         exp. cul. 25 mm., tars. ——.
    1 unsexed (Goodwin *in litt.*, 1972); wing 197 mm., tail 100 mm.,
                         exp. cul. 27 mm., tars. 20 mm.
    Confined to western Ecuador north of the Gulf of Guayaquil.

4. *A. a. diadema* (Spix).
ADULTS similar to *salvini*, but forehead crimson changing to dark purple-red on lores; crown lilac, more bluish anteriorly; feathers of occiput and nape green edged with greenish-yellow; feathers of hindneck green margined with lilac; cheeks yellowish-green; larger than *autumnalis*.
    3 males   wing 223–237 (229.0) mm., tail 110–121 (114.0) mm.,
            exp. cul. 31–32 (31.3) mm., tars. 24–26 (24.7) mm.
    2 females wing 235–239 (237.0) mm., tail 130–135 (132.5) mm.,
            exp. cul. 32–35 (33.5) mm., tars. 25–26 (25.5) mm.
    Often called the Diademed Amazon, this race is restricted to north-western Brazil between the Negro and upper Amazon Rivers.

GENERAL NOTES   Blake (1953) says that the Red-lored Amazon is common in the moist lowlands of eastern Mexico. Loetscher (1941) reports that in Veracruz it is a common to abundant resident of the humid tropical zone wherever there are woodlands, occurring locally throughout the whole length of the state and from sea level up to about 625 m.; in southern Veracruz he found it to be the commonest parrot, with the possible exception of the Aztec Conure (*Aratinga nana astec*). Dalquest found it to be the common parrot in the upper tropical zone of Veracruz (in Lowery and Dalquest, 1951). In north-eastern Oaxaca it is a common permanent resident of tropical evergreen forest between 30 and 330 m., ranging south to El Barrio on the Isthmus of Tehuantepec (Binford, 1968). Edwards and Lea (1955) report that along rivers in the Monserrate area, Chiapas, this species was seen almost daily in March and April, but seemed to be considerably less numerous in July and August. Paynter (1955) notes that it is found only along the southern base of Yucatán Peninsula, Mexico, where it inhabits rainforest, but winters, at least occasionally, in deciduous secondary growth within the rainforest zone; during the winter of 1948–1949, on the outskirts of Chetumal, Quintana Roo, large flocks were seen in old abandoned cornfields which contained much brush and large deciduous trees, and local people claimed that the parrots are to be found there every winter, but during the breeding season they move into the rainforest. Russell (1964) points out that it is a common and widely distributed resident of most parts of British Honduras, though possibly less numerous in the extreme south; it usually frequents plantation clearings and secondary growth in the immediate vicinity of tall rainforest, but also pentrates the forests and is not uncommon in the pine ridges. Monroe (1968) reports that in Honduras it occurs in and around lowland rainforest, and is the most common of the *Amazona* parrots in the humid Caribbean lowlands, ranging in the interior up to an elevation of 1,100 m.; flocks may be encountered also in more open, less humid parts of valleys along the Caribbean slope. Monroe also records it as being very common on Roatán and Barbareta, in the Bay Islands, but, during early May 1963, he failed to find it or any other parrot on Utila where previously this species had been recorded as being common in mangrove swamps (Bond, 1937). Land (1970) says that in Guatemala it is a fairly common resident of the Caribbean lowlands and the Petén from sea level up to 350 m., occurring in and around humid forest and out into disturbed woodland in humid areas. In the vicinity of Tikal, the Petén, it is fairly plentiful in the forest and in treetops along the edges of forests (Smithe, 1966). Huber (1933) found it to be common in the vicinity of Eden, north-eastern Nicaragua. Howell (1957) found it to be the most abundant parrot at El Recreo, eastern Nicaragua, and individuals, pairs, and flocks were seen daily in all habitats; he (1972) also reports that in north-eastern Nicaragua the species is equally common in lowland pine savannah and adjacent broad-leafed forest. Slud (1964) points out that in Costa Rica it is found in humid zones of the tropical belt, occasionally ascending to the lower subtropical along the Cordillera Central, but is absent from most of the dry-forested north-west and is generally less plentiful in the south-west, where it hardly ascends, if at all, above the tropical belt; it frequents extensively-forested areas, forest edges, secondary growth with emergent trees, patches of woodland, tree-lined borders of various kinds, and trees in plantations or clearings. It is a common resident throughout the tropical zone of Panama, including the Canal Zone, Isla Coiba, Isla Escudo de Veraguas, and the Archipiélago de las Perlas (Wetmore, 1968). Meyer de Schauensee (1964) says that in western Colombia it is found in forests in the tropical zone. Dugand (1947) reports that it is very rare in Atlántico, north-western Colombia, where he has seen it only a few times in heavily-forested areas. Olivares (1957) says that it is common in the vicinity of Guapí, Cauca, south-western Colombia. In Venezuela it is known only from the Sierra de Perija, extreme north-western Zulia, along the border with Colombia (Phelps and Phelps, 1958). There appears to be no published information on the status of this species in north-western Brazil, but the small numbers of specimens of *diadema* in collections suggests that it may not be common.

Red-lored Amazons are noisy birds and are usually seen in pairs or flocks of from about six to one hundred individuals; the pairs being readily discernible within these flocks. They are active in the morning and evening, and, to a lesser extent, on dull or rainy days, being seldom seen or heard during the warmer hours of the day unless disturbed from a roosting tree. They keep to the topmost branches of trees and are rather wary. At Paracoté, southern Panama, Aldrich and Bole (1937) noticed that when disturbed in fruit-bearing trees along the edge of the forest these parrots would invariably wait until the intruder had passed the tree before flying off with loud cries, but they always kept a screen of foliage between themselves and the intruder until well away from the immediate area. Once on the wing they nearly always fly long distances before settling again. They are most conspicuous when travelling from roosting places to feeding grounds in the morning and returning at dusk, the flying birds generally forming a loose company of individual pairs well separated from one another. Olivares has seen them flying at a great height over Guapí, south-western Colombia, their screeching call-notes attracting attention.

They feed on fruits, seeds, nuts, berries, buds, and blossoms, procured in the treetops. Olivares says that in south-western Colombia they are fond of the fruits of certain palm trees, and small fruits were found in the stomachs of specimens collected in that region. Russell reports that in British Honduras the parrots often raid ripening citrus and mango fruits.

CALL Harsh, raucous screeches syllabized as *ky-ake* . . . *ky-ake* . . . *ky-ake* and so on, or *yoik* . . . *yoik* and so on, enunciated quickly and often mixed with, or followed by warbling notes; also a rapid repetition of abrupt *ack-ack* or *chek-chek* notes (Slud, 1964).

NESTING On 9th February, Paynter collected a male with slightly enlarged testes near Aguada Seca, Campeche, southern Mexico. In British Honduras Russell has collected birds in breeding condition during February and March, while Peck found a nest containing two eggs on 16th March and hollows presumably occupied by nesting individuals as late as 20th May (in Russell, 1964). Smithe and Paynter (1963) state that specimens collected in the vicinity of Tikal, northern Guatemala, from March through to early June exhibited gonadal activity. On 12th April, Mays watched two parrots investigating hollows about 6 m. up in a dead tree standing in front of the Jungle Lodge at Tikal (*in litt.*, 1966). Olivares reports that in south-western Colombia nests are in hollows in the trunks of trees, and females collected in December had developed ovaries and fresh plumage, while a male taken on 12th January had well-developed testes and slightly-worn plumage.

Vane (1957) records a successful hatching in captivity using a foster parent, namely a female Grey Parrot (*Psittacus erithacus*), and says that the incubation period was twenty-five to twenty-six days.

EGGS Rounded; 2 eggs in the British Museum Collection measure 39.2 (37.6–40.8) × 30.5 (30.4–30.5) mm. [Harrison and Holyoak, 1970].

531

RED-TAILED AMAZON

Amazona brasiliensis (Linné)

Illustrated on page 537.

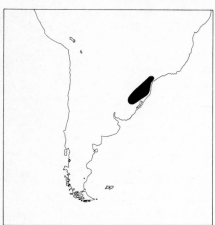

DESCRIPTION

Length 37 cm.

ADULTS general plumage green, paler on underparts; forehead and lores dull red; crown and nape pink-red, feathers tipped with dull violet and showing yellowish bases; chin, cheeks, ear-coverts, and neck dull pink-blue, feathers edged with dull mauve; under tail-coverts yellowish-green; carpal edge red; upper wing-coverts and innermost secondaries conspicuously edged with pale yellowish-green; primary-coverts green; primaries and secondaries green becoming blue towards tips; under wing-coverts yellowish-green; undersides of flight feathers slightly tinged with bluish-green on bases of inner webs; central tail feathers green, lateral feathers green tipped with greenish-yellow and subterminally banded with deep red, outer three feathers also banded with purple-blue; bill horn-coloured; iris brown; legs grey.

IMMATURES undescribed.

4 males   wing 209–215 (212.5) mm., tail 108–112 (110.0) mm.,
   exp. cul. 27–30 (29.3) mm., tars. 25–26 (25.3) mm.

2 females   wing 208–209 (208.5) mm., tail 101–107 (104.0) mm.,
   exp. cul. 28–29 (28.5) mm., tars. 26–27 (26.5) mm.

Confined to south-eastern Brazil from south-eastern São Paulo to Rio Grande do Sul.

DISTRIBUTION

SUBSPECIES

Camargo (1962) treats *brasiliensis* as a race within a polytypic species that also includes *dufresniana* and *rhodocorytha*, but I do not favour this arrangement. I do not doubt that *brasiliensis* is allied to *rhodocorytha*, but because of certain unique features of its plumage colouration, particularly the absence of a coloured wing-speculum and the conspicuous pale edgings to the wing-coverts, I prefer to follow Peters (1937) and give it specific status.

GENERAL NOTES

The Red-tailed Amazon formerly occurred throughout the littoral forests of south-eastern Brazil, but because of widespread deforestation it is now rare and is listed by Sick (1969) as a threatened species. Little is known of its habits. It is generally seen in pairs or small flocks, and sometimes associates with Red-spectacled Amazons (*Amazona pretrei*) in *Araucaria* forests.

BLUE-CHEEKED AMAZON

Amazona dufresniana (Shaw)

DESCRIPTION

Length 34 cm.

ADULTS general plumage dark green, slightly paler on underparts; feathers of neck and back strongly edged with dusky black, those of underparts very faintly edged with dusky black; forehead and lores orange-yellow; feathers of crown and occiput yellow broadly edged with dull green; cheeks, ear-coverts, and sides of neck violet-blue; under tail-coverts yellowish-green; carpal edge pale yellowish-green; well-defined wing-speculum across bases of first four secondaries yellowish-orange; primaries black slightly tinged with violet-blue towards tip of outer webs; under wing-coverts and undersides of flight feathers green; tail green tipped with yellowish-green, faint orange marking on inner webs of four outer feathers; bill grey with pink-red at base of upper mandible; iris orange-red; legs grey.

IMMATURES undescribed, but probably similar to adults.

DISTRIBUTION

Guianas and south-eastern Venezuela, and central-eastern Brazil.

SUBSPECIES

1. *A. d. dufresniana* (Shaw).   *Illustrated on page 540.*

 8 males   wing 218–225 (220.9) mm., tail 109–124 (115.1) mm.,
   exp. cul. 33–37 (34.9) mm., tars. 26–28 (26.6) mm.

 6 females   wing 200–226 (215.0) mm., tail 103–117 (109.2) mm.,
   exp. cul. 32–34 (33.0) mm., tars. 23–25 (24.2) mm.

 Confined to the Guianas and to the Gran Sabana in south-eastern Bolívar, Venezuela.

2. *A. d. rhodocorytha* (Salvadori).   *Illustrated on page 540.*

 ADULTS general plumage paler green than in *dufresniana*; forehead and crown red, some feathers on latter tipped with dull greenish-blue; feathers of occiput dull reddish-purple tipped with dusky black and tinged with blue; feathers of nape green tinged with dull reddish-purple and tipped with dusky black; lores orange tinged with red; throat and anterior of cheeks pink-red; ear-coverts and posterior of cheeks blue suffused with green; bases of first three secondaries red bordered with purple-blue; tail green tipped with yellowish-green, lateral feathers strongly marked with red.

 IMMATURES crown green tinged with red; red on bases of secondaries less extensive and restricted to first two feathers; red on lateral tail-feathers much reduced.

 6 males   wing 215–229 (221.7) mm., tail 99–119 (111.5) mm.,
   exp. cul. 30–36 (33.0) mm., tars. 24–26 (25.0) mm.

5 females wing 209–226 (215.6) mm., tail 107–116 (110.4) mm.,
exp. cul 29–32 (30.8) mm., tars. 25–26 (25.2) mm.,
This distinctive isolate is known as the Red-crowned Amazon. It occurs in central-eastern Brazil from Alagoas south to Rio de Janeiro.

GENERAL NOTES The Blue-cheeked Amazon is fairly common in Surinam and is generally seen in small flocks in the treetops (Haverschmidt, 1968); during July and August small flocks come into forests along the coastal sand ridges. Snyder (1966) says that in Guyana it is uncommon, though fairly widespread in interior forests. McLoughlin (1970) notes that it seems to be restricted mainly to the cooler, elevated forests of the interior of Guyana; in August 1967, he saw two pairs of what was almost certainly this species at Imbaimadai, a diamond mining centre in the interior. In eastern Brazil, *rhodocorytha* is becoming rare as forest is cleared from many parts of its range (Sick, 1969). It is probably already extinct in the state of Rio de Janeiro. Pinto (1935) found it to be very common in riverine forests in southern Bahia, particularly along the Gongogy and the Jucurucú, and was told that it was abundant in the vicinity of Camamú. In winter it moves into estuarine mangroves along the Brazilian coast, as also does the Orange-winged Amazon (*Amazona amazonica*).

During the day pairs or small flocks of these parrots are usually found feeding or resting among the topmost branches of tall forest trees, but at dusk they congregate in large flocks to go to roost. Pinto recalls that along the banks of the Gongogy River, not far from Bôa Nova, Bahia, large flocks were roosting in the highest trees and their raucous cries greeted the dawn of each new day. They feed on fruits, seeds, nuts, berries and buds, procured in the treetops.

CALL An almost incessant, raucous *caa-ua . . . caa-ua . . . caa-ua* (Pinto, 1935).

NESTING No records.

EGGS Undescribed.

FESTIVE AMAZON
Amazona festiva (Linné)

DESCRIPTION Length 34 cm.
ADULTS general plumage green, feathers of neck faintly edged with dusky black and those of wings narrowly edged with yellowish-green; lores and narrow frontal band dark red; blue above and behind eyes, and sometimes across occiput; cheeks bright yellowish-green; chin blue; under tail-coverts yellowish-green; lower back and rump scarlet; carpal edge pale yellowish-green; primary-coverts violet-blue narrowly edged with green; primaries violet-blue; tail green tipped with yellowish-green; bill grey; iris orange; legs pale greenish-grey.
IMMATURES blue above and behind eyes, on chin, and on occiput much paler and more restricted; lower back and rump green with one or two red feathers; red markings on bases of some lateral tail feathers.

DISTRIBUTION From north-western Guyana to eastern Ecuador, north-eastern Peru, and north-western Brazil.

SUBSPECIES

1. *A. f. festiva* (Linné).   *Illustrated on page 541.*
10 males wing 202–222 (211.2) mm., tail 94–110 (99.1) mm.,
exp. cul. 30–34 (31.5) mm., tars. 25–28 (26.4) mm.
11 females wing 195–216 (204.5) mm., tail 89–100 (95.2) mm.,
exp. cul. 29–32 (30.8) mm., tars. 25–27 (26.0) mm.
Ranges from eastern Ecuador, north-eastern Peru, and south-eastern Colombia east through the Amazon Basin to the lower Madeira River in eastern Amazonas, Brazil.

2. *A. f. bodini* (Finsch).
ADULTS general plumage more yellowish than in *festiva*, particularly on underparts; red of frontal band extended on to forehead and forecrown; feathers of crown and occiput edged with dull purple; feathers of hindneck more strongly edged with dusky black; lores blackish; feathers of cheeks edged with violet-blue; carpal edge yellowish; primary-coverts and outer webs of primaries green.
2 males wing 201–214 (207.5) mm., tail 111–112 (111.5) mm.,
exp. cul. 31–34 (32.5) mm., tars. 26–27 (26.5) mm.
4 females wing 197–203 (200.3) mm., tail 98–106 (102.5) mm.,
exp. cul. 30–32 (30.8) mm., tars. 24–26 (24.8) mm.
Known only from north-western Guyana and from central Venezuela along the Orinoco from Delta Amacuro west to the Meta River.

GENERAL NOTES The Festive Amazon is very abundant along the upper Amazon River and its tributaries, but is locally distributed in other parts of its range. Snyder (1966) points out that in Guyana it is known only from unconfirmed sightings made during 1948–1949 and from a couple of records dating from the middle of last century. In Venezuela it is very locally distributed along the Orinoco

River (Phelps and Phelps, 1958). Early this century Cherrie (1916) found it to be abundant along the middle stretches of the Orinoco River, especially about Altagracia and Caicara, Bolívar, Venezuela. Dugand and Borrero (1946) note that along the banks of the upper Amazon this species is one of the most abundant members of its genus, so it is not surprising that it should occur in south-eastern Colombia.

These parrots keep to the treetops in riverine forest, where their predominantly green plumage blends extremely well with the foliage, and it is only while flying above the forest canopy, screeching all the while, that they are conspicuous. They are generally seen in pairs or small flocks, though at times large numbers will congregate to feed. Regular roosting places are used by large flocks which build up in the late afternoon and disperse soon after sunrise. They feed on fruits, seeds, nuts, berries, blossoms and buds, procured in the treetops.

CALL A loud, metallic screech (in captivity).

NESTING No records.

EGGS Undescribed.

YELLOW-FACED AMAZON
Amazona xanthops (Spix)   *Illustrated on page 544.*

Length 27 cm.

DESCRIPTION

ADULTS head and neck yellow; some feathers on nape and hindneck green edged with dark green and narrowly tipped with dusky black; ear-coverts yellowish-orange; feathers of upper breast green broadly edged with dark green, in old birds suffused with yellow; lower breast and upper abdomen deep yellow becoming orange towards sides of body and axillaries; thighs and lower abdomen green, feathers edged with dark green; under and upper tail-coverts yellowish-green; back and wings green; outermost wing-coverts, inner secondaries and lower tertials edged with yellowish-green; carpal edge pale yellowish-green; primary-coverts green narrowly edged with dull blue; primaries and secondaries green very narrowly edged with greenish-yellow; under wing-coverts green; undersides of flight feathers bluish-green; tail green, lateral feathers yellowish-green basally banded with orange-red; bill horn-coloured with grey along top of upper mandible; iris yellow; legs pale grey.

IMMATURES yellow restricted to crown, periophthalmic region, ear-coverts, and cheeks; remainder of head green, feathers edged with dark bluish-green and tipped with dusky black; entire under-parts green, feathers edged with dark green; iris brown.

9 males   wing 189–201 (194.6) mm., tail 71–83 (75.4) mm.,
          exp. cul. 26–28 (27.0) mm., tars. 21–22 (21.4) mm.
2 females wing 188–193 (190.5) mm., tail 72–77 (74.5) mm.,
          exp. cul. 26 (26.0) mm., tars. 21–22 (21.5) mm.

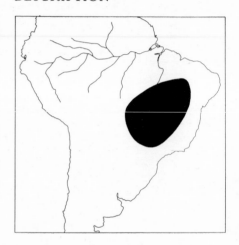

Eastern and central Brazil from southern Piauí and Goiás south to Mato Grosso and the interior of São Paulo.

DISTRIBUTION

Sick (1965) points out that the Yellow-faced Amazon is confined to the inland plateau of eastern Brazil, where it is typically an inhabitant of cerrado, which is a specialized vegetation community dominated by low semi-deciduous trees. Hellmayr (1929) reports that early in the century the Vienna Academy Expedition found it in great numbers in the vicinity of Parnaguá, southern Piauí. Pinto (1946) says that it is very common in the hills of southern Mato Grosso and Goiás, and it frequently raids guava plantations to feed on unripe fruit. Stager (1961) notes that it is rather locally distributed in central Goiás, where the Machris Expedition met with it only on the Chapada dos Veadeiros; a male was collected from atop a dead tree standing in a cultivated clearing in gallery forest, and a flock of approximately thirty-five was found feeding in fruit trees on an old abandoned farm.

GENERAL NOTES

CALL Undescribed.

NESTING No records.

EGGS Elliptical; 2 eggs 40.5 (40.0–40.9) × 31.9 (30.8–33.0) mm. [Schönwetter, 1964].

YELLOW-SHOULDERED AMAZON
Amazona barbadensis (Gmelin)

Length 33 cm.

DESCRIPTION

ADULTS general plumage green, feathers edged with dusky black; underparts slightly tinged with blue; forehead, forecrown, and lores white; hindcrown, periophthalmic region, and upper cheeks yellow; feathers of lower cheeks and throat green strongly suffused with blue and edged with dusky black; thighs yellow; under tail-coverts yellowish-green tinged with blue; bend of wing yellow; carpal edge pale yellowish-green; red wing-speculum across bases of outer four secondaries; primary-coverts green; primaries and secondaries green becoming violet-blue on outer webs towards tips; under wing-coverts green; undersides of flight feathers bluish-green; tail green tipped with yellowish-green, concealed orange-red markings towards bases of lateral feathers and outer webs of outermost feathers strongly suffused with blue; bill horn-coloured; iris orange; legs pale grey.

IMMATURES similar to adults, but underparts not tinged with blue.

DISTRIBUTION   Coastal Venezuela, islands off the coast, and the Netherlands Antilles.

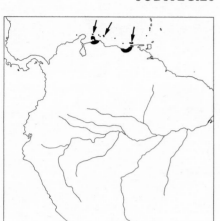

SUBSPECIES   1. *A. b. barbadensis* (Gmelin).   *Illustrated on page 541.*
      3 males   wing 201–205 (202.7) mm., tail 114–121 (116.3) mm.,
            exp. cul. 28–31 (29.7) mm., tars. 21–23 (22.3) mm.
      1 female   wing 201 mm., tail 120 mm.,
            exp. cul. 26 mm., tars. 21 mm.
      Locally distributed along the coast of Venezuela and on Aruba in the Netherlands Antilles; not recorded on Aruba since 1955 so may be extinct there.

2. *A. b. rothschildi* (Hartert).
      ADULTS like *barbadensis*, but yellow of head less extensive; yellow on bend of wing much reduced and intermixed with a variable amount of red.
      20 males   wing 207–228 (218.5) mm., tail 118–138 (128.6) mm.,
            exp. cul. 28–32 (30.3) mm., tars. 22–25 (23.5) mm.
      11 females wing 193–216 (208.2) mm., tail 107–133 (121.5) mm.,
            exp. cul. 27–30 (28.4) mm., tars. 21–23 (22.5) mm.
      Occurs on Bonaire in the Netherlands Antilles, and on Blanquilla and Margarita Islands off the coast of Venezuela.
      Voous (1957) points out that the differences between *barbadensis* and *rothschildi* are not constant, and there is some overlap of characters in specimens from Aruba and Bonaire. Furthermore, specimens from the coast of Venezuela are more or less intermediate. I examined specimens from all parts of the range and came to the same conclusions, so it would seem that *rothschildi* is not separable.

GENERAL NOTES   The Yellow-shouldered Amazon has been recorded from two localities in arid regions along the coast of Venezuela, namely Casigua, Falcón, and Barcelona, Anzoátegui (Phelps and Phelps, 1958). Early in the century Lowe (1907a and 1907b) found it to be common on Blanquilla Island, where several fairly large flocks were seen, while on Margarita Island he saw birds in high trees above El Valle and several parties in the vicinity of the lagoon at the western end of the island.
      In recent years there has been concern about the decline of this species in the Netherlands Antilles. Voous points out that it is still present on Bonaire, but on Aruba numbers seem to have been decreasing rapidly since the turn of the century, probably because of the loss of suitable habitat through expansion of the oil-refining industry. Voous also documents the change in status as recorded by several field observers. In 1892, Hartert found it to be common in wooded and rocky parts of Aruba, though it was timid and specimens were difficult to collect. When Ferry visited the island in 1908 it was still common, but once again its shyness was considered worth mentioning. In 1930, Rutten found it at Fontein, near a freshwater well in Rooi Prins, and in the neighbourhood of the Hooiberg; he came to the conclusion that it was rather rare. De Jong, in 1943, considered the species to be rare, and in 1948 he estimated the entire breeding population on the island at only a few pairs. Voous searched unsuccessfuly for it in 1952 and subsequently listed it as being extinct on Aruba, but in late November 1955 two birds were observed on the island; there have been no records since that date. Rooth (1968) spent some time on Bonaire in 1959–1960 and estimated that there were more than one hundred pairs on the island. In the spring of 1966 he made another short survey, but counted only a few birds. In January 1968, he again searched intensively in many parts of the island, but saw only twenty-three birds, mostly in pairs, which was contrary to former sightings of many flocks of tens of birds; the estimated population was closer to fifty than to one hundred pairs. The Pan American Section of the International Council for Bird Preservation pointed out to the Government of the Netherlands Antilles that capture and illegal exportation of parrots from Bonaire was the principal cause of an alarming decrease in numbers (see *President's Letter*, no. 1, 1963). An assurance that protection measures would be strictly enforced was given in reply, but Rooth says that in 1968 many birds were still being kept as pets and exported for this purpose to neighbouring islands.
      During his visit to Bonaire in 1951–1952 Voous found Yellow-shouldered Amazons exclusively in the northern hilly part of the island, especially in well-timbered places and in close proximity to rocky escarpments. They were often seen resting in the shade of the crowns of *Acacia*, *Caesalpinia* and *Bursera* trees in what appeared to be secondary seasonal forest and cactus vegetation. They frequently congregated in flocks of from six to ten, or even up to sixty or eighty individuals when feeding on the fruits of organpipe cacti (*Cereus repandus*) and those of *Casearia bonairensis*, the latter being available during November. They were also regular visitors to the fruit plantation at Fontein, where they seemed to be particularly fond of mangoes (*Mango mangifera*) and the fruits of *Achras sapota*. Stomach contents from three specimens consisted of nothing but the remains of cactus fruits.

CALL A harsh screeching note (in captivity).

NESTING Rooth says that on Bonaire these parrots probably breed in April and May, and nests are in hollows in trees, particularly in *Spondias lutea* and *Capparis flexuosa*, or in cavities and clefts in rocky escarpments.

EGGS. Ovate; 2 eggs, 36.7 (36.4–37.0) × 26.1 (25.8–26.3) mm. [Harrison and Holyoak, 1970].

BLUE-FRONTED AMAZON
Amazona aestiva (Linné)

DESCRIPTION Length 37 cm.
ADULTS general plumage green; feathers edged with dusky black, particularly on neck and back; forehead and anterior of lores blue; forecrown yellow tinged with white; hindcrown, periopthalmic region, ear-coverts, anterior of cheeks, and throat yellow; thighs green variably suffused with yellow; under and upper tail-coverts yellowish-green; bend of wing red; primary-coverts dark green tipped with violet-blue; primaries green becoming violet-blue towards tips; pronounced red wing-speculum across bases of five outer secondaries; secondaries green becoming violet-blue towards tips; secondary-coverts green narrowly edged with yellowish-green; under wing-coverts green; undersides of flight feathers bluish-green; tail green tipped with yellowish-green, lateral feathers basally barred with red and outermost feathers edged with blue; bill grey; iris orange; legs grey.
IMMATURES (variation in plumage); generally like adults, but with blue and yellow on head much reduced; in some birds the head is almost entirely green; iris dark brown.

DISTRIBUTION North-eastern Brazil south to Paraguay and northern Argentina.

SUBSPECIES 1. *A. a. aestiva* (Linné).　　　　　　　　　　　　　　　　　　　　*Illustrated on page 545.*
　　　8 males　wing 214–232 (221.4) mm., tail 112–140 (124.3) mm.,
　　　　　　　exp. cul. 30–34 (31.5) mm., tars. 24–27 (25.5) mm.
　　　7 females　wing 199–218 (211.6) mm., tail 106–121 (114.9) mm.,
　　　　　　　exp. cul. 29–32 (30.1) mm., tars. 24–26 (24.9) mm.
　　　Occurs in eastern Brazil from Piauí south to Rio Grande do Sul and south-eastern Mato Grosso.

2. *A. a. xanthopteryx* (Berlepsch).
ADULTS similar to *aestiva*, but yellow variably intermixed with red on bend of wing; in some birds red is entirely replaced by yellow.
　　　10 males　wing 222–238 (230.0) mm., tail 115–135 (125.0) mm.,
　　　　　　　exp. cul. 29–32 (30.5) mm., tars. 24–27 (25.3) mm.
　　　7 females　wing 221–229 (225.0) mm., tail 114–134 (122.6) mm.,
　　　　　　　exp. cul. 29–33 (30.7) mm., tars. 24–25 (24.4) mm.
　　　Ranges from northern and eastern Bolivia, and south-western Mato Grosso, Brazil, south through Paraguay to northern Argentina, as far as Santa Fe and occasionally to northernmost Buenos Aires.

GENERAL NOTES The Blue-fronted Amazon is one of the best-known of the amazons, being very popular as a pet in its homeland and in many countries of the world; it has a good reputation as a 'talker'. It is still common throughout most of its extensive range, though in some areas deforestation has adversely affected its status. Lamm (1948) observed it on four or five occasions in wooded areas in the interior of north-eastern Brazil, principally near the São Francisco River in southern Pernambuco. Stager (1961) found it to be common throughout the Serra Dourada and Chapada dos Veadeiros areas, central Goiás, where small flocks inhabited all cultivated clearings. Pinto (1946) points out that in forests along the Paraná and lower Rio Grande Rivers, São Paulo, the species was abundant up until the 1940s when presumably there was large-scale land-clearance for settlement. Cherrie recorded it as being common about Descalvados, south-western Mato Grosso, during November and December, and at Fort Wheeler, western Paraguay, in September (in Naumburg, 1930). Also in the Descalvados district, Rehn observed this species and the Orange-winged Amazon (*Amazona amazonica*) in small flocks either in flight or feeding in the treetops, and on one occasion in early September he saw both species in flocks only a short distance from one another (in Stone and Roberts, 1935). Eisentraut (1935) found it to be very common in both moist and dry forest throughout the Chaco region of south-eastern Bolivia. To the west of Puerto Pinasco, Paraguay, Wetmore (1926) found it to be common, and pairs were usually seen in palm groves where they fed on the palm seeds. Unger says that during May, June, and July this species wanders into eastern Paraguay (in Steinbacher, 1962). Pereyra (1942) says that in northern Argentina it inhabits forests and frequently comes out into more open country to feed.

Pairs or small flocks of these parrots spend most of the day feeding and resting in the crowns of trees, and here their plumage blends extremely well with the foliage so the only indication of their presence may be falling debris and pieces of fruit. While feeding they are tame and will

Red-tailed Amazon *Amazona brasiliensis* **1**
MP. 14982 ad. ♂

Red-lored Amazon **2**
Amazona autumnalis· autumnalis
ANSP. 63683 ad. ♂

generally allow a close appraoch, but if the disturbance persists they will eventually fly off in pairs, screeching loudly as they go. In flight they are very conspicuous, due mainly to their constant screeching, and this is demonstrated forcibly during the daily flights to and from roosting places. Eisentraut describes such flights that took place in south-eastern Bolivia. Every morning large numbers of parrots left their roosting trees and flew in a particular direction towards the feeding areas, returning along the same route in the evening. Only two flight paths were in evidence, and presumably this meant that the birds were using two roosting sites; in the morning birds came down from the mountains flying toward the south-east and also from the north flying directly south. As the flocks passed overhead paired birds were readily discernible because they flew close together; occasionally groups of three were seen, prabably a young or unattached bird accompanying a pair, but single birds or groups of more than three were not observed. Wetmore notes that in the early morning when the sunlight chances to strike the parrots at the right angle their beautifully variegated colours of red, yellow, and green show clearly, but at midday they appear as dark silhouettes or, if flying close by, plain green.

Food is procured in the treetops and consists of fruits, berries, seeds, nuts, blossoms and leaf buds. Pinto reports that at times the parrots attack crops, often causing considerable damage.

CALL Wetmore says that from a distance the loud calls given in flight resemble cries of *help . . .help.*

NESTING There is little published information about the breeding habits of this widespread and common species. Pinto says that in inland Brazil the breeding season is from October to March. Orfila (1938) says that nests are in hollows in old trees, and the same site may be used year after year.

Boosey (1939) records a successful breeding in captivity, but gives few details; it was estimated that the eggs must have been laid about the end of the first week in April and the first of five young vacated the nest on 20th July. Smith (1942) reports a successful hatching in captivity, but the young bird was reared by hand; only the female brooded and incubation lasted twenty-nine days.

EGGS Ovate; 8 eggs, 38.1 (36.1–40.8) × 29.6 (28.0–30.6) mm. [Schönwetter, 1964].

YELLOW-CROWNED AMAZON   *Illustrated on page 548.*
Amazona ochrocephala (Gmelin)

DESCRIPTION

Length 35 cm.

ADULTS general plumage green, paler and more yellowish on underparts; forehead and lores yellow, variably marked with green; crown yellow; some yellow feathers around eyes; ear-coverts and cheeks bright emerald green; feathers of nape and hindneck green edged with dusky black; thighs green variably suffused with yellow; bend of wing red; carpal edge yellowish-green; primaries and secondaries green becoming violet-blue towards tips; prominent red wing speculum across bases of five outer secondaries; under wing-coverts and undersides of flight feathers green; tail green tipped with yellowish-green, lateral feathers basally marked with red on inner webs and outermost feathers edged with blue; bill dark grey with orange on sides of upper mandible; iris orange; legs pale grey.

IMMATURES slightly duller green than adults and with more pronounced dusky black edging to feathers of nape and hindneck; yellow on crown and red on bend of wing generally less extensive; bill entirely dark grey; iris dark brown.

DISTRIBUTION

Central Mexico south to the Amazon Basin and eastern Peru; also on Trinidad.

SUBSPECIES

1. *A. o. ochrocephala* (Gmelin).
   10 males   wing 210–220 (213.8) mm., tail 109–121 (115.4) mm.,
              exp. cul. 32–37 (33.6) mm., tars. 25–28 (26.5) mm.
   8 females wing 199–220 (210.3) mm., tail 109–124 (114.6) mm.,
              exp. cul. 31–33 (32.4) mm., tars. 25–28 (26.0) mm.
   Ranges from the Guianas and the vicinity of Caxiricatuba, on the Tapajós River, Pará, northern Brazil, west through Venezuela, except southern Bolívar and Amazonas, and middle Amazonia to the Eastern Andes in Norte de Santander and Meta, Colombia; also occurs on Trinidad.

2. *A. o. xantholaema* Berlepsch.
   ADULTS differs from *ochrocephala* by having cheeks and ear-coverts yellow; narrow, well-defined frontal band green; yellow of crown extends further back over nape; thighs yellow; larger size.
   No specimens examined.
   1 male (**type**) (Steinbacher, *in litt.*, 1972); wing 233 mm., tail 122 mm.,
                                                     exp. cul. 36 mm., tars. 25 mm.
   1 female (Steinbacher, *in litt.*, 1972);   wing 223 mm., tail 121 mm.,
                                                     exp. cul. 34 mm., tars. 23 mm.
   Known only from two specimens collected on Marajó Island at the mouth of the Amazon

River, Pará, northern Brazil. Further specimens are needed to establish the validity of thisrace.

3. *A. o. nattereri* (Finsch).

ADULTS like *ochrocephala*, but with broad frontal band, cheeks, ear-coverts, and throat green strongly suffused with blue; underparts sometimes tinged with blue.
8 males   wing 221–235 (227.3) mm., tail 115–120 (117.0) mm.,
       exp. cul. 32–35 (33.4) mm., tars. 27–29 (28.0) mm.
7 females wing 211–221 (217.0) mm., tail 110–125 (116.6) mm.,
       exp. cul. 32–36 (33.9) mm., tars. 25–29 (26.7) mm.

Distributed from about Morelia and Florencia, Caquetá, southern Colombia, south through eastern Ecuador and eastern Peru to Acre and north-western Mato Grosso, Brazil. Dugand and Borrero (1948) point out that this race approaches to within 100 km. of *ochrocephala* in Cacquetá, southern Colombia, so it may be assumed that *nattereri* comes north along the foothills of the Andes, without departing much from the mountainous region and gradually becoming even more restricted as it reaches its northern limit.

4. *A. o. panamensis* (Cabanis).

ADULTS forehead, forecrown, and anterior of lores yellow; above eyes and hindcrown, bordering yellow area, bluish-green; less red on bend of wing; thighs generally green, but sometimes suffused with yellow; smaller than *ochrocephala*.
8 males   wing 191–215 (200.4) mm., tail 94–109 (100.9) mm.,
       exp. cul. 29–33 (30.8) mm., tars. 24–27 (24.9) mm.
8 females wing 190–210 (199.5) mm., tail 93–107 (99.0) mm.,
       exp. cul. 29–33 (30.8) mm., tars. 23–26 (24.8) mm.,

Distributed from northern Colombia, between Magdalena and Santander in the east and the upper Atrato River, Chocó, in the west, to western Panama; present on the Archipiélago de las Perlas, Panama.

5. *A. o. auropalliata* (Lesson).   *Illustrated on page 548.*

ADULTS forehead and crown green; variable yellow band across lower nape and hindneck; no red on bend of wing; no yellow on thighs; bill dark grey becoming paler towards base of upper mandible.
10 males   wing 219–234 (228.5) mm., tail 106–125 (115.4) mm.,
       exp. cul. 34–37 (35.4) mm., tars. 26–29 (27.4) mm.
10 females wing 209–224 (216.2) mm., tail 110–125 (114.5) mm.,
       exp. cul. 34–35 (34.2) mm., tars. 25–29 (26.5) mm.

Ranges along the Pacific slope of Central America from eastern Oaxaca, southern Mexico, south to north-western Costa Rica. This race is known as the Yellow-naped Amazon and is often treated as a separate species.

Red-crowned Amazon **1**
Amazona dufresniana rhodocorytha
MZSP. 38954 ad. ♀

Blue-cheeked Amazon **2**
Amazona dufresniana dufresniana
RMNH. Cat. 4, Reg. 33867 ad. ♂

6. *A. o. parvipes* Monroe and Howell.

ADULTS like *auropalliata*, but with red on bend of wing; bill generally paler and less heavily pigmented.
4 males   wing 213–238 (222.3) mm., tail 110–124 (117.0) mm.,
       exp. cul. 31–34 (33.0) mm., tars. 24–27 (25.8) mm.
2 females wing 213–220 (216.5) mm., tail 102–112 (107.0) mm.,
       exp. cul. 33–34 (33.5) mm., tars. 25 (25.0) mm.

Confined to Roatán, Barbareta, and Guanaja, in the Bay Islands, Honduras, and the Caribbean slope in easternmost Honduras and north-eastern Nicaragua.

Monroe (1968) points out that apparently two colour types of parrots, namely the yellow-naped and yellow-crowned, are present in the Sula Valley, north-western Honduras. Four Sula Valley specimens, two of each colour type, have been taken within 35 km. of each other. In 1962, Hamilton collected a female yellow-crowned bird from a flock of about fifty individuals, and noted that the few he observed closely were of the yellow-crowned type. Monroe suggests that on the basis of existing records the yellow-crowned type is native to the Sula Valley and probably represents an undescribed subspecies; the two yellow-naped specimens could have been extralimital vagrants or escaped cage birds.

7. *A. o. belizensis* Monroe and Howell.

ADULTS forehead, crown, lores, periophthalmic region, ear-coverts, and upper cheeks yellow; some birds have scattered yellow feathers on throat and hindcrown; otherwise similar to *oratrix*.
3 males   wing 216–222 (218.7) mm., tail 113–120 (117.7) mm.,
       exp. cul. 34–36 (35.0) mm., tars. 25–27 (25.7) mm.
3 females wing 205–217 (209.7) mm., tail 97–109 (103.7) mm.,
       exp. cul. 32–33 (32.3) mm., tars. 25–27 (26.0) mm.
Known only from British Honduras.

8. *A. o. oratrix* Ridgway.

ADULTS entire head and throat yellow; bend of wing pale red intermixed with yellow; carpal edge and thighs yellow; bill horn-coloured tinged with grey towards base of upper mandible.
IMMATURES head entirely green except for a patch of yellow on forehead; bend of wing green; carpal edge yellowish-green.

W.T. Cooper. 72.

15 males wing 222–244 (232.7) mm., tail 104–135 (118.2) mm.,
exp. cul. 30–37 (33.9) mm., tars. 25–28 (26.9) mm.
13 females wing 206–233 (222.4) mm., tail 105–126 (114.2) mm.,
exp. cul. 30–36 (31.7) mm., tars. 23–27 (25.5) mm.

This race is called the Yellow-headed Amazon, and is sometimes treated as a distinct species. It occurs in Colima and Guerrero, on the Pacific slope of central Mexico, and on the Caribbean slope from southern Nuevo León and Tamaulipas south to eastern Oaxaco, Tabasco, and possibly Yucatán. There is a tendency for birds from the Caribbean slope to be larger than those from the Pacific side, but in my opinion the populations cannot be separated subspecifically because there is too much overlap in size.

Monroe and Howell (1966) point out that specimens which appear to be typical *oratrix* and *auropalliata*, respectively, have been taken in eastern Oaxaca, and there seems to be no known examples of intermediates between these two forms. If a zone of integradation does exist, then it must be quite narrow. Binford says that both forms are scarce in the region where their ranges approach closely (in Monroe and Howell, 1966).

9. *A. o. tresmariae* Nelson.   *Illustrated on page 545.*

ADULTS similar to *oratrix*, but yellow of head extending down on to neck and upper breast; upperparts slightly paler green; underparts slightly tinged with blue; averages larger in size and with longer tail.

10 males wing 226–245 (241.2) mm., tail 118–136 (129.2) mm.,
exp. cul. 32–35 (34.3) mm., tars. 26–28 (27.2) mm.
4 females wing 229–232 (230.5) mm., tail 116–130 (124.3) mm.,
exp. cul. 31–33 (32.5) mm., tars. 25–26 (25.5) mm.

Confined to the Tres Marías Islands, off the coast of Nayarit, western Mexico.

The Yellow-crowned Amazon is a well-known member of the genus, and in all parts of its extensive range is very popular as a pet because of its prowess as a 'talker'. On Maria Madre, in the Tres Marías Islands, western Mexico, McLellan found it to be fairly common, pairs or flocks being seen on all parts of the island. Stager (1961) found it to be common on all four islands of the Tres Marías. Schaldach (1963) reports that it is an uncommon resident of Colima, western Mexico, where it seems to be mainly confined to the dense thorn forest and tall tropical deciduous forest at the base of the Cerro del Sacate, and the other mountain massifs of the the central portion of the state; the persistent taking of nestlings for the pet market could account for its apparent scarcity in the region. According to Loetscher (1941) it is a common to abundant resident of Veracruz, eastern Mexico, being locally distributed throughout timbered parts of the tropical zone below 500 m. Dalquest found it to be common in arid areas of the tropical zone of Veracruz (in Lowery and Dalquest, 1951). Binford (1968) says that in Oaxaca, southern Mexico, it is an uncommon and local resident of tropical deciduous and humid gallery forests up to approximately 330 m. Paynter (1955) points out that there are no reliable records from the Yucatán Peninsula, though the species could be expected to occur there. In Guatemala it is a fairly common resident of the Pacific lowlands up to 600 m., and occurs in dry open woodland, along the edges of woodland; and in open country adjoining woodland (Land, 1970); there is one record from the Petén. Tashian (1953) found it to be moderately common in savannah and along the forest edge at Finca El Cacahuito, south-eastern Guatemala. According to Russell (1964) it is locally distributed in British Honduras, being common only in the vicinity of Hill Bank and Ycacos Lagoons and along the lower reaches of the Sibun and Sittee Rivers; it roosts and nests in the pine ridges, but during the day feeds in nearby tall, humid forest. Monroe (1968) says that in Honduras it has not been recorded above 750 m. and is fairly common in lowland pine savannah in the north-east and on Bay Islands, and in arid scrub along the Pacific lowlands, but in the Sula Valley, in the north-west, it is a rare to uncommon resident of the drier open, scrubby areas. In El Salvador, Dickey and van Rossem (1938) found it to be a common resident of the arid lower tropical zone below 470 m., with the centre of abundance on the coastal plain. Howell (1972) reports that in north-eastern Nicaragua, as in neighbouring north-eastern Honduras, this species is an inhabitant of the distinctive savannah dominated by *Pinus caribaea*, though it feeds along the edges of riparian broad-leaved forest. Slud (1964) points out that in north-western Costa Rica it occurs as a typical member of the arid Pacific avifauna, being centred in the tropical dry forest and ascending up the adjacent lower slopes of the Guanacaste Cordillera. In Guanacaste it is perhaps most common in the lower Tempisque Basin where scrubby grazing lands alternate with marshlands, though it is also seen commonly throughout the rest of the dry-forested lowlands, including the more humid agricultural sector at the mainland entrance to the Gulf of Nicoya. Wetmore (1944) found it to be common in the vicinity of Liberia, northern Guanacaste, Costa Rica. In Panama the species is locally distributed in the tropical zone, mainly on the Pacific slope, but is not common, being absent altogether from considerable parts of its range (Wetmore, 1968); it seems to prefer gallery forest and seldom enters more humid habitats. Eisenmann and Loftin (1968) report that it is now rare in the Panama Canal Zone.

In Colombia this species is a resident of the tropical zone (Meyer de Schauensee, 1964). Dugand (1947) says that it is the most common *Amazona* species in Atlántico, northern Colombia. Olivares (1969) suggests that it is probably common along both banks of the upper Magdalena River, central Colombia, because he has observed it frequently on the left bank at Honda and La Dorada, Tolima, especially in tall palms. In the vicinity of Villavieja, Huila, also on the upper Magdalena River, Miller (1947) found it in the crowns of large trees along the river bank, and noticed that a

GENERAL NOTES

Festive Amazon *Amazona festiva festiva* **1**
AMNH. 237765 ad. unsexed

Yellow-shouldered Amazon **2**
Amazona barbadensis barbadensis
COP. 14783 ad. ♂

favoured kind of tree was one that grew to a height of more than 30 m. and bore conspicuous, large orange flowers. Terborgh and Weske (1969) report that at a locality on the left bank of the Apurímac River, Ayacucho, central Peru, the species was observed in a tract of primary forest and in an adjoining mature coffee plantation, and in matorral, which is a distinctive riparian woodland of varied composition. Novaes (1957) points out that a specimen from São Salvador, north-western Acre, Brazil, was collected in riverine forest along the Grajaú River. Pinto (1966) says that in Brazilian Amazonia the species does not usually extend farther south than the lower reaches of tributaries along the right bank of the Amazon River; it is extremely common in the Branco River region, Roraima, northern Brazil. In Venezuela it is generally distributed in forests of the tropical zone (Phelps and Phelps, 1958). Schafer and Phelps (1954) claim that it wanders, and the few sight records from mountain forests in the vicinity of the Rancho Grande Reserve, northern Venezuela, are probably of vagrants from the lowland plains where it is very common. Smith found it to be the common large parrot of the wooded areas in north-eastern Venezuela, and he noticed that it seemed to prefer dry forest while the Orange-winged Amazon (*Amazona amazonica*) was more abundant in moist forest, though at times both were encountered in the same locality (in Friedmann and Smith, 1950). Snyder (1966) says that the species occurs in wooded areas in Guyana, and is more common inland than along the coast. McLoughlin (1970) confirms this by saying that wild birds, presumably as distinct from escaped cage birds, are not often seen in coastal areas, though flocks may occasionally appear. In May 1971, I found it to be the only amazon occurring in the vicinity of Mabaruma, north-western Guyana, but it was not plentiful. Large numbers were being offered for sale in the marketplace at Georgetown, but they had been brought down from the interior. In Surinam it occurs in the interior and is common on the sand ridges of the coastal region where its forest habitat overlaps that of *Amazona amazonica*, though the latter species is much more plentiful (Haverschmidt, 1968). Herklots (1961) says that it is a rare resident in Trinidad.

Dalquest recalls that in early March 1947, near Jimba, Veracruz, eastern Mexico, large numbers of Yellow-crowned Amazons were seen flying from their feeding grounds in the jungles to roosting places out on the coastal plain, and for an hour before dusk from a few to a hundred or more parrots were in sight at all times, in pairs and small flocks, all flying toward the east. On Maria Cleofas, in the Tres Marías Islands, western Mexico, Stager found a flock of about twenty birds roosting in a heavy stand of agaves; late each afternoon the flock would come into the roosting area and, after perching atop the tall flowering stems of the agaves for a short while, the birds would descend into the lower spiny leaves of the plants to within 2 m. of the ground, where they remained until sunrise when all individuals would reassemble as a flock and fly off toward the forested slopes of the island. Russell reports that at Hill Bank Lagoon, British Honduras, pairs and loose groups of several pairs of loudly screeching parrots flew across the lagoon every evening, making their way to the pine ridges where they roosted in the highest branches of tall pines, one or two pairs to a tree. I did not observe any spectacular evening or early morning flights at Mabaruma, north-western Guyana, and all birds seen during the day were in small groups, usually flying above the forest canopy or quietly feeding in the treetops. I found that they were tame and approachable while feeding. I also noticed that when a parrot had finished eating fruits growing near the extremity of one branch it would walk with slow deliberate steps along that branch toward the main trunk of the tree, where it would climb to another branch and then return to the outer foliage to get at more fruits. If flushed from a feeding tree these parrots fly out from the opposite side of the crown, and although there is an audible flapping of wings as they leave there is no screeching until they are well away from the tree. Miller notes that along the Magdalena River, central Colombia, they moved from the crown of one tree to the crown of another, characteristically in pairs, and occasionally were seen in long flights across open country. They are strong fliers and fly quite high when travelling long distances. Wetmore (1968) reports that at sunrise one morning on Isla Parida, in the Archipiélago de las Perlas, a flock of about twenty birds was observed flying off toward the mainland, thus indicating that either they crossed to the mainland to feed or to the island to roost. Wetmore also points out that in Panama these amazons occur in the same feeding areas as other large parrots, but do not mix with them, except in a casual manner.

They feed on fruits, seeds, nuts, berries, blossoms and probably leaf buds. In north-eastern Venezuela, Smith observed them eating the ripe fruits of *Pereskia guamacho* and *Curatella americana* (in Friedmann and Smith, 1955). In May 1971, at Mabaruma, north-western Guyana, I watched five of these parrots feeding alongside a pair of Brown-throated Conures (*Aratinga pertinax*) in a kanakudiballi tree (*Cochlospermum orinocense*); the conures simply perched beside fruits and picked out seeds with their bills, but the amazons were biting off the entire fruit, holding it in one foot, and scooping out the seeds with the lower mandible. Land says that the parrots will attack corn crops.

Yellow-faced Amazon *Amazona xanthops* 1
NHM. 44930 ad. ♂

Yellow-faced Amazon *Amazona xanthops* 2
NHM. 41146 imm. ♂

CALL A reiterated screeching *kurr-owk* (Slud, 1964); also a variety of metallic shrieks and whistling notes.

NESTING Grant (1966) notes that breeding has been recorded from the Tres Marías Islands in February and from the nearby mainland of western Mexico in May. In British Honduras, Peck found nests containing eggs in March, and in May he found a nest holding a young bird (in Russell, 1964). At Puerto del Triunfo, El Salvador, a pair was observed working industriously at a hollow in a live tree, carrying out small chips and pieces of rotten wood, and when collected, on 7th January, the female was ready to lay (Dickey and van Rossem, 1938). At Cantaura, north-

eastern Venezuela, Smith collected a female with slightly enlarged gonads on 10th February, and during March and April fledglings were brought to him by local people (in Friedmann and Smith, 1950).

Beebe and Beebe (1910) describe a nest found in northern Venezuela. It was in a hollow in a rotten palm stump, about 2 m. from the ground. Tne entrance was rectangular in shape and measured 15 × 7 cm. At the bottom of the hollow, on a layer of chips, were three eggs and a nestling covered with white down.

Smith gives details of the nesting behaviour of a pair of hand-reared, tame birds kept at semi-liberty in north-eastern Venezuela, and points out that observations on the nesting behaviour of wild birds confirmed his findings (in Friedmann and Smith, 1955). Copulation occurred daily, often three or four times a day, throughout February, March, and April, generally in the early morning. Work on the nest cavity commenced within three days of the initial copulation. The female generally worked while the male remained outside, but at times both worked together. Work continued sporadically, usually in the morning, for about a month and then the eggs were laid. On all three occasions the clutch comprised three eggs. Only the female incubated; the male generally remained in the immediate vicinity, often at the entrance, but was not seen to enter the hollow once incubation had commenced. The female left the nest in the early morning and late afternoon, and, together with the male, flew in circles around the nesting tree, screeching loudly all the while. At times before the commencement of incubation, and continuously thereafter, the male fed the female by regurgitation. All eggs were infertile.

Smith (1970) records a successful breeding in captivity. Four eggs were laid within a week and incubation commenced with the laying of the first egg. The sound of young being fed was first heard twenty-nine days after the laying of the first egg and two months later two young birds left the nest.

EGGS Ovate, glossy; 3 eggs, 41.8 (41.0–43.2) × 30.9 (30.4–31.3) mm. [Belcher and Smooker, 1936].

Blue-fronted Amazon *Amazona aestiva aestiva* **1**
AM. 030571 ad. ♂

Yellow-headed Amazon **2**
Amazona ochrocephala tresmariae
LACM. 29685 ad. ♀

ORANGE-WINGED AMAZON
Amazona amazonica (Linné)

DESCRIPTION
Length 31 cm.
ADULTS general plumage green, feathers of hindneck and mantle lightly edged with dusky black; crown and anterior of cheeks yellow; lores and superciliary band violet-blue; ear-coverts and posterior of cheeks bright green; throat yellowish-green tinged with blue; under tail-coverts yellowish-green; primaries green becoming violet-blue and then black towards tips; prominent orange wing-speculum across bases of outer three secondaries; secondaries green tipped with violet-blue; carpal edge yellowish-green; under wing-coverts and undersides of flight feathers green; tail green tipped with yellowish-green, lateral feathers strongly tinged with orange-red and centrally barred with dark green, outermost feathers edged with blue; bill horn-coloured becoming grey towards tip; iris orange; legs pale grey.
IMMATURES similar to adults, but iris dark brown.

DISTRIBUTION
Colombia, Venezuela, and the Guianas south to eastern Peru and southern Brazil; also on Trinidad and Tobago.

SUBSPECIES

1. *A. a. amazonica* (Linné).   *Illustrated on page 549.*
   23 males   wing 189–221 (204.9) mm., tail 86–110 (98.2) mm.,
               exp. cul. 27–33 (30.3) mm., tars. 23–26 (24.4) mm.
   20 females wing 180–214 (195.8) mm., tail 82–112 (95.2) mm.,
               exp. cul. 26–32 (28.9) mm., tars. 22–26 (23.9) mm.
   Ranges from Colombia, mainly east of the Andes, Venezuela, except the mountains in the north-west, and the Guianas south through eastern Ecuador and eastern Peru to northern Bolivia, and through Brazil to south-western Mato Grosso and Paraná.
   There is a tendency for birds from the Guianas to be small and those from northern Bolivia to be large, but in my opinion these differences do not warrant subspecific separation so I have synonymized *micra* with *amazonica*.

2. *A. a. tobagensis* Cory.
ADULTS similar to *amazonica*, but with orange wing-speculum across bases of outer four secondaries instead of outer three.
   5 males   wing 196–213 (207.0) mm., tail 98–103 (100.4) mm.,
              exp. cul. 30–32 (31.4) mm., tars. 23–24 (23.4) mm.
   5 females wing 182–205 (197.4) mm., tail 94–102 (97.8) mm.,
              exp. cul. 29–31 (30.2) mm., tars. 23–26 (24.2) mm.
   Confined to Trinidad and Tobago Islands.
   Griscom and Greenway (1937) point out that the species shows striking individual variation in plumage and the orange wing-speculum may be present on the bases of the outer three to five secondaries. This indicates that *tobagensis* is probably not valid. Unfortunately, I did not look at this aspect when examining specimens.

Herklots (1961) says that the Orange-winged Amazon is very numerous in Trinidad, and is a swamp and forest-dwelling bird, ranging from sea level up to about 625 m.; it is also plentiful on Tobago. Bond (1970) reports that on Tobago it is particularly abundant at higher elevations near the Roxborough–Bloody Bay road. Haverschmidt (1968) says that it is the most numerous of the parrots found in Surinam, and it inhabits mangrove forests, timbered sand ridges in the coastal region, savannah forests, and the extensive forests of the interior. He also points out that in the vicinity of settlements numbers have declined because of constant shooting, especially by 'sportsmen' assembled at points where evening flights to roosting sites pass low overhead (Haverschmidt, 1958). In Guyana it is widespread and abundant in lowland forests and along coastal rivers (Snyder, 1966). In May 1971, I found it to be extremely plentiful in the Georgetown district, coastal Guyana. In Venezuela it is generally distributed in forests of the tropical zone (Phelps and Phelps, 1958). Smith reports that in north-eastern Venezuela this species and *Amazona ochrocephala* were sometimes encountered in the same locality, but it seemed that the former generally preferred moist forest while the latter was more a bird of dry woodland (in Friedmann and Smith, 1950); at Caicara, Monagas, he found it to be common in deciduous seasonal forest. Schafer and Phelps (1954) state that in the vicinity of the Rancho Grande Reserve, northern Venezuela, it does not ascend the mountains, being found only along the coast up to 200 m., especially in the cacao plantations of Turiamo and Ocumare. In Colombia it is widespread and fairly common in the tropical zone east of the Andes, though in the north it also occurs on the western side and to the south it has been recorded from south-eastern Nariño (see Meyer de Schauensee, 1952). Dugand (1947) reports that this species may be as common as the Yellow-crowned Amazon (*Amazona ochrocephala*) in Atlántico, northern Colombia, but he has recorded it with certainty only at Los Pendales, in the mangroves at Las Flores, and along the Magdalena River in Ponedera. Pinto (1946) indicates that in the interior of eastern Brazil it has declined in numbers because of widespread deforestation. Sick and Pabst (1968) point out that in winter it moves into estuarine mangroves along the coast of Brazil, often in the company of the Red-crowned Amazon (*Amazona dufresniana rhodocorytha*). In the Descalvados district, Mato Grosso, Brazil, Rehn found this species and the Blue-fronted Amazon (*Amazona aestiva*) in small flocks either in flight or feeding in the treetops, and on one occasion in early September he saw both species in flocks a short distance from one another (in Stone and Roberts, 1935).

Nottebohm and Nottebohm (1969) describe a basic pattern of daily activity observed during their study of these parrots in Nariva Swamp Sanctuary, Trinidad. At dawn the parrots commence to screech as they congregate in large groups in the treetops. These early morning gatherings take place every day and seem to be important to the very sociable birds. During the day they are generally seen in pairs flying above the forest canopy or in the crowns of tall trees foraging for fruits and seeds. In the evening pairs converge on a particular clump of trees or bamboos to roost communally, up to more than six hundred birds together. Attendance at these roosting places declines during the breeding season.

In May 1971, near Georgetown, Guyana, I watched many thousands of Orange-winged Amazons going to roost in a large clump of bamboos situated in the centre of neglected farmland a short distance from the Demerara River. From late afternoon until after nightfall hundreds of parrots, in pairs and flocks, could be seen in the air at all times as they came in to the roosting site from all directions. As the flocks passed overhead I detected occasional pairs of Mealy Amazons (*Amazona farinosa*). Birds coming from across the river almost invariably paused in a congregating tree, a huge deciduous tree standing on the near bank, and here they indulged in playful antics; I frequently saw screeching birds flapping their wings while hanging upside down, sometimes holding the branch by only one foot. So numerous were the parrots that the giant bamboo stems bent over with their weight. The overall effect of this remarkable scene was greatly intensified by the incessant screeching that continuously built up to reach deafening proportions. In flight the movement of wings below body level and the shallow, rapid wingbeats are very marked in this species.

Food is normally procured in the treetops, and consists of fruits, seeds, nuts, berries, blossoms and leaf buds. Herklots says that the parrots feed mainly in the early morning and late afternoon, and in Trinidad they are fond of the seeds of palms and the fruits of the hog plum. McLoughlin (1970) mentions the claim that in Guyana they eat the flowers and seeds of the swamp immortell (*Erythrina* sp.). Poonai (1969) points out that in Guyana they attack cultivated fruits, particularly oranges and mangoes. In some districts they have acquired a taste for cacao beans and can be troublesome in plantations. Seeds of *Curatella americana* were found in the crop of a specimen collected at Caicara, Monagas, north-eastern Venezuela (Friedmann and Smith, 1955). Stomach contents from a specimen collected on the Urubu River, Amazonas, Brazil, comprised remains of seeds, and the stomach from a specimen collected on the Mearim River, Maranhão, Brazil, contained remains of fruits and seeds with a total volume of 7 cc. (Schubart *et al.*, 1965).

CALL A shrill, disyllabic *kee-ik* . . . *kee-ik* . . . *kee-ik*; also a variety of harsh screeches and whistling notes.

NESTING Belcher and Smooker (1936) report that on Trinidad a clutch of five eggs was taken in mid-May and another clutch of five was taken at the beginning of June. Haverschmidt (1968) notes that in Surinam breeding has been recorded in February–March. Schafer and Phelps claim that in northern Venezuela breeding takes place in May and June.

McLoughlin describes a nest found in Guyana. It was in a dead tree, approximately 16 m. from the ground, and the nesting hollow was about 1.6 m. deep. It contained three young birds,

Yellow-naped Amazon 1
Amazona ochrocephala auropalliata
LSUMZ. 29067 ad. ♂

Yellow-crowned Amazon 2
Amazona ochrocephala ochrocephala
RMNH. Cat. 5, Reg. 3713 ad. unsexed

two of which were almost ready to fly but the third was much smaller and largely unfeathered.

Nottebohm and Nottebohm report that on Trinidad the breeding seasons seems to be well-defined, and in 1968, while they were studying the birds, most eggs were laid in March. Nests are in hollows in trees, mainly in the trunks of rotting palms. Two to four eggs constitute the normal clutch. Incubation lasts approximately three weeks and only the female broods. She leaves the nest for short periods when the male comes to feed her; as soon as he arrives the female joins him and both fly to a nearby tree where he feeds her by regurgitation. During the day the male remains in close proximity to the nest, but at dusk, while the hen stays in the nest with her eggs or chicks, he flies off to the communal roost which may be several kilometres away. After hatching, the young remain in the nest for two months.

EGGS Elliptical to ovate, slightly glossy or without gloss; 11 eggs, 37.4 (35.6–39.1) × 29.1 (27.7–32.5) mm. [Hellebrekers, 1941].

Scaly-naped Amazon **1**
Amazona mercenaria canipalliata
ANSP. 162824 ad. ♂

Orange-winged Amazon **2**
Amazona amazonica amazonica
AM. B5775 ad. unsexed

SCALY-NAPED AMAZON
Amazona mercenaria (Tschudi)

Length 34 cm.

ADULTS general plumage green, paler and brighter on forehead, cheeks, and underparts; feathers of crown, occiput, and nape dark green edged with dull greyish-blue and tipped with dusky black; feathers of hindneck and sides of neck dull green distinctly tipped with dusky black; upper and under tail-coverts yellowish-green; red wing-speculum across bases of outer three secondaries; primaries and secondaries green becoming violet-blue towards tips; carpal edge yellow variably marked with orange-red; under wing-coverts and undersides of flight feathers green; central tail feathers green tipped with yellowish-green; lateral feathers green, subterminally banded with red and tipped with yellowish-green; bill grey with horn-coloured marking at base of upper mandible; iris red; legs greenish-grey.

IMMATURES undescribed, but probably similar to adults.

DISTRIBUTION   Mountains of north-western Venezuela and western Colombia, south through Ecuador and Peru to northern Bolivia.

SUBSPECIES

1. *A. m. mercenaria* (Tschudi).
   8 males   wing 204–217 (210.0) mm., tail 90–101 (96.0) mm.,
      exp. cul. 26–29 (27.3) mm., tars. 21–23 (22.1) mm.
   8 females wing 195–217 (208.0) mm., tail 86–100 (94.9) mm.,
      exp. cul. 27–31 (28.1) mm., tars. 21–24 (22.4) mm.
   Ranges from the mountains of northern Bolivia north along the eastern slopes of the Andes in Peru. Bond (1955) points out that a specimen from Leimebamba, Amazonas, northern Peru, has less red on the wing-speculum, thus showing an approach to *canipalliata*.

2. *A. m. canipalliata* (Cabanis).   *Illustrated on page 549.*
   ADULTS similar to *mercenaria*, but red wing-speculum replaced by concealed maroon markings on bases of outer three secondaries.
   11 males   wing 200–214 (208.0) mm., tail 93–103 (98.4) mm.,
      exp. cul. 26–31 (28.8) mm., tars. 20–23 (21.8) mm.
   10 females wing 202–217 (208.2) mm., tail 96–107 (100.9) mm.,
      exp. cul. 26–30 (28.0) mm., tars. 20–22 (21.0) mm.
   Occurs along the eastern slopes of the Andes in Ecuador, in the Western, Central, and Eastern Andes, Colombia, and in the mountains of north-western Venezuela.

GENERAL NOTES   In north-western Venezuela the Scaly-naped Amazon is locally distributed in forests of the upper subtropical and temperate zones along the Sierra de Perijá, Zulia, and the southern sector of the Cordillera de Mérida (Phelps and Phelps, 1958). Meyer de Schauensee (1964) says that in Colombia it inhabits forest from the tropical up to the upper temperate zone. Todd and Carriker (1922) report that in the Santa Marta Mountains, northern Colombia, it was common wherever woodland remained above 2,500 m., and thence up to the lower borders of open alpine country at about 3,450 m. In the vicinity of Rio Frio, also in the Santa Marta Mountains, Darlington (1931) found it to be common in forest above 2,500 m. during both February and July. Olivares (1969) suspects that it may no longer occur in Cundinamarca, central Colombia, at least on the western slopes of the Eastern Andes, because he has not been able to locate it in the La Aguadita region despite intensive searching. In Nariño, south-western Colombia, Carriker (1959) found it to be quite common around La Guayacana. Bond and Meyer de Schauensee (1943) point out that in northern Bolivia specimens have been collected at localities between 800 and 2,500 m. above sea level.

There is little published information on the habits of this species. Todd and Carriker report that in the Santa Marta Mountains it was a very shy bird and difficult to collect, except in the early morning; it became necessary to camp for several nights at 2,800 m. elevation on the Cerro de Caracas so that birds could be collected while they roosted at the edge of the forest. On San Lorenzo Mountain, also in the Santa Marta region, a flock of about twelve birds was repeatedly

seen and heard around the highest peak, at about 2,900 m. elevation, in the late evening and at dawn, thus indicating that there was a roost in the immediate vicinity (in Todd and Carriker, 1922).

CALL Undescribed.

NESTING No records.

EGGS Ovate; 4 eggs, 35.4 (34.5–36.3) × 28.0 (26.8–31.0) mm. [Schönwetter, 1964].

MEALY AMAZON
Amazona farinosa (Boddaert)

Length 38 cm.

ADULTS general plumage green, upperparts with pronounced glaucous suffusion, and underparts paler green; variable yellow patch on crown, in some birds this is prominent and well-defined while in others it is represented by only a few scattered yellow feathers; feathers of occiput, nape, and hindneck dull green broadly edged with greyish-blue and strongly tipped with dusky black; upper and under tail-coverts yellowish-green; carpal edge red, often marked with yellowish-green; red wing-speculum across bases of outer secondaries, primaries and secondaries green becoming violet-blue towards tips; under wing-coverts and undersides of flight feathers green; tail green broadly tipped with yellowish-green, lateral feathers sometimes lightly marked with red and outermost feathers edged with blue; bill yellowish-horn at base becoming dark grey towards tips; iris red; legs pale grey.

IMMATURES like adults, but iris dark brown.

Vinaceous Amazon *Amazona vinacea* 1
ANSP. 769344 ad. ♀

Mealy Amazon *Amazona farinosa inornata* 2
NMV. 61425 ad. unsexed

DISTRIBUTION Southern Mexico south to northern Bolivia and central-eastern Brazil.

SUBSPECIES Gyldenstolpe (1951) points out that differences claimed to exist between subspecies in South America do not appear to be constant. I agree entirely with his comments, and suggest that because of individual variation in plumage and size all birds occuring south of western Panama are probably best treated as *farinosa*.

1. *A. f. farinosa* (Boddaert).
     15 males   wing 226–248 (241.2) mm., tail 107–143(129.3) mm.,
                  exp. cul. 34–43 (38.5) mm., tars. 27–31 (28.6) mm.
     8 females wing 222–252 (238.8) mm., tail 120–136 (128.5) mm.,
                  exp. cul. 35–39 (37.1) mm., tars. 28–31 (29.3) mm.
     Ranges from the Guianas, Bolívar in southern Venezuela, and possibly easternmost Vaupés, south-eastern Colombia, south through Amazonia to eastern São Paulo, Brazil, and northern Bolivia; intergrades with *chapmani* in northern Bolivia.

2. *A. f. inornata* (Salvadori).   *Illustrated on page 552.*
     ADULTS like *farinosa*, but upperparts with less pronounced glaucous suffusion; crown green, sometimes with scattered yellow feathers.
     12 males   wing 232–262 (243.4) mm., tail 124–146 (135.8) mm.,
                  exp. cul. 36–42 (39.1) mm., tars. 26–33 (29.3) mm.
     8 females wing 232–247 (238.6) mm., tail 126–136 (130.8) mm.,
                  exp. cul. 35–37 (36.3) mm., tars. 27–29 (28.0) mm.
     Distributed from Veraguas, Panama, east to north-western Venezuela, and south through Colombia, west of the Andes, to north-western Ecuador, and east of the Andes to Meta, eastern Colombia, and Amazonas, southern Venezuela; probably not distinct from *farinosa*.

3. *A. f. chapmani* Traylor.
     ADULTS similar to *inornata*, but larger.
     6 males   wing 255–279 (261.0) mm., tail 132–150 (142.6) mm.,
                  exp. cul. 39–42 (40.5) mm., tars. 27–32 (29.8) mm.
     1 female   wing 260 mm., tail 131 mm.,
                  exp. cul. 39 mm., tars. 29 mm.
     Known from Putumayo and Vaupés, south-eastern Colombia, the eastern slopes of the Andes in Ecuador, the Huallaga River, San Martín, northern Peru, and north-eastern Bolivia.
     This is a most unsatisfactory subspecies. The type is an abnormally large specimen, but all other specimens could be referred to *inornata*.

4. *A. f. virenticeps* (Salvadori).
     ADULTS like *farinosa*, but carpal edge greenish-yellow, sometimes slightly marked with red; general plumage more yellowish-green, particularly on underparts; crown green; forehead and lores green tinged with blue.
     5 males   wing 232–250 (237.6) mm., tail 118–136 (126.2) mm.,
                  exp. cul. 32–37 (34.4) mm., tars. 27–29 (28.2) mm.

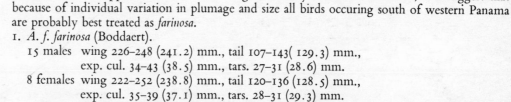

5 females wing 228–233 (230.6) mm., tail 115–125 (120.0) mm.,
exp. cul. 34–36 (34.8) mm., tars. 26–29 (27.2) mm.

Ranges from westernmost Panama, in western Chiriquí and western Bocas del Toro, north through Costa Rica and Nicaragua.

5. *A. f. guatemalae* (Sclater).
ADULTS similar to *virenticeps*, but forehead, lores, crown, and superciliary band extending down side of head blue; carpal edge greenish-yellow.
6 males   wing 231–248 (240.3) mm., tail 116–137 (128.8) mm.,
exp. cul. 36–38 (36.8) mm., tars. 28–29 (28.8) mm.
6 females wing 221–246 (236.8) mm., tail 127–136 (132.3) mm.,
exp. cul. 35–38 (37.0) mm., tars. 28–30 (29.3) mm.

Occurs along the Caribbean slope from Honduras north to Oaxaca and southern Veracruz, Mexico. Monroe (1968) points out that a specimen collected on Cerro Santa Bárbara, Honduras, shows some approach to *virenticeps*.

Blake (1953) points out that the Mealy Amazon is probably the least common of the amazons occurring in Mexico. Loetscher (1941) says that in southern Veracruz, Mexico, it is an uncommon and probably local resident of wooded habitats from near sea level up to about 600 m. Dalquest found it only once in Veracruz, when an Indian guide showed him a pair sitting in a tall tree in deep forest along the Coatzacoalcos River (in Lowery and Dalquest, 1951); the local people had not seen the species before. In Oaxaca, Mexico, it is a fairly common, permanent resident of heavy tropical evergreen forest in the Atlantic Region, between 30 and 300 m. elevation (Binford, 1968). Paynter (1955) reports that on the Yucatán Peninsula, Mexico, it inhabits rainforest, and near Escárcega, Campeche, he observed a feeding flock of several hundred birds. In British Honduras it is a moderately common resident of tall humid forests (Russell, 1964). Monroe (1968) says that it is an uncommon resident of tropical lowland rainforest on the Caribbean slope of Honduras, occurring up into low montane rainforest as high as 1,200 m. In the Caribbean lowlands and the Petén, Guatemala, it is a fairly common resident of undisturbed humid forest and the edges of forest from sea level up to 350 m., and at times it can be quite numerous locally (Land, 1970). Smithe (1966) reports that in the vicinity of Tikal, the Petén, northern Guatemala, it is common, though not as plentiful as the White-capped Parrot (*Pionus senilis*), and is found along the edges of clearings, roads, and trails in heavily forested areas. Slud (1964) says that in Costa Rica it occurs on both humid forested slopes, primarily the Caribbean because on the Pacific side it is generally scarce though locally abundant; it probably no longer occurs on the central plateau. In Costa Rica this species is almost completely sympatric geographically and ecologically with the Red-lored Amazon (*Amazona autumnalis*), but is appreciably more plentiful in wetter parts of the range and in the subtropical belt; in general, it is most numerous in heavily timbered areas, yet is not a true inhabitant of forest because it shows a preference for the borders of forest and adjacent clearings and plantations with tall trees. Orians (1969) recorded it in well-drained forest in north-eastern Costa Rica, and in almost pure stands of *Mora oleifera* bordering littoral mangrove forests on the Osa Peninsula in the south-west. Wetmore (1968) points out that it is the most common of the three species of *Amazona* found in Panama, where it inhabits forested areas throughout the tropical zone and ranges in mountain regions up to the lower edge of the subtropical zone. Eisenmann (1952) says that it is common in forest on Barro Colorado Island, Panama Canal Zone, and every day pairs were seen flying over the clearing which surrounds the biological laboratory. Wetmore (1957) found it to be a conspicuous parrot on Isla Coiba, Panama, where pairs and flocks ranged everywhere through the forest. It has also been recorded from Isla Ranchería, near Isla Coiba, and from Isla Coibita and Isla Canal de Afuera, Panama (Wetmore, 1968).

Meyer de Schauensee (1964) says that in Colombia this species inhabits forest in the tropical zone. Olivares (1957) reports that in the Guapí district, Cauca, western Colombia, it frequents dense forest, but is not as numerous as the Red-lored Amazon (*Amazona autumnalis*), a species with which it often associates. In north-western and southern Venezuela it is locally distributed in forests of the tropical zone (Phelps and Phelps, 1958). Snyder (1966) says that in Guyana it occurs in lowland forest in the interior and along coastal rivers, but is not as common as either the Orange-winged or Yellow-crowned Amazons (*Amazona amazonica* or *A. ochrocephala*). In May 1971, near Georgetown, Guyana, I observed a few pairs amongst thousands of Orange-winged Amazons going to roost. Haverschmidt (1968) reports that it is rather common in the forests of Surinam, and during July and August flocks come into forests on the coastal sand ridges where they live in the treetops. Bond found it to be common in the vicinity of Castanhal, Pará, north-eastern Brazil (in Stone, 1929). In Bahia, eastern Brazil, Pinto (1935) found that it was probably confined to the southern forests, where it was fairly common, though apparently not as plentiful as the Red-crowned Amazon (*Amazona dufresniana rhodocorytha*).

Mealy Amazons are generally observed in the early morning and late afternoon, when pairs and flocks fly high above the forest canopy on their way from roosting places to feeding grounds and then back again, their continuous screeching always attracting attention. Near the lower Jesusito River, Darién, eastern Panama, Barbour found a roost occupied by great numbers of birds (in Bangs and Barbour, 1922); at about 0800 hrs. every morning the parrots flew toward the hills, returning in the late afternoon, occasionally accompanied by a few pairs of macaws. Wetmore (1957) observed that on Isla Coiba, Panama, they flew about in the early morning until they had located a suitable feeding area and there they remained for the day. He also noted that for two hours or so after sunrise, while the parrots were flying from their roosts, men were stationed around fields of ripening corn to move the birds along to the forest by shouting and making other noise, because if not driven away these parrots caused much damage to crops. During the day small noisy groups may be seen flying from tree to tree or across open country intersecting forest, but generally they are quiet and unobtrusive as they feed or rest in the treetops, where their plumage blends extremely well with the foliage. It has been reported that in districts where these parrots are not common they frequently associate with other, more abundant amazons. In coastal Guyana, I had no trouble detecting occasional pairs intermingled with flocks of Orange-winged Amazons (*Amazona amazonica*), because the distinctive call-notes and large size were reliable guides to identification.

They feed on fruits, seeds, nuts, berries, blossoms and leaf buds, procured in the treetops. Near Escárcega, Campeche, southern Mexico, Paynter observed several hundred birds eating the fruits of ramón trees (*Brosimum alicastrum*). Wetmore (1968) reports that to the west of Puerto Armuelles, Chiriquí, western Panama, these parrots were present in forest where figs were ripening. Large green seeds were found in the stomach of a specimen collected at Casa Largo, Panama Canal Zone (Hallinan, 1924).

CALL In flight loud disyllabic notes resembling *catch-it . . . catch-it . . . catch-it*, or trisyllabic notes sounding like *taa-kaa-ee . . . taa-kaa-ee . . . taa-kaa-ee* accented on the higher-pitched middle syllable (Eisenmann, 1952; Smithe, 1966); also a series of bell-like notes, *kwok-kwok-kwok-kwok*, on a descending scale, usually given immediately after alighting. While resting or preening these parrots frequently emit soft, disyllabic clucking notes. All call-notes given by this species are less raucous than those of other amazons and have a distinct mellow tone.

NESTING Smithe and Paynter (1963) report that at Tikal, the Petén, Guatemala, a male with enlarged testes was collected in mid-May. Specimens showing a slight enlargement of the gonads were collected in the Guapí district, Cauca, western Colombia, during the last days of December and at the beginning of January (Olivares, 1957).

McLoughlin (1970) describes a nest found in Guyana. It was about 3 m. from the ground, in a hollow in the trunk of a cabbage palm. The hollow was deep and the entrance was through the decayed top of the trunk. It contained three nestlings, one much smaller than the other two.

On 15th April 1966, Mays found a nest in a crevice in a stone wall on top of Temple IV, one of the Mayan ruins at Tikal, the Petén, Guatemala (*in litt.*, 1966). The crevice was approximately 60 cm. deep, and there was a scattering of green leaves along the passageway. At the end of the crevice three newly-hatched nestlings were huddled together. Two of the nestlings were considerably larger than the third.

EGGS Broadly elliptical; 3 eggs, 37.7 (37.4–38.0) × 29.0 (28.4–29.4) mm. [Schönwetter, 1964].

VINACEOUS AMAZON
Amazona vinacea (Kuhl)

Illustrated on page 552.

DESCRIPTION

Length 30 cm.
ADULTS general plumage green, feathers strongly tipped with dusky black; lores and frontal band red; chin pink-red; long feathers of hindneck and sides of neck green broadly edged with pale blue and strongly tipped with dusky black; upper tail-coverts pale green; feathers of breast dull mauve-red tipped with dusky black; feathers of upper abdomen pale green with dull mauve-red bases and tipped with dusky black; feathers of lower abdomen yellowish-green faintly tipped with dusky black; under tail-coverts pale yellowish-green; carpal edge green variably marked with yellow and red; red wing-speculum across bases of outer three secondaries; primaries green becoming blue towards tips; under wing-coverts and undersides of flight feathers green; tail green narrowly tipped with yellowish-green, lateral feathers basally barred with red; bill dull pink-red becoming horn-coloured towards tip; iris red; legs pale grey.
IMMATURES duller and less extensive red frontal band; breast suffused with green; carpal edge greenish-yellow; bill horn-coloured with dull pink-red at base of upper mandible; iris brown.
13 males   wing 204–220 (210.2) mm., tail 98–120 (109.9) mm.,
          exp. cul. 24–29 (26.9) mm., tars. 21–24 (22.8) mm.
11 females wing 203–217 (207.9) mm., tail 101–115 (108.2) mm.,
          exp. cul. 24–29 (26.5) mm., tars. 22–24 (22.8) mm.

DISTRIBUTION

Occurs in south-eastern Brazil from southern Bahia south to Rio Grande do Sul, in eastern Paraguay, and in Misiones, north-eastern Argentina.

I did not see the Vinaceous Amazon in Rio Grande do Sul, south-eastern Brazil, during my brief visit in May 1971, but at Bom Jesus, in the north-east of the state, I was told by a local resident, who had a bird in captivity, that at times it was quite common in the district. It sometimes associates with the Red-spectacled Amazon (*Amazona pretrei*) and the Scaly-headed Parrot (*Pionus maximiliani*) to feed on ripe *Araucaria* seeds. Olrog (1959) says that in Misiones, north-eastern Argentina, it frequents subtropical forests. There is very little recorded information on the habits of this seemingly common species.

CALL Undescribed.

NESTING Von Ihering (1902) reports receiving an egg from a Sr Ch. Enslen, of São Lourenco, Rio Grande do Sul. It had been taken from a hollow, 2 m. in depth, situated high up in a huge myrtle tree.

EGGS Oval-shaped, smooth, and slightly glossy; 2 eggs, 38.1 (38.0–38.1) × 28.7 (27.5–30.0) mm. [Schönwetter, 1964; Von Ihering, 1902].

ST. LUCIA AMAZON.
Amazona versicolor (P. L. S. Müller)

Illustrated on page 556.

DESCRIPTION Length 43 cm.
ADULTS general plumage green, feathers strongly tipped with black; forehead, lores, and fore-crown violet-blue merging into paler blue on hindcrown, ear-coverts, and upper cheeks; red band across throat, extending down to centre of upper breast; feathers of lower breast green edged with reddish-brown and tipped with black; feathers of upper abdomen reddish-brown with green bases and faintly tipped with dusky black; thighs and lower abdomen pale green; under and upper tail-coverts yellowish-green; carpal edge yellowish-green; red wing-speculum across bases of outer secondaries; primary-coverts green tinged with violet-blue; primaries violet-blue; secondaries green becoming violet-blue towards tips; tail green broadly tipped with yellowish-green, lateral feathers basally barred with blue and with concealed red markings at bases; under wing-coverts yellowish-green tipped with dusky black; undersides of flight feathers greenish-blue; bill grey; iris orange; legs pale grey.
IMMATURES undescribed, but probably like adults though with brown iris.
6 males   wing 275–288 (280.3) mm., tail 165–171 (167.3) mm.,
                exp. cul. 34–36 (34.7) mm., tars. 28–30 (29.3) mm.
6 females wing 258–275 (265.5) mm., tail 165–170 (167.0) mm.,
                exp. cul. 31–34 (32.8) mm., tars. 26–29 (27.3) mm.

DISTRIBUTION Confined to the Island of St. Lucia, in the Caribbean Lesser Antilles.

GENERAL NOTES St. Lucia Amazons are inhabitants of mountain forest, and, although formerly widespread, are apparently now restricted to the central part of the island (Bond, 1971a). Diamond recently spent some time on the island and found that the parrots are indeed restricted to rainforest, but as there is a good stand of rainforest left in the south the parrots are reasonably common there (Lack *in litt.*, 1971). Wingate reports that the status of the parrots is not as critical as had been feared, but they are endangered, and in view of imminent developments on the island there is an urgent need for the implementation of conservation measures (*in litt.*, 1968). He says that the tract of rainforest still permanently inhabited by parrots is only about 50 sq. km., and the birds seem to be common in approximately half of this area, mainly to the east of Morne Gimie and north across the head-waters of the Cul de Sac River to the southern portion of the Barre de l'Isle Ridge. It seems that the main danger at present is hunting pressure not loss of habitat, though the latter is the basic reason for the present extremely restricted distribution. The parrots are legally protected, but this is not rigidly enforced and as many as forty are probably shot each year. Wingate quotes a report claiming that one hunter shot thirteen parrots between January and May 1966. Only strong enforcement of the law and protection of the remaining stands of mountain forests can ensure the survival of these splendid birds.

Little is known of their habits. Wingate reports that in April 1968 parties of up to six and many pairs were seen or heard flying overhead in the early morning and at intervals during the day. They were usually very quiet while feeding and often the only indication of their presence was the discarded pieces of fruit falling to the ground. Bond (1929b) found that the parrots appeared to be most active in the late afternoon, flying in small bands to their feeding grounds. Danforth (1935) reports that during a visit to St. Lucia in 1931 he observed parrots only on Piton Lacombe, where on top of the ridge, early one morning in July, twelve birds, in two flocks, were found feeding on the fruits of trees. Despite their size they were difficult to see in the treetops even at close range. Occasionally they emitted soft sounds when feeding and this betrayed their presence. While feeding they were quite tame and allowed a close approach. When disturbed they flew off in a flock, uttering loud screams. A male collected by Danforth had in its stomach small un-identified fruits and their seeds.

St. Lucia Amazon *Amazona versicolor*
AMNH. 475373 ad. ♀

CALL In flight a raucous, harsh screeching.

NESTING No records.

EGGS Undescribed.

RED-NECKED AMAZON

Amazon arausiaca (P. L. S. Müller)

Illustrated on page 557.

DESCRIPTION

Length 40 cm.

ADULTS general plumage green, feathers of nape, neck, and mantle tipped with dusky black; forehead, forecrown, lores, periophthalmic region, and anterior of cheeks violet-blue; red foreneck, in some birds extending to upper breast; under tail-coverts yellowish-green; carpal edge yellowish-green; primary-coverts dark green; primaries dark green becoming dull violet-blue towards tips; outer three secondaries red merging into yellow and then tipped with violet-blue; fourth secondary yellow tinged with green and tipped with violet-blue; under wing-coverts green; undersides of flight feathers blue; tail green tipped with yellowish-green, lateral feathers with concealed red marking on inner web near base; bill horn-coloured with grey tip; iris orange; legs grey.

IMMATURES undescribed, but presumably similar to adults though with brown iris.

10 males wing 237–260 (250.1) mm., tail 124–148 (137.1) mm.,
           exp. cul. 29–36 (32.2) mm., tars. 25–28 (26.8) mm.
8 females wing 240–256 (246.3) mm., tail 136–144 (139.5) mm.,
           exp cul. 29–31 (30.0) mm., tars. 25–27 (26.5) mm.

Restricted to the Island of Dominica, in the Caribbean Lesser Antilles.

DISTRIBUTION

GENERAL NOTES

Bond (1971a) says that the Red-necked Amazon occurs in mountain forest, for the most part at lower-elevations than the Imperial Amazon (*Amazona imperialis*). Fisher *et al.* (1969) claim that it lives mostly in forests on lower mountain slopes, and although reported as being fairly common and widespread in the 1940s it has suffered considerably from forest destruction, shooting and trapping, so is now quite rare. Wingate reports that both this species and the Imperial Amazon are still fairly widely distributed in the interior of Dominica (*in litt.*, 1966). They are threatened, not so much by loss of suitable habitat as by land-clearance for banana culture and by road-building projects which make the birds more accessible to hunters. The main factor at present limiting numbers is unquestionably hunting pressure, and it is *A. arausiaca* which is in greater danger because it prefers low elevations where settlements and the accompanying increase in hunting are widespread. It may have disappeared altogether from the southern sector of the island where roads and plantations have extended higher up the mountains. It is also scarce throughout tracts of the interior forest which are within half a days walk of roads and plantations and are, therefore, so accessible to hunters. Wingate also points out that roads are being pushed into the interior to open up the forests for timber production and this will undoubtedly result in increased hunting. There is a large area, perhaps 130 sq. km., surrounding Diablotin, especially to the east, where undisturbed virgin forests at low elevation extend for 5 to 8 km. toward the sea, and here Red-necked Amazons are probably still common. Strict protection from hunting and preservation of low altitude forest in reserves are essential to the survival of the Red-necked Amazon.

There is very little recorded information about the habits of these parrots. Porter (1929) observed pairs and small parties, sometimes in the company of Imperial Amazons, feeding in the tops of forest trees.

Red-necked Amazon *Amazona arausiaca*
AMNH. 475378 ad. ♂

CALL Undescribed.

NESTING Bond (1941) quotes a report claiming that nests are in holes in tall trees. Nothing further is known of the breeding habits.

EGGS Undescribed.

ST. VINCENT AMAZON

Amazona guildingii (Vigors)

Illustrated on page 560.

DESCRIPTION

Length 40 cm.

ADULTS (plumage variable); forehead, forecrown, lores and periophthalmic region creamy-white, merging into orange on hindcrown, anterior of cheeks, and throat; ear-coverts and posterior of cheeks violet-blue; long feathers of nape and hindneck olive-green tinged with dull blue and distinctly tipped with black; foreneck orange; feathers of underparts bronze-brown narrowly tipped with dusky black; abdomen suffused with green; under tail-coverts greenish-yellow; mantle, scapulars, back, and upper tail-coverts bronze-brown, last narrowly tipped with green; upper tertials dark green tinged with brown, lower tertials dark green tinged with violet-blue and sometimes faintly tipped with yellow; carpal edge orange; outer primary-coverts dark green edged with dull violet-blue, inner primary-coverts green; primaries black with conspicuous orange-yellow bases and centrally tinged with violet-blue; outer secondaries violet-blue with orange bases and centrally banded with green, inner secondaries dark green becoming violet-blue towards tips; secondary-coverts orange-brown with concealed green bases; median and lesser wing-coverts light bronze-brown; lesser under wing-coverts bronze-brown edged with green and sometimes tinged with pale blue; greater under wing-coverts and undersides of flight feathers yellow; tail feathers orange at base, with wide central band of dark violet-blue, and broadly tipped with orange-yellow; bill horn-coloured tinged with olive-green and marked with grey at base; iris orange; legs pale grey.

IMMATURES upperparts, including rump and upper tail-coverts, brownish-green; under wing-coverts and undersides of flight feathers green; iris brown.

5 males   wing 253–275 (265.4) mm., tail 160–170 (162.2) mm.,
            exp. cul. 33–39 (36.0) mm., tars. 27–31 (29.2) mm.
8 females wing 261–273 (266.6) mm., tail 148–162 (155.9) mm.,
            exp. cul. 32–36 (35.1) mm., tars. 27–30 (28.6) mm.

DISTRIBUTION   Confined to the Island of St. Vincent, in the Caribbean Lesser Antilles.

GENERAL NOTES   Bond (1971a) says that the St. Vincent Amazon occurs chiefly in mountain forest, though it has been found nesting not far above sea level near the windward coast. In 1927 he found it to be locally distributed on the island and more plentiful than had been expected, the total population at that time probably comprising up to several hundred birds (Bond, 1929b). Fisher *et al.* (1969) claim that this species does not seem to have decreased quite so fast as has the St. Lucia Amazon (*Amazona versicolor*), from neighbouring St. Lucia Island, perhaps because St. Vincent, though smaller, is less cultivated, and the parrot does not appear to be so dependent on montane forest; it was locally common at all heights in the late 1960s when Robert Porter Allen estimated that several hundred might still exist, mostly in the north but some also in the southern hills. In 1968, Wingate found it to be fairly common and tame, even near settlements, and birds could be observed without leaving the car (*in litt.*, 1972). Lack reports finding it to be fairly common high up in the rainforest along various valleys leading up to the central mountain block, but as far as he could ascertain it is not present on the mountains themselves because these are covered with dwarf forest (*in litt.*, 1971). He suggests that the species is threatened because of its restriction to the few remaining areas of rainforest. Kirby warns that estimates of the present population on St. Vincent can be very inaccurate, due largely to the difficulty of counting birds when groups move so freely back and forth across each valley (*in litt.*, 1972); at times the birds appear to be plentiful while at other times in the same year few are seen. He is confident that the population is viable and should remain stable, except for natural dynamic fluctuations. The species inhabits rainforest and the main requirement seems to be the presence of large trees in close proximity to each other. This habitat is more or less stable and no further alienation of forest is to be permitted. Factors still adversely affecting the population, namely illicit hunting, trapping, and felling of nesting trees to obtain nestlings for sale, have been prevalent during the past fifty years, but are now on the decline (Kirby *in litt.*, 1972); it is hoped that this decline will continue.

Kirby says that these amazons are noisy. They are intensely gregarious and groups of up to twenty or thirty can be seen feeding in the treetops, though pairs keep together and are readily discernible either in the trees or when flying overhead. Unless persistently disturbed, they are somewhat reluctant to leave an area in which they are feeding. Kirby recalls that on one occasion he was on a particular ridge and parrots could be heard calling from both sides, about 20 m. down from the crest. As he approached they flew off, one flock going into one valley and the other into the opposite valley. After a time they returned and alighted in the same general areas. On his way down from the ridge he walked through the area occupied by one flock and the birds dispersed, but some individuals stayed nearby; one watched him from about 50 m. away, even climbing down the branch to get a better view, and did not fly off until he was within 10 m. of the tree. In districts where hunting is prevalent the birds are not so confiding, and when disturbed fly off screeching loudly. The flight is direct and strong with rapid, jerky wingbeats.

Food is procured in the treetops and comprises fruits, seeds, berries and probably blossoms. Kirby says that the parrots eat the fruits of pennypiece (*Pouteria multiflora*) and the sweet, fibrous pericarp from bullet fruits (*Manikara bidentata*).

CALL Kirby reports that these parrots make a loud noise while feeding, sometimes a squeak like the turning of a rusty lock, at other times like a group of people squabbling. In flight the call emitted is a loud *quaw . . . quaw.*

NESTING According to Kirby breeding takes place toward the end of the dry season, that is about April. The nest is in a hollow in a very large tree, preferably a gommier (*Dacryodes excelsa*); a hole in a decayed limb or part of the trunk is enlarged by the birds to allow them to enter. Two young are reared—presumably only two eggs are laid—and these are about the same size at feathering.

Berry gives details of the first successful breeding in captivity, which took place at the Houston Zoological Gardens, U.S.A., in 1972 (*in litt.*, 1972). The clutch consisted of two eggs, only one of which proved to be fertile. They were laid on 28th March and 1st April, with incubation commencing on the appearance of the second egg. The fertile egg was chipped on 23rd April and the chick had hatched by the 25th. Only the female was observed incubating. The young bird developed rapidly and fourteen days after hatching its eyes commenced to open. At this point the male was observed entering the next-box. The young bird fledged sixty-seven days after hatching.

From the specimens that I have examined it seems that the plumage of a small proportion of young birds is similar to, though duller than, that of adults. On the other hand, it is apparent that some adult birds retain the green or 'immature' plumage. I have no evidence at all suggesting that there are two colour morphs and plumage does not change with age, but this is possible.

St. Vincent Amazon *Amazona guildingii*
LSUMZ. 69139 ad. ♂

EGGS An egg in the British Museum Collection measures 46.6 × 38.8 mm. [Harrison and Holyoak, 1970].

IMPERIAL AMAZON
Amazona imperialis Richmond

Illustrated on page 561.

DESCRIPTION

Length 45 cm.

ADULTS feathers of head, except cheeks and ear-coverts, dark maroon-purple variably suffused with greenish-blue and tipped with black; ear-coverts reddish-brown; feathers of cheeks brownish-maroon faintly edged with dusky black; feathers of breast and abdomen purple strongly margined with black; feathers of flanks and thighs green tipped with greenish-blue; under tail-coverts olive-green, each feather tipped with dull greenish-blue; mantle, back, rump, and upper tail-coverts green, feathers faintly edged with dusky black; wings green; carpal edge red; dark maroon wing-speculum across bases of outer secondaries; primaries dull violet-blue with green bases and brown tips; secondaries green becoming violet-blue towards tips; under wing-coverts green tipped with blue; undersides of flight feathers green; tail dull reddish-brown tipped with greenish-blue, central feathers and bases of lateral feathers suffused with green; bill greyish-horn; iris yellow to orange-red; legs grey.

IMMATURES occiput, nape and hindneck green; posterior of cheeks tinged with green; iris brown.

8 males   wing 270–293 (285.8) mm., tail 158–176 (168.9) mm.,
           exp. cul. 36–42 (39.4) mm., tars. 29–34 (31.3) mm.
10 females wing 275–299 (284.0) mm., tail 153–179 (166.3) mm.,
           exp. cul. 37–41 (39.2) mm., tars. 30–33 (31.9) mm.

DISTRIBUTION

Restricted to the Island of Dominica, in the Caribbean Lesser Antilles.

GENERAL NOTES

Bond (1971a) points out that the Imperial Amazon, probably the most spectacular species in the genus, inhabits mountain forest, chiefly at high elevations. In 1927, he found it in some numbers on the windward side of Dominica, particularly in dense forests to the south and south-east of Morne Diablotin (Bond, 1929b). Wingate says that although it is scarce, probably numbers were always low because it occupies high mountain forest, usually above 625 m., and such areas are of limited extent on the island (*in litt.*, 1966). Furthermore, the high forests are largely beyond the reach of settlements and plantations so there has been no destruction of the original habitat. While hunting has undoubtedly reduced numbers, the species still appears to occupy most of its former range, which includes all of the higher mountains, and it may be less changed in status than the Red-necked Amazon (*Amazona arausiaca*) from forests at lower elevations. However, Wingate hastens to emphasize that there must be concern for the future because heavy road-making equipment is being used to open up areas of the interior never previously accessible except on foot, and this will almost certainly bring about a dramatic increase in the hunting pressure. Kepler failed to see the Imperial Parrot during a visit to Dominica and reports that it seems to be confined to the forests around Morne Diablotin (*in litt.*, 1971). It is said that persons from neighbouring Guadeloupe, as well as local residents, are hunting these parrots, and if this is true the species is probably gravely threatened because, as rightly pointed out by Kepler, large conspicuous birds can be extirpated from an island even though the habitat is preserved. Only strict enforcement of legal protection and preservation of habitat in forest reserves will ensure the survival of this magnificent parrot.

These parrots are generally seen in pairs or small parties, sometimes in the company of Red-necked Amazons, feeding in the treetops or flying above the forest canopy. They are very shy and difficult to approach. Ober noticed that in the morning and toward dusk birds called to each other for about an hour, but during the remainder of the day they were quiet, except for an occasional cry (in Lawrence, 1878); when alarmed by the firing of a gun they screeched loudly and then abruptly became silent. When feeding in the treetops they are difficult to see, so well does their plumage blend with the foliage. Porter (1929) records watching two birds in a large fruit-bearing forest tree; one was eating the dark purple, pomegranate-like fruits, continually dropping pieces to the ground below, while the other was walking up and down the bare branch of a creeper.

They feed on fruits and seeds, especially those of gommier trees (*Dacryodes excelsa*) and mountain palms, nuts, berries, blossoms and buds, including the leaf buds of mountain palms (in Wood, 1924).

CALL In flight or when alarmed a raucous, harsh screeching; also a variety of shrill whistles and shrieks (in Wood, 1924). Wingate says that while at rest the parrots occasionally emit trumpet-like squawks (*in litt.*, 1972).

NESTING Virtually nothing is known of the nesting habits. Nests are said to be in hollows high up in tall trees, and only two eggs are laid (Frost, 1959).

Imperial Amazon *Amazona imperialis*
BM. 89.1.30.306 ad. ♀

EGGS Bond (1941) reports that an egg in the Rothschild Collection, presumably now in the American Museum of Natural History, measures approximately 45.5 × 40.0 mm. An egg in the British Museum Collection measures 45.6 × 37.3 mm. [Harrison and Holyoak, 1970].

Genus DEROPTYUS Wagler

The relationships of this monotypic genus are obscure. In taxonomic lists it is generally placed after *Amazona* and before *Triclaria*, but I doubt that it has affinities with either of these genera. Many authors have pointed out that some *Amazona* species have long, partly erectile feathers on the nape and hindneck, a feature which reaches maximum development in *Deroptyus*, but probably this is of little significance. *Deroptyus* may be allied to *Pionites* and *Pyrrhura*.

The species is a medium-sized parrot with a rather long rounded tail. The bill is fairly large and there is a distinct notch in the upper mandible. The feathers of the nape and hindneck are long and can be raised to form a ruff. There is no sexual dimorphism and young birds resemble adults.

HAWK-HEADED PARROT
Deroptyus accipitrinus (Linné)   *Illustrated on page 564.*

DESCRIPTION

Length 35 cm.
ADULTS forehead and crown buff-white; lores dark brown; feathers of occiput and sides of head brown shaft-streaked with buff-white; long feathers of nape and hindneck dark red broadly edged with blue; upperparts green; feathers of breast and abdomen dark red broadly edged with blue; thighs, flanks, and under tail-coverts green; primary-coverts and primaries brownish-black; secondaries green tipped with brownish-black and slightly tinged with blue; under wing-coverts green; undersides of flight and tail feathers grey-black; tail above green tinged with blue towards tip and edged with blue on outer webs of outermost feathers, concealed maroon spot at base of inner web of each lateral feather; bill grey-black; iris yellow; legs grey.
IMMATURES forehead creamy-buff; crown brown shaft-streaked with buff-white and suffused with green towards hindcrown; feathers of breast dark red edged with greenish-blue; iris greyish-brown.

DISTRIBUTION

Amazon Basin from the Guianas and eastern Pará, northern Brazil, west to south-eastern Colombia and north-eastern Peru.

SUBSPECIES

1. *D. a. accipitrinus* (Linné).
    8 males   wing 188–201 (194.1) mm., tail 131–153 (141.1) mm.,
                 exp. cul. 28–33 (31.4) mm., tars. 21–24 (21.9) mm.
    8 females wing 187–192 (189.8) mm., tail 114–142 (131.8) mm.,
                 exp. cul. 28–32 (30.0) mm., tars. 20–24 (21.9) mm.
    Occurs north of the Amazon River from Amapá, northernmost Brazil, west through the Guianas and southern Venezuela to south-eastern Colombia, south of the Meta River, north-eastern Peru, and possibly eastern Ecuador.

2. *D. a. fuscifrons* Hellmayr.
    ADULTS similar to *accipitrinus*, but forehead and crown dusky brown faintly shaft-streaked with buff-white; sides of head darker brown with buff-white shaft-streaks; no maroon spot at base of inner web of lateral tail-feathers.
    8 males   wing 193–203 (196.9) mm., tail 134–142 (138.4) mm.,
                 exp. cul. 30–32 (30.9) mm., tars. 21–24 (22.4) mm.
    5 females wing 189–197 (192.4) mm., tail 138–142 (140.2) mm.,
                 exp. cul. 30–31 (30.2) mm., tars. 22–23 (22.2) mm.
    Found south of the Amazon River in north-eastern Brazil, from eastern Pará, and possibly western Maranhão, west to the Tapajós River and south to northern Mato Grosso.

Hawk-headed Parrot
Deroptyus accipitrinus accipitrinus
RMNH. Cat. 10, Reg. 33621 ad. ♀

GENERAL NOTES

Haverschmidt (1968) reports that in Surinam the Hawk-headed Parrot is common in forests along coastal sand ridges, in savannah forests, and in the forests of the interior. According to Snyder (1966) it is uncommon in forests in Guyana. In southern Venezuela it is locally distributed in forests of the tropical zone (Phelps and Phelps, 1958). Lehmann (1957) reports that in the Mitú district Vaupés, south-eastern Colombia, this species is highly prized as a pet because of its beautiful plumage, but as far as he could ascertain it is not common.

These parrots associate in pairs or small flocks of up to twenty, and spend most of the day feeding or resting in the treetops. They normally fly low through the forest rather than above the canopy, and in flight their long, rounded tails are spread, thus producing a distinctive silhouette. Haverschmidt says that they roost singly in trees.

They feed on fruits, seeds, nuts, berries and possibly buds. McLoughlin (1970) quotes a report claiming that in Guyana the parrots eat the fruits of two species of black palm, and often visit small settlements to feed on guavas and *Inga* fruits. Stomach contents from a specimen collected on the Negro River, Amazonas, Brazil, comprised seeds, probably of an Anonaceae, and one large fruit (Schubart *et al.*, 1965).

CALL A wailing *chen-chen-chen . . . ee-yah . . . ee-yah*; also a nasal *angha-angha* and a harsh *chak-chak-chak* (McLoughlin, 1970; Snyder, 1966).

NESTING Haverschmidt reports that on 13th February 1948, in Surinam, he watched a party of five birds apparently displaying. All five birds flew upwards with very rapid wingbeats. On reaching a certain height the wingbeats stopped and the parrots glided downward with outstretched wings, ascending again with rapid wingbeats at the end of the downward glide. The flight resembled the display flight of some pigeons.

Nests are in old woodpeckers' holes in trees. McLoughlin describes an occupied nest found in Guyana on 13th March 1970. It was in what appeared to be an old woodpeckers' hole in a limb of a dead tree, about 20 m. from the ground. Another nest, that had been in use for several years until the tree fell, was in a hole in the trunk of a large dead tree, just below the base of the first branch and a little over 10 m. from the ground. In Surinam a sitting female was found on 19th April and a half-grown nestling was obtained during the last ten days of April (Haverschmidt, 1968). Snethlage (1935) reports that in mid-February an egg was taken from a nest at Inhanga, on the Marapanin River, Pará, Brazil.

Small (1966) records a series of successful breedings in captivity, but the data presented are not precise. The incubation period was not determined. The young remained in the nest for approximately eight to nine weeks after hatching.

EGGS Ovate to elliptical; 3 eggs, 36.0 (33.3–37.4) × 25.8 (24.7–26.8) mm. [Penard, 1927].

Genus TRICLARIA Wagler

The species in this monotypic genus is a medium-sized, stocky parrot with a fairly long, rounded tail. The bill is quite large and there is a distinct notch in the narrow, strongly ridged upper mandible. Sexual dimorphism is present and young birds resemble adults.

PURPLE-BELLIED PARROT
Triclaria malachitacea (Spix)

Illustrated on page 565.

Length 28 cm.

MALE general plumage green, slightly paler and more yellowish on head and underparts; chin and thighs slightly tinged with blue; centre of abdomen and lower breast purple; outer web of first primary violet-blue, remaining primaries green tinged with blue toward tips; undersides of flight feathers and tail feathers bluish-green; tail above green tinged with blue toward tips and edged with blue on outer webs of outer feathers; bill horn-coloured; iris brown; legs grey.

FEMALE like male, but centre of abdomen and lower breast green.

IMMATURES similar to adults, but males show little purple on centre of abdomen and have centre of lower breast green.

10 males   wing 151–165 (160.0) mm., tail 106–115 110.9) mm.,
           exp. cul 22–26 (23.2) mm., tars. 17–19 (18.2) mm.

10 females   wing 152–160 (156.1) mm., tail 107–114 (110.0) mm.,
           exp. cul. 21–22 (21.5) mm., tars. 17–19 (17.9) mm.

DISTRIBUTION   Occurs in south-eastern Brazil from southern Bahia south to Rio Grande do Sul.

GENERAL NOTES   The Purple-bellied Parrot seems to be quite common in the remaining forests of south-eastern Brazil, yet very little has been recorded about its habits. Pinto (1946) notes that it is abundant in mountainous regions of Espírito Santo, and recalls observing its frequent visits to an orchard on an estate where he was staying. Sick (1968) points out that there is a post-breeding movement from the Serra do Mar down into the coastal flats, where the species appears at localities such as Paratí, in the state of Rio de Janeiro, and is caught in great numbers. I did not see it during my visit to south-eastern Brazil in May 1971, but at São Paulo I was told by local residents that at times it occurs in woodlands and gardens on the outskirts of the city.

While resting in the treetops these parrots are quite inconspicuous because their green colouration blends very well with the foliage. Their flight is buoyant and swift. They feed on fruits, seeds, nuts, berries, nectar, buds, and possibly insects and their larvae, generally procured in the treetops. Sick says that they are particularly fond of juicy citron fruits (*Citrus medica*).

CALL   Murray (1969) says that the call is distinctive and difficult to describe, but is quite musical and unparrot-like.

NESTING   I know of no published reports of nesting in the wild.

Murray records an unsuccessful breeding attempt in captivity. The female incubated for approximately three weeks and one chick hatched. Although the chick died when about a week old the parents continued to follow what appeared to be their normal nesting behaviour. While sitting the female did not feed herself and rarely left the nest. About a fortnight after the chick had hatched she did come out periodically, but never ventured more than a metre or so away from the nest-box. As far as could be determined she made no attempt to feed herself or search for food until the young bird would have been about a month old had it lived.

Purple-bellied Parrot *Triclaria malachitacea*
NMV. 22469 ad. ♂

EGGS   Undescribed.

REFERENCES CITED

Abdulali, H., 1964, The birds of the Andaman and Nicobar Islands, *J. Bombay nat. Hist. Soc.*, **61**, pp. 483–571.

——, 1967, The birds of the Nicobar Islands, with notes on some Andaman birds, *ibid.*, **64**, pp. 139–190.

Aldrich, J. W., and B. J. Bole, Jr, 1937, The birds and mammals of the western slope of the Azuero Peninsula (Republic of Panama), *Scient. Publs Cleveland Mus. nat. Hist.*, **7**, pp, 1–96.

Ali, S., 1934, The Hyderabad State ornitholigical survey, Part IV, *J. Bombay nat. Hist. Soc.*, **37**, pp. 124–142.

——, 1943, The birds of Mysore, Part IV, *ibid.*, **44**, pp. 9–26.

——, 1946, *The Book of Indian Birds*, 4th ed., Bombay. Bombay Natural History Society Press.

——, 1949, *Indian Hill Birds*, Bombay. Cumberlege and Oxford University Press.

——, 1953, *The Birds of Travancore and Cochin*, Bombay. Cumberlege and Oxford University Press.

——, 1964, in A. L. Thomson, ed., *A New Dictionary of Birds*, London. Nelson.

——, 1969, *Birds of Kerala*, Madras. Oxford University Press.

——, and H. Abdulali, 1938, The birds of Bombay and Salsette, Part IV, *J. Bombay nat. Hist. Soc.*, **40**, pp. 148–173.

——, and S. D. Ripley, 1969, *Handbook of the Birds of India and Pakistan*, vol. 3, Bombay. Oxford University Press.

Allen, G. H., 1950, Birds as a biotic factor in the environment of pastures with particular reference to Galahs (*Cacatua roseicapilla*), *J. Aust. Inst. agric. Sci.*, **16**, pp. 18–25.

Allen, M. T., 1924, Breeding the Lesser Sulphur-crested Cockatoo, *Avicult. Mag.*, 4th ser., **2**, pp. 257–258.

Amadon, D., 1942, Birds collected during the Whitney South Sea Expedition: notes on some non-passerine genera, *Am. Mus. Novit.*, no. 1176, pp. 1–21.

——, 1953, Avian systematics and evolution in the Gulf of Guinea, *Bull. Am. Mus. nat. Hist.*, **100**, art. 3, pp. 393–452.

——, 1970, Taxonomic categories below the level of genus: theoretical and practical aspects, *J. Bombay nat. Hist. Soc.*, **67**, pp. 1–13.

——, and S. G. Jewett, Jr, 1946, Notes on Philippine birds, *Auk*, **63**, pp. 541–559.

——, and D. R. Eckelberry, 1955, Observations on Mexican birds, *Condor*, **57**, pp. 65–80.

——, and A. Basilio, 1957, Notes on the birds of Fernando Poo Island, Spanish Equatorial Africa, *Am. Mus. Novit.*, no. 1846, pp. 1–8.

Andrews, F. W., 1883, Notes on the Night Parrot, *Proc. R. Soc. S. Aust.*, **6**, pp. 29–30.

Andrle, R. F., 1967, Birds of the Sierra de Tuxtla in Veracruz, Mexico, *Wilson Bull.*, **79**, pp. 163–187.

Anon., 1970, First breeding of the Long-billed Corella, *Bird Keeping in Australia*, **12**, p. 50.

Archer, G., and E. M. Godman, 1961, *The Birds of British Somaliland and the Gulf of Aden*, vol. 3, Edinburgh. Oliver and Boyd.

Armstrong, J. S., 1932, *Hand-List to the Birds of Samoa*, London. Bale and Danielsson.

Ashby, E., 1907, Parrakeets moulting, *Emu*, **6**, pp. 193–194.

Attiwill, A. R., 1960, The Red-tailed Black Cockatoo in south-east of South Australia, *S. Aust. Orn.*, **23**, pp. 37–38.

Audubon, J. J., 1831, *Ornithological Biography*, vol. 1, Edinburgh. Adam Black.

Austin, O. L., Jr, 1961, *Birds of the World*, New York. Golden Press.

Backus, G. J., 1967, Changes in the avifauna of Fanning Island, central Pacific, between 1924 and 1963, *Condor*, **69**, pp. 207–209.

Bahr. P. H., 1912, On a journey to the Fiji Islands, with notes of the present status of their avifauna, made during a year's stay in the group, 1910–1911, *ibid*, 9th ser., **6**, pp. 282–314.

Baker, R. H., 1951, The avifauna of Micronesia; its origin, evolution and distribution, *Univ. Kans. Publs Mus. nat. Hist.*, **3**, pp. 1–359.

Bangs, O., 1916, A collection of birds from the Cayman Islands, *Bull. Mus. comp. Zool. Harv.*, **60**, pp. 303–320.

——, and W. R. Zappey, 1905, Birds of the Isle of Pines, *Am. Nat.*, **39**, pp. 179–215.

——, and T. E. Penard, 1918, Notes on a collection of Surinam birds, *Bull. Mus. comp. Zool. Harv.*, **62**, pp. 25–93.

——, and T. Barbour, 1922, Birds from Darién, *ibid.*, **65**, pp. 191–229.

——, and J. L. Peters, 1928, A collection of birds from Oaxaca, *ibid.*, **68**, pp. 385–404.

——, and A. Loveridge, 1933, Reports on the scientific results of an expedition to the south-western highlands of Tanganyika Territory, *ibid.*, **75**, pp. 143–221.

Bannerman, D. A., 1951, *The Birds of Tropical West Africa*, vol. 8, Edinburgh. Oliver and Boyd.

——, 1953, *The Birds of West and Equatorial Africa*, vol. 1, Edinburgh. Oliver and Boyd.

——, and W. M. Bannerman, 1968, *History of the Birds of the Cape Verde Islands: Birds of the Atlantic Islands*, vol. 4, Edinburgh. Oliver and Boyd.

Barattini, L. P., 1945, Las aves de Paysandú, *Anales Lic. Dptal. Pays.*, año 1, pp. 1–53. [Not cited.]

Barbour, T., 1943, Cuban ornithology, *Mem. Nuttall orn. Club*, no. 9, pp. 1–144.

Barros, R., 1934, Una excursión ornitológica a las Cordilleras del Estero Peuco, *Revta chil. Hist. nat.*, **38**, pp. 134–141.

Bates, G. L., 1930, *Handbook of the Birds of West Africa*, London. Bale and Danielsson.

——, 1934, Birds of the southern Sahara and adjoining countries in French West Africa, Part III, *ibid*, 13th ser., **4**, pp. 213–239.

Beckett, D. C., 1964, Keeping and breeding the Sierra or Andean Parrakeet, *Foreign Birds*, **30**, pp. 234–235.

Bedford, Duke of, 1954, *Parrots and Parrot-like Birds*, Fond du Lac. All-Pets Books.

Beebe, C. W., 1916, Notes on the birds of Pará, Brazil, *Zoologica, N.Y.*, **2**, pp. 55–106.

——, 1947, Avian migration at Rancho Grande in north-central Venezuela, *ibid.*, **32**, pp. 153–168.

Beebe, M. B., and W. Beebe, 1910, *Our Search for A Wilderness*, London. Constable.

Belcher, C., and G. D. Smooker, 1936, Birds of the colony of Trinidad and Tobago, Part III, *Ibis*, 13th ser., **6**, pp. 1–35.

Bell, H. L., 1966, Some feeding habits of the Rainbow Lorikeet, *Emu*, **66**, pp. 71–72.

——, 1968, A further note on the feeding of lorikeets, *ibid*, **68**, pp. 221–222.

——, 1969, Field notes on the birds of the Ok Tedi River drainage, New Guinea, *ibid.*, **69**, pp. 193–211.

——, 1970a, Field notes on the birds of Amazon Bay, Papua, *ibid.*, **70**, pp. 23–26.

——, 1970b, Field notes on birds of the Nomad River sub-district, Papua, *ibid.*, **70**, pp. 97–104.

——, 1970c, Notes on the Red-cheeked Parrot, *Geoffroyus geoffroyi*, in New Guinea, *Aust. Bird Watcher*, **3**, pp. 213–218.

——, 1970d, Additions to the avifauna of Goodenough Island, Papua, *Emu*, **70**, pp. 179–182.

Bendire, C., 1895, Life histories of North American birds, *Spec. Bull. U.S. natn. Mus.*, no. 5, pp. 1–508.

Benson, C. W., 1940, Further notes on Nyasaland birds (with particular reference to those of the Northern Province), Part II, *ibid*, 14th ser., **4**, pp. 387–483.

——, 1942, Additional notes on Nyasaland birds, *ibid.*, 14th ser., **6**, pp. 197–224

——, 1945, Notes on the birds of southern Abyssinia, *ibid.*, **87**, pp. 489–509.

——, 1960, The birds of the Comoro Islands: results of the British Ornithologists' Union Centenary Expedition 1958, *ibid.*, **103B**, pp. 5–106.

——, and F. M. Benson, 1942, Notes from southern Nyasaland, *ibid.*, **90**, pp. 388–394

——, and C. M. N. White, 1957, *Check List of the Birds of Northern Rhodesia*, Lusaka, Government Printer.

——, and M. P. Stuart Irwin, 1967, A contribution to the ornithology of Zambia, *Zambia Mus. Pap.*, no. 1, pp. 1–137.

Bent, A. C., 1940, Life histories of North American cuckoos, goatsuckers, hummingbirds and their allies, *Bull. U.S. natn. Mus.*, no. 176, pp. 1–506.

Bergman, S., 1960, The smallest parrots of the world, *Avicult. Mag.*, **66**, pp. 209–215.

Berlioz, J., 1941, Recherches osteologiques sur le crâne de perroquets. *Oiseau Revue fr. Orn.*, **11**, pp. 17–36.

——, 1959, Etude d'une nouvelle collection d'oiseaux du Gabon, *Bull. Mus. Hist. nat.*, Paris, 2nd ser., **31**, pp. 395–400.

——, and J. Roche, 1963, Etude d'une collection d'oiseaux de la Somalie, *ibid.*, 2nd ser., **35**, pp. 580–592.

Bernath, E. L., 1965, Observations in southern Chile in the southern hemisphere autumn. *Auk*, **82**, pp. 95–101.

Bertagnolio, P., 1970, Breeding of the Ornamental Lorikeet, *Parrot Soc. Mag.*, **4**, pp. 288–291.

Betts, F. N., 1951, The birds of Coorg, Part II, *J. Bombay nat. Hist. Soc.*, **50**, pp. 224–263.

Binford, L. C., 1968, A preliminary survey of the avifauna of the Mexican state of Oaxaca, vol. 1, Ph.D. thesis, Louisiana State University, pp. 1–597.

Biswas, B., 1951, Revisions of Indian birds, *Am. Mus. Novit.*, no. 1500, pp. 1–12.

——, 1959, On the parakeet *Psittacula intermedia* (Rothschild) [Aves: Psittacidae], *J. Bombay nat. Hist. Soc.*, **56**, pp. 558–562.

——, 1960, The birds of Nepal, Part II, *ibid.*, **57**, pp. 516–546.

Blackburn, A., 1971, Some notes on Fijian birds, *Notornis*, **18**, pp. 147–174.

Blake, E. R., 1953, *Birds of Mexico: A Guide for Field Identification*, Chicago. University of Chicago Press.

——, 1958, Birds of Volcán de Chiriquí, Panama, *Fieldiana, Zool.*, **36**, pp. 499–577.

——, 1962, Birds of the Sierra Macarena, eastern Colombia, *ibid.*, **44**, pp. 69–112.

——, and H. C. Hanson, 1942, Notes on a collection of birds from Michoacán, Mexico, *Publs Field Mus. nat. Hist., Zool. ser.*, **22**, pp. 513–551.

——, and M. A. Traylor, Jr, 1947, The subspecies of *Aratinga acuticaudata*, *Fieldiana, Zool.*, **31**, pp. 163–169.

Blancou, L., 1939, Contribution à l'étude des oiseaux de L'Oubangui-Chari Occidentale, *Oiseaux Revue fr. Orn.*, **9**, pp. 58–88, 255–277, 410–485.

Bloom, R. T., 1960, The breeding of Hanging Parrots in the new bird house at Chester Zoo, *Avicult. Mag.*, **66**, pp. 21–23.

Bó, N. A., 1965, Notas preliminares sobre la avifauna del nordeste de San Luis, *Hornero*, **10**, pp. 251–268.

Boehm, E. F., 1959, Parrots and cockatoos of the Mount Mary Plains, South Australia, *Emu*, **59**, pp. 83–87.

Boorer, W., 1964, Some notes on the behaviour and breeding of the Celestial Parrotlet, *Avicult. Mag.*, **70**, pp. 23–25.

Boosey, E., 1939, The breeding of Blue-fronted Amazon Parrots for the first time in Great Britain, *ibid.*, 5th ser., **4**, pp. 393–396.

——, 1957, The breeding of the Cuban Amazon Parrot, *ibid.*, **63**, pp. 17–19.

Bond, J., 1929a, The distribution and habits of the birds of the Republic of Haiti, *Proc. Acad. nat. Sci. Philad.*, **80**, pp. 483–521.

——, 1929b, On the birds of Dominica, St. Lucia, St. Vincent, and Barbados, B.W.I., *ibid.*, **80**, pp. 523–545.

——, 1937, Resident birds of the Bay Islands of Spanish Honduras, *ibid.*, **88**, pp. 353–364.

——, 1941, Nidification of the birds of Dominica, B.W.I., *Auk*, **58**, pp. 364–375.

——, 1946, The birds of Mona Island, *Notul. Nat.*, no. 176, pp. 1–10.

——, 1952, *Second Supplement to the Check-List of Birds of the West Indies* (1950), pp. 1–24, Philadelphia. Academy of Natural Sciences.

——, 1955, Additional notes on Peruvian birds, Part I, *Proc. Acad. nat. Sci. Philad.*, **107**, pp. 207–244.

——, 1956, *Check-List of Birds of the West Indies*, 4th ed., Philadelphia, Academy of Natural Sciences.

——, 1958, *Third Supplement to the Check-List of Birds of the West Indies* (1956), Philadelphia. Academy of Natural Sciences.

——, 1963, Derivation of the Antillean avifauna, *Proc. Acad. nat. Sci. Philad.*, **115**, pp. 79–98.

——, 1970, *Native and Winter Resident Birds of Tobago*, Philadelphia. Academy of Natural Sciences.

——, 1971a, *Birds of the West Indies*, 2nd ed., London. Collins.

——, 1971b, *Sixteenth Supplement to the Check-List of Birds of the West Indies* (1956), Philadelphia. Academy of Natural Sciences.

——, and R. Meyer de Schauensee, 1943, The birds of Bolivia, Part II, *Proc. Acad. nat. Sci. Philad.*, **95**, pp. 167–221.

Bouet, G., 1961, Oiseaux de l'Afrique tropicale, Part II, *Faune Un. fr.*, **17**, pp. 421–798.

Bourke, P. A., and A. F. Austin, 1947, Notes on the Red-browed Lorilet, *Emu*, **46**, pp. 286–294.

Bowen, W. W., 1932, East African birds collected during the Gray African expedition—1929, *Proc. Acad. nat. Sci. Philad.*, **83**, pp. 11–79.

Bradbourne, Lord, 1914, Aviculture in Paraguay, *Avicult. Mag.*, 3rd ser., **5**, pp. 185–191.

Bradley, D., and T. Wolff, 1956, The birds of Rennell Island, *The Natural History of Rennell Island, British Solomon Islands* (Scientific results of the Danish Rennell expedition, 1951, and the British Museum expedition, 1953), vol. 1, pp. 85–120.

Brattstrom, B. H., and T. R. Howell, 1956, The birds of the Revilla Gigedo Islands, Mexico, *Condor*, **58**, pp. 107–120.

Brereton, J. L., 1963, Evolution within the Psittaciformes, *Proc. XIIIth int. Orn. Congr.*, pp. 499–517.

——, and K. Immelmann, 1962, Head-scratching in the Psittaciformes, *Ibis*, **104**, pp. 169–175.

Brodkorb, P., 1937, Some birds of the Amazonian Islands of Caviana and Marajó, *Occ. Pap. Mus. Zool. Univ. Mich.*, no. 349, pp. 1–7.

Brook, E. J., 1907, Successful breeding of the White-eared Conure, *Avicult. Mag.*, new ser., **5**, pp. 59–60.

——, 1910a, The breeding of the Black Lory, *ibid.*, 3rd ser., **1**, pp. 28–29.

——, 1910b, Breeding of Stella's Lories, *Bird Notes*, new ser., **1**, pp. 237–238.

——, 1914, Breeding of the Fair Lorikeet, *Avicult. Mag.*, 3rd ser., **6**, pp. 29–30.

Brooks, F., and P. Brooks, Blue and Gold Macaws, *Parrot Soc. Mag.*, **4**, p. 117.

Brosset, A., 1964, Les Oiseaux de Pacaritambo (ouest de L'Ecuador), *Oiseaux Revue fr. Orn.*, **34**, pp. 1–24, 112–135.

Brunel, J., and J. M. Thiollay, 1969, Liste préliminaire des oiseaux de Côte-d'-Ivorie, *Alauda*, **37**, pp. 230–254.

Buckley, F. G., 1968, Behaviour of the Blue-crowned Hanging Parrot with comparative notes on the Vernal Hanging Parrot, *ibid*, **110**, pp. 145–164.

Buller, W. L., 1888, *A History of the Birds of New Zealand*, 2nd ed., 2 vols, London. The author.

——, 1894, Notes on the ornithology of New Zealand; with an exhibition of rare specimens, *Trans. N.Z. Inst.*, **27**, pp. 104–126.

Bump, G., 1971, The South American Monk, Quaker, or Grey-headed Parakeet, *Wildlife Leaflet*, no. 496, U.S. Dept. Interior Fish and Wildlife Service, Bureau of Sport, Fisheries and Wildlife, pp. 1–4.

Burgess, M. A., 1921, Breeding the Black-capped Lory, *Avicult. Mag.*, new ser., **12**, pp. 116–118.

Burleigh, T. D., and G. H. Lowery, Jr, 1942, Notes on the birds of southeastern Coahuila, *Occ. Pap. Mus. Zool. La St. Univ.*, no. 12, pp. 185–212.

Burnet, F. M., 1939, A note on the occurrence of fatal psittacosis in parrots living in the wild state, *Med. J. Aust.*, **1**, pp. 545–546.

Butler, A. G., 1905, The duration of the period of incubation, *Avicult. Mag.*, new ser., **3**, pp. 151–164.

Cain, A. J., 1955, A revision of *Trichoglossus haematodus* and of the Australian platycercine parrots, *ibid* **97**, pp. 432–479.

——, and I. C. J. Galbraith, 1956, Field notes on birds of the eastern Solomon Islands, *ibid.*, **98**, pp. 100–134.

Caldwell, J., 1876, Notes on the zoology of Rodriguez, *Proc. zool. Soc. Lond.* [1875], pp. 644–647.

Camargo, H. F. de A., 1962, Sôbre as raças geográficas Brasileiras de *Amazona brasiliensis* (L., 1758) (Aves, Psittacidae), *Papéis Dep. Zool. S Paulo*, **15**, pp. 67–77.

Carrick, R., 1956, The Little Corella, *Kakatoe sanguinea* G., and rice cultivation in the Kimberley Region, W.A., *C.S.I.R.O. Wildl. Res.*, **1**, pp. 69–71.

Carriker, M. A., Jr, 1910, An annotated list of the birds of Costa Rica including Cocos Island, *Ann. Carneg. Mus.*, **6**, pp. 314–970.

——, 1933, Descriptions of new birds from Peru, with notes on other little-known species, *Proc. Acad. nat. Sci. Philad.*, **85**, pp. 1–38.

——, 1959, New records of rare birds from Nariño and Cauca and notes on others, *Noved. colomb.*, **1**, (4), pp. 196–199.

Carter, T., 1912, Notes on *Licmetis pastinator* (Western Long-billed Cockatoo), *ibid*, 9th ser., **6**, pp. 627–634.

Cave, F. O., and J. D. Macdonald, 1955, *Birds of the Sudan: Their Identification and Distribution*, Edinburgh. Oliver and Boyd.

Cawkell, E. M., and R. E. Moreau, 1963, Notes on birds in the Gambia, *ibid*, **105**, pp. 156–178.

Chapin, J. P., 1939, The birds of the Belgian Congo, Part II, *Bull. Am. Mus. nat. Hist.*, **75**, pp. 1–632.

Chapman, F. M., 1917, The distribution of bird-life in Colombia: a contribution to a biological survey of South America, *ibid.*, **36**, pp. 1–729.

——, 1921, The distribution of bird life in the Urubamba Valley of Peru, *Bull. U.S. natn. Mus.*, no. 117, pp. 1–138.

——, 1926, The distribution of bird-life in Ecuador: a contribution to the study of the origin of Andean birdlife, *Bull. Am. Mus. nat. Hist.*, **55**, pp. 1–784.

——, 1929, Descriptions of new birds from Mt. Duida, Venezuela, *Am. Mus. Novit.*, no. 380, pp. 1–27.

Chasen, F. N., 1939, *The Birds of the Malay Peninsula*, vol. 4: *Birds of the Low-country Jungle and Scrub*, London. Witherby.

——, and A. Hoogerwerf, 1941, The birds of the Netherlands Indian Mt. Leuser Expedition 1937 to North Sumatra, *Treubia*, **18** suppl., pp. 1–125.

Cheesman, R. E., and W. L. Sclater, 1935, On a collection of birds from north-western Abyssinia, Part II, *ibid*, 13th ser., **5**, pp. 297–329.

Cheng, T., 1963, in T. Cheng, ed., *China's Economic Fauna: Birds*, [Chung-kuo ching-chi tung-wu chih-niao lei].

Cherrie, G. K., 1916, A contribution to the ornithology of the Orinoco region, *Mus. Brooklyn Inst. Arts Sci. Bull.*, **2**, pp. 133a–374.

Chisholm, E. C., 1934, Birds of the Comboyne Plateau, 1922–1934, *Emu*, **34**, pp. 8–23.

Christison, P., A. Buxton, and A. M. Emmet, 1946, Field notes on the birds of coastal Arakan and the foothills of the Yomas, *J. Bombay nat. Hist. Soc.*, **46**, pp. 13–32.

Chubb, C., 1910, On the birds of Paraguay, Part II, *ibid*, 9th ser., **4**, pp. 263–285.

——, 1916, *Birds of British Guiana*, vol. 1, London. Bernard Quaritch.

Churchill, D. M., and P. Christensen, 1970, Observations on pollen harvesting by brush-tongued lorikeets, *Aust. J. Zool.*, **18**, pp. 427–437.

Clancey, P. A., 1964, *The Birds of Natal and Zululand*, Edinburgh. Oliver and Boyd.

——, 1965, A catalogue of birds of the South African sub-region, Part II: Families Glareolidae–Pittidae, *Durban Mus. Novit.*, **7**, pp. 305–386.

Clarke, C. M. H., 1970, Observations on population, movements and food of the Kea (*Nestor notabilis*), *Notornis*, **17**, pp. 105–114.

Clay, T., 1964, in A. L. Thomson, ed., *A New Dictionary of Birds*, London. Nelson.

Cleland, J. B., 1918, The food of Australian birds, *N.S.W. Dept. Agr., Sci. Bull.*, no. 15, pp. 1–112.

——, 1919, The birds of Pilliga Scrub, New South Wales, *Emu*, **18**, pp. 272–285.

Collard, W. H., 1965, Breeding of the Chattering Lory, *Avicult. Mag.*, **71**, pp. 111–112.

Condon, H. T., 1941, The Australian broadtailed parrots, *Rec. S. Aust. Mus.*, **7**, pp. 117–144.

——, 1968, *A Handlist of the Birds of South Australia*, 2nd ed., Adelaide. South Australian Ornithological Association.

Conway, W. G., 1965, Apartment-building and cliff-dwelling parrots, *Anim. Kingd.*, **68**, pp. 40–46.

Coomans de Ruiter, L., 1951, Vogels van het dal van de Bodjo-rivier (Zuid-Celebes), *Ardea*, **39**, pp. 261–318.

——, and L. L. A. Maurenbrecher, 1948, Stadsvogels van Makassar (Zuid-Celebes), *ibid.*, **36**, pp. 163–198.

Costin, A. B., 1971, in A. B. Costin and H. J. Frith, eds., *Conservation*, Ringwood (Vic.). Penguin Books.

Cottam, C., and P. Knappen, 1939, Food of some uncommon North American birds, *Auk*, **56**, pp. 138–169.

Cuello, J., and E. Gerzenstein, 1962, Las aves del Uruguay, *Comun. zool. Mus. Hist. nat. Montev.*, **6** (93), pp. 1–191.

Cunningham, J. M., 1948, Number of Keas, *Notornis*, **2**, p. 154.

Cunningham-van Someren, 1948, G. R., *Agapornis swinderniana*, *ibid*, **90**, pp. 603–604.

——, 1969, Escapes of *Psittacula krameri* and *Agapornis* spp. breeding in Kenya, *Bull. Br. Orn. Club*, **89**, pp. 137–139.

Curr, D., 1971, Breeding of Malabar Bluewings, *Parrot Soc. Mag.*, **5**, pp. 263–266.

Curry-Lindahl, K., 1960, Ecological studies on mammals, birds, reptiles and amphibians in the eastern Belgian Congo, Part II, *Annls. Mus. r. Congo belge Sér., Sci. zool.*, **87**, pp. 1–170.

Dalborg-Johansen, J., 1954, Breeding Red-bellied Conures, *Avicult. Mag.*, **60**, p. 40.

Danforth, S. T., 1928, Birds observed in Jamaica during the summer of 1926. *Auk*, **45**, pp. 480–491.

——, 1929, Notes on the birds of Hispaniola, *ibid.*, **46**, pp. 358–375.

——, 1935, The birds of St. Lucia, *Univ. Puerto Rico Monogr.*, ser. B, no. 3, pp. 1–129.

Darlington, P. J., Jr, 1931, Notes on the birds of Rio Frio (near Santa Marta), Magdalena, Colombia, *Bull. Mus. comp. Zool. Harv.*, **71**, pp. 349–421.

Da Rosa Pinto, A. A., 1968, Algumas formas novas para Angola e outras para a Ciência descobertas no distrito do Cuando–Cubango (Angola), *Bonn. zool. Beitr.*, **19**, pp. 280–288.

Davies, S. J. J. F., 1966, The movements of the White-tailed Black Cockatoo (*Calyptorhynchus baudinii*) in south-western Australia, *W. Aust. Nat.*, **10**, pp. 33–42.

Davis, D. E., 1941, Notes on Cuban birds, *Wilson Bull.*, **53**, pp. 37–40.

Davis, L. I., 1952, Winter bird census at Xilitla, San Luis Potosí, Mexico, *Condor*, **54**, pp. 345–355.

Davis, W. B., 1944, Notes on summer birds of Guerrero, *ibid.*, **46**, pp. 9–14.

——, 1945, Notes on Veracruzan birds, *Auk*, **62**, pp. 272–286.

Dawson, E.W., 1959, The supposed occurrence of Kakapo, Kaka and Kea in the Chatham Islands, *Notornis*, **8**, pp. 106–115.

Dean, W. R. J., 1971, Breeding data for the birds of Natal and Zululand, *Durban Mus. Novit.*, **9**, pp. 59–91.

Deignan, H. G., 1945, The birds of northern Thailand, *Bull. U.S. natn. Mus.*, no. 186, pp. 1–616.

Dekeyser, P. L., and J. H. Derviot, 1966, Les oiseaux de L'Ouest Africain, Fasc. 1, *Init. étude afr.*, no. 19, pp. 1–507.

Delacour, J., 1966, *Guide des Oiseaux de la Nouvelle Calédonie et de ses Dependances*, Neuchâtel (Switzerland). Delachaux et Niestlé.

——, and E. Mayr, 1946, *Birds of the Philippines*, New York. Macmillan.

Descarpentries, A., and A. Villiers, 1969, Sur une collection d'oiseaux du sahel Sénégalais, *Bull. Mus. Hist. nat., Paris*, 2nd ser., **41**, pp. 385–394.

Diamond, J. M., 1967, New subspecies and records of birds from the Karimui Basin, New Guinea, *Am. Mus. Novit.*, no. 2284, pp. 1–17.

Dickey, D. R., and A. J. van Rossem, 1938, The birds of El Salvador, *Publs Field Mus. nat. Hist., Zool. ser.*, **23**, pp. 1–609.

Dietz, R. S., and J. C. Holden, 1970, The breakup of Pangaea, *Scient. Am.*, **223** (4,), pp. 30–41.

Dilger, W. C., 1954, Electrocution of parakeets at Agra, India, *Condor*, **56**, pp. 102–103.

——, 1960, The comparative ethology of the African parrot genus *Agapornis*, *Z. Tierpsychol.*, **17**, pp. 649–685.

Donaghho, W. R., 1950, Observations of some birds of Guadalcanal and Tulagi, *Condor*, **52**, pp. 127–132.

Dorst, J., 1956, Etude d'une collection d'oiseaux rapportée des hauts plateaux Andins du Pérou méridional, *Bull. Mus. Hist. nat., Paris*, 2nd ser., **28**, pp. 435–445.

——, 1961, Etude d'une collection d'oiseaux rapportée de la Vallée de Sandia, Pérou méridional, *ibid.*, 2nd ser., **33**, pp. 563–570.

Dove, R. S., and H. J. Goodhart, 1955, Field observations from the colony of Hong Kong, *ibid*, **97**, pp. 311–340.

Dugand, A., 1945, Notas ornitologicas Colombianas, I, *Caldasia*, **3** (13), pp. 337–341.

——, 1947, Aves del departmento del Atlántico, Colombia, *ibid.*, **4** (20), pp. 499–648.

——, 1948, Notas ornitologicas Colombianas, IV, *ibid.*, **5** (21), pp. 157–199.

——, and J. I. Borrero, 1946, Aves de la ribera Colombiana del Amazonas, *ibid.*, **4** (17), pp. 131–167.

——, and ——, 1948, Aves de la confluencia del Eagueta y Orteguaza (base aerea de Tres Esquinas), *ibid.*, **5** (21), pp. 115–156.

Dyck, J., 1971, Structure and spectral reflectance of green and blue feathers of the Rose-faced Lovebird (*Agapornis roseicollis*), *Biol. Skr. Dan. Vid. Selsk*, **18**, part 2, pp. 1–67.

Dyson, R. F., 1969, Captive hatching and development of a Thick-billed Parrot at Arizona–Sonora Desert Museum, *Int. Zoo Yb.*, no. 9, pp. 127–129.

Eates, K. R., 1937, The distribution and identification of the Large Indian Paroquet (*Psittacula. eupatria nipalensis* [Hodgs.]) in Sind, *J. Bombay nat. Hist. Soc.*, **39**, pp. 414–418.

Eaves, W. L., 1945, Breeding of the Plum-headed Parrakeet, *Avicult. Mag.*, 5th ser., **10**, pp. 14–15

Eckelberry, D. R., 1965, A note on the parrots of northeastern Argentina, *Wilson Bull.*, **77**, p. 111.

Edwards, E. P., and R. B. Lea, 1955, Birds of the Monserrate area, Chiapas, Mexico, *Condor*, **57**, pp. 31–54.

Edworthy, T., 1968, The breeding of Red Lories at Paignton Zoo, *Avicult. Mag.*, **74**, pp. 198–199.

Eisenmann, E., 1952, Annotated list of birds of Barro Colorado Island, Panama Canal Zone, *Smithson. misc. Collns*, **117** (5), pp. 1–62.

——, 1955, The species of Middle American birds, *Trans. Linn. Soc. N.Y.*, **7**, pp. 1–128.

——, 1957, Notes on birds of the province of Bocas del Toro, Panama, *Condor*, **59**, pp. 247–262.

——, 1961, Favourite foods of neotropical birds: flying termites and *Cecropia* catkins, *Auk*, **78**, pp. 636–638.

——, and H. Loftin, 1968, Birds of the Panama Canal Zone area, *Fla. Nat.*, **41**, pp. 57–60, 95.

Eisentraut, M., 1935, Biologische studien im bolivianischen Chaco, VI. Beitrag zur biologie der vogelfauna, *Mitt. zool. Mus. Berl.*, **20**, pp. 367–443.

Enehjelm, C. af, 1951, Breeding of the Green-rumped Parrotlet, *Avicult. Mag.*, **57**, pp. 53–56.

Etchecopar, R. D., 1969, L'extension de *Psittacula krameri* (la Perruche à collier rose) au Moyen-Orient, *Oiseau Revue fr. Orn.*, **39**, pp. 178–181.

——, and F. Hüe, 1967, *The Birds of North Africa*, 1st English ed., Edinburgh. Oliver and Boyd.

Ezra, A., 1933, Successful rearing of a young Derbyan Parrakeet, *Avicult. Mag.*, 4th ser., **11**, p. 236.

Falla, R. A., R. B. Sibson, and E. G. Turbott, 1966, *A Field Guide to the Birds of New Zealand*, 1st ed., London. Collins.
Favaloro, N. J., 1931, Notes of a trip to the Macpherson Range, south-eastern Queensland, *Emu*, **31**, pp. 48–59.
Ffrench, R. P., and M. Ffrench, 1966, Recent records of birds in Trinidad and Tobago, *Wilson Bull.*, **78**, pp. 5–11.
Fisher, A. K., and A. Wetmore, 1931, Report on birds recorded by the Pinchot Expedition of 1929 to the Caribbean and Pacific, *Proc. U.S. natn. Mus.*, **79**, art. 10, pp. 1–66.
Fisher, J., N. Simon, and J. Vincent, 1969, *The Red Book: Wildlife in Danger*, London. Collins
Fleming, R. L., Jr, 1967, The birds of Mussoorie, U.P., India. A distributional and ecological study, Ph.D. thesis (unpublished), Michigan State University, pp. 1–246.
Fleming, R. L., and R. H. Baker, 1963, Notes on the birds of Durango, Mexico, *Publs Mich. St. Univ. Mus., Biol. ser.*, **2**, pp. 275–303.
——, and M. A. Traylor, 1968, Distributional notes on Nepal birds, *Fieldiana, Zool.*, **53**, pp. 147–203.
Forbes, W. A., 1879, On the systematic position of the genus *Lathamus*, *Proc. zool. Soc. Lond.*, pp. 166–174.
Forbes-Watson, A. D., 1969, Notes on birds observed in the Comoros on behalf of the Smithsonian Institution, *Atoll Res. Bull.*, no. 128, pp. 1–23.
Forshaw, J. M., 1964, Some field observations on the Great Palm Cockatoo, *Emu*, **63**, pp. 327–331.
——, 1965, Brief field observations on the Mexican Parrotlet, *Avicult. Mag.*, **71**, pp. 101–103.
——, 1966, Observations and systematic notes on the Red-cheeked Parrot, *Mem. Qd Mus.*, **14**, pp. 175–180.
——, 1967, The subspecies of the Fig Parrot, *Opopsitta diophthalma*, *ibid.*, **15**, pp. 43–52.
——, 1969a, *Australian Parrots*, Melbourne. Lansdowne Press.
——, 1969b, in H. J. Frith, ed. *Birds in the Australian High Country*, Sydney. Reed.
——, 1971, Status of *Lorius amabilis* Stresemann, *Bull. Br. Orn. Club*, **91**, pp. 64–65.
Friedmann, H., 1927, Notes on some Argentina birds, *Bull. Mus. comp. Zool. Harv.*, **68**, pp. 139–236.
——, 1930, Birds collected by the Childs Frick Expedition to Ethiopia and Kenya Colony, Part I, Non-passeres, *Bull. U.S. natn. Mus.*, no. 153, pp. 1–516.
——, 1948, Birds collected by the National Geographic Society's expedition to northern Brazil and southern Venezuela, *Proc. U.S. natn. Mus.*, **97**, pp. 373–569.
——, and M. Davis, 1938, 'Left-handedness' in parrots, *Auk*, **55**, pp. 478–480.
——, L. Griscom, and R. T. Moore, 1950, Distributional check-list of the birds of Mexico, Part I, *Pacif. Cst Avifauna*, no. 29, pp. 1–202.
——, and F. D. Smith, Jr, 1950, A contribution to the ornithology of northeastern Venezuela, *Proc. U.S. natn. Mus.*, **100**, pp. 411–538.
——, and ——, 1955, A further contribution to the ornithology of north-eastern Venezuela, *ibid.*, **104**, pp. 463–524.
——, and J. G. Williams, 1969, The birds of the Sango Bay forests, Buddu County, Masaka District, Uganda, *Contr. Sci., Los Angeles Count. Mus.*, no. 162, pp. 1–48.
Frith, H. J., and J. H. Calaby, 1953, The Superb Parrot in southern New South Wales, *Emu*, **53**, pp. 324–330.
Frome, N. F., 1947, The birds of Delhi and district, *J. Bombay nat. Hist. Soc.*, **47**, pp. 277–300.
Frost, K. D., 1959, Three amazon parrots, *Avicult. Mag.*, **65**, pp. 84–85.
Fry, C. H., 1970, Ecological distribution of birds in north-eastern Mato Grosso state, Brazil, *An. Acad. brasil. Ciênc.*, **42**, pp. 275–318.
Fuggles-Couchman, N. R., 1939, Notes on some birds of the eastern province of Tanganyika Territory, *ibid*, 14th ser., **3**, pp. 76–106.

Galbraith, I. C. J., and E. H. Galbraith, 1962, Land birds of Guadalcanal and the San Cristoval Group, eastern Solomon Islands, *Bull. Br. Mus. nat. Hist.*, **9**, pp. 1–86.
Gallagher, M. D., 1960, Bird notes from Christmas Island, Pacific Ocean, *ibid*, **102**, pp. 490–502.
Garrido, O. H., and A. Schwartz, 1968, Anfibios, reptiles y aves de la península de Guanahacabibes, Cuba, *Poeyana*, ser. A, no. 53, pp. 1–68.
Gates, A. F., 1971, Breeding of the Hispaniolan or Salle's Amazon Parrot, *Avicult. Mag.*, **77**, pp. 185–187.
Gaymer, R., R. A. A. Blackman, P. G. Dawson, M. Penny, and C. M. Penny, 1969, The endemic birds of Seychelles, *ibid*, **111**, pp. 157–176.
Gibson, E., 1919, Further ornithological notes from the neighbourhood of Cape San Antonio, province of Buenos Ayres, Part II. *Trochilidae–Plataleidae*, *ibid*, 11th ser., **1**, pp. 495–537.
Gibson-Hill, C. A., 1949, An annotated checklist of the birds of Malaya, *Bull. Raffles Mus.*, no. 20, pp. 5–299.
——, 1950, A checklist of the birds of Singapore Island, *ibid.*, no. 21, pp. 132–183.
——, 1952, New Records for Singapore Island, *ibid.*, no. 24, pp. 321–326.
Gill, F. B., 1967, Birds of Rodriguez Island (Indian Ocean), *ibid*, **109**, pp. 383–390.
Gill, H. B., 1970, Birds of Innisfail and hinterland, *Emu*, **70**, pp. 105–116.
Gilliard, E. T., 1950, Notes on a collection of birds from Bataan, Luzon, Philippine Islands, *Bull. Am. Mus. nat. Hist.*, **94**, pp. 457–504.
——, and M. LeCroy, 1966, Birds of the middle Sepik region, New Guinea, *ibid.*, **132**, pp. 245–276.
——, and ——, 1967a, Results of the 1958–1959 Gilliard New Britain Expedition: 4. Annotated list of birds of the Whiteman Mountains, New Britain, *ibid.*, **135**, pp. 173–216.
——, and ——, 1967b, Annotated list of birds of the Adelbert Mountains, New Guinea, *ibid.*, **138**, pp. 51–82.
Glenister, A. G., 1951, *The Birds of the Malay Peninsula, Singapore and Penang*, London. Oxford University Press.
Glenny, F. H., 1954, Antarctica as a center of origin of birds, *Ohio J. Sci.*, **54**, pp. 307–314.
——, 1957, A revised classification of the Psittaciformes based on the carotid artery arrangement patterns, *Ann. Zool., Agra*, **2**, pp. 47–56.
Goddard, G. K., 1927, Breeding the Blue-rumped Parrotlet, *Avicult. Mag.*, 4th ser., **5**, pp. 338–339.
Goodfellow, W., 1900, A naturalist's notes in Ecuador, *ibid.*, **6**, pp. 65–72, 89–99, 120–128, 169–177, 221–228, 262–270.
——, 1902, Results of an ornithological journey through Colombia and Ecuador, Part V, *ibid*, 8th ser., **2**, pp. 207–233.
——, 1906, Notes on Mrs Johnstone's Lorikeet, *Avicult. Mag.*, new ser., **4**, pp. 83–87.
——, 1933, Some reminiscences of a collector (cont.), *ibid.*, 4th ser., **11**, pp. 414–423.
Gore, M. E. J., 1968, A check-list of the birds of Sabah, Borneo, *ibid*, **110**, pp. 165–196.
Gosse, P. H., 1847, *The Birds of Jamaica*, London. John Van Voorst.
Gould, J., 1865, *Handbook to the Birds of Australia*, vol. 2, London. The author.
Grant, P. R., 1966, Late breeding on the Tres Marías Islands, *Condor*, **68**, pp. 249–252.
——, and I. McT. Cowan, 1964, A review of the avifauna of the Tres Marías Islands, Nayarit, Mexico, *ibid.*, **66**, pp. 221–228.
Green, R. H., 1959, *A Catalogue of Tasmanian Birds*, Launceston. Foot and Playsted.
——, 1969, The birds of Flinders Island, *Rec. Queen Vict. Mus.*, no. 34, pp. 1–32.
——, and J.W. Swift, 1965, Rosellas as insect eaters, *Emu*, **65**, p. 75.
Greenway, J. C., Jr, 1935, Birds from the coastal range between the Markham and Waria Rivers, northeastern New Guinea, *Proc. New Engl. zool. Club*, **14**, pp. 15–106.
——, 1967, *Extinct and Vanishing Birds of the World*, revised ed., New York. Dover Publications.
Greenway, K. W., 1967, Breeding Meyer's Parrot (*Poicephalus meyeri*), *Avicult. Mag.*, **73**, pp. 195–196.
Griffiths, A. V., 1965, Breeding the Blue-eyed Cockatoo, *ibid.*, **71**, pp. 109–111.
Griscom, L., 1926, The ornithological results of the Mason-Spinden Expedition to Yucatán, Part II. Chinchorro Bank and Cozumel Island, *Am. Mus. Novit.*, no. 236, pp. 1–13.
——, 1932, The distribution of bird-life in Guatemala, *Bull. Am. Mus. nat. Hist.*, **64**, pp. 1–439.
——, 1950, Distribution and origin of the birds of Mexico, *Bull. Mus. comp. Zool. Harv.*, **103**, pp. 341–382.
——, and J. C. Greenway, Jr 1937, Critical notes on new neotropical birds, *ibid.*, **81**, pp. 417–437.
——, and ——, 1941, Birds of lower Amazonia, *ibid.*, **88**, pp. 83–344.
Guichard, K. M., and D. Goodwin, 1952, Notes on birds collected and observed in Oman and Hadhramaut, *ibid*, **94**, pp. 294–305.
Guinn, D. S., 1970, Umbrella Crested Cockatoo (*Kakatoë alba*), *Avicult. Bull.*, April issue.
Gundlach, J., 1876, *Contribución a la Ornitología Cubana*, Havana. [Not cited.]
Gyldenstolpe, N., 1945, The bird fauna of Rio Jurúa in western Brazil, *K. Sv. Vet. Akad. Handl.*, **22** (3), pp. 1–338.
——, 1951, The ornithology of the Rio Purús region in western Brazil, *Arkiv. Zool.*, **2**, pp. 1–320.
——, 1955a, Notes on a collection of birds made in the Western Highlands, central New Guinea, 1951, *ibid.*, ser. 2, **8**, pp. 1–181.
——, 1955b, Birds collected by Dr Sten Bergman during his expedition to Dutch New Guinea 1948–1949, *ibid.*, ser. 2, **8**, pp. 183–397.
Gysels, H., 1964, A biochemical evidence for the heterogeneity of the family Psittacidae, *Bull. Soc. r. Zool. Anvers*, no. 33, pp. 29–41.

Hachisuka, Marquis, 1934, *The Birds of the Philippine Islands, With Notes on the Mammal Fauna*, Part 3, London. Witherby.
——, 1953, *The Dodo and Kindred Birds or the Extinct Birds of the Mascarene Islands*, London. Witherby.
Haffer, J., 1959, Notas sobre las aves de la region de Urabá, *Lozania*, no. 12, pp. 1–49.
——, 1961, Notas sobre la avifauna de la Peninsula de la Guajira, *Noved. colomb.*, **1**, pp. 374–396.
——, 1967a, Zoogeographical notes on the 'nonforest' lowland bird faunas of northwestern South America, *Hornero*, **10**, pp. 315–333.
——, 1967b, On birds from the northern Chocó region, NW-Colombia, *Veröff zool. StSamml., Münch.*, **11**, pp. 123–149.
——, 1970, Art-Entstehung bei einigen Waldvögeln Amazoniens, *J. Orn.*, **111**, pp. 285–331.
Hald-Mortensen, P., 1971, A collection of birds from Liberia and Guinea, *Steenstrupia*, **1** (12), pp. 115–125.
Hallinan, T., 1924, Notes on some Panama Canal Zone birds with special reference to their food, *Auk*, **41**, pp. 304–326.
Hamel, J., 1970, Hybridization of Eastern and Crimson Rosellas in Otago, *Notornis*, **17**, pp. 126–129.
Hampe, H., 1939, Brotogerys parrakeets, *Avicult. Mag.*, 5th ser., **4**, pp. 402–406.
Hardy, J. W., 1963, Epigamic and reproductive behavior of the Orange-fronted Parakeet, *Condor*, **65**, pp. 169–199.
——, 1965, Flock social behavior of the Orange-fronted Parakeet, *ibid.*, **67**, pp. 140–156.
——, 1967, *Rhynchopsitta terrisi* is probably a valid species: a reassessment, *ibid.*, **69**, pp. 527–528.
——, and R. W. Dickerman, 1955, The taxonomic status of the Maroon-fronted Parrot, *ibid.*, **57**, pp. 305–306.
Hargrave, L. L., 1939, Bird bones from abandoned Indian dwellings in Arizona and Utah, *ibid.*, **41**, pp. 206–210.
Hargreaves, J. E., 1960, Breeding of the Blossom-headed Parrakeet, *Avicult. Mag.*, **66**, p. 27.
Harrison, C. J. O., and D. T. Holyoak, 1970, Apparently undescribed parrot eggs in the collection of the British Museum (Natural History), *Bull. Br. Orn. Club*, **90**, pp. 42–46.
Harrison, M., 1970, The Orange-fronted Parakeet (*Cyanoramphus malherbi*), *Notornis*, **17**, pp. 115–125.
Hartert, E., 1893, On the birds of the Islands of Aruba, Curaçao and Bonaire, *ibid*, 6th ser., **5**, pp. 289–338.
——, 1898, On a collection of birds from north-western Ecuador, *Novit. zool.*, **5**, pp. 477–505.
——, 1924, Types of birds in the Tring Museum, *ibid.*, **31**, pp. 112–134.
——, 1926a, On the birds of the district of Talasea in New Britain, *ibid.*, **33**, pp. 122–145.
——, 1926b, On the birds of the French Islands, north of New Britain, *ibid.*, **33**, pp. 171–178.
——, 1930, On a collection of birds made by Dr Ernst Mayr in northern Dutch New Guinea, *ibid.*, **36**, pp. 18–128.
——, and S. Venturi, 1909, Notes sur les oiseaux de la République Argentine, *ibid.*, **16**, pp. 159–267.
Harvey, W. G., and I. D. Harrison, 1970, The birds of the Mole Game Reserve, Part I. Non-passerines, *Niger. Orn. Soc. Bull.*, **7** (27), pp. 43–52.
Haverschmidt, F., 1954, Evening flights of Southern Everglade Kite and the Blue and Yellow Macaw in Surinam, *Wilson Bull.*, **66**, pp. 264–265.
——, 1958, Bird protection in Surinam, *Bull. int. Comm. Bird Preserv.*, **7**, pp. 234–236.
——, 1963, Dusky Parrot at sea near the coast of Surinam, *Ardea*, **51**, p. 253.
——, 1968, *Birds of Surinam*, Edinburgh. Oliver and Boyd.
——, 1972, Bird records from Surinam, *Bull. Br. Orn. Club*, **92**, pp. 49–53.
Heinrich, G., 1958, Zur verbreitung und lebensweise der vögel von Angola, Part II, *J. Orn.*, **99**, pp. 322–362.
Hellebrekers, W. P. J., 1941, Revision of the Penard oological collection from Surinam, *Zoöl. Meded., Leiden*, **23**, pp. 240–275.
——, and A. Hoogerwerf, 1967, A further contribution to our oological knowledge of the Island of Java (Indonesia), *Zool. Verh., Leiden*, no. 88, pp. 1–164.
Hellmayr, C., 1929, A contribution to the ornithology of north-eastern Brazil, *Publs Field Mus. nat. Hist., Zool. ser.*, **12**, pp. 235–501.
Henry, G. M., 1971, *A Guide to the Birds of Ceylon*, 2nd ed., London, Oxford University Press.
Herklots, G. A. C., 1940, The birds of Hong Kong, Part XXXV, *Hongkong Nat.*, **10**, pp. 75–78.
——, 1961, *The Birds of Trinidad and Tobago*, London. Collins.
Heydon, C., 1929, Alexandrine Parrakeets: incubation period, *Avicult. Mag.*, 4th ser., **7**, p. 151.
Hill, W. C. O., 1939, Breeding of the Queen of Bavaria's Conure (*Eupsittula guarouba* (Gmelin)), in captivity, *ibid.*, 5th ser., **4**, pp. 388–389.
Hinsby, K. B., 1947, The Orange-bellied Parrakeet, *Emu*, **47**, pp. 67–68.
Hoesch, W., 1940, Ueber den einflues der zivilisation auf das brutverhalten der vögel und über abweichende brutgewohnheiten (Beobachtungen aus Süd-West-Afrika), *J. Orn.*, **88**, pp. 576–586.
Holyoak, D. T., 1970a, The status of *Eos goodfellowi*, *Bull. Br. Orn. Club*, **90**, p. 91.
——, 1970b, The relation of the parrot genus *Opopsitta* to *Psittaculirostris*, *Emu*, **70**, p. 198.
——, 1970c, Structural characters for supporting the recognition of the genus *Eolophus* for *Cacatua roseicapilla*, *ibid.*, **70**, p. 200.
——, 1971a, Comments on the extinct parrot *Lophopsittacus mauritianus*, *Ardea*, **59**, pp. 50–51.
——, 1971b, The supposed fossil of *Conurus* from the Pleistocene of Buenos Aires, *ibid.*, **59**, pp. 51–52.
Honegger, R. E., 1966, Ornithologische beobachtungen von den Seychellen, *Natur Mus.*, **96**, pp. 481–490.
Hood, R., 1961, Tovi Parrakeets, *Foreign Birds*, **27**, p. 74.

Hoogerwerf, A., 1947, Contribution to the knowledge of the distribution of birds on the Island of Java, *Treubia*, **19**, pp. 83–137.
——, 1949, *De Avifauna van Tjibodas en Omgeving (Java)*, Buitenzorg. De Kon. Plantentuin van Indonesië.
——, 1964, On birds new for New Guinea or with a larger range than previously known (continued), *Bull. Br. Orn. Club*, **84**, pp. 153–161.
——, 1971, On a collection of birds from the Vogelkop, near Manokwari, north-western New Guinea, *Emu*, **71**, pp. 1–12.
——, and R. H. Siccama, 1938, De avifauna van Batavia en omstreken (cont.), *Ardea*, **27**, pp. 41–92.
Hopkinson, E., 1910, The Brown-necked Parrot, *Avicult. Mag.*, 3rd ser., **1**, pp. 107–112.
Housse, P. E., 1949, Notes sur l'avifaune du Chili, *Alauda*, **17**, pp. 1–15.
Howell, T. R., 1957, Birds of a second-growth rain forest area of Nicaragua, *Condor*, **59**, pp. 73–111.
——, 1964, Birds collected in Nicaragua by Bernardo Ponsol, *ibid.*, **66**, pp. 151–158.
——, 1972, An ecological study of the birds of the lowland pine savanna and adjacent rain forest in northeastern Nicaragua, *Living Bird*, 10th annual, pp. 185–242.
Hoy, G., 1968 Uber brutbiologie und eier einiger vögel aus nordwest-Argentina, *J. Orn.*, **109**, pp. 425–433.
Huber, W., 1933, Birds collected in northeastern Nicaragua in 1922, *Proc. Acad. nat. Sci. Philad.*, **84**, pp. 205–249.
Hudson, C., 1930, A list of some birds of the Seven Hills of Naini Tal, U.P., *J. Bombay nat. Hist. Soc.*, **34**, pp. 821–827.
Hudson, W. H., 1920, *Birds of La Plata*, vol. 2, New York. Dutton.
Hüe, F., and R. D. Etchecopar, 1970, *Les Oiseaux du Proche et du Moyen Orient*, Paris. N. Boubée et Cie.
Hughes, R. A., 1970, Notes on the birds of the Mollendo district, southwest Peru, *ibid*, **112**, pp. 229–241.
Humphrey, P. S., D. Bridge, P. W. Reynolds, and R. T. Peterson, 1970, *Birds of Isla Grande (Tierra del Fuego)*, Lawrence, Kansas. University of Kansas Museum of Natural History for Smithsonian Institution.
Husain, K. Z., 1959a, Taxonomic status of the Burmese Slaty-headed Parakeet, *ibid*, **101**, pp. 249–250.
——, 1959b, Is *Psittacula intermedia* (Rothschild) a valid species?, *Bull. Br. Orn. Club*, **79**, pp. 89–92.
Hutson, H. P. W., and D. A. Bannerman, 1931, The birds of northern Nigeria, Part III, *ibid*, 13th ser., **1**, pp. 147–203.

Immelmann, K., 1968, *Australian Parakeets*, 2nd rev. ed., Wittemberg. A.·Ziemsen.
Indge, H. J., 1953, Breeding account of the Red-sided Eclectus Parrot, *Avicult. Mag.*, **59**, pp. 66–67.
Irving Gass, M. D., 1954, Gold coast bird notes, Part I, *Niger. Fld.*, **29**, pp. 23–30.

Jackson, F. J., 1938, *The Birds of Kenya Colony and the Uganda Protectorate*, vol. 1, London. Gurney and Jackson.
Jackson, J. R., 1960, Keas at Arthur's Pass, *Notornis*, **9**, pp. 39–58.
——, 1962a, The life of the Kea, *Canterbury Mountaineer*, **31**, pp. 120–123.
——, 1962b, Do Keas attack sheep?, *Notornis*, **10**, pp. 33–38.
——, 1963a, Studies at a Kaka's nest, *ibid.*, **10**, pp. 168–176.
——, 1963b, The nesting of Keas, *ibid.*, **10**, pp. 334–337.
Jarman, H., 1965, The Orange-breasted Parrot, *Aust. Bird Watcher*, **2**, pp. 155–167.
Jayewardene, E. D. W., 1963, Breeding the Malabar or Indian Blue-winged Parrakeet, *Avicult. Mag.*, **69**, pp. 136–138.
Jindasa, G. P., 1961, Layard's Parrakeet bred, *Foreign Birds*, **27**, p. 224.
Johansen, H., 1966, Die vögel Feuerlands (Tierra del Fuego), *Vidensk. Meddr dansk naturh. Foren.*, **129**, pp. 215–260.
Johnson, A. W., 1967, *The Birds of Chile*, vol. 2, Buenos Aires, Platt Establecimientos Gráficos S.A.
Johnson, R., 1955, Breeding of the Purple-crowned Lorikeet, *Foreign Birds*, **21**, pp. 86–87.
Johnston, D. W., Blake, C. H., and Buden, D. W., 1971, Avifauna of the Cayman Islands, *Q. Jl Fla Acad. Sci.*, **34**, pp. 141–156.
Johnstone, E. J., 1907, The nesting of *Trichoglossus johnstoniae*, *Avicult. Mag.*, new ser., **5**, pp. 44–46.
Jones, V. D., 1955, Jendaya (or Yellow-headed) Conure, *ibid.*, **61**, pp. 26–27.
Junge, G. C. A., 1953, Zoological results of the Dutch New Guinea Expedition 1939. No. 5 The birds, *Zool. Verh., Leiden*, no. 20, pp. 1–77.

Keast, A., 1968, Moult in birds of the Australian dry country relative to rainfall and breeding, *J. Zool., Lond.*, **155**, pp. 185–200.
Kendall, S. B., 1956, Breeding the Timor Cockatoo, *Avicult. Mag.*, **62**, pp. 6–9.
Kepler, C. B., 1970, The Puerto Rican Parrot, in Chapter E–14: Preliminary comparison of bird species diversity and density in Luquillo and Guanica Forests, H. T. Odum, ed., *A Tropical Rain Forest*, Oak Ridge, Tenn. U.S. Atomic Energy Commission Division of Technical Information.
Kirby, H., Jr, 1925, The birds of Fanning Island, central Pacific Ocean, *Condor*, **27**, pp. 185–196.
Klaas, E. E., 1968, Summer birds from the Yucatán Peninsula, Mexico, *Univ. Kans. Publs Mus. nat. Hist.*, **17**, pp. 579–611.
Kloss, C. B. 1930, The birds of Mangalum and Mantanani Islands off the west coast of British North Borneo, *Bull. Raffles Mus.*, no. 4, pp. 117–123.
Koepcke, H. W., 1963, Probleme des vogelzuges in Peru, *Proc. XIIIth. Int. Orn. Congr.*, pp. 396–411.
Koepcke, M., 1961, Birds of the western slope of the Andes of Peru, *Am. Mus. Novit.*, no. 2028, pp. 1–31.
——, 1970, *The Birds of the Department of Lima, Peru*, rev. English ed., Wynnewood. Livingston.
Kuroda, N., 1936, *Birds of the Island of Java*, vol. 2, Tokyo. The author.

Lamba, B. S., 1966, Nidification of some common Indian birds, 10. The Rose-ringed Parakeet, *Psittacula krameri* Scopoli, *Proc. zool. Soc., Calcutta*, **19**, pp. 77–85.
Lamm, D. W., 1948, Notes on the birds of the states of Pernambuco and Paraiba, Brazil, *Auk*, **65**, pp. 261–283.
Land, H. C., 1962a, A collection of birds from the Sierra de las Minas, Guatemala, *Wilson Bull.*, **74**, pp. 267–283.
——, 1962b, A collection of birds from the arid interior of eastern Guatemala, *Auk*, **79**, pp. 1–11.
——, 1970, *Birds of Guatemala*, Wynnewood. Livingston.
Lang, E. M., 1969, Some observations on the Cape Parrot, *Avicult. Mag.*, **75**, pp. 84–86.
Langberg, W., 1958, Successful breeding of African Grey Parrots in Denmark, *ibid.*, **64**, pp. 57–64.
La Touche, J. D. D., 1931, *A Handbook of the Birds of Eastern China*, vol. 2, part I, London. Taylor and Francis.
Laubmann, A., 1930, *Wissenschaftliche Ergebnisse der Deutschen Gran Chaco-Expedition; Vögel*, Stuttgart. Strecker und Schröder.
——, 1932, Zur kenntnis von *Pyrrhura borellii* Salvadori, *Anz. orn. Ges. Bayern*, **2**, pp. 212–219.
Lavery, H. J., 1970, Sorghum damage by lorikeets, *Qd agric. J.*, **96**, pp. 785–786.
Lawrence, G. N., 1878, Catalogue of the birds of Dominica from collections made for the Smithsonian Institution by Frederick A. Ober, together with his notes and observations, *Proc. U.S. natn. Mus.*, **1**, pp. 48–69.
Laycock, G., 1969, The last parakeet, *Audubon*, **71** (2), pp. 21–25.
Lea, A. M., and J. T. Gray, 1935, The food of Australian birds, an analysis of the stomach contents, *Emu*, **34**, pp. 275–292; **35**, pp. 63–98.
Leck, C. F., and S. Hilty, 1968, A feeding congregation of local and migratory birds in the mountains of Panama, *Bird-Banding*, **39**, p. 318.
Lee, G., 1935, Breeding Kuhl's Lory, *Vini kuhli* (*Psittacula kuhli*), *Aviculture*, 3rd ser., **5**, pp. 47–48.
Legrand, H., 1964, Le perroquet noir de l'Isle de Praslin (Archipel de Seychelles), *Oiseaux Revue fr. Orn.*, **34**, pp. 154–158.
Lehmann, F. C., 1957, Contribuciones al estudio de la fauna de Colombia XII, *Noved. colomb.*, no. 3, pp. 101–156.
——, 1960, Contribuciones al estudio de la fauna de Colombia XV, *ibid.*, **1**, pp. 256–276.
Lekagul, B., 1968, *Bird Guide of Thailand*, Bangkok. Association for Conservation of Wildlife.
Lendon, A. H., 1946, Memories of the Moluccas, *Avicult. Mag.*, **52**, pp. 206–213.
——, 1951, *Australian Parrots in Captivity*, London. Avicultural Society.
——, 1965, Some birds of the Northern Territory of Australia, *Avicult. Mag.*, **71**, pp. 40–50.
Leopold, N. F., 1963, Checklist of birds of Puerto Rico and the Virgin Islands, *Bull. Puerto Rico agric. Exp. Stn insular Stn Río Piedras*, no. 168, pp. 1–119.
Lewis, T. H., 1971, Field notes on the dry season birds of Nayarit, *Tex. J. Sci.*, **23**, pp. 57–66.
Licht, L. E., 1968, Age of a female *Amazona festiva* at sexual maturity, *Wilson Bull.*, **80**, p. 106.
Lint, K. C., 1951, Breeding of the Rose-crested Cockatoo, *Avicult. Mag.*, **57**, pp. 223–224.
——, 1952, Breeding of the Finsch's Amazon, *ibid.*, **58**, pp. 23–24.
——, 1966, Thick-billed Parrots breed in captivity, *Zoonooz*, **39** (2), pp. 3–6.
——, 1969, Breeding New Guinea's Black Lory, *ibid.*, **42** (11), pp. 4–9.
Lister, U. G., 1962, African Grey Parrots breeding in captivity, *Niger. Fld*, **27**, pp. 127–134.
Loetscher, F. W., Jr, 1941, Ornithology of the Mexican state of Veracruz with an annotated list of the birds, Ph.D. Thesis, Cornell University, pp. 1–989.
Lönnberg, E., 1903, On a collection of birds from north-western Argentina and the Bolivian Chaco, *ibid*, 8th ser., **3**, pp. 441–471.
Lovell-Keays, L., 1914a, The breeding of Cactus Conures, *Avicult. Mag.*, 3rd ser., **6**, pp. 41–43.
——, 1914b, The breeding of All-Green Parrakeets (*Brotogeris tirica*) and Cactus Conures (*Conurus cactorum*), *Bird Notes*, new ser., **5**, pp. 347–349.
Loveridge, A., 1922, Notes on East African birds (chiefly nesting habits and stomach contents) collected 1915–1919, *Proc. zool. Soc., Lond.*, pp. 837–862.
Low, R., 1967, The Pearly Conure, *Avicult. Mag.*, **73**, pp. 4–7.
——, 1968, *Pyrrhura* conures and others, *ibid.*, **74**, pp. 47–48.
Lowe, P. R., 1907a, On the birds of Blanquilla Island, Venezuela, *ibid*, 9th ser., **1**, pp. 111–122.
——, 1907b, On the birds of Margarita Island, Venezuela, *ibid.*, 9th ser., **1**, pp. 547–570.
Lowery, G. H., Jr, and W. W. Dalquest, 1951, Birds from the state of Veracruz, Mexico, *Univ. Kans. Publs Mus. nat. Hist.*, **3**, pp. 531–649.
Lowther, E. H. N., 1940, Notes on some Indian birds, IV—The Manbhum district, *J. Bombay nat. Hist. Soc.*, **41**, pp. 526–547.
Ludlow, F., 1944, The birds of south-eastern Tibet, *ibid*, **86**, pp. 348–389.
——, 1951, The birds of Kongbo and Pome, south-east Tibet, *ibid.*, **93**, pp. 547–578.

Macdonald, J. D., 1957, *Contribution to the Ornithology of Western South Africa. Results of the British Museum (Natural History) South West Africa Expedition, 1949–1950*, London. British Museum (Natural History).
Macgillivray, W., 1914, Notes on some north Queensland birds, *Emu*, **13**, pp. 132–186.
——, 1918, Ornithologists in north Queensland, Part III, *ibid.*, **17**, pp. 180–212.
Mackay, R. D., 1970, *Handlist of the Birds of Port Moresby and District, Papua*, Melbourne. Nelson.
——, 1971, Observations for September, *New Guinea Bird Soc. Newsl.*, no. 71, p. 3.
Mackworth-Praed, C. W., and C. H. B. Grant, 1952, *Birds of Eastern and North-Eastern Africa. African Handbook of Birds*, ser. 1, vol. 1, London. Longmans, Green and Co.
——, and ——, 1962, *Birds of the Southern Third of Africa. African Handbook of Birds*, ser. 2, vol. 1, London. Longmans, Green and Co.
Maclaren, P. I. R., 1952, The sea and creek birds of Nigeria, Part I, *Niger. Fld*, **17**, pp. 160–174.
Maddison, N. E., 1910, Bird notes from the upper Goulburn, *Emu*, **9**, pp. 255–256.
Marchant, S., 1942, Some birds of the Owerri Province, S. Nigeria, *ibid*, 14th ser., **6**, pp. 137–196.
——, 1958, The birds of the Santa Elena Peninsula, S.W. Ecuador, *ibid.*, **100**, pp. 349–387.
——, 1960, The breeding of some S.W. Ecuadorian birds, *ibid.*, **102**, pp. 349–382.
——, 1961, Iraq bird notes–1960, *Bull. Iraq nat. Hist. Mus.*, **1** (4), pp. 1–37.
Marien, D., and K. F. Koopman, 1955, The relationships of the West Indian species of *Aratinga* (Aves, Psittacidae), *Am. Mus. Novit.*, no. 1712, pp. 1–20.
Marshall, A. J., and D. L. Serventy, 1958, The internal rhythm of reproduction in xerophilous birds under conditions of illumination and darkness, *J. exp. Biol.*, **35**, pp. 666–670.
Marshall, J. T., Jr, 1957, Birds of pine-oak woodland in southern Arizona and adjacent Mexico, *Pacif. Cst Avifauna*, no. 32, pp. 1–125.
Martin, P. S., C. R. Robins, and W. B. Heed, 1954, Birds and biogeography of the Sierra de Tamaulipas, an isolated pine-oak habitat, *Wilson Bull.*, **66**, pp. 38–57.
Mathews, G. M., 1917, *The Birds of Australia*, vol. 6, London. Witherby.
Mayr, E., 1931, Birds collected during the Whitney South Seas Expedition, XIII. A systematic list of the birds of Rennell Island with descriptions of new species and sub-species, *Am. Mus. Novit.*, no. 486, pp. 1–29.
——, 1937, Birds collected during the Whitney South Seas Expedition, XXXVI. Notes on New Guinea birds—III, *ibid.*, pp. 1–11.
——, 1940, Speciation phenomena in birds, *Am. Nat.*, **74**, pp. 249–278.
——, 1942, *Systematics and the Origin of Species*, New York. Columbia University Press.
——, 1944, The birds of Timor and Sumba, *Bull. Am. Mus. nat. Hist.*, **83**, art. 2, pp. 123–194.
——, 1945, *Birds of the Southwest Pacific*, New York. Macmillan.
——, 1953, Report of the standing committee on distribution of terrestrial faunas in the inner Pacific, *Proc. 7th Pacif. Sci. Congr.*, **4**, pp. 5–11.
——, 1963, *Animal Species and Evolution*, London. Oxford University Press.
——, 1964, in A. L. Thomson, ed., *A New Dictionary of Birds*, London. Nelson.
——, and E. T. Gilliard, 1954, Birds of central New Guinea, *Bull. Am. Mus. nat. Hist.*, **103**, art. 4, pp. 311–374.
——, and R. Meyer de Schauensee, 1939a, Zoological results of the Denison–Crockett Expedition to the South Pacific for the Academy of Natural Sciences of Philadelphia, 1937–1938, Part I. The birds of the Island of Biak, *Proc. Acad. nat. Sci. Philad.*, **91**, pp. 1–37.
——, and ——, 1939b, Zoological results of the Denison-Crockett Expedition to the South Pacific for the Academy of Natural Sciences of Philadelphia, 1937–1938, Part IV. Birds from north-western New Guinea, *ibid.*, **91**, pp. 97–144.
——, and ——, 1939c, Zoological results of the Denison-Crockett Expedition to the South Pacific for the Academy of Natural Sciences of Philadelphia, 1937–1938, Part V. Birds from the western Papuan Islands, *ibid.*, **91**, pp. 145–163.
——, and W. H. Phelps, 1967, The origin of the bird fauna of the south Venezuelan highlands, *Bull. Am. Mus. nat. Hist.*, **136**, art. 5, pp. 269–328.
——, and A. L. Rand, 1937, Results of the Archbold Expeditions, XIV. Birds of the 1933–1934

Papuan Expedition, *ibid.*, **73**, art. 1, pp. 1–248.
McClure, H. E., 1968, *Migratory Animal Pathological Survey, Annual Progress Report 1967*, San Francisco. U.S. Army Research and Development Group, Far East.
McGilp, J. N., 1931, *Geopsittacus occidentalis*, Night-Parrot, *S. Aust. Orn.*, **11**, pp. 68–70.
McKinley, D., 1960, The Carolina Parakeet in pioneer Missouri, *Wilson Bull.*, **72**, pp. 274–287.
——, 1966, The gay life and sad end of America's parakeet, *Explorer*, **8** (1), pp. 20–23.
McLachlan, G. R., and R. Liversidge, 1970, *Roberts Birds of South Africa*, 3rd rev. ed., Cape Town. Trustees of the John Voelcker Bird Book Fund.
McLellan, M. E., 1927, Notes on the birds of Sinaloa and Nayarit, Mexico, in the fall of 1925, *Proc. Calif. Acad. Sci.*, 4th ser., **16** (1), pp. 1–51.
McLoughlin, E., 1970, Field notes on the breeding and diet of some South American parrots, *Foreign Birds*, **36**, pp. 169–171, 210–213.
McNeil, R., J. R. Rodriguez S., and D. M. Figuera B., 1971, Handedness in the Brown-throated Parakeet *Aratinga pertinax* in relation with skeletal asymmetry, *ibid*, **113**, pp. 494–499.
Mees, G. F., 1957, Over het belang van Temminck's 'Discours Preliminaire' voor de zoologische nomenclatuur, *Zoöl. Meded., Leiden*, **35**, pp. 217–222.
——, 1964, Notes on two small collections of birds from New Guinea, *Zool. Verh., Leiden*, no. 66, pp. 1–37.
——, 1965, The avifauna of Misool, *Nova Guinea, Zool. ser.*, **31**, pp. 139–203.
——, in press, Die vögel der Insel Gebe, *Zoöl. Meded., Leiden*.
Meinertzhagen, R., 1937, Some notes on the birds of Kenya Colony, with especial reference to Mount Kenya, *ibid*, 14 th ser., **1**, pp. 731–760.
Mercer, R., 1967, A field guide to Fiji birds, *Fiji Mus. Spec. Publs*, no. 1, pp. 1–39.
Meyer, A. B., and L. W. Wiglesworth, 1898, *The Birds of the Celebes and the Neighbouring Islands*, vol. 1, Berlin. R. Friedländer.
Meyer de Schauensee, R., 1933, A collection of birds from southwestern Africa, *Proc. Acad. nat. Sci. Philad.* **84**, pp. 145–202.
——, 1944, Notes on Colombian parrots, *Notul. Nat.*, no. 140, pp. 1–5.
——, 1949, The birds of the Republic of Colombia (cont.), *Caldasia*, **5** (23), pp. 381–644.
——, 1950, Colombian zoological survey, Part VII. A collection of birds from Bolívar, Colombia, *Proc. Acad. nat. Sci. Philad.*, **102**, pp. 111–139.
——, 1952, Colombian zoological survey, Part X. A collection of birds from southeastern Nariño, Colombia, *ibid.*, **104**, pp. 1–33.
——, 1964, *The Birds of Colombia*, Narbeth. Livingston Publishing Company for Academy of Natural Sciences of Philadelphia.
——, 1966, *The Species of Birds of South America*, Narbeth. Livingston Publishing Company for Academy of Natural Sciences of Philadelphia.
——, 1970, *A Guide to the Birds of South America*, Wynnewood. Livingston Publishing Company for Academy of Natural Sciences of Philadelphia.
——, and J. E. Du Pont, 1962, Birds from the Philippine Islands, *Proc. Acad. nat. Sci. Philad.*, **114**, pp. 149–173.
——, and S. D. Ripley, 1940, Zoological results of the George Vanderbilt Sumatran Expedition, 1936–1939, Part III. Birds from Nias Island, *ibid.*, **91**, pp. 399–413.
——, and ——, 1953, Birds from Oman and Muscat, *ibid.*, **105**, pp. 71–90.
Miles, J. A. R., 1959, Ornithosis research in Australia, in *Biogeography and Ecology in Australia*, edited by A. Keast, R. L. Crocker, and C. S. Christian, *Monograpiae biol.*, **8**, pp. 412–426.
Miller, A. H., 1947, The tropical avifauna of the Upper Magdalena Valley, Colombia, *Auk*, **64**, pp. 351–381.
Mitchell, M. H., 1957, *Observations on Birds of Southeastern Brazil*, Toronto. University of Toronto Press.
Monroe, B. L., Jr, 1968, A distributional survey of the birds of Honduras, *Am. Orn. Un. Orn. Monogr.*, no. 7, pp. 1–457.
——, and T. R. Howell, 1966, Geographic variation in Middle American parrots of the *Amazona ochrocephala* complex, *Occ. Pap. Mus. Zool. La St. Univ.*, no. 34, pp. 1–18.
Moreau, R. E., 1945, The dwarf parrots (*Agapornis*) of Tanganyika, *Tanganyika Notes Rec.*, **19**, pp. 22–23.
——, 1948, Aspects of evolution in the parrot genus *Agapornis*, *ibid*, **90**, pp. 206–239, 449–460.
——, 1964, in A. L. Thomson, ed., *A New Dictionary of Birds*, London. Nelson.
Morrison, A., 1948, Notes on the birds of the Pampas River Valley, south Peru, *ibid*, **90**, pp. 119–126.
Mullick, P., 1969, Severe or Brown-fronted Macaw, *Foreign Birds*, **35**, pp. 100–101.
Munro, G. C., 1960, *Birds of Hawaii*, 2nd rev. ed., Rutland. Tuttle.
Murray, H., 1969, Breeding notes—season 1968, *Avicult. Mag.*, **75**, pp. 17–20.

Naumburg, E. M., 1930, The birds of Matto Grosso; a report on the birds secured by the Roosevelt-Rondon Expedition, *Bull. Am. Mus. nat. Hist.*, **60**, pp. 1–432.
Newton, A., 1875, Note on *Palaeornis exsul*, *ibid*, 3rd ser., **5**, pp. 342–343.
——, and E. Newton, 1876, On the Psittaci of the Mascarene Islands, *ibid.*, 3rd ser., **23**, pp. 281–289.
Newton, E., 1867, On the land-birds of the Seychelles Archipelago, *ibid.*, new ser., **3**, pp. 335–360.
Niceforo, H., 1945, Notas sobre aves de Colombia I, *Caldasia*, **3** (14), pp. 367–395.
——, and A. Olivares, 1966, Adiciones a la avifauna Colombiana, III (Columbidae–Caprimulgidae), *Boln Soc. venez. Cienc. nat.*, **26** (110), pp. 370–393.
Nieremberg, A., 1972, The Kissi-Kissi, *Parrot Soc. Mag.*, **6**, pp. 136–139.
Nicholls, E. G., 1905, A trip to the west, *Emu*, **5**, pp. 78–82.
Nichols, R. A., 1943, The breeding birds of St. Thomas and St. John, Virgin Islands, *Mem. Soc. cub. Hist. nat.*, **17**, pp. 23–37.
Nicholson, D. J., 1948, Escaped paroquets found breeding in Florida, *Auk*, **65**, p. 139.
Nielsen, A. V., 1964, Breeding the Red-faced Lovebird in Denmark, *Avicult. Mag.*, **70**, pp. 39–46.
Niethammer, G., 1953, Zur vogelwelt Boliviens, *Bonn. zool. Beitr.*, **4**, pp. 195–303.
——, and J. Niethammer, 1967, Neunachweise für Afghanistans vogelwelt, *J. Orn.*, **108**, pp. 76–80.
Norgaard-Olesen, E., 1968, The Blue-crowned Hanging Parakeet (*Loriculus galgulus*), *Avicult. Mag.*, **74**, pp. 215–216.
Norris, K. A., 1954, Colour change in the beaks of young Derbyan Parrakeets, *ibid.*, **60**, p. 98.
North, A. J., 1896, Aves, in *Report on the Work of the Horn Scientific Expedition to Central Australia*, Part 2. Zoology, London. Dulau and Co.
Nottebohm, F., and M. Nottebohm, 1969, The parrots of Bush Bush, *Anim. Kingd.*, **72**, pp. 19–23.
Novaes, F. C., 1957, Contribuição à ornitologia do noroeste do Acre, *Boln Mus. Paraense Emilio Goeldi*, no. 9, pp. 1–30.
Nowotny, Dr, 1898, The breeding of the Carolina Paroquet in captivity, *Auk*, **15**, pp. 28–32.

O'Connor, N., 1971, Letter to the Editor, *Parrot Soc. Mag.*, **5**, p. 184.
Oelke, H., 1968, Vogelsiedlungsdichten in den Tropen (Insel Jamaika, Karabische See), *Vogelwelt*, **89**, pp. 201–215.
Ogilvie-Grant, W. R., 1906, On the birds collected by Mr Walter Goodfellow on the Volcano of Apo and in its vicinity, in south-east Mindanao, Philippine Islands, *ibid*, 8th ser., **6**, pp. 465–505.
——, 1915, Report on the birds collected by the British Ornithologists' Union Expedition and the Wollaston Expedition in Dutch New Guinea, *ibid.*, Jubilee suppl., pp. 1–236.
Olivares, A., 1957, Aves de la costa del Pacifico Municipio de Guapi, Cauca, Colombia, II, *Caldasia*, **8** (36), pp. 33–93.
——, 1969, *Aves de Cundinamarca*, Univ. Nacional de Colombia: Direccion de Divulgacion Cultural.
Oliver, W. R. B., 1955, *New Zealand Birds*, 2nd ed., Wellington. Reed.
Olrog, C. C., 1948, Observaciones sobre la avifauna de Tierra del Fuego y Chile, *Acta zool. lilloana*, **5**, pp. 437–531.
——, 1959, *Las Aves Argentinas: Una Guia de Campo*, Buenos Aires. Instituto 'Miguel Lillo'.
——, 1968, *Las Aves Sudamericanas: Una Guia de Campo*, vol. 1, Buenos Aires. Instituto 'Miguel Lillo'.
Olsen, S. J., 1967, Osteology of the macaw and Thick-billed Parrot, *Kiva*, **32**, pp. 57–72.
Olson, S. L., and K. E. Blum, 1968, Avian dispersal of plants in Panama, *Ecology*, **49**, pp. 565–566.
O'Neill, J. P., 1969, Distributional notes on the birds of Peru, including twelve species previously unreported from the Republic, *Occ. Pap. Mus. Zool. La St. Univ.*, no. 37, pp. 1–11.
Orfila, R. N., 1936, Los Psittaciformes Argentinos, *Hornero*, **6**, pp. 197–225.
——, 1937, Los Psittaciformes Argentinos (cont.), *ibid.*, **6**, pp. 365–382
——, 1938, Los Psittaciformes Argentinos (cont.), *ibid.*, **7**, pp. 1–21.
Orians, G. H., 1969, The number of bird species in some tropical forests, *Ecology*, **50**, pp. 783–801.

Parker, S. A., 1970, Critical notes on the status of some Northern Territory birds, *S. Aust. Orn.*, **25**, pp. 115–125.
Parkes, K. C., 1960, Geographic and seasonal variation in the Black-collared Lovebird, *Agapornis swinderniana*, *Bull. Br. Orn. Club*, **80**, pp. 3–6.
——, 1963, Notes on some birds from Cuba and the Isle of Pines, *Ann. Carneg. Mus.*, **36**, pp. 129–132.
Partridge, W. R., 1964, Breeding the Greater Patagonian Conure, *Avicult. Mag.*, **70**, pp. 109–110.
Patten, R. A., 1941, Observations on the Solitary Lory in captivity, *Avicult. Mag.*, 5th ser., **6**, pp. 72–74.
——, 1947, Observations on Kuhl's Ruffed Lory (*Vini kuhli*) in captivity, *ibid.*, **53**, pp. 40–43.
Payne, C. M., 1956, Breeding the Derbyan Parrakeet, *ibid.*, **62**, pp. 53–55.
Paynter, R. A., Jr, 1955, The ornithogeography of the Yucatán Peninsula, *Bull. Peabody Mus. nat. Hist.*, no. 9, pp. 1–347.
——, 1956, Avifuana of the Jorullo region, Michoacán, Mexico, *Postilla*, no. 25, pp. 1–12.
——, 1957, Biological investigations in the Selva Lacandona, Chiapas, Mexico, VII. Birds of Laguna Ocotal, *Bull. Mus. comp. Zool. Harv.*, **116**, pp. 249–285.
Peña, L. E., 1961, Results of research in the Antofagasta Ranges of Chile and Bolivia, Part II. Annotated list of birds collected or observed, *Postilla*, No. 49, pp. 28–42.
Penard, R. P., and A. P. Penard, 1908, *De Vogels van Guyana*, vol. 1, Paramaribo, Wed. F. P. Penard.
Penard, T., 1927, Eggs of the Sun Parrot, *Auk*, **44**, pp. 420–421.
Penny, M., 1968, Endemic birds of the Seychelles, *Oryx*, **9**, pp. 267–275.
Pereyra, J. A., 1937, Contribucion al estudio y observaciones ornitologicas de la zona norte de las Gobernacion de La Pampa, *Mems Jard. zool., La Plata*, **7**, pp. 198–326.
——, 1938, Aves de la zona riberina nordeste de la provincia de Buenos Aires, *ibid.*, **9**, pp. 1–304.
——, 1942 Avifauna Argentina (contribucion a la ornitologia), *ibid.*, **10**, pp. 172–274.
Peters, J. L., 1923, Notes on some summer birds of northern Patagonia, *Bull. Mus. comp. Zool. Harv.*, **65**, pp. 277–337.
——, 1928, The races of *Amazona leucocephala* (Linn.), *Auk*, **45**, pp. 342–344.
——, 1937, *Check-List of Birds of the World*, vol. 3, Cambridge. Harvard University Press.
——, and C. H. Blake, 1948, *Microsittace* not generically different from *Enicognathus*, *Auk*, **65**, pp. 288–289.
——, and J. A. Griswold, Jr, 1943, Birds of the Harvard Peruvian Expedition, *Bull. Mus. comp. Zool. Harv.*, **92**, pp. 281–327.
Petersen, G., 1957, Breeding the Senegal Parrot, *Avicult. Mag.*, **63**, pp. 62–63.
Phelps, W. H., and W. H. Phelps, Jr, 1958, Lista de las aves de Venezuela con su distribucion, Part I. No Passeriformes, *Boln Soc. venez. Cienc. nat.*, **19** (90), pp. 1–317.
Phillips, A., J. Marshall, and G. Monson, 1964, *The Birds of Arizona*, Tucson. University of Arizona Press.
Pinto, O. M. de O., 1935, Aves da Bahia, *Revta Mus. paul.*, **19**, pp. 1–325.
——, 1945, Sôbre as formas Brasileiras do gênero *Forpus*, *Revta argent. Zoogeogr.*, **5**, pp. 11–19.
——, 1946, Aves brasileiras da família dos papagaios, *Relat. a. Inst. Bot., S Paulo*, pp. 126–129.
——, 1947, Contribuicão à ornitologiá do Baixo Amazonas, *Arq. Zool. Est. S Paulo*, **5**, pp. 311–482.
——, 1950, Miscelânea ornitològica (V), *Papéis Dep. Zool. S Paulo*, **9**, pp. 361–365.
——, 1954, Sôbre a coleção Carlos Estevão; de peles, ninhos e ovos das aves de Belém (Pará), *ibid.*, **11**, pp. 111–222.
——, 1966, *Cadernos da Amazônia*, **8**. *Estudo Critico e Catalogo Remissivo das Aves do Território Federal de Roraima*, Manaus. Instituto Nacional de Pesquisas da Amazônia.
——, and E. A. de Camargo, 1948, Sôbre uma coleção de aves do Rio das Mortes (Estado de Mato Grosso), *Papéis Dep. Zool. S Paulo*, **8**, pp. 287–336.
——, and ——, 1955, Lista anotada de aves colecionadas nos limites ocidentais do Estado do Paraná, *ibid.*, **12**, pp. 215–234.
——, and ——, 1957, Sôbre uma coleção de aves da região de Cachimbo (sul do Estado do Pará), *ibid.*, **13**, pp. 51–69.
Pitman, C. R. S., 1928, Some notes on *Poicephalus gulielmi massaicus*, *Bataleur*, **1**, pp. 17–23.
Plath, K., 1951, Breeding of the Goldie's Lorikeet, *Avicult. Mag.*, **57**, pp. 133–135.
Poltimore, Lady, 1936, Breeding of the Black-headed and White-breasted Caiques, *ibid.*, 5th ser., **1**, pp. 294–296.
Poonai, N. O., 1969, Nature conservation in tropical South America, Part III. Bird and man in the tropics, *Fla Nat.*, **42**, pp. 128–130, 142.
Porter, S., 1927, Notes from Portuguese East Africa, *Avicult. Mag.*, 4th ser., **5**, pp. 208–215.
——, 1929, In search of the Imperial Parrot, *ibid.*, 4th ser., **7**, pp. 240–246, 267–275.
——, 1935, Notes on birds of Fiji, *ibid.*, 4th ser., **13**, pp. 90–104.
——, 1936, A West Indian diary (continued), *ibid.*, 5th ser., **1**, pp. 66–82.
Potter, N. S., 1953, The birds of Calicoan, Philippine Islands, *Wilson Bull.*, **65**, pp. 252–270.
Potts, T. H., 1869, On the birds of New Zealand, *Trans. N.Z. Inst.*, **2**, pp. 40–78.
Power, D. M., 1966, Antiphonal dueting and evidence for auditory reaction time in the Orange-chinned Parakeet, *Auk*, **83**, pp. 314–319.
——, 1967, Epigamic and reproductive behavior of Orange-chinned Parakeets in captivity, *Condor*, **69**, pp. 28–41.
Prestwich, A. A., 1954, Breeding of the Lineolated Parakeet, *Avicult. Mag.*, **60**, pp. 1–4.
——, 1955, East African Brown-headed Parrot (*Poicephalus cryptoxanthus*), *ibid.*, **61**, pp. 1–2.
Prozesky, O. P. M., 1970. *A Field Guide to the Birds of Southern Africa*, London, Collins.
Puget, A., 1970, Observations sur les psittacidés vivant en Afghanistan, *Alauda*, **38**, pp. 306–309.

Rand, A. L., 1936, The distribution and habits of Madagascar birds; summary of the field notes of the Mission Zoologique Franco-Anglo-Américaine à Madagascar, *Bull. Am. Mus. nat. Hist.*, **72**, art. 5, pp. 143–499.
——, 1938, Results of the Archbold Expeditions, No. XIX. On some non-passerine New Guinea birds, *Am Mus. Novit.*, no. 990, pp. 1–15.
——, 1942a, Results of the Archbold Expeditions, No. 42. Birds of the 1936–1937 New Guinea expedition, *Bull. Am. Mus. nat. Hist.*, **79**, art. 4, pp. 289–366.
——, 1942b, Results of the Archbold Expeditions, No. 43. Birds of the 1938–1939 New Guinea expedition, *ibid.*, **79**, art. 7, pp. 425–516.

—, 1951, Birds from Liberia, *Fieldiana, Zool.*, **32**, pp. 561–653.

—, 1959, Late records of the Cebu Golden-backed Hanging Parrakeet, *Avicult. Mag.*, **65**, pp. 177–178.

—, and R. L. Fleming, 1957, Birds from Nepal, *Fieldiana, Zool.*, **41**, pp. 1–218.

—, and E. T. Gilliard, 1967, *Handbook of New Guinea Birds*, London. Weidenfield and Nicholson.

—, and D. S. Rabor, 1960, Birds of the Philippine Islands: Siquijor, Mount Malindang, Bohol, and Samar, *Fieldiana, Zool.*, **35**, pp. 223–441.

Reichenow, A., 1913, *Die Vögel, Handbuch der Systematischen Ornithologie*, bd. 1, Stuttgart. F. Enke.

Reid, B. E., 1970, Kakapo, in *Wildlife 1969: A Review*, Wellington. New Zealand Wildlife Service, Dept. Internal Affairs.

Rensch, B., 1930, Beitrag zur kenntnis der vogelwelt Balis, *Mitt. zool. Mus. Berl.*, **16**, pp. 530–542.

—, 1931, Die vogelwelt von Lombok, Sumbawa und Flores, *ibid.*, **17**, pp. 451–637.

Restall, R. L., 1970, Breeding Emma's Conure, *Foreign Birds*, **36**, pp. 45–47.

Rhodes, B., 1970, Breeding the Black-tailed Conure, *Avicult. Mag.*, **76**, pp. 141–142.

Ridpath, M. G., and R. E. Moreau, 1966, The birds of Tasmania: ecology and evolution, *ibid*, **108**, pp. 348–393.

Rigge, J. S., 1963, Breeding of the Crimson or Green-winged Macaw, *Avicult. Mag.*, **69**, pp. 34–35.

Riney, T., J. S. Watson, C. Bassett, E. G. Turbott, and W. E. Howard, 1959, Lake Monk Expedition: an ecological study in southern Fiordland, *Bull. N.Z. Dep. scient. ind. Res.*, no. 135, pp. 1–75.

Ripley, S. D., 1944, The bird fauna of the west Sumatra Islands, *Bull. Mus. comp. Zool. Harv.*, **94**, pp. 307–431.

—, 1950, Birds from Nepal, 1947–1949, *J. Bombay nat. Hist. Soc.*, **49**, pp. 355–417.

—, 1951, Migrants and introduced species in the Palau Archipelago, *Condor*, **53**, pp. 299–300.

—, 1961, *A Synopsis of the Birds of India and Pakistan*, Bombay. Bombay Natural History Society.

—, 1964, A systematic and ecological study of birds of New Guinea, *Bull. Peabody Mus. nat. Hist.*, no. 19, pp. 1–85.

—, and D. S. Rabor, 1958, Notes on a collection of birds from Mindoro Island, Philippines, *ibid.*, no. 13, pp. 1–83.

—, and ——, 1961, The avifauna of Mount Katanglad, *Postilla*, no. 50. pp. 1–20.

—, and G. E. Watson, 1956, Cuban bird notes, *ibid.*, no. 26, pp. 1–6.

Risdon, D. H. S., 1965, The breeding of a Blue and Yellow Macaw at the Tropical Bird Gardens, Rode, *Avicult. Mag.*, **71**, pp. 84–87.

—, 1968, The breeding of a young Umbrella Cockatoo, *ibid.*, **74**, pp. 15–16.

Roberts, R. V., 1953, Some birds of the Mokohinau Group, *Notornis*, **5**, pp. 197–198.

Robinson, H. C., 1927, *The Birds of the Malay Peninsula*, vol. 1: *The Commoner Birds*, London. Witherby.

Rodriguez-Vidal, J. A., 1959, Puerto Rican Parrot study, *Monogr. Dep. Agric. Com. P. Rico*, no. 1, pp. 1–15.

Rooth, J., 1968, Over het voorkomen van de Geelvleugelamazone, *Amazona barbadensis rothschildi*, op Bonaire, *Ardea*, **56**, pp. 281–283.

Rostron, A., 1969, Rosella parrots: New Zealand's most beautiful pests, *N.Z. agric. J.*, March issue, p. 40.

Rothschild, W., 1907, *Extinct Birds*, London. Hutchinson.

—, 1931, On a collection of birds made by Mr F. Shaw Mayer in the Weyland Mountains, Dutch New Guinea, in 1930, *Novit. zool.*, **36**, pp. 250–278.

—, and E. Hartert, 1901, List of a collection of birds from Kulambangra and Florida Islands, in the Solomons Group, *ibid.*, **8**, pp. 179–189.

—, E. Stresemann, and K. Paludan, 1932, Ornithologische ergebnisse der Expedition Stein 1931–1932, *ibid.*, **38**, pp. 127–247.

Rountree, F. R., R. Guerin, S. Pelte, and J. Vinson, 1952, Catalogue of the birds of Mauritius, *Bull. Maurit. Inst.*, no. 3, pp. 155–217.

Rowley, J. S., 1966, Breeding records of birds of the Sierra Madre del Sur, Oaxaca, Mexico, *Proc. West. Found. Vert. zool.*, **1**, pp. 107–204.

Russell, K., 1971, Breeding of the Perfect or Plain Lorikeet, *Avicult. Mag.*, **77**, pp. 115–116.

Russell, S. M., 1964, A distributional study of the birds of British Honduras, *Am. Orn. Un. Orn. Monogr.*, no. 1, pp. 1–95.

Ruwet, J. C., 1964, Notes écologiques et éthologiques sur les oiseaux des plaines de la Lufira supérieure (Katanga), II. Des Accipitres aux Pici, *Revue Zool. Bot. afr.*, **69**, pp. 1–63.

Salvadori, T., 1891, *Catalogue of Birds in the British Museum*, vol. 20. Psittaci, London. British Museum (Natural History).

—, 1900, On some additional species of parrots in the Genus *Pyrrhura*, *ibid*, 7th ser., **6**, pp. 667–674.

Salvan, J., 1968, Contribution a l'étude des oiseaux du Tchad (suite), *Oiseau Revue fr. Orn.*, **38**, pp. 127–150.

Sander, F., 1956, A list of birds of Lagos and its environs with brief notes on their status, Part I, *Niger. Fld*, **21**, pp. 147–162.

Sarasin, F., 1913, Die vögel Neu-Caledoniens und der Loyalty-Inseln, in F. Sarasin and J. Roux, *Nova Caledonia*, vol. 1, Wiesbaden. C. W. Kreidels Verlag.

Sassi, M., 1947, *Touit purpurata viridiceps* Chapman, *Alauda*, **54**, p. 178.

Schafer, E., and W. H. Phelps, 1954, Las aves del Parque Nacional 'Henri Pittier' (Rancho Grande) y sus funciones ecologicas, *Boln Soc. venez. Cienc nat.*, **16** (83), pp. 3–167.

Schaldach, W. J., Jr, 1963, The avifauna of Colima and adjacent Jalisco, Mexico, *Proc. West. Found. Vert. zool.*, **1** (1), pp. 1–100.

Schmidt, C. R., 1971, Breeding Keas at Zurich Zoo, *Int. Zoo Yb.*, vol. 11, pp. 137–140.

Schodde, R., and W. B. Hitchcock, 1968, Contributions to Papuasian ornithology, 1. Report on the birds of the Lake Kutubu area, Territory of Papua and New Guinea, *C.S.I.R.O. Div. Wildl. Res.*, *Tech. Pap.*, no. 13, pp. 1–73.

Schönwetter, M., 1964, *Handbuch der oologie*, bd. 1, lief. 9, Berlin. Akademie-Verlag.

Schubart, O., A. C. Aguirre, and H. Sick, 1965, Contribuição para o conhecimento da alimentação das aves Brasileiras, *Arq. Zool. Est. S Paulo*, **12**, pp. 95–249.

Schwartz, A., 1970, Land birds of Isla Saona, República Dominicana, *Q. Jl Fla Acad. Sci.*, **32**, pp. 291–306.

Sclater, P. L., 1860, List of the first collection of birds made by Mr Louis Fraser at Pallatanga, Ecuador, with notes and descriptions of new species, *Proc. zool. Soc., Lond.* [1859], pp. 135–149.

—, 1871, On two new or little-known parrots living in the Society's Gardens, *ibid.*, pp. 499–500.

Scott, W. E., 1946, Birds observed on Espiritu Santo, New Hebrides, *Auk*, **63**, pp. 362–368.

Sedgwick, E. H., 1952, Bird life at Leonora, Western Australia, *Emu*, **52**, pp. 285–296.

Serle, W., 1954, A second contribution to the ornithology of the British Cameroons, *ibid*, **96**, pp. 47–80.

—, 1957, A contribution to the ornithology of the eastern region of Nigeria, *ibid.*, **99**, pp. 371–418.

—, 1965, A third contribution to the ornithology of the British Cameroons, *ibid.*, **107**, pp. 60–94.

Serventy, D. L., 1964, in A. L. Thomson, ed., *A New Dictionary of Birds*, London. Nelson.

—, and H. M. Whittell, 1967, *Birds of Western Australia*, 4th. ed., Perth. Lamb Publications.

Seth-Smith, D., 1903, The Racket-tailed Parrot, *Prioniturus platurus* (Vieillot), *Avicult. Mag.*, new ser., **1**, pp. 345–347.

Shanahan, P. J., 1969, The Buffy-faced Pygmy Parrot, *Aust. Avicult.*, **23**, pp. 120–122.

Sharland, M., 1956, Birds of Tasman Peninsula, Tasmania, *Emu*, **56**, pp. 69–75.

—, 1958, *Tasmanian Birds*, 3rd ed., Sydney. Angus and Robertson.

Sharratt, G. W., and G. M. Sharratt, 1965, Hand-rearing Yellow-backed Lories, *Avicult. Mag.*, **71**, pp. 81–82.

Shore-Baily, W., 1915, The breeding of the Brown-eared Conures, *Bird Notes*, new ser., **6**, pp. 306–308.

—, 1925, The breeding of the Red-headed Conure, *Avicult. Mag.*, 4th ser., **3**, pp. 318–320.

Sibley, C. G., 1951, Notes on the birds of New Georgia, central Solomon Islands, *Condor*, **53**, pp. 81–92.

Sibson, R. B., 1947, A visit to Little Barrier Island, *Notornis*, (N.Z. Bird Notes), **2**, pp. 134–144.

Sick, H., 1965, A fauna do cerrado, *Arq. Zool Est. S Paulo*, **12**, pp. 71–93.

—, 1968, Vogelwanderungen im kontinentalen Südamerika, *Vogelwarte*, **24**, pp. 217–243.

—, 1969, Aves Brasileiras ameaçadas de extinção e noçoes gerais de conservação de aves no Brasil, *An. Acad. brasil. Ciênc.*, **41** suppl., pp. 205–229.

—, and L. F. Pabst, 1968, As aves do Rio de Janeiro (Guanabara) (Lista sistemática anotada), *Arq. Mus. nac., Rio de J.*, **53**, pp. 99–160.

Siebers, H. C., 1930, Fauna Buruana: Aves, *Treubia*, **7** suppl., pp. 165–303.

Sims, R. W., 1956, Birds collected by Mr F. Shaw-Mayer in the Central Highlands of New Guinea, *Bull. Br. Mus. nat. Hist.*, **3**, pp. 389–438.

Skead, C. J., 1964, The overland flights and the feeding habits of the Cape Parrot, *Poicephalus robustus* (Gmelin), in the Eastern Cape Province, *Ostrich*, **35**, pp. 202–223.

—, 1971, The Cape Parrot in the Transkei and Natal, *ibid.*, suppl. no. 9, pp. 165–178.

Slud, P., 1964, The birds of Costa Rica: distribution and ecology, *Bull. Am. Mus. nat. Hist.*, **128**, pp. 1–430.

Small, R. C., 1966, Breeding the Hawk-headed Parrot, *Avicult. Mag.*, **72**, pp. 71–72.

Smith, A. P., 1907, The Thick-billed Parrot in Arizona, *Condor*, **9**, p. 104.

Smith, C., 1970, Breeding the Double Yellow-headed Amazon, *Avicult. Mag.*, **76**, pp. 234–235.

Smith, E. T., 1960, Review of *Pionus maximiliani* (Kuhl), *Fieldiana, Zool.*, **39**, pp. 379–385.

Smith, G. A., 1971a, The use of the foot in feeding, with especial reference to parrots, *Avicult. Mag.*, **77**, pp. 93–100.

—, 1971b, Black-headed Caiques, *ibid.*, **77**, pp. 202–218.

Smith, G. D., 1942, Breeding and rearing Blue-fronted Amazon Parrots, *ibid.*, 5th ser., **7**, pp. 149–150.

Smith, K. D., 1957, An annotated check list of the birds of Eritrea (cont.), *ibid*, **99**, pp. 307–337.

Smithe, F. B., 1966, *The Birds of Tikal*, New York. Natural History Press.

—, and R. A. Paynter, Jr, 1963, Birds of Tikal, Guatemala, *Bull. Mus. comp. Zool. Harv.*, **128**, pp. 247–324.

Smithers, C. N., and H. J. de S. Disney, 1969, The distribution of terrestrial and freshwater birds on Norfolk Island, *Aust. Zool.*, **15**, pp. 127–140.

Smithers, R. H. N., 1964, *A Check-List of the Birds of the Bechuanaland Protectorate and the Caprivi Strip, With Data on Ecology and Breeding*, Bulawayo. National Museums of Southern Rhodesia.

—, M. P. Stuart Irwin, and M. L. Paterson, 1957, *A Check List of the Birds of Southern Rhodesia*, Bulawayo. Rhodesian Ornithological Society.

Smythies, B. E., 1953, *The Birds of Burma*, 2nd ed., Edinburgh. Oliver and Boyd.

—, 1968, *The Birds of Borneo*, 2nd ed., Edinburgh. Oliver and Boyd.

Snethlage, E., 1935, Beitrage zur brutbiologie brasilianischer vögel, *J. Orn.*, **83**, pp. 532–562.

Snyder, D. E., 1966, *The Birds of Guyana*, Salem. Peabody Museum.

Spence, T., 1955, Breeding of the Purple-capped Lory, *Avicult. Mag.*, **61**, pp. 14–17.

Stager, K. E., 1954, Birds of the Barranca de Cobre region of southwestern Chihuahua, Mexico, *Condor*, **56**, pp. 21–32.

—, 1957, The avifauna of the Tres Marías Islands, Mexico, *Auk*, **74**, pp. 413–432.

—, 1961, The Machris Brazilian Expedition, Ornithology: non-passerines, *Contr. Sci., Los Angeles County Mus.*, no. 41, pp. 1–27.

Stanford, J. K., 1935, Notes on the birds of the Sittang-Irrawaddy Plain, Lower Burma, *J. Bombay nat. Hist. Soc.*, **37**, pp. 859–889.

Steinbacher, G., 1934, Zur kenntnis des magens blütenbesuchender papageien, *Orn. Mber.*, **42**, pp. 80–84.

—, 1935, Zur anatomie von *Micropsitta*, *ibid.*, **43**, pp. 139–144.

Steinbacher, J., 1962, Beiträge zur kenntnis der vögel von Paraguay, *Abh. senckenb. naturforsch. Ges.*, **502**, pp. 1–106.

Stevens, H., 1925, Notes on the birds of the Sikkim Himalayas, Part IV, *J. Bombay nat. Hist. Soc.*, **30**, pp. 664–685.

Stone, W., 1929, On a collection of birds from the Pará region, eastern Brazil, *Proc. Acad. nat. Sci. Philad.*, **80**, pp. 149–176.

—, 1933, The birds of Honduras with special reference to a collection made in 1930 by John T. Emlen, Jr, and C. Brooke Worth, *ibid.*, **84**, pp. 291–342.

—, and H. R. Roberts, 1935, Zoological results of the Matto Grosso Expedition to Brazil in 1931, II. Birds, *ibid.*, **86**, pp. 363–397.

Stoner, C. R., 1952, Distribution of Lord Derby's Parakeet, *ibid*, **94**, p. 162.

Storr, G. M., 1967, List of Northern Territory birds, *Spec. Publs W. Aust. Mus.*, no. 4, pp. 1–90.

Stresemann, E., 1912, Ornithologische miszellen aus dem Indo-Australischen Gebiet, *Novit. zool.*, **19**, pp. 311–351.

—, 1913, Exhibition of some parrots collected in the Moluccas, *Bull. Br. Orn. Club*, **31**, p. 15.

—, 1914, Die vögel von Seran (Ceram), *Novit. zool.*, **21**, pp. 25–153.

—, 1927–1934, Aves, in *Kukenthal-Handbuch der Zoologie*, bd. 7, lief. 2, Berlin. Walter de Gruyter and Company.

—, 1940, Die vögel von Celebes, Teil III. Systematik und biologie, *J. Orn.* **88**, pp. 389–487.

—, and V. Stresemann, 1966, Die mauser der vögel, *ibid.*, **107** sonderheft, pp. 1–445.

Stuart Baker, E. C., 1927, *The Fauna of British India: Birds*, vol. 4, London. Taylor and Francis.

—, 1934, *The Nidification of Birds of the Indian Empire*, vol. 3, London. Taylor and Francis.

Such, J. D., 1964, Quaker Parrakeet, *Foreign Birds*, **30**, p. 235.

Sudbury, A., 1969, My trip to New Guinea, Part I, *Bird Obs., Melb.*, no. 450, pp. 5–8.

Sutton, G. M., and T. D. Burleigh, 1940a, Birds of Valles, San Luis Potosí, *Condor*, **42**, pp. 259–262.

—, and ——, 1940b, Birds of Tamazunchale, San Luis Potosí, *Wilson Bull.*, **52**, pp. 221–233.

—, and O. S. Pettingill, Jr, 1942, Birds of the Gomez Farias region, southwestern Tamaulipas, *Auk*, **59**, pp. 1–34.

Tarboton, W. R., 1968, *Check List of Birds of the South Central Transvaal*, Johannesburg. Witwatersrand Bird Club.

Tashian, R. E., 1952, Some birds from the Palenque region of northeastern Chiapas, Mexico, *Auk*, **69**, pp. 60–66.

—, 1953, The birds of southeastern Guatemala, *Condor*, **55**, pp. 198–210.

Tavistock, Marquis of, 1929a, The Derbyan Parrot, *ibid*, 12th ser., **5**, pp. 562–563.

—, 1929b, Moult of the Malabar Parrot, *ibid.*, 12th ser., **5**, p. 731.

—, 1931a, The nesting of the Halmahera Hanging Parrot (*Loriculus amabilis*), *Avicult. Mag.*, 4th ser., **9**, pp. 238–239.

—, 1931b, Plumage and bill-changes in parrakeets, *ibid*, 13th ser., **1**, p. 136.

—, 1936, First breeding in Great Britain of the Swift Lorikeet (or Parrakeet), *Foreign Birds*, **2**, p. 110.

—, 1938a, The breeding of the Tahiti Blue Lory, *Avicult. Mag.*, 5th ser., **3**, pp. 34–38.

——, 1938b, Exhibiting an egg of the Tahiti Blue Lory and remarks, *Bull. Br. Orn. Club*, **58**, pp. 55–56.
——, 1939, The breeding of the Ultramarine Lory, *Avicult. Mag.*, 5th ser., **4**, pp. 292–294.
——, 1950, The nesting of Musschenbroek's Lorikeet, *ibid.*, **56**, pp. 211–213.
——, 1954, *Parrots and Parrot-Like Birds*, 1st ed., Fond du Lac. All-Pets Books.
Taylor, G. F., 1971, The aviary breeding of black cockatoos, *Aust. Avicult.*, **25**, pp. 176–177.
Terborgh, J., and J. S. Weske, 1969, Colonization of secondary habitats by Peruvian birds, *Ecology*, **50**, pp. 765–782.
Thayer, J. E., 1906, Eggs and nests of the Thick-billed Parrot, *Auk*, **23**, pp. 223–224.
Thesigner, W., and M. Meynell, 1935, On a collection of birds from Danakil, Abyssinia, *ibid*, 13th ser., **5**, pp. 774–807.
Thomas, D. G., 1970, Swift Parrots wintering in Tasmania, *Tasm. Nat.*, no. 23, p. 4.
Thompson, D. W., 1900, On characteristic points in the cranial osteology of the parrots, *Proc. zool. Soc. Lond.*, [1899], pp. 9–46.
Thompson, M. C., 1962, Noteworthy records of birds from the Republic of Mexico, *Wilson Bull.*, **74**, pp. 173–176.
——, 1966, Birds from north Borneo, *Univ. Kans. Publs nat. Hist.*, **17**, pp. 377–433.
Thomson, A. L., ed., 1964, *A New Dictionary of Birds*, London. Nelson.
Thomson, D. F., 1935, *Birds of Cape York Peninsula: Ecological Notes, Field Observations, and Catalogue of Specimens Collected on Three Expeditions to North Queensland*, Melbourne. Government Printer.
Tily, I., 1951, Dunedin Naturalists' Field Club Notes, *Notornis*, **4**, pp. 149–150.
Todd, W. E. C., 1916, The birds of the Isle of Pines, *Ann, Carneg. Mus.*, **10** pp. 146–296.
——, and M. A. Carriker, Jr, 1922, The birds of the Santa Marta region of Colombia: a study in altitudinal distribution, *ibid.*, **14**, pp. 3–611.
Townsend, C. H., and A. Wetmore, 1919, Reports on the scientific results of the expedition to the tropical Pacific in charge of Alexander Agassiz on the 'Albatross', 1899–1900, XXI. The birds, *Bull. Mus. comp. Zool. Harv.*, **63**, pp. 151–225.
Traylor, M. A., 1958, Birds of northeastern Peru, *Fieldiana, Zool.*, **35**, pp. 87–141.
——, 1963, Check-list of Angolan birds, *Publ. cult. Cia Diament. Angola*, no. 61, pp. 1–250.
——, 1965, A collection of birds from Barotseland and Bechuanaland, *ibid*, **107**, pp. 138–172.
——, and D. Parelius, 1967, A collection of birds from the Ivory Coast, *Fieldiana, Zool.*, **51**, pp. 91–117.
Tubb, J. A., 1945, Field notes on some New Guinea birds, *Emu*, **44**, pp. 249–273.
Turbott, E. G., 1961, Little Barrier Island (Hauturu): Birds, *Bull. N.Z. Dep. scient. ind. Res.*, no. 137, pp. 136–175.
Turner, G. T., 1940, The first European breeding of the Queen of Bavaria Conure, *Foreign Birds*, **6**, pp. 88–90.
Turner, J. S., C. N. Smithers, and R. D. Hoogland, 1968, The conservation of Norfolk Island, *Spec. Publ. Aust. conserv. Found.*, no. 1, pp. 1–41.
Turner, M., and C. R. S., Pitman, 1965, The nesting habits and eggs of the Rufous-tailed Weaver, *Histurgops ruficauda* Reichenow, *Bull. Br. Orn. Club*, **85**, pp. 10–14.

Urban, E., 1959, Birds from Coahuila, Mexico, *Univ. Kans. Publs Mus. nat. Hist.*, **11**, pp. 443–516.
——, 1966, *Shell Guide to Ethiopian Birds*, Addis Ababa. Eto Publication.

Van Bemmel, A. C. V., and K. H. Voous, 1951, On the birds of the Islands of Muna and Buton, S. E. Celebes, *Treubia*, **21**, pp. 27–104.
Vane, E. N. T., 1950, Noble Macaws (*Ara nobilis cumanensis*), *Avicult. Mag.*, **56**, pp. 10–16.
——, 1953, Breeding the Moustache Parrakeet, *ibid.*, **59**, pp. 151–155.
——, 1954, Breeding the Canary-winged Parrakeet, *ibid.*, **60**, pp. 227–231.
——, 1957, Rearing the Yellow-cheeked Amazon, *ibid.*, **63**, pp. 183–188.
Van Rossem, A. J., 1945, A distributional survey of the birds of Sonora, Mexico, *Occ. Pap. Mus. Zool. La St. Univ.*, no. 21, pp. 1–379.
Van Tyne, J., 1935, The birds of northern Petén, Guatemala, *Misc. Publs Mus. Zool. Univ. Mich.*, no. 27, pp. 1–46.
——, 1950, Bird notes from Barro Colorado Island, Canal Zone, *Occ. Pap. Mus. Zool. Univ. Mich.*, no. 525, pp. 1–12.
Vaughan, J. H., 1930, The birds of Zanzibar and Pemba, *ibid*, 12th ser., **6**, pp. 1–48.
Vaurie, C., 1965, *The Birds of the Palearctic Fauna: Non Passeriformes*, London. Witherby.
Verheijen, J. A. J., 1964, Breeding season on the Island of Flores, Indonesia, *Ardea*, **52**, pp. 194–201.
Verheyen, R., 1956, Analyse du potentiel morphologique et projet d'une nouvelle classification des Psittaciformes, *Bull. Inst. r. Sci. nat. Belg.*, **32** (55), pp. 1–54.
Vevers, G. H., 1964, in A. L. Thomson, ed., *A New Dictionary of Birds*, London. Nelson.
Vielliard, J., 1969, Données biogeographiques sur l'avifaune d'Asie Occidentale, I. Afghanistan (premiére partie), *Alauda*, **37**, pp. 273–300.
Vincent, A. W., 1946, On the breeding habits of some African birds, *ibid*, **88**, pp. 48–67.
Vincent, J., 1934, The birds of northern Portuguese East Africa: comprising a list of, and observations on, the collections made during the British Museum Expedition of 1931–1932, Part V, *ibid*, 13th ser., **4**, pp. 757–799.
——, 1967, Birds in danger of extinction. Threatened species of birds: general report, *Bull. int. Coun. Bird Preserv.*, no. 10, pp. 82–100.
Vlasblom, A. G., 1953, The lower jaw of the parrots in relation to the architecture of the skull, *Proc. Sect. Sci. K. ned. Akad. Wet.*, **56**, ser. C, pp. 486–507.
Volker, O., 1937, Ueber fluoreszierende, gelbe Federpigmente bei papageien, eine neue Klasse von Federfarbstoffen, *J. Orn.*, **85**, pp. 136–146.
Von Hagen, W., 1938, A contribution to the biology of *Nasutitermes* (sensu stricto), *Proc. zool. Soc. Lond.*, **108A**, pp. 39–49.
Von Ihering, H., 1902, Contribuições para conhecimento da ornithologia de São Paulo, II. Descripção de novos ninhos e ovos, *Revta Mus. paul.*, **5**, pp. 291–303.
Voous, K. H., 1955, *De Vogels van de Nederlandse Antillen/Birds of the Netherlands Antilles*, Curaçao. Natuurwetenschappelijke Werkgroep Nederlandse Antillen. (Fauna Nederlandse Antillen, no. 1).
——, 1957, The birds of Aruba, Curaçao, and Bonaire, *Stud. Fauna Curaçao*, **7** (29), pp. 1–260.
——, 1965, Specimens of Lear's Macaw in the Zoological Museum of Amsterdam, *Oiseau Revue fr. Orn.*, **35** (no. spécial), pp. 153–155.

Wait, W. E., 1925, *Manual of the Birds of Ceylon*, Colombo. Colombo Museum.
Walkinshaw, L. H., and B. W. Baker, 1946, Notes on the birds of the Isle of Pines, Cuba, *Wilson Bull.*, **58**, pp. 133–142.
Ward, P., 1968, Origin of the avifauna of urban and suburban Singapore, *ibid*, **110**, pp. 239–255.
——, and B. Wood, 1967, Parrot damage to oil-palm fruit in Johore, *Planter, Kuala Lumpur*, **43**, pp. 101–103.
Warham, J., 1955, The nesting of the Rock Parrot, *Emu*, **55**, pp. 81–84.
Warner, D. W., 1947, The ornithology of New Caledonia and the Loyalty Islands, Ph.D. Thesis (unpublished), Cornell University, New York, pp. 1–228.
Watson, J., 1905, Breeding Passerine Parrotlets, *Avicult. Mag.*, new ser., **3**, pp. 34–35.
Wetmore, A., 1926, Observations on the birds of Argentina, Paraguay, Uruguay, and Chile, *Bull. U.S. natn. Mus.*, no. 133, pp. 1–448.
——, 1927, The birds of Porto Rico and the Virgin Islands—Psittaciformes to Passeriformes, *Scient. Surv. P. Rico*, **9** (4), pp. 409–598.
——, 1931, Early record of birds in Arizona and New Mexico, *Condor*, **33**, p. 35.
——, 1935, The Thick-billed Parrot in southern Arizona, *ibid.*, **37**, pp. 18–21.
——, 1939, Observations on the birds of northern Venezuela, *Proc. U.S. natn. Mus.*, **87**, pp. 173–260.
——, 1941, Notes on birds of the Guatemalan highlands, *ibid.*, **89**, pp. 523–581.
——, 1944, A collection of birds from Guanacaste, Costa Rica, *ibid.*, **95**, pp. 25–80.
——, 1957, The birds of Isla Coiba, Panama, *Smithson. misc. Collns*, **134** (9), pp. 1–105.
——, 1968, *The Birds of the Republic of Panama*, part 2. *Columbidae* (*Pigeons*) *to Picidae* (*Woodpeckers*), Washington. Smithsonian Institution Press.
——, and B. H. Swales, 1931, The birds of Haiti and the Dominican Republic, *Bull. U.S. natn. Mus.*, no. 155, pp. 1–483.
White, C. M. N., 1942, Notes on the birds of Fort Jameson district, Northern Rhodesia, *ibid*, 14th ser. **6**, pp. 435–437.
——, 1945, The ornithology of the Kaonde-Lunda Province, Northern Rhodesia, Part III, *ibid*, **87**, pp. 309–345.
——, 1953, Systematic notes on African birds, *Bull. Br. Orn. Club*, **73**, pp. 94–96.
White, H. L., 1922, A collecting trip to Cape York Peninsula, *Emu*, **22**, pp. 99–116.
Whitehead, J., 1899, Field-notes on birds collected in the Philippine Islands, Part III, *ibid*, 7th ser., **5**, pp. 381–399.
Whitlock, F. L., 1924, Journey to central Australia in search of the Night Parrot, *Emu*, **23**, pp. 248–281.
Wildash, P., 1968, *Birds of South Vietnam*, Rutland. Charles E. Tuttle.
Wildboer, Dr, 1926, The breeding of the Guiana Parrotlet, *Avicult. Mag.*, 4th ser., **4**, pp. 244–246.
Williams, C. B., 1922, Trinidad birds: notes on the food and habits of some Trinidad birds, *Bull. Dep. Agric. Trin. Tobago*, **20**, parts 2–4, pp. 123–185.
Williams, G. R., 1956, The Kakapo (*Strigops habroptilus*, Gray): a review and re-appraisal of a near-extinct species, *Notornis*, **7**, pp. 29–56.
——, 1960, The birds of the Pitcairn Islands, central South Pacific Ocean, *Ibid*, **102** pp. 58–70.
Williams, J. G., 1963, *A Field-Guide to the Birds of East and Central Africa*, London. Collins.
——, 1967, *A Field-Guide to the National Parks of East Africa*, London. Collins.
Wilson, C. E., 1949, Birds causing crop damage in The Sudan, *Sudan Notes Rec.*, **29**, pp. 161–173.
Wilson, H., 1937, Notes on the Night Parrot, with references to recent occurrences, *Emu*, **37**, pp. 79–87.
Wilson, S. B., 1907, Notes on birds of Tahiti and the Society Group, *ibid*, 9th ser., **1**, pp. 373–379.
Winterbottom, J. M., 1942, A contribution to the ornithology of Barotseland, *ibid*, 14th ser., **6**, pp. 337–389.
——, 1949, *Agapornis*, *ibid.*, **91**, pp. 170–171.
——, 1969, On the birds of the Sandveld Kalahari of South West Africa, *Ostrich*, **40**, pp. 182–204.
Wodzicki, K., 1969, A preliminary survey of rats and other land vertebrates of Niue Island, South Pacific, 2nd November–4th December, 1968, *Processed Report Prepared for the Niue Island Administration in Association with the Departments of Maori and Island Affairs and Scientific and Industrial Research*, Wellington, New Zealand.
Wood, C. A., 1924, My quest of the Imperial Parrot, *Avicult. Mag.*, 4th ser., **2**, pp. 57–59, 77–81.
——, and A. Wetmore, 1926, A collection of birds from the Fiji Islands, Part III. Field observations, *ibid*, 12th ser., **2**, pp. 91–136.
Wooldridge, T. R., 1969, Breeding of Meyer × Ruppell Parrot hybrid, *Parrot Soc. Mag.*, **3**, p. 27.
Wright, M. D., 1957, Notes on the birds of a selected area of Dehra Dun—June 1946 to July 1951, *J. Bombay nat. Hist. Soc.*, **54**, pp. 627–662.

Yaldwyn, J. C., 1952, Notes on the present status of Samoan birds, *Notornis*, **5**, pp. 28–30.
Yealland, H., 1935, The hand-rearing of the White-capped Parrot, *Avicult. Mag.*, 4th ser., **13**, pp. 11–16.
Yealland, J., 1940, The Blue Lories, *ibid.*, 5th ser., **5**, pp. 308–313.
Yepez, G., 1953, Estudio sobre la region de Perijá y sus habitantes, XI. El indio y las aves. *Publnes Univ. Zulia*, pp. 221–223.
Young, C. G., 1929, A contribution to the ornithology of the coastland of British Guiana, *ibid*, 12th ser., **5**, pp. 1–38.

Zapata, A., 1969, Aves observadas en el Golfo San Jorge, provincias de Chubut y Santa Cruz, Argentina, *Zool. Platense*, **1**, pp. 21–27.
Zimmer, J. T., 1930, Birds of the Marshall Field Peruvian Expedition, *Publs Field Mus. nat. Hist., Zool.*, **17**, pp. 233–480.
Zimmerman, D. A., 1967, *Agapornis fischeri*, *Lybius guifsobalito*, and *Stiphrornis erythrothorax* in Kenya, *Auk*, **84**, pp. 594–595.
——, and G. B. Harry ,1951, Summer birds of Autlán, Jalisco, *Wilson Bull.*, **63**, pp. 302–314.

Index of Scientific Names

Page numbers in parentheses indicate illustrations

Index of English Names

Page numbers in parentheses indicate illustrations.

6/94 Section on Macaws
p. 360 - 374 missing

Sections on the Amazons
missing